About Pearson

Pearson is the world's learning company, with presence across 70 countries worldwide. Our unique insights and world-class expertise comes from a long history of working closely with renowned teachers, authors and thought leaders, as a result of which, we have emerged as the preferred choice for millions of teachers and learners across the world.

We believe learning opens up opportunities, creates fulfilling careers and hence better lives. We hence collaborate with the best of minds to deliver you class-leading products, spread across the Higher Education and K12 spectrum.

Superior learning experience and improved outcomes are at the heart of everything we do. This product is the result of one such effort.

Your feedback plays a critical role in the evolution of our products and you can contact us – reachus@pearson.com. We look forward to it.

Table of Contents

Chapter 1

Displaying the Order in a Group of Numbers Using Tables and Graphs

Welcome to *Statistics for Psychology*. We imagine you to be like other students we have known who have taken this course. You have chosen to major in psychology or a related field because you are fascinated by people: fascinated by their visible behaviors and inner lives, as well as perhaps by your own psychology. Some of you are highly scientific sorts; others are more intuitive. Some of you are fond of math; others are less so. Whatever your style, we welcome you.

More importantly, we want to assure you that whatever your reason for studying psychology or a related field, this course is not a waste of time. Learning about statistics helps you to read the work of other psychologists, to do your own research if you so choose, and to hone both your reasoning and intuition. It also helps you to evaluate reports of scientific research in the media. Statistics really can make an important contribution to the next phase of your life.

Formally, **statistics** is a branch of mathematics that focuses on the organization, analysis, and interpretation of a group of numbers. But really what is statistics? Think of statistics as a tool that has evolved from a basic thinking process employed by every human: you observe a thing; you wonder what it means or what caused it; you have an insight or make an intuitive guess; you observe again, but now in detail, or you try making little changes in the process to test your intuition. Then you face the eternal problem: was your hunch confirmed or not? What are the chances that what you observed this second time will happen again and again, so that you can announce your insight to the world as something probably true?

In other words, statistics is a method of pursuing truth. At a minimum, statistics can tell you the likelihood that your hunch is true in this time and place and with these sorts of people. This type of pursuit of truth, especially in the form of an event's future likelihood, is the essence of psychology, of science, and of human evolution. Think of the first research questions: What will the mammoths do next spring? What will happen if I eat this root? It is easy to see how the early accurate "researchers" survived. You are here today because your ancestors exercised brains as well as brawn. Do those who come after you the same favor: think carefully about outcomes. Statistics is one good way to do that.

Psychologists use statistical methods to help them make sense of the numbers they collect when conducting research. Psychologists usually use statistical software to carry out statistical procedure. However, the best way to develop a solid understanding of statistics is actually to do the procedures by hand for a while (with the help of a calculator—it's not the multiplying and adding that you learn from, but the going through all the steps). To minimize the amount of mindless figuring you have to do, we use relatively small groups of simple numbers in each chapter's examples and practice problems. All of this allows you to focus on the *underlying principles and logic* of the statistical procedures as you manipulate the numbers. Having said that, we also recognize the importance for many of you of learning how to do statistical procedures on a computer so that, for example, you can some day conduct your own research, maybe starting with a senior project. Therefore, at the end of the chapter there is a section called Using SPSS. SPSS statistical software is commonly used by psychologists and other behavioral and social scientists to carry out statistical analyses. Check with your instructor to see if you have access to SPSS at your institution. (There are also a number of other statistical programs used by researchers, and many basic statistical procedures can be carried out using standard spreadsheet programs such as Excel; for those of you not using SPSS, the SPSS sections will still be helpful in giving you the general idea of how one does such problems on a computer.)

statistics branch of mathematics that focuses on the organization, analysis, and interpretation of a group of numbers.

descriptive statistics procedures for summarizing a group of scores or otherwise making them more understandable.

inferential statistics procedures for drawing conclusions based on the scores collected in a research study but going beyond them.

The Two Branches of Statistical Methods

There are two main branches of statistical methods.

1. **Descriptive statistics:** Psychologists use descriptive statistics to summarize and describe a group of numbers from a research study.
2. **Inferential statistics:** Psychologists use inferential statistics to draw conclusions and to make inferences that are based on the numbers from a research study but that go beyond the numbers. For example, inferential statistics

allow researchers to make inferences about a large group of individuals based on a research study in which a much smaller number of individuals took part.

In this chapter, we focus on descriptive statistics. This topic is important in its own right, but it also prepares you to understand inferential statistics.

In this chapter we introduce you to some basic concepts, and then you will learn to use tables and graphs to describe a group of numbers. The purpose of descriptive statistics is to make a group of numbers easy to understand. As you will see, tables and graphs help a great deal.

Some Basic Concepts

Variables, Values, and Scores

As part of a larger study (Aron, Paris, & Aron, 1995), researchers gave a questionnaire to students in an introductory statistics class during the first week of the course. One question asked was, "How stressed have you been in the last 2½ weeks, on a scale of 0 to 10, with 0 being *not at all stressed* and 10 being *as stressed as possible?*" (How would *you* answer?) In this study, the researchers used a survey to examine students' level of stress. Other methods that researchers use to study stress include creating stress with laboratory tasks (such as having to be videotaped giving a talk for humans or swimming in water for rats) and measuring stress-related hormones or brain changes.

In this example, level of stress is a **variable**, which can have **values** from 0 to 10, and the value of any particular person's answer is the person's **score**. If you answered 6, your score is 6; your score has a value of 6 on the variable called "level of stress."

More formally, a variable is a condition or characteristic that can have different values. In short, it can *vary*. In our example, the variable was level of stress, which can have the values of 0 through 10. Height is a variable, social class is a variable, score on a creativity test is a variable, type of psychotherapy received by patients is a variable, speed on a reaction time test is a variable, number of people absent from work on a given day is a variable, and so forth.

A value is just a number, such as 4, –81, or 367.12. A value can also be a category, such as male or female, or a psychiatric diagnosis—major depression, post-traumatic stress disorder—and so forth.

Finally, on any variable, each person studied has a particular number or *score* that is his or her value on the variable. As we've said, your score on the stress variable might have a value of 6. Another student's score might have a value of 8.

Psychology research is about variables, values, and scores (see Table 1). The formal definitions are a bit abstract, but in practice, the meaning is usually clear.

variable characteristic that can have different values.

values possible number or category that a score can have.

score particular person's value on a variable.

Table 1	Some Basic Terminology	
Term	**Definition**	**Examples**
Variable	Condition or characteristic that can have different values	Stress level; age; gender; religion
Value	Number or category	0, 1, 2, 3, 4; 25, 85; female; Catholic
Score	A particular person's value on a variable	0, 1, 2, 3, 4; 25, 85; female; Catholic

Levels of Measurement (Kinds of Variables)

Most of the variables psychologists use are like those in the stress ratings example: the scores are numbers that tell you how much there is of what is being measured. In the stress ratings example, the higher the number is, the more stress there is. This is an example of a **numeric variable**. Numeric variables are also called *quantitative variables*.

There are several kinds of numeric variables. In psychology research the most important distinction is between two types: equal-interval variables and rank-order variables. An **equal-interval variable** is a variable in which the numbers stand for approximately equal amounts of what is being measured. For example, grade point average (GPA) is a roughly equal-interval variable, since the difference between a GPA of 2.5 and 2.8 means about as much as the difference between a GPA of 3.0 and 3.3 (each is a difference of 0.3 of a GPA). Most psychologists also consider scales like the 0-to-10 stress ratings as roughly equal interval. So, for example, a difference between stress ratings of 4 and 6 means about as much as the difference between 7 and 9.

Some equal-interval variables are measured on what is called a **ratio scale**. An equal-interval variable is measured on a ratio scale if it has an *absolute zero point.* An absolute zero point means that the value of zero on the variable indicates a complete absence of the variable. Most counts or accumulations of things use a ratio scale. For example, the number of siblings a person has is measured on a ratio scale, because a zero value means having no siblings. With variables that are measured on a ratio scale, you can make statements about the difference in magnitude between values. So, we can say that a person with four siblings has twice as many siblings as a person with two siblings. Other examples of variables that are measured on a ratio scale include distance, time, and weight. However, most of the variables in psychology are not on a ratio scale.

The other main type of numeric variable, a **rank-order variable**, is a variable in which the numbers stand only for relative ranking. (Rank-order variables are also called *ordinal variables*.) A student's standing in his or her graduating class is an example. The amount of difference in underlying GPA between being second and third in class standing could be very unlike the amount of difference between being eighth and ninth.

A rank-order variable provides less information than an equal-interval variable. That is, the difference from one rank to the next doesn't tell you the exact difference in amount of what is being measured. However, psychologists often use rank-order variables because they are the only information available. Also, when people are being asked to rate something, it is sometimes easier and less arbitrary for them to make rank-order ratings. For example, when rating how much you like each of your friends, it may be easier to rank them by how much you like them than to rate your liking for each of them on a scale. Yet another reason researchers often use rank-order variables is that asking people to do rankings forces them to make distinctions. For example, if asked to rate how much you like each of your friends on a 1-to-10 scale, you might rate several of them at exactly the same level, but ranking would avoid such ties.

Another major type of variable used in psychology research, which is not a numeric variable at all, is a **nominal variable** in which the values are names or categories. The term *nominal* comes from the idea that its values are names. (Nominal variables are also called *categorical variables* because their values are categories.) For example, for the nominal variable gender, the values are female and male. A person's "score" on the variable gender is one of these two values. Another example is psychiatric diagnosis, which has values such as major depression, post-traumatic stress disorder, schizophrenia, and obsessive-compulsive disorder.

These different kinds of variables represent different **levels of measurement** (see Table 2). Researchers sometimes have to decide how they will measure a particular

numeric variable   variable whose values are numbers (as opposed to a nominal variable). Also called *quantitative variable*.

equal-interval variable   variable in which the numbers stand for approximately equal amounts of what is being measured.

ratio scale   an equal-interval variable is measured on a ratio scale if it has an *absolute zero point,* meaning that the value of zero on the variable indicates a complete absence of the variable.

rank-order variable   numeric variable in which the values are ranks, such as class standing or place finished in a race. Also called *ordinal variable.*

nominal variable   variable with values that are categories (that is, they are names rather than numbers). Also called *categorical variable.*

levels of measurement   types of underlying numerical information provided by a measure, such as equal-interval, rank-order, and nominal (categorical).

Table 2 Levels of Measurement		
Level	**Definition**	**Example**
Equal-interval	Numeric variable in which differences between values correspond to differences in the underlying thing being measured	Stress level; age
Rank-order	Numeric variable in which values correspond to the relative position of things measured	Class standing; position finished in a race
Nominal	Variable in which the values are categories	Gender; religion

variable. For example, they might use an equal-interval scale, a rank-order scale, or a nominal scale. The level of measurement selected affects the type of statistics that can be used with a variable. Suppose a researcher is studying the effects of a particular type of brain injury on being able to recognize objects. One approach the researcher might take would be to measure the number of different objects an injured person can observe at once. This is an example of an equal-interval level of measurement. Alternately, the researcher might rate people as able to observe no objects (rated 0), only one object at a time (rated 1), one object with a vague sense of other objects (rated 2), or ordinary vision (rated 3). This would be a rank-order approach. Finally, the researcher might divide people into those who can identify the location of an object but not what the object is (rated L), those who can identify what the object is but not locate it in space (rated I), those who can both locate and identify an object but have other abnormalities of object perception (rated O), those who are completely blind (rated B), and those with normal visual perception (rated N). This is a nominal level of measurement.

In this chapter, as in most psychology research, we focus mainly on numeric, equal-interval variables (or variables that roughly approximate equal-interval variables).

Another distinction that researchers sometimes make is between discrete variables and continuous variables. A **discrete variable** is one that has specific values and cannot have values between the specific values. For example, the number of times you went to the dentist in the last 12 months is a discrete variable. You may have gone 0, 1, 2, 3, or more times, but you can't have gone 1.72 times or 2.34 times. Nominal variables, such as gender, religious affiliation, and college major can also be considered to be discrete variables. With a **continuous variable**, there are in theory an infinite number of values between any two values. So, even though we usually answer the question "How old are you?" with a specific age, such as 19 or 20, you could also answer it by saying that you are 19.26 years old. Height, weight, and time are examples of other continuous variables.

discrete variable   variable that has specific values and that cannot have values between these specific values.

continuous variable   variable for which, in theory, there are an infinite number of values between any two values.

How are you doing?

1. A father rates his daughter as a 2 on a 7-point scale (from 1 to 7) of crankiness. In this example, (a) what is the variable, (b) what is the score, and (c) what is the range of values?
2. What is the difference between a numeric and a nominal variable?
3. Give the level of measurement of each of the following variables: (a) a person's nationality (Mexican, Chinese, Ethiopian, Australian, etc.), (b) a person's score on a standard IQ test, (c) a person's place on a waiting list (first in line, second in line, etc.).
4. What is the difference between a discrete and a continuous variable?

Answers

1. (a) crankiness, (b) 2, (c) 1 to 7.
2. A numeric variable has values that are numbers that tell you the degree or extent of what the variable measures; a nominal variable has values that are different categories and have no particular numerical order.
3. (a) nominal, (b) equal-interval, (c) rank-order.
4. A discrete variable has specific values and has no values between the specific values. A continuous variable has, in theory, an infinite number of values between any two values.

BOX 1   Important Trivia for Poetic Statistics Students

The word *statistics* comes from the Italian word *statista,* a person dealing with affairs of state (from *stato,* "state"). It was originally called "state arithmetic," involving the tabulation of information about nations, especially for the purpose of taxation and planning the feasibility of wars.

Statistics were needed in ancient times to figure the odds of shipwrecks and piracy for marine insurance that would encourage voyages of commerce and exploration to far-flung places. The modern study of mortality rates and life insurance descended from the 17th-century plague pits—counting the bodies of persons cut down in the bloom of youth. The theory of errors began in astronomy, that is, with stargazing; the theory of correlation has its roots in biology, from the observation of parent and child differences. Probability theory arose in the tense environs of the gambling table. The theory of analysis of experiments began in breweries and out among waving fields of wheat, where correct guesses determined not only the survival of a tasty beer but of thousands of marginal farmers. Theories of measurement and factor analysis derived from personality psychology, where the depths of human character were first explored with numbers. And chi-square came to us from sociology, where it was often a question of class.

In the early days of statistics, it was popular to use the new methods to prove the existence of God. For example, John Arbuthnot discovered that more male than female babies were born in London between 1629 and 1710. In what is considered the first use of a statistical test, he proved that the male birthrate was higher than could be expected by chance (assuming that 50:50 was chance) and concluded that there was a plan operating, since males face more danger to obtain food for their families, and only God, he said, could do such planning.

In 1767, John Michell also used probability theory to prove the existence of God when he argued that the odds were 500,000 to 1 against six stars being placed as close together as those in the constellation Pleiades; so their placement had to have been a deliberate act of the Creator.

Statistics in the "state arithmetic" sense are legally endorsed by most governments today. For example, the first article of the U.S. Constitution requires a census. And statistics helped the United States win the Revolutionary War. John Adams obtained critical aid from Holland by pointing out certain vital statistics, carefully gathered by the clergy in local parishes, demonstrating that the colonies had doubled their population every 18 years, adding 20,000 fighting men per annum. "Is this the case of our enemy, Great Britain?" Adams wrote. "Which then can maintain the war the longest?"

Similar statistics were observed by U.S. President Thomas Jefferson in 1786. He wrote that his people "become uneasy" when there are more of them than 10 per square mile and that given the population growth of the new country, within 40 years these restless souls would fill up all of their country's "vacant land." Some 17 years later, Jefferson doubled the size of the United States' "vacant" land through the Louisiana Purchase.

Frequency Tables

An Example

Let's return to the stress ratings example. Recall that in this study, students in an introductory statistics class during the first week of the course answered the question, "How stressed have you been in the last 2½ weeks, on a scale of 0 to 10, with 0 being *not at all stressed* and 10 being *as stressed as possible?*" The actual study included scores from 151 students. To ease the learning for this example, we are going to use a representative subset of scores from 30 of the 151 students (this also saves you time if you want to try it for yourself). The 30 students' scores (their ratings on the scale) are:

8, 7, 4, 10, 8, 6, 8, 9, 9, 7, 3, 7, 6, 5, 0, 9, 10, 7, 7, 3, 6, 7, 5, 2, 1, 6, 7, 10, 8, 8.

Looking through all these scores gives some sense of the overall tendencies, but this is hardly an accurate method. One solution is to make a table showing how many students used each of the 11 values that the ratings can have (0, 1, 2, and so on, through 10). That is, the number of students who used each particular rating is the *frequency* of that value. We have done this in Table 3. We also figured the percentage that each value's frequency is of the total number of scores. Tables like this sometimes give only the raw-number frequencies, not the percentages, or only the percentages and not the raw-number frequencies.

In addition, some frequency tables include, for each value, the total number of scores with that value and all values preceding it. These are called *cumulative frequencies* because they tell how many scores are accumulated up to this point on the table. If percentages are used, cumulative percentages also may be included (for an example, see Figure 19 in the Using SPSS section). Cumulative percentages give, for each value, the percentage of scores up to and including that value. The cumulative percentage for any given value (or for a score having that value) is also called a *percentile*. Cumulative frequencies and cumulative percentages allow you to see where a particular score falls in the overall group of scores.

Table 3 is called a **frequency table** because it shows how frequently (how many times) each score was used. A frequency table makes the pattern of numbers easy to see. In this example, you can see that most of the students rated their stress level around 7 or 8, with few rating it very low.

Table 3 Frequency Table of Number of Students Rating Each Value of the Stress Scale

Stress Rating	Frequency	Percent
0	1	3.3
1	1	3.3
2	1	3.3
3	2	6.7
4	1	3.3
5	2	6.7
6	4	13.3
7	7	23.3
8	5	16.7
9	3	10.0
10	3	10.0

Source: Data based on Aron et al. (1995).

How to Make a Frequency Table

There are four steps in making a frequency table.

❶ **Make a list down the page of each possible value, from lowest to highest.** In the stress ratings results, the list goes from 0, the lowest possible rating, up to 10, the highest possible rating.[1] Note that even if one of the ratings between 0 and 10 is not used, you still include that value in the listing, showing it as having a frequency of 0. For example, if no one gave a stress rating of 2, you still include 2 as one of the values on the frequency table.

❷ **Go one by one through the scores, making a mark for each next to its value on your list.** This is shown in Figure 1.

❸ **Make a table showing how many times each value on your list is used.** That is, add up the number of marks beside each value.

❹ **Figure the percentage of scores for each value.** To do this, take the frequency for that value, divide it by the total number of scores, and multiply by 100. You may need to round off the percentage. We recommend that you

frequency table ordered listing of number of individuals having each of the different values for a particular variable.

Figure 1   Making a frequency table for the stress ratings scores. (Data based on Aron, Paris, and Aron, 1995.)

round percentages to one decimal place. Note that because of the rounding, your percentages do not usually add up to exactly 100% (but the total should be very close to 100%).

Frequency Tables for Nominal Variables

The preceding steps assume you are using numeric variables, the most common situation. However, you can also use a frequency table to show the number of scores for each value (that is, for each category) of a nominal variable. For example, researchers (Aron, Aron, & Smollan, 1992) asked 208 students to name the closest person in their life. As shown in Table 4, 33 students selected a family member, 76 a nonromantic friend, 92 a romantic partner, and 7 selected some other person. Also in Table 4, the values listed on the left hand side of the frequency table are the values (the categories) of the variable.

Table 4   Frequency Table for a Nominal Variable: Closest Person in Life for 208 Students

Closest Person	Frequency	Percent
Family member	33	15.9
Nonromantic friend	76	36.5
Romantic partner	92	44.2
Other	7	3.4

Source: Data from Aron et al. (1992).

Another Example

Tracy McLaughlin-Volpe and her colleagues (2001) had 94 introductory psychology students keep a diary of their social interactions for a week during the regular semester. Each time a participant had a social interaction lasting 10 minutes or longer, he or she would fill out a card. The card had questions about various aspects of the conversation and the conversation partner. Excluding family and work situations, the number of social interactions 10 minutes or longer over a week for these students were as follows:

48, 15, 33, 3, 21, 19, 17, 16, 44, 25, 30, 3, 5, 9, 35, 32, 26, 13, 14, 14, 47, 47, 18, 11, 5, 19, 24, 17, 6, 25, 8, 18, 29, 1, 18, 22, 3, 22, 29, 2, 6, 10, 29, 10, 29, 21, 38, 41, 16, 17, 8, 40, 8, 10, 18, 7, 4, 4, 8, 11, 3, 23, 10, 19, 21, 13, 12, 10, 4, 17, 11, 21, 9, 8, 7, 5, 3, 22, 14, 25, 4, 11, 10, 18, 1, 28, 27, 19, 24, 35, 9, 30, 8, 26.

Now, let's follow our four steps for making a frequency table.

❶ **Make a list down the page of each possible value, from lowest to highest.** The lowest possible number of interactions is 0. In this study, the highest number of interactions could be any number. However, the highest actual number in this group is 48; so we can use 48 as the highest value. Thus, the first step is to list these values down a page. (It might be good to use several columns so that you can have all the scores on a single page.)

❷ **Go one by one through the scores, making a mark for each next to its value on your list.** Figure 2 shows the results of this step.

❸ **Make a table showing how many times each value on your list is used.** Table 5 is the result.

❹ **Figure the percentage of scores for each value.** We have *not* done so in this example because it would not help much for seeing the pattern of scores. However, if you want to check your understanding of this step, the first five percentages would be 0.0%, 2.1%, 1.1%, 5.3%, and 4.3%. (These are the percentages for frequencies of 0, 2, 1, 5, and 4, rounded to one decimal place.)

Grouped Frequency Tables

Sometimes there are so many possible values that an ordinary frequency table is too awkward to give a simple picture of the scores. The last example was a bit like that, wasn't it? The solution is to make groupings of values that include all values in a certain range. Consider the stress ratings example. Instead of having a separate frequency figure for the group of students who rated their stress as 8 and another for those who rated it as 9, you could have a combined category of 8 and 9. This combined category is a range of values that includes these two values. A combined category like this is called an **interval**. This particular interval of 8 and 9 has a frequency of 8 (the 5 scores with a value of 8 plus the 3 scores with a value of 9).

A frequency table that uses intervals is called a **grouped frequency table**. Table 6 is a grouped frequency table for the stress ratings example. (Note that in this example the full frequency table has only 11 different values. Thus, a grouped

0 -	17 - ////	34 -
1 - //	18 - 𝖳𝖧𝖫	35 - //
2 - /	19 - ////	36 -
3 - 𝖳𝖧𝖫	20 -	37 -
4 - ////	21 - ////	38 - /
5 - ///	22 - ///	39 -
6 - //	23 - /	40 - /
7 - //	24 - //	41 - /
8 - 𝖳𝖧𝖫 /	25 - ///	42 -
9 - ///	26 - //	43 -
10 - 𝖳𝖧𝖫 /	27 - /	44 - /
11 - ////	28 - /	45 -
12 - /	29 - ////	46 -
13 - //	30 - //	47 - //
14 - ///	31 -	48 - /
15 - /	32 - /	
16 - //	33 - /	

Figure 2 Making a frequency table of students' social interactions over a week. (Data from McLaughlin-Volpe et al., 2001.)

TIP FOR SUCCESS

Be sure to check your work by adding the frequencies for all of the scores. This sum should equal the total number of scores you started with.

Table 5	Frequency Table for Number of Social Interactions During a Week for 94 College Students				
Score	**Frequency**	**Score**	**Frequency**	**Score**	**Frequency**
0	0	17	4	34	0
1	2	18	5	35	2
2	1	19	4	36	0
3	5	20	0	37	0
4	4	21	4	38	1
5	3	22	3	39	0
6	2	23	1	40	1
7	2	24	2	41	1
8	6	25	3	42	0
9	3	26	2	43	0
10	6	27	1	44	1
11	4	28	1	45	0
12	1	29	4	46	0
13	2	30	2	47	2
14	3	31	0	48	1
15	1	32	1		
16	2	33	1		

Source: Data from McLaughlin-Volpe et al. (2001).

Table 6	Grouped Frequency Table for Stress Ratings	
Stress Rating Interval	**Frequency**	**Percent**
0–1	2	6.7
2–3	3	10.0
4–5	3	10.0
6–7	11	36.7
8–9	8	26.7
10–11	3	10.0

Source: Data based on Aron et al. (1995).

interval range of values in a grouped frequency table that are grouped together. (For example, if the interval size is 10, one of the intervals might be from 10 to 19.)

grouped frequency table frequency table in which the number of individuals (frequency) is given for each interval of values.

Table 7 Grouped Frequency Table for Numbers of Social Interactions During a Week for 94 College Students

Interval	Frequency	Percent
0–4	12	12.8
5–9	16	17.0
10–14	16	17.0
15–19	16	17.0
20–24	10	10.6
25–29	11	11.7
30–34	4	4.3
35–39	3	3.2
40–44	3	3.2
45–49	3	3.2

Source: Data from McLaughlin-Volpe et al. (2001).

frequency table is not really necessary.) Table 7 is a grouped frequency table for the 94 students' number of social interactions over a week.

A grouped frequency table can make information even more directly understandable than an ordinary frequency table can. Of course, the greater understandability of a grouped frequency table is at a cost. You lose some information: the details of the breakdown of frequencies in each interval.

When you are setting up a grouped frequency table, it makes a big difference how many intervals you use. There are guidelines to help researchers with this, but in practice it is done automatically by the researcher's computer (see this chapter's Using SPSS section for instructions on how to create frequency tables using statistical software). However, should you have to make a grouped frequency table on your own, the key is to experiment with the interval size until you come up with one that is a round number (such as 2, 3, 5, or 10) and that creates about 5 to 15 intervals. Then, when actually setting up the table, be sure you set the start of each interval to a multiple of the interval size and the top end of each interval to the number just below the start of the next interval. For example, Table 6 uses six intervals with an interval size of 2. The intervals are 0–1, 2–3, 4–5, 6–7, 8–9, and 10–11. Note that each interval starts with a multiple of 2 (0, 2, 4, 6, 8, 10) and the top end of each interval (1, 3, 5, 7, 9) is the number just below the start of the next interval (2, 4, 6, 8, 10). Table 7 uses 10 intervals with an interval size of 5. The intervals are 0–4, 5–9, 10–14, 15–19, and so on, with a final interval of 45–49. Note that each interval starts with a multiple of 5 (0, 5, 10, 15, and so on) and that the top end of each interval (4, 9, 14, 19, and so on) is the number just below the start of the next interval (5, 10, 15, 20, and so on).

How are you doing?

1. What is a frequency table?
2. Why would a researcher want to make a frequency table?
3. Make a frequency table for the following scores: 5, 7, 4, 5, 6, 5, 4.
4. What does a grouped frequency table group?

Answers

1. A frequency table is a systematic listing of the number of scores (the frequency) of each value in the group studied.
2. A frequency table makes it easy to see the pattern in a large group of scores.

3. Value	Frequency	Percent
4	2	28.6
5	3	42.9
6	1	14.3
7	1	14.3

4. A grouped frequency table groups the frequencies of adjacent values into intervals.

Histograms

histogram barlike graph of a frequency distribution in which the values are plotted along the horizontal axis and the height of each bar is the frequency of that value; the bars are usually placed next to each other without spaces, giving the appearance of a city skyline.

A graph is another good way to make a large group of scores easy to understand. A picture may be worth a thousand words, but it is also sometimes worth a thousand numbers. A straightforward approach is to make a graph of the frequency table. One kind of graph of the information in a frequency table is a kind of bar chart called a **histogram**. In a histogram, the height of each bar is the frequency of each value in the frequency table. Ordinarily, in a histogram, all the bars are put next to each other with no space in between. The result is that a histogram looks a bit like

a city skyline. Figure 3 shows two histograms based on the stress ratings example
(one based on the ordinary frequency table and one based on the grouped frequency
table). Figure 4 shows a histogram based on the grouped frequency table for the example of the numbers of students' social interactions in a week.

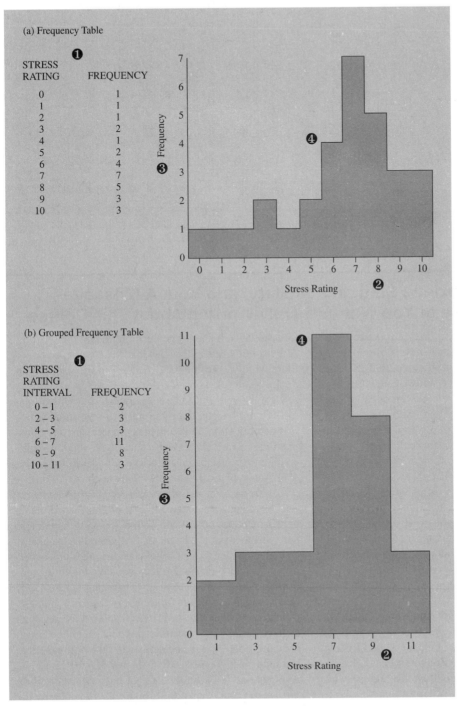

Figure 3 Histograms based on (a) frequency table and (b) a grouped frequency for the
stress ratings example. (Data based on Aron et al., 1995.)

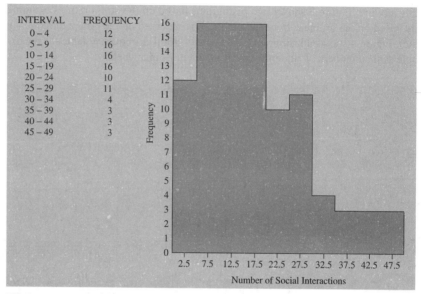

INTERVAL	FREQUENCY
0 – 4	12
5 – 9	16
10 – 14	16
15 – 19	16
20 – 24	10
25 – 29	11
30 – 34	4
35 – 39	3
40 – 44	3
45 – 49	3

Figure 4   Histogram for number of social interactions during a week for 94 college students, based on grouped frequencies. (Data from McLaughlin-Volpe et al., 2001.)

BOX 2   Math Anxiety, Statistics Anxiety, and You: A Message for Those of You Who Are Truly Worried About This Course

Many of you are probably not looking forward to this course, and some of you may even have a certain degree of "statistics anxiety" (Onwuegbuzie, 2000; Zeidner, 1991). You are not alone. The study of statistics anxiety is a growing field. There are even questionnaire measures of statistics anxiety (e.g., Statistical Anxiety Rating Scale; Cruise, Cash, & Bolton, 1985) and the *Statistical Education Research Journal*, begun in 2002, devotes many articles to the problem and how instructors can reduce it. What can you do?

First, take hope. In fact, several studies of statistics anxiety actually bring home the importance of hope (e.g., Kauer, 2010; Onwuegbuzie & Snyder, 2000). There's reason for hope because this course is a chance for a fresh start with digits. Your past performance in (or avoidance of) geometry, trigonometry, calculus, or similar courses need not influence in any way how well you comprehend statistics. This is largely a different subject.

Second, a little anxiety is not a bad thing. A study of statistics anxiety at Auburn University (Keeley, Zayac, & Correia, 2008) confirmed one of the most solid findings in psychology, the Yerkes-Dodson (1908) law. That law says that performance and comfort are highest when you are at your optimal level of arousal, neither under aroused and bored or over aroused and anxious, but just

right. (Maybe it should be the Goldilocks' Law.) In the Auburn study, students with some anxiety out performed those with too much anxiety and also those with too little. So go ahead, worry a little.

If, however, your anxiety is interfering with studying or taking tests, then you need to determine where it is coming from. Is it statistics anxiety, anxiety about math in general, test anxiety, general anxiety, low self-confidence? Each can play its role (Cooper & Robinson, 1989; Dwinell & Higbee, 1991; Onwuegbuzie, 2000).

Is your problem statistics anxiety or general math anxiety? If you only fear statistics, we promise it will be no harder than any other math course (actually, much *less* purely mathematical than most). For general math anxiety, go to the Internet. A search will yield hundreds of wonderful books and Web sites to help you. We highly recommend Sheila Tobias's classics, *Overcoming Math Anxiety* (1995) and *Succeed with Math: Every Student's Guide to Conquering Math Anxiety* (1987). Tobias, a former math avoider herself, suggests that your goal should be "math mental health," which she defines as "the willingness to learn the math you need when you need it" (1995, p. 12). Another fine book on the subject is *Conquering Math Anxiety* by Carol Arem (2009). Both authors emphasize the importance of looking back over your history with math to when it became a problem. They also teach ways to deal with the emotions as they rise up while you are studying.

Is your problem test anxiety? Test taking can easily push you out of your optimal level of arousal, especially when the test is timed. Your mind starts to race, creating more anxiety, more arousal, and so on. Maybe the thought comes that you are "no good and never will be." So think through that thought right now so that you can forget it. You are in college. You are definitely "good." If you have had some low grades, that may reflect your problems with tests more than your abilities.

What more can you do about test anxiety? There are many ways to reduce anxiety and arousal in general, such as learning to breathe properly and to take a brief break to relax deeply. Your counseling center should be able to help you or direct you to some good books on the subject. Again, many Web sites deal with reducing anxiety.

We think that test anxiety is best solved by over preparing for a few tests, so that you go in with the certainty that you cannot possibly fail, no matter how aroused you become. The ideal time to begin applying this tactic is the first test of this course. There will be no old material to review, success will not depend on having understood previous material, and initial success will help you do well throughout the course.

You also might enlist the sympathy of your instructor or teaching assistant about your test anxiety. Bring in a list of what you have studied, explain why you are being so exacting, and ask if you have missed anything. Your preparation must be ridiculously thorough, but only for a few exams. After these successes, your test anxiety should decline. Also, reduce your arousal by making the testing situation more familiar. Create a practice test situation as similar to a real test as possible, making a special effort to duplicate the aspects that bother you most. If feeling rushed is the troubling part, once you think you are well prepared, set yourself a time limit for solving some homework problems. Make yourself write out answers fully and legibly—this may be part of what makes you feel slow during a test. If the presence of others bothers you—the sound of their scurrying pencils while yours is frozen in midair—do your practice test with others in your course. If the sense of competition is behind your fear, add the twist of making it an explicit contest—then laugh about it afterwards.

Is your problem a general lack of confidence? Maybe something else in your life is causing you to worry or feel bad about yourself. In that case, it is time you tried your friendly college counseling center.

Lastly, could you be highly sensitive? A final word about anxiety and arousal. About 20% of us seem to be born "highly sensitive" (Aron, Aron, & Jagiellowicz, 2012). Traditionally seen as shyness, hesitancy, or introversion (Eysenck, 1981; Kagan, 1994), this temperament trait actually seems due to a preference to observe, notice subtle stimulation, and process this information deeply, along with having a heightened emotionality that serves to motivate that processing (Aron, 1996; Aron & Aron, 1997; Jagiellowicz et al., 2011). This trait is normal and found in over one hundred other species (Wolf, van Doorn, & Weissing, 2008). Highly sensitive persons (HSPs) tend to be very intuitive or even gifted. But they are more easily over aroused by high levels of stimulation, like tests.

You might want to find out if you are an HSP (at *www.hsperson.com*). If you are, appreciate the trait's assets and make some allowances for its one disadvantage, this tendency to become easily over aroused, which can affect test performance. What matters is what you actually know, which is probably quite a bit. This simple act of self-acceptance—that you are *not* less smart but *are* more sensitive—may in itself help ease your arousal when trying to express your statistical knowledge.

More generally. Is there still a lingering feeling that you are "no good" at math? That some people are just naturally good at math and you are not one of them? A study cited by Tobias (1995) compared students in Asia and the United States on an international mathematics test and found the U.S. students were thoroughly outperformed. Why? Interviews revealed that Asian students saw math as an ability fairly equally distributed among people and thought that differences in performance were due to hard work. In contrast, U.S. students thought some people are just born better at math; so hard work matters little.

Learn from those good at math. Do not feel nervous when you are stuck. Stay calm and go back to the last place where you understood things, or ask for help from someone who will not make you nervous. One of the worst feelings is having someone explain something, and you still don't get it. But if that happens, remember that it is just that you are getting anxious and over aroused, not that you are "bad at math." Keep looking for the right kind of help. Some people love to teach and know the importance of praising you when you get it right. Find them. Then, once you understand something, try to explain it to someone else right away. Teaching is a great way to really grasp an idea.

And breathe deeply. Stay calm. Maybe you can actually enjoy the process of becoming someone who truly understands this subject.

How to Make a Histogram

There are four steps in making a histogram.

❶ **Make a frequency table (or grouped frequency table).**

❷ **Put the values along the bottom of the page, from left to right, from lowest to highest.** If you are making a histogram from a grouped frequency table, the values you put along the bottom of the page are the interval midpoints. The midpoint of an interval is halfway between the start of that interval and the start of the next highest interval. So, in Figure 4, the midpoint for the 0–4 interval is 2.5, because 2.5 is halfway between 0 (the start of the interval) and 5 (the start of the next highest interval). For the 5–9 interval, the midpoint is 7.5 because 7.5 is halfway between 5 (the start of the interval) and 10 (the start of the next highest interval). Do this for each interval. When you get to the last interval, find the midpoint between the start of the interval and the start of what would be the next highest interval. So, in Figure 4, the midpoint for the 45–49 interval is halfway between 45 (the start of the interval) and 50 (the start of what would be the next interval), which is 47.5.

❸ **Make a scale of frequencies along the left edge of the page that goes from 0 at the bottom to the highest frequency for any value.**

❹ **Make a bar above each value with a height for the frequency of that value.** For each bar, make sure that the middle of the bar is above its value.

When you have a nominal variable, the histogram is called a *bar graph*. Since the values of a nominal variable are not in any particular order, you leave a space between the bars. Figure 5 shows a bar graph based on the frequency table in Table 4.

> **TIP FOR SUCCESS**
>
> Now try this yourself! Work out the interval midpoints for the grouped frequency table for the stress ratings example shown in Table 6. Remember, you are not finding the middle point of the interval, but rather the middle point between where one interval starts and the next one begins. Your answers should be the same as the values shown along the bottom of Figure 3b.

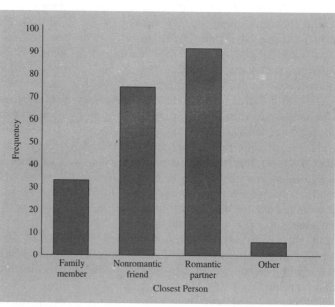

Figure 5   Bar graph for the closest person in life for 208 students (see Table 4). (Data from Aron et al., 1995.)

How are you doing?

1. Why do researchers make histograms?
2. When making a histogram from a frequency table, (a) what goes along the bottom, (b) what goes along the left edge, and (c) what goes above each value?
3. Make a histogram based on the following frequency table:

Value	Frequency
1	3
2	4
3	8
4	5
5	2

4. How is a histogram based on a nominal variable different from one based on a numeric equal-interval variable?

Answers

1. Researchers make histograms to show the pattern visually in a frequency table.
2. (a) The values, from lowest to highest go along the bottom; (b) the frequencies from 0 at the bottom to the highest frequency of any value at the top go along the left edge; (c) above each value is a bar with a height of the frequency for that value.
3. See Figure 6.

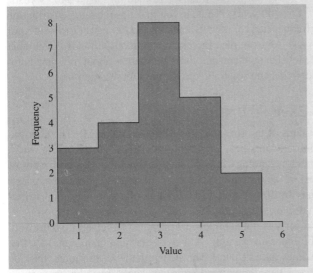

Figure 6
Histogram for "How are you doing?" question 3.

4. A histogram based on a nominal variable has gaps between the bars and is called a bar graph.

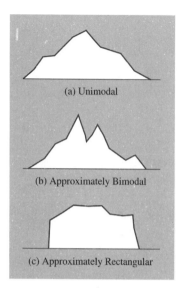

Figure 7 Examples of (a) unimodal, (b) approximately bimodal, and (c) approximately rectangular frequency polygons.

frequency distribution pattern of frequencies over the various values; what a frequency table, histogram, or frequency polygon describes.

unimodal distribution frequency distribution with one value clearly having a larger frequency than any other.

bimodal distribution frequency distribution with two approximately equal frequencies, each clearly larger than any of the others.

multimodal distribution frequency distribution with two or more high frequencies separated by a lower frequency; a bimodal distribution is the special case of two high frequencies.

rectangular distribution frequency distribution in which all values have approximately the same frequency.

symmetrical distribution distribution in which the pattern of frequencies on the left and right side are mirror images of each other.

skewed distribution distribution in which the scores pile up on one side of the middle and are spread out on the other side; distribution that is not symmetrical.

Shapes of Frequency Distributions

A **frequency distribution** shows the pattern of frequencies over the various values. A frequency table or histogram describes a frequency distribution because each shows the pattern or shape of how the frequencies are spread out, or "distributed." Psychologists also describe this shape in words. Describing the shape of a distribution is important.

Unimodal and Bimodal Frequency Distributions

One question is whether a distribution's shape has only one main high point: one high "tower" in the histogram. For example, in the stress ratings study, the most frequent value is 7, giving a graph only one very high area. This is a **unimodal distribution**. If a distribution has two fairly equal high points, it is a **bimodal distribution**. Any distribution with two or more high points is called a **multimodal distribution**. (Strictly speaking, a distribution is bimodal or multimodal only if the peaks are exactly equal. However, psychologists use these terms more informally to describe the general shape.) Finally, a distribution with values of all about the same frequency is a **rectangular distribution**. Figure 7 shows examples of these frequency distribution shapes. As you will see, the graphs in Figure 7 are not histograms, but special line graphs called *frequency polygons,* which are another way to graph a frequency table. In a frequency polygon, the line moves from point to point. The height of each point shows the number of scores with that value. This creates a mountain-peak skyline.

The scores from most psychology studies are usually an approximately unimodal distribution. Bimodal and other multimodal distributions occasionally turn up. A bimodal example is the distribution of the ages of people in a toddlers' play area in a park, who are mostly either toddlers of ages around 2 to 4 years or caretakers with ages of 20 to 40 years or so (with few infants, a few siblings aged 5 to 19 years, and a few grandparents above 40 years). Thus, if you make a frequency distribution of these ages, the large frequencies are at the values for toddler ages (2 to 4) and for higher ages (20 to 40 or so). An example of a rectangular distribution is the number of children at each grade level at an elementary school; there is about the same number in first grade, second grade, and so on. Figure 8 shows these examples.

Symmetrical and Skewed Distributions

Look again at the histograms of the stress ratings example (Figure 3). The distribution is lopsided, with more scores near the high end. This is somewhat unusual. Most things we measure in psychology have about equal numbers on both sides of the middle. That is, most of the time in psychology, the scores follow an approximately **symmetrical distribution** (if you fold the graph of a symmetrical distribution in half, the two halves look the same).

A distribution that clearly is not symmetrical is called a **skewed distribution**. The stress ratings distribution is an example. A skewed distribution has one side that is long and spread out, somewhat like a tail. The side with the *fewer* scores (the side that looks like a tail) is considered the direction of the skew. Thus, the stress study example, which has too few scores at the low end, is skewed to the left. However, the social interactions example, which has too few scores at the high end, is skewed to the right (see Figure 4). Figure 9 shows examples of approximately symmetrical and skewed distributions.

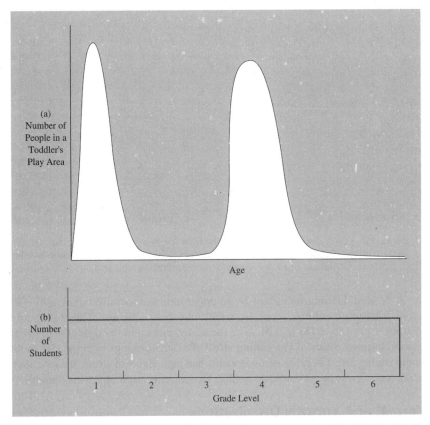

Figure 8 Fictional examples of distributions that are not unimodal: (a) A bimodal distribution showing the possible frequencies for people of different ages in a toddler's play area. (b) A regular distribution showing the possible frequencies of students at different grade levels in an elementary school.

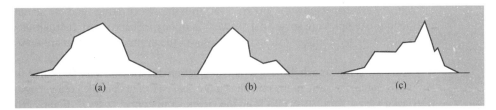

Figure 9 Examples of frequency polygons of distributions that are (a) approximately symmetrical, (b) skewed to the right (positively skewed), and (c) skewed to the left (negatively skewed).

A distribution that is skewed to the right is also called *positively skewed*. A distribution skewed to the left is also called *negatively skewed*.

Strongly skewed distributions come up in psychology research mainly when what is being measured has some upper or lower limit. For example, a family cannot have fewer than zero children. When many scores pile up at the low end because it is impossible to have a lower score, the result is called a **floor effect**. A skewed distribution caused by a lower limit is shown in Figure 10a.

TIP FOR SUCCESS

It helps you remember the direction of the skew to know that the word *skew* comes from the French *queue*, which means line or tail. Thus, the direction of the skew is the side that has the long line, or tail.

floor effect situation in which many scores pile up at the low end of a distribution (creating skewness to the right) because it is not possible to have any lower score.

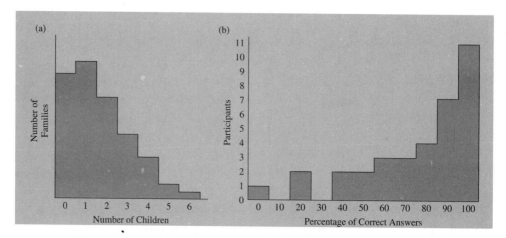

Figure 10 (a) A distribution skewed to the right due to a floor effect: fictional distribution of the number of children in families. (b) A distribution skewed to the left due to a ceiling effect: fictional distribution of adults' scores on a multiplication table test.

A skewed distribution caused by an upper limit is shown in Figure 10b. This is a distribution of adults' scores on a multiplication table test. This distribution is strongly skewed to the left. Most of the scores pile up at the right, the high end (a perfect score). This shows a **ceiling effect**. The stress ratings example also shows a mild ceiling effect because many students had high levels of stress, the maximum rating was 10, and people often do not like to use ratings right at the maximum.

Normal and Kurtotic Distributions

Psychologists also describe a distribution in terms of whether the middle of the distribution is particularly peaked or flat. The standard of comparison is a bell-shaped curve. In psychology research and in nature generally, distributions often are similar to this bell-shaped standard, called the **normal curve**. However, the important thing is that the normal curve is a unimodal, symmetrical curve with an average peak—the sort of bell shape shown in Figure 11a. Both the stress ratings and the social interactions examples are somewhat skewed. In our experience, most distributions that result from psychology research are closer to the normal curve than are these two examples.

Kurtosis is how much the shape of a distribution differs from a normal curve in terms of whether its curve in the middle is more peaked or flat than the normal curve (DeCarlo, 1997). Kurtosis comes from the Greek word *kyrtos*, "curve." Figure 11b shows a kurtotic distribution with a more extreme peak than the normal curve. Figure 11c shows an extreme example of a kurtotic distribution, one with a very flat distribution. (A rectangular distribution would be even more extreme.)

Distributions that are more peaked or flat than a normal curve also tend to have a different shape in the tails. Those with a very peaked curve usually have more scores in the tails of the distribution than the normal curve (see Figure 11b). It is as if the normal curve got pinched in the middle and some of it went up into a sharp peak and the rest spread out into thick tails. Distributions with a flatter curve usually have fewer scores in the tails of the distribution than the normal curve (see Figure 11c). It is as if the tails and the top of the curve both got sucked in toward the middle on both sides. Although it is often easiest to identify kurtosis in terms of how peaked or flat the distribution is, the number of scores in the tails is what matters.

ceiling effect situation in which many scores pile up at the high end of a distribution (creating skewness to the left) because it is not possible to have a higher score.

normal curve specific, mathematically defined, bell-shaped frequency distribution that is symmetrical and unimodal; distributions observed in nature and in research commonly approximate it.

kurtosis extent to which a frequency distribution deviates from a normal curve in terms of whether its curve in the middle is more peaked or flat than the normal curve.

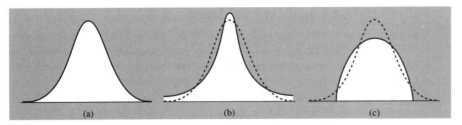

Figure 11 Examples of (a) normal, (b) heavy-tailed, and (c) light-tailed distributions. The normal distribution is shown as a dashed line in (b) and (c).

Source: Adapted from DeCarlo, T. (1997). On the meaning and use of kurtosis. *Psychological Methods, 3*, 292–307. Copyright © 1997 by the American Psychological Association. Adapted with permission. The use of APA information does not imply endorsement by APA.

How are you doing?

1. Describe the difference between a unimodal and multimodal distribution in terms of (a) a frequency graph and (b) a frequency table.
2. What does it mean to say that a distribution is skewed to the left?
3. What kind of skew is created by (a) a floor effect and (b) a ceiling effect?
4. When a distribution is described as being peaked or flat, what is it being compared to?

Answers

1. (a) A unimodal distribution has one main high point; a multimodal distribution has more than one main high point. (b) A unimodal distribution has one value with a higher frequency than all the other frequencies; a multimodal distribution has more than one value with large frequencies compared to the values around it.
2. When a distribution is skewed to the left, fewer scores have low values than have high values.
3. (a) A floor effect creates a distribution that is skewed to the right; (b) a ceiling effect creates a distribution that is skewed to the left.
4. The distribution is being compared to a normal curve.

Controversy: Misleading Graphs

The most serious controversy about frequency tables and histograms is not among psychologists, but among the general public. The misuse of these procedures by some public figures, advertisers, and the media seems to have created skepticism about the trustworthiness of statistics in general and of statistical tables and charts in particular. Everyone has heard that "statistics lie."

Of course, people can and do lie with statistics. It is just as easy to lie with words, but you may be less sure of your ability to recognize lies with numbers. In this section, we note two ways in which frequency tables and graphs can be mis-used and tell how to recognize such misuses. Much of this material is based on the classic discussion of these issues in Tufte (1983). There is also a substantial research literature on the misuse of graphs in corporate and government technical reports on an array of important scientific and social topics (e.g., Jones, 2011).

Failure to Use Equal Interval Sizes

A key requirement of a grouped frequency table or graph is that the size of the intervals be equal. If they are not equal, the table or graph can be very misleading. Tufte (1983) gives an example, shown in Figure 12, from the respectable (and usually very accurate) *New York Times*. This chart gives the impression that commissions paid to travel agents dropped dramatically in 1978. However, a close reading of the graph shows that the third bar for each airline is for only the first half of 1978. Thus, only half a year is being compared to each of the preceding full years. Assuming that the second half of 1978 was like the first half, the information in this graph actually tells us that 1978 shows an increase rather than a decrease. For example, Delta Airlines estimated a full-year 1978 figure of $72 million, much higher than 1977's $57 million.

Exaggeration of Proportions

The height of a histogram or bar graph (or frequency polygon) usually begins at 0 or the lowest value of the scale and continues to the highest value of the scale. Figure 13a shows a bar graph that does not follow this standard. The bar graph shows the mean housing price in a particular region over a 4-year period (from 2008 to 2011). By starting the vertical axis at $150,000 (instead of 0, as is customary), the graph appears to exaggerate the changes in housing price over time. Figure 13b shows the same results with the vertical axis starting at $0. You can still see the changes in housing price from year to year in Figure 13b but the figure does a better job of showing the size of those changes.

The overall proportion of a histogram or bar graph should be about 1 to 1.5 times as wide as it is tall, as in Figure 14a for the stress ratings example. But look what

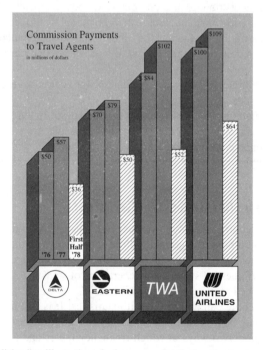

Figure 12   Misleading illustration of a frequency distribution due to unequal interval sizes.

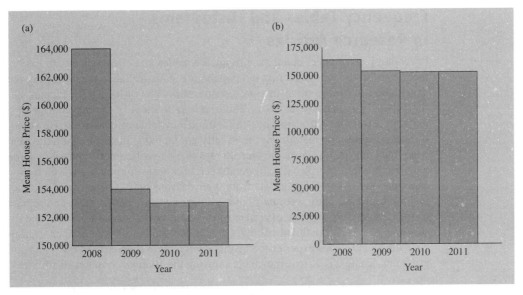

Figure 13 Misleading bar graph due to not starting at zero. The vertical axis starts at $150,000 for figure (a) compared to $0 for figure (b).

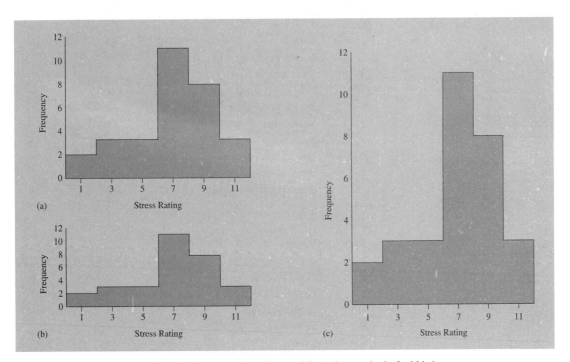

Figure 14 Histogram of students' stress ratings distorted from the standard of width 1 to 1.5 times height. (Data based on Aron et al., 1995.)

happens if we make the graph much shorter or taller, as shown in Figures 14b and 14c. The effect is like using computer software to alter a photograph of a person: the true picture is distorted. Any particular shape of the histogram is in a sense accurate. But the 1-to-1.5 proportion has been adopted to give people a standard for comparison. Changing this proportion misleads the eye.

Frequency Tables and Histograms in Research Articles

Psychology researchers mainly use frequency tables and histograms as an important first step before conducting more elaborate statistical analyses. Knowing the distribution of the variables in your research study can influence the type of statistical analysis that you conduct. The best way to identify the distribution of a variable is to look at it visually, using a frequency table or histogram. However, frequency tables and histograms are usually not included in research articles, and when they are, just because they are so rare, they are often not standard in some way. Hether and Murphy (2010) conducted an interesting study, in which they examined the health-related plots from three seasons of 10 prime-time U.S. television programs. They were particularly interested in whether male and female characters on the programs experienced different types of health issues. The researchers devised a detailed coding scheme that graduate students then used to code the health issues experienced by male and female characters in the television programs. Table 8 is a frequency table showing the 10 most common health issues

Table 8	Ten Most Common Health Issues for Male and Female Characters		
Rank	**Health Issue**	**Freq**	**% Within Sex**
Males			
1	Homicide	245	33
2	Unusual illness/disease	107	15
3	Unintentional injury	43	6
4	Motor vehicle related	37	5
5	Illegal substance abuse	30	4
6	Heart disease	28	4
7	Mental health	23	3
8	Toxic substance exposure	22	3
9	Unintentional falls	20	3
10	Prescription medication abuse	19	3
N		732	
Females			
1	Homicide	151	27
2	Unusual illness/disease	89	16
3	Pregnancy related	47	9
4	Rape/sexual assault	29	5
5	Unintentional injury	23	4
6	Mental health	22	4
7	Cancer	21	4
8	Motor vehicle related	21	4
9	Heart disease	16	3
10	Alcohol abuse	14	3
		554	

Source: Hether, H. J., & Murphy, S. T. (2010). Sex roles in health storylines on prime time television: A content analysis. *Sex Roles, 62*, 810–821. Reprinted by permission of Springer publishers.

faced by the male and female characters. The table shows, for example, that the most common health issue was homicide, which represented 33% and 27% of the health issues experienced by male and female characters, respectively.

Histograms are even more rare in research articles (except in articles *about* statistics), but they do appear occasionally. Maggi and colleagues (2007) conducted a study of age-related changes in cigarette smoking behaviors in Canadian adolescents. As shown in Figure 15, they created a histogram—from a grouped frequency table—to display their results. Their histogram shows the results from the two samples they studied (one shown in the light colored bars and the other in the dark colored bars). As you can see in the figure, less than 10% of the 10- and 11-year-olds reported that they had tried smoking, but more than half of the 16- and 17-year-olds said they had tried smoking. As already mentioned, such figures are often not standard in some way. In this example, the researchers drew the histogram with gaps between the bars, whereas it is standard not to use gaps (unless you are drawing a bar graph for a nominal variable). However, the histogram still does a good job of showing the distribution. Also, the researchers, to allow for a fair comparison of how the rate of smoking differed among adolescents of varying ages, plotted the percentage of adolescents on the vertical axis instead of the actual number of adolescents. (This was a very appropriate change from the standard in this case. Plotting the actual number of adolescents who reported smoking would have been misleading, because there were not the same number of individuals in each of the age groups.)

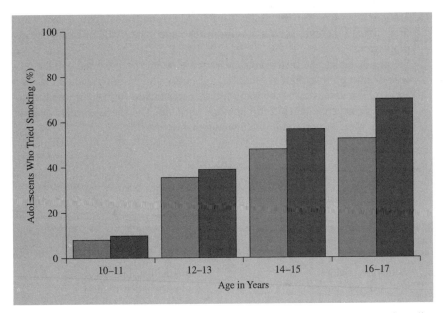

Figure 15   Change in the percentage of adolescents surveyed in the Canadian National Longitudinal Survey of Children and Youth longitudinal sample ($N = 9,667$; light blue) and cross-sectional sample ($N = 7,965$; dark blue), who had tried smoking between the ages of 10 and 17 years.

Source: Maggi, S., Hertzman, C., & Vaillancourt, T. (2007). Changes in smoking behaviors from late childhood to adolescence: Insights from the Canadian National Longitudinal Survey of Children and Youth. *Health Psychology, 26*, 232–240. Published by the American Psychological Association. Reprinted with permission.

Learning Aids

Summary

1. Psychologists use descriptive statistics to describe and summarize a group of numbers from a research study.
2. A value is a number or category; a variable is a characteristic that can have different values; a score is a particular person's value on the variable.
3. Most variables in psychology research are numeric with approximately equal intervals. However, some numeric variables are rank-ordered (the values are ranks), and some variables are not numeric at all (the values are categories).
4. A frequency table organizes the scores into a table of each of the possible values with the frequency and percentage of scores with that value.
5. When there are many different values, a grouped frequency table is useful. It is like an ordinary frequency table except that the frequencies are given for intervals that include a range of values.
6. The pattern of frequencies in a distribution can be shown visually with a histogram (or bar graph for a nominal variable), in which the height of each bar is the frequency for a particular value.
7. The general shape of a histogram can be unimodal (having a single peak), bimodal (having two peaks), multimodal (including bimodal), or rectangular (having no peak); it can be symmetrical or skewed (having a long tail) to the right or the left; and, compared to the bell-shaped normal curve, it can be kurtotic (having a peaked or flat distribution).
8. Statistical graphs for the general public are sometimes distorted in ways that mislead the eye, such as failing to use equal intervals or exaggerating proportions.
9. Frequency tables and histograms are very important for researchers in the process of interpreting their results, but are rarely shown in published research articles. When they are, they often follow nonstandard formats or involve frequencies (or percentages) for a nominal variable. The shapes of distributions (normal, skewed, and so on) are more often described.

Key Terms

statistics	nominal variable	bimodal distribution
descriptive statistics	levels of measurement	multimodal distribution
inferential statistics	discrete variable	rectangular distribution
variable	continuous variable	symmetrical distribution
values	frequency table	skewed distribution
score	interval	floor effect
numeric variable	grouped frequency table	ceiling effect
equal-interval variable	histogram	normal curve
ratio scale	frequency distribution	kurtosis
rank-order variable	unimodal distribution	

Example Worked-Out Problems

Ten first-year university students rated their interest in graduate school on a scale from 1 = *no interest at all* to 6 = *high interest.* Their scores were as follows: 2, 4, 5, 5, 1, 3, 6, 3, 6, 6.

Making a Frequency Table

See Figure 16.

Interest in Graduate School	Frequency	Percent	
1	1	10	/
2	1	10	/
3	2	20	//
4	1	10	/
5	2	20	//
6	3	30	///

2, 4, 5, 5, 1, 3, 6, 3, 6, 6

Figure 16   Answer to Example Worked-Out Problem for making a frequency table. ❶ Make a list down the page of each possible value, from lowest to highest. ❷ Go one by one through the scores, making a mark for each next to its value on your list. ❸ Make a table showing how many times each value on your list is used. ❹ Figure the percentage of scores for each value.

Making a Histogram

See Figure 17.

Interest in Graduate School	Frequency
1	1
2	1
3	2
4	1
5	2
6	3

Figure 17   Answer to Example Worked-Out Problem for making a histogram. ❶ Make a frequency table. ❷ Put the values along the bottom of the page (from left to right, from lowest to highest). ❸ Make a scale of frequencies along the left edge of the page (going from 0 at the bottom to the highest frequency for any value). ❹ Make a bar for each value (with a height for the frequency of that value).

These problems involve tabulation and making graphs. Most real-life statistics problems are done with special statistical software. Even if you have such software, do these problems by hand to ingrain the method in your mind. To learn how to use a computer to solve statistics problems like those in this chapter, refer to the Using SPSS section at the end of this chapter.

All data are fictional unless an actual citation is given.

Set I

1. A client rates her satisfaction with her vocational counselor as a 3 on a 4-point scale from 1 = *not at all satisfied* to 4 = *very satisfied*. What is the (a) variable, (b) possible values, and (c) this client's score?
2. Give the level of measurement for each of the following variables: (a) ethnic group to which a person belongs, (b) number of times a mouse makes a wrong turn in a laboratory maze, and (c) position a runner finishes in a race.
3. A particular block in a suburban neighborhood has 20 households. The number of children in these households is as follows:

$$2, 4, 2, 1, 0, 3, 6, 0, 1, 1, 2, 3, 2, 0, 1, 2, 1, 0, 2, 2$$

Make (a) a frequency table and (b) a histogram. Then (c) describe the general shape of the distribution.
4. Fifty students were asked how many hours they studied this weekend. Here are their answers:

$$11, 2, 0, 13, 5, 7, 1, 8, 12, 11, 7, 8, 9, 10, 7, 4, 6, 10, 4, 7, 8, 6, 7, 10, 7, 3,$$
$$11, 18, 2, 9, 7, 3, 8, 7, 3, 13, 9, 8, 7, 7, 10, 4, 15, 3, 5, 6, 9, 7, 10, 6$$

Make (a) a frequency table and (b) a histogram. Then (c) describe the general shape of the distribution.
5. These are the scores on a test of sensitivity to smell taken by 25 chefs attending a national conference:

$$96, 83, 59, 64, 73, 74, 80, 68, 87, 67, 64, 92, 76, 71, 68, 50, 85,$$
$$75, 81, 70, 76, 91, 69, 83, 75$$

Make (a) a frequency table and (b) histogram. (c) Make a grouped frequency table using intervals of 50–59, 60–69, 70–79, 80–89, and 90–99. Based on the grouped frequency table, (d) make a histogram and (e) describe the general shape of the distribution.
6. The following data are the number of minutes it took each of a group of 34 10-year-olds to do a series of abstract puzzles:

$$24, 83, 36, 22, 81, 39, 60, 62, 38, 66, 38, 36, 45, 20, 20, 67, 41, 87,$$
$$41, 82, 35, 82, 28, 80, 80, 68, 40, 27, 43, 80, 31, 89, 83, 24$$

Make (a) a frequency table and (b) a grouped frequency table using intervals of 20–29, 30–39, 40–49, 50–59, 60–69, 70–79, and 80–89. Based on the grouped frequency table, (c) make a histogram and (d) describe the general shape of the distribution.

7. Describe the shapes of the three distributions illustrated.

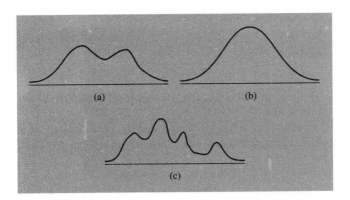

8. Make up and draw an example of each of the following distributions: (a) symmetrical, (b) rectangular, and (c) skewed to the right.
9. Explain to a person who has never had a course in statistics what is meant by (a) a symmetrical unimodal distribution and (b) a negatively skewed unimodal distribution. (Be sure to include in your first answer an explanation of what *distribution* means.)

Set II

10. A participant in a cognitive psychology study is given 50 words to remember and later asked to recall as many of the words as she can. She recalls 17 words. What is the (a) variable, (b) possible values, and (c) score?

11. Explain and give an example for each of the following types of variables: (a) equal-interval, (b) rank-order, (c) nominal, (d) ratio scale, (e) continuous; (f) discrete.

12. An organizational psychologist asks 20 employees in a company to rate their job satisfaction on a 5-point scale from 1 = *very unsatisfied* to 5 = *very satisfied*. The ratings are as follows:

$$3, 2, 3, 4, 1, 3, 3, 4, 5, 2, 3, 5, 2, 3, 3, 4, 1, 3, 2, 4$$

Make (a) a frequency table and (b) a histogram. Then (c) describe the general shape of the distribution.

13. A social psychologist asked 15 college students how many times they "fell in love" before they were 11 years old. The numbers of times were as follows:

$$2, 0, 6, 0, 3, 1, 0, 4, 9, 0, 5, 6, 1, 0, 2$$

Make (a) a frequency table and (b) a histogram. Then (c) describe the general shape of the distribution.

14. Following are the speeds of 40 cars clocked by radar on a particular road in a 35-mph zone on a particular afternoon:

30, 36, 42, 36, 30, 52, 36, 34, 36, 33, 30, 32, 35, 32, 37, 34, 36, 31, 35, 20, 24, 46, 23, 31, 32, 45, 34, 37, 28, 40, 34, 38, 40, 52, 31, 33, 15, 27, 36, 40

Make (a) a grouped frequency table and (b) a histogram based on the grouped frequency table. Then (c) describe the general shape of the distribution.

15. Here are the number of holiday gifts purchased by 25 families randomly interviewed at a local mall at the end of the holiday season:

22, 18, 22, 26, 19, 14, 23, 27, 2, 18, 28, 28, 11, 16, 34, 28, 13, 21, 32, 17, 6, 29, 23, 22, 19

Make (a) a frequency table and (b) a grouped frequency table using intervals of 0–4, 5–9, 10–14, 15–19, 20–24, 25–29, and 30–34. Based on the grouped frequency table, (c) make a histogram and (d) describe the general shape of the distribution.

16. Pick a book and a page number of your choice. (Select a page with at least 30 lines; *do not pick a textbook or any book with tables or illustrations.*) Make a list of the number of words on each line; use that list as your group of scores. Make (a) a frequency table and (b) a histogram. Then (c) describe the general shape of the distribution. (Be sure to give the name, author, publisher, and year of the book you used, along with the page number, with your answer.)

17. Explain to a person who has never taken a course in statistics the meaning of a grouped frequency table.

18. Make up and draw an example of each of the following distributions: (a) bimodal, (b) approximately rectangular, and (c) skewed to the right. Do not use an example given in class.

19. Find an example in a newspaper, magazine, or news website of a graph that misleads by failing to use equal interval sizes or by exaggerating proportions.

20. Raskauskas and Stoltz (2007) asked a group of 84 adolescents about their involvement in traditional and electronic bullying. The researchers defined electronic bullying as "... a means of bullying in which peers use electronics [such as text messages, emails, and defaming Web sites] to taunt, threaten,

Table 9	Incidence of Traditional and Electronic Bullying and Victimization ($N = 84$)	
Form of Bullying	**N**	**%**
Electronic victims	41	48.8
Text-message victim	27	32.1
Internet victim (Web sites, chatrooms)	13	15.5
Picture-phone victim	8	9.5
Traditional victims	60	71.4
Physical victim	38	45.2
Teasing victim	50	59.5
Rumors victim	32	38.6
Exclusion victim	30	50.0
Electronic bullies	18	21.4
Text-message bully	18	21.4
Internet bully	11	13.1
Traditional bullies	54	64.3
Physical bully	29	34.5
Teasing bully	38	45.2
Rumor bully	22	26.2
Exclusion bully	35	41.7

Source: Raskauskas, J., & Stoltz, A. D. (2007). Involvement in traditional and electronic bullying among adolescents. *Developmental Psychology, 43*, 564–575. Published by the American Psychological Association. Reprinted with permission.

harass, and/or intimidate a peer" (p. 565). Table 9 is a frequency table showing the adolescents' reported incidence of being victims or perpetrators of traditional and electronic bullying. (a) Using this table as an example, explain the idea of a frequency table to a person who has never had a course in statistics. (b) Explain the general meaning of the pattern of results.

Using SPSS

The ☞ in the following steps indicates a mouse click. (We used SPSS version 19.0 to carry out these analyses. The steps and output may be slightly different for other versions of SPSS.)

Creating a Frequency Table

❶ Enter the scores from your distribution in one column of the data window.

❷ ☞ *Analyze.*

❸ ☞ *Descriptive statistics.*

❹ ☞ *Frequencies.*

❺ ☞ the variable you want to make a frequency table of and then ☞ the arrow.

❻ ☞ *OK.*

Practice the preceding steps by creating a frequency table for the social interactions example in this chapter (the scores are also listed). After Step ❺, your screen should look like Figure 18. Your output window (which appears after you ☞ *OK* in Step ❻) should look like Figure 19. As you will see, SPSS automatically produces a column with the cumulative percentage (or percentile) for each value. (Note that it is possible to create grouped frequency tables in SPSS, but since it is not a straightforward process, we do not cover it here.)

Figure 18   SPSS data window and frequencies window for the social interactions example. (Data from McLaughlin-Volpe et al., 2001.)

Creating a Histogram

❶ Enter the scores from your distribution in one column of the data window.

❷ ✍ *Analyze.*

❸ ✍ *Descriptive statistics.*

❹ ✍ *Frequencies.*

❺ ✍ the variable you want to make a histogram of and then ✍ the arrow.

❻ ✍ *Charts,* ✍ *Histograms,* ✍ *Continue.*

❼ Optional: To instruct SPSS *not* to produce a frequency table, ✍ the box labeled *Display frequency tables* (this *un*checks the box).

❽ ✍ *OK.*

Practice these steps by creating a histogram for the social interactions example in this chapter (the scores are also listed). Your output window should look like Figure 20. Notice that SPSS automatically creates a histogram based on a grouped frequency table. (Should you wish, you can change the number of intervals or the

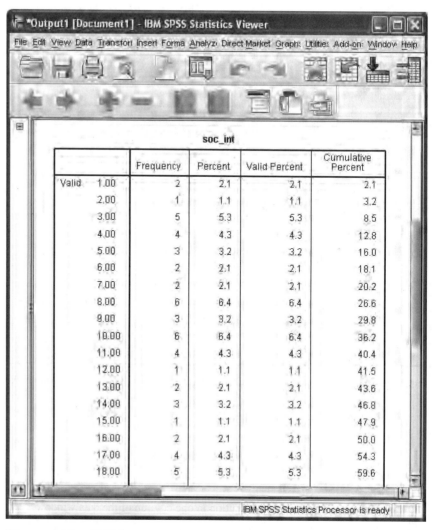

Figure 19   SPSS frequency table for the social interactions example. (Data from McLaughlin-Volpe et al., 2001.)

interval size for the histogram by doing the following: Place your mouse cursor on the histogram and double ✑ to bring up a Chart Editor window; place your mouse cursor over one of the bars in the histogram and double ✑ to bring up a Properties window; ✑ *Custom;* ✑ *Number of intervals* or ✑ *Interval Width*; then enter the number of intervals or the interval size you want; ✑ *Apply.* If you want a nongrouped histogram, type in "1" for the interval width.)

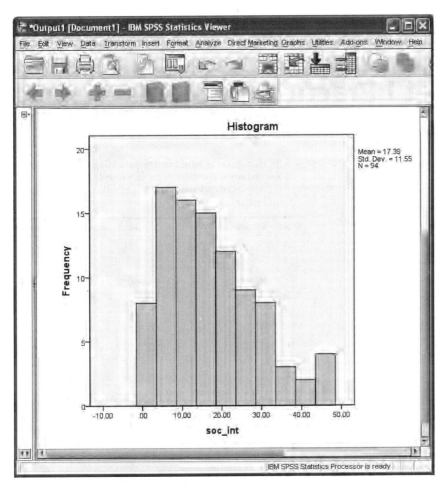

Figure 20 SPSS histogram for the social interactions example. (Data from McLaughlin-Volpe et al., 2001.)

Chapter Note

1. Most research articles follow the procedure we recommend here: going from lowest at the top to highest at the bottom. However, some statistics authorities recommend going from highest at the top to lowest at the bottom.

Answers to Set I Practice Problems

Chapter 1

1. (a) Satisfaction with the vocational counselor; (b) 1, 2, 3, or 4; (c) 3.
2. (a) Nominal (or categorical); (b) numeric (or quantitative)—more precisely, equal interval; (c) numeric (or quantitative)—more precisely, rank order (or ordinal).
3. (a) Frequency table:

Number of Children	Frequency	Percent
0	4	20
1	5	25
2	7	35
3	2	10
4	1	5
5	0	0
6	1	5

(b) Histogram:

(c) Unimodal, skewed to the right.
4. (a) Frequency table:

Hours	Frequency	Percent	Hours	Frequency	Percent
0	1	2	10	5	10
1	1	2	11	3	6
2	2	4	12	1	2
3	4	8	13	2	4
4	3	6	14	0	0
5	2	4	15	1	2
6	4	8	16	0	0
7	11	22	17	0	0
8	5	10	18	1	2
9	4	8			

(b) Histogram is based on the preceding frequency table. See answer to question 3b for an example.
(c) Approximately unimodal, slightly skewed to the right.
5. (a) Frequency table:

Score	Frequency	Percent	Score	Frequency	Percent
50	1	4	74	1	4
51	0	0	75	2	8
52	0	0	76	2	8
53	0	0	77	0	0
54	0	0	78	0	0
55	0	0	79	0	0
56	0	0	80	1	4
57	0	0	81	1	4
58	0	0	82	0	0
59	1	4	83	2	8
60	0	0	84	0	0
61	0	0	85	1	4
62	0	0	86	0	0
63	0	0	87	1	4
64	2	8	88	0	0
65	0	0	89	0	0
66	0	0	90	0	0
67	1	4	91	1	4
68	2	8	92	1	4
69	1	4	93	0	0
70	1	4	94	0	0
71	1	4	95	0	0
72	0	0	96	1	4
73	1	4			

(b) Based on the preceding frequency table. See answer to question 3b for an example.
(c) Grouped frequency table:

Interval	Frequency	Percent
50–59	2	8
60–69	6	24
70–79	8	32
80–89	6	24
90–99	3	12

(d) Based on frequency table in (c) above. See answer to question 3b for an example.
(e) Unimodal, approximately symmetrical (slightly skewed to the left).
6. (a) Similar to question 5a.
(b) Grouped frequency table:

Interval	Frequency	Percent
20–29	7	20.6
30–39	7	20.6
40–49	5	14.7
50–59	0	0.0
60–69	5	14.7
70–79	0	0.0
80–89	10	29.4

(c) Histogram:

(d) Roughly rectangular.

7. (a) Bimodal; (b) approximately normal (or unimodal or symmetrical); (c) multimodal.
8. (a) Any distribution that is symmetrical (that is, the pattern of frequencies on the left and right side of the distribution are mirror images of each other); (b) any distribution in which all values have approximately the same frequency; (c) any distribution in which the scores are piled up on the left side of the distribution and are spread out on the right side of the distribution.
9. (a) A distribution is the way a group of numbers is spread out over the possible values the numbers can have. You can describe such a distribution with a graph, called a histogram—a kind of bar graph with one bar for each possible value with one unit of height for each time its particular value occurs. In a histogram, a symmetrical distribution has a symmetrical shape (the right and left halves are mirror images). A unimodal distribution is one in which this graph has a single high point, with the other values gradually decreasing around it.
(b) A negatively skewed unimodal distribution has a single high point, is not symmetrical, and its tail—the long, low side—extends to the left (where the negative scores go on the graph).

Chapter 2

Central Tendency and Variability

Chapter 2

Central Tendency and Variability

Chapter Outline

- ❖ Central Tendency
- ❖ Variability
- ❖ Controversy: The Tyranny of the Mean
- ❖ Central Tendency and Variability in Research Articles

- ❖ Learning Aids
  - ❖ Summary
  - ❖ Key Terms
  - ❖ Example Worked-Out Problems
  - ❖ Practice Problems
  - ❖ Using SPSS
- ❖ Chapter Notes

Several recent studies have asked students to record their dreams each morning for a week or two (e.g., Mikulincer, Shaver, & Avihou-Kanza, 2011). In a typical study, the total number of dreams per week for 10 students might be as follows: 7, 8, 8, 7, 3, 1, 6, 9, 3, 8. How might you make this group of scores more understandable?

One way to gain that understanding is to use the tables and graphs. Another way, which you will learn in this chapter, is to use numbers to describe and summarize a group of scores such as this.

First, you can describe a group of scores in terms of a *representative* (or *typical*) *value,* such as an average. A representative value gives the *central tendency* of a group of scores. A representative value is a simple way, with a single number, to describe a group of scores (and there may be hundreds—or even thousands—of scores). The main representative value we consider is the *mean.* Next, we focus on ways of describing how the numbers are spread out in a group of scores. In other words, we consider the amount of variation, or *variability,* among the scores. The two measures of variability you will learn about are called the *variance* and *standard deviation.*

In this chapter, you will use statistical formulas. Such formulas are not here to confuse you. Hopefully, you will come to see that they actually simplify things and provide a very straightforward, concise way of describing statistical procedures. To help you grasp what such formulas mean in words, whenever we present formulas, we always also give the "translation" in ordinary English.

Central Tendency

The **central tendency** of a group of scores (a distribution) refers to the middle of the group of scores. You will learn about three measures of central tendency: *mean, mode,* and *median.* Each measure of central tendency uses its own method to come up with a single number describing the middle of a group of scores. We start with the mean, the most commonly used measure of central tendency. Understanding the mean is also an important foundation for much of what you learn later.

The Mean

Usually the best measure of central tendency is the ordinary average, the sum of all the scores divided by the number of scores. In statistics, this is called the **mean**. The average, or mean, of a group of scores is a representative value. Consider again the example from the start of the chapter, in which 10 students recorded their total number of dreams during the last weeks. The mean of the 10 scores (7, 8, 8, 7, 3, 1, 6, 9, 3, 8) is 6 (the sum of 60 dreams divided by 10 students). That is, on the average, each student had 6 dreams in the past week. The information for the 10 students is thus summarized by the single number 6.

You can think of the mean as a kind of balancing point for the distribution of scores. Try it by visualizing a board balanced over a log, like a rudimentary teeter-totter. Imagine piles of blocks set along the board according to their values, one for each score in the distribution (like a histogram made of blocks). The mean is the point on the board where the weight of the blocks on one side balances exactly with the weight on the other side. Figure 1 shows this for the number of dreams for the 10 students.

Mathematically, you can think of the mean as the point at which the total distance to all the scores above that point equals the total distance to all the scores below that point. Let's first figure the total distance from the mean to all the scores above the mean for the dreams example shown in Figure 1. There are two scores of 7, each of which is 1 unit above 6 (the mean). There are three scores of 8, each of which is 2 units above 6. And, there is one score of 9, which is 3 units above 6. This gives a total distance of 11 units $(1 + 1 + 2 + 2 + 2 + 3)$ from the mean to all the scores above the mean. Now, let's look at the scores below the mean. There are two scores of 3, each of which is 3 units below 6 (the mean). And there is one score of 1, which is 5 units below 6. This gives a total distance of 11 units $(3 + 3 + 5)$ from the mean to all of the scores below the mean. Thus, you can see that the total distance from the mean to the scores above the mean is the same as the total distance from the mean to the scores below the mean. The scores above the mean balance out the scores below the mean (and vice-versa).

central tendency   typical or most representative value of a group of scores.

mean   arithmetic average of a group of scores; sum of the scores divided by the number of scores.

$M = 6$

1   2   3   4   5   6   7   8   9

Figure 1   Mean of the distribution of the number of dreams during a week for 10 students, illustrated using blocks on a board balanced on a log.

Figure 2 Means of various distributions illustrated with blocks on a board balanced on a log.

Some other examples are shown in Figure 2. Notice that there doesn't have to be a block right at the balance point. That is, the mean doesn't have to be a score actually in the distribution. The mean is the average of the scores, the balance point. The mean can be a decimal number, even if all the scores in the distribution have to be whole numbers (a mean of 2.30 children, for example). For each distribution in Figure 2, the total distance from the mean to the scores above the mean is the same as the total distance from the mean to the scores below the mean. (By the way, this analogy to blocks on a board, in reality, works out precisely only if the board has no weight of its own.)

Formula for the Mean and Statistical Symbols

The rule for figuring the mean is to add up all the scores and divide by the number of scores. Here is how this rule is written as a formula:

> The mean is the sum of the scores divided by the number of scores.

$$M = \frac{\sum X}{N} \tag{1}$$

M is a symbol for the mean. An alternative symbol, $\overline{X}$ ("X-bar"), is sometimes used. However, M is almost always used in published research articles, as recommended by the style guidelines of the American Psychological Association (2009). You will see $\overline{X}$ used mostly in advanced statistics books and in articles *about* statistics. In fact, there is not a standard agreement for many of the symbols used in statistics. (In this text we generally use the symbols most widely found in psychology research articles.)

$\sum$, the capital Greek letter sigma, is the symbol for "sum of." It means "add up all the numbers for whatever follows." It is the most common special arithmetic symbol used in statistics.

X stands for the scores in the distribution of the variable X. We could have picked any letter. However, if there is only one variable, it is usually called X.

$\sum X$ is "the sum of X." This tells you to add up all the scores in the distribution of the variable X. Suppose X is the number of dreams of our 10 students: $\sum X$ is $7 + 8 + 8 + 7 + 3 + 1 + 6 + 9 + 3 + 8$, which is 60.

TIP FOR SUCCESS

Think of each formula as a statistical recipe, with statistical symbols as ingredients. Before you use each formula, be sure you know what each symbol stands for. Then carefully follow the formula to come up with the end result.

M mean.

$\sum$ sum of; add up all the scores following this symbol.

X scores in the distribution of the variable *X*.

N stands for number—the number of scores in a distribution. In our example, there are 10 scores. Thus, N equals 10.[1]

Overall, the formula says to divide the sum of all the scores in the distribution of the variable X by the total number of scores, N. In the dreams example, this means you divide 60 by 10. Put in terms of the formula,

$$M = \frac{\Sigma X}{N} = \frac{60}{10} = 6$$

Additional Examples of Figuring the Mean

Consider the following example: The stress ratings of the 30 students in the first week of their statistics class (based on Aron et al., 1995) were:

8, 7, 4, 10, 8, 6, 8, 9, 9, 7, 3, 7, 6, 5, 0, 9, 10, 7, 7, 3, 6, 7, 5, 2, 1, 6, 7, 10, 8, 8

You can now summarize all this information as a single number by figuring the mean. Figure the mean by adding up all the stress ratings and dividing by the number of stress ratings. That is, you add up the 30 stress ratings: $8 + 7 + 4 + 10 + 8 + 6 + 8 + 9 + 9 + 7 + 3 + 7 + 6 + 5 + 0 + 9 + 10 + 7 + 7 + 3 + 6 + 7 + 5 + 2 + 1 + 6 + 7 + 10 + 8 + 8$, for a total of 193. Then you divide this total by the number of scores, 30. In terms of the formula,

$$M = \frac{\Sigma X}{N} = \frac{193}{30} = 6.43$$

This tells you that the average stress rating was 6.43 (after rounding off). This is clearly higher than the middle of the 0–10 scale. You can also see this on a graph. Think again of the histogram as a pile of blocks on a board and the mean of 6.43 as the point where the board balances on the fulcrum (see Figure 3). This single representative value simplifies the information in the 30 stress scores.

N number of scores in a distribution.

Figure 3   Analogy of blocks on a board balanced on a fulcrum showing the means for 30 statistics students' ratings of their stress level. (Data based on Aron et al., 1995.)

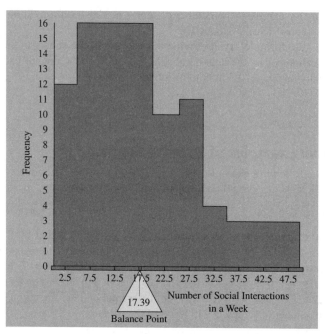

Figure 4   Analogy of blocks on a board balanced on a fulcrum illustrating the mean for number of social interactions during a week for 94 college students. (Data from McLaughlin-Volpe et al., 2001.)

Similarly, consider example of students' social interactions (McLaughlin-Volpe et al., 2001). The actual number of interactions over a week for the 94 students are as follows: 48, 15, 33, 3, 21, 19, 17, 16, 44, 25, 30, 3, 5, 9, 35, 32, 26, 13, 14, 14, 47, 47, 18, 11, 5, 19, 24, 17, 6, 25, 8, 18, 29, 1, 18, 22, 3, 22, 29, 2, 6, 10, 29, 10, 29, 21, 38, 41, 16, 17, 8, 40, 8, 10, 18, 7, 4, 4, 8, 11, 3, 23, 10, 19, 21, 13, 12, 10, 4, 17, 11, 21, 9, 8, 7, 5, 3, 22, 14, 25, 4, 11, 10, 18, 1, 28, 27, 19, 24, 35, 9, 30, 8, 26. We can now take those same 94 scores, add them up, and divide by 94 to figure the mean:

$$M = \frac{\sum X}{N} = \frac{1{,}635}{94} = 17.39$$

This tells us that during this week these students had an average of 17.39 social interactions. Figure 4 shows the mean of 17.39 as the balance point for the 94 social interaction scores.

Steps for Figuring the Mean

Figure the mean in two steps.

➊ **Add up all the scores.** That is, figure $\sum X$.
➋ **Divide this sum by the number of scores.** That is, divide $\sum X$ by N.

The Mode

The **mode** is another measure of central tendency. The mode is the most common single value in a distribution. In our dreams example, the mode is 8. This is because there are three students with 8 dreams and no other particular number of dreams

mode   value with the greatest frequency in a distribution.

Figure 5 Mode as the high point in a distribution's histogram, using the example of the number of dreams during a week for 10 students.

with as many students. Another way to think of the mode is that it is the particular value with the largest frequency in a frequency table, the high point or peak of a distribution's histogram (as shown in Figure 5).

In a perfectly symmetrical unimodal distribution, the mode is the same as the mean. However, what happens when the mean and the mode are not the same? In that situation, the mode is usually not a very good way of describing the central tendency of the scores in the distribution. In fact, sometimes researchers compare the mode to the mean to show that the distribution is *not* perfectly symmetrical. Also, the mode can be a particularly poor representative value because it does not reflect many aspects of the distribution. For example, you can change some of the scores in a distribution without affecting the mode—but this is not true of the mean, which is affected by any changes in the scores in the distribution (see Figure 6).

Figure 6 Effect on the mean and on the mode of changing some scores, using the example of the number of dreams during a week for 10 students.

Figure 7   The median is the middle score when scores are lined up from lowest to highest, using the example of the number of dreams during a week for 10 students.

On the other hand, the mode *is* the usual way of describing the central tendency for a nominal variable. For example, if you know the religions of a particular group of people, the mode tells you for this group which religion has the most people in it. However, when it comes to figuring central tendency for numerical variables in psychology research, the mode is rarely used.

The Median

Another alternative to the mean is the **median**. If you line up all the scores from lowest to highest, the middle score is the median. Figure 7 shows the scores for the number of dreams lined up from lowest to highest. In this example, the fifth and sixth scores (the two middle ones) are both 7s. Either way, the median is 7.

When you have an even number of scores, the median can be between two different scores. In that situation, the median is the average (the mean) of those two scores.

TIP FOR SUCCESS

When figuring the median, remember that the first step is to line up the scores from lowest to highest. Forgetting to do this is the most common mistake students make when figuring the median.

Steps for Finding the Median

Finding the median takes three steps.

➊ **Line up all the scores from lowest to highest.**
➋ **Figure how many scores there are to the middle score by adding 1 to the number of scores and dividing by 2.** For example, with 29 scores, adding 1 and dividing by 2 gives you 15. The 15th score is the middle score. If there are 50 scores, adding 1 and dividing by 2 gives you 25.5. Because there are no half scores, the 25th and 26th scores (the scores on either side of 25.5) are the middle scores.
➌ **Count up to the middle score or scores.** If you have one middle score, this is the median. If you have two middle scores, the median is the average (the mean) of these two scores.

Comparing the Mean, Mode, and Median

Sometimes, the median is better than the mean (or mode) as a representative value for a group of scores. This happens when a few extreme scores would strongly affect the mean but would not affect the median. Reaction time scores are a common example in psychology research. Suppose you are asked to press a key as quickly as possible when a picture of a particular political candidate is shown on the computer screen. On five showings of the candidate, your times (in seconds) to respond are .74, .86, 2.32, .79, and .81. The mean of these five scores is 1.1040: that is, $(\sum X)/N = 5.52/5 = 1.1040$. However, this mean is very much influenced by the one very long time (2.32 seconds). (Perhaps you were distracted just when the candidate's picture was shown.) The median is much less affected by the extreme score. The median of these five scores is .81—a value that is much more representative of most of the scores. Thus, using the median deemphasizes the one extreme time, which is probably appropriate. An extreme score like this is called an **outlier**. In this example, the outlier was much higher than the other scores, but in other cases an outlier may be much lower than the other scores in the distribution.

median   middle score when all the scores in a distribution are arranged from lowest to highest.

outlier   score with an extreme value (very high or very low) in relation to the other scores in the distribution.

The importance of whether you use the mean, mode, or median can be seen in a controversy among psychologists studying the evolutionary basis of human mate choice. One set of theorists (e.g., Buss & Schmitt, 1993) argued that over their lives, men should prefer to have many partners, but women should prefer to have just one reliable partner. This is because a woman can have only a small number of children in a lifetime and her genes are most likely to survive if those few children are well taken care of. Men, however, can have a great many children in a lifetime. Therefore, according to the theory, a shotgun approach is best for men, because their genes are most likely to survive if they have a great many partners. Consistent with this assumption, evolutionary psychologists have found that men report wanting far more partners than do women.

Other theorists (e.g., Miller & Fishkin, 1997), however, have questioned this view. They argue that women and men should prefer about the same number of partners. This is because individuals with a basic predisposition to seek a strong intimate bond are most likely to survive infancy. This desire for strong bonds, they argue, remains in adulthood. These theorists also asked women and men how many partners they wanted. They found the same result as the previous researchers when using the mean: men wanted an average of 64.3 partners, women an average of 2.8 partners. However, the picture looks drastically different if you look at the median or mode (see Table 1). Figure 8, taken directly from their article, shows why. Most women and most men want

Table 1 Responses of 106 Men and 160 Women to the Question, "How many partners would you ideally desire in the next 30 years?"

	Mean	Median	Mode
Women	2.8	1	1
Men	64.3	1	1

Source: Data from Miller & Fishkin (1997).

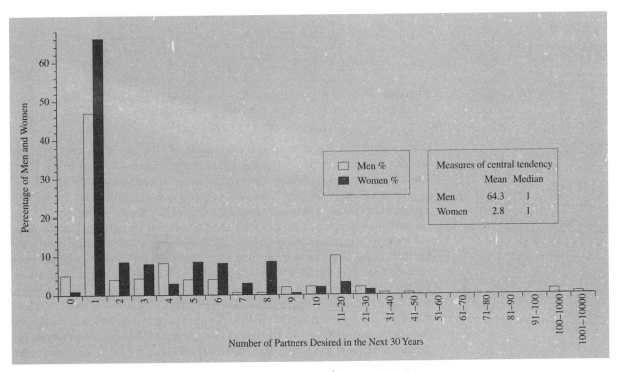

Figure 8 Distributions for men and women for the ideal number of partners desired over 30 years. *Note:* To include all the data, we collapsed across categories farther out on the tail of these distributions. If every category represented a single number, it would be more apparent that the tail is very flat and that distributions are even more skewed than is apparent here.

Source: Miller, L. C., & Fishkin, S. A. (1997). On the dynamics of human bonding and reproductive success: Seeking windows on the adapted-for-human-environmental interface. In J. Simpson & D. T. Kenrick (Eds.), *Evolutionary social psychology* (pp. 197–235). Mahwah, NJ: Erlbaum.

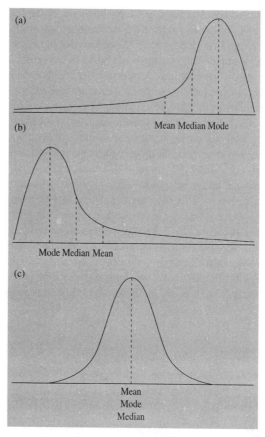

Figure 9 Locations of the mean, mode, and median on (a) a distribution skewed to the left, (b) a distribution skewed to the right, and (c) a normal curve.

just one partner. A few want more, some many more. The big difference is that there are a lot more men in the small group that want many more than one partner. These results have also been replicated in subsequent studies (Pedersen et al., 2002).

So, which theory is right? You could argue either way from these results. (For a more recent discussion of this controversy regarding the theoretical and statistical issues, see Smith & Konik, 2011.) The point is that focusing just on the mean can clearly misrepresent the reality of the distribution. As this example shows, the median is most likely to be used when a few extreme scores would make the mean unrepresentative of the main body of scores. Figure 9 illustrates this point, by showing the relative location of the mean, mode, and median for three types of distribution. The distribution in Figure 9a is skewed to the left (negatively skewed); the long tail of the distribution points to the left. The mode in this distribution is the highest point of the distribution, which is on the far right hand side of the distribution. The median is the point at which half of the scores are above that point and half are below. As you can see, for that to happen, the median must be a lower value than the mode. Finally, the mean is strongly influenced by the very low scores in the long tail of the distribution and is thus a lower value than the median. Figure 9b shows the location of the mean, mode, and median for a distribution that is skewed to the right (positively skewed). In this case, the mean is a higher value than either the mode or median because the mean is strongly influenced by the very *high* scores in the long tail of the distribution. Again, the mode is the highest point of the distribution, and

Table 2 Summary of Measures of Central Tendency

Measure	Definition	When Used
Mean	Sum of the scores divided by the number of scores	• With equal-interval variables • Very commonly used in psychology research
Mode	Value with the greatest frequency in a distribution	• With nominal variables • Rarely used in psychology research
Median	Middle score when all the scores in a distribution are arranged from lowest to highest	• With rank-ordered variables • When a distribution has one or more outliers • Rarely used in psychology research

the median is between the mode and the mean. In Figures 9a and 9b, the mean is not a good representative value of the scores, because it is overly influenced by the extreme scores.

Figure 9c shows a normal curve. As for any distribution, the mode is the highest point in the distribution. For a normal curve, the highest point falls exactly at the midpoint of the distribution. This midpoint is the median value, since half of the scores in the distribution are below that point and half are above it. The mean also falls at the same point because the normal curve is symmetrical about the midpoint, and every score in the left hand side of the curve has a matching score on the right hand side. So, for a perfect normal curve, the mean, mode, and median are always the same value.

In some situations, psychologists use the median as part of more complex statistical methods. Also, the median is the usual way of describing the central tendency for a rank-order variable. Otherwise, unless there are extreme scores, psychologists almost always use the mean as the representative value of a group of scores. In fact, as you will learn, the mean is a fundamental building block for most other statistical techniques.

A summary of the mean, mode, and median as measures of central tendency is shown in Table 2.

How are you doing?

1. Name and define three measures of central tendency.
2. Write the formula for the mean and define each of the symbols.
3. Figure the mean of the following scores: 2, 3, 3, 6, and 6.
4. For the following scores, find (a) the mean, (b) the mode, and (c) the median: 5, 3, 2, 13, 2. (d) Why is the mean different from the median?

Answers

1. The mean is the ordinary average, the sum of the scores divided by the number of scores. The mode is the most frequent score in a distribution. The median is the middle score; that is, if you line the scores up from lowest to highest, it is the halfway score.
2. The formula for the mean is $M = (\Sigma X)/N$. M is the mean; Σ is the symbol for "sum of"—add up all the scores that follow; X is the variable whose scores you are adding up; N is the number of scores.
3. $M = (\Sigma X)/N = (2 + 3 + 3 + 6 + 6)/5 = 4$.
4. (a) The mean is 5; (b) the mode is 2; (c) the median is 3; (d) The mean is different from the median because the extreme score (13) makes the mean higher than the median.

Variability

Researchers also want to know how spread out the scores are in a distribution. This shows the amount of variability in the distribution. For example, suppose you were asked, "How old are the students in your statistics class?" At a city-based university with many returning and part-time students, the mean age might be 29 years. You could answer, "The average age of the students in my class is 29." However, this would not tell the whole story. You could have a mean of 29 because every student in the class was exactly 29 years old. If this is the case, the scores in the distribution are not spread out at all. In other words, there is no variation, or *variability*, among the scores. You could also have a mean of 29 because exactly half the class members were 19 and the other half 39. In this situation, the distribution is much more spread out; there is considerable variability among the scores in the distribution.

You can think of the variability of a distribution as the amount of spread of the scores around the mean. In other words, how close or far from the mean are the scores in a distribution? If the scores are mostly quite close to the mean, then the distribution has less variability than if the scores are further from the mean. Distributions with the same mean can have very different amounts of spread around the mean; Figure 10a shows histograms for three different frequency distributions with the same mean but different amounts of spread around the mean. A real-life example of this is shown in Figure 11, which shows the distributions of the housing prices in two

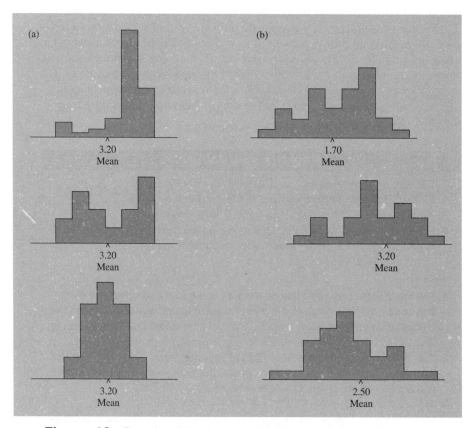

Figure 10 Examples of distributions with (a) the same mean but different amounts of spread, and (b) different means but the same amount of spread.

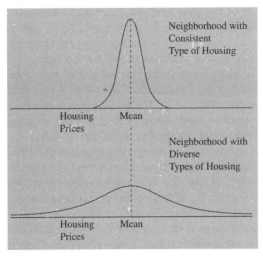

Figure 11 Example of two distributions with the same mean but different amounts of spread: housing prices for a neighborhood with diverse types of housing and for a neighborhood with a consistent type of housing.

neighborhoods: one with diverse housing types and the other with a consistent type of housing. As with Figure 10a, the mean housing price is the same in each neighborhood. However, the distribution for the neighborhood with diverse housing types is much more spread out around the mean than the distribution for the neighborhood that has a consistent type of housing. This tells you that there is much greater variability in the prices of housing in the neighborhood with diverse types of housing than in the neighborhood with a consistent housing type. Also, distributions with different means can have the same amount of spread around the mean. Figure 10b shows three different distributions with different means but the same amount of spread. So, although the mean provides a representative value of a group of scores, it doesn't tell you about the variability of the scores. You will now learn about two measures of the variability of a group of scores: the *variance* and *standard deviation.*[2]

The Variance

The **variance** of a group of scores is one kind of number that tells you how spread out the scores are around the mean. To be precise, the variance is the average of each score's squared difference from the mean.

Here are the four steps to figure the variance:

❶ **Subtract the mean from each score.** This gives each score's **deviation score**, which is how far away the score is from the mean.
❷ **Square each of these deviation scores** (multiply each by itself). This gives each score's **squared deviation score**.
❸ **Add up the squared deviation scores.** This total is called the **sum of squared deviations**.
❹ **Divide the sum of squared deviations by the number of scores.** This gives the average (the mean) of the squared deviations, called the variance.

Suppose one distribution is more spread out than another. The more spread-out distribution has a larger variance because being spread out makes the deviation scores bigger. If the deviation scores are bigger, the squared deviation scores and the average of the squared deviation scores (the variance) are also bigger.

variance   measure of how spread out a set of scores are; average of the squared deviations from the mean.

deviation score   score minus the mean.

squared deviation score   square of the difference between a score and the mean.

sum of squared deviations   total of each score's squared difference from the mean.

In the example of the class in which everyone was exactly 29 years old, the variance would be exactly 0. That is, there would be no variance (which makes sense, because there is no variability among the ages). (In terms of the numbers, each person's deviation score would be $29 - 29 = 0$; 0 squared is 0. The average of a bunch of zeros is 0.) By contrast, the class of half 19-year-olds and half 39-year-olds would have a rather large variance of 100. (The 19-year-olds would each have deviation scores of $19 - 29 = -10$. The 39-year-olds would have deviation scores of $39 - 29 = 10$. All the squared deviation scores, which are either -10 squared or 10 squared, come out to 100. The average of all 100s is 100.)

The variance is extremely important in many statistical procedures you will learn about later. However, the variance is rarely used as a *descriptive statistic*. This is because the variance is based on *squared* deviation scores, which do not give a very easy-to-understand sense of how spread out the actual, nonsquared scores are. For example, a class with a variance of 100 clearly has a more spread-out distribution than one whose variance is 10. However, the number 100 does not give an obvious insight into the actual variation among the ages, none of which is anywhere near 100 years away from the others.[3]

The Standard Deviation

The most widely used number to *describe* the spread of a group of scores is the **standard deviation**. The standard deviation is simply the square root of the variance. There are two steps in figuring the standard deviation.

❶ **Figure the variance.**
❷ **Take the square root.** The standard deviation is the *positive* square root of the variance. (Any number has both a positive and a negative square root. For example, the square root of 9 is both $+3$ and -3. But for the standard deviation we always use the positive square root.)

If the variance of a group of scores is 100, the standard deviation is 10. If the variance is 9, the standard deviation is 3.

The variance is about squared deviations from the mean. Therefore, its square root, the standard deviation, is about direct, ordinary, not-squared deviations from the mean. *Roughly speaking, the standard deviation is the average amount that scores differ from the mean.* For example, consider a class where the ages have a standard deviation of 10 years. This tells you that the ages are spread out, on the average, about 10 years in each direction from the mean. Knowing the standard deviation gives you a general sense of the degree of spread.[4]

The standard deviation does not, however, perfectly describe the shape of the distribution. For example, suppose the distribution of the number of children in families in a particular country has a mean of 4 and standard deviation of 1. Figure 12 shows several possibilities of the distribution of number of children, all with a mean of 4 and a standard deviation of 1.

Formulas for the Variance and the Standard Deviation

We have seen that the variance is the average squared deviation from the mean. Here is the formula for the variance.

standard deviation   square root of the average of the squared deviations from the mean; the most common descriptive statistic for variation; approximately the average amount that scores in a distribution vary from the mean.

The variance is the sum of the squared deviations of the scores from the mean, divided by the number of scores.

$$SD^2 = \frac{\Sigma(X - M)^2}{N} \qquad (2)$$

Figure 12   Some possible distributions for family size in a country where the mean is 4 and the standard deviation is 1.

SD^2 is the symbol for the *variance*. This may seem surprising. SD is short for *standard deviation*. The symbol SD^2 emphasizes that the variance is the standard deviation squared. (Later, you will learn other symbols for the variance, S^2 and σ^2—the lowercase Greek letter sigma squared. The different symbols are for different situations in which the variance is used. In some cases, it is figured slightly differently.)

The top part of the formula is the *sum of squared deviations*. X is for each score and M is the mean. Thus, $X - M$ is the score minus the mean, the deviation score. The superscript number (^{2}) tells you to square each deviation score. Finally, the sum sign (Σ) tells you to add up all these squared-deviation scores.

The sum of squared deviations of the scores from the mean, which is called the **sum of squares** for short, has its own symbol, SS. Thus, the variance formula can be written using SS instead of $\Sigma(X - M)^2$:

$$SD^2 = \frac{SS}{N} \qquad (3)$$

Whether you use the simplified symbol SS or the full description of the sum of squared deviations, the bottom part of the formula is just N, the number of scores. That is, the formula says to divide the sum of the squared deviation scores by the number of scores in the distribution.

SD^2 variance.

SD standard deviation.

sum of squares (SS)   sum of squared deviations.

TIP FOR SUCCESS

The sum of squared deviations is an important part of many of the procedures you will learn later; so be sure that you fully understand it, as well as how it is figured.

The variance is the sum of squares divided by the number of scores.

The standard deviation is the square root of the variance. So, if you already know the variance, the formula is

The standard deviation is the square root of the variance.

$$SD = \sqrt{SD^2} \tag{4}$$

The formula for the standard deviation, starting from scratch, is the square root of what you figure for the variance:

The standard deviation is the square root of the result of taking the sum of the squared deviations of the scores from the mean divided by the number of scores.

$$SD = \sqrt{\frac{\sum(X - M)^2}{N}} \tag{5}$$

or

The standard deviation is the square root of the result of taking the sum of squares divided by the number of scores.

$$SD = \sqrt{\frac{SS}{N}} \tag{6}$$

Examples of Figuring the Variance and Standard Deviation

Table 3 shows the figuring for the variance and standard deviation for the number of dreams example. (The table assumes you have already figured the mean to be 6 dreams.) Usually, it is easiest to do your figuring using a calculator, especially one with a square-root key. The standard deviation of 2.57 tells you that roughly speaking, on the average, the number of dreams vary by about 2½ from the mean of 6.

Table 4 shows the figuring for the variance and standard deviation for the example of students' number of social interactions during a week (McLaughlin-Volpe et al., 2001). (To save space, the table shows only the first few and last few scores.) Roughly speaking, this result tells you that a student's number of social interactions in a week varies from the mean (of 17.39) by an average of 11.49 social interactions. This can also be shown on a histogram (see Figure 13).

Measures of variability, such as the variance and standard deviation, are heavily influenced by the presence of one or more outliers (extreme values) in a distribution.

TIP FOR SUCCESS

Always check that your answers make *intuitive sense*. For example, looking at the scores for the dreams example, a standard deviation—which, roughly speaking, represents the average amount that the scores vary from the mean—of 2.57 makes sense. If your answer had been 31.23, however, it would mean that, on average, the number of dreams varied by more than 30 from the mean of 6. Looking at the group of scores, that just couldn't be true.

TIP FOR SUCCESS

Notice that in Table 3 that the deviation scores (shown in the third column) add up to 0. The sum of the deviation scores is *always* 0 (or very close to 0, allowing for rounding error). So, to check your figuring, always sum the deviation scores. If they do not add up to 0, do your figuring again!

Table 3　Figuring the Variance and Standard Deviation in the Number of Dreams Example

Score (Number of Dreams)	−	Mean Score (Mean Number of Dreams)	=	Deviation Score	Squared Deviation Score
7		6		1	1
8		6		2	4
8		6		2	4
7		6		1	1
3		6		−3	9
1		6		−5	25
6		6		0	0
9		6		3	9
3		6		−3	9
8		6		2	4
				Σ: 0	66

$$\text{Variance} = SD^2 = \frac{\sum(X - M)^2}{N} = \frac{SS}{N} = \frac{66}{10} = 6.60$$

$$\text{Standard deviation} = SD = \sqrt{SD^2} = \sqrt{6.60} = 2.57$$

Table 4 Figuring the Variance and Standard Deviation for Number of Social Interactions During a Week for 94 College Students

Number of Interactions	−	Mean Number of Interactions	=	Deviation Score	Squared Deviation Score
48		17.39		30.61	936.97
15		17.39		−2.39	5.71
33		17.39		15.61	243.67
3		17.39		−14.39	207.07
21		17.39		3.61	13.03
-		-		-	-
-				-	-
-				-	-
35		17.39		17.61	310.11
9		17.39		−8.39	70.39
30		17.39		12.61	159.01
8		17.39		−9.39	88.17
26		17.39		8.61	74.13
				Σ: 0.00	12,406.44

$$\text{Variance} = SD^2 = \frac{\Sigma(X - M)^2}{N} = \frac{12,406.44}{94} = 131.98$$

$$\text{Standard deviation} = \sqrt{SD^2} = \sqrt{131.98} = 11.49$$

Source: Data from McLaughlin-Volpe et al. (2001).

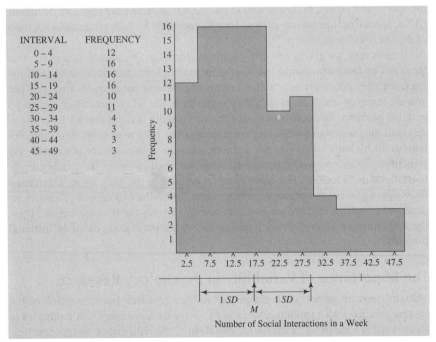

INTERVAL	FREQUENCY
0 – 4	12
5 – 9	16
10 – 14	16
15 – 19	16
20 – 24	10
25 – 29	11
30 – 34	4
35 – 39	3
40 – 44	3
45 – 49	3

Figure 13 The standard deviation as the distance along the base of a histogram, using the example of number of social interactions in a week. (Data from McLaughlin-Volpe et al., 2001.)

The variance is the sum of the squared scores minus the result of taking the sum of all the scores, squaring this sum and dividing by the number of scores, and then taking this whole difference and dividing it by the number of scores.

The scores in the number of dreams example were 7, 8, 8, 7, 3, 1, 6, 9, 3, 8, and we figured the standard deviation of the scores to be 2.57. Now imagine that one additional person is added to the study and that the person reports having 21 dreams in the past week. The standard deviation of the scores would now be 4.96; adding this single score almost doubled the size of the standard deviation.

Computational and Definitional Formulas

In actual research situations, psychologists must often figure the variance and the standard deviation for distributions with many scores, often involving decimals or large numbers. In the days before computers, this could make the whole process quite time-consuming, even with a calculator. To deal with this problem, in the old days researchers developed various shortcuts to simplify the figuring. A shortcut formula of this type is called a **computational formula**.

The traditional computational formula for the variance (of the kind we are discussing in this chapter) is as follows:

$$SD^2 = \frac{\sum X^2 - [(\sum X)^2/N]}{N} \qquad (7)$$

$\sum X^2$ means that you square each score and then take the sum of the squared scores. However, $(\sum X)^2$ means that you first add up all the scores and then take the square of this sum. Although this sounds complicated, this formula was actually easier to use than the one you learned before if a researcher was figuring the variance for a lot of numbers by hand or even with an old-fashioned handheld calculator, because the researcher did not have to first find the deviation score for each score.

However, these days computational formulas are mainly of historical interest. In fact, today, even many handheld calculators are set up so that you need only enter the scores and press a button or two to get the variance and the standard deviation. (Also, spreadsheet programs such as Excel commonly include procedures for most of the statistical procedure.)

In this text, we give a few computational formulas, because you may run into them and be confused should you look at an old book on statistical methods. However, we very definitely recommend *not* using the computational formulas when you are learning statistics, even if they might save you a few minutes of figuring a practice problem. The computational formulas usually make it much harder to understand the *meaning* of what you are figuring. The only reason for figuring problems at all by hand when you are learning statistics is to reinforce the underlying principles. Thus, you would be undermining the whole point of the practice problems if you use a formula that had a complex relation to the basic logic. The formulas we give you for the practice problems and for all the examples in this text are designed to help strengthen your understanding of what the figuring *means*. Thus, the usual formula we give for each procedure is what statisticians call a **definitional formula**.

computational formula equation mathematically equivalent to the definitional formula. Easier to use for figuring by hand, it does not directly show the meaning of the procedure.

definitional formula equation for a statistical procedure directly showing the meaning of the procedure.

The Importance of Variability in Psychology Research

Variability is an important topic in psychology research because much of the research focuses on explaining variability. We will use a couple of examples to show what we mean by "explaining variability." As you might imagine, different students experience different levels of stress with regard to learning statistics: Some experience little stress; for other students, learning statistics can be a source of great stress. So, in this example, explaining variability means identifying the factors that explain why students differ in the amount of stress they experience. Perhaps how much experience students have had with math explains some of the variability. That is, according to this explanation, the differences (the variability) among students in amount of stress are partially due to the differences (the variability) among students in the amount of experience they have had with math. Thus, the variation in math experience partially explains, or accounts for, the variation in stress. What factors might explain the variation in students' number of weekly social interactions? Perhaps a factor is variation in the extraversion of students, with more extraverted students tending to have more interactions. Or perhaps it is variation in gender, with one gender having consistently more interactions than the other.

The Variance as the Sum of Squared Deviations Divided by $N - 1$

Researchers often use a slightly different kind of variance. We have defined the variance as the average of the squared deviation scores. Using that definition, you divide the sum of the squared deviation scores by the number of scores (that is, the variance is SS/N). For many purposes it is better to define the variance as the sum of squared deviation scores divided by *1 less than the number of scores*. In other words, for those purposes the variance is the sum of squared deviations divided by $N - 1$ (that is, variance is $SS/[N - 1]$). (You use this dividing by $N - 1$ approach when you have scores from a particular group of people and you want to estimate what the variance would be for the larger group of people whom these individuals represent.)

The variances and standard deviations given in research articles are usually figured using $SS/(N - 1)$. Also, when calculators or computers give the variance or the standard deviation automatically, they are usually figured in this way (for example, see the Using SPSS section at the end of this chapter). But don't worry. The approach you are learning in this chapter of dividing by N (that is, figuring variance as SS/N) is entirely correct for our purpose here, which is to use descriptive statistics to describe the variation in a particular group of scores. We mention this other approach (variance as $SS/[N - 1]$) now only so that you will not be confused if you read about variance or standard deviation in other places or if your calculator or a computer program gives a surprising result.

How are you doing?

1. (a) Define the variance and (b) indicate what it tells you about a distribution and how this is different from what the mean tells you.
2. (a) Define the standard deviation; (b) describe its relation to the variance; and (c) explain what it tells you approximately about a group of scores.
3. Give the full formula for the variance and indicate what each of the symbols means.
4. Figure the (a) variance and (b) standard deviation for the following scores: 2, 4, 3, and 7 ($M = 4$).
5. Explain the difference between a definitional formula and a computational formula.

6. What is the difference between the formula for the variance you learned in this chapter and the formula that is typically used to figure the variance in research articles?

Answers

1. (a) The variance is the average of the squared deviation of each score from the mean. (b) The variance tells you about how spread out the scores are (that is, their variability), while the mean tells you the central tendency of the distribution.

2. (a) The standard deviation is the square root of the average of the squared deviations from the mean. (b) The standard deviation is the square root of the variance. (c) The standard deviation tells you approximately the average amount that scores differ from the mean.

3. $SD^2 = [\Sigma(X - M)^2]/N$. SD^2 is the variance. Σ tells you to take the sum of what follows. X is for the scores for the variable being studied. M is the mean of the scores. N is the number of scores.

4. (a) Variance: $SD^2 = [\Sigma(X - M)^2]/N = [(2 - 4)^2 + (4 - 4)^2 + (3 - 4)^2 + (7 - 4)^2]/4 = 14/4 = 3.50$.
(b) Standard deviation: $SD = \sqrt{SD^2} = \sqrt{3.50} = 1.87$.

5. A definitional formula is the standard formula in the straightforward form that shows the meaning of what the formula is figuring. A computational formula is a mathematically equivalent variation of the definitional formula. However, the computational formula tends not to show the underlying meaning. Computational formulas were often used before computers were available and researchers had to do their figuring by hand with a lot of scores.

6. The formula for the variance in this chapter divides the sum of squares by the number of scores (that is, SS/N). The variance in research articles is usually figured by dividing the sum of squares by one less than the number of scores (that is, $SS/[N - 1]$).

BOX 1   The Sheer Joy (Yes, Joy) of Statistical Analysis

You are learning statistics for the fun of it, right? No? Or maybe so, after all. If you become a psychologist, at some time or other you will form a hypothesis, gather data, and analyze them. (Even if you plan a career as a psychotherapist or other mental health practitioner, you will probably eventually wish to test an idea about the nature of your patients and their difficulties.) That hypothesis—your own original idea—and the data you gather to test it are going to be very important to you. Your heart may well be pounding with excitement as you analyze the data.

Consider some of the comments of social psychologists we interviewed some years ago for our book *The Heart of Social Psychology* (Aron & Aron, 1989). Deborah Richardson, who studies interpersonal aggression, confided that her favorite part of being a social psychologist is looking at the statistical output of the computer analyses:

It's like putting together a puzzle. . . . It's a highly arousing, positive experience for me. I often go through periods of euphoria. Even when the data don't do what I want them to do . . . [there's a] physiological response. . . . It's exciting to see the numbers come off—Is it actually the way I thought it would be?—then thinking about the alternatives.

Harry Reis, recent President of the Society for Personality and Social Psychology, sees his profession the same way:

By far the most rewarding part is when you get a new data set and start analyzing it and things pop out, partly a confirmation of what led you into the study in the first place, but then also other things . . . . "Why is that?" Trying to make sense of it. The kind of ideas that come from data. . . . I love analyzing data.

Bibb Latane, winner (twice!) of the Behavioral Science Award from the American Association for the Advancement of Science, is known for, among other things, his work on why people don't always intervene to help others who are in trouble. He reports eagerly awaiting

. . . the first glimmerings of what came out . . . [and] using them to shape what the next question should be . . . You need to use everything you've got, . . . every bit of your experience and intuition. It's where you have the biggest effect, it's the least routine. You're in the room with the tiger, face to face with the core of what you are doing, at the moment of truth.

Bill Graziano, at Purdue University, whose work integrates developmental, personality, and social psychology, calls the analysis of his data "great fun, just great fun." And in the same vein, Margaret Clark, at Yale University, who studies emotion and close relationships, declares that "the most fun of all is getting the data and looking at them."

So, you see? Statistics in the service of your own creative ideas can be a pleasure indeed.

Controversy: The Tyranny of the Mean

Looking in the behavioral and social science research journals, you would think that statistical methods are their sole tool and language, but there have also been rebellions against the reign of statistics. We are most familiar with this issue in psychology, where the most unexpected opposition came from the leader of behaviorism, the school in the history of psychology most dedicated to keeping the field strictly scientific.

Behaviorism opposed the study of inner states because inner events are impossible to observe objectively. (Today most research psychologists claim to measure inner events indirectly but objectively.) Behaviorism's most famous advocate, B. F. Skinner, was quite opposed to statistics. Skinner even said, "I would much rather see a graduate student in psychology taking a course in physical chemistry than in statistics. And I would include [before statistics] other sciences, even poetry, music, and art" (Evans, 1976, p. 93).

Skinner was constantly pointing to the information lost by averaging the results of a number of cases. For instance, Skinner (1956) cited the example of three overeating mice—one naturally obese, one poisoned with gold, and one whose hypothalamus had been altered. Each had a different curve for learning to press a bar for food. If these learning curves had been merged statistically, the result would have represented no actual eating habits of any real mouse. As Skinner said, "These three individual curves contain more information than could probably ever be generated with measures requiring statistical treatment, yet they will be viewed with suspicion by many psychologists because they are single cases" (p. 232).

In clinical psychology and the study of personality, voices have always been raised in favor of the in-depth study of one person instead of or as well as the averaging of persons. The philosophical underpinnings of the in-depth study of individuals can be found in phenomenology, which began in Europe after World War I (Husserl, 1970). This viewpoint has been important throughout the social sciences, not just in psychology.

Today, the rebellion in psychology is led by qualitative research methodologists (e.g., Willig & Stainton-Rogers, 2008), an approach that is much more prominent in other behavioral and social sciences, such as communication. The qualitative research methods, developed mainly in cultural anthropology, can involve long interviews or observations of a few individuals. The highly skilled researcher decides, as the event is taking place, what is important to remember, record, and pursue through more questions or observations. The mind of the researcher is the main tool because, according to this approach, only that mind can find the important relationships among the many categories of events arising in the respondent's speech.

Many who favor qualitative methods argue for a blend: First, discover the important categories through a qualitative approach. Then, determine their incidence in the larger population through quantitative methods. Too often, these advocates argue, quantitative researchers jump to conclusions about a phenomenon without first exploring the human experience of it through free-response interviews or observations.

Finally, Carl Jung, founder of Jungian psychology, sometimes spoke of the "statistical mood" and its effect on a person's feeling of uniqueness. Jung had no problem with statistics—he used them in his own research. He was concerned about the cultural impact of this "statistical mood"—much like the impact of being on a jammed subway and observing the hundreds of blank faces and feeling diminished, "one of a crowd." He held that the important contributions to culture tend to come from people who feel unique and not ordinary. As we increasingly describe ourselves statistically—"90% of men under thirty think . . ."—we tend to do just that, think like 90% of men under thirty. To counteract this mood, Jungian analyst Marie Louise von Franz (1979) wrote, "An act of loyalty is required towards one's own feelings" (pp. IV-18). Feeling "makes your life and your relationships and deeds feel unique and gives them a definite value" (pp. IV-18–IV-19). Your beloved is like no one else. Your own death is a face behind a door. And the meaning of 'civilian deaths this month due to the war were 20,964' is unfathomable horror—not a number.

In short, there have been many who have questioned an exclusively statistical view of our subject matter, and their voices should be considered too as you proceed with your study of what has become the predominant, but not exclusive, means of doing psychology research.

BOX 2   Gender, Ethnicity, and Math Performance

From time to time someone tries to argue that because some groups of people score better on standardized math tests and make careers out of mathematics, these groups have a genetic advantage in math (or statistics), implying others are innately inferior at it. The issue comes up about gender, about racial and ethnic groups, and of course in arguments about overall intelligence as well as math. There's little evidence for such genetic differences (a must-see classic article is Block, 1995), but the stereotypes persist.

The impact of these stereotypes was well established in research by Steele and his colleagues (e.g., 1997), who have done numerous studies on what they call "stereotype threat," the risk of confirming, as a self-characteristic, a negative stereotype about a group you happen to belong to. Steele argues that it is not so much that you have internalized a negative attitude about yourself, but that certain situations create the threat. A typical experiment creating stereotype threat (Spencer et al., 1999) involved women taking a difficult math test. Half were told that men generally do better on the test, and the other half that women generally do equally well. Those who were told that women do worse did indeed score substantially lower than the other group. In the

other condition, there was no difference. (In fact, in two separate studies, men performed a little worse when they were told there was no gender difference, as if they had lost some of their confidence.)

In another typical experiment creating stereotype threat, fifth- and sixth-grade students were randomly assigned to fill out a form asking for their race before taking their end-of-year mathematics test (Alter et al., 2010). African American students who filled out this form only answered about half as many math questions correctly as African American students who did not.

Stereotype threat has also been found to occur in the United States for Latinos (Gonzales et al., 2002) and the poor (Croizet & Claire, 1998), but they can occur in any culture, to any subgroup that is the target of negative stereotypes. Stereotype threat plays the main role in lower test scores among minorities (Suzuki & Aronson, 2005). For example, the same difference of 15 IQ points between a dominant and minority group has been found all over the world, even when there is no genetic difference between the groups. And in cases where opportunities for a group have changed, such as when they emigrate, differences have rapidly disappeared (Block, 1995). Hyde and

Mertz (2009) found that the more gender equality there is in a society, the more that women are equal to men in their math performance, and the greater likelihood that women are found to have "profound mathematical talent."

What Can You Do for Yourself?

Thanks to a better understanding of the brain, psychologists (e.g., Forbes & Schmader, 2010) are learning more about how stereotype threat works to hurt your performance by looking separately at the effects of attitudes (occurring in parts of the brain associated with emotions) and stereotypes (affecting parts of the brain that interpret experience, a constant activity). Sometimes it is said that minorities fail because they give up or have a "negative attitude," but this research sorts that out. In a series of experiments involving "implicit association," women were trained without being aware of it to have a more positive attitude towards math or to have a more positive stereotype of women as good at math. The goal was to sort out attitude and stereotype. The study found that positive attitude did not help with math performance. In fact, when under stereotype threat (a man tells them they are going to take a math test and asks them their gender), these women were even more interested in math and more motivated to do it than when not threatened.

Additional experiments revealed that scores improved only when the women were taught to believe (through implicit retraining) that, as a woman, they could actually do math equally as well as men.

Stereotypes, not attitudes, were the problem because countering stereotypes, unlike maintaining a positive attitude, requires constant mental effort. Stereotypes operate in the part of the brain where you are continually interpreting experience, so you have to keep telling yourself, "I can do this." That takes up some of your working memory, and the less working memory, the more difficult it is to solve math problems.

Change Those Beliefs

This research says that you *must* work on your wrong belief that because of being part of some minority you cannot do math as well as others. This is the only protection against those conditions that remind you of the negative stereotypes about your group and math. To begin that project, let's look at some facts. There is no indication that, on average, men and women differ in their math abilities. In a recent comprehensive review, Lindberg and colleagues (2010) combined the results of 242 studies that together included data from more

than 1 million men and women. Overall, they found no evidence of gender differences in mathematics performance. However, it is true that there are currently more men than women employed in math-intensive academic careers, such as engineering, physics, chemistry, and mathematics. Why might that be? According to a recent analysis by Ceci and Williams (2010), it does not appear to be due to gender differences in math ability or current gender discrimination (although discrimination in the past likely helps to explain historical trends). Instead, men and women's different preferences and choices seem to be the primary reason why fewer women pursue a career in math-intensive fields. As adolescents, fewer girls than boys are interested in math-intensive careers. And among individuals who pursue graduate level education in math-intensive fields, women are more likely to switch fields or drop out than men.

As for African-Americans in the United States, Steele (1997) found that differences in performance from the majority all had to do with the situation. For example, when African American students were enrolled in a transition-to-college program emphasizing that they were the cream of the crop and much was expected of them, their grades rose substantially. African American students at the same school who were enrolled in a remedial program for minorities received considerable attention, but their grades improved very little, and many more of them dropped out of school than in the other group. Steele argues that the very idea of a remedial program exposed those students to a subtle stereotype threat.

Treat Stereotype Threat as Another Form of Anxiety

While you are working on changing your stereotypes, you can try to be alert to stereotype threat. But research on stereotypes shows that they can be activated without our awareness (Fiske, 1998), so another approach is to try to counter its effects on working memory, which are the same as those caused by any form of test anxiety. Cognitive research on stereotype threat has demonstrated that it most affects math problems relying on long-term memory, and it spills over into subsequent tasks not normally affected by stereotype threat (Beilock et al., 2007). That means that what you have studied can be easily forgotten unless you over prepare, and that in turn can make you doubt your ability even to add 2 + 2. So do all that you can to keep yourself in an optimal level of arousal, such as making the testing situation familiar, associated with success, and even comfortable. You know you can do it.

Be Empowered

Finally, although increasing your motivation alone does not help very much, it can't hurt. Fight for your right to know this subject. Consider these words from the former president of the Mathematics Association of America:

The paradox of our times is that as mathematics becomes increasingly powerful, only the powerful seem to benefit from it [italics added]. The ability to think mathematically—broadly interpreted—is absolutely

crucial to advancement in virtually every career. Confidence in dealing with data, skepticism in analyzing arguments, persistence in penetrating complex problems, and literacy in communicating about technical matters are the enabling arts offered by the new mathematical sciences. (Steen, 1987, p. xviii)

Do not let anyone take away your power to change the world, which most emphatically requires you to know how to use and interpret statistics.

Central Tendency and Variability in Research Articles

The mean and the standard deviation are very commonly reported in research articles. However, the mode, median, and variance are only occasionally reported. Sometimes, the mean and standard deviation are included in the text of an article. For our dreams example, the researcher might write, "The mean number of dreams in the last week for the 10 students was 6.00 ($SD = 2.57$)." Means and standard deviations are also often listed in tables, especially if a study includes several groups or several different variables. For example, Kujath (2011) conducted a study with 183 college students who reported using Facebook or MySpace. As shown in Table 5 (reproduced from Kujath's article), the students reported on their use of each social networking site. Notice that the table is one of those relatively rare examples that includes the median as well as the mean and standard deviation (usually just the mean and standard deviation are shown). As the table shows, students reported using MySpace for a greater amount of time per day (mean = 67.4 minutes) than Facebook (mean = 39.1 minutes). Also notice that there was greater variability in the total time per day students spent on MySpace ($SD = 112.7$ minutes) compared to Facebook ($SD = 77.0$). How does your usage of social networking sites compare to the usage reported in this study?

Another interesting example is shown in Table 6 (reproduced from Norcross et al., 2005). The table shows the application and enrollment statistics for psychology doctoral programs in the United States, broken down by area of psychology and by year (1973, 1979, 1992, and 2003). The table does not give standard deviations, but it does give both means and medians. For example, in 2003 the mean number of applicants to doctoral counseling psychology programs was 71.0, but the median was only 59. This suggests that some programs had very high numbers of applicants that skewed the distribution. In fact, you can see from the table that for almost every

Table 5　Facebook and MySpace Utilization

	Facebook			MySpace		
	Mn	Mdn	SD	Mn	Mdn	SD
Membership months	21.9	24.0	13.4	28.2	24.0	15.5
Times used per day	1.2	1.0	1.3	1.6	1.0	1.5
Minutes spent per use	31.5	17.5	58.8	38.8	30.0	57.1
Total minutes per day	39.1	15.0	77.0	67.4	30.0	112.7

Source: Kujath, C. L. (2011). Facebook and MySpace: Complement or substitute for face-to-face interaction? *Cyberpsychology, Behavior, and Social Networking, 14*, 75–78. Reprinted by permission of Mary Ann Liebert, Inc. publishers.

Table 6 Application and Enrollment Statistics by Area and Year: Doctoral Programs

Program	N of programs				Applications								Enrollments			
					M				Mdn				M		Mdn	
	1973	1979	1992	2003	1973	1979	1992	2003	1973	1979	1992	2003	1992	2003	1992	2003
Clinical	105	130	225	216	314.4	252.6	191.1	142.0	290	234	168	126	12.0	15.4	8	8
Clinical neuro				20				72.3				37		10.7		6
Community	4	2	5	13	90.5		24.4	23.5	60		23	21	3.2	3.3	2	3
Counseling	29	43	52	66	133.4	90.9	120.2	71.0	120	84	110	59	7.3	6.8	6	7
Health			7	13			40.7	71.2			30	56	4.4	6.7	5	4
School	30	39	56	57	78.5	54.0	31.3	38.7	53	34	32	31	5.4	6.9	5	5
Other health service provider subfield				52				83.5				48		9.2		7
Cognitive			57	104			24.6	30.1			22	22	2.6	3.4	2	3
Developmental	56	72	77	111	54.1	38.9	27.6	25.5	41	30	24	22	2.8	3.4	2	3
Educational	23	28	30	35	67.8	39.7	20.0	19.7	34	26	12	13	6.0	4.9	4	4
Experimental	118	127	78	40	56.2	33.2	31.3	26.7	42	25	26	17	4.4	4.1	3	3
I/O	20	25	49	60	39.9	54.7	66.2	46.9	37	48	70	41	4.9	4.7	4	4
Neuroscience				53				22.0				16		2.8		2
Personality	23	15	10	18	42.5	24.7	12.3	47.8	33	17	6	31	1.0	2.8	1	2
Psychobiological/ physiological				18				21.1				17		2.4		2
Quantitative	40	43	26	17	33.2	29.3	20.0	11.2	29	24	20	11	3.9	1.9	2	1
Social	58	72	59	85	48.7	30.9	47.1	43.1	40	24	37	35	3.3	3.2	3	3
Other fields	60	47	28	101	61.6	74.1	26.6	26.0	27	25	15	17	3.3	3.8	2	3
Total	566	645	1,039	1,079	106.1	85.2	69.4	59.6			31	33	5.6	6.7	4	4

Note. The academic years correspond to the 1975–1976, 1981–1982, 1994 and 2005 editions of *Graduate Study in Psychology*, respectively. Clinical neuro = clinical neuropsychology; I/O = industrial-organizational.

Source. Norcross, J. C., Kohout, J. L., & Wicherski, M. (2005). Graduate study in psychology: 1971 to 2004. *American Psychologist, 60*, 959–975. Published by the American Psychological Association. Reprinted with permission.

kind of program and for both applications and enrollments, the means are typically higher than the medians. You may also be struck by just how competitive it is to get into doctoral programs in many areas of psychology. It is our experience that one of the factors that makes a lot of difference is doing well in statistics courses!

Learning Aids

Summary

1. The mean is the most commonly used measure of central tendency of a distribution of scores. The mean is the ordinary average—the sum of the scores divided by the number of scores. In symbols, $M = (\Sigma X)/N$.
2. Other, less commonly used ways of describing the central tendency of a distribution of scores are the mode (the most common single value) and the median (the value of the middle score when all the scores are lined up from lowest to highest).
3. The variability of a group of scores can be described by the variance and the standard deviation.
4. The variance is the average of the squared deviation of each score from the mean. In symbols, $SD^2 = [\Sigma(X - M)^2]/N$. The sum of squared deviations, $\Sigma(X - M)^2$, is also symbolized as SS. Thus $SD^2 = SS/N$.
5. The standard deviation is the square root of the variance. In symbols, $SD = \sqrt{SD^2}$. It is approximately the average amount that scores differ from the mean.
6. There have always been a few psychologists who have warned against statistical methodology because in the process of creating averages, knowledge about the individual case is lost.
7. Means and standard deviations are often given in research articles in the text or in tables.

Key Terms

central tendency	median	standard deviation (SD)
mean (M)	outlier	SD^2
Σ (sum of)	variance	SD
X	deviation score	sum of squares (SS)
N (number of scores)	squared deviation score	computational formula
mode	sum of squared deviations	definitional formula

Example Worked-Out Problems

Figuring the Mean

Find the mean for the following scores: 8, 6, 6, 9, 6, 5, 6, 2.

Answer

You can figure the mean using the formula or the steps.

Using the formula: $M = (\Sigma X)/N = 48/8 = 6$.

Using the steps:

❶ **Add up all the scores.** $8 + 6 + 6 + 9 + 6 + 5 + 6 + 2 = 48$.
❷ **Divide this sum by the number of scores.** $48/8 = 6$.

Finding the Median

Find the median for the following scores: $1, 7, 4, 2, 3, 6, 2, 9, 7$.

Answer

❶ **Line up all the scores from lowest to highest.** $1, 2, 2, 3, 4, 6, 7, 7, 9$.
❷ **Figure how many scores there are to the middle score by adding 1 to the number of scores and dividing by 2.** There are 9 scores; so the middle score is the result of adding 1 to 9 and then dividing by 2, which is 5. The middle score is the fifth score.
❸ **Count up to the middle score or scores.** The fifth score from the bottom is 4; so the median is 4.

Figuring the Sum of Squares and the Variance

Find the sum of squares and the variance for the following scores: $8, 6, 6, 9, 6, 5, 6, 2$. (These are the same scores used in the previous example for the mean: $M = 6$.)

Answer

You can figure the sum of squares and the variance using the formulas or the steps.
Using the formulas:

$$SS = \Sigma(X - M)^2 = (8 - 6)^2 + (6 - 6)^2 + (6 - 6)^2$$
$$+ (9 - 6)^2 + (6 - 6)^2 + (5 - 6)^2 + (6 - 6)^2 + (2 - 6)^2$$
$$= 2^2 + 0^2 + 0^2 + 3^2 + 0^2 + -1^2 + 0^2 + -4^2$$
$$= 4 + 0 + 0 + 9 + 0 + 1 + 0 + 16$$
$$= 30$$
$$SD^2 = SS/N = 30/8 = 3.75.$$

Table 7 shows the figuring, using the following steps:

❶ **Subtract the mean from each score.**
❷ **Square each of these deviation scores.**

Table 7 Figuring for Example Worked-Out Problem for the Sum of Squares and Variance Using Steps

Score	Mean	❶ Deviation	❷ Squared Deviation
8	6	2	4
6	6	0	0
6	6	0	0
9	6	3	9
6	6	0	0
5	6	−1	1
6	6	0	0
2	6	−4	16
			$\Sigma = SS = 30$ ❸

❹ Variance $= 30/8 = 3.75$

❸ **Add up the squared deviation scores.** This gives the sum of squares (SS).
❹ **Divide the sum of squared deviations by the number of scores.** This gives the variance (SD^2).

Figuring the Standard Deviation

Find the standard deviation for the following scores: 8, 6, 6, 9, 6, 5, 6, 2. (These are the same scores used above for the mean, sum of squares, and variance. $SD^2 = 3.75$.)

Answer

You can figure the standard deviation using the formula or the steps.
　　Using the formula: $SD = \sqrt{SD^2} = \sqrt{3.75} = 1.94$.
　　Using the steps:

❶ **Figure the variance.** The variance (from above) is 3.75.
❷ **Take the square root.** The square root of 3.75 is 1.94.

Outline for Writing Essays on Finding the Mean, Variance, and Standard Deviation

1. Explain that the mean is a measure of the central tendency of a group of scores. Mention that the mean is the ordinary average, the sum of the scores divided by the number of scores.
2. Explain that the variance and standard deviation both measure the amount of variability (or spread) among a group of scores.
3. The variance is the average of each score's squared difference from the mean. Describe the steps for figuring the variance.
4. Roughly speaking, the standard deviation is the average amount that scores differ from the mean. Explain that the standard deviation is directly related to the variance and is figured by taking the square root of the variance.

Practice Problems

These problems involve figuring. Most real-life statistics problems are done with special statistical software. Even if you have such software, do these problems by hand to ingrain the method in your mind. To learn how to use a computer to solve statistics problems like those in this chapter, refer to the Using SPSS section at the end of this chapter.

　　All data are fictional unless an actual citation is given.

Set I

1. For the following scores, find the (a) mean, (b) median, (c) sum of squared deviations, (d) variance, and (e) standard deviation:

$$32, 28, 24, 28, 28, 31, 35, 29, 26$$

2. For the following scores, find the (a) mean, (b) median, (c) sum of squared deviations, (d) variance, and (e) standard deviation:

$$6, 1, 4, 2, 3, 4, 6, 6$$

3. For the following scores, find the (a) mean, (b) median, (c) sum of squared deviations, (d) variance, and (e) standard deviation:

$$2.13, 6.01, 3.33, 5.78$$

4. Here are the noon temperatures (in degrees Celsius) in a particular Canadian city on Thanksgiving Day for the 10 years from 2002 through 2011: 0, 3, 6, 8, 2, 9, 7, 6, 4, 5. Describe the typical temperature and the amount of variation to a person who has never had a course in statistics. Give three ways of describing the representative temperature and two ways of describing its variation, explaining the differences and how you figured each.

5. A researcher is studying the amygdala (a part of the brain involved in emotion). Six participants in a particular fMRI (brain scan) study are measured for the increase in activation of their amygdala while they are viewing pictures of violent scenes. The activation increases are .43, .32, .64, .21, .29, and .51. Figure the (a) mean and (b) standard deviation for these six activation increases. (c) Explain what you have done and what the results mean to a person who has never had a course in statistics.

6. Describe and explain the location of the mean, mode, and median for a normal curve.

7. A researcher studied the number of anxiety attacks recounted over a two-week period by 30 people in psychotherapy for an anxiety disorder. In an article describing the results of the study, the researcher reports: "The mean number of anxiety attacks was 6.84 $(SD = 3.18)$." Explain these results to a person who has never had a course in statistics.

8. In a study by Gonzaga et al. (2001), romantic couples answered questions about how much they loved their partner and also were videotaped while revealing something about themselves to their partner. The videotapes were later rated by trained judges for various signs of affiliation. Table 8 shows some of the results. Explain to a person who has never had a course in statistics the results for self-reported love for the partner and for the number of seconds "leaning toward the partner."

Set II

9. (a) Describe and explain the difference between the mean, median, and mode. (b) Make up an example (not in your lectures) in which the median would be the preferred measure of central tendency.

Table 8 Mean Levels of Emotions and Cue Display in Study 1

Indicator	Women ($n = 60$)		Men ($n = 60$)	
	M	SD	M	SD
Emotion reports				
Self-reported love	5.02	2.16	5.11	2.08
Partner-estimated love	4.85	2.13	4.58	2.20
Affiliation-cue display				
Affirmative head nods	1.28	2.89	1.21	1.91
Duchenne smiles	4.45	5.24	5.78	5.59
Leaning toward partner	32.27	20.36	31.36	21.08
Gesticulation	0.13	0.40	0.25	0.77

Note: Emotions are rated on a scale of 0 (*none*) to 8 (*extreme*). Cue displays are shown as mean seconds displayed per 60 s.

Source: Gonzaga, G. C., Keltner, D., Londahl, E. A., & Smith, M. D. (2001). Love and the commitment problem in romantic relationships and friendship. *Journal of Personality and Social Psychology, 81,* 247–262. Published by the American Psychological Association. Reprinted with permission.

10. (a) Describe the variance and standard deviation. (b) Explain why the standard deviation is more often used as a descriptive statistic than the variance.

11. For the following scores, find the (a) mean, (b) median, (c) sum of squared deviations, (d) variance, and (e) standard deviation:

2, 2, 0, 5, 1, 4, 1, 3, 0, 0, 1, 4, 4, 0, 1, 4, 3, 4, 2, 1, 0

12. For the following scores, find the (a) mean, (b) median, (c) sum of squared deviations, (d) variance, and (e) standard deviation:

1,112; 1,245; 1,361; 1,372; 1,472

13. For the following scores, find the (a) mean, (b) median, (c) sum of squared deviations, (d) variance, and (e) standard deviation:

3.0, 3.4, 2.6, 3.3, 3.5, 3.2

14. For the following scores, find the (a) mean, (b) median, (c) sum of squared deviations, (d) variance, and (e) standard deviation:

8, −5, 7, −10, 5

15. Make up three sets of scores: (a) one with the mean greater than the median, (b) one with the median and the mean the same, and (c) one with the mode greater than the median. (Each made-up set of scores should include at least five scores.)

16. A psychologist interested in political behavior measured the square footage of the desks in the official office of four U.S. governors and of four chief executive officers (CEOs) of major U.S. corporations. The figures for the governors were 44, 36, 52, and 40 square feet. The figures for the CEOs were 32, 60, 48, and 36 square feet. (a) Figure the means and standard deviations for the governors and for the CEOs. (b) Explain, to a person who has never had a course in statistics, what you have done. (c) Note the ways in which the means and standard deviations differ, and speculate on the possible meaning of these differences, presuming that they are representative of U.S. governors and large corporations' CEOs in general.

17. A developmental psychologist studies the number of words that seven infants have learned at a particular age. The numbers are 10, 12, 8, 0, 3, 40, and 18. Figure the (a) mean, (b) median, and (c) standard deviation for the number of words learned by these seven infants. (d) Explain what you have done and what the results mean to a person who has never had a course in statistics.

18. Describe and explain the location of the mean, mode, and median of a distribution of scores that is strongly skewed to the left.

19. You figure the variance of a distribution of scores to be –4.26. Explain why your answer cannot be correct.

20. A study involves measuring the number of days absent from work for 216 employees of a large company during the preceding year. As part of the results, the researcher reports, "The number of days absent during the preceding year ($M = 9.21; SD = 7.34$) was . . . ." Explain what is written in parentheses to a person who has never had a course in statistics.

21. Selwyn (2007) conducted a study of gender-related perceptions of information and communication technologies (such as video game systems, DVD players, and cell phones). The researcher asked 406 college students in Wales to rate 8 technologies in terms of their level of masculinity or femininity. The students rated each technology using a 7-point response scale, from –3 for very feminine to

+3 for very masculine, with a midpoint of 0 for neither masculine or feminine. Table 9 (reproduced from Selwyn's article) shows the mean, standard deviation, and variance of the students' ratings of each technology. Explain the results to a person who has never had a course in statistics. (Be sure to explain some specific numbers, as well as the general principle of the mean, standard deviation, and variance.)

Table 9 Mean Scores for Each Technology

	N	Mean	S.D.	Variance
Games machine (e.g., Playstation)	403	1.92	1.00	.98
DVD Player	406	.44	.85	.73
Personal Computer (PC)	400	.36	.82	.68
Digital radio (DAB)	399	.34	.99	.98
Television set	406	.26	.78	.62
Radio	404	−.01	.81	.65
Mobile phone	399	−.19	.88	.77
Landline telephone	404	−.77	1.03	1.07

Note: Mean scores range from −3 (*very feminine*) to +3 (*very masculine*). The midpoint score of .0 denotes "neither masculine nor feminine."

Source: Selwyn, N. (2007). Hi-tech = guy-tech? An exploration of undergraduate students' gendered perceptions of information and communication technologies. *Sex Roles, 56,* 525–536. Copyright © 2007. Reprinted by permission of Springer Science and Business Media.

Using SPSS

The ✍ in the following steps indicates a mouse click. (We used SPSS version 19.0 to carry out these analyses. The steps and output may be slightly different for other versions of SPSS.)

Finding the Mean, Mode, and Median

❶ Enter the scores from your distribution in one column of the data window.
❷ ✍ *Analyze.*
❸ ✍ *Descriptive statistics.*
❹ ✍ *Frequencies.*
❺ ✍ the variable for which you want to find the mean, mode, and median, and then ✍ the arrow.
❻ ✍ *Statistics.*
❼ ✍ *Mean,* ✍ *Median,* ✍ *Mode,* ✍ *Continue.*
❽ Optional: To instruct SPSS *not* to produce a frequency table, ✍ the box labeled *Display frequency tables* (this *un*checks the box).
❾ ✍ *OK.*

Practice the preceding steps by finding the mean, mode, and median for the number of dreams example at the start of the chapter (the scores are 7, 8, 8, 7, 3, 1, 6, 9, 3, 8). Your output window should look like Figure 14. (If you instructed SPSS not to show the frequency table, your output will show only the mean, median, and mode.)

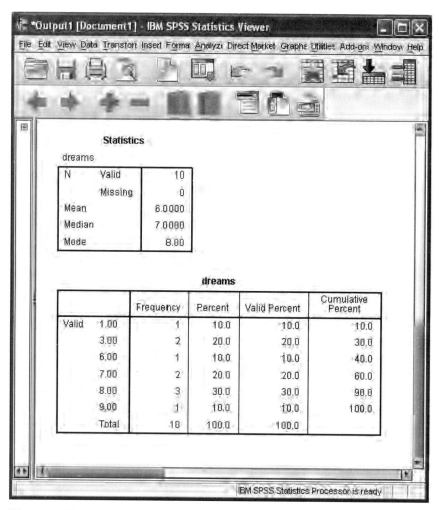

Figure 14 Using SPSS to find the mean, median, and mode for the number of dreams example.

Finding the Variance and Standard Deviation

As mentioned earlier in the chapter, most calculators and computer software—including SPSS—calculate the variance and standard deviation using a formula that involves dividing by $N - 1$ instead of N. So, if you request the variance and standard deviation directly from SPSS (for example, by clicking *Variance* and *Std. deviation* in Step ❼), the answers provided by SPSS will be slightly different from the answers in this chapter.[5] The following steps show you how to use SPSS to figure the variance and standard deviation using the dividing-by-N method you learned in this chapter. It is easier to learn these steps using actual numbers; so we will use the number of dreams example again.

❶ Enter the scores for which you want to compute the variance and standard deviation in one column of the data window (the scores are 7, 8, 8, 7, 3, 1, 6, 9, 3, 8). We will call this variable "dreams." (This is the same first step for finding the mean of a distribution of scores.)

Figure 15 SPSS compute variable window for Step ❸ of finding the variance and standard deviation for the number of dreams example.

❷ Find the mean of the scores by following the preceding steps for Finding the Mean, Mode, and Median. The mean of the dreams variable is 6.

❸ You are now going to create a new variable that shows each score's squared deviation from the mean. ✍ *Transform,* ✍ *Compute Variable.* You could call the new variable any name you want, but we will call it "squared_deviation". So, type *squared_deviation* in the box labeled *Target Variable.* You are now going to tell SPSS how to figure this new variable called *squared_deviation.* In the box labeled *Numeric Expression,* write $(dreams - 6) * (dreams - 6)$. (The asterisk is how you show *multiplication* in SPSS.) As you can see, this formula takes each score's deviation score and multiplies it by itself to give the squared deviation score. Your Compute Variable window should look like Figure 15. ✍ *OK.* You will see that a new variable called *squared_deviation* has been added to the data window (see Figure 16). The scores are the squared deviations of each score from the mean.

❹ As you learned in this chapter, the variance is figured by dividing the sum of the squared deviations by the number of scores. This is the same as taking the mean of the squared deviation scores. So, to find the variance of the dreams scores, follow the steps shown earlier to find the mean of the *squared_deviation* variable. This comes out to 6.60; so the variance of the dreams scores is 6.60.

❺ To find the standard deviation, use a calculator to find the square root of 6.60, which is 2.57.

If you were conducting an actual research study in which you were testing a group of people in order to make generalizations to people like those tested in

Figure 16   SPSS data window after Step ❸ for finding the variance and standard deviation for the number of dreams example.

general, you would usually request the variance and standard deviation directly from SPSS (using its $N - 1$ approach). However, for our purpose in this chapter (describing the variation in a group of scores for its own sake), the steps we just outlined are entirely appropriate.

Chapter Notes

1. In more formal, mathematical statistics writing, the symbols can be more complex. This complexity allows formulas to handle intricate situations without confusion. However, in books on statistics for psychologists, even fairly advanced texts, the symbols are kept simple. The simplified form rarely creates ambiguities in the kinds of statistical formulas psychologists use.

2. This section focuses on the variance and standard deviation as indicators of spread, or variability. Another way to describe the spread of a group of scores is in terms of the *range*—the highest score minus the lowest score. Suppose that in a particular class the oldest student is 39 years of age and the youngest is 19; the range is 20 (that is, $39 - 19 = 20$). Psychology researchers rarely use the range because it is such an imprecise way to describe the spread; it does not take into account how clumped together or spread out the scores are within the range.

3. Why don't statisticians use the deviation scores themselves, make all deviations positive, and just use their average? In fact, the average of the deviation scores (treating all deviations as positive) has a formal name—the *average deviation* or *mean deviation*. This procedure was actually used in the past, and some psychologists have noted subtle advantages of the average deviation (Catanzaro & Taylor, 1996). However, the average deviation does not work out very well as part of more complicated statistical procedures.

4. It is important to remember that the standard deviation in most cases is not *exactly* the average amount that scores differ from the mean. To be precise, the standard deviation is the square root of the average of scores' squared deviations from the mean. This squaring, averaging, and then taking the square root can give a slightly different result from simply averaging the scores' deviations from the mean. Still, the result of this approach has technical advantages that outweigh the slight disadvantage of giving only an approximate description of the average variation from the mean.

5. Note that if you request the variance from SPSS, you can convert it to the variance as we figure it in this chapter by multiplying the variance from SPSS by $N - 1$ (that is, the number of scores minus 1) and then dividing the result by N (the number of scores). That is, the variance as we are figuring it in this chapter comes out to SPSS's variance multiplied by $(N - 1)/N$. Taking the square root of the resulting value will give you the standard deviation (using the formula you learned in this chapter). We use a slightly longer approach to figuring the variance and standard deviation to reinforce the basic logic of the variance and standard deviation, and also to show you how to create new variables in SPSS.

Answers to Set I Practice Problems

Chapter 2

1. (a) $M = (\sum X)/N = 261/9 = 29$; (b) 28; (c) $\sum(X - M)^2 =$ $(32 - 29)^2 + (28 - 29)^2 + (24 - 29)^2 + (28 - 29)^2 +$ $(28 - 29)^2 + (31 - 29)^2 + (35 - 29)^2 + (29 - 29)^2 +$ $(26 - 29)^2 = 86$; (d) $SD^2 = [\sum(X - M)^2]/N = 86/9 = 9.56$; (e) $SD = \sqrt{SD^2} = \sqrt{9.56} = 3.09$.

2. (a) 4; (b) 4; (c) 26; (d) 3.25; (e) 1.80.

3. (a) 4.3125; (b) 4.5550; (c) 10.7637; (d) 2.6909; (e) 1.6404.

4. The average temperature, in the sense of adding up the 10 temperatures and dividing by 10, was 5 degrees Celsius. This is the *mean*. However, if you line up the temperatures from lowest to highest, the middle two numbers are 5 and 6. The middle number in a distribution is called the *median*. In a situation like this, when you have two middle numbers, the median is the mean of those two numbers. Therefore, the median temperature is 5.5 degrees. The specific temperature that came up most often is the *mode*; the mode is 6 degrees.

   As for the variation (the amount of variability), one approach is the *variance*—the average of each temperature's squared deviation from the mean temperature, which is 7.0. You get a more direct sense of how much a group of numbers vary among themselves if you take the square root of the variance, which gives the standard deviation; the square root of 7.0 is 2.65. This means, roughly, that on an average day the temperature differs by 2.65 degrees from the average of 5 degrees.

5. (a) .4000; (b) .1446; (c) similar to question 4.

6. The mean, mode, and median for a normal curve are all located at the same midpoint of the curve (this is also the highest point in the distribution). The mode is the highest point in the distribution, which for a normal curve falls exactly at the midpoint of the distribution. This midpoint is the median value, since half of the scores in the distribution are below that point and half are above that point. The mean also falls at the same point because the normal curve is symmetrical about the midpoint, and every score in the left hand side of the curve has a matching score on the right hand side.

7. The mean is the ordinary arithmetic average: add up the total number of anxiety attacks and divide by the number of people. The mean number of anxiety attacks over a two-week period was 6.84. The *SD* (standard deviation), roughly speaking, is the average amount that the number of anxiety attacks are spread out from their average—in this case, by 3.18 attacks. This is quite a lot of spread. To be more precise, you figure the standard deviation by taking each person's number of anxiety attacks and subtracting 6.84 from it and squaring this difference; the standard deviation is the square root of the average of these differences.

8. Like the answer to question 7, focusing on means of 5.02, 5.11, 32.27, and 31.36 and on standard deviations of 2.16, 2.08, 20.36, and 21.08.

Chapter 3

Some Key Ingredients for Inferential Statistics

Chapter 3

Some Key Ingredients for Inferential Statistics

Z Scores, the Normal Curve, Sample versus Population, and Probability

Chapter Outline

- ❖ Z Scores
- ❖ The Normal Curve
- ❖ Sample and Population
- ❖ Probability
- ❖ Controversies: Is the Normal Curve Really So Normal? and Using Nonrandom Samples
- ❖ Z Scores, Normal Curves, Samples and Populations, and Probabilities in Research Articles

- ❖ Advanced Topic: Probability Rules and Conditional Probabilities
- ❖ Learning Aids
  - ❖ Summary
  - ❖ Key Terms
  - ❖ Example Worked-Out Problems
  - ❖ Practice Problems
  - ❖ Using SPSS
- ❖ Chapter Notes

TIP FOR SUCCESS

Before beginning this chapter, be sure that you have mastered the shapes of distributions and the mean and standard deviation.

Ordinarily, psychologists conduct research to test a theoretical principle or the effectiveness of a practical procedure. For example, a psychophysiologist might measure changes in heart rate from before to after solving a difficult problem. The measurements are then used to test a theory predicting that heart rate should change following successful problem solving. An applied social psychologist might examine the effectiveness of a program of neighborhood meetings intended to promote water conservation. Such studies are carried out with a particular group of research participants. But researchers use inferential statistics to make more general conclusions about the theoretical principle or procedure being studied. These conclusions go *beyond* the particular group of research participants studied.

This chapter introduces inferential statistics. In this chapter, we consider four topics: Z scores, the normal curve, sample versus population, and probability.

Z Scores

You know how to describe a group of scores in terms of the mean and variation around the mean. In this section you learn how to describe a particular score in terms of where it fits into the overall group of scores. That is, you learn how to use the mean and standard deviation to create a Z score; a Z score describes a score in terms of how much it is above or below the average.

Suppose you are told that a student, Jerome, is asked the question, "To what extent are you a morning person?" Jerome responds with a 5 on a 7-point scale, where 1 = *not at all* and 7 = *extremely*. Now suppose that we do not know anything about how other students answer this question. In this situation, it is hard to tell whether Jerome is more or less of a morning person in relation to other students. However, suppose that we know for students in general, the mean rating (*M*) is 3.40 and the standard deviation (*SD*) is 1.47. (These values are the actual mean and standard deviation that we found for this question in a large sample of students in statistics classes at eight different universities across the United States and Canada.) With this knowledge, we can see that Jerome is more of a morning person than is typical among students. We can also see that Jerome is above the average (1.60 units more than average; that is, 5 − 3.40 = 1.60) by a bit more than students typically vary from the average (that is, students typically vary by about 1.47, the standard deviation). This is all shown in Figure 1.

What Is a Z Score?

A **Z score** makes use of the mean and standard deviation to describe a particular score. Specifically, a Z score is the number of standard deviations the actual score is above or below the mean. If the actual score is above the mean, the Z score is positive. If the actual score is below the mean, the Z score is negative. The standard deviation now becomes a kind of yardstick, a unit of measure in its own right.

In our example, Jerome has a score of 5, which is 1.60 units above the mean of 3.40. One standard deviation is 1.47 units; so Jerome's score is a little more than 1

Z score   number of standard deviations that a score is above (or below, if it is negative) the mean of its distribution; it is thus an ordinary score transformed so that it better describes the score's location in a distribution.

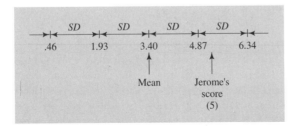

Figure 1   Score of one student, Jerome, in relation to the overall distribution on the measure of the extent to which students are morning people.

Figure 2   Scales of Z scores and raw scores for the example of the extent to which students are morning people.

standard deviation above the mean. To be precise, Jerome's Z score is $+1.09$ (that is, his score of 5 is 1.09 standard deviations above the mean). Another student, Ashley, has a score of 2. Her score is 1.40 units below the mean. Therefore, her score is a little less than 1 standard deviation below the mean (a Z score of $-.95$). So, Ashley's score is below the average by about as much as students typically vary from the average.

Z scores have many practical uses. As you will see later in this chapter, they are especially useful for showing exactly where a particular score falls on the normal curve.

Z Scores as a Scale

Figure 2 shows a scale of Z scores lined up against a scale of raw scores for our example of the degree to which students are morning people. A **raw score** is an ordinary score as opposed to a Z score. The two scales are something like a ruler with inches lined up on one side and centimeters on the other.

Changing a number to a Z score is a bit like converting words for measurement in various obscure languages into one language that everyone can understand—inches, cubits, and zingles (we made up that last one), for example, into centimeters. It is a very valuable tool.

Suppose that a developmental psychologist observed 3-year-old Jacob in a laboratory situation playing with other children of the same age. During the observation, the psychologist counted the number of times Jacob spoke to the other children. The result, over several observations, is that Jacob spoke to other children about 8 times per hour of play. Without any standard of comparison, it would be hard to draw any conclusions from this. Let's assume, however, that it was known from previous research that under similar conditions, the mean number of times children speak is 12, with a standard deviation of 4. With that information, we can see that Jacob spoke less often than other children in general, but not extremely less often. Jacob would have a Z score of -1 ($M = 12$ and $SD = 4$, thus a score of 8 is 1 SD below M), as shown in Figure 3.

Suppose Ryan were observed speaking to other children 20 times in an hour. Ryan would clearly be unusually talkative, with a Z score of $+2$ (see Figure 3). Ryan speaks not merely more than the average but more by twice as much as children tend to vary from the average!

raw score   ordinary score (or any number in a distribution before it has been made into a Z score or otherwise transformed).

Figure 3   Number of times each hour that two children spoke, shown as raw scores and Z scores.

Formula to Change a Raw Score to a Z Score

A Z score is the number of standard deviations by which the raw score is above or below the mean. To figure a Z score, subtract the mean from the raw score, giving the deviation score. Then divide the deviation score by the standard deviation. The formula is

$$Z = \frac{X - M}{SD} \qquad (1)$$ ← A Z score is the raw score minus the mean, divided by the standard deviation.

For example, using the formula for Jacob, the child who spoke to other children 8 times in an hour (where the mean number of times children speak is 12 and the standard deviation is 4),

$$Z = \frac{8 - 12}{4} = \frac{-4}{4} = -1$$

Steps to Change a Raw Score to a Z Score

❶ Figure the deviation score: subtract the mean from the raw score.
❷ Figure the Z score: divide the deviation score by the standard deviation.

Using these steps for Jacob, the child who spoke with other children 8 times in an hour,

❶ Figure the deviation score: subtract the mean from the raw score.
$8 - 12 = -4$.
❷ Figure the Z score: divide the deviation score by the standard deviation.
$-4/4 = -1$.

Formula to Change a Z Score to a Raw Score

To change a Z score to a raw score, the process is reversed: multiply the Z score by the standard deviation and then add the mean. The formula is

$$X = (Z)(SD) + M \qquad (2)$$ ← The raw score is the Z score multiplied by the standard deviation, plus the mean.

Suppose a child has a Z score of 1.5 on the number of times spoken with another child during an hour. This child is 1.5 standard deviations above the mean. Because the standard deviation in this example is 4 raw score units (times spoken), the child is 6 raw score units above the mean, which is 12. Thus, 6 units above the mean is 18. Using the formula,

$$X = (Z)(SD) + M = (1.5)(4) + 12 = 6 + 12 = 18.$$

Steps to Change a Z Score to a Raw Score

❶ Figure the deviation score: multiply the Z score by the standard deviation.
❷ Figure the raw score: add the mean to the deviation score.

Using these steps for the child with a Z score of 1.5 on the number of times spoken with another child during an hour:

❶ Figure the deviation score: multiply the Z score by the standard deviation.
$(1.5)(4) = 6$.
❷ Figure the raw score: add the mean to the deviation score. $6 + 12 = 18$.

Figure 4   Scales of Z scores and raw scores for the example of the extent to which students are morning people, showing the scores of two sample students.

Additional Examples of Changing Z Scores to Raw Scores and Vice Versa

Consider again the example from the start of the chapter in which students were asked the extent to which they were a morning person. Using a scale from 1 (*not at all*) to 7 (*extremely*), the mean was 3.40 and the standard deviation was 1.47. Suppose a student's raw score is 6. That student is well above the mean. Specifically, using the formula,

$$Z = \frac{X - M}{SD} = \frac{6 - 3.40}{1.47} = \frac{2.60}{1.47} = 1.77$$

That is, the student's raw score is 1.77 standard deviations above the mean (see Figure 4, Student 1). Using the 7-point scale (from 1 = *not at all* to 7 = *extremely*), to what extent are *you* a morning person? Now figure the Z score for your rating (your raw score).

Another student has a Z score of -1.63, a score well below the mean. (This student is much less of a morning person than is typically the case for students.) You can find the exact raw score for this student using the formula

$$X = (Z)(SD) + M = (-1.63)(1.47) + 3.40 = -2.40 + 3.40 = 1.00$$

That is, the student's raw score is 1.00 (see Figure 4, Student 2).

Let's also consider some examples from the study of students' stress ratings. The mean stress rating of the 30 statistics students (using a 0–10 scale) was 6.43, and the standard deviation was 2.56. Figure 5 shows the raw score and Z score scales. Suppose a student's stress raw score is 10. That student is well above the mean. Specifically, using the formula

$$Z = \frac{X - M}{SD} = \frac{10 - 6.43}{2.56} = \frac{3.57}{2.56} = 1.39$$

The student's stress level is 1.39 standard deviations above the mean (see Figure 5, Student 1). On a scale of 0–10, how stressed have *you* been in the last 2½ weeks? Figure the Z score for your raw stress score.

Figure 5   Scales of Z scores and raw scores for 30 statistics students' ratings of their stress level, showing the scores of two sample students. (Data based on Aron et al., 1995.)

Another student has a Z score of -1.73, a stress level well below the mean. You can find the exact raw stress score for this student using the formula:

$$X = (Z)(SD) + M = (-1.73)(2.56) + 6.43 = -4.43 + 6.43 = 2.00$$

That is, the student's raw stress score is 2.00 (see Figure 5, Student 2).

The Mean and Standard Deviation of Z Scores

The mean of any distribution of Z scores is always 0. This is so because when you change each raw score to a Z score, you take the raw score minus the mean. So the mean is subtracted out of all the raw scores, making the overall mean come out to 0. In other words, in any distribution, the sum of the positive Z scores must always equal the sum of the negative Z scores. Thus, when you add them all up, you get 0.

The standard deviation of any distribution of Z scores is always 1. This is because when you change each raw score to a Z score, you divide the score by one standard deviation. As you work through the examples that follow, this will become increasingly intuitive. It is important to note that the shape of a distribution is not changed when raw scores are converted to Z scores. So, for example, if a distribution of raw scores is positively skewed, the distribution of Z scores will also be positively skewed.

A Z score is sometimes called a *standard score*. There are two reasons: Z scores have standard values for the mean and the standard deviation, and, as we saw earlier, Z scores provide a kind of standard scale of measurement for any variable. (However, sometimes the term *standard score* is used only when the Z scores are for a distribution that follows a normal curve.)

How are you doing?

1. How is a Z score related to a raw score?
2. Write the formula for changing a raw score to a Z score, and define each of the symbols.
3. For a particular group of scores, $M = 20$ and $SD = 5$. Give the Z score for (a) 30, (b) 15, (c) 20, and (d) 22.5.
4. Write the formula for changing a Z score to a raw score, and define each of the symbols.
5. For a particular group of scores, $M = 10$ and $SD = 2$. Give the raw score for a Z score of (a) +2, (b) +.5, (c) 0, and (d) −3.
6. Suppose a person has a Z score for overall health of +2 and a Z score for overall sense of humor of +1. What does it mean to say that this person is healthier than she is funny?

Answers

1. A Z score is the number of standard deviations a raw score is above or below the mean.
2. $Z = (X - M)/SD$. Z is the Z score; X is the raw score; M is the mean; SD is the standard deviation.
3. (a) $Z = (X - M)/SD = (30 - 20)/5 = 10/5 = 2$; (b) −1; (c) 0; (d) .5.
4. $X = (Z)(SD) + M$. X is the raw score; Z is the Z score; SD is the standard deviation; M is the mean.
5. (a) $X = (Z)(SD) + M = (2)(2) + 10 = 4 + 10 = 14$; (b) 11; (c) 10; (d) 4.
6. This person is more above the average in health (in terms of how much people typically vary from average in health) than she is above the average in humor (in terms of how much people typically vary from the average in humor).

The Normal Curve

The graphs of the distributions of many of the variables that psychologists study follow a unimodal, roughly symmetrical, bell-shaped curve. These bell-shaped smooth histograms approximate a precise and important mathematical distribution called the **normal distribution**, or, more simply, the **normal curve**.[1] The normal curve is a mathematical (or theoretical) distribution. Researchers often compare the actual distributions of the variables they are studying (that is, the distributions they find in research studies) to the normal curve. They don't expect the distributions of their variables to match the normal curve *perfectly* (since the normal curve is a theoretical distribution), but researchers often check whether their variables *approximately* follow a normal curve. (The normal curve or normal distribution is also often called a *Gaussian distribution* after the astronomer Karl Friedrich Gauss. However, if its discovery can be attributed to anyone, it should really be to Abraham de Moivre—see Box 1.) An example of the normal curve is shown in Figure 6.

Why the Normal Curve Is So Common in Nature

Take, for example, the number of different letters a particular person can remember accurately on various testings (with different random letters each time). On some testings the number of letters remembered may be high, on others low, and on most somewhere in between. That is, the number of different letters a person can recall on various testings probably approximately follows a normal curve. Suppose that the person has a basic ability to recall, say, seven letters in this kind of memory task. Nevertheless, on any particular testing, the actual number recalled will be affected by various influences—noisiness of the room, the person's mood at the moment, a combination of random letters similar to a familiar name, and so on.

These various influences add up to make the person recall more than seven on some testings and less than seven on others. However, the particular combination of such influences that come up at any testing is essentially random; thus, on most testings, positive and negative influences should cancel out. The chances are not very good of all the random negative influences happening to come together on a testing when none of the random positive influences show up. Thus, in general, the person remembers a middle amount, an amount in which all the opposing influences cancel each other out. Very high or very low scores are much less common.

This creates a unimodal distribution with most of the scores near the middle and fewer at the extremes. It also creates a distribution that is symmetrical, because the number of letters recalled is as likely to be above as below the middle. Being a unimodal symmetrical curve does not guarantee that it will be a normal curve; it could be too flat or too pointed. However, it can be shown mathematically that in the long run, if the influences are truly random, and the number of different influences being

normal distribution   frequency distribution that follows a normal curve.

normal curve   specific, mathematically defined, bell-shaped frequency distribution that is symmetrical and unimodal; distributions observed in nature and in research commonly approximate it.

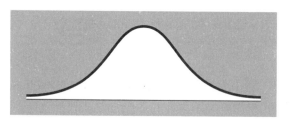

Figure 6   A normal curve.

BOX 1   de Moivre, the Eccentric Stranger Who Invented the Normal Curve

The normal curve is central to statistics and is the foundation of most statistical theories and procedures. If any one person can be said to have discovered this fundamental of the field, it was Abraham de Moivre. He was a French Protestant who came to England at the age of 21 because of religious persecution in France, which in 1685 denied Protestants all their civil liberties. In England, de Moivre became a friend of Isaac Newton, who was supposed to have often answered questions by saying, "Ask Mr. de Moivre—he knows all that better than I do." Yet because he was a foreigner, de Moivre was never able to rise to the same heights of fame as the British-born mathematicians who respected him so greatly.

Abraham de Moivre was mainly an expert on chance. In 1733, he wrote a "method of approximating the sum of the terms of the binomial expanded into a series." His paper essentially described the normal curve. The description was only in the form of a law, however; de Moivre never actually drew the curve itself. In fact, he was not very interested in it.

Credit for discovering the normal curve is often given to Pierre Laplace, a Frenchman who stayed home; or Karl Friedrich Gauss, a German; or Thomas Simpson, an Englishman. All worked on the problem of the distribution of errors around a mean, even going so far as describing the curve or drawing approximations of it. But even without drawing it, de Moivre was the first to compute the areas under the normal curve at 1, 2, and 3 standard deviations, and Karl Pearson, a distinguished later statistician, felt strongly that de Moivre was the true discoverer of this important concept.

In England, de Moivre was highly esteemed as a man of letters as well as of numbers, being familiar with all the classics and able to recite whole scenes from his beloved Molière's *The Misanthrope*. But for all his feelings for his native France, the French Academy elected him a *foreign* member of the Academy of Sciences just before his death. In England, he was ineligible for a university position because he was a foreigner there, as well. He remained in poverty, unable even to marry. In his earlier years, he worked as a traveling teacher of mathematics. Later, he was famous for his daily sittings in Slaughter's Coffee House in Long Acre, making himself available to gamblers and insurance underwriters (two professions equally uncertain and hazardous before statistics were refined), who paid him a small sum for figuring odds for them.

De Moivre's unusual death generated several legends. He worked a great deal with infinite series, which always converge to a certain limit. One story has it that de Moivre began sleeping 15 more minutes each night until he was asleep all the time, then died. Another version claims that his work at the coffeehouse drove him to such despair that he simply went to sleep until he died. At any rate, in his 80s he could stay awake only four hours a day, although he was said to be as keenly intellectual in those hours as ever. Then his wakefulness was reduced to 1 hour, then none at all. At the age of 87, after eight days in bed, he failed to wake and was declared dead from "somnolence" (sleepiness).

Sources: Pearson (1978); Tankard (1984).

---

combined is large, a precise normal curve will result. Mathematical statisticians call this principle the *central limit theorem*.

The Normal Curve and the Percentage of Scores Between the Mean and 1 and 2 Standard Deviations from the Mean

The shape of the normal curve is standard. Thus, there is a known percentage of scores above or below any particular point. For example, exactly 50% of the scores in a normal curve are below the mean, because in any symmetrical distribution half the scores are below the mean. More interestingly, as shown in Figure 7, approximately 34% of the scores are always between the mean and 1 standard deviation from the mean.

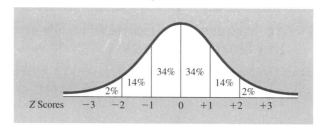

Figure 7 Normal curve with approximate percentages of scores between the mean and 1 and 2 standard deviations above and below the mean.

Consider IQ scores. On many widely used intelligence tests, the mean IQ is 100, the standard deviation is 15, and the distribution of IQs is roughly a normal curve (see Figure 8). Knowing about the normal curve and the percentage of scores between the mean and 1 standard deviation above the mean tells you that about 34% of people have IQs between 100, the mean IQ, and 115, the IQ score that is 1 standard deviation above the mean. Similarly, because the normal curve is symmetrical, about 34% of people have IQs between 100 and 85 (the score that is 1 standard deviation below the mean), and 68% (34% + 34%) have IQs between 85 and 115.

There are many fewer scores between 1 and 2 standard deviations from the mean than there are between the mean and 1 standard deviation from the mean. It turns out that about 14% of the scores in a normal curve are between 1 and 2 standard deviations above the mean (see Figure 7). (Similarly, about 14% of the scores are between 1 and 2 standard deviations below the mean.) Thus, about 14% of people have IQs between 115 (1 standard deviation above the mean) and 130 (2 standard deviations above the mean).

You will find it very useful to remember the 34% and 14% figures. These figures tell you the percentages of people above and below any particular score whenever you know that score's number of standard deviations above or below the mean. You can also reverse this approach and figure out a person's number of standard deviations from the mean from a percentage. Suppose you are told that a person scored in the top 2% on a test. Assuming that scores on the test are approximately normally distributed, the person must have a score that is at least 2 standard deviations above the mean. This is because a total of 50% of the scores are above the mean, but 34% are between the mean and 1 standard deviation above the mean, and another 14% are between 1 and 2 standard deviations above the mean. That leaves 2% of scores (that is, 50% − 34% − 14% = 2%) that are 2 standard deviations or more above the mean.

Figure 8 Distribution of IQ scores on many standard intelligence tests (with a mean of 100 and a standard deviation of 15).

Similarly, suppose you were selecting animals for a study and needed to consider their visual acuity. Suppose also that visual acuity was normally distributed and you wanted to use animals in the middle two-thirds (a figure close to 68%) for visual acuity. In this situation, you would select animals that scored between 1 standard deviation above and 1 standard deviation below the mean. (That is, about 34% are between the mean and 1 standard deviation above the mean and another 34% are between the mean and 1 standard deviation below the mean.) Also, remember that a Z score is the number of standard deviations that a score is above or below the mean—which is just what we are talking about here. Thus, if you knew the mean and the standard deviation of the visual acuity test, you could figure out the raw scores (the actual level of visual acuity) for being 1 standard deviation below and 1 standard deviation above the mean (that is, Z scores of −1 and +1). You would do this using the methods of changing raw scores to Z scores and vice versa that you learned earlier in this chapter, which are $Z = (X - M)/SD$ and $X = (Z)(SD) + M$.

The Normal Curve Table and Z Scores

The 50%, 34%, and 14% figures are important practical rules for working with a group of scores that follow a normal distribution. However, in many research and applied situations, psychologists need more accurate information. Because the normal curve is a precise mathematical curve, you can figure the exact percentage of scores between any two points on the normal curve (not just those that happen to be right at 1 or 2 standard deviations from the mean). For example, exactly 68.59% of scores have a Z score between +.62 and −1.68; exactly 2.81% of scores have a Z score between +.79 and +.89; and so forth. Statisticians have worked out tables for the normal curve that give the percentage of scores between the mean (a Z score of 0) and any other Z score (as well as the percentage of scores in the tail for any Z score).

We have included a **normal curve table** in the Appendix (Table A-1).[2] Table 1 shows the first part of the full table. The first column in the table lists the Z score. The second column, labeled "% Mean to Z," gives the percentage of scores between the mean and that Z score. The shaded area in the curve at the top of the column gives a visual reminder of the meaning of the percentages in the column. The third column, labeled "% in Tail," gives the percentage of scores in the tail for that Z score. The shaded tail area in the curve at the top of the column shows the meaning of the percentages in the column. Notice that the table lists only positive Z scores. This is because the normal curve is perfectly symmetrical. Thus, the percentage of scores between the mean and, say, a Z of +.98 (which is 33.65%) is exactly the same as the percentage of scores between the mean and a Z of −.98 (again 33.65%); and the percentage of scores in the tail for a Z score of +1.77 (3.84%) is the same as the percentage of scores in the tail for a Z score of −1.77 (again, 3.84%). Notice that for each Z score, the "% Mean to Z" value and the "% in Tail" value sum to 50.00. This is because exactly 50% of the scores are above the mean for a normal curve. For example, for the Z score of .57, the "% Mean to Z" value is 21.57% and the "% in Tail" value is 28.43%, and 21.57% + 28.43% = 50.00%.

Suppose you want to know the percentage of scores between the mean and a Z score of .64. You just look up .64 in the "Z" column of the table and the "% Mean to Z" column tells you that 23.89% of the scores in a normal curve are between the mean and this Z score. These values are highlighted in Table 1.

TIP FOR SUCCESS

Remember that negative Z scores are scores below the mean, and positive Z scores are scores above the mean.

normal curve table   table showing percentages of scores associated with the normal curve; the table usually includes percentages of scores between the mean and various numbers of standard deviations above the mean and percentages of scores more positive than various numbers of standard deviations above the mean.

Table 1   Normal Curve Areas: Percentage of the Normal Curve Between the Mean and the Scores Shown and Percentage of Scores in the Tail for the Z Scores Shown (First part of table only: full table is Table A-1 in the Appendix. Highlighted values are examples from the text.)

Z	% Mean to Z	% in Tail	Z	% Mean to Z	% in Tail
.00	.00	50.00	.45	17.36	32.64
.01	.40	49.60	.46	17.72	32.28
.02	.80	49.20	.47	18.08	31.92
.03	1.20	48.80	.48	18.44	31.56
.04	1.60	48.40	.49	18.79	31.21
.05	1.99	48.01	.50	19.15	30.85
.06	2.39	47.61	.51	19.50	30.50
.07	2.79	47.21	.52	19.85	30.15
.08	3.19	46.81	.53	20.19	29.81
.09	3.59	46.41	.54	20.54	29.46
.10	3.98	46.02	.55	20.88	29.12
.11	4.38	45.62	.56	21.23	28.77
.12	4.78	45.22	.57	21.57	28.43
.13	5.17	44.83	.58	21.90	28.10
.14	5.57	44.43	.59	22.24	27.76
.15	5.96	44.04	.60	22.57	27.43
.16	6.36	43.64	.61	22.91	27.09
.17	6.75	43.25	.62	23.24	26.76
.18	7.14	42.86	.63	23.57	26.43
.19	7.53	42.47	.64	23.89	26.11
.20	7.93	42.07	.65	24.22	25.78
.21	8.32	41.68	.66	24.54	25.46

TIP FOR SUCCESS

Notice that the table repeats the basic three columns twice on the page. Be sure to look across to the columns you need.

You can also reverse the process and use the table to find the Z score for a particular percentage of scores. For example, imagine that 30% of ninth-grade students had a creativity score higher than Samantha's. Assuming that creativity scores follow a normal curve, you can figure out her Z score as follows: if 30% of students scored higher than she did, then 30% of the scores are in the tail above her score. This is shown in Figure 9. So, you would look at the "% in Tail" column of the table until you found the percentage that was closest to 30%. In this example, the closest is 30.15%. Finally, look at the "Z" column to the left of this percentage, which lists a Z score of .52 (these values of 30.15% and .52 are highlighted in Table 1). Thus, Samantha's Z score for her level of creativity is .52. If you know the mean and standard deviation for ninth-grade students' creativity scores, you can figure out Samantha's actual raw score on the test by changing her Z score of .52 to a raw score using the usual formula, $X = (Z)(SD) + (M)$.

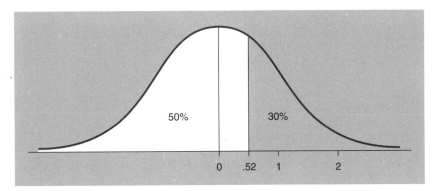

Figure 9 Distribution of creativity test scores showing area for top 30% of scores and Z score where this area begins.

Steps for Figuring the Percentage of Scores Above or Below a Particular Raw Score or Z Score Using the Normal Curve Table

Here are the five steps for figuring the percentage of scores.

❶ **If you are beginning with a raw score, first change it to a Z score.** Use the usual formula, $Z = (X - M)/SD$.

❷ **Draw a picture of the normal curve, decide where the Z score falls on it, and shade in the area for which you are finding the percentage.** When marking where the Z score falls on the normal curve, be sure to put it in the right place above or below the mean according to whether it is a positive or negative Z score.

❸ **Make a rough estimate of the shaded area's percentage based on the 50%– 34%–14% percentages.** You don't need to be very exact; it is enough just to estimate a range in which the shaded area has to fall, figuring it is between two particular whole Z scores. This rough estimate step is designed not only to help you avoid errors (by providing a check for your figuring), but also to help you develop an intuitive sense of how the normal curve works.

❹ **Find the exact percentage using the normal curve table, adding 50% if necessary.** Look up the Z score in the "Z" column of Table A-1 and find the percentage in the "% Mean to Z" column or "% in Tail" column next to it. If you want the percentage of scores between the mean and this Z score, or if you want the percentage of scores in the tail for this Z score, the percentage in the table is your final answer. However, sometimes you need to add 50% to the percentage in the table. You need to do this if the Z score is positive and you want the total percentage below this Z score, or if the Z score is negative and you want the total percentage above this Z score. However, you don't need to memorize these rules. It is much easier to make a picture for the problem and reason out whether the percentage you have from the table is correct as is, or if you need to add 50%.

❺ **Check that your exact percentage is within the range of your rough estimate from Step ❸.**

Examples

Here are two examples using IQ scores where $M = 100$ and $SD = 15$.

Example 1: If a person has an IQ of 125, what percentage of people have higher IQs?

Figure 10   Distribution of IQ scores showing percentage of scores above an IQ score of 125 (shaded area).

❶ **If you are beginning with a raw score, first change it to a Z score.** Using the usual formula, $Z = (X - M)/SD, Z = (125 - 100)/15 = +1.67$.

❷ **Draw a picture of the normal curve, decide where the Z score falls on it, and shade in the area for which you are finding the percentage.** This is shown in Figure 10 (along with the exact percentages figured later).

❸ **Make a rough estimate of the shaded area's percentage based on the 50%–34%–14% percentages.** If the shaded area started at a Z score of 1, it would have 16% above it. If it started at a Z score of 2, it would have only 2% above it. So, with a Z score of 1.67, the number of scores above it has to be somewhere between 16% and 2%.

❹ **Find the exact percentage using the normal curve table, adding 50% if necessary.** In Table A-1, 1.67 in the "Z" column goes with 4.75 in the "% in Tail" column. Thus, 4.75% of people have IQ scores higher than 125. This is the answer to our problem. (There is no need to add 50% to the percentage.)

❺ **Check that your exact percentage is within the range of your rough estimate from Step ❸.** Our result, 4.75%, is within the 16-to-2% range we estimated.

Example 2: If a person has an IQ of 95, what percentage of people have higher IQs?

❶ **If you are beginning with a raw score, first change it to a Z score.** Using the usual formula, $Z = (95 - 100)/15 = -.33$.

❷ **Draw a picture of the normal curve, decide where the Z score falls on it, and shade in the area for which you are finding the percentage.** This is shown in Figure 11 (along with the percentages figured later).

Figure 11   Distribution of IQ scores showing percentage of scores above an IQ score of 95 (shaded area).

❸ **Make a rough estimate of the shaded area's percentage based on the 50%–34%–14% percentages.** You know that 34% of the scores are between the mean and a Z score of −1. Also, 50% of the curve is above the mean. Thus, the Z score of −.33 has to have between 50% and 84% of scores above it.

❹ **Find the exact percentage using the normal curve table, adding 50% if necessary.** The table shows that 12.93% of scores are between the mean and a Z score of .33. Thus, the percentage of scores above a Z score of −.33 is the 12.93% between the Z score and the mean plus the 50% above the mean, which is 62.93%.

❺ **Check that your exact percentage is within the range of your rough estimate from Step ❸.** Our result of 62.93% is within the 50-to-84% range we estimated.

Figuring *Z* Scores and Raw Scores from Percentages Using the Normal Curve Table

Going from a percentage to a Z score or raw score is similar to going from a Z score or raw score to a percentage. However, you reverse the procedure when figuring the exact percentage. Also, any necessary changes from a Z score to a raw score are done at the end.

Here are the five steps.

❶ **Draw a picture of the normal curve, and shade in the approximate area for your percentage using the 50%–34%–14% percentages.**

❷ **Make a rough estimate of the Z score where the shaded area stops.**

❸ **Find the exact Z score using the normal curve table (subtracting 50% from your percentage if necessary before looking up the Z score).** Looking at your picture, figure out either the percentage in the shaded tail or the percentage between the mean and where the shading stops. For example, if your percentage is the bottom 35%, then the percentage in the shaded tail is 35%. Figuring the percentage between the mean and where the shading stops will sometimes involve subtracting 50% from the percentage in the problem. For example, if your percentage is the top 72%, then the percentage from the mean to where that shading stops is 22% ($72\% - 50\% = 22\%$).

Once you have the percentage, look up the closest percentage in the appropriate column of the normal curve table ("% Mean to Z" or "% in Tail") and find the Z score for that percentage. That Z will be your answer—except it may be negative. The best way to tell if it is positive or negative is by looking at your picture.

❹ **Check that your exact Z score is within the range of your rough estimate from Step ❷.**

❺ **If you want to find a raw score, change it from the Z score.** Use the usual formula, $X = (Z)(SD) + M$.

Examples

Here are three examples. Once again, we use IQ for our examples, with $M = 100$ and $SD = 15$.

Example 1: What IQ score would a person need to be in the top 5%?

❶ **Draw a picture of the normal curve, and shade in the approximate area for your percentage using the 50%–34%–14% percentages.** We wanted the top 5%. Thus, the shading has to begin above (to the right of) 1 *SD* (there are

Figure 12   Finding the Z score and IQ raw score for where the top 5% of scores start.

16% of scores above 1 *SD*). However, it cannot start above 2 *SD* because only 2% of all the scores are above 2 *SD*. But 5% is a lot closer to 2% than to 16%. Thus, you would start shading a small way to the left of the 2 *SD* point. This is shown in Figure 12.

❷ **Make a rough estimate of the Z score where the shaded area stops.** The Z score is between +1 and +2.

❸ **Find the exact Z score using the normal curve table (subtracting 50% from your percentage if necessary before looking up the Z score).** We want the top 5%, which means we can use the "% in Tail" column of the normal curve table. Looking in that column, the closest percentage to 5% is 5.05% (or you could use 4.95%). This goes with a Z score of 1.64 in the "Z" column.

❹ **Check that your exact Z score is within the range of your rough estimate from Step ❷.** As we estimated, +1.64 is between +1 and +2 (and closer to 2).

❺ **If you want to find a raw score, change it from the Z score.** Using the formula, $X = (Z)(SD) + M = (1.64)(15) + 100 = 124.60$. In sum, to be in the top 5%, a person would need an IQ of at least 124.60.

Example 2:   What IQ score would a person need to be in the top 55%?

❶ **Draw a picture of the normal curve and shade in the approximate area for your percentage using the 50%–34%–14% percentages.** You want the top 55%. There are 50% of scores above the mean. So, the shading has to begin below (to the left of) the mean. There are 34% of scores between the mean and 1 *SD* below the mean; so the score is between the mean and 1 *SD* below the mean. You would shade the area to the right of that point. This is shown in Figure 13.

Figure 13   Finding the IQ score for where the top 55% of scores start.

❷ **Make a rough estimate of the Z score where the shaded area stops.** The Z score has to be between 0 and −1.

❸ **Find the exact Z score using the normal curve table (subtracting 50% from your percentage if necessary before looking up the Z score).** Being in the top 55% means that 5% of people have IQs between this IQ and the mean (that is, 55% − 50% = 5%). In the normal curve table, the closest percentage to 5% in the "% Mean to Z" column is 5.17%, which goes with a Z score of .13. Because you are below the mean, this becomes −.13.

❹ **Check that your exact Z score is within the range of your rough estimate from Step ❷.** As we estimated, −.13 is between 0 and −1.

❺ **If you want to find a raw score, change it from the Z score.** Using the usual formula, $X = (-.13)(15) + 100 = 98.05$. So, to be in the top 55% on IQ, a person needs an IQ score of 98.05 or higher.

Example 3: What range of IQ scores includes the 95% of people in the middle range of IQ scores?

This kind of problem, of finding the middle percentage, may seem odd at first. However, it is actually a very common situation used in procedures.

Think of this kind of problem in terms of finding the scores that go with the upper and lower ends of this percentage. Thus, in this example, you are trying to find the points where the bottom 2.5% ends and the top 2.5% begins (which, out of 100%, leaves the middle 95%).

❶ **Draw a picture of the normal curve, and shade in the approximate area for your percentage using the 50%–34%–14% percentages.** Let's start where the top 2.5% begins. This point has to be higher than 1 *SD* (16% of scores are higher than 1 *SD*). However, it cannot start above 2 *SD* because there are only 2% of scores above 2 *SD*. But 2.5% is very close to 2%. Thus, the top 2.5% starts just to the left of the 2 *SD* point. Similarly, the point where the bottom 2.5% comes in is just to the right of −2 *SD*. The result of all this is that we will shade in two tail areas on the curve: one starting just above −2 *SD* and the other starting just below +2 *SD*. This is shown in Figure 14.

❷ **Make a rough estimate of the Z score where the shaded area stops.** You can see from the picture that the Z score for where the shaded area stops above the mean is just below +2. Similarly, the Z score for where the shaded area stops below the mean is just above −2.

❸ **Find the exact Z score using the normal curve table (subtracting 50% from your percentage if necessary before looking up the Z score).** Being in the top 2.5% means that 2.5% of the IQ scores are in the upper tail. In the normal curve table, the closest percentage to 2.5% in the "% in Tail" column is exactly

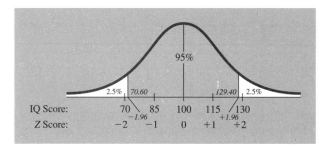

Figure 14   Finding the IQ scores for where the middle 95% of scores begins and ends.

2.50%, which goes with a Z score of $+1.96$. The normal curve is symmetrical. Thus, the Z score for the lower tail is -1.96.

❹ **Check that your exact Z score is within the range of your rough estimate from Step ❷.** As we estimated, $+1.96$ is between $+1$ and $+2$ and is very close to $+2$, and -1.96 is between -1 and -2 and very close to -2.

❺ **If you want to find a raw score, change it from the Z score.** For the high end, using the usual formula, $X = (1.96)(15) + 100 = 129.40$. For the low end, $X = (-1.96)(15) + 100 = 70.60$. In sum, the middle 95% of IQ scores run from 70.60 to 129.40.

How are you doing?

1. Why is the normal curve (or at least a curve that is symmetrical and unimodal) so common in nature?
2. Without using a normal curve table, about what percentage of scores on a normal curve are (a) above the mean, (b) between the mean and 1 SD above the mean, (c) between 1 and 2 SDs above the mean, (d) below the mean, (e) between the mean and 1 SD below the mean, and (f) between 1 and 2 SDs below the mean?
3. Without using a normal curve table, about what percentage of scores on a normal curve are (a) between the mean and 2 SDs above the mean, (b) below 1 SD above the mean, (c) above 2 SDs below the mean?
4. Without using a normal curve table, about what Z score would a person have who is at the start of the top (a) 50%, (b) 16%, (c) 84%, (d) 2%?
5. Using the normal curve table, what percentage of scores are (a) between the mean and a Z score of 2.14, (b) above 2.14, (c) below 2.14?
6. Using the normal curve table, what Z score would you have if (a) 20% are above you and (b) 80% are below you?

Answers

1. It is common because any particular score is the result of the random combination of many effects, some of which make the score larger and some of which make the score smaller. Thus, on average these effects balance out near the middle, with relatively few at each extreme, because it is unlikely for most of the increasing and decreasing effects to come out in the same direction.
2. (a) Above the mean: 50%; (b) between the mean and 1 SD above the mean: 34%; (c) between 1 and 2 SDs above the mean: 14%; (d) below the mean: 50%; (e) between the mean and 1 SD below the mean: 34%; (f) between 1 and 2 SDs below the mean: 14%.
3. (a) Between the mean and 2 SDs above the mean: 48%; (b) below 1 SD above the mean: 84%; (c) above 2 SDs below the mean: 98%.
4. (a) 50%: 0; (b) 16%: 1; (c) 84%: -1; (d) 2%: 2.
5. (a) Between the mean and a Z score of 2.14: 48.38%; (b) above 2.14: 1.62%; (c) below 2.14: 98.38%.
6. (a) 20% above you: .84; (b) 80% below you: .84.

population   entire group of people to which a researcher intends the results of a study to apply; larger group to which inferences are made on the basis of the particular set of people (sample) studied.

sample   scores of the particular group of people studied; usually considered to be representative of the scores in some larger population.

Sample and Population

We are going to introduce you to some important ideas by thinking of beans. Suppose you are cooking a pot of beans and taste a spoonful to see if they are done. In this example, the pot of beans is a **population**, the entire set of things of interest. The spoonful is a **sample**, the part of the population about which you actually have

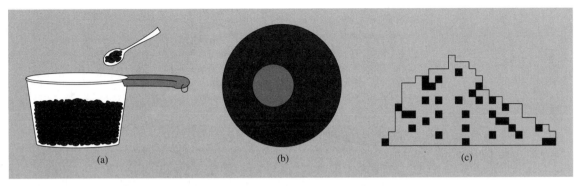

Figure 15   Populations and samples: (a) The entire pot of beans is the population, and the spoonful is the sample. (b) The entire larger circle is the population, and the circle within it is the sample. (c) The histogram is of the population, and the particular shaded scores make up the sample.

information. This is shown in Figure 15a. Figures 15b and 15c are other ways of showing the relation of a sample to a population.

In psychology research, we typically study samples of individuals to make inferences about some larger group (a population). A sample might consist of the scores of 50 Canadian women who participate in a particular experiment, whereas the population might be intended to be the scores of all Canadian women. In an opinion survey, 1,000 people might be selected from the voting-age population of a particular country and asked for whom they plan to vote. The opinions of these 1,000 people are the sample. The opinions of the larger voting public in that country, to which the pollsters apply their results, is the population (see Figure 16).

Why Psychologists Study Samples Instead of Populations

If you want to know something about a population, your results would be most accurate if you could study the entire population rather than a subgroup from it. However, in most research situations this is not practical. More important, the whole point of research usually is to be able to make generalizations or predictions about events beyond your reach. We would not call it scientific research if we tested three particular cars to see which gets better gas mileage—unless you hoped to say something about the gas mileage of those models of cars in general. In other words, a researcher might do an experiment on how people store words in short-term memory using 20 students as the participants in the experiment. But the purpose of the experiment is not to find out how these *particular* 20 students respond to the experimental versus the control condition. Rather, the purpose is to learn something about human memory under these conditions *in general.*

The strategy in almost all psychology research is to study a sample of individuals who are believed to be representative of the general population (or of some particular population of interest). More realistically, researchers try to study people who do not differ from the general population in any systematic way that should matter for that topic of research.

The sample is what is studied, and the population is an unknown about which researchers draw conclusions based on the sample.

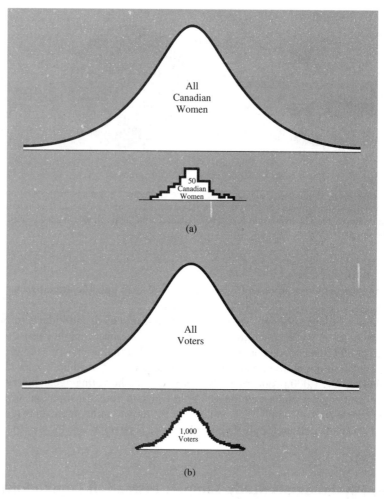

Figure 16 Additional examples of populations and samples: (a) The population is the scores of all Canadian women, and the sample is the scores of the 50 Canadian women studied. (b) The population is the voting preferences of the entire voting-age population, and the sample is the voting preferences of the 1,000 voting-age people who were surveyed.

TIP FOR SUCCESS

For more detailed information about methods of sampling, see Box 2 as well as Web Chapter W1 (*Overview of the Logic and Language of Psychology Research,* available at *www.pearsoned.co.in/prc/home.*

random selection   method for selecting a sample that uses truly random procedures (usually meaning that each person in the population has an equal chance of being selected); one procedure is for the researcher to begin with a complete list of all the people in the population and select a group of them to study using a table of random numbers.

Methods of Sampling

Usually, the ideal method of picking out a sample to study is called **random selection**. The researcher starts with a complete list of the population and randomly selects some of them to study. An example of random selection is to put each name on a table tennis ball, put all the balls into a big hopper, shake it up, and have a blindfolded person select as many as are needed. (In practice, most researchers use a computer-generated list of random numbers. Just how computers or persons can create a list of truly random numbers is an interesting question in its own right.)

It is important not to confuse truly random selection with what might be called *haphazard selection;* for example, just taking whoever is available or happens to be first on a list. When using haphazard selection, it is surprisingly easy to pick accidentally a group of people that is very different from the population as a whole. Consider a survey of attitudes about your statistics instructor. Suppose you give your questionnaire only to other students sitting near you in class. Such a survey would be affected by all the things that influence where students choose to sit, some of which have to do with just what your survey is about—how much students like the instructor or the class. Thus, asking students who sit near you would likely result in opinions more like your own than a truly random sample would.

Unfortunately, it is often impractical or impossible to study a truly random sample. Much of the time, in fact, studies are conducted with whoever is willing or available to be a research participant. At best, as noted, a researcher tries to study

BOX 2   Surveys, Polls, and 1948's Costly "Free Sample"

It is time to make you a more informed reader of polls in the media. Usually the results of properly done public polls are accompanied, somewhere in fine print, by a statement such as, "From a telephone survey of 1,000 American adults taken on June 4 and 5. Sampling error ±3%." What does a statement like this mean?

The Gallup poll is as good an example as any (Gallup, 1972; see also *www.gallup.com*), and there is no better place to begin than in 1948, when all three of the major polling organizations—Gallup, Crossley (for Hearst papers), and Roper (for *Fortune*)—wrongly predicted Thomas Dewey's victory over Harry Truman for the U.S. presidency. Yet Gallup's prediction was based on 50,000 interviews and Roper's on 15,000. By contrast, to predict Barack Obama's 2008 U.S. presidential victory, Gallup used only 3,050. Since 1952, the pollsters have never used more than 8,144—but with very small error and no outright mistakes. What has changed?

The method used before 1948, and never repeated since, was called "quota sampling." Interviewers were assigned a fixed number of persons to interview, with strict quotas to fill in all the categories that seemed important, such as residence, sex, age, race, and economic status. Within these specifics, however, they were free to interview whomever they liked. Republicans generally tended to be easier to interview. They were more likely to have telephones and permanent addresses and to live in better houses and better neighborhoods. In 1948, the election was very close, and the Republican bias produced the embarrassing mistake that changed survey methods forever.

Since 1948, all survey organizations have used what is called a "probability method." Simple random sampling is the purest case of the probability method, but simple random sampling for a survey about a U.S. presidential election would require drawing names from a list of all the eligible voters in the nation—a lot of people. Each person selected would have to be found, in diversely scattered locales. So instead, "multistage cluster sampling" is used. The United States is divided into seven size-of-community groupings, from large cities to rural open

country; these groupings are divided into seven geographic regions (New England, Middle Atlantic, and so on), after which smaller equal-sized groups are zoned, and then city blocks are drawn from the zones, with the probability of selection being proportional to the size of the population or number of dwelling units. Finally, an interviewer is given a randomly selected starting point on the map and is required to follow a given direction, taking households in sequence.

Actually, telephoning is the favored method for polling today. Phone surveys cost about one-third of door-to-door polls. Since most people now own phones, this method is less biased than in Truman's time. Phoning also allows computers to randomly dial phone numbers and, unlike telephone directories, this method calls unlisted numbers. However, survey organizations in the United States typically do not call cell phone numbers. Thus, U.S. households that use a cell phone for all calls and do not have a home phone are not usually included in telephone opinion polls. Most survey organizations consider the current cell-phone-only rate to be low enough not to cause large biases in poll results (especially since the demographic characteristics of individuals without a home phone suggest that they are less likely to vote than individuals who live in households with a home phone). However, there is increasing concern in the research community about the issue and how to adjust for it (e.g., Peytchev et al., 2011). Survey organizations are also starting to explore the use of other polling methods, such as email and the Internet.

Whether by telephone or face to face, there will be about 35% nonrespondents after three attempts. This creates yet another bias, dealt with through questions about how much time a person spends at home, so that a slight extra weight can be given to the responses of those reached but usually at home less, to make up for those missed entirely.

Now you know quite a bit about opinion polls, but we have left two important questions unanswered: Why are only about 1,000 included in a poll meant to describe all U.S. adults, and what does the term *sampling error* mean? For these answers, refer to Box 1 of *Hypothesis Tests with Means of Samples.*

a sample that is not systematically unrepresentative of the population in any known way. For example, suppose a study is about a process that is likely to differ for people of different age groups. In this situation, the researcher may attempt to include people of all age groups in the study. Alternatively, the researcher would be careful to draw conclusions only about the age group studied.

Statistical Terminology for Samples and Populations

The mean, variance, and standard deviation of a population are called **population parameters**. A population parameter usually is unknown and can be estimated only from what you know about a sample taken from that population. You do not taste all the beans, just the spoonful. "The beans are done" is an inference about the whole pot.

Population parameters are usually shown as Greek letters (e.g., μ). (This is a statistical convention with origins tracing back more than 2,000 years to the early Greek mathematicians.) The symbol for the mean of a population is μ, the Greek letter mu. The symbol for the variance of a population is σ^2, and the symbol for its standard deviation is σ, the lowercase Greek letter sigma. You won't see these symbols often, except while learning statistics. This is because, again, researchers seldom know the population parameters.

The mean, variance, and standard deviation you figure for the scores in a sample are called **sample statistics**. A sample statistic is figured from known information. Sample statistics are what we have been figuring all along and are expressed with the Roman letters: M, SD^2, and SD. The population parameter and sample statistic symbols for the mean, variance, and standard deviation are summarized in Table 2.

The use of different types of symbols for population parameters (Greek letters) and sample statistics (Roman letters) can take some getting used to; so don't worry if it seems tricky at first. It's important to know that the *statistical concepts* you are learning—such as the mean, variance, and standard deviation—are the same for both a population and a sample. So, for example, you have learned that the standard deviation provides a measure of the variability of the scores in a distribution—whether we are talking about a sample or a population. (The variance and standard deviation are sometimes *figured* in a slightly different way for a population than for a sample, but the *concepts* do not change). We use different symbols for population parameters and sample statistics to make it clear whether we are referring to a population or a sample.

population parameter   actual value of the mean, standard deviation, and so on, for the population; usually population parameters are not known, though often they are estimated based on information in samples.

μ population mean.

σ^2 population variance.

σ population standard deviation.

sample statistics   descriptive statistics, such as the mean or standard deviation, figured from the scores in a group of people studied.

Table 2   Population Parameters and Sample Statistics

	Population Parameter (Usually Unknown)	Sample Statistic (Figured from Known Data)
Basis:	Scores of entire population	Scores of sample only
Symbols:		
Mean	μ	M
Standard deviation	σ	SD
Variance	σ^2	SD^2

How are you doing?

1. Explain the difference between the population and a sample for a research study.
2. Why do psychologists usually study samples and not populations?
3. Explain the difference between random sampling and haphazard sampling.
4. Explain the difference between a population parameter and a sample statistic.
5. Give the symbols for the population parameters for (a) the mean and (b) the standard deviation.
6. Why are different symbols (Greek versus Roman letters) used for population parameters and sample statistics?

Answers

1. The population is the entire group to which results of a study are intended to apply. The sample is the particular, smaller group of individuals actually studied.
2. Psychologists usually study samples and not populations because it is not practical in most cases to study the entire population.
3. In random sampling, the sample is chosen from among the population using a completely random method, so that each individual has an equal chance of being included in the sample. In haphazard sampling, the researcher selects individuals who are easily available or who are convenient to study.
4. A population parameter is about the population (such as the mean of all the scores in the population); a sample statistic is about a particular sample (such as the mean of the scores of the people in the sample).
5. (a) Mean: μ; (b) standard deviation: σ.
6. Using different symbols for population parameters and sample statistics ensures that there is no confusion as to whether a symbol refers to a population or a sample.

Probability

The purpose of most psychological research is to examine the truth of a theory or the effectiveness of a procedure. But scientific research of any kind can only make that truth or effectiveness seem more or less likely; it cannot give us the luxury of knowing for certain. Probability is very important in science. In particular, probability is very important in inferential statistics, the methods psychologists use to go from results of research studies to conclusions about theories or applied procedures.

Probability has been studied for centuries by mathematicians and philosophers. Yet even today the topic is full of controversy. Fortunately, however, you need to know only a few key ideas to understand and carry out the inferential statistical procedures. These few key points are not very difficult; indeed, some students find them to be quite intuitive.

Interpretations of Probability

In statistics, we usually define **probability** as the expected relative frequency of a particular outcome. An **outcome** is the result of an experiment (or just about any situation in which the result is not known in advance, such as a coin coming up heads or it raining tomorrow). *Frequency* is how many times something happens. The *relative frequency* is the number of times something happens relative to the

probability expected relative frequency of an outcome; the proportion of successful outcomes to all outcomes.

outcome term used in discussing probability for the result of an experiment (or almost any event, such as a coin coming up heads or it raining tomorrow).

number of times it could have happened; that is, relative frequency is the proportion of times something happens. (A coin might come up heads 8 times out of 12 flips, for a relative frequency of 8/12, or 2/3.) **Expected relative frequency** is what you expect to get in the long run if you repeat the experiment many times. (In the case of a coin, in the long run you would expect to get 1/2 heads). This is called the **long-run relative-frequency interpretation of probability**. You may find it helpful to think of probability in terms of the likelihood of a particular outcome occurring. If the probability is very low, then the outcome is unlikely to occur, but if the probability is higher, then it is more likely that the outcome will happen.

We also use probability to express how certain we are that a particular thing will happen. This is called the **subjective interpretation of probability**. Suppose that you say there is a 95% chance that your favorite restaurant will be open tonight. You could be using a kind of relative frequency interpretation. This would imply that if you were to check whether this restaurant was open many times on days like today, you would find it open on 95% of those days. However, what you mean is probably more subjective: on a scale of 0% to 100%, you would rate your confidence that the restaurant is open at 95%. To put it another way, you would feel that a fair bet would have odds based on a 95% chance of the restaurant's being open.

The interpretation, however, does not affect how probability is figured. We mention these interpretations because we want to give you a deeper insight into the meaning of the term *probability,* which is such a prominent concept throughout statistics.

Figuring Probabilities

Probabilities are usually figured as the proportion of successful possible outcomes—the number of possible successful outcomes divided by the number of *all* possible outcomes. That is,

$$\text{Probability} = \frac{\text{Possible successful outcomes}}{\text{All possible outcomes}}$$

Consider the probability of getting heads when flipping a coin. There is one possible successful outcome (getting heads) out of two possible outcomes (getting heads or getting tails). This makes a probability of 1/2, or .5. In a throw of a single die, the probability of a 2 (or any other particular side of the six-sided die) is 1/6, or .17. This is because there can be only one successful outcome out of six possible outcomes. The probability of throwing a die and getting a number 3 or lower is 3/6, or .5. There are three possible successful outcomes (a 1, a 2, or a 3) out of six possible outcomes.

Now consider a slightly more complicated example. Suppose a class has 200 people in it, and 30 are seniors. If you were to pick someone from the class at random, the probability of picking a senior would be 30/200, or .15. This is because there are 30 possible successful outcomes (getting a senior) out of 200 possible outcomes.

Steps for Finding Probabilities

There are three steps for finding probabilities.

❶ Determine the number of possible successful outcomes.
❷ Determine the number of all possible outcomes.

expected relative frequency number of successful outcomes divided by the number of total outcomes you would expect to get if you repeated an experiment a large number of times.

long-run relative-frequency interpretation of probability understanding of probability as the proportion of a particular outcome that you would get if the experiment were repeated many times.

subjective interpretation of probability way of understanding probability as the degree of one's certainty that a particular outcome will occur.

❸ **Divide the number of possible successful outcomes (Step ❶) by the number of all possible outcomes (Step ❷).**

Let's apply these three steps to the probability of getting a number 3 or lower on a throw of a die.

❶ **Determine the number of possible successful outcomes.** There are three outcomes of 3 or lower: 1, 2, or 3.

❷ **Determine the number of all possible outcomes.** There are six possible outcomes in the throw of a die: 1, 2, 3, 4, 5, or 6.

❸ **Divide the number of possible successful outcomes (Step ❶) by the number of all possible outcomes (Step ❷).** $3/6 = .5$.

Range of Probabilities

A probability is a proportion, the number of possible successful outcomes to the total number of possible outcomes. A proportion cannot be less than 0 or greater than 1. In terms of percentages, proportions range from 0% to 100%. Something that has no chance of happening has a probability of 0, and something that is certain to happen has a probability of 1. Notice that when the probability of an event is 0, the event is completely *impossible;* it cannot happen. But when the probability of an event is low, say 5% or even 1%, the event is *improbable* or *unlikely,* but not impossible.

Probabilities Expressed as Symbols

Probability is usually symbolized by the letter p. The actual probability number is usually given as a decimal, though sometimes fractions or percentages are used. A 50-50 chance is usually written as $p = .5$, but it could also be written as $p = 1/2$

BOX 3 Pascal Begins Probability Theory at the Gambling Table, Then Learns to Bet on God

In England, statistics were used to keep track of death rates and to prove the existence of God. The French and Italians, however, developed statistics at the gaming table. In particular, there was the "problem of points"—the division of the stakes in a game after it has been interrupted. If a certain number of plays were planned, how much of the stakes should each player walk away with, given the percentage of plays completed?

The problem was discussed at least as early as 1494 by Luca Pacioli, a friend of Leonardo da Vinci. But it was unsolved until 1654, when it was presented to Blaise Pascal by the Chevalier de Méré. Pascal, a French child prodigy, attended meetings of the most famous adult French mathematicians and at 15 proved an important theorem in geometry. In correspondence with Pierre de Fermat, another famous French mathematician, Pascal solved the problem of points and in so doing began the field of probability theory and the work that would lead to

the normal curve. (For more information on the problem of points, including its solution, see *http://mathforum. org/isaac/problems/prob1.html*).

Not long after solving this problem, Pascal became as religiously devout as the English statisticians. He was in a runaway horse-drawn coach on a bridge and was saved from drowning by the traces (the straps between the horses and the carriage) breaking at the last possible moment. He took this as a warning to abandon his mathematical work in favor of religious writings and later formulated "Pascal's wager": that the value of a game is the value of the prize times the probability of winning it; therefore, even if the probability is low that God exists, we should gamble on the affirmative because the value of the prize is infinite, whereas the value of not believing is only finite worldly pleasure.

Source: Tankard (1984).

or $p = 50\%$. It is also common to see probability written as being less than some number, using the "less than" sign. For example, $p < .05$ means "the probability is less than .05."

Probability Rules

As already noted, our discussion only scratches the surface of probability. One of the topics we have not considered is the rules for figuring probabilities for multiple outcomes: for example, what is the chance of flipping a coin twice and both times getting heads? These are called probability rules, and they are important in the mathematical foundation of many aspects of statistics. However, you don't need to know these probability rules to understand what we cover in this chapter. Also, the rules are rarely used directly in analyzing results of psychology research. Nevertheless, you occasionally see such procedures referred to in research articles. Thus, the most widely mentioned probability rules are described in the Advanced Topics section toward the end of this chapter.

Probability, *Z* Scores, and the Normal Distribution

So far, we mainly have discussed probabilities of specific events that might or might not happen. We also can talk about a range of events that might or might not happen. The throw of a die coming out 3 or lower is an example (it includes the range 1, 2, and 3). Another example is the probability of selecting someone on a city street who is between the ages of 30 and 40.

If you think of probability in terms of the proportion of scores, probability fits in well with frequency distributions. In the frequency distribution shown in Figure 17, 3 of the total of 50 people scored 9 or 10. If you were selecting people from this group of 50 at random, there would be 3 chances (possible successful outcomes) out of 50 (all possible outcomes) of selecting one that was 9 or 10. Thus, $p = 3/50 = .06$.

You can also think of the normal distribution as a probability distribution. With a normal curve, the percentage of scores between any two Z scores is known. The percentage of scores between any two Z scores is the same as the probability of selecting a score between those two Z scores. As you saw earlier in this chapter, approximately 34% of scores in a normal curve are between the mean and one standard deviation from the mean. You should therefore not be surprised to learn that the probability of a score being between the mean and a Z score of $+1$ is about .34 (that is, $p = .34$).

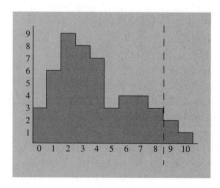

Figure 17   Frequency distribution (shown as a histogram) of 50 people, in which $p = .06$ (3/50) of randomly selecting a person with a score of 9 or 10.

In a previous IQ example in the normal curve section of this chapter, we figured that 95% of the scores in a normal curve are between a Z score of $+1.96$ and a Z score of -1.96 (see Figure 14). Thus, if you were to select a score at random from a distribution that follows a normal curve, the probability of selecting a score *between* Z scores of $+1.96$ and -1.96 is .95 (that is, a 95% chance). This is a very high probability. Also, the probability of selecting a score from such a distribution that is either *greater* than a Z score of $+1.96$ or *less than* a Z score of -1.96 is .05 (that is, a 5% chance). This is a very low probability. It helps to think about this visually. If you look back to Figure 14, the .05 probability of selecting a score that is either *greater* than a Z score of $+1.96$ or *less than* a Z score of -1.96 is represented by the tail areas in the figure.

Probability, Samples, and Populations

Probability is also relevant to samples and populations. In this chapter, we will use an example to give you a sense of the role of probability in samples and populations. Imagine you are told that a sample of one person has a score of 4 on a certain measure. However, you do not know whether this person is from a population of women or of men. You are told that a population of women has scores on this measure that are normally distributed with a mean of 10 and a standard deviation of 3. How likely do you think it is that your sample of 1 person comes from this population of women? From your knowledge of the normal curve (see Figure 7), you know there are very few scores as low as 4 in a normal distribution that has a mean of 10 and a standard deviation of 3. So there is a very low likelihood that this person comes from the population of women. Now, what if the sample person had a score of 9? In this case, there is a much greater likelihood that this person comes from the population of women because there are many scores of 9 in that population. This kind of reasoning provides an introduction to the process of *hypothesis testing*.

How are you doing?

1. The probability of an event is defined as the expected relative frequency of a particular outcome. Explain what is meant by (a) relative frequency and (b) outcome.
2. List and explain two interpretations of probability.
3. Suppose you have 400 coins in a jar and 40 of them are more than 9 years old. You then mix up the coins and pull one out hoping to get one that is more than 9 years old. (a) What is the number of possible successful outcomes? (b) What is the number of all possible outcomes? (c) What is the probability of getting one that is more than 9 years old?
4. Suppose people's scores on a particular personality test are normally distributed with a mean of 50 and a standard deviation of 10. If you were to pick a person completely at random, what is the probability you would pick someone with a score on this test higher than 60?
5. What is meant by $p < .01$?

Answers

1. (a) Relative frequency is the number of times something happens in relation to the number of times it could have happened. (b) An outcome is the result of an experiment—what happens in a situation where what will happen is not known in advance.

2. (a) The long-run relative frequency interpretation of probability is that probability is the proportion of times we expect something to happen (relative to how often it could happen) if the situation were repeated a very large number of times. (b) The subjective interpretation of probability is that probability is our sense of confidence that something will happen rated on a 0% to 100% scale.

3. (a) The number of possible successful outcomes is 40. (b) The number of all possible outcomes is 400. (c) The probability of getting one that is more than 9 years old is $40/400 = .10$.

4. The probability you would pick someone with a score on this test higher than 60 is $p = .16$ (since 16% of the scores are more than one standard deviation above the mean).

5. The probability is less than .01.

Controversies: Is the Normal Curve Really So Normal? And Using Nonrandom Samples

Basic though they are, there is considerable controversy about the topics we have introduced in this chapter. In this section we consider a major controversy about the normal curve and nonrandom samples.

Is the Normal Curve Really So Normal?

We've said that real distributions in the world often closely approximate the normal curve. Just how often real distributions closely follow a normal curve turns out to be very important, not just because normal curves make Z scores more useful. The main statistical methods psychologists use assume that the samples studied come from populations that follow a normal curve. Researchers almost never know the true shape of the population distribution; so if they want to use the usual methods, they have to just *assume* it is normal, making this assumption because most populations are normal. Yet there is a long-standing debate in psychology about just how often populations really are normally distributed. The predominant view has been that, given how psychology measures are developed, a bell-shaped distribution "is almost guaranteed" (Walberg et al., 1984, p. 107). Or, as Hopkins and Glass (1978) put it, measurements in all disciplines are such good approximations to the curve that one might think, "God loves the normal curve!"

On the other hand, there has been a persistent line of criticism about whether nature really packages itself so neatly. In a classic study, Micceri (1989) showed that many measures commonly used in psychology are *not* normally distributed "in nature." His study included achievement and ability tests (such as the SAT and the GRE) and personality tests (such as the Minnesota Multiphasic Personality Inventory, MMPI). Micceri examined the distributions of scores of 440 psychological and educational measures that had been used on very large samples. All of the measures he examined had been studied in samples of over 190 individuals, and the majority had samples of over 1,000 (14.3% even had samples of 5,000 to 10,293). Yet large samples were of no help. No measure he studied had a distribution that passed all checks for normality (mostly, Micceri looked for skewness, kurtosis, and "lumpiness"). Few measures had distributions that even came reasonably close to looking like the normal curve. Nor were these variations predictable: "The distributions studied here exhibited almost every conceivable type of contamination" (p. 162), although some were more common with certain types of tests. Micceri discusses many obvious reasons for this nonnormality, such as ceiling or floor effects.

How much has it mattered that the distributions for these measures were so far from normal? According to Micceri, the answer is just not known. And until more is known, the general opinion among psychologists will no doubt remain supportive of traditional statistical methods, with the underlying mathematics based on the assumption of normal population distributions.

What is the reason for this nonchalance in the face of findings such as Micceri's? It turns out that under most conditions in which the standard methods are used, they give results that are reasonably accurate even when the formal requirement of a normal population distribution is not met (e.g., Sawilowsky & Blair, 1992). In this chapter, we generally adopt this majority position favoring the use of the standard methods in all but the most extreme cases. But you should be aware that a vocal minority of psychologists disagrees. Some of the alternative statistical techniques they favor (ones that do not rely on assuming a normal distribution in the population) include the use of *nonparametric statistics* that do not have assumptions about the shape of the population distribution.

Francis Galton (1889), one of the major pioneers of statistical methods, said of the normal curve, "I know of scarcely anything so apt to impress the imagination.... [It] would have been personified by the Greeks and deified, if they had known of it. It reigns with serenity and in complete self-effacement amidst the wild confusion" (p. 66). Ironically, it may be true that in psychology, at least, it truly reigns in pure and austere isolation, with no even close-to-perfect real-life imitators.

Using Nonrandom Samples

Most of the procedures you learn later are based on mathematics that assume the sample studied is a random sample of the population. As we pointed out, however, in most psychology research the samples are nonrandom, including whatever individuals are available to participate in the experiment. Most studies are done with college students, volunteers, convenient laboratory animals, and the like.

Some psychologists are concerned about this problem and have suggested that researchers need to use different statistical approaches that make generalizations only to the kinds of people that are actually being used in the study.[3] For example, these psychologists would argue that, if your sample has a particular nonnormal distribution, you should assume that you can generalize only to a population with the same particular nonnormal distribution.

Sociologists, as compared to psychologists, are much more concerned about the representativeness of the groups they study. Studies reported in sociology journals (or in sociologically oriented social psychology journals) are much more likely to use formal methods of random selection and large samples, or at least to address the issue in their articles.

Why are psychologists more comfortable with using nonrandom samples? The main reason is that psychologists are mainly interested in the *relationships* among variables. If in one population the effect of experimentally changing X leads to a change in Y, this relationship should probably hold in other populations. This relationship should hold even if the actual levels of *Y* differ from population to population. Suppose that a researcher conducts an experiment testing the relation of number of exposures to a list of words to number of words remembered. Suppose further that this study is done with undergraduates taking introductory psychology and that the result is that the greater the number of exposures is, the greater is the number of words remembered. The actual number of words remembered from the list might well be different for people other than introductory psychology students. For example, chess masters (who probably have highly developed memories) may recall more words; people who have just been upset may recall fewer words. However, even in these groups, we would expect that the more times someone is exposed to the list, the more words will be remembered. That is, the *relation* of number of exposures to number of words recalled will probably be about the same in each population.

In sociology, political science, certain areas of medicine, and some other fields, the representativeness of samples is much more important. This is because researchers in these fields are more concerned with the actual mean and variance of a variable in a particular society or population group. For example, a sociologist might be interested in the average attitude towards older people in the population of a particular country. For this purpose, how sampling is done is extremely important. Indeed, even in psychology, random samples are sometimes used. For example, in a random telephone survey of U.S. households, O'Leary et al. (2012) found that 40.3% of individuals married more than 10 years reported that they were "very intensely in love" with their spouse.

Z Scores, Normal Curves, Samples and Populations, and Probabilities in Research Articles

You need to understand the topics we covered in this chapter to learn what comes next. However, the topics of this chapter are rarely mentioned directly in research articles (except in articles *about* methods or statistics). Although *Z* scores are extremely important as steps in advanced statistical procedures, they are rarely reported directly in research articles. Sometimes you will see the normal curve mentioned, usually when a researcher is describing the pattern of scores on a particular variable.

Research articles will sometimes briefly mention the method of selecting the sample from the population. For example, Morgenstern and colleagues (2009) conducted a survey study among children and adolescents in Germany and the United States to test whether individuals from lower socioeconomic status backgrounds may be more at risk for obesity because they engage in more sedentary behaviors, such as watching television. With regard to the German sample, they described the method of their study as follows:

> Forty-two public schools from the state of Schleswig-Holstein were randomly selected and invited to take part in an investigation of media use and child/adolescent behavior; 27 schools (64%) agreed to participate. All students (*N* = 6607) in grades 6 to 8 were recruited for the study. Eight hundred thirty-six students (12.7%) were excluded because of missing parental consent forms, 145 (2.2%) were absent on the day of data collection, and 816 (12.4%) were excluded because of missing or inconsistent/implausible data..., which provided a final sample of 4810 children and adolescents. (p. 732)

With regard to the U.S. sample, they described the recruitment method as follows:

> Using random-digit-dial methods, 6522 children and adolescents aged 10 to 14 years were recruited.... The baseline sample was representative of the US population with respect to region of the country, ethnicity and family income. (p. 732)

Whenever possible, researchers report the proportion of individuals approached for the study who actually participated in the study. This is called the *response rate*. For this study, Morgenstern and colleagues (2009) noted the response rate for the German schools (64%), as well as the percentage of students who provided usable survey data (4810/6607 = 73%).

Researchers sometimes also check whether their sample is similar to the population as a whole, based on any information they may have about the overall population. For example, Morgenstern and colleagues (2009) noted that the U.S. sample was consistent with the population in terms of geographic region, ethnicity, and family income. However, 10.8% of the U.S. sample was found to be overweight, which "...compares with a nationwide prevalence of overweight for the US population from the National Health and Nutrition Examination Survey of 17.6% in 12- to 19-year-old children (2003-2006), so the sample was biased toward leaner children (or there were some who underreported their weight)" (p. 733).

However, even survey studies typically are not able to use such rigorous methods and have to rely on more haphazard methods of getting their samples. For example, in a study of relationship distress and partner abuse (Heyman et al., 2001), the researchers describe their method of gathering research participants to interview as follows: "Seventy-four couples of varying levels of relationship adjustment were recruited through community newspaper advertisements" (p. 336). In a study of this kind, one cannot very easily recruit a random sample of abusers since there is no list of all abusers to recruit from. This could be done with a very large national random sample of couples, who would then include a random sample of abusers. Indeed, the authors of this study are very aware of the issues. At the end of the article, when discussing "cautions necessary when interpreting our results," they note that before their conclusions can be taken as definitive "our study must be replicated with a representative sample" (p. 341).

Finally, probability is rarely discussed directly in research articles, except in relation to statistical significance. In almost any article you look at, the results section will be strewn with descriptions of various methods having to do with statistical significance, followed by something like "$p < .05$" or "$p < .01$." The p refers to probability, but the probability of what?

Advanced Topic: Probability Rules and Conditional Probabilities

This advanced topic section provides additional information on probability, focusing specifically on probability rules and conditional probabilities. Probability rules are procedures for figuring probabilities in more complex situations than we have considered so far. This section considers the two most widely used such rules and also explains the concept of conditional probabilities that is used in advanced discussions of probability.

Addition Rule

The *addition rule* (also called the *or rule*) is used when there are two or more *mutually exclusive outcomes*. "Mutually exclusive" means that, if one outcome happens, the others can't happen. For example, heads or tails on a single coin flip are mutually exclusive because the result has to be one or the other, but can't be both. With mutually exclusive outcomes, the total probability of getting either outcome is the sum of the individual probabilities. Thus, on a single coin flip, the total chance of getting either heads (which is .5) or tails (also .5) is 1.0 (.5 plus .5). Similarly, on a single throw of a die, the chance of getting either a 3 (1/6) or a 5 (1/6) is 1/3 (1/6 + 1/6). If you are picking a student at random from your university in which 30% are seniors and 25% are juniors, the chance of picking someone who is either a senior or a junior is 55%.

Even though we have not used the term *addition rule,* we have already used this rule in many of the examples we considered in this chapter. For example, we used this rule when we figured that the chance of getting a 3 or lower on the throw of a die is .5.

Multiplication Rule

The *multiplication rule* (also called the *and rule*), however, is completely new. You use the multiplication rule to figure the probability of getting *both* of two (or more) *independent outcomes.* Independent outcomes are those for which getting one has no effect on getting the other. For example, getting a head or tail on one flip of a coin is an independent outcome from getting a head or tail on a second flip of a coin. The probability of getting both of two independent outcomes is the product of (the result of multiplying) the individual probabilities. For example, on a single coin flip, the chance of getting a head is .5. On a second coin flip, the chance of getting a head (regardless of what you got on the first flip) is also .5. Thus, the probability of getting heads on *both* coin flips is .25 (.5 multiplied by .5). On two throws of a die, the chance of getting a 5 on *both* throws is 1/36—the probability of getting a 5 on the first throw (1/6) multiplied by the probability of getting a 5 on the second throw (1/6). Similarly, on a multiple choice exam with four possible answers to each item, the chance of getting both of two questions correct just by guessing is 1/16—that is, the chance of getting one question correct just by guessing (1/4) multiplied by the chance of getting the other correct just by guessing (1/4). To take one more example, suppose you have a 20% chance of getting accepted into one graduate school and a 30% chance of getting accepted into another graduate school. Your chance of getting accepted at *both* graduate schools is just 6% (that is, 20% $\times$ 30% = 6%).

Conditional Probabilities

There are several other probability rules, some of which are combinations of the addition and multiplication rules. Most of these other rules have to do with what are called *conditional probabilities.* A conditional probability is the probability of one outcome, assuming some other outcome will happen. That is, the probability of the one outcome depends on—is *conditional* on—the probability of the other outcome. Thus, suppose that college A has 50% women and college B has 60% women. If you select a person at random, what is the chance of getting a woman? If you know the person is from college A, the probability is 50%. That is, the probability of getting a woman, conditional upon her coming from college A, is 50%.

Learning Aids

Summary

1. A *Z* score is the number of standard deviations that a raw score is above or below the mean.
2. The scores on many variables in psychology research approximately follow a bell-shaped, symmetrical, unimodal distribution called the normal curve. Because the shape of this curve follows an exact mathematical formula, there is a specific percentage of scores between any two points on a normal curve.

3. A useful working rule for normal curves is that 50% of the scores are above the mean, 34% are between the mean and 1 standard deviation above the mean, and 14% are between 1 and 2 standard deviations above the mean.

4. A normal curve table gives the percentage of scores between the mean and any particular Z score, as well as the percentage of scores in the tail for any Z score. Using this table, and knowing that the curve is symmetrical and that 50% of the scores are above the mean, you can figure the percentage of scores above or below any particular Z score. You can also use the table to figure the Z score for the point where a particular percentage of scores begins or ends.

5. A sample is an individual or group that is studied—usually as representative of some larger group or population that cannot be studied in its entirety. Ideally, the sample is selected from a population using a strictly random procedure. The mean (M), variance (SD^2), standard deviation (SD), and so forth of a sample are called sample statistics. When referring to a population, the sample statistics are called population parameters and are symbolized by Greek letters—μ for mean, σ^2 for variance, and σ for standard deviation.

6. Most psychology researchers consider the probability of an event to be its expected relative frequency. However, some think of probability as the subjective degree of belief that the event will happen. Probability is figured as the proportion of successful outcomes to total possible outcomes. It is symbolized by p and has a range from 0 (event is impossible) to 1 (event is certain). The normal curve provides a way to know the probabilities of scores being within particular ranges of values.

7. There are controversies about many of the topics in this chapter. One is about whether normal distributions are truly typical of the populations of scores for the variables we study in psychology. In another controversy, some researchers have questioned the use of standard statistical methods in the typical psychology research situation that does not use strict random sampling.

8. Research articles rarely discuss Z scores, normal curves (except briefly when a variable being studied seems not to follow a normal curve), or probability (except in relation to statistical significance). Procedures of sampling, particularly when the study is a survey, are sometimes described, and the representativeness of a sample may also be discussed.

9. ADVANCED TOPIC: In situations where there are two or more mutually exclusive outcomes, probabilities are figured following an addition rule, in which the total probability is the sum of the individual probabilities. A multiplication rule (in which probabilities are multiplied together) is followed to figure the probability of getting both of two (or more) independent outcomes. A conditional probability is the probability of one outcome, assuming some other particular outcome will happen.

Key Terms

Z score
raw score
normal distribution
normal curve
normal curve table
population
sample

random selection
population parameter
μ (population mean)
σ^2 (population variance)
σ (population standard deviation)
sample statistics
probability (p)

outcome
expected relative frequency
long-run relative-frequency interpretation of probability
subjective interpretation of probability

Example Worked-Out Problems

Changing a Raw Score to a Z Score

A distribution has a mean of 80 and a standard deviation of 20. Find the Z score for a raw score of 65.

Answer

You can change a raw score to a Z score using the formula or the steps.
   Using the formula: $Z = (X - M)/SD = (65 - 80)/20 = -15/20 = -.75.$
   Using the steps:

❶ **Figure the deviation score: subtract the mean from the raw score.** $65 - 80 = -15.$
❷ **Figure the Z score: divide the deviation score by the standard deviation.** $-15/20 = -.75.$

Changing a Z Score to a Raw Score

A distribution has a mean of 200 and a standard deviation of 50. A person has a Z score of 1.26. What is the person's raw score?

Answer

You can change a Z score to a raw score using the formula or the steps.
   Using the formula: $X = (Z)(SD) + M = (1.26)(50) + 200 = 63 + 200 = 263.$
   Using the steps:

❶ **Figure the deviation score: multiply the Z score by the standard deviation.** $1.26 \times 50 = 63.$
❷ **Figure the raw score: add the mean to the deviation score.** $63 + 200 = 263.$

Outline for Writing Essays Involving Z Scores

1. If required by the question, explain the mean, variance, and standard deviation (using the points in the essay outlined in *Central Tendency and Variability*).
2. Describe the basic idea of a Z score as a way of describing where a particular score fits into an overall group of scores. Specifically, a Z score shows the number of standard deviations a score is above or below the mean.
3. Explain the steps for figuring a Z score from a raw (ordinary) score.
4. Mention that changing raw scores to Z scores puts scores that are for different variables onto the same scale, which makes it easier to make comparisons between scores on the variables.

Figuring the Percentage Above or Below a Particular Raw Score or Z Score

Suppose a test of sensitivity to violence is known to have a mean of 20, a standard deviation of 3, and a normal curve shape. What percentage of people have scores above 24?

Answer

❶ **If you are beginning with a raw score, first change it to a Z score.** Using the usual formula, $Z = (X - M)/SD, Z = (24 - 20)/3 = 1.33.$

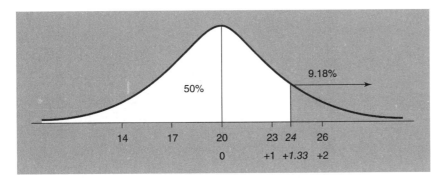

Figure 18 Distribution of sensitivity to violence scores showing the percentage of scores above a score of 24 (shaded area).

❷ **Draw a picture of the normal curve, decide where the Z score falls on it, and shade in the area for which you are finding the percentage.** This is shown in Figure 18.

❸ **Make a rough estimate of the shaded area's percentage based on the 50%–34%–14% percentages.** If the shaded area started at a Z score of 1, it would include 16%. If it started at a Z score of 2, it would include only 2%. So with a Z score of 1.33, it has to be somewhere between 16% and 2%.

❹ **Find the exact percentage using the normal curve table, adding 50% if necessary.** In Table A-1 (in the Appendix), 1.33 in the "Z" column goes with 9.18% in the "% in Tail" column. This is the answer to our problem: 9.18% of people have a higher score than 24 on the sensitivity to violence measure. (There is no need to add 50% to the percentage.)

❺ **Check that your exact percentage is within the range of your rough estimate from Step ❸.** Our result, 9.18%, is within the 16% to 2% range estimated.

Note: If the problem involves Z scores that are all exactly 0, 1, or 2 (or −1 or −2), you can work out the problem entirely using the 50%−34%−14% figures and without using the normal curve table (although you should still draw a figure and shade in the appropriate area).

Figuring Z Scores and Raw Scores From Percentages

Consider the same situation: A test of sensitivity to violence is known to have a mean of 20, a standard deviation of 3, and a normal curve shape. What is the minimum score a person needs to be in the top 75%?

Answer

❶ **Draw a picture of the normal curve, and shade in the approximate area for your percentage using the 50%–34%–14% percentages.** The shading has to begin between the mean and 1 *SD* below the mean. (There are 50% above the mean and 84% above 1 *SD* below the mean). This is shown in Figure 19.

❷ **Make a rough estimate of the Z score where the shaded area stops.** The Z score has to be between 0 and −1.

❸ **Find the exact Z score using the normal curve table (subtracting 50% from your percentage if necessary before looking up the Z score).** Since 50% of people have sensitivity to violence scores above the mean, for the top 75% you

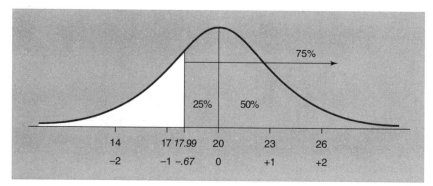

Figure 19   Finding the sensitivity to violence raw score for where the top 75% of scores start.

need to include the 25% below the mean (that is, $75\% - 50\% = 25\%$). Looking in the "% Mean to Z" column of the normal curve table, the closest figure to 25% is 24.86, which goes with a Z of .67. Since we are interested in below the mean, we want $-.67$.

❹ **Check that your exact Z score is within the range of your rough estimate from Step ❷.** $-.67$ is between 0 and -1.

❺ **If you want to find a raw score, change it from the Z score.** Using the formula $X = (Z)(SD) + M$, $X = (-.67)(3) + 20 = -2.01 + 20 = 17.99$. That is, to be in the top 75%, a person needs to have a score on this test of at least 18.

Note: If the problem instructs you not to use a normal curve table, you should be able to work the problem using just the 50%–34%–14% figures (although you should still draw a figure and shade in the appropriate area).

Outline for Writing Essays on the Logic and Computations for Figuring a Percentage from a Z Score and Vice Versa

1. Note that the normal curve is a mathematical (or theoretical) distribution, describe its shape (be sure to include a diagram of the normal curve), and mention that many variables in nature and in research approximately follow a normal curve.
2. If required by the question, explain the mean and standard deviation (using the points in the essay outlined in *Central Tendency and Variability*).
3. Describe the link between the normal curve and the percentage of scores between the mean and any Z score. Be sure to include a description of the normal curve table and show how it is used.
4. Briefly describe the steps required to figure a percentage from a Z score or vice versa (as required by the question). Be sure to draw a diagram of the normal curve with appropriate numbers and shaded areas marked on it from the relevant question (e.g., the mean, one and two standard deviations above/below the mean, shaded area for which percentage or Z score is to be determined).

Finding a Probability

A candy dish has four kinds of fruit-flavored candy: 20 apple, 20 strawberry, 5 cherry, and 5 grape. If you close your eyes and pick one piece of candy at random, what is the probability it will be either cherry or grape?

Answer

❶ **Determine the number of possible successful outcomes.** There are 10 possible successful outcomes—5 cherry and 5 grape.

❷ **Determine the number of all possible outcomes.** There are 50 possible outcomes overall: $20 + 20 + 5 + 5 = 50$.

❸ **Divide the number of possible successful outcomes (Step ❶) by the number of all possible outcomes (Step ❷).** $10/50 = .2$. Thus, the probability of picking either a cherry or grape candy is .2.

Practice Problems

These problems involve figuring. Most real-life statistics problems are done with special statistical software. Even if you have such software, do these problems by hand to ingrain the method in your mind. To learn how to use a computer to solve statistics problems like those in this chapter, refer to the Using SPSS section at the end of this chapter.

All data are fictional unless an actual citation is given.

Set I

1. On a measure of anxiety, the mean is 79 and the standard deviation is 12. What are the Z scores for each of the following raw scores? (a) 91, (b) 68, and (c) 103.
2. On an intelligence test, the mean number of raw items correct is 231 and the standard deviation is 41. What are the raw (actual) scores on the test for people with IQs of (a) 107, (b) 83, and (c) 100? To do this problem, first figure the Z score for the particular IQ score; then use that Z score to find the raw score. Note that IQ scores have a mean of 100 and a standard deviation of 15.
3. Six months after a divorce, the former wife and husband each take a test that measures divorce adjustment. The wife's score is 63, and the husband's score is 59. Overall, the mean score for divorced women on this test is 60 ($SD = 6$), the mean score for divorced men is 55 ($SD = 4$). Which of the two has adjusted better to the divorce in relation to other divorced people of the same gender? Explain your answer to a person who has never had a course in statistics.
4. Suppose the people living in a city have a mean score of 40 and a standard deviation of 5 on a measure of concern about the environment. Assume that these concern scores are normally distributed. Using the 50%−34%−14% figures, approximately what percentage of people have a score (a) above 40, (b) above 45, (c) above 30, (d) above 35, (e) below 40, (f) below 45, (g) below 30, and (h) below 35?
5. Using the information in problem 4 and the 50%−34%−14% figures, what is the minimum score a person has to have to be in the top (a) 2%, (b) 16%, (c) 50%, (d) 84%, and (e) 98%?
6. A psychologist has been studying eye fatigue using a particular measure, which she administers to students after they have worked for 1 hour writing on a computer. On this measure, she has found that the distribution follows a normal curve. Using a normal curve table, what percentage of students have Z scores (a) below 1.5, (b) above 1.5, (c) below −1.5, (d) above −1.5, (e) above 2.10, (f) below 2.10, (g) above .45, (h) below −1.78, and (i) above 1.68?
7. In the previous problem, the test of eye fatigue has a mean of 15 and a standard deviation of 5. Using a normal curve table, what percentage of students have scores (a) above 16, (b) above 17, (c) above 18, (d) below 18, (e) below 14?

8. In the eye fatigue example of problems 6 and 7, using a normal curve table, what is the lowest score on the eye fatigue measure a person has to have to be in (a) the top 40%, (b) the top 30%, (c) the top 20%?

9. Using a normal curve table, give the percentage of scores between the mean and a Z score of (a) .58, (b) .59, (c) 1.46, (d) 1.56, (e) −.58.

10. Consider a test of coordination that has a normal distribution, a mean of 50, and a standard deviation of 10. (a) How high a score would a person need to have to be in the top 5%? (b) Explain your answer to someone who has never had a course in statistics.

11. Berger and colleagues (2011) conducted a telephone survey of energy drink consumption and alcohol use among adults in Milwaukee. In the method section of their article, they explain that "[t]he study sample was comprised of individuals aged 18 or older who participated in the 2008 Greater Milwaukee Survey, a semiannual cross-sectional random-digit-dial landline telephone survey of household residents in the Milwaukee, Wisconsin Metropolitan Statistical Area. In total, 946 adults aged 18 to 92 participated in the survey for a response rate . . . of 20.9%" (p. 517). Explain to a person who has never had a course in statistics or research methods what it means to use a random-digit-dial method and why it is important.

12. The following numbers of individuals in a company received special assistance from the personnel department last year:

Drug/alcohol	10
Family crisis counseling	20
Other	20
Total	50

If you were to select someone at random from the records for last year, what is the probability that the person would be in each of the following categories: (a) drug/alcohol, (b) family, (c) drug/alcohol or family, (d) any category except "Other," or (e) any of the three categories? (f) Explain your answers to someone who has never had a course in statistics.

Set II

13. On a measure of artistic ability, the mean for college students in New Zealand is 150 and the standard deviation is 25. Give the Z scores for New Zealand college students who score (a) 100, (b) 120, (c) 140, and (d) 160. Give the raw scores for persons whose Z scores on this test are (e) −1, (f) −.8, (g) −.2, and (h) 1.38.

14. On a standard measure of hearing ability, the mean is 300 and the standard deviation is 20. Give the Z scores for persons who score (a) 340, (b) 310, and (c) 260. Give the raw scores for persons whose Z scores on this test are (d) 2.4, (e) 1.5, (f) 0, and (g) −4.5.

15. A person scores 81 on a test of verbal ability and 6.4 on a test of quantitative ability. For the verbal ability test, the mean for people in general is 50 and the standard deviation is 20. For the quantitative ability test, the mean for people in general is 0 and the standard deviation is 5. Which is this person's stronger ability: verbal or quantitative? Explain your answer to a person who has never had a course in statistics.

16. The amount of time it takes to recover physiologically from a certain kind of sudden noise is found to be normally distributed with a mean of 80 seconds and a standard deviation of 10 seconds. Using the 50%−34%−14% figures, approximately what percentage of scores (on time to recover) will be (a) above 100, (b) below 100, (c) above 90, (d) below 90, (e) above 80, (f) below 80, (g) above 70, (h) below 70, (i) above 60, and (j) below 60?

17. Using the information in problem 16 and the 50%−34%−14% figures, what is the longest time to recover that a person can take and still be in the bottom (a) 2%, (b) 16%, (c) 50%, (d) 84%, and (e) 98%?

18. Suppose that the scores of architects on a particular creativity test are normally distributed. Using a normal curve table, what percentage of architects have Z scores (a) above .10, (b) below .10, (c) above .20, (d) below .20, (e) above 1.10, (f) below 1.10, (g) above −.10, and (h) below −.10?

19. In the example in problem 18, using a normal curve table, what is the minimum Z score an architect can have on the creativity test to be in the (a) top 50%, (b) top 40%, (c) top 60%, (d) top 30%, and (e) top 20%?

20. In the example in problem 18, assume that the mean is 300 and the standard deviation is 25. Using a normal curve table, what scores would be the top and bottom scores to find (a) the middle 50% of architects, (b) the middle 90% of architects, and (c) the middle 99% of architects?

21. Suppose that you are designing an instrument panel for a large industrial machine. The machine requires the person using it to reach 2 feet from a particular position. The reach from this position for adult women is known to have a mean of 2.8 feet with a standard deviation of .5. The reach for adult men is known to have a mean of 3.1 feet with a standard deviation of .6. Both women's and men's reach from this position is normally distributed. If this design is implemented, (a) what percentage of women will not be able to work on this instrument panel? (b) What percentage of men will not be able to work on this instrument panel? (c) Explain your answers to a person who has never had a course in statistics.

22. Suppose you want to conduct a survey of the attitude of psychology graduate students studying clinical psychology toward psychoanalytic methods of psychotherapy. One approach would be to contact every psychology graduate student you know and ask them to fill out a questionnaire about it. (a) What kind of sampling method is this? (b) What is a major limitation of this kind of approach?

23. A large study evaluating a national mass media smoking cessation campaign in the United States recruited participants using a "…random-digit-dial method, from February 5 through April 15, 2008, prior to the national launch of the…media campaign" (Vallone et al., 2011, p. S39). Explain to a person who has never had a course in statistics (a) why this method of sampling might be used and (b) why it may be a problem if not everyone called agreed to be interviewed.

24. Suppose that you were going to conduct a survey of visitors to your campus. You want the survey to be as representative as possible. (a) How would you select the people to survey? (b) Why would that be your best method?

25. You are conducting a survey at a college with 800 students, 50 faculty members, and 150 administrators. Each of these 1,000 individuals has a single email address listed in the online campus directory. Suppose you were to select one email address at random. What is the probability it would be (a) a student, (b) a faculty member, (c) an administrator, (d) a faculty member or administrator, and (e) anyone except an administrator? (f) Explain your answers to someone who has never had a course in statistics.

26. You apply to 20 graduate programs, 10 of which are in clinical psychology, 5 of which are in counseling psychology, and 5 of which are in social work. You get a message from home that you have a letter from one of the programs you applied to, but nothing is said about which one. Give the probabilities it is from (a) a clinical psychology program, (b) a counseling psychology program, (c) from any program other than social work. (d) Explain your answers to someone who has never had a course in statistics.

The ✐ in the following steps indicates a mouse click. (We used SPSS version 19.0 to carry out these analyses. The steps and output may be slightly different for other versions of SPSS.)

Changing Raw Scores to Z Scores

It is easier to learn these steps using actual numbers, so we will use the number of dreams example from *Central Tendency and Variability.*

❶ Enter the scores from your distribution in one column of the data window (the scores are 7, 8, 8, 7, 3, 1, 6, 9, 3, 8). We will call this variable "dreams."

❷ Find the mean and standard deviation of the scores. You learned how to do this in the Using SPSS section of *Central Tendency and Variability.* The mean is 6, and the standard deviation is 2.57.

❸ You are now going to create a new variable that shows the Z score for each raw score. ✐ *Transform,* ✐ *Compute Variable.* You can call the new variable any name that you want, but we will call it "zdreams." So, type *zdreams* in the box labeled *Target Variable.* In the box labeled *Numeric Expression,* type $(dreams - 6)/2.57$. As you can see, this formula creates a deviation score (by subtracting the mean from the raw score) and divides the deviation score by the standard deviation. ✐ *OK.* You will see that a new variable called *zdreams* has been added to the data window. The scores for this *zdreams* variable are the Z scores for the dreams variable.[4] Your data window should now look like Figure 20.

Figure 20   Using SPSS to change raw scores to Z scores for the number of dreams.

Chapter Notes

1. The formula for the normal curve (when the mean is 0 and the standard deviation is 1) is

$$f(x) = \frac{1}{\sqrt{2\pi}} e^{-x^2/2}$$

where $f(x)$ is the height of the curve at point x and π and e are the usual mathematical constants (approximately 3.14 and 2.72, respectively). However, psychology researchers almost never use this formula because it is built into the statistics software that do calculations involving normal curves. When work must be done by hand, any needed information about the normal curve is provided in tables in statistics books (for example, Table A-1 in the Appendix).

2. The exact percentage of scores between any two Z scores can also be calculated using statistics or spreadsheet software (for example, using the normal curve function in Excel).

3. Frick (1998) argued that in most cases psychology researchers should not think in terms of samples and populations at all. Rather, he argues, researchers should think of themselves as studying processes. An experiment examines some process in a group of individuals. Then the researcher evaluates the probability that the pattern of results could have been caused by chance factors. For example, the researcher examines whether a difference in means between an experimental and a control group could have been caused by factors other than by the experimental manipulation. Frick claims that this way of thinking is much closer to the way researchers actually work, and argues that it has various advantages in terms of the subtle logic of inferential statistical procedures.

4. You can also request the Z scores directly from SPSS. However, SPSS figures the standard deviation based on the dividing by $N - 1$ formula for the variance. Thus, the Z scores figured directly by SPSS will be different from the Z scores as you learn to figure them. Here are the steps for figuring Z scores (based on the dividing by $N - 1$ formula) directly from SPSS: ❶ Enter the scores from your distribution in one column of the data window. ❷ ✎ *Analyze*, ✎ *Descriptive statistics*, ✎ *Descriptives*. ❸ ✎ on the variable for which you want to find the Z scores, and then ✎ the arrow. ❹ ✎ the box labeled *Save standardized values as variables* (this checks the box). ❺ ✎ *OK*. A new variable is added to the data window. The values for this variable are the Z scores for your variable (based on the dividing by $N - 1$ formula). (You can ignore the output window, which by default will show descriptive statistics for your variable.)

Appendix: Tables

Table A-1 Normal Curve Areas: Percentage of the Normal Curve Between the Mean and the *Z* Scores Shown and Percentage of Scores in the Tail for the *Z* Scores Shown

Z	% Mean to Z	% in Tail	Z	% Mean to Z	% in Tail
.00	0.00	50.00	.30	11.79	38.21
.01	0.40	49.60	.31	12.17	37.83
.02	0.80	49.20	.32	12.55	37.45
.03	1.20	48.80	.33	12.93	37.07
.04	1.60	48.40	.34	13.31	36.69
.05	1.99	48.01	.35	13.68	36.32
.06	2.39	47.61	.36	14.06	35.94
.07	2.79	47.21	.37	14.43	35.57
.08	3.19	46.81	.38	14.80	35.20
.09	3.59	46.41	.39	15.17	34.83
.10	3.98	46.02	.40	15.54	34.46
.11	4.38	45.62	.41	15.91	34.09
.12	4.78	45.22	.42	16.28	33.72
.13	5.17	44.83	.43	16.64	33.36
.14	5.57	44.43	.44	17.00	33.00
.15	5.96	44.04	.45	17.36	32.64
.16	6.36	43.64	.46	17.72	32.28
.17	6.75	43.25	.47	18.08	31.92
.18	7.14	42.86	.48	18.44	31.56
.19	7.53	42.47	.49	18.79	31.21
.20	7.93	42.07	.50	19.15	30.85
.21	8.32	41.68	.51	19.50	30.50
.22	8.71	41.29	.52	19.85	30.15
.23	9.10	40.90	.53	20.19	29.81
.24	9.48	40.52	.54	20.54	29.46
.25	9.87	40.13	.55	20.88	29.12
.26	10.26	39.74	.56	21.23	28.77
.27	10.64	39.36	.57	21.57	28.43
.28	11.03	38.97	.58	21.90	28.10
.29	11.41	38.59	.59	22.24	27.76

(continued)

Table A-1 (continued)

Z	% Mean to Z	% in Tail	Z	% Mean to Z	% in Tail
.60	22.57	27.43	1.03	34.85	15.15
.61	22.91	27.09	1.04	35.08	14.92
.62	23.24	26.76	1.05	35.31	14.69
.63	23.57	26.43	1.06	35.54	14.46
.64	23.89	26.11	1.07	35.77	14.23
.65	24.22	25.78	1.08	35.99	14.01
.66	24.54	25.46	1.09	36.21	13.79
.67	24.86	25.14	1.10	36.43	13.57
.68	25.17	24.83	1.11	36.65	13.35
.69	25.49	24.51	1.12	36.86	13.14
.70	25.80	24.20	1.13	37.08	12.92
.71	26.11	23.89	1.14	37.29	12.71
.72	26.42	23.58	1.15	37.49	12.51
.73	26.73	23.27	1.16	37.70	12.30
.74	27.04	22.96	1.17	37.90	12.10
.75	27.34	22.66	1.18	38.10	11.90
.76	27.64	22.36	1.19	38.30	11.70
.77	27.94	22.06	1.20	38.49	11.51
.78	28.23	21.77	1.21	38.69	11.31
.79	28.52	21.48	1.22	38.88	11.12
.80	28.81	21.19	1.23	39.07	10.93
.81	29.10	20.90	1.24	39.25	10.75
.82	29.39	20.61	1.25	39.44	10.56
.83	29.67	20.33	1.26	39.62	10.38
.84	29.95	20.05	1.27	39.80	10.20
.85	30.23	19.77	1.28	39.97	10.03
.86	30.51	19.49	1.29	40.15	9.85
.87	30.78	19.22	1.30	40.32	9.68
.88	31.06	18.94	1.31	40.49	9.51
.89	31.33	18.67	1.32	40.66	9.34
.90	31.59	18.41	1.33	40.82	9.18
.91	31.86	18.14	1.34	40.99	9.01
.92	32.12	17.88	1.35	41.15	8.85
.93	32.38	17.62	1.36	41.31	8.69
.94	32.64	17.36	1.37	41.47	8.53
.95	32.89	17.11	1.38	41.62	8.38
.96	33.15	16.85	1.39	41.77	8.23
.97	33.40	16.60	1.40	41.92	8.08
.98	33.65	16.35	1.41	42.07	7.93
.99	33.89	16.11	1.42	42.22	7.78
1.00	34.13	15.87	1.43	42.36	7.64
1.01	34.38	15.62	1.44	42.51	7.49
1.02	34.61	15.39	1.45	42.65	7.35

Table A-1 (*continued*)

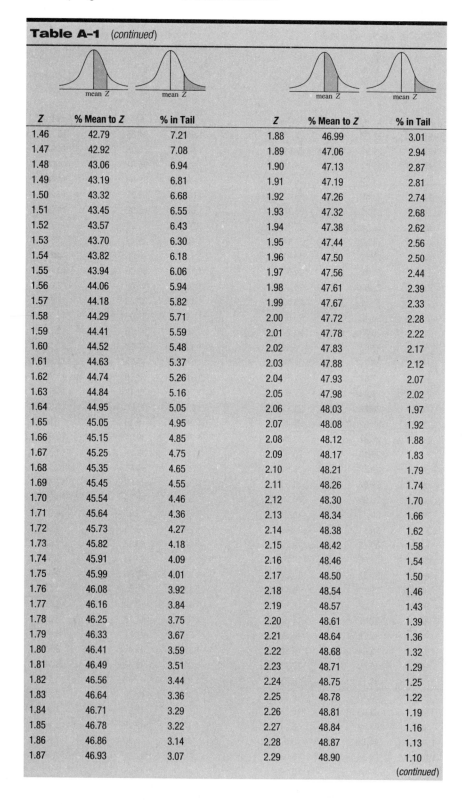

Z	% Mean to Z	% in Tail	Z	% Mean to Z	% in Tail
1.46	42.79	7.21	1.88	46.99	3.01
1.47	42.92	7.08	1.89	47.06	2.94
1.48	43.06	6.94	1.90	47.13	2.87
1.49	43.19	6.81	1.91	47.19	2.81
1.50	43.32	6.68	1.92	47.26	2.74
1.51	43.45	6.55	1.93	47.32	2.68
1.52	43.57	6.43	1.94	47.38	2.62
1.53	43.70	6.30	1.95	47.44	2.56
1.54	43.82	6.18	1.96	47.50	2.50
1.55	43.94	6.06	1.97	47.56	2.44
1.56	44.06	5.94	1.98	47.61	2.39
1.57	44.18	5.82	1.99	47.67	2.33
1.58	44.29	5.71	2.00	47.72	2.28
1.59	44.41	5.59	2.01	47.78	2.22
1.60	44.52	5.48	2.02	47.83	2.17
1.61	44.63	5.37	2.03	47.88	2.12
1.62	44.74	5.26	2.04	47.93	2.07
1.63	44.84	5.16	2.05	47.98	2.02
1.64	44.95	5.05	2.06	48.03	1.97
1.65	45.05	4.95	2.07	48.08	1.92
1.66	45.15	4.85	2.08	48.12	1.88
1.67	45.25	4.75	2.09	48.17	1.83
1.68	45.35	4.65	2.10	48.21	1.79
1.69	45.45	4.55	2.11	48.26	1.74
1.70	45.54	4.46	2.12	48.30	1.70
1.71	45.64	4.36	2.13	48.34	1.66
1.72	45.73	4.27	2.14	48.38	1.62
1.73	45.82	4.18	2.15	48.42	1.58
1.74	45.91	4.09	2.16	48.46	1.54
1.75	45.99	4.01	2.17	48.50	1.50
1.76	46.08	3.92	2.18	48.54	1.46
1.77	46.16	3.84	2.19	48.57	1.43
1.78	46.25	3.75	2.20	48.61	1.39
1.79	46.33	3.67	2.21	48.64	1.36
1.80	46.41	3.59	2.22	48.68	1.32
1.81	46.49	3.51	2.23	48.71	1.29
1.82	46.56	3.44	2.24	48.75	1.25
1.83	46.64	3.36	2.25	48.78	1.22
1.84	46.71	3.29	2.26	48.81	1.19
1.85	46.78	3.22	2.27	48.84	1.16
1.86	46.86	3.14	2.28	48.87	1.13
1.87	46.93	3.07	2.29	48.90	1.10

(*continued*)

Table A-1 *(continued)*

Z	% Mean to Z	% in Tail	Z	% Mean to Z	% in Tail
2.30	48.93	1.07	2.67	49.62	.38
2.31	48.96	1.04	2.68	49.63	.37
2.32	48.98	1.02	2.69	49.64	.36
2.33	49.01	.99	2.70	49.65	.35
2.34	49.04	.96	2.71	49.66	.34
2.35	49.06	.94	2.72	49.67	.33
2.36	49.09	.91	2.73	49.68	.32
2.37	49.11	.89	2.74	49.69	.31
2.38	49.13	.87	2.75	49.70	.30
2.39	49.16	.84	2.76	49.71	.29
2.40	49.18	.82	2.77	49.72	.28
2.41	49.20	.80	2.78	49.73	.27
2.42	49.22	.78	2.79	49.74	.26
2.43	49.25	.75	2.80	49.74	.26
2.44	49.27	.73	2.81	49.75	.25
2.45	49.29	.71	2.82	49.76	.24
2.46	49.31	.69	2.83	49.77	.23
2.47	49.32	.68	2.84	49.77	.23
2.48	49.34	.66	2.85	49.78	.22
2.49	49.36	.64	2.86	49.79	.21
2.50	49.38	.62	2.87	49.79	.21
2.51	49.40	.60	2.88	49.80	.20
2.52	49.41	.59	2.89	49.81	.19
2.53	49.43	.57	2.90	49.81	.19
2.54	49.45	.55	2.91	49.82	.18
2.55	49.46	.54	2.92	49.82	.18
2.56	49.48	.52	2.93	49.83	.17
2.57	49.49	.51	2.94	49.84	.16
2.58	49.51	.49	2.95	49.84	.16
2.59	49.52	.48	2.96	49.85	.15
2.60	49.53	.47	2.97	49.85	.15
2.61	49.55	.45	2.98	49.86	.14
2.62	49.56	.44	2.99	49.86	.14
2.63	49.57	.43	3.00	49.87	.13
2.64	49.59	.41	3.50	49.98	.02
2.65	49.60	.40	4.00	50.00	.00
2.66	49.61	.39	4.50	50.00	.00

Answers to Set I Practice Problems

Chapter 3

1. (a) $Z = (X - M)/SD = (91 - 79)/12 = 1$; (b) $-.92$; (c) 2.
2. (a) If IQ = 107, $Z = (X - M)/SD = (107 - 100)/15 = .47$; $X = (Z)(SD) + M = (.47)(41) + 231 = 250$. (We rounded off to a whole number because the actual score on the test is the number of items correct, which cannot be a fraction.) (b) $Z = -1.13$; $X = 185$; (c) $Z = 0$; $X = 231$.
3. Wife: $Z = (X - M)/SD = (63 - 60)/6 = .5$. Husband: $Z = (59 - 55)/4 = 1$. The husband has adjusted better in relation to other divorced men than the wife has adjusted in relation to other divorced women.

   For wives, a score of 63 is 3 points better than the average of 60 for divorced women in general. (The mean in the problem is the ordinary average—the sum of the scores divided by the number of scores.) There is, of course, some variation in scores among divorced women. The approximate average amount that women's scores differ from the average is 6 points; this is the *SD* (standard deviation) referred to in the problem. (*SD* is only approximately the average amount scores differ from the mean. To be precise, *SD* is the square root of the average of the square of the difference of each score from the mean.) Thus, this divorced woman's score of 63 (which is 3 points above the mean of 60) is only half as far as above the mean of wives' scores. This gives her what is called a *Z* score of +.5, which gives her location on a scale that compares her score to that of divorced women in general. Using the same logic, the husband's divorce adjustment is as much above the mean as the average amount that men differ from the mean; that is, he has a *Z* score of +1. What this all means is that both have adjusted better than average for their gender, but the husband has adjusted better in relation to other divorced men than the wife has adjusted in relation to other divorced women.
4. (a) 50%; (b) 16%; (c) 98%; (d) 84%; (e) 50%; (f) 84%; (g) 2%; (h) 16%.
5. (a) 50; (b) 45; (c) 40; (d) 35; (e) 30.
6. (a) From the normal curve table, 43.32% (.4332) have *Z* scores between the mean and 1.5. By definition, 50% have *Z* scores below the mean. Thus, the total percentage below 1.5 is 50% + 43.32% = 93.32%; (b) 6.68%; (c) 6.68%; (d) 93.32%; (e) 1.79%; (f) 98.21%; (g) 32.64%; (h) 3.75%; (i) 4.65%.
7. (a) $Z = (16 - 15)/5 = .2$; from the normal curve table, percentage in the tail for a *Z* score of .2 = 42.07%; (b) 34.46%; (c) 27.43%; (d) 72.57%; (e) 42.07%.
8. (a) Top 40% means 40% in the tail; the nearest *Z* score from the normal curve table for 40% in the tail is .25; a *Z* score of .25 equals a raw score of $(.25)(5) + 15 = 16.25$; (b) 17.6; (c) 19.2.
9. (a) 21.90%; (b) 22.24%; (c) 42.79%; (d) 44.06%; (e) 21.90%.
10. (a) Needed $Z = 1.64$; this corresponds to a raw score of $(1.64)(10) + 50 = 66.4$. (b) The scores for many things you measure, in nature and in psychology, tend approximately to follow the particular pattern shown in the figure shown here, called a "normal curve." In a normal curve, most of the scores are near the middle, with fewer numbers of scores at each extreme. Because the normal curve is mathematically defined, the precise proportion of scores in any particular section of it can be calculated, and these have been listed in special tables. (Then explain mean and standard deviation as in answers to Chapter 2 problems, and *Z* scores as in question 3.) The normal curve table tells the percentage of score in the normal curve between the mean and any particular *Z* score, and the percentage of scores in the tail beyond it for any *Z* score.

The coordination test scores are known to follow a normal curve. Thus, you can look up in the table the *Z* score for the point on the normal curve at which 5% of the scores are in the tail. This is a *Z* score of 1.64 (actually, there is not an exact point on the table for 5% in the tail; so I could have used either 1.64 or 1.65). With a standard deviation of 10, a *Z* score of 1.64 is 16.4 points above the mean; adding that to the mean of 50 makes the score needed to be in the top 5% turn out to 66.4.
11. A *sample* is a group of people studied that represents the entire group to which the results are intended to apply, called the *population*. (In this example, the population is adults in Milwaukee.) You study a sample because it would be impractical or impossible to test the entire population. One way of ensuring that the sample is not systematically unrepresentative is to select the sample randomly. This does not mean haphazardly. For example, just taking adults who are easily available to test would be haphazard sampling. But this would not be a good method because whatever factors make them easily available—such as living in a nearby town—might make them unrepresentative of the population as a whole. By using randomly selected telephone numbers

to select the sample, the researchers are trying to produce a sample that is representative of the whole population.

12. (a) 10/50: $p = 10/50 = .2$; (b) .4; (c) $(10 + 20)/50 = .6$; (d) .6; (e) 1. (f) The probability of a particular thing happening is usually defined as the number of possible ways the thing could happen (the number of *possible successful outcomes*) divided by the number of possible ways things like this could happen (the number of *all possible outcomes*). For part (a) there are 10 different drug/alcohol people you might pick out of a total of 50 people you are picking from. Thus, the probability is $10/50 = .2$. The same principle applies for parts (b) through (e).

Chapter 4

Introduction to Hypothesis Testing

Chapter 4

Introduction to Hypothesis Testing

Chapter Outline

- ❖ A Hypothesis-Testing Example
- ❖ The Core Logic of Hypothesis Testing
- ❖ The Hypothesis-Testing Process
- ❖ One-Tailed and Two-Tailed Hypothesis Tests
- ❖ Controversy: Should Significance Tests Be Banned?

- ❖ Hypothesis Tests in Research Articles
- ❖ Learning Aids
  - ❖ Summary
  - ❖ Key Terms
  - ❖ Example Worked-Out Problems
  - ❖ Practice Problems
- ❖ Chapter Notes

hypothesis testing procedure for deciding whether the outcome of a study (results for a sample) supports a particular theory or practical innovation (which is thought to apply to a population).

hypothesis prediction, often based on informal observation, previous research, or theory, that is tested in a research study.

theory set of principles that attempt to explain one or more facts, relationships, or events; psychologists often derive specific predictions from theories that are then tested in research studies.

In this chapter, we introduce the crucial topic of **hypothesis testing**. A **hypothesis** is a prediction intended to be tested in a research study. The prediction may be based on informal observation (as in clinical or applied settings regarding a possible practical innovation), on related results of previous studies, or on a broader *theory* about what is being studied. You can think of a **theory** as a set of principles that attempt to explain an important psychological process. A theory usually leads to various specific hypotheses that can be tested in research studies.

This chapter focuses on the basic logic for analyzing results of a research study to test a hypothesis. The central theme of hypothesis testing has to do with the important distinction between sample and population discussed in *Some Key Ingredients for Inferential Statistics*. Hypothesis testing is a systematic procedure for deciding whether the results of a research study, which examines a sample, support a hypothesis which applies to a population. Hypothesis testing is the central theme in most research in psychology and related fields.

Many students find the most difficult part of the course to be mastering the basic logic of this chapter. This chapter in particular requires some mental gymnastics. Even if you follow everything the first time through, you will be wise to review the chapter thoroughly. Hypothesis testing involves grasping ideas that make little sense covered separately; so in this chapter you learn several new ideas all at once.

However, once you understand the material in this chapter, your mind will be used to this sort of thing, and the rest of the course should seem easier.

At the same time, we have kept this introduction to hypothesis testing as simple as possible. For example, real-life psychology research involves samples of many individuals. However, to minimize how much you have to learn at one time, this chapter's examples are about studies in which the sample is a single individual. To do this, we use some odd examples. Just remember that you are building a foundation that will prepare you to understand hypothesis testing as it is actually done in real research.

A Hypothesis-Testing Example

Here is our first necessarily odd example that we made up to keep this introduction to hypothesis testing as straightforward as possible. A large research project has been going on for several years. In this project, new babies are given a particular vitamin, and then the research team follows their development during the first 2 years of life. So far, the vitamin has not speeded up the development of the babies. The ages at which these and all other babies start to walk are shown in Figure 1. The mean is 14 months ($\mu = 14$), the standard deviation is 3 months ($\sigma = 3$), and the ages follow a normal curve. Based on the normal curve percentages, you can figure that only about 2% of babies start walking before 8 months of age; these are the babies who are more than 2 standard deviations below the mean. (This fictional distribution is close to the true distribution researchers have found for babies in multiple countries; WHO Multicentre Growth Reference Study Group, 2006.)

One of the researchers working on the project has an idea. If the vitamin the babies are taking could be more highly refined, perhaps its effect would be dramatically increased: babies taking the highly purified version should start walking much earlier than other babies. (We will assume that the purification process could not possibly make the vitamin harmful.) However, refining the vitamin in this way is extremely expensive for each dose; so the research team decides to try the procedure with just enough purified doses for one baby. A newborn in the project is then randomly selected to take the highly purified version of the vitamin, and the researchers then follow this baby's progress for 2 years. What kind of result should

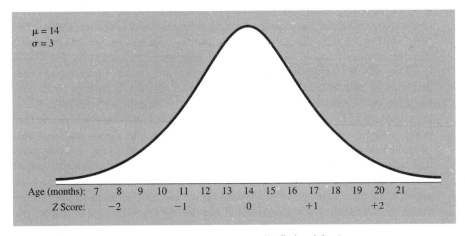

Figure 1   Distribution of when babies begin to walk (fictional data).

lead the researchers to conclude that the highly purified vitamin allows babies to walk earlier?

This is a hypothesis-testing problem. The researchers want to draw a general conclusion about whether the purified vitamin allows babies *in general* to walk earlier. The conclusion will be about babies in general (a population of babies). However, the conclusion will be based on results of studying a sample. In this example, the sample consists of a single baby.

The Core Logic of Hypothesis Testing

There is a standard way researchers approach any hypothesis-testing problem. For this example, it works as follows. Consider first the population of babies in general (those who are not given the specially purified vitamin). In this population, the chance of a baby's starting to walk at age 8 months or earlier would be only about 2%. (As shown in Figure 1, the mean walking age is 14 months with a standard deviation of 3 months.) Thus, walking at 8 months or earlier is highly unlikely among such babies. But what if the randomly selected sample of one baby in our study does start walking by 8 months? Suppose the specially purified vitamin had no effect on this particular baby's walking age, which means that the baby's walking age should be similar to that of babies who were not given the vitamin. In that case, it is highly unlikely (only about a 2% chance) that the particular baby we selected at random would start walking by 8 months. So, if the baby in our study does in fact start walking by 8 months, we *reject* the idea that the specially purified vitamin has *no* effect. And if we reject the idea that the specially purified vitamin has no effect, then we must also *accept* the idea that the specially purified vitamin *does* have an effect.

Using the same reasoning, if the baby starts walking by 8 months, we reject the idea that this baby comes from a population of babies like that of the general population with a mean walking age of 14 months. We then conclude that babies given the specially purified vitamin will on the average start to walk before 14 months. Our explanation for the baby's early walking age in the study is that the specially purified vitamin speeded up the baby's development.

In this example, the researchers first spelled out what would have to happen for them to conclude that the special purification procedure makes a difference. Having laid this out in advance, the researchers then conducted their study. Conducting the study in this case meant giving the specially purified vitamin to a randomly selected baby and watching to see how early that baby walked. We supposed that the result of the study is that the baby started walking before 8 months. The researchers then concluded that it is *unlikely* the specially purified vitamin makes *no* difference; therefore, they concluded that it *does* make a difference.

This kind of testing, with its opposite-of-what-you-predict, roundabout reasoning, is at the heart of inferential statistics in psychology. It is something like a double negative. One reason for this approach is that we have the information to figure the probability of getting a particular experimental result if the situation of there being *no difference* is true. In the purified vitamin example, the researchers know what the probabilities are of babies walking at different ages if the specially purified vitamin does not have any effect. The probabilities of babies walking at various ages are already known from studies of babies in general—that is, babies who have not received the specially purified vitamin. If the specially purified vitamin has no effect, then the ages at which babies start walking are the same with or without the specially purified vitamin. Thus, the distribution is that shown in Figure 1, based on ages at which babies start walking in general.

Without such a tortuous way of going at the problem, in most cases you could not test hypotheses scientifically at all. In almost all psychology research, we base our conclusions on the question, "What is the probability of getting our research results if the opposite of what we are predicting were true?" That is, we usually predict an effect of some kind. However, we decide on whether there *is* such an effect by seeing if it is unlikely that there is *not* such an effect. If it is highly unlikely that we would get our research results if the opposite of what we are predicting were true, that finding is our basis for rejecting the opposite prediction. If we reject the opposite prediction, we are able to accept our prediction. However, if it is likely that we would get our research results if the opposite of what we are predicting were true, we are not able to reject the opposite prediction. If we are not able to reject the opposite prediction, we are not able to accept our prediction.

The Hypothesis-Testing Process

Let's look at our example again, this time going over each step in some detail. Along the way, we cover the special terminology of hypothesis testing. Most important, we introduce the five steps of hypothesis testing.

Step ❶: Restate the Question as a Research Hypothesis and a Null Hypothesis About the Populations

Our researchers are interested in the effects on babies in general (not just on this particular baby). That is, the purpose of studying samples is to know about populations. Thus, it is useful to restate the research question in terms of populations. In our example, we can think of two populations of babies:

Population 1: Babies who take the specially purified vitamin.
Population 2: Babies in general (that is, babies who do not take the specially purified vitamin).

Population 1 consists of babies who receive the experimental treatment (the specially purified vitamin). In our example, we use a sample of one baby to draw a conclusion about the age at which babies in Population 1 start to walk. Population 2 is a kind of comparison baseline of what is already known about babies in general.

The prediction of our research team is that Population 1 babies (those who take the specially purified vitamin) will on the average walk earlier than Population 2 babies (babies in general who do not take the specially purified vitamin). This prediction is based on the researchers' theory of how these vitamins work. A prediction like this about the difference between populations is called a **research hypothesis**. Put more formally, the prediction is that the mean of Population 1 is lower (babies receiving the special vitamin walk earlier) than the mean of Population 2. In symbols, the research hypothesis for this example is $\mu_1 < \mu_2$.

The opposite of the research hypothesis is that the populations are not different in the way predicted. Under this scenario, Population 1 babies (those who take the specially purified vitamin) will on the average *not* walk earlier than Population 2 babies (babies in general—those who do not take the specially purified vitamin). That is, the prediction is that there is no difference in the ages at which Population 1 and Population 2 babies start walking. On the average, they start at the same time. A statement like this, about a lack of difference between populations, is the crucial *opposite* of the research hypothesis. It is called a **null hypothesis**. It has this name because it states the situation in which there is no difference (the difference is "null") between the populations. In symbols, the null hypothesis is $\mu_1 = \mu_2$.[1]

research hypothesis statement in hypothesis testing about the predicted relation between populations (often a prediction of a difference between population means).

null hypothesis statement about a relation between populations that is the opposite of the research hypothesis; statement that in the population there is no difference (or a difference opposite to that predicted) between populations; contrived statement set up to examine whether it can be rejected as part of hypothesis testing.

The research hypothesis and the null hypothesis are complete opposites: if one is true, the other cannot be. In fact, the research hypothesis is sometimes called the *alternative hypothesis*—that is, it is the alternative to the null hypothesis. This term is a bit ironic. As researchers, we care most about the research hypothesis. But when doing the steps of hypothesis testing, we use this roundabout method of seeing whether or not we can reject the null hypothesis so that we can decide about its alternative (the research hypothesis).

Step ❷: Determine the Characteristics of the Comparison Distribution

Recall that the overall logic of hypothesis testing involves figuring out the probability of getting a particular result if the null hypothesis is true. Thus, you need to know what the situation would be if the null hypothesis were true. In our example, we start out knowing the key information about Population 2, babies in the general population (see Figure 1): we know it follows a normal curve, $\mu = 14$, and $\sigma = 3$. If the null hypothesis is true, Population 1 and Population 2 are the same; in our example, this would mean for Populations 1 and 2, $\mu = 14$ and $\sigma = 3$, and both follow a normal curve.

In the hypothesis-testing process, you want to find out the probability that you could have gotten a sample score as extreme as what you got (say, a baby walking very early) if your sample were from a population with a distribution of the sort you would have if the null hypothesis were true. We call this distribution a **comparison distribution**. (The comparison distribution is sometimes called a *sampling distribution*.) That is, in the hypothesis-testing process, you compare the actual sample's score to this comparison distribution.

In our vitamin example, the null hypothesis is that there is no difference in walking age between babies who take the specially purified vitamin (Population 1) and babies in general who do not take the specially purified vitamin (Population 2). The comparison distribution is the distribution for Population 2, since this population represents the walking age of babies if the null hypothesis is true. There are different types of comparison distributions, but the same principle applies in all cases: The comparison distribution is the distribution that represents the population situation if the null hypothesis is true.

Step ❸: Determine the Cutoff Sample Score on the Comparison Distribution at Which the Null Hypothesis Should Be Rejected

Ideally, before conducting a study, researchers set a target against which they will compare their result: how extreme a sample score they would need to decide against the null hypothesis, that is, how extreme the sample score would have to be for it to be too unlikely that they could get such an extreme score if the null hypothesis were true. This is called the **cutoff sample score**. (The cutoff sample score is also known as the *critical value*.)

Consider our purified vitamin example, in which the null hypothesis is that walking age is not influenced by whether babies take the specially purified vitamin. The researchers might decide that, if the null hypothesis were true, a randomly selected baby walking before 8 months would be very unlikely. With a normal

comparison distribution   distribution used in hypothesis testing. It represents the population situation if the null hypothesis is true. It is the distribution to which you compare the score based on your sample's results.

cutoff sample score   point in hypothesis testing, on the comparison distribution at which, if reached or exceeded by the sample score, you reject the null hypothesis. Also called *critical value*.

distribution, being 2 or more standard deviations below the mean (walking by 8 months) could occur less than 2% of the time. Thus, based on the comparison distribution, the researchers set their cutoff sample score even before doing the study. They decide in advance that *if* the result of their study is a baby who walks by 8 months, they will reject the null hypothesis.

But what if the baby does not start walking until after 8 months? If that happens, the researchers will not be able to reject the null hypothesis.

When setting in advance how extreme a sample's score needs to be to reject the null hypothesis, researchers use Z scores and percentages. In our purified vitamin example, the researchers might decide that if a result were less likely than 2%, they would reject the null hypothesis. Being in the bottom 2% of a normal curve means having a Z score of about -2 or lower. Thus, the researchers would set -2 as their Z-score cutoff point on the comparison distribution for deciding that a result is extreme enough to reject the null hypothesis. So, if the actual sample Z score is -2 or lower, the researchers will reject the null hypothesis. However, if the actual sample Z score is greater than -2, the researchers will not reject the null hypothesis.

Suppose that the researchers are even more cautious about too easily rejecting the null hypothesis. They might decide that they will reject the null hypothesis only if they get a result that could occur by chance 1% of the time or less. They could then figure out the Z-score cutoff for 1%. Using the normal curve table, to have a score in the lower 1% of a normal curve, you need a Z score of -2.33 or less. (In our example, a Z score of -2.33 means 7 months.) In Figure 2, we have shaded the 1% of the comparison distribution in which a sample would be considered so extreme that the possibility that it came from a distribution like this would be rejected. Now the researchers will reject the null hypothesis only if the actual sample Z score is -2.33 or lower—that is, if it falls in the shaded area in Figure 2. If the sample Z score falls outside the shaded area in Figure 2, the researchers will *not* reject the null hypothesis.

In general, psychology researchers use a cutoff on the comparison distribution with a probability of 5% that a score will be at least that extreme if the null hypothesis were true. That is, researchers reject the null hypothesis if the probability of getting a sample score this extreme (if the null hypothesis were true) is less than 5%. This probability is usually written as $p < .05$. However, in some areas of research, or when researchers want to be especially cautious, they use a cutoff of 1% ($p < .01$).[2]

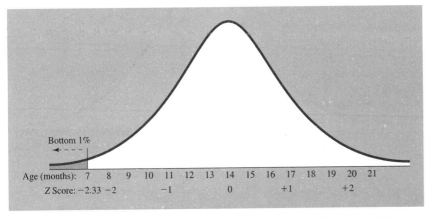

Figure 2   Distribution of when babies begin to walk, with bottom 1% shaded (fictional data).

These are called **conventional levels of significance**. They are described as the *.05 significance level* and the *.01 significance level.* We also refer to them as the 5% significance level and the 1% significance level. When a sample score is so extreme that researchers reject the null hypothesis, the result is said to be **statistically significant** (or just *significant,* as it is often abbreviated).

Step ❹: Determine Your Sample's Score on the Comparison Distribution

The next step is to carry out the study and get the actual results for your sample. Once you have the results for your sample, you figure the Z score for the sample's raw score based on the population mean and standard deviation of the comparison distribution.

Assume that the researchers did the study and the baby who was given the specially purified vitamin started walking at 6 months. The mean of the comparison distribution to which we are comparing these results is 14 months and the standard deviation is 3 months. That is, $\mu = 14$ and $\sigma = 3$. Thus, a baby who walks at 6 months is 8 months below the population mean. This puts the baby $2^{2/3}$ standard deviations below the population mean. The Z score for this sample baby on the comparison distribution is thus -2.67 [that is, $Z = (6 - 14)/3 = -2.67$]. Figure 3 shows the score of our sample baby on the comparison distribution.

Step ❺: Decide Whether to Reject the Null Hypothesis

To decide whether to reject the null hypothesis, compare your actual sample's Z score (from Step ❹) to the cutoff Z score (from Step ❸). In our example, the actual result was -2.67. Let's suppose the researchers had decided in advance that they would reject the null hypothesis if the sample's Z score was below -2. Since -2.67 is below -2, the researchers would reject the null hypothesis.

Alternatively, suppose the researchers had used the more conservative 1% significance level. The needed Z score to reject the null hypothesis would then have been -2.33 or lower. But, again, the actual Z for the randomly selected baby

conventional levels of significance ($p < .05, p < .01$) levels of significance widely used in psychology.

statistically significant conclusion that the results of a study would be unlikely if in fact the sample studied represents a population that is no different from the population in general; an outcome of hypothesis testing in which the null hypothesis is rejected.

Figure 3 Distribution of when babies begin to walk, showing both the bottom 1% and the single baby who is the sample studied (fictional data).

was -2.67 (a more extreme score than -2.33). Thus, even with this more conservative cutoff, they would still reject the null hypothesis. This situation is shown in Figure 3. As you can see in the figure, the bottom 1% of the distribution is shaded. We recommend that you always draw such a picture of the distribution. Be sure to shade in the part of the distribution that is *more extreme* (that is, farther out in the tail) than the cutoff sample score. If your actual sample Z score falls within the shaded region, you can reject the null hypothesis. Since the sample Z score (-2.67) in this example falls within the shaded tail region, the researchers can reject the null hypothesis.

If the researchers reject the null hypothesis, what remains is the research hypothesis. In this example, the research team would conclude that the results of their study support the research hypothesis that babies who take the specially purified vitamin walk earlier than babies in general.

Implications of Rejecting or Failing to Reject the Null Hypothesis

It is important to emphasize two points about the conclusions you can make from the hypothesis-testing process. First, when you reject the null hypothesis, all you are saying is that your results support the research hypothesis (as in our example). You would not go on to say that the results *prove* the research hypothesis or that the results show that the research hypothesis is *true.* Terms such as *prove* and *true* are too strong because the results of research studies are based on probabilities. Specifically, they are based on the probability being low of getting your result if the null hypothesis were true. *Proven* and *true* are acceptable terms in logic and mathematics, but to use these words in conclusions from scientific research is unprofessional. (It is all right to use *true* when speaking hypothetically—for example, "*if* this hypothesis *were* true, then..."—but not when speaking of conclusions about an actual result.) What you do say when you reject the null hypothesis is that the results are *statistically significant.* You can also say that the results "support" or "provide evidence for" the research hypothesis.

Second, when a result is not extreme enough to reject the null hypothesis, you do not say that the result *supports* (or *proves*) the null hypothesis. You simply say the result is *not statistically significant.* A result that is not strong enough to reject the null hypothesis means the study was inconclusive. The results may not be extreme enough to reject the null hypothesis, but the null hypothesis might still be false (and the research hypothesis true). Suppose in our example that the specially purified vitamin had only a slight but still real effect. In that case, we would not expect to find a baby who is given the purified vitamin to be walking a lot earlier than babies in general. Thus, we would not be able to reject the null hypothesis, even though it is false.

Showing the null hypothesis to be true would mean showing that there is absolutely no difference between the populations. It is always possible that there is a difference between the populations but that the difference is much smaller than the particular study was able to detect. Therefore, when a result is not extreme enough to reject the null hypothesis, the results are said to be *inconclusive.* Sometimes, however, if studies have been done using large samples and accurate measuring procedures, evidence may build up in support of something close to the null hypothesis—that there is at most very little difference between the populations. (We have more to say on this important issue later in this chapter.) The core logic of

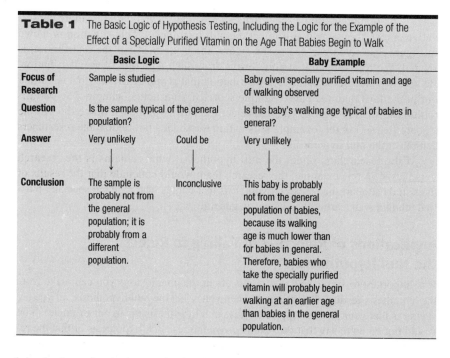

Table 1 The Basic Logic of Hypothesis Testing, Including the Logic for the Example of the Effect of a Specially Purified Vitamin on the Age That Babies Begin to Walk

	Basic Logic		Baby Example
Focus of Research	Sample is studied		Baby given specially purified vitamin and age of walking observed
Question	Is the sample typical of the general population?		Is this baby's walking age typical of babies in general?
Answer	Very unlikely	Could be	Very unlikely
	↓	↓	↓
Conclusion	The sample is probably not from the general population; it is probably from a different population.	Inconclusive	This baby is probably not from the general population of babies, because its walking age is much lower than for babies in general. Therefore, babies who take the specially purified vitamin will probably begin walking at an earlier age than babies in the general population.

hypothesis testing is summarized in Table 1, which also includes the logic for our example of a baby who is given a specially purified vitamin.

Summary of Steps of Hypothesis Testing

Here is a summary of the five steps of hypothesis testing.

❶ **Restate the question as a research hypothesis and a null hypothesis about the populations.**
❷ **Determine the characteristics of the comparison distribution.**
❸ **Determine the cutoff sample score on the comparison distribution at which the null hypothesis should be rejected.**
❹ **Determine your sample's score on the comparison distribution.**
❺ **Decide whether to reject the null hypothesis.**

A Second Example

Here is another fictional example (based on results of actual studies). Two happy-go-lucky personality psychologists are examining the theory that happiness comes from positive experiences. In particular, these researchers argue that if people have something very fortunate happen to them, they become very happy and will still be happy 6 months later. So the researchers plan the following experiment: a person will be randomly selected from the North American adult public and given $10 million. Six months later, the person's happiness will be measured. It is already known (in this fictional example) what the distribution of happiness is like in the general population of North American adults, and this is shown in Figure 4. On the test being used, the mean happiness score is 70, the standard deviation is 10, and the distribution is approximately normal.

The psychologists now carry out the hypothesis-testing procedure. That is, the researchers consider how happy the person would have to be before they can

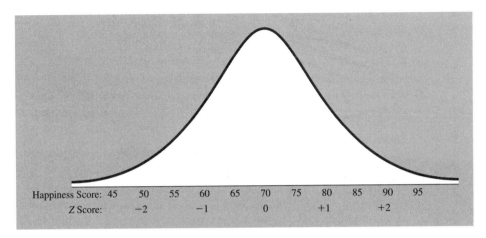

Happiness Score: 45   50   55   60   65   70   75   80   85   90   95
Z Score: −2   −1   0   +1   +2

Figure 4   Distribution of happiness sources (fictional data).

confidently reject the null hypothesis that receiving so much money does *not* make people happier 6 months later. If the researchers' result shows a very high level of happiness, the psychologists will *reject* the null hypothesis and conclude that getting $10 million probably *does* make people happier 6 months later. But if the result is not very extreme, the researchers would not be able to conclude anything one way or the other about the effects. That is, because there is not sufficient evidence to reject the null hypothesis, the results of the experiment would be inconclusive.

Now let us consider the hypothesis-testing procedure in more detail in this example, following the five steps.

❶ **Restate the question as a research hypothesis and a null hypothesis about the populations.** There are two populations of interest:

Population 1: People who 6 months ago received $10 million.
Population 2: The general population (consisting of people who 6 months ago did not receive $10 million).

The prediction of the personality psychologists, based on their theory of happiness, is that Population 1 people will on the average be happier than Population 2 people: in symbols, $\mu_1 > \mu_2$. The null hypothesis is that Population 1 people (those who get $10 million) will not be happier than Population 2 people (people in general who do not get $10 million).

❷ **Determine the characteristics of the comparison distribution.** The comparison distribution is the distribution that represents the population situation if the null hypothesis is true. If the null hypothesis is true, the distributions of Populations 1 and 2 are the same. We know Population 2's distribution (it is normally distributed with $\mu = 70$ and $\sigma = 10$), so we can use it as the comparison distribution.

❸ **Determine the cutoff sample score on the comparison distribution at which the null hypothesis should be rejected.** What kind of result would be extreme enough to convince us to reject the null hypothesis? In this example, assume that the researchers decided the following in advance: they will reject the null hypothesis as too unlikely if the results would occur less than 5% of the time if this null hypothesis were true. We know that the comparison distribution is a normal curve. Thus, we can figure that the top 5% of scores from the normal curve table begin at a Z score of about 1.64. So the researchers set as the cutoff point for rejecting the null hypothesis a result in which the sample's Z score on the comparison distribution is at or above 1.64. (The mean of the comparison distribution is 70 and the standard deviation is 10. Therefore, the null hypothesis will be rejected if the sample result is at or above 86.4.)

❹ **Determine your sample's score on the comparison distribution.** Now for the results: six months after giving the randomly selected person $10 million, the now very wealthy research participant takes the happiness test. The person's score is 80. As you can see from Figure 4, a score of 80 has a Z score of $+1$ on the comparison distribution.

❺ **Decide whether to reject the null hypothesis.** The Z score of the sample individual is $+1$. The researchers set the minimum Z score to reject the null hypothesis at $+1.64$. Thus, the sample score is not extreme enough to reject the null hypothesis. The experiment is inconclusive; researchers would say the results are "not statistically significant." Figure 5 shows the comparison distribution with the top 5% shaded and the location of the sample participant who received $10 million.

You may be interested to know that Brickman et al. (1978) carried out a more elaborate study based on the same question. They studied lottery winners as examples of people suddenly having a very positive event happen to them. Their results were similar to those in our fictional example: those who won the lottery were not much happier 6 months later than people who did not win the lottery. Also, another group they studied, people who had become paraplegics through a random accident, were not much less happy than other people 6 months later. These researchers concluded that if a major event does have a lasting effect on happiness, it is probably not a very big one. This conclusion is consistent with the findings of more recent studies (e.g., Suh et al., 1996). There is also evidence that people's happiness may be determined by how they spend their money, regardless of how much money they have. For example, Dunn and colleagues (2008) have shown that when people spend money on other people, it makes them happier than if they spend the money

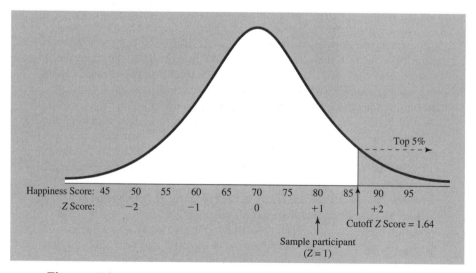

Figure 5   Distribution of happiness scores with upper 5% shaded and showing the location of the sample participant (fictional data).

on themselves. Indeed, in recent years, a great deal of research has examined what factors contribute to people's level of happiness. If you are interested in knowing more about this topic, we highly recommend an article by Diener and colleagues (2006), Diener and Biswas-Diener's book, *Happiness: Unlocking the Mysteries of Psychological Wealth* (2008), and social psychologist Daniel Gilbert's (2006) engaging best seller, *Stumbling on Happiness.*

How are you doing?

1. A sample of rats in a laboratory is given an experimental treatment intended to make them learn a maze faster than other rats. State (a) the null hypothesis and (b) the research hypothesis.
2. (a) What is a comparison distribution? (b) What role does it play in hypothesis testing?
3. What is the cutoff sample score?
4. Why do we say that hypothesis testing involves a double negative logic?
5. What can you conclude when (a) a result is so extreme that you reject the null hypothesis and (b) a result is not very extreme so that you cannot reject the null hypothesis?
6. A training program to increase friendliness is tried on one individual randomly selected from the general public. Among the general public (who do not get this training program), the mean on the friendliness measure is 30 with a standard deviation of 4. The researchers want to test their hypothesis at the 5% significance level. After going through the training program, this individual takes the friendliness measure and gets a score of 40. What should the researchers conclude?

Answers

1. (a) Null hypothesis: The population of rats like those that get the experimental treatment score the same on the time to learn the maze as the population of rats in general that do not get the experimental treatment. (b) Research hypothesis: The population of rats like those that get the experimental treatment learn the maze faster than the population of rats in general that do not get the experimental treatment.
2. (a) A comparison distribution is a distribution to which you compare the results of your study. (b) In hypothesis testing, the comparison distribution is the distribution for the situation when the null hypothesis is true. To decide whether to reject the null hypothesis, check how extreme the score of your sample is on this comparison distribution—how likely it would be to get a sample with a score this extreme if your sample came from this comparison distribution.
3. The cutoff sample score is the Z score at which, if the sample's Z score is more extreme than it is on the comparison distribution, you reject the null hypothesis.
4. We say that hypothesis testing involves a double negative logic because we are interested in the research hypothesis, but we test whether it is true by seeing if we can reject its opposite, the null hypothesis.
5. (a) The research hypothesis is supported when a result is so extreme that you reject the null hypothesis; the result is statistically significant. (b) The result is not statistically significant when a result is not very extreme; the result is inconclusive.

6. The training program increases friendliness. The cutoff sample Z score on the comparison distribution is 1.64. The actual sample's Z score of 2.50 is more extreme—that is, farther in the tail—than the cutoff Z score. Therefore, reject the null hypothesis; the research hypothesis is supported; the result is statistically significant.

One-Tailed and Two-Tailed Hypothesis Tests

In our examples so far, the researchers were interested in only one direction of result. In our first example, researchers tested whether babies given the specially purified vitamin would walk *earlier* than babies in general. In the happiness example, the personality psychologists predicted the person who received $10 million would be *happier* than other people. The researchers in these studies were not interested in the possibility that giving the specially purified vitamin would cause babies to start walking *later* or that people getting $10 million might become *less* happy.

Directional Hypotheses and One-Tailed Tests

The purified vitamin and happiness studies are examples of testing a **directional hypothesis**. Both studies focused on a specific direction of effect. When a researcher makes a directional hypothesis, the null hypothesis is also, in a sense, directional. Suppose the research hypothesis is that getting $10 million will make a person happier than the general population. The null hypothesis, then, is that the money will either have no effect or make the person less happy. [In symbols, if the research hypothesis is $\mu_1 > \mu_2$, then the null hypothesis is $\mu_1 \leq \mu_2$ ("$\leq$" is the symbol for less than or equal to).] Thus, in Figure 5, to reject the null hypothesis, the sample has to have a score in one tail of the comparison distribution: the upper extreme or tail (in this example, the top 5%) of the comparison distribution. (When it comes to rejecting the null hypothesis with a directional hypothesis, a score at the other tail is the same as a score in the middle; that is, such a score does not allow you to reject the null hypothesis.) For this reason, the test of a directional hypothesis is called a **one-tailed test**. A one-tailed test can be one-tailed in either direction. In the happiness study example, the tail for the predicted effect was at the high end. In the baby study example, the tail for the predicted effect was at the low end (that is, the prediction tested was that babies given the specially purified vitamin would start walking unusually *early*).

Nondirectional Hypotheses and Two-Tailed Tests

Sometimes, a research hypothesis states that an experimental procedure will have an effect, without saying whether it will produce a very high score or a very low score. Suppose an organizational psychologist is interested in how a new social skills program will affect productivity. The program could either improve productivity by making the working environment more pleasant or hurt productivity by encouraging people to socialize instead of work. The research hypothesis is that the social skills program *changes* the level of productivity; the null hypothesis is that the program does not change productivity one way or the other. In symbols, the research hypothesis is $\mu_1 \neq \mu_2$ ("$\neq$" is the symbol for not equal); the null hypothesis is $\mu_1 = \mu_2$.

When a research hypothesis predicts an effect but does not predict a direction for the effect, it is called a **nondirectional hypothesis**. To test the significance of a nondirectional hypothesis, you have to consider the possibility that the sample could be extreme at either tail of the comparison distribution. Thus, this is called a **two-tailed test**.

directional hypothesis   research hypothesis predicting a particular direction of difference between populations—for example, a prediction that the population like the sample studied has a higher mean than the population in general.

one-tailed test   hypothesis-testing procedure for a directional hypothesis; situation in which the region of the comparison distribution in which the null hypothesis would be rejected is all on one side (tail) of the distribution.

nondirectional hypothesis   research hypothesis that does not predict a particular direction of difference between the population like the sample studied and the population in general.

two-tailed test   hypothesis-testing procedure for a nondirectional hypothesis; the situation in which the region of the comparison distribution in which the null hypothesis would be rejected is divided between the two sides (tails) of the distribution.

Determining Cutoff Scores with Two-Tailed Tests

There is a special complication in a two-tailed test. You have to divide the significance percentage between the two tails. For example, with a 5% significance level, you reject a null hypothesis only if the sample is so extreme that it is in either the top 2.5% or the bottom 2.5% of the comparison distribution. This keeps the overall level of significance at a total of 5%.

Note that a two-tailed test makes the cutoff Z scores for the 5% level +1.96 and −1.96. For a one-tailed test at the 5% level, the cutoff is not so extreme: only +1.64 or −1.64. But with a one-tailed test, only one side of the distribution is considered. These situations are shown in Figure 6a.

Using the 1% significance level, a two-tailed test (.5% at each tail) has cutoffs of +2.58 and −2.58, whereas a one-tailed test's cutoff is either +2.33 or −2.33. These situations are shown in Figure 6b. The Z score cutoffs for one-tailed and two-tailed tests for the .05 and .01 significance levels are also summarized in Table 2.

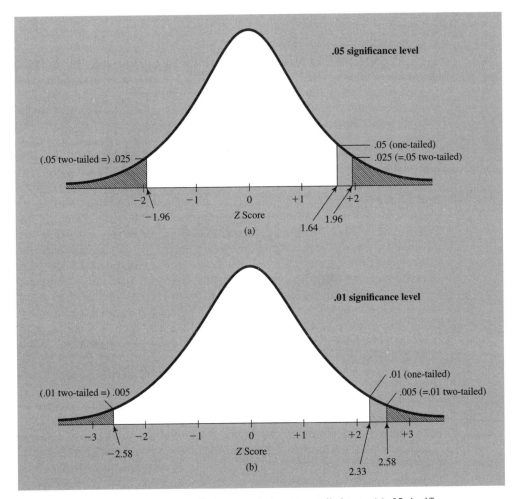

Figure 6 Significance level cutoffs for one-tailed and two-tailed tests: (a) .05 significance level; (b) .01 significance level. (The one-tailed tests in these examples assume the prediction was for a high score. You could instead have a one-tailed test where the prediction is for the lower, left tail.)

Table 2   One-Tailed and Two-Tailed Cutoff Z Scores for the .05 and .01 Significance Levels

		Type of Test	
		One-Tailed	Two-Tailed
Significance	*.05*	−1.64 *or* 1.64	−1.96 *and* 1.96
Level	*.01*	−2.33 *or* 2.33	−2.58 *and* 2.58

When to Use One-Tailed or Two-Tailed Tests

If the researcher decides in advance to use a one-tailed test, then the sample's score does not need to be so extreme to be significant compared to what would be needed with a two-tailed test. Yet there is a price. If the result is extreme in the direction opposite to what was predicted—no matter how extreme—the result cannot be considered statistically significant.

In principle, you plan to use a one-tailed test when you have a clearly directional hypothesis and a two-tailed test when you have a clearly nondirectional hypothesis. In practice, the decision is not so simple. Even when a theory clearly predicts a particular result, the actual result may come out opposite to what you expected. Sometimes, the opposite may be more interesting than what you had predicted. (For example, what if, as in all the fairy tales about wish-granting genies and fish, receiving $10 million and being able to fulfill almost any material desire had made that individual miserable?) By using one-tailed tests, we risk having to ignore possibly important results.

For these reasons, researchers disagree about whether one-tailed tests should be used, even when there is a clearly directional hypothesis. To be safe, most researchers use two-tailed tests for both nondirectional and directional hypotheses. If the two-tailed test is significant, then the researcher looks at the result to see the direction and considers the study significant in that direction. In practice, always using two-tailed tests is a conservative procedure because the cutoff scores are more extreme for a two-tailed test and so it is less likely that a two-tailed test will give a significant result. Thus, if you do get a significant result with a two-tailed test, you are more confident about the conclusion. In fact, in most psychology research articles, unless the researcher specifically states that a one-tailed test was used, it is assumed that the test was two-tailed. The use of one- versus two-tailed tests varies across different areas of research. In many fields, one-tailed tests are almost never used; in others, such as neuroimaging, they are very common. One recent paper actually counted how many one-tailed tests were used in its field: "A review of 85 published evaluations of school-based drug prevention curricula...revealed that 20% employed one-tailed tests" (Ringwalt et al., 2011, p. 135).

In practice, however, our experience is that most research results are either so extreme that they will be significant whether you use a one-tailed or two-tailed test or so far from extreme that they would not be significant in either kind of test. But what happens when a result is less certain? The researcher's decision about one- or two-tailed tests now can make a big difference. In this situation the researcher tries to use the type of test that will give the most accurate and noncontroversial conclusion. The idea is to let nature—not a researcher's decisions—determine the conclusion as much as possible. Further, whenever a result is less than completely clear one way or the other, most researchers are not comfortable drawing strong conclusions until more research is done.

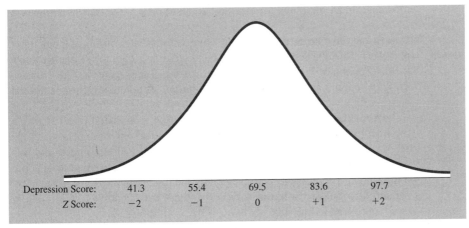

Figure 7 Distribution of depression scores at 4 weeks after admission for diagnosed depressed psychiatric patients receiving the standard therapy (fictional data).

Example of Hypothesis Testing with a Two-Tailed Test

Here is one more fictional example, this time using a two-tailed test. Clinical psychologists at a residential treatment center have developed a new type of therapy to reduce depression that they believe is more effective than the current therapy. However, as with any treatment, it could make patients' depression worse. Thus, the clinical psychologists make a nondirectional hypothesis.

The psychologists randomly select an incoming patient to receive the new form of therapy instead of the usual therapy. (In a real study, of course, more than one patient would be selected, but let's assume that only one person has been trained to do the new therapy and she has time to treat only one patient.) After 4 weeks, the patient fills out a standard depression scale that is given automatically to all patients after 4 weeks. The standard scale has been given at this treatment center for a long time. Thus, the psychologists know in advance the distribution of depression scores at 4 weeks for those who receive the usual therapy: it follows a normal curve with a mean of 69.5 and a standard deviation of 14.1. (These figures correspond roughly to the depression scores found in a national survey of 75,000 psychiatric patients given a widely used standard test; Dahlstrom et al., 1986). This distribution is shown in Figure 7.

The clinical psychologists then carry out the five steps of hypothesis testing.

❶ **Restate the question as a research hypothesis and a null hypothesis about the populations.** There are two populations of interest:

Population 1: Patients diagnosed as depressed who receive the new therapy.
Population 2: Patients diagnosed as depressed in general (who receive the usual therapy).

The research hypothesis is that when measured on depression 4 weeks after admission, patients who receive the new therapy (Population 1) will on the average score differently from patients who receive the current therapy (Population 2). In symbols, the research hypothesis is $\mu_1 \neq \mu_2$. The opposite of the research hypothesis, the null hypothesis, is that patients who receive the new therapy will have the same average depression level as the patients who receive the usual therapy. (That is, the depression level measured after 4 weeks will have the same mean for Populations 1 and 2.) In symbols, the null hypothesis is $\mu_1 = \mu_2$.

❷ **Determine the characteristics of the comparison distribution.** If the null hypothesis is true, the distributions of Populations 1 and 2 are the same. We know the distribution of Population 2 (it is the one shown in Figure 7). Thus, we can use Population 2 as our comparison distribution. As noted, it follows a normal curve, with $\mu = 69.5$ and $\sigma = 14.1$.

❸ **Determine the cutoff sample score on the comparison distribution at which the null hypothesis should be rejected.** The clinical psychologists select the 5% significance level. They have made a nondirectional hypothesis and will therefore use a two-tailed test. Thus, they will reject the null hypothesis only if the patient's depression score is in either the top or bottom 2.5% of the comparison distribution. In terms of Z scores, these cutoffs are $+1.96$ and -1.96 (see Figure 6 and Table 2).

❹ **Determine your sample's score on the comparison distribution.** The patient who received the new therapy was measured 4 weeks after admission. The patient's score on the depression scale was 41, which is a Z score on the comparison distribution of -2.02. That is, $Z = (X - M)/SD = (41 - 69.5)/14.1 = -2.02$. Figure 8 shows the distribution of Population 2 for this study, with the upper and lower 2.5% areas shaded; the depression score of the sample patient is also shown.

❺ **Decide whether to reject the null hypothesis.** A Z score of -2.02 is slightly more extreme than a Z score of -1.96, which is where the lower 2.5% of the comparison distribution begins. Notice in Figure 8 that the Z score of -2.02 falls within the shaded area in the left tail of the comparison distribution. This Z score of -2.02 is a result so extreme that it is unlikely to have occurred if this patient were from a population no different from Population 2. Therefore, the clinical psychologists reject the null hypothesis. The result is statistically significant, and it supports the research hypothesis that depressed patients receiving the new therapy have different depression levels than depressed patients in general who receive the usual therapy.

TIP FOR SUCCESS

When carrying out the five steps of hypothesis testing, always draw a figure like Figure 8. Be sure to include the cutoff score(s) and shade the appropriate tail(s). If the sample score falls inside a shaded tail region, you can reject the null hypothesis and the result is statistically significant. If the sample score does not fall inside a shaded tail region, you cannot reject the null hypothesis.

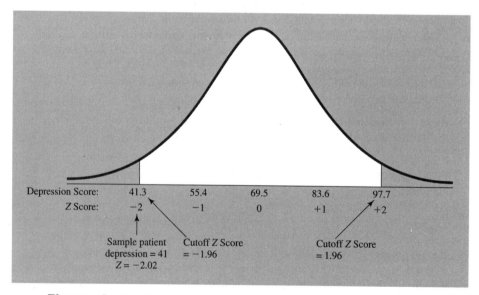

Figure 8   Distribution of depression scores with upper and lower 2.5% shaded and showing the sample patient who received the new therapy (fictional data).

How are you doing?

1. What is a nondirectional hypothesis test?
2. What is a two-tailed test?
3. Why do you use a two-tailed test when testing a nondirectional hypothesis?
4. What is the advantage of using a one-tailed test when your theory predicts a particular direction of result?
5. Why might you use a two-tailed test even when your theory predicts a particular direction of result?
6. A researcher predicts that making people hungry will affect how well they do on a coordination test. A randomly selected person is asked not to eat for 24 hours before taking a standard coordination test and gets a score of 400. For people in general of this age group and gender, tested under normal conditions, coordination scores are normally distributed with a mean of 500 and a standard deviation of 40. Using the .01 significance level, what should the researcher conclude?

Answers

1. A nondirectional hypothesis test is a hypothesis test in which you do not predict a particular direction of difference.
2. A two-tailed test is one in which the overall percentage for the cutoff is divided between the two tails of the comparison distribution. A two-tailed test is used to test the significance of a nondirectional hypothesis.
3. You use a two-tailed test when testing a nondirectional hypothesis because an extreme result in either direction supports the research hypothesis.
4. The cutoff for a one-tailed test is not so extreme; thus, if your result comes out in the predicted direction, it is more likely to be significant. The cutoff is not so extreme because the entire percentage (say 5%) is put in one tail instead of being divided between two tails.
5. You might use a two-tailed test even if your theory predicts a particular direction of result because it lets you count as significant an extreme result in either direction. If you used a one-tailed test and the result came out opposite to the prediction, it could not be called statistically significant.
6. The cutoffs are $+2.58$ and -2.58. The sample person's Z score is $(400 - 500)/40 = -2.5$. The result is not significant; the study is inconclusive.

Controversy: Should Significance Tests Be Banned?

In the last couple of decades, there has been a major controversy about significance testing itself, with a concerted movement on the part of a small but vocal group of psychologists to ban significance tests completely! This is a radical suggestion with far-reaching implications: for at least half a century, nearly every research study in psychology has used significance tests. More has probably been written in major psychology journals in the last 20 years about this controversy than ever before about any statistics issue.

The discussion has been so heated that one article began as follows:

> It is not true that a group of radical activists held 10 statisticians and six editors hostage at the ... convention of the American Psychological Society and chanted, "Support the total test ban!" and "Nix the null!" (Abelson, 1997, p. 12)

This is by far the most important controversy regarding statistics used in psychology. In this chapter, we focus on some basic challenges to hypothesis testing.

First, be reassured that you are not learning about hypothesis testing for nothing. Whatever happens in the future, you absolutely have to understand hypothesis testing to make sense of virtually every research article published in the past. Further, in spite of the controversy that has raged for more than two decades, it is very rare to see new articles that do not use significance testing. Thus, it is doubtful that any major shifts will occur in the near future. Finally, even if hypothesis testing is one day completely abandoned, the alternatives likely to replace it require that you understand virtually all of the logic and procedures you are learning in this course.

So, what is the big controversy? Some of the debate concerns subtle points of logic. For example, does it make sense to worry about rejecting the null hypothesis when it is extremely unlikely to be true that there was no effect at all? Another issue is about the foundation of hypothesis testing, populations, and samples. In most experiments, the samples we use are not actually randomly selected from any definable population as they ought to be according to the "pure" version of how to test a hypothesis. Finally, there is an issue about the logic of using the assertion that the results of a study are not likely if the null hypothesis is true (what we look at in significance testing) as the basis for concluding that the null hypothesis is unlikely. (That is, does the probability of our result, given the null hypothesis, tell us the probability of the null hypothesis given our result? For a discussion of the issues here, see Gorard, 2010.) This controversy becomes rather technical, and the majority view at the moment appears to be that with some minor adjustments to how research results are reported, the way researchers in psychology use hypothesis testing is reasonable (Balluerka et al., 2005; Iacobucci, 2005; Nickerson, 2000).

At the same time, however, very recently, there has been a dramatic revival of interest in a completely different approach to hypothesis testing, called Bayesian analysis (e.g., Kruschke, 2011). This approach is named after Thomas Bayes, an early 18th-century English clergyman who developed a probability law now known as Bayes theorem. The theorem can be proved mathematically and is not controversial. However, its applications are hotly debated. The current flurry of interest has been generated in part by a controversial article (Bem, 2011) on "precognition" (that the future can influence how we behave in the present) published in a top psychology journal. Using standard methods of significance testing, the results of the research are quite strong. However, using Bayesian methods, the results are much less strong (Rouder & Morey, 2011; Wagenmakers, Wetzels, Borsboom, & Van der Maas, 2011), although this conclusion about what Bayesian methods show about the research results has been contested by Bem and two Bayesian statistician collaborators (Bem, Utts, & Johnson, 2011). Even before the controversial Bem paper was published, Bayesian methods were already starting to gain substantial attention.

What can a Bayesian approach do? When analyzing the results of a study, one can actually compute the odds of the research hypothesis being more likely than the null hypothesis. These odds are called a "Bayes factor" (if the prior belief is that the two hypotheses are equally likely). In a sense, the Bayes factor odds agree with the conclusions from standard significance testing. Wetzels and colleagues (2011) calculated the Bayes factor for each of 855 recently published psychology studies. They found that when a result was significant using the standard method at $p < .05$, the Bayes factor odds almost always favored the research hypothesis; when the results were not significant, the Bayes factor odds almost always favored the null hypothesis. However, there was one big difference. As you have learned in this chapter, researchers traditionally consider $p < .05$ to be "significant." But Wetzels et al. found that studies with p values between .05 and .01 had odds of only about 2 to 1 that the research hypothesis is more likely than the null. Thus, the standard approach may be too liberal, permitting us to be convinced by findings that should not be very convincing.

Perhaps even more important, the Bayesian approach offers a way to examine the odds that the null hypothesis is more likely than the research hypothesis. This is something impossible to examine with the standard significance testing. This possibility is particularly likely to be appealing to researchers because it provides an opportunity to do something that we have long wanted to do—directly test the plausibility of the null hypothesis.

The exact null hypothesis may only be possible in very special cases. However, in practice, we are often quite interested in testing whether groups are *not different* (such as women and men or different cultures or ethnicities); or that some procedure that is otherwise beneficial does *not* have any adverse effects; or that two approaches or theories about something have essentially *equal* effects (Gallistel, 2009). Further, software and even online calculators (e.g., Rouder et al., 2009) have now become available that make it practical to figure the Bayes factor in common research designs.

Indeed, the combination of the opportunity to test directly the plausibility of the null and the ready availability of software to carry it out has led to one of the first (and still very rare) papers to use this Bayesian method in a standard research situation. Weinberg and Hajcak (2011) conducted a study of brain activity in response to different kinds of emotional pictures. Most of their results were examined using standard significance testing. However, one particularly important prediction of their research was that a previously found difference between responses to positive and negative pictures would disappear when the pictures of each type excluded certain unusual images. That is, they were predicting a non-difference, the null hypothesis. In their results section, they report: "Because comparisons of the reconstituted pleasant and unpleasant categories amount to an attempt to support the null hypothesis, two Bayes-factor...tests were also conducted...[T]he odds...were greater than 6:1 favoring the null hypothesis,...Because the odds favor the null hypothesis, we cautiously conclude that there may in fact be no difference between the [brain response] elicited by the reconstituted pleasant and unpleasant categories..." (p. 777).

So, perhaps the ideas originated by Reverend Bayes will be the wave of the future. On the other hand, in spite of the current great excitement about this Bayesian revival in articles about statistical methods, it seems unlikely (perhaps 10 to 1?) that it will become the standard method in the very near future.

Potential long-term future directions aside, the biggest complaint today against significance tests, and the one that has received almost universal agreement, is that their standard meaning is interpreted incorrectly (e.g., Balluerka et al., 2005). In fact, opponents of significance tests argue that even if there were no other problems with the tests, they should be banned simply because they are so often and so badly misused. One major misuse of significance tests is the tendency for researchers to decide that, if a result is not significant, the null hypothesis is shown to be true. We have emphasized that when you can't reject the null hypothesis, the results are simply inconclusive. The error of concluding the null hypothesis is true from failing to reject it is extremely serious, because important theories and methods may be considered false just because a particular study did not get strong enough results.

What should be done? The general consensus at the moment seems to be that we should keep significance tests, but better train our students not to misuse them.

We should not throw the baby out with the bathwater. To address this controversy, the American Psychological Association (APA) established a committee of eminent psychologists renowned for their statistical expertise. The committee met over a two-year period, circulated a preliminary report, and considered reactions to it from a large number of researchers. In the end, they strongly condemned various misuses of significance testing such as the kind we just discussed, but they left its use up to the decision of each researcher. In their report they concluded:

> Some had hoped that this task force would vote to recommend an outright ban on the use of significance tests in psychology journals. Although this might eliminate some abuses, the committee thought there were enough counterexamples (e.g., Abelson, 1997) to justify forbearance. (Wilkinson & Task Force on Statistical Inference, 1999, pp. 602–603)

Balluerka and colleagues (2005) reviewed the arguments for and against significance testing. Their conclusion, was that "...rigorous research activity requires the use of...[significance testing] in the appropriate context, the complementary

BOX 1   Jacob Cohen, the Ultimate New Yorker: Funny, Pushy, Brilliant, and Kind

New Yorkers can be proud of Jacob Cohen, who introduced to behavioral and social scientists some of our most important statistical tools. Never worried about being popular—although he was—Cohen almost single-handedly forced the current debate over significance testing, which he liked to joke was entrenched like a "secular religion." About the asterisk that accompanies a significant result, he said the religion must be "of Judeo-Christian derivation, as it employs as its most powerful icon a six-pointed cross" (1990, p. 1307).

Jacob went to City College of New York at age 15, but excelled only at table tennis. In fact, he failed calculus. However, in 1947, after World War II, he entered graduate school at New York University (NYU) in clinical psychology and three years later had earned a masters and a doctorate. He then worked in rather lowly roles for the Veterans Administration, doing research on various practical topics, until he returned to NYU in 1959. There he became a very famous faculty member because of his creative, off-beat ideas about statistics. Amazingly, he made his contributions having no mathematics training beyond high school algebra.

But a lack of formal training may have been Jacob Cohen's advantage because he emphasized looking at data and thinking about them, not just applying a standard analysis. In particular, he demonstrated that the standard methods were not working very well, especially for the "soft" fields of psychology such as clinical, personality, and social psychology. Many of his ideas were hailed as great breakthroughs. Starting in the 1990s, he really began to

force the issue of the mindless use of significance testing. But he still used humor to tease behavioral and social scientists for their failure to see the problems inherent in the arbitrary yes-no decision feature of null hypothesis testing. For example, he liked to remind everyone that significance testing came out of Sir Ronald Fisher's work in agriculture, in which the decisions were yes-no matters such as whether a crop needed manure. He pointed out that behavioral and social scientists "do not deal in manure, at least not knowingly" (Cohen, 1990, p. 1307)! He really disliked the fact that Fisher-style decision making is used to determine the fate of not only doctoral dissertations, research funds, publications, and promotions, "but whether to have a baby just now" (1990, p. 1307). And getting more serious, he charged that significance testing's "arbitrary unreasonable tyranny has led to data fudging of varying degrees of subtlety, from grossly altering data to dropping cases where there 'must have been' errors" (p. 1307).

Cohen was active in many social causes, especially desegregation in the schools and fighting discrimination in police departments. He cared passionately about everything he did. He was deeply loved. And he suffered from major depression, becoming incapacitated by it four times in his life.

Got troubles? Got no more math than high school algebra? It doesn't have to stop you from contributing to science.

Sources: P. Cohen (2005); Shrout (2001).

use of other methods which provide information about aspects not addressed by ...
[significance testing], and adherence to a series of recommendations which promote
its rational use in psychological research" (p. 55). If you become a research psychologist, congratulations on being among those who have learned to be "rigorous."

Hypothesis Tests in Research Articles

In general, hypothesis testing is reported in research articles using one of the specific methods of hypothesis testing. For each result of interest, the researcher usually first indicates whether the result was statistically significant. (Note that, as
with the first of the following examples, the researcher will not necessarily use the
word *significant;* so look out for other indicators, such as reporting that scores on
a variable decreased, increased, or were associated with scores on another variable.) Next, the researcher usually gives the symbol associated with the specific
method used in figuring the probability that the result would have occurred if the
null hypothesis was true, such as t, F, or χ^2. Finally, there will be an indication of
the significance level, such as $p < .05$ or $p < .01$. (The researcher will usually
also provide other information, such as the mean and standard deviation of sample
scores.) For example, in the study of health-related plots in prime time American
television programs, Hether and Murphy (2010) reported: "... of all the prevention
information depicted, there was significantly more when the ill or injured character was male, as opposed to female: (60% versus 40%, $\chi^2(1) = 4.00, p < .05$)"
(p. 817). The key thing to understand now about this result is the "$p < .05$." This
means that the probability of the results if the null hypothesis were true is less
than .05 (5%).

When a result is close but does not reach the significance level chosen, it may
be reported anyway as a "near significant trend" or as having "approached significance." When a result is not even close to being extreme enough to reject the null
hypothesis, it may be reported as "not significant," or the abbreviation *ns* will be
used. Finally, whether or not a result is significant, it is increasingly common (and
now recommended in the 6th edition of the *Publication Manual of the American
Psychological Association,* 2009) for researchers to report the exact p level, such
as $p = .03$ or $p = .27$. (These are given in computer outputs of hypothesis testing
results.) The p reported in this case is based on the exact proportion of the comparison distribution that is more extreme than the sample score information that you
could figure from the Z score for your sample and a normal curve table.

A researcher will usually note if he or she used a one-tailed test. When reading
research articles in most fields, you can assume the researcher used a two-tailed
test if nothing is said otherwise. Even though a researcher has chosen a significance level in advance, such as .05, the researcher may note that results meet more
rigorous standards. Thus, in the same article, you may see some results noted as
"$p < .05$," others as "$p < .01$," and still others as "$p < .001$."

Finally, researchers often show hypothesis testing results only as asterisks
(stars) in a table of results. In such tables, a result with an asterisk means it is significant, while a result without an asterisk is not. For example, Table 3 shows the results
of part of a study by Colley and colleagues (2010) comparing how male and female
university students in England use camera phones. The table gives figures for means
and standard deviations of men and women's ratings of the importance of using a
camera phone for different purposes. The important things to look at in the table are

Table 3 Means and Standard Deviations of Ratings of Personal Importance of Different Purposes of Using a Camera Phone

	Men		Women	
	Mean	**SD**	**Mean**	**SD**
Record special events for myself	5.09	1.53	5.29	1.58
Record special events to share with others present	5.02	1.54	4.98	1.60
Record special events to share with others not present	5.09	1.50	5.27	1.62
Use as a visual note of something for myself	3.79	1.81	4.43	1.80
Use as a visual note to use in a task with others	3.05	1.48	3.41	1.67
Send news to family or friends	4.18	1.91	4.23	1.91
Record something that captures my interest for myself	5.23	1.51	5.02	1.54
Record something that captures my interest to share with others	5.03	1.35	5.12	1.52
Record images of people who are important to me for myself	5.18	1.67	5.81**	1.29
Record images of people who are important to me to share with others	4.75	1.51	5.37**	1.30

Rating scale from 1 = not at all important to 7 = very important. Differences between adjacent cells relating to male and female participants significant at $p < .01$ (adjusted level) shown as **. No results were significant at the lower level of $p < .05$.

Source: Colley, A., Todd, Z., White, A., & Turner-Moore, T. (2010). Communication using camera phones among young men and women: Who sends what to whom? *Sex Roles, 63*, 348–360. Reproduced with permission of Springer publishers.

the asterisks (and the note at the bottom of the table that goes with them). The asterisks tell you the significance level for the various comparisons between men and women's ratings. The table shows that women rated two purposes of using a camera phone as being more important than men did: "recording images of people who are important to me for myself" and "recording images of people who are important to me to share with others." The asterisks show that the differences were significant at the .01 (one in a hundred) level. The lack of asterisks for the other rows tells you that the importance ratings for those camera phone purposes did not show a statistically significant difference between men and women.

In reporting results of significance testing, researchers rarely talk explicitly about the research hypothesis or the null hypothesis, nor do they describe any of the other steps of the process in detail. It is assumed that readers of psychology research understand all of this very well.

Learning Aids

Summary

1. Hypothesis testing considers the probability that the result of a study could have come about even if the experimental procedure had no effect. If this probability is low, the scenario of no effect is rejected and the hypothesis behind the experimental procedure is supported.
2. The expectation of an effect is the research hypothesis, and the hypothetical situation of no effect is the null hypothesis.

3. When a result (that is, a sample score) is so extreme that the result would be very unlikely if the null hypothesis were true, the researcher rejects the null hypothesis and describes the research hypothesis as supported. If the result is not that extreme, the researcher does not reject the null hypothesis, and the study is inconclusive.

4. Psychologists usually consider a result too extreme if it is less likely than 5% (that is, a significance level of $p < .05$) to have come about if the null hypothesis were true. Psychologists sometimes use a more extreme 1% ($p < .01$ significance level), or even .1% ($p < .001$ significance level), cutoff.

5. The cutoff percentage is the probability of the result being extreme in a predicted direction in a directional or one-tailed test. The cutoff percentages are the probability of the result being extreme in either direction in a nondirectional or two-tailed test.

6. The five steps of hypothesis testing are:
   ❶ **Restate the question as a research hypothesis and a null hypothesis about the populations.**
   ❷ **Determine the characteristics of the comparison distribution.**
   ❸ **Determine the cutoff sample score on the comparison distribution at which the null hypothesis should be rejected.**
   ❹ **Determine your sample's score on the comparison distribution.**
   ❺ **Decide whether to reject the null hypothesis.**

7. There has been much controversy about significance tests, including critiques of the basic logic and arguments in favor of an alternative Bayesian approach that gives odds of the relative plausibility of the research and null hypotheses. The major critique, however, is that significance testing is often seriously misused, such as by incorrectly interpreting not rejecting the null hypothesis as demonstrating that the null hypothesis is true.

8. Research articles typically report the results of hypothesis testing by saying a result was or was not significant and giving the probability level cutoff (usually 5% or 1%, although sometimes giving an exact figure) that the decision was based on.

Key Terms

hypothesis testing	comparison distribution	directional hypothesis
hypothesis	cutoff sample score	one-tailed test
theory	conventional levels of significance	nondirectional hypothesis
research hypothesis	($p < .05, p < .01$)	two-tailed test
null hypothesis	statistically significant	

Example Worked-Out Problems

A randomly selected individual, after going through an experimental treatment, has a score of 27 on a particular measure. The scores of people in general on this measure are normally distributed with a mean of 19 and a standard deviation of 4. The researcher predicts an effect, but does not predict a particular direction of effect. Using the 5% significance level, what should you conclude? Solve this problem explicitly using all five steps of hypothesis testing and illustrate your answer with a sketch showing the comparison distribution, the cutoff (or cutoffs), and the score of the sample on this distribution.

Answer

❶ **Restate the question as a research hypothesis and a null hypothesis about the populations.** There are two populations of interest:

Population 1: People who go through the experimental procedure.
Population 2: People in general (that is, people who do not go through the experimental procedure).

The research hypothesis is that Population 1 will score differently than Population 2 on the particular measure. The null hypothesis is that the two populations are not different on the measure.

❷ **Determine the characteristics of the comparison distribution:** $\mu = 19$, $\sigma = 4$, normally distributed.

❸ **Determine the cutoff sample score on the comparison distribution at which the null hypothesis should be rejected.** For a two-tailed test at the 5% level (2.5% at each tail), the cutoff scores are $+1.96$ and -1.96 (see Figure 6 or Table 2).

❹ **Determine your sample's score on the comparison distribution.** $Z = (27 - 19)/4 = 2$.

❺ **Decide whether to reject the null hypothesis.** A Z score of 2 is more extreme than the cutoff Z of ± 1.96. Reject the null hypothesis; the result is significant. The experimental procedure affects scores on this measure. The diagram is shown in Figure 9.

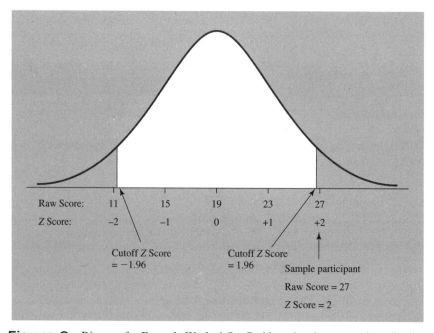

Figure 9　Diagram for Example Worked-Out Problem showing comparison distribution, cutoffs (2.5% shaded area in each tail), and sample score.

Outline for Writing Essays for Hypothesis-Testing Problems Involving a Single Sample of One Participant and a Known Population

1. Describe the core logic of hypothesis testing. Be sure to explain terminology such as research hypothesis and null hypothesis, and explain the concept of providing support for the research hypothesis when the study results are strong enough to reject the null hypothesis.
2. Explain the concept of the comparison distribution. Be sure to mention that it is the distribution that represents the population situation if the null hypothesis is true. Note that the key characteristics of the comparison distribution are its mean, standard deviation, and shape.
3. Describe the logic and process for determining (using the normal curve) the cutoff sample scores on the comparison distribution at which you should reject the null hypothesis.
4. Describe how to figure the sample's score on the comparison distribution.
5. Explain how and why the scores from Steps ❸ and ❹ of the hypothesis-testing process are compared. Explain the meaning of the result of this comparison with regard to the specific research and null hypotheses being tested.

Practice Problems

These problems involve figuring. Most real-life statistics problems are done with special statistical software. Even if you have such software, do these problems by hand to ingrain the method in your mind.

All data are fictional unless an actual citation is given.

Set I

1. Define the following terms in your own words: (a) hypothesis-testing procedure, (b) .05 significance level, and (c) two-tailed test.
2. When a result is not extreme enough to reject the null hypothesis, explain why it is wrong to conclude that your result supports the null hypothesis.
3. For each of the following, (a) say which two populations are being compared, (b) state the research hypothesis, (c) state the null hypothesis, and (d) say whether you should use a one-tailed or two-tailed test and why.
   i. Do Canadian children whose parents are librarians score higher than Canadian children in general on reading ability?
   ii. Is the level of income for residents of a particular city different from the level of income for people in the region?
   iii. Do people who have experienced an earthquake have more or less self-confidence than the general population?
4. Based on the information given for each of the following studies, decide whether to reject the null hypothesis. For each, give (a) the Z-score cutoff (or cutoffs) on the comparison distribution at which the null hypothesis should be rejected, (b) the Z score on the comparison distribution for the

sample score, and (c) your conclusion. Assume that all populations are normally distributed.

	Population				
Study	μ	σ	Sample Score	p	Tails of Test
A	10	2	14	.05	1 (high predicted)
B	10	2	14	.05	2
C	10	2	14	.01	1 (high predicted)
D	10	2	14	.01	2
E	10	4	14	.05	1 (high predicted)

5. Based on the information given for each of the following studies, decide whether to reject the null hypothesis. For each, give (a) the Z-score cutoff (or cutoffs) on the comparison distribution at which the null hypothesis should be rejected, (b) the Z score on the comparison distribution for the sample score, and (c) your conclusion. Assume that all populations are normally distributed.

	Population				
Study	μ	σ	Sample Score	p	Tails of Test
A	70	4	74	.05	1 (high predicted)
B	70	1	74	.01	2
C	70	2	76	.01	2
D	72	2	77	.01	2
E	72	2	68	.05	1 (low predicted)

6. A psychologist studying the senses of taste and smell has carried out many studies in which students are given each of 20 different foods (apricot, chocolate, cherry, coffee, garlic, and so on). She administers each food by dropping a liquid on the tongue. Based on her past research, she knows that for students overall at the university, the mean number of the 20 foods that students can identify correctly is 14, with a standard deviation of 4, and the distribution of scores follows a normal curve. The psychologist wants to know whether people's accuracy on this task has more to do with smell than with taste. In other words, she wants to test whether people do *worse* on the task when they are only able to taste the liquid compared to when they can both taste and smell it (note that this is a directional hypothesis). Thus, she sets up special procedures that keep a person from being able to use the sense of smell during the task. The psychologist then tries the procedure on one randomly selected student. This student is able to identify only 5 correctly. (a) Using the .05 significance level, what should the psychologist conclude? Solve this problem explicitly using all five steps of hypothesis testing and illustrate your answer with a sketch showing the comparison distribution, the cutoff (or cutoffs), and the score of the sample on this distribution. (b) Then explain your answer to someone who has never had a course in statistics (but who is familiar with mean, standard deviation, and Z scores).

7. A psychologist is working with people who have had a particular type of major surgery. This psychologist proposes that people will recover from the operation more quickly if friends and family are in the room with them for the first 48 hours after the operation. It is known that time to recover from this kind of surgery is normally distributed with a mean of 12 days and a standard deviation

of 5 days. The procedure of having friends and family in the room for the period after the surgery is tried with a randomly selected patient. This patient recovers in 18 days. (a) Using the .01 significance level, what should the researcher conclude? Solve this problem explicitly using all five steps of hypothesis testing, and illustrate your answer with a sketch showing the comparison distribution, the cutoff (or cutoffs), and the score of the sample on this distribution. (b) Then explain your answer to someone who has never had a course in statistics (but who is familiar with mean, standard deviation, and Z scores).

8. What is the effect of going through a natural disaster on the attitude of police chiefs about the goodness of the people in their city? A researcher studying this expects a more positive attitude (because of the many acts of heroism and helping of neighbors), but a more negative attitude is also possible (because of looting and scams). It is known that, using a 1-to-10 scale (from 1 = extremely negative attitude to 10 = extremely positive attitude), in general police chiefs' attitudes about the goodness of the people in their cities is normally distributed, with a mean of 6.5 and a standard deviation of 2.1. A major earthquake has just occurred in an isolated city, and shortly afterward the researcher is able to give the attitude questionnaire to the police chief of that city. The chief's score is 8.2. (a) Using the .05 significance level, what should the researcher conclude? Solve this problem explicitly using all five steps of hypothesis testing and illustrate your answer with a sketch showing the comparison distribution, the cutoff (or cutoffs), and the score of the sample on this distribution. (b) Then explain your answer to someone who has never had a course in statistics (but who is familiar with mean, standard deviation, and Z scores).

9. Robins and John (1997) carried out a study on narcissism (self-love), comparing people who scored high versus low on a narcissism questionnaire. (An example item was, "If I ruled the world it would be a better place.") They also had other questionnaires, including one that had an item about how many times the participant looked in the mirror on a typical day. In their results section, the researchers noted "... as predicted, high-narcissism individuals reported looking at themselves in the mirror more frequently than did low narcissism individuals (Ms = 5.7 vs. 4.8),... $p < .05$" (p. 39). Explain this result to a person who has never had a course in statistics. (Focus on the meaning of this result in terms of the general logic of hypothesis testing and statistical significance.)

10. Reber and Kotovsky (1997), in a study of problem solving, described one of their results comparing a specific group of participants within their overall control condition as follows: "This group took an average of 179 moves to solve the puzzle, whereas the rest of the control participants took an average of 74 moves, $t(19) = 3.31, p < .01$" (p. 183). Explain this result to a person who has never had a course in statistics. (Focus on the meaning of this result in terms of the general logic of hypothesis testing and statistical significance.)

Set II

11. List the five steps of hypothesis testing, and explain the procedure and logic of each.
12. When a result is significant, explain why it is wrong to say the result "proves" the research hypothesis.

13. For each of the following, (a) state which two populations are being compared, (b) state the research hypothesis, (c) state the null hypothesis, and (d) say whether you should use a one-tailed or two-tailed test and why.

   i. In an experiment, people are told to solve a problem by focusing on the details. Is the speed of solving the problem different for people who get such instructions compared to the speed for people who are given no special instructions?

   ii. Based on anthropological reports in which the status of women is scored on a 10-point scale, the mean and standard deviation across many cultures are known. A new culture is found in which there is an unusual family arrangement. The status of women is also rated in this culture. Do cultures with the unusual family arrangement provide higher status to women than cultures in general?

   iii. Do people who live in big cities develop more stress-related conditions than people in general?

14. Based on the information given for each of the following studies, decide whether to reject the null hypothesis. For each, give (a) the Z-score cutoff (or cutoffs) on the comparison distribution at which the null hypothesis should be rejected, (b) the Z score on the comparison distribution for the sample score, and (c) your conclusion. Assume that all populations are normally distributed.

Study	Population μ	σ	Sample Score	p	Tails of Test
A	5	1	7	.05	1 (high predicted)
B	5	1	7	.05	2
C	5	1	7	.01	1 (high predicted)
D	5	1	7	.01	2

15. Based on the information given for each of the following studies, decide whether to reject the null hypothesis. For each, give (a) the Z-score cutoff (or cutoffs) on the comparison distribution at which the null hypothesis should be rejected, (b) the Z score on the comparison distribution for the sample score, and (c) your conclusion. Assume that all populations are normally distributed.

Study	Population μ	σ	Sample Score	p	Tails of Test
A	100.0	10.0	80	.05	1 (low predicted)
B	100.0	20.0	80	.01	2
C	74.3	11.8	80	.01	2
D	16.9	1.2	80	.05	1 (low predicted)
E	88.1	12.7	80	.05	2

16. A researcher wants to test whether a certain sound will make rats do worse on learning tasks. It is known that an ordinary rat can learn to run a particular maze correctly in 18 trials, with a standard deviation of 6. (The number of trials to learn this maze is normally distributed.) The researcher now tries an ordinary rat in the maze, but with the sound. The rat takes 38 trials to learn the maze. (a) Using the .05 level, what should the researcher conclude? Solve this

problem explicitly using all five steps of hypothesis testing, and illustrate your answer with a sketch showing the comparison distribution, the cutoff (or cutoffs), and the score of the sample on this distribution. (b) Then explain your answer to someone who has never had a course in statistics (but who is familiar with mean, standard deviation, and Z scores).

17. A family psychologist developed an elaborate training program to reduce the stress of childless men who marry women with adolescent children. It is known from previous research that such men, one month after moving in with their new wife and her children, have a stress level of 85 with a standard deviation of 15, and the stress levels are normally distributed. The training program is tried on one man randomly selected from all those in a particular city who during the preceding month have married a woman with an adolescent child. After the training program, this man's stress level is 60. (a) Using the .05 level, what should the researcher conclude? Solve this problem explicitly using all five steps of hypothesis testing and illustrate your answer with a sketch showing the comparison distribution, the cutoff (or cutoffs), and the score of the sample on this distribution. (b) Then explain your answer to someone who has never had a course in statistics (but who is familiar with mean, standard deviation, and Z scores).

18. A researcher predicts that listening to music while solving math problems will make a particular brain area more active. To test this, a research participant has her brain scanned while listening to music and solving math problems, and the brain area of interest has a percentage signal change of 58. From many previous studies with this same math problems procedure (but not listening to music), it is known that the signal change in this brain area is normally distributed with a mean of 35 and a standard deviation of 10. (a) Using the .01 level, what should the researcher conclude? Solve this problem explicitly using all five steps of hypothesis testing, and illustrate your answer with a sketch showing the comparison distribution, the cutoff (or cutoffs), and the score of the sample on this distribution. (b) Then explain your answer to someone who has never had a course in statistics (but who is familiar with mean, standard deviation, and Z scores).

19. Pecukonis (1990), as part of a larger study, measured ego development (a measure of overall maturity) and ability to empathize with others among a group of 24 aggressive adolescent girls in a residential treatment center. The girls were divided into high- and low-ego development groups, and the empathy ("cognitive empathy") scores of these two groups were compared. In his results section, Pecukonis reported, "The average score on cognitive empathy for subjects scoring high on ego development was 22.1 as compared with 16.3 for low scorers,... $p < .005$" (p. 68). Explain this result to a person who has never had a course in statistics. (Focus on the meaning of this result in terms of the general logic of hypothesis testing and statistical significance.)

20. Bohnert and colleagues (2007) conducted a study comparing various aspects of social adjustment to college of male and female students during the summer before their first year of college (Time 1) and 10 months later (Time 2). Table 4 shows the results of the study. The "$t(83)$" column gives details of the specific hypothesis testing procedure used in this study called a t test. In this study, the t test was used to compare the different types of social adjustment (such as friendship quality and loneliness) between male and female students. Considering just the first two rows of the table (the ratings of friendship quality

Table 4 Means and Standard Deviation for Main Study Variables by Gender

	Total (n = 85)		Males (n = 31)		Females (n = 54)		
	M	SD	M	SD	M	SD	t (83)
Adolescence (Time 1)							
Friendship quality	2.70	0.40	2.49	0.46	2.82	0.32	13.98***
Loneliness	36.39	8.71	39.30	9.98	34.78	7.56	5.47*
Emerging adulthood (Time 2)							
Friendship quality	3.10	0.48	2.84	0.57	3.21	0.38	11.31***
Loneliness	35.84	9.98	37.88	11.38	34.71	9.21	1.76
Activities: Intensity	8.09	8.27	10.00	10.19	7.18	7.18	0.98
Activities: Breadth	1.71	1.06	1.84	1.18	1.65	1.01	0.51

$*p < .05. **p < .01. ***p < .001.$

Source: Bohnert, A. M., Aikins, J. W., & Edidin, J. (2007). The role of organized activities in facilitating social adaptation across the transition to college. *Journal of Adolescent Research, 22*, 189–208. Sage Publications, Ltd. Reprinted by permission of Sage Publications, Thousands Oaks, London, and New Delhi.

and loneliness at Time 1), explain what these results mean to a person who has never had a course in statistics. (Focus on the meaning of the results in terms of the general logic of hypothesis testing and statistical significance.)

Chapter Notes

1. We are simplifying a bit to make the initial learning easier. The research hypothesis is that one population will walk earlier than the other, $\mu_1 < \mu_2$. Thus, to be precise, its opposite is that the other group will either walk at the same time or later. That is, the opposite of the research hypothesis in this example includes both no difference and a difference in the direction opposite to what we predicted. In terms of symbols, if our research hypothesis is $\mu_1 < \mu_2$, then its opposite is $\mu_1 \geq \mu_2$ (the symbol "≥" means "greater than or equal to"). We discuss this issue in some detail later in the chapter.
2. In practice, since hypothesis testing is usually done using a computer program, you have to decide in advance only on the cutoff probability. The program output usually includes the exact probability of getting your result if the null hypothesis were true. You then just compare the program output's probability to see if it is less than the cutoff probability level you set in advance. However, to *understand* what these probability levels mean, you need to learn the entire process, including how to figure the Z score for a particular cutoff probability.

Answers to Set I Practice Problems

Chapter 4

1. (a) Hypothesis-testing procedure: the logical, statistical procedure for determining the likelihood of your study having gotten a particular pattern of results if the null hypothesis is true. (b) .05 Significance level: the situation in hypothesis testing in which you decide to reject the null hypothesis because the probability of getting your particular results if the null hypothesis were true is less than 5%. (c) Two-tailed test: a procedure used in hypothesis testing when the research hypothesis does not specify a particular direction of difference; it tests for extreme results that are either higher or lower than would be expected if the null hypothesis were true.
2. It is possible that the research hypothesis is correct but the result in the particular sample was not extreme enough to be able to reject the null hypothesis.
3. i. (a) Population 1: Canadian children of librarians; Population 2: All Canadian children. (b) Population 1 children have a higher average reading ability than Population 2 children. (c) Population 1's average reading ability is not higher than Population 2's. (d) One-tailed, because the question is whether they "score higher"; only one direction of difference is of interest.
   ii. (a) Population 1: People who live in a particular city; Population 2: All people who live in the region. (b) Populations 1 and 2 have different mean incomes. (c) Populations 1 and 2 have the same mean income. (d) Two-tailed, because the question is whether the income of the people in the city is "different" from those in the region as a whole; a difference in either direction would be of interest.
  iii. (a) Population 1: People who have experienced an earthquake; Population 2: People in general. (b) Populations 1 and 2 have different mean levels of self-confidence. (c) Populations 1 and 2 have the same mean level of self-confidence. (d) Two-tailed, because the question specifies "more or less"; a difference in either direction would be of interest.

4.

Study	Cutoff	Z Score on Comparison Distribution	Decision
A	+1.64	2	Reject null hypothesis
B	±1.96	2	Reject null hypothesis
C	+2.33	2	Inconclusive
D	±2.58	2	Inconclusive
E	+1.64	1	Inconclusive

5.

Study	Cutoff	Z Score on Comparison Distribution	Decision
A	+1.64	1	Inconclusive
B	±2.58	4	Reject null hypothesis
C	±2.58	3	Reject null hypothesis
D	±2.58	2.5	Inconclusive
E	−1.64	−2	Reject null hypothesis

6. (a) ❶ **Restate the question as a research hypothesis and a null hypothesis about the populations.** There are two populations of interest:
Population 1: Students who are prevented from using their sense of smell.
Population 2: Students in general.

The research hypothesis is that students prevented from using their sense of smell (Population 1) will do worse on the taste task than students in general (Population 2). The null hypothesis is that students prevented from using their sense of smell (Population 1) will not do worse on the taste task than students in general (Population 2).
❷ **Determine the characteristics of the comparison distribution.** The comparison distribution will be the same as Population 2. As stated in the problem, $\mu = 14$ and $\sigma = 4$. We assume it follows a normal curve.
❸ **Determine the cutoff sample score on the comparison distribution at which the null hypothesis should be rejected.** For a one-tailed test at the .05 level, the cutoff is −1.64. (The cutoff is a *negative value*, because the research hypothesis is that Population 1 will *do worse* on the task than Population 2—that is, Population 1 will have a *lower score* on the task than Population 2.)
❹ **Determine your sample's score on the comparison distribution.** The sample's score was 5. $Z = (5 - 14)/4 = -2.25$.
❺ **Decide whether to reject the null hypothesis.** A Z score of −2.25 is more extreme than the cutoff of −1.64. Thus, you can reject the null hypothesis. The research hypothesis is supported—not having a sense of smell makes for fewer correct identifications.
(b) In brief, you solve this problem by considering the likelihood that being without a sense of smell makes no difference. If the sense of smell made no difference, the probability of the student studied getting any particular number correct

is simply the probability of students in general getting any particular number correct. We know the distribution of the number correct that students get in general. Thus, you can figure that probability. It turns out that it would be fairly unlikely to get only five correct; so the researcher concludes that not having the sense of smell does make a difference.

To go into the details a bit, the key issue is determining these probabilities. We assumed that the number correct for the students in general follows a normal curve—a specific bell-shaped mathematical pattern in which most of the scores are in the middle and there are fewer scores as the number correct gets higher or lower. There are tables showing exactly what proportions are more extreme than any particular Z score on the normal curve.

When considering what to conclude from a study, researchers often use a convention that, if a result could have happened by chance less than 5% of the time under a particular scenario, the scenario will be considered unlikely. The normal curve tables show that the top 5% of the normal curve begins with a Z score of 1.64. The normal curve is completely symmetrical; thus, the bottom 5% includes all Z scores below -1.64. Therefore, the researcher would probably set the following rule: the scenario in which being without the sense of smell makes no difference will be rejected as unlikely if the number correct (converted to a Z score using the mean and standard deviation for students in general) is less than -1.64.

The actual number correct for the student who could not use the sense of smell was 5. The normal curve for students in general had a mean of 14 and a standard deviation of 4. Getting 5 correct is 9 below the mean of 14; in terms of standard deviations of 4 each, it is 9/4 below the mean. A Z score of -2.25 is more extreme than -1.64. Thus, the researcher concludes that the scenario in which being

without smell has no effect is unlikely. This is shown in what I have drawn here:

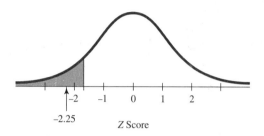

7. Cutoff (.01 level, one-tailed) $= -2.33$; Z score on comparison distribution for patient studied $= 1.20$; the experiment is inconclusive. Hypothesis testing steps, explanation, and sketch are similar to those of question 6.
8. Cutoff (.05 level, two-tailed) $= \pm 1.96$; Z score on comparison distribution for the police chief studied $= .81$; the experiment is inconclusive. Hypothesis testing steps, explanation, and sketch similar to question 6.
9. The two Ms (5.7 and 4.8) and the $p < .05$ are crucial. M stands for *mean*, the average of the scores in a particular group. The average number of times per day the high narcissism participants looked in the mirrors was 5.7, while the average for the low narcissism participants was only 4.8. The $p < .05$ tells us that this difference is statistically significant at the .05 level. This means that, if a person's level of narcissism made no difference in how often the person looked in the mirror, the chances of getting two groups of participants who were this different on looking in the mirror just by chance would be 5%. Hence, you can reject that possibility as unlikely and conclude that the level of narcissism does make a difference in how often people look in the mirror.
10. Similar to question 9.

Chapter 5

Hypothesis Tests with Means of Samples

The basic logic of hypothesis testing involves use of a sample of a single individual as examples. However, in actual practice, psychology research almost always involves a sample of many individuals. In this chapter, we consider hypothesis testing with a sample of more than one individual. For example, a social psychologist is interested in the potential effect of perceptions of people's personality on perceptions of their physical attractiveness. The researcher's theory predicts that, if you are told that a person has positive personality qualities (such as kindness, warmth, a sense of humor, and intelligence), you will rate that person as more attractive than if no mention had been made of the person's personality qualities. From extensive previous research (in which no mention was made of personality qualities), the researcher has established the population mean and standard deviation of the attractiveness rating of a photo of a particular person. The researcher then recruits a sample of 64 individuals to rate the attractiveness of the person in the photograph. However, prior to rating the person, each individual is told that the person whose photograph they are going to rate has many positive personality qualities. In this chapter, you will learn how to test hypotheses in situations such as those presented in this example, situations in which the population has a *known mean and standard deviation* and in which a sample has *more than one individual.* Mainly, this requires examining in some detail a new kind of distribution, called a "distribution of means." (We will return to this example later in the chapter.)

The Distribution of Means

Hypothesis testing in the usual research situation, where you are studying a sample of many individuals, is exactly the same as you learned in *Introduction to Hypothesis Testing*—with an important exception. When you have more than one person in your sample, there is a special problem with Step ❷, determining the characteristics of the comparison distribution. In each of our examples so far, the comparison distribution has been a distribution of *individual scores* (such as the population of ages when individual babies start walking). A distribution of individual scores has been the correct comparison distribution because we have used examples with a sample of *one individual.* That is, there has been a match between the type of sample score we have been dealing with (a score from *one individual*) and the comparison distribution (a distribution of *individual scores*).

Now, consider the situation when you have a sample of, say, 64 individuals (as in the attractiveness rating example). You now have a *group of 64 scores* (an attractiveness rating from each of the 64 people in the study). The mean is a very useful representative value of a group of scores. Thus, the score you care about most when there is more than one individual in your sample is the *mean of the group of scores.* In this example, you would focus on the mean of the 64 individuals' scores. Suppose you were to compare the mean of this sample of 64 individuals' scores to a distribution of a population of individual scores. This would be a mismatch—like comparing apples to oranges. *Instead, when you are interested in the mean of a sample of 64 scores, you need a comparison distribution that is a distribution of means of samples of 64 scores.* We call such a comparison distribution a **distribution of means.** So, the scores in a distribution of means are *means,* not scores of single individuals.

A distribution of means is a distribution of the means of lots and lots of samples of the same size, with each sample randomly taken from the same population of individuals. (Statisticians also call this distribution of means a *sampling distribution of the mean.* In this chapter, however, we use the term *distribution of means* to keep it clear that we are talking about populations of *means,* not samples or a distribution of samples.)

The distribution of means is the correct comparison distribution when there is more than one person in a sample. Thus, in most research situations, determining the characteristics of a distribution of means is necessary for Step ❷ of the hypothesis-testing procedure, determining the characteristics of the comparison distribution.

Building a Distribution of Means

distribution of means   distribution of means of samples of a given size from a population (also called a *sampling distribution of the mean*); comparison distribution when testing hypotheses involving a single sample of more than one individual.

To help you understand the idea of a distribution of means, we consider how you could build up such a distribution from an ordinary population distribution of individual scores. Suppose our population of individual scores was of the grade levels of the 90,000 elementary and junior-high schoolchildren in a particular region. Suppose further (to keep the example simple) that there are exactly 10,000 children at each grade level, from first through ninth grade. This population distribution would

Figure 1 Distribution of grade levels among 90,000 schoolchildren (fictional data).

Figure 2 Distribution of the means of three randomly taken samples of two schoolchildren's grade levels, each from a population of grade levels of 90,000 schoolchildren (fictional data).

be rectangular, with a mean of 5, a variance of 6.67, and a standard deviation of 2.58 (see Figure 1).

Next, suppose that you wrote each child's grade level on a table tennis ball and put all 90,000 balls into a giant tub. The tub would have 10,000 balls with a 1 on them, 10,000 with a 2 on them, and so forth. You stir up the balls in the tub and then take two of them out. You have taken a random sample of two balls. Suppose one ball has a 2 on it and the other has a 9 on it. The mean grade level of this sample of two children's grade levels is 5.5, the average of 2 and 9. Now you put the balls back, mix up all the balls, and select two balls again. Maybe this time you get two 4s, making the mean of your second sample 4. Then you try again; this time you get a 2 and a 7, making your mean 4.5. So far you have three means: 5.5, 4, and 4.5.

Each of these three numbers is a mean of a sample of grade levels of two school children. And these three means can be thought of as a small distribution in its own right. The mean of this little distribution of means is 4.67 (the sum of 5.5, 4, and 4.5, divided by 3). The variance of this distribution of means is .39 (the variance of 5.5, 4, and 4.5). The standard deviation of this distribution of means is .62 (the square root of .39). A histogram of this distribution of your three means is shown in Figure 2.

Suppose you continued selecting samples of two balls and taking the mean of the numbers on each pair of balls. The histogram of means would continue to grow. Figure 3 shows examples of distributions of means varying from a sample with just 50 means, up to a sample with 1,000 means (with each mean being of a sample of two randomly drawn balls). (We actually made the histograms shown in Figure 3 using a computer to make the random selections instead of using 90,000 table tennis balls and a giant tub.)

As you can imagine, the method we just described is not a practical way of determining the characteristics of a distribution of means. Fortunately, however, you can figure out the characteristics of a distribution of means directly, using some simple rules, without taking even one sample. The only information you need is (a) the characteristics of the distribution of the population of individuals and (b) the number of scores in each sample. (Don't worry for now about how you could know the characteristics of the population of individuals.) The laborious method of building up a distribution of means in the way we have just considered and the concise method you will learn shortly give the same result. We have had you think of the process in terms of the painstaking method only to help you understand the idea of a distribution of means.

TIP FOR SUCCESS

Be sure you fully understand the idea of a distribution of means (and why it is the correct comparison distribution when a sample contains more than one individual). You may need to go through this chapter a couple of times to achieve full understanding of this crucial concept.

Figure 3 Histograms of means of two grade levels randomly selected from a large group of students with equal numbers of grades 1 through 9. Histograms are shown for 50 such means, 200 such means, 400 such means, 600 such means, 800 such means, and 1,000 such means. Notice that the histograms become increasingly like a normal curve as the number of means increases.

Determining the Characteristics of a Distribution of Means

Recall that Step ❷ of hypothesis testing involves determining the characteristics of the comparison distribution. The three key characteristics of the comparison distribution that you need to determine are:

1. Its mean.
2. Its spread (which you measure using the variance and standard deviation).
3. Its shape.

Notice three things about the distribution of means we built in our example, as shown in Figure 3:

1. The mean of the distribution of means is about the same as the mean of the original population of individuals (both are 5).
2. The spread of the distribution of means is less than the spread of the distribution of the population of individuals.
3. The shape of the distribution of means is approximately normal.

The first two observations, regarding the mean and the spread, are true for all distributions of means. The third, regarding the shape, is true for most distributions of means. These three observations, in fact, illustrate three basic rules you can use to find the mean, the spread (that is, the variance and standard deviation), and the shape of any distribution of means without having to write on plastic balls and take endless samples.

Now let's look at the three rules more closely. The first is for the **mean of a distribution of means**.

mean of a distribution of means the mean of a distribution of means of samples of a given size from a population; it comes out to be the same as the mean of the population of individuals.

Rule 1: The mean of a distribution of means is the same as the mean of the population of individuals.   Stated as a formula,

$$\mu_M = \mu \qquad (1)$$

← The mean of a distribution of means is equal to the mean of the population of individuals.

μ_M is the mean of the distribution of means. μ is the mean of the population of individuals (it is a Greek letter because the distribution of means is also a kind of population).

Each sample is based on a group of randomly selected individuals from the population of individuals. Thus, the mean of a sample will sometimes be higher and sometimes lower than the mean of the whole population of individuals. However, because the selection process is random and we are taking a very large number of samples, eventually the high means and the low means perfectly balance each other out.

In Figure 3, as the number of sample means in the distributions of means increases, the mean of the distribution of means becomes more similar to the mean of the population of individuals, which in this example was 5. It can be proven mathematically that, if you took an infinite number of samples, the mean of the distribution of means of these samples would come out to be exactly the same as the mean of the distribution of individuals.

The second rule is about spread. Rule 2a is for the **variance of a distribution of means**.

Rule 2a: The variance of a distribution of means is the variance of the population of individuals divided by the number of individuals in each sample.   A distribution of means will be less spread out than the distribution of individuals from which the samples are taken. If you are taking a sample of two scores, it is less likely that *both* scores will be extreme. Further, for a particular random sample to have an extreme mean, the two extreme scores would both have to be extreme in the same direction (both very high or both very low). Thus, having more than a single score in each sample has a moderating effect on the mean of such samples. In any one sample, the extremes tend to be balanced out by a middle score or by an extreme in the opposite direction. This makes each sample mean tend toward the middle and away from extreme values. With fewer extreme means, the variance of the means is less than the variance of the population of individuals.

Consider our example again. There were plenty of 1s and 9s in the population, making a fair amount of spread. That is, about a ninth of the time, if you were taking samples of single scores, you would get a 1, and about a ninth of the time you would get a 9. If you are taking samples of two at a time, you would get a sample with a mean of 1 (that is, in which *both* balls were 1s) or a mean of 9 (both balls 9s) much less often. Getting two balls that average out to a middle value such as 5 is much more likely. (This is because several combinations could give this result—1 and 9, 2 and 8, 3 and 7, 4 and 6, or two 5s).

The more individuals in each sample, the less spread out the means of the samples will be. This is because, the more scores in each sample, the rarer it will be for extremes in any particular sample not to be balanced out by middle scores or extremes in the other direction. In terms of the table tennis balls in our example, we rarely got a mean of 1 when taking samples of two balls at a time. If we were taking three balls at a time, getting a sample with a mean of 1 (all three balls would have to be 1s) is even less likely. Getting middle values for the means becomes even more likely.

Using samples of two balls at a time, the variance of the distribution of means came out to about 3.34. This is half of the variance of the population of individuals,

μ_M mean of a distribution of means.

variance of a distribution of means   variance of the population divided by the number of scores in each sample.

which was 6.67. If we had built up a distribution of means using samples of three balls each, the variance of the distribution of means would have been 2.22. This is one-third of the variance of our population of individuals. Had we randomly selected five balls for each sample, the variance of the distribution of means would have been one-fifth of the variance of the population of individuals.

These examples follow a general rule—our Rule 2a for the distribution of means: the variance of a distribution of means is the variance of the population of individuals divided by the number of individuals in each of the samples. This rule holds in all situations and can be proven mathematically.

Here is Rule 2a stated as a formula:

> The variance of a distribution of means is the variance of the population of individuals divided by the number of individuals in each sample.

$$\sigma_M^2 = \frac{\sigma^2}{N} \qquad (2)$$

σ_M^2 is the variance of the distribution of means. σ^2 is the variance of the population of individuals, and N is the number of individuals in each sample.

In our example, the variance of the population of individual children's grade levels was 6.67, and there were two children's grade levels in each sample. Thus,

$$\sigma_M^2 = \frac{\sigma^2}{N} = \frac{6.67}{2} = 3.34$$

To use a different example, suppose a population had a variance of 400 and you wanted to know the variance of a distribution of means of 25 individuals each:

$$\sigma_M^2 = \frac{\sigma^2}{N} = \frac{400}{25} = 16$$

The second part of this rule tells us about the **standard deviation of a distribution of means**.

Rule 2b: The standard deviation of a distribution of means is the square root of the variance of the distribution of means.   Stated as a formula,

> The standard deviation of a distribution of means is the square root of the variance of the distribution of means and also the square root of the result of dividing the variance of the population of individuals by the number of individuals in each sample.

$$\sigma_M = \sqrt{\sigma_M^2} = \sqrt{\frac{\sigma^2}{N}} \qquad (3)$$

σ_M is the standard deviation of the distribution of means.[1]

The standard deviation of the distribution of means also has a special name of its own, the **standard error of the mean (SEM)**, or the **standard error (SE)**, for short. (Thus, σ_M also stands for the standard error.) It has this name because it tells you how much the means of samples are typically "in error" as estimates of the mean of the population of individuals. That is, it tells you how much the various means in the distribution of means tend to deviate from the mean of the population. We have more to say about the standard error later in the chapter.

Finally, the third rule for finding the characteristics of a distribution of means focuses on its shape.

Rule 3: The shape of a distribution of means is approximately normal if either (a) each sample is of 30 or more individuals or (b) the distribution of the population of individuals is normal.   Whatever the shape of the distribution of the population of individuals, the distribution of means tends to be unimodal and symmetrical. In the grade-level example, the population distribution was rectangular. (It had an equal number at each value.) However, the shape of the distribution of

---

TIP FOR SUCCESS

When you figure the variance of a distribution of means (σ_M^2), be sure to divide the *population variance* (σ^2) by the number of individuals in each sample. In many real research situations you know the population standard deviation (σ) and not the population variance (σ^2). Thus, before you use Formula 2, you first have to remember to square the population standard deviation to find the population variance (σ^2). Then you can use the formula to find the variance of the distribution of means (σ_M^2).

σ_M^2 variance of a distribution of means.

standard deviation of a distribution of means   square root of the variance of a distribution of means; also called *standard error of the mean (SEM)* and *standard error (SE)*.

σ_M standard deviation of a distribution of means.

standard error of the mean (SEM)   same as *standard deviation of a distribution of means;* also called *standard error (SE)*.

standard error (SE)   same as *standard deviation of a distribution of means;* also called *standard error of the mean (SEM)*.

1,000 sample means (see Figure 3) was roughly that of a bell—unimodal and symmetrical. Had we taken many more than 1,000 samples, the shape would have been even more clearly unimodal and symmetrical.

A distribution of means tends to be unimodal because of the same basic process of extremes balancing each other out that we noted in the discussion of the variance: middle scores for means are more likely, and extreme means are less likely. A distribution of means tends to be symmetrical because a lack of symmetry (skew) is caused by extremes. With fewer extremes, there is less asymmetry. In our grade-level example, the distribution of means we built up also came out so clearly symmetrical because the population distribution of individual grade levels was symmetrical. Had the population distribution of individuals been skewed to one side, the distribution of means would have still been skewed, but not as much.

The more individuals in each sample, the closer the distribution of means will be to a normal curve. Although the distribution of means will rarely be an exactly normal curve, with samples of 30 or more individuals (even with a nonnormal population of individuals), the approximation of the distribution of means to a normal curve is very close and the percentages in the normal curve table will be extremely accurate.[2,3] (That is, samples that are larger than 30 make for even slightly better approximations, but for most practical research purposes, the approximation with 30 is quite good enough.) Finally, whenever the population distribution of individuals is normal, the distribution of means will be normal, regardless of the number of individuals in each sample.

Summary of Rules and Formulas for Determining the Characteristics of a Distribution of Means

Rule 1: The mean of a distribution of means is the same as the mean of the population of individuals:

$$\mu_M = \mu$$

Rule 2a: The variance of a distribution of means is the variance of the population of individuals divided by the number of individuals in each sample:

$$\sigma_M^2 = \frac{\sigma^2}{N}$$

Rule 2b: The standard deviation of a distribution of means is the square root of the variance of the distribution of means:

$$\sigma_M = \sqrt{\sigma_M^2} = \sqrt{\frac{\sigma^2}{N}}$$

Rule 3: The shape of a distribution of means is approximately normal if either (a) each sample is of 30 or more individuals or (b) the distribution of the population of individuals is normal.   Figure 4 shows these three rules graphically.

These three rules are based on the *central limit theorem,* a fundamental principle in mathematical statistics. A notable strength of the central limit theorem is that it provides the key characteristics (central tendency, variability, and shape) of a distribution of means for a population with a distribution *of any shape.*

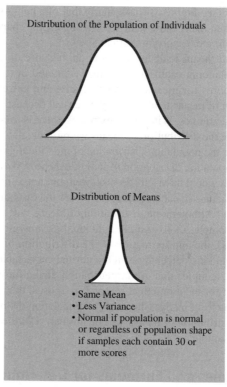

Figure 4   Comparing the distribution of the population of individuals (upper curve) and the distribution of means (lower curve).

Example of Determining the Characteristics of a Distribution of Means

Think back to the example from the start of the chapter in which students rated the attractiveness of a person in a photograph. Consider the population of students' ratings of the person in the photograph (when students are told nothing about the personality characteristics of the person in the photograph). Suppose the distribution is approximately normal with a mean of 200 and a standard deviation of 48. What will be the characteristics of the distribution of means for samples of 64 students?

Rule 1: The mean of a distribution of means is the same as the mean of the population of individuals.   The mean of the population is 200. Thus, the mean of the distribution of means will also be 200. That is, $\mu_M = \mu = 200$.

Rule 2a: The variance of a distribution of means is the variance of the population of individuals divided by the number of individuals in each sample.   The standard deviation of the population of individuals is 48; thus, the variance of the population of individuals is 48^2, which is 2,304. The variance of the distribution of means is therefore 2,304 divided by 64 (the size of the sample). This comes out to 36. That is, $\sigma_M^2 = \sigma^2/N = 2{,}304/64 = 36$.

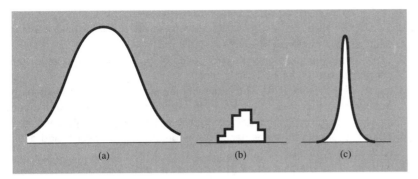

Figure 5   Three kinds of distributions: (a) the distribution of a population of individuals, (b) the distribution of a particular sample taken from that population, and (c) the distribution of means.

Rule 2b: The standard deviation of a distribution of means is the square root of the variance of the distribution of means.   The standard deviation of the distribution of means is the square root of 36, which is 6. That is, $\sigma_M = \sqrt{\sigma_M^2} = \sqrt{36} = 6$.

Rule 3: The shape of a distribution of means is approximately normal if either (a) each sample is of 30 or more individuals or (b) the distribution of the population of individuals is normal.   Our situation meets both of these conditions—the sample of 64 students is more than 30, and the population of individuals follows a normal distribution. Thus, the distribution of means will follow a normal curve. (It would have been enough even if only one of the two conditions had been met.)

Review of the Three Kinds of Distributions

We have considered three kinds of distributions: (1) the distribution of a population of individuals, (2) the distribution of a particular sample of individuals from that population, and (3) the distribution of means. Figure 5 shows these three kinds of distributions graphically and Table 1 describes them.

Table 1 Comparison of Three Types of Distributions			
	Population's Distribution	**Particular Sample's Distribution**	**Distribution of Means**
Content	Scores of all individuals in the population	Scores of the individuals in a single sample	Means of samples randomly taken from the population
Shape	Could be any shape; often normal	Could be any shape	Approximately normal if samples have ≥ 30 individuals in each or if population is normal
Mean	μ	$M = (\sum X)/N$	$\mu_M = \mu$
Variance	σ^2	$SD^2 = [\sum(X - M)^2]/N$	$\sigma_M^2 = \sigma^2/N$
Standard deviation	σ	$SD = \sqrt{SD^2}$	$\sigma_M = \sqrt{\sigma_M^2}$

1. What is a distribution of means?
2. Explain how you could create a distribution of means by taking a large number of samples of four individuals each.
3. (a) Why is the mean of the distribution of means the same as the mean of the population of individuals? (b) Why is the variance of a distribution of means smaller than the variance of the distribution of the population of individuals?
4. Write the formula for the variance of the distribution of means, and define each of the symbols.
5. (a) What is the standard error? (b) Why does it have this name?
6. A population of individuals that follows a normal curve has a mean of 60 and a standard deviation of 10. What are the characteristics of a distribution of means from this population for samples of four scores each?

Answers

1. A distribution of means is a distribution of the means of a very large number of samples of the same size randomly taken from a population of individuals.
2. Take a random sample of four scores from the population and figure its mean. Do this a very large number of times. Make a distribution of all of these means.
3. (a) With randomly taken samples, some will have higher means and some lower means than those of the population of individuals; in the long run these have to balance out. (b) In any one sample, you are less likely to get several scores with an extreme mean than you are to get a single extreme score. This is because in any random sample it is highly unlikely to get several extremes in the same direction; extreme scores tend to be balanced out by middle scores or extremes in the opposite direction. Thus, with fewer extreme scores and more middle scores, there is less variance.
4. The formula for the variance of the distribution of means is: $\sigma_M^2 = \sigma^2/N$. σ_M^2 is the variance of the distribution of means; σ^2 is the variance of the population of individuals; N is the number of individuals in your sample.
5. (a) The standard error is the standard deviation of the distribution of means. (b) It has this name because it tells you about how much means of samples typically (standardly) differ from the population mean, and thus tells you the typical (standard) amount that the means of samples are in error as estimates of the population mean.
6. The characteristics of the distribution of means for samples of four scores each are as follows: $\mu_M = \mu = 60$; $\sigma_M^2 = \sigma^2/N = 10^2/4 = 25$; $\sigma_M = 5$; shape = normal.

Hypothesis Testing with a Distribution of Means: The Z Test

Now we are ready to turn to hypothesis testing when there is more than one individual in the study's sample. The hypothesis testing procedure you will learn is called a Z test.

The Distribution of Means as the Comparison Distribution in Hypothesis Testing

In the usual research situation, a psychologist studies a sample of more than one person. In this situation, the distribution of means is the comparison distribution. It is the distribution whose characteristics you need to determine for Step ❷ of the hypothesis-testing

BOX 1 More About Polls: Sampling Errors and Errors in Thinking About Samples

If you think back to Box 3 in *Some Key Ingredients for Inferential Statistics* on surveys and the Gallup poll, you will recall that we left two important questions unanswered about fine print included with the results of a poll, saying something like, "From a telephone survey of 1,000 American adults taken on June 4 and 5. Sampling error ± 3%." First, you might wonder how such small numbers, like 1,000 (but rarely much less), can be used to predict the opinion of the entire U.S. population. Second, after working through the material in this chapter on the standard deviation of the distribution of means, you may wonder what the term *sampling error* means when a sample is not randomly sampled but rather selected by the complicated probability method used for polls.

Regarding sample size, you know from this chapter that large sample sizes, like 1,000, greatly reduce the standard deviation of the distribution of means. That is, the curve becomes very high and narrow, gathered all around the population mean. The mean of any sample of that size is very close to being the population mean.

When a sample is only a small part of a very large population, the sample's *absolute size* is the only determiner

of accuracy. This absolute size determines the impact of the random errors of measurement and selection. What remains important is reducing bias or systematic error, which can be done only by careful planning.

As for the term *sampling error,* it is worked out according to past experience with the sampling procedures used. It is given in tables for different sample sizes (usually below 1,000, because that is where error increases dramatically).

So the number of people polled is not very important (provided that it is at least 1,000 or so), but what matters very much are the methods of sampling and estimating error, which will not be reported in the detail necessary to judge whether the results are reliable. The reputation of the organization doing the survey is probably the best criterion. If the sampling and error-estimating approach is not revealed at all, be cautious. For more information about how polls are conducted, go to *http://media.gallup.com/PDF/FAQ/HowArePolls.pdf* (note that sampling error is referred to as "margin of error" on the Web site).

process. The distribution of means is the distribution to which you compare your sample's mean. It is this comparison that tells you how likely it is that you could have selected a sample with a mean that is this extreme *if the null hypothesis were true.*

Figuring the Z Score of a Sample's Mean on the Distribution of Means

There can be some confusion in figuring the location of your sample on the comparison distribution in hypothesis testing with a sample of more than one. In this situation, you are finding a Z score of your sample's mean on a distribution of means. (Before, you were finding the Z score of a single individual on a distribution of single individuals.) The method of changing the sample's mean to a Z score is the same as the usual way of changing a raw score to a Z score. However, you have to be careful not to get mixed up because more than one mean is involved. It is important to remember that you are treating the sample mean like a single score. Recall that the ordinary formula for changing a raw score to a Z score is $Z = (X - M)/SD$. In the present situation, you are actually using the following formula:

$$Z = \frac{M - \mu_M}{\sigma_M}$$ (4)

The Z score for the sample's mean on the distribution of means is the sample's mean minus the mean of the distribution of means, divided by the standard deviation of the distribution of means.

For example, suppose your sample's mean is 18 and the distribution of means has a mean of 10 and a standard deviation of 4. The Z score of this sample mean is +2. Using the formula,

$$Z = \frac{M - \mu_M}{\sigma_M} = \frac{18 - 10}{4} = \frac{8}{4} = 2$$

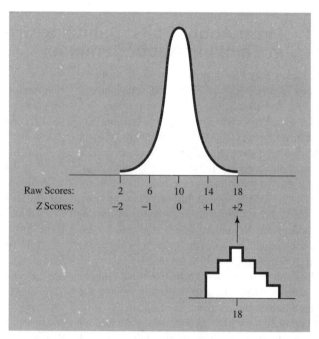

Figure 6   Z score for the mean of a particular sample on the distribution of means.

This is shown in Figure 6.

The hypothesis test you are learning in this chapter is called a **Z test**, because you figure the Z score for your sample's mean.

Example

Let's return again to our example of whether being told a person has positive personality qualities increases ratings of the physical attractiveness of that person. The social psychologist asks 64 randomly selected students to rate the attractiveness of a particular person in a photograph. Prior to rating the attractiveness of the person, each student is told that the person has positive personality qualities (kindness, warmth, a sense of humor, and intelligence). On a scale of 0 (the lowest possible attractiveness) to 400 (the highest possible attractiveness), the mean attractiveness rating given by the 64 students is 220. From extensive previous research, the psychologist knows the distribution of attractiveness ratings of the person in the photograph (when there has been no mention of the person's personality qualities). Those ratings when nothing is mentioned about the personality have a mean of 200 and a standard deviation of 48, and they follow an approximately normal distribution. This distribution is shown in Figure 7a.[4]

Now let's carry out the Z test by following the five steps of hypothesis testing:

❶ **Restate the question as a research hypothesis and a null hypothesis about the populations.** The two populations are these:

Population 1: Students who are told that the person has positive personality qualities.
Population 2: Students in general (who are told nothing about the person's personality qualities).

TIP FOR SUCCESS

Population 2 is the population for the comparison distribution, which is the distribution that shows the population situation if the null hypothesis is true.

Z **test**   hypothesis-testing procedure in which there is a single sample and the population variance is known.

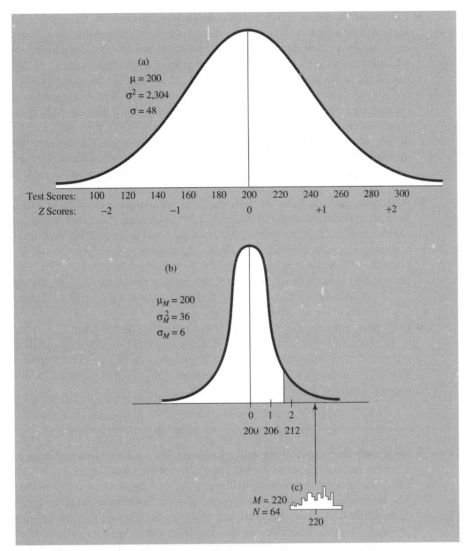

Figure 7　For the fictional study of positive personality qualities and ratings of physical attractiveness, (a) the distribution of the population of individuals, (b) the distribution of means (the comparison distribution), and (c) the sample's distribution. The shaded area in the distribution of means is the rejection region—the area in which the null hypothesis will be rejected if the study's sample mean turns out to be in that area.

The research hypothesis is that the population of students who are told that the person has positive personality qualities will on the average give higher attractiveness scores for that person than the population of students who are told nothing about the person's personality qualities: $\mu_1 > \mu_2$. The null hypothesis is that Population 1's scores will not on the average be higher than Population 2's: $\mu_1 \leq \mu_2$. Note that these are directional hypotheses. The researcher wants to know if being told that the person has positive personality qualities will increase attractiveness scores; a result in the opposite direction would not be relevant to the theory the researcher is testing.

❷ **Determine the characteristics of the comparison distribution.** The result of the study will be a mean of a sample of 64 individuals (students in this case). Thus, the comparison distribution has to be the distribution of means of samples of 64 individuals each. This comparison distribution will have a mean of 200 (the same as the population mean). That is, as we saw earlier in the chapter, $\mu_M = 200$. Its variance will be the population variance divided by the number of individuals in the sample. The population variance, σ^2, is 2,304 (the population standard deviation of 48 squared); the sample size is 64. Thus, the variance of the distribution of means, σ_M^2 will be 2,304/64, or 36. The standard deviation of the distribution of means, σ_M is the square root of 36, or 6. Finally, because there are more than 30 individuals in the sample, the shape of the distribution of means will be approximately normal. Figure 7b shows this distribution of means.

❸ **Determine the cutoff sample score on the comparison distribution at which the null hypothesis should be rejected.** Let's assume the researcher decides to use the standard 5% significance level. As we noted in Step ❶, the researcher is making a directional prediction. Hence, the researcher will reject the null hypothesis if the result is in the top 5% of the comparison distribution. The comparison distribution (the distribution of means) is a normal curve. Thus, the top 5% can be found from the normal curve table. It starts at a Z of +1.64. This top 5% is shown as the shaded area in Figure 7b.

❹ **Determine your sample's score on the comparison distribution.** The result of the (fictional) study is that the 64 students told that the person has positive personality qualities gave a mean attractiveness rating of 220. (This sample's distribution is shown in Figure 7c.) A mean of 220 is 3.33 standard deviations above the mean of the distribution of means:

$$Z = \frac{M - \mu_M}{\sigma_M} = \frac{220 - 200}{6} = \frac{20}{6} = 3.33$$

❺ **Decide whether to reject the null hypothesis.** We set the minimum Z score to reject the null hypothesis to +1.64. The Z score of the sample's mean is +3.33. Thus, the social psychologist will reject the null hypothesis and conclude that the research hypothesis is supported. To put this another way, the result of the Z test is statistically significant at the $p < .05$ level. You can see this in Figure 7b. Note how extreme the sample's mean is on the distribution of means (the distribution that would apply if the null hypothesis were true). The final conclusion is that, among students, being told that a person has positive personality qualities does increase the attractiveness ratings of that person. (Results of actual studies show this effect, as well as showing that if you have heard negative information about a person, you then rate them as less physically attractive; e.g., Lewandowski, Aron, & Gee, 2007.)

A Second Example

Suppose a researcher wants to test the effect of a communication skills workshop on students' use of verbal fillers during a presentation. Verbal fillers are words such as "um," "uh," and "you know" that people commonly use in conversations and when giving presentations. The researcher conducts a study in which 25 students attend communication skills workshops and then give a half-hour presentation on a topic of their choice. The presentations are recorded and the researcher later counts the number of verbal fillers each student used during his or her presentation. In this fictional example, we assume it is known from previous studies that students typically

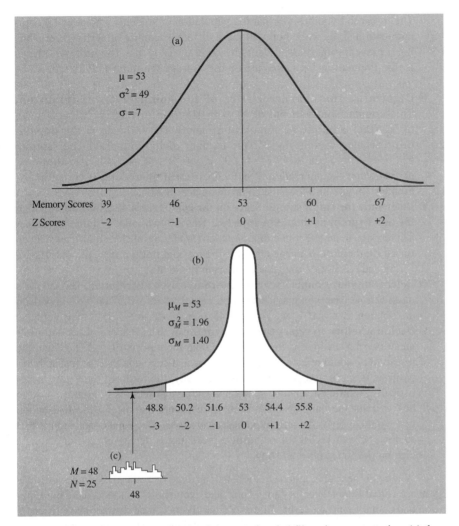

Figure 8 For the fictional study of the use of verbal filters in a presentation, (a) the distribution of the population of individuals, (b) the distribution of means (the comparison distribution), and (c) the sample's distribution. The shaded areas in the distribution of means are the rejection regions—the areas in which the null hypothesis will be rejected if the study's sample mean turns out to be in that area.

use a mean of 53 verbal fillers during a half-hour presentation of this kind, with a standard deviation of 7, and the distribution of verbal fillers follows a normal curve (see Figure 8a). The 25 students who took a communication skills workshop used a mean of 48 verbal fillers. The researcher wants to carry out the Z test using the 1% significance level, and an effect in either direction would be important (that is, the researcher is interested in whether communications workshops could increase or decrease the use of verbal fillers).

❶ **Restate the question as a research hypothesis and a null hypothesis about the populations.** The two populations are:

Population 1: Students who attend a communication skills workshop.
Population 2: Students in general (who do not attend a communication skills workshop).

The research hypothesis is that the population of students who attend a communication skills workshop will use a different number of verbal fillers during a presentation than students in general: $\mu_1 \neq \mu_2$. The null hypothesis is that Population 1's scores are on the average the same as Population 2's: $\mu_1 = \mu_2$.

❷ **Determine the characteristics of the comparison distribution.** This comparison distribution is a distribution of means. It has a mean of 53 (the same as the population mean). Its variance is the population variance divided by 25, the number of individuals in the sample: $\sigma_M^2 = \sigma^2/N = 7^2/25 = 49/25 = 1.96$; $\sigma_M = \sqrt{1.96} = 1.40$. Its shape is normal, since the population of individual verbal filler scores is normally distributed. (Figure 8b shows the comparison distribution.)

❸ **Determine the cutoff sample score on the comparison distribution at which the null hypothesis should be rejected.** This is a two-tailed test (the researcher is interested in an effect in either direction) at the overall 1% significance level. Based on the normal curve table for the top and bottom .5%, the cutoffs are +2.58 and −2.58 (see tiny shaded areas in Figure 8b).

❹ **Determine your sample's score on the comparison distribution.** The sample's mean was 48 (see Figure 8c). This comes out to a Z of −3.57 on the comparison distribution: $Z = (M - \mu_M)/\sigma_M = (48 - 53)/1.40 = -5/1.40 = -3.57$.

❺ **Decide whether to reject the null hypothesis.** The Z score of the sample's mean is −3.57, which is more extreme than the cutoffs of ±2.58. Thus, the researchers would reject the null hypothesis and conclude that the research hypothesis is supported. To put this another way, the result of the Z test is statistically significant at the $p < .01$ level. You can see this in Figure 8b. Note how extreme the sample's mean is on the distribution of means (the distribution that would apply if the null hypothesis were true). The final conclusion is that students' use of verbal fillers during a presentation decreases after attending a communication skills workshop.

When you next give a presentation, ask a friend to count the number of times you use verbal fillers (such as "um," "uh," and "you know"), or record the presentation and count your own verbal fillers. Verbal fillers can be distracting to listeners and may hurt the quality of a presentation. Communications specialists recommend replacing verbal fillers with brief pauses (that allow you to gather your thoughts) (O'Hair et al., 2009).

How are you doing?

1. How is hypothesis testing with a sample of more than one person different from hypothesis testing with a sample of a single person?
2. How do you find the Z score for the sample's mean on the distribution of means?
3. A team of researchers predict that showing a certain film will change people's attitudes toward alcohol. The researchers then randomly select 36 people, show them the film, and give them an attitude questionnaire. The mean score on the attitude test for these 36 people is 70. The score for people in general on this test is 75, with a standard deviation of 12. Using the five steps of hypothesis testing and the 5% significance level, carry out a Z test to see if viewing the film changes people's attitudes toward alcohol.

Answers

1. In hypothesis testing with a sample of more than one person, the comparison distribution is a distribution of means.
2. You use the usual formula for changing a raw score to a Z score, but using the mean and standard deviation of the distribution of means. The formula is $Z = (M - \mu_M)/\sigma_M$.
3. ❶ **Restate the question as a research hypothesis and a null hypothesis about the populations.** The two populations are:
   Population 1: People shown the film.
   Population 2: People in general (who are not shown the film).
   The research hypothesis is that the mean attitude of the population shown the film is different from the mean attitude of the population of people in general: $\mu_1 \neq \mu_2$. The null hypothesis is that the populations have the same mean attitude score: $\mu_1 = \mu_2$.
   ❷ **Determine the characteristics of the comparison distribution.** $\mu_M = \mu = 75$; $\sigma_M^2 = \sigma^2/N = 12^2/36 = 144/36 = 4$; $\sigma_M = 2$; shape is normal.
   ❸ **Determine the cutoff sample score on the comparison distribution at which the null hypothesis should be rejected.** Two-tailed cutoffs, 5% significance levels are $+1.96$ and -1.96.
   ❹ **Determine your sample's score on the comparison distribution.** $Z = (M - \mu_M)/\sigma_M = (70 - 75)/2 = -2.50$.
   ❺ **Decide whether to reject the null hypothesis.** The Z score of the sample's mean is -2.50, which is more extreme than -1.96; reject the null hypothesis. Seeing the film does appear to change attitudes.

Controversy: Marginal Significance

A long-standing controversy regarding significance testing is what to do when a result does not make the cutoff value at the usual 5% level but comes very close (say, $p < .10$). This is often called "marginal significance," "approaching significance," or a "near significant trend." A few years ago, the controversy was spotlighted on an email listserv for social and personality psychologists. The discussion began when the following note was posted by Todd Nelson (California State University Stanislaus):

> Throughout my ph.d. training . . . it was common parlance to refer to . . . P-values of between .05 and .10 as "marginally significant." It was a very common term in all the major social psychological journals . . . and among my professors.
>
> The other day, in a thesis defense I was chairing, I was dumfounded when the other thesis committee members strongly objected to the term "marginally significant" in the student's results section . . . both saying they had NEVER heard of the term (!).
>
> Wanting to make sure I was still on planet Earth, I consulted several statistics and research textbooks in my office, and found a few that referred to "marginal significance" and several articles by noted statisticians who make the case for discussing results in the .05–.10 range . . .
>
> [H]ave you heard of this term . . .? Do you use it and teach it? If so, why? If not, what is your objection?

Almost immediately, there were more than 100 responses! First, it quickly became clear that calling results that are close "marginally significant" is indeed a common practice in many areas of psychology. As Frank LoSchiavo

(Ohio University) put it, "It sounds like it is the other committee members who are not on Earth."

But it also became clear that while it may be fairly common, many think it is a bad idea. Charles Stangor (University of Maryland) called it a "completely bogus concept...used to make us poor scientists feel better when our results are close but no cigar." Tricia Yurak (Rowan University) called it "a fudge term that I won't use" adding that "even if I get a p value of .07, I will report it as not significant." Richard St. Jean (University of Prince Edward Island) recalls "one of my stats professors said calling a finding marginally significant is like calling a woman marginally pregnant! The principle is that it is an all or none decision..." David Washburn (Georgia State University) explains the logic: "One decides in advance or by convention to call $p < .05$ effects 'significant'.... [T]erms like 'marginally significant' are counterfactuals—like saying you 'almost did' something that you didn't do." As several of the email posts noted, the argument was spelled out in some detail in an article by Chet Insko (2002; University of North Carolina):

> ... null-hypothesis testing depends on traditional two-valued logic. Thus, one either rejects or fails to reject the null hypothesis, and rejection of the null hypothesis allows for acceptance of the logical contradictory of the null hypothesis, the research hypothesis. The crucial point here is that deductive logic is two valued; for example, Socrates is or is not mortal.... A logician would not, for example, conclude that Socrates is marginally mortal. Since null-hypothesis testing depends on logic, only two-valued distinctions can be made, and this, of course, requires a single cut point to differentiate significant test statistics from nonsignificant test statistics. (p. 1331)

However, the majority opinion among those responding was expressed by Warren Thorngate (Carleton University): "...people who adhere to the '0.05 or nothing!' philosophy either need to be reeducated or enter therapy." Phoebe Ellsworth (University of Michigan) added that "to act as though there is a gulf between .05 and .06 is not maintaining high standards; it is idiocy." The point here is that .05 is an arbitrary convention. Indeed, many quoted a comment in an influential article by Rosnow and Rosenthal (1989) "...surely God loves the .06 nearly as much as the .05" (p. 1277). In addition, many noted that it is more important to emphasize the size of the effect and the power of the study. Also, several mentioned that such "near significant results" may be appropriate particularly when there are related results that are clearly significant (for example, if a study of the effects on stress is significant when using a questionnaire measure and is also near significant when using a physiological measure). Finally, quite a few people emphasized that the acceptability of reporting such results varies considerably among different specialty areas of psychology.

Hypothesis Tests About Means of Samples (Z Tests) and Standard Errors in Research Articles

As we have noted several times, research in which there is a known population mean and standard deviation is quite rare in psychology. Thus, you will not often see a Z test in a research article. We have asked you to learn about this situation mainly as another crucial building block for understanding hypothesis testing in more common research situations. Still, Z tests do show up now and then.

Here is an example. As part of a larger study, Wiseman (1997) gave a loneliness test to a group of college students in Israel. As a first step in examining the results, Wiseman checked that the average score on the loneliness test was not significantly different from a known population distribution based on a large U.S. study of university students that had been conducted earlier by Russell and colleagues (1980). Wiseman reported:

> ...[T]he mean loneliness scores of the current Israeli sample were similar to those of Russell et al.'s (1980) university sample for both males (Israeli: $M = 38.74, SD = 9.30$; Russell: $M = 37.06, SD = 10.91$; $z = 1.09$, NS) and females (Israeli: $M = 36.39$, $SD = 8.87$; Russell: $M = 36.06, SD = 10.11$; $z = .25$, NS). (p. 291)

In this example, the researcher gives the standard deviation for both the sample studied (the Israeli group) and the population (the data from Russell). However, in the steps of figuring each Z (the sample's score on the distribution of means), the researcher would have used the standard deviation only of the population. Notice also that the researcher took the nonsignificance of the difference as support for the sample means being "similar" to the population means. However, the researcher was very careful not to claim that these results showed there was "no difference."

Of the topics we have covered in this chapter, the one you are most likely to see in a research article is the standard deviation of the distribution of means, used to describe the amount of variation that might be expected among means of samples of a given size from this population. In this context, it is usually called the *standard error* (*SE*) or *standard error of the mean* (*SEM*). Standard errors are typically shown in research articles as the lines that go above (and sometimes also below) the tops of the bars in a bar graph; these lines are called *error bars*. For example, Ginoa and Flynn (2011) examined whether gift recipients are more appreciative of a gift they requested compared to one that they did not request. In one of their studies, 198 married adults completed an online survey about giving and receiving wedding gifts. The participants were randomly assigned to recall wedding gifts in one of four conditions: (a) receiving a gift at their own wedding that was not on their gift registry, (b) receiving a gift at their own wedding they had requested on their gift registry, (c) giving a gift at someone else's wedding that was not on the receipient's gift registry, and (d) giving a gift at someone else's wedding that was on the recipient's gift registry. The participants then answered five questions (on a scale from $1 = not\ at\ all$ to $7 = to\ a\ great\ extent$) about how much they appreciated receiving the gift or how much they think the recipient appreciated the gift. Each participant's responses across the five questions were averaged to create a measure of overall appreciation. Their results are shown in Figure 9, which includes error bars. Interestingly, the results showed that gift recipients reported greater appreciation for requested than unrequested gifts. However, gift givers indicated that they thought the recipients of their gifts were equally appreciative, regardless of whether the gift had been requested or not. The title of the article nicely summarized the main findings of Ginoa and Flynn's (2011) research: "Give them what they want: The benefits of explicitness in gift exchange."

Error bars have been standard on bar graphs in certain areas of psychology, such as perception and neuroscience for a long time, but in recent years their use has become increasingly common throughout the field (Cumming et al., 2007).

Figure 9   Appreciation ratings by condition, Study I. Error bars represent standard errors.

Source: Ginoa, F., & Flynn, F. J. (2011). Give them what they want: The benefits of explicitness in gift exchange. *Journal of Experimental Social Psychology, 47*, 915–922. Reproduced by permission of Elsevier publishers.

Advanced Topic: Estimation, Standard Errors, and Confidence Intervals

Hypothesis testing is our main focus in this chapter. However, there is another kind of statistical question related to the distribution of means that is also important in psychology: estimating the population mean based on the scores in a sample. Traditionally, this has been very important in survey research. However, it is often also important in experimental research (e.g., Wilkinson and Task Force on Statistical Inference, 1999) and can even serve as an alternative approach to hypothesis testing.

Estimating the Population Mean When It Is Unknown

When the population mean is unknown, *the best estimate of the population mean is the sample mean.* In the study of students who were told about a person's positive personality qualities, the mean attractiveness rating given to that person by the sample of 64 students was 220. Thus, 220 is the best estimate of the mean attractiveness rating that would be given by the unknown population of students who would ever be told about a person's positive personality qualities.

How accurate is the sample mean as an estimate of the population mean? A way to get at this question is to ask, "How much do means of samples from a population vary?" Fortunately we have already thought about this question when considering the distribution of means. The variation in means of samples from a population is the variation in the distribution of means. The standard deviation of this distribution of means, the standard error of the mean, is thus a measure of how much the means of samples vary from the overall population mean. (As we noted earlier, just because researchers are often interested in using a mean of a sample to estimate the population mean, this variation in the distribution of means is thought of as "error" and we give the name "standard error of the mean" to the standard deviation of a distribution of means.)

In our example, the accuracy of our estimate of 220 for the mean of the population of students who are told about the person's positive personality qualities is the standard error, which we figured earlier to be 6.

Range of Possible Means Likely to Include the Population Mean

You may also want to estimate the *range* of possible means that are likely to include the population mean. Consider our estimate of 220 with a standard error of 6. Now follow this closely: suppose you took a mean from our distribution of means; it is 34% likely you would get a mean between 220 (the mean of the distribution of means) and 226 (one standard error above 220). This is because the distribution of means is a normal curve. Thus, the standard error is 1 standard deviation on that curve, and 34% of a normal curve is between the mean and 1 standard deviation above the mean. From this reasoning, we could also figure that another 34% should be between 220 and 214 (1 standard error below 220). Putting this together, we have a region from 214 to 226 that we are 68% confident should include the population mean if our sample was randomly taken from this population.[5] (See Figure 10a.)

This is an example of a **confidence interval** (usually abbreviated CI). We would call it the "68% confidence interval." The upper and lower ends of a confidence interval are called **confidence limits**. In this example, the confidence limits for the 68% confidence interval are 214 and 226 (see Figure 10a).

Let's review the logic: based on our knowledge of a sample's mean, we are trying to estimate the mean of the population that sample came from. Our best estimate of the population mean has to be our sample mean. What we don't know is how

confidence interval (CI) roughly speaking, the range of scores (that is, the scores between an upper and lower value) that is likely to include the true population mean; more precisely, the range of possible population means from which it is not highly unlikely that you could have obtained your sample mean.

confidence limit upper or lower value of a confidence interval.

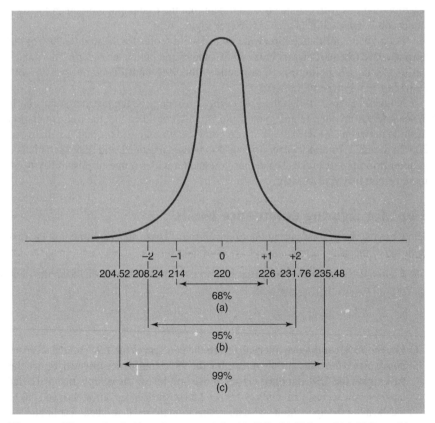

Figure 10 A distribution of means and the (a) 68%, (b) 95%, and (c) 99% confidence intervals for students rating the physical attractiveness of a person after being told that the person has positive personality qualities (fictional data).

good an estimate it is. If sample means from that population could vary a lot, then we cannot be very confident that our estimate is close to the true population mean. But if the sample means are likely all to be very close to the true population mean, we can assume our estimate is pretty close. To get a sense of how accurate our estimate is, we can use our knowledge of the normal curve to estimate the *range* of possible means that are likely to include the population mean. This estimate of the range of means is called a confidence interval.

The 95% and 99% Confidence Intervals

Normally, you would want to be more than 68% confident about your estimates. Thus, when figuring confidence intervals, psychologists use 95% or even 99% confidence intervals. These are figured based on the distribution of means for the area that includes the middle 95% or middle 99%. For the **95% confidence interval**, you want the area in a normal curve on each side between the mean and the Z score that includes 47.5% (47.5% plus 47.5% adds up to 95%). The normal curve table shows this to be 1.96. Thus, in terms of Z scores, the 95% confidence interval is from -1.96 to $+1.96$ on the distribution of means. Changing these Z scores to raw scores for the attractiveness ratings example gives an interval of 208.24 to 231.76 (see Figure 10b). That is, for the lower confidence limit, $(-1.96)(6) + 220 = 11.76 + 220 = 208.24$; for the upper confidence limit, $(1.96)(6) + 220 = 11.76 + 220 = 231.76$. In sum, based on the sample of 64 students who were told about the person's positive personality qualities, you can be 95% confident that the true population mean for such students is between 208.24 and 231.76 (see Figure 10b).

For a **99% confidence interval**, you use the Z scores for the middle 99% of the normal curve (the part that includes 49.5% above and below the mean). This comes out to ± 2.58. Changing this to raw scores, the 99% confidence interval is from 204.52 to 235.48 (see Figure 10c).

Notice in Figure 10 that the greater the confidence is, the broader is the confidence interval. In our example, you could be 68% confident that the true population mean is between 214 and 226; but you could be 95% confident that it is between 208.24 and 231.76 and 99% confident it is between 204.52 and 235.48. This is a general principle. It makes sense that you need a wider range of possibility to be more certain that you are right.

Steps for Figuring Confidence Limits

There are two steps for figuring confidence limits. These steps assume that the distribution of means is approximately a normal distribution.

❶ **Figure the standard error.** That is, find the standard deviation of the distribution of means in the usual way:

$$\sigma_M = \sqrt{\sigma_M^2} = \sqrt{\frac{\sigma^2}{N}}$$

❷ **For the 95% confidence interval, figure the raw scores for 1.96 standard errors above and below the sample mean; for the 99% confidence interval, figure the raw scores for 2.58 standard errors above and below the sample mean.** To figure these raw scores, first multiply 1.96 or 2.58 by the standard error, then add this to the mean for the upper limit and subtract this from the mean for the lower limit.

In terms of the overall figuring, once you know the standard error, the upper limit of the 95% confidence interval is equal to the sample mean *plus* 1.96 multiplied by the standard error of the mean: upper limit $= M + (1.96)(\sigma_M)$; the lower limit is the sample mean *minus* 1.96 multiplied by the standard error:

95% confidence interval confidence interval in which, roughly speaking, there is a 95% chance that the population mean falls within this interval.

99% confidence interval confidence interval in which, roughly speaking, there is a 99% chance that the population mean falls within this interval.

lower limit $= M - (1.96)(\sigma_M)$. For the 99% CI, the computation for the upper limit is: $M + (2.58)(\sigma_M)$; the lower 99% CI limit is $M - (2.58)(\sigma_M)$.

Example Let's find the 99% confidence interval for the verbal fillers example from earlier in the chapter. Recall that, in that example, the number of verbal fillers used by students in the general population (that is, students who had not attended a communication skills workshop) was normally distributed with a mean of 53 and a standard deviation of 7. The 25 students who attended a communication skills workshop used a mean of 48 fillers.

❶ **Figure the standard error.** $\sigma_M = \sqrt{\dfrac{\sigma^2}{N}} = \sqrt{\dfrac{7^2}{25}} = \sqrt{1.96} = 1.40.$

❷ **For the 95% confidence interval, figure the raw scores for 1.96 standard errors above and below the sample mean; for the 99% confidence interval, figure the raw scores for 2.58 standard errors above and below the sample mean.** You want the 99% confidence interval. Thus, first multiply 2.58 by 1.40 to get 3.61, which is how far the confidence limit is from the mean. For the upper confidence limit, add this distance to the sample mean: $48 + 3.61 = 51.61$. In terms of the overall calculations, upper limit $= M + (2.58)(\sigma_M) = 48 + (2.58)(1.40) = 51.61$. For the lower confidence limit, subtract 3.61 (the results of multiplying 2.58 by 1.40) from 48, the mean of the sample, which gives 44.39. In terms of the overall calculations, lower limit $= 48 - (2.58)(1.40) = 44.39$.

Thus, based on this sample of 25 students, you can be 99% confident that an interval from 44.39 to 51.61 includes the true population mean.

The Subtle Logic of Confidence Intervals

If you understand the preceding explanation, it will be sufficient for practical purposes in working with confidence intervals. Basically, confidence intervals tell you the range of means that you can be pretty sure include the true population mean. However, if you want to think deeply about the situation, there is a subtle issue about precisely what these numbers mean. (What follows is kind of an "advanced, advanced" topic section!)

Strictly speaking, consider what we are figuring to be, say, a 95% confidence interval. We are figuring it as the range of means that are 95% likely to come from a population *with a true mean that happens to be the mean of our sample.* However, what we really want to know is the range that is 95% likely to include the true population mean. This we cannot know. That is, we are figuring one thing and really want to know another. Read this paragraph again and think about it. It is easy to miss this subtle but logically significant twist.

The way this awkward situation has been dealt with traditionally by most researchers is just to ignore this subtlety. Researchers who are more sophisticated statistically are comfortable with the situation by emphasizing that what we actually say is that we are 95% *confident* that the true mean is in this range. That is, by using this language, we are acknowledging that what we are doing is really a bit backward, but it is the best we can do! "Confidence" is closer to the subjective interpretation of probability. In fact, "confidence" is meant to be a slightly vaguer term than probability. Nevertheless, it is not completely vague. What we are doing does have a solid basis.

Here is how to understand this: suppose in our attractiveness ratings example, the true mean was indeed 220. As we have seen, this would give a 95% confidence interval of 208.24 to 231.76, as shown in Figure 11a. We don't know what the true population mean is. But suppose the true population mean was 208.24. The range that includes 95% of sample means from this population's distribution of means would be from 196.48 to 220.00, as shown in Figure 11b. (You can work this out yourself

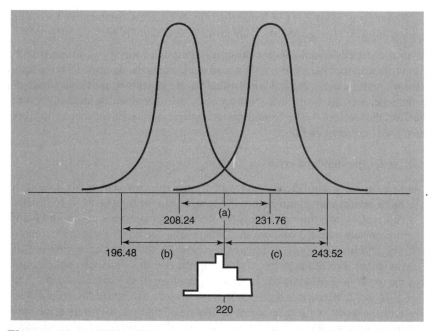

Figure 11   (a) 95% confidence interval based on sample mean of 220 for students rating the physical attractiveness of a person after being told that the person has positive personality qualities (fictional data); (b) range including 95% of sample means, based on distribution of means shown above it with μ_{Mb} = lower limit of the 95% confidence interval for $M = 220$; (c) range including 95% of sample means, based on distribution of means above it with μ_{Mc} = upper limit of the 95% confidence interval for $M = 220$.

following the two steps for figuring confidence limits.) Similarly, for the population with a mean of 231.76, the range that includes 95% of sample means from this population's distribution of means is from 220.00 to 243.52, as shown in Figure 11c.

What this shows is a general principle: for a 95% confidence interval, the lower confidence limit is the lowest possible population mean that would have a 95% probability of including our sample mean; the upper confidence limit is the highest possible population mean that would have a 95% probability of including our sample mean.

This convoluted logic is a bit like the double-negative logic behind hypothesis testing. This is no accident, since both are making inferences from samples to populations using the same information.

Confidence Intervals and Hypothesis Testing

A practical implication of the link of confidence intervals and hypothesis testing is that you can use confidence intervals to do hypothesis testing! If the confidence interval does not include the mean of the null hypothesis distribution, then the result is statistically significant. For example, in the attractiveness ratings study, the 95% confidence interval for those who were told that the person has positive personality qualities was from 208.24 to 231.76. However, the population that was told nothing about the person's personality qualities had a mean of 200. This population mean is outside the range of the confidence interval. Thus, if you are 95% confident that the true range is 208.24 to 231.76 and the population mean for those who were told nothing about the person's personality qualities is not in this range, you are 95% confident that that population is not the same as the one your sample came from.

Another way to understand this is in terms of the idea that the confidence limits are the points at which a more extreme true population would not include your sample mean 95% of the time. The population mean for those who were told nothing about the person's personality qualities was 200. If this were the true mean also for the group that was told about the person's positive personality qualities, 95% of the time it would not produce a sample mean as high as the one we got.

How are you doing?

1. (a) What is the best estimate of a population mean? (b) Why?
2. (a) What number is used to indicate the accuracy of an estimate of the population mean? (b) Why?
3. What is a 95% confidence interval?
4. A researcher predicts that showing a certain film will change people's attitudes toward alcohol. The researchers then randomly select 36 people, show them the film, and give them an attitude questionnaire. The mean score on the attitude test for these 36 people is 70. The score on this test for people in the general population (who do not see the film) is 75, with a standard deviation of 12. (a) Find the best estimate of the mean of people in general who see the film and (b) its 95% confidence interval. (c) Compare this result to the conclusion you drew for this same situation when you used this example in the "How are you doing?" section for hypothesis testing with a distribution of means.
5. (a) Why is it wrong to say that the 95% confidence interval is the region in which there is a 95% probability of finding the true population mean? (b) What is the basis for our 95% confidence?

Answers

1. (a) The best estimate of a population mean is the sample mean. (b) It is more likely to have come from a population with the same mean than from any other population.
2. (a) The standard error (or standard deviation of the distribution of means) is used to indicate the accuracy of an estimate of the population mean. (b) The standard error (or standard deviation of the distribution of means) is roughly the average amount that means vary from the mean of the distribution of means.
3. A 95% confidence interval is the range of values that you are 95% confident includes the population mean, estimated based on the scores in a sample.
4. (a) The best estimate is the sample mean: 70.
   (b) Standard error (σ_M) is $\sqrt{\sigma^2/N} = \sqrt{144/36} = 2$. The lower confidence limit $= M - (1.96)(\sigma_M) = 70 - (1.96)(2) = 70 - 3.92 = 66.08$; upper confidence limit $= M + (1.96)(\sigma_M) = 70 + (1.96)(2) = 70 + 3.92 - 73.92$. The 95% confidence interval is from 66.08 to 73.92.
   (c) The 95% confidence interval does not include the mean of the general population (which was 75). Thus, you can reject the null hypothesis that the two populations are the same. This is the same conclusion as when using this example for hypothesis testing.
5. (a) It is wrong to say that the 95% confidence interval is the region in which there is a 95% probability of finding the true population mean because you do not know the true population mean; so you have no way of knowing for sure what to start with when figuring 95% probability.
   (b) The lower confidence limit is the point at which a true population any lower would not have a 95% probability of including a sample with our mean; similarly, the upper confidence limit is the point at which a true population any higher would not have a 95% probability of including a sample with our mean.

Advanced Topic Controversy: Confidence Intervals versus Significance Tests

For a number of years there has been a lively debate among psychologists about significance testing. Among the major issues in that debate is a proposal that psychologists should use confidence intervals instead of significance tests.

Those who favor replacing significance tests with confidence intervals (e.g., Cohen, 1994; Coulsen, Healey, Fidler, & Cumming, 2010; Hunter, 1997; Schmidt, 1996) cite several major advantages. First, as we noted above, confidence intervals contain all the key information in a significance test,[6] but also give additional information—the estimation of the range of values that you can be quite confident include the true population mean. A second advantage is that they focus attention on the estimation of effects instead of on hypothesis testing. Some researchers argue that the goal of science is to provide numeric estimates of effects (and the accuracy of those estimates), not just decisions as to whether an effect is different from zero.

Confidence intervals are particularly valuable when the results are not significant (Frick, 1995). This is because knowing the confidence interval gives you an idea of just how far from no effect you can be confident that the true mean is to be found. If the results are not significant and the entire confidence interval is near to no effect, you can feel confident that, even if there is some true effect, it is probably small. However, if the results are not significant and the confidence interval, while including no effect, also spreads out to include means far from no effect, it would tell us that the study is really very inconclusive: it is possible that there is little or no effect, but it is also possible that there is a substantial effect.

A third advantage claimed by proponents of confidence intervals over significance testing is that researchers are less likely to misuse them (Coulsen et al., 2010). A common error in the use of significance tests is to conclude that a nonsignificant result means there is no effect. With confidence intervals, it is harder to fall into this kind of error.

In light of these various advantages, the *Publication Manual of the American Psychological Association* (2009) now strongly recommends that confidence intervals be routinely included in research articles. However, it is still relatively uncommon to find confidence intervals in research articles. For example, in a survey of studies that were published in 2005 and 2006, confidence intervals were reported in only about 10% of articles (Cumming et al., 2007). The survey also found that is was rare to find confidence intervals without also seeing significance tests. In part, this is probably due to tradition and to most psychologists having been trained with significance tests and having become used to them.

Other researchers (e.g., Abelson, 1997; Harris, 1997; Nickerson, 2000) emphasize two reasons for not abandoning significance testing in favor of confidence intervals. First, for some advanced statistical procedures, it is possible to do significance testing but not to figure confidence intervals. Second, just as it is possible to make mistakes with significance tests, it is also possible to make other kinds of mistakes with confidence intervals—especially since most research psychologists are less experienced in using them.

Whatever the eventual outcome of this controversy about confidence intervals, it is valuable to understand them, since you will run into them when reading research literature, and you are likely to see them more often in the future. On the other hand, there is no sign that they are likely to replace significance testing any time soon. For this reason (and to keep the amount of material to be learned manageable), we have made confidence intervals an advanced topic and decided not to emphasize them further .

Advanced Topic: Confidence Intervals in Research Articles

As we noted, confidence intervals (usually abbreviated as CI) are sometimes reported in research articles. For example, Morey and colleagues (2009) conducted a study to test a diet and exercise intervention for overweight individuals age 65 years and older who had been diagnosed with cancer. Participants were randomly assigned to be in the intervention group (a 12-month program of mailed materials and telephone counseling) or a control group (no intervention until the study was done). Morey et al. reported the following results: "Participants in the intervention group reported a mean weight loss of 2.06 kg (95% CI, 1.69–2.43 kg), which was more than twice that reported by the control group (0.92 kg; 95% CI, 0.51–1.33 kg)" (p. 1888). This means that we can be 95% confident that the true amount of weight lost on average by participants in the intervention group was between 1.69 kg and 2.43 kg, and for control group participants it was between 0.51 kg and 1.33 kg. As another example, an organizational psychologist might explain that the average number of overtime hours per week worked in a particular industry is 3.7 with a 95% confidence interval of 2.5 to 4.9. This would tell you that the true average number of overtime hours is probably somewhere between 2.5 and 4.9.

A shortcut that many researchers find helpful in reading research articles that give standard errors but not confidence intervals is that the 95% confidence interval is approximately 2 standard errors in both directions (it is exactly 1.96 *SE*s) and the 99% confidence interval is approximately 2.5 standard errors in both directions (it is exactly 2.58 *SE*s).

Finally, we should note that although standard errors are the most common when error bars are included in graphs, about 15% of the time the error bars actually refer to confidence intervals (Cumming et al., 2007). Because confidence intervals are 2 to 2.5 times wider than standard errors, this makes a huge difference in interpreting them. Thus, when you see error bars on a graph, you should be sure to read the figure caption to see whether they are standard errors or confidence intervals (and if they are confidence intervals, check whether they are for 95% or 99% intervals).

Learning Aids

Summary

1. When studying a sample of more than one individual, the comparison distribution in the hypothesis-testing process is a distribution of means. It can be thought of as what would result from (a) taking a very large number of samples, each of the same number of scores taken randomly from the population of individuals, and then (b) making a distribution of the means of these samples.
2. The distribution of means has the same mean as the corresponding population of individuals. However, it has a smaller variance because the means of samples are less likely to be extreme than individual scores. (In any one sample, extreme scores are likely to be balanced by middle scores or extreme scores in the other

direction.) Specifically, the variance of the distribution of means is the variance of the population of individuals divided by the number of individuals in each sample. Its standard deviation is the square root of its variance. The shape of the distribution of means approximates a normal curve if either (a) the samples are each of 30 or more scores or (b) the population of individuals follows a normal curve.

3. Hypothesis tests with a single sample of more than one individual and a known population are called Z tests and are·done the same way as the hypothesis tests that are done using a single individual compared to a population of individuals. The main exception is that the comparison distribution in a hypothesis test with a single sample of more than one individual and a known population is a distribution of means.

4. There is some controversy about the use of terms such as *marginal significance, approaching significance,* and *near significant trend* to describe results that come close to the significance cutoff value. Critics of these terms note that hypothesis testing is an all or nothing decision. However, other researchers advocate for greater flexibility and point out that the .05 and .01 significance levels are arbitrary conventions.

5. The kind of hypothesis testing described in this chapter (the Z test) is rarely used in research practice; you have learned it as another stepping-stone. The standard deviation of the distribution of means (the standard error) is commonly used to describe the expected variability of means, particularly in bar graphs in which the standard error may be shown as the length of a line above (and sometimes below) the top of each bar.

6. ADVANCED TOPIC: The sample mean is the best estimate for the population mean when the population mean is unknown. The accuracy of the estimate is the standard deviation of the distribution of means (also known as the standard error), which tells you roughly the amount by which means vary. Based on the distribution of means, you can figure the range of possible means that are likely to include the population mean. If we assume the distribution of means follows a normal curve, the 95% confidence interval includes the range from 1.96 standard deviations below the sample mean (the lower confidence limit) to 1.96 standard deviations above the sample mean (the upper confidence limit). Strictly speaking, the 95% confidence interval around a sample mean is the range in which the lower limit is the mean of the lowest population that would have a 95% probability of including a sample with this sample mean, and the upper limit is the corresponding mean of the highest population. The 99% confidence interval includes the range from 2.58 standard deviations below the sample mean (the lower confidence limit) to 2.58 standard deviations above the sample mean (the upper confidence limit).

7. ADVANCED TOPIC: An aspect of the ongoing controversy about significance tests is whether researchers should replace them with confidence intervals. Proponents of confidence intervals argue that they provide additional information, put the focus on estimation, and reduce misuses common with significance tests. Confidence intervals have become more common in recent years in psychology research articles, but they are still relatively uncommon, and it is very rare to see them entirely replacing significance tests. Opponents of relying exclusively on confidence intervals argue that they cannot be used in some advanced procedures, estimation is not always the goal, and they can have misuses of their own. When confidence intervals are reported in research articles, it is usually with the abbreviation CI.

Key Terms

distribution of means
mean of a distribution of means
μ_M
variance of a distribution of means
σ_M^2

standard deviation of a distribution
   of means
σ_M
standard error of the mean (*SEM*)
standard error (*SE*)

Z test
confidence interval (CI)
confidence limit
95% confidence interval
99% confidence interval

Example Worked-Out Problems

Figuring the Standard Deviation of the Distribution of Means

Find the standard deviation of the distribution of means for a population with $\sigma = 13$ and a sample size of 20.

Answer

Using Rules 2a and 2b for the characteristics of a distribution of means: **The variance of a distribution of means is the variance of the population of individuals divided by the number of individuals in each sample. The standard deviation of a distribution of means is the square root of the variance of the distribution of means.** The variance of the population is 169 (that is, 13 squared is 169); dividing this by 20 gives a variance of the distribution of means of 8.45. The square root of this, 2.91, is the standard deviation of the distribution of means.

Using the formula,

$$\sigma_M = \sqrt{\frac{\sigma^2}{N}} = \sqrt{\frac{13^2}{20}} = \sqrt{\frac{169}{20}} = \sqrt{8.45} = 2.91$$

Hypothesis Testing with a Sample of More Than One: The *Z* Test

A sample of 75 people was given an experimental treatment and had a mean of 16 on a particular measure. The general population of individuals has a mean of 15 on this measure and a standard deviation of 5. Carry out a *Z* test using the five steps of hypothesis testing with a two-tailed test at the .05 significance level, and make a drawing of the distributions involved.

Answer

❶ **Restate the question as a research hypothesis and a null hypothesis about the populations.** The two populations are:

Population 1: Those given the experimental treatment.
Population 2: People in the general population (who are not given the experimental treatment).

The research hypothesis is that the population given the experimental treatment will have a different mean on the particular measure from the mean of people in the general population (who are not given the experimental treatment): $\mu_1 \neq \mu_2$. The null hypothesis is that the populations have the same mean score on this measure: $\mu_1 = \mu_2$.

❷ **Determine the characteristics of the comparison distribution.** $\mu_M = \mu = 15$; $\sigma_M = \sqrt{\dfrac{\sigma^2}{N}} = \sqrt{\dfrac{5^2}{75}} = \sqrt{.33} = .57$; shape is normal (sample size is greater than 30).

❸ **Determine the cutoff sample score on the comparison distribution at which the null hypothesis should be rejected.** Two-tailed cutoffs, 5% significance level, are $+1.96$ and -1.96.

❹ **Determine your sample's score on the comparison distribution.** Using the formula, $Z = (M - \mu_M)/\sigma_M$, $Z = (16 - 15)/.57 = 1/.57 = 1.75$.

❺ **Decide whether to reject the null hypothesis.** The sample's Z score of 1.75 is *not* more extreme than the cutoffs of ± 1.96; do not reject the null hypothesis. Results are inconclusive. The distributions involved are shown in Figure 12.

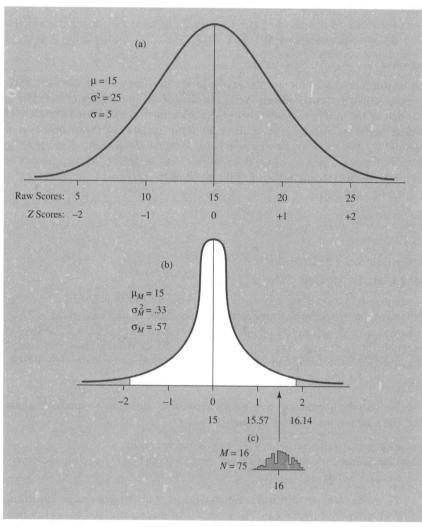

Figure 12   Answer to the hypothesis-testing problem in Example Worked-Out Problems: (a) the distribution of the population of individuals, (b) the distribution of means (the comparison distribution), and (c) the sample's distribution.

Outline for Writing Essays for Hypothesis-Testing Problems Involving a Single Sample of More Than One and a Known Population (Z Test)

1. Describe the core logic of hypothesis testing in this situation. Be sure to explain the meaning of the research hypothesis and the null hypothesis in this situation where we focus on the mean of a sample and compare it to a known population mean. Explain the concept of support being provided for the research hypothesis when the study results allow the null hypothesis to be rejected.

2. Explain the concept of the comparison distribution. Be sure to mention that, with a sample of more than one, the comparison distribution is a distribution of means because the information from the study is a mean of a sample. Mention that the distribution of means has the same mean as the population mean because there is no reason for random samples in the long run to have a different mean. And mention the distribution of means has a smaller variance (the variance of the population divided by the number in each sample) because it is harder to get extreme means than extreme individual cases by chance, and the larger the samples are, the rarer it is to get extreme means.

3. Describe the logic and process for determining (using the normal curve) the cutoff sample score(s) on the comparison distribution at which the null hypothesis should be rejected.

4. Describe how and why you figure the Z score of the sample mean on the comparison distribution.

5. Explain how and why the scores from Steps ❸ and ❹ of the hypothesis-testing process are compared. Explain the meaning of the result of this comparison with regard to the specific research and null hypotheses being tested.

Advanced Topic: Finding Confidence Intervals

Find the 99% confidence interval for the sample mean in the study just described.

Answer

❶ **Figure the standard error.** The standard error is the standard deviation of the distribution of means. In the preceding problem, it was .57.

❷ **For the 95% confidence interval, figure the raw scores for 1.96 standard errors above and below the sample mean; for the 99% confidence interval, figure the raw scores for 2.58 standard errors above and below the sample mean.** For the 99% confidence interval, upper limit $= M + (2.58)(\sigma_M) = 16 + (2.58)(.57) = 16 + 1.47 = 17.47$;   lower limit $= M - (2.58)(\sigma_M) = 16 - (2.58)(.57) = 16 - 1.47 = 14.53$. Thus, the 99% confidence interval is from 14.53 to 17.47.

Advanced Topic: Outline for Writing Essays for Finding Confidence Intervals

1. Explain that a confidence interval is an estimate (based on your sample's mean and the standard deviation of the distribution of means) of the range of values that is likely to include the true population mean for the group studied (Population 1). Be sure to mention that the 95% (or 99%) confidence interval is the range of values you are 95% (or 99%) confident include the true population mean.

2. Explain that the first step in figuring a confidence interval is to estimate the population mean (for which the best estimate is the sample mean), and figure the standard deviation of the distribution of means.
3. Mention that you next find the Z scores that go with the confidence interval that you want.
4. Describe how to change the Z scores to raw scores to find the confidence interval.

Practice Problems

These problems involve figuring. Most real-life statistics problems are done with special statistical software. Even if you have such software, do these problems by hand to ingrain the method in your mind.

All data are fictional unless an actual citation is given.

Set I

1. Why is the standard deviation of the distribution of means generally smaller than the standard deviation of the distribution of the population of individuals?
2. For a population that has a standard deviation of 10, figure the standard deviation of the distribution of means for samples of size (a) 2, (b) 3, (c) 4, and (d) 9.
3. For a population that has a standard deviation of 20, figure the standard deviation of the distribution of means for samples of size (a) 2, (b) 3, (c) 4, and (d) 9.
4. ADVANCED TOPIC: Figure the 95% confidence interval (that is, the lower and upper confidence limits) for each part of problem 2. Assume that in each case the researcher's sample has a mean of 100 and that the population of individuals is known to follow a normal curve.
5. ADVANCED TOPIC: Figure the 99% confidence interval (that is, the lower and upper confidence limits) for each part of problem 3. Assume that in each case the researcher's sample has a mean of 10 and that the population of individuals is known to follow a normal curve.
6. For each of the following samples that were given an experimental treatment, test whether the samples represent populations that are different from the general population: (a) a sample of 10 with a mean of 44, (b) a sample of 1 with a mean of 48. The general population of individuals has a mean of 40, a standard deviation of 6, and follows a normal curve. For each sample, carry out a Z test using the five steps of hypothesis testing with a two-tailed test at the .05 significance level, and make a drawing of the distributions involved. (c) ADVANCED TOPIC: Figure the 95% confidence interval for parts (a) and (b).
7. For each of the following samples that were given an experimental treatment, test whether they represent populations that score significantly higher than the general population: (a) a sample of 100 with a mean of 82, (b) a sample of 10 with a mean of 84. The general population of individuals has a mean of 81, a standard deviation of 8, and follows a normal curve. For each sample, carry out a Z test using the five steps of hypothesis testing with a one-tailed test at the .01 significance level, and make a drawing of the distributions involved. (c) ADVANCED TOPIC: Figure the 99% confidence interval for parts (a) and (b).

8. Twenty-five women between the ages of 70 and 80 were randomly selected from the general population of women their age to take part in a special program to decrease reaction time (speed). After the course, the women had an average reaction time of 1.5 seconds. Assume that the mean reaction time for the general population of women of this age group is 1.8, with a standard deviation of .5 seconds. (Also assume that the population is approximately normal.) What should you conclude about the effectiveness of the course? (a) Carry out a Z test using the five steps of hypothesis testing (use the .01 level). (b) Make a drawing of the distributions involved. (c) Explain your answer to someone who is familiar with the general logic of hypothesis testing, the normal curve, Z scores, and probability, but not with the idea of a distribution of means. (d) ADVANCED TOPIC: Figure the 99% confidence interval and explain your answer to someone who is familiar with the general logic of hypothesis testing, the normal curve, Z scores, probability, and the idea of a distribution of means, but has not heard of confidence intervals.

9. A large number of people were shown a particular video of an automobile collision between a moving car and a stopped car. Each person then filled out a questionnaire about how likely it was that the driver of the moving car was at fault, on a scale from $0 = $ *not at fault* to $10 = $ *completely at fault.* The distribution of ratings under ordinary conditions follows a normal curve with $\mu = 5.5$ and $\sigma = .8$. Sixteen randomly selected individuals are tested in a condition in which the wording of the question is changed so that the question asks, "How likely is it that the driver of the car who crashed into the other was at fault?" (The difference is that in this changed condition, instead of describing the event in a neutral way, the question uses the phrase "crashed into.") Using the changed instruction, these 16 research participants gave a mean at-fault rating of 5.9. Did the changed instructions significantly increase the rating of being at fault? (a) Carry out a Z test using the five steps of hypothesis testing (use the .05 level). (b) Make a drawing of the distributions involved. (c) Explain your answer to someone who has never taken statistics. (d) ADVANCED TOPIC: Figure the 95% confidence interval.

10. Lee and colleagues (2000) tested a theory of the role of distinctiveness in face perception. In their study, participants indicated whether they recognized each of 48 faces of male celebrities when they were shown rapidly on a computer screen. A third of the faces were shown in caricature form, in which facial features were electronically modified so that distinctive features were exaggerated; a third were shown in veridical form, in which the faces were not modified at all; and a third were shown in anticaricature form, in which facial features were modified to be slightly more like the average of the celebrities' faces. The average percentage correct across their participants is shown in Figure 13. Explain the meaning of the error bars in this figure to a person who understands mean, standard deviation, and variance, but nothing else about statistics.

11. ADVANCED TOPIC: Christakis and Fowler (2007) studied more than 12,000 people over a 32-year period to examine if people's chances of becoming obese are related to whether they have friends and family who become obese. They reported that "A person's chance of becoming obese increased by 57% (95% confidence interval [CI], 6 to 123) if he or she had a friend who became obese in a given interval" (p. 370). Explain what the 95% confidence interval reported in this study means to a person who understands hypothesis testing with the mean of a sample of more than one, but who has never heard of confidence intervals.

Figure 13 Identification accuracy as a function of image type. Standard error bars are shown.

Source: Lee, K., Byatt, G., & Rhodes, G. (2000). Caricature effects, distinctiveness, and identification: Testing the face-space framework. *Psychological Science, 11*, 379–385. Copyright © 2000 by Blackwell Publishing. Reprinted by permission of Sage Publications.

Set II

12. Under what conditions is it reasonable to assume that a distribution of means will follow a normal curve?
13. Indicate the mean and the standard deviation of the distribution of means for each of the following situations.

	Population		Sample Size
	Mean	Variance	N
(a)	100	40	10
(b)	100	30	10
(c)	100	20	10
(d)	100	10	10
(e)	50	10	10
(f)	100	40	20
(g)	100	10	20

14. Figure the standard deviation of the distribution of means for a population with a standard deviation of 20 and sample sizes of (a) 10, (b) 11, (c) 100, and (d) 101.
15. ADVANCED TOPIC: Figure the 95% confidence interval (that is, the lower and upper confidence limits) for each part of problem 13. Assume that in each case the researcher's sample has a mean of 80 and the population of individuals is known to follow a normal curve.
16. ADVANCED TOPIC: Figure the 99% confidence interval (that is, the lower and upper confidence limits) for each part of problem 14. Assume that in each case the researcher's sample has a mean of 50 and that the population of individuals is known to follow a normal curve.
17. For each of the following studies, the samples were given an experimental treatment and the researchers compared their results to the general population. (Assume all populations are normally distributed.) For each, carry out a Z test using the five steps of hypothesis testing for a two-tailed test, and make a drawing of the distributions involved. ADVANCED TOPIC: Figure the 95% confidence interval for each study.

	Population		Sample Size	Sample Mean	Significance Level
	μ	σ	N		
(a)	36	8	16	38	.05
(b)	36	6	16	38	.05
(c)	36	4	16	38	.05
(d)	36	4	16	38	.01
(e)	34	4	16	38	.01

18. For each of the following studies, the samples were given an experimental treat-ment and the researchers compared their results to the general population. For each, carry out a Z test using the five steps of hypothesis testing for a two-tailed test at the .01 level, and make a drawing of the distributions involved. ADVANCED TOPIC: Figure the 99% confidence interval for each study.

	Population		Sample Size	Sample Mean
	μ	σ	N	
(a)	10	2	50	12
(b)	10	2	100	12
(c)	12	4	50	12
(d)	14	4	100	12

19. A researcher is interested in whether people are able to identify emotions correctly when they are extremely tired. It is known that, using a particular method of measurement, the accuracy ratings of people in the general population (who are not extremely tired) are normally distributed with a mean of 82 and a variance of 20. In the present study, however, the researcher arranges to test 50 people who had no sleep the previous night. The mean accuracy for these 50 individuals was 78. Using the .05 level, what should the researcher conclude? (a) Carry out a Z test using the five steps of hypothesis testing. (b) Make a drawing of the distributions involved. (c) Explain your answer to someone who knows about hypothesis testing with a sample of a single individual but who knows nothing about hypothesis testing with a sample of more than one individual. (d) ADVANCED TOPIC: Figure the 95% confidence interval and explain your answer to someone who is familiar with the general logic of hypothesis testing, the normal curve, Z scores, probability, and the idea of a distribution of means, but who has not heard of confidence intervals.

20. A psychologist is interested in the conditions that affect the number of dreams per month that people report in which they are alone. We will assume that based on extensive previous research, it is known that in the general population the number of such dreams per month follows a normal curve, with $\mu = 5$ and $\sigma = 4$. The researcher wants to test the prediction that the number of such dreams will be greater among people who have recently experienced a trau-matic event. Thus, the psychologist studies 36 individuals who have recently experienced a traumatic event, having them keep a record of their dreams for a month. Their mean number of alone dreams is 8. Should you conclude that people who have recently had a traumatic experience have a significantly different number of dreams in which they are alone? (a) Carry out a Z test using the five steps of hypothesis testing (use the .05 level). (b) Make a drawing of the distributions involved. (c) Explain your answer to a person who has never had a course in statistics. (d) ADVANCED TOPIC: Figure the 95% confidence interval.

21. A government-sponsored telephone counseling service for adolescents tested whether the length of calls would be affected by a special telephone system that had a better sound quality. Over the past several years, the lengths of telephone calls (in minutes) were normally distributed with $\mu = 18$ and $\sigma = 8$. They arranged to have the special phone system loaned to them for one day. On that day, the mean length of the 46 calls they received was 21 minutes. Test whether the length of calls has changed using the 5% significance level. (a) Carry out a Z test using the five steps of hypothesis testing. (b) Make a drawing of the distributions involved. (c) Explain your answer to someone who knows about hypothesis testing with a sample of a single individual but who knows nothing about hypothesis testing with samples of more than one individual. (d) ADVANCED TOPIC: Figure the 95% confidence interval.

22. Stankiewicz and colleagues (2006) examined how limitations in human perception and memory (and other factors) affect people's ability to find their way in indoor spaces. In one of their experiments, eight students used a computer keyboard to move through a virtual indoor space of corridors and hallways shown on a computer monitor. The researchers calculated how efficiently students moved through the space, with efficiency ranging from 0 (extremely inefficient) to 1 (extremely efficient). The researchers compared the efficiency of moving through the space when students had a limited view of the space versus when they had a clear (or unlimited) view of the space. Their results are shown in Figure 14. In the figure caption, they note that "Error bars represent 1 standard error of the mean." Explain the meaning of this statement, using one of the error bars as an example, to a person who understands mean and standard deviation, but knows nothing else about statistics.

23. Maier and colleagues (2008) conducted a study to examine whether the perception of the color red can adversely affect intellectual performance. The researchers based their hypothesis on a theory that, in achievement situations, red is associated with the risk of failure, such as when teachers use red ink to correct students' errors. To test their hypothesis, the researchers asked 20 German high

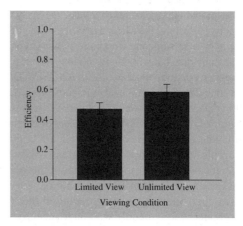

Figure 14   The mean navigation efficiency when navigating in the unlimited and limited viewing condition in Experiment 2. In the limited-view condition, visual information was available as far as the next intersection (further details were obscured by "fog"). In the unlimited-view condition, visual information was available to the end of the corridor. Error bars represent 1 standard error of the mean.

Source: Stankiewicz, B. J., Legge, G. E., Mansfield, J. S., & Schlicht, E. J. (2006). Lost in virtual space: Studies in human and ideal spatial navigation. *Journal of Experimental Psychology: Human Perception and Performance, 32*, 688–704. Copyright © 2006 by the American Psychological Association.

Figure 15   The effect of color on IQ test (numeric subtest) performance in Experiment 1. NOTE: Mean and standard error of the number of correctly solved items by color on the cover of the test.

Source: Maier, M. A., Elliot, A. J., & Lichtenfeld, S. (2008). Mediation of the negative effect of red on intellectual performance. *Personality and Social Psychology Bulletin, 34*, 1530–1540. Copyright © 2008, Society for Personality and Social Psychology, Inc. Reprinted by permission of Sage Publications.

school students to take a 20-item numeric IQ test and randomly assigned them to one of two experimental conditions. In one condition, a large red rectangle appeared on the cover page of the test. In the other condition, the rectangle was a gray color. The results are shown in Figure 15, which includes standard error bars. Explain what the standard error bars mean, using one of the error bars as an example, to a person who understands mean and standard deviation, but knows nothing else about statistics. (You may be interested to know that the results supported the researchers' hypothesis: Students who viewed the red rectangle solved fewer of the IQ items than students who viewed the gray rectangle.)

24. Cut up 90 small slips of paper, and write each number from 1 to 9 on 10 slips each. Put the slips in a large bowl and mix them up. (a) Take out a slip, write down the number on it, and put it back. Do this 20 times. Make a histogram, and figure the mean and the variance of the result. You should get an approximately rectangular distribution. (b) Take two slips out, figure out their mean, write it down, and put the slips back.[7] Repeat this process 20 times. Make a histogram; then figure the mean and the variance of this distribution of means. The variance should be about half of the variance of the distribution of individual scores. (c) Repeat the process again, this time taking three slips at a time. Again, make a histogram and figure the mean and the variance of the distribution of means. The distribution of means of three slips each should have a variance of about a third of the distribution of individual scores. Also note that as the sample size increases, your distributions get closer to normal. (Had you begun with a normally distributed distribution of slips, your distributions of means would have been fairly close to normal regardless of the number of slips in each sample.)

Chapter Notes

1. The formula for figuring the standard deviation of a distribution of means can also be written as $\sigma_M = \dfrac{\sigma}{\sqrt{N}}.$ We prefer to use Formula 3, because it provides a reminder of the basic logic that the variance of a distribution of means is

figured by dividing the variance of the population of individuals by the number of individuals in each sample.

2. We have ignored the fact that a normal curve is a smooth theoretical distribution, whereas in most real-life distributions, scores are only at specific numbers, such as a child being in a particular grade and not in a fraction of a grade. So, one difference between our example distribution of means and a normal curve is that the normal curve is smooth. However, in psychology research, even when our measurements are at specific numbers, we usually treat the situation as if the underlying thing being measured is continuous.

3. We have already considered this principle of a distribution of means tending toward a normal curve. Though we had not yet discussed the distribution of means, we still used this principle to explain why the distribution of so many things in nature follows a normal curve. We can explain it as the various influences balancing each other out, to make an averaged influence come out with most of the scores near the center and a few at either extreme. Now we have made the same point using the terminology of a distribution of means. Think of any distribution of individual scores in nature as a situation in which each score is actually an average of a random set of influences on that individual. Consider the distribution of weights of pebbles. Each pebble's weight is a kind of average of all the different forces that went into making the pebble have a particular weight.

4. This fictional study would be much better if the social psychologist also had another group of students who were randomly assigned to rate the attractiveness of the person after being told nothing about the person's personality qualities. Relying on the attractiveness ratings for a known population of students is a bit hazardous. This is because the circumstances in the experiment might be somewhat different from that of the usual situation in which students rated the attractiveness of the person. However, we have taken liberties with this example to help introduce the hypothesis-testing process to you one step at a time. In this example and the others in this chapter, we use situations in which a single sample is contrasted with a "known" population. The hypothesis-testing procedure can be extended to more realistic research situations, those involving more than one group of participants and those involving populations whose characteristics are not known.

5. Strictly speaking, being 68% confident that the population mean is within a certain interval of scores refers to the fact that if you created a series of intervals based on samples of the same sample size, about 68% of those intervals would include the actual population mean. See the later "Subtle Logic" section for more discussion of this issue.

6. Some proponents of confidence intervals over significance testing argue that we should ignore the link with hypothesis testing altogether. This is the most radical antisignificance-test position. That is, these psychologists argue that our entire focus should be on estimation, and significance testing of any kind should be irrelevant.

7. Technically, when taking the samples of two slips, this should be done by taking one, writing it down, putting it back, then taking the next, writing it down, and putting it back. You would consider these two scores as one sample for which you figure a mean. The same applies for samples of three slips. This is called sampling *with replacement*. However, with 90 slips in the bowl, taking two or three slips at a time and putting them back will be a close enough approximation for this exercise and will save you some time.

Answers to Set I Practice Problems

Chapter 5

1. The standard deviation of the distribution of means is generally smaller than the standard deviation of the distribution of the population of individuals because there is less variation among means of samples of more than one score than there are among individual scores. This is because the likelihood of two extreme scores in the same direction randomly ending up in the same sample is less than the probability of each of those extreme scores being chosen individually.

2. (a) $\sigma^2 = 10^2 = 100$; $\sigma_M^2 = \sigma^2/N = 100/2 = 50$; $\sigma_M = \sqrt{\sigma_M^2} = \sqrt{50} = 7.07$; (b) 5.77; (c) 5; (d) 3.33.

3. (a) $\sigma^2 = 20^2 = 400$; $\sigma_M^2 = \sigma^2/N = 400/2 = 200$; $\sigma_M = \sqrt{\sigma_M^2} = \sqrt{200} = 14.14$; (b) 11.55; (c) 10; (d) 6.67.

4. (a) The best estimate of the population mean is the sample mean of 100. From question 2a, the standard deviation of the distribution of means (σ_M) is 7.07. For the 95% confidence limits, the Z scores you want are -1.96 and $+1.96$. Lower limit $= (-1.96)(7.07) + 100 = 86.14$; upper limit $= (1.96)(7.07) + 100 = 113.86$; (b) 88.69, 111.31; (c) 90.2, 109.8; (d) 93.47, 106.53.

5. (a) The best estimate of the population mean is the sample mean of 10. From question 3a, the standard deviation of the distribution of means (σ_M) is 14.14. For the 99% confidence limits, the Z scores you want are -2.58 and $+2.58$. Lower limit $= (-2.58)(14.14) + 10 = -26.48$; upper limit $= (2.58)(14.14) + 10 = 46.48$; (b) -19.80, 39.80; (c) -15.80, 35.80; (d) -7.21, 27.21.

6. (a) ❶ **Restate the question as a research hypothesis and a null hypothesis about the populations.** There are two populations of interest:

Population 1: People given the experimental treatment.
Population 2: People in general (who do not get the experimental treatment).

The research hypothesis is that the population given the experimental treatment (Population 1) has a different mean score than people in general (Population 2). The null hypothesis is that Population 1's mean is the same as Population 2's.
❷ **Determine the characteristics of the comparison distribution.** Comparison distribution is a distribution of means of samples of 10 taken from the distribution of Population 2. $\mu_M = \mu = 40$; $\sigma_M^2 = \sigma^2/N = 6^2/10 = 3.6$; $\sigma_M = \sqrt{\sigma_M^2} = \sqrt{3.6} = 1.90$. Because the population is normal, the distribution of means is normal.
❸ **Determine the cutoff sample score on the comparison distribution at which the null hypothesis should be**

rejected. For a two-tailed test at the .05 level, the cutoffs are -1.96 and 1.96.
❹ **Determine your sample's score on the comparison distribution.** $Z = (44 - 40)/1.90 = 2.11$.
❺ **Decide whether to reject the null hypothesis.** 2.11 is more extreme than 1.96. Thus, you can reject the null hypothesis. The research hypothesis is supported; those who receive the experimental treatment score differently from the general population. The distributions involved are shown on the next page.
(b) Hypothesis-testing steps similar to part (a). $\sigma_M = 6$; $Z = (48 - 40)/6 = 1.33$; do not reject null hypothesis; study is inconclusive as to whether those who receive the experimental treatment are different from those in the general population. (c) For part (a), 95% confidence interval: Lower limit $= (-1.96)(1.9) + 44 = 40.28$; upper limit $= (1.96)(1.9) + 44 = 47.72$. For part (b), 95% confidence interval: 36.24 to 59.76.

7. Hypothesis-testing steps and drawing similar to question 6. (a) $\sigma_M = .8$; $Z = (82 - 81)/.8 = 1.25$; do not reject null hypothesis. (b) $\sigma_M = 2.53$; $Z = (84 - 81)/2.53 = 1.19$; do not reject null hypothesis. (c) For part (a), 99% confidence interval: 79.94 to 84.06. For part (b), 99% confidence interval: 77.47 to 90.53.

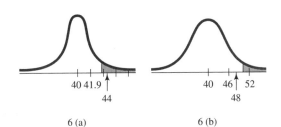

6 (a)   6 (b)

8. (a) and (b) Hypothesis-testing steps and drawing similar to question 6. $\sigma_M = .1$; $Z = (1.5 - 1.8)/.1 = -3$; reject the null hypothesis.

(c) This is a standard hypothesis-testing problem, with one exception. You can't compare directly the reaction times for the group of 25 women tested to a distribution of reaction times for individual women. The probability of a group of scores having an extreme mean just by chance is much less than the probability of any single individual having an extreme score just by chance. (When taking a group of scores at random, any extreme individual scores are likely to be balanced out by less extreme or oppositely extreme scores.) Thus, you need to compare the mean of the group of 25 reaction times to a distribution of what would happen if you were to take many random groups of 25 reaction time scores and find the mean of each group of 25 scores.

Such a distribution of many means of samples has the same mean as the original distribution of individual scores (there is no reason for it to be higher or lower). However, it is a narrower curve. This is because the chances of extremes are less. In fact, its variance will be exactly the variance of the original distribution of individuals divided by the number of scores in each sample. In this example, this makes a distribution of means with a mean of 1.8 and a standard deviation of .1 (that is, .1 is the square root of the result of $.5^2$ divided by 25). This will be a normal distribution because a distribution of many means from a normally distributed population is also normal.

The cutoff for significance, using the .01 level and a one-tailed test, is -2.33. The mean reaction time of the group of 25 women who received the special program, 1.5, was 3 standard deviations below the mean of the distribution of means, making it clearly more extreme than the cutoff. Thus, you can reject the null hypothesis and conclude that the results support the hypothesis that elderly women who take part in the special program have lower reaction times.

(d) 99% confidence interval: 1.24 to 1.76. The confidence interval is an estimate (based on your sample's mean and the standard deviation of the distribution of means) of the range of values that is likely to include the true population mean for the group studied (Population 1: in this example, women who receive the special reaction-time program). A 99% confidence interval is the range of values you are 99% confident include the true population mean. The lower limit of this interval is the mean of the lowest distribution of means that would have a 99% chance of including this sample mean; its upper limit is the mean of the highest distribution of means that would have a 99% chance of including this sample mean.

To figure the confidence interval, you first consider that the best single estimate of the mean of Population 1 is the sample's mean (in this case, 1.5). You then assume that the standard deviation of the distribution of means for this population is the same as for the known population (which we figured earlier to be .1). Based on this information, if the true population mean was 1.5, 99% of the time, sample means would fall between a Z score of -2.58 (the point on the normal curve that includes 49.5% of the scores below the mean) and $+2.58$. In our example, these Z scores correspond to raw scores of 1.24 and 1.76.

It turns out that the values figured in this way are the limits of the confidence interval. Why? Suppose the true population mean was 1.24. In this case, there would be a .5% chance of getting a mean as large as or larger than 1.5. (That is, with a mean of 1.24 and a standard deviation of .1, 1.5 is exactly 2.58 standard deviations above the mean, which is the point that corresponds to the cutoff for the top .5% of this curve.) Similarly, if the true population mean was 1.76, there would only be a .5% chance of getting a mean lower than 1.5.

9. (a) and (b) Hypothesis-testing steps and drawing similar to question 6. $\sigma_M = .2$; $Z = (5.9 - 5.5)/.2 = 2$; reject the null hypothesis. (c) Similar to question 8c, plus an explanation of material from previous chapter on hypothesis testing, normal curve, means, and standard deviations. (d) 95% confidence interval: 5.51 to 6.29.

10. The error bars are the lines that go above and below the top of each bar. The error bars show, for each particular group, the standard deviation of the distribution of means for people like those in this group. (Then explain a distribution of means as in question 8c.)

11. Similar to question 8d.

Chapter 6

Making Sense of Statistical Significance
Decision Errors, Effect Size, and Statistical Power

S tatistical significance is extremely important in psychology research, but sophisticated researchers and readers of research understand that there is more to the story of a study's result than $p < .05$ or *ns* (not significant). This chapter helps you become sophisticated about making sense of significance. Gaining this sophistication means learning about three interrelated issues: decision errors, effect size, and statistical power.

Decision Errors

A crucial topic for making sense of statistical significance is the kinds of errors that are possible in the hypothesis-testing process. The kind of errors we consider here are about how, in spite of doing all your figuring correctly, your conclusions from hypothesis testing can still be incorrect. It is *not* about making mistakes in calculations or even about using the wrong procedures. That is, **decision errors** are situations in which the *right procedures* lead to the *wrong decisions*.

TIP FOR SUCCESS

This chapter builds directly on *Introduction to Hypothesis Testing* and *Hypothesis Tests with Means of Samples*. We do not recommend embarking on this chapter until you have a good understanding of the key material in those texts, especially hypothesis testing and the distribution of means.

decision errors incorrect conclusions in hypothesis testing in relation to the real (but unknown) situation, such as deciding the null hypothesis is false when it is really true.

195

Decision errors are possible in hypothesis testing because you are making decisions about populations based on information in samples. The whole hypothesis-testing process is based on probabilities; it is set up to make the probability of decision errors as small as possible, but it can not eliminate the possibility of errors entirely. For example, we decide to reject the null hypothesis only if a sample's mean is so extreme that there is a very small probability (say, less than 5%) that we could have gotten such an extreme sample if the null hypothesis is true. But a very small probability is not the same as a zero probability! Thus, in spite of your best intentions, decision errors are always possible.

There are two kinds of decision errors in hypothesis testing: Type I error and Type II error.

Type I Error

You make a **Type I error** when you conclude that the study supports the research hypothesis when in reality the research hypothesis is false. Or, to put it in terms of the null hypothesis, you make a Type I error if you reject the null hypothesis when in fact the null hypothesis is true. A medical analogy for a Type I error would be when it is believed a medicine will help a patient, but in fact it is of no value.

Suppose you carried out a study in which you had set the significance level cutoff at a very lenient probability level, such as 20%. This would mean that it would not take a very extreme result to reject the null hypothesis. If you did many studies like this, you would often (about 20% of the time) be deciding to consider the research hypothesis supported when you should not. That is, you would have a 20% chance of making a Type I error.

Even when you set the probability at the conventional .05 or .01 levels, you will still make a Type I error sometimes (5% or 1% of the time). Consider the example of giving a new therapy being tested to a depressed patient. Suppose the new therapy is in general about equally effective as the usual therapy. However, in randomly picking a sample of one depressed patient to study, the clinical psychologists might just happen to pick a patient whose depression would respond unusually well to the new therapy. Randomly selecting a sample patient like this is *unlikely*. But such extreme samples are possible. Should this happen, the clinical psychologists would reject the null hypothesis and conclude that the new therapy is different than the usual therapy. Their decision to reject the null hypothesis would be wrong—a Type I error. Of course, the researchers could not know they had made a decision error of this kind. What reassures researchers is that they know from the logic of hypothesis testing that the probability of getting a sample like this if there really is no difference, and thus making a Type I error, is kept low (less than 5% if you use the .05 significance level).

Still, the fact that Type I errors can happen at all is of serious concern to psychologists, who might construct entire theories and research programs, not to mention practical applications, based on a conclusion from hypothesis testing that is in fact mistaken. It is because these errors are of such serious concern that they are called Type I.

As we have noted, researchers cannot tell when they have made a Type I error. However, they can try to carry out studies so that the chance of making a Type I error is as small as possible.

What is the chance of making a Type I error? It is the same as the significance level you set. If you set the significance level at $p < .05$, you are saying you will

Type I error rejecting the null hypothesis when in fact it is true; getting a statistically significant result when in fact the research hypothesis is not true.

reject the null hypothesis if there is less than a 5% (.05) chance that you could have gotten your result if the null hypothesis were true. When rejecting the null hypothesis in this way, you are allowing up to a 5% chance that you got your results even though the null hypothesis was actually true. That is, you are allowing a 5% chance of a Type I error.

The significance level, which is the chance of making a Type I error, is called **alpha** (the Greek letter α). The lower the alpha, the smaller the chance of a Type I error. Researchers who do not want to take a lot of risk set alpha lower than .05, such as $p < .001$. In this way, the result of a study has to be very extreme for the hypothesis-testing process to reject the null hypothesis.

Using a .001 significance level is like buying insurance against making a Type I error. However, as when buying insurance, the better the protection, the higher the cost. There is a cost in setting the significance level at too extreme a level. We turn to that cost next.

Type II Error

If you set a very extreme significance level, such as $p < .001$, you run a different kind of risk: you may carry out a study in which, in reality, the research hypothesis is true but the result does not come out extreme enough to reject the null hypothesis. Thus, the decision error you would make here is when the hypothesis-testing procedure leads you to decide that the results of the study are inconclusive when in reality the research hypothesis is true. To put this in terms of the null hypothesis, this kind of decision error is in *not* rejecting the null hypothesis when in reality the null hypothesis is false. This is called a **Type II error**. The probability of making a Type II error is called **beta** (the Greek letter β). (Do not confuse this beta with the standardized regression coefficient, which is also called beta.) A medical analogy for a Type II error would be when it is decided that a medicine will not help a patient (that the medicine will be ineffective for the patient; this is like the null hypothesis) when in fact it really would help.

Consider again our depression therapy example. Suppose that, in truth, the new therapy is better at treating depression than the usual therapy. However, in conducting your study, the results for the sample patient are not strong enough to allow you to reject the null hypothesis. Perhaps the random sample patient that you selected to try out the new therapy happened to be a rare person who responds to the new therapy about the same as people in general respond to the usual therapy. The results would not be significant and you would decide the research hypothesis (that the new therapy is different from the usual therapy) is not supported. However, by not rejecting the null hypothesis, and thus refusing to draw a conclusion, without knowing it, you would be making a Type II error.

Type II errors especially concern psychologists interested in practical applications. This is because a Type II error could mean that a valuable practical procedure (such as a new therapy) is not used.

As with a Type I error, you cannot know when you have made a Type II error. But researchers can try to carry out studies so as to reduce the chance of making one. One way of buying insurance against a Type II error is to set a very lenient significance level, such as $p < .10$ or even $p < .20$. In this way, even if a study produces only a very small effect, this effect has a good chance of being significant. There is a cost to this insurance policy, too.

alpha (α)   probability of making a Type I error; same as *significance level.*

Type II error   failing to reject the null hypothesis when in fact it is false; failing to get a statistically significant result when in fact the research hypothesis is true.

beta (β)   probability of making a Type II error.

Relationship Between Type I and Type II Errors

When it comes to setting significance levels, protecting against one kind of decision error increases the chance of making the other. The insurance policy against Type I error (setting a significance level of, say, .001) has the cost of increasing the chance of making a Type II error. (This is because with an extreme significance level like .001, even if the research hypothesis is true, the results have to be quite strong for you to reject the null hypothesis.) The insurance policy against Type II error (setting a significance level of, say, .20) has the cost of increasing the chance of making a Type I error. (This is because, with a level of significance like .20, even if the null hypothesis is true, it is fairly easy—it would happen about 20% of the time—to get a significant result just by accidentally getting a sample that is higher or lower than the general population before doing the study.)

The trade-off between these two conflicting concerns usually is worked out by compromise—thus the standard 5% ($p < .05$) and 1% ($p < .01$) significance levels.

Summary of Possible Outcomes of Hypothesis Testing

The entire issue of possibly correct or mistaken conclusions in hypothesis testing is shown in Table 1. Along the top of this table are the two possibilities about whether the null hypothesis or the research hypothesis is really true. (Remember, you never actually know this.)

Along the side is whether, after hypothesis testing, you decide that the research hypothesis is supported (reject the null hypothesis) or decide that the results are inconclusive (do not reject the null hypothesis). Table 1 shows that there are two ways to be correct and two ways to be in error in any hypothesis-testing situation.

Table 1 Possible Correct and Incorrect Decisions in Hypothesis Testing

	Real Situation (in practice, unknown)	
	Null Hypothesis True	Research Hypothesis True
Research hypothesis supported (reject null hypothesis)	Error (Type I) α	Correct decision
Study is inconclusive (do not reject null hypothesis)	Correct decision	Error (Type II) β

Conclusion Using Hypothesis-testing Procedure

How are you doing?

1. What is a decision error?
2. (a) What is a Type I error? (b) Why is it possible? (c) What is its probability? (d) What is this probability called?
3. (a) What is a Type II error? (b) Why is it possible? (c) What is its probability called?
4. If you set a lenient alpha level (say .25), what is the effect on the probability of (a) Type I error and (b) Type II error?
5. If you set an extreme alpha level (say .001), what is the effect on the probability of (a) Type I error and (b) Type II error?

Answers

1. A decision error is a conclusion from hypothesis testing that does not match reality.
2. (a) A Type I error is rejecting the null hypothesis (and thus supporting the research hypothesis) when the null hypothesis is actually true (and the research hypothesis is actually false). (b) You reject the null hypothesis when a sample's result is so extreme that it is unlikely you would have gotten that result if the null hypothesis is true. However, even though it is unlikely, it is still possible that the null hypothesis is true. (c) The probability of a Type I error is the significance level (such as .05). (d) The probability is called alpha.
3. (a) A Type II error is failing to reject the null hypothesis (and thus failing to support the research hypothesis) when the null hypothesis is actually false (and the research hypothesis is actually true). (b) You reject the null hypothesis when a sample's result is so extreme it is unlikely you would have gotten that result if the null hypothesis is true. However, the null hypothesis could be false, but the particular sample may happen not to be extreme enough to reject the null hypothesis. (c) A Type II error's probability is called beta.
4. (a) The probability is high; (b) the probability is low.
5. (a) The probability is low; (b) the probability is high.

Effect Size

Consider an example, in which people rated the physical attractiveness of a person after being told that the person has positive personality qualities. In the hypothesis-testing procedure for this example (the Z test), we compared two populations:

Population 1: Students who are told that the person has positive personality qualities.
Population 2: Students in general (who are told nothing about the person's personality qualities).

The research hypothesis was that Population 1 would on the average give higher attractiveness ratings to the person in the photograph than Population 2. Population 2 is known to have a mean of 200. In the example, we said the researcher found that the sample of 64 students who were told that the person has positive personality qualities gave a mean attractiveness rating of 220. Following the hypothesis-testing procedure, we rejected the null hypothesis that the two populations are the same. This was because it was extremely unlikely that we would get a sample with a score as high as 220 from a population like Population 2 (see Figure 1). Thus, we could conclude the result is "statistically significant." In this example, the best estimate of the mean of Population 1 is the sample's mean, which is 220. Thus, we can estimate that telling students about the person's positive personality qualities has an average effect of increasing the students' ratings of the physical attractiveness of the person by 20 points.

Now look again at Figure 1. Suppose the sample's score had been only 210. This would have given a Z score of 1.67 (that is, $[210 - 200]/6 = 1.67$). This is more extreme than the cutoff in this example, which was 1.64, so the result would still have been significant. However, in this situation we would estimate that the average effect of telling students about the person's positive personality qualities was only 10 points.

Notice that both results are significant, but in one example the effect is twice as big as in the other example. The point is that knowing statistical significance does not give you much information about the *size* of the effect. Significance tells us that the results of the experiment should convince us that there is an effect. But significance does not tell us how *big* this effect is.

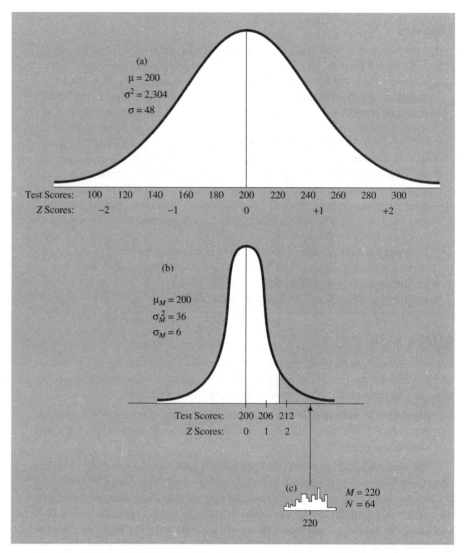

Figure 1   For the fictional study of positive personality qualities and ratings of physical attractiveness, (a) the distribution of the population of individuals, (b) the distribution of means for Population 2 (the comparison distribution), and (c) the sample's distribution. The shaded area in the distribution of means is the rejection region—the area in which the null hypothesis will be rejected if the study's sample mean turns out to be in that area.

Put another way, **effect size** is a measure of the difference between population means. You can think of effect size as how much something changes after a specific intervention. Effect size indicates the extent to which two populations do *not* overlap—that is, how much they are separated due to the experimental procedure. In the attractiveness ratings example, Population 2 (the known population) had a mean of 200; based on our original sample's mean of 220, we estimated that Population 1 (those told that the person has positive personality qualities) would have a mean of 220. The left curve in Figure 2 is the distribution (*of individual scores*) for Population 2; the right curve is the distribution for Population 1. Now look at Figure 3. Again, the left curve is for Population 2 and is the same as in Figure 2. However, this time the

effect size   standardized measure of difference (lack of overlap) between populations. Effect size increases with greater differences between means.

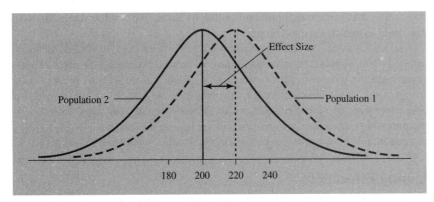

Figure 2   The distributions for the fictional study of positive personality qualities and ratings of physical attractiveness. Right curve: Population 1, those students told that the person has positive personality qualities. Left curve: Population 2, students told nothing about the person's personality. Population 1's mean is estimated based on the sample mean of 220; its standard deviation of 48 is assumed to be the same as Population 2's, which is known.

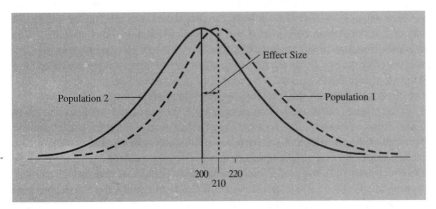

Figure 3   The distributions for the fictional study of positive personality qualities and ratings of physical attractiveness. Right curve: Population 1, those students told that the person has positive personality qualities. Left curve: Population 2, students told nothing about the person's personality. Population 1's mean is estimated based on a sample mean of 210; its standard deviation of 48 is assumed to be the same as Population 2's, which is known.

right curve for Population 1 is estimated based on a sample (the sample told that the person has positive personality qualities) with a mean of 210. Here you can see that the effect size is smaller and that the two populations overlap even more.

We often want to know not only whether a result is significant, but how big the effect is. As we will discuss later, an effect could well be statistically significant but not of much practical significance. That is, suppose an increase of only 10 points on the attractiveness measure is not considered important. Further, we may want to compare the results of this procedure to that of other procedures studied in the past. (You might think that psychologists could just compare studies using significance levels. And it is true that we are more confident of a result if it is significant at the .01 level than at the .05 level. However, significance, including whether you make the .01 or .05 level, is influenced by both the effect size and the number of people in the study. Thus, a study that is significant at the .05 level with a sample of 20 people would have had to have a much bigger effect size to be significant than a study of

1000 people that came out significant at the .01 level. We discuss these issues in some detail in the later section on power.)

For these reasons, the *Publication Manual of the American Psychological Association* (2009), the accepted standard for how to present psychology research results, recommends that some measure of effect size is included along with the results of significance tests. Thus, whenever you use a hypothesis-testing procedure, you should also figure effect size. You can think of it as a sixth step in our standard hypothesis-testing procedure: *figure the effect size*. As you will see later in this chapter, effect size plays an important role in two other important statistical topics: meta-analysis and power.

Figuring Effect Size

You just learned that effect size is a measure of the difference between two population means.[1] In Figure 2, the effect size is shown as the difference between the Population 1 mean and the Population 2 mean, which is 20 (that is, $220 - 200 = 20$). This effect size of 20 is called a *raw score effect size*, because the effect size is given in terms of the raw score on the measure (which in this case is a measure of attractiveness, from a low of 0 to a high of 400). But what if you want to compare this effect size with the result of a similar study that used a different measure of attractiveness? This similar study used a measure with a 1-to-10 scale, and the researchers reported an estimated Population 2 mean of 5, a Population 1 mean of 6, and a population standard deviation of 2. The raw score effect size in this study is 1 (that is, $6 - 5 = 1$). How do we compare this raw score effect size of 1 with the raw score effect size of 20 in our original study? The solution to this problem is to use a *standardized effect size*—that is, to divide the raw score effect size for each study by its respective population standard deviation.

In the original attractiveness ratings example, the population standard deviation (of individuals) was 48. Thus, a raw score of effect size of 20 gives a standardized effect size of 20/48, which is .42. That is, the effect of knowing positive personality qualities was to increase attractiveness ratings by .42 of a standard deviation. The raw score effect size of 1 in the similar study (which had a population standard deviation of 2) is a standardized effect size of $1/2 = .50$. Thus, in this study, the effect was to increase the ratings by .50 (half) of a standard deviation. So, in this case the effect size in our original example is smaller than the effect size in the similar study. Usually, when psychologists refer to an effect size in a situation like we are considering, they mean a standardized effect size.

Stated as a formula,

$$d = \frac{\mu_1 - \mu_2}{\sigma} \tag{1}$$

In this formula, d (also known as *Cohen's d*) is a symbol for effect size. μ_1 is the mean of Population 1 (the mean for the population that receives the experimental manipulation); μ_2 is the mean of Population 2 (the known population, the basis for the comparison distribution); and σ is the population standard deviation. The numerator of the formula is the difference between the population means. Therefore, the larger this difference is, the larger the effect size is.

Notice that when figuring effect size, you don't use σ_M, the standard deviation of the distribution of means. Instead, you use σ, the standard deviation of the population of individuals. Also notice that you are only concerned with one population's standard deviation. This is because in hypothesis testing you usually assume that both populations have the same standard deviation.

TIP FOR SUCCESS

Notice that what you are doing here is basically the same as figuring *Z* scores. And, as when figuring *Z* scores, you can compare apples to oranges in the sense that you can compare results on different measures with different means and standard deviations.

The **standardized effect size** is the difference between the population means divided by the population's standard deviation.

---

d effect size

Consider again the attractiveness ratings example shown in Figure 1. The mean of Population 1 was 220, the mean of Population 2 was 200, and the population standard deviation was 48. (In hypothesis-testing situations you don't know the mean of Population 1, so you actually use an *estimated mean*. Thus, you are actually figuring an *estimated effect size*.) Using these numbers,

$$d = (\mu_1 - \mu_2)/\sigma = (220 - 200)/48 = 20/48 = .42.$$

For the example in which the sample mean was 210, we estimated Population 1's mean to be 210. Thus,

$$d = (\mu_1 - \mu_2)/\sigma = (210 - 200)/48 = 10/48 = .21.$$

However, suppose the procedure actually reduced the score, so that those who were given the special instructions had a mean of 170:

$$d = (\mu_1 - \mu_2)/\sigma = (170 - 200)/48 = -30/48 = -.63.$$

The minus sign means that the effect is a decrease.

Effect Size Conventions

What should you consider to be a "big" effect, and what is a "small" effect? Jacob Cohen (1988, 1992), a renowned psychologist, helped solve this problem. Cohen came up with some **effect size conventions** based on the effects found in psychology research in general. Specifically, Cohen recommended that, for the kind of situation we are considering in this chapter, we should think of a small effect size as about .20. With a d of .20, the populations of individuals have an overlap of about 85%. This small effect size of .20 is, for example, the average difference in height between 15- and 16-year-old girls (see Figure 4a), which is about a half-inch difference with a standard deviation of about 2.1 inches. Cohen considered a

effect size conventions   standard rules about what to consider a small, medium, and large effect size, based on what is typical in psychology research; also known as Cohen's conventions.

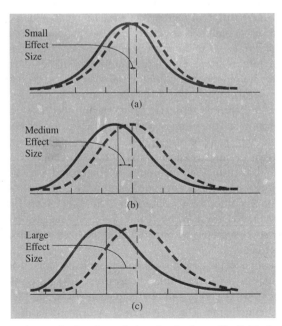

Figure 4   Comparisons of pairs of population distributions of individuals showing Cohen's conventions for effect size: (a) small effect size ($d = .20$), (b) medium effect size ($d = .50$), (c) large effect size ($d = .80$).

Table 2 Summary of
Cohen's Effect Size Conventions for
Mean Differences

Verbal Description	Effect Size (d)
Small	.20
Medium	.50
Large	.80

medium effect size to be .50, which means an overlap of about 67%. This is about the average difference in heights between 14- and 18-year-old girls (see Figure 4b). Finally, Cohen defined a large effect size as .80. This is only about a 53% overlap. It is about the average difference in height between 13- and 18-year-old girls (see Figure 4c). These three effect size conventions are summarized in Table 2. (Note that these effect size conventions apply in the same way to both positive and negative effect sizes. So, −.20 is a small effect size, −.50 is a medium effect size, and −.80 is a large effect size.)

Consider another example. Many IQ tests have a standard deviation of 15 points. An experimental procedure with a small effect size would create an increase in IQ of 3 IQ points. (A difference of 3 IQ points between the mean of the population who goes through the experimental procedure and the mean of the population that does not, divided by the population standard deviation of 15, gives an effect size of .20. That is, $d = 3/15 = .20$.) An experimental procedure with a medium effect size would increase IQ by 7.5 points. An experimental procedure with a large effect size would increase IQ by 12.0 points.

Cohen's effect size conventions provide a guide for deciding on the importance of the effect of a study in relation to what is typical in psychology. However, they are only *a guide*. That is, when evaluating a particular effect size, it is important to consider the magnitude of effect that is typically found in that specific area of research, as well as the potential practical or clinical implications of such an effect.

Meta-Analysis

Meta-analysis is an important development in statistics that has had a profound effect on psychology, especially clinical and social psychology, and on many other scientific fields, such as medicine, public health, education, and organizational behavior. This procedure combines results from different studies, even results using different methods of measurement. When combining results, the crucial results combined are *effect sizes*. As an example, a social psychologist might be interested in the effects of cross-race friendships on prejudice, a topic on which there has been a large number of studies. Using meta-analysis, the social psychologist could combine the results of these studies. This would provide an overall effect size. It would also tell how effect sizes differ for studies done in different countries or about prejudice toward different ethnic groups. (For an example of such a meta-analysis, see Davies and colleagues, 2011. For another example of meta-analysis, see Box 1.) An educational psychologist might be interested in the effects of different educational methods on students' educational achievement. Walberg and Lai (1999) carried out a large meta-analysis on this very topic and provided effect size estimates for 275 educational methods and conditions. The effect sizes for selected general educational methods are shown in Table 3. As you can see in the table, many of the methods are associated with medium effect sizes and several have large (or very large) effect sizes.

Reviews of the collection of studies on a particular topic that use meta-analysis are an alternative to the traditional "narrative" literature review article. Such traditional reviews describe and evaluate each study and then attempt to draw some overall conclusion. The first formal meta-analysis in psychology, which

meta-analysis   statistical method for combining effect sizes from different studies.

BOX 1 Effect Sizes for Relaxation and Meditation: A Restful Meta-Analysis

In the 1970s and 1980s, the results of research on meditation and relaxation were the subject of considerable controversy. Eppley, Abrams, and Shear (1989) decided to look at the issue systematically by conducting a meta-analysis of the effects of various relaxation techniques on trait anxiety (that is, ongoing anxiety as opposed to a temporary state). Eppley and colleagues chose trait anxiety for their meta-analysis because it is a definite problem related to many other mental health issues, yet in itself is fairly consistent from test to test.

Following the usual procedure, the researchers searched the scientific literature for studies—not only research journals, but books and doctoral dissertations. Finding all the relevant research studies is one of the most difficult parts of meta-analysis.

To find the "bottom line," the researchers compared effect sizes for each of the four widely studied methods of meditation and relaxation. The result was that the average effect size for the 35 transcendental meditation (TM) studies was .70 (meaning an average difference of .70 standard deviations in anxiety scores between those who practiced this meditation procedure and those in the control groups). This effect size was significantly larger than the average effect size of .28 for the 44 studies on all other types of meditation, the average effect size of .38 for the 30 studies on "progressive relaxation" (a widely used method at the time by clinical psychologists), and the average effect size of .40 for the 37 studies on other forms of relaxation.

Looking at different populations of research participants, they discovered that people who were screened to be highly anxious contributed more to the effect size, and prison populations and younger participants seemed to gain more from TM. There was no significant impact on effect size of the skill of the instructors, expectations of the participants, whether participants had volunteered or been randomly assigned to conditions, experimenter bias (the TM results were actually stronger when any apparently pro-TM researchers' studies were eliminated), the various measures of anxiety, and the research designs.

The researchers thought that one clue to TM's high performance might be that techniques involving concentration produced a significantly smaller effect, whereas TM makes a point of teaching an "effortless, spontaneous" method. Also, TM uses Sanskrit mantras (special sounds) said to come from a very old tradition and selected for each student by the instructor. Results were lower for methods employing randomly selected Sanskrit sounds or personally selected English words.

Whatever the reasons, the authors concluded that there are "grounds for optimism that at least some current treatment procedures can effectively reduce trait anxiety" (p. 973). So, if you are prone to worry about matters like statistics exams, consider these results. (For a more recent meta-analyses of TM effects, in this case on blood pressure, see Anderson, Liu, & Kryscio, 2008. For some more recent examples of meta-analyses of relaxation training and stress reduction techniques in general, see Chiesa & Serretti, 2009, and Manzoni et al., 2008.)

focused on the effects of psychotherapy, was published more than 30 years ago (Smith & Glass, 1977). Since then, meta-analysis has become an increasingly popular statistical procedure. To get a sense of the popularity of meta-analysis, we used a research database commonly used by psychologists (called PsycINFO) to search for publications on meta-analysis in the psychological research literature during different time periods. From 1977 to 1979, there were 18 research publications (research articles, books, book chapters, and dissertations) on meta-analysis. From 2009 to 2011, there were more than 3500 research publications on meta-analysis in the literature.

Table 3 Effect Sizes of Selected General Educational Methods	
Elements of Instruction	
Cues	1.25
Reinforcement	1.17
Corrective feedback	.94
Engagement	.88
Mastery Learning	.73
Computer-Assisted Instruction	
For early elementary students	1.05
For handicapped students	.66
Teaching	
Direct instruction	.71
Comprehension instruction	.55
Teaching Techniques	
Homework with teacher comments	.83
Graded homework	.78
Frequent testing	.49
Pretests	.48
Adjunct questions	.40
Goal setting	.40
Assigned homework	.28
Explanatory Graphics	.75

Source: Adapted from Walberg, H. J., & Lai, J. S. (1999). Meta-analytic effects for policy. In G. J. Cizek (Ed.). *Handbook of Educational Policy* (pp. 419–453). San Diego, CA. Academic Press. Copyright © 1999 by Elsevier. Reprinted by permission of Elsevier.

How are you doing?

1. What does effect size add to just knowing whether a result is significant?
2. Why do researchers usually use a *standardized* effect size?
3. Write the formula for effect size in the situation we have been considering, and define each of the symbols.
4. On a standard test, the population is known to have a mean of 500 and a standard deviation of 100. Those receiving an experimental treatment have a mean of 540. What is the effect size?
5. (a) Why are effect size conventions useful? (b) What are the effect size conventions for *d*?
6. (a) What is meta-analysis? (b) What is the role of effect size in a meta-analysis?

Answers

1. A significant result can be just barely big enough to be significant or much bigger than necessary to be significant. Thus, knowing effect size tells you how big the effect is.
2. A standardized effect size makes results of studies using different measures comparable.
3. The formula for effect size is $d = (\mu_1 - \mu_2)/\sigma$. d is effect size; μ_1 is the mean of Population 1 (the mean for the population that receives the experimental

manipulation); μ_2 is the mean of Population 2 (the known population, the basis for the comparison distribution); and σ is the population standard deviation.

4. The effect size is $d = (\mu_1 - \mu_2)/\sigma = (540 - 500)/100 = .40$.
5. (a) Effect size conventions allow you to compare the effect size of a study to what is typically found in psychology research. (b) The effect size conventions for d are small $= .20$, medium $= .50$, large $= .80$.
6. (a) Meta-analysis is a systematic procedure for combining results of different studies. (b) Meta-analyses usually come up with average effect sizes across studies and compare effect sizes for different subgroups of studies.

Statistical Power

Power is the ability to achieve your goals. A goal of a researcher conducting a study is to get a significant result—but only *if* the research hypothesis really is true. The **statistical power** of a research study is the probability that the study will produce a statistically significant result if the research hypothesis is true. Power is *not* the probability that a study will produce a statistically significant result; it is the probability that a study will produce a statistically significant result, *if the research hypothesis is true*. The "if" is the key here. When the research hypothesis is false, you do not want to get significant results. (That would be a Type I error, as you learned earlier in the chapter.) Remember, however, even when the research hypothesis is true, a study will not automatically give a significant result; the sample that happens to be selected from the population may not turn out to be extreme enough to reject the null hypothesis.

Statistical power is important for several reasons. As you will learn later in the chapter, figuring power when planning a study helps you decide how many participants you need. As you will also learn later in the chapter, understanding power is extremely important when you read a research article, particularly for making sense of results that are not significant or results that are statistically but not practically significant.

Consider once again our example in which students rated the physical attractiveness of a person after being told that the person has positive personality qualities. Recall that we compared two populations:

Population 1: Students who are told that the person has positive personality qualities.
Population 2: Students in general (who are told nothing about the person's personality qualities).

Also recall that the research hypothesis was that Population 1 would give higher attractiveness ratings than Population 2.

The curve in Figure 5 shows the distribution of means for Population 2. (Be careful: when discussing effect size, we showed figures, such as Figures 2 and 3, for populations of individuals; now we are back to focusing on distributions of means.) This curve is the comparison distribution, the distribution of means that you would expect for both populations if the null hypothesis were true. The mean of this distribution of means is 200 and its standard deviation is 6. Using the 5% significance level, one-tailed, you need a Z score for the mean of your sample of at least 1.64 to reject the null hypothesis. Using the formula for converting Z scores to raw scores, this comes out to a raw score of 209.84; that is, $(1.64)(6) + 200 = 209.84$. Therefore, we have shaded the tail of the distribution above a raw score of 209.84 (a Z score of 1.64 on this distribution). This is the area where you would reject the

TIP FOR SUCCESS

If you are at all unsure about Type I and Type II errors, take some time now to review the Decision Errors section earlier in the chapter. As a brief reminder, you make a Type I error if the hypothesis-testing procedure leads you to decide that a study supports the research hypothesis when in reality the research hypothesis is false. You make a Type II error if the hypothesis-testing procedure leads you to decide that the results of a study are inconclusive when in reality the research hypothesis is true.

statistical power probability that the study will give a significant result if the research hypothesis is true.

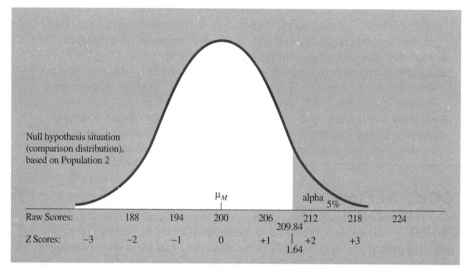

Null hypothesis situation
(comparison distribution),
based on Population 2

μ_M alpha 5%

Raw Scores: 188   194   200   206   212   218   224
                                              209.84

Z Scores: −3   −2   −1   0   +1 | +2   +3
                                                  1.64

Figure 5   For the fictional study of positive personality qualities and ratings of physical attractiveness, distribution of means for Population 2 (the comparison distribution), students told nothing about the person's personality. Significance cutoff score (209.84) shown for $p < .05$, one-tailed.

null hypothesis if, as a result of your study, the mean of your sample was in this area. This shaded area is labeled "alpha" because alpha is a name for the significance level (which in this example is 5%, or $p < .05$).

Imagine that the researcher predicts that telling students about the positive personality qualities of the person will increase the attractiveness rating of the person to 208. (This is an increase of 8 points from the mean of 200; 200 being the mean when no mention is made about the person's personality). If this prediction is correct, the research hypothesis is true and the mean of Population 1 (the population of students who are told about the person's positive personality qualities) is indeed greater than the mean of Population 2. The distribution of means for Population 1 for this *hypothetical predicted situation* is shown in the top part of Figure 6. Notice that the distribution has a mean of 208.

Now take a look at the curve shown in the bottom part of Figure 6. This curve is exactly the same as the one shown in Figure 5: the comparison distribution, the distribution of means for Population 2. Notice that the distribution of means for Population 1 (the top curve) is set off to the right of the distribution of means for Population 2 (the bottom curve). This is because the researcher predicts the mean of Population 1 to be higher (a mean of 208) than the mean of Population 1 (which we know is 200). (If Population 1's mean is predicted to be *lower* than Population 2's mean, then Population 1 would be set off to the *left*.) If the null hypothesis is true, the true distribution for Population 1 is the same as the distribution based on Population 2. Thus, the Population 1 distribution would be lined up directly above the Population 2 distribution and would not be set off to the right (or the left).

Recall that the cutoff score for rejecting the null hypothesis in this example is 209.84. Thus, the shaded rejection area for Population 2's distribution of means (shown in the bottom curve in Figure 6) starts at 209.84. We can also create a rejection area for the distribution of means for Population 1. This rejection area will also start at 209.84 (see the shaded area in the top curve in Figure 6). Remember that, in this example, Population 1's distribution of means represents the possible sample

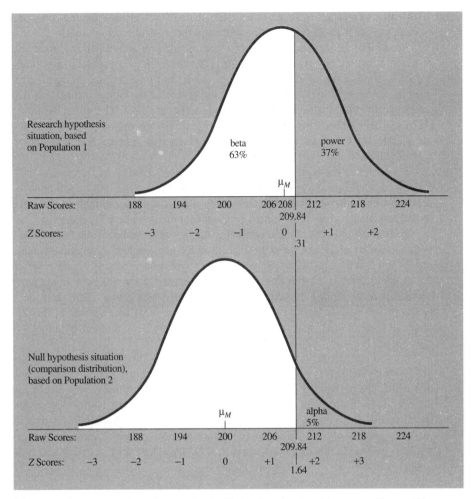

Figure 6   Distributions of means for the fictional study of positive personality qualities and ratings of physical attractiveness. Upper curve: Population 1 based on predicted population mean of 208. Lower curve: Population 2 (the comparison distribution) based on known population mean of 200. Significance cutoff score (209.84) shown for $p < .05$, one-tailed. Power = 37%.

means that we would get if we randomly selected 64 students from a population of students with a mean of 208 (and a standard deviation of 48).

Now, suppose the researcher carries out the study. The researcher randomly selects a sample of 64 students, tells them that a particular person has positive personality qualities, and then asks them to rate the attractiveness of that person. The researcher finds the mean of the attractiveness ratings given by the sample of 64 students in the study. And suppose this sample's mean turns out to be in the shaded area of the distributions (that is, a mean of 209.84 or higher). If that happens, the researcher will reject the null hypothesis. What Figure 6 shows us is that most of the means from Population 1's distribution of means (assuming that its mean is 208) will not be large enough to reject the null hypothesis. Less than half of the upper distribution is shaded. Put another way, if the research hypothesis is true, as the researcher predicts, the sample studied is a random sample from this Population 1 distribution of means. However, there is less than a 50-50 chance that the mean of a random sample from this distribution will be in the shaded rejection area.

Recall that the statistical power of a study is the probability that the study will produce a statistically significant result if the research hypothesis is true. Since we are assuming the research hypothesis is true in this example, the shaded region in the upper distribution represents the power of the study. It turns out that the power for this situation (shown in Figure 6) is only 37%. Therefore, assuming the researcher's prediction is correct, the researcher has only a 37% chance that the sample of 64 students will have a mean high enough to make the result statistically significant.

Suppose that the particular sample of 64 students studied had a mean of 203. Since you would need a mean of at least 209.84 to reject the null hypothesis, the result of this study would not be statistically significant, even though the research hypothesis really is true. This is how you would come to make a Type II error.

It is entirely possible that the researcher might select a sample from Population 1 with a mean far enough to the right (that is, with a high enough mean attractiveness rating) to be in the shaded rejection area. However, given the way we have set up the example, there is a better than even chance that the study will *not* turn out to be significant, *even though we know the research hypothesis is true*. (Of course, once again, the researcher would not know this.) When a study like the one in this example has only a small chance of being significant even if the research hypothesis is true, we say the study has *low power*.

As you learned earlier in the chapter, you make a Type II error if you do *not* get a significant result when in fact the research hypothesis is true. You learned that *beta* is the probability of making a Type II error—that is, the probability of *not* getting a significant result when the research hypothesis is true. Notice that power, the probability of getting a significant result if the research hypothesis is true, is just the *opposite* of beta. Thus, beta + power = 100%, which means that beta is 100% − power. In this example, power is 37%. Thus, beta for this example is 63% (that is, 100% − 37% = 63%) (see Figure 6).

Determining Statistical Power

The statistical power of a study can be figured. In a situation like the attractiveness ratings example (when you have a known population and a single sample), figuring power involves figuring out the area of the shaded portion of the upper distribution in Figure 6 (for more details, see the Advanced Topic section later in this chapter). The research situations faced by researchers are usually more complex than our current example, and figuring power is much more complicated. Thus, researchers do not usually figure power by hand and instead rely on computer programs or tables.

Researchers can use a power software package to determine power. There are also power calculators available on the Internet. When using a power software package or Internet power calculator, the researcher puts in the values for the various aspects of the research study (such as the known population mean, the predicted population mean, the population standard deviation, the sample size, the significance level, and whether the test is one- or two-tailed), and the figuring is done automatically.

Finally, researchers can find the power of a study using special charts, called **power tables**. [Such tables have been prepared by Cohen (1988) and by Kraemer & Thiemann (1987), among others.]

power table   table for a hypothesis-testing procedure showing the statistical power of a study for various effect sizes and sample sizes.

How are you doing?

1. (a) What is statistical power? (b) How is it different from just the probability of getting a significant result? (c) What is the probability of getting a significant result if the research hypothesis is false?
2. Give two reasons why statistical power is important.
3. (a) What is the relationship of power to beta? (b) How is beta figured?
4. (a) Name three approaches that researchers typically use to determine power. (b) Why do researchers use these approaches, as opposed to figuring power themselves by hand?

Answers

1. (a) Statistical power is the probability of getting a significant result if the research hypothesis is true. (b) It is the probability *if the research hypothesis is true*. (c) The probability of getting a significant result if the research hypothesis is false is alpha, the significance level (that is, the probability of making a Type I error).
2. Statistical power is important because (i) it can help you determine how many participants are needed for a study you are planning, and (ii) understanding power can help you make sense of results that are not significant or results that are statistically but not practically significant.
3. (a) Beta, the probability of *not* getting a significant result if the research hypothesis is true, is the opposite of power, the probability of getting a significant result if the research hypothesis is true. (b) Beta is 100% minus power.
4. (a) Three approaches that researchers typically use to determine power are (i) power software packages, (ii) Internet power calculators, and (iii) power tables. (b) In common hypothesis-testing situations, figuring power by hand is very complicated.

What Determines the Power of a Study?

It is very important that you understand what power is about. It is especially important to understand the factors that affect the power of a study and how to use power when planning a study and when making sense of a study you read.

The statistical power of a study depends on two main factors: (1) how big an effect (the effect size) the research hypothesis predicts and (2) how many participants are in the study (the sample size). Power is also affected by the significance level chosen, whether a one-tailed or two-tailed test is used, and the kind of hypothesis-testing procedure used.

Effect Size

Figure 6 shows the situation in our attractiveness ratings example in which the researcher had reason to predict that students told that the person has positive personality qualities (Population 1, the upper curve) would have a mean score *8 points higher* than students who were not told anything about the person's personality (Population 2, the lower curve). Figure 7 shows the same study for a situation in which the researcher would have reason to expect that Population 1 would have a mean score *16 points higher* than Population 2. Comparing Figure 7 to Figure 6, you are more likely to get a significant result in the situation shown in Figure 7. In fact, we noted earlier that the Figure 6 situation, in which the researcher had reason to predict a mean of only 208, has a power of 37%. However, the Figure 7 situation, in which there was a basis for the researcher to predict a mean of 216, comes out to a power of 85%. In any study, the bigger

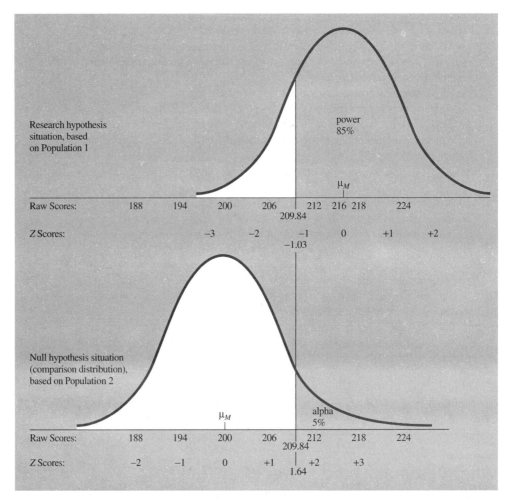

Figure 7   Distributions of means for the fictional study of positive personality qualities and ratings of physical attractiveness. Upper curve: Population 1, based on predicted population mean of 216. Bottom curve: Population 2 (the comparison distribution), based on the known population mean of 200. Significance cutoff score (209.84) shown for $p < .05$, one-tailed. Power = 85%. Compare with Figure 6, in which the predicted population mean was 208 and power was 37%.

the difference that your theory or previous research says you should expect between the two populations, the more power there is in the study. That is, if in fact there is a big mean difference in the population, you have more chance of getting a significant result in the study. So if you predict a bigger mean difference, the power you figure based on that prediction will be greater. (Thus, if you figure power based on a prediction that is unrealistically big, you are just fooling yourself about the power of the study.)

The difference in the means between populations we saw earlier is part of what goes into effect size. Thus, the bigger the effect size is, the greater the power is. The effect size for the situation in Figure 6, in which the researcher predicted Population 1 to have a mean of 208, is .17. That is, $d = (\mu_1 - \mu_2)/\sigma = (208 - 200)/48 = 8/48 = .17$. The effect size for the situation in Figure 7, in which the researcher predicted Population 1 to have a mean of 216, is .33. That is, $d = (\mu_1 - \mu_2)/\sigma = (216 - 200)/48 = .33$.

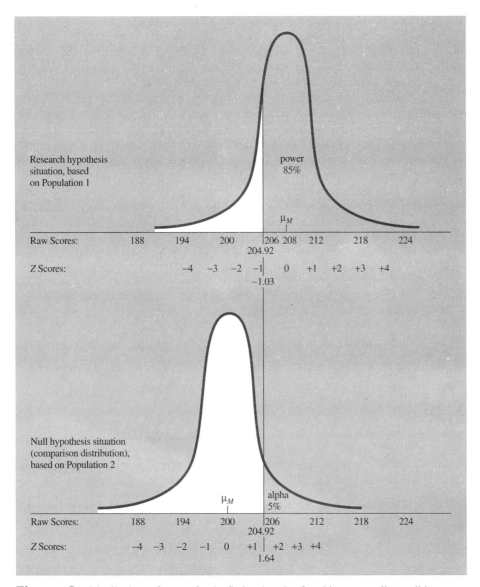

Figure 8 Distributions of means for the fictional study of positive personality qualities and ratings of physical attractiveness. Upper curve: Population 1, based on predicted population mean of 208. Bottom curve: Population 2 (the comparison distribution), based on the known population mean of 200. In this example, the population standard deviation is half as large as that shown for this example in previous figures. Significance cutoff score (204.92) shown for $p < .05$, one-tailed. Power = 85%. Compare with Figure 6, which had the original population standard deviation and power was 37%.

Effect size, however, is also affected by the population standard deviation. The smaller the standard deviation is, the bigger the effect size is. In terms of the effect size formula, this is because, if you divide by a smaller number, the result is bigger. In terms of the actual distributions, this is because, if two distributions that are separated are narrower, they *overlap less*. Figure 8 shows two distributions of means based on the same example. However, this time we have changed the example so that the population standard deviation is exactly half of what it was. In this version, the predicted mean is the original 208. However, both distributions of means are much narrower. Therefore, there is much less overlap between the upper curve and the lower curve (the comparison distribution). The result is that the power is 85%, much higher than the power of 37% in the original situation shown in Figure 6. The idea here is that the smaller the population standard deviation becomes, the greater the power is.

Overall, these examples illustrate the general principle that the less overlap between the two distributions, the more likely it is that a study will give a significant result. Two distributions might have little overlap either because there is a large difference between their means (as in Figure 7) or because they have such a small standard deviation, that even with a small mean difference they do not overlap much (see Figure 8). This principle is summarized more generally in Figure 9.

Notice that these two factors, the difference between the means and the standard deviation of the population, are exactly what goes into figuring effect size. That is, effect size is the difference between the means divided by the population standard deviation: $d = (\mu_1 - \mu_2)/\sigma$. Thus, the larger the expected difference is between the two population means (that is, the larger $\mu_1 - \mu_2$ is), the greater the effect size becomes; and the smaller the standard deviation is within the two populations

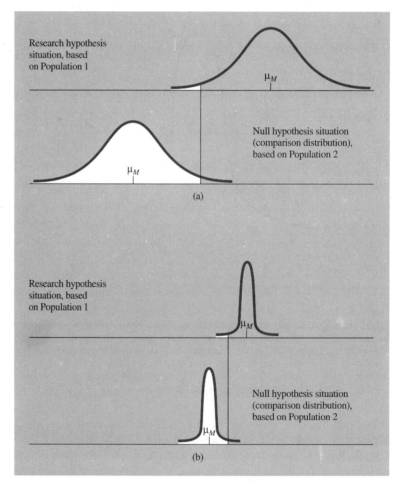

Figure 9   The predicted and comparison distributions of means might have little overlap (and thus the study would have high power) because either (a) the two means are very different or (b) the population standard deviation is very small.

(that is, the smaller σ^2 is and thus the smaller σ is), the greater the effect size becomes. And the greater the effect size is, the greater the power is.

When figuring power in advance of doing a study, the difference between the means of the two populations is the difference between the known population mean (Population 2) and the researcher's prediction for the population to be given the experimental manipulation (Population 1). This prediction is based on a precise theory, on previous experience with research of this kind, or on what would be the smallest difference that would be useful. In the situations we have considered so far, the population standard deviation, the other number you need to figure the effect size, is known in advance.

Determining Power from Predicted Effect Sizes

Sometimes, instead of predicting a particular mean, researchers predict an effect size. Especially when studying something for the first time, researchers make this prediction using Cohen's conventions. That is, they may have only a fairly vague idea of how big an effect to expect, so if they expect a small effect, for example, they use a predicted effect size of .20.

Once the researchers have predicted an effect size, in whatever way, they can use their predicted effect size to figure the predicted mean (the mean for Population 1), and then find the power in the usual way (using a power software package, an Internet power calculator, or a power table, or using the figuring shown in the Advanced Topic section later in this chapter). Consider our example in which the known population (Population 2) has a mean of 200 and a standard deviation of 48. Suppose the researcher predicts an effect size of .20 (a small effect size, using Cohen's conventions). In this situation, the predicted mean has to be enough higher than 200 so that the overall effect size, after dividing by 48, comes out to .20. That is, the mean difference has to increase by .20 standard deviations. In the example, .20 of 48 is 9.60. Thus, the predicted mean has to be 9.60 higher than the known mean. In this example, the known mean is 200; so the predicted mean for an effect size of .20 would be 209.60.

Stating this principle in terms of a formula,

$$\text{Predicted } \mu_1 = \mu_2 + (d)(\sigma) \tag{2} \leftarrow$$

The predicted mean of the population to which the experimental procedure will be applied is the known population mean plus the result of multiplying the predicted effect size by the known population standard deviation.

Using the formula for our attractiveness ratings example with a predicted effect size of .20 (a small effect size),

$$\text{Predicted } \mu_1 = \mu_2 + (d)(\sigma) = 200 + (.20)(48) = 200 + 9.60 = 209.60.$$

Using the formula for our attractiveness ratings example with a predicted effect size of .50 (a medium effect size),

$$\text{Predicted } \mu_1 = \mu_2 + (d)(\sigma) = 200 + (.50)(48) = 200 + 24.00 = 224.00.$$

Figure 10 shows, for our attractiveness ratings example, the distributions of means for small (middle curve) and medium (upper curve) predicted effect sizes, along with the power for each situation.

Sample Size

The other major influence on power, besides effect size, is the number of people in the sample studied, the sample size. Basically, the more people there are in the study, the more power there is. Indeed, in most cases, sample size matters even more than effect size (and is a factor over which the researcher usually has more control).

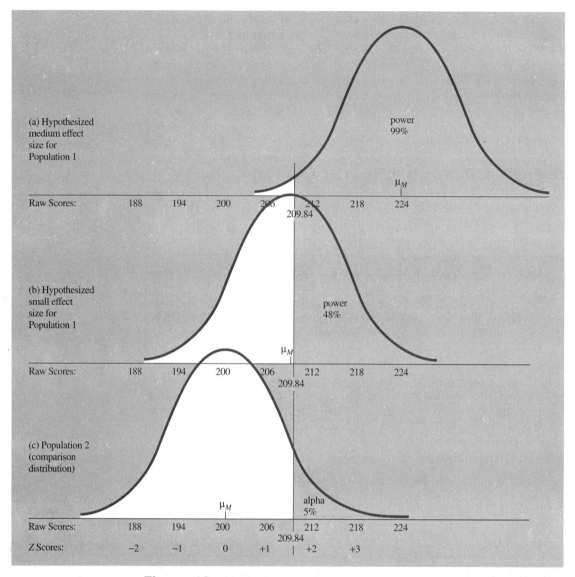

(a) Hypothesized medium effect size for Population 1

power 99%

μ_M

Raw Scores: 188   194   200   206   212   218   224
                                   209.84

(b) Hypothesized small effect size for Population 1

power 48%

μ_M

Raw Scores: 188   194   200   206   212   218   224
                                   209.84

(c) Population 2 (comparison distribution)

μ_M

alpha 5%

Raw Scores: 188   194   200   206   212   218   224
                                   209.84
Z Scores: −2   −1   0   +1   +2   +3

Figure 10 Distributions of means for the fictional study of positive personality qualities and ratings of physical attractiveness: (a) and (b) are based on predicted distributions of
populations of individuals; (c) is based on a known distribution of population of individuals.
Significance cutoff score (209.84) shown for $p < .05$, one-tailed. In this example, (a) is the
predicted distribution with a medium effect size ($d = .50$, power = 99%); and (b) is the
predicted distribution with a small effect size ($d = .20$, power = 48%).

Sample size affects power because, the larger the sample size is, the smaller
the standard deviation of the distribution of means becomes. If these distributions
have a smaller standard deviation, they are narrower. And if they are narrower, there
is less overlap between them. Figure 11 shows the situation for our attractiveness
ratings example if the study included 100 students, instead of the 64 in the original
example, with a predicted mean of 208 and a population standard deviation of 48.
The power now is 51%. (It was 37% with 64 students.) With 500 participants in the
study, power is 99% (see Figure 12).

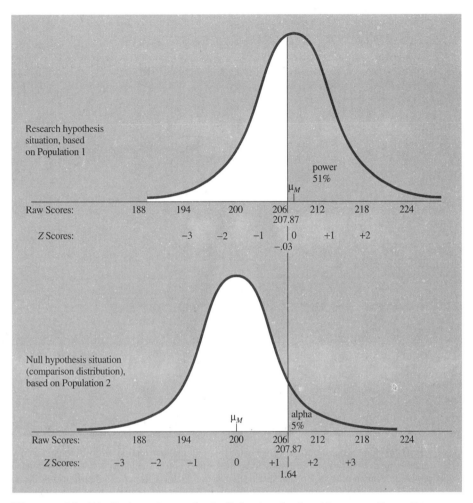

Figure 11 Distributions of means for the fictional study of positive personality qualities and ratings of physical attractiveness. Upper curve: Population 1, based on predicted population mean of 208. Bottom curve: Population 2 (the comparison distribution), based on the known population mean of 200. In this example, the sample size is 100, compared to 64 in the original example. Significance cutoff score (207.87) shown for $p < .05$, one-tailed. Power $= 51\%$. Compare with Figure 6, which had the original sample size and power was 37%.

Don't get mixed up. The distributions of means can be narrow (and thus have less overlap and more power) for two very different reasons. One reason is that the population of individuals may have a small standard deviation; this has to do with effect size. The other reason is that the sample size is large. This reason is completely separate. Sample size has nothing to do with effect size. Both effect size and sample size affect power. However, as we will see shortly, these two different influences on power lead to completely different kinds of practical steps for increasing power when planning a study.

Figuring Needed Sample Size for a Given Level of Power

When planning a study, the main reason researchers consider power is to help decide how many participants to include in the study. Sample size has an important influence on power. Thus, a researcher wants to be sure to have enough people in the study for the study to have fairly high power. (Too often, researchers carry out

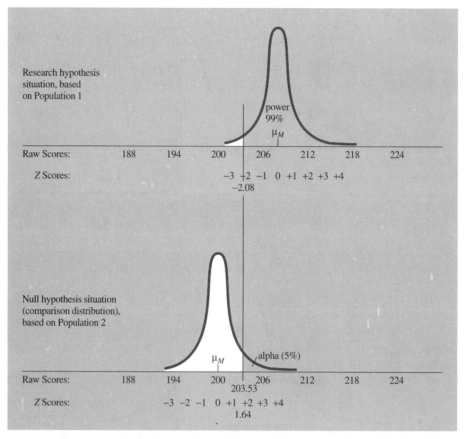

Figure 12 Distributions of means for the fictional distribution of positive personality qualities and ratings of physical attractiveness. Upper curve: Population 1, based on predicted population mean of 208. Bottom curve: Population 2 (the comparison distribution), based on the known population mean of 200. In this example, the sample size is 500, compared to 64 in the original example. Significance cutoff score (203.53) shown for $p < .05$, one-tailed. Power = 99%. Compare with Figure 6, which had the original sample size and power was 37%, and with Figure 7, which had a sample of 100 and a power of 51%.

studies in which the power is so low that it is unlikely they will get a significant result even if the research hypothesis is true. See Box 2.)

A researcher can figure out the needed number of participants by turning the steps of figuring power on their head. You begin with the level of power you want—say, 80%—and then figure how many participants you need to get that level of power. Suppose the researcher in our attractiveness ratings example was planning the study and wanted to figure out how many students to include in the sample. Let us presume that based on previous research for a situation like this, the researcher predicts a mean difference of 8 and there is a known population standard deviation of 48. In this case, it turns out that the researcher would need 222 students to have 80% power. We won't go into the computational details here. (However, if you read the Advanced Procedures section later in the chapter, you might want to try figuring this out on your own. See if you can get the same answer as we did, starting with 80% power and following the steps backward to get the number of participants needed.)

In practice, researchers use power software packages, Internet power calculators, or special power tables that tell you how many participants you need in a study

BOX 2   The Power of Typical Psychology Experiments

More than four decades ago, Jacob Cohen (1962), a psychologist specializing in statistical methods, published in the *Journal of Abnormal and Social Psychology* a now well-known analysis of the statistical power of studies. He had observed that great attention was given to significance, or the issue of whether a Type I error had been made (that the research hypothesis was mistakenly supported when in fact the null hypothesis was true; that an effect was being assumed from the results that in fact did not exist). But essentially no attention was given to the possibility of a Type II error (that a real effect had been mistakenly missed; that the null hypothesis had mistakenly not been rejected and a real effect was ignored—indeed, often treated as nonexistent—because of inconclusive results). Power was not even mentioned in the studies he was discussing.

Cohen computed the power for the results in these articles. Not being familiar with the many content areas involved, he looked at power under three assumptions of effect size: small, medium, and large. If small, he found that the studies published had only one chance in six of detecting a significant effect if the research hypothesis were true because of their small sample sizes. Not one of the studies he reviewed had a better than 50-50 chance. If he assumed a medium effect in the population, the studies had a slightly better than 50-50 chance of getting a significant result. One quarter still had less than one chance in three. Only if one assumes large effect sizes did the studies as they were designed have a good chance of reaching statistical significance. As Cohen (1962) put it, "A generation of researchers could be suitably employed in repeating interesting studies which originally used inadequate sample sizes" (p. 153).

These experiments that "failed," when in fact their hypotheses were never adequately tested, represented tremendous knowledge that may have been lost, perhaps never to be explored again. And this loss was simply because of a failure to be concerned about power—most often a failure to calculate, through a consideration of effect size, significance level, and power, the sample size that would best test the hypothesis.

In 1969, Cohen published a handbook for analyzing power in the social sciences, and a revised version appeared in 1988. Still, in an article published in 1989, Sedlmeier and Gigerenzer observed that Cohen's admonitions apparently had had no effect during the

intervening years. In fact, the power of studies in the same journal that Cohen had studied (now the *Journal of Abnormal Psychology*) had actually decreased over those years. And low power still went unnoticed. Only 2 of 64 experiments even discussed power, and these two had not estimated it. Meanwhile, in 11% of the studies published in that issue, nonsignificance was considered a confirmation of the null hypothesis. Yet Sedlmeier and Gigerenzer found that the median power in these particular studies was only 25%. Certainly, if we are to consider it valuable information in itself when results favor the null hypothesis, it can be taken that way only when power is high enough so that, if the research hypothesis was true, the study would at least have an even chance of showing it.

A number of analyses of the power of studies in specific journals and research fields suggest that many studies are still conducted with low power (e.g., Bezeau and Graves's 2001 analysis of three clinical neuropsychology journals, Clark-Carters's 1997 study of the *British Journal of Psychology,* and the 2006 study by Woods et al. of the cognitive effect of subthalamic nucleus deep brain stimulation in Parkinson's disease). However, this trend may not hold for all areas of psychological research. For example, Shen et al. (2011) reported that studies published in *The Journal of Applied Psychology* from 1995 to 2008 had, on average, enough power to identify effect sizes of interest to applied psychologists. Still, the stubborn failure by many researchers to consider power is a bit shocking. More often than not, it means that researchers are going through all their work for nothing. The odds are against their finding what they seek, even if it is true. But in an article in *American Psychologist* titled, "Things I Have Learned (So Far)," Jacob Cohen (1990) looked back over the decades philosophically:

I do not despair. I remember that W. S. Gosset, the fellow who worked in a brewery and appeared in print modestly as "Student," published the *t* test a decade before we entered World War I, and the test didn't get into the psychological statistics textbooks until after World War II.

These things take time. So, if you publish something that you think is really good, and a year or a decade or two go by and hardly anyone seems to have taken notice, remember the *t* test, and take heart. (p. 1311) to have a high level of power, given a certain predicted effect size. We provide simplified versions of power tables for each of the main hypothesis-testing procedures you learn.

Other Influences on Power

Three other factors, besides effect size and sample size, affect power.

1. **Significance level (alpha).** Less extreme significance levels (such as $p < .10$ or $p < .20$) mean more power. More extreme significance levels ($p < .01$ or $p < .001$) mean less power. Less extreme significance levels result in more power because the shaded rejection area on the lower curve is bigger. Thus, more of the area in the upper curve is shaded. More extreme significance levels result in less power because the shaded rejection region on the lower curve is smaller. Suppose in our attractiveness ratings example we had used the .01 significance level instead. The power would have dropped from 37% to only 16% (see Figure 13).

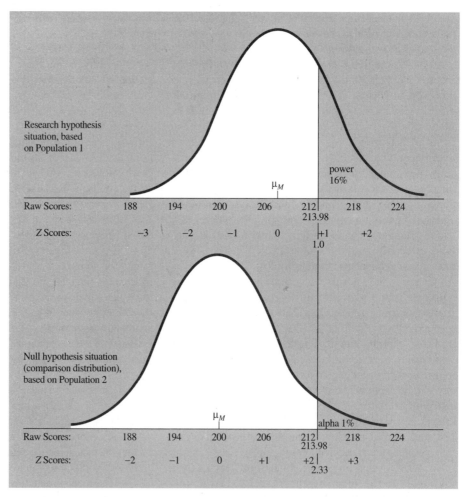

Figure 13 Distributions of means for the fictional study of positive personality qualities and ratings of physical attractiveness. Upper curve: Population 1, based on predicted population mean of 208. Bottom curve: Population 2 (the comparison distribution), based on the known population mean of 200. Significance cutoff score (213.98) now shown for $p < .01$, one-tailed. Power = 16%. Compare with Figure 6, which used a significance level of $p < .05$, one-tailed, and power was 37%.

It is important to bear in mind that using a less extreme significance level (such as $p < .10$ or $p < .20$) increases the chance of making a Type I error. Also, using an extreme significance level (such as $p < .01$ or $p < .001$) increases the chance of making a Type II error.

2. **One- versus two-tailed tests.** Using a two-tailed test makes it harder to get significance on any one tail. Thus, keeping everything else the same, power is less with a two-tailed test than with a one-tailed test. Suppose in our attractiveness ratings example we had used a two-tailed test instead of a one-tailed test (but still using 5% overall). As shown in Figure 14, power would be only 26% (compared to 37% in the original one-tailed version).

3. **Type of hypothesis-testing procedure.** Sometimes the researcher has a choice of more than one hypothesis-testing procedure to use for a particular study.

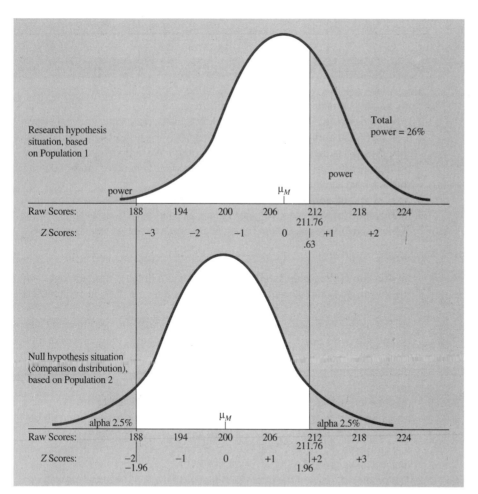

Figure 14 Distributions of means for the fictional study of positive personality qualities and ratings of physical attractiveness. Upper curve: Population 1, based on predicted population mean of 208. Bottom curve: Population 2 (the comparison distribution), based on the known population mean of 200. Significance cutoff score (211.76) now shown for $p < .05$, two-tailed. Power = 26%. Compare with Figure 6, which used a significance level of $p < .05$, one-tailed, and power was 37%.

Summary of Influences on Power

Table 4 summarizes the effects of various factors on the power of a study.

Table 4 Influences on Power

Feature of the Study	Increases Power	Decreases Power
Effect size (d) ($d = [\mu_1 - \mu_2]/\sigma$)	Large d	Small d
Effect size combines the following two features:		
Predicted difference between population means ($\mu_1 - \mu_2$)	Large differences	Small differences
Population standard deviation (σ)	Small (σ)	Large (σ)
Sample size (N)	Large N	Small N
Significance level (α)	Lenient, high α (such as .05 or .10)	Extreme, low α (such as .01 or .001)
One-tailed versus two-tailed test	One-tailed	Two-tailed
Type of hypothesis-testing procedure used	Varies	Varies

How are you doing?

1. (a) What are the two factors that determine effect size? For each factor [(b) and (c)], explain how and why it affects power.
2. In a planned study involving a standard test, the population is known to have a mean of 500 and a standard deviation of 100. The researchers predict that their planned experimental procedure will produce a large effect (that is, they predict an effect size of .80). What is the predicted mean of the population that will be given the experimental procedure?
3. (a) How and (b) why does sample size affect power?
4. (a) How and (b) why does the significance level used affect power?
5. (a) How and (b) why does using a one-tailed versus a two-tailed test affect power?

Answers

1. (a) The two factors that determine effect size are (i) the difference between the known and predicted population means and (ii) the population standard deviation.
   (b) The more difference there is between the means, the larger the effect size is, and the more power. This is because it drives the distributions of means farther apart and thus they have less overlap; so the area in the predicted distribution that is more extreme than the cutoff in the known distribution is greater.
   (c) The smaller the population standard deviation is, the larger the effect size becomes, and the greater the power. This is because it makes the distributions of means narrower and thus have less overlap. Therefore, the area in the predicted distribution that is more extreme than the cutoff in the known distribution is greater.
2. The predicted mean of the population that will be given the experimental procedure is predicted $\mu_1 = \mu_2 + (d)(\sigma) = 500 + (.80)(100) = 580$.
3. (a) The larger the sample size is, the more power there is. (b) This is because a larger sample size makes the distributions of means narrower (because the

standard deviation of a distribution of means is the square root of the result of dividing the population variance by the sample size) and thus have less overlap; so the area in the predicted distribution that is more extreme than the cutoff in the known distribution is greater.

4. (a) The more lenient the significance level is (for example, .10 versus .05), the more power there is. (b) This is because it makes the cutoff in the known distribution less extreme; so the corresponding area that is more extreme than this cutoff in the predicted distribution of means is larger.

5. (a) A study with a one-tailed test has more power (for a result in the predicted direction) than a two-tailed test. (b) This is because with a one-tailed test, the cutoff in the predicted direction in the known distribution is less extreme; so the corresponding area that is more extreme than this cutoff in the predicted distribution of means is larger. There is an added cutoff in the opposite side with a two-tailed test, but this is so far out on the distribution that it has little effect on power.

The Role of Power When Planning a Study

Determining power is very important when planning a study. If you do a study in which the power is low, even if the research hypothesis is true, the study will probably not give statistically significant results. Thus, the time and expense of carrying out the study, as it is currently planned, would probably not be worthwhile. So when the power of a planned study is found to be low, researchers look for practical ways to increase the power to an acceptable level.

What is an acceptable level of power? A widely used rule is that a study should have 80% power to be worth doing (see Cohen, 1988). Power of 80% means that there is an 80% (8 out of 10) chance that the study will produce a statistically significant result if the research hypothesis is true. Obviously, the more power the better. However, the costs of greater power, such as studying more people, often make even 80% power beyond your reach.

How can you increase the power of a planned study? In principle, you can do so by changing any of the factors summarized in Table 4. Let's consider each.

1. **Increase effect size by increasing the predicted difference between population means.** You can't just arbitrarily predict a bigger effect. There has to be a sound basis for your prediction. Thus, to increase the predicted difference, your method in carrying out the study must make it reasonable to expect a bigger effect. Consider again our example of the experiment about the impact of telling students about the positive personality characteristics of a person on the attractiveness ratings of that person. One way to increase the expected mean difference might be to use a more intense experimental procedure (such as telling students that the person has a great many positive personality qualities and does not have a single negative personality quality). A disadvantage of this approach of increasing the impact of the experimental procedure is that you may have to use an experimental procedure that is not like the one to which you want the results of your study to apply. It can also sometimes be difficult or costly. In some studies, another way to increase the expected mean difference might be to make the instructions more elaborate, spending more time explaining them, perhaps allowing time for practice, and so forth.

2. **Increase effect size by decreasing the population standard deviation.** You can decrease the population standard deviation in a planned study in at least two ways. One way is to study a population that has less variance within it than the one originally planned. For example, in a study of fifth-graders' performance on a test, you might only use fifth-graders in a particular suburban school system. The disadvantage is that your results will then apply only to the more limited population.

   Another way to decrease the population standard deviation is to use conditions of testing that are more standardized and measures that are more precise. For example, testing in a controlled laboratory setting usually makes for less variation among scores in results (meaning a smaller standard deviation). Similarly, using measures and tests with very clear wording also reduces variation. When practical, this is an excellent way to increase power, but often the study is already as rigorous as it can be.

3. **Increase the sample size.** The most straightforward way to increase power is to study more people. Of course, if you are studying billionaires who have made their fortune by founding a tech company, there is a limit to how many are available. Also, using a larger sample size often adds to the time and cost of conducting the research study. In most research situations, though, increasing sample size is the main way to change a planned study to raise its power.

4. **Use a less extreme level of significance (such as $p < .10$ or $p < .20$).** Ordinarily, the level of significance you use should be the least extreme that reasonably protects against Type I error. Normally, in psychology research, this will be $p < .05$. In general, we don't recommend using a less extreme significance level to increase power because this increases the chances of making a Type I error. Also, most psychology research journals consider $p < .05$ to be the standard cutoff for determining statistical significance. Thus, if you use a less extreme level of significance, it may be hard to get the results of your study published.

5. **Use a one-tailed test.** Whether you use a one- or two-tailed test depends on the logic of the hypothesis being studied (and in many areas of psychology one-tailed tests are frowned upon under any circumstances). As with significance level, it is rare that you have much of a choice about this factor.

Table 5 Summary of Practical Ways of Increasing the Power of a Planned Study

Feature of the Study	Practical Way of Raising Power	Disadvantages
Predicted difference between population means ($\mu_1 - \mu_2$)	Increase the intensity of experimental procedure.	May not be practical or may distort study's meaning.
Standard deviation (σ)	Use a less diverse population.	May not be available; decreases generalizability.
	Use standardized, controlled circumstances of testing or more precise measurement.	Not always practical.
Sample size (N)	Use a larger sample size.	Not always practical; can be costly.
Significance level (α)	Use a more lenient level of significance (such as .10).	Raises alpha, the probability of Type I error.
One-tailed versus two-tailed test	Use a one-tailed test.	May not be appropriate for the logic of the study.
Type of hypothesis-testing procedure	Use a more sensitive procedure.	None may be available or appropriate.

6. **Use a more sensitive hypothesis-testing procedure.** This is fine if alternatives are available. Usually, however, the researcher begins with the most sensitive method available; so little more can be done.

Table 5 summarizes some practical ways to increase the power of a planned experiment.

The Role of Power When Interpreting the Results of a Study

Understanding statistical power and what affects it is very important in drawing conclusions from the results of research.

When a Result Is Statistically Significant: Statistical Significance versus Practical Significance

You have learned that a study with a larger effect size is more likely to come out statistically significant. It also is possible for a study with a very small effect size to come out significant. This is likely to happen when a study has high power due to other factors, especially a large sample size. Consider a sample of 10,000 adults who complete a new Internet-based counseling program designed to increase their level of happiness. At the end of the program, their mean happiness score is 100.6, compared to the mean happiness score of 100 ($\sigma = 10$) for adults in general. This result would be significant at the .001 level. So the researchers would be confident that the new program increases people's level of happiness. But the effect size is a tiny .06. This means that the new program increases happiness by only a very small amount. Such a small increase is unlikely to make a noticeable difference in people's lives and thus the researchers might conclude that the effect of the program is statistically significant but has little practical significance.

Clinical and applied psychologists (as well as researchers and practitioners in other behavioral, social, and medical fields) often distinguish between a result being statistically significant versus clinically significant. The latter phrase, clinically significant, means that the result is big enough to make a difference that matters in treating people. Chambless and Hollon (1998) stated the issue quite simply: "If a treatment is to be useful to practitioners it is not enough for treatment effects to be statistically significant: they also need to be large enough to be clinically meaningful" (p. 11).

The message here is that when judging a study's results, there are two questions. First, is the result statistically significant? If it is, we consider it to be a *real effect*. The next question is whether the effect size is large enough for the result to be *useful or interesting*. This second question is especially important if the study has practical implications. (Sometimes, in a study testing purely theoretical issues, it may be enough just to be confident that there is an effect at all in a particular direction. We have more to say about this later when discussing controversies.)

If the sample was small, you can assume that a statistically significant result is probably also practically important. (That is, with a small sample size, the only way to get a statistically significant result using standard procedures is if the effect size is fairly large.) On the other hand, if the sample size is very large, you must consider the effect size directly, because it is quite possible that the effect size is too small to be useful. As Bakeman (2006) succinctly noted: ". . . statistical significance should not overly impress us. After all, even the most miniscule effect can achieve statistical significance if the sample size is large enough" (pp. 136–137). What we just said may seem a bit of a paradox. Most people assume that the more people there are in the study, the more important its results will be. In a sense, just the reverse is true. All other things being equal, if a study with only a few participants manages to be significant, that significance must be due to a large effect size. A study with a large number of people that is statistically significant may or may not have a large effect size. This is why the American Psychological Association (2009) urges researchers to include effect sizes when they describe the results of studies in research articles.

Also notice that it is usually not a good idea to compare the significance level of two studies to see which has the more important result. For example, a study with a small number of participants that is significant at the .05 level is likely to have a large effect size. However, a study with a large number of participants that is significant even at the .001 level might well have a small effect size.

The level of significance does tell you something. It tells you how confident you can be that these results could not have been found if the null hypothesis were true. The more extreme (lower) the p level is, the stronger the evidence is for a nonzero effect size (Frick, 1996). However, it is definitely *not* the case that the more extreme (smaller) the p level is, the larger the effect size will be. If two studies were identical in every other way, a more extreme (smaller) p level would mean a bigger effect. But if the studies differ, especially if they differ in sample size, p level is ambiguous in its relation to effect size. A small p level could be due to a large effect size, but it could just as well be due to a large sample size. Thus, the p level tells you about the strength of our confidence that there is a nonzero effect, but it does not tell you how big that nonzero effect is.

The most important lesson from all this is that the word *significant* in statistically significant has a very special meaning. It means that you can be pretty confident that there is some real effect. But it does *not* tell you much about whether that real effect is significant in a practical sense, that it is important or noteworthy.

Role of Power When a Result Is Not Statistically Significant

We know that a result that is not statistically significant is inconclusive. Often, however, we really would like to conclude that there is little or no difference between the populations. Can we ever do that?

Consider the relationship of power to a nonsignificant result. Suppose you carried out a study that had low power and did not get a significant result. In this situation, the result is entirely inconclusive. Not getting a significant result may have come about because the research hypothesis was false or because the study had too little power (for example, because it had too few participants).

On the other hand, suppose you carried out a study that had high power and you did not get a significant result. In this situation, it seems unlikely that the research hypothesis is true. In this situation (where there is high power), a nonsignificant result is a fairly strong argument against the research hypothesis. This does not mean that all versions of the research hypothesis are false. For example, it is possible that the research hypothesis is true and the populations are only very slightly different (and you figured power based on predicting a large difference).

In sum, a nonsignificant result from a study with low power is truly inconclusive. However, a nonsignificant result from a study with high power does suggest either that the research hypothesis is false or that there is less of an effect than was predicted when figuring power.

Summary of the Role of Power When Evaluating Results of a Study

Table 6 summarizes the role of significance and sample size in interpreting research results.

Table 6   Role of Significance and Sample Size in Interpreting Research Results

Result Statistically Significant	Sample Size	Conclusion
Yes	Small	Important result
Yes	Large	Might or might not have practical importance
No	Small	Inconclusive
No	Large	Research hypothesis probably false

How are you doing?

1. (a) What are the two basic ways of increasing the effect size of a planned study? For each [(b) and (c)], how can it be done, and what are the disadvantages?
2. What is usually the easiest way to increase the power of a planned study?
3. What are the disadvantages of increasing the power of a planned study by using (a) a more lenient significance level or (b) a one-tailed test rather than a two-tailed test?
4. Why is statistical significance not the same as practical importance?
5. You are comparing two studies in which one is significant at $p < .01$ and the other is significant at $p < .05$. (a) What can you conclude about the two studies? (b) What can you *not* conclude about the two studies?
6. When a result is significant, what can you conclude about effect size if the study had (a) a very large sample size or (b) a very small sample size?
7. When a result is not significant, what can you conclude about the truth of the research hypothesis if the study had (a) a very large sample size or (b) a very small sample size?

Answers

1. (a) The two basic ways of increasing the effect size of a planned study are: (i) increase the predicted difference between population means, and (ii) reduce the population standard deviation.
   (b) You can increase the predicted difference by making the experimental procedure more impactful. The disadvantages are that it may change the meaning of the procedure you really want to study and it might not be practical.
   (c) You can decrease the population standard deviation by using a less diverse population (which has the disadvantage of not permitting you to apply your results to a more general population) and by using more standardized procedures or more accurate measurement (which may not be practical).
2. Usually, the easiest way to increase the power of a planned study is to increase the sample size.
3. (a) Increasing the power of a planned study by using a more lenient significance level increases the probability of a Type I error (and will make it harder

to get your study results published in a journal). (b) A one-tailed test rather than a two-tailed test may not be appropriate to the logic of the study, may not be acceptable in a particular area of psychology, and if the result comes out opposite to predictions, in principle, it would have to be considered nonsignificant.

4. A statistically significant result means that you can be confident the effect would be unlikely to happen if the null hypothesis were true; it does not, however, mean that it is a large or substantial effect.

5. (a) We can be more confident for the first study than for the second study in rejecting the null hypothesis. (b) We *cannot* conclude which one has the bigger effect size.

6. (a) Given a very large sample size, the effect size could be small or large. (b) Given a very small sample size, the effect size is probably large.

7. (a) The research hypothesis is probably not true (or has a much smaller effect size than predicted). (b) You can conclude very little about the truth of the research hypothesis.

Controversy: Statistical Significance Versus Effect Size

There is an ongoing, heated controversy about the value of significance tests. Significance tests are misused in two main ways that seriously concern psychologists. One of them is that nonsignificant results are unthinkingly interpreted as showing there is in fact no effect. In light of this chapter, you should be able to see even more clearly why this mistake is a problem: nonsignificant results could be due either to little or no true effect or simply to the low power of the experiment.

We will now discuss how significance tests are often misused the other way. This misuse occurs when a significant result is unthinkingly interpreted as being an "important" result; that is, significance is confused with a large effect size.

Loosely speaking, statistical significance is about the probability that we could have gotten our pattern of results by chance if the null hypothesis were true. As Frick (1996) put it, significance is about the strength of the evidence that we have a nonzero effect. If our result is significant at the .05 level, that is pretty good evidence; if it is significant at the .01 level, that is even better evidence.

However, as we have seen in this chapter, a significant result may not be important in the sense of meaning a large effect size or having practical importance. For example, if the sample size was large, a result with a tiny effect size could be statistically significant at $p < .001$. In this situation we would be very confident that the true effect was other than zero. But the size of this true nonzero effect would still be very small. We would be concluding that we have a real, but slight, effect. Similarly, if the sample size was small enough, a result with a huge effect size might not be statistically significant at all. In this situation, our best estimate of the size of the effect is that it is large. But we would have no confidence that this effect is really there at all; it could be that the true effect is very small or even in the opposite direction.

Several researchers have observed that the word *significant* is the cause of some confusion. Fidler and colleagues (2005) noted: "Confusion of clinical and statistical significance often manifests itself in ambiguous language: Researchers describe their results as *significant* or *nonsignificant* without distinguishing whether they are speaking statistically or substantively" (p. 137). One solution might be to change the term *statistically significant,* but it is unlikely that this will happen anytime soon. Thus, it is important that when reading or conducting psychology research, you keep in mind the distinction between the special way the word *significance* is used in psychology versus the way it is used in ordinary language. Most psychologists do not see the misuses as a reason to abandon significance testing. Instead, they argue, we should make more of an effort to prevent such misuse.

However, this is not the end of the matter. Many of those who oppose significance testing argue that, even if properly used, significance testing misses the point. What psychology is fundamentally about, they argue, is effect size. It is not about whether a result is nonzero. The full version of that proposal is that researchers should really be reporting effect sizes (ideally, with confidence intervals around the effect sizes).

Proponents of emphasizing effect size argue that effect sizes provide information that can be compared to other studies and used in accumulating information over independent studies as research in a field progresses. Effect sizes are crucial ingredients in meta-analysis, and many of the proponents of effect size see meta-analysis as *the* wave of the future of psychology.

There are, however, counterarguments in favor of significance testing (and against using effect sizes alone). One such counterargument is that, when sample size is small, it is still possible for a study to come out with a large effect size just by chance. Thus, if we are interested in the result of a particular study that used a small sample, significance tests protect against taking the results of such a study too seriously. Similarly, at times a very small effect size is nevertheless important. In such a situation, it is crucial to know whether the result should be trusted as very unlikely if the null hypothesis were true. Still, many of those making these counterarguments agree that significance has been overemphasized. Most hold that significance should always be reported but that effect size should also be given more emphasis in the discussion of results.

There is yet another view: in some circumstances effect sizes are actually misleading, and we should rely only on significance testing. Chow (1988, 1996), for example, makes a distinction between applied and theoretically oriented research. In applied research, psychologists want to know the actual amount of effect a particular program has or how big is the actual difference between two particular groups. In these circumstances, Chow agrees, effect size is a good idea. However, when doing theoretical research, Chow argues, the situation is quite different. In this situation, he says, effect sizes can be irrelevant and even misleading.

Consider an experiment on the effect of familiarity on recognizing information. The point of such a study is to examine the basic way that familiarity affects information processing. A particular study might show people a series of familiar and unfamiliar words to see how many milliseconds it takes to recognize them. The effect size of such a study would tell us very little to help interpret the results of the study. It depends on all sorts of details of how the study was done, such as just how familiar and unfamiliar the words were, the specific way the words were presented, and so forth. What matters in a study like this, Chow says, is that (a) the prediction of a difference in recognizing familiar versus unfamiliar words was based on theory, (b) the results were consistent with what was predicted (as shown by the statistical significance), and (c) the theory was thus supported. On the other hand, if many studies are done using similar procedures but with meaningfully different aspects (for example, different kinds of familiarity), it may be very valuable to be able to compare effect sizes.

The current balance of the use of significance tests and effect sizes is probably just what one might expect from the points that Chow makes. In applied areas of psychology, there is an increasing emphasis on effect size. But in more theoretical areas of psychology, explicit mentions of effect size are less common. (For example, Sun et al., 2010, analyzed 1243 research articles published in mainstream journals in education and psychology between 2005 and 2007. In the education journals, which typically focus on relatively applied studies, 73% of articles included effect sizes; at the same time, psychology journals, which include many journals that emphasize more theoretical issues, only 40% included effect sizes.) Nevertheless, the prevailing view among statistics experts in psychology seems to be that, even in theoretically oriented research, the potential loss (due to misplaced emphasis) by including effect size is probably offset by, among other benefits, the usefulness to future researchers of having such information to help them in figuring power when planning their own studies and, most important, for future meta-analysts who will combine the results of this study with other related studies.

Decision Errors, Effect Size, and Power in Research Articles

Decision errors (Type I or Type II) are rarely mentioned in research articles. They might be mentioned if the study did not find statistically significant results and also had low power. In this situation, the researchers might mention that the lack of significant results may represent a Type II error. Since most academic journals generally avoid publishing such studies, you will seldom see such discussions. However, as noted earlier, it is increasingly common for articles to mention effect size, especially in applied research. For example, Morehouse and Tobler (2000) studied the effectiveness of an intervention program for "high-risk, multiproblem, inner-city, primarily African-American and Latino youth." The authors reported, "Youth who received 5–30 hours of intervention ([the high dosage group], $n = 101$) were compared with those who received 1–4 hours (the low-dosage group, $n = 31$). . . . The difference between the groups in terms of reduction in [alcohol and drug] use was highly significant. A between-groups effect size of .68 was achieved for the high-dosage group when compared with the low-dosage group." (Their wording about the study is a bit confusing; they are using *dosage* here to mean the amount of intervention, not the amount of drugs anyone was taking!) The meaning of the .68 effect size is that the group getting 5 to 30 hours of intervention was .68 standard deviations higher in terms of reduction on their drug and alcohol use than the group getting only 1 to 4 hours of the intervention. This is a medium to large effect size.

Effect size is most commonly reported in meta-analyses, in which results from different articles are being combined and compared. We have given several examples of such meta-analytic studies, including one in Box 1. As an example of how these studies actually describe results in terms of effect size, consider a meta-analysis conducted by Hostetter (2011), which tested whether gesturing when speaking improves communication. The meta-analysis included results from 38 research studies (some of which provided results for several different samples) that examined whether people's understanding of a message differs when speech is presented with gestures compared to when it is not. As noted in the article, "Cohen's d, a standardized estimate of effect size, was calculated for each unique sample in each study" (p. 304). In terms of the overall result of the meta-analysis, Hostetter reported: ". . . [T]he mean effect size was calculated as .61 . . . and shows that, across studies, gestures do have a moderate, beneficial effect on communication" (p. 306). As shown in Table 7, the article also reported the effect size for several different subgroups. The standardized effect sizes (d) are shown in the column labeled "Mean effect size." (The final column of the table presents information that is beyond our discussion of meta-analysis.) Effect sizes in the table that are significantly greater than zero at $p < .05$ are shown by an asterisk. From the table, you can see that almost all of the effect sizes were significantly greater than zero and most fell within the small to large range of Cohen's effect size conventions. Hostetter conducted additional analyses and found that the magnitude of effect size differed according to three factors. "First, effects of gesture differ as a function of gesture topic, such that gestures that depict motor actions are more communicative than those that depict abstract topics. Second, effects of gesture on communication are larger when the gestures are not completely redundant with the accompanying speech; effects are smaller when there is more overlap between the information conveyed in the 2 modalities. Third, the size of the effect of gesture is dependent on the age of the listeners, such that children benefit more from gestures than do adults" (p. 297).

Table 7   Descriptive Information About the Effect Sizes of Each Subgroup

Moderator	Subgroup	Number of samples	Mean effect size	Standard error of effect size
Speaking topic	Abstract	8	0.31	0.18
	Spatial	32	0.57*	0.10
	Motor	23	0.77*	0.11
Gesture-speech redundancy	Redundant	54	0.55*	0.07
	Nonredundant	9	1.04*	0.21
Listener's age	Adults	42	0.51*	0.09
	Children	21	0.84*	0.13
Special population	Typical	55	0.61*	0.07
	Special	8	0.66*	0.22
Speech controlled	Controlled	57	0.63*	0.07
	Not controlled	6	0.45	0.23
Gesture spontaneity	Spontaneous	24	0.47*	0.11
	Scripted	39	0.70*	0.09
Face visibility in control condition	Visible	45	0.69*	0.09
	Not Visible	18	0.46*	0.12
Dependent variable	Comprehension	28	0.59*	0.11
	Memory	20	0.56*	0.12
	Learning	15	0.72*	0.14

Note. Effect size is significantly greater than zero, at * $p < .05$.

Source: Hostetter, A. B. (2011). When do gestures communicate? A meta-analysis. *Psychological Bulletin, 137,* 297–315. Reproduced by permission of the American Psychological Association.

You mainly think about power when planning research. (Power, for example, is often a major topic in grant proposals requesting funding for research and in thesis proposals; an estimate of the power of a planned study is also usually required in an application to a university's human subjects review board for permission to conduct the planned study.) As for research articles, power is sometimes mentioned in the final section of an article where the author discusses the meaning of the results or in discussions of results of other studies. In either situation, the emphasis tends to be on the meaning of nonsignificant results. Also, when power is discussed, it may be explained in some detail because psychologists have been slow to be knowledgeable about power.

For example, Denenberg (1999), in discussing the basis for his own study, makes the following comments about a relevant previous study by Mody, Kennedy, and Brady (1997) that had not found significant results.

> [T]hey were confronted with the serious problem of having to accept the null hypothesis. . . . we can view this issue in terms of statistical power. . . . A minimal statistical power of .80 [80%] is required before one can consider the argument that the lack of significance may be interpreted as evidence that Ho [the null hypothesis] is true. To conduct a power analysis, it is necessary to specify an expected mean difference, the alpha level, and whether a one-tailed or two-tailed test will be used. Given a power requirement of .80 [80%], one can then determine the N necessary. Once these conditions are satisfied, if the experiment fails to find a significant difference, then one can make the following kind of a statement: "We have designed an experiment with a .8 probability of finding a significant difference, if such exists in the population. Because we failed to find a significant effect, we think it quite unlikely that one exists. Even if it does exist, its contribution would appear to be minimal. . . ."
>
> Mody et al. never discussed power, even though they interpreted negative findings as proof of the validity of the null hypothesis in all of their experiments. . . . Because the participants were split in this experiment, the *ns* [sample sizes] were reduced to 10 per group. Under such conditions one would not expect to find a significant difference, unless the experimental variable was very powerful. In other words, it is more difficult to reject the null hypothesis when working with small *ns* [sample sizes]. The only meaningful conclusion that can be drawn from this study is that no meaningful interpretation can be made of the lack of findings. (pp. 380–381)

Here is another example. Huey and Polo (2008) conducted a review of research on psychological treatments for a variety of emotional and behavioral problems (such as anxiety, depression, and substance abuse) among ethnic minority youth. In discussing their results, they noted the following: "[a] concern is whether sample sizes have been sufficient to test key hypotheses. The absence of difference does not necessarily indicate group equivalence, and may suggest that studies lack adequate statistical power" (p. 295). They went on to state that: "larger samples are needed to better answer key questions of theoretical interest to minority mental health researchers. Although there are other methods for maximizing statistical power (e.g., using more sensitive measures, adjusting alpha [significance] level), increasing sample size is perhaps the most practical approach" (p. 295).

Advanced Topic: Figuring Statistical Power

In this section, you will learn how to figure statistical power by hand for research situations in which the mean and standard deviation of the comparison distribution are known and a mean is predicted for the population of individuals receiving the experimental procedure. Learning to figure power by hand will greatly deepen your understanding of this important topic.

Consider again the attractiveness ratings example shown in Figure 6. The population of individuals who were not told anything about the person's positive personality qualities (Population 1) had a mean of 200 and a standard deviation of 48 (a variance of 2,304). The researcher studied a sample of 64 students. Thus, we figured the standard deviation of the distribution of means to be 6; that is, $\sigma_M = \sqrt{\dfrac{\sigma^2}{N}} = \sqrt{\dfrac{2,304}{64}} = 6$. We have presumed that the researcher predicted that telling students that the person had positive personality qualities would raise the mean attractiveness rating to 208.

You learned earlier that the power of the study is represented by the shaded region in the upper curve in Figure 6, the distribution of means for Population 1. Thus, figuring the percentage of the curve in that shaded area will tell us the power of the study. Recall that the cutoff Z score on Populations 2's distribution of means (the lower distribution in Figure 6) was 1.64. This corresponded to a raw score cutoff of 209.84. Now, look at the top curve in Figure 6, the distribution of means for Population 1. This raw score cutoff of 209.84 corresponds to a Z score on that distribution of .31; that is, $Z = (M - \mu_M)/\sigma_M = (209.84 - 208)/6 = .31$.

The normal curve table (Table A-1 in the Appendix) shows that 38% of a normal curve is in the tail region above a Z of .31. In other words, 38% of the means in predicted Population 1's distribution of means are above a Z score of .31 (and therefore 38% of the means are above a raw score of 209.84). Thus, the power of the study is 38%. (The exact percentage shown in the table is 37.83%, but we can round power to the nearest whole percentage.) Recall that we told you earlier the power for the study was 37%. This difference between 37% and 37.83% occurs due to rounding error (the 37% we reported was rounding off based on using a computer program that kept multiple decimal places).

Notice that the way we figured power had nothing to do with the actual results of the study. It was based on predictions. In fact, researchers usually figure power *before* doing the study.

Steps for Figuring Power

In our situation (the mean of a single sample compared to a known population), there are four steps to figure power:

❶ **Gather the needed information: the mean and standard deviation of Population 2's distribution of means (the comparison distribution) and the predicted mean of Population 1's distribution of means (the population that is given the experimental procedure).** The mean of Population 2's distribution of means is 200 and its standard deviation is 6. The predicted mean of Population 1's distribution of means is 208.

❷ **Figure the raw-score cutoff point on the comparison distribution to reject the null hypothesis.** For the 5% significance level, one-tailed, the Z score cutoff is +1.64. A Z of +1.64 is a raw score of 209.84. Thus, in the lower curve (the comparison distribution) in Figure 6, we have shaded the area to the right of 209.84. This is the alpha region.

❸ **Figure the Z score for this same point, but on the distribution of means for the population that receives the experimental procedure (Population 1).** On this distribution (based on the predicted scores for Population 1), a raw score of 209.84 is the same as a Z score of .31; that is, $Z = (M - \mu_M)/\sigma_M = (209.84 - 208)/6 = .31$. Thus, in the upper curve in

Figure 6, we have shaded the area to the right of .31. This shaded area shows the power of the study, the area in which a mean of an actual sample would produce statistically significant results for the study.

❹ **Using the normal curve table, figure the probability of getting a score more extreme than that Z score.**[2] The normal curve table shows 38% in the tail region above a Z of .31. The power of this study is 38%. (Beta is thus $100\% - 38\% = 62\%$.)

How are you doing?

1. In a planned study, the population is known to have a mean of 500 and a standard deviation of 100. The researchers will give the experimental treatment to 60 people and predict that the mean for those 60 will be 540. They will use the .05 significance level. (a) Figure the power of this study and (b) sketch the distributions involved. (c) What is beta in this study?

Answer

1. (a) ❶ **Gather the needed information.** The mean of the comparison distribution is 500. The predicted mean of the population that receives the experimental procedure is 540. The standard deviation of the distribution of means, σ_M, is $\sqrt{\sigma^2/N} = \sqrt{100^2/60} = 12.91$.

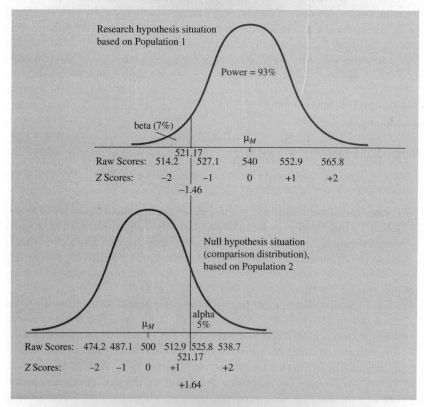

Figure 15 Distributions of means for "How are you doing?" question 1. Upper curve: Predicted. Lower curve: Known.

❷ **Figure the raw-score cutoff point on the comparison distribution to reject the null hypothesis.** A Z of $+1.64$ (for the 5% significance level) gives a raw score of 521.17.

❸ **Figure the Z score for this same point, but on the distribution of means for the population that receives the experimental procedure (Population 1).** A raw score of 521.17 on this distribution is a Z score of -1.46.

❹ **Using the normal curve table, figure the probability of getting a score more extreme than that Z score.** Power = 93% (that is, 43% between the mean and a Z of -1.46, plus 50% above the mean).

(b) The distributions involved are shown in Figure 15.

(c) Beta is 7%: that is, 100% $-$ 93% $=$ 7%.

Learning Aids

Summary

1. There are two kinds of possible decision errors in hypothesis testing. A Type I error is when a researcher rejects the null hypothesis, but the null hypothesis is actually true. A Type II error is when a researcher does not reject the null hypothesis, but the null hypothesis is actually false.

2. Effect size is a measure of the difference between population means. In the hypothesis-testing situations you learned about in this chapter, you can think of effect size as how much something changes after a specific intervention. A widely used standardized measure of effect size, Cohen's d, is the difference between population means divided by the population standard deviation. Cohen's effect size conventions consider a small effect to be .20, a medium effect to be .50, and a large effect to be .80.

3. Meta-analysis is a procedure for systematically combining and comparing effect sizes of separate studies.

4. The statistical power of a study is the probability that it will give a statistically significant result *if the research hypothesis is true.*

5. The larger the effect size is, the greater the power is. This is because the greater the difference is between means or the smaller the population standard deviation is (the two ingredients in effect size), the less overlap there is between the known and predicted populations' distributions of means. Thus, the area in the predicted distribution that is more extreme than the cutoff in the known distribution is greater. Also, if you know or predict the effect size, you can figure the predicted mean; it will be the known mean plus the result of multiplying the effect size by the population standard deviation. You can then use this to figure power.

6. The larger the sample size is, the greater the power is. This is because the larger the sample is, the smaller is the variance of the distribution of means. So, for a given effect size, there is less overlap between distributions of means.

7. Power is also affected by significance level (the more extreme, such as .01, the lower the power), by whether a one-tailed or two-tailed test is used (with less

power for a two-tailed test), and by the type of hypothesis-testing procedure used (in the occasional situation where there is a choice of procedure).

8. Statistically significant results from a study with high power (such as one with a large sample size) may not have practical importance. Results that are not statistically significant from a study with low power (such as one with a small sample size) leave open the possibility that significant results might show up if power were increased.

9. Psychologists disagree about whether statistical significance or effect size is more important in interpreting experimental results; theoretically oriented psychologists are more likely to emphasize statistical significance; applied researchers, effect size.

10. Research articles in all areas increasingly report effect size (in addition to significance), and effect sizes are almost always reported in meta-analyses. Research articles sometimes include discussions of power, especially when evaluating nonsignificant results.

11. ADVANCED TOPIC: To figure power (in the situation of a known population and a single sample), you first find the cutoff point for significance, in raw-score terms, on the comparison distribution. Based on a specific predicted mean, you can find the Z score for this cutoff on the distribution of means for the population given the experimental procedure. Power is the probability of exceeding this Z score, the area greater than this Z score, which you can find from the normal curve table.

Key Terms

decision errors	beta (β)	meta-analysis
Type I error	effect size (d)	statistical power
alpha (α)	d	power table
Type II error	effect size conventions	

Example Worked-Out Problems

Each problem below is based on a known population with a normal distribution, $\mu = 40$, and $\sigma = 10$.

Figuring the Effect Size

A sample given an experimental treatment has a mean of 37. What is the effect size? Is this approximately small, medium, or large?

Answer

$d = (\mu_1 - \mu_2)/\sigma = (37 - 40)/10 = -3/10 = -.30$; approximately small.

Find the Predicted Mean from an Effect Size

The researcher predicts a small negative effect size. What is the predicted mean?

Answer

A small negative effect size is $-.20$. Predicted $\mu_1 = \mu_2 + (d)(\sigma) = 40 + (-.20)$ $(10) = 40 + (-2) = 38$.

Outline for Writing Essays on Effect Size and Power for Studies Involving a Sample of More Than One Individual and a Known Population

1. Explain the idea of effect size as the degree of overlap between distributions, noting how this overlap is a function of mean difference and population standard deviation (and describing precisely how it is figured and why it is figured that way). If required by the question, discuss the effect size conventions.
2. Explain the idea of power as the probability of getting significant results if the research hypothesis is true. Be sure to mention that the standard minimum acceptable level of power for a research study is 80%. Explain the role played by power when you are interpreting the results of a study (both when a study is and is not significant), taking into account significance levels and sample size in relation to the likely effect size.
3. Explain the relationship between effect size and power.

Advanced Topic: Figuring Power

The researcher plans to conduct a new study with a sample of 25 and predicts that, when given a new experimental treatment, this group will have a mean of 49. The researcher plans to use the 1% significance level (one-tailed). What is the power of the planned study? What is beta in this study? Make a diagram of the distributions on which you show the areas for alpha, beta, and power.

Answer

❶ **Gather the needed information: the mean and standard deviation of Population 2's distribution of means (the comparison distribution) and the predicted mean of Population 1's distribution of means (the population given the experimental procedure).** The mean of the comparison distribution is 40. The predicted mean of the distribution of means for the population that receives the experimental procedure is 49. The standard deviation of the distribution of means, σ_M, is $\sqrt{10^2/25} = \sqrt{100/25} = \sqrt{4} = 2$.

❷ **Figure the raw-score cutoff point on the comparison distribution to reject the null hypothesis.** A Z of $+2.33$ (for the 1% significance level) gives a raw score of $40 + (2.33)(2) = 44.66$.

❸ **Figure the Z score for this same point, but on the distribution of means for the population that receives the experimental procedure (Population 1).** A raw score of 44.66 on the distribution that will be given the experimental treatment is a Z score of $(44.66 - 49)/2 = -4.34/2 = -2.17$.

❹ **Using the normal curve table, figure the probability of getting a score more extreme than that Z score.** From the normal curve table, the area between the mean and a Z of 2.17 is 48.5%. Since -2.17 is below the mean, and there is another 50% above the mean, power = 98.5%, which we can round to 99%. The distributions involved are shown in Figure 16. Beta is 100% $-$ power. Thus, beta = 100% $-$ 99% = 1%.

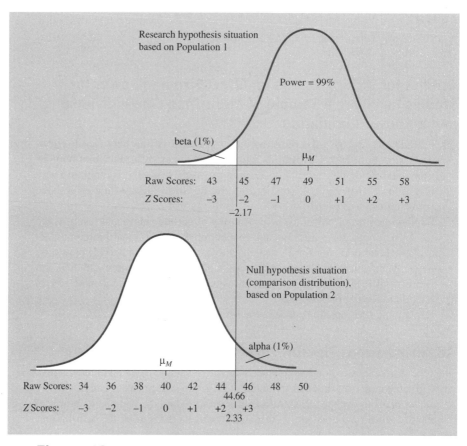

Figure 16 Distributions of means for Example Worked-Out Problem for figuring power. Upper curve: Predicted. Bottom curve: Known.

Practice Problems

These problems involve figuring. Most real-life statistics problems are done on a computer with special statistical software. Even if you have such software, do these problems by hand to ingrain the method in your mind.

All data are fictional unless an actual citation is given.

Set I

1. Define alpha and beta.
2. For each of the following studies, make a chart of the four possible correct and incorrect decisions, and explain what each would mean. Each chart should be laid out like Table 1, but put into the boxes the possible results, using the names of the variables involved in the study.
   (a) A study of whether increasing the amount of recess time improves school-children's in-class behavior.
   (b) A study of whether color-blind individuals can distinguish gray shades better than the population at large.
   (c) A study comparing individuals who have ever been in psychotherapy to the general public to see if they are more tolerant of other people's upsets than is the general population.

3. In a completed study, there is a known population with a normal distribution, $\mu = 25$, and $\sigma = 12$. What is the estimated effect size if a sample given an experimental procedure has a mean of (a) 19, (b) 22, (c) 25, (d) 30, and (e) 35? For each part, also indicate whether the effect is approximately small, medium, or large.

4. In a planned study, there is a known population with a normal distribution, $\mu = 50$, and $\sigma = 5$. What is the predicted effect size (d) if the researchers predict that those given an experimental treatment have a mean of (a) 50, (b) 52, (c) 54, (d) 56, and (e) 47? For each part, also indicate whether the effect is approximately small, medium, or large.

5. In a planned study, there is a known population with a normal distribution, $\mu = 15$, and $\sigma = 2$. What is the predicted mean if the researcher predicts (a) a small positive effect size, (b) a medium negative effect size, (c) a large positive effect size, (d) an effect size of $d = .35$, and (e) an effect size of $d = -1.50$?

6. Here is information about several possible versions of a planned experiment. Figure effect size for each; sketch the distributions involved, showing the area for alpha, beta, and power. (Assume all populations have a normal distribution.) ADVANCED TOPIC: Figure the power for each version.

	Population		Predicted Mean	N	Significance Level	One- or Two-Tailed
	μ	σ				
(a)	90	4	91	100	.05	1
(b)	90	4	92	100	.05	1
(c)	90	2	91	100	.05	1
(d)	90	4	91	16	.05	1
(e)	90	4	91	100	.01	1
(f)	90	4	91	100	.05	2

7. You read a study in which the result is significant ($p < .05$). You then look at the size of the sample. If the sample is very large (rather than very small), how should this affect your interpretation of (a) the probability that the null hypothesis is actually true and (b) the practical importance of the result? (c) Explain your answers to a person who understands hypothesis testing but has never learned about effect size or power.

8. Aron and colleagues (1997) placed strangers in pairs and asked them to talk together following a series of instructions designed to help them become close. At the end of 45 minutes, individuals privately answered some questions about how close they now felt to their partners. (The researchers combined the answers into a "closeness composite.") One key question was whether closeness would be affected by either (a) matching strangers based on their attitude agreement or (b) leading participants to believe that they had been put together with someone who would like them. The result for both agreement and expecting to be liked was that "there was no significant differences on the closeness composite" (p. 367). The researchers went on to argue that the results suggested that there was little true effect of these variables on closeness:

> There was about 90% power in this study of achieving significant effects . . . for the two manipulated variables if in fact there were a large effect of this kind ($d = .8$). Indeed, the power is about 90% for finding at least a near-significant ($p < .10$) medium-sized effect ($d = .5$). Thus, it seems unlikely that we would have obtained the present results if in fact there is more than a small effect. . . . (p. 367)

Explain this result to a person who understands hypothesis testing but has never learned about power or effect size.

9. How does each of the following affect the power of a planned study?
   (a) A larger predicted difference between the means of the populations.
   (b) A larger population standard deviation.
   (c) A larger sample size.
   (d) Using a more extreme significance level (e.g., .01 instead of .05).
   (e) Using a two-tailed test instead of a one-tailed test.
10. List two situations in which it is useful to consider power, indicating what the use is for each.
11. ADVANCED TOPIC: Based on a particular theory of creativity, a psychologist predicts that artists will be greater risk takers than the general population. The general population is normally distributed with a mean of 50 and a standard deviation of 12 on the risk-taking questionnaire this psychologist plans to use. The psychologist expects that artists will score, on the average, 55 on this questionnaire. The psychologist plans to study 36 artists and test the hypothesis at the .05 level. (a) What is the power of this study? (b) Sketch the distributions involved, showing the areas for alpha, beta, and power. (c) Explain your answer to someone who understands hypothesis testing with means of samples but has never learned about power.
12. ADVANCED TOPIC: On a memory task in which words are learned in a random order, it is known that people can recall a mean of 11 words with a standard deviation of 4 and that the distribution follows a normal curve. A cognitive psychologist, to test a theory, modifies that task so that the words are presented in a way in which words that have a related meaning are presented together. The cognitive psychologist predicts that, under these conditions, people will recall so many more words that there will be a large effect size. She plans to test this with a sample of 20 people, using the .01 significance level, two-tailed. (a) What is the power of this study? (b) Sketch the distributions involved, showing the areas for alpha, beta, and power. (c) Explain your answer to someone who understands hypothesis testing involving means of samples but has never learned about effect size or power.

Set II

13. For each of the following studies, make a chart of the four possible correct and incorrect decisions, and explain what each would mean. (Each chart should be laid out like Table 1, but put into the boxes the possible results, using the names of the variables involved in the study.)
    (a) A study of whether infants born prematurely begin to recognize faces later than do infants in general.
    (b) A study of whether high school students who receive an AIDS prevention program in their school are more likely to practice safe sex than are other high school students.
    (c) A study of whether memory for abstract ideas is reduced if the information is presented in distracting colors.
14. In a completed study, there is a known population with a normal distribution, $\mu = 122$, and $\sigma = 8$. What is the estimated effect size if a sample given an experimental procedure has a mean of (a) 100, (b) 110, (c) 120, (d) 130, and (e) 140? For each part, also indicate whether the effect is approximately small, medium, or large.

15. In a planned study, there is a known population with a normal distribution, $\mu = 0$, and $\sigma = 10$. What is the predicted effect size (d) if the researchers predict that those given an experimental treatment have a mean of (a) -8, (b) -5, (c) -2, (d) 0, and (e) 10? For each part, also indicate whether the effect is approximately small, medium, or large.

16. In a planned study, there is a known population with a normal distribution, $\mu = 17.5$, and $\sigma = 3.2$. What is the predicted mean if the researcher predicts (a) a small positive effect size, (b) a medium negative effect size, (c) an effect size of $d = .40$, (d) an effect size of $d = -.40$, (e) an effect size of $d = 3$?

17. Here is information about several possible versions of a planned experiment, each with a single sample. Figure effect size for each; then sketch the distributions involved, showing the areas for alpha, beta, and power. (Assume all populations have a normal distribution.) ADVANCED TOPIC: Figure the power for each version.

	Population		Predicted Mean	N	Significance Level	One- or Two-Tailed
	μ	σ				
(a)	0	.5	.1	50	.05	1
(b)	0	.5	.5	50	.05	1
(c)	0	.5	1.0	50	.05	1
(d)	0	.5	.5	100	.05	1
(e)	0	.5	.5	200	.05	1
(f)	0	.5	.5	400	.05	1

18. You read a study that just barely fails to be significant at the .05 level. That is, the result is not significant. You then look at the size of the sample. If the sample is very large (rather than very small), how should this affect your interpretation of (a) the probability that the null hypothesis is actually true and (b) the probability that the null hypothesis is actually false? (c) Explain your answers to a person who understands hypothesis testing but has never learned about power.

19. In the Decision Errors, Effect Size, and Power in Research Articles section earlier in this chapter, you read about a review study conducted by Huey and Polo (2008) that examined psychological treatments for clinical problems among ethnic minority youth. As part of their review, the researchers identified twenty-five studies that compared the effect of a psychotherapy treatment versus a control treatment on youths' clinical problems. They conducted a meta-analysis of the twenty-five studies and reported the results as follows:

> [T]he mean effect size was $d = .44$. Because coefficients of .20 or lower represent" "small" effects, coefficients around .50 "medium" effects, and coefficients of .80 or higher "large effects", the overall d reported here falls somewhat below the standard for a "medium" effect (Cohen, 1988). (p. 282)

Explain the purpose and results of this meta-analysis to someone who is familiar with effect size but has never heard of meta-analysis.

20. Caspi and colleagues (1997) analyzed results from a large-scale longitudinal study of a sample of children born around 1972 in Dunedin, New Zealand. As one part of their study, the researchers compared the 94 in their sample who were, at age 21, alcohol dependent (clearly alcoholic) versus the 863 who were not alcohol dependent. The researchers compared these two groups in terms of

personality test scores from when they were 18 years old. After noting that all results were significant, they reported the following results:

> Young adults who were alcohol dependent at age 21 scored lower at age 18 on Traditionalism ($d = .49$), Harm Avoidance ($d = .44$), Control ($d = .64$), and Social Closeness ($d = .40$), and higher on Aggression ($d = .86$), Alienation ($d = .66$), and Stress Reaction ($d = .50$).

Explain these results, including why it was especially important for the researchers in this study to give effect sizes, to a person who understands hypothesis testing but has never learned about effect size or power.

21. Tsang and colleagues (2009) conducted a review to examine the statistical power of studies that had compared patients' experiences of serious adverse events (such as a life-threatening medical event) during randomized controlled trials of medical treatments. They identified six studies that reported the results of statistical analyses to test whether the number of adverse effects experienced by patients receiving one medical treatment differed from the number experienced by those receiving a different treatment. Tsang et al. summarized their results as follows: "Three of the six studies included in this analysis reported non-statistically significant differences in serious adverse event rates, and concluded that there was no difference in risk despite [having power] of less than 0.37 to detect the reported differences" (p. 610). They also noted that: "A high probability of type II error may lead to erroneous clinical inference resulting in harm. The statistical power for nonsignificant tests should be considered in the interpretation of results" (p. 609). Explain the results of this review to a person who understands hypothesis testing and decision errors but has never learned about effect size or power.

22. You are planning a study that you compute as having quite low power. Name six things that you might do to increase power.

23. ADVANCED TOPIC: A psychologist is planning a study on the effect of motivation on performance on an attention task. In this task, participants try to identify target letters in a stream of letters passing by at a rapid rate. The researcher knows from long experience that, under ordinary experimental conditions, the population of students who participate in this task identify a mean of 71 of the key letters, that the standard deviation is 10, and that the distribution is approximately normal. The psychologist predicts that, if the participant is paid a dollar for each letter identified correctly, the number correctly identified will increase to 74. The psychologist plans to test 20 participants under these conditions, using the .05 level. (a) What is the power of this study? (b) Sketch the distributions involved, showing the areas for alpha, beta, and power. (c) Explain your answer to someone who understands hypothesis testing involving means of samples but has never learned about power.

24. ADVANCED TOPIC: An organizational psychologist predicts that assembly workers will have a somewhat higher level of job satisfaction if they are given a new kind of incentive program (that is, he predicts a medium effect size). On a standard job satisfaction scale, for assembly workers in this company overall, the distribution is normal, with $\mu = 82$ and $\sigma = 7$. The psychologist plans to provide the new incentive program to 25 randomly selected assembly workers. (a) What is the power of this study (using $p < .01$)? (b) Sketch the distributions involved, showing the areas for alpha, beta, and power. (c) Explain your answer to someone who understands hypothesis testing involving means of samples but has never learned about effect size or power.

Chapter Notes

1. Effect size can refer to other kinds of effects, such as the overall extent to which there is variation among means of several different populations, or the extent to which two variables in a population are related to each other.
2. This method of figuring power (which is the only method for figuring power by hand) assumes that the distributions of means are normally distributed.

Appendix: Tables

Table A-1 Normal Curve Areas: Percentage of the Normal Curve Between the Mean and the Z Scores Shown and Percentage of Scores in the Tail for the Z Scores Shown

Z	% Mean to Z	% in Tail	Z	% Mean to Z	% in Tail
.00	0.00	50.00	.30	11.79	38.21
.01	0.40	49.60	.31	12.17	37.83
.02	0.80	49.20	.32	12.55	37.45
.03	1.20	48.80	.33	12.93	37.07
.04	1.60	48.40	.34	13.31	36.69
.05	1.99	48.01	.35	13.68	36.32
.06	2.39	47.61	.36	14.06	35.94
.07	2.79	47.21	.37	14.43	35.57
.08	3.19	46.81	.38	14.80	35.20
.09	3.59	46.41	.39	15.17	34.83
.10	3.98	46.02	.40	15.54	34.46
.11	4.38	45.62	.41	15.91	34.09
.12	4.78	45.22	.42	16.28	33.72
.13	5.17	44.83	.43	16.64	33.36
.14	5.57	44.43	.44	17.00	33.00
.15	5.96	44.04	.45	17.36	32.64
.16	6.36	43.64	.46	17.72	32.28
.17	6.75	43.25	.47	18.08	31.92
.18	7.14	42.86	.48	18.44	31.56
.19	7.53	42.47	.49	18.79	31.21
.20	7.93	42.07	.50	19.15	30.85
.21	8.32	41.68	.51	19.50	30.50
.22	8.71	41.29	.52	19.85	30.15
.23	9.10	40.90	.53	20.19	29.81
.24	9.48	40.52	.54	20.54	29.46
.25	9.87	40.13	.55	20.88	29.12
.26	10.26	39.74	.56	21.23	28.77
.27	10.64	39.36	.57	21.57	28.43
.28	11.03	38.97	.58	21.90	28.10
.29	11.41	38.59	.59	22.24	27.76

(continued)

Table A-1 (continued)

Z	% Mean to Z	% in Tail	Z	% Mean to Z	% in Tail
.60	22.57	27.43	1.03	34.85	15.15
.61	22.91	27.09	1.04	35.08	14.92
.62	23.24	26.76	1.05	35.31	14.69
.63	23.57	26.43	1.06	35.54	14.46
.64	23.89	26.11	1.07	35.77	14.23
.65	24.22	25.78	1.08	35.99	14.01
.66	24.54	25.46	1.09	36.21	13.79
.67	24.86	25.14	1.10	36.43	13.57
.68	25.17	24.83	1.11	36.65	13.35
.69	25.49	24.51	1.12	36.86	13.14
.70	25.80	24.20	1.13	37.08	12.92
.71	26.11	23.89	1.14	37.29	12.71
.72	26.42	23.58	1.15	37.49	12.51
.73	26.73	23.27	1.16	37.70	12.30
.74	27.04	22.96	1.17	37.90	12.10
.75	27.34	22.66	1.18	38.10	11.90
.76	27.64	22.36	1.19	38.30	11.70
.77	27.94	22.06	1.20	38.49	11.51
.78	28.23	21.77	1.21	38.69	11.31
.79	28.52	21.48	1.22	38.88	11.12
.80	28.81	21.19	1.23	39.07	10.93
.81	29.10	20.90	1.24	39.25	10.75
.82	29.39	20.61	1.25	39.44	10.56
.83	29.67	20.33	1.26	39.62	10.38
.84	29.95	20.05	1.27	39.80	10.20
.85	30.23	19.77	1.28	39.97	10.03
.86	30.51	19.49	1.29	40.15	9.85
.87	30.78	19.22	1.30	40.32	9.68
.88	31.06	18.94	1.31	40.49	9.51
.89	31.33	18.67	1.32	40.66	9.34
.90	31.59	18.41	1.33	40.82	9.18
.91	31.86	18.14	1.34	40.99	9.01
.92	32.12	17.88	1.35	41.15	8.85
.93	32.38	17.62	1.36	41.31	8.69
.94	32.64	17.36	1.37	41.47	8.53
.95	32.89	17.11	1.38	41.62	8.38
.96	33.15	16.85	1.39	41.77	8.23
.97	33.40	16.60	1.40	41.92	8.08
.98	33.65	16.35	1.41	42.07	7.93
.99	33.89	16.11	1.42	42.22	7.78
1.00	34.13	15.87	1.43	42.36	7.64
1.01	34.38	15.62	1.44	42.51	7.49
1.02	34.61	15.39	1.45	42.65	7.35

Table A-1 (continued)

Z	% Mean to Z	% in Tail	Z	% Mean to Z	% in Tail
1.46	42.79	7.21	1.88	46.99	3.01
1.47	42.92	7.08	1.89	47.06	2.94
1.48	43.06	6.94	1.90	47.13	2.87
1.49	43.19	6.81	1.91	47.19	2.81
1.50	43.32	6.68	1.92	47.26	2.74
1.51	43.45	6.55	1.93	47.32	2.68
1.52	43.57	6.43	1.94	47.38	2.62
1.53	43.70	6.30	1.95	47.44	2.56
1.54	43.82	6.18	1.96	47.50	2.50
1.55	43.94	6.06	1.97	47.56	2.44
1.56	44.06	5.94	1.98	47.61	2.39
1.57	44.18	5.82	1.99	47.67	2.33
1.58	44.29	5.71	2.00	47.72	2.28
1.59	44.41	5.59	2.01	47.78	2.22
1.60	44.52	5.48	2.02	47.83	2.17
1.61	44.63	5.37	2.03	47.88	2.12
1.62	44.74	5.26	2.04	47.93	2.07
1.63	44.84	5.16	2.05	47.98	2.02
1.64	44.95	5.05	2.06	48.03	1.97
1.65	45.05	4.95	2.07	48.08	1.92
1.66	45.15	4.85	2.08	48.12	1.88
1.67	45.25	4.75	2.09	48.17	1.83
1.68	45.35	4.65	2.10	48.21	1.79
1.69	45.45	4.55	2.11	48.26	1.74
1.70	45.54	4.46	2.12	48.30	1.70
1.71	45.64	4.36	2.13	48.34	1.66
1.72	45.73	4.27	2.14	48.38	1.62
1.73	45.82	4.18	2.15	48.42	1.58
1.74	45.91	4.09	2.16	48.46	1.54
1.75	45.99	4.01	2.17	48.50	1.50
1.76	46.08	3.92	2.18	48.54	1.46
1.77	46.16	3.84	2.19	48.57	1.43
1.78	46.25	3.75	2.20	48.61	1.39
1.79	46.33	3.67	2.21	48.64	1.36
1.80	46.41	3.59	2.22	48.68	1.32
1.81	46.49	3.51	2.23	48.71	1.29
1.82	46.56	3.44	2.24	48.75	1.25
1.83	46.64	3.36	2.25	48.78	1.22
1.84	46.71	3.29	2.26	48.81	1.19
1.85	46.78	3.22	2.27	48.84	1.16
1.86	46.86	3.14	2.28	48.87	1.13
1.87	46.93	3.07	2.29	48.90	1.10

(continued)

Table A-1 (continued)

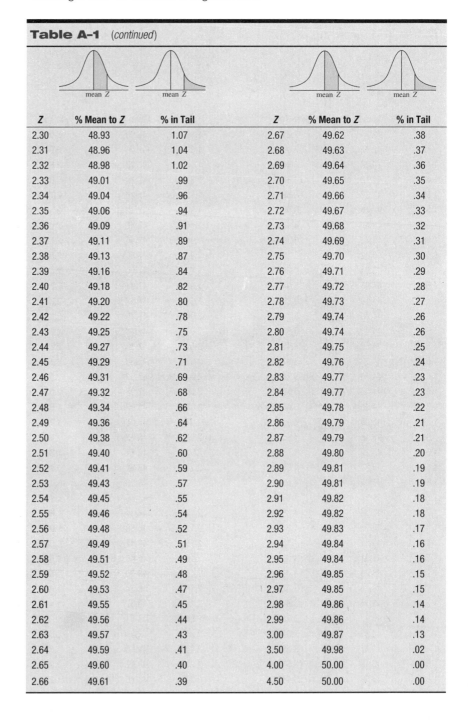

Z	% Mean to Z	% in Tail	Z	% Mean to Z	% in Tail
2.30	48.93	1.07	2.67	49.62	.38
2.31	48.96	1.04	2.68	49.63	.37
2.32	48.98	1.02	2.69	49.64	.36
2.33	49.01	.99	2.70	49.65	.35
2.34	49.04	.96	2.71	49.66	.34
2.35	49.06	.94	2.72	49.67	.33
2.36	49.09	.91	2.73	49.68	.32
2.37	49.11	.89	2.74	49.69	.31
2.38	49.13	.87	2.75	49.70	.30
2.39	49.16	.84	2.76	49.71	.29
2.40	49.18	.82	2.77	49.72	.28
2.41	49.20	.80	2.78	49.73	.27
2.42	49.22	.78	2.79	49.74	.26
2.43	49.25	.75	2.80	49.74	.26
2.44	49.27	.73	2.81	49.75	.25
2.45	49.29	.71	2.82	49.76	.24
2.46	49.31	.69	2.83	49.77	.23
2.47	49.32	.68	2.84	49.77	.23
2.48	49.34	.66	2.85	49.78	.22
2.49	49.36	.64	2.86	49.79	.21
2.50	49.38	.62	2.87	49.79	.21
2.51	49.40	.60	2.88	49.80	.20
2.52	49.41	.59	2.89	49.81	.19
2.53	49.43	.57	2.90	49.81	.19
2.54	49.45	.55	2.91	49.82	.18
2.55	49.46	.54	2.92	49.82	.18
2.56	49.48	.52	2.93	49.83	.17
2.57	49.49	.51	2.94	49.84	.16
2.58	49.51	.49	2.95	49.84	.16
2.59	49.52	.48	2.96	49.85	.15
2.60	49.53	.47	2.97	49.85	.15
2.61	49.55	.45	2.98	49.86	.14
2.62	49.56	.44	2.99	49.86	.14
2.63	49.57	.43	3.00	49.87	.13
2.64	49.59	.41	3.50	49.98	.02
2.65	49.60	.40	4.00	50.00	.00
2.66	49.61	.39	4.50	50.00	.00

Answers to Set I Practice Problems

Chapter 6

1. *Alpha* is the probability of rejecting the null hypothesis when the null hypothesis is actually true (that is, alpha is the probability of making a Type I error). *Beta* is the probability of failing to reject the null hypothesis when in fact the null hypothesis is false (that is, beta is the probability of making a Type II error).

2. (a)

		Real Situation	
		Null Hypothesis True	**Research Hypothesis True**
Research Hypothesis Supported (Reject null)		*Type I Error* Decide more recess time improves behavior, but it really doesn't	*Correct Decision* Decide more recess time improves behavior, and it really does
Study Inconclusive (Do not reject null)		*Correct Decision* Decide effect of recess time on behavior is not shown in this study; actually more recess time doesn't improve behavior	*Type II Error* Decide effect of recess time on behavior is not shown in this study; actually more recess time improves behavior

(Left side label: Conclusion from Hypothesis Testing)

(b) and (c) Answers are similar to those of question 2a.

3. (a) $d = (\mu_1 - \mu_2)/\sigma = (19 - 25)/12 = -.50$, medium; (b) $-.25$. small; (c) 0, no effect; (d) .42, medium; (e) .83, large.

4. (a) $d = (\mu_1 - \mu_2)/\sigma = (50 - 50)/5 = 0$, no effect; (b) .40, medium; (c) .80, large; (d) 1.20, large; (e) $-.60$, medium.

5. A small positive effect size is .20. Predicted $\mu_1 = \mu_2 + (d)(\sigma) = 15 + (.20)(2) = 15.4$; (b) 14; (c) 16.6; (d) 15.7; (e) 12.

6.

	Z Needed for Significance	σ_M	**Score for Significance**
(a)	1.64	.4	90.66
(b)	1.64	.4	90.66
(c)	1.64	.2	90.33
(d)	1.64	1.0	91.64
(e)	2.33	.4	90.93
(f)	1.96	.4	90.78

	Z for Significance on the Predicted Population	**Beta**	**Power**	**Effect Size**
(a)	$(90.66 - 91)/.4 = -.85$	.20	.80	.25
(b)	$(90.66 - 92)/.4 = -3.35$	<.01	>.99	.50
(c)	$(90.33 - 91)/.2 = -3.35$	<.01	>.99	.50
(d)	$(91.64 - 91)/1 = .64$	.74	.26	.25
(e)	$(90.93 - 91)/.4 = -.18$	.43	.57	.25
(f)	$(90.78 - 91)/.4 = -.55$	.29	.71	.25

Drawing of overlapping distributions for part (a) follows.

7. (a) Not affected; (b) possibly of small importance; (c) regarding situation (a), the significance tells you the probability of getting your results if the null hypothesis is true; sample size is already taken into account in figuring the significance. Regarding situation (b), it is possible to get a significant result with a large sample even when the actual practical effect is slight, such as when the mean of your sample (which is your best estimate of the mean of the population that gets the experimental treatment) is only slightly higher than the mean of the known population. This is possible because significance is based on the difference between the mean of your sample and the known population mean divided by the standard deviation of the distribution of means. If the sample size is very large, then the standard deviation of the distribution of means is very small (because it is figured by taking the square root of the result of dividing the population variance by the sample size). Thus, even a small difference between the means when divided by a very small denominator can give a large overall result, making the study significant.

8. Power is the chance of rejecting the null hypothesis if the research hypothesis is true. In other words, the power of a study represents the likelihood that you will get a statistically significant result in your study, if in fact the research hypothesis is true. Ideally, a study should have power of 80% or more. If a study has low power and does not get a statistically significant result, the result of the study is entirely inconclusive. This is because it is not clear whether the nonsignificant result is due to the low power of the study or because the research hypothesis is in fact false.

Effect size can be thought of as the degree to which populations do not overlap. The larger the effect size is, the greater the power will be. As noted by Aron and colleagues, their study had a high level of power (about 90%) for detecting both large and medium-sized effects. Given this high level of power, the researchers were able to conclude that the most likely reason for the nonsignificant study results is that the research hypothesis is in fact false. As the researchers noted, with such a high level of power, it is very unlikely that the results of the study would be nonsignificant if there were in fact a medium-sized or large effect in the population. Since smaller effect sizes are associated with lower power, the researchers were careful not to rule out the possibility that there is in fact a small effect in the population (which may not have been detected in the study due to the lower power for identifying a small effect size).

9. (a) Increases power; (b) decreases power; (c) increases power; (d) decreases power; (e) decreases power.

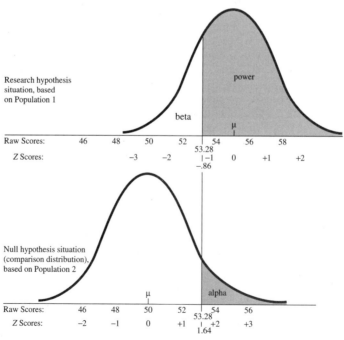

10. (i) When planning an experiment, to permit changes of various kinds (or even abandon the project) if power is too low (or possibly to make the study less costly, for example by reducing the number of participants, if power is higher than reasonably needed). (ii) After a study is done that had nonsignificant results, to evaluate whether the result should be attributed to the null hypothesis being true (in the high-power situation) or to inadequate power so that it is still reasonable to think that future research might have a chance of being significant. (Also, in the case of a significant result with a large sample, if power is very high, this suggests that a small effect size is possible, so that, although the result is significant, it may not be very important.)

11. (a) ❶ $\sigma_M = 2$; ❷ significance cutoff: $Z = 1.64$; raw $= 50 + (1.64)(2) = 53.28$; ❸ corresponding Z on predicted distribution $= (53.28 - 55)/2 = -.86$; ❹ from Z table, power $= .81$, beta $= .19$.
(b)
(c) Power is the chance of rejecting the null hypothesis if the research hypothesis is true. To find power, you first need the standard deviation of the comparison distribution (2 here) and the cutoff to reject the null hypothesis in raw score terms (this is a one-tailed test at the .05 level; so it is a Z of 1.64, which for this distribution's mean and standard deviation is 53.28). You also have to be able to assume that the distributions of both the known population (Population 2) and the distribution for the population based on the research hypothesis (Population 1) follow a normal curve and have the same variance. Then comes the power figuring. The researcher hypothesizes that the mean of the population of artists (Population 1) is 55. The distribution of means from this population would be normal with mean $= 55$ and $\sigma_M = 2$. We already figured that any mean above 53.28 will be significant in terms of the comparison distribution. But a score of 53.28 has a Z score of only $-.86$ on the distribution of means based on the researcher's hypothesis. Using the normal curve table, 81% is above $-.86$. Assuming that the research's predictions are correct, there is an 81% chance that a sample of 36 artists will produce a result high enough to reject the null hypothesis. That is, power is 81%.

12. (a) ❶ predicted $\mu_1 = \mu_2 + (d)(\sigma) = 11 + (.80)(4) = 14.2$. ❷ $\sigma_M = .89$; significance cutoff: $Z = 2.58$; raw $= 11 + (2.58)(.89) = 13.3$; ❸ corresponding Z on predicted distribution $= (13.3 - 14.2)/.89 = -1.01$; ❹ from Z table, power $= .84$, beta $= .16$. (b) and (c) are similar to questions 11b and c, with an additional explanation of effect size.

Chapter 7
Introduction to *t* Tests

Chapter 7

Introduction to *t* Tests

Single Sample and Dependent Means

At this point, you may think you know all about hypothesis testing. Here's a surprise: what you know will not help you much as a researcher. Why? The procedures for testing hypotheses described up to this point were, of course, absolutely necessary for what you will now learn. However, these procedures involved comparing a group of scores to a *known population*. In real research practice, you often compare two or more groups of scores to each other, without any direct information about populations. For example, you may have two scores for each person in a group of people, such as scores on an anxiety test before and after psychotherapy or number of familiar versus unfamiliar words recalled in a memory experiment. Or you might have one score per person for two groups of people, such as an experimental group and a control group in a study of the effect of sleep loss on problem solving, or comparing the self-esteem test scores of a group of 10-year-old girls to a group of 10-year-old boys.

These kinds of research situations are among the most common in psychology, where usually the only information available is from samples. Nothing is known about the populations that the samples are supposed to come from. In particular, the researcher does not know the variance of the populations involved, which is a crucial ingredient in Step ❷ of the hypothesis-testing process (determining the characteristics of the comparison distribution).

In this chapter, we first look at the solution to the problem of not knowing the population variance by focusing on a special situation: comparing the mean of a single sample to a population with a known mean but an unknown variance. Then, after describing how to handle this problem of not knowing the population variance, we go on to consider the situation in which there is no known population at all—the situation in which all we have are two scores for each of a number of people.

The hypothesis-testing procedures you learn in this chapter, those in which the population variance is unknown, are examples of *t* **tests**. The *t* test is sometimes called "Student's *t*" because its main principles were originally developed by William S. Gosset, who published his research articles anonymously using the name "Student" (see Box 1).

The *t* Test for a Single Sample

Let's begin with an example. Suppose your college newspaper reports an informal survey showing that students at your college study an average of 17 hours per week. However, you think that the students in your dormitory study much more than that. You randomly pick 16 students from your dormitory and ask them on an anonymous questionnaire how much they study each day. Your result is that these 16 students study an average of 21 hours per week. Should you conclude that students in your dormitory study more than the college average? Or should you conclude that your results are close enough to the college average that the small difference of 4 hours might well be due to your having picked, purely by chance, 16 of the more studious residents in your dormitory?

In this example you have scores for a sample of individuals and you want to compare the mean of this sample to a population for which you know the mean but not the variance. Hypothesis testing in this situation is called a *t* **test for a single sample**. (It is also called a *one-sample t test*.) The *t* test for a single sample works basically the same way as the *Z* test. Consider an example where you have scores for a sample of individuals (such as a group of 64 students rating the attractiveness of a person in a photograph after being told that the person has positive personality qualities) and you want to compare the mean of this sample to a population of students not told about the person's personality qualities). In this case, you know both the mean and variance of the general population to which you are going to compare your sample. In the situations we are now going to consider, everything is the same, but you don't know the population variance. This presents two important new wrinkles affecting the details of how you carry out two of the steps of the hypothesis-testing process.

The first important new wrinkle is in Step ❷. Because the population variance is not known, you have to estimate it. So the first new wrinkle we consider is how to estimate an unknown population variance. The other important new wrinkle affects both Steps ❷ and ❸. When the population variance has to be estimated, the shape of the comparison distribution is not quite a normal curve; so the second new wrinkle

***t* test** hypothesis-testing procedure in which the population variance is unknown; it compares *t* scores from a sample to a comparison distribution called a *t* distribution.

***t* test for a single sample** hypothesis-testing procedure in which a sample mean is being compared to a known population mean and the population variance is unknown.

BOX 1   William S. Gosset, Alias "Student": Not a Mathematician, But a Practical Man

The Granger Collection

William S. Gosset graduated from Oxford University in 1899 with degrees in mathematics and chemistry. It happened that in the same year the Guinness brewers in Dublin, Ireland, were seeking a few young scientists to take a first-ever scientific look at beer making. Gosset took one of these jobs and soon had immersed himself in barley, hops, and vats of brew.

The problem was how to make beer of a consistently high quality. Scientists such as Gosset wanted to make the quality of beer less variable, and they were especially interested in finding the cause of bad batches. A proper scientist would say, "Conduct experiments!" But a business such as a brewery could not afford to waste money on experiments involving large numbers of vats, some of which any brewer worth his hops knew would fail. So Gosset was forced to contemplate the probability of, say, a certain strain of barley producing terrible beer when the experiment could consist of only a few batches of each strain. Adding to the problem was that he had no idea of the variability of a given strain of barley—perhaps some fields planted with the same strain grew better barley. (Does this sound familiar? Poor Gosset, like today's psychologists, had no idea of his population's variance.)

Gosset was up to the task, although at the time only he knew that. To his colleagues at the brewery, he was

a professor of mathematics and not a proper brewer at all. To his statistical colleagues, mainly at the Biometric Laboratory at University College in London, he was a mere brewer and not a proper mathematician.

So Gosset discovered the *t* distribution and invented the *t* test—simplicity itself (compared to most of statistics)—for situations when samples are small and the variability of the larger population is unknown. However, the Guinness brewery did not allow its scientists to publish papers, because one Guinness scientist had revealed brewery secrets. To this day, most statisticians call the *t* distribution "Student's *t*" because Gosset wrote under the anonymous name "Student." A few of his fellow statisticians knew who "Student" was, but apparently meetings with others involved the secrecy worthy of a spy novel. The brewery learned of his scientific fame only at his death, when colleagues wanted to honor him.

In spite of his great achievements, Gosset often wrote in letters that his own work provided "only a rough idea of the thing" or so-and-so "really worked out the complete mathematics." He was remembered as a thoughtful, kind, humble man, sensitive to others' feelings. Gosset's friendliness and generosity with his time and ideas also resulted in many students and younger colleagues making major breakthroughs based on his help.

To learn more about William Gosset, go to *http://www-history.mcs.st-andrews.ac.uk/Biographies/Gosset.html*.

Sources: Peters (1987); Salsburg (2001); Stigler (1986); Tankard (1984).

we consider is the shape of the comparison distribution (for Step ❷) and how to use a special table to find the cutoff (Step ❸) on what is a slightly differently shaped distribution.

Let's return to the amount of studying example. Step ❶ of the hypothesis-testing procedure is to restate the problem as hypotheses about populations. There are two populations:

Population 1: The kind of students who live in your dormitory.
Population 2: The kind of students in general at your college.

The research hypothesis is that Population 1 students study more than Population 2 students; the null hypothesis is that Population 1 students do not study more than Population 2 students.

Step ❷ is to determine the characteristics of the comparison distribution. In this example, its mean will be 17, what the survey found for students at your college generally (Population 2).

The next part of Step ❷ is finding the variance of the distribution of means. Now you face a problem. Up to now in this text, you have always known the variance of the population of individuals. Using that variance, you then figured the variance of the distribution of means. However, in the present example, the variance of the number of hours studied for students at your college (the Population 2 students) was not reported in the newspaper article. So you email the paper. Unfortunately, the reporter did not figure the variance, and the original survey results are no longer available. What to do?

Basic Principle of the *t* Test: Estimating the Population Variance from the Sample Scores

If you do not know the variance of the population of individuals, you can *estimate* it from what you do know—the scores of the people in your sample.

In the logic of hypothesis testing, you consider the group of people you study to be a random sample from a particular population. The variance of this sample ought to reflect the variance of that population. If the scores in the population have *a lot* of variation, then the scores in a sample randomly selected from that population should also have *a lot* of variation. If the population has *very little* variation, the scores in a sample from that population should also have *very little* variation. Thus, it should be possible to use the variation among the scores in the sample to make an informed guess about the spread of the scores in the population. That is, you could figure the variance of the sample's scores, and that should be *similar* to the variance of the scores in the population. (See Figure 1.)

There is, however, one small hitch. The variance of a sample will generally be slightly smaller than the variance of the population from which it is taken. For this reason, the variance of the sample is a **biased estimate** of the population variance.[1]

biased estimate   estimate of a population parameter that is likely systematically to overestimate or underestimate the true value of the population parameter. For example, SD^2 would be a biased estimate of the population variance (it would systematically underestimate it).

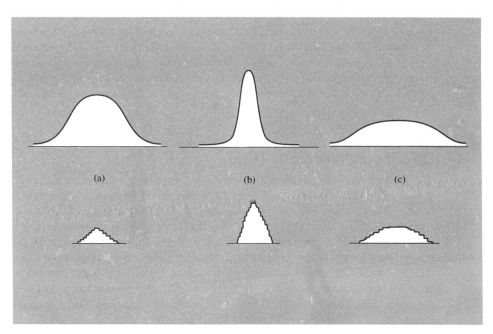

Figure 1   The variation in a sample's scores (shown in the lower distributions) is similar to the variation of scores in the population from which the sample is taken (shown in the upper distributions).

It is a *biased estimate* because it consistently slightly *underestimates* the actual variance of the population. (For example, if a population has a variance of 180, a typical sample of 20 scores might have a variance of only 171.) If we used a biased estimate of the population variance in our research studies, our results would not be accurate. Therefore, we need to identify an *unbiased estimate* of the population variance.

Fortunately, you can figure an **unbiased estimate of the population variance** by slightly changing the ordinary variance formula. The ordinary variance formula is the sum of the squared deviation scores divided by the number of scores. The changed formula still starts with the sum of the squared deviation scores, but divides this by the number of scores *minus 1*. Dividing by a slightly smaller number makes the result slightly larger. Dividing by the number of scores minus 1 makes the variance you get just enough larger to make it an *unbiased estimate* of the population variance. (This unbiased estimate is our best estimate of the population variance. However, it is still an *estimate,* so it is unlikely to be exactly the same as the true population variance. But what we can count on is that our unbiased estimate of the population variance is equally likely to be too high as it is to be too low. This is what makes our estimate *unbiased.*)

The symbol we will use for the unbiased estimate of the population variance is S^2. The formula is the usual variance formula, but now dividing by $N - 1$:

The estimated population variance is the sum of the squared deviation scores divided by the number of scores minus 1.

$$S^2 = \frac{\sum(X - M)^2}{N - 1} = \frac{SS}{N - 1} \tag{1}$$

The estimated population standard deviation is the square root of the estimated population variance.

$$S = \sqrt{S^2} \tag{2}$$

Let's return again to the example of hours spent studying and figure the estimated population variance from the sample's 16 scores. First, you figure the sum of squared deviation scores. (Subtract the mean from each of the scores, square those deviation scores, and add them.) Presume in our example that this comes out to 694 (that is, $SS = 694$). To get the estimated population variance, you divide this sum of squared deviation scores by the number of scores minus 1. In this example, you divide 694 by $16 - 1$; 694 divided by 15 comes out to 46.27. In terms of the formula,

$$S^2 = \frac{\sum(X - M)^2}{N - 1} = \frac{SS}{N - 1} = \frac{694}{16 - 1} = \frac{694}{15} = 46.27$$

Degrees of Freedom

The number you divide by (the number of scores minus 1) to get the estimated population variance has a special name. It is called the **degrees of freedom** (and is abbreviated as *df*). It has this name because it is the number of scores in a sample that are "free to vary." The idea is that, when figuring the variance, you first have to know the mean. If you know the mean and all but one of the scores in the sample, you can figure out the one you don't know with a little arithmetic. For example, suppose we know that two scores have a mean of 6 and one of the scores is a 4. The other score has to be an 8 (since the mean of 4 and 8 is 6). Even though there are two scores, if we know the mean, the number of scores "free to vary" is just one. So in this kind of situation the degrees of freedom are the number of scores minus 1. In terms of a formula,

Table 1   Summary of Different Types of Standard Deviations and Variances

Statistical Term	Symbol
Sample standard deviation	SD
Population standard deviation	σ
Estimated population standard deviation	S
Standard deviation of the distribution of means (based on an estimated population variance)	S_M
Sample variance	SD^2
Population variance	σ^2
Estimated population variance	S^2
Variance of the distribution of means (based on an estimated population variance)	S_M^2

The degrees of freedom are the number of scores in the sample minus 1.

$$df = N - 1 \tag{3}$$

df is the degrees of freedom.

In our example, $df = 16 - 1 = 15$. (In some situations, the degrees of freedom are figured a bit differently. This is because in those situations, the number of scores free to vary is different. For all the situations you learn about in this chapter, $df = N - 1$.)

The formula for the estimated population variance is often written using df instead of $N - 1$:

$$S^2 = \frac{\Sigma(X - M)^2}{df} = \frac{SS}{df} \qquad \textbf{(4)}$$

The estimated population variance is the sum of squared deviations divided by the degrees of freedom.

The Standard Deviation of the Distribution of Means

When you have a sample of more than one, the comparison distribution is a *distribution of means,* and the variance of a distribution of means is the variance of the population of individuals divided by the sample size. You have just estimated the variance of the population. Thus, you can estimate the variance of the distribution of means by dividing the estimated population variance by the sample size. The standard deviation of the distribution of means is the square root of its variance. Stated as formulas,

$$S_M^2 = \frac{S^2}{N} \qquad \textbf{(5)}$$

The variance of the distribution of means based on an estimated population variance is the estimated population variance divided by the number of scores in the sample.

$$S_M = \sqrt{S_M^2} \qquad \textbf{(6)}$$

The standard deviation of the distribution of means based on an estimated population variance is the square root of the variance of the distribution of means based on an estimated population variance.

Note that, with an estimated population variance, the symbols for the variance and standard deviation of the distribution of means use S instead of σ.

In our example, the sample size was 16 and we worked out the estimated population variance to be 46.27. The variance of the distribution of means, based on that estimate, will be 2.89. That is, 46.27 divided by 16 equals 2.89. The standard deviation is 1.70, the square root of 2.89. In terms of the formulas,

$$S_M^2 = \frac{S^2}{N} = \frac{46.27}{16} = 2.89$$

$$S_M = \sqrt{S_M^2} = \sqrt{2.89} = 1.70$$

At this point, you have now seen several different types of standard deviation and variance (that is, for a sample, for a known population, and unbiased estimates when the population standard deviation or variance are not known), and each of these types has used a different symbol. To help you keep them straight, a summary of the types of standard deviation and variance is shown in Table 1.

The Shape of the Comparison Distribution When Using an Estimated Population Variance: The *t* Distribution

It can be recalled that when the population distribution follows a normal curve, the shape of the distribution of means will also be a normal curve. However, this changes when you do hypothesis testing with an estimated population variance. When you are using an estimated population variance, you have less true information and more room for error. The mathematical effect is that there are likely to be

TIP FOR SUCCESS

Be sure that you fully understand the difference between S^2 and S_M^2. These terms look similar, but they are quite different. S^2 is the estimated variance of the population of individuals. S_M^2 is the estimated variance of the distribution of means (based on the estimated variance of the population of individuals, S^2).

slightly more extreme means than in an exact normal curve. Further, the smaller your sample size, the bigger this tendency. This is because, with a smaller sample size, your estimate of the population variance is based on less information.

The result of all this is that, when doing hypothesis testing using an estimated variance, your comparison distribution will not be a normal curve. Instead, the comparison distribution will be a slightly different curve called a *t* **distribution**.

Actually, there is a whole family of *t* distributions. They all have the same general shape of a slightly more spread out normal curve, but vary in terms of how much more spread out they are based on the number of degrees of freedom you used to estimate the population variance. However, for any particular degrees of freedom, there is only one *t* distribution.

Generally, as noted, *t* distributions look to the eye like a normal curve—bell-shaped, symmetrical, and unimodal. A *t* distribution differs subtly in having heavier tails (that is, slightly more scores at the extremes). This slight difference in shape affects how extreme a score you need to reject the null hypothesis. As always, to reject the null hypothesis, your sample mean has to be in an extreme section of the comparison distribution of means, such as the top 5%. However, if the comparison distribution has more of its means in the tails than a normal curve would have, then the point where the top 5% begins has to be farther out on this comparison distribution. The result is that it takes a slightly more extreme sample mean to get a significant result when using a *t* distribution than when using a normal curve.

Just how much the *t* distribution differs from the normal curve depends on the degrees of freedom, the amount of information used in estimating the population variance. The *t* distribution differs most from the normal curve (that is, it is most spread out and has the thickest tails) when the degrees of freedom are low. (This is because your estimate of the population variance is based on a very small sample.) For example, using the normal curve, you may recall that 1.64 is the cutoff for a one-tailed test at the .05 level. On a *t* distribution with 7 degrees of freedom (that is, with a sample size of 8), the cutoff is 1.895 for a one-tailed test at the .05 level. If your estimate is based on a larger sample, say a sample of 25 (so that $df = 24$), the cutoff is 1.711, a cutoff much closer to that for the normal curve. If your sample size is infinite, the *t* distribution is the same as the normal curve. (Of course, if your sample size were infinite, it would include the entire population!) But even with sample sizes of 30 or more, the *t* distribution is nearly identical to the normal curve. Figure 2 shows how *t* distributions with different degrees of freedom compare to a normal curve. As you can see in the figure, the *t* distribution with 20 degrees of freedom is more similar to the normal curve than the *t* distribution with just 2 degrees of freedom.

Shortly, you will learn how to find the cutoff using a *t* distribution, but let's first return briefly to the example of how much students in your dorm study each week. You finally have everything you need for Step ❷ about the characteristics of the

t **distribution**   mathematically defined curve that is the comparison distribution used in a *t* test.

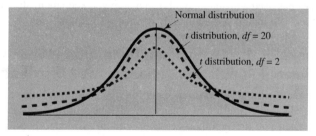

Figure 2   *t* distributions (dashed blue lines) compared to the normal curve (solid black line).

comparison distribution. We have already seen that the distribution of means in this example has a mean of 17 hours and a standard deviation of 1.70. You can now add that the shape of the comparison distribution will be a *t* distribution with 15 degrees of freedom.[2]

The Cutoff Sample Score for Rejecting the Null Hypothesis: Using the *t* Table

Step ❸ of hypothesis testing is determining the cutoff for rejecting the null hypothesis. There is a different *t* distribution for any particular degrees of freedom. However, to avoid taking up pages and pages with tables for each possible *t* distribution, you use a simplified table that gives only the crucial cutoff points. We have included such a **t table** in the Appendix (Table A-2). Just as with the normal curve table, the *t* table shows only positive *t* scores. If you have a one-tailed test, you need to decide whether your cutoff score is a positive *t* score or a negative *t* score. If your one-tailed test is testing whether the mean of Population 1 is greater than the mean of Population 2, the cutoff *t* score is positive. However, if your one-tailed test is testing whether the mean of Population 1 is less than the mean of Population 2, the cutoff *t* score is negative.

In the hours-studied example, you have a one-tailed test. (You want to know whether students in your dorm study *more* than students in general at your college study.) You will probably want to use the 5% significance level, because the cost of a Type I error (mistakenly rejecting the null hypothesis) is not great. You have 16 participants, making 15 degrees of freedom for your estimate of the population variance.

t table   table of cutoff scores on the *t* distribution for various degrees of freedom, significance levels, and one- and two-tailed tests.

Table 2   Cutoff Scores for *t* Distributions with 1 Through 17 Degrees of Freedom (Highlighting Cutoff for Hours-Studied Example)

	One-Tailed Tests			Two-Tailed Tests		
df	.10	.05	.01	.10	.05	.01
1	3.078	6.314	31.821	6.314	12.706	63.657
2	1.886	2.920	6.965	2.920	4.303	9.925
3	1.638	2.353	4.541	2.353	3.182	5.841
4	1.533	2.132	3.747	2.132	2.776	4.604
5	1.476	2.015	3.365	2.015	2.571	4.032
6	1.440	1.943	3.143	1.943	2.447	3.708
7	1.415	1.895	2.998	1.895	2.365	3.500
8	1.397	1.860	2.897	1.860	2.306	3.356
9	1.383	1.833	2.822	1.833	2.262	3.250
10	1.372	1.813	2.764	1.813	2.228	3.170
11	1.364	1.796	2.718	1.796	2.201	3.106
12	1.356	1.783	2.681	1.783	2.179	3.055
13	1.350	1.771	2.651	1.771	2.161	3.013
14	1.345	1.762	2.625	1.762	2.145	2.977
15	1.341	1.753	2.603	1.753	2.132	2.947
16	1.337	1.746	2.584	1.746	2.120	2.921
17	1.334	1.740	2.567	1.740	2.110	2.898

Table 2 shows a portion of the *t* table from Table A-2 in the Appendix. Find the column for the .05 significance level for one-tailed tests and move down to the row for 15 degrees of freedom. The crucial cutoff is 1.753. In this example, you are testing whether students in your dormitory (Population 1) study *more* than students in general at your college (Population 2). In other words, you are testing whether students in your dormitory have a higher *t* score than students in general. This means that the cutoff *t* score is positive. Thus, you will reject the null hypothesis if your sample's mean is 1.753 or more standard deviations above the mean on the comparison distribution. (If you were using a known variance, you would have found your cutoff from a normal curve table. The *Z* score to reject the null hypothesis based on the normal curve would have been 1.645.)

One other point about using the *t* table: In the full *t* table in the Appendix, there are rows for each degree of freedom from 1 through 30, then for 35, 40, 45, and so on up to 100. Suppose your study has degrees of freedom between two of these higher values. To be safe, you should use the nearest degrees of freedom to yours given on the table that is less than yours. For example, in a study with 43 degrees of freedom, you would use the cutoff for *df* = 40.

The Sample Mean's Score on the Comparison Distribution: The *t* Score

Step ❹ of hypothesis testing is figuring your sample mean's score on the comparison distribution. Earlier, this meant finding the *Z* score on the comparison distribution—the number of standard deviations your sample's mean is from the mean on the distribution. You do exactly the same thing when your comparison distribution is a *t* distribution. The only difference is that, instead of calling this a *Z* score, because it is from a *t* distribution, you call it a **t score**. In terms of a formula,

> The *t* score is your sample's mean minus the population mean, divided by the standard deviation of the distribution of means.

$$t = \frac{M - \mu}{S_M} \tag{7}$$

In the example, your sample's mean of 21 is 4 hours from the mean of the distribution of means, which amounts to 2.35 standard deviations from the mean (4 hours divided by the standard deviation of 1.70 hours).[3] That is, the *t* score in the example is 2.35. In terms of the formula,

$$t = \frac{M - \mu}{S_M} = \frac{21 - 17}{1.70} = \frac{4}{1.70} = 2.35$$

Deciding Whether to Reject the Null Hypothesis

Step ❺ of hypothesis testing is deciding whether to reject the null hypothesis. This step is exactly the same with a *t* test. In the example, the cutoff *t* score was 1.753 and the actual *t* score for your sample was 2.35. Conclusion: reject the null hypothesis. The research hypothesis is supported that students in your dorm study more than students in the college overall.

Figure 3 shows the various distributions for this example.

Summary of Hypothesis Testing When the Population Variance Is Not Known

t score   on a *t* distribution, number of standard deviations from the mean (like a *Z* score, but on a *t* distribution).

Table 3 compares the hypothesis-testing procedure we just considered (for a *t* test for a single sample) with the hypothesis-testing procedure for a *Z* test where you know the population's mean *and* you know its variance.

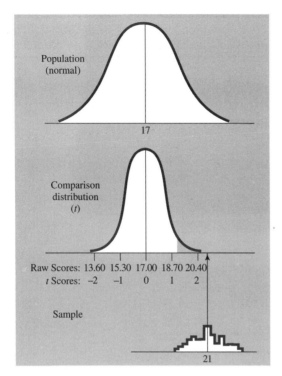

Figure 3   Distributions for the hours-studied example.

Another Example of a *t* Test for a Single Sample

Consider another fictional example. Suppose a researcher was studying the psychological effects of a devastating flood in a small rural community. Specifically, the researcher was interested in how hopeful (versus unhopeful) people felt after the flood. The researcher randomly selected 10 people from this community to complete a short questionnaire. The key item on the questionnaire asked how hopeful they

Table 3   Hypothesis Testing with a Single Sample Mean When Population Variance Is Unknown (*t* Test for a Single Sample) Compared to When Population Variance Is Known (*Z* Test)

Steps in Hypothesis Testing	Difference From When Population Variance Is Known
❶ Restate the question as a research hypothesis and a null hypothesis about the populations.	No difference in method.
❷ Determine the characteristics of the comparison distribution:	
Population mean	No difference in method.
Population variance	*Estimate* from the sample.
Standard deviation of the distribution of sample means	No difference in method (but based on *estimated* population variance).
Shape of the comparison distribution	Use the *t* distribution with $df = N - 1$.
❸ Determine the significance cutoff.	Use the *t* table.
❹ Determine your sample's score on the comparison distribution.	No difference in method (but called a *t* score).
❺ Decide whether to reject the null hypothesis.	No difference in method.

Table 4 Results and Figuring for a Single-Sample *t* Test for a Study of 10 People's Ratings of Hopefulness Following a Devastating Flood (Fictional Data)

Rating (X)	Difference From the Sample's Mean (X − M)	Squared Difference From the Sample's Mean (X − M)²
5	.30	.09
3	−1.70	2.89
6	1.30	1.69
2	−2.70	7.29
7	2.30	5.29
6	1.30	1.69
7	2.30	5.29
4	−.70	.49
2	−2.70	7.29
5	.30	.09
Σ: 47		32.10

$M = (\Sigma X)/N = 47/10 = 4.70$
$df = N - 1 = 10 - 1 = 9$
$\mu = 4.00$
$S^2 = SS/df = 32.10/(10 - 1) = 32.10/9 = 3.57$
$S_M^2 = S^2/N = 3.57/10 = .36$
$S_M = \sqrt{S_M^2} = \sqrt{.36} = .60$
t with $df = 9$ needed for 1% significance level, two-tailed $= \pm 3.250$
Actual sample $t = (M - \mu)/S_M = (4.70 - 4.00)/.60 = .70/.60 = 1.17$
Decision: Do not reject the null hypothesis.

felt, using a 7-point scale from *extremely unhopeful* (1) to *neutral* (4) to *extremely hopeful* (7). The researcher wanted to know whether the ratings of hopefulness for people who had been through the flood would be consistently above or below the neutral point on the scale (4).

Table 4 shows the results and figuring for the *t* test for a single sample; Figure 4 shows the distributions involved. Here are the steps of hypothesis testing.

❶ **Restate the question as a research hypothesis and a null hypothesis about the populations.** There are two populations:

Population 1: People who experienced the flood.
Population 2: People who are neither hopeful nor unhopeful.

The research hypothesis is that the two populations will score differently. The null hypothesis is that they will score the same.

❷ **Determine the characteristics of the comparison distribution.** If the null hypothesis is true, the mean of both populations is 4. The variance of these populations is not known, so you have to estimate it from the sample. As shown in Table 4, the sum of the squared deviations of the sample's scores from the sample's mean is 32.10. Thus, the estimated population variance is 32.10 divided by 9 degrees of freedom (10 − 1), which comes out to 3.57.

The distribution of means has a mean of 4 (the same as the population mean). Its variance is the estimated population variance divided by the sample size (3.57 divided by 10 equals .36). The square root of this, the standard deviation of the distribution of means, is .60. Its shape will be a *t* distribution for $df = 9$.

TIP FOR SUCCESS

Be careful. To find the variance of a distribution of means, you always divide the population variance by the sample size. This is true whether the population's variance is known or only estimated. It is only when making the estimate of the population variance that you divide by the sample size minus 1. That is, the degrees of freedom are used only when estimating the variance of the population of individuals, not when going to the next step of figuring the variance of the distribution of means.

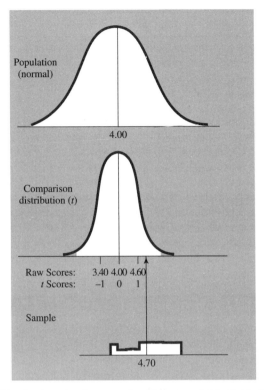

Figure 4 Distributions for the example of how hopeful individuals felt following a devastating flood.

❸ **Determine the cutoff sample score on the comparison distribution at which the null hypothesis should be rejected.** The researcher wanted to be very cautious about mistakenly concluding that the flood made a difference. Thus, she decided to use the .01 significance level. The hypothesis was nondirectional (that is, no specific direction of difference from the mean of 4 was specified; either result would have been of interest); so the researcher used a two-tailed test. The researcher looked up the cutoff in Table 2 (or Table A-2 in the Appendix) for a two-tailed test and 9 degrees of freedom. The cutoff given in the table is 3.250. Thus, to reject the null hypothesis, the sample's score on the comparison distribution must be 3.250 or higher, or −3.250 or lower.

❹ **Determine your sample's score on the comparison distribution.** The sample's mean of 4.70 is .70 scale points from the null hypothesis mean of 4.00. That makes it 1.17 standard deviations on the comparison distribution from that distribution's mean (.70/.60 = 1.17); $t = 1.17$.

❺ **Decide whether to reject the null hypothesis.** The t of 1.17 is not as extreme as the needed t of ±3.250. Therefore, the researcher cannot reject the null hypothesis. The study is inconclusive. (If the researcher had used a larger sample, giving more power, the result might have been quite different.)

Summary of Steps for a *t* Test for a Single Sample

Table 5 summarizes the steps of hypothesis testing when you have scores from a single sample and a population with a known mean but an unknown variance.[4]

Table 5   Steps for a *t* Test for a Single Sample

❶ **Restate the question as a research hypothesis and a null hypothesis about the populations.**
❷ **Determine the characteristics of the comparison distribution.**
 a. The mean is the same as the known population mean.
 b. The standard deviation is figured as follows:
   ❹ Figure the estimated population variance: $S^2 = SS/df$.
   ❺ Figure the variance of the distribution of means: $S_M^2 = S^2/N$.
   ❻ Figure the standard deviation of the distribution of means: $S_M = \sqrt{S_M^2}$.
 c. The shape will be a *t* distribution with $N - 1$ degrees of freedom.
❸ **Determine the cutoff sample score on the comparison distribution at which the null hypothesis should be rejected.**
 a. Decide the significance level and whether to use a one-tailed or a two-tailed test.
 b. Look up the appropriate cutoff in a *t* table.
❹ **Determine your sample's score on the comparison distribution:** $t = (M - \mu)/S_M$.
❺ **Decide whether to reject the null hypothesis:** Compare the scores from Steps ❸ and ❹.

How are you doing?

1. In what sense is a sample's variance a biased estimate of the variance of the population the sample is taken from? That is, in what way does a sample's variance typically differ from the population's?
2. What is the difference between the usual formula for figuring the variance and the formula for estimating a population's variance from the scores in a sample (that is, the formula for an unbiased estimate of the population variance)?
3. (a) What are degrees of freedom? (b) How do you figure the degrees of freedom in a *t* test for a single sample? (c) What do they have to do with estimating the population variance? (d) What do they have to do with the *t* distribution?
4. (a) How does a *t* distribution differ from a normal curve? (b) How do degrees of freedom affect this? (c) What is the effect of the difference on hypothesis testing?
5. List three differences in how you do hypothesis testing for a *t* test for a single sample versus for the *Z* test.
6. A population has a mean of 23. A sample of 4 is given an experimental procedure and has scores of 20, 22, 22, and 20. Test the hypothesis that the procedure produces a lower score. Use the .05 significance level. (a) Use the steps of hypothesis testing and (b) make a sketch of the distributions involved.

Answers

1. The sample's variance will in general be slightly smaller than the variance of the population the sample is taken from.
2. In the usual formula you divide by the number of participants (*N*); in the formula for estimating a population's variance from the scores in a sample, you divide by the number of participants in the sample minus 1 (that is, $N - 1$).
3. (a) The degrees of freedom are the number of scores free to vary. (b) The degrees of freedom in a *t* test for a single sample are the number of scores in the sample minus 1. (c) In estimating the population variance, the formula is the sum of squared deviations divided by the degrees of freedom. (d) *t* distributions differ slightly from each other according to the degrees of freedom.

4. (a) A *t* distribution differs from a normal curve in that it has heavier tails; that is, it has more scores at the extremes. (b) The more degrees of freedom, the closer the shape (including the tails) is to a normal curve. (c) The cutoffs for significance are more extreme for a *t* distribution than for a normal curve.

5. In the *t* test you (a) estimate the population variance from the sample (it is not known in advance); (b) you look up the cutoff on a *t* table in which you also have to take into account the degrees of freedom (you don't use a normal curve table); and (c) your sample's score on the comparison distribution, which is a *t* distribution (not a normal curve), is called a *t* score (not a *Z* score).

6. (a) Steps of hypothesis testing:

❶ **Restate the question as a research hypothesis and a null hypothesis about the populations.** There are two populations:

Population 1: People who are given the experimental procedure.
Population 2: The general population.

The research hypothesis is that Population 1 will score lower than Population 2. The null hypothesis is that Population 1 will not score lower than Population 2.

❷ **Determine the characteristics of the comparison distribution.**
  a. The mean of the distribution of means is 23.
  b. The standard deviation is figured as follows:
    ❹ Figure the estimated population variance. You first need to figure the sample mean, which is $(20 + 22 + 22 + 20)/4 = 84/4 = 21$. The

Figure 5 Distributions for answer to "How are you doing?" question 6b.

estimated population variance is $S^2 = SS/(N-1) = [(20-21)^2 + (22-21)^2 + (22-21)^2 + (20-21)^2]/(4-1) = (-1^2 + 1^2 + 1^2 + -1^2)/3 = (1+1+1+1)/3 = 4/3 = 1.33.$

❷ Figure the variance of the distribution of means:

$$S_M^2 = S^2/N = 1.33/4 = .33$$

❸ Figure the standard deviation of the distribution of means:

$$S_M = \sqrt{S_M^2} = \sqrt{.33} = .57$$

c. The shape of the comparison distribution will be a *t* distribution with $df = 3$.

❸ **Determine the cutoff sample score on the comparison distribution at which the null hypothesis should be rejected.** From Table A-2, the cutoff for a one-tailed *t* test at the .05 level for $df = 3$ is -2.353. The cutoff *t* score is negative because the research hypothesis is that the procedure produces a *lower* score.

❹ **Determine your sample's score on the comparison distribution.** $t = (M - \mu)/S_M = (21-23)/.57 = -2/.57 = -3.51.$

❺ **Decide whether to reject the null hypothesis.** The *t* of -3.51 is more extreme than the needed *t* of -2.353. Therefore, reject the null hypothesis; the research hypothesis is supported.

(b) Sketches of distributions are shown in Figure 5.

The *t* Test for Dependent Means

The situation you just learned about (the *t* test for a single sample) is for when you know the population mean but not its variance and you have a single sample of scores. It turns out that in most research you do not even know the population's *mean;* plus, in most research situations you usually have not one set, but *two* sets, of scores. These two things, not knowing the population mean and having two sets of scores, are very, very common.

The rest of this chapter focuses specifically on this important research situation in which you have two scores from each person in your sample. (Finally, we are at the point where you are learning a method used in lots of real studies.) This kind of research situation is called a **repeated measures design** (also known as a *within-subjects design*). A common example is when you measure the same people before and after some psychological or social intervention. For example, a psychologist might measure the quality of men's communication before and after receiving premarital counseling. (For additional information on repeated measures designs, be sure to read our Web Chapter W1, "Overview of the Logic and Language of Psychology Research," which is available at *www.pearsoned.co.in/prc/home.*

repeated measures design research strategy in which each person is tested more than once; same as *within-subjects design.*

t test for dependent means hypothesis-testing procedure in which there are two scores for each person and the population variance is not known; it determines the significance of a hypothesis that is being tested using difference or change scores from a single group of people.

The hypothesis-testing procedure for the situation in which each person is measured twice (that is, for the situation in which we have a repeated measures design) is a *t* **test for dependent means**. It has the name "dependent means" because the mean for each group of scores (for example, a group of before-scores and a group of after-scores) are dependent on each other in that they are both from the same people. (There can be situations in which you compare scores from two different groups of people, a research situation you analyze using a *t* test for *independent* means.)

You do a *t* test for dependent means exactly the same way as a *t* test for a single sample, except that (a) you use something called *difference scores,* and (b) you assume that the population mean (of the difference scores) is 0. We will now consider each of these two new aspects.

Difference Scores

With a repeated measures design, your sample includes two scores for each person instead of just one. The way you handle this is to make the two scores per person into one score per person! You do this magic by creating **difference scores**: For each person, you subtract one score from the other. If the difference is before versus after, difference scores are also called *change scores.*

Consider the example of the quality of men's communication before and after receiving premarital counseling. The psychologist subtracts the communication quality score before the counseling from the communication quality score after the counseling. This gives an after-minus-before difference score for each man. When the two scores are a before-score and an after-score, we usually take the after-score minus the before-score to indicate the *change.*

Once you have the difference score for each person in the study, you do the rest of the hypothesis testing with difference scores. That is, you treat the study as if there were a single sample of scores (scores that in this situation happen to be difference scores).

Population of Difference Scores with a Mean of 0

So far in the research situations considered, you have always known the mean of the population to which you compared your sample's mean. For example, in the college dormitory survey of hours studied, you knew the population mean was 17 hours. However, now we are using difference scores, and we usually don't know the mean of the population of difference scores.

Here is the solution. Ordinarily, the null hypothesis in a repeated measures design is that on the average there is *no difference* between the two groups of scores. For example, the null hypothesis in a study of the quality of men's communication before and after receiving premarital counseling is that on the average there is no difference between communication quality before and after the counseling. What does no *difference* mean? Saying there is on the average no difference is the same as saying that the mean of the population of the difference scores is 0. Therefore, when working with difference scores, you are comparing the population of difference scores that your sample of difference scores comes from to a population of difference scores with a mean of 0. In other words, with a *t* test for dependent means, what we call Population 2 will ordinarily have a mean of 0 (that is, it is a population of difference scores that has a mean of 0).

Example of a *t* Test for Dependent Means

How can engaged couples improve their chances of a happy marriage? Here is an early study testing the effect of a communication skills course that is a good example (because of its small sample size) for understanding the *t* test for dependent means. Olthoff (1989) tested the communication quality of couples three months before and again three months after marriage. One group studied was 19 couples who had received ordinary (very minimal) premarital counseling from the ministers who were going to marry them. (To keep the example simple, we will focus on just this one group, and only on the husbands in the group. Scores for wives were similar, though somewhat more varied, making it a more complicated example for learning the *t* test procedure.)

The scores for the 19 husbands are listed in the "Before" and "After" columns in Table 6, followed by all the *t* test figuring. (The distributions involved are shown in Figure 6.) The crucial column for starting the analysis is the difference scores. For example, the first husband, whose communication quality was 126 before marriage and 115 after had a difference of -11. (We figured after minus before, so

difference scores difference between a person's score on one testing and the same person's score on another testing; often an after-score minus a before-score, in which case it is also called a *change* score.

Table 6   *t* Test for Communication Quality Scores Before and After Marriage for 19 Husbands Who Received Ordinary Premarital Counseling

Husband	Communication Quality		Difference (After − Before)	Deviation (Difference − *M*)	Squared Deviation
	Before	*After*			
A	126	115	−11	1.05	1.10
B	133	125	−8	4.05	16.40
C	126	96	−30	−17.95	322.20
D	115	115	0	12.05	145.20
E	108	119	11	23.05	531.30
F	109	82	−27	−14.95	223.50
G	124	93	−31	−18.95	359.10
H	98	109	11	23.05	531.30
I	95	72	−23	−10.95	119.90
J	120	104	−16	−3.95	15.60
K	118	107	−11	1.05	1.10
L	126	118	−8	4.05	16.40
M	121	102	−19	−6.95	48.30
N	116	115	−1	11.05	122.10
O	94	83	−11	1.05	1.10
P	105	87	−18	−5.95	35.40
Q	123	121	−2	10.05	101.00
R	125	100	−25	−12.95	167.70
S	128	118	−10	2.05	4.20
Σ:	2,210	1,981	−229		2,762.90

For difference scores:

$M = -229/19 = -12.05$

$\mu = 0$ (assumed as a no-change baseline of comparison)

$S^2 = SS/df = 2{,}762.90/(19 - 1) = 153.49$

$S_M^2 = S^2/N = 153.49/19 = 8.08$

$S_M = \sqrt{S_M^2} = \sqrt{8.08} = 2.84$

t with $df = 18$ needed for 5% level, two-tailed $= \pm 2.101$

$t = (M - \mu)/S_M = (-12.05 - 0)/2.84 = -4.24$

Decision: Reject the null hypothesis.

Source: Data from Olthoff (1989).

that an increase is positive and a decrease, as for this husband, is negative.) The mean of the difference scores is −12.05. That is, on the average, these 19 husbands' communication quality decreased by about 12 points.

Is this decrease significant? In other words, how likely is it that this sample of difference scores is a random sample from a population of difference scores whose mean is 0?

❶ **Restate the question as a research hypothesis and a null hypothesis about the populations.** There are two populations:

Population 1: Husbands who receive ordinary premarital counseling.
Population 2: Husbands whose communication quality does not change from before to after marriage. (In other words, it is a population of husbands

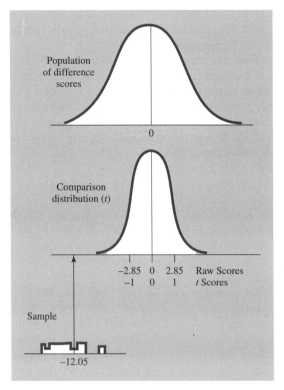

Figure 6   Distributions for the Olthoff (1989) example of a *t* test for dependent means.

whose mean difference in communication quality from before to after marriage is 0.)

The research hypothesis is that Population 1's mean difference score (communication quality after marriage minus communication quality before marriage) is different from Population 2's mean difference score (of zero). That is, the research hypothesis is that husbands who receive ordinary premarital counseling, like the husbands Olthoff studied, *do* change in communication quality from before to after marriage. The null hypothesis is that the populations are the same—that the husbands who receive ordinary premarital counseling *do not* change in their communication quality from before to after marriage.

Notice that you have no actual information about Population 2 husbands. The husbands in the study are a sample of Population 1 husbands. For the purposes of hypothesis testing, you set up Population 2 as a kind of straw man comparison group. That is, for the purpose of the analysis, you set up a comparison group of husbands who, if measured before and after marriage, would on the average show no difference.

❷ **Determine the characteristics of the comparison distribution.** If the null hypothesis is true, the mean of the population of difference scores is 0. The variance of the population of difference scores can be estimated from the sample of difference scores. As shown in Table 6, the sum of squared deviations of the difference scores from the mean of the difference scores is 2,762.90. With

19 husbands in the study, there are 18 degrees of freedom. Dividing the sum of squared deviation scores by the degrees of freedom gives an estimated population variance of difference scores of 153.49.

The distribution of means (from this population of difference scores) has a mean of 0, the same as the mean of the population of difference scores. The variance of the distribution of means of difference scores is the estimated population variance of difference scores (153.49) divided by the sample size (19), which gives 8.08. The standard deviation of the distribution of means of difference scores is 2.84, the square root of 8.08. Because Olthoff was using an estimated population variance, the comparison distribution is a *t* distribution. The estimate of the population variance of difference scores is based on 18 degrees of freedom, so this comparison distribution is a *t* distribution for 18 degrees of freedom.

❸ **Determine the cutoff sample score on the comparison distribution at which the null hypothesis should be rejected.** Olthoff used a two-tailed test to allow for either an increase or decrease in communication quality. Using the .05 significance level and 18 degrees of freedom, Table A-2 shows cutoff *t* scores of $+2.101$ and -2.101.

❹ **Determine your sample's score on the comparison distribution.** Olthoff's sample had a mean difference score of -12.05. That is, the mean was 12.05 points below the mean of 0 on the distribution of means of difference scores. The standard deviation of the distribution of means of difference scores is 2.84. Thus, the mean of the difference scores of -12.05 is 4.24 standard deviations below the mean of the distribution of means of difference scores. So Olthoff's sample of difference scores has a *t* score of -4.24.

❺ **Decide whether to reject the null hypothesis.** The *t* of -4.24 for the sample of difference scores is more extreme than the needed *t* of ± 2.101. Thus, you can reject the null hypothesis: Olthoff's husbands are from a population in which husbands' communication quality is different after marriage from what it was before (it is lower).

Olthoff's actual study was more complex. You may be interested to know that he found that the wives also showed this decrease in communication quality after marriage. But a group of similar engaged couples who were given special communication skills training by their ministers (much more than the usual short session) had no significant decline in marital communication quality after marriage. In fact, there is a great deal of research showing that on the average marital happiness declines steeply over time (Umberson et al., 2006; VanLaningham et al., 2001), but it is certainly not inevitable for all couples (O'Leary et al., 2012). And many studies have now shown the value of a full course of premarital communications training. For example, a recent representative survey of 3,344 adults in the United States showed that those who had attended a premarital communication program had significantly greater marital satisfaction, had less marital conflict, and were 31% less likely to divorce (Stanley et al., 2006; similarly strong results have also been found in controlled random assignment experiments; e.g., Stanley et al., 2010). Furthermore, benefits were greatest for those with a university education! (No one has yet tested it, but perhaps benefits are greatest of all for those who took a statistics course as part of their education?)

Summary of Steps for a *t* Test for Dependent Means

Table 7 summarizes the steps for a *t* test for dependent means.[5]

Table 7   Steps for a *t* Test for Dependent Means

❶ **Restate the question as a research hypothesis and a null hypothesis about the populations.**

❷ **Determine the characteristics of the comparison distribution.**

   a. Make each person's two scores into a difference score. Do all the remaining steps using these difference scores.

   b. Figure the mean of the difference scores.

   c. Assume a mean of the distribution of means of difference scores of 0: $\mu = 0$.

   d. The standard deviation of the distribution of means of difference scores is figured as follows:

      Ⓐ Figure the estimated population variance of difference scores: $S^2 = SS/df$.

      Ⓑ Figure the variance of the distribution of means of difference scores: $S_M^2 = S^2/N$.

      Ⓒ Figure the standard deviation of the distribution of means of difference scores: $S_M = \sqrt{S_M^2}$.

   e. The shape is a *t* distribution with $df = N - 1$.

❸ **Determine the cutoff sample score on the comparison distribution at which the null hypothesis should be rejected.**

   a. Decide the significance level and whether to use a one-tailed or a two-tailed test.

   b. Look up the appropriate cutoff in a *t* table.

❹ **Determine your sample's score on the comparison distribution:** $t = (M - \mu)/S_M$.

❺ **Decide whether to reject the null hypothesis:** Compare the scores from Steps ❸ and ❹.

A Second Example of a *t* Test for Dependent Means

Here is another example. A team of researchers examined the brain systems involved in human romantic love (Aron et al., 2005). One issue was whether romantic love engages a part of the brain called the ventral tegmental areas (VTA for short; a brain area that is engaged when people win money, are given cocaine, and other such "rewards"). Thus, the researchers recruited people who had very recently fallen "madly in love." (For example, to be in the study participants had to think about their partner at least 80% of their waking hours.) Participants brought a picture of their beloved with them, plus a picture of a familiar, neutral person of the same age and sex as their beloved. Participants then went in to the functional magnetic resonance imaging (fMRI) machine and their brain was scanned while they looked at the two pictures—30 seconds at the neutral person's picture, 30 seconds at their beloved, 30 seconds at the neutral person, and so forth.

Table 8 shows average brain activations (mean fMRI scanner values) in the VTA area of interest during the two kinds of pictures. (We have simplified the example for teaching purposes, including using only 10 participants when the actual study had 17.) It also shows the figuring of the difference scores and all the other figuring for the *t* test for dependent means. Figure 7 shows the distributions involved. Here are the steps of hypothesis testing:

❶ **Restate the question as a research hypothesis and a null hypothesis about the populations.** There are two populations:

Population 1: Individuals like those tested in this study.
Population 2: Individuals whose brain activation in the VTA area of interest is the same when looking at a picture of their beloved and a picture of a familiar, neutral person.

The research hypothesis is that Population 1's mean difference score (brain activation when viewing the beloved's picture minus brain activation when

Table 8 *t* Test for a Study of Romantic Love and Brain Activation in the VTA

Student	Brain Activation		Difference (Beloved − Control)	Deviation (Difference − M)	Squared Deviation
	Beloved's photo	*Control photo*			
1	1487.8	1487.2	.6	−.800	.640
2	1329.4	1328.1	1.3	−.100	.010
3	1407.9	1405.9	2.0	.600	.360
4	1236.1	1234.0	2.1	.700	.490
5	1299.8	1298.2	1.6	.200	.040
6	1447.2	1444.7	2.5	1.100	1.210
7	1354.1	1354.3	−.2	−1.600	2.560
8	1204.6	1203.7	.9	−.500	.250
9	1322.3	1320.8	1.5	.100	.010
10	1388.5	1386.8	1.7	.300	.090
Σ:	13477.7	13463.7	14.0		5.660

For difference scores:

$M = 14.0/10 = 1.400$

$\mu = 0$ (assumed as a no-change baseline of comparison)

$S^2 = SS/df = 5.660/(10 - 1) = 5.660/9 = .629$

$S_M^2 = S^2/N = .629/10 = .063$

$S_M = \sqrt{S_M^2} = \sqrt{.063} = .251$

t with $df = 9$ needed for 5% level, one-tailed $= 1.833$

$t = (M - \mu)/S_M = (1.400 - 0)/.251 = 5.58$

Decision: Reject the null hypothesis.

Source: Data based on Aron et al. (2005).

viewing the neutral person's picture) is greater than Population 2's mean difference score (of no difference). That is, the research hypothesis is that brain activation in the VTA area of interest is greater when viewing the beloved person's picture than when viewing the neutral person's picture. The null hypothesis is that Population 1's mean difference score is not greater than Population 2's. That is, the null hypothesis is that brain activation in the VTA area of interest is not greater when viewing the beloved person's picture than when viewing the neutral person's picture.

❷ **Determine the characteristics of the comparison distribution.**

a. Make each person's two scores into a difference score. This is shown in the column labeled "Difference" in Table 8. You do all the remaining steps using these difference scores.

b. Figure the mean of the difference scores. The sum of the difference scores (14.0) divided by the number of difference scores (10) gives a mean of the difference scores of 1.400. So, $M = 1.400$.

c. Assume a mean of the distribution of means of difference scores of 0: $\mu = 0$.

d. The standard deviation of the distribution of means of difference scores is figured as follows:

   ❶ Figure the estimated population variance of difference scores: $S^2 = SS/df = 5.660/(10 - 1) = .629$.

   ❷ Figure the variance of the distribution of means of difference scores: $S_M^2 = S^2/N = .629/10 = .063$.

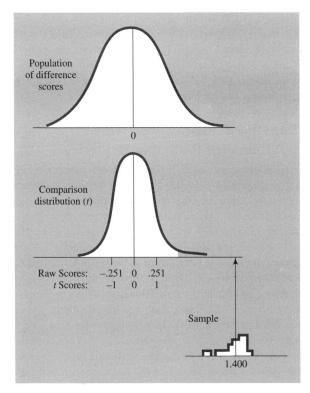

Figure 7 Distributions for the example of romantic love and brain activation in the VTA.

    ❹ Figure the standard deviation of the distribution of means of difference scores: $S_M = \sqrt{S_M^2} = \sqrt{.063} = .251$.

    e. The shape is a *t* distribution with $df = N - 1$. Therefore, the comparison distribution is a *t* distribution for 9 degrees of freedom. It is a *t* distribution because we figured its variance based on an estimated population variance. It has 9 degrees of freedom because there were 9 degrees of freedom in the estimate of the population variance.

❸ **Determine the cutoff sample score on the comparison distribution at which the null hypothesis should be rejected.**

    a. We will use the standard .05 significance level. This is a one-tailed test because the researchers were interested only in a specific direction of difference.

    b. Using the .05 significance level with 9 degrees of freedom, Table A-2 shows a cutoff *t* of 1.833. In Table 8, the difference score is figured as brain activation when viewing the beloved's picture minus brain activation when viewing the neutral person's picture. Thus, the research hypothesis predicts a positive difference score, which means that our cutoff is +1.833.

❹ **Determine your sample's score on the comparison distribution.** $t = (M - \mu)/S_M = (1.400 - 0)/.251 = 5.58$. The sample's mean difference of 1.400 is 5.58 standard deviations (of .251 each) above the mean of 0 on the distribution of means of difference scores.

❺ **Decide whether to reject the null hypothesis.** The sample's *t* score of 5.58 is more extreme than the cutoff *t* of 1.833. You can reject the null hypothesis. Brain activation in the VTA area of interest is greater when viewing a beloved's picture than when viewing a neutral person's picture. The results of this study are not limited to North Americans or to individuals who have recently fallen in love. The study has now been replicated several times, for example, with virtually identical results in Beijing with Chinese students who were intensely in love (Xu et al., 2011). Perhaps especially encouraging, another recent study replicated the results with a group of long-term married couples who reported being very intensely in love (Acevedo et al., 2012).

t Test for Dependent Means with Scores from Pairs of Research Participants

The *t* test for dependent means is also called a *paired-samples t test, t test for correlated means, t test for matched samples,* and *t test for matched pairs.* Each of these names comes from the same idea that in this kind of *t* test you are comparing two sets of scores that are related to each other in a direct way. In the *t* test for dependent means examples in this chapter, the two sets of scores have been related because each individual had a score in both sets of scores (for example, a score before a procedure and a score after a procedure). However, you can also use a *t* test for dependent means with scores from *pairs of research participants,* considering each pair as if it were one person, and figuring the difference score for each pair. For example, suppose you have 30 married couples and want to test whether wives consistently do more housework than husbands. You could figure for each couple a difference score of the wife's hours of housework per week minus her husband's number of hours of housework per week. There are also situations in which experimenters *create* pairs. For example, a researcher might put participants into pairs to do a puzzle task together and, for each pair, assign one to be a leader and one a follower. At the end of the study, participants privately fill out a questionnaire about how much they enjoyed the interaction. The procedure for analyzing this study would be to create a difference score for each pair by taking the enjoyment rating of the leader minus the enjoyment rating of the follower.

Review and Comparison of *Z* Test, *t* Test for a Single Sample, and *t* test for Dependent Means

In this chapter you have learned about the *t* test for a single sample and the *t* test for dependent means. Table 9 provides a review and comparison of the *Z* test, the *t* test for a single sample, and the *t* test for dependent means.

Table 9 Review of the *Z* Test, the *t* Test for a Single Sample, and the *t* Test for Dependent Means

Features	Type of Test		
	Z Test	*t* Test for a Single Sample	*t* Test for Dependent Means
Population variance is known	Yes	No	No
Population mean is known	Yes	Yes	No
Number of scores for each participant	1	1	2
Shape of comparison distribution	*Z* distribution	*t* distribution	*t* distribution
Formula for degrees of freedom	Not applicable	$df = N - 1$	$df = N - 1$
Formula	$Z = (M - \mu_M)/\sigma_M$	$t = (M - \mu)/S_M$	$t = (M - \mu)/S_M$

1. Describe the situation in which you would use a *t* test for dependent means.
2. When doing a *t* test for dependent means, what do you do with the two scores you have for each participant?
3. In a *t* test for dependent means, (a) what is usually considered to be the mean of the "known" population (Population 2). (b) Why?
4. Five individuals are tested before and after an experimental procedure; their scores are given in the following table. Test the hypothesis that there is no change, using the .05 significance level. (a) Use the steps of hypothesis testing and (b) sketch the distributions involved.

Person	Before	After
1	20	30
2	30	50
3	20	10
4	40	30
5	30	40

5. What about the research situation makes the difference in whether you should carry out a *Z* test or a *t* test for a single sample?
6. What about the research situation makes the difference in whether you should carry out a *t* test for a single sample or a *t* test for dependent means?

Answers

1. A *t* test for dependent means is used when you are doing hypothesis testing and you have two scores for each participant (such as a before-score and an after-score) and the population variance is unknown. It is also used when a study compares participants who are organized into pairs.
2. When doing a *t* test for dependent means, subtract one score from the other to create a difference (or change) score for each person. The *t* test is then done with these difference (or change) scores.
3. (a) The mean of the "known" population (Population 2) is 0. (b) You are comparing your sample to a situation in which there is no difference—a population of difference scores in which the average difference is 0.
4. (a) Steps of hypothesis testing (all figuring is shown in Table 10):

   ❶ **Restate the question as a research hypothesis and a null hypothesis about the populations.** There are two populations:

   Population 1: People like those tested before and after the experimental procedure.
   Population 2: People whose scores are the same before and after the experimental procedure.
   The research hypothesis is that Population 1's mean change score (after minus before) is different from Population 2's. The null hypothesis is that Population 1's mean change score is the same as Population 2's.

   ❷ **Determine the characteristics of the comparison distribution.** The mean of the distribution of means of difference scores (the comparison distribution) is 0; the standard deviation of the distribution of means of difference scores is 6; it is a *t* distribution with 4 degrees of freedom.

Table 10   Figuring for Answer to "How Are You Doing?" Question 4

Person	Score Before	Score After	Difference (After − Before)	Deviation (Difference − *M*)	Squared Deviation
1	20	30	10	6	36
2	30	50	20	16	256
3	20	10	−10	−14	196
4	40	30	−10	−14	196
5	30	40	10	6	36
Σ:	140	160	20		720

For difference scores:

$M = 20/5 = 4.00$

$\mu = 0$

$S^2 = SS/df = 720/(5 - 1) = 720/4 = 180$

$S_M^2 = S^2/N = 180/5 = 36$

$S_M = \sqrt{S_M^2} = \sqrt{36} = 6$

t for *df* = 4 needed for 5% significance level, two-tailed = ±2.776

$t = (M - \mu)/S_M = (4 - 0)/6 = .67$

Decision: Do not reject the null hypothesis.

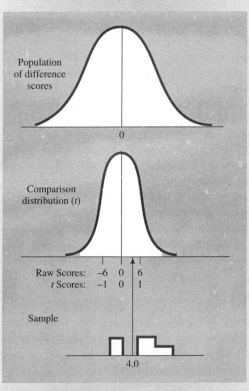

Figure 8   Distributions for answer to "How are you doing?" question 4.

   ❸ **Determine the cutoff sample score on the comparison distribution at which the null hypothesis should be rejected.** For a two-tailed test at the .05 level, the cutoff sample scores are +2.776 and −2.776.

   ❹ **Determine your sample's score on the comparison distribution.** $t = (4 - 0)/6 = .67$.

   ❺ **Decide whether to reject the null hypothesis.** The sample's *t* score of .67 is not more extreme than the cutoff *t* of ± 2.776. Therefore, do *not* reject the null hypothesis.

   (b) The distributions are shown in Figure 8.

5. As shown in Table 9, whether the population variance is known determines whether you should carry out a *Z* test or a *t* test for a single sample. You use a *Z* test when the population variance is known and you use the *t* test for a single sample when it is not known.

6. As shown in Table 9, when the population variance is not known, you do a *t* test. You use a *t* test for a single sample when you know the population mean and you have one score for each participant; you use the *t* test for dependent means when you do not know the population mean and there are two scores for each participant.

Assumptions of the *t* Test for a Single Sample and the *t* Test for Dependent Means

As we have seen, when you are using an estimated population variance, the comparison distribution is a *t* distribution. However, the comparison distribution will be exactly a *t* distribution only if the distribution of individuals follows a normal curve. Otherwise, the comparison distribution will follow some other (usually unknown) shape.

Thus, strictly speaking, a normal population is a requirement within the logic and mathematics of the *t* test. A requirement like this for a hypothesis-testing procedure is called an **assumption**. That is, a normal population distribution is one assumption of the *t* test. The effect of this assumption is that if the population distribution is not normal, the comparison distribution will be some indeterminate shape other than a *t* distribution—and thus the cutoffs on the *t* table will be incorrect.

Unfortunately, when you do a *t* test, you don't know whether the population is normal. This is because, when doing a *t* test, usually all you have to go on are the scores in your sample. Fortunately, however, distributions in psychology research quite often approximate a normal curve. (This also applies to distributions of difference scores.) Also, statisticians have found that, in practice, you get reasonably accurate results with *t* tests even when the population is rather far from normal. In other words, the *t* test is said to be *robust* over moderate violations of the assumption of a normal population distribution. How statisticians figure out the **robustness** of a test is an interesting topic.

The only very common situation in which using a *t* test for dependent means is likely to give a seriously distorted result is when you are using a one-tailed test and the population is highly skewed (is very asymmetrical, with a much longer tail on one side than the other). Thus, you need to be cautious about your conclusions when doing a one-tailed test if the sample of difference scores is highly skewed, suggesting the population it comes from is also highly skewed.

assumption condition, such as a population's having a normal distribution, required for carrying out a particular hypothesis-testing procedure; a part of the mathematical foundation for the accuracy of the tables used in determining cutoff values.

robustness extent to which a particular hypothesis-testing procedure is reasonably accurate even when its assumptions are violated.

Effect Size and Power for the *t* Test for Dependent Means

Effect Size

You can figure the effect size for a study using a *t* test for dependent means.[6] *d* is the difference between the population means divided by the population standard deviation: $d = (\mu_1 - \mu_2)/\sigma$. When using this formula for a *t* test for dependent means, μ_1 is for the predicted mean of the population of difference scores, μ_2 (the "known" population mean) is almost always 0, and σ usually stands for the standard deviation of the population of difference scores. The conventions for effect size for a *t* test for dependent means are also the same as for the situation considered in *Making Sense of Statistical Significance*: A small effect size is .20, a medium effect size is .50, and a large effect size is .80.

Consider an example. A sports psychologist plans a study on attitudes toward teammates before versus after a game. She will administer an attitude questionnaire twice, once before and once after a game. Suppose that the smallest before-after difference that would be of any importance is 4 points on the questionnaire. Also suppose that, based on related research, the researcher figures that the standard deviation of difference scores on this attitude questionnaire is about 8 points. Thus, $\mu_1 = 4$ and $\sigma = 8$. Applying the effect size formula, $d = (\mu_1 - \mu_2)/\sigma = (4 - 0)/8 = .50$. In terms of the effect size conventions, her planned study has a medium effect size.

To estimate the effect size after a study, use the actual mean of your sample's difference scores as your estimate of μ_1, and use S (for the population of difference scores) as your estimate of σ. Consider our first example of a *t* test for dependent means, the study of husbands' change in communication quality. In that study, the mean of the difference scores was -12.05. The estimated population standard deviation of the difference scores would be 12.41. That is, we figured the estimated variance of the difference scores (S^2) to be 153.49; $\sqrt{S^2} = 12.39$. Therefore, the estimated effect size is $d = (\mu_1 - \mu_2)/\sigma = (M - 0)/S = (-12.05 - 0)/12.39 = -.97$. This is a very large effect size. (The negative sign for the effect size means that the large effect was a decrease.)

Power

Power for a *t* test for dependent means can be determined using a power table, a power software package, or an Internet power calculator. Table 11 gives the approximate power at the .05 significance level for small, medium, and large effect sizes and one-tailed and two-tailed tests. In the sports psychology example, the researcher expected a medium effect size ($d = .50$). If she planned to conduct the study using the .05 level, two-tailed, with 20 participants, the study would have a power of .59. This means that, if the research hypothesis is true and has a medium effect size, there is a 59% chance that this study will come out significant.

The power table (Table 11) is also useful when you are reading about a nonsignificant result in a published study. Suppose that a study using a *t* test for dependent means has a nonsignificant result. The study tested significance at the .05 level, was two-tailed, and had 10 participants. Should you conclude that there is in fact no difference at all in the populations? Probably not. Even assuming a medium effect size, Table 11 shows that there is only a 32% chance of getting a significant result in this study.

Consider another study that was not significant. This study also used the .05 significance level, two-tailed. This study had 100 research participants. Table 11 tells you that

Table 11 Approximate Power for Studies Using the *t* Test for Dependent Means for Testing Hypotheses at the .05 Significance Level

Difference Scores in Sample (*N*)	Small (*d* = .20)	Medium (*d* = .50)	Large (*d* = .80)
One-tailed test			
10	.15	.46	.78
20	.22	.71	.96
30	.29	.86	*
40	.35	.93	*
50	.40	.97	*
100	.63	*	*
Two-tailed test			
10	.09	.32	.66
20	.14	.59	.93
30	.19	.77	.99
40	.24	.88	*
50	.29	.94	*
100	.55	*	*

*Power is nearly 1.

there would be a 55% chance of the study's coming out significant if there were even a true small effect size in the population. If there were a medium effect size in the population, the table indicates that there is almost a 100% chance that this study would have come out significant. Thus, in this study with 100 participants, we could conclude from the results that in the population there is probably at most a small difference.

To keep Table 11 simple, we have given power figures for only a few different numbers of participants (10, 20, 30, 40, 50, and 100). This should be adequate for the kinds of rough evaluations you need to make when evaluating results of research articles.[7]

Planning Sample Size

Table 12 gives the approximate number of participants needed for 80% power for a planned study. (Eighty percent is a common figure used by researchers for the minimum power to make a study worth doing.) Suppose you plan a study in which you expect a large effect size and you use the .05 significance level, two-tailed. The table shows you would only need 14 participants to have 80% power. On the other hand, a study using the same significance level, also two-tailed, but in which you expect only a small effect size would need 196 participants for 80% power.[8]

Table 12 Approximate Number of Research Participants Needed for 80% Power for the *t* Test for Dependent Means in Testing Hypotheses at the .05 Significance Level

	Small (*d* = .20)	Medium (*d* = .50)	Large (*d* = .80)
One-tailed	156	26	12
Two-tailed	196	33	14

How are you doing?

1. (a) What is an assumption in hypothesis testing? (b) Describe a specific assumption for a *t* test for dependent means. (c) What is the effect of violating this assumption? (d) What does it mean to say that the *t* test for dependent means is robust? (e) Describe a situation in which it is not robust.
2. How can you tell if you have violated the normal curve assumption for a *t* test for dependent means?
3. (a) Write the formula for effect size; (b) describe each of its terms as they apply to a planned *t* test for dependent means; (c) describe what you use for each of its terms in figuring effect size for a completed study that used a *t* test for dependent means.
4. You are planning a study in which you predict the mean of the population of difference scores to be 40, and the population standard deviation is 80. You plan to test significance using a *t* test for dependent means, one-tailed, with an alpha of .05. (a) What is the predicted effect size? (b) What is the power of this study if you carry it out with 20 participants? (c) How many participants would you need to have 80% power?

Answers

1. (a) An assumption is a requirement that you must meet for the results of the hypothesis testing procedure to be accurate. (b) The population of individuals' difference scores is assumed to be a normal distribution. (c) The significance level cutoff from the *t* table is not accurate. (d) Unless you very strongly violate the assumption (that is, unless the population distribution is very far from normal), the cutoff is fairly accurate. (e) The *t* test for dependent means is not robust when you are doing a one-tailed test and the population distribution is highly skewed.
2. You look at the distribution of the sample of difference scores to see if it is dramatically different from a normal curve.
3. (a) $d = (\mu_1 - \mu_2)/\sigma$. (b) d is the effect size; μ_1 is for the predicted mean of the population of difference scores; μ_2 is the mean of the known population, which for a population of difference scores is almost always 0; σ is for the standard deviation of the population of difference scores. (c) To estimate μ_1, you use M, the actual mean of your sample's difference scores; μ_2 remains as 0; and for σ, you use S, the estimated standard deviation of the population of difference scores.
4. (a) Predicted effect size: $d = (\mu_1 - \mu_2)/\sigma = (40 - 0)/80 = .50$. (b) Power of this study: .71. (c) Using Table 12, 26 participants are needed for 80% power.

Controversy: Advantages and Disadvantages of Repeated Measures Designs

The main controversies about *t* tests have to do with their relative advantages and disadvantages compared to various alternatives. There is, however, one consideration that we want to comment on now. It is about all research designs in which the same participants are tested before and after some experimental intervention (the kind of situation the *t* test for dependent means is often used for).

Studies using difference scores (that is, studies using a repeated measures design) often have much larger effect sizes for the same amount of expected difference between means than other kinds of research designs. That is, testing each of a group of participants twice (once under one condition and once under a different condition) usually produces a study with high power. In particular, this kind of study gives more power than dividing the participants up into two groups and testing each group once (one group tested under one condition and the other tested under another condition). In fact, studies using difference scores usually have even more power than those in which you have twice as many participants, but each is tested only once.

Why do repeated measures designs have so much power? The reason is that the standard deviation of difference scores is usually quite low. (The standard deviation of difference scores is what you divide by to get the effect size when using difference scores.) This produces a large effect size, which increases the power. In a repeated measures design, the only variation is in the difference scores. Variation among participants on each testing's scores is not part of the variation involved in the analysis. As an example, look back at Table 8 from our romantic love and brain imaging study. Notice that there were very great differences between the scores (fMRI scanner activation values) for each participant. The first participant's scores were around 1,487, the second's was around 1,328, and so forth. Each person has a quite different overall level of activation. But the *differences* between the two conditions were relatively small. What we see in this example is that, because difference scores are all comparing participants to themselves, the variation in them is much less (and does not include the variation between participants). William S. Gosset, who essentially invented the *t* test (see Box 1), made much of the higher power of repeated measures studies in a historically interesting controversy over an experiment about milk, which is described in Box 2.

On the other hand, testing a group of people before and after an experimental procedure, without any kind of control group that does not go through the procedure, is a weak research design (Cook & Campbell, 1979). Even if such a study produces a significant difference, it leaves many alternative explanations for that difference. For example, the research participants might have matured or improved during that period anyway, or perhaps other events happened between tests, or the participants not getting benefits may have dropped out. It is even possible that the initial test itself caused changes.

Note, however, that the difficulties of research that tests people before and after some intervention are shared only slightly with the kind of study in which participants are tested under two conditions, such as viewing a beloved person's picture and a neutral person's picture, with half tested first viewing the beloved's picture and half tested first viewing the neutral person's picture. Another example would be a study examining the hand-eye coordination of a group of surgeons under both quiet and noisy conditions (not while doing surgery, of course). Each surgeon would perform the test of hand-eye coordination during quiet conditions and noisy conditions. Ideally, any effects of practice or fatigue from taking the test twice would be equalized by testing half of the surgeons under noisy conditions first, and half under quiet conditions first.

Single Sample *t* Tests and Dependent Means *t* Tests in Research Articles

Research articles usually describe *t* tests in a fairly standard format that includes the degrees of freedom, the *t* score, and the significance level. For example, "$t(24) = 2.80$, $p < .05$" tells you that the researcher used a *t* test with 24 degrees

BOX 2   The Power of Studies Using Difference Scores: How the Lanarkshire Milk Experiment Could Have Been Milked for More

In 1930, a major health experiment was conducted in Scotland involving 20,000 schoolchildren. Its main purpose was to compare the growth of a group of children who were assigned to drink milk regularly to those who were in a control group. The results were that those who drank milk showed more growth.

However, William Gosset, a contemporary statistician and inventor of the *t* test (see Box 1), was appalled at the way the experiment was conducted. It had cost about £7,500, which in 1930 was a huge amount of money, and was done wrong! Large studies such as this were very popular among statisticians in those days because they seemed to imitate the large numbers found in nature. Gosset, by contrast, being a brewer, was forced to use very small numbers in his studies—experimental batches of beer were too costly. And he was often chided by the "real statisticians" for his small sample sizes. But Gosset argued that no number of participants was large enough when strict random assignment was not followed. And in this study, teachers

were permitted to switch children from group to group if they took pity on a child whom they felt would benefit from receiving milk!

However, even more interesting in light of the present chapter, Gosset demonstrated that the researchers could have obtained the same result with 50 pairs of identical twins, flipping a coin to determine which of each pair was in the milk group (and sticking to it). Of course, the statistic you would use is the *t* test as taught in this chapter—the *t* test for dependent means.

More recently, the development of power analysis has thoroughly vindicated Gosset. It is now clear just how surprisingly few participants are needed when a researcher can find a way to set up a repeated measures design in which difference scores are the basic unit of analysis. (In this case, each *pair* of twins would be one "participant.") As Gosset could have told them, studies that use the *t* test for dependent means can be extremely sensitive.

Sources: Peters (1987); Tankard (1984).

of freedom, found a *t* score of 2.80, and the result was significant at the .05 level. Whether a one-tailed or two-tailed test was used may also be noted. (If not, assume that it was two-tailed.) Usually the means, and sometimes the standard deviations, are given for each testing. Rarely does an article report the standard deviation of the difference scores.

Had our student in the dormitory example reported the results in a research article, she would have written something like this: "The sample from my dormitory studied a mean of 21 hours ($SD = 6.80$). Based on a *t* test for a single sample, this was significantly different from the known mean of 17 for the college as a whole, $t(15) = 2.35, p < .05$, one-tailed." The researchers in our fictional flood victims example might have written up their results as follows: "The reported hopefulness of our sample of flood victims ($M = 4.70, SD = 1.89$) was not significantly different from the midpoint of the scale, $t(9) = 1.17$."

As we noted earlier, psychologists only occasionally use the *t* test for a single sample. We introduced it mainly as a stepping-stone to the more widely used *t* test for dependent means. Nevertheless, one sometimes sees the *t* test for a single sample in research articles. For example, Soproni and colleagues (2001), as part of a larger study, had pet dogs respond to a series of eight trials in which the owner would look at one of two bowls of dog food and the researchers measured whether the dog went to the correct bowl. (The researchers called these "at trials" because the owner looked directly *at* the target.) For each dog, this produced an average percentage correct that was compared to chance, which would be 50% correct. Here is part of their results: "During the eight test trials for gesture, dogs performed significantly above chance on at target trials: one sample *t* test, $t(13) = 5.3, p < .01...$" (p. 124).

As we have said, the *t* test for dependent means is much more commonly used. Olthoff (1989) might have reported the result of his study of husbands' communication quality as follows: "There was a significant decline in communication quality, dropping from a mean of 116.32 before marriage to a mean of 104.26 after marriage, $t(18) = -4.24, p < .05$."

As another example, Rashotte and Webster (2005) carried out a study about people's general expectations about the abilities of men and women. In the study, the researchers showed 174 college students photos of women and men (referred to as the female and male targets, respectively). The students rated the person in each photo in terms of that person's general abilities (e.g., in terms of the person's intelligence, abstract abilities, capability at most tasks, and so on). For each participant, these ratings were combined to create a measure of the perceived status of the female targets and of the male targets. The researchers then compared the status ratings given for the female targets and male targets. Since each participant in the study rated *both* the female and the male targets, the researchers compared the status ratings assigned to the female and male targets using a *t* test for dependent means. Table 13 shows the results. The row entitled "Whole sample $(N = 174)$"gives the result of the *t* test for all 174 participants and shows that the status rating assigned to the male targets was significantly higher than the rating assigned to the female targets $(t = 3.46, p < .001)$. As shown in the table, the researchers also conducted two additional *t* tests to see if this effect was the same among the female participants and the male participants. The results showed that both the female and the male participants assigned higher ratings to the male targets.

Often the results of a *t* test for dependent means will be given in the text and not in a table. For example, Song and Schwarz (2009) asked 20 university students to rate the harm of food additives that were either easy to pronounce (e.g., Magnalroxate) or hard to pronounce (e.g., Hnegripitrom). (In case you are wondering, these are not real food additives!) Each student rated all of the food additives using a scale from 1 = *very safe* to 7 = *very harmful*. Here is how Song and Schwarz reported the results of their *t* test for dependent means: "As predicted, participants...rated substances with hard-to-pronounce names $(M = 4.12, SD = 0.78)$ as more harmful than substances with easy-to-pronounce names $(M = 3.7, SD = 0.74)$, $t(19) = 2.41, p < .03$" (p. 136).

Table 13 Status Scale: Mean (and *SE*) General Expectations for Female and Male Targets

Respondents	Mean Score (*SE*)		M − F Target Difference	*t* (1-tailed *p*)
	Female Target	Male Target		
Whole sample ($N = 174$)	5.60 (.06)	5.85 (.07)	.25	3.46 (<.001)
Female respondents ($N = 111$)	5.62 (.07)	5.84 (.081)	.22	2.62 (<.05)
Male respondents ($N = 63$)	5.57 (.10)	5.86 (.11)	.29	2.26 (<.05)

Source: Rashotte, L. S., & Webster, M., Jr. (2005). Gender status beliefs. *Social Science Research, 34,* 618–633. Copyright © 2005 by Elsevier. Reprinted by permission of Elsevier.

Example Worked-Out Problems

t Test for a Single Sample

Eight participants are tested after being given an experimental procedure. Their scores are 14, 8, 6, 5, 13, 10, 10, and 6. The population of people not given this procedure is normally distributed with a mean of 6. Using the .05 level, two-tailed, does the experimental procedure make a difference? (a) Use the five steps of hypothesis testing and (b) sketch the distributions involved.

Answer

(a) Steps of hypothesis testing:

❶ **Restate the question as a research hypothesis and a null hypothesis about the populations.** There are two populations:

Population 1: People who are given the experimental procedure.
Population 2: The general population.

The research hypothesis is that the Population 1 will score differently than Population 2. The null hypothesis is that Population 1 will score the same as Population 2.

❷ **Determine the characteristics of the comparison distribution.** The mean of the distribution of means is 6 (the known population mean). To figure the estimated population variance, you first need to figure the sample mean, which is $(14 + 8 + 6 + 5 + 13 + 10 + 10 + 6)/8 = 72/8 = 9$. The estimated population variance is $S^2 = SS/df = 78/7 = 11.14$; the variance of the distribution of means is $S_M^2 = S^2/N = 11.14/8 = 1.39$. The standard deviation of the distribution of means is $S_M = \sqrt{S_M^2} = \sqrt{1.39} = 1.18$. Its shape will be a t distribution for $df = 7$.

❸ **Determine the cutoff sample score on the comparison distribution at which the null hypothesis should be rejected.** From Table A-2, the cutoffs for a two-tailed t test at the .05 level for $df = 7$ are $+2.365$ and -2.365.

❹ **Determine your sample's score on the comparison distribution.** $t = (M - \mu)/S_M = (9 - 6)/1.18 = 3/1.18 = 2.54$.

❺ **Decide whether to reject the null hypothesis.** The t of 2.54 is more extreme than the needed t of ± 2.365. Therefore, reject the null hypothesis; the research hypothesis is supported. The experimental procedure does make a difference.

(b) Sketches of distributions are shown in Figure 9.

t Test for Dependent Means

A researcher tests 10 individuals before and after an experimental procedure. The results are as follows:

Participant	Before	After
1	10.4	10.8
2	12.6	12.1
3	11.2	12.1
4	10.9	11.4
5	14.3	13.9
6	13.2	13.5
7	9.7	10.9
8	11.5	11.5
9	10.8	10.4
10	13.1	12.5

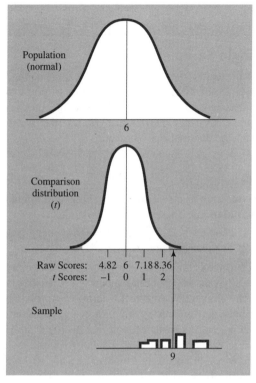

Figure 9 Distributions for answer to Example Worked-Out Example Problem for *t* test for a single sample.

Test the hypothesis that there is an increase in scores, using the .05 significance level. (a) Use the five steps of hypothesis testing and (b) sketch the distributions involved.

Answer

(a) Table 14 shows the results, including the figuring of difference scores and all the other figuring for the *t* test for dependent means. Here are the steps of hypothesis testing:

❶ **Restate the question as a research hypothesis and a null hypothesis about the populations.** There are two populations:

Population 1: People like those who are given the experimental procedure.
Population 2: People who show no change from before to after.

The research hypothesis is that Population 1's mean difference score (figured using "after" scores minus "before" scores) is greater than Population 2's mean difference score. The null hypothesis is that Population 1's mean difference score is not greater than Population 2's.

❷ **Determine the characteristics of the comparison distribution.** Its population mean is 0 difference. The estimated population variance of difference

Table 14 Figuring for Answer to Example Worked-Out Problem for *t* Test for Dependent Means

Participant	Score		Difference (After − Before)	Deviation (Difference − M)	Squared Deviation
	Before	After			
1	10.4	10.8	.4	.260	.068
2	12.6	12.1	−.5	−.640	.410
3	11.2	12.1	.9	.760	.578
4	10.9	11.4	.5	.360	.130
5	14.3	13.9	−.4	−.540	.292
6	13.2	13.5	.3	.160	.026
7	9.7	10.9	1.2	1.060	1.124
8	11.5	11.5	0.0	−.140	.020
9	10.8	10.4	−.4	−.540	.292
10	13.1	12.5	−.6	−.740	.548
Σ:	117.7	119.1	1.4		3.488

For difference scores:

$M = 1.4/10 = .140$

$\mu = 0$

$S^2 = SS/df = 3.488/(10 - 1) = 3.488/9 = .388$

$S_M^2 = S^2/N = .388/10 = .039$

$S_M = \sqrt{S_M^2} = \sqrt{.039} = .197$

t for $df = 9$ needed for 5% significance level, one-tailed $= 1.833$

$t = (M - \mu)/S_M = (.140 - 0)/.197 = .71$

Decision: Do not reject the null hypothesis.

scores, S^2, is shown in Table 14 to be .388. As shown in Table 14, the standard deviation of the distribution of means of difference scores, S_M, is .197. Therefore, the comparison distribution has a mean of 0 and a standard deviation of .197. It will be a *t* distribution for $df = 9$.

❸ **Determine the cutoff sample score on the comparison distribution at which the null hypothesis should be rejected.** For a one-tailed test at the .05 level with $df = 9$, the cutoff is 1.833. (The cutoff is positive as the research hypothesis is that Population 1's mean difference score will be *greater* than Population 2's.)

❹ **Determine your sample's score on the comparison distribution.** The sample's mean change of .140 is .71 standard deviations (of .197 each) on the distribution of means above that distribution's mean of 0. That is, $t = (M - \mu)/S_M = (.140 - 0)/.197 = .71$.

❺ **Decide whether to reject the null hypothesis.** The sample's *t* of .71 is less extreme than the needed *t* of 1.833. Thus, you cannot reject the null hypothesis. The study is inconclusive.

(b) Sketches of distributions are shown in Figure 10.

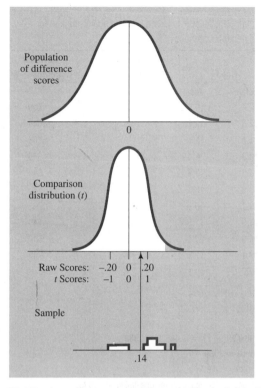

Figure 10   Distributions for answer to Example Worked-Out Problem for *t* test for dependent means.

Outline for Writing Essays for a *t* Test for a Single Sample

1. Describe the core logic of hypothesis testing in this situation. Be sure to mention that the *t* test for a single sample is used for hypothesis testing when you have scores for a sample of individuals and you want to compare the mean of this sample to a population for which the mean is known but the variance is unknown. Be sure to explain the meaning of the research hypothesis and the null hypothesis in this situation.

2. Outline the logic of estimating the population variance from the sample scores. Explain the idea of biased and unbiased estimates of the population variance, and describe the formula for estimating the population variance and why it is different from the ordinary variance formula.

3. Describe the comparison distribution (the *t* distribution) that is used with a *t* test for a single sample, noting how it is different from a normal curve and why. Explain why a *t* distribution (as opposed to the normal curve) is used as the comparison distribution.

4. Describe the logic and process for determining the cutoff sample score(s) on the comparison distribution at which the null hypothesis should be rejected.

5. Describe how and why you figure the *t* score of the sample mean on the comparison distribution.

6. Explain how and why the scores from Steps ❸ and ❹ of the hypothesis-testing process are compared. Explain the meaning of the result of this comparison with regard to the specific research and null hypotheses being tested.

Outline for Writing Essays for a *t* Test for Dependent Means

1. Describe the core logic of hypothesis testing in this situation. Be sure to mention that the *t* test for dependent means is used for hypothesis testing when you have two scores from each person in your sample. Be sure to explain the meaning of the research hypothesis and the null hypothesis in this situation. Explain the logic and procedure for creating difference scores.
2. Explain why you use 0 as the mean for the comparison distribution.
3. Outline the logic of estimating the population variance of difference scores from the sample scores. Explain the idea of biased and unbiased estimates of the population variance, and describe the formula for estimating the population variance. Describe how to figure the standard deviation of the distribution of means of difference scores.
4. Describe the comparison distribution (the *t* distribution) that is used with a *t* test for dependent means. Explain why a *t* distribution (as opposed to the normal curve) is used as the comparison distribution.
5. Describe the logic and process for determining the cutoff sample score(s) on the comparison distribution at which the null hypothesis should be rejected.
6. Describe how and why you figure the *t* score of the sample mean on the comparison distribution.
7. Explain how and why the scores from Steps ❸ and ❹ of the hypothesis-testing process are compared. Explain the meaning of the result of this comparison with regard to the specific research and null hypotheses being tested.

Practice Problems

These problems involve figuring. Most real-life statistics problems are done with special statistical software. Even if you have such software, do these problems by hand to ingrain the method in your mind. To learn how to use a computer to solve statistics problems like those in this chapter, refer to the Using SPSS section at the end of this chapter.

All data are fictional unless an actual citation is given.

Set I

1. In each of the following studies, a single sample's mean is being compared to a population with a known mean but an unknown variance. For each study, decide whether the result is significant. (Be sure to show all of your calculations.)

	Sample Size (*N*)	Population Mean (μ)	Estimated Population Variance (*S*²)	Sample Mean (*M*)	Tails	Significance Level (α)
(a)	64	12.40	9.00	11.00	1 (low predicted)	.05
(b)	49	1,006.35	317.91	1,009.72	2	.01
(c)	400	52.00	7.02	52.41	1 (high predicted)	.01

2. Suppose a candidate running for sheriff in a rural community claims that she will reduce the average speed of emergency response to less than 30 minutes,

which is thought to be the average response time with the current sheriff. There are no past records; so the actual standard deviation of such response times cannot be determined. Thanks to this campaign, she is elected sheriff, and careful records are now kept. The response times for the first month are 26, 30, 28, 29, 25, 28, 32, 35, 24, and 23 minutes.

Using the .05 level of significance, did she keep her promise? (a) Use the steps of hypothesis testing. (b) Sketch the distributions involved. (c) Explain your answer to someone who has never taken a course in statistics.

3. A researcher tests five individuals who have seen paid political ads about a particular issue. These individuals take a multiple-choice test about the issue in which people in general (who know nothing about the issue) usually get 40 questions correct. The number correct for these five individuals was 48, 41, 40, 51, and 50.

Using the .05 level of significance, two-tailed, do people who see the ads score differently on this test? (a) Use the steps of hypothesis testing. (b) Sketch the distributions involved. (c) Explain your answer to someone who is familiar with the Z test but is unfamiliar with *t* tests.

4. For each of the following studies using difference scores, test the significance using a *t* test for dependent means.

	Number of Difference Scores in Sample	Mean of Difference Scores in Sample	Estimated Population Variance of Difference Scores	Tails	Significance Level
(a)	20	1.7	8.29	1 (high predicted)	.05
(b)	164	2.3	414.53	2	.05
(c)	15	−2.2	4.00	1 (low predicted)	.01

5. A program to decrease littering was carried out in four cities in California's Central Valley starting in August 2011. The amount of litter in the streets (average pounds of litter collected per block per day) was measured during July before the program started and then the next July, after the program had been in effect for a year. The results were as follows:

City	July 2011	July 2012
Fresno	9	2
Merced	10	4
Bakersfield	8	9
Stockton	9	1

Using the .01 level of significance, was there a significant decrease in the amount of litter? (a) Use the five steps of hypothesis testing. (b) Sketch the distributions involved. (c) Explain your answer to someone who understands mean, standard deviation, and variance, but knows nothing else about statistics.

6. A researcher assesses the level of a particular hormone in the blood in five patients before and after they begin taking a hormone treatment program. Results for the five patients are as follows:

Patient	Before	After
A	.20	.18
B	.16	.16
C	.24	.23
D	.22	.19
E	.17	.16

Using the .05 significance level, was there a significant change in the level of this hormone? (a) Use the steps of hypothesis testing. (b) Sketch the distributions involved. (c) Explain your answer to someone who understands the *t* test for a single sample but is unfamiliar with the *t* test for dependent means.

7. Figure the estimated effect size and indicate whether it is approximately small, medium, or large, for each of the following studies:

	Mean Change	S
(a)	20	32
(b)	5	10
(c)	.1	.4
(d)	100	500

8. What is the power of each of the following studies, using a *t* test for dependent means (based on the .05 significance level)?

	Effect Size	N	Tails
(a)	Small	20	One
(b)	Medium	20	One
(c)	Medium	30	One
(d)	Medium	30	Two
(e)	Large	30	Two

9. About how many participants are needed for 80% power in each of the following planned studies that will use a *t* test for dependent means with $p < .05$?

	Predicted Effect Size	Tails
(a)	Medium	Two
(b)	Large	One
(c)	Small	One

10. Weller and Weller (1997) conducted a study of the tendency for the menstrual cycles of women who live together (such as sisters) to become synchronized. For their statistical analysis, they compared scores on a measure of synchronization of pairs of sisters living together versus the degree of synchronization that would be expected by chance (lower scores mean more synchronization).

Their key results (reported in a table not reproduced here) were synchrony scores of 6.32 for the 30 roommate sister pairs in their sample compared to an expected synchrony score of 7.76; they then reported a *t* score of 2.27 and a *p* level of .011 for this difference. Explain this result to a person who is familiar with hypothesis testing with a known population variance, but not with the *t* test for a single sample.

11. A psychologist conducts a study of perceptual illusions under two different lighting conditions. Twenty participants were each tested under both of the two different conditions. The experimenter reported: "The mean number of effective illusions was 6.72 under the bright conditions and 6.85 under the dimly lit conditions, a difference that was not significant, $t(19) = 1.62$." Explain this result to a person who has never had a course in statistics. Be sure to use sketches of the distributions in your answer.

12. A study was done of personality characteristics of 100 students who were tested at the beginning and end of their first year of college. The researchers reported the results in the following table:

Personality Scale	Fall M	SD	Spring M	SD	Difference M	SD
Anxiety	16.82	4.21	15.32	3.84	1.50**	1.85
Depression	89.32	8.39	86.24	8.91	3.08**	4.23
Introversion	59.89	6.87	60.12	7.11	−.23	2.22
Neuroticism	38.11	5.39	37.22	6.02	.89*	4.21

*$p < .05$, **$p < .01$.

(a) Focusing on the difference scores, figure the *t* values for each personality scale. (Assume that *SD* in the table is for what we have called *S*, the unbiased estimate of the population standard deviation.)
(b) Explain to a person who has never had a course in statistics what this table means.

Set II

13. In each of the following studies, a single sample's mean is being compared to a population with a known mean but an unknown variance. For each study, decide whether the result is significant.

	Sample Size (N)	Population Mean (μ)	Estimated Population Standard Deviation (S)	Sample Mean (M)	Tails	Significance Level (α)
(a)	16	100.31	2.00	100.98	1 (high predicted)	.05
(b)	16	.47	4.00	.00	2	.05
(c)	16	68.90	9.00	34.00	1 (low predicted)	.01

14. Evolutionary theories often emphasize that humans have adapted to their physical environment. One such theory hypothesizes that people should spontaneously follow a 24-hour cycle of sleeping and waking—even if they are not

exposed to the usual pattern of sunlight. To test this notion, eight paid volunteers were placed (individually) in a room in which there was no light from the outside and no clocks or other indications of time. They could turn the lights on and off as they wished. After a month in the room, each individual tended to develop a steady cycle. Their cycles at the end of the study were as follows: 25, 27, 25, 23, 24, 25, 26, and 25.

Using the .05 level of significance, what should we conclude about the theory that 24 hours is the natural cycle? (That is, does the average cycle length under these conditions differ significantly from 24 hours?) (a) Use the steps of hypothesis testing. (b) Sketch the distributions involved. (c) Explain your answer to someone who has never taken a course in statistics.

15. In a particular country, it is known that college seniors report falling in love an average of 2.20 times during their college years. A sample of five seniors, originally from that country but who have spent their entire college career in the United States, were asked how many times they had fallen in love during their college years. Their numbers were 2, 3, 5, 5, and 2. Using the .05 significance level, do students like these who go to college in the United States fall in love more often than those from their country who go to college in their own country? (a) Use the steps of hypothesis testing. (b) Sketch the distributions involved. (c) Explain your answer to someone who is familiar with the Z test but is unfamiliar with the t test for a single sample.

16. For each of the following studies using difference scores, test the significance using a t test for dependent means.

	Number of Difference Scores in Sample	Mean of Difference Scores	S^2 for Difference Scores	Tails	Significance Level
(a)	10	3.8	50	One (high)	.05
(b)	100	3.8	50	One (high)	.05
(c)	100	1.9	50	One (high)	.05
(d)	100	1.9	50	Two	.05
(e)	100	1.9	25	Two	.05

17. Four individuals with high levels of cholesterol went on a special crash diet, avoiding high-cholesterol foods and taking special supplements. Their total cholesterol levels before and after the diet were as follows:

Participant	Before	After
J. K.	287	255
L. M. M	305	269
A. K.	243	245
R. O. S.	309	247

Using the .05 level of significance, was there a significant change in cholesterol level? (a) Use the steps of hypothesis testing. (b) Sketch the distributions involved. (c) Explain your answer to someone who has never taken a course in statistics.

18. Five people who were convicted of speeding were ordered by the court to attend a workshop. A special device put into their cars kept records of their speeds for two weeks before and after the workshop. The maximum speeds for each person during the two weeks before and the two weeks after the workshop follow.

Participant	Before	After
L. B.	65	58
J. K.	62	65
R .C.	60	56
R. T.	70	66
J. M.	68	60

Using the .05 significance level, should we conclude that people are likely to drive more slowly after such a workshop? (a) Use the steps of hypothesis testing. (b) Sketch the distributions involved. (c) Explain your answer to someone who is familiar with hypothesis testing involving known populations, but has never learned anything about *t* tests.

19. The amount of oxygen consumption was measured in six individuals over two 10-minute periods while sitting with their eyes closed. During one period, they listened to an exciting adventure story; during the other, they heard restful music.

Participant	Story	Music
1	6.12	5.39
2	7.25	6.72
3	5.70	5.42
4	6.40	6.16
5	5.82	5.96
6	6.24	6.08

Based on the results shown, is oxygen consumption less when listening to the music? Use the .01 significance level. (a) Use the steps of hypothesis testing. (b) Sketch the distributions involved. (c) Explain your answer to someone who understands mean, standard deviation, and variance but knows nothing else about statistics.

20. Five sophomores were given an English achievement test before and after receiving instruction in basic grammar. Their scores are shown below.

Student	Before	After
A	20	18
B	18	22
C	17	15
D	16	17
E	12	9

Is it reasonable to conclude that future students would show higher scores after instruction? Use the .05 significance level. (a) Use the steps of hypothesis

testing. (b) Sketch the distributions involved (c) Explain your answer to someone who understands mean, standard deviation, and variance but knows nothing
else about statistics.

21. Figure the predicted effect size and indicate whether it is approximately small,
medium, or large, for each of the following planned studies:

	Predicted Mean Change	σ
(a)	8	30
(b)	8	10
(c)	16	30
(d)	16	10

22. What is the power of each of the following studies, using a *t* test for dependent
means (based on the .05 significance level)?

	Effect Size	N	Tails
(a)	Small	50	Two
(b)	Medium	50	Two
(c)	Large	50	Two
(d)	Small	10	Two
(e)	Small	40	Two
(f)	Small	100	Two
(g)	Small	100	One

23. About how many participants are needed for 80% power in each of the following planned studies that will use a *t* test for dependent means with $p < .05$?

	Predicted Effect Size	Tails
(a)	Small	Two
(b)	Medium	One
(c)	Large	Two

24. A study compared union activity of employees in 10 plants during two different decades. The researchers reported "a significant increase in union activity, $t(9) = 3.28, p < .01$." Explain this result to a person who has never had a
course in statistics. Be sure to use sketches of the distributions in your answer.

25. Baker and Moore (2008) surveyed 58 people when they first started using
MySpace (the researchers called this "Time 0") and again 2 months later (referred to as "Time 1" by the researchers). At both time points, the participants
completed a measure of social integration (a sense of belonging to a group
of friends). Also, at Time 1, the researchers examined participants' MySpace
profiles to see whether they had started blogging in the past 2 months. The
researchers used *t* tests for dependent means (which they refer to as *paired sample t tests*) to test whether bloggers and nonbloggers differed in their level of
social integration from Time 0 to Time 1. Here is how the researchers reported

the results: "Paired samples *t* tests showed bloggers were significantly higher in social integration at Time 1 than Time 0, $t(30) = 3.19, p < .01, \ldots$ with no difference for nonbloggers, $t(26) = -0.370, p > .05$." Explain these results to someone who is familiar with the *t* test for a single sample but not with the *t* test for dependent means.

26. Table 15 (reproduced from a study by Larson et al., 2001) shows ratings of various aspects of work and home life of 100 middle-class men in India who were fathers. Pick three rows of interest to you and explain the results to someone who is familiar with the mean, variance, and Z scores but knows nothing else about statistics.

Table 15 Comparison of Fathers' Mean Psychological States in the Job and Home Spheres ($N = 100$)

Scale	Range	Work	Home	Work vs. Home
Important	0–9	5.98	5.06	6.86***
Attention	0–9	6.15	5.13	7.96***
Challenge	0–9	4.11	2.41	11.49***
Choice	0–9	4.28	4.74	−3.38***
Wish doing else	0–9	1.50	1.44	0.61
Hurried	0–3	1.80	1.39	3.21**
Social anxiety	0–3	0.81	0.64	3.17**
Affect	1–7	4.84	4.98	−2.64**
Social climate	1–7	5.64	5.95	4.17***

Note: Values for column 3 are *t* scores; $df = 90$ for all *t* tests.
**p < .01.
***p < .001.
Source: Larson, R., Dworkin, J., & Verma, S. (2001). Men's work and family lives in India: The daily organization of time and emotions. *Journal of Family Psychology, 15,* 206–224. Copyright © 2001 by the American Psychological Association.

Using SPSS

The ✑ in the following steps indicates a mouse click. (We used SPSS version 19 for Windows to carry out these analyses. The steps and output may be slightly different for other versions of SPSS.)

t Test for a Single Sample

❶ Enter the scores from your distribution in one column of the data window.
❷ ✑ *Analyze*.
❸ ✑ *Compare means*.
❹ ✑ *One-sample T test* (this is the name SPSS uses for a *t* test for a single sample).
❺ ✑ on the variable for which you want to carry out the *t* test and then ✑ the arrow.
❻ Enter the population mean in the "Test Value" box.
❼ ✑ *OK*.

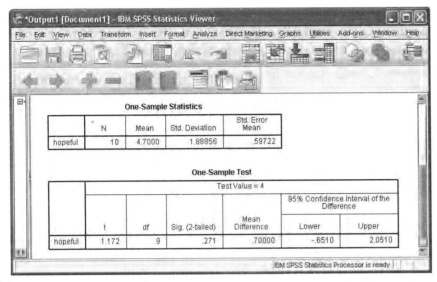

Figure 11 Using SPSS to carry out a *t* test for a single sample for the example of 10 people's ratings of hopefulness after a flood.

Practice these steps by carrying out a single sample *t* test for the example shown earlier in this chapter of 10 people's ratings of hopefulness after a flood. The sample scores, population mean, and figuring for that study are shown in Table 4. Your SPSS output window should look like Figure 11. The first table provides information about the variable: the number of scores ("N"); the mean of the scores ("Mean"); the estimated population standard deviation, S ("Std. Deviation"); and the standard deviation of the distribution of means, S_M ("Std. Error Mean"). Check that the values in that table are consistent (allowing for rounding error) with the values in Table 4.

The second table in the SPSS output window gives the outcome of the *t* test. Compare the values of *t* and *df* in that table and the values shown in Table 4. The exact two-tailed significance level of the *t* test is given in the "Sig. (2-tailed)" column. In this study, the researcher was using the .01 significance level. The significance level given by SPSS (.271) is not more extreme than .01, which means that the researcher cannot reject the null hypothesis and the study is inconclusive.

t Test for Dependent Means

❶ Enter one set of scores (for example, the "before" scores) in the first column of the data window. Then enter the second set of scores (for example, the "after" scores) in the second column of the data window. (Be sure to enter the scores in the order they are listed.) Since each row in the SPSS data window represents a separate person, it is important that you enter each person's scores in two separate columns (for example, a "before" column and an "after" column).

❷ ✍ *Analyze.*

❸ ✍ *Compare means.*

❹ ✍ *Paired-Samples T Test* (this is the name SPSS uses for a *t* test for dependent means).

❺ ✑ on one of the variables, such as the "after" variable (this will highlight the variable). ✑ the arrow. The variable will now appear as "Variable 1" for "Pair 1" in the "Paired Variables" box. ✑ on the second variable, such as the "before" variable (this will highlight the variable). ✑ the arrow. The variable will now appear as "Variable 2" for "Pair 1".

❻ ✑ *OK.*

Practice these steps by carrying out a *t* test for dependent means for Olthoff's (1989) study of communication quality of 19 men who received ordinary premarital counseling. The scores and figuring for that study are shown in Table 6. Your SPSS output window should look like Figure 12. The key information is contained in the third table (labeled "Paired Samples Test"). The final three columns of this table give the *t* score (–4.240), the degrees of freedom (18), and the two-tailed significance level (.000 in this case) of the *t* test. The significance level is so small that, even after rounding to three decimal places, it is less than .001. Because the significance level is more extreme than the .05 significance level we set for this study, you can reject the null hypothesis. By looking at the means for the "after" variable and the "before" variable in the first table (labeled "Paired Samples Statistics"), you can see that the husbands' communication quality was lower after marriage (a mean of 104.2632) than before marriage (a mean of 116.3158).

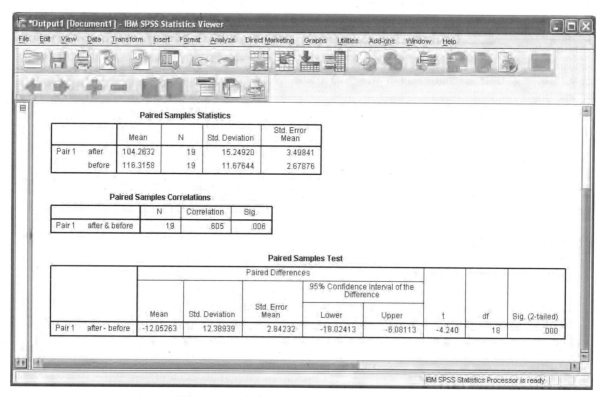

Figure 12 Using SPSS to carry out a *t* test for dependent means for Olthoff's (1989) study of communication quality of 19 men who received ordinary premarital counseling.

Chapter Notes

1. A sample's variance is slightly smaller than the population's because it is based on deviations from the sample's mean. A sample's mean is the optimal balance point for its scores. Thus, deviations of a sample's scores from its mean will be smaller than deviations from any other number. The mean of a sample generally is not exactly the same as the mean of the population it comes from. Thus, deviations of a sample's scores from its mean will generally be smaller than deviations of that sample's scores from the population mean.

2. Statisticians make a subtle distinction in this situation between the comparison distribution and the distribution of means. (We avoid this distinction to simplify your learning of what is already fairly difficult.) The general procedure of hypothesis testing can be described as calculating a Z score for your sample's mean, where $Z = (M - \mu)/\sigma_M$, and then comparing this Z score to a cutoff Z score from the normal curve table. We described this process as using the distribution of means as your comparison distribution. Statisticians would say that actually you are comparing the Z score you figured for your sample mean to a distribution of Z scores (which is simply a standard normal curve). Similarly, for a t test, statisticians think of the procedure as figuring a t score (like a Z score, but figured using an estimated standard deviation), where $t = (M - \mu)/S_M$, and then comparing your computed t score to a cutoff t score from a t distribution table. Thus, according to the formal statistical logic, the comparison distribution is a distribution of t scores, not of means.

3. The symbol μ in the formula should read μ_M, since it refers to the population mean of a *distribution of means*. The μ_M terminology can be used to emphasize the conceptual difference between the mean of a population of individuals and the mean of a population of means. But μ and μ_M are always equal. Thus, to keep the terminology as straightforward as possible in this chapter, we refer to the mean of a distribution of means as μ. (If we were even more formal, we might use μ_2 or even μ_{M_2} because we are referring to the mean of Population 2.)

4. The steps of carrying out a t test for a single sample can be combined into a computational formula for t based on difference scores. For learning purposes in your class, you should use the steps as we have discussed them in this chapter. In a real research situation, the figuring is usually all done by computer (see this chapter's Using SPSS section). Should you ever have to do a t test for a single sample for an actual research study by hand, you may find the following formula useful:

$$ t = \frac{M - \mu}{\sqrt{\dfrac{\Sigma X^2 - ((\Sigma X)^2/N)}{(N-1)(N)}}} \longleftarrow $$

The *t* score for a *t* test for a single sample is the result of subtracting the population mean from the sample mean and dividing that difference by the square root of the following: the sum of the squared scores minus the result of taking the sum of all the scores, squaring this sum and dividing by the number of scores, then taking this whole difference and dividing it by the result of multiplying the number of scores minus 1 by the number of scores.

5. The steps of carrying out a t test for dependent means can be combined into a computational formula for t based on difference scores. For learning purposes in your class, you should use the steps as we have discussed them in this chapter. In a real research situation, the figuring is usually all done by computer (see the Using SPSS section at the end of this chapter). However, if you ever have to

The *t* score for a *t* test for dependent means is the result of dividing the sum of the difference scores by the number of difference scores and then dividing that result by the square root of the following: the sum of the squared difference scores minus the result of taking the sum of all the difference scores, squaring this sum and dividing by the number of difference scores, then taking this whole difference and dividing it by the result of multiplying the number of difference scores minus 1 by the number of difference scores.

do a *t* test for dependent means for an actual research study by hand, you may find the formula useful:

$$t = \frac{(\Sigma D)/N}{\sqrt{\dfrac{\Sigma D^2 - ((\Sigma D)^2/N)}{(N-1)(N)}}}$$

6. Single sample *t* tests are quite rare in practice; so we didn't include a discussion of effect size or power for them in the main text. However, the effect size for a single sample *t* test can be figured using the approach for figuring effect size for the *t* test for dependent means. It is the difference between the population means divided by the population standard deviation: $d = (\mu_1 - \mu_2)/\sigma$. When using this formula for a *t* test for a single sample, μ_1 is the predicted mean of Population 1 (the population from which you are studying a sample), μ_2 is the mean of the "known" population, and σ is the population standard deviation. The conventions for effect size for a *t* test for a single sample are the same as for the situation considered in *Making Sense of Statistical Significance*: A small effect size is .20, a medium effect size is .50, and a large effect size is .80.

7. Cohen (1988, pp. 28–39) provides more detailed tables in terms of numbers of participants, levels of effect size, and significance levels. If you use his tables, note that the *d* referred to is actually based on a *t* test for independent means. To use these tables for a *t* test for dependent means, first multiply your effect size by 1.4. For example, if your effect size is .30, for purposes of using Cohen's tables, you would consider it to be .42 (that is, .30 × 1.4 = .42). The only other difference from our table is that Cohen describes the significance level by the letter *a* (for "alpha level"), with a subscript of either 1 or 2, referring to a one-tailed or two-tailed test. For example, a table that refers to "$a_1 = .05$" at the top means that this is the table for $p < .05$, one-tailed.

8. More detailed tables, giving the needed numbers of participants for levels of power other than 80% (and also for effect sizes other than .20, .50, and .80 and for other significance levels) are provided in Cohen (1988, pp. 54–55). However, see Chapter Note 7 about using Cohen's tables for a *t* test for dependent means.

Appendix: Table

Table A-2 Cutoff Scores for the *t* Distribution

df	One-Tailed Tests .10	.05	.01	Two-Tailed Tests .10	.05	.01
1	3.078	6.314	31.821	6.314	12.706	63.657
2	1.886	2.920	6.965	2.920	4.303	9.925
3	1.638	2.353	4.541	2.353	3.182	5.841
4	1.533	2.132	3.747	2.132	2.776	4.604
5	1.476	2.015	3.365	2.015	2.571	4.032
6	1.440	1.943	3.143	1.943	2.447	3.708
7	1.415	1.895	2.998	1.895	2.365	3.500
8	1.397	1.860	2.897	1.860	2.306	3.356
9	1.383	1.833	2.822	1.833	2.262	3.250
10	1.372	1.813	2.764	1.813	2.228	3.170
11	1.364	1.796	2.718	1.796	2.201	3.106
12	1.356	1.783	2.681	1.783	2.179	3.055
13	1.350	1.771	2.651	1.771	2.161	3.013
14	1.345	1.762	2.625	1.762	2.145	2.977
15	1.341	1.753	2.603	1.753	2.132	2.947
16	1.337	1.746	2.584	1.746	2.120	2.921
17	1.334	1.740	2.567	1.740	2.110	2.898
18	1.331	1.734	2.553	1.734	2.101	2.879
19	1.328	1.729	2.540	1.729	2.093	2.861
20	1.326	1.725	2.528	1.725	2.086	2.846
21	1.323	1.721	2.518	1.721	2.080	2.832
22	1.321	1.717	2.509	1.717	2.074	2.819
23	1.320	1.714	2.500	1.714	2.069	2.808
24	1.318	1.711	2.492	1.711	2.064	2.797
25	1.317	1.708	2.485	1.708	2.060	2.788
26	1.315	1.706	2.479	1.706	2.056	2.779
27	1.314	1.704	2.473	1.704	2.052	2.771
28	1.313	1.701	2.467	1.701	2.049	2.764
29	1.312	1.699	2.462	1.699	2.045	2.757
30	1.311	1.698	2.458	1.698	2.043	2.750
35	1.306	1.690	2.438	1.690	2.030	2.724
40	1.303	1.684	2.424	1.684	2.021	2.705

(*continued*)

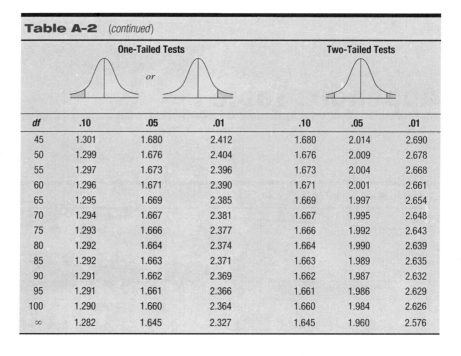

Table A-2 *(continued)*

df	One-Tailed Tests			Two-Tailed Tests		
	.10	.05	.01	.10	.05	.01
45	1.301	1.680	2.412	1.680	2.014	2.690
50	1.299	1.676	2.404	1.676	2.009	2.678
55	1.297	1.673	2.396	1.673	2.004	2.668
60	1.296	1.671	2.390	1.671	2.001	2.661
65	1.295	1.669	2.385	1.669	1.997	2.654
70	1.294	1.667	2.381	1.667	1.995	2.648
75	1.293	1.666	2.377	1.666	1.992	2.643
80	1.292	1.664	2.374	1.664	1.990	2.639
85	1.292	1.663	2.371	1.663	1.989	2.635
90	1.291	1.662	2.369	1.662	1.987	2.632
95	1.291	1.661	2.366	1.661	1.986	2.629
100	1.290	1.660	2.364	1.660	1.984	2.626
∞	1.282	1.645	2.327	1.645	1.960	2.576

Answers to Set I Practice Problems

Chapter 7

1. (a) t needed ($df = 63, p < .05$, one-tailed) $= -1.671$; $S_M^2 = S^2/N = 9/64 = .141$. $S_M = \sqrt{S_M^2} = \sqrt{.141} = .38$; $t = (M - \mu)/S_M = (11 - 12.40)/.38 = -3.68$; reject null hypothesis. (b) t needed $= -2.690, 2.690$; $S_M = 2.55$; $t = 1.32$; do not reject null hypothesis. (c) t needed $= 2.364$; $S_M = .13$; $t = 3.15$; reject null hypothesis.

2. (a) ❶ **Restate the question as a research hypothesis and a null hypothesis about the populations.** There are two populations of interest:

   Population 1: Response times under the new sheriff.
   Population 2: Response times under the old sheriff.

   The research hypothesis is that the two populations are different. The null hypothesis is that the two populations are the same.

❷ **Determine the characteristics of the comparison distribution.** Population 2: shape $=$ assumed normal; $\mu = 30$; The estimated population variance is $S^2 = [\sum (X - M)^2]/df = (124)/(10 - 1) = 13.78$. Distribution of means: shape $= t(df = 9)$; mean of the distribution of means $= 30$; variance of the distribution of means is $S_M^2 = S^2/N = 13.78/10 = 1.378$; standard deviation of the distribution of means is $S_M = \sqrt{S_M^2} = \sqrt{1.378} = 1.17$.

❸ **Determine the cutoff sample score on the comparison distribution at which the null hypothesis should be rejected.** t needed ($df = 9, p < .05$, one-tailed) $= -1.833$.

❹ **Determine your sample's score on the comparison distribution.** $M = (\sum X)/N = 280/10 = 28$; $t = (M - \mu)/S_M = (28 - 30)/1.17 = -1.71$.

❺ **Decide whether to reject the null hypothesis.** -1.71 is not more extreme than -1.833; do not reject the null hypothesis.

(b)

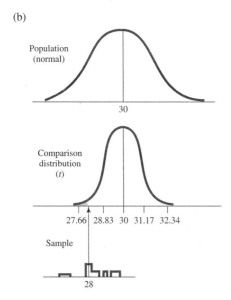

(c) Similar to question 5c, except, instead of difference scores, actual scores are used here, and the expected population mean is the 30 minutes that the sheriff had promised to do better than the current sheriff.

3. (a) and (b) Hypothesis testing steps and sketch similar to questions 2a and b; *t* needed $= -2.776, 2.776$; $t = (M - \mu)/S_M = (46 - 40)/2.3 = 2.61$; do not reject the null hypothesis. (c) Similar to question 5c, except, instead of difference scores, actual scores are used here, and the expected population mean is the 40 questions that people usually get correct.

4. (a) *t* needed $(df = 19, p < .05, \text{one-tailed}) = 1.729$; $S_M^2 = S^2/N = 8.29/20 = .415$; $S_M = \sqrt{S_M^2} = \sqrt{.415} = .64$; $t = (M - \mu)/S_M = (1.7 - 0)/.64 = 2.66$; reject null hypothesis. (b) *t* needed $= -1.984, 1.984$; $S_M^2 = S^2/N = 414.53/164 = 2.53$; $S_M = \sqrt{S_M^2} = \sqrt{2.53} = 1.59$; $t = (2.3 - 0)/1.59 = 1.45$; do not reject null hypothesis. (c) *t* needed $= -2.625$; $S_M^2 = S^2/N = 4/15 = .27$; $S_M = \sqrt{S_M^2} = \sqrt{.27} = .52$; $t = -4.23$; reject null hypothesis.

5. (a) ❶ **Restate the question as a research hypothesis and a null hypothesis about the populations.** There are two populations of interest:

Population 1: Cities like those who participated in the antilittering program.
Population 2: Cities that do not change in the amount of litter over a one-year period.

The research hypothesis is that Population 1 has a greater mean decrease in litter than Population 2. The null hypothesis is that Population 1 doesn't have a greater mean decrease in litter than Population 2.

❷ **Determine the characteristics of the comparison distribution.** Population 2: shape = assumed normal; $\mu = 0$; the estimated population variance is $S^2 = [\Sigma(X - M)^2]/df = (50)/(4 - 1) = 16.67$. Distribution of means: shape $= t(df = 3)$; mean of the distribution of means of difference scores $= 0$; variance of the distribution of means of difference

scores is $S_M^2 = S^2/N = 16.67/4 = 4.17$; standard deviation of the distribution of means of difference scores is $S_M = \sqrt{S_M^2} = \sqrt{4.17} = 2.04$.

❸ **Determine the cutoff sample score on the comparison distribution at which the null hypothesis should be rejected.** *t* needed $(df = 3, p < .01, \text{one-tailed}) = -4.541$.

❹ **Determine your sample's score on the comparison distribution.** Change scores $= -7, -6, 1, -8$; $M = -20/4 = -5$; $t = (M - \mu)/S_M = (-5 - 0)/2.04 = -2.45$.

❺ **Decide whether to reject the null hypothesis.** -2.45 (from Step ❹) is not more extreme than the cutoff of -4.541 (from Step ❸); do not reject the null hypothesis.

(b)

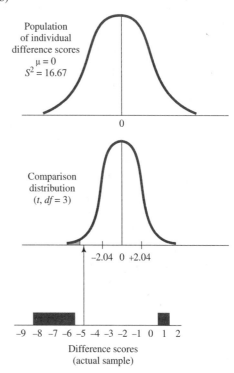

(c) The first thing I did was to simplify things by converting the numbers to difference scores—postprogram (2012) litter minus preprogram (2011) litter for each city. Then I found the mean of these difference scores, which was -5. That is, there is an average decrease of five pounds of litter per block per day.

The next step was to see whether this result, found in these four cities, indicates some real difference more generally due to being in this program. The alternative is the possibility that this much change could have happened in four randomly selected cities just by chance even if in general the program has no real effect. That is, we imagine that the average change for cities in general is actually 0, and maybe this study just happened to pick four cities that would have decreased this much anyway.

I then considered just how much a group of four cities would have to change before I could conclude that they have changed too much to chalk it up to chance. This required figuring out the characteristics of this imagined population of cities in which, on the average, there is no change. An average of no change is the same as saying it has a mean of 0 change. Since I didn't know the variance of this hypothetical distribution of cities that don't change, I estimated it from the information in the sample of four cities. If the sample cities were just a chance drawn from the hypothetical distribution of no change, the variance of these cities should reflect the variance of this distribution (which would be the distribution they come from). However, the variance figured from a particular group (sample) from a larger population will in general be slightly smaller than the true population's variance. Thus, I had to modify the variance formula to take this into account: instead of dividing the sum of the squared deviations by the number of scores, I divided it by the degrees of freedom, which is the number of scores minus 1—in this case, 3. (This adjustment exactly accounts for the tendency of the variance in the sample to underestimate the true population variance.) As shown in the calculations in the steps of hypothesis testing, this gave an estimated population variance (S^2) of 16.67.

I was interested not in individual cities but in a group of four. Thus, what I really needed to know was the characteristics of a distribution of means of samples of four taken from this hypothetical population of individual city change scores. Such a distribution of means will have the same mean of 0 (since there is no reason to expect the means of such groups of four drawn randomly to be systematically higher or lower than 0). However, such a distribution will have a much smaller variance (because the average of a group of four scores is a lot less likely to be extreme than any individual score). Fortunately, it is known (and can be proved mathematically) that the variance of a distribution of means is the variance of the distribution of individuals divided by the number of individuals in each sample. In our example, this works out to 16.67 divided by 4, which is 4.17. The standard deviation of this distribution is thus the square root of 4.17, or 2.04.

It also turns out that if we assume that the hypothetical population of individual cities' change scores is normally distributed (and we have no reason to think otherwise), the distribution of means of samples from that distribution can

be thought of as having a precise known shape, called a *t* distribution (which has slightly thicker tails than a normal curve). Thus, I looked in a table for a *t* distribution for the situation in which there are 3 degrees of freedom used to estimate the population variance. The table shows that there is less than a 1% chance of getting a score that is −4.541 standard deviations from the mean of this distribution.

The mean change score for the sample of four cities was −5, which is 2.45 (that is, −5/2.04) standard deviations below the mean of 0 change on this distribution of means of change scores. This is not as extreme as −4.541. Thus, there is more than a 1% chance that these results could have come from a hypothetical distribution with no change. Therefore, the researcher would not rule out that possibility, and the study would be considered inconclusive.

6. (a), (b), and (c). Hypothesis-testing steps, sketch, and explanation similar to question 5. *t* needed = −2.776, 2.776; $t = (M - \mu)/S_M = (-.014 - 0)/.005 = -2.8$; reject the null hypothesis. (*Note*: This result is very close to the cutoff level; if you round off slightly, your result might not be significant. This is one of those rare situations in which different ways of rounding can produce different results.)

7. (a) $d = (\mu_1 - \mu_2)/\sigma = (20 - 0)/32 = .63$, medium effect size; (b) .50, medium; (c) .25, small; (d) .20, small.

8. From Table 7-11: (a) .22; (b) .71; (c) .86; (d) .77; (e) .99.

9. From Table 7-12: (a) 33; (b) 12; (c) 156.

10. Similar to question 5c, except focusing on this study and the simpler situation involving just a single sample; you also do not need to explain the basic logic of hypothesis testing (only what is added when you have an unknown population variance).

11. Similar to questions 5b and 5c, except the explanation should focus on this study; also, material on mean, standard deviation, and variance should be added, as in the answers to Chapter 2 problems.

12. (a) Anxiety: $S_M^2 = S^2/N = 1.85^2/100 = .0342$; $S_M = \sqrt{S_M^2} = \sqrt{.0342} = .185$; $t = 1.50/.185 = 8.11$. Depression: $S_M = .423$; $t = 7.28$; Introversion: $S_M = .222$; $t = -1.04$; Neuroticism: $S_M = .421$; $t = 2.11$.

(b) Similar to question 5c, except focusing on this study; also, material on mean, standard deviation, and variance should be added, as in the answers to Chapter 2 problems.

Chapter 8

The *t* Test for Independent Means

In this chapter, you learn how to compare two sets of scores, one from each of *two entirely separate groups of people*. This is a very common situation in psychology research. For example, a study may compare the scores from individuals in an experimental group to the scores from individuals in a control group (or from a group of men and a group of women). This is a *t* test situation because you don't know the population variances (so they must be estimated). The scores of the two groups are independent of each other; so the test you learn in this chapter is called a ***t* test for independent means**.

Let's consider an example. A team of researchers is interested in whether writing one's thoughts and feelings associated with traumatic life events can affect physical health. This kind of writing is called expressive writing. Suppose the researchers recruit undergraduate students to take part in a study and randomly

t test for independent means
hypothesis-testing procedure in which there are two separate groups of people tested and in which the population variance is not known.

assign them to be in an expressive writing group or a control group. Students in the expressive writing group are instructed to write four 20-minute essays, one over each of four consecutive days, about their most traumatic life experiences. Students in the control group also write four 20-minute essays over four consecutive days, but their essays are each about their plans for that day. One month later, the researchers ask the students to rate their overall level of physical health (on a scale from 0 = *very poor health* to 100 = *perfect health*). Since the expressive writing and the control group contain different students, a *t* test for independent means is the appropriate test of the effect of expressive writing on physical health. We will return to this example later in the chapter. But first, you will learn about the logic of the *t* test for independent means, which involves learning about a new kind of distribution (called the *distribution of differences between means*).

The Distribution of Differences Between Means

distribution of differences between means   distribution of differences between means of pairs of samples such that, for each pair of means, one is from one population and the other is from a second population; the comparison distribution in a *t* test for independent means.

In the situation you face in this chapter, the scores in one group are for different people than the scores in the other group. So you don't have any pairs of scores, as you do when the same group of people each had two scores. Thus, it wouldn't be possible to create difference scores in any meaningful way, so you can't use difference scores for the hypothesis-testing procedure in this chapter. Instead, when the scores in one group are for different people than the scores in the other group, what you can compare is the *mean* of one group to the *mean* of the other group.

So the *t* test for independent means focuses on the *difference between the means* of the two groups. The hypothesis-testing procedure, however, for the most part works just like the hypothesis-testing procedures you have already learned. The main difference is that the focus is now on the difference between means, so the comparison distribution is a **distribution of differences between means**.

A distribution of differences between means is, in a sense, two steps removed from the populations of individuals: First, there is a distribution of means from each population of individuals; second, there is a distribution of differences between pairs of means, one of each pair of means taken from its particular distributions of means.

Think of this distribution of differences between means as being built up as follows: (a) randomly select one mean from the distribution of means for the first group's population, (b) randomly select one mean from the distribution of means for the second group's population, and (c) subtract. (That is, take the mean from the first distribution of means and subtract the mean from the second distribution of means.) This gives a difference score between the two selected means. Then repeat the process. This creates a second difference score, a difference between the two newly selected means. Repeating this process a large number of times creates a distribution of differences between means. You would never actually create a distribution of differences between means using this lengthy method (there is a simpler mathematical rule that accomplishes the same thing). But it shows clearly what makes up the distribution.

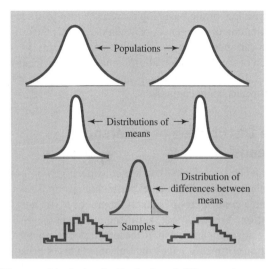

Figure 1   Diagram of the logic of a distribution of differences between means.

The Overall Logic and a Visual Picture of the Distribution of Differences Between Means

Figure 1 shows the entire logical construction for a distribution of differences between means. At the top are the two population distributions. We do not know the characteristics of these population distributions, but we do know that if the null hypothesis is true, the two population means are the same. That is, the null hypothesis is that $\mu_1 = \mu_2$. We also can estimate the variance of these populations based on the sample information (these estimated variances will be S_1^2 and S_2^2).

Below each population distribution is the distribution of means for that population. Using the estimated population variance and knowing the size of each sample, you can figure the variance of each distribution of means in the usual way. (It is the estimated variance of its parent population divided by the size of the sample from that population that is being studied.)

Below these two distributions of means, and built from them, is the crucial *distribution of differences between means*. This distribution's variance is ultimately based on estimated population variances. Thus, we can think of it as a *t* distribution. The goal of a *t* test for independent means is to decide whether the difference between the means of your two actual samples is a more extreme difference than the cutoff difference on this distribution of differences between means. The two actual samples are shown (as histograms) at the bottom.

Remember, this whole procedure is really a kind of complicated castle in the air. It exists only in our minds to help us make decisions based on the results of an actual experiment. The only concrete reality in all of this is the actual scores in the two samples. You estimate the population variances from these sample scores. The variances of the two distributions of means are based entirely on these estimated population variances (and the sample sizes). And, as you will see shortly, the characteristics of the distribution of differences between means are based on these two distributions of means.

Still, the procedure is a powerful one. It has the power of mathematics and logic behind it. It helps you develop general knowledge based on the specifics of a particular study.

With this overview of the basic logic, we now turn to six key details: (1) the mean of the distribution of differences between means, (2) the estimated population variance, (3) the variance of the two distributions of means, (4) the variance and standard deviation of the distribution of differences between means, (5) the shape of the distribution of differences between means, and (6) the *t* score for the difference between the two means being compared.

Mean of the Distribution of Differences Between Means

In a *t* test for independent means, you are considering two populations: for example, one population from which an experimental group is taken and one population from which a control group is taken. In practice, you don't know the mean of either population. You do know that if the null hypothesis is true, these two populations have equal means. Also, if these two populations have equal means, the two distributions of means have equal means. (This is because each distribution of means has the same mean as its parent population of individuals.) Finally, if you take random samples from two distributions with equal means, the differences between the means of these random samples, in the long run, balance out to 0. The result of all this is the following: whatever the specifics of the study, you know that, if the null hypothesis is true, the distribution of differences between means has a mean of 0.

Estimating the Population Variance

Population variance is the sum of squared deviation scores divided by the degrees of freedom (the number in the sample minus 1). To do a *t* test for independent means, it has to be reasonable to assume that the populations the two samples come from have the same variance (which, in statistical terms, is called *homogeneity of variance*). (If the null hypothesis is true, they also have the same mean. However, whether or not the null hypothesis is true, you must be able to assume that the two populations have the same variance.) Therefore, when you estimate the variance from the scores in either sample, you are getting two separate estimates of what should be the same number. In practice, the two estimates will almost never be exactly identical. Since they are both supposed to be estimating the same thing, the best solution is to average the two estimates to get the best single overall estimate. This is called the **pooled estimate of the population variance (S^2_{Pooled})**.

In making this average, however, you also have to take into account that the two samples may not be the same size. If one sample is larger than the other, the estimate it provides is likely to be more accurate (because it is based on more information). If both samples are exactly the same size, you could just take an ordinary average of the two estimates. On the other hand, when they are not the same size, you need to make some adjustment in the averaging to give more weight to the larger sample. That is, you need a **weighted average**, an average weighted by the amount of information each sample provides.

Also, to be precise, the amount of information each sample provides is not its number of scores, but its degrees of freedom (its number of scores minus 1). Thus, your weighted average needs to be based on the degrees of freedom each sample provides. To find the weighted average, you figure out what proportion of the total degrees of freedom each sample contributes and multiply that proportion by the

pooled estimate of the population variance (S^2_{Pooled}) in a *t* test for independent means, weighted average of the estimates of the population variance from two samples (each estimate weighted by the proportion consisting of its sample's degrees of freedom divided by the total degrees of freedom for both samples).

weighted average average in which the scores being averaged do not have equal influence on the total, as in figuring the pooled variance estimate in a *t* test for independent means.

population variance estimate from that sample. Finally, you add up the two results, and that is your weighted, pooled estimate. In terms of a formula,

$$S^2_{Pooled} = \frac{df_1}{df_{Total}}(S^2_1) + \frac{df_2}{df_{Total}}(S^2_2) \qquad (1)$$

In this formula, S^2_{Pooled} is the pooled estimate of the population variance. df_1 is the degrees of freedom in the sample from Population 1, and df_2 is the degrees of freedom in the sample from Population 2. (Remember, each sample's df is its number of scores minus 1.) df_{Total} is the total degrees of freedom ($df_{Total} = df_1 + df_2$). S^2_1 is the estimate of the population variance based on the scores in Population 1's sample; S^2_2 is the estimate based on the scores in Population 2's sample.

Consider a study in which the population variance estimate based on an experimental group of 11 participants is 60, and the population variance estimate based on a control group of 31 participants is 80. The estimate from the experimental group is based on 10 degrees of freedom (11 participants minus 1), and the estimate from the control group is based on 30 degrees of freedom (31 minus 1). The total information on which the estimate is based is the total degrees of freedom—in this example, 40 (that is, $10 + 30$). Thus, the experimental group provides one-quarter of the total information ($10/40 = 1/4$) and the control group provides three-quarters of the total information ($30/40 = 3/4$).

You then multiply the estimate from the experimental group by 1/4, making 15 (that is, $60 \times 1/4 = 15$), and you multiply the estimate from the control group by 3/4, making 60 (that is, $80 \times 3/4 = 60$). Adding the two gives an overall estimate of 15 plus 60, which is 75. Using the formula,

$$S^2_{Pooled} = \frac{df_1}{df_{Total}}(S^2_1) + \frac{df_2}{df_{Total}}(S^2_2) = \frac{10}{40}(60) + \frac{30}{40}(80)$$

$$= \frac{1}{4}(60) + \frac{3}{4}(80) = 15 + 60 = 75.$$

Notice that this procedure does not give the same result as ordinary averaging (without weighting).

Ordinary averaging would give an estimate of 70 [that is, $(60 + 80)/2 = 70$]. Your weighted, pooled estimate of the population variance of 75 is closer to the estimate based on the control group alone than to the estimate based on the experimental group alone. This is as it should be, because the control group estimate in this example was based on more information.

Figuring the Variance of Each of the Two Distributions of Means

The pooled estimate of the population variance is the best estimate for both populations. (Remember, to do a *t* test for independent means, you have to be able to assume that the two populations have the same variance.) However, even though the two populations have the same variance, if the samples are not the same size, the distributions of means taken from them do not have the same variance. That is because the variance of a distribution of means is the population variance divided by the sample size. In terms of formulas,

$$S^2_{M_1} = \frac{S^2_{Pooled}}{N_1} \qquad (2)$$

The variance of the distribution of means for the second population (based on an estimated population variance) is the pooled estimate of the population variance divided by the number of participants in the sample from the second population.

$$S^2_{M_2} = \frac{S^2_{\text{Pooled}}}{N_2} \qquad (3)$$

Consider again the study with 11 in the experimental group and 31 in the control group. We figured the pooled estimate of the population variance to be 75. For the experimental group, the variance of the distribution of means would be 75/11, which is 6.82. For the control group, the variance would be 75/31, which is 2.42. Using the formulas,

$$S^2_{M_1} = \frac{S^2_{\text{Pooled}}}{N_1} = \frac{75}{11} = 6.82$$

$$S^2_{M_2} = \frac{S^2_{\text{Pooled}}}{N_2} = \frac{75}{31} = 2.42.$$

TIP FOR SUCCESS

Remember that when figuring estimated variances, you divide by the degrees of freedom. But when figuring the variance of a distribution of means, which does not involve any additional estimation, you divide by the actual number in the sample.

The Variance and Standard Deviation of the Distribution of Differences Between Means

The **variance of the distribution of differences between means** ($S^2_{\text{Difference}}$) is the variance of Population 1's distribution of means plus the variance of Population 2's distribution of means. (This is because, in a difference between two numbers, the variation in each contributes to the overall variation in their difference. It is like subtracting a moving number from a moving target.) Stated as a formula,

$$S^2_{\text{Difference}} = S^2_{M_1} + S^2_{M_2} \qquad (4)$$

The **standard deviation of the distribution of differences between means** ($S_{\text{Difference}}$) is the square root of the variance:

$$S_{\text{Difference}} = \sqrt{S^2_{\text{Difference}}} \qquad (5)$$

The variance of the distribution of differences between means is the variance of the distribution of means for the first population (based on an estimated population variance) plus the variance of the distribution of means for the second population (based on an estimated population variance).

In the example we have been considering, the variance of the distribution of means for the experimental group was 6.82, and the variance of the distribution of means for the control group was 2.42; the variance of the distribution of the difference between means is thus 6.82 plus 2.42, which is 9.24. This makes the standard deviation of this distribution the square root of 9.24, which is 3.04. In terms of the formulas,

$$S^2_{\text{Difference}} = S^2_{M_1} + S^2_{M_2} = 6.82 + 2.42 = 9.24$$

$$S_{\text{Difference}} = \sqrt{S^2_{\text{Difference}}} = \sqrt{9.24} = 3.04.$$

The standard deviation of the distribution of differences between means is the square root of the variance of the distribution of differences between means.

You have learned about several new types of variance in this chapter. For a summary of all of the types of variance that are used in a *t* test for independent means, see Table 1.

variance of a distribution of differences between means ($S^2_{\text{Difference}}$) one of the numbers figured as part of a *t* test for independent means; it equals the sum of the variances of the distributions of means associated with each of the two samples.

standard deviation of the distribution of differences between means ($S_{\text{Difference}}$) in a *t* test for independent means, square root of the variance of the distribution of differences between means.

Steps to Find the Standard Deviation of the Distribution of Differences Between Means

❶ **Figure the estimated population variances based on each sample.** That is, figure one estimate for each population using the formula $S^2 = SS/(N - 1)$.

❷ **Figure the pooled estimate of the population variance:**

$$S^2_{\text{Pooled}} = \frac{df_1}{df_{\text{Total}}}(S^2_1) + \frac{df_2}{df_{\text{Total}}}(S^2_2)$$

$$(df_1 = N_1 - 1 \text{ and } df_2 = N_2 - 1; \, df_{\text{Total}} = df_1 + df_2)$$

Table 1 Summary of Different Types of Variance Used for the *t* Test for Independent Means

Type of Variance	Symbol
Estimated population variance for the first population	S_1^2
Estimated population variance for the second population	S_2^2
Pooled estimate of the population variance	S_{Pooled}^2
Variance of the distribution of means for the first population (based on an estimated population variance)	$S_{M_1}^2$
Variance of the distribution of means for the second population (based on an estimated population variance)	$S_{M_2}^2$
Variance of the distribution of differences between means	$S_{Difference}^2$

❿ **Figure the variance of each distribution of means:** $S_{M_1}^2 = S_{Pooled}^2/N_1$ and $S_{M_2}^2 = S_{Pooled}^2/N_2$.

⓫ **Figure the variance of the distribution of differences between means:** $S_{Difference}^2 = S_{M_1}^2 + S_{M_2}^2$.

⓬ **Figure the standard deviation of the distribution of differences between means:** $S_{Difference} = \sqrt{S_{Difference}^2}$.

The Shape of the Distribution of Differences Between Means

The distribution of differences between means is based on estimated population variances. Thus, the distribution of differences between means (the comparison distribution) is a *t* distribution. The variance of this distribution is figured based on population variance estimates from two samples. Therefore, the degrees of freedom for this *t* distribution are the sum of the degrees of freedom of the two samples. In terms of a formula,

$$df_{Total} = df_1 + df_2 \qquad (6)$$

> The total degrees of freedom for a *t* test for independent means is the degrees of freedom in the first sample plus the degrees of freedom in the second sample.

In the example we have been considering with an experimental group of 11 and a control group of 31, we saw earlier that the total degrees of freedom is 40 (that is, $11 - 1 = 10$; $31 - 1 = 30$; and $10 + 30 = 40$). To find the *t* score needed for significance, you look up the cutoff point in the *t* table in the row with 40 degrees of freedom. Suppose you are conducting a one-tailed test using the .05 significance level. The *t* table in the Appendix (Table A-2) shows a cutoff of 1.684 for 40 degrees of freedom. That is, for a result to be significant, the difference between the means has to be at least 1.684 standard deviations above the mean difference of 0 on the distribution of differences between means.

The *t* Score for the Difference Between the Two Actual Means

Here is how you figure the *t* score for Step ❹ of the hypothesis testing: First, figure the difference between your two actual samples' means. (That is, subtract one from the other). Then, figure out where this difference is on the distribution of differences between means. You do this by dividing your difference by the standard deviation of this distribution. In terms of a formula,

$$t = \frac{M_1 - M_2}{S_{Difference}} \qquad (7)$$

> The *t* score is the difference between the two sample means divided by the standard deviation of the distribution of differences between means.

For our example, suppose the mean of the first sample is 198 and the mean of the second sample is 190. The difference between these two means is 8 (that is, $198 - 190 = 8$). Earlier we figured the standard deviation of the distribution of differences between means in this example to be 3.04. That would make a *t* score of 2.63 (that is, $8/3.04 = 2.63$). In other words, in this example the difference between the two means is 2.63 standard deviations above the mean of the distribution of differences between means. In terms of the formula,

$$t = \frac{M_1 - M_2}{S_{\text{Difference}}} = \frac{198 - 190}{3.04} = \frac{8}{3.04} = 2.63$$

How are you doing?

1. (a) When would you carry out a *t* test for independent means? (b) How is this different from the situation in which you would carry out a *t* test for dependent means?
2. (a) What is the comparison distribution in a *t* test for independent means? (b) Explain the logic of going from scores in two samples to an estimate of the variance of this comparison distribution. (c) Illustrate your answer with sketches of the distributions involved. (d) Why is the mean of this distribution 0?
3. Write the formula for each of the following: (a) pooled estimate of the population variance, (b) variance of the distribution of means for the first population, (c) variance of the distribution of differences between means, and (d) *t* score in a *t* test for independent means. (e) Define all the symbols used in these formulas.
4. Explain (a) why a *t* test for independent means uses a single pooled estimate of the population variance, and (b) why and (c) how this estimate is "weighted."
5. For a particular study comparing means of two samples, the first sample has 21 participants and an estimated population variance of 100; the second sample has 31 participants and an estimated population variance of 200. (a) What is the standard deviation of the distribution of differences between means? (b) What is its mean? (c) What will be its shape? (d) Illustrate your answer with sketches of the distributions involved.

Answers

1. (a) You carry out a *t* test for independent means when you have done a study in which you have scores from two samples of different individuals and you do not know the population variance.
   (b) In a *t* test for dependent means you have two scores from each of several individuals.
2. (a) The comparison distribution in a *t* test for independent means is a distribution of differences between means.
   (b) You estimate the population variance from each sample's scores. Since you assume the populations have the same variance, you then pool the two estimates (giving proportionately more weight in this averaging to the sample that has more degrees of freedom in its estimate). Using this pooled estimate, you figure the variance of the distribution of means for each sample's population by dividing this pooled estimate by the sample's number of participants. Finally, since your interest is in a difference between means, you create a comparison distribution of differences between means. This comparison distribution will have a variance equal to the sum of the variances of the two distributions of means. (Because the distribution of differences between means is made up of pairs of means, one

taken from each distribution of means, the variance of both of these distributions of means contributes to the variance of the comparison distribution.)

(c) Your sketch should look like Figure 1.

(d) The mean of this distribution will be zero because, if the null hypothesis is true, the two populations have the same mean. So differences between means would on the average come out to zero.

3. (a) Pooled estimate of the population variance:

$$S^2_{Pooled} = \frac{df_1}{df_{Total}}(S^2_1) + \frac{df_2}{df_{Total}}(S^2_2).$$

(b) Variance of the distribution of means for the first population:

$$S^2_{M_1} = \frac{S^2_{Pooled}}{N_1}.$$

(c) Variance of the distribution of differences between means:

$$S^2_{Difference} = S^2_{M_1} + S^2_{M_2}.$$

(d) *t* score in a *t* test for independent means: $t = \dfrac{M_1 - M_2}{S_{Difference}}$.

(e) S^2_{Pooled} is the pooled estimate of the population variance; df_1 and df_2 are the degrees of freedom in the samples from the first and second populations, respectively; df_{Total} is the total degrees of freedom (the sum of df_1 and df_2); S^2_1 and S^2_2 are the population variance estimates based on the samples from the first and second populations, respectively; $S^2_{M_1}$ is the variance of the distribution of means for the first population based on an estimated variance of the population of individuals; N_1 is the number of participants in the sample from the first population; $S^2_{Difference}$ is the variance of the distribution of differences between means based on estimated variances of the populations of individuals; *t* is the *t* score for a *t* test for independent means (the number of standard deviations from the mean on the distribution of differences between means); M_1 and M_2 are the means of the samples from the first and second populations, respectively; and $S_{Difference}$ is the standard deviation of the distribution of differences between means based on estimated variances of the populations of individuals.

4. (a) You assume that both populations have the same variance; thus the estimates from the two samples should be estimates of the same number.

(b) We weight (give more influence to) an estimate from a larger sample because, being based on more information, it is likely to be more accurate.

(c) The actual weighting is done by multiplying each sample's estimate by the degrees of freedom for that sample divided by the total degrees of freedom; you then sum these two products.

5. (a) Standard deviation of the distribution of differences between means:

$$S^2_{Pooled} = (20/50)(100) + (30/50)(200) = 40 + 120 = 160.$$
$$S^2_{M_1} = 160/21 = 7.62; S^2_{M_2} = 160/31 = 5.16;$$
$$S^2_{Difference} = 7.62 + 5.16 = 12.78;$$
$$S_{Difference} = \sqrt{12.78} = 3.57.$$

(b) Mean: 0; (c) Shape: *t* distribution with $df = 50$; (d) Should look like Figure 1 with numbers written in (see Figure 2 for an example).

Hypothesis Testing with a *t* Test for Independent Means

Considering the five steps of hypothesis testing, there are three new wrinkles for a *t* test for independent means: (1) the comparison distribution is now a distribution of differences between means (this affects Step ❷); (2) the degrees of freedom for finding the cutoff on the *t* table is based on two samples (this affects Step ❸); and (3) your sample's score on the comparison distribution is based on the difference between your two means (this affects Step ❹).

Example of a *t* Test for Independent Means

Let's return to the expressive writing study that we introduced at the start of the chapter. Twenty students were recruited to take part in the study. The 10 students randomly assigned to the expressive writing group wrote about their thoughts and feelings associated with their most traumatic life events. The 10 students randomly assigned to the control group wrote about their plans for the day. One month later, all of the students rated their overall level of physical health on a scale from $0 = $ *very poor health* to $100 = $ *perfect health*. (Although this example is based on actual studies, we made up the details we use here to be an easier example to follow for learning. Mainly, actual studies usually have large samples. Real studies on this kind of topic also often use more objective measures of health, such as number of physician visits or days missed from school.)

The scores and figuring for the *t* test are shown in Table 2. Figure 2 shows the distributions involved. Let's go through the five steps of hypothesis testing.

Table 2 *t* Test for Independent Means for a Fictional Study of the Effect of Expressive Writing on Physical Health

Expressive Writing Group			Control Writing Group		
Score	Deviation from Mean (Score − *M*)	Squared Deviation from Mean	Score	Deviation from Mean (Score − *M*)	Squared Deviation from Mean
77	−2	4	87	19	361
88	9	81	77	9	81
77	−2	4	71	3	9
90	11	121	70	2	4
68	−11	121	63	−5	25
74	−5	25	50	−18	324
62	−17	289	58	−10	100
93	14	196	63	−5	25
82	3	9	76	8	64
79	0	0	65	−3	9
Σ:790		850	680		1002

$M_1 = 79.00$; $S_1^2 = 850/9 = 94.44$; $M_2 = 68.00$; $S_2^2 = 1002/9 = 111.33$

$N_1 = 10$; $df_1 = N_1 - 1 = 9$; $N_2 = 10$; $df_2 = N_2 - 1 = 9$

$df_{Total} = df_1 + df_2 = 9 + 9 = 18$

$S_{Pooled}^2 = \dfrac{df_1}{df_{Total}}(S_1^2) + \dfrac{df_2}{df_{Total}}(S_2^2) = \dfrac{9}{18}(94.44) + \dfrac{9}{18}(111.33) = 47.22 + 55.67 = 102.89$

$S_{M_1}^2 = S_{Pooled}^2/N_1 = 102.89/10 = 10.29$

$S_{M_2}^2 = S_{Pooled}^2/N_2 = 102.89/10 = 10.29$

$S_{Difference}^2 = S_{M_1}^2 + S_{M_2}^2 = 10.29 + 10.29 = 20.58$

$S_{Difference} = \sqrt{S_{Difference}^2} = \sqrt{20.58} = 4.54$

Needed *t* with $df = 18$, 5% level, two-tailed $= \pm 2.101$

$t = (M_1 - M_2)/S_{Difference} = (79.00 - 68.00)/4.54 = 2.42$

Decision: Reject the null hypothesis.

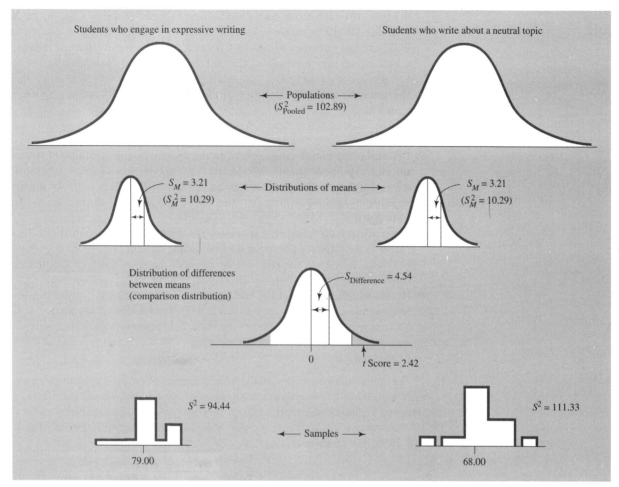

Figure 2   Distributions for a *t* test for independent means for the expressive writing example.

❶ **Restate the question as a research hypothesis and a null hypothesis about the populations.** There are two populations:

Population 1: Students who engage in expressive writing.
Population 2: Students who write about a neutral topic (their plans for the day).

The researchers were interested in identifying a positive or a negative health effect of expressive writing. Thus, the research hypothesis was that Population 1 students would rate their health differently from Population 2 students: $\mu_1 \neq \mu_2$. The null hypothesis was that Population 1 students would rate their health the same as Population 2 students: $\mu_1 = \mu_2$.

❷ **Determine the characteristics of the comparison distribution.** The comparison distribution is a distribution of differences between means. (a) Its mean is 0 (as it almost always is in a *t* test for independent means, because we are interested in whether there is more than 0 difference between the two populations). (b) Regarding its standard deviation,

  ❹ **Figure the estimated population variances based on each sample.** As shown in Table 2, S_1^2 comes out to 94.44 and $S_2^2 = 111.33$.
  ❺ **Figure the pooled estimate of the population variance:** As shown in Table 2, the figuring for S_{Pooled}^2 gives a result of 102.89.

❹ **Figure the variance of each distribution of means:** Dividing S^2_{Pooled} by the N in each sample, as shown in Table 2, gives $S^2_{M_1} = 10.29$ and $S^2_{M_2} = 10.29$.

❺ **Figure the variance of the distribution of differences between means:** Adding up the variances of the two distributions of means, as shown in Table 2, comes out to $S^2_{\text{Difference}} = 20.58$.

❻ **Figure the standard deviation of the distribution of differences between means:** $S_{\text{Difference}} = \sqrt{S^2_{\text{Difference}}} = \sqrt{20.58} = 4.54$.

(c) The shape of this comparison distribution will be a *t* distribution with a total of 18 degrees of freedom.

❸ **Determine the cutoff sample score on the comparison distribution at which the null hypothesis should be rejected.** This requires a two-tailed test because the researchers were interested in an effect in either direction. As shown in Table A-2 (in the Appendix), the cutoff *t* scores at the .05 level are 2.101 and −2.101.

❹ **Determine your sample's score on the comparison distribution.** The *t* score is the difference between the two sample means (79.00 − 68.00, which is 11.00), divided by the standard deviation of the distribution of differences between means (which is 4.54). This comes out to 2.42.

❺ **Decide whether to reject the null hypothesis.** The *t* score of 2.42 for the difference between the two actual means is larger than the cutoff *t* score of 2.101. You can reject the null hypothesis. The research hypothesis is supported: students who engage in expressive writing report a higher level of health than students who write about a neutral topic.

The actual numbers in this study were fictional. However, the results are consistent with those from many actual studies that have shown beneficial effects of expressive writing on self-reported health outcomes, as well as additional outcomes, such as number of doctor visits and psychological well-being (e.g., Pennebaker & Beall, 1986; Wallander et al., 2011; see also Frattaroli, 2006).

Summary of Steps for a *t* Test for Independent Means

Table 3 summarizes the steps for a *t* test for independent means.[1]

A Second Example of a *t* Test for Independent Means

Suppose a researcher wants to study the effectiveness of a new job skills training program for people who have not been able to hold a job. Fourteen people who have not been able to hold a job agree to be in the study. The researcher randomly picks 6 of these volunteers to be an experimental group that will go through the special training program. The other 8 volunteers are put in a control group that will go through an ordinary job skills training program. After finishing their training program (of whichever type), all 14 are placed in similar jobs.

A month later, each volunteer's employer is asked to rate how well the new employee is performing, using a 9-point scale. The scores and figuring for the *t* test are shown in Table 4. The distributions involved are shown in Figure 3. Let's carry out the analysis, following the five steps of hypothesis testing.

❶ **Restate the question as a research hypothesis and a null hypothesis about the populations.** There are two populations:

Population 1: Individuals who could not hold a job, who then participate in the special job skills program.

Table 3 Steps for a *t* Test for Independent Means

❶ **Restate the question as a research hypothesis and a null hypothesis about the populations.**

❷ **Determine the characteristics of the comparison distribution.**
a. Its mean will be 0.
b. Figure its standard deviation.
   Ⓐ **Figure the estimated population variances based on each sample.** For each population,
   $$S^2 = SS/(N - 1)$$
   Ⓑ **Figure the pooled estimate of the population variance:**
   $$S^2_{Pooled} = \frac{df_1}{df_{Total}}(S^2_1) + \frac{df_2}{df_{Total}}(S^2_2)$$
   $(df_1 = N_1 - 1$ and $df_2 = N_2 - 1; df_{Total} = df_1 + df_2)$
   Ⓒ **Figure the variance of each distribution of means:**
   $$S^2_{M_1} = S^2_{Pooled}/N_1 \text{ and } S^2_{M_2} = S^2_{Pooled}/N_2$$
   Ⓓ **Figure the variance of the distribution of differences between means:**
   $$S^2_{Difference} = S^2_{M_1} + S^2_{M_2}$$
   Ⓔ **Figure the standard deviation of the distribution of differences between means:**
   $$S_{Difference} = \sqrt{S^2_{Difference}}$$
c. Determine its shape: It will be a *t* distribution with df_{Total} degrees of freedom.

❸ **Determine the cutoff sample score on the comparison distribution at which the null hypothesis should be rejected.**
a. Determine the degrees of freedom (df_{Total}), desired significance level, and tails in the test (one or two).
b. Look up the appropriate cutoff in a *t* table. If the exact *df* is not given, use the *df* below it.

❹ **Determine your sample's score on the comparison distribution:**
$$t = (M_1 - M_2)/S_{Difference}$$

❺ **Decide whether to reject the null hypothesis:** Compare the scores from Steps ❸ and ❹.

Table 4 Figuring for a *t* Test for Independent Means for the Job Skills Example

Experimental Group (Receiving Special Program)			Control Group (Receiving Ordinary Program)		
Score	Deviation from Mean	Squared Deviation from Mean	Score	Deviation from Mean	Squared Deviation from Mean
6	0	0	6	3	9
4	−2	4	1	−2	4
9	3	9	5	2	4
7	1	1	3	0	0
7	1	1	1	−2	4
3	−3	9	1	−2	4
Σ: 36	0	24	4	1	1
			3	0	0
			Σ: 24	0	26

$M_1 = 36/6; S^2_1 = 24/5 = 4.8; M_2 = 24/8 = 3; S^2_2 = 26/7 = 3.71$

$N_1 = 6; df_1 = 6 - 1 = 5; N_2 = 8; df_2 = 8 - 1 = 7$

$df_{Total} = df_1 + df_2 = 5 + 7 = 12$

$S^2_{Pooled} = \dfrac{df_1}{df_{Total}}(S^2_1) + \dfrac{df_2}{df_{Total}}(S^2_2) = \dfrac{5}{12}(4.8) + \dfrac{7}{12}(3.71) = 2 + 2.16 = 4.16$

$S^2_{M_1} = S^2_{Pooled}/N_1 = 4.16/6 = 0.69$

$S^2_{M_2} = S^2_{Pooled}/N_2 = 4.16/8 = 0.52$

$S^2_{Difference} = S^2_{M_1} + S^2_{M_2} = 0.69 + 0.52 = 1.21$

$S_{Difference} = \sqrt{S^2_{Difference}} = \sqrt{1.21} = 1.10$

Needed *t* with $df = 12$, 5% level, two-tailed $= \pm 2.179$

$t = (M_1 - M_2)/S_{Difference} = (6 - 3)/1.10 = 3/1.10 = 2.73$

Decision: Reject the null hypothesis, the research hypothesis is supported.

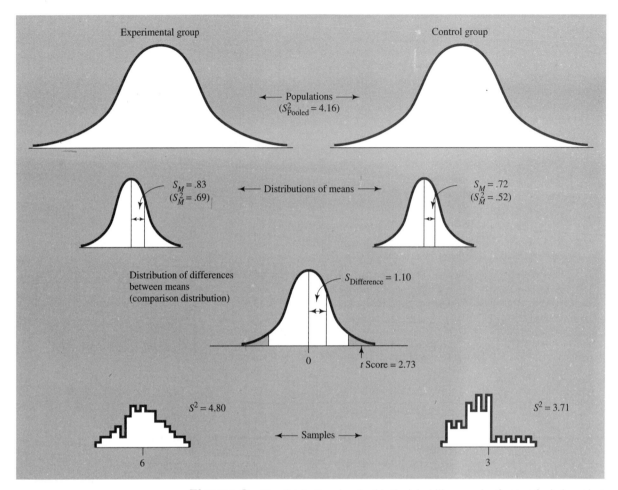

Figure 3   The distributions involved in the job skills example of a *t* test for independent means.

Population 2: Individuals who could not hold a job, who then participate in an ordinary job skills program.

It is possible for the special program to have either a positive or a negative effect compared to the ordinary program, and either result would be of interest. Thus, the research hypothesis is that the means of Population 1 and Population 2 are different: $\mu_1 \neq \mu_2$. This is a nondirectional hypothesis. The null hypothesis is that the means of Population 1 and Population 2 are the same: $\mu_1 = \mu_2$.

❷ **Determine the characteristics of the comparison distribution.**

a. Its mean will be 0.

b. Figure its standard deviation. See Table 4 for the figuring for each step below.

   ❶ **Figure the estimated population variances based on each sample.** $S_1^2 = 4.80$ and $S_2^2 = 3.71$.

   ❷ **Figure the pooled estimate of the population variance.** $S_{\text{Pooled}}^2 = 4.16$.

   ❸ **Figure the variance of each distribution of means.** Dividing S_{Pooled}^2 by the N in each sample gives $S_{M_1}^2 = .69$ and $S_{M_2}^2 = .52$.

❶ **Figure the variance of the distribution of differences between means.** Adding up the variances of the two distribution of means comes out to $S^2_{\text{Difference}} = 1.21$.

❷ **Figure the standard deviation of the distribution of differences between means.** $S_{\text{Difference}} = \sqrt{1.21} = 1.10$

c. It is a *t* distribution with $df_{\text{Total}} = 12$.

❸ **Determine the cutoff sample score on the comparison distribution at which the null hypothesis should be rejected.** The cutoff you need is for a two-tailed test (because the research hypothesis is nondirectional) at the usual .05 level, with 12 degrees of freedom. Looking this up on the *t* table in the Appendix (Table A-2), the cutoff *t* scores are 2.179 and −2.179.

❹ **Determine your sample's score on the comparison distribution.** The *t* score is the difference between the two sample means, divided by the standard deviation of the distribution of differences between means. This comes out to a *t* of 2.73. (That is, $t = 3.00/1.10 = 2.73$.)

❺ **Decide whether to reject the null hypothesis.** The *t* score of 2.73 is more extreme than the cutoff *t* score of 2.179. Thus, the researchers can reject the null hypothesis. The research hypothesis is supported: The new special job skills program is more effective than the ordinary job skills program.

How are you doing?

1. List the ways in which hypothesis testing for a *t* test for independent means is different from a *t* test for dependent means in terms of (a) Step ❷, (b) Step ❸, and (c) Step ❹.
2. Using the .05 significance level, figure a *t* test for independent means for an experiment in which scores in an experimental condition are predicted to be lower than scores in a control condition. For the experimental condition, with 26 participants, $M = 5$, $S^2 = 10$; for the control condition, with 36 participants, $M = 8$, $S^2 = 12$. (a) Use the steps of hypothesis testing. (b) Sketch the distributions involved.

Answers

1. (a) The comparison distribution for a *t* test for independent means is a distribution of differences between means.
   (b) The degrees of freedom for a *t* test for independent means is the sum of the degrees of freedom for the two samples.
   (c) The *t* score for a *t* test for independent means is based on differences between means (divided by the standard deviation of the distribution of differences between means).
2. (a) Steps of hypothesis testing:
   ❶ **Restate the question as a research hypothesis and a null hypothesis about the populations.** There are two populations.

   Population 1: People given the experimental procedure.
   Population 2: People given the control procedure.

   The research hypothesis is that the mean of Population 1 is less than the mean of Population 2: $\mu_1 < \mu_2$. The null hypothesis is that the mean of Population 1 is not less than the mean of Population 2: $\mu_1 \geq \mu_2$.
   ❷ **Determine the characteristics of the comparison distribution.**
   (a) Its mean will be 0.

(b) Figure its standard deviation,

Ⓐ Figure the estimated population variances based on each sample. $S_1^2 = 10$; $S_2^2 = 12$.

Ⓑ Figure the pooled estimate of the population variance: $S_{Pooled}^2 = (25/60)(10) + (35/60)(12) = 4.17 + 7.00 = 11.17$.

Ⓒ Figure the variance of each distribution of means: $S_{M_1}^2 = 11.17/26 = .43$ and $S_{M_2}^2 = 11.17/36 = .31$.

Ⓓ Figure the variance of the distribution of differences between means: $S_{Difference}^2 = .43 + .31 = .74$.

Ⓔ Figure the standard deviation of the distribution of differences between means: $S_{Difference} = \sqrt{S_{Difference}^2} = \sqrt{.74} = .86$.

(c) The shape is a *t* distribution with $df_{Total} = 60$.

❸ Determine the cutoff sample score on the comparison distribution at which the null hypothesis should be rejected. The *t* cutoff for .05 level, one-tailed, $df_{Total} = 60$ is -1.671. (The cutoff is a negative

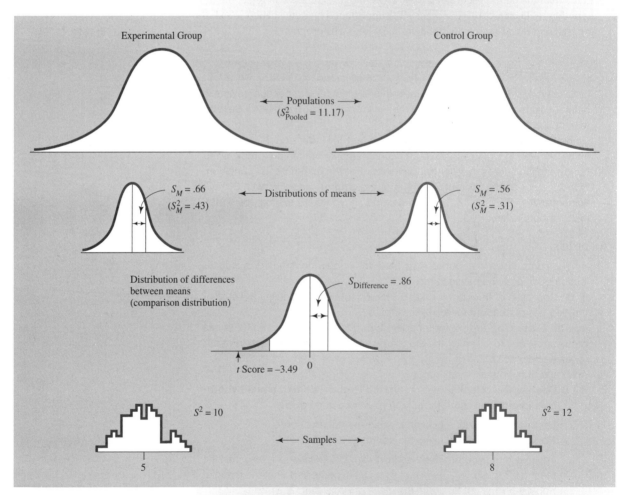

Figure 4 Distributions for a *t* test for independent means for the answer to "How are you doing?" question 2.

t score, because the research hypothesis is that the mean of Population 1 will be *lower* than the mean of Population 2.)

❹ **Determine your sample's score on the comparison distribution.**
$t = (M_1 - M_2)/S_{Difference} = (5 - 8)/.86 = -3.49$.

❺ **Decide whether to reject the null hypothesis.** The t of -3.49 is more extreme than the cutoff t of -1.671. Therefore, reject the null hypothesis.

(b) The distributions involved are shown in Figure 4.

Assumptions of the *t* Test for Independent Means

The first assumption for a *t* test for independent means is the same as that for any *t* test: each of the population distributions is assumed to follow a normal curve. In practice, this is only a problem if you have reason to think that the two populations are dramatically skewed distributions and in opposite directions. The *t* test holds up well even when the shape of the population distributions is fairly far from normal.

In a *t* test for independent means, you also have to be able to assume that the two populations have the same variance. (As you learned earlier in the chapter, this assumption is called *homogeneity of variance*.) Once again, however, it turns out that in practice the *t* test gives pretty accurate results even when there are fairly large differences in the population variances, particularly when there are equal or near equal numbers of scores in the two samples. (How do we know that the *t* test holds up well to moderate violations of its assumptions? See Box 1 for a description of what are called Monte Carlo methods.)

However, the *t* test can give quite misleading results if (a) the scores in the samples suggest that the populations are very far from normal, (b) the variances are very different, or (c) there are both problems. In these situations, there are alternatives to the ordinary *t* test procedure.

Many computer programs for figuring the *t* test for independent means actually provide two sets of results. One set of results figures the *t* test assuming the population variances are equal. This method is the standard one, the one you have learned in this chapter. A second set of results uses a special alternative procedure that takes into account that the population variances may be unequal. (But it still assumes that the populations follow a normal distribution.) An example of these two sets of results is shown in the Using SPSS section at the end of this chapter (see Figure 7). However, in most situations we can assume that the population variances are equal. Thus, researchers usually use the standard method. Using the special alternative procedure has the advantage that you don't have to worry about whether you met the equal population variance assumption. But it has the disadvantage that if you have met that assumption, with this special method you have less power. That is, when you do meet the assumption, you are slightly less likely to get a significant result using the special method.

A final assumption of the *t* test for independent means is that the scores are independent from each other. In other words, none of the scores within each group or between the groups can be paired or matched up in any way (as this would make the scores dependent on each other to some degree). (Of course we can allow that those in each group are similar, in that they have the same experimental condition or the same characteristic that put them into the two groups.) For example, consider a study comparing the effects of a cognitive therapy to an emotion-based therapy with

BOX 1   Monte Carlo Methods: When Mathematics Becomes Just an Experiment, and Statistics Depend on a Game of Chance

The name for the methods, *Monte Carlo* (after the famous casino resort city in Monaco), has been adopted only in recent years. But the approach itself dates back at least a few centuries to when mathematicians would set down their pens or chalk and go out and try an actual experiment to test a particular understanding of a probability problem. For example, in 1777 Buffon described, in his *Essai d'Arithmétique morale,* a method of computing the ratio of the diameter of a circle to its circumference by tossing a needle onto a flat surface containing parallel lines. Assuming that the needle fell randomly into any position, one could figure the odds of its taking certain positions, such as touching the lines or not and lying at certain angles. The term *Monte Carlo* no doubt reflects the early understanding of mathematicians and statisticians that many of their problems were like those involving games of chance.

Wide use of Monte Carlo methods by statisticians became possible with the advent of computers. This is because the essence of Monte Carlo studies is the interaction of randomness and probabilities, which means testing out a great many possibilities. Indeed, the first application of Monte Carlo methods was in neutron physics because the behavior of particles when scattered by a neutron beam is so complicated and so close to random that solving the problem mathematically from equations was practically impossible. But by artificially simulating the statistical conditions of what were essentially physical experiments, the physical world could be understood—or at least approximated in an adequate way.

Do you remember being shown Brownian motion in your chemistry or physics class in high school? Its study is a good example of a Monte Carlo problem. Here are atomic particles, more or less, this time in fluids, free to do an almost limitless number of almost random things. In fact, Brownian motion has been likened to a "random walk" of a drunkard. At any moment, the drunkard could move in any direction. But the problem is simplified by limiting the drunkard (or particle) to an imaginary grid.

Picture the grid of a city's streets. Further imagine that there is a wall around the city that the drunkard cannot escape (just as all particles must come to a limit; they cannot go on forever). At the limit, the wall, the drunkard must pay a fine, which also varies randomly. The point of this example is how much is random—all the movements and also all the ultimate consequences. So the number of possible paths is enormous.

The random walk example brings us to the main feature of Monte Carlo methods: they require the use of random numbers.

Now, let's return to what interests us here: the use of Monte Carlo studies to check out what will be the result of the violations of assumptions of statistical tests. For example, the computer may set up two populations with identical means, but the other parameters are supplied by the statistical researcher so that these violate an important assumption. Perhaps the populations are skewed a certain way or the two populations have different variances.

Then, samples are randomly selected from each of these two offbeat populations (remember, they were invented by the computer). The means of these samples are compared using the usual *t*-test procedure with the usual *t* tables with all their assumptions. A large number, often around 10,000, of such pairs of samples are selected, and a *t* test is figured for each. The question is, "How many of these 10,000 *t* tests will come out significant at the 5% significance level?" Ideally, the result would be about 5%, or 50 of the 10,000. But what if 10% (1,000) of these supposedly 5%-level tests come out significant? What if only 1% do? If these kinds of results arise, then this particular violation of the assumptions of the *t* test cannot be tolerated. But, in fact, most violations (except for very extreme ones) checked with these methods do not create very large changes in the *p* values.

Monte Carlo methods are a boon to statistics, but like everything else, they have their drawbacks as well and consequently their critics. One problem is that the ways in which populations can violate assumptions are almost limitless in their variations. But even computers have their limits; Monte Carlo studies are tried on only a representative set of those variations. A more specific problem is that there is good reason to think that some of the variations that are not studied are far more like the real world than those that have been studied. Finally, when we are deciding whether to use a particular statistic in any specific situation, we have no idea about the population our sample came from; is it like any on which there has been a Monte Carlo study performed, or not? Simply knowing that Monte Carlo studies have shown some statistic to be robust in the face of many kinds of assumption violations does not prove that it is robust in a given situation. We can only hope that it increases the chances that using the statistic is safe and justifiable.

At any rate, Monte Carlo studies are a perfect example of how the computer has changed science. Shreider (1966) expressed it this way:

Computers have led to a novel revolution in mathematics. Whereas previously an investigation of a random process was regarded as complete as soon as it was reduced to an analytic description, nowadays it is convenient in many cases to solve an analytic problem by reducing it to a corresponding random process and then simulating that process. (p. vii)

In other words, instead of math helping us analyze experiments, experiments are helping us analyze math.

25 clients receiving each type of therapy. And suppose that the 25 people receiving cognitive therapy consist of 5 seeing therapist Jones, 10 seeing therapist Gonzales, and 10 seeing therapist Johnson. The people seeing therapist Jones are likely to have more similar effects from their therapy to each other than they are to those seeing one of the other therapists. Thus, their scores on the effects of therapy are especially closely linked together and are not truly independent. Using a standard *t* test would treat these as 25 different people receiving cognitive therapy. However, these 25 are not really separate people drawn from the population. In technical terms, the *t* test would be giving a result that is based on too many degrees of freedom. The result would be a more extreme level of significance than is truly warranted. There are special procedures for handling situations like this, called multilevel modeling. But here, the main point is that this kind of situation is one that seriously distorts the results of a standard *t* test.

Effect Size and Power for the *t* Test for Independent Means
Effect Size

Effect size for the *t* test for independent means is figured in basically the same way as we have been using all along:

$$d = \frac{\mu_1 - \mu_2}{\sigma} \tag{8}$$

The effect size is the difference between the population means divided by the population's standard deviation.

Cohen's (1988) conventions for the *t* test for independent means are the same as in all the situations we have considered so far: .20 for a small effect size, .50 for a medium effect size, and .80 for a large effect size.

Suppose that an environmental psychologist is working in a city with high levels of air pollution. This psychologist plans a study of the number of problems completed on a creativity test over a one-hour period. The study compares performance under two conditions. In the experimental condition, each participant takes the test in a room with a special air purifier. In the control condition, each participant takes the test in a room without the air purifier. The researcher expects that the control group will probably score like others who have taken this test in the past, which is a mean of 21. But the researcher expects that the experimental group will perform better, scoring about 29. This test is known from previous research to have a standard deviation of about 10. Thus, $\mu_1 = 29$, $\mu_2 = 21$, and $\sigma = 10$. Given these figures, $d = (\mu_1 - \mu_2)/\sigma = (29 - 21)/10 = .80$, a large effect size.

When you have the results of a completed study, you estimate the effect size as the difference between the sample means divided by the pooled estimate of the population standard deviation (the square root of the pooled estimate of the population variance). You use the sample means because they are the best estimate of the population means, and you use S_{Pooled} because it is the best estimate of σ. Stated as a formula,

> The estimated effect size is the difference between the sample means divided by the pooled estimate of the population's standard deviation.

$$\text{Estimated } d = \frac{M_1 - M_2}{S_{Pooled}} \qquad (9)$$

Consider Valenzuela's (1997) study of the quality of instructional assistance provided by mothers of poor children. The mean for the sample of mothers of the adequately nourished children was 33.10; the mean for the sample of mothers of chronically undernourished children was 27.00. We figured the pooled estimate of the population variance to be 168.77; the standard deviation is thus 12.99. The difference in means of 6.10, divided by 12.99, gives an effect size of .47—a medium effect size. In terms of the formula,

$$\text{Estimated } d = \frac{M_1 - M_2}{S_{Pooled}} = \frac{33.10 - 27.00}{12.99} = \frac{6.10}{12.99} = .47$$

Power

Power for a *t* test for independent means can be determined using a power table, a power software package, or an Internet power calculator. The power table shown in Table 5 gives the approximate power for the .05 significance level for small, medium, and large effect sizes, and one-tailed or two-tailed tests.[2] Consider again the environmental psychology example of a planned study, where the researchers expected a large effect size $(d = .80)$. Suppose this researcher plans to use the .05 level, one-tailed, with 10 participants. Based on Table 5, the study would have a

Table 5 Approximate Power for Studies Using the *t* Test for Independent Means Testing Hypotheses at the .05 Significance Level

Number of Participants in Each Group	Effect Size		
	Small (.20)	Medium (.50)	Large (.80)
One-tailed test			
10	.11	.29	.53
20	.15	.46	.80
30	.19	.61	.92
40	.22	.72	.97
50	.26	.80	.99
100	.41	.97	*
Two-tailed test			
10	.07	.18	.39
20	.09	.33	.69
30	.12	.47	.86
40	.14	.60	.94
50	.17	.70	.98
100	.29	.94	*

*Nearly 1.

Table 6	Approximate Number of Participants Needed in Each Group (Assuming Equal Sample Sizes) for 80% Power for the *t* Test for Independent Means, Testing Hypotheses at the .05 Significance Level		
	Effect Size		
	Small (.20)	**Medium (.50)**	**Large (.80)**
One-tailed	310	50	20
Two-tailed	393	64	26

power of .53. This means that, even if the research hypothesis is in fact true and has a large effect size, there is only a 53% chance that the study will come out significant.

Now consider an example of a completed study. Suppose you have read a study using a *t* test for independent means that had a nonsignificant result using the .05 significance level, two-tailed. There were 40 participants in each group. Should you conclude that there is in fact no difference at all in the populations? This conclusion seems quite unjustified. Table 5 shows a power of only .14 for a small effect size. This suggests that even if such a small effect does indeed exist in the populations, this study would probably not come out significant. Still, we can also conclude that, if there is a true difference in the populations, it is probably not large. Table 5 shows a power of .94 for a large effect size. This suggests that, if a large effect exists, it almost surely would have produced a significant result.

Planning Sample Size

Table 6 gives the approximate number of participants needed for 80% power for estimated small, medium, and large effect sizes, using one-tailed and two-tailed tests, all using the .05 significance level.[3] Suppose you plan a study in which you expect a medium effect size and will use the .05 significance level, one-tailed. Based on Table 6, you need 50 people in each group (100 total) to have 80% power. However, if you did a study using the same significance level but expected a large effect size, you would need only 20 people in each group (40 total).

How are you doing?

1. List two assumptions for the *t* test for independent means. For each, give the situations in which violations of these assumptions would be seriously problematic.
2. Why do you need to assume the populations have the same variance?
3. What is the meaning of the assumption of independent scores for the *t* test for independent means?
4. What is the effect size for a planned study in which Population 1 is predicted to have a mean of 17, Population 2 is predicted to have a mean of 25, and the population standard deviation is assumed to be about 20?
5. What is the power of a study using a *t* test for independent means, with a two-tailed test at the .05 significance level, in which the researchers predict a large effect size and there are 20 participants in each group?
6. How many participants do you need in each group for 80% power in a planned study in which you predict a small effect size and will be using a *t* test for independent means, one-tailed, at the .05 significance level?

Answers

1. One assumption is that the two populations are normally distributed; this is mainly a problem if you have reason to think the two populations are strongly skewed in opposite directions. A second assumption is that the two populations have the same variance; this is mainly a problem if you believe the two distributions have quite different variances *and* the sample sizes are different.
2. You need to assume the populations have the same variance because you make a pooled estimate of the population variance. The pooling would not make sense if the estimates from the two samples were for populations with different variances.
3. The assumption of independent scores is that the scores within and between the two groups cannot be matched or paired in any way.
4. The effect size is $d = (17 - 25)/20 = -8/20 = -.40$.
5. The power is .69.
6. You need 310 participants.

Review and Comparison of the Three Kinds of *t* Tests

You have now learned about three kinds of *t* tests: In this chapter you learned about the *t* test for independent means. Table 7 provides a review and comparison of the three kinds of *t* tests.

As you can see in Table 7, the population variance is not known for each test, and the shape of the comparison distribution for each test is a *t* distribution. The single sample *t* test is used for hypothesis testing when you are comparing the mean of a single sample to a known population mean. However, in most research in psychology, you do not know the population mean. With an unknown population mean, the *t* test for dependent means is the appropriate *t* test when each participant has two

TIP FOR SUCCESS

We recommend that you spend some time carefully going through Table 7. Test your understanding of the three kinds of *t* tests by covering up portions of the table and trying to recall the hidden information. If you are at all unsure about any information in the table, be sure to review the relevant material in this chapter and in *Introduction to t Tests*.

Table 7   Review of the Three Kinds of *t* Tests

Feature of the *t* Tests	Single Sample	Dependent Means	Independent Means
		Type of *t* Test	
Population variance is known	No	No	No
Population mean is known	Yes	No	No
Number of scores for each participant	1	2	1
t test carried out on difference scores	No	Yes	No
Shape of comparison distribution	*t* distribution	*t* distribution	*t* distribution
Formula for degrees of freedom	$df = N - 1$	$df = N - 1$	$df_{Total} = df_1 + df_2$ $(df_1 = N_1 - 1; df_2 = N_2 - 1)$
Formula for *t*	$t = (M - \mu)/S_M$	$t = (M - \mu)/S_M$	$t = (M_1 - M_2)/S_{Difference}$

scores (such as a before-score and an after-score) and you want to see if, on average, there is a difference between the participants' pairs of scores. The *t* test for independent means is used for hypothesis testing when you are comparing the mean of scores from one group of individuals (such as an experimental group) with the mean of scores from a different group of individuals (such as a control group).

Controversy: The Problem of Too Many *t* Tests

A long-standing controversy is what is usually called the problem of "too many *t* tests." The basic issues come up in all types of hypothesis testing, not just in the *t* test. However, we introduce this problem now because it has traditionally been brought up in this context.

Suppose you do a large number of *t* tests for the same study. For example, you might compare two groups on each of 17 different measures, such as different indicators of memory on a recall task, various intelligence test subscales, or different aspects of observed interactions between infants. When you do several *t* tests in the same study, the chance of any one of them coming out significant at, say, the 5% level is really greater than 5%. If you make 100 independent comparisons, on the average five of them will come out significant at the 5% level just by chance. That is, about five will come out significant even if there is no true difference at all between the populations the *t* tests are comparing.

The fundamental issue is not controversial. Everyone agrees that there is a problem in a study involving a large number of comparisons. And everyone agrees that in a study like this, if only a few results come out significant, these differences should be viewed very cautiously. The controversy is about how cautious to be and about how few is "only a few." One reason there is room for controversy is that, in most cases, the many comparisons being made are not independent; the chance of one coming out significant is related to the chance of another coming out significant.

Here is an example. A study compares a sample of lawyers to a sample of doctors on 100 personality traits. Now suppose the researcher simply conducts 100 *t* tests. If these 100 *t* tests were truly independent, we would expect that on the average five would come out significant just by chance. In fact, tables exist that tell you quite precisely the chance of any particular number of *t* tests coming out significant. The problem, however, is that in practice these 100 *t* tests are *not* independent. Many of the various personality traits are probably related: if doctors and lawyers differ on assertiveness, they probably also differ on self-confidence. Thus, certain sets of comparisons may be more or less likely to come out significant by chance so that 5 in 100 may not be what you should expect by chance.

There is yet another complication: in most cases, differences on some of the variables are more important than on others. Some comparisons may directly test a theory or the effectiveness of some practical procedure; other comparisons may be more "exploratory."

Here is another kind of example. In studies using brain imaging procedures (such as functional magnetic resonance imagery [fMRI]), the way the analysis works for a typical study is like this: a person's brain is scanned every few seconds over a 10- or 15-minute period. During this time, the person is sometimes looking at one kind of image, say a picture of a person smiling, and at other times is looking at a different kind of image, say a picture of the same person frowning. For each little area of the brain, the fMRI produces a number for how active that area was during each 2- to 3-second scan. Thus, for each little area of the brain, you might have 60 numbers for activation when looking at the smile and 60 numbers for when looking at the frown. Thus, for each little area, you can figure a *t* test for dependent means. In fact, this is exactly what is done in this kind of research. The problem, however, is that you have a great many little areas of the brain. (Typically, in fMRI research, each little area may be about a 1/4-inch cube or smaller.) Thus, you have several thousand *t* tests, and you would expect some of them to be significant just by chance. This whole situation is further complicated by the issue that some brain areas might be expected to be more likely to show different levels of activity for this kind of image. In addition, the situation is still further complicated by the fact that you might want to pay more attention when two or more little areas that are right next to each other show significant differences.

In these various examples, there are a variety of contending solutions. One solution is the Bonferroni procedure where we consider a related situation, one that comes up in studies comparing more than two groups. However, the issue remains at the forefront of work on the development of statistical methods. (Aron et al. [2005] used one of the more conservative methods in the study that was the basis of the example in *Introduction to t Tests*; so they were very confident of their results—but, using that method, they might have missed finding even more differences.) In the fMRI research literature, this issue has been a particularly lively discussion topic (e.g., Nichols & Hayasaka, 2003; Zhang, Fan, & Yu, 2011).

The *t* Test for Independent Means in Research Articles

A *t* test for independent means is usually described in a research article by giving the means (and sometimes the standard deviations) of the two samples, plus the usual way of reporting any kind of *t* test—for example, $t(38) = 4.72, p < .01$ (recall that the number in parentheses is the degrees of freedom). The result of the study of the health effects of expressive writing might be written up as follows: "The mean level of self-reported health in the expressive writing group was 79.00 ($SD = 9.72$), and the mean for the control writing group was 68.00 ($SD = 10.55$); $t(18) = 2.42, p < .05$, two-tailed."

Here is another example. Muise and colleagues (2009) conducted a study of the use of the social networking Web site Facebook among 308 university students. The students completed survey items about their use of Facebook, including a 27-item measure of Facebook jealousy (with scores ranging from a low of 1 to a high of 7) created by the researchers (e.g., "How likely are you to monitor your partner's activities on Facebook?"). Here is an excerpt from the results section of the study: "Participants in the current sample reported spending an average of 38.93 minutes on Facebook each day ($SD = 32.13$) and had between 25 and 1,000 Facebook friends ($M = 296.19, SD = 173.04$). . . . Women, $M = 40.57, SD = 26.76$, in our sample spent significantly more time on Facebook than men, $M = 29.83, SD = 23.73$; $t(305) = -3.32, p < 0.01$, and women, $M = 3.29, SD = 1.24$, score significantly higher on Facebook jealousy than men, $M = 2.81, SD = 1.09$; $t(305) = -3.32, p < 0.01$" (p. 442). How do these results compare to the experiences that you and your friends have using Facebook?

Table 8 is an example in which the results of several *t* tests are given in a table. This table is taken from a series of studies conducted by McConnell and colleagues (2011) that examined whether people who own pets differ from those who don't in terms of their well-being, personality, and attachment styles (that is, their

Table 8 Mean Differences Between Pet Owners and Nonowners in Study 1 on Well-Being, Personality, and Attachment Style Measures in Study 1

Variable	Owners	Nonowners	*t* (215)
Well-being measures			
Depression	30.00	31.72	1.29
Loneliness	38.64	41.64	1.79[†]
Self-esteem	34.27	32.21	2.59*
Physical illnesses and symptoms	3.98	4.21	0.45
Subjective happiness	5.20	5.06	0.66
Exercise and fitness	4.40	3.94	2.64**
Personality factors			
Openness	4.06	3.98	0.81
Agreeableness	3.98	3.88	1.02
Conscientiousness	4.03	3.68	3.52**
Extraversion	3.52	3.25	2.13*
Neuroticism	2.16	2.23	0.67
Attachment style endorsement			
Secure	4.62	4.50	0.40
Fearful	3.16	3.72	1.77[†]
Preoccupied	2.53	3.06	1.90[†]
Dismissing	3.64	3.10	2.64**

[†] $p < .08$. * $p < .05$. ** $p < .01$.

Source: McConnell, A. R., Brown, C. M., Shoda, T. M., Stayton, L. E., & Martin, C. E. (2011). Friends with benefits: On the positive consequences of pet ownership. *Journal of Personality and Social Psychology, 101*, 1239–1252. Reproduced by permission of the American Psychological Association.

general expectations about close relationships). A total of 217 people completed the survey measures, 167 of whom reported owning a pet. As shown in Table 8, the researchers used *t* tests for independent means to compare the responses of pet owners and nonowners on each of the variables of interest. The results showed that, compared to nonowners, pet owners had higher self-esteem, greater levels of exercise and fitness, and higher levels of conscientiousness and extraversion. Pet owners also more strongly endorsed a dismissive attachment style, which according to the researchers, indicated that they have "…an ability to 'take or leave' human relationships." As shown by the [†] symbol in the table, several of the other results were close to being statistically significant (they had *p* values of less than .08), but they did not reach the standard $p < .05$ cutoff.

Advanced Topic: Power for the *t* Test for Independent Means When Sample Sizes Are Not Equal

For a study with any given total number of participants, power is greatest when the participants are divided into two equal groups. Recall the example from earlier in this chapter where the 42 participants were divided into 11 in the experimental group and 31 in the control group. This study has much less power than it would have if the researchers had been able to divide their 42 participants into 21 in each group.

There is a practical problem in figuring power from tables when sample sizes are not equal. (Power software packages and Internet power calculators require you to specify the sample sizes, which are then taken into account when they figure power.) Like most power tables, Table 5 assumes equal numbers in each of the two groups. What do you do when your two samples have different numbers of people in them? It turns out that in terms of power, the **harmonic mean** of the numbers of participants in two unequal sample sizes gives the equivalent sample size for what you would have with two equal samples. There are several accounts as to the origin of the harmonic mean, but it seems most likely that it originated from ancient Greek times (around 350 BCE) in the context of music and harmonious tones. The harmonic mean sample size is given by this formula:

> The harmonic mean is two times the first sample size times the second sample size, all divided by the sum of the two sample sizes.

$$\text{Harmonic mean} = \frac{(2)(N_1)(N_2)}{N_1 + N_2} \tag{10}$$

In our example with 11 in one group and 31 in the other, the harmonic mean is 16.24:

$$\text{Harmonic mean} = \frac{(2)(N_1)(N_2)}{N_1 + N_2} = \frac{(2)(11)(31)}{11 + 31} = \frac{682}{42} = 16.24$$

harmonic mean   special average influenced disproportionately by smaller numbers; in a *t* test for independent means when the number of scores in the two groups differ, the harmonic mean is used as the equivalent of each group's sample size when determining power.

Thus, even though you have a total of 42 participants, the study has the power of a study with equal sample sizes of only about 16 in each group. (This means that a study with a total of 32 participants divided equally would have had about the same power.)

How are you doing?

1. What is the approximate power of a study using a *t* test for independent means, with a two-tailed test at the .05 significance level, in which the researchers predict a large effect size, and there are 6 participants in one group and 34 participants in the other group?

Answer

1. Harmonic mean = (2)(6)(34)/(6 + 34) = 408/40 = 10.20. Power for a study like this with 10 in each group = .39 (see Table 5).

Learning Aids

Summary

1. A *t* test for independent means is used for hypothesis testing with scores from two entirely separate groups of people. The comparison distribution for a *t* test for independent means is a distribution of differences between means of samples. This distribution can be thought of as being built up in two steps: each population of individuals produces a distribution of means, and then a new distribution is created of differences between pairs of means selected from these two distributions of means.

2. The distribution of differences between means has a mean of 0 and is a *t* distribution with the total of the degrees of freedom from the two samples. Its standard deviation is figured in several steps:
   - Ⓐ **Figure the estimated population variances based on each sample.**
   - Ⓑ **Figure the pooled estimate of the population variance.**
   - Ⓒ **Figure the variance of each distribution of means.**
   - Ⓓ **Figure the variance of the distribution of differences between means.**
   - Ⓔ **Figure the standard deviation of the distribution of differences between means.**
3. Assumptions of the *t* test for independent means include that the two populations are normally distributed and have the same variance. However, the *t* test gives fairly accurate results when the true situation is moderately different from the assumptions. Additionally, the scores must be entirely independent from each other.
4. Effect size for a *t* test for independent means is the difference between the means divided by the population standard deviation. Power for a *t* test for independent means can be determined using a table (see Table 5), a power software package, or an Internet power calculator.
5. When you carry out many significance tests in the same study, such as a series of *t* tests comparing two groups on various measures, the possibility that any one of the comparisons may turn out significant at the .05 level by chance is greater than .05. There is controversy about how to adjust for this problem, though most agree that results should be interpreted cautiously in a situation of this kind.
6. *t* tests for independent means are usually reported in research articles with the means of the two groups plus the degrees of freedom, *t* score, and significance level. Results may also be reported in a table in which each significant difference may be shown by asterisks.
7. ADVANCED TOPIC: Power is greatest when the sample sizes of the two groups are equal. When they are not equal, you use the harmonic mean of the two sample sizes when looking up power in a table.

Key Terms

t test for independent means
distribution of differences between means
pooled estimate of the population variance (S^2_{Pooled})
weighted average
variance of the distribution of differences between means ($S^2_{Difference}$)
standard deviation of the distribution of differences between means ($S_{Difference}$)
harmonic mean

Example Worked-Out Problems

Figuring the Standard Deviation of the Distribution of Differences Between Means

Figure $S_{Difference}$ for the following study: $N_1 = 40$, $S^2_1 = 15$; $N_2 = 60$; $S^2_2 = 12$.

Answer

❶ **Figure the estimated population variances based on each sample:**
$S_1^2 = 15; S_2^2 = 12.$

❷ **Figure the pooled estimate of the population variance:**

$$df_1 = N_1 - 1 = 40 - 1 = 39; df_2 = N_2 - 1 = 60 - 1 = 59;$$

$$df_{\text{Total}} = df_1 + df_2 = 39 + 59 = 98$$

$$S_{\text{Pooled}}^2 = \frac{df_1}{df_{\text{Total}}}(S_1^2) + \frac{df_2}{df_{\text{Total}}}(S_2^2) = (39/98)(15) + (59/98)(12) = 13.19$$

❸ **Figure the variance of each distribution of means:**

$$S_{M_1}^2 = S_{\text{Pooled}}^2/N_1 = 13.19/40 = .33$$
$$S_{M_2}^2 = S_{\text{Pooled}}^2/N_2 = 13.19/60 = .22$$

❹ **Figure the variance of the distribution of differences between means:**

$$S_{\text{Difference}}^2 = S_{M_1}^2 + S_{M_2}^2 = .33 + .22 = .55$$

❺ **Figure the standard deviation of the distribution of differences between means:**

$$S_{\text{Difference}} = \sqrt{S_{\text{Difference}}^2} = \sqrt{.55} = .74$$

Hypothesis Testing Using the *t* Test for Independent Means

A researcher randomly assigns five individuals to receive a new experimental procedure and five to a control condition. At the end of the study, all 10 are measured. Scores for those in the experimental group were 7, 6, 9, 7, and 6. Scores for those in the control group were 5, 2, 4, 3, and 6. Carry out a *t* test for independent means using the .05 level of significance, two-tailed. Use the five steps of hypothesis testing and sketch the distributions involved.

Answer

The figuring is shown in Table 9; the distributions are shown in Figure 5. Here are the steps of hypothesis testing.

❶ **Restate the question as a research hypothesis and a null hypothesis about the populations.** There are two populations:

Population 1: People like those who receive the experimental procedure.
Population 2: People like those who receive the control procedure.

The research hypothesis is that the means of the two populations are different: $\mu_1 \neq \mu_2$. The null hypothesis is that the means of the two populations are the same: $\mu_1 = \mu_2$.

❷ **Determine the characteristics of the comparison distribution.**
(a) The distribution of differences between means has a mean of 0. (b) Regarding its standard deviation,

❶ **Figure the estimated population variances based on each sample:**
$S_1^2 = 1.50; S_2^2 = 2.50.$

Table 9   Figuring for Example Worked-Out Problem for Hypothesis Testing Using the *t* Test for Independent Means

	Experimental Group			Control Group	
Score	Deviation From Mean	Squared Deviation From Mean	Score	Deviation From Mean	Squared Deviation From Mean
7	0	0	5	1	1
6	−1	1	2	−2	4
9	2	4	4	0	0
7	0	0	3	−1	1
6	−1	1	6	2	4
Σ: 35	0	6	20	0	10

$M_1 = 7; S_1^2 = 6/4 = 1.50; M_2 = 4; S_2^2 = 10/4 = 2.50$

$N_1 = 5; df_1 = N_1 - 1 = 4; N_2 = 5; df_2 = N_2 - 1 = 4$

$df_{Total} = df_1 + df_2 = 4 + 4 = 8$

$S_{Pooled}^2 = \dfrac{df_1}{df_{Total}}(S_1^2) + \dfrac{df_2}{df_{Total}}(S_2^2) = \dfrac{4}{8}(1.50) + \dfrac{4}{8}(2.50) = .75 + 1.25 = 2.00$

$S_{M_1}^2 = S_{Pooled}^2/N_1 = 2.00/5 = .40$

$S_{M_2}^2 = S_{Pooled}^2/N_2 = 2.00/5 = .40$

$S_{Difference}^2 = S_{M_1}^2 + S_{M_2}^2 = .40 + .40 = .80$

$S_{Difference} = \sqrt{S_{Difference}^2} = \sqrt{.80} = .89$

Needed *t* with $df = 8$, 5% level, two-tailed $= \pm 2.306$

$t = (M_1 - M_2)/S_{Difference} = (7 - 4)/.89 = 3/.89 = 3.37$

Decision: Reject the null hypothesis; the research hypothesis is supported.

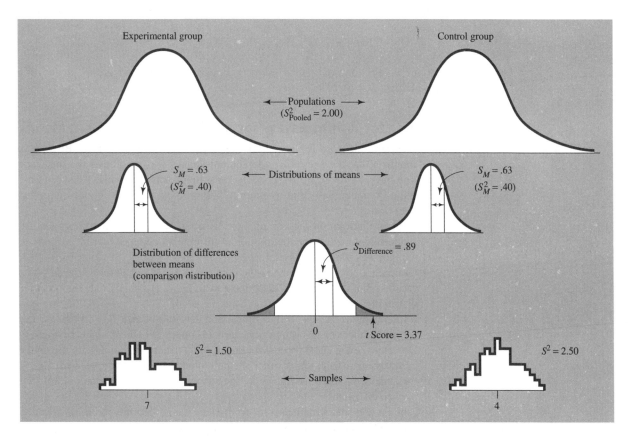

Figure 5   The distributions in the Example Worked-Out Problem for hypothesis testing using the *t* test for independent means.

❸ **Figure the pooled estimate of the population variance:** $S^2_{\text{Pooled}} = 2.00$.
❹ **Figure the variance of each distribution of means:** $S^2_{M_1} = .40$; $S^2_{M_2} = .40$.
❺ **Figure the variance of the distribution of differences between means:** $S^2_{\text{Difference}} = .80$.
❻ **Figure the standard deviation of the distribution of differences between means:** $S_{\text{Difference}} = .89$.

(c) The shape of the comparison distribution is a *t* distribution with $df_{\text{Total}} = 8$

❸ **Determine the cutoff sample score on the comparison distribution at which the null hypothesis should be rejected.** With $df_{\text{Total}} = 8$, .05 significance level, two-tailed test, the cutoffs are 2.306 and -2.306.

❹ **Determine the sample's score on the comparison distribution.** $t = (7 - 4)/.89 = 3.37$.

❺ **Decide whether to reject the null hypothesis.** The *t* of 3.37 is more extreme than the cutoffs of ± 2.306. Thus, you can reject the null hypothesis. The research hypothesis is supported.

Advanced Topic: Finding Power When Sample Sizes Are Unequal

A planned study with a predicted small effect size has 22 in one group and 51 in the other. What is the approximate power for a one-tailed test at the .05 significance level?

Answer

$$\text{Harmonic mean} = \frac{(2)(N_1)(N_2)}{N_1 + N_2} = \frac{(2)(22)(51)}{22 + 51} = \frac{2244}{73} = 30.7$$

From Table 5, for a one-tailed test with 30 participants in each group, power for a small effect size is .19.

Outline for Writing Essays for a *t* Test for Independent Means

1. Describe the core logic of hypothesis testing in this situation. Be sure to mention that the *t* test for independent is used for hypothesis testing when you have scores from two entirely separate groups of people. Be sure to explain the meaning of the research hypothesis and the null hypothesis in this situation.
2. Explain the logic of the comparison distribution that is used with a *t* test for independent means (the distribution of differences between means). Be sure to explain why you use 0 as its mean.
3. Outline the logic of estimating the population variance and the variance of the two distributions of means. Describe how to figure the standard deviation of the distribution of differences between means.
4. Explain why the shape of the comparison distribution that is used with a *t* test for independent means is a *t* distribution (as opposed to the normal curve).
5. Describe the logic and process for determining the cutoff sample score(s) on the comparison distribution at which the null hypothesis should be rejected.
6. Describe why and how you figure the *t* score of the sample mean on the comparison distribution.
7. Explain how and why the scores from Steps ❸ and ❹ of the hypothesis-testing process are compared. Explain the meaning of the result of this comparison with regard to the specific research and null hypotheses being tested.

Practice Problems

These problems involve figuring. Most real-life statistics problems are done with special statistical software. Even if you have such software, do these problems by hand to ingrain the method in your mind. To learn how to use a computer to solve statistics problems like those in this chapter, refer to the Using SPSS section at the end of this chapter.

All data are fictional unless an actual citation is given.

Set I

1. For each of the following studies, say whether you would use a *t* test for dependent means or a *t* test for independent means.
   (a) A researcher randomly assigns a group of 25 unemployed workers to receive a new job skills program and 24 other workers to receive the standard job skills program, and then measures how well they all do on a job skills test.
   (b) A researcher measures self-esteem in 21 students before and after taking a difficult exam.
   (c) A researcher tests reaction time of each member of a group of 14 individuals twice, once while in a very hot room and once while in a normal-temperature room.
2. Figure $S_{\text{Difference}}$ for each of the following studies:

	N_1	S_1^2	N_2	S_2^2
(a)	20	1	20	2
(b)	20	1	40	2
(c)	40	1	20	2
(d)	40	1	40	2
(e)	40	1	40	4

3. For each of the following experiments, decide whether the difference between conditions is statistically significant at the .05 level (two-tailed).

	Experimental Group			Control Group		
	N	M	S^2	N	M	S^2
(a)	30	12.0	2.4	30	11.1	2.8
(b)	20	12.0	2.4	40	11.1	2.8
(c)	30	12.0	2.2	30	11.1	3.0

4. A social psychologist studying mass communication randomly assigned 82 volunteers to one of two experimental groups. Sixty-one were instructed to get their news for a month only from television, and 21 were instructed to get their news for a month only from the Internet. (Why the researcher didn't assign equal numbers to the two conditions is a mystery!) After the month was up, all participants were tested on their knowledge of several political issues. The researcher did not have a prediction as to which news source would make people more knowledgeable. That is, the researcher simply

predicted that there is some kind of difference. These were the results of the study. TV group: $M = 24$, $S^2 = 4$; Internet group: $M = 26$, $S^2 = 6$. Using the .01 level, what should the social psychologist conclude? (a) Use the steps of hypothesis testing, (b) sketch the distributions involved, and (c) explain your answers to someone who is familiar with the *t* test for a single sample, but not with the *t* test for independent means.

5. An educational psychologist was interested in whether using a student's own name in a story affected children's attention span while reading. Six children were randomly assigned to read a story under ordinary conditions (using names like Dick and Jane). Five other children read versions of the same story, but with each child's own name substituted for one of the children in the story. The researcher kept a careful measure of how long it took each child to read the story. The results are shown in the following table. Using the .05 level, does including the child's name make any difference? (a) Use the steps of hypothesis testing, (b) sketch the distributions involved, and (c) explain your answers to someone who has never had a course in statistics.

Ordinary Story		Own-Name Story	
Student	Reading Time	Student	Reading Time
A	2	G	4
B	5	H	16
C	7	I	11
D	9	J	9
E	6	K	8
F	7		

6. A developmental psychologist compares 4-year-olds and 8-year-olds on their ability to understand the analogies used in stories. The scores for the five 4-year-olds tested were 7, 6, 2, 3, and 8. The scores for the three 8-year-olds tested were 9, 2, and 5. Using the .05 level, do older children do better? (a) Use the steps of hypothesis testing, (b) sketch the distributions involved, and (c) explain your answers to someone who understands the *t* test for a single sample but does not know anything about the *t* test for independent means.

7. Figure the estimated effect size for problems (a) 4, (b) 5, and (c) 6. (d) Explain what you have done in part (a) to someone who understands the *t* test for independent means but knows nothing about effect size.

8. Figure the approximate power of a *t* test for independent means for each of the following planned studies:

	Number of People in Each Group	One- or Two-Tailed	Effect Size
(a)	30	1	Small (.20)
(b)	100	2	Large (.80)
(c)	40	1	Medium (.50)
(d)	40	1	Large (.80)

9. ADVANCED TOPIC: Figure the approximate power of each of the following planned studies, all using a *t* test for independent means at the .05 significance level, one-tailed, with a predicted small effect size:

	N_1	N_2
(a)	3	57
(b)	10	50
(c)	20	40
(d)	30	30

10. What are the approximate numbers of participants needed for each of the following planned studies to have 80% power, assuming equal numbers in the two groups and all using the .05 significance level? (Be sure to give the total number of participants needed, not just the number needed for each group.)

		Expected		
	μ_1	μ_2	σ	Tails
(a)	107.0	149.0	84.0	1
(b)	22.5	16.2	31.5	2
(c)	14.0	12.0	2.5	1
(d)	480.0	520.0	50.0	2

11. Van Aken and Asendorpf (1997) studied 139 German 12-year-olds. All of the children completed a general self-worth questionnaire and were interviewed about the supportiveness they experienced from their mothers, fathers, and classmates. The researchers then compared the self-worth of those with high and low levels of support of each type. The researchers reported that "lower general self-worth was found for children with a low-supportive mother $(t(137) = 4.52, p < .001, d = 0.78)$ and with a low-supportive father $(t(137) = 4.03, p < .001, d = 0.69)$.... A lower general self-worth was also found for children with only low supportive classmates $(t(137) = 2.04, p < .05, d = 0.35)$." (a) Explain what these results mean to a person who has never had a course in statistics. (b) Include a discussion of effect size and power. (When figuring power, you can assume that the two groups in each comparison had about equal sample sizes.)

12. Gallagher-Thompson and her colleagues (2001) compared 27 wives who were caring for their husbands who had Alzheimer's disease to 27 wives in which neither partner had Alzheimer's. The two groups of wives were otherwise similar in terms of age, number of years married, and social economic status. Table 10 (reproduced from their Table 1) shows some of their results. Focusing on the Geriatric Depression Scale (the first row of the table) and the Mutuality Scale for Shared Values (the last row in the table), explain these results to a person who knows about the *t* test for a single sample but is unfamiliar with the *t* test for independent means.

Table 10   Comparison of Caregiving and Noncaregiving Wives on Select Psychosocial Variables

	Caregiving Wives ($n = 27$)			Noncaregiving Wives ($n = 27$)				
	M	**SD**	**Range**	**M**	**SD**	**Range**	**t**	**p**
Geriatric Depression Scale[a]	9.42	6.59	1–25	2.37	2.54	0–8	5.14	.0001
Perceived Stress Scale[b]	22.29	8.34	6–36	15.33	6.36	7–30	3.44	.001
Hope questionnaire[c]								
Agency	11.88	1.63	9–16	13.23	1.39	10–16	3.20	.002
Resilience	11.89	0.91	10–14	13.08	1.60	10–16	3.31	.002
Total	23.77	2.03	21–29	26.31	2.56	22–31	3.97	.0001
Mutuality Scale[d]								
Closeness	3.51	.81	.33–4	3.70	.41	2.67–4	−1.02	.315
Reciprocity	2.25	1.19	.17–4	3.25	.55	1.67–4	−3.68	.001
Shared pleasures	2.65	1.00	0–4	3.52	.61	1.75–4	−3.66	.001
Shared values	3.15	.89	0–4	3.46	.45	2.4–4	−1.51	.138

Note: For all measures, higher scores indicate more of the construct being measured.

[a]Maximum score is 30.
[b]Maximum score is 56.
[c]Four questions in each subscale, with a maximum total score of 32.
[d]Maximum mean for each subscale is 4.

Source: Gallagher-Thompson, D., Dal Canto, P. G., Jacob, T., & Thompson, L. W. (2001). A comparison of marital interaction patterns between couples in which the husband does or does not have Alzheimer's disease. *The Journals of Gerontology Series B: Psychology Sciences and Social Sciences, 56*, 5140–5150. Copyright © 2001 by the Gerontological Society of America. Reprinted by permission of Oxford University Press.

Set II

13. Make up two examples of studies (not from your lectures) that would be tested with a *t* test for independent means.

14. For each of the following studies, say whether you would use a *t* test for dependent means or a *t* test for independent means.
    (a) A researcher measures the heights of 40 university students who are the firstborn in their families and compares the 15 who come from large families to the 25 who come from smaller families.
    (b) A researcher tests performance on a math skills test of each of 250 individuals before and after they complete a one-day seminar on managing test anxiety.
    (c) A researcher compares the resting heart rate of 15 individuals who have been taking a particular drug to the resting heart rate of 48 other individuals who have not been taking the drug.

15. Figure $S_{\text{Difference}}$ for each of the following studies:

	N_1	S_1^2	N_2	S_2^2
(a)	30	5	20	4
(b)	30	5	30	4
(c)	30	5	50	4
(d)	20	5	30	4
(e)	30	5	20	2

16. For each of the following experiments, decide whether the difference between conditions is statistically significant at the .05 level (two-tailed).

	Experimental Group			Control Group		
	N	*M*	*S²*	*N*	*M*	*S²*
(a)	10	604	60	10	607	50
(b)	40	604	60	40	607	50
(c)	10	604	20	40	607	16

17. A psychologist theorized that people can hear better when they have just eaten a large meal. Six individuals were randomly assigned to eat either a large meal or a small meal. After eating the meal, their hearing was tested. The hearing ability scores (high numbers indicate greater ability) are given in the following table. Using the .05 level, do the results support the psychologist's theory? (a) Use the steps of hypothesis testing, (b) sketch the distributions involved, and (c) explain your answers to someone who has never had a course in statistics.

Big Meal Group		Small Meal Group	
Subject	Hearing	Subject	Hearing
A	22	D	19
B	25	E	23
C	25	F	21

18. Twenty students randomly assigned to an experimental group receive an instructional program; 30 in a control group do not. After 6 months, both groups are tested on their knowledge. The experimental group has a mean of 38 on the test (with an estimated population standard deviation of 3); the control group has a mean of 35 (with an estimated population standard deviation of 5). Using the .05 level, what should the experimenter conclude? (a) Use the steps of hypothesis testing, (b) sketch the distributions involved, and (c) explain your answer to someone who is familiar with the *t* test for a single sample but not with the *t* test for independent means.

19. A study of the effects of color on easing anxiety compared anxiety test scores of participants who completed the test printed on either soft yellow paper or on harsh green paper. The scores for five participants who completed the test printed on the yellow paper were 17, 19, 28, 21, and 18. The scores for four participants who completed the test on the green paper were 20, 26, 17, and 24. Using the .05 level, one-tailed (predicting lower anxiety scores for the yellow paper), what should the researcher conclude? (a) Use the steps of hypothesis testing, (b) sketch the distributions involved, and (c) explain your answers to someone who is familiar with the *t* test for a single sample but not with the *t* test for independent means.

20. Figure the estimated effect size for problems (a) 16, (b) 17, and (c) 18. (d) Explain your answer to part (a) to a person who understands the *t* test for independent means but is unfamiliar with effect size.

21. Figure the approximate power of a *t* test for independent means for each of the following planned studies:

	Number of People in Each Group	One- or Two-Tailed	Effect Size
(a)	60	1	Small (.20)
(b)	60	2	Large (.80)
(c)	10	2	Medium (.50)
(d)	100	2	Medium (.50)

22. ADVANCED TOPIC: What is the approximate power of each of the following planned studies, all using a *t* test for independent means at the .05 significance level, two-tailed, with a predicted medium effect size?

	N_1	N_2
(a)	90	10
(b)	50	50
(c)	6	34
(d)	20	20

23. What are the approximate numbers of participants needed for each of the following planned studies to have 80% power, assuming equal numbers in the two groups and all using the .05 significance level? (Be sure to give the total number of participants needed, not just the number needed for each group.)

	Expected			
	μ_1	μ_2	σ	Tails
(a)	10	15	25	1
(b)	10	30	25	1
(c)	10	30	40	1
(d)	10	15	25	2

24. Gibbons and colleagues (2006) surveyed 152 college students in Guatemala on their beliefs about machismo (a strong sense of masculinity), their attitudes toward women, and their beliefs about adoption. As shown in Table 11, the researchers used three *t* tests for independent means to examine whether female and male students differed on these beliefs and attitudes. The scales were scored so that higher scores were for more positive attitudes about machismo, more egalitarian (equal) gender beliefs (which were measured using the Attitudes Towards Women Scale for Adolescents, abbreviated as AWSA in Table 11), and more favorable beliefs about adoption. Explain the study results to a person who has never had a course in statistics. ADVANCED TOPIC: Include a discussion of effect size and power.

25. Jackson and colleagues (2001) gave a questionnaire about Internet usage to university students. Table 12 shows their results comparing men and women.

Table 11 Mean and Standard Deviation of Scores for Women and Men on Measures of Machismo, Attitudes Toward Women, and Adoption Beliefs

	Women ($n = 64$)	Men ($n = 88$)	*t*	*p*
Machismo	$1.17 \pm .15$	$1.32 \pm .20$	4.77	<.001
AWSA	$3.26 \pm .31$	$2.98 \pm .35$	5.00	<.001
Adoption	$3.10 \pm .39$	$2.85 \pm .41$	3.07	<.01

Source: Gibbons, J. L., Wilson, S. L., & Rufener, C. A. (2006). Gender attitudes mediate gender differences in attitudes towards adoption in Guatemala. *Sex Roles, 54*, 139–145. Copyright © 2006. Reprinted by permission of Springer Science and Business Media.

Table 12   Gender Differences in Internet Use and Potential Mediators

	Males[a]	Females[b]	*t*-value	*df*	*p*-value
E-mail use	4.16 (0.66)	4.30 (0.57)	2.81	626	.005
Web use	3.57 (0.67)	3.30 (0.67)	−4.84	627	.000
Overall Internet use	3.86 (0.58)	3.80 (0.53)	−1.44	627	.130
Computer anxiety	1.67 (0.56)	1.80 (0.57)	4.03	612	.000
Computer self-efficacy	3.89 (0.52)	3.71 (0.62)	−3.49	608	.001
Loneliness	2.06 (0.64)	1.96 (0.64)	−1.88	607	.061
Depression	1.22 (0.32)	1.28 (0.34)	2.36	609	.019
E-mail privacy	4.04 (0.78)	4.10 (0.69)	−0.97	609	.516
E-mail trust	3.50 (0.77)	3.46 (0.75)	−0.65	610	.516
Web privacy	4.06 (0.74)	4.09 (0.71)	0.62	623	.534
Web trust	3.14 (0.73)	3.12 (0.73)	−0.28	624	.780
Web search success	4.05 (0.85)	4.13 (0.81)	1.12	568	.262
Importance of computer skills	2.54 (1.03)	2.31 (0.90)	−2.57	477	.011
Computers cause health problems	2.67 (1.00)	3.00 (1.08)	3.36	476	.001
Gender stereotypes about computer skills	3.45 (1.15)	4.33 (0.96)	−8.95	476	.000
Racial/ethnic stereotypes about computer skills	3.63 (1.17)	3.99 (1.07)	3.40	477	.001
Computers are taking over	3.08 (1.19)	2.87 (1.08)	−1.89	476	.059

Note: For the attitude items, 1 = strongly agree, 2 = strongly disagree. For gender, 1 = male, 2 = female. Numbers in parentheses are standard deviations.

[a] n = 227.

[b] n = 403.

Source: Jackson, L. A., Ervin, K. S., Gardner, P. D., & Schmitt, N. (2004). Gender and the Internet Women communicating and men searching. *Sex Roles, 44*, 363–379. Copyright © 2004. Reprinted by permission of Springer Science and Business Media.

(a) Select one significant and one nonsignificant result and explain these two results to a person who understands the *t* test for a single sample but does not know anything about the *t* test for independent means. (b) ADVANCED TOPIC: Include a discussion of effect size and power (note that the sample sizes for the male and female groups are shown in the table footnote).

Using SPSS

The ✑ in the following steps indicates a mouse click. (We used SPSS version 19 for Windows to carry out these analyses. The steps and output may be slightly different for other versions of SPSS.)

t Test for Independent Means

It is easier to learn these steps using actual numbers, so we will use the expressive writing example from earlier in the chapter. The scores for that example are shown in Table 2.

❶ Enter the scores into SPSS. SPSS assumes that all scores in a row are from the same person. In this example, each person is in only one of the two groups (*either* the expressive writing group *or* the control writing group). Thus, to tell

SPSS which person is in each group, you should enter the numbers as shown in Figure 6. In the first column (labeled "group"), we used the number "1" to indicate that a person is in the expressive writing group and the number "2" to indicate that a person is in the control writing group. Each person's score on the health measure is listed in the second column (labeled "health"). (For the *t* test for dependent

Figure 6 SPSS data editor window for the expressive writing example (in which 20 students were randomly assigned to be in an expressive writing or a control writing group).

means in the *Introduction to t-Tests*, you set up the SPSS data with a before-scores column and an after-scores column so that both scores for a particular person were on the same line. In this example, you have only one score per person; so you have one column of scores and another column to show which experimental group each person is in; that is, you have a score column and a group column.)

❷ ⬧ *Analyze.*

❸ ⬧ *Compare means.*

❹ ⬧ *Independent-Samples T Test* (this is the name SPSS uses for a *t* test for independent means).

❺ ⬧ on the variable called "health" and then ⬧ the arrow next to the box labeled "Test Variable(s)." This tells SPSS that the *t* test should be carried out on the scores for the "health" variable.

❻ ⬧ the variable called "group" and then ⬧ the arrow next to the the box labeled "Grouping Variable." This tells SPSS that the variable called "group" shows which person is in which group. ⬧ *Define Groups.* You now tell SPSS the values you used to label each group. Put 1 in the Group 1 box and put 2 in the Group 2 box. ⬧ *Continue.*

❼ ⬧ *OK.* Your SPSS output window should look like Figure 7.

The first table in the SPSS output provides information about the two variables. The first column gives the levels of the grouping variable (1 and 2, which indicate the expressive writing group and the control writing group, respectively). The second, third, and fourth columns give, respectively, the number of individuals (N), mean (M), and estimated population standard deviation (S) for each group. The fifth column, labeled "Std. error mean," is the standard deviation of the distribution of means, S_M, for each group. Note that these values for the standard error of the mean are based on each population variance estimate and not on the pooled estimate; so they are not quite the same for each group as the square root of each S_M^2 figured in the text. (See Table 2 for the figuring for this example.)

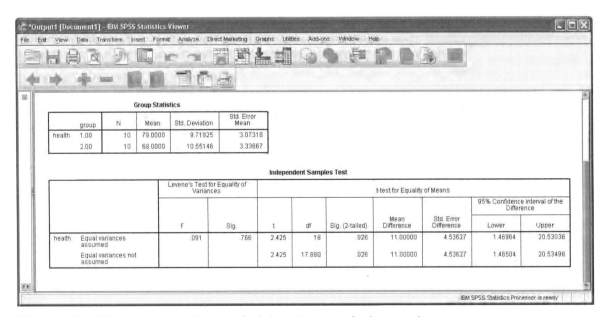

Figure 7 SPSS output window for a *t* test for independent means for the expressive writing example.

The second table in the SPSS output shows the actual results of the *t* test for independent means. Before the *t* test results, SPSS shows the results of "Levene's Test for Equality of Variances," which is a test of whether the *variances* of the two populations are the same. This test is important mainly as a check on whether you have met the assumption of equal population variances (called "homogeneity of variance"). If this test is significant (that is, the value in the "Sig." column is less than .05), this assumption is brought into question. However, in this example, the result is clearly not significant (.766 is not below .05), so we have no reason to doubt the assumption of equal population variances. Thus, we can feel more confident that whatever conclusion we draw from the *t* test will be accurate.

The *t* test results begin with the column labeled "*t*." Note that there are two rows of *t* test results. The first row (a *t* of 2.425, *df* of 18, and so on), labeled "Equal variances assumed" (on the left hand side of the table), shows the *t* test results assuming the population variances are equal. The second row (a *t* of 2.425, *df* of 17.880, and so on), labeled "Equal variances not assumed," shows the *t* test results if we do not assume that the population variances are equal. In the present example (as in most real-life cases), the Levene test was not significant; so we use the *t* test results assuming equal population variances. Notice that the values for "*t*" (the sample's *t* score), "*df*" (degrees of freedom), and "Std. Error Difference" (the standard deviation of the distribution of differences between means, $S_{\text{Difference}}$) in Figure 7 are the same (within rounding error) as their respective values we figured by hand in Table 2. The column labeled "Sig. (2-tailed)" shows the exact significance level of the sample's *t* score. The significance level of .026 is less than our .05 cutoff for this example, which means that you can reject the null hypothesis and the research hypothesis is supported. (You can ignore the final two columns of the table, listed under the heading "95% Confidence Interval of the Difference." These columns refer to the raw scores corresponding to the *t* scores at the bottom 2.5% and the top 2.5% of the *t* distribution). Note that SPSS does not know if you are doing a one-tailed or a two-tailed test. So it always gives results for a two-tailed test. If you are doing a one-tailed test, the true significance level is exactly half of what is given by SPSS.

You can use the information from the SPSS output to calculate the effect size for the *t* test for independent means. Specifically, the first table shows the estimated population standard deviation for each group (*S*). This allows you to calculate S^2_{Pooled}, using the

formula $S^2_{\text{Pooled}} = \dfrac{df_1}{df_{\text{Total}}}(S^2_1) + \dfrac{df_2}{df_{\text{Total}}}(S^2_2) = \dfrac{9}{18}(94.44) + \dfrac{9}{18}(111.33) = 102.89.$

The formula for the effect size for a *t* test for independent means from a completed study is: Estimated $d = \dfrac{M_1 - M_2}{S_{\text{Pooled}}} = \dfrac{79 - 68}{\sqrt{102.89}} = 1.08.$ This is a very large effect size.

Chapter Notes

1. In a real research situation, the figuring for a *t* test for independent means is usually all done by computer (see this chapter's Using SPSS section). However, if you ever have to do a *t* test for independent means for an actual research

study with a fairly large sample size by hand (or with just a calculator), you may find the following formula useful:

$$t = \frac{M_1 - M_2}{\sqrt{\dfrac{(N_1 - 1)(S_1^2) + (N_2 - 1)(S_2^2)}{N_1 + N_2 - 2}\left(\dfrac{1}{N_1} + \dfrac{1}{N_2}\right)}}$$ ←

2. Cohen (1988, pp. 28–39) provides more detailed tables in terms of number of participants, levels of effect size, and significance levels. Note that Cohen describes the significance level by the letter *a* (for "alpha level"), with a subscript of either 1 or 2, referring to a one-tailed or two-tailed test. For example, a table that refers to "$a_1 = .05$" at the top means that this is the table for $p < .05$, one-tailed.
3. Cohen (1988, pp. 54–55) provides fuller tables, indicating needed numbers of participants for levels of power other than 80%; for effect sizes other than .20, .50, and .80; and for other significance levels. If you just need a rough approximation, Dunlap and Myers (1997) have developed a shortcut for finding the approximate number of participants needed for studies using the *t* test for independent means. For 50% power, the number of participants needed per group is approximately $(8/d^2) + 1$. For 80%–90% power, $(16/d^2) + 2$.

The *t* score for a *t* test for independent means is the result of subtracting Sample 2's mean from Sample 1's mean and dividing that difference by the square root of the following: multiplying one less than the number of scores in Sample 1 by Population 1's estimated population variance and adding this product to the result of multiplying one less than the number of scores in Sample 2 by Population 2's estimated population variance, and then dividing this summed result by two less than the sum of the number of scores in Sample 1 and the number of scores in Sample 2, and then taking the result of this division and multiplying it by the result of adding one divided by the number of scores in Sample 1 to one divided by the number of scores in Sample 2.

Appendix: Table

Table A-2 Cutoff Scores for the *t* Distribution

	One-Tailed Tests			Two-Tailed Tests		
df	.10	.05	.01	.10	.05	.01
1	3.078	6.314	31.821	6.314	12.706	63.657
2	1.886	2.920	6.965	2.920	4.303	9.925
3	1.638	2.353	4.541	2.353	3.182	5.841
4	1.533	2.132	3.747	2.132	2.776	4.604
5	1.476	2.015	3.365	2.015	2.571	4.032
6	1.440	1.943	3.143	1.943	2.447	3.708
7	1.415	1.895	2.998	1.895	2.365	3.500

(continued)

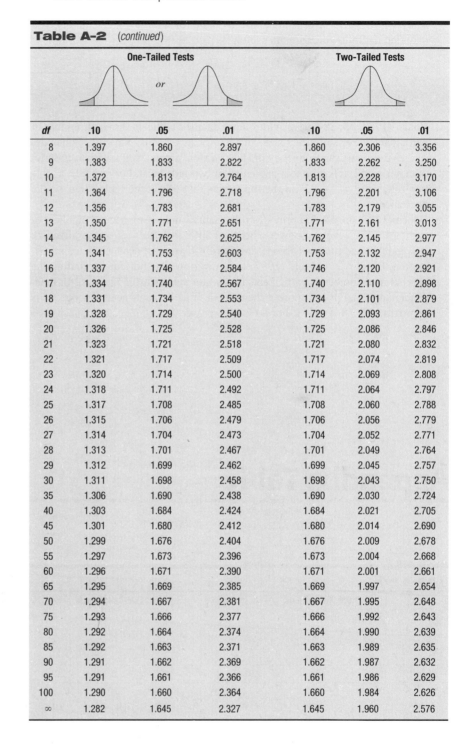

Table A-2 *(continued)*

df	One-Tailed Tests .10	.05	.01	Two-Tailed Tests .10	.05	.01
8	1.397	1.860	2.897	1.860	2.306	3.356
9	1.383	1.833	2.822	1.833	2.262	3.250
10	1.372	1.813	2.764	1.813	2.228	3.170
11	1.364	1.796	2.718	1.796	2.201	3.106
12	1.356	1.783	2.681	1.783	2.179	3.055
13	1.350	1.771	2.651	1.771	2.161	3.013
14	1.345	1.762	2.625	1.762	2.145	2.977
15	1.341	1.753	2.603	1.753	2.132	2.947
16	1.337	1.746	2.584	1.746	2.120	2.921
17	1.334	1.740	2.567	1.740	2.110	2.898
18	1.331	1.734	2.553	1.734	2.101	2.879
19	1.328	1.729	2.540	1.729	2.093	2.861
20	1.326	1.725	2.528	1.725	2.086	2.846
21	1.323	1.721	2.518	1.721	2.080	2.832
22	1.321	1.717	2.509	1.717	2.074	2.819
23	1.320	1.714	2.500	1.714	2.069	2.808
24	1.318	1.711	2.492	1.711	2.064	2.797
25	1.317	1.708	2.485	1.708	2.060	2.788
26	1.315	1.706	2.479	1.706	2.056	2.779
27	1.314	1.704	2.473	1.704	2.052	2.771
28	1.313	1.701	2.467	1.701	2.049	2.764
29	1.312	1.699	2.462	1.699	2.045	2.757
30	1.311	1.698	2.458	1.698	2.043	2.750
35	1.306	1.690	2.438	1.690	2.030	2.724
40	1.303	1.684	2.424	1.684	2.021	2.705
45	1.301	1.680	2.412	1.680	2.014	2.690
50	1.299	1.676	2.404	1.676	2.009	2.678
55	1.297	1.673	2.396	1.673	2.004	2.668
60	1.296	1.671	2.390	1.671	2.001	2.661
65	1.295	1.669	2.385	1.669	1.997	2.654
70	1.294	1.667	2.381	1.667	1.995	2.648
75	1.293	1.666	2.377	1.666	1.992	2.643
80	1.292	1.664	2.374	1.664	1.990	2.639
85	1.292	1.663	2.371	1.663	1.989	2.635
90	1.291	1.662	2.369	1.662	1.987	2.632
95	1.291	1.661	2.366	1.661	1.986	2.629
100	1.290	1.660	2.364	1.660	1.984	2.626
∞	1.282	1.645	2.327	1.645	1.960	2.576

Answers to Set I Practice Problems

Chapter 8

1. (a) Independent; (b) dependent; (c) dependent.
2. (a) $S_{\text{Pooled}}^2 = (df_1/df_{\text{Total}})(S_1^2) + (df_2/df_{\text{Total}})(S_2^2) = (19/38)$ $(1) + (19/38)(2) = 1.5; S_{M_1}^2 = S_{\text{Pooled}}^2/N_1 = 1.5/20 = .075;$ $S_{M_2}^2 = .075; S_{\text{Difference}}^2 = S_{M_1}^2 + S_{M_2}^2 = .075 + .075 = .15;$ $S_{\text{Difference}} = .39.$ (b) .35; (c) .32; (d) .27; (e) .35.
3. (a) t needed $(df = 58, p < .05, \text{two-tailed}) = -2.004, 2.004;$ $S_{\text{Pooled}}^2 = (df_1/df_{\text{Total}})(S_1^2) + (df_2/df_{\text{Total}})(S_2^2) = (29/58)$ $(2.4) + (29/58)(2.8) = 2.6; S_{M_1}^2 = S_{\text{Pooled}}^2/N_1 = 2.6/30 = .087; S_{M_2}^2 = .087; S_{\text{Difference}}^2 = S_{M_1}^2 + S_{M_2}^2 = .087 + .087 = .174. S_{\text{Difference}} = .417; t = (M_1 - M_2)/S_{\text{Difference}} = (12 - 11.1)/.417 = 2.16.$ Conclusion: Reject the null hypothesis. The difference is significant.
   (b) $S_{\text{Pooled}}^2 = 2.67; S_{\text{Difference}} = .45; t = 2.00;$ do not reject the null hypothesis. (c) $S_{\text{Pooled}}^2 = 2.60; S_{\text{Difference}} = .417; t = 2.16;$ reject the null hypothesis.
4. (a) ❶ **Restate the question as a research hypothesis and a null hypothesis about the populations.** There are two populations of interest:

Population 1: People who get their news from TV.
Population 2: People who get their news from the Internet.

The research hypothesis is that the two populations have different means. The null hypothesis is that the two populations have the same mean.
❷ **Determine the characteristics of the comparison distribution.** $S_{\text{Pooled}}^2 = (60/80)(4) + (20/80)(6) = 4.5;$ mean of the comparison distribution (distribution of difference between means) $= 0; S_{\text{Difference}} = .54;$ Shape $= t(df = 80).$
❸ **Determine the cutoff sample score on the comparison distribution at which the null hypothesis should be rejected.** t needed $(df = 80, p < .01, \text{two-tailed}) = -2.639, 2.639.$
❹ **Determine your sample's score on the comparison distribution.** $t = (24 - 26)/.54 = -3.70.$
❺ **Decide whether to reject the null hypothesis.** -3.70 is more extreme than $-2.639;$ reject the null hypothesis; the prediction is supported by the experiment.
(b)

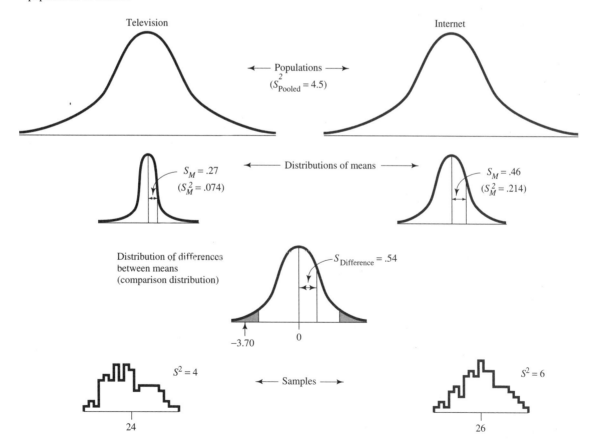

(c) In this situation, I am testing whether the two samples come from identical populations. I have two estimates of those identical populations, one from each sample. Thus, to get the most accurate overall estimate of the population variance, I can average the two estimates of the population variance. To give more weight to the estimate based on the larger degrees of freedom, I figure a weighted average, multiplying each estimate by its proportion of the total degrees of freedom and adding up the results. This pooled estimate of the population variance comes out to 4.5.

Because I was interested not in individual scores but in the difference between the mean of a group of 61 and the mean of another group of 21, I needed to figure out what would be the characteristics of a distribution of differences between means of groups of 61 and 21 that are randomly taken from the two identical populations whose variance I just estimated. This required two steps. First, I figured the characteristics of the distribution of means in the usual way for the population associated with each sample, but using my pooled estimate for the variance of each population of individuals. This came out to .074 for the TV group and .214 for the Internet group. The second step is directly about the distribution of differences between means. It is like a distribution you would get if you took a mean from the distribution of means for the TV group, took one from the distribution of means for the Internet group, and figured their difference. After doing this many times, the distribution of these differences would make up a new distribution, called a distribution of differences between means. Because we are assuming (if Internet versus TV made no difference) that the two original populations have the same means, on average, the difference between a mean taken from the TV group and a mean taken from the Internet group should come out to 0 (because sometimes one will be bigger and sometimes the other, but in the long run these random fluctuations should balance out). The variance of this distribution of differences between means is affected by the variation in both distributions of means; in fact, it is just the sum of the two. Thus, its variance is .074 plus .214, or .288. Its square root, the standard deviation of the distribution of differences between means, is .54.

Because this whole process is based on estimated variances, the distribution of means is a *t* distribution with degrees of freedom equal to the total number of degrees of freedom that went into the two estimates; thus $df = 80$. Looking this up on the *t* table for .01 two-tailed gives a cut-off needed of -2.639 and 2.639. The *t* for my sample is the difference between the two groups divided by the standard deviation of the distribution of differences between means: $(24 - 26)/.54 = -3.70$. This is more extreme than the cutoff; so I can reject the null hypothesis.

5. (a), (b), and (c). Hypothesis-testing steps, sketch, and explanation similar to question 4 [except part (c) also needs to include basic material as in answers to previous chapters' problems]. *t* needed $= -2.262, 2.262; S^2_{Pooled} = (5/9)(5.6) + (4/9)(19.3) = 11.69; S^2_{Difference} = 1.95 + 2.34 = 4.29; S_{Difference} = 2.07; t = (6 - 9.6)/2.07 = -1.74$. Do not reject the null hypothesis; the experiment is inconclusive as to whether including the child's name makes a difference. (*Note:* The scores in this problem seem to violate the assumption of equal population variances. However, because the result was not significant even using the

ordinary procedure, it would probably not be significant using a modified procedure.)

6. (a), (b), and (c). Hypothesis-testing steps, sketch, and explanation similar to question 4. *t* needed $= 1.943; S^2_{Pooled} = (4/6)(6.7) + (2/6)(12.33) = 8.58; S^2_{Difference} = 2.86 + 1.72 = 4.58; S_{Difference} = 2.14; t = (5.33 - 5.2)/2.14 = .06$. Do not reject the null hypothesis; the experiment is inconclusive as to whether older children do better.

7. (a) Estimated $d = (M_1 - M_2)/S_{Pooled} = (24 - 26)/\sqrt{4.5} = -.94$; (b) -1.05; (c) .04. (d) Effect size represents the degree to which two populations do not overlap. The less that two populations overlap, the larger the effect size will be. In psychology, we often want to know not just whether a result is significant, but how big the effect is; effect size provides a measure of how big the effect is. Effect size for the *t* test for independent means is the difference between the population means divided by the standard deviation of the population of individuals. However, you do not know the population means; so you estimate them using the sample means. You also do not know the standard deviation of the population of individuals; so you estimate it by using the pooled estimate of the population standard deviation. So, in part (a), the effect size was the difference between the sample means (24 minus 26, which gives -2), divided by the pooled estimate of the population standard deviation (which was the square root of 4.5, or 2.12). This gave an estimated effect size of $-.94$, which is a large effect size according to Cohen's effect size conventions for the *t* test for independent means.

8. From Table 8-5: (a) .19; (b) nearly 1; (c) .72; (d) .97.

9. (a) Harmonic mean $= 2(N_1)(N_2)/(N_1 + N_2) = (2)(3)(57)/(3 + 57) = 5.7$; from Table 8-5 approximate power $= .11$; (b) harmonic mean $= 16.7$, power $= .15$; (c) harmonic mean $= 26.7$, power $= .19$; (d) harmonic mean $= 30$, power $= .19$.

10. (a) Estimated $d = (M_1 - M_2)/S_{Pooled} = (107 - 149)/84 = -.50$, medium effect size; needed N (from Table 8-6) $= 50$ per group, 100 total. (b) Estimated $d = .20$; needed $N = 393$ per group, 786 total. (c) Estimated $d = .80$; needed $N = 20$ per group, 40 total. (d) Estimated $d = -.80$; needed $N = 26$ per group, 52 total.

11. Along with the following, include a full explanation of all terms and concepts as in question 4c and answers to previous chapters' explanation problems. (a) and (b) This study shows that using a conventional .05 significance level, German children who receive low levels of support—whether from their mother, father, or classmates—showed lower levels of self-worth. Further, the effect sizes were fairly large (.78 and .69) with regard to support from mother or father; however, the effect size was only small to moderate (.35) with regard to support from classmates. This would seem to imply that support from parents is more important than support from classmates in terms of a child's feeling of self-worth. The power of the study for a large effect size is .98. (This assumes there were about equal numbers of children in the high and low support groups, that the test is two-tailed, and uses the figure for 50 in each group.) The power for a medium effect size is .70. Because we already know that the results are significant and we know the effect sizes, the power calculations are not very important.

12. Similar to question 4c, focusing on the results of this study.

Chapter 9
Introduction to the Analysis of Variance

Chapter 9

Introduction to the Analysis of Variance

TIP FOR SUCCESS

This chapter assumes you understand the logic of hypothesis testing and the *t* test (particularly estimated population variance and the distribution of means). So be sure you understand the relevant material in *Introduction to Hypothesis Testing, Hypothesis Tests with Means of Samples, Introduction to t Tests,* and *The t Test for Independent Means* before starting this chapter.

In this chapter, you will learn about a procedure for comparing *more than two groups of scores,* each of which is from an *entirely separate group of people.*

Let's begin with an example. In a classic study, Cindy Hazan and Philip Shaver (1987) arranged to have the *Rocky Mountain News,* a large Denver area newspaper, print a mail-in survey. The survey included the question shown in Table 1 to measure what is called attachment style. (How would *you* answer this item?) Those who selected the first choice are "secure"; those who selected the second, "avoidant"; and those who selected the third, "anxious-ambivalent." These attachment styles are thought to be different ways of behaving and thinking in close relationships that develop from a person's experience with early caretakers (Mikulincer &

Table 1 Question Used in Hazan and Shaver (1987) Newspaper Survey

Which of the following best describes your feelings? [Check one]

[ ] I find it relatively easy to get close to others and am comfortable depending on them and having them depend on me. I don't often worry about being abandoned or about someone getting too close to me.

[ ] I am somewhat uncomfortable being close to others; I find it difficult to trust them completely, difficult to allow myself to depend on them. I am nervous when anyone gets too close, and often, love partners want me to be more intimate than I feel comfortable being.

[ ] I find that others are reluctant to get as close as I would like. I often worry that my partner doesn't really love me or won't want to stay with me. I want to merge completely with another person, and this desire sometimes scares people away.

Source: Hazan and Shaver (1987, p. 515).

Shaver, 2007). (Of course, this single item is only a very rough measure that works for a large survey but is certainly not definitive in any particular person.) Readers also answered questions about various aspects of love, including an item about their level of jealousy in their current or most recent relationship. Hazan and Shaver then compared the amount of jealousy reported by people with the three different attachment styles.

With a *t* test for independent means, Hazan and Shaver could have compared the mean jealousy scores of any two of the attachment styles. Instead, they were interested in the overall difference among all three attachment styles. The statistical procedure for testing variation among the means of *more than two groups* is called the **analysis of variance**, abbreviated as **ANOVA**. (You could use the analysis of variance for a study with only two groups, but the simpler *t* test gives the same result.)

In this chapter, we introduce the analysis of variance, focusing on the situation in which the different groups being compared each have the same number of scores. In an Advanced Topic section later in the chapter, we describe a more flexible way of thinking about analysis of variance that allows groups to have different numbers of scores. Later, we may also consider situations in which the different groups are arrayed across more than one dimension. For example, in the same analysis we might consider both gender and attachment style, making six groups in all (female secure, male secure, female avoidant, etc.), arrayed across the two dimensions of gender and attachment style. That situation is known as a *factorial analysis of variance*. To emphasize the difference from factorial analysis of variance, what you learn in this chapter is often called a *one-way analysis of variance*.

Basic Logic of the Analysis of Variance

The null hypothesis in an analysis of variance is that the several populations being compared all have the same mean. For example, in the attachment style example, the null hypothesis is that the populations of secure, avoidant, and anxious-ambivalent people all have the same degree of jealousy. The research hypothesis would be that the degree of jealousy differs among these three populations.

Hypothesis testing in analysis of variance is about whether the means of the samples differ more than you would expect if the null hypothesis were true. This question about *means* is answered, surprisingly, by analyzing *variances* (hence the

analysis of variance (ANOVA) hypothesis-testing procedure for studies with three or more groups.

name *analysis of variance*). Among other reasons, you focus on variances because, when you want to know how several means differ, you are asking about the variation among those means.

Thus, to understand the logic of analysis of variance, we consider variances. In particular, we begin by discussing *two different ways* of estimating population variances. As you will see, the analysis of variance is about a comparison of the results of these two different ways of estimating population variances.

Estimating Population Variance from Variation Within Each Sample

With the analysis of variance, as with the *t* test, you do not know the true population variances. However, as with the *t* test, you can estimate the variance of each of the populations from the scores in the samples. Also, as with the *t* test, you assume in the analysis of variance that all populations have the *same* variance. This allows you to average the estimates from each sample into a single pooled estimate, called the **within-groups estimate of the population variance**. It is an average of estimates figured entirely from the scores *within* each of the samples.

One of the most important things to remember about this within-groups estimate is that it is not affected by whether the null hypothesis is true. This estimate comes out the same whether the means of the populations are all the same (the null hypothesis is true) or the means of the populations are not all the same (the null hypothesis is false). This estimate comes out the same because it focuses only on the variation *inside* each population. Thus, it doesn't matter how far apart the means of the different populations are.

If the variation in scores within each sample is not affected by whether the null hypothesis is true, what determines the level of within-group variation? The answer is that chance factors (that is, factors that are unknown to the researcher) account for why different people in a sample have different scores. These chance factors include the fact that different people respond differently to the same situation or treatment and that there may be some experimental error associated with the measurement of the variable of interest. Thus, we can think of the within-groups population variance estimate as an estimate based on chance (or unknown) factors that cause different people in a study to have different scores.

Estimating the Population Variance from Variation Between the Means of the Samples

There is also a second way to estimate the population variance. Each sample's mean is a number in its own right. If there are several samples, there are several such numbers, and these numbers will have some variation among them. The variation among these means gives another way to estimate the variance in the populations that the samples come from. Just how this works is a bit tricky; so follow the next two sections closely.

When the Null Hypothesis Is True   First, consider the situation in which the null hypothesis is true. In this situation, all samples come from populations that have the same mean. Remember, we are always assuming that all populations have the same variance (and also that they are all normal curves). Thus, if the null hypothesis is true, all populations are identical and thus they have the same mean, variance, and shape.

within-groups estimate of the population variance estimate of the variance of the population of individuals based on the variation among the scores in each of the actual groups studied.

However, even when the populations are identical (that is, even when the null hypothesis is true), samples from the different populations will each be a little different. How different can the sample means be? That depends on how much variation there is in each population. If a population has very little variation in the scores in it, then the means of samples from that population (or any identical population) will tend to be very similar to each other. When the null hypothesis is true, the variability among the sample means is influenced by the same chance factors that influence the variability among the scores within each sample.

What if several identical populations (with the same population mean) have a lot of variation in the scores within each? In that situation, if you take one sample from each population, the means of those samples could easily be very different from each other. Being very different, the variance of these means will be large. The point is that the more variance within each of several identical populations, the more variance there will be among the means of samples when you take a random sample from each population.

Suppose you were studying samples of six children from each of three large playgrounds (the populations in this example). If each playground had children who were all either 7 or 8 years old, the means of your three samples would all be between 7 and 8. Thus, there would not be much variance among those means. However, if each playground had children ranging from 3 to 12 years old, the means of the three samples would probably vary quite a bit. What this shows is that the variation among the means of samples is related directly to the amount of variation in each of the populations from which the samples are taken. The more variation in each population, the more variation there is among the means of samples taken from those populations.

This principle is shown in Figure 1. The three identical populations on the left have small variances, and the three identical populations on the right have large variances. In each set of three identical populations, even though the *means of the populations* (shown by triangles) are exactly the same, the *means of the samples* from those populations (shown by Xs) are not exactly the same. Most important, the sample means from the populations that each have a small amount of variance are closer together (have less variance among them). The sample means from the populations that each have more variance are more spread out (have more variance among them).

We have now seen that the variation among the means of samples taken from identical populations is related directly to the variation of the scores in each of those populations. This has a very important and perhaps surprising implication: it should be possible to estimate the variance in each population from the variation among the means of our samples.

Such an estimate is called a **between-groups estimate of the population variance**. (It has this name because it is based on the variation between the means of the samples, the "groups." Grammatically, it ought to be *among* groups, but *between* groups is traditional.) You will learn how to figure this estimate later in the chapter.

So far, all of this logic we have considered has assumed that the null hypothesis is true, so that there is no variation among the means of the *populations*. In this situation, the between-groups estimate of the population variance (which reflects variability in the means of the samples) is influenced by the chance factors that cause different people in the same sample to have different scores. Let's now consider what happens when the null hypothesis is not true, when instead the research hypothesis is true.

When the Null Hypothesis Is Not True If the null hypothesis is not true (and thus the research hypothesis is true), the populations themselves have different means. In this situation, variation among the means of samples taken from these

between-groups estimate of the population variance estimate of the variance of the population of individuals based on the variation among the means of the groups studied.

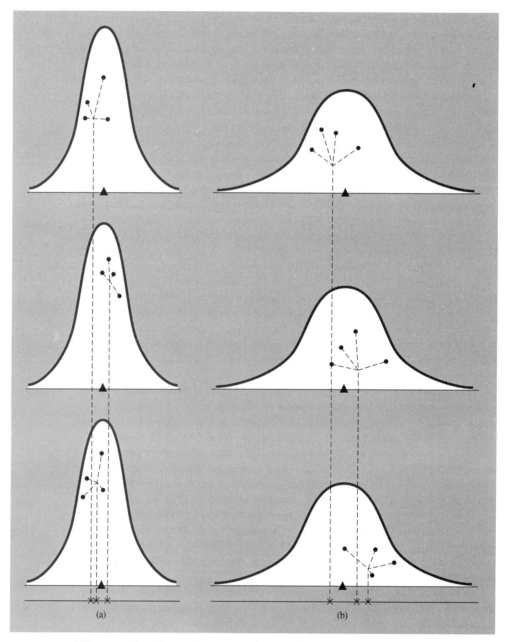

Figure 1 Means of samples from identical populations will not be identical.
(a) Sample means from populations with less variation will vary less. (b) Sample means from
populations with more variation will vary more. (The scores in each sample are shown by
dots, population means are indicated by a triangle, and sample means are shown by an X.)

populations is still caused by the chance factors that cause variation within the
populations. So the larger the variation within the populations, the larger the variation will be among the means of samples taken from the populations. However, in
this situation, in which the research hypothesis is true, variation among the means
of the samples *also* is caused by variation among the population means. You can

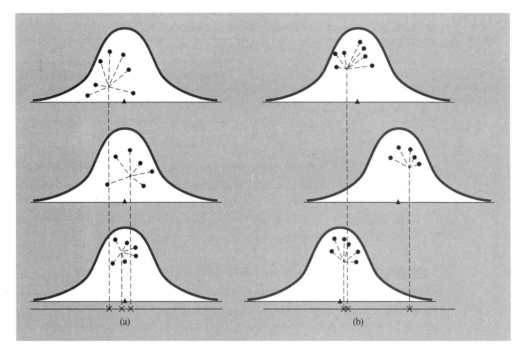

Figure 2 Means of samples from populations whose means differ (b) will vary more than sample means taken from populations whose means are the same (a). (The scores in each sample are shown by dots, population means are indicated by a triangle, and sample means are shown by an X.)

think of this variation among population means as resulting from a treatment effect—that is, the different treatment received by the groups (as in an experiment) causes the groups to have different means. So, when the research hypothesis is true, the means of the samples are spread out for two different reasons: (1) because of variation in each of the populations (due to chance factors) and (2) because of variation among the population means (that is, a treatment effect). The left side of Figure 2 shows populations with the same means (shown by triangles) and the means of samples taken from them (shown by Xs). (This is the same situation as in both sides of Figure 1.) The right side of Figure 2 shows three populations with different means (shown by triangles) and the means of samples taken from them (shown by Xs). (This is the situation we have just been discussing.) Notice that the means of the samples are more spread out in the situation on the right side of Figure 2. This is true even though the variations in the populations are the same for the situation on both sides of Figure 2. This additional spread (variance) for the means on the right side of Figure 2 is due to the populations having different means.

In summary, the between-groups estimate of the population variance is figured based on the variation among the means of the samples. If the null hypothesis is true, this estimate gives an accurate indication of the variation within the populations (that is, the variation due to chance factors). But if the null hypothesis is false, this method of estimating the population variance is influenced both by the variation within the populations (the variation due to chance factors) and the variation among the population means (the variation due to a treatment effect). It will not give an accurate estimate of the variation within the populations because it also will be affected by the variation among the populations. This difference between the two situations has

Table 2 Sources of Variation in Within-Groups and Between-Groups Variance Estimates

	Variation Within Populations (Due to Chance Factors)	Variation Between Populations (Due to a Treatment Effect)
Null hypothesis is true		
Within-groups estimate reflects	✓	
Between-groups estimate reflects	✓	
Research hypothesis is true		
Within-groups estimate reflects	✓	
Between-groups estimate reflects	✓	✓

important implications. It is what makes the analysis of variance a method of testing hypotheses about whether there is a difference among means of populations.

Comparing the Within-Groups and Between-Groups Estimates of Population Variance

Table 2 summarizes what we have seen so far about the within-groups and between-groups estimates of population variance, both when the null hypothesis is true and when the research hypothesis is true. When the null hypothesis is true, the within-groups and between-groups estimates are based on the same thing (that is, the chance variation within populations). Literally, they are estimates of the same population variance. Therefore, when the null hypothesis is true, both estimates should be about the same. (Only *about* the same; these are estimates). Here is another way of describing this similarity of the between-groups estimate and the within-groups estimate when the null hypothesis is true: In this situation, the ratio of the between-groups estimate to the within-groups estimate should be approximately one to one. For example, if the within-groups estimate is 107.5, the between-groups estimate should be around 107.5, so that the ratio would be about 1. (A ratio is found by dividing one number by the other; thus $107.5/107.5 = 1$.)

Now let's turn to the bottom half of Table 2, regarding when the research hypothesis is true (and thus, the null hypothesis is not true). The situation is quite different here. When the research hypothesis is true, the between-groups estimate is influenced by two sources of variation: (1) the variation of the scores in each population (due to chance factors), and (2) the variation of the means of the populations from each other (due to a treatment effect). Yet, even when the research hypothesis is true, the within-groups estimate still is influenced *only* by the variation in the populations. Therefore, when the research hypothesis is true, the between-groups estimate should be *larger* than the within-groups estimate. In this situation, because the research hypothesis is true, the ratio of the between-groups estimate to the within-groups estimate should be greater than 1. For example, the between-groups estimate might be 638.9 and the within-groups estimate 107.5, making a ratio of 638.9 to 107.5, or 5.94. In this example, the between-groups estimate is nearly six times bigger (5.94 times to be exact) than the within-groups estimate.

This is the central principle of the analysis of variance: *When the null hypothesis is true, the ratio of the between-groups population variance estimate to the within-groups population variance estimate should be about 1. When the research hypothesis is true, this ratio should be greater than 1.* If you figure this ratio and it comes out much greater than 1, you can reject the null hypothesis. That is, it is

BOX 1   Sir Ronald Fisher, Caustic Genius of Statistics

Hulton Archive/Getty Images

Ronald A. Fisher, a contemporary of William Gosset and Karl Pearson, was probably the brightest and certainly the most productive of this close-knit group of British statisticians. In the process of writing 300 papers and seven books, he developed many of the modern field's key concepts: variance, analysis of variance, significance levels, the null hypothesis, and almost all of our basic ideas of research design, including the fundamental importance of randomization. In fact, he has been described as producing the "scaffolding onto which the discipline [of statistics] was built" (Wright, 2009, p. 588). For good measure, he was also a major contributor to the field of genetics.

A family legend is that little Ronald, born in 1890, was so fascinated by math that one day, at age 3, when put into his highchair for breakfast, he asked his nurse, "What is a half of a half?" Told it was a quarter, he asked, "What's half of a quarter?" To that answer he wanted to know what was half of an eighth. At the next answer he purportedly thought a moment and said, "Then I suppose that a half of a sixteenth must be a thirty-toof." Ah, baby stories.

As a grown man, however, Fisher seems to have been anything but darling. Some observers ascribe this to a cold and unemotional mother, but whatever the reason, throughout his life he was embroiled in bitter feuds, even with scholars who had previously been his closest allies and who certainly ought to have been comrades in research.

Fisher's thin ration of compassion extended to his readers as well; not only was his writing hopelessly obscure, but it often simply failed to supply important assumptions and proofs. Gosset said that when Fisher began a sentence with "Evidently," it meant two hours of hard work before one could hope to see why the point was evident.

Indeed, his lack of empathy extended to all of humankind. Like Galton, Fisher was fond of eugenics, favoring anything that might increase the birthrate of the upper and professional classes and skilled artisans. Not only did he see contraception as a poor idea—fearing that the least desirable persons would use it least—but he defended infanticide as serving an evolutionary function. It may be just as well that his opportunities to experiment with breeding never extended beyond the raising of his own children and some crops of potatoes and wheat.

Although Fisher eventually became the Galton Professor of Eugenics at University College, his most influential appointment probably came when he was invited to Iowa State College in Ames for the summers of 1931 and 1936 (where he was said to be so put out with the terrible heat that he stored his sheets in the refrigerator all day). At Ames, Fisher greatly impressed George Snedecor, an American professor of mathematics also working on agricultural problems. Consequently, Snedecor wrote a textbook of statistics for agriculture that borrowed heavily from Fisher's work. The book so popularized Fisher's ideas about statistics and research design that its second edition sold 100,000 copies.

You can learn more about Fisher at the following Web site: *http://www-groups.dcs.st-and.ac.uk/~history/Biographies/Fisher.html.*

Sources: Peters (1987); Salsburg (2001); Stigler (1986); Tankard (1984); Wright (2009).

---

unlikely that the null hypothesis could be true and the between-groups estimate be a lot bigger than the within-groups estimate.

The *F* Ratio

This crucial ratio of the between-groups to the within-groups population variance estimate is called an ***F* ratio**. (The *F* is for Sir Ronald Fisher, an eminent statistician who developed the analysis of variance; see Box 1.)

The *F* Distribution and the *F* Table

We have said that if the crucial ratio of between-groups estimate to within-groups estimate (the *F* ratio) is a lot larger than 1, you can reject the null hypothesis. The next question is, "Just how much bigger than 1 should it be?"

***F* ratio**   ratio of the between-groups population variance estimate to the within-groups population variance estimate.

Statisticians have developed the mathematics of an **F distribution** and have prepared tables of F ratios. For any given situation, you merely look up in an **F table** how extreme an F ratio is needed to reject the null hypothesis at, say, the .05 level. (You learn to use the F table later in the chapter.)

For an example of an F ratio, let's return to the attachment style study from the start of the chapter. The results of that study, for jealousy, were as follows: The between-groups population variance estimate was 23.27, and the within-groups population variance estimate was .53. (You learn shortly how to figure these estimates on your own.) The ratio of the between-groups to the within-groups variance estimates (23.27/.53) came out to 43.91; that is, $F = 43.91$. This F ratio is considerably larger than 1. The F ratio needed to reject the null hypothesis at the .05 level in this study is only 3.01. Thus, the researchers confidently rejected the null hypothesis and concluded that the amount of jealousy is not the same for the three attachment styles. (Mean jealousy ratings were 2.17 for secures, 2.57 for avoidants, and 2.88 for anxious-ambivalents. The question was "I [loved/love] _____ so much that I often felt/feel jealous." The blank was for the respondent's current or most recent relationship partner's name. Responses were on a 1 to 4 scale, from *strongly disagree* to *strongly agree*.)

An Analogy

Some students find an analogy helpful in understanding the analysis of variance. The analogy is to what engineers call the signal-to-noise ratio. For example, your ability to make out the words in a cell phone conversation with poor reception depends on the strength of the signal versus the amount of random noise. With the F ratio in the analysis of variance, the difference among the means of the samples is like the signal; it is the information of interest. The variation within the samples is like the noise. When the variation among the samples is sufficiently great in comparison to the variation within the samples, you conclude that there is a significant effect.

TIP FOR SUCCESS

These "How are you doing?" questions and answers provide a useful summary of the logic of the analysis of variance. Be sure to review them (and the relevant sections in the text) as many times as necessary to fully understand this logic.

F distribution   mathematically defined curve that is the comparison distribution used in an analysis of variance.

F table   table of cutoff scores on the F distribution.

How are you doing?

1. When can you use an analysis of variance?
2. (a) What is the within-groups population variance estimate based on? (b) How is it affected by the null hypothesis being true or not? (c) Why?
3. (a) What is the between-groups population variance estimate based on? (b) How is it affected by the null hypothesis being true or not? (c) Why?
4. What are two sources of variation that can contribute to the between-groups population variance estimate?
5. (a) What is the F ratio; (b) why is it usually about 1 when the null hypothesis is true; and (c) why is it usually larger than 1 when the null hypothesis is false?

Answers

1. Analysis of variance can be used when you are comparing means of samples from more than two populations.
2. (a) The within-groups population variance estimate is based on the variation among the scores in each of the samples. (b) It is not affected. (c) Whether the null hypothesis is true has to do with whether the means of the populations differ. Thus, the within-groups estimate is not affected by whether the null hypothesis is true because the variation *within* each population (which is the basis for the variation in each sample) is not affected by whether the population means differ.

3. (a) The between-groups population variance estimate is based on the variation among the means of the samples. (b) It is larger when the null hypothesis is false. (c) Whether the null hypothesis is true has to do with whether the means of the populations differ. When the null hypothesis is false, the means of the populations differ. Thus, the between-groups estimate is bigger when the null hypothesis is false, because the variation among the means of the populations (which is one basis for the variation among the means of the samples) is greater when the population means differ.

4. Two sources of variation that can contribute to the between-groups population variance estimate are (1) variation among the scores in each of the populations (that is, variation due to chance factors), and (2) variation among the means of the populations (that is, variation due to a treatment effect).

5. (a) The F ratio is the ratio of the between-groups population variance estimate to the within-groups population variance estimate. (b) Both estimates are based entirely on the same source of variation—the variation among the scores in each of the populations (that is, due to chance factors). (c) The between-groups estimate is also influenced by the variation among the means of the populations (that is, a treatment effect) whereas the within-groups estimate is not. Thus, when the null hypothesis is false (and thus the means of the populations are not the same), the between-groups estimate will be bigger than the within-groups estimate.

Carrying Out an Analysis of Variance

Now that we have considered the basic logic of the analysis of variance, we will go through an example to illustrate the details. (We use a fictional study to keep the numbers simple.)

Suppose a social psychologist is studying the influence of knowledge of previous criminal record on juries' perceptions of the guilt or innocence of defendants. The researcher recruits 15 volunteers who have been selected for jury duty (but have not yet served at a trial). The researcher shows them a DVD of a four-hour trial in which a woman is accused of passing bad checks. Before viewing the video, however, all of the research participants are given a "background sheet" with age, marital status, education, and other such information about the accused woman. The sheet is the same for all 15 participants, with one difference. For five of the participants, the last section of the sheet says that the woman has been convicted several times before of passing bad checks; we will call those participants the Criminal Record group. For five other participants, the last section of the sheet says the woman has a completely clean criminal record—the Clean Record group. For the remaining five participants, the sheet does not mention anything about criminal record one way or the other—the No Information group.

The participants are randomly assigned to the groups. After viewing the video of the trial, all 15 participants make a rating on a 10-point scale, which runs from completely sure she is innocent (1) to completely sure she is guilty (10). The results of this fictional study are shown in Table 3. As you can see, the means of the three groups are different (8, 4, and 5). Yet there is also quite a bit of variation within each of the three groups. Population variance estimates from the scores in each of these three groups are 4.5, 5.0, and 6.5.

You need to figure the following numbers to test the hypothesis that the three populations are different: (a) a population variance estimate based on the variation of the scores within each of the samples, (b) a population variance estimate based on

Table 3   Results of the Criminal Record Study (Fictional Data)

Criminal Record Group			Clean Record Group			No Information Group		
Rating	Deviation from Mean	Squared Deviation from Mean	Rating	Deviation from Mean	Squared Deviation from Mean	Rating	Deviation from Mean	Squared Deviation from Mean
10	2	4	5	1	1	4	−1	1
7	−1	1	1	−3	9	6	1	1
5	−3	9	3	−1	1	9	4	16
10	2	4	7	3	9	3	−2	4
8	0	0	4	0	0	3	−2	4
Σ: 40	0	18	20	0	20	25	0	26

$M = 40/5 = 8$

$S^2 = 18/4 = 4.5$

$M = 20/5 = 4$

$S^2 = 20/4 = 5.0$

$M = 25/5 = 5$

$S^2 = 26/4 = 6.5$

the differences between the group means, and (c) the ratio of the two, the F ratio. (In addition, you need the significance cutoff F from an F table.)

Figuring the Within-Groups Estimate of the Population Variance

You can estimate the population variance from any one group (that is, from any one sample) using the usual method of estimating a population variance from a sample. First, you figure the sum of the squared deviation scores. That is, you take the deviation of each score from its group's mean, square that deviation score, and sum all the squared deviation scores. Second, you divide that sum of squared deviation scores by that group's degrees of freedom. (The degrees of freedom for a group are the number of scores in the group minus 1.) For the example, as shown in Table 3, this gives an estimated population variance of 4.5 based on the Criminal Record group's scores, an estimate of 5.0 based on the Clean Record group's scores, and an estimate of 6.5 based on the No Information group's scores.

Once again, in the analysis of variance, as with the t test, we assume that the populations have the same variance and that the estimates based on each sample's scores are all estimating the same true population variance. The sample sizes are equal in this example; so the estimate for each group is based on an equal amount of information. Thus, you can pool these variance estimates by straight averaging. This gives an overall estimate of the population variance based on the variation within groups of 5.33 (that is, the sum of 4.5, 5.0, and 6.5, which is 16, divided by 3, the number of groups).

To summarize, the two steps for figuring the within-groups population variance estimate are:

Ⓐ **Figure population variance estimates based on each group's scores.**
Ⓑ **Average these variance estimates.** The estimated population variance based on the variation of the scores within each of the groups is the within-groups variance estimate. This is symbolized as S^2_{Within} or MS_{Within}. MS_{Within} is short for *mean squares within.* The term *mean squares* is another name for the variance, because the variance is the mean of the squared deviations. (S^2_{Within} or MS_{Within} is also sometimes called the error variance and symbolized as S^2_{Error} or MS_{Error}.)

S^2_{Within} **or** MS_{Within} within-groups estimate of the population variance.

In terms of a formula,

$$S^2_{\text{Within}} \text{ or } MS_{\text{Within}} = \frac{S_1^2 + S_2^2 + \cdots + S_{\text{Last}}^2}{N_{\text{Groups}}} \qquad (1)$$

The within-groups population variance estimate is the sum of the population variance estimates based on each sample, divided by the number of groups.

In this formula, S_1^2 is the estimated population variance based on the scores in the first group (the group from Population 1), S_2^2 is the estimated population variance based on the scores in the second group, and S_{Last}^2 is the estimated population variance based on the scores in the last group. (The dots, or ellipsis, in the formula show that you are to fill in a population variance estimate for as many other groups as there are in the analysis.) N_{Groups} is the number of groups.

Using this formula for our figuring, we get

$$S^2_{\text{Within}} = \frac{S_1^2 + S_2^2 + \cdots + S_{\text{Last}}^2}{N_{\text{Groups}}} = \frac{4.5 + 5.0 + 6.5}{3} = \frac{16}{3} = 5.33$$

Figuring the Between-Groups Estimate of the Population Variance

Figuring the between-groups estimate of the population variance also involves two steps (though quite different ones from the within-groups estimate). First estimate, from the means of your samples, the variance of a distribution of means. Second, based on the variance of this distribution of means, figure the variance of the population of individuals. Here are the two steps in more detail:

❶ **Estimate the variance of the distribution of means:** Add up the sample means' squared deviations from the overall mean (the mean of all the scores) and divide this by the number of means minus 1.

You can think of the means of your samples as taken from a distribution of means. Follow the standard procedure of using the scores in a sample to estimate the variance of the population from which these scores are taken. In this situation, you think of the means of your samples as the scores and the distribution of means as the population from which these scores come. What this all boils down to are the following procedures. You begin by figuring the sum of squared deviations. (You find the mean of your sample means, figure the deviation of each sample mean from this mean of means, square each of these deviations, and finally sum these squared deviations.) Then, divide this sum of squared deviations by the degrees of freedom, which is the number of means minus 1. In terms of a formula (when sample sizes are all equal),

grand mean (GM) overall mean of all the scores, regardless of what group they are in; when group sizes are equal, mean of the group means.

$$S_M^2 = \frac{\sum (M - GM)^2}{df_{\text{Between}}} \qquad (2)$$

The estimated variance of the distribution of means is the sum of each sample mean's squared deviation from the grand mean, divided by the degrees of freedom for the between-groups population variance estimate.

In this formula, S_M^2 is the estimated variance of the distribution of means (estimated based on the means of the samples in your study). M is the mean of each of your samples. GM is the **grand mean**, the overall mean of all your scores, which is also the mean of your means. df_{Between} is the degrees of freedom in the between-groups estimate, the number of groups minus 1. Stated as a formula,

$$df_{\text{Between}} = N_{\text{Groups}} - 1 \qquad (3)$$

The degrees of freedom for the between-groups population variance estimate is the number of groups minus 1.

In the criminal record example, the three means are 8, 4, and 5. The figuring of S_M^2 is shown in Table 4.

| | Deviation from | Squared Deviation |
Sample Means	Grand Mean	from Grand Mean
(M)	$(M - GM)$	$(M - GM)^2$
4	-1.67	2.79
8	2.33	5.43
5	$-.67$	.45
Σ 17		8.67

Table 4 Estimated Variance of the Distribution of Means Based on Means of the Three Experimental Groups in the Criminal Record Study (Fictional Data)

$$GM = (\Sigma M)/N_{\text{Groups}} = 17/3 = 5.67; \quad S_M^2 = \Sigma(M - GM)^2/df_{\text{Between}} = 8.67/2 = 4.34$$

❺ Figure the estimated variance of the population of individual scores: Multiply the variance of the distribution of means by the number of scores in each group.

What we just figured in Step **❹**, from a sample of a few means, is the estimated variance of a distribution of means. From this we want to estimate the variance of the population (the distribution of individuals) on which the distribution of means is based. We know that the variance of a distribution of means is smaller than the variance of the population (the distribution of individuals) that it is based on. This is because means are less likely to be extreme than are individual scores (because any one sample is unlikely to include several scores that are extreme in the same direction). Specifically, the variance of a distribution of means is the variance of the distribution of individual scores divided by the number of scores in each sample.

Now you are going to figure the variance of the distribution of individuals by *multiplying* the variance of the distribution of means by the sample size (see Table 5). That is, to come up with the variance of the population of individuals, you multiply your estimate of the variance of the distribution of means by the sample size in each of the groups. The result of all this is the between-groups variance estimate. Stated as a formula (for when sample sizes are equal),

The between-groups population variance estimate (or mean squares between) is the estimated variance of the distribution of means multiplied by the number of scores in each group.

$$S_{\text{Between}}^2 \quad \text{or} \quad MS_{\text{Between}} = S_M^2(n) \qquad (4)$$

In this formula, S_{Between}^2 or MS_{Between} is the estimate of the population variance based on the variation between the means (the between-groups population variance estimate). n is the number of participants in each sample.

S_{Between}^2 **or** MS_{Between} between-groups estimate of the population variance.

Let's return to our example in which there were five participants in each sample and an estimated variance of the distribution of means of 4.34. In this example,

Table 5 Comparison of Figuring the Variance of a Distribution of Means from the Variance of a Distribution of Individuals, and the Reverse

- From distribution of individuals to distribution of means: $S_M^2 = S^2/n$
- From distribution of means to distribution of individuals: $S^2 = (S_M^2)(n)$

multiplying 4.34 by 5 gives a between-groups population variance estimate of 21.70. In terms of the formula,

$$S^2_{\text{Between}} \text{ or } MS_{\text{Between}} = (S^2_M)(n) = (4.34)(5) = 21.70$$

Figuring the *F* Ratio

The *F* ratio is the ratio of the between-groups to the within-groups estimate of the population variance. Stated as a formula,

$$F = \frac{S^2_{\text{Between}}}{S^2_{\text{Within}}} \quad \text{or} \quad \frac{MS_{\text{Between}}}{MS_{\text{Within}}} \qquad (5) \leftarrow$$

The *F* ratio is the between-groups population variance estimate (or mean squares between) divided by the within-groups population variance estimate (or mean squares within).

In the example, the ratio of between to within is 21.70 to 5.33. Carrying out the division gives an *F* ratio of 4.07. In terms of the formula,

$$F = \frac{S^2_{\text{Between}}}{S^2_{\text{Within}}} \quad \text{or} \quad \frac{MS_{\text{Between}}}{MS_{\text{Within}}} = \frac{21.70}{5.33} = 4.07$$

The *F* Distribution

You are not quite done. You still need to find the cutoff for the *F* ratio that is large enough to reject the null hypothesis. This requires a distribution of *F* ratios that you can use to figure out what is an extreme *F* ratio.

In practice, you simply look up the needed cutoff on a table (or read the exact significance from the computer output). To understand where that number on the table comes from, you need to understand the *F* distribution. The easiest way to understand this distribution is to think about how you would go about making one.

Start with three identical populations. Next, randomly select five scores from each. Then, on the basis of these three samples (of five scores each), figure the *F* ratio. (That is, use these scores to make a within-groups estimate and a between-groups estimate, then divide the between estimate by the within estimate.) Let's say that you do this and the *F* ratio you come up with is 1.36. Now you select three new random samples of five scores each and figure the *F* ratio using these three samples. Perhaps you get an *F* of .93. If you do this whole process many, many times, you will eventually get a lot of *F* ratios. The distribution of all possible *F* ratios figured in this way (from random samples from identical populations) is called the *F* distribution. Figure 3 shows an example of an *F* distribution. (There are many different *F* distributions, and each has a slightly different shape. The exact shape depends on how many samples you take each time and how many scores are in each sample. The general shape is like that shown in the figure.)

No one actually goes about making *F* distributions in this way. It is a mathematical distribution whose exact characteristics can be found from a formula. Statisticians can also prove that the formula gives exactly the same result as if you had the patience to follow this procedure of taking random samples and figuring the *F* ratio of each for a very long time.

As you can see in Figure 3, the *F* distribution is not symmetrical but has a long tail on the right. The reason for the positive skew is that an *F* distribution is a distribution of ratios of variances. Variances are always positive numbers. (A variance is an average of squared deviations, and anything squared is a positive number.) A ratio of a positive number to a positive number can never be less than 0. Yet there is nothing to stop a ratio from being a very high number. Thus, the *F* ratio's

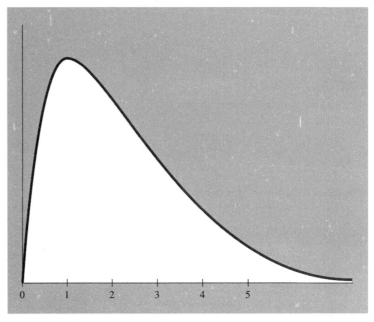

Figure 3 An F distribution.

distribution cannot be lower than 0 and can rise quite high.[1] (Most F ratios pile up near 1, but they spread out more on the positive side, where they have more room to spread out.)

between-groups (or numerator) degrees of freedom ($df_{Between}$) degrees of freedom used in the between-groups estimate of the population variance in an analysis of variance (the numerator of the F ratio); number of scores free to vary (number of means minus 1) in figuring the between-groups estimate of the population variance.

within-groups (or denominator) degrees of freedom (df_{Within}) degrees of freedom used in the within-groups estimate of the population variance in an analysis of variance, denominator of the F ratio; number of scores free to vary (number of scores in each group minus 1, summed over all the groups) in figuring the within-groups population variance estimate.

The degrees of freedom for the within-groups population variance estimate is the sum of the degrees of freedom used in making estimates of the population variance from each sample.

The F Table

The F table is a little more complicated than the t table. This is because there is a different F distribution according to both the degrees of freedom used in the between-groups variance estimate and the degrees of freedom used in the within-groups variance estimate. That is, you have to take into account two different degrees of freedom to look up the needed cutoff. One is the **between-groups degrees of freedom**. It is also called the *numerator degrees of freedom*. This is the degrees of freedom you use in the between-groups variance estimate, the numerator of the F ratio. As shown earlier in Formula 3, the degrees of freedom for the between-groups population variance estimate is equal to the number of groups minus 1 ($df_{Between} = N_{Groups} - 1$).

The other type of degrees of freedom is the **within-groups degrees of freedom**, also called the *denominator degrees of freedom*. This is the sum of the degrees of freedom from each sample you use when figuring out the within-groups variance estimate, the denominator of the F ratio.

Stated as a formula,

$$df_{Within} = df_1 + df_2 + \cdots + df_{Last} \tag{6}$$

In the criminal record study example, the between-groups degrees of freedom is 2. (There are 3 means, minus 1.) In terms of the formula,

$$df_{Between} = N_{Groups} - 1 = 3 - 1 = 2$$

Table 6 Selected Cutoffs for the F Distribution (with Values Highlighted for the Criminal Record Study)

Denominator Degrees of Freedom	Significance Level	Numerator Degrees of Freedom					
		1	2	3	4	5	6
10	.01	10.05	7.56	6.55	6.00	5.64	5.39
	.05	4.97	4.10	3.71	3.48	3.33	3.22
	.10	3.29	2.93	2.73	2.61	2.52	2.46
11	.01	9.65	7.21	6.22	5.67	5.32	5.07
	.05	4.85	3.98	3.59	3.36	3.20	3.10
	.10	3.23	2.86	2.66	2.54	2.45	2.39
12	.01	9.33	6.93	5.95	5.41	5.07	4.82
	.05	4.75	3.89	3.49	3.26	3.11	3.00
	.10	3.18	2.81	2.61	2.48	2.40	2.33
13	.01	9.07	6.70	5.74	5.21	4.86	4.62
	.05	4.67	3.81	3.41	3.18	3.03	2.92
	.10	3.14	2.76	2.56	2.43	2.35	2.28

Note: Full table is Table A-3 in the Appendix.

The within-groups degrees of freedom is 12. This is because each of the groups has 4 degrees of freedom on which the estimate is based (5 scores minus 1) and there are 3 groups overall, making a total of 12 degrees of freedom. In terms of the formula,

$$df_{Within} = df_1 + df_2 + \cdots + df_{Last} = (5 - 1) + (5 - 1) + (5 - 1)$$
$$= 4 + 4 + 4 = 12$$

You would look up the cutoff for an F distribution "with 2 and 12" degrees of freedom. As shown in Table 6, for the .05 level, you need an F ratio of 3.89 to reject the null hypothesis. (The full F table is Table A-3 in the Appendix.)

How are you doing?

For part (c) of each question, use the following scores involving three samples: The scores in Sample A are 5 and 7 ($M = 6$), the scores in Sample B are 6 and 9 ($M = 7.5$), and the scores in Sample C are 8 and 9 ($M = 8.5$).

1. (a) Write the formula for the within-groups population variance estimate and (b) define each of the symbols. (c) Figure the within-groups population variance estimate for these scores.

2. (a) Write the formula for the variance of the distribution of means when using it as part of an analysis of variance and (b) define each of the symbols. (c) Figure the variance of the distribution of means for these scores.

3. (a) Write the formula for the between-groups population variance estimate based on the variance of the distribution of means and (b) define each of the symbols and explain the logic behind this formula. (c) Figure the between-groups population variance estimate for these scores.

4. (a) Write the formula for the F ratio and (b) define each of the symbols and explain the logic behind this formula. (c) Figure the F ratio for these scores.

5. (a) Write the formulas for the between-groups and within-groups degrees of freedom and (b) define each of the symbols. (c) Figure the between-groups and within-groups degrees of freedom for these scores.

6. (a) What is the F distribution? (b) Why is it skewed to the right? (c) What is the cutoff F for these scores for the .05 significance level?

Answers

1. (a) Formula for the within-groups population variance estimate:

$$S^2_{\text{Within}} = (S^2_1 + S^2_2 + \cdots + S^2_{\text{Last}})/(N_{\text{Groups}}).$$

(b) S^2_{Within} is the within-groups population variance estimate; S^2_1 is the estimated population variance based on the scores in the first group (Sample A); S^2_2 is the estimated population variance based on the scores in the second group; S^2_{Last} is the estimated population variance based on the scores in the last group; the dots show that you are to fill in a population variance estimate for as many other groups as there are in the analysis; N_{Groups} is the number of groups.

(c) Figuring for the within-groups population variance estimate:

$$S^2_1 = [(5 - 6)^2 + (7 - 6)^2]/(2 - 1) = (1 + 1)/1 = 2;$$
$$S^2_2 = [(6 - 7.5)^2 + (9 - 7.5)^2]/(2 - 1) = (2.25 + 2.25)/1 = 4.5;$$
$$S^2_3 = [(8 - 8.5)^2 + (9 - 8.5)^2]/(2 - 1) = (.25 + .25)/1 = .5;$$
$$S^2_{\text{Within}} = (S^2_1 + S^2_2 + \cdots + S^2_{\text{Last}})/N_{\text{Groups}} = (2 + 4.5 + .5)/3 = 7/3 = 2.33.$$

2. (a) Formula for the variance of the distribution of means when using it as part of an analysis of variance: $S^2_M = \Sigma(M - GM)^2/df_{\text{Between}}$.

(b) S^2_M is the estimated variance of the distribution of means (estimated based on the means of the samples in your study). M is the mean of each of your samples. GM is the grand mean, the overall mean of all your scores, which is also the mean of your means. df_{Between} is the degrees of freedom in the between-groups estimate, the number of groups minus 1.

(c) Grand mean (GM) is $(6 + 7.5 + 8.5)/3 = 7.33$.

$$\begin{aligned} S^2_M &= \Sigma(M - GM)^2/df_{\text{Between}} \\ &= [(6 - 7.33)^2 + (7.5 - 7.33)^2 + (8.5 - 7.33)^2]/3 - 1 \\ &= (1.77 + .03 + 1.37)/2 = 3.17/2 = 1.59. \end{aligned}$$

3. (a) Formula for the between-groups population variance estimate based on the variance of the distribution of means: $S^2_{\text{Between}} = (S^2_M)(n)$.

(b) S^2_{Between} is the between-groups population variance estimate; S^2_M is the estimated variance of the distribution of means (estimated based on the means of the samples in your study); n is the number of participants in each sample. The goal is to have a variance of a distribution of individuals based on the variation among the means of the groups. S^2_M is the estimate of the variance of a distribution of means from the overall population based on the means of the samples. To go from the variance of a distribution of means to the variance of a distribution of individuals, you multiply by the size of each sample. This is because the variance of the distribution of means is always smaller than the distribution of individuals (because means of samples are less likely to be extreme than are individual scores); the exact relation is that the variance of distribution of means is the variance of the distribution of individuals divided by the sample size; thus you reverse that process here.

(c) $S^2_{\text{Between}} = (S^2_M)(n) = (1.59)(2) = 3.18$.

4. (a) Formula for the F ratio: $F = S^2_{\text{Between}}/S^2_{\text{Within}}$.

(b) F is the F ratio; S^2_{Between} is the between-groups population variance estimate; S^2_{Within} is the within-groups population variance estimate. The null hypothesis is that all the samples come from populations with the same mean. If the null hypothesis is true, the F ratio should be about 1. This is because the two population variance estimates are based on the same thing, the variation within each of the populations (due to chance factors). If the research hypothesis is true, so that the samples come from populations with different means, the F ratio should be larger than 1. This is because the between-groups estimate is now influenced by the variation both within the populations (due to chance factors) and among them (due to a treatment effect). But the within-groups estimate is still affected only by the variation within each of the populations.

(c) $F = S^2_{Between}/S^2_{Within} = 3.18/2.33 = 1.36$.

5. (a) Formulas for the between-groups and within-groups degrees of freedom: $df_{Between} = N_{Groups} - 1$ and $df_{Within} = df_1 + df_2 + \cdots + df_{Last}$.

(b) $df_{Between}$ is the between-groups degrees of freedom; N_{Groups} is the number of groups; df_{Within} is the within-groups degrees of freedom; df_1 is the degrees of freedom for the population variance estimate based on the scores in the first sample; df_2 is the degrees of freedom for the population variance estimate based on the scores in the second sample; df_{Last} is the degrees of freedom for the population variance estimate based on the scores in the last sample; the dots show that you are to fill in the population degrees of freedom for as many other samples as there are in the analysis.

(c) $df_{Between} = N_{Groups} - 1 = 3 - 1 = 2$; $df_{Within} = df_1 + df_2 + \cdots + df_{Last} = 1 + 1 + 1 = 3$.

6. (a) The F distribution is the distribution of F ratios you would expect by chance. (b) F ratios, because they are a ratio of variances (which as averages of squared numbers have to be positive), are ratios of two positive numbers, which always have to be positive. Thus, they can't be less than 0. But there is no limit to how high an F ratio can be. Thus, the scores bunch up at the left (near 0) and spread out to the right. (c) Cutoff F for the .05 significance level: 9.55.

Hypothesis Testing with the Analysis of Variance

Here are the five steps of hypothesis testing for the criminal record study. The distributions involved are shown in Figure 4.

❶ **Restate the question as a research hypothesis and a null hypothesis about the populations.** There are three populations:

Population 1: Jurors told that the defendant has a criminal record.
Population 2: Jurors told that the defendant has a clean record.
Population 3: Jurors given no information about the defendant's record.

The null hypothesis is that these three populations have the same mean ($\mu_1 = \mu_2 = \mu_3$). The research hypothesis is that the populations' means are not the same.

❷ **Determine the characteristics of the comparison distribution.** The comparison distribution is an F distribution with 2 and 12 degrees of freedom.

❸ **Determine the cutoff sample score on the comparison distribution at which the null hypothesis should be rejected.** Using the F table for the .05 significance level, the cutoff F ratio is 3.89.

❹ **Determine your sample's score on the comparison distribution.** In the analysis of variance, the comparison distribution is an F distribution, and the sample's score on that distribution is thus its F ratio. In the example, the F ratio was 4.07.

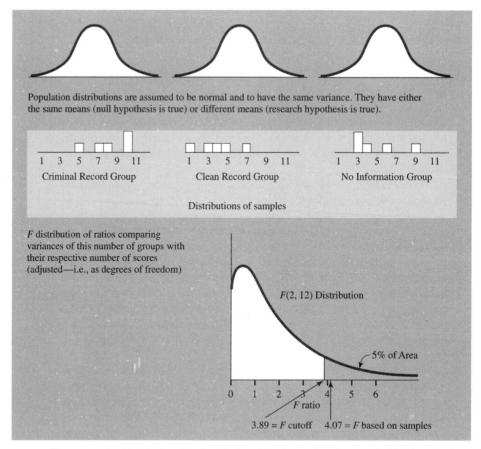

Figure 4   Distributions involved in the criminal record study example (fictitious data).

❺ **Decide whether to reject the null hypothesis.** In the example, the F ratio of 4.07 is more extreme than the .05 significance level cutoff of 3.89. Thus, the researcher would reject the null hypothesis that the three groups come from populations with the same mean. This suggests that they come from populations with different means: that people exposed to different kinds of information (or no information) about the criminal record of a defendant in a situation of this kind will differ in their ratings of the defendant's guilt.

You may be interested to know that several real studies have looked at whether knowing a defendant's prior criminal record affects the likelihood of conviction (Steblay et al., 2006). The overall conclusion seems to be reasonably consistent with that of the fictional study described here.

Another Example

Mikulincer (1998) conducted a series of studies in Israel using the same attachment style classification measure we discussed earlier in the chapter (see Table 1). One of his studies included 30 university students (10 of each attachment style), all of whom were in serious romantic relationships. As part of the study, each evening the students wrote down whether during that day their partner had done something to violate their trust. Participants noted such events as the partner being very late for a

Table 7	Number of Trust Violation Events by Romantic Partners Over 3 Weeks Reported by Individuals of Three Attachment Styles		

	Attachment Style		
	Secure	**Avoidant**	**Anxious-Ambivalent**
n	10	10	10
M	2.10	3.70	4.20
S	1.66	1.89	1.93
S^2	2.76	3.57	3.72

F distribution:

$df_{Between} = N_{Groups} - 1 = 3 - 1 = 2$

$df_{Within} = df_1 + df_2 + \cdots + df_{Last} = (10-1) + (10-1) + (10-1) = 9 + 9 + 9 = 27$

F needed for significance at .05 level from F table, $df = 2, 27$: 3.36

Between-groups population variance estimate:

Table for finding S^2 for the three means

	M	Deviation	Squared Deviation
Secure	2.10	−1.23	1.51
Avoidant	3.70	.37	.14
Anxious-Ambivalent	4.20	.87	.76
	Σ: 10.00		$\Sigma(M - GM)^2$: 2.41
	GM: 3.33		

$S_M^2 = \Sigma(M - GM)^2/df_{Between} = 2.41/2 = 1.205$

$S_{Between}^2$ or $MS_{Between} = (S_M^2)(n) = (1.205)(10) = 12.05$

Within-groups population variance estimate:

S_{Within}^2 or $MS_{Within} = \dfrac{S_1^2 + S_2^2 + \cdots + S_{Last}^2}{N_{groups}} = \dfrac{2.76 + 3.57 + 3.72}{3} = \dfrac{10.05}{3} = 3.35$

F ratio: $F = S_{Between}^2/S_{Within}^2$ or $MS_{Between}/MS_{Within} = 12.05/3.35 = 3.60$

Decision: Reject the null hypothesis.

Source: Data from Mikulincer (1998).

promised meeting or "forgetting" to tell the participant about some important plan. The results, along with the analysis of variance figuring, are shown in Table 7. The distributions involved are shown in Figure 5. The steps of the hypothesis testing follow.

❶ **Restate the question as a research hypothesis and a null hypothesis about the populations.** There are three populations.

Population 1: Students with a secure attachment style.
Population 2: Students with an avoidant attachment style.
Population 3: Students with an anxious-ambivalent attachment style.

The null hypothesis is that these three populations have the same mean $(\mu_1 = \mu_2 = \mu_3)$. The research hypothesis is that their means are not the same.

❷ **Determine the characteristics of the comparison distribution.** The comparison distribution will be an F distribution. Its degrees of freedom are figured as follows: the between-groups variance estimate is based on three groups, making 2 degrees of freedom. The within-groups estimate is based on 9 degrees of freedom (10 participants) in each of the three groups, making a total of 27 degrees of freedom.

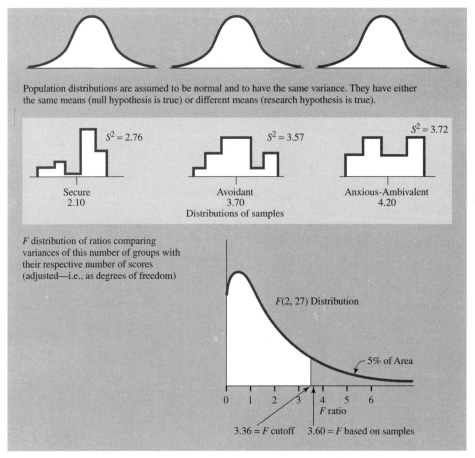

Population distributions are assumed to be normal and to have the same variance. They have either the same means (null hypothesis is true) or different means (research hypothesis is true).

$S^2 = 2.76$ $S^2 = 3.57$ $S^2 = 3.72$

Secure
2.10

Avoidant
3.70

Anxious-Ambivalent
4.20

Distributions of samples

F distribution of ratios comparing variances of this number of groups with their respective number of scores (adjusted—i.e., as degrees of freedom)

$F(2, 27)$ Distribution

5% of Area

0   1   2   3   4   5   6
F ratio

3.36 = F cutoff   3.60 = F based on samples

Figure 5   Distributions involved in the attachment style example. (*Source:* Data from Mikulincer, 1998.)

❸ **Determine the cutoff sample score on the comparison distribution at which the null hypothesis should be rejected.** Using Table A-3 in the Appendix, look down the column for 2 degrees of freedom in the numerator and stop at the row for our denominator degrees of freedom of 27. We will use the .05 significance level. This gives a cutoff F of 3.36.

❹ **Determine your sample's score on the comparison distribution.** This step requires determining the sample's F ratio. You find the between-groups variance estimate (the numerator of the F ratio) in two steps.

  Ⓐ **Estimate the variance of the distribution of means:** Add up the sample means' squared deviations from the grand mean, and divide by the number of means minus 1. From Table 7, this comes out to 1.205.

  Ⓑ **Figure the estimated variance of the population of individual scores:** Multiply the variance of the distribution of means by the number of scores in each group. From Table 7, this comes out to 12.05.

  You find the within-groups variance estimate (the denominator of the F ratio) in two steps.

  Ⓐ **Figure population variance estimates based on each group's scores:** As shown in Table 7, the population variance estimates are 2.76, 3.57, and 3.72.

Table 8   Steps for the Analysis of Variance (When Sample Sizes Are Equal)

❶ **Restate the question as a research hypothesis and a null hypothesis about the populations.**

❷ **Determine the characteristics of the comparison distribution.**
  a. The comparison distribution is an F distribution.
  b. The between-groups (numerator) degrees of freedom is the number of groups minus 1:
     $df_{Between} = N_{Groups} - 1$.
  c. The within-groups (denominator) degrees of freedom is the sum of the degrees of freedom in each group (the number in the group minus 1):
     $df_{Within} = df_1 + df_2 + \cdots + df_{Last}$.

❸ **Determine the cutoff sample score on the comparison distribution at which the null hypothesis should be rejected.**
  a. Decide the significance level.
  b. Look up the appropriate cutoff in an F table, using the degrees of freedom from Step ❷.

❹ **Determine your sample's score on the comparison distribution.** This will be an F ratio.
  a. Figure the between-groups population variance estimate ($S^2_{Between}$ or $MS_{Between}$).
     Figure the means of each group.
     ❶ **Estimate the variance of the distribution of means:** $S^2_M = \Sigma(M - GM)^2/df_{Between}$.
     ❷ **Figure the estimated variance of the population of individual scores:**
        $S^2_{Between}$ or $MS_{Between} = (S^2_M)(n)$
  b. Figure the within-groups population variance estimate (S^2_{Within} or MS_{Within}).
     ❶ **Figure population variance estimates based on each group's scores:** For each group,
        $S^2 = \Sigma(X - M)^2/(n - 1) = SS/df$.
     ❷ **Average these variance estimates:**
        S^2_{Within} or $MS_{Within} = (S^2_1 + S^2_2 + \cdots + S^2_{Last})/N_{Groups}$.
  c. Figure the F ratio: $F = S^2_{Between}/S^2_{Within}$ or $F = MS_{Between}/MS_{Within}$.

❺ **Decide whether to reject the null hypothesis:** Compare the scores from Steps ❸ and ❹.

❷ **Average these variance estimates:** The average of 2.76, 3.57, and 3.72 comes out to 3.35. The F ratio is the between-groups variance estimate divided by the within-groups variance estimate, which comes out to 3.60 (that is, 12.05/3.35 = 3.60).

❺ **Decide whether to reject the null hypothesis.** The F ratio of 3.60 is more extreme than the .05 significance level cutoff F of 3.36. Therefore, Mikulincer (1998) rejected the null hypothesis. He was able to conclude that students having the three attachment styles differ in the number of trust violations by their romantic partners they reported over a 3-week period. This conclusion was consistent with Mikulincer's hypotheses based on attachment theory.

Summary of Steps for Hypothesis Testing with the Analysis of Variance

Table 8 summarizes the steps of an analysis of variance of the kind we have been considering in this chapter.

Assumptions in the Analysis of Variance

The assumptions for the analysis of variance are basically the same as for the t test for independent means. That is, the cutoff F ratio from the table (or the exact p level from the computer output) is strictly accurate only when the populations follow a normal curve and have equal variances. As with the t test, in practice the cutoffs are reasonably accurate even when your populations are moderately far from normal and have moderately different variances. As a general rule, if the variance estimate of the group with the largest estimate is no more than four or five times that of the smallest and the sample sizes are equal, the conclusions using the F distribution should be adequately accurate. As with the t test for independent means, the type of analysis of variance you are learning about in this chapter assumes that all of the scores in the groups are independent from each other (that is, none of the scores within each group or across the groups are paired or matched in any way).

How are you doing?

1. A study compares the effects of three experimental treatments, A, B, and C, by giving each treatment to 16 participants and then assessing their performance on a standard measure. The results on the standard measure are as follows. Treatment A group: $M = 20$, $S^2 = 8$; Treatment B group: $M = 22$, $S^2 = 9$; Treatment C group: $M = 18$, $S^2 = 7$. Using the .01 significance level, do the three experimental treatments create any difference among the populations these groups represent? (a) Use the steps of hypothesis testing and (b) sketch the distributions involved.
2. Give three assumptions for the analysis of variance.
3. Why do we need the equal variance assumption?
4. What is the general rule about when violations of the equal variance assumption are likely to lead to serious inaccuracies in results?

Answers

1. (a) Steps of hypothesis testing:
   ❶ **Restate the question as a research hypothesis and a null hypothesis about the populations.** There are three populations.

   Population 1: People given experimental treatment A.
   Population 2: People given experimental treatment B.
   Population 3: People given experimental treatment C.

   The null hypothesis is that these three populations have the same mean ($\mu_1 = \mu_2 = \mu_3$). The research hypothesis is that their means are not the same.
   ❷ **Determine the characteristics of the comparison distribution.** The comparison distribution will be an F distribution. Its degrees of freedom are figured as follows: The between-groups variance estimate is based on three groups, making 2 degrees of freedom. The within-groups estimate is based on 15 degrees of freedom (16 participants) in each of the three groups, making 45 degrees of freedom.
   ❸ **Determine the cutoff sample score on the comparison distribution at which the null hypothesis should be rejected.** Using Table A-3 in the Appendix, the cutoff F for numerator $df = 2$ and denominator $df = 45$ at the .01 significance level is 5.11.
   ❹ **Determine your sample's score on the comparison distribution.**
   (a) Figure the between-groups population variance estimate ($S^2_{Between}$): First, figure the mean of each group. The group means are 20, 22, and 18.
      ❶ **Estimate the variance of the distribution of means:** Add up the sample means' squared deviations from the grand mean and divide by the number of means minus 1:
      $$S^2_M = [(20 - 20)^2 + (22 - 20)^2 + (18 - 20)^2]/(3 - 1)$$
      $$= (0 + 4 + 4)/2 = 4$$

ⓑ **Figure the estimated variance of the population of individual scores:** Multiply the variance of the distribution of means by the number of scores in each group.

$$S^2_{\text{Between}} = (4)(16) = 64$$

(b) Figure the within-groups population variance estimate (S^2_{Within}):

Ⓐ **Figure population variance estimates based on each group's scores:** Treatment A group, $S^2 = 8$; Treatment B group, $S^2 = 9$; Treatment C group, $S^2 = 7$.

Ⓑ **Average these variance estimates:** $S^2_{\text{Within}} = (8 + 9 + 7)/3 = 8$. The F ratio is the between-groups estimate divided by the within-groups estimate: $F = 64/8 = 8.00$.

⑤ **Decide whether to reject the null hypothesis.** The F of 8.00 is more extreme than the .01 cutoff F of 5.11. Therefore, reject the null hypothesis. The research hypothesis is supported; the different experimental treatments do produce different effects on the standard performance measure.

(b) The distributions involved are shown in Figure 6.

2. The assumptions for the analysis of variance are that the populations are assumed each to be normally distributed with equal variances and the scores are independent of each other.

3. We need the equal variance assumption to be able to justify averaging the estimates from each sample into an overall within-groups population variance estimate.

4. The analysis can lead to inaccurate results when the variance estimate from the group with the largest estimate is more than four or five times the smallest variance estimate.

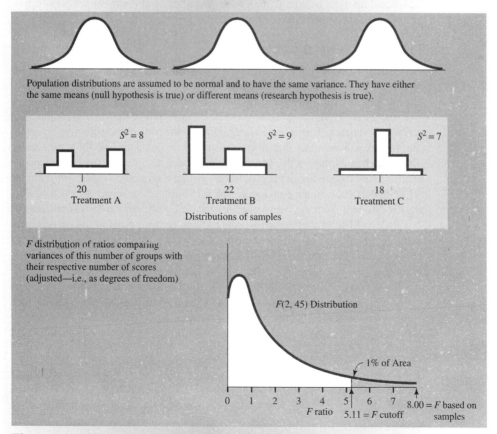

Population distributions are assumed to be normal and to have the same variance. They have either the same means (null hypothesis is true) or different means (research hypothesis is true).

$S^2 = 8$ $S^2 = 9$ $S^2 = 7$

20 22 18
Treatment A Treatment B Treatment C

Distributions of samples

F distribution of ratios comparing variances of this number of groups with their respective number of scores (adjusted—i.e., as degrees of freedom)

$F(2, 45)$ Distribution

1% of Area

0 1 2 3 4 5 6 7

F ratio

$5.11 = F$ cutoff

$8.00 = F$ based on samples

Figure 6   Distributions for "How are you doing?" question 1.

Planned Contrasts

When you reject the null hypothesis in an analysis of variance, this implies that the population means are not all the same. What is not clear, however, is which population means differ from which. For example, in the criminal record study, the Criminal Record group jurors had the highest ratings for the defendant's guilt ($M = 8$); the No Information group jurors, the second highest ($M = 5$); and the Clean Record group jurors, the lowest ($M = 4$). From the analysis of variance results, we concluded that the true means of the three populations these groups represent are not all the same. (That is, the overall analysis of variance was significant.) However, we do not know which populations' means are significantly different from each other.

In practice, in most research situations involving more than two groups, our real interest is not in an overall, or *omnibus,* difference among the several groups, but rather in more specific comparisons. For example, in the criminal record study, the researchers' prediction in advance would probably have been that the Criminal Record group would rate the defendant's guilt higher than both the No Information group and the Clean Record group. If, in fact, the researchers had made such predictions, these predictions would be examples of what are called **planned contrasts**. (They are called "contrasts" because they contrast the results from specific groups.)

Researchers use planned contrasts to look at some particular, focused differences between groups that directly follow from a theory or that are related directly to some practical application. Planned contrasts are also sometimes called *a priori comparisons* because they have been planned in advance (*a priori*) of the study. They may also be called *planned comparisons* because they were planned in advance. Finally, a general name you may see for most contrasts you would figure (whether planned in advance or not) is *linear contrasts.*

Figuring Planned Contrasts

The procedure to compare the means of a particular pair of groups is a direct extension of what you already know: figure a between-groups population variance estimate, a within-groups population variance estimate, and an F.

The within-groups population variance estimate will be the same as for the overall analysis of variance. This is because, regardless of the particular groups you are comparing, you are still assuming that all groups are from populations with the same variance. Thus, your best estimate of that variance is the one that makes use of the information from all the groups, the average of the population variance estimates from each of the samples.

The between-groups population variance estimate, however, in a planned contrast is different from the between-groups variance estimate in the overall analysis. It is different because in a planned contrast you are interested in the variation only between a particular pair of means. Specifically, in a planned contrast between two group means, you figure the between-groups population variance estimate with the usual two-step procedure, but using just the two means of interest.[2]

Once you have the two variance estimates for the planned contrast, you figure the F in the usual way, and compare it to a cutoff from the F table based on the df that go into the two estimates, which are the same as the overall analysis for df_{Within} and are usually exactly 1 for df_{Between} (because the between estimate is based on two means, and $2 - 1 = 1$).

planned contrast comparison in which the particular means to be compared were decided in advance. Also called *planned comparison.*

An Example

Consider the planned contrast of the Criminal Record group ($M = 8$) to the No Information group ($M = 5$).

The within-groups population variance estimate for a planned contrast is always the same as the within-groups estimate from the overall analysis: In the criminal record example S^2_{Within} was 5.33.

For the between-groups population variance estimate, you follow the usual two-step procedure, but using only the two means you plan to compare.

❹ Estimate the variance of the distribution of means: Add up the sample means' squared deviations from the grand mean and divide by the number of means minus 1. The grand mean for these two means would be 6.5 [that is, $(8 + 5)/2 = 6.5$] and df_{Between} when there are two means being compared is $2 - 1 = 1$. Thus,

$$S^2_M = \Sigma(M - GM)^2/df_{\text{Between}} = [(8 - 6.5)^2 + (5 - 6.5)^2]/1$$
$$= [1.5^2 + (-1.5)^2]/1 = 2.25 + 2.25 = 4.5.$$

❺ Figure the estimated variance of the population of individual scores: Multiply the variance of the distribution of means by the number of scores in each group. There are five scores in each group in this study. Thus,

$$S^2_{\text{Between}} = (S^2_M)(n) = (4.5)(5) = 22.5$$

Thus, for this planned contrast, $F = S^2_{\text{Between}}/S^2_{\text{Within}} = 22.5/5.33 = 4.22$. The .05 cutoff F for $df = 1, 12$ is 4.75. Thus, the planned contrast is not significant. You can conclude that the three means differ overall (from the original analysis of variance, which was significant), but you cannot conclude specifically that the Criminal Record condition makes a person rate guilt differently from being in the No Information condition.

A Second Example

What about the other planned contrast of the Criminal Record Group ($M = 8$) to the Clean Record group ($M = 4$)?

For the between-groups population variance estimate,

❹ Estimate the variance of the distribution of means: Add the sample means' squared deviations from the grand mean and divide by the number of means minus 1. The grand mean for these two means is $(8 + 4)/2 = 6.0$ and $df_{\text{Between}} = 2 - 1 = 1$. Thus,

$$S^2_M = [(8 - 6.0)^2 + (4 - 6.0)^2]/1 = [2.0^2 + (-2.0^2)]/1 = 4.0 + 4.0 = 8.0$$

❺ Figure the estimated variance of the population of individual scores: Multiply the variance of the distribution of means by the number of scores in each group:

$$S^2_{\text{Between}} = (S^2_M)(n) = (8)(5) = 40.0$$

The within-groups estimate, again, is the same as we figured for the overall analysis—5.33.

Thus, $F = S^2_{\text{Between}}/S^2_{\text{Within}} = 40.0/5.33 = 7.50$. This F of 7.50 is larger than 4.75 (the .05 cutoff F for $df = 1, 12$), which means that the planned contrast is significant. Thus, you can conclude that the Criminal Record condition makes a person rate guilt differently from the Clean Record condition.

The Bonferroni Procedure

There is a problem when you carry out several planned contrasts. Normally, when you set the .05 significance level, this means you have selected a cutoff so extreme that you have only a .05 chance of getting a significant result if the null hypothesis is true. However, with multiple contrasts, if you use the .05 cutoff, you can actually have much *more* than a .05 chance of getting a significant result if the null hypothesis is true!

The reason is this: if you are making several contrasts (comparisons), each at the .05 level, the chance of any one of them coming out significant is more than .05. (It is like flipping coins. If you flip any one coin, it has only a 50% chance of coming up heads. But if you flip five coins, there is a lot better than 50% chance at least one of them will come up heads.) In fact, if you make two contrasts, each at the .05 significance level, there is about a .10 chance that at least one will come out significant just by chance (that is, that at least one would come out significant even if the null hypothesis is true). If you make three planned contrasts at the .05 level, there is about a .15 chance.

A widely used approach for dealing with this problem with planned contrasts is the **Bonferroni procedure**. (It is also known as *Dunn's test*.) The idea of the Bonferroni procedure is that you use a more stringent significance level for each contrast. The result is that the overall chance of any one of the contrasts being mistakenly significant is still reasonably low. For example, if each of two planned contrasts used the .025 significance level, the overall chance of any one of them being mistakenly significant would still be less than .05. (That is, .05/2 = .025.) With three planned contrasts, you could use the .017 level (.05/3 = .017).

The general principle is that the Bonferroni corrected cutoff you use is the true significance level you want divided by the number of planned contrasts. Thus, if you want to test your hypothesis at the .01 level and you will make three planned contrasts, you would test each planned contrast using the .0033 significance level. That is, .01/3 = .0033.

If you are doing your analyses on a computer, it gives exact significance probabilities as part of the output—that is, it might give a p of .037 or .0054, not just whether you are beyond the .05 or .01 level. However, if you are using tables, normally only the .01 or .05 cutoffs would be available. Thus, even though almost all researchers use computers for their analyses, this situation has led to some traditions that are still followed today. Specifically, for simplicity, when the Bonferroni corrected cutoff might be .017 or even .025, researchers often use the .01 significance level. Also, if there are only two planned contrasts (or even three), it is common for researchers not to correct at all.

How are you doing?

1. (a) What is a planned contrast? (b) Why do researchers make them?
2. How is the procedure for figuring a planned contrast between two particular groups different from the overall analysis of variance?
3. A study has three groups of 25 participants each in the overall analysis of variance, and S^2_{Within} is 100. The researcher makes a single planned contrast between a group that has a mean of 10 and another group that has a mean of 16. Is it significant? (Use the .05 significance level.)
4. (a) Why do researchers making multiple planned contrasts need to make the Bonferroni correction? (b) What is the principle of the Bonferroni correction?
5. If a researcher is making four planned contrasts using the .05 significance level, what would be the Bonferroni corrected significance level?

Bonferroni procedure multiple-comparison procedure in which the total alpha percentage is divided among the set of comparisons so that each is tested at a more stringent significance level.

Answers

1. (a) A planned contrast is a focused comparison of two groups in an over-all analysis of variance that the researcher planned in advance of the study based on a theory or practical issue.
   (b) Researchers make planned contrasts because they are more likely to be of theoretical or practical interest than the overall difference among means.
2. The procedure for figuring a planned contrast between two particular groups is the same except that you make the between-groups estimate using only the means of the two groups being compared.
3. The planned contrast is significant. For the between-groups population variance estimate for the planned contrast,
   ❹ **Estimate the variance of the distribution of means:**

   $GM = (10 + 16)/2 = 13; df_{Between} = 2 - 1 = 1.$

   $S_M^2 = [(10 - 13)^2 + (16 - 13)^2]/1 = 18$

   ❸ **Figure the estimated variance of the population of individual scores:**

   $$S_{Between}^2 = (18)(25) = 450$$

   The within-groups estimate is the same as the overall within-groups estimate, 100.

   $$F = 450/100 = 4.5.$$

   The cutoff for $df = 1, 72$ (actually 1, 70, since 1, 72 is not in the table) is 3.98. You can reject the null hypothesis. The planned contrast is significant.
4. (a) Researchers make a Bonferroni correction with multiple planned contrasts because the chance of any one coming out significant is greater than the direct significance level used.
   (b) To carry out a Bonferroni correction, you divide your overall desired true significance level by the number of contrasts. This way, the chance of any one of them coming out significant is taken into account.
5. The Bonferroni corrected significance level is $.05/4 = .0125$.

Post Hoc Comparisons

As we have noted, rejecting the null hypothesis in an analysis of variance implies that the population means are not all the same, but it does not tell you which population means differ from which. As you learned in the preceding section on planned contrasts, researchers often plan specific comparisons based on theory or practical considerations. Sometimes, however, researchers take a more exploratory approach, for example, comparing all the different pairings of means to discover which ones do and do not differ significantly. (We call this making *pairwise comparisons,* because you are comparing all possible pairings of means.) That is, after the study is done, the researcher is fishing through the results to see which groups differ from each other. These are called **post hoc comparisons** (or *a posteriori comparisons*) because they are after the fact and not planned in advance.

In post hoc comparisons, all possible comparisons have to be taken into account when figuring the overall chance of any one of them turning out significant. Using the Bonferroni procedure for post hoc comparisons is safe, in the sense that you are confident you won't get too many results significant by chance. But in post hoc comparisons there are often so many comparisons to consider that the overall

post hoc comparisons multiple comparisons, not specified in advance; procedure conducted as part of an exploratory analysis after an analysis of variance.

significance level is divided into such a small number by the Bonferroni procedure that getting any one comparison to come out significant would be a long shot.
For example, with four groups, there are six possible pairs to compare; so using a
Bonferroni correction and an overall significance level of .05, you would have to
test each comparison at .05/6 or .0083. If there are five groups, there are 10 possible
comparisons; .05 overall becomes .005 for each comparison. And so forth. Thus, the
power for any one comparison becomes very low.

Of course, you might think, "I'll just test the pairs of means that have the biggest difference so that the number of comparisons won't be so great." Unfortunately, this strategy won't work. Since you did not decide in advance which pairs
of means would be compared, when exploring after the fact, you have to take into
account that any of the pairs might have been the biggest ones. So unless you made
specific predictions in advance—and had a sound theoretical or practical basis for
those predictions—all the possible pairings have to be counted.

For this reason, statisticians have developed a variety of procedures to use in
these fishing expeditions. These procedures attempt to keep the overall risk of a Type I
error at some level like .05, while at the same time not too drastically reducing statistical power. You may see some of these referred to in articles you read, described
by the names of their developers; the **Scheffé test** and *Tukey test* are the most widely
used, with the *Neuman-Keuls* and *Duncan* procedures almost as common. Which
procedure is best under various conditions remains a topic of dispute. You can learn
the details about the possibilities and controversies in intermediate statistics.

The Scheffé Test

As a post hoc test, the Scheffé method has the advantage of being the most widely
applicable method. We say that because it is the only one that can be used when
you are making relatively simple comparisons (such as the ones we have considered in which two groups are being compared), as well as when you are making
more complex comparisons (for example, comparing the average of two groups to
a third group). Its disadvantage, however, is that, compared to the Tukey and other
procedures, it is the most conservative. That is, for any given post hoc comparison, its chance of being significant using the Scheffé is usually still better than the
Bonferroni, but worse than the Tukey or any of the other post hoc contrasts.

To use the Scheffé test, you first figure the F for your comparison in the usual
way. But then you divide that F by the overall study's $df_{Between}$ (the number of groups
minus 1). You then compare this much smaller F to the overall study's F cutoff.

Here is an example. Recall that for the comparison of the Criminal Record
group versus the No Information group, we figured an F of 4.22. Since the overall
$df_{Between}$ in that study was 2 (there were three groups), for a Scheffé test, you would
actually consider the F for this contrast to be an F of only $4.22/2 = 2.11$. You would
then compare this Scheffé corrected F of 2.11 to the cutoff F for the overall between
effect (in this example, the F for $df = 2, 12$), which was 3.89. Thus, the comparison
is not significant using the Scheffé test.

How are you doing?

1. (a) What are post hoc comparisons? (b) Why do researchers make them?
2. (a) Why do researchers typically not use the Bonferroni procedure for post
hoc comparisons?
(b) What is the advantage over the Bonferroni procedure of procedures such
as the Tukey and Scheffé tests?

Scheffé test method of figuring the
significance of post hoc comparisons
that takes into account all possible
comparisons that could be made.

3. What are the (a) advantages and (b) disadvantages of the Scheffé procedure versus other post hoc tests (such as the Tukey)?
4. How do you carry out the Scheffé procedure?
5. Suppose in a study with four groups of 50 participants each, for a particular contrast, you figure an F of 12.60. Using a Scheffé test, is this significant at the .05 significance level?

Answers

1. (a) Post hoc comparisons are comparisons figured after an analysis of variance, such as between two groups, that were not planned in advance.
   (b) Researchers make them as an exploratory procedure to see what patterns of relations among populations are suggested by the data over and above any comparisons that were planned in advance.
2. (a) In any follow-up analysis, there are usually so many possible post hoc comparisons that, if you used the Bonferroni procedure, your corrected significance level would be so extreme that it would be very hard for any result to be significant.
   (b) The effect of the Tukey and Scheffé tests, and others like them, when doing multiple post hoc comparisons and correctly adjusting for the many comparisons being made, is that a result does not have to be quite so extreme to be significant.
3. (a) You can use the Scheffé procedure for any number of comparisons, including complex comparisons.
   (b) The Scheffé procedure is more conservative: the chance of any comparison being significant is less.
4. Figure the comparison in the usual way, but divide the F by the overall study's df_{Between} and use the overall study's F cutoff.
5. Overall study's $df_{\text{Between}} = 4 - 1 = 3$; $df_{\text{Within}} = 49 + 49 + 49 + 49 = 196$. Scheffé corrected $F = 12.60/3 = 4.20$. Overall study's .05 cutoff F ($df = 3$, 196; closest on table $= 3$, 100) is 2.70. Thus, even with the Scheffé correction, this comparison is significant.

Effect Size and Power for the Analysis of Variance

Effect Size

Effect size for the analysis of variance is a little more complex than for a t test. With the t test, you took the difference between the two means and divided by the standard deviation. In the analysis of variance, you have more than two means; so it is not obvious just what is the equivalent to the difference between the means—the numerator in figuring effect size.[3] Thus, in this section we consider a quite different approach to effect size, the **proportion of variance accounted for (R^2)**.

To be precise, R^2 is the proportion of the total variation of scores from the grand mean that is accounted for by the variation between the means of the groups. (In other words, you consider how much of the variance in the measured variable—such as ratings of guilt—is accounted for by the variable that divides up the groups—such as what experimental condition one is in.) In terms of a formula,

$$R^2 = \frac{(S^2_{\text{Between}})(df_{\text{Between}})}{(S^2_{\text{Between}})(df_{\text{Between}}) + (S^2_{\text{Within}})(df_{\text{Within}})} \qquad (7)$$

proportion of variance accounted for (R^2) proportion of the total variation of scores from the grand mean that is accounted for by the variation between the means of the groups.

The proportion of variance accounted for is the between-groups population variance estimate multiplied by the between-groups degrees of freedom, divided by the sum of the between-groups population variance estimate multiplied by the between-groups degrees of freedom, plus the within-groups population variance estimate multiplied by the within-groups degrees of freedom.

The between- and within-groups degrees of freedom are included in the formula to take into account the number of participants and the number of groups used in the study. But this formula looks more complicated than it really is. Basically the numerator is a version of the between-groups variance estimate, and the denominator is a version of the total variance (between plus within). Consider once again the criminal record study. In that example, $S_{Between}^2 = 21.70$, $df_{Between} = 2$, $S_{Within}^2 = 5.33$, and $df_{Within} = 12$. Thus, the proportion of the total variation accounted for by the variation between groups is $(21.70)(2)/[(21.70)(2) + (5.33)(12)]$, which is .40 (or 40%). In terms of the formula,

$$R^2 = \frac{(S_{Between}^2)(df_{Between})}{(S_{Between}^2)(df_{Between}) + (S_{Within}^2)(df_{Within})}$$

$$= \frac{(21.70)(2)}{(21.70)(2) + (5.33)(12)} = \frac{43.40}{107.36} = .40$$

What if the between-groups and within-groups variance estimates are not available, as is often true in published studies? It is also possible to figure R^2 directly from F and the degrees of freedom. The formula is

> The proportion of variance accounted for is the F ratio multiplied by the between-groups degrees of freedom (the degrees of freedom for the between-groups population variance estimate), divided by the sum of the F ratio multiplied by the between-groups degrees of freedom, plus the degrees of freedom for the within-groups population variance estimate.

$$R^2 = \frac{(F)(df_{Between})}{(F)(df_{Between}) + df_{Within}} \tag{8}$$

For example, in the criminal record study,

$$R^2 = \frac{(F)(df_{Between})}{(F)(df_{Between}) + df_{Within}} = \frac{(4.07)(2)}{(4.07)(2) + 12} = \frac{8.14}{20.14} = .40$$

You should also know that another common name for this measure of effect size (besides R^2) is η^2, the Greek letter *eta squared*; η^2 is also known as the *correlation ratio*.

The proportion of variance accounted for is a useful measure of effect size because it has the direct meaning suggested by its name. (Further, researchers are familiar with R^2 from its use in regression and its square root, R, is a kind of correlation coefficient that is very familiar to most researchers.)

R^2 has a minimum of 0 and a maximum of 1. However, in practice it is rare in most psychology research for an analysis of variance to have an R^2 even as high as .20. Cohen's (1988) conventions for R^2 are .01, a small effect size; .06, a medium effect size; and .14, a large effect size.

Power

Table 9 shows the approximate power for the .05 significance level for small, medium, and large effect sizes; sample sizes of 10, 20, 30, 40, 50, and 100 per group; and three, four, and five groups.[4]

Consider a planned study with five groups of 10 participants each and an expected large effect size (.14). Using the .05 significance level, the study would have a power of .56. Thus, even if the research hypothesis is in fact true and has a large effect size, there is only a little greater than even chance (56%) that the study will come out significant.

Determining power is especially useful when interpreting the practical implication of a nonsignificant result. For example, suppose that you have read a study using an analysis of variance with four groups of 30 participants each, and there is a nonsignificant result at the .05 level. Table 9 shows a power of only .13 for a small effect size. This suggests that even if such a small effect exists in the population, this study would

eta squared (η^2)   common name for the R^2 measure of effect size for the analysis of variance. Also called *correlation ratio*.

Table 9 Approximate Power for Studies Using the Analysis of Variance Testing Hypotheses at the .05 Significance Level

Participants per Group (n)	Effect Size Small ($R^2 = .01$)	Medium ($R^2 = .06$)	Large ($R^2 = .14$)
Three groups ($df_{Between} = 2$)			
10	.07	.20	.45
20	.09	.38	.78
30	.12	.55	.93
40	.15	.68	.98
50	.18	.79	.99
100	.32	.98	*
Four groups ($df_{Between} = 3$)			
10	.07	.21	.51
20	.10	.43	.85
30	.13	.61	.96
40	.16	.76	.99
50	.19	.85	*
100	.36	.99	*
Five groups ($df_{Between} = 4$)			
10	.07	.23	.56
20	.10	.47	.90
30	.13	.67	.98
40	.17	.81	*
50	.21	.90	*
100	.40	*	*

*Nearly 1.

be very unlikely to have come out significant. But the table shows a power of .96 for a large effect size. This suggests that if a large effect existed in the population, it almost surely would have shown up in that study.

Planning Sample Size

Table 10 gives the approximate number of participants you need in each group for 80% power at the .05 significance level for estimated small, medium, and large effect sizes for studies with three, four, and five groups.[5]

Table 10 Approximate Number of Participants Needed in Each Group (Assuming Equal Sample Sizes) for 80% Power for the One-Way Analysis of Variance Testing Hypotheses at the .05 Significance Level

	Effect Size Small ($R^2 = .01$)	Medium ($R^2 = .06$)	Large ($R^2 = .14$)
Three groups ($df_{Between} = 2$)	322	52	21
Four groups ($df_{Between} = 3$)	274	45	18
Five groups ($df_{Between} = 4$)	240	39	16

For example, suppose you are planning a study involving four groups and you expect a small effect size (and will use the .05 significance level). For 80% power, you would need 274 participants in each group, a total of 1,096 in all. However, suppose you could adjust the research plan so that it was now reasonable to predict a large effect size (perhaps by using more accurate measures and a stronger experimental procedure). Now you would need only 18 in each of the four groups, for a total of 72.

How are you doing?

1. (a) Why is the method of figuring effect size for analysis of variance quite different from that used for the t tests? (b) Explain the logic of why proportion of variance accounted for can serve as an effect size in analysis of variance.
2. (a) Write the formula for effect size in analysis of variance using $S^2_{Between}$ and S^2_{Within}; (b) define each of the symbols; (c) give an alternative symbol for R^2; and (d) figure the effect size for a study in which $S^2_{Between} = 12.22$, $S^2_{Within} = 7.20$, $df_{Between} = 2$, and $df_{Within} = 8$.
3. (a) Write the formula for effect size in analysis of variance from a study in which only the F ratio and degrees of freedom are available; (b) define each of the symbols; and (c) figure the effect size for a study with 18 participants in each of the three groups and an F of 4.50.
4. What is the power of a study with four groups of approximately 40 participants each to be tested at the .05 significance level, in which the researchers predict a large effect size?
5. About how many participants do you need in each group for 80% power in a planned study with five groups in which you predict a medium effect size and will be using the .05 significance level?

Answers

1. (a) With t tests, your focus is on the difference between two means; there is no direct equivalent in the analysis of variance. (b) You are figuring the percentage of the total variation among the scores that is accounted for by which group the participant is in.
2. (a) The formula for effect size in analysis of variance: $R^2 = (S^2_{Between})(df_{Between})/[(S^2_{Between})(df_{Between}) + (S^2_{Within})(df_{Within})]$. (b) R^2 is the proportion of variance accounted for; $S^2_{Between}$ is the between-groups population variance estimate; $df_{Between}$ is the between-groups degrees of freedom (number of groups minus 1); S^2_{Within} is the within-groups population variance estimate; df_{Within} is the within-groups degrees of freedom (the sum of the degrees of freedom for each group's population variance estimate). (c) η^2. (d) Effect size: .30.
3. (a) $R^2 = (F)(df_{Between})/[(F)(df_{Between}) + df_{Within}]$. (b) R^2 is the proportion of variance accounted for; F is the F ratio from the study; $df_{Between}$ is the between-groups degrees of freedom; and df_{Within} is the within-groups degrees of freedom. (c) Effect size:

$$df_{Between} = 3 - 1 = 2; df_{Within} = 17 + 17 + 17 = 51.$$
$$R^2 = (F)(df_{Between})/[(F)(df_{Between}) + df_{Within}]$$
$$= (4.5)(2)/[(4.5)(2) + 51] = 9/[9 + 51] = 9/60 = .15.$$

4. The power of the study is .99.
5. The number of participants needed in each group is 39.

Controversy: Omnibus Tests versus Planned Contrasts

The analysis of variance is commonly used in situations comparing three or more groups. (If you are comparing two groups, you can use a *t* test.) However, following the logic we introduced earlier, Rosnow and Rosenthal (1989) argue that such diffuse or omnibus tests are not very useful. They say that, in almost all cases when we test the overall difference among three or more groups, "we have tested a question in which we almost surely are not interested" (p. 1281). In which questions *are* we interested? We are interested in specific comparisons, such as between two particular groups.

Rosnow and Rosenthal (1989; see also Furr & Rosenthal, 2003) advocate that, when figuring an analysis of variance, you should analyze *only* planned contrasts. These should replace entirely the overall *F* test (that is, the diffuse or omnibus *F* test) for whether you can reject the hypothesis of no difference among population means. Traditionally, planned contrasts, when used at all, are a supplement to the overall *F* test. So this has been a rather revolutionary idea.

Consider an example. Orbach and colleagues (1997) compared a group of suicidal mental hospital patients (individuals who had made serious suicide attempts), nonsuicidal mental hospital patients with similar diagnoses, and a control group of volunteers from the community. The purpose of the study was to test the theory that suicidal individuals have a higher tolerance for physical pain. The idea is that their higher pain threshold makes it easier for them to do the painful acts usually involved in suicide. The researchers carried out standard pain threshold and other sensory tests and administered a variety of questionnaires to all three groups. Here is how they describe their analysis:

> To examine the study hypothesis, we performed a set of two linear contrasts for each pain measure.... The first linear contrast, *suicidality contrast,* compared the suicidal group with the two nonsuicidal groups (psychiatric inpatients and control participants). The second contrast compared the two nonsuicidal groups.... We did not make a previous omnibus *F* because we conducted preplanned group comparisons testing the study hypothesis. Because of multiple comparisons needed, the critical alpha was set at .01, to avoid Type I error....
>
> The suicidality contrast was significant for thermal sensation threshold, $F(1, 95) = 21.64, p < .01$; pain threshold, $F(1, 95) = 23.65, p < .01$; pain tolerance $F(1, 95) = 6.55, p < .01$; and maximum tolerance $F(1, 95) = 16.05$. No significant difference was found between the suicidal and nonsuicidal groups in the magnitude estimate measure. An examination of the means... supports our main hypothesis: Suicidal participants, as expected, had high sensation and pain thresholds, high pain tolerance, and were more likely to tolerate the maximum temperature administered than inpatients and control participants. Interestingly, the second set of contrasts revealed no significant differences between the psychiatric inpatients and control participants in any of the five pain measures. (p. 648)

The study by Orbach and colleagues study exemplifies Rosnow and Rosenthal's advice to use planned contrasts instead of an overall analysis of variance. But, although the idea was originally proposed more than two decades ago, this approach has not yet been widely adopted and is still controversial. The main concern is regarding one-tailed and two-tailed tests. If we adopt the highly targeted, planned contrasts recommended by Rosnow and Rosenthal, critics argue, we lose out on finding unexpected differences not initially planned, and we put too much control of what is found in the hands of the researcher (versus nature).

Analyses of Variance in Research Articles

Analyses of variance (of the kind we have considered in this chapter) are usually described in a research article by giving the F, the degrees of freedom, and the significance level. For example, "$F(3, 68) = 5.21, p < .01$." The means for the groups usually are given in a table, although if there are only a few groups and only one or a few measures, the means may be given in the regular text of the article. Usually, there is some report of additional analyses, such as planned contrasts.

Returning again to the criminal record study example, we could describe the analysis of variance results this way: "The means for the Criminal Record, Clean Record, and No Information groups were 8.0, 4.0, and 5.0, respectively. These were significantly different, $F(2, 12) = 4.07, p < .05$. We also carried out two planned contrasts: The Criminal Record versus the No Information condition, $F(1, 12) = 4.22, p < .10$; and the Criminal Record versus the Clean Record condition, $F(1, 12) = 7.50, p < .05$. Although the first contrast approached significance, after a Bonferroni correction (for two planned contrasts), it does not even reach the .10 level."

Note that it is also common for researchers to report planned contrasts using t tests. These are not ordinary t tests for independent means, but rather special t tests for the comparisons that are mathematically equivalent to the method we described—that is, the results in terms of significance are identical.

Researchers often report results of post hoc comparisons among all pairs of means. The most common method of doing this is by putting small letters by the means in the tables. Usually, means with the same letter are *not* significantly different from each other; those with different letters are. For example, Table 11 presents the actual results on the love experience measures in the Hazan and Shaver (1987)

		Anxious/		
Scale Name	**Avoidant**	**Ambivalent**	**Secure**	**$F(2, 571)$**
Happiness	3.19_a	3.31_a	3.51_b	14.21***
Friendship	3.18_a	3.19_a	3.50_b	22.96***
Trust	3.11_a	3.13_a	3.43_b	16.21***
Fear of closeness	2.30_a	2.15_a	1.88_b	22.65***
Acceptance	2.86_a	3.03_b	3.01_b	4.66**
Emotional extremes	2.75_a	3.05_b	2.36_c	27.54***
Jealousy	2.57_a	2.88_b	2.17_c	43.91***
Obsessive preoccupation	3.01_a	3.29_b	3.01_a	9.47***
Sexual attraction	3.27_a	3.43_b	3.27_a	4.08*
Desire for union	2.81_a	3.25_b	2.69_a	22.67***
Desire for reciprocation	3.24_a	3.55_b	3.22_a	14.90***
Love at first sight	2.91_a	3.17_b	2.97_a	6.00**

Table 11   Love Subscale Means for the Three Attachment Types (Newspaper Sample)

Note: Within each row, means with different subscripts differ at the .05 level of significance according to a Scheffé test.*$p < .05$; **$p < .01$; ***$p < .001$.

Source: Hazan, C., & Shaver, P. (1987). Romantic love conceptualized as an attachment process. *Journal of Personality and Social Psychology, 52,* 511–524. Published by the American Psychological Association. Reprinted with permission.

study (our example at the start of the chapter). Consider the first row (the happiness results). The avoidant and anxious-ambivalent groups are not significantly different from each other, since they have the same letter (*a*). But both are significantly different on happiness compared to the secure group, which has a different letter (*b*). In the jealousy row, however, all three groups differ from one another.

When reading results of post hoc comparisons, you will see many different procedures named. For example, Table 11 (from the Hazan and Shaver study) explicitly mentions that the results are "according to a Scheffé test."

Advanced Topic: The Structural Model in the Analysis of Variance

This chapter introduced the basic logic of the analysis of variance. Building on this understanding, we now briefly describe an alternative but mathematically equivalent way of understanding the analysis of variance. This alternative is called the **structural model**. The core logic you learned earlier in the chapter still applies. However, the structural model provides a different and more flexible way of figuring the two population variance estimates. Understanding the structural model provides deeper insights into the underlying logic of the analysis of variance, including helping you understand the way analysis of variance results are laid out in computer printouts. Also, the structural method more easily handles the situation in which the number of individuals in each group is not equal. Finally, the structural model method is related to a fundamental mathematical approach to which we want to expose those of you who might be going on to more advanced statistics courses.

Principles of the Structural Model
Dividing Up the Deviations

The structural model is all about deviations. To start with, there is the deviation of a score from the grand mean. In the criminal record example earlier in the chapter (see Tables 3 and 4), the grand mean of the 15 scores was $85/15 = 5.67$.

The deviation from the grand mean is just the beginning. You then think of this deviation from the grand mean as having two parts: (a) the deviation of the score from the mean of its group and (b) the deviation of the mean of its group from the grand mean. Consider a participant in the criminal record study who rated the defendant's guilt as a 10. The grand mean of all participants' guilt ratings was 5.67. This person's score has a total deviation of 4.33 (that is, $10 - 5.67 = 4.33$). The mean of the Criminal Record group by itself was 8. Thus, the deviation of this person's score from his or her group's mean is 2 (that is, $10 - 8 = 2$), and the deviation of that group's mean from the grand mean is 2.33 (that is, $8 - 5.67 = 2.33$). Note that these two deviations (2 and 2.33) add up to the total deviation of 4.33. This is shown in Figure 7. We encourage you to study this figure until you grasp it well.

Summing the Squared Deviations

The next step in the structural model is to square each of these deviation scores and add up the squared deviations of each type for all the participants. This gives a *sum of squared deviations* for each type of deviation score. It turns out that the sum of squared deviations of each score from the grand mean is equal to (a) the sum of the squared deviations of each score from its group's mean plus (b) the sum of the

structural model way of understanding the analysis of variance as a division of the deviation of each score from the overall mean into two parts: the variation in groups (its deviation from its group's mean) and the variation between groups (its group's mean's deviation from the overall mean); an alternative (but mathematically equivalent) way of understanding the analysis of variance.

Figure 7   Example from the fictional criminal record study of the deviation of one individual's score from the grand mean being that individual's score's deviation from his or her group's mean plus that individual's group's mean's deviation from the grand mean.

The sum of squared deviations of each score from the grand mean is the sum of squared deviations of each score from its group's mean plus the sum of squared deviations of each score's group's mean from the grand mean.

squared deviations of each score's group's mean from the grand mean. This principle can be stated as a formula:

$$\Sigma(X - GM)^2 = \Sigma(X - M)^2 + \Sigma(M - GM)^2 \quad \text{or}$$
$$SS_{\text{Total}} = SS_{\text{Within}} + SS_{\text{Between}} \tag{9}$$

In this formula, $\Sigma(X - GM)^2$ or $\textbf{SS}_{\textbf{Total}}$ is the sum of squared deviations of each score from the grand mean, completely ignoring the group a score is in. $\Sigma(X - M)^2$ or $\textbf{SS}_{\textbf{Within}}$ is the sum of squared deviations of each score from its group's mean, added up for all participants. $\Sigma(M - GM)^2$ or $\textbf{SS}_{\textbf{Between}}$ is the sum of squared deviations of each score's group's mean from the grand mean—again, added up for all participants.

This rule applies only to the *sums* of the squared deviations. For each individual score, the deviations themselves, but not the squared deviations, always add up.

$\textbf{SS}_{\textbf{Total}}$ sum of squared deviations of each score from the overall mean of all scores, completely ignoring the group a score is in.

$\textbf{SS}_{\textbf{Within}}$ sum of squared deviations of each score from its group's mean.

$\textbf{SS}_{\textbf{Between}}$ sum of squared deviations of each score's group's mean from the grand mean.

From the Sums of Squared Deviations to the Population Variance Estimates

Now we are ready to use these sums of squared deviations to figure the needed population variance estimates for an analysis of variance. To do this, you divide each sum of squared deviations by an appropriate degrees of freedom. The between-groups population variance estimate (S^2_{Between} or MS_{Between}) is the sum of squared deviations of each score's group's mean from the grand mean (SS_{Between}) divided by the degrees of freedom on which it is based (df_{Between}, the number of groups minus 1). Stated as a formula,

The between-groups population variance estimate is the sum of squared deviations of each score's group's mean from the grand mean divided by the degrees of freedom for the between-groups population variance estimate.

$$S^2_{\text{Between}} = \frac{\Sigma(M - GM)^2}{df_{\text{Between}}} \quad \text{or} \quad MS_{\text{Between}} = \frac{SS_{\text{Between}}}{df_{\text{Between}}} \tag{10}$$

The within-groups population variance estimate (S^2_{Within} or MS_{Within}) is the sum of squared deviations of each score from its group's mean (SS_{Within}) divided by the total degrees of freedom on which this is based (df_{Within}; the sum of the degrees of freedom over all the groups—the number of scores in the first group minus 1, plus the number in the second group minus 1, etc.). Stated as a formula,

The within-groups population variance estimate is the sum of squared deviations of each score from its group's mean divided by the degrees of freedom for the within-groups population variance estimate.

$$S^2_{\text{Within}} = \frac{\Sigma(X - M)^2}{df_{\text{Within}}} \quad \text{or} \quad MS_{\text{Within}} = \frac{SS_{\text{Within}}}{df_{\text{Within}}} \tag{11}$$

Notice that we have ignored the sum of squared deviations of each score from the grand mean (SS_{Total}). This sum of squares is useful mainly for checking our arithmetic. Recall that $SS_{\text{Total}} = SS_{\text{Within}} + SS_{\text{Between}}$.

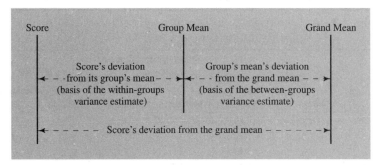

Figure 8   The score's deviations from its group's mean is the basis for the within-groups population variance estimate; the group's mean's deviation from the grand mean is the basis for the between-groups population variance estimate.

Figure 8 again shows the division of the deviation score into two parts, but this time emphasizes which deviations are associated with which population variance estimates.

Relation of the Structural Model Method to the Method You Learned Earlier in the Chapter

The methods we have just described for figuring the within-groups and between-groups population variance estimates using the structural model approach give exactly the same result as the methods you learned earlier in the chapter. (If you enjoy algebra, you might see whether you can derive the earlier formulas from the ones you have just learned.) However, the procedures you follow to figure those estimates are quite different. In the structural model method, when figuring the within-groups variance estimate method, you never actually figure the variance estimate for each group and average them. Similarly, for the between-groups estimate, with the structural model method, you never multiply anything by the number of scores in each sample. The point is that, with either method, you get the same within-groups and between-groups variance estimates, and thus the same F and the same overall result.

The deeper logic of the analysis of variance with the structural model is also essentially the same as what you learned earlier in the chapter, with a twist. The twist is one of emphasis. The method you learned earlier in the chapter emphasizes entire groups, comparing a variance based on differences among group means to a variance based on averaging variances of the groups. The structural model method emphasizes individual scores. It compares a variance based on deviations of individual scores' groups' means from the grand mean to a variance based on deviations of individual scores from their group's mean. The method earlier in the chapter focuses directly on what contributes to the overall population variance estimates; the structural model method focuses directly on what contributes to the divisions of the deviations of scores from the grand mean.

An Example

Table 12 shows all the figuring using the structural model for an analysis of variance for the criminal record study. This table shows all three types of deviations and squared deviations for each score. For example, for the first person, the deviation from the grand mean is 4.33 (the score of 10 minus the grand mean of 5.67). This

Table 12 Analysis of Variance for the Criminal Record Study (Fictional Data) Using the Structural Model Method (Compare to Tables 3 and 4)

Criminal Record Group

X	X − GM Deviation	X − GM Squared Deviation	X − M Deviation	X − M Squared Deviation	M − GM Deviation	M − GM Squared Deviation
10	4.33	18.75	2	4	2.33	5.43
7	1.33	1.77	−1	1	2.33	5.43
5	−.67	.45	−3	9	2.33	5.43
10	4.33	18.75	2	4	2.33	5.43
8	2.33	5.43	0	0	2.33	5.43
40		45.15		18		27.15

$M = 40/5 = 8$

Clean Record Group

X	X − GM Deviation	X − GM Squared Deviation	X − M Deviation	X − M Squared Deviation	M − GM Deviation	M − GM Squared Deviation
5	−.67	.45	1	1	−1.67	2.79
1	−4.67	21.81	−3	9	−1.67	2.79
3	−2.67	7.13	−1	1	−1.67	2.79
7	1.33	1.77	3	9	−1.67	2.79
4	−1.67	2.79	0	0	−1.67	2.79
20		33.95		20		13.95

$M = 20/5 = 4$

No Information Group

X	X − GM Deviation	X − GM Squared Deviation	X − M Deviation	X − M Squared Deviation	M − GM Deviation	M − GM Squared Deviation
4	−1.67	2.79	−1	1	−.67	.45
6	.33	.11	1	1	−.67	.45
9	3.33	11.09	4	16	−.67	.45
3	−2.67	7.13	−2	4	−.67	.45
3	−2.67	7.13	−2	4	−.67	.45
25		28.25		26		2.25

$M = 25/5 = 5$

Sums of squared deviations:

$\sum(X - GM)^2$ or $SS_{Total} = 45.15 + 33.95 + 28.25 = 107.35$

$\sum(X - M)^2$ or $SS_{Within} = 18 + 20 + 26 = 64$

$\sum(M - GM)^2$ or $SS_{Between} = 27.15 + 13.95 + 2.25 = 43.35$

Check ($SS_{Total} = SS_{Within} + SS_{Between}$):

$SS_{Total} = 107.35$; $SS_{Within} + SS_{Between} = 64 + 43.35 = 107.35$

Degrees of freedom:

$df_{Total} = N - 1 = 15 - 1 = 14$

$df_{Within} = df_1 + df_2 + \cdots + df_{Last} = (5 - 1) + (5 - 1) + (5 - 1) = 4 + 4 + 4 = 12$

$df_{Between} = N_{Groups} - 1 = 3 - 1 = 2$

Check ($df_{Total} = df_{Within} + df_{Between}$): $14 = 12 + 2$

Population variance estimates:

S^2_{Within} or $MS_{Within} = SS_{Within}/df_{Within} = 64/12 = 5.33$

$S^2_{Between}$ or $MS_{Between} = SS_{Between}/df_{Between} = 43.35/2 = 21.68$

F ratio: $F = S^2_{Between}/S^2_{Within}$ or $MS_{Between}/MS_{Within} = 21.68/5.33 = 4.07$

deviation squared is 18.75. The deviation of the score from its group's mean is 2; this deviation squared is 4. Finally, the deviation of the score's group's mean from the grand mean is 2.33; this deviation squared is 5.43. Notice that the deviations of each score's group's mean from the grand mean (in this case, 2.33) is the same number for all the scores in a group. At the bottom of each column, we have also summed the squared deviations of each type.

The bottom part of Table 12 shows the analysis of variance figuring. First, you figure the three sums of squared deviations (SS_{Total}, SS_{Within}, and $SS_{Between}$). The next step is to check for accuracy. You do this following the principle that the sum of squared deviations of each score from the grand mean comes out to the total of the other two kinds of sums of squared deviations.

The degrees of freedom, the next step shown in the table, is figured the same way as you learned earlier in the chapter. Then, the table shows the figuring of the two crucial population variance estimates. You figure them by dividing each sum of squared deviations by the appropriate degrees of freedom. Finally, the table shows the figuring of the F ratio in the usual way—dividing the between-groups variance estimate by the within-groups variance estimate. All these results, degrees of freedom, variance estimates, and F come out exactly the same (within rounding error) as we figured earlier in the chapter.

Analysis of Variance Tables

An **analysis of variance table** lays out the results of an analysis of variance based on the structural model method. These kinds of charts are automatically produced by most analysis of variance computer programs (see, for example, Figure 11 later in the chapter). A standard analysis of variance table has five columns. Table 13 shows an analysis of variance table for the criminal record study.

The first column in a standard analysis of variance table is labeled "Source"; it lists the type of variance estimate or deviation score involved ("between" [groups], "within" [groups], and "total"). The next column is usually labeled "SS"(sum of squares); it lists the different types of sums of squared deviations. The third column is "df" (the degrees of freedom of each type). The fourth column is "MS" (mean square); this refers to mean squares, that is, MS is SS divided by df, the variance estimate. MS is, as usual, the same thing as S^2. However, in an analysis of variance table the variance is almost always referred to as MS. The last column is "F," the F ratio. (In a computer printout there may be additional columns, listing the exact p value and possibly effect size or confidence intervals.) Each row of the table refers to one of the variance estimates. The first row is for the between-groups variance estimate. It is usually listed under Source as "Between" or "Group," although you will sometimes see it called "Model" or "Treatment." The second row is for the within-groups variance estimate, though it is sometimes labeled as "Error." The final row is for the sum of squares based on the total deviation of each score from the grand mean. Note, however, that computer printouts will sometimes use a different order for the columns and will sometimes omit either SS or MS, but not both.

analysis of variance table chart showing the major elements in figuring an analysis of variance using the structural model approach.

Table 13	Analysis of Variance Table for the Criminal Record Study (Fictional Data)			
Source	SS	df	MS	F
Between	43.35	2	21.68	4.07
Within	64	12	5.33	
Total	107.35	14		

Table 14   Hypothesis Testing Steps for an Analysis of Variance Using the Structural Model Approach (Equal- or Unequal-Sized Groups)

❶ **Restate the question as a research hypothesis and a null hypothesis about the populations.**

❷ **Determine the characteristics of the comparison distribution.**
   a. The comparison distribution will be an F distribution.
   b. The between-groups (numerator) degrees of freedom is the number of groups minus 1: $df_{Between} = N_{Groups} - 1$.
   c. The within-groups (denominator) degrees of freedom is the sum of the degrees of freedom in each group (the number of scores in the group minus 1): $df_{Within} = df_1 + df_2 + \cdots + df_{Last}$.
   d. Check the accuracy of your figuring by making sure that df_{Within} and $df_{Between}$ sum to df_{Total} (which is the total number of participants minus 1).

❸ **Determine the cutoff sample score on the comparison distribution at which the null hypothesis should be rejected.**
   a. Decide the significance level.
   b. Look up the appropriate cutoff in an F table, using the degrees of freedom from Step ❷.

❹ **Determine your sample's score on the comparison distribution.** This will be an F ratio.
   a. Figure the mean of each group and the grand mean of all scores.
   b. Figure the following deviations for each score:
      i. Its deviation from the grand mean $(X - GM)$.
      ii. Its deviation from its group's mean $(X - M)$.
      iii. Its group's mean's deviation from the grand mean $(M - GM)$.
   c. Square each of these deviation scores.
   d. Figure the sums of each of these three types of deviation scores (SS_{Total}, SS_{Within}, and $SS_{Between}$).
   e. Check the accuracy of your figuring by making sure that $SS_{Within} + SS_{Between} = SS_{Total}$.
   f. Figure the between-groups variance estimate: $SS_{Between}/df_{Between}$.
   g. Figure the within-groups variance estimate: SS_{Within}/df_{Within}.
   h. Figure the F ratio: $F = S^2_{Between}/S^2_{Within}$ or $F = MS_{Between}/MS_{Within}$.

❺ **Decide whether to reject the null hypothesis:** Compare scores from Steps ❸ and ❹.

TIP FOR SUCCESS

Check your understanding of the structural model method for analysis of variance by covering up portions of Table 15 and trying to recall the hidden material.

Table 15   Analysis of Variance Table Showing Symbols and Formulas for Figuring the Analysis of Variance

Symbols Corresponding to Each Part of an Analysis of Variance Table				
Source	**SS**	**df**	**MS**	**F**
Between	$SS_{Between}$	$df_{Between}$	$MS_{Between}$ (or $S^2_{Between}$)	F
Within	SS_{Within}	df_{Within}	MS_{Within} (or S^2_{Within})	
Total	SS_{Total}	df_{Total}		

Formulas for Each Part of an Analysis of Variance Table				
Source	**SS**	**df**	**MS**	**F**
Between	$\sum(M - GM)^2$	$N_{Groups} - 1$	$SS_{Between}/df_{Between}$	$MS_{Between}/MS_{Within}$
Within	$\sum(X - M)^2$	$df_1 + df_2 + \cdots + df_{Last}$	SS_{Within}/df_{Within}	
Total	$\sum(X - GM)^2$	$N - 1$		

Summary of Procedures for an Analysis of Variance Using the Structural Model

Table 14 summarizes the steps in an analysis of variance using the structural model method. Note that the only difference from what you learned earlier in this chapter is in Step ❹, substeps b through g (compare to Table 8). Table 15 shows an analysis of variance table with the symbols for all the parts put in each section where the numbers would usually go. It is followed by the same style of analysis of variance table with the various formulas filled in where the numbers would usually go.[6]

Learning Aids

Summary

1. The analysis of variance (ANOVA) is used to test hypotheses based on differences among means of more than two samples. The procedure compares two estimates of population variance. One, the within-groups estimate, is the average of the variance estimates from each of the samples. The other, the between-groups estimate, is based on the variation among the means of the samples.

2. The F ratio is the between-groups estimate divided by the within-groups estimate. The null hypothesis is that all the samples come from populations with the same mean. If the null hypothesis is true, the F ratio should be close to 1. This is because the two population variance estimates are based on the same thing, the variation within each of the populations (due to chance factors). If the research hypothesis is true, so that the samples come from populations with different means, the F ratio should be larger than 1. This is because the between-groups estimate is now influenced by the variation both within the populations (due to chance factors) and among them (due to a treatment effect). But the within-groups estimate is still affected only by the variation within each of the populations.

3. When the samples are of equal size, the within-groups population variance estimate is the ordinary average of the estimates of the population variance figured from each sample. The between-groups population variance estimate is done in two steps. First, you estimate the variance of the distribution of means based on the means of your samples. (This is figured with the usual formula for estimating population variance from sample scores.) Second, you multiply this estimate by the number of participants in each group. This step takes you from the variance of the distribution of means to the variance of the distribution of individual scores.

4. The distribution of F ratios when the null hypothesis is true is a mathematically defined distribution that is skewed to the right. Significance cutoffs are given on an F table according to the degrees of freedom for each population variance estimate: the between-groups (numerator) degrees of freedom is the number of groups minus 1, and the within-groups (denominator) degrees of freedom is the sum of the degrees of freedom within all samples.

5. The assumptions for the analysis of variance are the same as for the t test. The populations must be normally distributed, with equal variances. Like the t test, the analysis of variance is robust to moderate violations of these assumptions.

6. The overall results of an analysis of variance are often followed up by planned contrasts, based on theory or a specific practical need, that examine differences such as those between specific pairs of means. These contrasts (or comparisons) are figured using the usual analysis of variance method, but with the between-groups estimate based on the variation between the two means being compared.

7. When making more than one planned contrast, researchers often protect against the possibility of getting some contrasts significant just by chance by making a Bonferroni correction of the significance level (dividing the overall desired significance level by the number of contrasts).

8. An analysis of variance may be followed up by exploratory, post hoc comparisons. Such comparisons have to protect against the possibility of getting some significant results just by chance because of the great many comparisons that could be made. There are a number of methods for dealing with this problem that are not as severe as the Bonferroni correction. In one such method, the Scheffé test, you figure each comparison of interest in the usual way and then divide its F by the between-groups degrees of freedom from the overall analysis of variance.

9. The proportion of variance accounted for (R^2), also called "eta squared" (η^2), is a measure of analysis of variance effect size. R^2 represents how much of the variation in the measured variable is accounted for by the division into groups. Power depends on effect size, number of people in the study, significance level, and number of groups.

10. Some experts recommend that, instead of using an analysis of variance to make diffuse, overall comparisons among several means, researchers should plan in advance to conduct only specific planned contrasts, targeted directly to their theoretical or practical questions.

11. Analysis of variance results are reported in a standard fashion, such as $F(3, 68) = 5.21, p < .01$. Results of planned contrasts are also commonly reported (sometimes using special t tests instead of analysis of variance). Results of post hoc comparisons are usually shown by putting small letters by the means in tables.

12. ADVANCED TOPIC: An alternative approach to the analysis of variance uses the structural model. In the structural model method, the deviation of each score from the grand mean is divided into two parts: (a) the score's difference from its group's mean and (b) its group's mean's difference from the grand mean. These deviations, when squared, summed, and divided by the appropriate degrees of freedom, give the same within-groups and between-groups estimates as using the standard analysis of variance method you learned. However, the structural model is more flexible and can be applied to studies with unequal sample sizes. Computations using the structural model are usually summarized in an analysis of variance table, with a column for source of variation (between, within, and total), sums of squared deviations (SS), degrees of freedom (df), population variance estimates (MS, which equals SS/df), and F (which equals $MS_{\text{Between}}/MS_{\text{Within}}$).

Key Terms

analysis of variance (ANOVA)
within-groups estimate of the population variance (S^2_{Within} or MS_{Within})
between-groups estimate of the population variance (S^2_{Between} or MS_{Between})
F ratio
F distribution
F table

S^2_{Within} or MS_{Within}
grand mean (GM)
S^2_{Between} or MS_{Between}
between-groups (or numerator) degrees of freedom (df_{Between})
within-groups (or denominator) degrees of freedom (df_{Within})
planned contrasts

Bonferroni procedure
post hoc comparisons
Scheffé test
proportion of variance accounted for (R^2)
eta squared (η^2)
structural model
SS_{Total}, SS_{Within}, SS_{Between}
analysis of variance table

Example Worked-Out Problems

Overall Analysis of Variance

An experiment compares the effects of four treatments, giving each treatment to 20 participants and then assessing their performance on a standard measure. The results on the standard measure are as follows. Treatment 1: $M = 15, S^2 = 20$; Treatment 2: $M = 12, S^2 = 25$; Treatment 3: $M = 18, S^2 = 14$; Treatment 4: $M = 15, S^2 = 27$. Using the .05 significance level, does treatment matter? Use the five steps of hypothesis testing and sketch the distributions involved.

Answer

The distributions involved are shown in Figure 9.

❶ **Restate the question as a research hypothesis and a null hypothesis about the populations.** There are four populations.

Population 1: People given experimental treatment 1.
Population 2: People given experimental treatment 2.
Population 3: People given experimental treatment 3.
Population 4: People given experimental treatment 4.

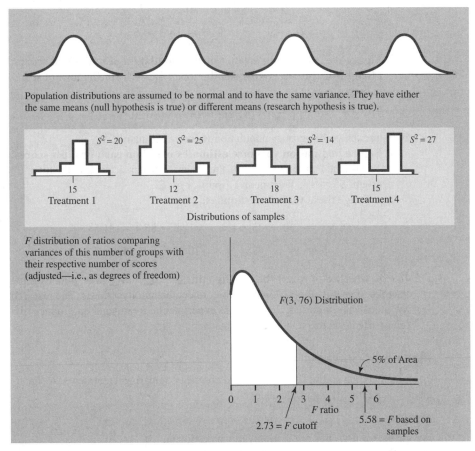

Figure 9 Distributions involved in Example Worked-Out Problem for overall analysis of variance.

The null hypothesis is that these four populations have the same mean ($\mu_1 = \mu_2 = \mu_3 = \mu_4$). The research hypothesis is that the four population means are not the same.

❷ **Determine the characteristics of the comparison distribution.** The comparison distribution will be an F distribution. $df_{Between} = N_{Groups} - 1 = 4 - 1 = 3$; $df_{Within} = df_1 + df_2 + \cdots + df_{Last} = 19 + 19 + 19 + 19 = 76$.

❸ **Determine the cutoff sample score on the comparison distribution at which the null hypothesis should be rejected.** Using Table A-3 in the Appendix for $df = 3, 75$ (the closest below 3, 76) at the .05 level, the cutoff F is 2.73.

❹ **Determine your sample's score on the comparison distribution.**

a. Figure the between-groups population variance estimate ($S^2_{Between}$):
Figure the mean of each group. The group means are 15, 12, 18, and 15.

 ❶ **Estimate the variance of the distribution of means:** Add up the sample means' squared deviations from the grand mean and divide by the number of means minus 1:

$$GM = (15 + 12 + 18 + 15)/4 = 15$$
$$S^2_M = \Sigma(M - GM)^2/df_{Between}$$
$$= [(15 - 15)^2 + (12 - 15)^2 + (18 - 15)^2$$
$$+ (15 - 15)^2]/(4 - 1)$$
$$= (0 + 9 + 9 + 0)/3 = 18/3 = 6.$$

 ❷ **Figure the estimated variance of the population of individual scores:** Multiply the variance of the distribution of means by the number of scores in each group.

$$S^2_{Between} = (S^2_M)(n) = (6)(20) = 120.$$

b. Figure the within-groups population variance estimate (S^2_{Within}):

 ❶ **Figure population variance estimates based on each group's scores:** Treatment 1 group, $S^2 = 20$; Treatment 2 group, $S^2 = 25$; Treatment 3 group, $S^2 = 14$; Treatment 4 group, $S^2 = 27$.

 ❷ **Average these variance estimates:**

$$S^2_{Within} = (20 + 25 + 14 + 27)/4 = 86/4 = 21.5.$$
$$F = S^2_{Between}/S^2_{Within} = 120/21.5 = 5.58.$$

❺ **Decide whether to reject the null hypothesis.** The F of 5.58 is more extreme than the .05 cutoff F of 2.73. Therefore, reject the null hypothesis. The research hypothesis is supported; the different experimental treatments do produce different effects on the standard performance measure.

Planned Contrasts

For the preceding study, figure a planned contrast comparing Treatment 2 to Treatment 3 using the .01 significance level.

Answer

For the between-groups population variance estimate,

 ❶ **Estimate the variance of the distribution of means:** Add up the sample means' squared deviations from the grand mean and divide by the number of means minus 1. The grand mean for these two means is $(12 + 18)/2 = 15$ and $df_{Between} = N_{Groups} - 1 = 2 - 1 = 1$.

$$S_M^2 = [\Sigma(M - GM)^2]/df_{Between}$$
$$= [(12 - 15)^2 + (18 - 15)^2]/1$$
$$= [(-3)^2 + 3^2]/1 = (9 + 9)/1 = 18.$$

❹ **Figure the estimated variance of the population of individual scores:** Multiply the variance of the distribution of means by the number of scores in each group.

$$S_{Between}^2 = (S_M^2)(n) = (18)(20) = 360$$
$$S_{Within}^2 \text{ (from the overall analysis)} = 21.5$$
$$F = S_{Between}^2/S_{Within}^2 = 360/21.5 = 16.74.$$

The cutoff F for .05, $df = 1, 75$ (the closest on the table below the true df of 1, 76) = 3.97.
Reject the null hypothesis; the contrast is significant.

Bonferroni Procedure

What is the Bonferroni corrected significance level for each of six planned contrasts at the overall .05 significance level?

Answer

Bonferroni corrected significance $= .05/6 = .0083$.

Post Hoc Comparisons Using the Scheffé Method

A study has five groups with 10 participants in each. Using a Scheffé test, is a comparison with a computed F of 11.21 significant at the .01 significance level?

Answer

The overall study's $df_{Between} = 5 - 1 = 4$; $df_{Within} = 9 + 9 + 9 + 9 + 9 = 45$. The Scheffé corrected F for this contrast is $11.21/4 = 2.80$. The overall study's .01 cutoff F ($df = 4, 45$) is 3.77. The contrast is not significant.

Figuring Effect Size for an Analysis of Variance

Figure the effect size for the overall analysis of variance Example Worked-Out Problem.

Answer

$$R^2 = (S_{Between}^2)(df_{Between})/[(S_{Within}^2)(df_{Between}) + (S_{Within}^2)(df_{Within})]$$
$$= (120)(3)/[(120)(3) + (21.5)(76)] = (360)/[(360) + (1634)] = .18.$$

Advanced Topic: Figuring an Analysis of Variance Using the Structural Model Method

A researcher at an alcohol treatment center conducts a study of client satisfaction with treatment methods A, B, and C. The researcher randomly assigns each of the available 10 clients to receive one of these treatments; four clients end up with Treatment A, three with Treatment B, and three with Treatment C. Two weeks later, the researcher measures client satisfaction with the three treatments on a scale from 1 (low satisfaction) to 20 (high satisfaction). Scores for Treatment A were 8, 13, 10, and 9. Scores for Treatment B were 7, 3, and 8. Scores for Treatment C were 6, 4, and 2. Use the steps of hypothesis testing and figure an analysis of variance (at the .05 level) using the structural model method. (Although the example we used for the structural model method earlier in the chapter had the same number of participants in each group, you can use the same method in this example with unequal sized groups. Just remember to figure the grand mean, GM, as the average of all of the scores across all of the groups.)

Answer

Table 16 shows the figuring and the analysis of variance table.

Table 16   Analysis of Variance Figuring and Analysis of Variance Table Problem for an Alcohol Treatment Study (Fictional Data)

Treatment A						Treatment B						Treatment C					
X	X − GM		X − M		M − GM		X	X − GM		X − M		M − GM		X	X − GM		X − M		M − GM		

X	Dev	Dev²	Dev	Dev²	Dev	Dev²	X	Dev	Dev²	Dev	Dev²	Dev	Dev²	X	Dev	Dev²	Dev	Dev²	Dev	Dev²
8	1	1	−2	4	3	9	7	0	0	1	1	−1	1	6	−1	1	2	4	−3	9
13	6	36	3	9	3	9	3	−4	16	−3	9	−1	1	4	−3	9	0	0	−3	9
10	3	9	0	0	3	9	8	1	1	2	4	−1	1	2	−5	25	−2	4	−3	9
9	2	4	−1	1	3	9														
40		50		14		36	18		17		14		3	12		35		8		27

$M = 40/4 = 10$ $M = 18/3 = 6$ $M = 12/3 = 4$

Note: Dev = Deviation; Dev² = Squared deviation.

$GM = (40 + 18 + 12)/10 = 70/10 = 7$

$df_{Total} = N - 1 = 10 - 1 = 9$

$df_{Within} = df_1 + df_2 + \cdots + df_{Last} = (4 - 1) + (3 - 1) + (3 - 1) = 3 + 2 + 2 = 7$

$df_{Between} = N_{Groups} - 1 = 3 - 1 = 2$

F needed for $df = 2, 7$ at the .05 level $= 4.74$

$SS_{Total} = 50 + 17 + 35 = 102$

$SS_{Within} = 14 + 14 + 8 = 36$

$SS_{Between} = 36 + 3 + 27 = 66$

ANALYSIS OF VARIANCE TABLE:

Source	SS	df	MS	F
Between	66	2	33	6.42
Within	36	7	5.14	
Total	102	9		

Decision: Reject the null hypothesis.

❶ **Restate the question as a research hypothesis and a null hypothesis about the populations.** There are three populations:

Population 1: Alcoholics receiving Treatment A.
Population 2: Alcoholics receiving Treatment B.
Population 3: Alcoholics receiving Treatment C.

The null hypothesis is that these three populations have the same mean ($\mu_1 = \mu_2 = \mu_3$). The research hypothesis is that they do not all have the same mean.

❷ **Determine the characteristics of the comparison distribution.** An F distribution; from Table 16, $df = 2, 7$.

❸ **Determine the cutoff sample score on the comparison distribution at which the null hypothesis should be rejected.** Using Table A-3, for $df = 2, 7$ and a .05 significance level, the cutoff F is 4.74.

❹ **Determine your sample's score on the comparison distribution.** From the figuring shown in Table 16, $F = 6.42$.

❺ **Decide whether to reject the null hypothesis.** The F ratio of 6.42 is more extreme than the .05 significance level cutoff F of 4.74. Thus, the researcher can reject the null hypothesis. If these were real data, the researcher could conclude that the three kinds of treatment have different effects on how satisfied clients like theirs are with their treatment.

Outline for Writing Essays for a One-Way Analysis of Variance

1. Explain that the one-way analysis of variance is used for hypothesis testing when you have scores from three or more entirely separate groups of people. Be sure to explain the meaning of the research hypothesis and the null hypothesis in this situation.

2. Describe the core logic of hypothesis testing in this situation. Be sure to mention that the analysis of variance involves comparing the results of two ways of estimating the population variance. One population variance estimate (the within-groups estimate) is based on the variation within each sample and the other estimate (the between-groups estimate) is based on the variation among the means of the samples. Be sure to describe these estimates in detail (including how they are figured, why they are figured that way, and how each is affected by whether the null hypothesis is true); explain how and why they are used to figure an F ratio.

3. Explain the logic of the comparison distribution that is used with a one-way analysis of variance (the F distribution).

4. Describe the logic and process for determining the cutoff sample F score on the comparison distribution at which the null hypothesis should be rejected.

5. Explain how and why the scores from Steps ❸ and ❹ of the hypothesis-testing process are compared. Explain the meaning of the result of this comparison with regard to the specific research and null hypotheses being tested.

Practice Problems

These problems involve figuring. Most real-life statistics problems are done with special statistical software. Even if you have such software, do these problems by hand to ingrain the method in your mind. To learn how to use a computer to solve

statistics problems like those in this chapter, refer to the Using SPSS section at the end of this chapter.

All data are fictional unless an actual citation is given.

Set I

1. For each of the following studies, decide whether you can reject the null hypothesis that the groups come from identical populations. Use the .05 level. Note that study (b) provides S, not S^2.

(a)	Group 1	Group 2	Group 3
n	10	10	10
M	7.4	6.8	6.8
S^2	.82	.90	.80

(b)	Group 1	Group 2	Group 3	Group 4
n	25	25	25	25
M	94	101	124	105
S	24	28	31	25

2. For each of the following studies, (a) and (b), decide whether you can reject the null hypothesis that the groups come from identical populations. Use the .01 level. (c) Figure the effect size for each study. (d) ADVANCED TOPIC: For study (a), carry out an analysis of variance using the structural model method.

(a)	Group 1	Group 2	Group 3
	8	6	4
	8	6	4
	7	5	3
	9	7	5

(b)	Group 1	Group 2	Group 3
	12	10	8
	4	2	0
	12	10	8
	4	2	0

3. A psychologist at a private psychiatric hospital was asked to determine whether there was any clear difference in the length of stay of patients with different categories of diagnosis. Looking at the last four patients in each of the three major categories, the results (in terms of weeks of stay) were as follows:

	Diagnosis Category	
Affective Disorders	Cognitive Disorders	Drug-Related Conditions
7	12	8
6	8	10
5	9	12
6	11	10

(a) Using the .05 level and the five steps of hypothesis testing, is there a significant difference in length of stay among diagnosis categories? (b) Sketch the distributions involved. (c) Figure the effect size for the study. (d) Explain your answer to part (a) to someone who understands everything involved in conducting a t test for independent means but is unfamiliar with the analysis of variance. (e) Test the significance of planned contrasts (using the .05 level without a Bonferroni correction) for affective disorders versus drug-related conditions and (f) cognitive disorders versus drug-related conditions. (g) Explain your answers to parts (e) and (f) to a person who understands analysis of variance but is unfamiliar with planned contrasts.

4. A study compared the felt intensity of unrequited love (loving someone who doesn't love you) among three groups: 50 individuals who were currently experiencing unrequited love who had a mean experienced intensity $= 3.5, S^2 = 5.2$; 50 who had previously experienced unrequited love and described their experiences retrospectively, $M = 3.2, S^2 = 5.8$; and 50 who had never experienced unrequited love but described how they thought they would feel if they were to experience it, $M = 3.8, S^2 = 4.8$. Determine the significance of the difference among groups, using the 5% level. (a) Use the steps of hypothesis testing; (b) sketch the distributions involved; (c) figure the effect size for the study; and (d) explain your answer to part (a) to someone who has never had a course in statistics.

5. A researcher studying genetic influences on learning compares the maze performance of four genetically different strains of mice, using eight mice per strain. Performance for the four strains were as follows:

Strain	Mean	S
J	41	3.5
M	38	4.6
Q	14	3.8
W	37	4.9

Using the .01 significance level, is there an overall difference in maze performance among the four strains? (a) Use the steps of hypothesis testing; (b) sketch the distributions involved; (c) figure the effect size for the study; and (d) explain your answer to part (a) to someone who is familiar with hypothesis testing with known populations but unfamiliar with the t test or the analysis of variance. (e) Test the significance of planned contrasts using the overall .05 level (with a Bonferroni correction for testing each of the five contrasts) for strain J versus strain M, (f) for strain J versus strain Q, (g) for strain J versus strain W, (h) for strain Q versus strain M, and (i) for strain Q versus strain W. (j) Explain your answers to parts (e) through (i) to a person who understands analysis of variance but is unfamiliar with planned contrasts and the Bonferroni correction.

6. What is the Bonferroni corrected significance level for each of the following situations?

Situation	(a)	(b)	(c)	(d)
Overall significance level	.05	.05	.01	.01
Number of planned contrasts	2	4	3	5

7. For each of the following studies, test whether a comparison in which the researcher figures an F of 17.21 would be significant using the Scheffé method.

	Number of Groups	Participants in Each Group	Significance Level
(a)	5	10	.05
(b)	6	10	.05
(c)	5	20	.05
(d)	5	10	.01

8. What is the power of each of the following planned studies, using the analysis of variance with $p < .05$?

	Predicted Effect Size	Number of Groups	Participants in Each Group
(a)	Small	3	20
(b)	Small	3	30
(c)	Small	4	20
(d)	Medium	3	20

9. About how many participants do you need in each group for 80% power in each of the following planned studies, using the analysis of variance with $p < .05$?

	Predicted Effect Size	Number of Groups
(a)	Small	3
(b)	Large	3
(c)	Small	4
(d)	Medium	3

10. Grilo and colleagues (1997) are clinical psychologists interested in the relationship of depression and substance use to personality disorders. Personality disorders are persistent, problematic traits and behaviors that exceed the usual range of individual differences. The researchers conducted interviews assessing personality disorders with adolescents who were psychiatric inpatients and had one of three diagnoses: (1) those with major depression, (2) those with substance abuse, and (3) those with both major depression and substance abuse. The mean number of disorders was as follows: major depression $M = 1.0$, substance abuse $M = .7$, those with both conditions $M = 1.9$. The researchers reported, "The three study groups differed in the average number of diagnosed personality disorders, $F(2, 112) = 10.18, p < .0001$." Explain this result to someone who is familiar with hypothesis testing with known populations but is unfamiliar with the t test or the analysis of variance.

11. A researcher wants to know whether the need for mental health care among prisoners varies according to the different types of prison facilities. The researcher randomly selects 40 prisoners from each of the three main types of prisons in a particular Canadian province and conducts exams to determine their need for mental health care. In the article describing the results, the researcher reported the means for each group and then added: "The need for mental health care

among prisoners in the three types of prison systems appeared to be clearly different, $F(2, 117) = 5.62, p < .01$. A planned comparison [contrast] of System 1 to System 2 was significant, $F(1, 117) = 4.03, p < .05$." Explain this result to a person who has never had a course in statistics.

12. Based on Table 11 from the Hazan and Shaver (1987) study, indicate for which variables, if any, (a) the Avoidants are significantly different from the other two groups, (b) the Anxious-Ambivalents are different from the other two groups, (c) the Secures are different from the other two groups, and (d) all three groups are different. (e) Explain, to a person who understands analysis of variance but does not know anything about post hoc comparisons, what is meant in the table note that the results are "according to a Scheffé test."

13. Which type of English word is longer: nouns, verbs, or adjectives? Go to a book of at least 400 pages and turn to random pages using the random numbers listed at the end of this paragraph. Go down the page until you come to a noun. Note its length (in number of letters). Do this for 10 different nouns. Do the same for 10 verbs and then for 10 adjectives. Using the .05 significance level, (a) carry out an analysis of variance comparing the three types of words, and (b) figure a planned contrast of nouns versus verbs. (Be sure also to give the full bibliographic information on the book you used: authors, title, year published, publisher, city.)

73, 320, 179, 323, 219, 176, 167, 102, 228, 352, 4, 335, 118, 12, 333, 123, 38, 49, 399, 17, 188, 264, 342, 89, 13, 77, 378, 223, 92, 77, 152, 34, 214, 75, 83, 198, 210

Set II

14. For each of the following studies, decide whether you can reject the null hypothesis that the groups come from identical populations. Use the .05 level.

(a)	Group 1	Group 2	Group 3
n	5	5	5
M	10	12	14
S^2	4	6	5

(b)	Group 1	Group 2	Group 3
n	10	10	10
M	10	12	14
S^2	4	6	5

15. For each of the following studies, (a) and (b), decide whether you can reject the null hypothesis that the groups come from identical populations. Use the .01 level. (c) Figure the effect size for each study. (d) ADVANCED TOPIC: Carry out an analysis of variance for study (a) using the structural model method.

(a)	Group 1	Group 2	Group 3
	1	1	8
	2	2	7
	1	1	8
	2	2	7

(b)	Group 1	Group 2	Group 3
	1	4	8
	2	5	7
	1	4	8
	2	5	7

16. An organizational psychologist was interested in whether individuals working in different sectors of a company differed in their attitudes toward the company. The results for the three people surveyed in development were 10, 12, and 11; for the three in the marketing department, 6, 6, and 8; for the three in accounting, 7, 4, and 4; and for the three in production, 14, 16, and 13 (higher numbers mean more positive attitudes). Was there a significant difference in attitude toward the company among employees working in different sectors of the company at the .05 level? (a) Use the steps of hypothesis testing; (b) sketch the distributions involved; (c) figure the effect size for the study; (d) explain your answer to part (a) to someone who understands everything involved in conducting a *t* test for independent means but is unfamiliar with the analysis of variance; (e) test the significance of planned contrasts using the overall .05 level (with a Bonferroni correction for testing each of the five contrasts) for engineering versus production, (f) marketing versus production, (g) accounting versus production, (h) development versus marketing, and (i) development versus accounting. (j) Explain your answers to parts (e) through (i) to a person who understands analysis of variance but is unfamiliar with planned contrasts or Bonferroni corrections. (k) ADVANCED TOPIC: Carry out an analysis of variance for the study using the structural model method.

17. Do students at various universities differ in how sociable they are? Twenty-five students were randomly selected from each of three universities in a region and were asked to report on the amount of time they spent socializing each day with other students. The result for University X was a mean of 5 hours and an estimated population variance of 2 hours; for University Y, $M = 4, S^2 = 1.5$; and for University Z, $M = 6, S^2 = 2.5$. What should you conclude? Use the .05 level. (a) Use the steps of hypothesis testing, (b) figure the effect size for the study; and (c) explain your answers to parts (a) and (b) to someone who has never had a course in statistics.

18. A psychologist studying artistic preference randomly assigns a group of 45 participants to one of three conditions in which they view a series of unfamiliar abstract paintings. The 15 participants in the Famous condition are led to believe that these are each famous paintings; their mean rating for liking the paintings is 6.5 ($S = 3.5$). The 15 in the Critically Acclaimed condition are led to believe that these are paintings that are not famous but are very highly thought of by a group of professional art critics; their mean rating is 8.5 ($S = 4.2$). The 15 in the Control condition are given no special information about the paintings; their mean rating is 3.1 ($S = 2.9$). Does what people are told about paintings make a difference in how well they are liked? Use the .05 level. (a) Use the steps of hypothesis testing; (b) sketch the distributions involved; (c) figure the effect size for the study; (d) explain your answer to part (a) to someone who is familiar with the *t* test for independent means but is unfamiliar with analysis of variance; (e) test the significance of planned contrasts (using the .05 significance level without a Bonferroni correction) for Famous versus Control and (f) Critically Acclaimed versus Control. (g) Explain your answers to parts (e) and (f) to

a person who understands analysis of variance but is unfamiliar with planned contrasts.

19. What is the Bonferroni corrected significance level for each of the following situations?

Situation	(a)	(b)	(c)	(d)
Overall significance level	.01	.01	.05	.05
Number of planned contrasts	4	2	4	3

20. For each of the following studies, test whether a comparison in which the researcher figures an F of 8.12 would be significant using the Scheffé method.

	Number of Groups	Participants in Each Group	Significance Level
(a)	4	30	.05
(b)	5	80	.05
(c)	4	5	.05
(d)	8	30	.01

21. What is the power of each of the following planned studies, using the analysis of variance with $p < .05$?

	Predicted Effect Size	Number of Groups	Participants in Each Group
(a)	Small	4	50
(b)	Medium	4	50
(c)	Large	4	50
(d)	Medium	5	50

22. About how many participants do you need in each group for 80% power in each of the following planned studies, using the analysis of variance with $p < .05$?

	Predicted Effect Size	Number of Groups
(a)	Small	5
(b)	Medium	5
(c)	Large	5
(d)	Medium	3

23. An experiment is conducted in which 60 participants each fill out a personality test, but not according to the way the participants see themselves. Instead, 15 are randomly assigned to fill it out according to the way they think their mothers see them (that is, the way they think their mothers would fill it out to describe the participants); 15 as their fathers would fill it out for them; 15 as their best friends would fill it out for them; and 15 as the professors they know best would fill it out for them. The main results appear in Table 17. Explain these results to a person who has never had a course in statistics.

24. Rosalie Friend (2001), an educational psychologist, compared three methods of teaching writing. Students were randomly assigned to three different experimental conditions involving different methods of writing a summary. At the end

Table 17   Means for Main Personality Scales for Each Experimental Condition (Fictional Data)

Scale	Mother	Father	Friend	Professor	$F(3, 56)$
Conformity	24	21	12	16	4.21**
Extroversion	14	13	15	13	2.05
Maturity	15	15	22	19	3.11*
Self-confidence	38	42	27	32	3.58*

*$p < .05$, **$p < .01$.

of the two days of instructions, participants wrote a summary. One of the ways it was scored was the percentage of specific details of information it included from the original material. Here is a selection from her article describing one of the findings:

> The effect of summarization method on inclusion of important information was significant: $F(2, 144) = 4.1032, p < .019$. The mean scores (with standard deviations in parentheses) were as follows: Argument Repetition, 59.6% (17.9); Generalization, 59.8% (15.2); and Self-Reflection, 50.2% (18.0). (p. 14)

(a) Explain these results to a person who has never had a course in statistics.
(b) Using the information in the preceding description, figure the effect size for the study.

25. Miller (1997) asked 147 female students to view slides of magazine ads that included, among other things, pictures of attractive men. The participants were measured for physiological arousal (skin conductance) while viewing the ads and also after viewing them; they were asked to rate the attractiveness and how much they would like to meet each person in the ads. As part of the analysis, Miller compared results for women dating no one, women in casual dating relationships, and women in exclusive dating relationships. Table 18 shows Miller's results. (a), (b), and (c) Describe the pattern of results on each variable. (d) Explain, to a person who understands analysis of variance but is unfamiliar with post hoc comparisons, what is meant in a general way by the table note that the results are based on "Duncan's multiple range test." (That is, you don't need to explain this specific test, but you do need to explain why a test like this was used and what it attempts to accomplish.)

Table 18   Effects of Relationship Status

Dependent measure	Relationship Status		
	Dating No One	Casual Dating	Exclusive Dating
Skin conductance	19.5b	19.1b	15.8a
Desire to meet target	14.6b	15.3b	11.2a
Perceived physical attractiveness of target	15.6b	17.1b	13.8a

Note: Higher numbers reflect greater arousal, desire to meet target, and perceived attractiveness; for the latter two items the possible range was 1–19. Within each row, means with different subscripts differ significantly ($p < .05$) by Duncan's multiple range test.

Source: Miller, R.S. (1997). Inattentive and contented: Relationship commitment and attention to alternatives. *Journal of Personality and Social Psychology, 73,* 758–766. Published by the American Psychological Association. Reprinted with permission.

Using SPSS

The ✑ in the following steps indicates a mouse click. (We used SPSS version 19 for Windows to carry out these analyses. The steps and output may be slightly different for other versions of SPSS.)

It is easier to learn these steps using actual numbers; so we will use the criminal record example from earlier in the chapter. The scores for that example are shown in Table 3.

Figuring a One-Way Analysis of Variance

❶ Enter the scores into SPSS. SPSS assumes that all scores across a row are from the same person. In this example, each person is in only one of the three groups (the Criminal Record group, the Clean Record group, or the No Information group). Thus, to tell SPSS which person is in each group, enter the numbers as shown in Figure 10. In the first column (labeled "group"), we used the number "1" to indicate that a person is in the Criminal Record group, the number "2" to indicate a person in the Clean Record group, and the number "3" to indicate a person in the No Information group.

❷ ✑ Analyze.

❸ ✑ Compare means.

❹ ✑ One-Way ANOVA.

❺ ✑ on the variable called "guilt" and then ✑ the arrow next to the box labeled "Dependent List." This tells SPSS that the analysis of variance should be carried out on the scores for the "guilt" variable.

❻ ✑ the variable called "group" and then ✑ the arrow next to the box labeled "Factor." This tells SPSS that the variable called "group" shows which person is in which group.

❼ ✑ Options. ✑ the box labeled Descriptive (this checks the box). This tells SPSS to provide descriptive statistics (such as the mean and standard deviation) for each group. ✑ Continue. (Step ❼ is optional, but we strongly recommend requesting descriptive statistics for any hypothesis testing situation.)

❽ ✑ OK. Your SPSS output window should look like Figure 11.

The first table in the SPSS output provides descriptive statistics (number of individuals, mean, estimated population standard deviation, and other statistics) for the "guilt" scores for each of the three groups.

The second table in the SPSS output shows the actual results of the one-way analysis of variance. The first column lists the types of population variance estimates (between groups and within groups). The second column lists the between groups and within groups sums of squares: these are described in the Advanced Topic section earlier in this chapter, but ignore this column if you did not read that section. The third column, "df," gives the degrees of freedom. In the between groups row, this corresponds to df_{Between}; in the within groups row, this corresponds to df_{Within}. The fourth column, "Mean Square," gives the population variance estimates (S^2_{Between} and S^2_{Within}), with the between-groups estimate first and then the within-groups estimate. The next column gives the F ratio for the analysis of variance. Allowing for rounding error, the values for "df," "Mean Square," and "F" (and "Sum of Squares") are the same as those reported earlier in the chapter. The final column, "Sig.," shows the exact significance level of the F ratio.

Figure 10　SPSS data editor window for the criminal record example (in which 15 individuals rated the guilt of a defendant after being randomly assigned to one of the three groups that were given different information about the defendant's previous criminal record).

The significance level of .045 is less than our .05 cutoff for this example. Thus, you can reject the null hypothesis and the research hypothesis is supported (that is, the result is statistically significant). You can also use the information in the table to calculate the effect size (R^2). For example, using formula 8,

$$R^2 = \frac{(F)(df_{\text{Between}})}{(F)(df_{\text{Between}}) + df_{\text{Within}}} = \frac{(4.063)(2)}{(4.063)(2) + 12} = .40.$$

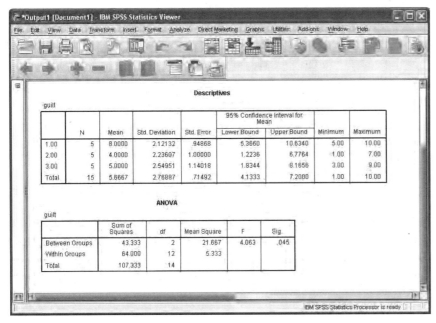

Figure 11 SPSS output window for a one-way analysis of variance for the criminal record example.

Figuring a Planned Contrast for a One-Way Analysis of Variance

We will again use the criminal record example that we used for the one-way analysis of variance. Note that, before going through the following steps, we went to the "Variable View" window in SPSS and entered value labels (in the "Values" column) for the "group" variable (1 = "criminal record"; 2 = "clean record"; 3 = "no information"). Doing this makes it easier to read the SPSS output for the planned contrast. We will use the example from earlier in the chapter in which we considered a planned contrast of the Criminal Record group to the No Information group.

First, follow Steps ❶ through ❼ shown above for a one-way analysis of variance.

❽ ✑ *Contrasts*. In order to tell SPSS which groups you would like to compare in the planned contrast, you assign special numbers, called "coefficients," to each group. In this example we are comparing the Criminal Record group (which had a value of "1" for the "group" variable) to the No Information group (which had a value of "3" for the "group" variable). When assigning coefficients to the groups to create the planned contrast, the main things to know are that any group assigned a coefficient of 0 is not included in the contrast and that the contrasts for all of the groups should sum to 0. In our example, we wish to compare the first group (the Criminal Record group) with the third group (the No Information group), so we can do that by using contrasts of: 1, 0, and −1. To do that, enter "1" in the box next to "Coefficients" and ✑ *Add*. Then enter "0" in the box next to "Coefficients" and ✑ *Add*. Finally, enter "−1" in the box next to "Coefficients" and ✑ *Add*. ✑ *Continue*.

❾ ✑ *OK*.

The first two tables shown in your SPSS output window will be the same as the tables shown in Figure 11. There will also be two new tables in your SPSS output window, which are shown in Figure 12. The first new table, labeled "Contrast Coefficients," shows which groups are being compared in the planned contrast. In our

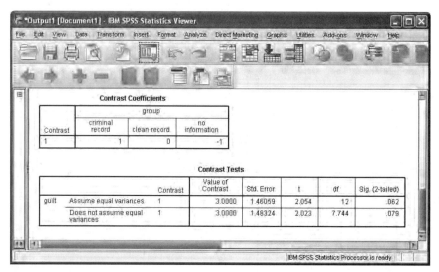

Figure 12 SPSS output window for a planned contrast for a one-way analysis of variance for the criminal record example.

example, the contrast coefficients confirm that the Criminal Record group and the No Information group are being compared. The second new table, labeled "Contrast Tests," shows the result of the planned contrast. SPSS calculates the contrast in two different ways, one assuming that the groups have equal population variance and the other assuming that they do not. We will assume that the groups have equal population variance, so we will focus on the first row of results in the table. The "Value of Contrast" of 3.0000 is the difference between the means of the two groups in the contrast (as shown in Figure 11, the Criminal Record group had a mean of 8 and the No Information group had a mean of 5). The "Sig. (2-tailed)" column shows a p value of .062 for the planned contrast. Since the p value is greater than the standard .05 cutoff, the planned contrast is not statistically significant. (Incidentally, don't worry that the contrast test shown in Figure 12 gives a t value instead of an F value, which is what you learned when calculating planned contrasts earlier in the chapter. When comparing two groups, which is what we are doing in this planned contrast, the t test and the F test are conceptually the same. It turns out that the value of t is the square root of the value of F. Thus, the t value of 2.054 shown in Figure 12 corresponds to an F value of 4.22, which is the F value that we calculated for this planned contrast earlier in the chapter. You can learn more about the relationship between the t test and the F test in Web Chapter W4, which is available at *www.pearsoned.co.in/ prc/home*.

Post Hoc Tests for a One-Way Analysis of Variance

We will again use the criminal record example that we used for the one-way analysis of variance. Note that, before going through the following steps, we went to the "Variable View" window in SPSS and entered value labels (in the "Values" column) for the "group" variable (1 = "criminal record"; 2 = "clean record"; 3 = "no information"). Doing this makes it easier to read the SPSS output for the post hoc tests.

First, follow Steps ❶ through ❼ shown earlier for a one-way analysis of variance.

Post Hoc Tests

Multiple Comparisons

guilt
Scheffe

(I) group	(J) group	Mean Difference (I-J)	Std. Error	Sig.	95% Confidence Interval Lower Bound	Upper Bound
criminal record	clean record	4.00000	1.46059	.054	-.0715	8.0715
	no information	3.00000	1.46059	.164	-1.0715	7.0715
clean record	criminal record	-4.00000	1.46059	.054	-8.0715	.0715
	no information	-1.00000	1.46059	.795	-5.0715	3.0715
no information	criminal record	-3.00000	1.46059	.164	-7.0715	1.0715
	clean record	1.00000	1.46059	.795	-3.0715	5.0715

IBM SPSS Statistics Processor is ready

Figure 13 SPSS output window for post hoc tests for a one-way analysis of variance for the criminal record example.

❽ ✑ *Post Hoc*. As you will see in the window that appears, there are many different types of post hoc tests available. In this chapter, we focused on the Scheffé test, so ✑ the box labeled *Scheffe* (this checks the box). ✑ *Continue*.

❾ ✑ *OK*.

The first two tables shown in your SPSS output window will be the same as the tables shown in Figure 11. There will also be two new tables in your SPSS output window; the first of these tables, labeled "Post Hoc Tests," is the most important and is shown in Figure 13. The table shows the results of all possible comparisons of the study groups (Criminal Record, No Record, and No Information). Let's start by looking at the first row of numbers, which shows the comparison of the Criminal Record group to the Clean Record group. The value of 4 in the "Mean Difference" column tells you that the difference between the means of these groups was 4. The "Sig." column tells you the exact significance level associated with a difference of that size. The value of .054 is not less than our standard .05 cutoff value, which tells you that the means of the Criminal Record and Clean Record groups are not significantly different. (For the current purposes, you do not need to worry about the columns labeled "Std. Error" or "95% Confidence Interval.") The second row of numbers shows the result of comparing the Criminal Record group to the No Information group. As you can see in the "Mean Difference" column, the difference between the means of these groups was 3; this difference is not statistically significant since the significance level of .164 is greater than our standard .05 cutoff. You can ignore the third row of numbers because it shows the result of comparing the Clean Record group to the Criminal Record group, and you have already seen the result of that comparison in the first row of the table. The only remaining comparison to consider is the difference between the Clean Record group and the No Information group. That comparison is shown in the fourth row of numbers. The difference between the means of those groups was −1 and the significance level of .795 tells you that this difference is not statistically significant. So, overall, none of the three Scheffé post hoc comparisons was statistically significant.

Chapter Notes

1. It is possible, by chance, for F to be larger or smaller than 1 in any particular situation. Both the between-groups and the within-groups estimates are only *estimates* and can each vary a fair amount even when the null hypothesis is perfectly true. If F is considerably larger than 1, you reject the null hypothesis that the populations all have the same mean. But what if F is substantially smaller than 1? This rarely happens. When it does, it could mean that there is *less* variation among the groups than would be expected by chance—something is restricting the variation between groups.

2. Why not just use a t test to compare the two groups? If you used an ordinary t test, your pooled estimate of the population variance would be based on only these two groups. Thus, you would be ignoring the information about the population variance provided by the scores in the other groups. One way to deal with this would be to do the ordinary t test in the usual way at every step, except wherever you would ordinarily use the pooled estimate, you would instead use the within-groups population variance estimate from the overall analysis of variance. Also, you would determine your significance cutoff using the df for the overall within-groups estimate. Actually, this modified t test procedure for a planned contrast and the one we describe using the F test are mathematically equivalent and give exactly the same final result in terms of whether or not your result is significant. (For a more general discussion of the relation of the t test to the analysis of variance, see Web Chapter W4, which is available at *www.pearsoned.co.in/prc/home.*) We emphasize the F test approach here because it is more straightforward in terms of the rest of the material in this chapter.

3. There actually *is* a kind of analysis of variance equivalent to the difference between means—the variation among the means. In fact, Cohen (1988) recommends using the standard deviation of the distribution of means. Thus, he defines what he calls f as an effect size for the analysis of variance, which is figured as the standard deviation of the distribution of means (estimated as S_M) divided by the standard deviation of the individuals (estimated as S_{Within}). However, this measure of effect size is rarely used in research articles and is less intuitively meaningful than the more common one we discuss here.

4. More detailed tables are provided in Cohen (1988, pp. 289–354). When using these tables, note that the value of u at the top of each of his tables refers to df_{Between}, which for a one-way analysis of variance is the number of groups minus 1, not the number of groups as used in our Table 9.

5. More detailed tables are provided in Cohen (1988, pp. 381–389). If you use these, see Chapter Note 4.

6. There are also computational formulas for figuring an analysis of variance with the structural model method. For learning purposes in your class, you should use the steps as we have discussed them in this Advanced Topic section. In a real research situation, the figuring is usually all done by computer (see this chapter's Using SPSS section). However, if you are ever in the unlikely situation of having to do a one-way analysis of variance for an actual research study by hand (or just using a hand calculator), you may find the following formulas useful:

$$SS_{\text{Total}} = \Sigma X^2 - \frac{(\Sigma X)^2}{N}$$

$$SS_{\text{Between}} = \frac{(\Sigma X_1)^2}{n_1} + \frac{(\Sigma X_2)^2}{n_2} + \cdots + \frac{(\Sigma X_{\text{Last}})^2}{n_{\text{Last}}} - \frac{(\Sigma X)^2}{N}$$

$$SS_{\text{Within}} = SS_{\text{Total}} - SS_{\text{Between}}$$

Appendix: Table

Table A-3 Cutoff Scores for the *F* Distribution

Denominator df	Significance Level	Numerator Degrees of Freedom					
		1	2	3	4	5	6
1	.01	4,052	5,000	5,404	5,625	5,764	5,859
	.05	162	200	216	225	230	234
	.10	39.9	49.5	53.6	55.8	57.2	58.2
2	.01	98.50	99.00	99.17	99.25	99.30	99.33
	.05	18.51	19.00	19.17	19.25	19.30	19.33
	.10	8.53	9.00	9.16	9.24	9.29	9.33
3	.01	34.12	30.82	29.46	28.71	28.24	27.91
	.05	10.13	9.55	9.28	9.12	9.01	8.94
	.10	5.54	5.46	5.39	5.34	5.31	5.28
4	.01	21.20	18.00	16.70	15.98	15.52	15.21
	.05	7.71	6.95	6.59	6.39	6.26	6.16
	.10	4.55	4.33	4.19	4.11	4.05	4.01
5	.01	16.26	13.27	12.06	11.39	10.97	10.67
	.05	6.61	5.79	5.41	5.19	5.05	4.95
	.10	4.06	3.78	3.62	3.52	3.45	3.41
6	.01	13.75	10.93	9.78	9.15	8.75	8.47
	.05	5.99	5.14	4.76	4.53	4.39	4.28
	.10	3.78	3.46	3.29	3.18	3.11	3.06
7	.01	12.25	9.55	8.45	7.85	7.46	7.19
	.05	5.59	4.74	4.35	4.12	3.97	3.87
	.10	3.59	3.26	3.08	2.96	2.88	2.83
8	.01	11.26	8.65	7.59	7.01	6.63	6.37
	.05	5.32	4.46	4.07	3.84	3.69	3.58
	.10	3.46	3.11	2.92	2.81	2.73	2.67
9	.01	10.56	8.02	6.99	6.42	6.06	5.80
	.05	5.12	4.26	3.86	3.63	3.48	3.37
	.10	3.36	3.01	2.81	2.69	2.61	2.55
10	.01	10.05	7.56	6.55	6.00	5.64	5.39
	.05	4.97	4.10	3.71	3.48	3.33	3.22
	.10	3.29	2.93	2.73	2.61	2.52	2.46
11	.01	9.65	7.21	6.22	5.67	5.32	5.07
	.05	4.85	3.98	3.59	3.36	3.20	3.10
	.10	3.23	2.86	2.66	2.54	2.45	2.39

(continued)

Table A-3 (continued)

Denominator df	Significance Level	Numerator Degrees of Freedom					
		1	2	3	4	5	6
12	.01	9.33	6.93	5.95	5.41	5.07	4.82
	.05	4.75	3.89	3.49	3.26	3.11	3.00
	.10	3.18	2.81	2.61	2.48	2.40	2.33
13	.01	9.07	6.70	5.74	5.21	4.86	4.62
	.05	4.67	3.81	3.41	3.18	3.03	2.92
	.10	3.14	2.76	2.56	2.43	2.35	2.28
14	.01	8.86	6.52	5.56	5.04	4.70	4.46
	.05	4.60	3.74	3.34	3.11	2.96	2.85
	.10	3.10	2.73	2.52	2.40	2.31	2.24
15	.01	8.68	6.36	5.42	4.89	4.56	4.32
	.05	4.54	3.68	3.29	3.06	2.90	2.79
	.10	3.07	2.70	2.49	2.36	2.27	2.21
16	.01	8.53	6.23	5.29	4.77	4.44	4.20
	.05	4.49	3.63	3.24	3.01	2.85	2.74
	.10	3.05	2.67	2.46	2.33	2.24	2.18
17	.01	8.40	6.11	5.19	4.67	4.34	4.10
	.05	4.45	3.59	3.20	2.97	2.81	2.70
	.10	3.03	2.65	2.44	2.31	2.22	2.15
18	.01	8.29	6.01	5.09	4.58	4.25	4.02
	.05	4.41	3.56	3.16	2.93	2.77	2.66
	.10	3.01	2.62	2.42	2.29	2.20	2.13
19	.01	8.19	5.93	5.01	4.50	4.17	3.94
	.05	4.38	3.52	3.13	2.90	2.74	2.63
	.10	2.99	2.61	2.40	2.27	2.18	2.11
20	.01	8.10	5.85	4.94	4.43	4.10	3.87
	.05	4.35	3.49	3.10	2.87	2.71	2.60
	.10	2.98	2.59	2.38	2.25	2.16	2.09
21	.01	8.02	5.78	4.88	4.37	4.04	3.81
	.05	4.33	3.47	3.07	2.84	2.69	2.57
	.10	2.96	2.58	2.37	2.23	2.14	2.08
22	.01	7.95	5.72	4.82	4.31	3.99	3.76
	.05	4.30	3.44	3.05	2.82	2.66	2.55
	.10	2.95	2.56	2.35	2.22	2.13	2.06
23	.01	7.88	5.66	4.77	4.26	3.94	3.71
	.05	4.28	3.42	3.03	2.80	2.64	2.53
	.10	2.94	2.55	2.34	2.21	2.12	2.05
24	.01	7.82	5.61	4.72	4.22	3.90	3.67
	.05	4.26	3.40	3.01	2.78	2.62	2.51
	.10	2.93	2.54	2.33	2.20	2.10	2.04
25	.01	7.77	5.57	4.68	4.18	3.86	3.63
	.05	4.24	3.39	2.99	2.76	2.60	2.49
	.10	2.92	2.53	2.32	2.19	2.09	2.03
26	.01	7.72	5.53	4.64	4.14	3.82	3.59
	.05	4.23	3.37	2.98	2.74	2.59	2.48
	.10	2.91	2.52	2.31	2.18	2.08	2.01

Table A-3 (continued)

Denominator df	Significance Level	Numerator Degrees of Freedom					
		1	2	3	4	5	6
27	.01	7.68	5.49	4.60	4.11	3.79	3.56
	.05	4.21	3.36	2.96	2.73	2.57	2.46
	.10	2.90	2.51	2.30	2.17	2.07	2.01
28	.01	7.64	5.45	4.57	4.08	3.75	3.53
	.05	4.20	3.34	2.95	2.72	2.56	2.45
	.10	2.89	2.50	2.29	2.16	2.07	2.00
29	.01	7.60	5.42	4.54	4.05	3.73	3.50
	.05	4.18	3.33	2.94	2.70	2.55	2.43
	.10	2.89	2.50	2.28	2.15	2.06	1.99
30	.01	7.56	5.39	4.51	4.02	3.70	3.47
	.05	4.17	3.32	2.92	2.69	2.53	2.42
	.10	2.88	2.49	2.28	2.14	2.05	1.98
35	.01	7.42	5.27	4.40	3.91	3.59	3.37
	.05	4.12	3.27	2.88	2.64	2.49	2.37
	.10	2.86	2.46	2.25	2.11	2.02	1.95
40	.01	7.32	5.18	4.31	3.83	3.51	3.29
	.05	4.09	3.23	2.84	2.61	2.45	2.34
	.10	2.84	2.44	2.23	2.09	2.00	1.93
45	.01	7.23	5.11	4.25	3.77	3.46	3.23
	.05	4.06	3.21	2.81	2.58	2.42	2.31
	.10	2.82	2.43	2.21	2.08	1.98	1.91
50	.01	7.17	5.06	4.20	3.72	3.41	3.19
	.05	4.04	3.18	2.79	2.56	2.40	2.29
	.10	2.81	2.41	2.20	2.06	1.97	1.90
55	.01	7.12	5.01	4.16	3.68	3.37	3.15
	.05	4.02	3.17	2.77	2.54	2.38	2.27
	.10	2.80	2.40	2.19	2.05	1.96	1.89
60	.01	7.08	4.98	4.13	3.65	3.34	3.12
	.05	4.00	3.15	2.76	2.53	2.37	2.26
	.10	2.79	2.39	2.18	2.04	1.95	1.88
65	.01	7.04	4.95	4.10	3.62	3.31	3.09
	.05	3.99	3.14	2.75	2.51	2.36	2.24
	.10	2.79	2.39	2.17	2.03	1.94	1.87
70	.01	7.01	4.92	4.08	3.60	3.29	3.07
	.05	3.98	3.13	2.74	2.50	2.35	2.23
	.10	2.78	2.38	2.16	2.03	1.93	1.86
75	.01	6.99	4.90	4.06	3.58	3.27	3.05
	.05	3.97	3.12	2.73	2.49	2.34	2.22
	.10	2.77	2.38	2.16	2.02	1.93	1.86
80	.01	6.96	4.88	4.04	3.56	3.26	3.04
	.05	3.96	3.11	2.72	2.49	2.33	2.22
	.10	2.77	2.37	2.15	2.02	1.92	1.85
85	.01	6.94	4.86	4.02	3.55	3.24	3.02
	.05	3.95	3.10	2.71	2.48	2.32	2.21
	.10	2.77	2.37	2.15	2.01	1.92	1.85

(continued)

Table A-3 (*continued*)

Denominator df	Significance Level	Numerator Degrees of Freedom					
		1	2	3	4	5	6
90	.01	6.93	4.85	4.01	3.54	3.23	3.01
	.05	3.95	3.10	2.71	2.47	2.32	2.20
	.10	2.76	2.36	2.15	2.01	1.91	1.84
95	.01	6.91	4.84	4.00	3.52	3.22	3.00
	.05	3.94	3.09	2.70	2.47	2.31	2.20
	.10	2.76	2.36	2.14	2.01	1.91	1.84
100	.01	6.90	4.82	3.98	3.51	3.21	2.99
	.05	3.94	3.09	2.70	2.46	2.31	2.19
	.10	2.76	2.36	2.14	2.00	1.91	1.83
∞	.01	6.64	4.61	3.78	3.32	3.02	2.80
	.05	3.84	3.00	2.61	2.37	2.22	2.10
	.10	2.71	2.30	2.08	1.95	1.85	1.78

Answers to Set I Practice Problems

Chapter 9

1. (a) F needed ($df = 2, 27; p < .05$) = 3.36; $S_M^2 = [\sum(M - GM)^2]/df_{\text{Between}}) = [(7.4 - 7)^2 + (6.8 - 7)^2 + (6.8 - 7)^2]/2 = .12$; $S_{\text{Between}}^2 = (S_M^2)(n) = (.12)(10) = 1.2$; $S_{\text{Within}}^2 = (S_1^2 + S_2^2 + \cdots + S_{\text{Last}}^2)/N_{\text{Groups}} = (.82 + .90 + .80)/3 = .84$; $F = 1.2/.84 = 1.43$; do not reject the null hypothesis.

(b) F needed ($df = 3, 96; p < .05$) = 2.70 (actually using $df = 3, 95$); $S_M^2 = 164.67$; $S_{\text{Between}}^2 = (164.67)(25) = 4116.75$; $S_{\text{Within}}^2 = 736.5$; $F = 5.59$; reject the null hypothesis.

2. (a) F needed ($df = 2, 9; p < .01$) = 8.02; Group 1: $M = 8$, $S^2 = .67$; Group 2: $M = 6$, $S^2 = .67$; Group 3: $M = 4$, $S^2 = .67$; $S_{\text{Between}}^2 = (4)(4) = 16$; $S_{\text{Within}}^2 = .67$; $F = 16/.67 = 23.88$; reject the null hypothesis.

(b) F needed ($df = 2, 9; p < .01$) = 8.02; Group 1: $M = 8$, $S^2 = 21.33$; Group 2: $M = 6$, $S^2 = 21.33$; Group 3: $M = 4$, $S^2 = 21.33$; $S_{\text{Between}}^2 = (4)(4) = 16$; $S_{\text{Within}}^2 = 21.33$; $F = 16/21.33 = .75$; do not reject the null hypothesis.

(c) For part (a), $R^2 = (S_{\text{Between}}^2)(df_{\text{Between}})/[(S_{\text{Between}}^2)(df_{\text{Between}}) + (S_{\text{Within}}^2)(df_{\text{Within}})] = (16)(2)/[(16)(2) + (.67)(9)] = .84$. For part (b), $R^2 = (S_{\text{Between}}^2)(df_{\text{Between}})/[(S_{\text{Between}}^2)(df_{\text{Between}}) + (S_{\text{Within}}^2)(df_{\text{Within}})] = (16)(2)/[(16)(2) + (21.33)(9)] = .14$.

(d)

Group 1						
	X − GM		X − M		M − GM	
X	Dev	Dev²	Dev	Dev²	Dev	Dev²
8	2	4	0	0	2	4
8	2	4	0	0	2	4
7	1	1	−1	1	2	4
9	3	9	1	1	2	4
Σ 32		18		2		16

$M = 32/4 = 8.$

Group 2						
	X − GM		X − M		M − GM	
X	Dev	Dev²	Dev	Dev²	Dev	Dev²
6	0	0	0	0	0	0
6	0	0	0	0	0	0
5	−1	1	−1	1	0	0
7	1	1	1	1	0	0
Σ 24		2		2		0

$M = 24/4 = 6.$

Group 3						
	X − GM		X − M		M − GM	
X	Dev	Dev²	Dev	Dev²	Dev	Dev²
4	−2	4	0	0	−2	4
4	−2	4	0	0	−2	4
3	−3	9	−1	1	−2	4
5	−1	1	1	1	−2	4
Σ 16		18		2		16

Overall analysis:

$M = 16/4 = 4.$

$GM = (32 + 24 + 16)/12 = 72/12 = 6.$

$SS_{\text{Total}} = 18 + 2 + 18 = 38.$

$SS_{\text{Within}} = 2 + 2 + 2 = 6.$

$SS_{\text{Between}} = 16 + 0 + 16 = 32.$

Analysis of variance table:

Source	SS	df	MS	F
Between	32	2	16	23.88
Within	6	9	.67	
Total	38	11		

Conclusion: Reject the null hypothesis

3. (a) ❶ **Restate the question as a research hypothesis and a null hypothesis about the populations.** There are three populations of interest:

Population 1: Patients with affective disorders.
Population 2: Patients with cognitive disorders.
Population 3: Patients with drug-related conditions

    The research hypothesis is that the three population means differ. The null hypothesis is that the three populations have the same mean.

❷ **Determine the characteristics of the comparison distribution.** F distribution with 2 and 9 degrees of freedom.

❸ **Determine the cutoff sample score on the comparison distribution at which the null hypothesis should be rejected.** 5% level, $F(df = 2, 9)$ needed = 4.26.

❹ **Determine your sample's score on the comparison distribution.** $S_{\text{Between}}^2 = (5.33)(4) = 21.32$; $S_{\text{Within}}^2 = (.67 + 3.33 + 2.67)/3 = 2.22$; $F = 21.32/2.22 = 9.60$.

❺ **Decide whether to reject the null hypothesis.** F from Step ❹ (9.60) is more extreme than cutoff F from Step ❸ (4.26); reject the null hypothesis.

(b)

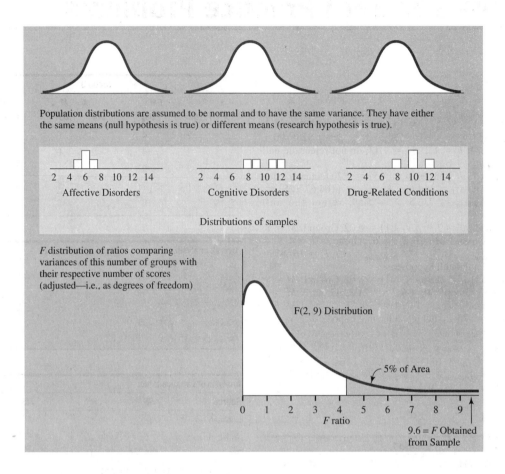

Population distributions are assumed to be normal and to have the same variance. They have either the same means (null hypothesis is true) or different means (research hypothesis is true).

2 4 6 8 10 12 14   2 4 6 8 10 12 14   2 4 6 8 10 12 14
Affective Disorders   Cognitive Disorders   Drug-Related Conditions

Distributions of samples

F distribution of ratios comparing variances of this number of groups with their respective number of scores (adjusted—i.e., as degrees of freedom)

F(2, 9) Distribution

5% of Area

0   1   2   3   4   5   6   7   8   9
F ratio

9.6 = F Obtained from Sample

(c) $R^2 = (S_{\text{Between}}^2)(df_{\text{Between}})/[(S_{\text{Between}}^2)(df_{\text{Between}}) + (S_{\text{Within}}^2)(df_{\text{Within}})] = (21.32)(2)/[(21.32)(2) + (2.22)(9)] = .68$.

(d) The null hypothesis is that the three groups are from populations of length-of-stay scores with equal means (and, as with a t test, we must be able to assume that they have equal variances). If this null hypothesis is true, then you can estimate the variance of these equal populations in two ways:

(i) You can estimate from the variation within each of the three groups and then average them. (This is just what you would do in a t test for independent means, except now you are averaging three variances instead of just two. Also in a t test you would weight these variances according to the degrees of freedom they contribute to the overall estimate. However, because all three groups have equal numbers, you can simply average them—in effect weighting them equally.) In this example, the three variance estimates were .67, 3.33, and 2.67, which gave a pooled estimate of 2.22. This is called the within-groups estimate of the population variance.

(ii) You can estimate the variance using the three means. If we assume the null hypothesis is true, the means of the three groups are based on samples taken from identical populations. Each of these identical populations will have an identical

distribution of means of samples taken from that population. If the null hypothesis were true, the means of our three samples would all be from identical populations, which is the same as if they were all from the same population. Thus, the amount of variation among our three means should reflect the variation in the distribution of means that they can be thought of as coming from. As a result, I can use these three means (6, 10, and 10) to estimate the variance in this distribution of means. Using the usual formula for estimating a population variance, I get 5.33.

However, what we want is the variance of a distribution of individuals. So the question is, what would be the distribution of individuals that would produce a distribution of means (of four scores each) with a variance of 5.33? To find the distribution of means from a distribution of individuals, you divide the variance of the distribution of individuals by the size of the samples. In this case, you want to do the reverse. Thus, you multiply the variance of the distribution of means by the size of the samples to get the variance of the distribution of individuals. This comes out to 5.33 times 4, or 21.32. This is called the between-groups estimate of the population variance.

If the null hypothesis is true, the within-groups and between-groups estimates of the population variance should be about the same because they are estimates of essentially the same population. Thus, the ratio of the between-groups estimate divided by the within-groups estimate should be about 1.

However, suppose the null hypothesis is false and the three populations from which these groups come have different means. In that situation, the estimate based on the variation among the group means will be bigger than the one based on the variation within the groups. The reason it will be bigger is as follows. If the null hypothesis is true, the only reason that the means of our groups vary is because of the variance inside of each of the three identical distributions of means. But if the null hypothesis is false, each of those distributions of means also has a different mean. Thus, the variation in our means is due to *both* the variation inside of each of these now *not* identical distributions of means, and also to the differences in the means of these distributions of means. Thus, there is an additional source of variation in the means of our groups. If you estimate the variance of the population using these three means, it will be larger than if the null hypothesis were true. On the other hand, the within-groups variance is not affected by whether the three groups have different means, because it considers variation only within each of the groups. The within-groups variance thus does not get any bigger if the null hypothesis is false. Therefore, when the null hypothesis is false, the ratio of the between-groups variance to the within-groups variance will be more than 1.

The ratio of the between-groups estimate to the within-groups estimate is called an F ratio. In this example, our F ratio is 21.32 to 2.22; $21.32/2.22 = 9.60$.

Statisticians have made tables of what happens when you figure F ratios based on the situation in which you randomly take a group of four scores from each of three identical populations. This is the situation in which the null hypothesis is true. Looking at these tables, it turns out that there is less than a 5% chance of getting an F ratio larger than 4.26. Because our actual F ratio is bigger than this, we can reject the null hypothesis.

(e) F needed $(df = 1, 9; p < .05) = 5.12$; $S^2_{Between}$ (for two means) $= (8)(4) = 32$; S^2_{Within} (from overall analysis) $= 2.22$; $F = 32/2.22 = 14.41$; reject the null hypothesis.

(f) $S^2_{Between} = (0)(4) = 0$; $F = 0/2.22 = 0$; do not reject the null hypothesis.

(g) In a study with more than two groups, researchers often make predictions for differences between specific pairs of groups; these are called planned contrasts. To test a planned contrast, you do a special analysis of variance in which the between-groups estimate is based on just the two groups being compared, but the within-groups estimate uses the information from all groups in the overall analysis of variance. (The variation in all populations is assumed to be the same, so this method lets you take advantage of the information in all the groups when figuring the within-groups population variance estimate.) Thus, for the first planned contrast (Affective versus Drug-Related Conditions), I figured the between-groups estimate using the estimated variance of the distribution of means based on means of these two groups (6 and 10, which came out to $S^2_M = 8$) and then multiplied this by the number in each group (4). The result was 32. Dividing this by the overall within-groups estimate I'd figured earlier in the problem, which was 2.22, gave an F ratio of 14.41. This was bigger than the needed F for df

of 1 (the number of df in figuring the between-groups estimate). Thus, I could reject the null hypothesis. Following the same procedure for the second planned contrast gave an F of 0, which of course was not significant.

4. (a), (b), (c), and (d). Hypothesis-testing steps, sketch of distributions, effect size, and explanation similar to question 3 [except (d) needs to include material similar to explanations from earlier chapters' practice problems]. F needed ($df = 2$, 147; $p < .05) = 3.09$ (actually using $df = 2, 100$); $S^2_{Between} = (.09)(50) = 4.5$; $S^2_{Within} = (5.2 + 5.8 + 4.8)/3 = 5.27$; $F = .85$; do not reject the null hypothesis. $R^2 = (4.5)(2)/[(4.5)(2) + (5.27)(147)] = .01$.

5. (a), (b), (c), and (d). Hypothesis-testing steps, sketch of distributions, effect size, and explanation similar to question 3 [except (d) needs to include material similar to explanations from earlier chapters' practice problems]. F needed ($df = 3, 28; p < .01) = 4.57$; $S^2_{Between} = (155)(8) = 1240$; $S^2_{Within} = (3.5^2 + 4.6^2 + 3.8^2 + 4.9^2)/4 = 17.97$; $F = 69.0$; reject the null hypothesis. $R^2 = (1240)(3)/[(1240)(3) + (17.97)(28)] = .88$.

(e) Bonferroni corrected significance level $= .05/5 = .01$; F needed ($df = 1, 28; p < .01) = 7.64$; $S^2_{Between}$ (for two means) $= (4.5)(8) = 36$, S^2_{Within} (from overall analysis) $= 17.97$, $F = 36/17.97 = 2.00$, do not reject the null hypothesis.

(f) $S^2_{Between} = (364.5)(8) = 2916$, $F = 2916/17.97 = 162.27$, reject the null hypothesis.

(g) $S^2_{Between} = (8)(8) = 64$, $F = 64/17.97 = 3.56$, do not reject the null hypothesis.

(h) $S^2_{Between} = (288)(8) = 2304$, $F = 2304/17.97 = 128.21$, reject the null hypothesis.

(i) $S^2_{Between} = (264.5)(8) = 2116$, $F = 2116/17.97 = 117.75$, reject the null hypothesis.

(j) (Explanation of planned contrasts similar to question 3d.) Bonferroni correction is done to take into account that, when testing many contrasts, the chance of any one of them coming out significant is greater than the supposed significance level. This is corrected by using for each contrast a significance level based on dividing the overall significance level by the number of contrasts. In this problem with five contrasts and an overall significance level of .05, each of the five contrasts is tested at the $.05/5 = .01$ level of significance.

6. (a) $.05/2 = .025$; (b) .0125; (c) .0033; (d) .002.

7. (a) Overall study's $df_{Between} = 5 - 1 = 4$; $df_{Within} = 9 + 9 + 9 + 9 + 9 - 45$. Scheffé corrected $F - 17.21/4 = 4.30$. Overall study's .05 cutoff $F(df = 4, 45)$ is 2.58. Thus, even with the Scheffé correction, this comparison is significant. (b) Scheffé corrected $F = 17.21/5 = 3.44$. Overall study's .05 cutoff F ($df = 5, 54$, actually using $df = 5, 50$ from the table) is 2.40, significant comparison. (c) Scheffé corrected $F = 17.21/4 = 4.30$. Overall study's .05 cutoff $F(df = 4, 95)$ is 2.47, significant comparison. (d) Scheffé corrected $F = 17.21/4 = 4.30$. Overall study's .01 cutoff $F(df = 4, 45)$ is 3.77, significant comparison.

8. From Table 9-9: (a) .09; (b) .12; (c) .10; (d) .38.

9. From Table 9-10: (a) 322; (b) 21; (c) 274; (d) 52.

10. Similar to question 3d (and also including material from Chapter 8), but focusing on this study's results.

11. Similar to questions 3d and 3g (and including material from previous chapters) but focusing on this study's results.

12. (a) Acceptance, emotional extremes, jealousy; (b) emotional extremes, jealousy, obsessive preoccupation, sexual attraction, desire for union, desire for reciprocation, love at first sight; (c) happiness, friendship, trust, fear of closeness, emotional extremes, jealousy; (d) emotional extremes, jealousy. (e) After conducting an overall analysis of variance among more than two groups, researchers often go on to conduct an exploratory analysis comparing each pair of groups; these are called post hoc (after the fact) comparisons. The problem is that, with many comparisons, it is possible that some will be significant just by chance more often than the supposed significance level of, say, 5%. When doing post hoc tests, special procedures have been developed to protect against this problem so that the researcher can be confident that any difference found will be truly no more likely to have occurred by, say, 5% (if that is the significance level chosen) if the null hypothesis is true. The Scheffé test is an example of this kind of procedure.

Chapter 10

Factorial Analysis of Variance

Chapter Outline

❖ Basic Logic of Factorial Designs and Interaction Effects

❖ Recognizing and Interpreting Interaction Effects

❖ Basic Logic of the Two-Way Analysis of Variance

❖ Assumptions in the Factorial Analysis of Variance

❖ Extensions and Special Cases of the Analysis of Variance

❖ Controversy: Dichotomizing Numeric Variables

❖ Factorial Analysis of Variance in Research Articles

❖ Advanced Topic: Figuring a Two-Way Analysis of Variance

❖ Advanced Topic: Power and Effect Size in the Factorial Analysis of Variance

❖ Learning Aids

   ❖ Summary

   ❖ Key Terms

   ❖ Example Worked-Out Problems

   ❖ Practice Problems

   ❖ Using SPSS

❖ Chapter Notes

Factorial analysis of variance is a method that provides a flexible and efficient approach to analyzing results of studies that use what is called a **factorial research design.** As you will learn in this chapter, in a factorial research design, the effects of *two or more variables* are examined at the same time by making groupings of every combination of the variables. Factorial research designs are widely used in psychology.

We first consider in depth the nature of the research approach used in these kinds of studies. We then go on to a discussion of the reasoning for, and basic logic of, a factorial analysis of variance. We also discuss some extensions to the analysis of variance. We present the computational procedures for a factorial analysis of variance in an Advanced Topic section. Power and effect size for a factorial analysis of variance are also covered in an Advanced Topic section. (We cover a particular type of advanced analysis of variance called *repeated measures analysis of variance* in a Web Chapter available at *www.pearsoned.co.in/prc/home.*

factorial analysis of variance analysis of variance for a factorial research design.

factorial research design way of organizing a study in which the effects of two or more variables are studied at once by making groupings of every combination of the variables.

419

Basic Logic of Factorial Designs and Interaction Effects

An Example

E. Aron and A. Aron (1997; see also E. Aron et al., 2012) proposed that people differ on a basic, inherited tendency they call "sensory-processing sensitivity" that is found in about a fifth of humans and in many animal species. People with this trait process information especially thoroughly. Table 1 gives six items from their Highly Sensitive Person Scale. If you score high on most of the items, you are probably among the 20% of people who are "highly sensitive." (See also Box 2.)

One implication of being a highly sensitive person, according to this model, is that such people are more affected than others by success and failure. This is because they process all experiences more completely. So one would expect highly sensitive people to feel especially good when they succeed and especially bad when they fail. To test this prediction, E. Aron, A. Aron, and Davies (2005, Study 4) conducted an experiment. In the experiment, students first completed the sensitivity questions in Table 1. (This permitted the researchers when analyzing the results to divide them into highly sensitive and not highly sensitive.) Later, as part of a series of tests on attitudes and other topics, everyone was given a timed test of their "applied reasoning ability," something important to most students. But without their knowing it, half took an extremely easy version and half took a version so difficult that some problems had no right answer.

The questionnaires were handed out to people in alternate seats (it was randomly determined where this process began in each row); so if you had the hard version of the test, the people on either side had an easy version and you were probably aware that they finished quickly while you were still struggling. On the other hand, if you had the easy version, you were probably aware that you had finished easily while the others around you were still working on what you presumed to be the same test.

Right after the test, everyone was asked some items about their mood, how depressed, anxious, and sad they felt at the moment. (The mood items were buried in other questions, so it was not obvious that testing mood was the purpose of the study.) Responses to the mood items were averaged to create a measure of overall negative mood.

In sum, the study looked at the effect of *two different factors* on negative mood: (1) whether the students were highly sensitive or not highly sensitive and (2) whether the students had taken the easy test (which caused them to feel they had succeeded) or the hard test (which caused them to feel they had failed).

Table 1 Selected Items from the Highly Sensitive Person Scale

1. Do you find it unpleasant to have a lot going on at once?
2. Do you find yourself wanting to withdraw during busy days, into bed or into a darkened room or any place where you can have some privacy and relief from stimulation?
3. Are you easily overwhelmed by things like bright lights, strong smells, coarse fabrics, or sirens close by?
4. Do you get rattled when you have a lot to do in a short amount of time?
5. Do changes in your life shake you up?
6. Are you bothered by intense stimuli, like loud noises and chaotic scenes?

Note: Each item is answered on a scale from 1 "Not at all" to 7 "Extremely."

Source: Aron, E., & Aron, A. (1997). Sensory-processing sensitivity and its relation to introversion and emotionality. *Journal of Personality and Social Psychology, 73,* 345–368. Published by the American Psychological Association. Reprinted with permission.

Aron and colleagues could have done two studies, one comparing highly sensitive versus not highly sensitive individuals and one comparing people who took the
easy test versus people who took the hard test. Instead, they studied the effects of
both sensitivity and test difficulty in a single study. With this setup there were four
groups of participants (see Table 2): (a) those who are not highly sensitive and took
the easy test, (b) those who are highly sensitive and took the easy test, (c) those who
are not highly sensitive and took the hard test, and (d) those who are highly sensitive
and took the hard test.

Factorial Research Design Defined

The Aron and colleagues (2005) study is an example of a factorial research design.
As you learned at the beginning of the chapter, in a factorial research design the
effects of *two or more variables* are examined at once by making groupings of every
combination of the variables. In this example, there are two levels of sensitivity (not
high and high) and two levels of test difficulty (easy and hard). This creates four
possible group combinations, and the researchers used all of them in their study.

A factorial research design has a major advantage over conducting separate
studies of each variable: efficiency. With a factorial design, you can study both variables at once, without needing twice as many participants. In the example, Aron
and colleagues were able to use a single group of participants to study the effects of
sensitivity and test difficulty on negative mood. (The two "studies" don't get in each
other's way because for each part of each comparison, there are equal numbers in
each part of the other conditions.)

Interaction Effects

There is, however, an even more important advantage of a factorial research design.
A factorial design lets you study the effects of *combining two or more variables*. In
this example, sensitivity and test difficulty might affect negative mood in a simple
additive way. By additive, we mean that their combined influence is the sum of
their separate influences; if you are more of one and also more of the other, then the
overall effect is the total of the two individual effects. For example, suppose being
highly sensitive makes you more likely to experience a negative mood; similarly,
suppose the test being hard makes you more likely to experience a negative mood.
If these two effects are additive, then participants in the high sensitivity, hard test
group will be most likely to experience a negative mood; participants who are not
highly sensitive and take the easy test will be the least likely to experience a negative mood; and those in the other two conditions would have an intermediate likelihood of experiencing a negative mood.

It could also be that one variable but not the other has an effect. Or perhaps neither variable has any effect. In the additive situation, or when only one variable or
neither has an effect, looking at the two variables in combination does not give any
interesting additional information.

However, it is also possible that the *combination of the two variables* changes
the result. In fact, as noted earlier, Aron and colleagues predicted that the effect of
being highly sensitive would be especially strong in the hard test condition. A situation where the *combination* of variables has a special effect is called an **interaction effect**. An interaction effect is an effect in which the effect of one variable that
divides the groups on the measured variable is different across the levels of the other
variable that divides the groups—a situation in which the "whole is greater than (or
less than!) the sum of the parts".

Table 2 Factorial Research
Design Employed by Aron and
colleagues (2005)

	Test Difficulty	
	Easy	Hard
Not High	a	c
High	b	d

(Sensitivity labels rows: Not High, High)

Source: Based on Aron, E., Aron, A., & Davies,
K. M. (2005). Adult shyness: The interaction of
temporal sensitivity and an adverse childhood
environment. *Personality and Social Psychology
Bulletin, 31,* 181–197. Copyright © 2005 by
Sage Publications, Inc. Reprinted by permission
of Sage Publications, Inc.

interaction effect situation in the
factorial analysis of variance in which a
combination of variables has an effect
that could not be predicted from the
effects of the two variables individually;
situation in which the effect of
one variable that divides the groups
on the measured variable is different
across the levels of the other variable
that divides the groups.

Table 3 Mean Levels of Negative Mood in the Aron and colleagues (2005) Study

		Test Difficulty	
		Easy	Hard
Sensitivity	Not High	2.43	2.56
	High	2.19	3.01

In the Aron and colleagues study, there was an interaction effect. Look at Table 3. The result was that the students in the High Sensitivity/Hard Test group had the most negative mood (remember, a high number means a more negative mood), and the students in the High Sensitivity/Easy Test group had the least negative mood. The level of negative mood in the other two groups (the Not High Sensitivity groups) was similar and in between that of the two High Sensitivity groups. These results show that the effect of test difficulty (on negative mood) is different according to the level of sensitivity: for students who are not highly sensitive, their level of negative mood is slightly higher with a hard test (2.56) compared to an easy test (2.43); but for students who are highly sensitive, their level of negative mood is much higher with a hard test (3.01) compared to an easy test (2.19).

Suppose the researchers had studied sensitivity and test difficulty in two separate studies. In the study of sensitivity (assuming equal numbers of students in each group), they would have concluded that sensitivity had little (if any) effect on negative mood: the average level of negative mood for students who are not highly sensitive is 2.50 (that is, the average of 2.43 and 2.56) and for highly sensitive students 2.60 (the average of 2.19 and 3.01). In the study of test difficulty (again assuming equal numbers of students in each group), they would have concluded that students experienced a lower level of negative mood when taking an easy test than a hard test: The average level of negative mood for students taking the easy test was 2.31 (the average of 2.43 and 2.19), and the average for those taking the hard test was 2.79 (the average of 2.56 and 3.01). Thus, following the approach of two separate studies, the researchers would have completely missed the most important result. The most important result had to do with the *combination of the two factors*.

Some Terminology

The Aron and colleagues study used a **two-way factorial research design**. It would be analyzed with what is called a **two-way analysis of variance** because it considers the effects of two variables that divide the groups. These variables are called **grouping variables**. By contrast, for some situations, we use a **one-way analysis of variance**. Such analyses are called *one-way* because they consider the effect of only one grouping variable (such as a person's attachment style or kind of information about a defendant's criminal record).

In a two-way analysis of variance, each grouping variable or "way" (each dimension in the diagram) is a possible **main effect**. If the result for a grouping variable, averaging across the other grouping variable(s), is significant, it is a *main effect*. This is entirely different from an *interaction effect,* which is based on the *combination of grouping variables*. In the two-way Aron and colleagues study, there was a possibility of two main effects and one interaction effect. The two possible main effects are one for sensitivity and one for test difficulty. The possible interaction effect is for the combination of sensitivity and test difficulty. In a two-way analysis of variance you are always testing two possible main effects and one possible interaction effect.

Each grouping combination in a factorial design is called a **cell**. The mean of the scores in each cell is a **cell mean**. In the Aron and colleagues study, there are four cells and thus four cell means, one for each combination of the levels of sensitivity and test difficulty. That is, one cell is Not High Sensitivity and an Easy Test (as shown in Table 3, its cell mean is 2.43); one cell is High Sensitivity and an Easy Test (2.19); one cell is Not High Sensitivity and a Hard Test (2.56); and one cell is High Sensitivity and a Hard Test (3.01).

two-way factorial research design factorial research design in analysis of variance with two variables that each divide the groups.

two-way analysis of variance analysis of variance for a two-way factorial research design.

grouping variable a variable that separates groups in analysis of variance.

one-way analysis of variance analysis of variance in which there is only one grouping variable.

main effect difference between groups on one grouping variable in a factorial design in analysis of variance; result for a grouping variable, averaging across the levels of the other grouping variable(s).

cell in a factorial design, particular combination of levels of the variables that divide the group.

cell mean mean of a particular combination of levels of the variables that divide the groups in a factorial design in analysis of variance.

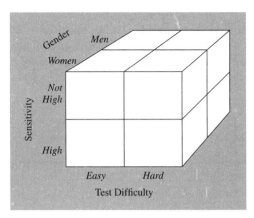

Figure 1   Possible three-way factorial research design for the Aron and colleagues (2005) study.

The means of one grouping variable alone are called **marginal means**. For example, in the Aron and colleagues study there are two marginal means for each grouping variable. For sensitivity, there is one marginal mean for all the students who are not highly sensitive (as we saw earlier, 2.50) and one for all the students who are highly sensitive (2.60). For the test difficulty grouping variable, there is one marginal mean for all the students who took the easy test (2.31) and one marginal mean for all the students who took the hard test (2.79). (Because we were mainly interested in the interaction, we did not show these marginal means in our tables.) To look at a main effect, you focus on the marginal means for each grouping variable. To look at the interaction effect, you focus on the pattern of individual cell means.

Some studies investigate the effect of three or more grouping variables at a time. For example, Aron and colleagues could have looked at whether their results were different for women and men. To do this, they would have divided each of their four groups into two subgroups, women and men. This would have created eight grouping combinations: Not High Sensitivity/Easy Test/Women; Not High Sensitivity/Easy Test/Men; Not High Sensitivity/Hard Test/Women; and so forth. The complete set of groupings is shown in Figure 1. This analysis would examine the influence of three grouping variables at one time: sensitivity, test difficulty, and gender. It takes three dimensions to diagram such a study. Thus, this is an example of a *three-way factorial design*. You can do studies with four-way and even higher factorial designs, though you can't diagram such studies in any simple way. However, most psychology research is limited to two-way and occasionally three-way factorial designs.

Factorial research designs are often described in terms of the number of grouping variables in the study and the number of levels that each grouping variable has. So, for example, consider a study of the effects of two grouping variables in which the first grouping variable has two levels (such as low and high) and the second grouping variable has three levels (such as small, medium, and large). This would be called a 2×3 *factorial design*: the 2 is for the number of levels of the first grouping variable and the 3 is for the number of levels of the second grouping variable. As another example, consider a study with three grouping variables, with the first grouping variable having two levels and the other two grouping variables each having three levels. This would be a $2 \times 3 \times 3$ design. The Aron and colleagues study used a 2×2 design.

marginal means   in a factorial design in analysis of variance, mean score for all the participants at a particular level of one of the grouping variables.

How are you doing?

1. (a) What is a factorial research design? (b) and (c) Give two advantages of a factorial research design over doing two separate studies.
2. In a factorial design, (a) what is a main effect, and (b) what is an interaction effect?
3. In the following table are the means from a study in which participants rated the originality of paintings under various conditions. For each mean, indicate its grouping and whether it is a cell or marginal mean.

	Contemporary	Renaissance	Overall
Landscape	6.5	5.5	6
Portrait	3.5	2.5	3
Overall	5	4	

4. In each of the following studies, participants' performance on a coordination task was measured under various conditions or compared for different groups. For each study, make a diagram of the research design and indicate whether it is a one-way, two-way, or three-way design: (a) a study in which people are assigned to either a high-stress condition or a low-stress condition, and, in each of these conditions, half are assigned to work alone and half to work in a room with other people; (b) a study comparing students majoring in physics, chemistry, or engineering; (c) a study comparing people doing a task in a hot room versus a cold room, with half in each room doing the task with their right hand and half with their left hand, and within each of these various temperature/ hand combinations, half are blindfolded and half are not.
5. Explain what it means to say that a study is using a 2 × 4 research design.

Answers

1. (a) A factorial research design is a research design in which the effect of two or more grouping variables is examined at once by making groupings of every combination of the variables.
   (b) A factorial research design is more efficient. For example, you can study the effects of two grouping variables at once with only a single group of participants.
   (c) A factorial research design makes it possible to see if there are interaction effects.
2. (a) A main effect in a factorial research design is the effect of one of the grouping variables, ignoring the pattern of results on the other grouping variable(s) (or a difference in the marginal means for the different levels of a particular grouping variable).
   (b) An interaction effect is the different effect of one grouping variable according to the level of the other grouping variable(s).
3. 6.5 = cell mean for Contemporary/Landscape group; 5.5 = cell mean for Renaissance/Landscape group; 6 = marginal mean for Landscape groups; 3.5 = cell mean for Contemporary/Portrait group; 2.5 = cell mean for Renaissance/Portrait group; 3 = marginal mean for Portrait groups; 5 = marginal mean for Contemporary groups; and 4 = marginal mean for Renaissance groups.
4. (a) Two-way.

	Stress	
Task	High	Low
Alone		
With Others		

(b) One-way.

Subject		
Physics	Chemistry	Engineering

(c) Three-way.

5. A study is using a 2 × 4 research design when it has two grouping variables, one that has two levels and one that has four levels.

Recognizing and Interpreting Interaction Effects

It is very important to understand interaction effects. In many experiments and other kinds of research (such as the combined effects of genetics and the environment on various behaviors), the interaction effect is the main point of the research. As we have seen, an interaction effect is an effect in which the impact of one grouping variable depends on the level of another grouping variable. You can think out and describe an interaction effect in three ways: in words, in numbers, or in a graph. Note that, in discussing the examples in this section on interaction effects, we will treat all differences that have the pattern of an interaction effect or of a main effect as if they were statistically significant. (In reality, you would carry out hypothesis testing steps to test whether the particular patterns were strong enough to be statistically significant.) We are taking this approach here to keep the focus on the *idea* of interaction effects while you are learning this fairly abstract notion.

Identifying Interaction Effects in Words and Numbers

You can think out an interaction effect in words by saying that you have an interaction effect when the effect of one grouping variable varies according to the level of another grouping variable. In the Aron and colleagues example, the effect of test difficulty (easy versus hard) varies according to the level of sensitivity (not high versus high). Another way of saying this is that the effect of test difficulty depends on the level of sensitivity (the effect of test difficulty is different for highly sensitive individuals than for individuals who are not highly sensitive). (You can also talk about this interaction effect by focusing on the other grouping variable first. So you could say that the effect of sensitivity varies according to the level of test difficulty, or that the effect of sensitivity depends on the level of test difficulty. Interaction effects are completely symmetrical in that you can describe them from the point of view of either grouping variable.)

You can see an interaction effect numerically by looking at the pattern of cell means. If there is an interaction effect, the *pattern of differences in cell means* across one row will not be the same as the patterns of differences in cell means across another row. (Again, all of this is symmetrical: you can also look at the differences in cell means for one column compared to another column, but we will focus here on rows.) Consider the Aron and colleagues example. In the Not High Sensitivity row, the cell mean for negative mood of the Easy Test students (2.43) was just slightly lower than the cell mean for negative mood of the Hard Test students (2.56). This is a difference of $-.13$ (that is, $2.43 - 2.56 = -.13$). However, now look at the High Sensitivity row. In this row, the cell mean for Easy Test students' negative mood (2.19) was a lot lower than the cell mean for negative mood for the Hard Test students (3.01). This difference of $-.82$ is not at all the same as the difference of $-.13$ in the Not High Sensitivity row; this *dissimilar pattern of differences in cell means* indicates an interaction effect.

Some Examples

Table 4 gives cell means and marginal means for six possible results of a fictional two-way factorial study on the relation of age and education (the grouping variables) to income (the measured variable) in North America. The grouping variable age has two levels (younger, such as 25 to 30, versus older, such as 40 to 45), and the grouping variable education has two levels (high school versus college). Thus, the study is using a 2×2 research design. These fictional results are exaggerated to make clear when there are interactions and main effects. Before you look at the six possible results, take a minute to think about what kind of results you might expect (and hope!) to see. For example, do you expect that people with a college education will earn less than or more than people with only a high school education? Would you expect younger people to earn more than or less than older people? Most

Table 4   Possible Means for Results of a Study of the Relation of Age and Education to Income (in Thousands of Dollars)

	Result A			Result B			Result C		
Age	High School	College	Overall	High School	College	Overall	High School	College	Overall
Younger	40	40	40	60	40	50	20	60	40
Older	40	60	50	40	60	50	40	80	60
Overall	40	50		50	50		30	70	

	Result D			Result E			Result F		
Age	High School	College	Overall	High School	College	Overall	High School	College	Overall
Younger	20	20	20	40	60	50	30	45	37.5
Older	120	120	120	40	80	60	35	60	47.5
Overall	70	70		40	70		32.5	52.5	

importantly (since we are focusing on interaction effects), what about the possibility of an interaction effect? Do you think that the effect of education (college versus high school) will be different according to age (younger versus older)? Let's take a look at the six possible results and then we'll tell you what the results of actual research show.

Result A Interaction. Note that in the Younger row, education makes no difference, but in the Older row, the college cell mean is much higher than the high-school cell mean. One way to say this is that for the younger group, education is unrelated to income; but for the older group, people with a college education earn much more than those with less education. There are also two main effects: overall, older people earn more than younger people, and overall, people with a college education earn more than those with only a high school education.

Result B Interaction. This is because, in the Younger row, the high school mean income is higher than the college mean income, but in the Older row the high-school mean income is lower. Put in words, among younger people, those with only a high school education make more money (perhaps because they entered the workplace earlier or the kinds of jobs they have start out at a higher level); but among older people, those with a college education make more money. (There are no main effects in Result B, since the marginal means for the two rows are the same and the marginal means for the two columns are the same.)

Result C No interaction. In the Younger row, the high-school mean is 40 lower than the college mean, and the same is true in the Older row. Whether young or old, people with college educations earn $40,000 more. (That is, there is a main effect for age and also a main effect for education.)

Result D No interaction. There is no difference in the pattern of income between the two rows. Regardless of education, older people earn $100,000 more. (That is, there is a main effect for age; but there is no main effect for education.)

Result E Interaction. In the Younger row, the college mean is 20 higher than the high-school mean, but in the Older row, the college mean is 40 higher than the high-school mean. So among young people, college-educated people earn a little more; but, among older people, those with a college education earn much more. (There are also main effects for both age and education.)

Result F Interaction. There is a smaller difference between the high school and college mean in the Younger row than in the Older row. As with Result E, for people with a college education, income increases more with age than it does for those with only a high school education. (There are also main effects for both age and education.)

Based on statistics from the U.S. Census Bureau, the actual situation in the United States is closest to Result F (Day & Newberger, 2002). People with a college education earn more than those with only a high school education in both age groups, but the difference is somewhat greater for the older group. You also may be interested to know that, based on data from 2009, individuals with a college degree in the United States earn an average of $30,000 more per year than those with only a high school education (U.S. Census Bureau, 2009). However, it is important to keep in mind that whether people receive a college education is

TIP FOR SUCCESS
Remember, you tell whether there is an interaction effect by looking at the *pattern of cell means*. There is an interaction effect if the pattern of cell means in one row is different from the pattern of cell means across another row.

TIP FOR SUCCESS
You tell whether there is a main effect by looking at the *marginal means*. The marginal means in Tables 4 and 5 are the means in the "Overall" columns and rows. There is a main effect for a particular grouping variable if the marginal means for the different levels of that grouping variable are not the same.

Table 5   Some Possible Results of an Experiment on the Effect of Task Difficulty and Arousal Level on Performance (Fictional Data)

	Result A				Result B				Result C			
	Manipulated Arousal				Manipulated Arousal				Manipulated Arousal			
Task	Low	Moderate	High	Overall	Low	Moderate	High	Overall	Low	Moderate	High	Overall
Easy	10	10	10	10	10	20	30	20	10	20	30	20
Hard	20	20	20	20	10	20	30	20	20	30	40	30
Overall	15	15	15		10	20	30		15	25	35	

Task	Result D				Result E				Result F			
Easy	10	20	30	20	10	20	10	13.3	10	20	30	20
Hard	10	20	60	30	20	10	20	16.7	30	20	10	20
Overall	10	20	45		15	15	15		20	20	20	

also related to the social class of their parents and other factors that may affect income as much as education does.

More Examples

Table 5 shows possible results of another fictional study. In this factorial experiment, the two experimentally manipulated variables are difficulty of the task (which has two levels: easy versus hard) and level of physiological arousal (which has three levels: low, moderate, or high). (This study is using a 2×3 research design.) Arousal in this study is how anxious the participant is made to feel about the importance of doing well. The variable being measured is how well the participant performs a set of arithmetic tasks. Let's consider each possible pattern of results.

Result A   No interaction. The pattern of cell means in the Easy row is the same as the pattern of cell means in the Hard row. In each row, the cell means are the same for each level of arousal. (There is one main effect: task difficulty affects performance; arousal does not.)

Result B   No interaction. The cell means in the Easy row increase by 10 from low to moderate and from moderate to high. The cell means in the Hard row do the same. (Again, there is only one main effect: arousal affects performance; task difficulty does not.)

Result C   No interaction. The cell means in the Easy row increase by 10 from low to moderate and from moderate to high; the cell means in the Hard row do the same. (In this example, there are two main effects: arousal affects performance and task difficulty affects performance.)

Result D   Interaction. The pattern of cell means in the Easy row is an increase of 10 from low to moderate and another increase of 10 from moderate to high. This pattern is not the same as the pattern of cell means in the Hard row, where there is again an increase of 10 from low to moderate, but there is an increase of 40 from moderate to high. Thus, in all cases, performance on easy and hard tasks tends to improve with greater arousal. However, the impact of high versus moderate arousal is much greater for hard than for easy tasks. (There are two main effects: arousal affects performance and task difficulty affects performance.)

Result E   Interaction. The pattern of cell means in the Easy row is an increase of 10 and then a decrease of 10. This is quite different from the Hard row, where the pattern is a decrease of 10 and then an increase of 10. For easy tasks, performance is best under moderate arousal, but, for hard tasks, performance is worst under moderate arousal. (There is only one main effect: task difficulty affects performance; arousal does not.)

Result F   Interaction. In the Easy row, the cell means increase as you go across; in the Hard row, they decrease as you go across. For easy tasks, the more arousal, the better; for hard tasks, arousal interferes with performance. (There are no main effects.) (Result F is closest to a well established finding in psychology known as the Yerkes-Dodson law.)

Identifying Interaction Effects Graphically

Another common way of making sense of interaction effects is by graphing the pattern of cell means. This is usually done with a bar graph, although a line graph is sometimes used. The bar graph in Figure 2 shows the results from Aron and colleagues' (2005) study. Figure 3 is a line graph that shows the same results as the bar graph in Figure 2. Figures 4 and 5 show the bar graphs for the fictional results we just considered from Tables 3 and 4, respectively.

One thing to notice about such graphs is this: whenever there is an interaction, the pattern of bars on one section of the graph is different from the pattern on the other section of the graph. Thus, in Figure 2, the pattern for not highly sensitive is a small step up, but the pattern for highly sensitive is a much larger step up. The bars having a different pattern is just a graphic way of saying that the pattern of differences between the cell means from row to row is not the same. In a line graph, such

Figure 2   Bar graph for level of negative mood as a function of sensitivity (not high versus high) and test difficulty (easy versus hard).

Source: Based on Aron, E., Aron, A., & Davies, K. M. (2005). Adult shyness: The interaction of temporal sensitivity and an adverse childhood environment. *Personality and Social Psychology Bulletin, 31*, 1–17. Copyright © 2005 by Sage Publications, Inc. Reprinted by permission of Sage Publications, Inc.

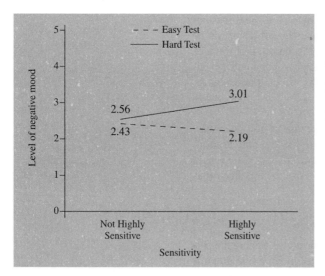

Figure 3 Line graph for level of negative mood as a function of sensitivity (not high versus high) and test difficulty (easy versus hard).

Source: Based on Aron, E., Aron, A., & Davies, K. M. (2005). Adult shyness: The interaction of temporal sensitivity and an adverse childhood environment. *Personality and Social Psychology Bulletin, 31,* 1–17. Copyright © 2005 by Sage Publications, Inc. Reprinted by permission of Sage Publications, Inc.

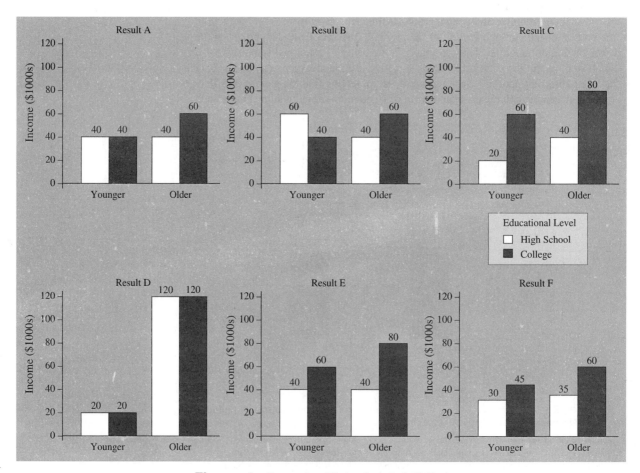

Figure 4 Bar graphs of fictional results in Table 4.

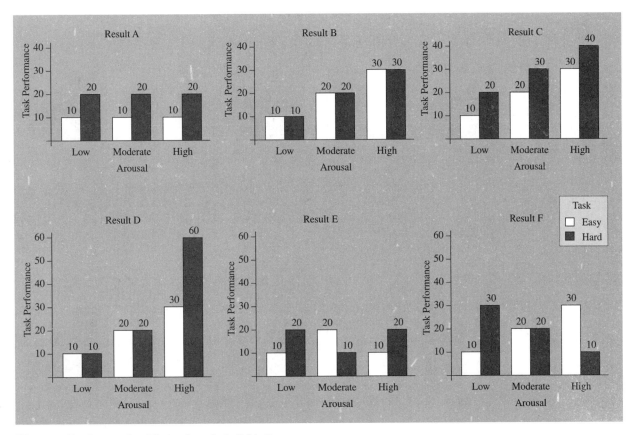

Figure 5   Bar graphs of fictional results in Table 5.

as Figure 3, you can tell there is an interaction by the *lines* not being parallel; as with a bar graph, this shows that there is a different pattern of cell means from row to row.

Consider Figure 4, based on the age and education examples. First look at Results C and D. In Result C, the younger and older sets of bars have the same pattern: both step up by 40. In Result D, both are flat. Within both Results C and D, the younger bars and the older bars have the same pattern. These were the examples that *did not have interactions.* All the other results, which did have interactions, have patterns of bars that are not the same for the younger and older groups. For example, in Result A, the two younger bars are flat, but the older bars show a step up. In Result B, the younger bars show a step down from high school to college, but the older bars show a step up from high school to college. In Results E and F, both younger and older bars show a step up, but the younger bars show a smaller step up than the older bars.

Consider Figure 5. Results A, B, and C show no interaction; within each result, the patterns of bars for low, moderate, and high arousal are the same. Result D is an interaction. You can see this in the figure as follows: the bars within low are flat and the bars within moderate are flat; but for the high arousal bars, there is a step up from easy to hard tasks. Result E's interaction shows steps up for low and high arousal, but a step down for moderate arousal. Result F's interaction is seen in there being a step up for low, flat for moderate, and a step down for hard.

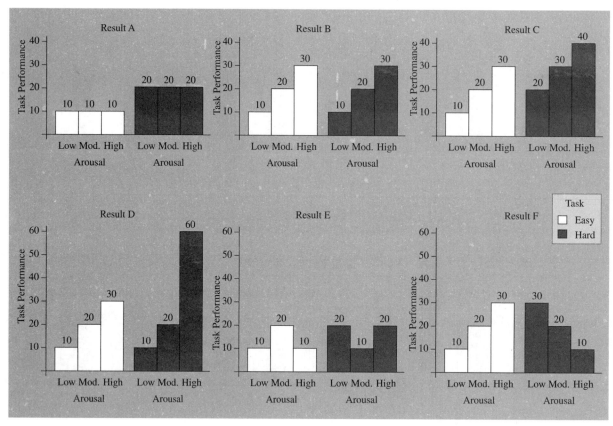

Figure 6   Alternative bar graphs (compared to Figure 5) of fictional results in Table 5.

Figure 6 shows an alternate way of graphing the results from Table 5 than shown in Figure 5. Here we have grouped the bars according to hard versus easy. The easy task bars for low, moderate, and high arousal are next to each other and the hard task bars for low, moderate, and high arousal are next to each other. This alternate way of grouping is completely equivalent in meaning and leads to exactly the same conclusions. For example, in Result A the three hard-task bars are flat and the three easy-task bars are flat. In Results B and C, where there is also no interaction, the three easy-task bars rise up in the same step pattern as the three hard task bars. However, consider Result D, where there is an interaction. The pattern of the easy task bars is different from the pattern of the hard task bars. There is a bigger step up from moderate to high arousal in the hard task bars than there is in the easy task bars.

You can also see *main effects* from these graphs. In Figure 4, a main effect for age would be shown by the bars for younger being overall higher or lower than the bars for older. For example, in Result C, the bars for older are clearly higher than the bars for younger. What about the main effect for the bars that are not grouped together—college versus high school in this example? With these bars, you have to see whether the overall step pattern goes up or down. For example, in Result C, there is also a main effect for education, because the general pattern of the bars for high school to college goes up, and it does this for both the younger and older bars. Result D shows a main effect for age (the older bars are higher than the younger bars). But Result D does not show a main effect for education; the pattern is flat for both the older and younger bars. Result A in Figure 5 shows a main effect for task difficulty but no main effect for arousal. This is because the average heights of the bars are the same for low, moderate, and high arousal, while within each arousal level, the bars step up from easy to hard.

Relation of Interaction and Main Effects

A study can have any combination of main and interaction effects. For example, you can have both main effects and the interaction, as in the pattern in Result F of Table 4. In this result, as you saw, older students earn more (a main effect for age), college students earn more (a main effect for level of education), and how much more college students earn depends on age (the interaction effect). Similarly, in Result D of Table 5, on the average people perform better at hard tasks (a main effect for task difficulty) and at higher levels of arousal (a main effect for arousal level), but the effect of task difficulty shows up only at high levels of arousal (the interaction). (Notice, however, that the main effect for task difficulty—the higher average for hard tasks—is entirely due to the high arousal condition. We have more to say about this kind of situation shortly.)

There can also be an interaction effect with no main effects. Result B of Table 4 is an example. The average level of income is the same for younger and older (no main effect for age), and it is the same for college and high school (no main effect for level of education). Similarly, in Result F of Table 5, the average performance is the same for low, moderate, and high arousal (no main effect for arousal level) and is the same for easy and hard tasks (no main effect for task difficulty). However, in both examples there are clear interactions.

It is also possible for there to be one main effect along with an interaction, one main effect by itself, or no main or interaction effects.

When there is no interaction, a main effect has a straightforward meaning. However, when there is an interaction along with a main effect, things are more complicated. Consider Result D in the arousal and task difficulty example (Table 5). There are two main effects and an interaction. But as we noted earlier, the main effect for task difficulty is entirely due to the high arousal hard task cell. It would be misleading to say anything about hard versus easy tasks overall without also saying that the effect really depends on the level of arousal. You should be especially cautious about the meaning of a main effect when the direction of the effect is reversed for some levels of the other grouping variable.

On the other hand, even when there is an interaction, sometimes the main effect clearly holds up over and above the interaction. That is, the main effect may be there at every level of the other grouping variable, but even more strongly at some points than at others. Consider again Result D in the arousal and task difficulty example (Table 5). In this result, the main effect for arousal holds up over and above the interaction. The effect for arousal is there for both easy and hard tasks; in both cases, low arousal produces the least performance, moderate the next most, and high arousal the most. (There is still an interaction because how much high arousal produces better performance than moderate arousal is more for hard than for easy tasks.)

How are you doing?

Questions 1 to 3 are based on the following results for a fictional study of the effects of vividness and length of examples (the grouping variables) on number of examples recalled (the measured variables).

| | Vividness | | |
Example Length	Low	High	Overall
Short	5	7	6
Long	3	1	2
Overall	4	4	

1. Describe the pattern of results in words.
2. Explain the pattern in terms of numbers.
3. (a) and (b) Make two bar graphs of these results.
4. For a two-way factorial research design, what are the possible combinations of main and interaction effects?
5. When there is both a main and an interaction effect, (a) under what conditions must you be careful in interpreting the main effect, and (b) under what conditions can you still be confident in the overall main effect?

Answers

1. There is a main effect in which short examples are recalled better, there is no main effect for vividness, and there is an interaction effect in which there is a bigger advantage of short over long examples when they are highly vivid.

Figure 7   Answer to "How are you doing?" question 3.

2. The main effect is that on the average people recall six short examples but only two long examples. There is no main effect for vividness because people on the average recall four examples, regardless of how vivid the examples are. The interaction effect is that for short examples, people recall two more highly vivid than low vivid; but for long examples, they recall two fewer highly vivid than low vivid.

3. See Figure 7.

4. All possible combinations: no main or interaction effects; either main effect only; the interaction only; both main effects but no interaction effect; an interaction effect with either main effect; or an interaction effect with both main effects.

5. (a) You should be careful in interpreting the main effect when it is found for only one level of the other grouping variable or when its direction is reversed at different levels of the other grouping variable.

   (b) You can still be confident in the overall main effect when it holds and is in the same direction at each level of the other grouping variable.

Basic Logic of the Two-Way Analysis of Variance

The statistical procedure for analyzing the results of a two-way factorial study is called a *two-way analysis of variance*. In any analysis of variance, you figure an *F* ratio, and this *F* ratio compares a population variance estimate based on the variation *between* the means of the groupings of interest to a population variance estimate based on variation *within* groups.

The Three *F* Ratios in a Two-Way Analysis of Variance

In a two-way analysis of variance, there are three *F* ratios: one for the grouping variable spread across the columns (the column main effect), one for the grouping variable spread across the rows (the row main effect), and one for the interaction effect. In the test difficulty and sensitivity example, there would be one *F* for the main effect for Test Difficulty, one *F* for main effect for Sensitivity, and one *F* for the interaction of Test Difficulty with Sensitivity.

The numerator of each of these three *F* ratios will be a between-groups population variance estimate based on the groupings being compared for the particular main or interaction effect. The within-groups variance estimate is the same for all three *F* ratios; it is always the average of the population variance estimates made from the scores in each of the cells. Since this within-groups variance estimate is based on estimates from each cell, it can also be called a *within-cells variance estimate*.

Logic of the *F* Ratios for the Column and Row Main Effects

One way of understanding how the analysis is done for main effects is as follows. Consider the main effect for the columns grouping variable. Figure the following *F* ratio: the numerator is a between-groups variance estimate based on the variation between the column marginal means. The denominator is a within-groups (within-cells) variance estimate based on averaging the variance estimates from each of the cells. Think again of the Aron and colleagues (2005) example. The *F* ratio for test difficulty (the columns grouping variable, as we have drawn the chart—see Table 6) is figured as follows. The numerator, the between-groups variance estimate, is based on the difference between the easy test difficulty marginal mean and

Table 6 Mean Levels of Negative Mood in the Aron and colleagues (2005) Study

		Test Difficulty	
		Easy	Hard
Sensitivity	Not High	2.43	2.56
	High	2.19	3.01

BOX 1   Personality and Situational Influences on Behavior: An Interaction Effect

In a certain sense, the study of statistics is training in a style of seeing the world.

Regardless of whether psychological researchers draw an explicit comparison between analysis of variance and the way they think, they probably often use the crisp model of analysis of variance as a guide to their own logic. They do this not only when analyzing data or even when designing research, but they probably also use the analysis of variance as a metaphor when theorizing as well.

An important example of how statistics has influenced the way psychologists think about their subject matter, not just their data, is in the history of the study of personality. In the 1960s, the field of personality was forever changed by the work of Walter Mischel (1968; for an insider's description, see Mischel, 2007). Mischel appeared to have demonstrated that, as a rule, *situation* (a street signal turning red, for example, or a well-dressed person asking for help) is a far better predictor of how a person will act than any *personality trait* (for example, that a person is by nature cautious or altruistic). The embattled personality theorists, typically trained in psychodynamics, struggled to defend themselves within the rules of the game as Mischel had defined them: how much of the variation in behavior could really be predicted by their personality measures? That is, personality theorists were forced to think statistically.

One result of this challenge was something called "interactionism" (e.g., Endler & Magnusson, 1976; for a recent discussion of the issue, see Reynolds et al., 2010). That is the idea that behavior is best predicted by the interaction of person and situation. You can instantly guess what statistical method has had its influence. (You are studying it in this chapter!)

For example, according to interactionism, neither the personality trait of anxiety nor the situation of taking the SAT is nearly as good a predictor of anxiety as knowing that a person with a given tendency toward anxiety perceives the taking of the SAT as an anxiety-producing situation. The emphasis is that behavior is being altered constantly by the individual's internal disposition interacting with his or her perception of the changing situation. (In fact, even Walter Mischel [2004] later proposed a theory of this kind.)

Let's follow an anxious man through some situations. He may feel even more—or perhaps less—anxiety while proceeding from the testing situation to a dark, empty parking lot, depending again on the interaction of his trait anxiety and his perception of this new situation. The same is true as he proceeds to drive home on the highway, to open the garage door, to enter an empty house.

According to interactionism, the person is not a passive component but an "intentional active agent in this interaction process" (Endler & Magnusson, 1976, p. 968).

The important part of the person aspect of the interaction is how a person thinks about a situation. The important part of the situation aspect of the interaction is, again, its meaning for the person. (Note that the Aron et al. [2005] study we have been using as an example in this chapter is a current version of just such an interaction of personality [sensitivity] with a situation [being faced with an easy or a hard test].) Some form of interactionism now appears to be true in general for explaining what people do and the idea continues to be highly important in personality psychology. For example, whether one is a "morning person" or a "night person" (the personality trait) interacts with one's work schedule in predicting one's alertness (Cavallera & Giudici, 2008). (It is now turning out that interactionism may even explain the way ordinary people typically *understand* other people's behavior [Kammrath et al., 2005]. That is, people may be intuitive statisticians!)

This influence of statistics on theory has been happening throughout the history of nearly every area of psychology. Indeed, the influence of recent statistical developments on thinking has become particularly important in recent years as new ideas are developed in statistical methods (such as multilevel modeling) and as new opportunities emerge as psychologists more thoroughly take into account the role of culture, genetics, and neural processes in predicting behavior. In a sense, we could say that pioneers in statistics are now determining not only the complexity of psychological research that is possible, but the depth of theorizing itself. They are carving out the channels through which psychologists' actual thinking patterns flow and therefore are shaping and directing much of our understanding of psychology.

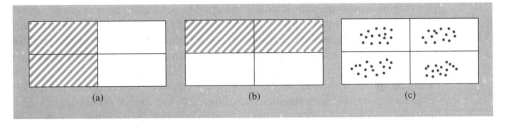

Figure 8 A diagram to help you understand a two-way factorial analysis of variance: (a) the column between-groups variance estimate as based on the difference between the mean of the participants in the first (shaded) and second (unshaded) columns; (b) the row between-groups variance estimate as based on the difference between the mean of the participants in the top (shaded) and bottom (unshaded) rows; and (c) the within-groups (within-cells) variance estimate as based on the variation among scores in each cell.

the hard test difficulty marginal mean. The denominator, the within-groups (within-cells) variance estimate, is based on averaging the population variance estimates from within each of the four cells.

The procedure for the row main effect is the same idea. You figure it using a between-groups variance estimate based on the difference between the two row marginal means. (The Aron and colleagues study was designed so that the row marginal means are the mean for all the nonhighly sensitive participants and the mean for all the highly sensitive participants.)

Figure 8a shows the column between-groups variance estimate as based on the difference between the mean of the scores in the first column (the shaded area) and the mean of the scores in the second column (the unshaded area). Figure 8b shows the row between-groups estimate as based on the difference between the mean of the scores in its top row (the shaded area) and the mean of the scores in the bottom row (the unshaded area). And Figure 8c shows the within-groups variance estimate (used for all the *F* ratios) as based on the variation among the scores in each of the cells.

Logic of the *F* Ratio for the Interaction Effect

The logic of the *F* ratio for the interaction effect is a bit more complex. One approach is to think of the interaction effect as the combinations left over after considering the row and column main effects. Consider a study with two grouping variables, each of which has two levels. (As you learned earlier, this is called a 2 × 2 research design.) In this study, the main effects have grouped the four cells into rows and columns. But it is also possible to divide the cells into other kinds of groupings. Figure 9, based on the Aron and colleagues (2005) study, shows a remaining possible organization of the four cells into two larger groupings: (a) one grouping of two cells consisting of the upper left cell (Not High Sensitivity/Easy Test Difficulty) along with the lower right cell (High Sensitivity/Hard Test Difficulty), and (b) another grouping of two cells consisting of the lower left cell (High Sensitivity/Easy Test Difficulty) and the upper right cell (Not High Sensitivity/Hard Test Difficulty). The between-groups variance estimate for the interaction effect can then be figured from the variation between the means of these two groupings. (In this example, these two groupings of cells are the diagonals.)

With a 2 × 2 design, there is only one organization of pairs of cells that is not already accounted for by the row and column organizations: the grouping pattern

Figure 9 Interaction as a comparison of scores in the shaded cells (easy test difficulty and high sensitivity; hard test difficulty and not high sensitivity) to the mean of the scores in the unshaded cells (easy test difficulty and not high sensitivity; hard test difficulty and high sensitivity) in the study by Aron and colleagues (2005).

(of diagonals) shown in the example in Figure 9. But the situation is not so simple with a larger two-way design, such as a 2×3 study (a study in which the first variable has two levels and the second variable has three levels, such as the study of task difficulty and arousal we considered earlier). In such a study, there is more than one way to make the groupings, and all must be taken into account. Thus, it can be quite complicated to figure the between-groups variance estimate for the interaction effect when dealing with situations other than a 2×2 design. Fortunately, it turns out that figuring the between-groups variance estimate for the interaction is much more straightforward when using the structural model approach. Thus, we describe the actual figuring for the factorial analysis of variance using the structural model approach in a later Advanced Topic section in this chapter. (But the procedures we have just described actually work quite well and simply when you have the very common 2×2 situation.)

Assumptions in the Factorial Analysis of Variance

The assumptions for a factorial analysis of variance are the same as for the one-way analysis of variance. However, in a factorial analysis of variance, the requirements of population normality and equal variances apply to the populations that go with each cell.

Extensions and Special Cases of the Analysis of Variance

The analysis of variance is an extremely versatile technique. We cannot, in this introductory text, go into the details of the statistical procedures for handling all the possibilities. (These are covered in most intermediate statistics texts in psychology as well as in what are often called "experimental design" textbooks.) However, it is possible to describe some of the main variations and to provide some insight into the basic modifications to what you have already learned.

Three-Way and Higher Analysis of Variance Designs

The most straightforward extension of the two-way analysis of variance is to studies involving three-way designs (in which there are three grouping variables) or even four-way and higher designs. The basic logic of such studies is the same as we have described in this chapter, except that there are additional main and interaction effects.

Sometimes a study involves secondary grouping variables, such as the order of the presentation of different parts of an experimental task or which of two experimenters conducted the study for each participant. Such secondary grouping variables are usually of interest only if they interact with the major grouping variables. In these situations, the researcher may start with a multiway factorial analysis of variance. If these grouping variables of secondary interest do not have significant interaction effects with the grouping variables of primary interest, you run the analysis again, ignoring these secondary variables. The design then becomes a more manageable two-way or three-way analysis of variance.

The resulting analysis is said to be *collapsed* over the variables that are being ignored.

Repeated Measures Analysis of Variance

In all the situations in this chapter, the different cells or groupings are based on scores from *different individuals.* Sometimes, however, a researcher measures the same individual in several different situations. (In a study with only one grouping variable of this kind that has two levels, such as the levels of before and after some treatment, you can use a *t* test for dependent means. But if there are more than two levels or if there is another grouping variable involved as well, you have to use analysis of variance.) Consider a study in which, for each participant, you measure speed of recognizing a syllable when embedded in three word types: familiar words, unfamiliar words, and nonword sounds. The result is that for each participant you have an average number of errors for each word type. Or suppose you do a study of psychotherapy effects testing patients on their depression before, immediately following, and again three months after therapy. In each of these examples, you have three groups of scores, but in each example, all three scores are from the same people. These studies are examples of repeated measures designs.

Repeated measures designs are analyzed with a **repeated measures analysis of variance**. It has this name because the same participants are being measured repeatedly. This kind of design and analysis is also called a *within-subjects design* or *within-subjects analysis of variance* because the comparison is within, not between, the different participants or subjects. (The American Psychological Association recommends the use of the term *participants* rather than "subjects.")

Sometimes a repeated measures variable is crossed in the same study with an ordinary between-subjects variable. For example, in the therapy study, there might be a control group not getting the therapy but tested at the same three points in time. This would be a *mixed* 2 (therapy versus control group) $\times$ 3 (before, after, 3 months after) design in which the first variable is the usual between-subjects type and the second is a repeated measures type. It is even possible to have two repeated measures factors or even more complicated combinations.

We cover *repeated measures analysis of variance* in more detail in a Web Chapter available at *www.pearsoned.co.in/prc/home.*

repeated measures analysis of variance analysis of variance for a repeated measures design in which each person is tested more than once so that the levels of the grouping variable(s) are different times or types of testing for the same persons.

How are you doing?

1. In a two-way analysis of variance, what is the numerator of the *F* ratio for the row main effect?
2. In a 2×2 analysis of variance, what is the numerator of the *F* ratio for the interaction effect?
3. In any two-way analysis of variance, what is the denominator of the *F* ratio for (a) each main effect and (b) the interaction?
4. What are the assumptions for a factorial analysis of variance?
5. (a) What does it mean when a research study reports that "results were collapsed over order of testing"? (b) How is a repeated measures analysis of variance different from an ordinary between-subjects analysis of variance? (c) What is a mixed design?

Answers

1. The numerator of the F ratio for the row main effect is the estimated population variance estimate based on the variation between the two row means.
2. The numerator of the F ratio for the interaction effect is the estimated population variance estimate based on the variation between the means of the two diagonals.
3. (a) The denominator of the F ratio for each main effect is the within-groups (within-cells) population variance estimate. (b) The denominator of the F ratio for the interaction is the same thing: within-groups (within-cells) population variance estimate.
4. The populations associated with each cell follow a normal distribution and all have the same variance.
5. (a) Which order of testing a participant was given is ignored in the analysis. (b) In a repeated measures analysis of variance, each participant has a score in each of the groups or cells of the analysis; in an ordinary, between-subjects analysis of variance, each participant has a score in only one group or cell. (c) One factor is a repeated measures factor and one factor is between-subjects.

Controversy: Dichotomizing Numeric Variables

Suppose a developmental psychologist measured anxiety and social skills in a group of children. The psychologist then observed their behavior in a playgroup with other children, focusing on their aggressive responses. To examine the results of this study, the researcher divided the children in half on their anxiety scores (making a high anxiety and a low anxiety group), then divided them in half on social skills (making a high and low social skills group). The combinations resulted in four groups: High Anxiety/High Social Skills; High Anxiety/Low Social Skills; and so forth. Having divided up the children in this way, the researcher then carried out a two-way (2×2) factorial analysis of variance, with grouping variables of anxiety (high versus low) and social skills (high versus low). With this analysis, the researcher could see whether there was a main effect of anxiety on aggression, a main effect of social skills on aggression, and/or an interaction effect of anxiety and social skills on aggression.

The thing to notice here is that the researcher divided up the children into two groups on anxiety and two groups on social skills. Consider anxiety first. In this study anxiety was a numeric, quantitative variable measured along a continuum. Nevertheless, the researcher ignored all the fine gradations and simply divided the group in half, making a high anxiety and a low anxiety grouping. This resulted in everyone in the high anxiety grouping being treated as having the same (high) level of anxiety and everyone in the low anxiety grouping being treated as having the same (low) level of anxiety.

This kind of division is called **dichotomizing**—making into a dichotomy, or two groupings. Since the dichotomizing is usually done by taking those above and below the median, it is also called making a *median split* of the scores. In this example, the researcher also dichotomized (made a median split) on social skills.

The advantage of dichotomizing numeric variables is that you can then do a factorial analysis of variance, with all of its advantages of efficiency and testing interaction effects. Also, most psychologists are familiar with factorial analysis of variance. Many psychologists are less familiar with alternative procedures that

dichotomizing dividing the scores for a variable into two groups. Also called *median split.*

accomplish much the same thing but do not require dichotomizing. (The alternative procedures one would use in these cases are mainly those based on multiple regression.)

A major disadvantage of dichotomizing is that you lose information when you reduce a whole range of scores to just two, high and low; it is just less accurate. Owen and Froman (2005) outlined the problem clearly (referring to dichotomizing by splitting the sample in half at the median): "With a median split, a person's score barely above the median is now put into the same category (*high*) as a person three standard deviations above the mean. That does not make good sense or good use of the data" (p. 499). One result is that the effect size and power of a study that dichotomizes is lower than when using the original scores (DeCoster, Iselin, & Gallucci, 2009; MacCallum et al., 2002; Taylor et al., 2006). Cohen (1983) calculated this reduction in power and effect size to be between 20% and 66%! It is equivalent, he suggested, to "discarding one-third to two-thirds of the sample" (p. 253).

On the other hand, many researchers dichotomize their variables, claiming that the effect is "conservative"—that, while it may increase the chance of a Type II error (failing to reject the null hypothesis when in fact it is false), it does not increase the chance of a Type I error (rejecting the null hypothesis when it is true). Put another way, dichotomizing reduces accuracy so that it is harder, not easier, to get significant results.

However, even assuming that, on the average, the effect of dichotomizing a single variable is conservative, there are still problems. One concern is that the analysis is now *overly* conservative in the sense that true results will go undiscovered (you will make Type II errors) and true effect sizes will be underestimated. There is also a general inaccuracy. Dichotomizing is conservative *on the average*. But in any particular case the inaccuracy in dichotomizing could happen to work in favor of the researcher's hypothesis, making a true nondifference come out significant in the study and a true large effect size come out smaller.

Indeed, Maxwell and Delaney (1993) have shown that, when both variables in a two-way factorial design are dichotomized (as in our example of anxiety and social skills), the effect is *not* automatically conservative. Under a number of common conditions in psychology research, dichotomizing two variables can produce the opposite of conservative effects even on the average. According to Maxwell and Delaney, you should be especially skeptical of the results of studies using a two-way analysis of variance in which both variables have been dichotomized.

There are, however, a few limited instances when dichotomization is appropriate. For example, MacCallum and colleagues (2002) note that it is appropriate when there is clear and convincing evidence that the two groups created by dichotomization represent very different types of people (see also DeCoster et al., 2009). Recall in the Aron and colleagues (2005) example that the researchers dichotomized scores on the measure of sensitivity to create a group of individuals who were not highly sensitive and a group who were highly sensitive. In their article, Aron and colleagues cited evidence from a variety of sources, including research on sensitivity in both infants and animals, indicating that sensitivity is best considered as a dichotomous variable rather than as a continuous variable. That is, the evidence is that people are essentially either highly sensitive or not, and variations along the scale are just due to the test's not being perfectly accurate.

Interestingly, dichotomizing can also be misleading to our understanding in important applied situations. Markon, Chmielewski, and Miller (2011) analyzed data from 58 studies (involving a total of 59,575 participants) focusing on different kinds of clinical conditions, such as depression and personality disorders. They found that across the many different kinds of mental illnesses studied, at least when using standard measurement procedures, it is more accurate to consider these conditions as continuous, running from none to some to a lot, rather than as a condition that a person either has or doesn't have.

In spite of the common problems of dichotomization, dichotomizing (even of both variables in two-way analysis of variance) is still surprisingly common in psychology research. It is our impression, however, that it is dying out.

Factorial Analysis of Variance in Research Articles

In a factorial analysis of variance, researchers usually give a description plus a table or figure. The text gives the F ratio and the information that goes with it for each main and interaction effect. The table gives the cell means and sometimes also the marginal means. If there is a significant interaction effect, there may also be a graph.

Van Prooijen and colleagues (2004) carried out a series of studies focusing on the effect of belongingness (whether a person feels included in, or excluded from, a group) and being able to voice one's opinion about a decision. The researchers examined the effect of these two variables on a person's satisfaction with the decision-making process (also known as *procedural satisfaction*). The participants were Dutch university students who were asked to imagine themselves as members of a team working on a project. They were then told that one member of the team would have to be excluded from a hypothetical project. Some students were told that they were not chosen to be excluded (the *inclusion* condition), other students were told that they were the person selected to be excluded from the project (the *exclusion* condition), and a final group of students were told that it was unclear whether they would be excluded (the *not yet known* condition). (Thus, the belongingness grouping variable had three levels: inclusion, exclusion, and not yet known.) Then, each student was either told that he or she would or would not be able to voice an opinion about a financial bonus to be received by the group (the *voice* condition and *no voice* condition, respectively). (Thus, the procedure grouping variable—as the researchers called it—had two levels: voice and no voice.) The researchers measured procedural satisfaction by asking the students to rate how satisfied they were with the way they were treated by the other people on their team. Here is how they reported the results:

> A 3 $\times$ 2 analysis of variance (ANOVA) on the procedural satisfaction scale showed main effects of both procedure, $F(1, 136) = 94.28, p < .01, \eta^2 = .41$, and group belongingness, $F(2, 136) = 3.70, p < .03, \eta^2 = .05$. More important . . . was that this analysis also yielded the predicted interaction effect, $F(2, 136) = 3.46, p < .04, \eta^2 = .05$. The cell means and standard deviations are shown in Table [7]. . . . Findings . . . showed that inclusion in a group leads to stronger effects of voice as opposed to no-voice procedures on participants' ratings of procedural satisfaction than exclusion from a group. (p. 70)

Note that van Prooijen and colleagues (2004) provided the effect size for each main effect and the interaction effect. The effect sizes were shown as values of eta squared, η^2, which is another name for R^2. In an Advanced Topic section later in this chapter, we describe how to figure R^2 for a factorial analysis of variance. Notice in Table 7 that the researchers used subscript letters ($_{a, b, c}$) to show the results of post hoc comparisons of the means.

Table 7 Means and Standard Deviations of Participants' Procedural Satisfaction Ratings as a Function of Group Belongingness and Procedure, Experiment 1

| Procedure | Group Belongingness | | | | | |
| | Inclusion | | Exclusion | | Not yet known | |
	M	*SD*	*M*	*SD*	*M*	*SD*
Voice	4.86_a	1.82	3.31_b	1.83	4.46_a	1.95
No voice	1.89_c	1.14	1.81_c	0.84	1.69_c	0.83

Note: Means are on 7-point scales, with higher values indicating more positive ratings of procedural satisfaction. Means with no subscript in common differ as indicated by a least significant difference test for multiple comparisons between means ($p < .05$).
Source: van Prooijen, J. W., van den Bos, K., & Wilke, H. A. M. (2004). Group belongingness and procedural justice: Social inclusion and exclusion by peers affects the psychology of voice. *Journal of Personality and Social Psychology, 87,* 66–79. Published by the American Psychological Association. Reprinted with permission.

As we mentioned earlier in the chapter, researchers sometimes show interaction effects using a kind of line graph. Consider an example. Shao and Skarlicki (2009) conducted a study to examine whether there was an interaction effect of mindfulness and gender (the two grouping or independent variables) on academic performance (the measured or dependent variable) among students in an MBA (Master's of Business Administration) program. Mindfulness can be defined as a person's tendency to be "attentive to and aware of what is taking place in the present" (Brown & Ryan, 2003, p. 822) and the researchers measured it using a 15-item survey. Based on previous neuroscience research on mindfulness and gender differences in activation of the left and right brain hemispheres, the researchers hypothesized that women would show a stronger positive association between mindfulness and academic performance than men. The results of the study are shown in the line graph in Figure 10. As you can see, the results supported the researchers' hypothesis: Women with higher mindfulness had better academic performance than women with lower mindfulness, but that was not the case among men (and in fact, the researchers noted that mindfulness was not significantly associated with performance among men). In a line graph, such as Figure 10, you can tell that there is an interaction by the lines not being parallel. As with a bar graph, this shows that there is a different pattern of cell means from row to row.

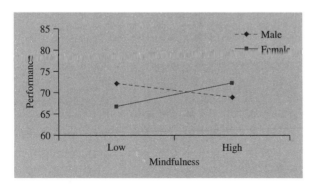

Figure 10 Two-way interaction of mindfulness and gender on performance.
Source: Shao, R., & Skarlicki, D. P. (2009). The role of mindfulness in predicting individual performance. *Canadian Journal of Behavioral Science, 41,* 195–201. Published by the American Psychological Association. Reprinted with permission.

Advanced Topic: Figuring a Two-Way Analysis of Variance

As we noted earlier, to figure the interaction effect in a factorial analysis of variance beyond a 2 × 2 design, it is much easier to use the structural model approach you learned in the Advanced Topic sections of *Introduction to the Analysis of Variance*. Rather than mix approaches, researchers carry out the entire factorial analysis of variance using the structural model approach. Thus, in this section we first consider the structural model approach as it applies to factorial analysis of variance and then go into the details of how to do the figuring for a full factorial analysis of variance. As you will soon see, this Advanced Topic section builds directly on the Advanced Topic section in *Introduction to the Analysis of Variance* on the structural model in the analysis of variance.

The Structural Model for the Two-Way Analysis of Variance

From the structural model perspective, each score's overall deviation from the grand mean of all scores can be divided into several parts. In a two-way analysis, there are four such parts of this overall deviation (see Figure 11):

1. The score's deviation from the mean of its cell (used for the within-groups population variance estimate).
2. The deviation of the score's row's mean from the grand mean (used for the between-groups population variance estimate for the main effect for the grouping variable that divides the rows).
3. The deviation of the score's column's mean from the grand mean (used for the between-groups population variance estimate for the main effect for the grouping variable that divides the columns).

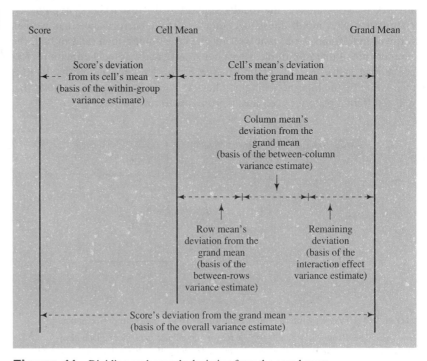

Figure 11 Dividing each score's deviation from the grand mean.

4. What remains after subtracting the other three deviations from the overall deviation from the grand mean (used for the between-groups estimate for the interaction effect).

Steps for the Two-Way Analysis of Variance

When figuring an analysis of variance using the structural model, you figure the F ratios as follows:

❹ **Figure the mean of each cell, row, and column, plus the grand mean of all scores.**

❸ **Figure all the deviation scores of each type.**

❷ **Square each deviation score.** This gives the squared deviations.

❶ **Add up the squared deviation scores of each type.** This gives the sums of squared deviations.

❺ **Divide each sum of squared deviations by its appropriate degrees of freedom.** This gives the variance estimates.

❻ **Divide the various between-groups variance estimates by the within-groups variance estimate.** This gives the F ratios.

In terms of formulas, the sums of squares are as follows:

$$SS_{\text{Rows}} = \Sigma(M_{\text{Row}} - GM)^2 \qquad (1)$$

The sum of squared deviations for rows is the sum of each score's row's mean's squared deviation from the grand mean.

$$SS_{\text{Columns}} = \Sigma(M_{\text{Column}} - GM)^2 \qquad (2)$$

The sum of squared deviations for columns is the sum of each score's column's mean's squared deviation from the grand mean.

$$SS_{\text{Interaction}} = \Sigma[(X - GM) - (X - M) - (M_{\text{Row}} - GM) \\ - (M_{\text{Column}} - GM)]^2 \qquad (3)$$

The sum of squared deviations for the interaction is the sum of the squares of each score's deviation from the grand mean minus its deviation from its cell's mean, minus its row's mean's deviation from the grand mean, minus its column's mean's deviation from the grand mean.

$$SS_{\text{Within}} = \Sigma(X - M)^2 \qquad (4)$$

The sum of squared deviations within groups (within cells) is the sum of each score's squared deviation from its cell's mean.

$$SS_{\text{Total}} = \Sigma(X - GM)^2 \qquad (5)$$

The sum of squared deviations total is the sum of each score's squared deviation from the grand mean.

In these formulas, SS_{Rows}, SS_{Columns}, $SS_{\text{Interaction}}$, and SS_{Within} are the sums of squared deviations for rows, columns, interaction, and within groups (within cells). The sum sign (Σ) tells you to add up over all scores (not just over all rows or columns or cells). GM is the grand mean; X is the score. M_{Row} and M_{Column} are the mean of a score's row or column, and M is the mean of a score's cell.

As was the case for the one-way analysis of variance, here too the different individual sums of squares add up to the total sums of squares. (You can use this as a check on your arithmetic.) Stated as a formula,

The sum of squared deviations total is the sum of squared deviations for rows, plus the sum of squared deviations for columns, plus the sum of squared deviations for the interaction, plus the sum of squared deviations within groups (within cells).

$$SS_{\text{Total}} = SS_{\text{Rows}} + SS_{\text{Columns}} + SS_{\text{Interaction}} + SS_{\text{Within}} \tag{6}$$

The formulas for the population variance estimates are, as was the case for the one-way analysis of variance using the structural model approach, the sums of squares divided by the degrees of freedom:

The population variance estimate based on the variation between rows is the sum of squared deviations for rows divided by the degrees of freedom for rows.

$$S^2_{\text{Rows}} \quad \text{or} \quad MS_{\text{Rows}} = \frac{SS_{\text{Rows}}}{df_{\text{Rows}}} \tag{7}$$

The population variance estimate based on the variation between columns is the sum of squared deviations for columns divided by the degrees of freedom for columns.

$$S^2_{\text{Columns}} \quad \text{or} \quad MS_{\text{Columns}} = \frac{SS_{\text{Columns}}}{df_{\text{Columns}}} \tag{8}$$

The population variance estimate based on the variation associated with the interaction is the sum of squared deviations for the interaction divided by the degrees of freedom for the interaction.

$$S^2_{\text{Interaction}} \quad \text{or} \quad MS_{\text{Interaction}} = \frac{SS_{\text{Interaction}}}{df_{\text{Interaction}}} \tag{9}$$

The population variance estimate based on the variation within groups (within cells) is the sum of squared deviations within groups (within cells) divided by the within-groups (within-cells) degrees of freedom.

$$S^2_{\text{Within}} \quad \text{or} \quad MS_{\text{Within}} = \frac{SS_{\text{Within}}}{df_{\text{Within}}} \tag{10}$$

The F ratios are the population variance estimates for the different effects, each divided by the within-groups population variance estimate:

The F ratio for the row main effect is the population variance estimate based on the variation between rows divided rows divided by the population variance estimate based on the variation within groups (within cells).

$$F_{\text{Rows}} = \frac{S^2_{\text{Rows}}}{S^2_{\text{Within}}} \quad \text{or} \quad \frac{MS_{\text{Rows}}}{MS_{\text{Within}}} \tag{11}$$

The F ratio for the column main effect is the population variance estimate based on the variation between columns divided by the population variance estimate based on the variation within groups (within cells).

$$F_{\text{Columns}} = \frac{S^2_{\text{Columns}}}{S^2_{\text{Within}}} \quad \text{or} \quad \frac{MS_{\text{Columns}}}{MS_{\text{Within}}} \tag{12}$$

$$F_{\text{Interaction}} = \frac{S^2_{\text{Interaction}}}{S^2_{\text{Within}}} \quad \text{or} \quad \frac{MS_{\text{Interaction}}}{MS_{\text{Within}}} \qquad (13)$$

> The F ratio for the interaction effect is the population variance estimate based on the variation associated with the interaction divided by the population variance estimate based on the variation within groups (within cells).

Degrees of Freedom in a Two-Way Analysis of Variance

Degrees of Freedom for Between-Groups Variance Estimates for the Main Effects The degrees of freedom for each main effect (each between-groups variance estimate) is the number of levels of the grouping variable minus 1. For example, if there are two levels to a grouping variable, as in each main effect in the Aron and colleagues (2005) study, there is one degree of freedom for each of these main effects. In the arousal levels and task difficulty examples we considered earlier, the columns grouping variable (arousal level) main effect had three levels. Thus, there were two degrees of freedom for this grouping variable's main effect.

Stated as formulas,

$$df_{\text{Rows}} = N_{\text{Rows}} - 1 \qquad (14)$$

> The degrees of freedom for the rows main effect is the number of rows minus 1.

$$df_{\text{Columns}} = N_{\text{Columns}} - 1 \qquad (15)$$

> The degrees of freedom for the columns main effect is the number of columns minus 1.

Degrees of Freedom for the Interaction Effect Variance Estimate The degrees of freedom for the variance estimate for the interaction effect is the total number of cells minus the number of degrees of freedom for both main effects, minus 1. In the Aron and colleagues (2005) study, there were four cells and one degree of freedom for each main effect. This leaves two degrees of freedom, minus 1 more, leaving one degree of freedom for the interaction. In the arousal level and task difficulty examples, there were six cells. There were two degrees of freedom for the column effect and one for the row effect (easy versus hard task). This leaves three degrees of freedom. When one more is subtracted, there are two degrees of freedom left for the interaction.

Stated as a formula,

$$df_{\text{Interaction}} = N_{\text{Cells}} - df_{\text{Rows}} - df_{\text{Columns}} - 1 \qquad (16)$$

> The degrees of freedom for the interaction effect is the number of cells minus the degrees of freedom for the row main effect minus the degrees of freedom for the column main effect minus 1.

Applying the formula to the Aron and colleagues study,

$$df_{\text{Interaction}} = N_{\text{Cells}} - df_{\text{Rows}} - df_{\text{Columns}} - 1 = 4 - 1 - 1 - 1 = 1.$$

Applying the formula to the arousal and task difficulty example,

$$df_{\text{Interaction}} = N_{\text{Cells}} - df_{\text{Rows}} - df_{\text{Columns}} - 1 = 6 - 1 - 2 - 1 = 2.$$

Degrees of Freedom for the Within-Groups Population Variance Estimate As usual, the within-groups degrees of freedom is the sum of the degrees of freedom for all the groups (in this case, all the cells). For each cell, you take its number of scores minus 1, then add up what you get for all the cells. In terms of a formula,

$$df_{\text{Within}} = df_1 + df_2 + \cdots + df_{\text{Last}} \qquad (17)$$

> The degrees of freedom for the within-groups (within-cells) population variance estimate is the sum of the degrees of freedom for all the cells.

In this formula, $df_1, df_2, \ldots, df_{Last}$ are the degrees of freedom for each cell (the number of scores in the cell minus 1), in succession, from the first cell to the last.

Total Degrees of Freedom   The total degrees of freedom, as usual, is the number of scores minus 1. In terms of a formula,

> The total degrees of freedom is the number of scores minus 1.

$$df_{Total} = N - 1 \qquad (18)$$

You can also figure the total degrees of freedom by adding up all the individual degrees of freedom (for columns, rows, interaction, and within). This provides a check of your arithmetic in figuring degrees of freedom. In terms of a formula,

> The total degrees of freedom are the degrees of freedom for the row main effect plus the degrees of freedom for the column main effect plus the degrees of freedom for the interaction effect plus the degrees of freedom for the within-groups (within-cells) population variance estimate.

$$df_{Total} = df_{Rows} + df_{Columns} + df_{Interaction} + df_{Within} \qquad (19)$$

Table for a Two-Way Analysis of Variance

The analysis of variance table in a two-way analysis is similar to the ones involving one-way analysis of variance. However, with a two-way analysis of variance there is a line in the table for each between-groups effect (that is, for the columns main effect, the rows main effect, and the interaction). Table 8 shows the layout.

Example   Let's return to the Aron and colleagues (2005) example, in which students, who were either highly sensitive or not highly sensitive, took an easy test or a hard test. The study was a 2×2 factorial design, with grouping variables of sensitivity and test difficulty. The variable measured was students' level of negative mood. There were 160 students in the original study, but, to keep the figuring simple, we have made up scores that give the same cell and marginal means, but with only five students per cell. The cell means and marginal means are shown in Table 9. The scores and the figuring for all the deviations are shown in Table 10. Table 11 shows the cutoff F values and the analysis of variance table. Figure 2 (earlier in the chapter) graphs the results. We can explore the example following the usual step-by-step hypothesis-testing procedure.

Table 9   Cell and Marginal Means for Level of Negative Mood

		Test Difficulty		
		Easy	Hard	
Sensitivity	Not High	2.43	2.56	2.50
	High	2.19	3.01	2.60
		2.31	2.79	

Source: Data from Aron et al. (2005).

Table 8   Layout of an Analysis of Variance Table for a Two-Way Analysis of Variance

Source	SS	df	MS	F
Between:				
Columns	$SS_{Columns}$	$df_{Columns}$	$MS_{Columns}$	$F_{Columns}$
Rows	SS_{Rows}	df_{Rows}	MS_{Rows}	F_{Rows}
Interaction	$SS_{Interaction}$	$df_{Interaction}$	$MS_{Interaction}$	$F_{Interaction}$
Within	SS_{Within}	df_{Within}	MS_{Within}	
Total	SS_{Total}	df_{Total}		

Table 10 Scores, Squared Deviations, and Sums of Squared Deviations for Fictional Data Based on the Aron and Colleagues (2005) Study

		Easy Test Difficulty						Hard Test Difficulty			
X	$(X - GM)^2$	$(X - M)^2$	$(M_{Row} - GM)^2$	$(M_{Column} - GM)^2$	INT^2	X	$(X - GM)^2$	$(X - M)^2$	$(M_{Row} - GM)^2$	$(M_{Column} - GM)^2$	INT^2
Not Highly Sensitive											
2.63	.01	.04	.00	.06	.03	2.69	.02	.02	.00	.06	.03
2.53	.00	.01	.00	.06	.03	2.31	.06	.06	.00	.06	.03
2.25	.09	.03	.00	.06	.03	2.45	.01	.01	.00	.06	.03
2.22	.11	.04	.00	.06	.03	2.80	.06	.06	.00	.06	.03
2.52	.00	.01	.00	.06	.03	2.55	.00	.00	.00	.06	.03
12.15	.21	.13	.00	.30	.15	12.80	.15	.15	.00	.30	.15
Highly Sensitive											
2.06	.24	.02	.00	.06	.03	3.21	.44	.04	.00	.06	.03
2.32	.05	.02	.00	.06	.03	3.21	.44	.04	.00	.06	.03
2.04	.26	.02	.00	.06	.03	2.77	.05	.06	.00	.06	.03
2.31	.06	.01	.00	.06	.03	2.83	.08	.03	.00	.06	.03
2.22	.11	.00	.00	.06	.03	3.03	.23	.00	.00	.06	.03
10.95	.72	.07	.00	.30	.15	15.05	1.24	.17	.00	.30	.15

GM = grand mean (mean of all the scores)
M = mean of the score's cell
M_{Row} = mean of the score's row
M_{Column} = mean of the score's column
INT = score's remaining deviation for the interaction

Examples of figuring of deviations, using the first score in the Not Highly Sensitive/Easy Test cell:

$$(X - GM)^2 = (2.63 - 2.55)^2 = .08^2 = .01$$
$$(X - M)^2 = (2.63 - 2.43)^2 = .20^2 = .04$$
$$(M_{Row} - GM)^2 = (2.50 - 2.55)^2 = -.05^2 = .00$$
$$(M_{Column} - GM)^2 = (2.31 - 2.55)^2 = -.24^2 = .06$$
$$INT^2 = [(X - GM) - (X - M) - (M_{Row} - GM) - (M_{Column} - GM)]^2$$
$$= [(.08) - (.20) - (-.05) - (-.24)]^2 = (.08 - .20 + .05 + .24)^2 = .17^2 = .03$$
$$SS_{Total} = .21 + .15 + .72 + 1.24 = 2.32$$
$$SS_{Within} = .13 + .15 + .07 + .17 = .52$$
$$SS_{Rows} = .00 + .00 + .00 + .00 = .00$$
$$SS_{Columns} = .30 + .30 + .30 + .30 = 1.20$$
$$SS_{Interaction} = .15 + .15 + .15 + .15 = .60$$

Accuracy check: $SS_{Total} = 2.32$, $SS_{Within} + SS_{Rows} + SS_{Columns} + SS_{Interaction} = .52 + .00 + 1.20 + .60 = 2.32$

Table 11 Factorial Analysis of Variance Based on the Aron and Colleagues (2005) Study (Fictional Data)

F needed for Sensitivity main effect ($df = 1, 16; p < .05$) = 4.49.
F needed for Test Difficulty main effect ($df = 1, 16; p < .05$) = 4.49.
F needed for Interaction effect ($df = 1, 16; p < .05$) = 4.49.

Source	SS	df	MS	F	Decision
Sensitivity	.00	1	.00	0.00	Do not reject the null hypothesis
Test Difficulty	1.20	1	1.20	40.00	Reject the null hypothesis
Sensitivity × Test Difficulty	.60	1	.60	20.00	Reject the null hypothesis
Within groups	.52	16	.03		

❶ **Restate the question as a research hypothesis and a null hypothesis about the populations for each main effect and the interaction effect.** There are four populations:

> **Population 1, 1:** People who are not highly sensitive and take an easy test.
> **Population 1, 2:** People who are not highly sensitive and take a hard test.
> **Population 2, 1:** People who are highly sensitive and take an easy test.
> **Population 2, 2:** People who are highly sensitive and take a hard test.

The first null hypothesis is that the combined populations for individuals who are not highly sensitive (Populations 1, 1 and 1, 2) have the same level of negative mood as the combined populations for individuals who are highly sensitive (Populations 2, 1 and 2, 2). This is the null hypothesis for testing the main effect for sensitivity (not highly sensitive versus highly sensitive). The research hypothesis is that the populations of not highly sensitive and highly sensitive individuals have different means.

The second null hypothesis is that the combined populations for those who take an easy test (Populations 1, 1 and 2, 1) have the same level of negative mood as the combined populations for those who take a hard test (Populations 1, 2 and 2, 2). This is the null hypothesis for testing the main effect for test difficulty (easy versus hard). The research hypothesis is that populations taking easy and hard tests have different means.

The third null hypothesis is that the difference between the level of negative mood of the two populations for individuals who are not highly sensitive (Population 1, 1 minus Population 1, 2) will be the same as the difference between the means of the two populations for individuals who are highly sensitive (Population 2, 1 minus Population 2, 2). This is the null hypothesis for testing the interaction effect. (We could also say the same thing, with no change in meaning, as the difference between the two populations for the easy test equaling the difference between the two populations for the hard test.) The research hypothesis is that these differences will not be the same.

❷ **Determine the characteristics of the comparison distributions.** The three comparison distributions will be F distributions. The denominator degrees of freedom are the sum of the degrees of freedom in each of the cells (the number of scores in the cell minus 1). In this example, there are five participants in each of the four cells. This makes four degrees of freedom per cell, for a total of 16 within-groups degrees of freedom. The numerator for the comparison distribution for the sensitivity main effect has one degree of freedom (two rows minus 1); the numerator for the test difficulty main effect also has one degree of freedom; and the numerator degrees of freedom for the interaction effect is, again, 1 (it is the number of cells, four, minus the degrees of freedom for columns, minus the degrees of freedom for rows, minus 1).

❸ **Determine the cutoff sample scores on the comparison distributions at which each null hypothesis should be rejected.** Using the .05 significance level, Table A-3 (in the Appendix) gives a cutoff for 1 and 16 degrees of freedom of 4.49. The degrees of freedom and the significance level are the same in this example for both main effects and the interaction, so the cutoff is the same for all three (see Table 11).

❹ **Determine your samples' scores on each comparison distribution.** This requires figuring three F ratios.

   ❹ **Figure the mean of each cell, row, and column, plus the grand mean of all scores.** The cell means, row means, and column means are shown in Table 9. The grand mean of all the scores (the sum of all the scores, divided by the total number of scores) is 2.55.

   ❺ **Figure all the deviation scores of each type.** To save space, Table 10 shows only the squared deviations. However, following the table of squared deviations, we show how we figured all the deviations for the first score. For example, the deviation of the first score from the grand mean is 2.63 minus 2.55.

   ❻ **Square each deviation score.** All of these squared deviations are shown in Table 10. For example, the first score's deviation of .12 from the grand mean, when squared, is .01.

   ❼ **Add up the squared deviation scores of each type.** For example, for the sum of squared deviations from the grand mean, the total in the first cell (Not Highly Sensitive/Easy Test) is .21; for the second cell, .15; for the third, .72; and for the fourth, 1.24. This adds up to a total of 2.32. That is, $SS_{\text{Total}} = 2.32$. Remember that the *sums* of the various squared deviations (SS_{Within}, SS_{Rows}, SS_{Columns}, $SS_{\text{Interaction}}$) add up to SS_{Total}.

   But within a single participant, the various squared deviations do not add up to the overall squared deviation of the score from the grand mean. Table 10 also shows the check for accuracy: The sum of the squared deviations from the grand mean equals the total of the sums of the other four kinds of squared deviations (within rounding error).

   ❽ **Divide each sum of squared deviations by its appropriate degrees of freedom.** This is shown in Table 11. For example, the population variance estimate for Test Difficulty (the columns) comes out to 1.20, the sum of squares of 1.20 divided by the degrees of freedom of 1.

   ❾ **Divide the various between-groups variance estimates by the within-groups variance estimate.** This gives the F ratios and is shown in Table 11. For example, the F for Test Difficulty comes out to 40.00, the between-rows population variance estimate of 1.20 divided by the within-groups population variance estimate of .03.

❺ **Decide whether to reject the null hypotheses.** The F ratio for the test difficulty main effect of 40.00 is much larger than the cutoff of 4.49. Thus, you can reject the null hypothesis that the populations of individuals who take an easy test and a difficult test have the same mean level of negative mood. That is, the test difficulty effect is significant. The F of 0.00 for the sensitivity main effect did not reach the necessary 4.49 cutoff. Finally, the interaction effect F of 20.00 is larger than 4.49; so the interaction effect is significant. As can be seen from the cell means in Table 9 (and from Figure 2), the test difficulty main effect is due to individuals taking the hard test having a higher level of negative mood than individuals who take the easy test. The interaction effect is due to a different effect of test difficulty on negative mood according to the level of sensitivity. The level of negative mood of students who are not highly sensitive is slightly higher with a hard test compared to an easy test; but the level of negative mood of students who are highly sensitive is much higher with a hard test compared to an easy test. You can see how using an analysis of variance to look at interaction effects uncovered an interesting relationship among the variables.

TIP FOR SUCCESS

When figuring the deviation for the interaction effect, keep close track of the signs of the deviations you are subtracting and remember that this interaction deviation, prior to squaring, is figured from the original unsquared deviations, not the squared deviations.

Summary of Procedures for a Two-Way Analysis of Variance   Table 12 summarizes the steps of hypothesis testing and Table 13 shows the analysis of variance table and the formulas for a two-way analysis of variance.

Table 12   Steps of Hypothesis Testing for a Two-Way Analysis of Variance

❶ **Restate the question as a research hypothesis and a null hypothesis about the populations for each main effect and the interaction effect.**

❷ **Determine the characteristics of the comparison distributions.**

   a. The numerator degrees of freedom for the F distribution for the columns main effect is the number of columns minus 1: $df_{Columns} = N_{Columns} - 1$.

   b. The numerator degrees of freedom for the F distribution for the rows main effect is the number of rows minus 1: $df_{Rows} = N_{Rows} - 1$.

   c. The numerator degrees of freedom for the F distribution for the interaction effect is the number of cells minus the degrees of freedom for columns minus the degrees of freedom for rows minus 1: $df_{Interaction} = N_{Cells} - df_{Columns} - df_{Rows} - 1$.

   d. The comparison distributions will be F distributions with denominator degrees of freedom equal to the sum of the degrees of freedom in each of the cells (the number of scores in the cell minus 1): $df_{Within} = df_1 + df_2 + \cdots + df_{Last}$.

   e. Check the accuracy of your figuring by making sure that all of the degrees of freedom add up to the total degrees of freedom:
$df_{Total} = N - 1 = df_{Within} + df_{Columns} + df_{Rows} + df_{Interaction}$.

❸ **Determine the cutoff sample scores on the comparison distributions at which each null hypothesis should be rejected.**

   a. Determine the desired significance levels.

   b. Look up the appropriate cutoffs in an F table (Table A-3 in the Appendix).

❹ **Determine your samples' scores on each comparison distribution.**

   Ⓐ **Figure the mean of each cell, row, and column, plus the grand mean of all scores.**

   Ⓑ **Figure all the deviation scores of each type. For each score figure:**

     i. Its deviation from the grand mean: $X - GM$.

     ii. Its deviation from its cell's mean: $X - M$.

     iii. Its row's mean's deviation from the grand mean: $M_{Row} - GM$.

     iv. Its column's mean's deviation from the grand mean: $M_{Column} - GM$.

     v. Its deviation from the grand mean minus all the other deviations: Interaction deviation $= (X - GM) - (X - M) - (M_{Row} - GM) - (M_{Column} - GM)$.

   Ⓒ **Square each deviation score.** This gives the squared deviations.

   Ⓓ **Add up the squared deviation scores of each type.** This gives the sums of squared deviations: SS_{Total}, SS_{Within}, $SS_{Columns}$, SS_{Rows}, and $SS_{Interaction}$.

   Ⓔ **Divide each sum of squared deviations by its appropriate degrees of freedom.** This gives the variance estimates. That is, $MS_{Columns}$ or $S^2_{Columns} = SS_{Columns}/df_{Columns}$; MS_{Rows} or $S^2_{Rows} = SS_{Rows}/df_{Rows}$; $MS_{Interaction}$ or $S^2_{Interaction} = SS_{Interaction}/df_{Interaction}$.

   Ⓕ **Divide the various between-groups variance estimates by the within-groups variance estimate.** This gives the F ratios: $F_{Columns} = S^2_{Columns}/S^2_{Within}$ or $MS_{Columns}/MS_{Within}$; $F_{Rows} = S^2_{Rows}/S^2_{Within}$ or MS_{Rows}/MS_{Within}; $F_{Interaction} = S^2_{Interaction}/S^2_{Within}$ or $MS_{Interaction}/MS_{Within}$.

❺ **Decide whether to reject the null hypotheses.** Compare scores in Steps ❸ and ❹.

Table 13   Analysis of Variance Table and Formulas for a Two-Way Analysis of Variance

Analysis of variance table:

Source	SS	df	MS	F
Between:				
Columns	$SS_{Columns}$	$df_{Columns}$	$MS_{Columns}$ (or $S^2_{Columns}$)	$F_{Columns}$
Rows	SS_{Rows}	df_{Rows}	MS_{Rows} (or S^2_{Rows})	F_{Rows}
Interaction	$SS_{Interaction}$	$df_{Interaction}$	$MS_{Interaction}$ (or $S^2_{Interaction}$)	$F_{Interaction}$
Within	SS_{Within}	df_{Within}	MS_{Within} (or S^2_{Within})	
Total	SS_{Total}	df_{Total}		

(continued)

Table 13 (*continued*)

Formulas for each section of the analysis of variance table:

Source	SS	df	MS	F
Between:				
Columns	$\sum(M_{Column} - GM)^2$	$N_{Columns} - 1$	$SS_{Columns}/df_{Columns}$	$MS_{Columns}/MS_{Within}$
Rows	$\sum(M_{Row} - GM)^2$	$N_{Rows} - 1$	SS_{Rows}/df_{Rows}	MS_{Rows}/MS_{Within}
Interaction	$\sum[(X - GM)$ $\quad -(X - M)$ $\quad -(M_{Row} - GM)$ $\quad -(M_{Column} - GM)]^2$	$N_{Cells} - df_{Columns} - df_{Rows} - 1$	$SS_{Interaction}/df_{Interaction}$	$MS_{Interaction}/MS_{Within}$
Within	$\sum(X - M)^2$	$df_1 + df_2 + \cdots + df_{Last}$	SS_{Within}/df_{Within}	
Total	$\sum(X - GM)^2$	$N - 1$		

Definitions of basic symbols:

$\sum$	= sum of the appropriate numbers for all *scores* (not all cells)
M	= mean of a score's cell
M_{Row}	= mean of a score's row
M_{Column}	= mean of a score's column
GM	= grand mean of all scores
N_{Cells}	= number of cells
N_{Rows}	= number of rows
$N_{Columns}$	= number of columns
X	= each score
N	= total number of scores in the study

How are you doing?

1. List the steps for figuring the F ratios in a two-way factorial analysis of variance.
2. Write the formula for the sum of squares for rows and define each of the symbols.
3. Write the formula for the sum of squares for the interaction and define each of the symbols.
4. Write the formula for the degrees of freedom for the interaction and define each of the symbols.
5. Here are the scores for participants A through H (a total of eight; two participants per cell) for the fictional study of the effects of vividness and length of examples on the number of examples recalled used in an earlier "How are you doing?" question. Find the three F ratios (and test their significance at $p < .05$).

Participant	Vividness Condition	Length Condition	Number Recalled
A	Low	Short	6
B	Low	Short	4
C	High	Short	9
D	High	Short	5
E	Low	Long	2
F	Low	Long	4
G	High	Long	1
H	High	Long	1

Answers

1. **Ⓐ** Figure the mean of each cell, row, and column, plus the grand mean of all scores.
   Ⓑ Figure all the deviation scores of each type.
   Ⓒ Square each deviation score.
   Ⓓ Add up the squared deviation scores of each type.
   Ⓔ Divide each sum of squared deviations by its appropriate degrees of freedom.
   Ⓕ Divide the various between-groups variance estimates by the within-groups variance estimate.

2. Formula for the sum of squares for rows: $SS_{Rows} = \Sigma(M_{Row} - GM)^2$.
   SS_{Rows} is the sum of squared deviations for rows; Σ tells you to add up what follows over all scores; M_{Row} is the mean of a score's row; and GM is the grand mean (the mean of all the scores).

3. Formula for the sum of squares for the interaction:
   $SS_{Interaction} = \Sigma[(X - GM) - (X - M) - (M_{Row} - GM) - (M_{Column} - GM)]^2$.
   $SS_{Interaction}$ is the sum of squared deviations for the interaction; Σ tells you to add up what follows over all scores; X is each score; GM is the grand

---

Table 14   Figuring for "How Are You Doing?" question 5

F needed for main effect for Vividness ($df = 1, 4; p < .05) = 7.71$.

F needed for main effect for Length ($df = 1, 4; p < .05) = 7.71$.

F needed for interaction effect ($df = 1, 4; p < .05) = 7.71$.

	Low Vividness						High Vividness					
X	$(X - GM)^2$	$(X - M)^2$	$(M_{Row} - GM)^2$	$(M_{Column} - GM)^2$	INT^2	X	$(X - GM)^2$	$(X - M)^2$	$(M_{Row} - GM)^2$	$(M_{Column} - GM)^2$	INT^2
Short											
6	4	1	4	0	1	9	25	4	4	0	1
4	0	1	4	0	1	5	1	4	4	0	1
	4	2	8	0	2		26	8	8	0	2
Long											
2	4	1	4	0	1	1	9	0	4	0	1
4	0	1	4	0	1	1	9	0	4	0	1
	4	2	8	0	2		18	0	8	0	2

SS_{Total} $= 4 + 26 + 4 + 18 = 52$

SS_{Within} $= 2 + 8 + 2 + 0 = 12$

SS_{Rows} $= 8 + 8 + 8 + 8 = 32$

$SS_{Columns}$ $= 0 + 0 + 0 + 0 = 0$

$SS_{Interaction}$ $= 2 + 2 + 2 + 2 = 8$

Accuracy check: $SS_{Total} = SS_{Within} + SS_{Rows} + SS_{Columns} + SS_{Interaction} = 12 + 32 + 0 + 8 = 52$

Source	SS	df	MS	F	Decision
Length (rows)	32	1	32	10.67	Reject the null hypothesis.
Vividness (columns)	0	1	0	0	Do not reject the null hypothesis.
Interaction (Length × Vividness)	8	1	8	2.67	Do not reject the null hypothesis.
Within groups	12	4	3		

mean (the mean of all the scores); M is the mean of a score's cell; and M_{Row} and M_{Column} are the means, respectively, of a score's row and column.

4. Formula for the degrees of freedom for the interaction:

$df_{\text{Interaction}} = N_{\text{Cells}} - df_{\text{Columns}} - df_{\text{Rows}} - 1$.

$df_{\text{Interaction}}$ is the degrees of freedom for the interaction effect; N_{Cells} is the number of cells; df_{Columns} is the degrees of freedom for columns (the number of columns -1); and df_{Rows} is the degrees of freedom for rows (the number of rows -1).

5. The major figuring is shown in Table 14. For the Length effect, $F = 10.67$; significant. For the Vividness effect, $F = 0$; not significant. For the interaction effect, $F = 2.67$; not significant.

Advanced Topic: Power and Effect Size in the Factorial Analysis of Variance

You figure power and effect size in a factorial analysis of variance using the same approach as for a one-way analysis of variance, except that you figure power and effect size separately for each main effect and the interaction.

Effect Size

You can figure the effect size for each main and interaction effect as an R^2, the proportion of variance accounted for (also called eta squared, symbolized as η^2) by the effect. The proportion of variance accounted for in a one-way analysis of variance can be described as the proportion of the total variation of scores from the grand mean that is accounted for by the variation between the means of the groups. In a one-way analysis of variance, $R^2 = (S^2_{\text{Between}})(df_{\text{Between}})/[(S^2_{\text{Between}})(df_{\text{Between}}) + (S^2_{\text{Within}})(df_{\text{Within}})]$. Now, consider the situation of the column effect in a two-way analysis of variance. We can certainly substitute S^2_{Columns} for S^2_{Between} and df_{Columns} for df_{Between} in the numerator of the equation. S^2_{Columns} (the sum of squared deviations of the columns' means from the grand mean) is the variance created by the effect of the grouping variable that divides the groups across the columns and is otherwise not accounted for.

However, what about the denominator—the baseline, which is the variance that is to be accounted for in the proportion of variance accounted for? In a two-way analysis, the squared deviations of each score from the grand mean are now partly accounted for by the column effect, the row effect, and the interaction effect. But the column effect should not be held responsible for variance already accounted for by the row and interaction effects; the squared deviations to be accounted for by columns should include only those squared deviations not already accounted for by rows or the interaction. Thus, we can substitute S^2_{Columns} for S^2_{Between} and df_{Columns} for df_{Between} in the denominator of the equation. To put this in terms of a formula,

$$R^2_{\text{Columns}} = \frac{(S^2_{\text{Columns}})(df_{\text{Columns}})}{(S^2_{\text{Columns}})(df_{\text{Columns}}) + (S^2_{\text{Within}})(df_{\text{Within}})}$$

(20) ←

The proportion of variance accounted for by variation between columns is the product of the F ratio for columns multiplied by its degrees of freedom divided by the sum of the F ratio for columns multiplied by its degrees of freedom plus the degrees of freedom within groups (within cells).

The proportion of variance accounted for by variation between rows is the population variance estimate based on the variation between rows multiplied by the degrees of freedom for the rows, divided by the sum of the population variance estimate based on the variation between rows multiplied by the degrees of freedom for the rows, plus the within-groups (within-cells) population variance estimate multiplied by the within-groups (within-cells) degrees of freedom.

The same principle holds for the row and interaction effects. Stated as formulas,

$$R^2_{\text{Rows}} = \frac{(S^2_{\text{Rows}})(df_{\text{Rows}})}{(S^2_{\text{Rows}})(df_{\text{Rows}}) + (S^2_{\text{Within}})(df_{\text{Within}})} \tag{21}$$

The proportion of variance accounted for by the interaction is the population variance estimate based on the variation associated with the interaction multiplied by the degrees of freedom for the interaction, divided by the sum of the population variance estimate based on the variation associated with the interaction multiplied by the degrees of freedom for the interaction, plus the within-groups (within-cells) population variance estimate multiplied by the within-groups (within-cells) degrees of freedom.

$$R^2_{\text{Interaction}} = \frac{(S^2_{\text{Interaction}})(df_{\text{Interaction}})}{(S^2_{\text{Interaction}})(df_{\text{Interaction}}) + (S^2_{\text{Within}})(df_{\text{Within}})} \tag{22}$$

Technically, each of these is a "partial" R^2 because it describes the proportion of variance accounted for by an effect after "partialing out" the other effects.

In our example based on the Aron and colleagues (2005) study, R^2 would be figured as follows:

$$R^2_{\text{Columns}}(\text{Test Difficulty}) = \frac{(S^2_{\text{Columns}})(df_{\text{Columns}})}{(S^2_{\text{Columns}})(df_{\text{Columns}}) + (S^2_{\text{Within}})(df_{\text{Within}})}$$

$$= \frac{(1.20)(1)}{(1.20)(1) + (.03)(16)} = .71$$

$$R^2_{\text{Rows}}(\text{Sensitivity}) = \frac{(S^2_{\text{Rows}})(df_{\text{Rows}})}{(S^2_{\text{Rows}})(df_{\text{Rows}}) + (S^2_{\text{Within}})(df_{\text{Within}})}$$

$$= \frac{(.00)(1)}{(.00)(1) + (.03)(16)} = .00$$

$$R^2_{\text{Interaction}}(\text{Interaction}) = \frac{(S^2_{\text{Interaction}})(df_{\text{Interaction}})}{(S^2_{\text{Interaction}})(df_{\text{Interaction}}) + (S^2_{\text{Within}})(df_{\text{Within}})}$$

$$= \frac{(.60)(1)}{(.60)(1) + (.03)(16)} = .56$$

Based on Cohen's conventions for R^2 in the analysis of variance (.01, small effect size; .06, medium effect size; .14, large effect size), there is an enormous effect size—a high R^2—for test difficulty and also an extremely large effect size for the interaction. The nonsignificant effect for affiliation had a zero effect size. (In the actual study, the effect sizes were much smaller. The effect sizes for test difficulty and the interaction are so large in the example because we made up scores with much less variance than in the actual study. We did this to help you see the patterns very clearly.)

Power

In a factorial analysis of variance, the power of each effect is influenced by the overall design. For example, a three-level column effect will have different power if it is crossed with a two-level row effect than if it is crossed with a three-level row effect. To keep things simple, we present power figures for only the three most common two-way analysis of situations: all effects in a 2×2 design, a two-level (two-row or two-column) main effect in a 2×3 design, and a three-level (three-row or three-column) main effect in a 2×3 design. (The power of the interaction in a 2×3 design is the same as for the three-level main effect.)

Table 15 presents approximate power at the .05 significance level for each of these situations for small, medium, and large effect sizes and for cell sizes of 10, 20, 30, 40, 50, and 100.[1]

Consider a planned 2×2 study with 30 participants in each cell and an expected medium effect size ($R^2 = .06$) for the row main effect (and using the

Table 15 Approximate Power for Studies Using 2×2 or 2×3 Analysis of Variance for Hypotheses Tested at the .05 Significance Level

	Effect Size		
	Small	Medium	Large
N Per Cell	($R^2 = .01$)	($R^2 = .06$)	($R^2 = .14$)
All effects in a 2×2 analysis:			
10	.09	.33	.68
20	.13	.60	.94
30	.19	.78	.99
40	.24	.89	*
50	.29	.94	*
100	.52	*	*
Two-level main effect in a 2×3 analysis:			
10	.11	.46	.84
20	.18	.77	.99
30	.26	.92	*
40	.34	.97	*
50	.41	.99	*
100	.70	*	*
Three-level main effect and interaction effect in a 2×3 analysis:			
10	.09	.36	.76
20	.14	.67	.98
30	.21	.86	*
40	.27	.94	*
50	.32	.98	*
100	.59	*	*

*Nearly 1.

Table 16   Approximate Number of Participants Needed in Each Cell (Assuming Equal Sample Sizes) for 80% Power for Studies Using a 2 × 2 or 2 × 3 Analysis of Variance, Testing Hypotheses at the .05 Significance Level

	Effect Size		
	Small $(R^2 = .01)$	Medium $(R^2 = .06)$	Large $(R^2 = .14)$
2 × 2: All effects	197	33	14
2 × 3: Two-level main effect	132	22	9
Three-level main effect and interaction	162	27	11

.05 significance level). The row main effect for this planned study would have a power of .78, meaning that, if the research hypothesis for this row main effect is in fact true and has a medium effect size, the chance that the study will come out significant is about 78%.

Or consider an example of a published study in which a nonsignificant result is found for an interaction effect in a 2 × 3 analysis of variance with 20 participants per cell. Based on the table, power is only .14 for a small effect size. This means that, even if such a small effect exists in the population, this study would be very unlikely to have come out significant. By contrast, the table shows a power of .98 for a large effect size. This means that if a large interaction effect existed in the population, it would almost certainly have been significant in this study.

Planning Sample Size

Table 16 gives the approximate number of participants *per cell* needed for 80% power at the .05 significance level for estimated small, medium, and large effect sizes for the same situations as were included in the power table.[2]

Suppose that you are planning a 2 × 3 analysis of variance in which you are predicting a large effect size for the main effect on the three-level variable and a medium effect size for the other main effect and interaction. For 80% power (at the .05 significance level), you need 11 participants per cell for the three-level main effect, 22 per cell for the two-level main effect, and 27 per cell for the interaction effect. Of course, you have to do the whole study at once. Thus, you need at least 27 per cell (unless you choose to risk lower power for the interaction effect). This would mean recruiting 162 participants (27 for each of the six cells of the 2 × 3 design).

How are you doing?

1. (a) Write the formula for the effect size for rows in a two-way analysis of variance, (b) define each of the symbols, and (c) figure the effect size for a study in which S^2_{Rows} is 9.45, S^2_{Within} is 3.67, df_{Rows} is 1, and df_{Within} is 36.
2. (a) What is the power of the two-level main effect in a 2 × 3 analysis of variance with approximately 40 participants in each group to be tested at the .05 significance level, in which the researchers predict a medium effect size? (b) About how many participants do you need in each cell for 80% power in a planned 2 × 2 study in which you predict a medium effect size and will be using the .05 significance level?

Answers

1. (a) Effect size for rows in a two-way analysis of variance:

$$R^2_{Rows} = \frac{(S^2_{Rows})(df_{Rows})}{(S^2_{Rows})(df_{Rows}) + (S^2_{Within})(df_{Within})}.$$

(b) R^2_{Rows} is the proportion of variance accounted for by variation between rows; S^2_{Rows} is the population variance estimate for rows; df_{Rows} is the degrees of freedom for rows (number of rows minus 1); S^2_{Within} is the within-groups population variance estimate; and df_{Within} is the degrees of freedom within groups (the number of scores in each cell minus 1, added up over all cells).

(c) $R^2_{Rows} = (9.45)(1)/[(9.45)(1) + (3.67)(36)] = 9.45/141.57 = .07$.

2. (a) Power: 97. (b) Number of participants per cell: 33.

Learning Aids

Summary

1. In a factorial research design, participants are put into groupings according to the combinations of the grouping variables whose effects are being studied. In such designs, you can study the effects of two grouping variables without needing twice as many participants. Also, such designs allow you to study the effects of combinations of the two grouping variables.
2. An interaction effect is when the impact of one grouping variable varies according to the level of the other grouping variable. A main effect is the impact of one grouping variable, ignoring the effect of the other grouping variable. Interaction effects and main effects can be described verbally, numerically, and graphically (usually on a graph with bars for each combination of the grouping variables, with the height of the bar being the score on the measured variable). When there is an interaction along with a main effect, you have to be cautious in drawing conclusions about the main effect.
3. In a two-way analysis of variance, there are three types of between-groups variance estimates: one for differences on the grouping variable dividing the rows, one for differences on the grouping variable dividing the columns, and one for the interaction of the row and column variables. Since the within-groups variance estimate is based on estimates from each cell, it can also be called a *within-cells* variance estimate.
4. The assumptions for a factorial analysis of variance are the same as for the one-way analysis of variance except that the requirements of population normality and equal variances apply to the populations that go with each cell.
5. The factorial analysis of variance can be extended beyond two-way designs and can also be used for repeated measures studies. (For more information on repeated measures analysis of variance, see the Web chapter available at *www.pearsoned.co.in/prc/home.*
6. There is a long-standing controversy about whether to dichotomize continuous variables to do an analysis of variance. This is a decreasingly common procedure; alternative procedures that use the full range of values of each variable are generally considered the better approach.

7. Results of factorial analyses of variance often include graphical descriptions of results, particularly when the interaction effect is significant. These are usually bar graphs but sometimes include line graphs.

8. ADVANCED TOPIC: The figuring for a two-way analysis of variance uses an expanded version of the structural model approach. The within-groups estimate is based on deviations of each score from its cell's mean. The row effect is based on deviations between row means and the grand mean; the column main effect, on deviations between column means and the grand mean. The interaction effect is based on the deviation of scores from the grand mean remaining after subtracting all the other deviations from the grand mean (deviations from the cell mean, the row means, and the column means). To get the actual population variance estimates, the various deviations (within, rows, columns, and interaction) are squared, summed, and divided by their degrees of freedom. The F ratios for row, column, and interaction effects are the population variance estimates for each of these divided by the within-groups (within-cells) population variance estimate.

9. ADVANCED TOPIC: In a factorial analysis of variance, you figure effect size and power separately for each main and interaction effect. R^2 is the variance estimate for that particular effect multiplied by the degrees of freedom for that effect, divided by the sum of the variance estimate for that particular effect multiplied by the degrees of freedom for that effect, plus the within-groups variance estimate multiplied by the within-groups degrees of freedom.

Key Terms

factorial analysis of variance	two-way analysis of variance	cell
factorial research design	grouping variable	cell mean
interaction effect	one-way analysis of variance	marginal means
two-way factorial research design	main effect	repeated measures analysis of variance
		dichotomizing

Example Worked-Out Problems

Recognizing and Interpreting Main Effects and Interaction Effects

Each of the following tables of means shows the result of a fictional study using a two-way factorial research design. Assuming that any differences are statistically significant, for each table, (a) indicate which effects (main and interaction), if any, are found, and (b) describe the meaning of the pattern of means (that is, any main or interaction effects or the lack thereof).

1. Measured variable: Level of happiness

		Stress		
		Low	High	Overall
Age	Young	8	4	6
	Old	8	4	6
	Overall	8	4	6

2. Measured variable: Symptoms of depression

	Therapy		
	No	Yes	Overall
Medication No	9	6	7.5
Yes	6	2	4
Overall	7.5	4	5.75

Answers

1. (a) Main effect for stress, no main effect for age, no interaction effect; (b) happiness is lower for people with high stress, but there is no difference in happiness between younger and older people, and each combination of stress and age has the level of happiness you would expect knowing the level of each variable.

2. (a) Main effects for therapy and medication, interaction effect; (b) fewer symptoms of depression are found for people who have therapy and people who take medication, and people who have therapy and take medication have an especially low number of symptoms.

Bar Graphs and Figuring a Two-Way Analysis of Variance

In a 3×2 experiment, Variable A has three levels (1, 2, and 3), and Variable B has two levels (1 and 2). Four participants are randomly assigned to each combination of Variables A and B and are then observed on the measured variable. Scores of the 24 participants follow:

	Variable B	
	Level 1	Level 2
Variable A Level 1	25	19
	20	24
	23	21
	24	20
Variable A Level 2	22	24
	19	18
	22	22
	21	20
Variable A Level 3	16	18
	19	21
	13	16
	16	17

(a) Make a table of cell and marginal means. (b) Make a bar graph of the cell means. (c) ADVANCED TOPIC: Are there any significant main or interaction effects (use the .05 significance level)?

Answers

(a)

		Variable B		
		Level 1	Level 2	Overall
Variable A	Level 1	23	21	22
	Level 2	21	21	21
	Level 3	16	18	17
	Overall	20	20	20

(b) See Figure 12.
(c) Table 17 shows the figuring and conclusions.

Outline for Writing Essays for a Two-Way Analysis of Variance

1. Explain that the two-way analysis of variance is used for hypothesis testing when a study uses a two-way factorial research design; with such a design, participants are put into groupings according to the combinations of the variables whose effects are being studied.
2. Describe the core logic of hypothesis testing in this situation. Be sure to explain what is meant by the terms *main effect* and *interaction effect*. Also, describe the three F ratios that are tested in a two-way analysis of variance, including how each F ratio is figured.
3. Describe the assumptions of a two-way analysis of variance.
4. ADVANCED TOPIC: Describe the structural model for the analysis of variance, including how each score's overall deviation from the grand mean can be divided into several components. Explain the logic of the comparison distributions that are used with the two-way analysis of variance. Describe the logic and process for determining the cutoff sample F scores at which each null hypothesis should be rejected. Explain how and why the scores from Steps ❸ and ❹ of the hypothesis-testing process are compared. Explain the meaning of the results of these comparisons with regard to the specific research and null hypotheses being tested.

Figure 12   Bar graph for Example Worked-Out Problem.

Table 17 Figuring for Two-Way Factorial Analysis of Variance Example Worked-Out Problem

F needed for main effect for Variable B ($df = 1, 18; p < .05$) = 4.41.

F needed for main effect for Variable A ($df = 2, 18; p < .05$) = 3.56.

F needed for interaction effect ($df = 2, 18; p < .05$) = 3.56.

| | Variable B Level 1 | | | | | | Variable B Level 2 | | | | |
X	$(X - GM)^2$	$(X - M)^2$	$(M_{Row} - GM)^2$	$(M_{Column} - GM)^2$	INT^2	X	$(X - GM)^2$	$(X - M)^2$	$(M_{Row} - GM)^2$	$(M_{Column} - GM)^2$	INT^2
Variable A Level 1											
25	25	4	4	0	1	19	1	4	4	0	1
20	0	9	4	0	1	24	16	9	4	0	1
23	9	0	4	0	1	21	1	0	4	0	1
24	16	1	4	0	1	20	0	1	4	0	1
	50	14	16	0	4		18	14	16	0	4
Variable A Level 2											
22	4	1	1	0	0	24	16	9	1	0	0
19	1	4	1	0	0	18	4	9	1	0	0
22	4	1	1	0	0	22	4	1	1	0	0
21	1	0	1	0	0	20	0	1	1	0	0
	10	6	4	0	0		24	20	4	0	0
Variable A Level 3											
16	16	0	9	0	1	18	4	0	9	0	1
19	1	9	9	0	1	21	1	9	9	0	1
13	49	9	9	0	1	16	16	4	9	0	1
16	16	0	9	0	1	17	9	1	9	0	1
	82	18	36	0	4		30	14	36	0	4

M = mean of the score's cell

M_{Row} = mean of the score's row

M_{Column} = mean of the score's column

INT = score's remaining deviation for the interaction

Sample figuring of deviations, using the first score in the Variable A Level 1/Variable B Level 1 cell:

$(X - GM)^2$ = $(25 - 20)^2 = 5^2 = 25$.

$(X - M)^2$ = $(25 - 23)^2 = 2^2 = 4$.

$(M_{Row} - GM)^2$ = $(22 - 20)^2 = 2^2 = 4$.

$(M_{Column} - GM)^2$ = $(20 - 20)^2 = 0^2 = 0$.

INT^2 = $[(X - GM) - (X - M) - (M_{Row} - GM) - (M_{Column} - GM)]^2 = (5 - 2 - 2 - 0)^2 = 1^2 = 1$

SS_{Total} = $50 + 18 + 10 + 24 + 82 + 30 = 214$

SS_{Within} = $14 + 14 + 6 + 20 + 18 + 14 = 86$

SS_{Column} = $0 + 0 + 0 + 0 + 0 + 0 = 0$

SS_{Row} = $16 + 16 + 4 + 4 + 36 + 36 = 112$

$SS_{Interaction}$ = $4 + 4 + 0 + 0 + 4 + 4 = 16$

Accuracy check: $SS_{Total} = 214$; $SS_{Within} + SS_{Rows} + SS_{Columns} + SS_{Interaction} = 86 + 0 + 112 + 16 = 214$

Source	SS	df	MS	F	Decision
Variable B (columns)	0	1	0	0.0	Do not reject the null hypothesis.
Variable A (rows)	112	2	56	11.7	Reject the null hypothesis.
Interaction (columns × rows)	16	2	8	1.7	Do not reject the null hypothesis.
Within groups	86	18	4.8		

Practice Problems

These problems involve figuring. Most real-life statistics problems are done with special statistical software. Even if you have such software, do these problems by hand to ingrain the method in your mind. To learn how to use a computer to solve statistics problems like those in this chapter, refer to the Using SPSS section at the end of this chapter.

All data are fictional unless an actual citation is given.

Set I

1. Each of the following is a table of means showing the results of a study using a factorial design. Assuming that any differences are statistically significant, for each table, (a) and (b) make two bar graphs showing the results (in one graph grouping the bars according to one variable and in the other graph grouping the bars according to the other variable); (c) indicate which effects (main and interaction), if any, are found; and (d) describe the meaning of the pattern of means (that is, any main or interaction effects or the lack thereof) in words.

   (i) Measured variable: Income (thousands of dollars)

   (ii) Measured variable: Grade point average

   (iii) Measured variable: Days sick per month

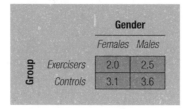

2. Each of the following is a table of means showing the results of a study using a factorial design. Assuming that any differences are statistically significant, for each table, (a) and (b) make two bar graphs showing the results (in one graph

grouping the bars according to one variable and in the other graph grouping the bars according to the other variable); (c) indicate which effects (main and inter-action), if any, are found; and (d) describe the meaning of the pattern of means (that is, any main or interaction effects or the lack thereof) in words.

(i) Measured variable: Conversation length

	Topic	
Relationship	Nonpersonal	Personal
Friend	16	20
Parent	10	6

(ii) Measured variable: Rated restaurant quality

	City		
Cost	New York	Chicago	Vancouver
Expensive	9	5	7
Moderate	6	4	6
Inexpensive	4	3	5

(iii) Measured variable: Ratings of flavor

	Coffee Brand		
Type	X	Y	Z
Regular	7	4	6
Decaf	5	2	6

3. A sports psychologist studied the effect of a motivational program on injuries among players of three different sports. The following chart shows the design. For each of the following possible patterns of results, make up a set of cell means, figure the marginal means, and make a bar graph of the results (assume that any differences are statistically significant): (a) a main effect for type of sport and no other main effect or interaction; (b) a main effect for program and no other main effect or interaction; (c) both main effects but no interaction; (d) a main effect for program and an interaction, but no main effect for type of sport; (e) both main effects and an interaction.

   Measured Variable: Number of injuries per person over 10 weeks

	Sport		
Sport	Baseball	Football	Basketball
With motivational program			
Without motivational program			

4. Kunda and Oleson (1997) studied the effect on stereotypes of counterinformation, learning about someone who is opposite to what you would expect from the stereotype. They predicted that extreme counterinformation may have a boomerang effect—making the stereotype even stronger. Participants were preselected to be in the study based on a questionnaire in which they rated public relations (PR) agents for their typical degree of extroversion: an "extreme-stereotype" group of participants who had rated PR agents as extremely extroverted and a "moderate-stereotype" group of participants who had rated PR agents as only moderately extroverted. During the actual study, some participants were given a description of a particular PR agent who was highly introverted, the extreme deviant condition; the other participants were given no special description, the control condition. Finally, all participants were asked about their beliefs about PR agents. Kunda and Oleson (1997) reported the results as follows:

> A 2 (prior stereotype) $\times$ 2 (condition) ANOVA yielded a significant interaction, $F(1, 42) = 5.69, p < .05$, indicating that the impact of the target on participants' stereotypes depended on their prior stereotypes. As can be seen in Figure 13, extreme-stereotype participants exposed to the highly introverted target came to view PR agents as even more extroverted than did extreme controls . . . [a] boomerang effect. . . . A different pattern was observed for the moderate-stereotype participants: Their stereotypes were unaffected by exposure to the same target . . . . The ANOVA also revealed a large effect for prior stereotypes, $F(1, 42) = 38.94, p < .0001$ indicating, not surprisingly, that extreme-stereotype participants continued to view PR agents as more extroverted than did moderate-stereotype participants. There was also a marginal effect for condition, $F(1, 42) = 2.89, p < .10$, which was clearly due entirely to the extreme-stereotype participants. (p. 974)

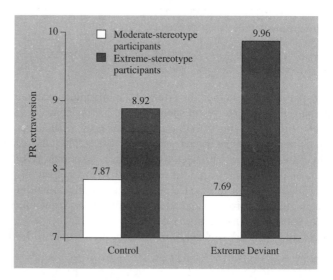

Figure 13   Mean ratings of the extraversion of public relations (PR) agents made by participants with moderate or extreme prior stereotypes who were exposed to an extremely introverted PR agent or to no target (controls). Higher numbers indicate a greater PR extraversion.

Source: Kunda, Z., & Oleson, K. C. (1997). When exceptions prove the rule: How extremity of deviance determines the impact of defiant examples on stereotypes. *Journal of Personality and Social Psychology, 72,* 965–979. Published by the American Psychological Association. Reprinted with permission.

Briefly describe the meaning of these results to a person who has never had a course in statistics. (Do not go into the computational details, just the basic logic of the pattern of means, the significant results, and issues of interpreting nonsignificant results.)

5. Yamagishi and Melara (2001) studied people's ability to separate visual images from the background. Participants were shown images differing from the background in either just chromaticity (color) or just luminescence (brightness). Also, they made the figures more difficult to identify by degrading (distorting) either the contour (shape of the edges) or the surface of the figure. The key measure was "difference in sensitivity from baseline," which the researchers abbreviated as Δd_a. Here is an excerpt from their results (note that MS_e refers to mean squared error, which is the same as MS_{Within}, the population variance estimate based on the variation within groups (within cells).

> The only factor to yield a significant main effect was task $[(F(1, 3) = 373.35, MS_e = 0.01, p < .001]$. Greater overall loss was observed in the chromacity tasks ($\Delta d_a = -0.86$) than in the luminance tasks ($\Delta d_a = -0.37$) . . . . [T]he critical effect is found in the interaction between degradation and task. This interaction, depicted in Figure 14, was highly significant $[F(1, 3) = 178.77, MS_e = 0.02, p < .001]$. As one can see, figural identification in the

Figure 14 Average difference in sensitivity from baseline (Δd_a) in luminance and chromaticity tasks under contour-degradation and surface-degradation conditions across Experiments IA and IB. Note the crossover interaction between degradation and task: performance in the luminance tasks was most disrupted by contour degradation, whereas performance in the chromaticity tasks was most disrupted by surface degradation.

Source: Yamagishi, N., & Melara, R. D. (2001). Informational primacy of visual dimensions: Specialized roles for luminance and chromaticity in figure-ground perception. *Perception and Psychophysics, 63*, 824–846. Reprinted with permission.

luminance tasks was disrupted by contour degradation, but not by surface degradation. On the other hand, figural identification in the chromacity task was disrupted by both forms of degradation; however, surface degradation was twice as harmful to performance in these tasks as contour degradation. (p. 831)

Describe the meaning of these results to a person who understands one-way analysis of variance but is completely unfamiliar with factorial designs or the two-way analysis of variance.

6. ADVANCED TOPIC: For each of the following data sets, carry out an analysis of variance, including making a table of cell and marginal means and making a bar graph of the cell means. Use the .05 significance level.

(a)	Experimental Condition	
	A	B
Group 1	0	3
	1	2
	1	3
Group 2	3	0
	2	1
	3	1

(b)	Experimental Condition	
	A	B
Group 1	0	0
	1	1
	1	1
Group 2	3	3
	2	2
	3	3

(c)	Experimental Condition	
	A	B
Group 1	0	3
	1	2
	1	3
Group 2	0	3
	1	2
	1	3

7. ADVANCED TOPIC: Patients with two kinds of diagnoses were randomly assigned to one of three types of therapy and the effectiveness of the therapy was measured on a 1-to-15 scale (with a higher number indicating greater effectiveness). There were two patients per cell. Based on the following results, (a) carry out the analysis of variance (use the .05 significance level), (b) make a table of cell and marginal means, (c) make a bar graph of the results, and (d) describe the results in words (indicate which effects are significant and, on the basis of the significant effects, how to understand the pattern of cell means).

	Therapy A	Therapy B	Therapy C
Diagnosis I	6	3	2
	2	1	4
Diagnosis II	11	7	8
	9	9	10

8. ADVANCED TOPIC: A psychologist who studies the legal system conducted a study of the effect of defendants' likability and nervousness on willingness to convict the defendant. Each participant read the same transcript, taken from an actual trial, in which the guilt or innocence of a male defendant was quite ambiguous. All participants also saw a brief videotape that supposedly showed the defendant on the witness stand. However, the way the actor played the part on the videotape differed for different participants, including the four possibilities of likable versus not and nervous versus not. After viewing the tape, participants rated the likelihood that the defendant is innocent (on a scale of 1, *very unlikely*, to 10, *very likely*). The results for the first 12 participants in the study were as follows:

	Likeable	Not Likeable
Nervous	7	3
	8	4
	6	2
Not nervous	3	7
	3	5
	3	9

(a) Carry out the analysis of variance (use the .05 significance level). (b) Make a table of cell and marginal means. (c) Make a bar graph of the results. (d) Explain the results and the way you arrived at them to someone who is familiar with the one-way analysis of variance (including the structural model approach) but not with the factorial analysis of variance.

9. ADVANCED TOPIC: Figure the effect size for each main and interaction effect for problems (a) 6a, (b) 6b, (c) 6c, (d) 7, and (e) 8.

10. ADVANCED TOPIC: What is the power of the effect in the following planned studies using the analysis of variance with $p < .05$?

	Predicted Effect Size	Overall Design	Number of Levels of the Effect	Participants Per Cell
(a)	Small	2 × 2	2	30
(b)	Small	2 × 2	2	50
(c)	Small	2 × 3	2	30
(d)	Small	2 × 3	3	30
(e)	Medium	2 × 2	2	30

11. ADVANCED TOPIC: About how many participants do you need in each cell for 80% power in each of the following planned studies, using the analysis of variance with $p < .05$?

	Predicted Effect Size	Design	Effect
(a)	Small	2 × 2	Main effect
(b)	Small	2 × 2	Interaction effect
(c)	Medium	2 × 2	Main effect
(d)	Small	2 × 3	Two-level main effect
(e)	Small	2 × 3	Three-level main effect
(f)	Small	2 × 3	Interaction effect

Set II

12. Each of the following tables of means shows the results of a study using a factorial design. Assuming that any differences are statistically significant, for each table (a) and (b), make two bar graphs showing the results (in one graph grouping the bars according to one variable and in the other graph grouping the bars according to the other variable); (c) indicate which effects (main and interaction), if any, are found; and (d) describe the meaning of the pattern of means (that is, any main or interaction effects or the lack thereof) in words.
(i) Measured variable: Degree of envy of another person's success

		Degree of Success	
		Great	Small
Status of Other	Friend	8	5
	Stranger	1	4

(ii) Measured variable: Observed engagement in the activity

		Play Activity	
		Blocks	Dress Up
Situation	Alone	4.5	2.5
	With playmate	2.5	4.5

(iii) Measured variable: Intensity of attention

		Program	
		Swan Lake	Modern
Type of Balletgoer	Regular	20	15
	Sometime	15	15
	Novice	10	5

13. Each of the following tables of means shows the results of a study using a factorial design. Assuming that any differences are statistically significant, for each table (a) and (b), make two bar graphs showing the results (in one graph grouping the bars according to one variable and in the other graph grouping the bars according to the other variable); (c) indicate which effects (main and

interaction), if any, are found; and (d) describe the meaning of the pattern of means (that is, any main or interaction effects or the lack thereof) in words.

(i) Measured variable: Right frontal neural activity in brain during memory task

		Items Remembered	
		Words	Pictures
Times Presented	Once	45	68
	Twice	30	30

(ii) Measured variable: Approval rating of the U.S. president

		Region			
		West	East	Midwest	South
Class	Middle	70	45	55	50
	Lower	50	25	35	30

(iii) Measured variable: Satisfaction with education

		Gender	
		Females	Males
Time After Obtaining BA	1 month	3	3
	1 year	4	4
	5 years	9	9

14. In this study, English-speaking participants were instructed to try to read a paragraph for a half hour in one of three languages they did not understand. They read the paragraph after either being told the main idea of the paragraph, told the main idea of the first sentence only, or not told anything about the meaning. They were given translations of some words. The researchers then measured how many of the other words they could correctly translate. The following chart shows the design. For each of the following possible patterns of results, make up a set of cell means, figure the marginal means, and make a bar graph of the results: (a) a main effect for language and no other main effect or interaction; (b) a main effect for knowledge of meaning and no other main effect or interaction; (c) both main effects but no interaction; (d) a main effect for language and an interaction, but no main effect for knowledge of meaning; (e) both main effects and an interaction.

Measured variable: Number of words not given that participant could correctly translate

		Language		
		Dutch	Rumanian	Swedish
Knowledge of Meaning	Paragraph			
	Sentence			
	None			

15. Brockner and colleagues (2001) studied the effect of cultural values about the appropriateness of power differentials on how employees feel about having input to managers about important decisions. Their participants were business students in China (a culture in which power differentials are considered appropriate and normal), a "high power distance" culture, and in the United States, a "low power distance" culture. The students were asked to imagine that they were working in a company and had just been put under the direction of a new manager; they were then assigned to one of three conditions: (1) the new manager discouraged input from them (the low voice condition), (2) the new manager encouraged input from them (high voice), or (3) no information was given about the manager's style (the control condition). They then had the students answer questions about how committed they would feel to the organization. Here is how the researchers reported the results:

> A two-factor ANOVA yielded a significant main effect of voice, $F(2, 245) = 26.30, p < .001$. As expected, participants responded less favorably in the low voice condition ($M = 2.93$) than in the high voice condition ($M = 3.58$). The mean rating in the control condition ($M = 3.34$) fell between these two extremes. Of greater importance, the interaction between culture and voice was also significant, $F(2, 245) = 4.11, p < .02$. . . . As can be seen in Table [18] the voice effect was more pronounced in the low power distance culture (the United States) than in the high power distance culture (the People's Republic of China). (p. 304)

Briefly describe the meaning of these results to a person who has never had a course in statistics. (Do not go into the computational details, just the basic logic of the pattern of means, the significant results, and issues of interpreting nonsignificant results.)

16. Sinclair and Kunda (2000) tested the idea that, if you want to think well of someone (for example, because he or she has said positive things about you), you are less influenced by the normal stereotypes when evaluating them. Participants filled out a questionnaire on their social skills, then either a male or female "manager in training" gave them feedback, rigged so that half the participants were given positive feedback and half, negative feedback. Finally, the participants rated the managers for their skill at evaluating them. The

Table 18 Mean Level of Organizational Commitment as a Function of Culture and Level of Voice (Study 1)

	Level of Voice		
Culture	Low	High	Control
United States (low power distance)	2.63 (0.72)	3.57 (0.56)	3.17 (0.66)
People's Republic of China (high power distance)	3.27 (0.68)	3.60 (0.43)	3.52 (0.55)

Note: Scores could range from 1 to 5, with higher scores reflecting greater organizational commitment. Standard deviations are in parentheses.
Source: Brockner, J., Ackerman, G., Greenberg, J., Gelfand, M. J., Francesco, A. M., Chen, Z. X., Leung, K., Bierbrauer, G., Gomez, C., Kirkman, B. L., & Shapiro, D. (2001). Culture and procedural justice: The influence of power distance on reactions to voice. Journal of Experimental Social Psychology, 37, 300–315. Copyright © 2001 with permission from Elsevier.

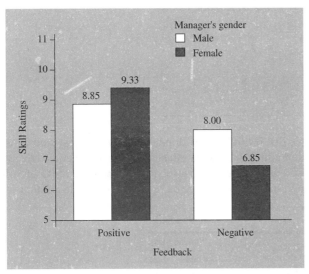

Figure 15 Participants' ratings of the manager's skill at evaluating them as a function of feedback favorability and the manager's gender (Study 2).

Source: Sinclair, L., & Kunda, Z. (2000). Motivated stereotyping of women: She's fine if she praised me but incompetent if she criticized me. *Personality and Social Psychology Bulletin, 26,* 1329–1342. Copyright © 2000 by Society for Personality and Social Psychology, Inc. Reprinted by permission of Sage Publications, Inc.

question was whether the usual tendency to stereotype women as less skillful managers would be undermined when people got positive ratings. Here are the results:

> Participants' ratings of the manager's skill at evaluating them were analyzed with a 2 (feedback) $\times$ 2 (manager gender) ANOVA. Managers who had provided positive feedback ($M = 9.08$) were rated more than were managers who had provided negative feedback ($M = 7.46$), $F(1, 46) = 19.44, p < .0001$. However, as may be seen in Figure 15, the effect was qualified by a significant interaction, $F(1, 46) = 4.71, p < .05$. (pp. 1335–1336)

Describe the meaning of these results to a person who understands one-way analysis of variance but is completely unfamiliar with factorial designs or the two-way analysis of variance.

17. ADVANCED TOPIC: For each of the following data sets, carry out an analysis of variance, including making a table of cell and marginal means and making a bar graph of the cell means. Use the .05 significance level.

(a)	Group	
	I	II
Experimental Condition A	8	8
	6	6
Experimental Condition B	3	3
	1	1

(b)	Group	
	I	II
Experimental Condition A	9	9
	5	5
Experimental Condition B	4	4
	0	0

18. ADVANCED TOPIC: A developmental psychologist studied the effects of loudness of a sudden noise on infants of different inherited temperaments. The infants were exposed either to a sudden loud noise or a sudden soft noise, then the infants' startle reactions were observed. The startle reaction scores were as follows:

	Sudden Noise	
	Loud	Soft
Temperament K	14	7
	10	5
	9	9
Temperament R	3	8
	8	8
	7	2

(a) Make a table of cell and marginal means; (b) draw a bar graph of them; (c) carry out the five steps of hypothesis testing (use the .05 significance level); and (d) describe the results in words (indicate which effects are significant and, on the basis of the significant effects, how to understand the pattern of cell means).

19. ADVANCED TOPIC: In a particular high school, three types of video teaching programs were each tried for English, history, and math. The researchers then measured amount learned. There were two students per cell. Based on the following results, (a) make a table of cell and marginal means, (b) draw a bar graph of them, (c) carry out the five steps of hypothesis testing (use the .05 significance level), and (d) explain the results and the way you arrived at them to someone who is familiar with the one-way analysis of variance (including the structural model approach), but not with the factorial analysis of variance.

	English	History	Math
Program Type A	3	15	2
	3	14	3
Program Type B	6	18	6
	8	10	5
Program Type C	1	13	2
	3	4	0

20. ADVANCED TOPIC: Figure the effect size for each main and interaction effect for problems (a) 17a, (b) 17b, (c) 18, and (d) 19.

21. ADVANCED TOPIC: What is the power of the effect in the following planned studies using the analysis of variance with $p < .05$?

	Predicted Effect Size	Overall Design	Number of Levels of the Effect	Participants Per Cell
(a)	Small	2 × 2	2	10
(b)	Medium	2 × 2	2	10
(c)	Large	2 × 2	2	10
(d)	Medium	2 × 3	3	10
(e)	Medium	2 × 3	3	20
(f)	Medium	2 × 2	Interaction	20

22. ADVANCED TOPIC: About how many participants do you need in each cell for 80% power in each of the following planned studies, using the analysis of variance with $p < .05$?

	Predicted Effect Size	Design	Effect
(a)	Medium	2 × 2	Main effect
(b)	Large	2 × 2	Main effect
(c)	Medium	2 × 2	Interaction effect
(d)	Medium	2 × 3	Three-level main effect
(e)	Large	2 × 3	Three-level main effect
(f)	Medium	2 × 3	Interaction effect

Using SPSS

The ✑ in the following steps indicates a mouse click. (We used SPSS version 19 for Windows to carry out these analyses. The steps and output may be slightly different for other versions of SPSS.)

Figuring a Two-Way Analysis of Variance

It is easier to learn these steps using actual numbers; so we will use the study of the effects of vividness (low versus high) and length of examples (short versus long) on the number of examples recalled. The scores for that example are shown in "How are you doing?" question 5, and the figuring is shown in Table 14.

❶ Enter the scores into SPSS. SPSS assumes that all scores in a row are from the same person. In this example, each person is in only one of the four cells. Further, we want to be able to tell SPSS what each score means in terms of the grouping variables. Thus, you should enter the numbers as shown in Figure 16. In the first column (labeled "vivid"), we used the number "1" to indicate that a person is in the low vividness condition and the number "2" to indicate a person is in the high vividness condition. That is, the first column is for the first grouping variable (vividness in this case), and we arbitrarily used a 1 or a 2 to show which level a person is in on this grouping variable (we could have used any two numbers, but 1 and 2 are simple). In the second column (labeled "length"), we used the number

Figure 16 SPSS data editor window for the fictional study of the effects of vividness and length of examples on the number of examples recalled.

"1" for a person being in the short length condition and "2" for a person being in the long length condition. In the third column (labeled "recall"), we put in each person's score on the measured variable (that is, the number of examples each person recalled).

❷ ✍ *Analyze*.

❸ ✍ *General Linear Model*.

❹ ✍ *Univariate*.

❺ ✍ the variable called "recall" and then ✍ the arrow next to the box labeled "Dependent Variable." This tells SPSS that the analysis of variance should be carried out on the scores for the "recall" variable. ("Dependent variable" is another name for the measured variable.)

❻ ✍ the variable called "length" and then ✍ the arrow next to the box labeled "Fixed Factor(s)." This tells SPSS that the grouping variable called "length" shows whether people saw examples that were short or long. ("Fixed factors" is another name for the kind of grouping variables usually used in a factorial analysis of variance.)

❼ ✍ the variable called "vivid" and then ✍ the arrow next to the box labeled "Fixed Factor(s)." This tells SPSS that the grouping variable called "vivid" shows whether people saw examples that had low or high vividness.

❽ ✐ *Options.* ✐ the box labeled *Descriptive statistics* (this checks the box). This tells SPSS to provide descriptive statistics (means, standard deviations, etc.) for each cell. ✐ the box labeled *Estimates of Effect Size* (this checks the box). ✐ *Continue.* (Step ❽ is optional, but we strongly recommend requesting descriptive statistics and effect size estimates for any hypothesis-testing situation.)

❾ ✐ *OK.* Your SPSS output window should look like Figure 17.

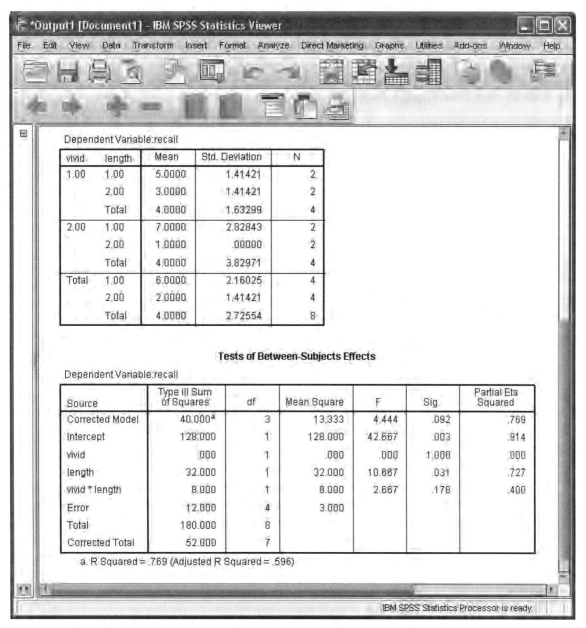

Dependent Variable:recall

vivid	length	Mean	Std. Deviation	N
1.00	1.00	5.0000	1.41421	2
	2.00	3.0000	1.41421	2
	Total	4.0000	1.63299	4
2.00	1.00	7.0000	2.82843	2
	2.00	1.0000	.00000	2
	Total	4.0000	3.82971	4
Total	1.00	6.0000	2.16025	4
	2.00	2.0000	1.41421	4
	Total	4.0000	2.72554	8

Tests of Between-Subjects Effects

Dependent Variable:recall

Source	Type III Sum of Squares	df	Mean Square	F	Sig.	Partial Eta Squared
Corrected Model	40.000[a]	3	13.333	4.444	.092	.769
Intercept	128.000	1	128.000	42.667	.003	.914
vivid	.000	1	.000	.000	1.000	.000
length	32.000	1	32.000	10.667	.031	.727
vivid * length	8.000	1	8.000	2.667	.178	.400
Error	12.000	4	3.000			
Total	180.000	8				
Corrected Total	52.000	7				

a. R Squared = .769 (Adjusted R Squared = .596)

Figure 17 SPSS output window for a two-way analysis of variance for the fictional study of the effects of vividness and length of examples on the number of examples recalled.

The first table in the SPSS output (which is not shown in Figure 17) gives the number of individuals in each level of the two grouping variables ("vivid" and "length"). Be sure to look at this closely to check that the analysis actually used the participants and variables you intended! The second table (labeled "Descriptive Statistics") provides descriptive statistics (mean, estimated population standard deviation, and number of individuals) for the "recall" scores for each cell. Knowing the mean value of each cell is important when it comes to interpreting significant results from an analysis of variance. This table also provides marginal means for each row and column and the overall mean. These are shown in the "Total" rows and "Total" section.

The third table in the SPSS output (labeled "Tests of Between-Subjects Effects") shows the actual results of the two-way analysis of variance. You can ignore the results shown in the rows labeled "Corrected Model," "Intercept," and "Corrected Total." The first column ("Source") lists the types of population variance estimates, including the effects for "vivid," "length," the interaction ("vivid * length"), and the within-groups estimate ("Error"). The second column lists the sums of squares: these are described in the Advanced Topic section earlier in this chapter, but ignore this column if you did not read that section. The third column, "df," gives each type of degrees of freedom. The fourth column, "Mean Square," gives the population variance estimates for each main effect (vivid, length), for the interaction, and for the within-groups (or "Error"). The next column gives the F ratio for each main effect and for the interaction. The values for "df," "Mean Square," and "F" (and "Sum of Squares") are consistent with those shown in Table 14, where we worked this out by hand using the procedures in the Advanced Topic section. The "Sig." column shows the exact significance level of each F ratio. The significance level of .031 for the "length" effect is less than our .05 cutoff for this example, which means that you can reject the null hypothesis and the research hypothesis is supported (that is, the result is statistically significant). For the "vivid" effect, the significance level of 1.000 is greater than our .05 cutoff, which means that you cannot reject the null hypothesis. The significance level of .178 for the interaction effect is also greater than our .05 cutoff, which means that you cannot reject the null hypothesis.

The effect size estimates are shown in the final column of table, labeled "Partial Eta Squared." As you learned earlier in the chapter, eta squared (η^2) is another name for R squared (R^2). (The eta squared values are referred to as being partial because they describe the proportion of variance accounted for by an effect after the other effects have been taken into account or "partialed out.") The most important effect size estimates to focus on are those for each of the main effects and for the interaction. The SPSS output also provides an effect size estimate for the overall analysis, which is shown in the "Corrected Model" row (eta squared = .769) as well as in a note underneath the table ("R squared = .769"). For more information on how to calculate effect size for a factorial analysis of variance, see the Advanced Topic section earlier in this chapter.

Making a Bar Graph of the Results of a Two-Way Analysis of Variance

As you learned earlier in the chapter, it is often helpful to make a bar graph to visualize the results of a two-way analysis of variance. We will use the same example from the preceding two-way analysis of variance to show how to create such a bar graph. Note that, before we undertook the following steps to produce the bar graph, we went to the "Variable View" window in SPSS and entered value labels (in the "Values"

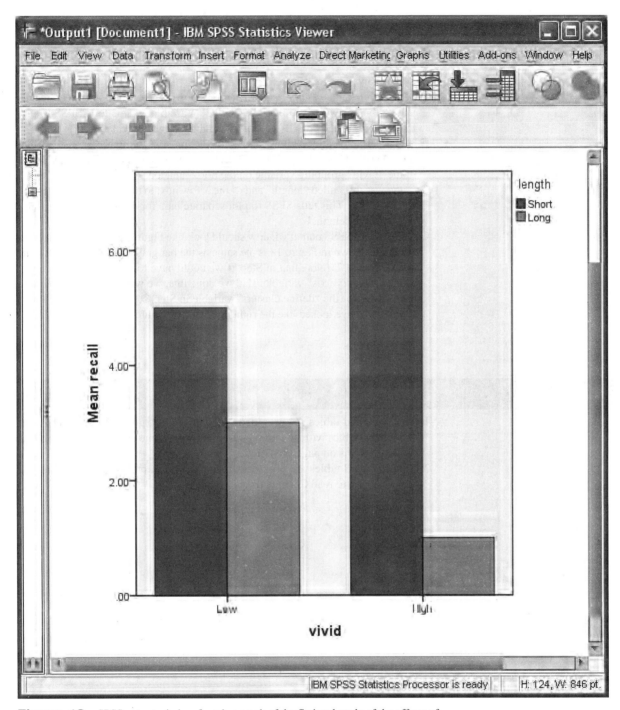

Figure 18 SPSS output window for a bar graph of the fictional study of the effects of vividness and length of examples on the number of examples recalled.

column) for the "vivid" (1 = "Low"; 2 = "High") and "length" (1 = "Short"; 2 = "Long") variables. This makes it easier to understand the bar graph, as these value labels are then shown on the graph.

❶ Enter the scores into SPSS as shown in Figure 16.

❷ ✐ *Graphs.*

❸ ✐ *Legacy Dialogs.*

❹ ✐ *Bar.*

❺ ✐ the graph next to "Clustered." ✐ *Define.*

❻ ✐ the circle labeled *Other statistic (e.g., mean).* ✐ the variable called "recall" and ✐ the arrow next to the box labeled "Variable:". This tells SPSS to plot mean scores of the "recall" grouping variable on the vertical axis.

❼ ✐ the variable called "vivid" and ✐ the arrow next to the box labeled "Category Axis:". This tells SPSS to plot separate sets of bars according to the levels of the "vivid" grouping variable on the horizontal axis.

❽ ✐ the variable called "length" and ✐ the arrow next to the box labeled "Defined Clusters by:". This tells SPSS to plot separate bars for each level of the grouping variable "length."

❾ ✐ *OK.* Your SPSS output window should look like Figure 18. As you can see, the bar graph shown in Figure 18 is the same as the bar graph shown in the left hand side of Figure 7. (Note that in Step ❼ we could have told SPSS to use "length" as the "category axis" variable. Had we done that, we would have also told it to use "vivid" for the "define clusters" variable in Step ❽. The resulting bar graph would then have looked like the right hand side of Figure 7.)

Chapter Notes

1. More detailed tables are provided in Cohen (1988, pp. 389–354). However, using these tables with a factorial design requires some preliminary figuring, as Cohen explains on pages 364–379.

2. More detailed tables are provided in Cohen (1988, pp. 381–389). If you use these, be sure to read Cohen's pages 396–403.

Appendix: Table

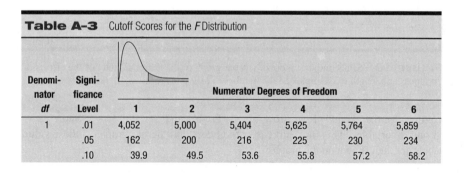

Table A-3 Cutoff Scores for the *F* Distribution

Denominator df	Significance Level	Numerator Degrees of Freedom					
		1	2	3	4	5	6
1	.01	4,052	5,000	5,404	5,625	5,764	5,859
	.05	162	200	216	225	230	234
	.10	39.9	49.5	53.6	55.8	57.2	58.2

Table A-3 *(continued)*

Denomi-nator df	Signi-ficance Level	\multicolumn{6}{c}{Numerator Degrees of Freedom}
		1	2	3	4	5	6
2	.01	98.50	99.00	99.17	99.25	99.30	99.33
	.05	18.51	19.00	19.17	19.25	19.30	19.33
	.10	8.53	9.00	9.16	9.24	9.29	9.33
3	.01	34.12	30.82	29.46	28.71	28.24	27.91
	.05	10.13	9.55	9.28	9.12	9.01	8.94
	.10	5.54	5.46	5.39	5.34	5.31	5.28
4	.01	21.20	18.00	16.70	15.98	15.52	15.21
	.05	7.71	6.95	6.59	6.39	6.26	6.16
	.10	4.55	4.33	4.19	4.11	4.05	4.01
5	.01	16.26	13.27	12.06	11.39	10.97	10.67
	.05	6.61	5.79	5.41	5.19	5.05	4.95
	.10	4.06	3.78	3.62	3.52	3.45	3.41
6	.01	13.75	10.93	9.78	9.15	8.75	8.47
	.05	5.99	5.14	4.76	4.53	4.39	4.28
	.10	3.78	3.46	3.29	3.18	3.11	3.06
7	.01	12.25	9.55	8.45	7.85	7.46	7.19
	.05	5.59	4.74	4.35	4.12	3.97	3.87
	.10	3.59	3.26	3.08	2.96	2.88	2.83
8	.01	11.26	8.65	7.59	7.01	6.63	6.37
	.05	5.32	4.46	4.07	3.84	3.69	3.58
	.10	3.46	3.11	2.92	2.81	2.73	2.67
9	.01	10.56	8.02	6.99	6.42	6.06	5.80
	.05	5.12	4.26	3.86	3.63	3.48	3.37
	.10	3.36	3.01	2.81	2.69	2.61	2.55
10	.01	10.05	7.56	6.55	6.00	5.64	5.39
	.05	4.97	4.10	3.71	3.48	3.33	3.22
	.10	3.29	2.93	2.73	2.61	2.52	2.46
11	.01	9.65	7.21	6.22	5.67	5.32	5.07
	.05	4.85	3.98	3.59	3.36	3.20	3.10
	.10	3.23	2.86	2.66	2.54	2.45	2.39
12	.01	9.33	6.93	5.95	5.41	5.07	4.82
	.05	4.75	3.89	3.49	3.26	3.11	3.00
	.10	3.18	2.81	2.61	2.48	2.40	2.33
13	.01	9.07	6.70	5.74	5.21	4.86	4.62
	.05	4.67	3.81	3.41	3.18	3.03	2.92
	.10	3.14	2.76	2.56	2.43	2.35	2.28
14	.01	8.86	6.52	5.56	5.04	4.70	4.46
	.05	4.60	3.74	3.34	3.11	2.96	2.85
	.10	3.10	2.73	2.52	2.40	2.31	2.24
15	.01	8.68	6.36	5.42	4.89	4.56	4.32
	.05	4.54	3.68	3.29	3.06	2.90	2.79
	.10	3.07	2.70	2.49	2.36	2.27	2.21
16	.01	8.53	6.23	5.29	4.77	4.44	4.20
	.05	4.49	3.63	3.24	3.01	2.85	2.74
	.10	3.05	2.67	2.46	2.33	2.24	2.18

(continued)

Table A-3 (continued)

Denomi- nator df	Signi- ficance Level	Numerator Degrees of Freedom					
		1	2	3	4	5	6
17	.01	8.40	6.11	5.19	4.67	4.34	4.10
	.05	4.45	3.59	3.20	2.97	2.81	2.70
	.10	3.03	2.65	2.44	2.31	2.22	2.15
18	.01	8.29	6.01	5.09	4.58	4.25	4.02
	.05	4.41	3.56	3.16	2.93	2.77	2.66
	.10	3.01	2.62	2.42	2.29	2.20	2.13
19	.01	8.19	5.93	5.01	4.50	4.17	3.94
	.05	4.38	3.52	3.13	2.90	2.74	2.63
	.10	2.99	2.61	2.40	2.27	2.18	2.11
20	.01	8.10	5.85	4.94	4.43	4.10	3.87
	.05	4.35	3.49	3.10	2.87	2.71	2.60
	.10	2.98	2.59	2.38	2.25	2.16	2.09
21	.01	8.02	5.78	4.88	4.37	4.04	3.81
	.05	4.33	3.47	3.07	2.84	2.69	2.57
	.10	2.96	2.58	2.37	2.23	2.14	2.08
22	.01	7.95	5.72	4.82	4.31	3.99	3.76
	.05	4.30	3.44	3.05	2.82	2.66	2.55
	.10	2.95	2.56	2.35	2.22	2.13	2.06
23	.01	7.88	5.66	4.77	4.26	3.94	3.71
	.05	4.28	3.42	3.03	2.80	2.64	2.53
	.10	2.94	2.55	2.34	2.21	2.12	2.05
24	.01	7.82	5.61	4.72	4.22	3.90	3.67
	.05	4.26	3.40	3.01	2.78	2.62	2.51
	.10	2.93	2.54	2.33	2.20	2.10	2.04
25	.01	7.77	5.57	4.68	4.18	3.86	3.63
	.05	4.24	3.39	2.99	2.76	2.60	2.49
	.10	2.92	2.53	2.32	2.19	2.09	2.03
26	.01	7.72	5.53	4.64	4.14	3.82	3.59
	.05	4.23	3.37	2.98	2.74	2.59	2.48
	.10	2.91	2.52	2.31	2.18	2.08	2.01
27	.01	7.68	5.49	4.60	4.11	3.79	3.56
	.05	4.21	3.36	2.96	2.73	2.57	2.46
	.10	2.90	2.51	2.30	2.17	2.07	2.01
28	.01	7.64	5.45	4.57	4.08	3.75	3.53
	.05	4.20	3.34	2.95	2.72	2.56	2.45
	.10	2.89	2.50	2.29	2.16	2.07	2.00
29	.01	7.60	5.42	4.54	4.05	3.73	3.50
	.05	4.18	3.33	2.94	2.70	2.55	2.43
	.10	2.89	2.50	2.28	2.15	2.06	1.99
30	.01	7.56	5.39	4.51	4.02	3.70	3.47
	.05	4.17	3.32	2.92	2.69	2.53	2.42
	.10	2.88	2.49	2.28	2.14	2.05	1.98
35	.01	7.42	5.27	4.40	3.91	3.59	3.37
	.05	4.12	3.27	2.88	2.64	2.49	2.37
	.10	2.86	2.46	2.25	2.11	2.02	1.95

Table A-3 (continued)

Denominator df	Significance Level	Numerator Degrees of Freedom					
		1	2	3	4	5	6
40	.01	7.32	5.18	4.31	3.83	3.51	3.29
	.05	4.09	3.23	2.84	2.61	2.45	2.34
	.10	2.84	2.44	2.23	2.09	2.00	1.93
45	.01	7.23	5.11	4.25	3.77	3.46	3.23
	.05	4.06	3.21	2.81	2.58	2.42	2.31
	.10	2.82	2.43	2.21	2.08	1.98	1.91
50	.01	7.17	5.06	4.20	3.72	3.41	3.19
	.05	4.04	3.18	2.79	2.56	2.40	2.29
	.10	2.81	2.41	2.20	2.06	1.97	1.90
55	.01	7.12	5.01	4.16	3.68	3.37	3.15
	.05	4.02	3.17	2.77	2.54	2.38	2.27
	.10	2.80	2.40	2.19	2.05	1.96	1.89
60	.01	7.08	4.98	4.13	3.65	3.34	3.12
	.05	4.00	3.15	2.76	2.53	2.37	2.26
	.10	2.79	2.39	2.18	2.04	1.95	1.88
65	.01	7.04	4.95	4.10	3.62	3.31	3.09
	.05	3.99	3.14	2.75	2.51	2.36	2.24
	.10	2.79	2.39	2.17	2.03	1.94	1.87
70	.01	7.01	4.92	4.08	3.60	3.29	3.07
	.05	3.98	3.13	2.74	2.50	2.35	2.23
	.10	2.78	2.38	2.16	2.03	1.93	1.86
75	.01	6.99	4.90	4.06	3.58	3.27	3.05
	.05	3.97	3.12	2.73	2.49	2.34	2.22
	.10	2.77	2.38	2.16	2.02	1.93	1.86
80	.01	6.96	4.88	4.04	3.56	3.26	3.04
	.05	3.96	3.11	2.72	2.49	2.33	2.22
	.10	2.77	2.37	2.15	2.02	1.92	1.85
85	.01	6.94	4.86	4.02	3.55	3.24	3.02
	.05	3.95	3.10	2.71	2.48	2.32	2.21
	.10	2.77	2.37	2.15	2.01	1.92	1.85
90	.01	6.93	4.85	4.01	3.54	3.23	3.01
	.05	3.95	3.10	2.71	2.47	2.32	2.20
	.10	2.76	2.36	2.15	2.01	1.91	1.84
95	.01	6.91	4.84	4.00	3.52	3.22	3.00
	.05	3.94	3.09	2.70	2.47	2.31	2.20
	.10	2.76	2.36	2.14	2.01	1.91	1.84
100	.01	6.90	4.82	3.98	3.51	3.21	2.99
	.05	3.94	3.09	2.70	2.46	2.31	2.19
	.10	2.76	2.36	2.14	2.00	1.91	1.83
∞	.01	6.64	4.61	3.78	3.32	3.02	2.80
	.05	3.84	3.00	2.61	2.37	2.22	2.10
	.10	2.71	2.30	2.08	1.95	1.85	1.78

Answers to Set I Practice Problems

Chapter 10

1. i. (a) and (b)

(c) Main effects for class and age, interaction effect; (d) income is greater in general for upper-class and for older individuals, but the combination of older and upper class has a higher income than would be expected just from the effects of either variable alone.

ii. (a) and (b) Graphs of the same kind as in part (i) (a) and (b); (c) no main effects, interaction effect; (d) neither type of college nor type of major, by itself, predicts grades, but there is a clear pattern if one considers the combinations: grades are highest for community college arts majors and for liberal arts college science majors.

iii. (a) and (b) Graphs of the same kind as in part (i) (a) and (b); (c) both main effects significant; no interaction; (d) females miss fewer days per month than males; those who exercise miss fewer days per month than controls. Each combination misses the number of days you would expect knowing their level of each variable separately.

2. i. (a) and (b) Graphs of the same kind as in question 1 (i) (a) and (b); (c) main effect for relationship and an interaction; (d) conversations are longer with friends, but the difference is much greater for personal than for nonpersonal topics.

ii. (a) and (b) Graphs of the same kind as in question 1 (i) (a) and (b); (c) main effect for city and cost, plus an interaction; (d) restaurant quality is different in different cities, with New York highest and Chicago lowest. Restaurant quality is different in different price ranges, with expensive the best and inexpensive the least. The two factors do not simply combine, however, because price makes more difference in New York than in other cities.

iii. (a) and (b) Graphs of the same kind as in question 1 (i) (a) and (b); (c) main effects for brand and type and an interaction; (d) flavor is rated on the average more positively for regular than decaf, and brands Z and X are rated more favorably than Y. However, there is an interaction in which there is no difference between regular and decaf for brand Z, but for brands Z and Y, regular is rated 2 points higher.

3. Example answers.

		Sport			
Condition	**(a)**	*Baseball*	*Football*	*Basketball*	
	With motivational program	10	5	6	7
	Without motivational program	10	5	6	7
		10	5	6	
Condition	**(b)**	*Baseball*	*Football*	*Basketball*	
	With motivational program	6	6	6	6
	Without motivational program	10	10	10	10
		8	8	8	
Condition	**(c)**	*Baseball*	*Football*	*Basketball*	
	With motivational program	6	7	8	7
	Without motivational program	8	9	10	9
		7	8	9	

(d)

Condition	Baseball	Football	Basketball	
With motivational program	6	7	8	7
Without motivational program	10	9	8	9
	8	8	8	

(e)

Condition	Baseball	Football	Basketball	
With motivational program	6	7	8	7
Without motivational program	6	8	10	8
	6	7.5	9	

4. As expected, participants with extreme stereotypes about PR agents being extroverted, compared to participants with only moderate stereotypes of this kind, described PR agents as more extroverted. This result was statistically significant, meaning that you can be reasonably confident that the pattern of the result applies not just to the particular people studied, but to people like those studied in general. (More precisely, the researchers were able to conclude that, if there was no average difference in the general population between extreme and moderate stereotype people, there is less than a .0001 chance that this experiment could have produced a result that strong.) In addition, and most important, this tendency was surprisingly much stronger for participants who were given a description of a particular PR agent who was highly introverted. This result was also statistically significant. (In this case, the chance was less than 5% of getting a result this strong if in the general population there was no average tendency of this kind.)

On average, those exposed to the extreme introvert tended to give higher ratings of extroversion. This result was of "marginal" statistical significance, meaning that it was on the borderline of being too unlikely to have come up if there were no true average difference in the population. More important, this result is not very interesting because, as you can see from the graph, it is entirely due to the extreme stereotype participants; if anything, the moderate stereotype participants showed an opposite pattern of effect.

5. Similar to question 4.
6. F needed for each effect in (a), (b), and (c) ($df = 1, 8, p < .05$) = 5.32. Graphs as the same kind as in question 1 (i) (a) or (b).

(a)

		Experimental Condition		
		A	B	Overall
Group	1	.67	2.67	1.67
	2	2.67	.67	1.67
Overall		1.67	1.67	

Source	SS	df	MS	F	
Group	0	1	0	0	Do not reject null.
Condition	0	1	0	0	Do not reject null.
Interaction	12	1	12	35.29	Reject null.
Within cells	2.68	8	.34		

(b)

		Experimental Condition		
		A	B	Overall
Group	1	.67	.67	.67
	2	2.67	2.67	2.67
Overall		1.67	1.67	

Source	SS	df	MS	F	
Group	12	1	12	35.29	Reject null.
Condition	0	1	0	0	Do not reject null.
Interaction	0	1	0	0	Do not reject null.
Within cells	2.68	8	.34		

(c)

		Experimental Condition		
		A	B	Overall
Group	1	.67	2.67	1.67
	2	.67	2.67	1.67
Overall		.67	2.67	

Source	SS	df	MS	F	
Group	0	1	0	0	Do not reject null.
Condition	12	1	12	35.29	Reject null.
Interaction	0	1	0	0	Do not reject null.
Within cells	2.68	8	.34		

7. (a) F needed for main effect for Diagnosis ($df = 1, 6$) = 5.99; for main effect for Therapy and interaction ($df = 2, 6$) = 5.14.

Source	SS	df	MS	F	
Therapy	8	2	4	1.33	Do not reject null.
Diagnosis	108	1	108	36	Reject null.
Interaction	0	2	0	0	Do not reject null.
Within cells	18	6	3		

(b) Means:

	A	B	C	
I	4	2	3	3
II	10	8	9	9
	7	5	6	

(c) Similar to question 1 (i) (a).
(d) There is a significant difference in effectiveness between the two diagnostic categories: therapy is more effective for those with Diagnosis II. However, there is no

significant difference among types of therapy, and the types of therapy are not significantly differentially effective for the different diagnostic types.

8. (a) F needed for each effect ($df = 1, 8$) = 5.32.

Source	SS	df	MS	F	
Likability	0	1	0	0	Do not reject null.
Nervousness	0	1	0	0	Do not reject null.
Interaction	48	1	48	32	Reject null.
Within cells	12	8	1.5		

(b) Means

	Likeable	Not Likeable	
Nervous	7	3	5
Not Nervous	3	7	5
	5	5	

(c) Similar to question 1 (i) (a).

(d) These results indicate that there is a significant interaction between nervousness and likability: The defendant who is likeable is more likely to be rated innocent if he is nervous; but the defendant who is not likeable is more likely to be rated innocent if he is not nervous. There was no overall significant effect for likeable or not or for nervous or not, though with the very small sample sizes involved, failures to reject the null hypothesis should not be taken as evidence that such an effect does not exist.

The figuring of the significance is like a one-way analysis of variance using the structural model approach. The within-groups sum of squares and degrees of freedom are figured in the usual way, considering each cell as its own group. However, the between-groups deviations from the mean are divided into three parts: one is the variation between likability versus not (based on each participant's liking versus not-liking group's mean minus the grand mean); another is the variation between nervous versus not. The degrees of freedom for each is the number of levels (2 in each case) minus 1.

However, following this procedure, some of the between-groups effect is left over—the variation between likability groups that is different according to which nervousness group they are in. This is an example of what is called an interaction effect. You figure its mean squares based on the deviation of the score from the overall grand mean minus the other three deviations (the score minus its group's mean from the grand mean). Its degrees of freedom are what are left over in the total between-groups degrees of freedom (with four subgroups, between-groups $df = 3$ minus 1 for likability and minus another 1 for nervousness).

9. (a) $R^2_{\text{Columns}} = (S^2_{\text{Columns}})(df_{\text{Columns}})/$
$[(S^2_{\text{Columns}})(df_{\text{Columns}}) + (S^2_{\text{Within}})(df_{\text{Within}})]$;
$R^2_{\text{Condition}} = (0)(1)/[(0)(1) + (.34)(8)] = 0$,
$R^2_{\text{Group}} = 0, R^2_{\text{Interaction}} = .82$; (b) $R^2_{\text{Condition}} = 0$,
$R^2_{\text{Group}} = .82, R^2_{\text{Interaction}} = 0$; (c) $R^2_{\text{Condition}} = .82$,
$R^2_{\text{Group}} = 0, R^2_{\text{Interaction}} = 0$; (d) $R^2_{\text{Therapy}} = .31$,
$R^2_{\text{Diagnosis}} = .86, R^2_{\text{Interaction}} = 0$; (e) $R^2_{\text{Likability}} = 0$,
$R^2_{\text{Nervousness}} = 0, R^2_{\text{Interaction}} = .80$.

10. From Table 10-15: (a) .19; (b) .29; (c) .26; (d) .21; (e) .78.

11. From Table 10-16: (a) 197; (b) 197; (c) 33; (d) 132; (e) 162; (f) 162.

Chapter 11

Correlation

This chapter is about a statistical procedure that allows you to look at the relationship between two groups of scores. To give you an idea of what we mean, let's consider some real-world examples. Among students, there is a relationship between high school grades and college grades. It isn't a perfect relationship, but generally speaking students with better high school grades tend to get better grades in college. Similarly, there is a relationship between parents' heights and the adult height of their children. Taller parents tend to give birth to children who grow up to be taller than the children of shorter parents. Again, the relationship isn't perfect, but the general pattern is clear. Now we'll look at an example in detail.

One hundred thirteen married people in the small college town of Santa Cruz, California, responded to a questionnaire in the local newspaper about their marriage. (This was part of a larger study reported by Aron and colleagues [2000].) As part of the questionnaire, they answered the question, "How exciting are the things you do together with your partner?" using a scale from 1 = *not exciting at all* to 5 = *extremely exciting*. The questionnaire also included a standard measure of marital satisfaction (that included items such as, "In general, how often do you think that things between you and your partner are going well?").

The researchers were interested in finding out the relationship between doing exciting things with a marital partner and the level of marital satisfaction people reported. In other words, they wanted to look at the relationship between two groups of scores: the group of scores for doing exciting things and the group of scores for marital satisfaction. As shown in Figure 1, the relationship between these two groups of scores can be shown very clearly using a graph. The horizontal axis is for people's answers to the question, "How exciting are the things you do together with your partner?" The vertical axis is for the marital satisfaction scores. Each person's score on the two variables is shown as a dot.

The overall pattern is that the dots go from the lower left to the upper right. That is, lower scores on the variable "doing exciting activities with your partner" most often go with lower scores on the variable "marital satisfaction," and higher most often with higher. So, in general, this graph shows that the less people did exciting activities with their partner, the less satisfied they were in their marriage; and the more they did exciting activities together, the more satisfied they were in their marriage. Even though the pattern is far from one to one, you can see a general trend. This general pattern is of low scores on one variable going with low scores on the other variable, high scores going with high scores, and mediums with mediums. This is an example of a **correlation**. (This finding that doing exciting activities with an established relationship partner is positively associated with good relationship quality has since been found in other surveys, as well as in longitudinal studies, daily diary report studies, and laboratory experiments; e.g., Aron et al., 2000; Tsapelas et al., 2009.)

correlation association between scores on two variables.

A correlation describes the relationship between two variables. More precisely, the usual measure of a correlation describes the relationship between *two*

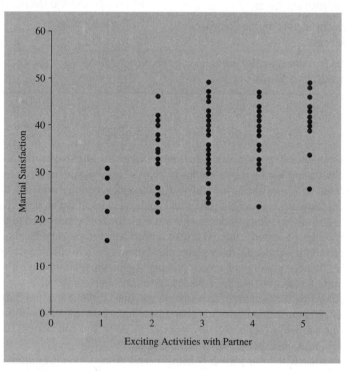

Figure 1 Scatter diagram showing the correlation for 113 married individuals between doing exciting activities with their partner and their marital satisfaction. (Data from Aron et al., 2000.)

equal-interval numeric variables. The differences between values for equal-interval numeric variables correspond to differences in the underlying thing being measured. (Most psychologists consider scales like a 1 to 10 rating scale as approximately equal-interval scales.) There are countless examples of correlations: in children, there is a correlation between age and coordination skills; among students, there is a correlation between amount of time studying and amount learned; in the marketplace, we often assume that a correlation exists between price and quality—that high prices go with high quality and low with low.

This chapter explores correlation, including how to describe it graphically, different types of correlations, how to figure the correlation coefficient (which gives a number for the degree of correlation), the statistical significance of a correlation coefficient, issues about how to interpret a correlation coefficient, and effect size and power for a correlation coefficient.

TIP FOR SUCCESS

If you're in any way unsure about what an equal-interval numeric variable is, be sure to review the material in *Displaying the Order in a Group of Numbers Using Tables and Graphs* on kinds of variables.

Graphing Correlations: The Scatter Diagram

Figure 1 shows the correlation between exciting activities and marital satisfaction and is an example of a **scatter diagram** (also called a *scatterplot*). A scatter diagram shows you at a glance the pattern of the relationship between the two variables.

How to Make a Scatter Diagram

There are three steps to making a scatter diagram:

❶ **Draw the axes and decide which variable goes on which axis.** Often, it doesn't matter which variable goes on which axis. However, sometimes the researchers are thinking of one of the variables as predicting or causing the other. In that case, the variable that is doing the predicting or causing goes on the horizontal axis and the variable that is being predicted about or caused goes on the vertical axis. In Figure 1, we put exciting activities on the horizontal axis and marital satisfaction on the vertical axis. This was because the study was based on a theory that the more exciting activities that an established couple does together, the more the couple is satisfied with their marriage. (We will have more to say about this later in the chapter when we discuss causality.)

❷ **Determine the range of values to use for each variable and mark them on the axes.** Your numbers should go from low to high on each axis, starting from where the axes meet. Your low value on each axis should be 0.

Each axis should continue to the highest value your measure can possibly have. When there is no obvious highest possible value, make the axis go to a value that is as high as people ordinarily score in the group of people of interest for your study. Note that scatter diagrams are usually made roughly square, with the horizontal and vertical axes being about the same length (a 1:1 ratio).

❸ **Mark a dot for each pair of scores.** Find the place on the horizontal axis for the first pair of scores on the horizontal-axis variable. Next, move up to the height for the score for the first pair of scores on the vertical-axis variable. Then mark a clear dot. Continue this process for the remaining pairs of scores. Sometimes the same pair of scores occurs twice (or more times). This means that the dots for these pairs would go in the same place. When this happens, you can put a second dot as near as possible to the first—touching, if possible—but making it clear that there are in fact two dots in the one place. Alternatively, you can put the number 2 in that place.

scatter diagram graph showing the relationship between two variables: the values of one variable are along the horizontal axis and the values of the other variable are along the vertical axis; each score is shown as a dot in this two-dimensional space.

Table 1 Hours Slept Last Night and Happy Mood Example (Fictional Data)	
Hours Slept	**Happy Mood**
5	2
7	4
8	7
6	2
6	3
10	6

An Example

Suppose a researcher is studying the relationship of sleep to mood. As an initial test, the researcher asks six students in her morning seminar two questions:

1. How many hours did you sleep last night?
2. How happy do you feel right now on a scale from 0 = *not at all happy* to 8 = *extremely happy?*

The (fictional) results are shown in Table 1. (In practice, a much larger group would be used in this kind of research. We are using an example with just six to keep things simple for learning. In fact, we have done a real version of this study. Results of the real study are similar to what we show here, except not as strong as the ones we made up to make the pattern clear for learning.)

❶ **Draw the axes and decide which variable goes on which axis.** Because sleep comes before mood in this study, it makes most sense to think of sleep as the predictor. Thus, as shown in Figure 2a, we put hours slept on the horizontal axis and happy mood on the vertical axis.

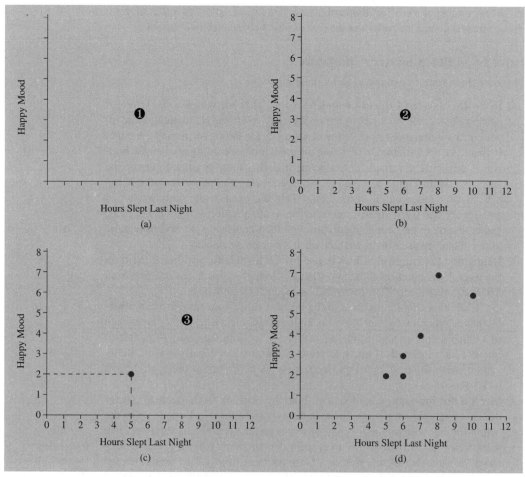

Figure 2 Steps for making a scatter diagram. (a) ❶ Draw the axes and decide which variable goes on which axis—the predictor variable (Hours Slept Last Night) on the horizontal axis, the other (Happy Mood) on the vertical axis. (b) ❷ Determine the range of values to use for each variable and mark them on the axes. (c) ❸ Mark a dot for the pair of scores for the first student. (d) ❸ continued: Mark dots for the remaining pairs of scores.

❷ **Determine the range of values to use for each variable and mark them on the axes.** For the horizontal axis, we start at 0 as usual. We do not know the maximum possible, but let us assume that students rarely sleep more than 12 hours. The vertical axis goes from 0 to 8, the lowest and highest scores possible on the happiness question. See Figure 2b.

❸ **Mark a dot for each pair of scores.** For the first student, the number of hours slept last night was 5. Move across to 5 on the horizontal axis. The happy mood rating for the first student was 2, so move up to the point across from the 2 on the vertical axis. Place a dot at this point, as shown in Figure 2c. Do the same for each of the other five students. The result should look like Figure 2d.

How are you doing?

1. What does a scatter diagram show, and what does it consist of?
2. (a) Which variable goes on the horizontal axis when one variable in a study can be thought of as predicting another variable? (b) Which goes on the vertical axis?
3. Make a scatter diagram for the following scores for four people who were each tested on two variables, X and Y. X is the variable we are predicting from; it can have scores ranging from 0 to 6. Y is the variable being predicted; it can have scores from 0 to 7.

Person	X	Y
A	3	4
B	6	7
C	1	2
D	4	6

Figure 3   Scatter diagram for scores in "How are you doing?" question 3.

Answers

1. A scatter diagram is a graph that shows the relation between two variables. One axis is for one variable; the other axis, for the other variable. The graph has a dot for each individual's pair of scores. The dot for each pair is placed above that of the score for that pair on the horizontal axis variable and directly across from the score for that pair on the vertical axis variable.
2. (a) The variable that is doing the predicting goes on the horizontal axis. (b) The variable that is being predicted goes on the vertical axis.
3. See Figure 3.

Patterns of Correlation

Linear and Curvilinear Correlations

In each example so far, the pattern in the scatter diagram very roughly approximates a straight line. Thus, each is an example of a **linear correlation**. In the scatter diagram for the study of happy mood and sleep (Figure 2d), you could draw a line showing the general trend of the dots, as we have done in Figure 4. Notice that the scores do not all fall right on the line. Notice also, however, that the line does describe the general tendency of the scores.

Sometimes, however, the general relationship between two variables does not follow a straight line at all, but instead follows the more complex pattern of a **curvilinear correlation**. Consider, for example, the relationship between your satisfaction with a romantic relationship and how much your partner idealizes you (how positively you believe your partner sees you minus how positively you see yourself). Up to a point we like being idealized (and we certainly don't like being seen less positively by a partner than we see ourselves!). However, what the latest studies have shown is that there can be too much of a good thing (Tomlinson et al., 2011). That

linear correlation relation between two variables that shows up on a scatter diagram as the dots roughly following a straight line.

curvilinear correlation relation between two variables that shows up on a scatter diagram as dots following a systematic pattern that is not a straight line.

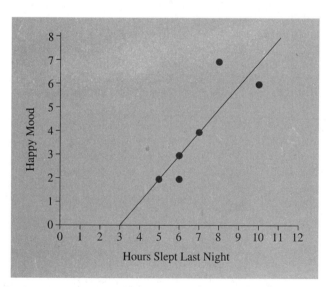

Figure 4   Scatter diagram from Figure 2d with a line drawn to show the general trend.

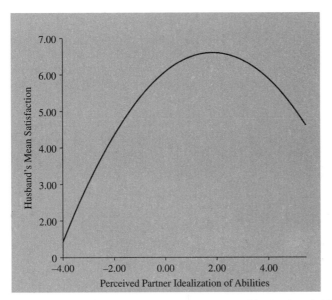

Figure 5 Association of satisfaction with perceived partner idealization of abilities (extent to which wife is perceived to see self's abilities more positively than one sees one's own abilities) ($N = 89$).

Source: Tomlinson, J. M., Aron, A., Carmichael, C. L., Reis, H. T., & Holmes, J. G. (2011). *The effects of feeling over-idealized in dating and married relationships.* Presented at the International Association for Relationships Research Mini Conference, Tucson, AZ.

is, when feeling over-idealized, we feel less satisfied with the relationship. It is as if we are being put on a pedestal, that our autonomy is threatened, that our partner will eventually find out we are not as wonderful as he or she thinks we are, or that we simply don't have to try as hard in the relationship because we are seen as so wonderful. This particular curvilinear pattern is shown in Figure 5. As shown in the figure, up to a certain point, husbands with a higher perceived partner idealization of their abilities were more satisfied with their relationship. However, husbands' level of relationship satisfaction starts to decrease among those with the highest levels of perceived partner idealization. Notice that you could not draw a straight line to describe this pattern. More generally, a recent review described how a number of positive characteristics, such as generosity, happiness, and even conscientiousness, can have negative effects at very high levels, and that psychologists need to pay more attention to the possibility of curvilinear relationships (Grant & Schwartz, 2011). Some other examples of curvilinear relationships are shown in Figure 6.

The usual way of figuring the correlation (the one you learn shortly in this chapter) gives the degree of *linear* correlation. If the true pattern of association is curvilinear, figuring the correlation in the usual way could show little or no correlation. Thus, it is important to look at scatter diagrams to identify these richer relationships rather than automatically figuring correlations in the usual way, assuming that the only possible relationship is a straight line.

No Correlation

It is also possible for two variables to be essentially unrelated to each other. For example, if you were to do a study of income and shoe size, your results might appear as shown in Figure 7. The dots are spread everywhere, and there is no line,

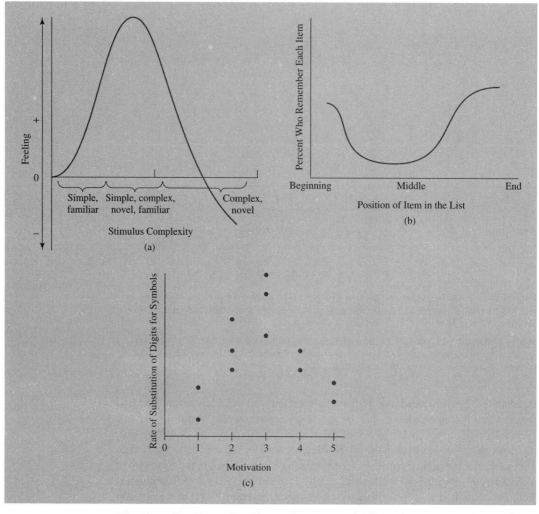

Figure 6 Examples of curvilinear relationships: (a) the way we feel and the complexity of a stimulus; (b) the number of people who remember an item and its position on a list; and (c) children's rate of and motivation for substituting digits for symbols.

no correlation no systematic relationship between two variables.

positive correlation relation between two variables in which high scores on one go with high scores on the other, mediums with mediums, and lows with lows; on a scatter diagram, the dots roughly follow a straight line sloping up and to the right.

negative correlation relation between two variables in which high scores on one go with low scores on the other, mediums with mediums, and lows with highs; on a scatter diagram, the dots roughly follow a straight line sloping down and to the right.

straight or otherwise, that is any reasonable representation of a trend. There is simply **no correlation**.

Positive and Negative Linear Correlations

In the examples so far of linear correlations, such as exciting activities and marital satisfaction, high scores go with high scores, lows with lows, and mediums with mediums. This is called a **positive correlation**. (One reason for the term "positive" is that in geometry, the slope of a line is positive when it goes up and to the right on a graph like this. Notice that in Figure 4 the positive correlation between happy mood and sleep is shown by a line that goes up and to the right.)

Sometimes, however, high scores on one variable go with low scores on the other variable and low scores with high scores. This is called a **negative correlation**. For example, in the newspaper survey about marriage, the researchers also asked

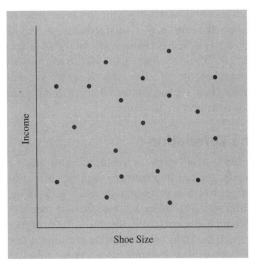

Figure 7 Two variables with no association with each other: income and shoe size (fictional data).

about boredom with the relationship and the partner. Not surprisingly, the more bored a person was, the *lower* was the person's marital satisfaction. That is, low scores on one variable went with high scores on the other. Similarly, the less bored a person was, the higher the marital satisfaction. This is shown in Figure 8, where we also put in a line to emphasize the general trend. You can see that as it goes from left to right, the line slopes slightly downward.

Another example of a negative correlation is from organizational psychology. A well established finding in that field is that absenteeism from work has a negative linear correlation with satisfaction with the job (e.g., Mirvis & Lawler, 1977). That

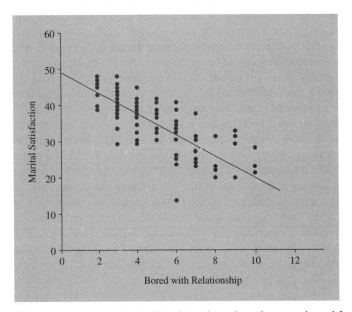

Figure 8 Scatter diagram with the line drawn in to show the general trend for a negative correlation between two variables: greater boredom with the relationship goes with lower marital satisfaction. (Data from Aron et al., 2000.)

is, the higher the level of job satisfaction, the lower the level of absenteeism. Put another way, the *lower* the level of job satisfaction is, the *higher* the absenteeism becomes. Research on this topic has continued to show this pattern all over the world (e.g., Punnett et al., 2007), and the same pattern is found for university classes: the *more* satisfied students are, the *less* they miss class (Yorges et al., 2007). (Perhaps also, the less you miss class, the more satisfied you will be! Again, we'll turn to the issue of what causes what later in the chapter.)

Strength of the Correlation

What we mean by the *strength of the correlation* is how much there is a clear pattern of some particular relationship between two variables. For example, we saw that a positive linear correlation is when high scores go with highs, mediums with mediums, lows with lows. The strength (or degree) of such a correlation, then, is *how much* highs go with highs, and so on. Similarly, the strength of a negative linear correlation is how much the highs on one variable go with the lows on the other, and so forth. To put this another way, the strength of a linear correlation can be seen in a scatter diagram by how close the dots fall to a simple straight line. There is a "large" (or "strong") linear correlation if the dots fall close to a straight line (the line sloping up or down depending on whether the linear correlation is positive or negative). A perfect linear correlation means all the dots fall exactly on the straight line. There is a "small" (or "weak") correlation when you can barely tell there is a correlation at all; the dots fall far from a straight line. The correlation is "moderate" (also called a "medium" correlation) if the pattern of dots is somewhere between a small and a large correlation.

Importance of Identifying the Pattern of Correlation

The procedure you learn in the next main section is for figuring the direction and strength of linear correlation. As we suggested earlier, the best approach to such a problem is *first* to make a scatter diagram and to identify the pattern of correlation. If the pattern is curvilinear, then you would not go on to figure the linear correlation. This is important because figuring the linear correlation when the true correlation is curvilinear would be misleading. (For example, you might conclude that there is little or no correlation when in fact there is a quite strong relationship; it is just not a linear relationship.) It is however reasonable to assume that a correlation is linear unless the scatter diagram shows a curvilinear correlation. We say this, because when the linear correlation is small, the dots will fall far from a straight line. In such situations, it can sometimes be hard to imagine a straight line that roughly shows the pattern of dots, and it is best to assume that if there is a pattern it is the simplest (most "parsimonious") pattern, which is a straight line.

If you can see from the dots even a vague linear pattern, it is also valuable to eyeball the scatter diagram a bit more. The idea is to note the direction (positive or negative) of the linear correlation and also to make a rough guess as to the strength of the correlation. Scatter diagrams with varying directions and strengths of correlation are shown in Figure 9. You can see that Figure 9a is a large positive correlation (because the dots go up and to the right and all fall close to what would be a simple straight line, 9b is a large negative correlation, 9c seems more of a moderate positive correlation, 9d seems more of a small to moderate negative correlation, and 9e and 9f appear either very small or no correlation. Using a scatter diagram to examine the direction and approximate strength of correlation is important because it lets you check to see whether you have made a major mistake when you then do the figuring you learn in the next section.

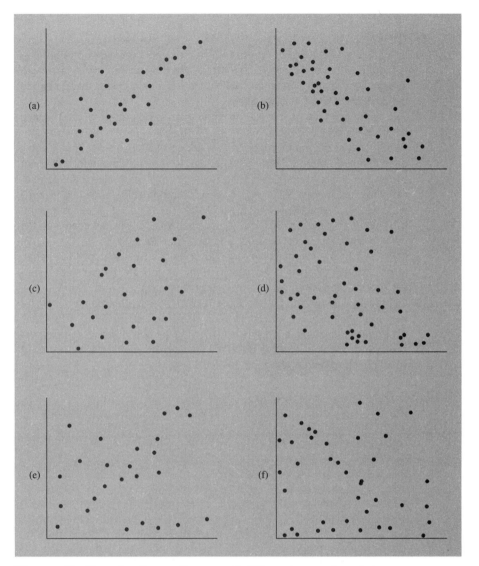

Figure 9 Examples of scatter diagrams with different degrees of correlation.

How are you doing?

1. What is the difference between a linear and curvilinear correlation in terms of how they appear in a scatter diagram?
2. What does it mean to say that two variables have no correlation?
3. What is the difference between a positive and negative linear correlation? Answer this question in terms of (a) the patterns in a scatter diagram and (b) what those patterns tell you about the relationship between the two variables.
4. For each of the scatter diagrams shown in Figure 10, say whether the pattern is roughly linear, curvilinear, or no correlation. If the pattern is roughly linear, also say if it is positive or negative, and whether it is large, moderate, or small.
5. Give two reasons why it is important to identify the pattern of correlation in a scatter diagram before figuring the precise correlation.

Answers

1. In a linear correlation, the pattern of dots roughly follows a straight line (although with a small correlation, the dots will be spread widely around a straight line); in a curvilinear correlation, there is a clear systematic pattern to the dots, but it is not a straight line.
2. Two variables have no correlation when there is no pattern of relationship between them.
3. (a) In a scatter diagram for a positive linear correlation, the line that roughly describes the pattern of dots goes up and to the right; in a negative linear correlation, the line goes down and to the right. (b) In a positive linear correlation, the basic pattern is that high scores on one variable go with high scores on the other, mediums go with mediums, and lows go with lows; in a negative linear correlation, high scores on one variable go with low scores on the other, mediums go with mediums, and lows go with highs.
4. In Figure 10: (a) linear, negative, large; (b) curvilinear; (c) linear, positive, large; (d) no correlation (it may at first look one way or the other to you; but try seeing it as the other direction and you will see that too!).
5. Identifying whether the pattern of correlation in a scatter diagram is linear tells you whether it is appropriate to use the standard procedures for figuring a linear correlation. If it is linear, identifying the direction and approximate strength of correlation before doing the figuring lets you check the results of your figuring when you are done.

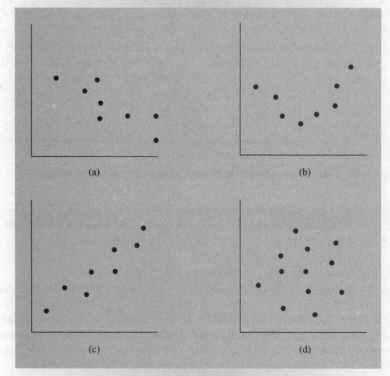

(a)   (b)

(c)   (d)

Figure 10   Scatter diagrams for "How are you doing?" question 4.

The Correlation Coefficient

Looking at a scatter diagram gives you a rough idea of the relationship between two variables, but it is not a very precise approach. What you need is a number that gives the exact correlation (in terms of its direction and strength).

Logic of Figuring the Linear Correlation

A linear correlation (when it is positive) means that highs go with highs and lows with lows. Thus, the first thing you need in figuring the linear correlation is some way to measure what is a high score and what is a low score. This means comparing scores on different variables in a consistent way. You can solve this problem of comparing apples and oranges by using Z scores.

To review, a Z score is the number of standard deviations that a score is from the mean. Whatever the range of values of the variable, if you change your raw scores to Z scores, a raw score that is high (i.e., above the mean of the scores on that variable) will always have a positive Z score. Similarly, a raw score that is low (below the mean) will always have a negative Z score. Furthermore, regardless of the particular measure used, Z scores tell you in a very standard way just how high or low each score is. A Z score of 1 is always exactly 1 standard deviation above the mean, and a Z score of 2 is twice as many standard deviations above the mean. Z scores on one variable are directly comparable to Z scores on another variable.

There is an additional reason why Z scores are so useful when figuring the exact correlation. It has to do with what happens if you multiply a score on one variable by a score on the other variable, which is called a *cross-product*. When using Z scores, this is called a **cross-product of Z scores**. If you multiply a high Z score by a high Z score, you will always get a positive cross-product. This is because no matter what the variable, scores above the mean are positive Z scores, and any positive number multiplied by any positive number has to be a positive number. Furthermore—and here is where it gets interesting—if you multiply a low Z score by a low Z score, you also always get a positive cross-product. This is because no matter what the variable, scores below the mean are negative Z scores, and a negative multiplied by a negative gives a positive.

If highs on one variable go with highs on the other, and lows on the one go with lows on the other, the cross-products of Z scores always will be positive. Considering a whole distribution of scores, suppose you take each person's Z score on one variable and multiply it by that person's Z score on the other variable. The result of doing this when highs go with highs, and lows with lows, is that the multiplications all come out positive. If, for all the people in the study, you add up these cross-products of Z scores, which are all positive, you will end up with a large positive number.

On the other hand, with a negative correlation, highs go with lows and lows with highs. In terms of Z scores, this would mean positives with negatives and negatives with positives. Multiplied out, that gives all negative cross-products. If you add all these negative cross-products together, you get a large negative number.

Finally, suppose there is no linear correlation. In this situation, for some people highs on one variable would go with highs on the other variable (and some lows would go with lows), making positive cross-products. For other people, highs on one variable would go with lows on the other variable (and some lows would go with highs), making negative cross-products. Adding up these cross-products for all the people in the study would result in the positive cross-products and the negative cross-products cancelling each other out, giving a result of 0 (or close to 0).

cross-product of Z scores   the result of multiplying a person's Z score on one variable by the person's Z score on another variable.

In each situation, we changed all the scores to Z scores, multiplied each person's two Z scores by each other, and added up these cross-products. The result was a *large positive number* if there was a *positive linear correlation*, a *large negative number* if there was a *negative linear correlation*, and *a number near 0* if there was *no linear correlation*.

Table 2 summarizes the logic up to this point. The table shows the effect on the correlation of different patterns of raw scores and resulting Z scores. For example, the first row shows a high score on X going with a high score on Y. In this situation, the Z score for variable X is a positive number (since X is a high number, above the mean of X), and similarly the Z score for variable Y is a positive number (since Y is a high number, above the mean of Y). Thus, the product of these two positive Z scores must be a positive number (since a positive number multiplied by a positive number always gives a positive number). The overall effect is that when a high score on X goes with a high score on Y, the pair of scores contribute toward making a positive correlation. The table shows that positive products of Z scores contribute toward making a positive correlation, negative products of Z scores contribute toward making a negative correlation, and products of Z scores that are zero (or close to zero) contribute toward making a correlation of zero.

However, you are still left with the problem of figuring the *strength* of a positive or negative correlation on some standard scale. The larger the number (either positive or negative), the bigger the correlation. But how large is large, and how large is not very large? You can't judge the strength of the correlation from the sum of the cross-products alone, because it gets bigger just by adding the cross-products of more people together. (That is, a study with 100 people would have a larger sum of cross-products than the same study with only 25 people, even if the two studies had the same degree of correlation.) The solution is to divide this sum of the cross-products by the number of people in the study. That is, you figure the *average of the cross-products of Z scores*. It turns out that because of the nature of Z scores, this average can never be more than $+1$, which would be a positive linear perfect correlation. It can never be less than -1, which would be a negative linear perfect correlation. In the situation of no linear correlation, the average of the cross-products of Z scores is 0.

For a positive linear correlation that is not perfect, which is the usual situation, the average of the cross-products of Z scores is between 0 and $+1$. To put it another way, if the general trend of the dots is upward and to the right, but they do not fall exactly on a single straight line, this number is between 0 and $+1$. The same rule holds for negative correlations: They fall between 0 and -1. So, overall, a correlation varies from -1 to $+1$.

Table 2   The Effect on the Correlation of Different Patterns of Raw Scores and Z Scores

Pair of Raw Scores		Pair of Z Scores		Cross-Product of Z Scores	Effect on Correlation
X	Y	Z_X	Z_Y	$Z_X Z_Y$	
High	High	$+$	$+$	$+$	Contributes to positive correlation
Low	Low	$-$	$-$	$+$	Contributes to positive correlation
High	Low	$+$	$-$	$-$	Contributes to negative correlation
Low	High	$-$	$+$	$-$	Contributes to negative correlation
Middle	Any	0	$+$, $-$, or 0	0	Makes correlation near 0
Any	Middle	$+$, $-$, or 0	0	0	Makes correlation near 0

Note: $+$ indicates a positive number, $-$ indicates a negative number.

Interpreting the Correlation Coefficient

The result of dividing the sum of the products of Z scores by the number of people in the study is called the **correlation coefficient**. It is also called the Pearson correlation coefficient (or the Pearson product-moment correlation coefficient, to be very traditional). It is named after Karl Pearson. Pearson, along with Francis Galton (see Box 1 in this chapter), played a major role in developing the correlation coefficient. The correlation coefficient is abbreviated by the letter r, which is short for regression, an idea closely related to correlation.

The sign ($+$ or $-$) of a correlation coefficient tells you the *direction* of the linear correlation between two variables (a positive correlation or a negative correlation). The actual value of the correlation coefficient—from a low of 0 to a high of 1, ignoring the sign of the correlation coefficient—tells you the *strength* of the linear correlation. So, a correlation coefficient of $+.85$ represents a larger linear correlation than a correlation of $+.42$. Similarly, a correlation of $-.90$ represents a larger linear correlation than $+.85$ (since .90 is bigger than .85). Another way of thinking of

correlation coefficient (r) measure of degree of linear correlation between two variables ranging from -1 (a perfect negative linear correlation) through 0 (no correlation) to $+1$ (a perfect positive correlation).

BOX 1   Galton: Gentleman Genius

Corbiss/Bettman

Sir Francis Galton is credited with inventing the correlation statistic. (Karl Pearson worked out the formulas, but Pearson was a student of Galton and gave Galton all the credit.) Statistics at this time (around the end of the 19th century) was a tight little British club. In fact, most of science was an only slightly larger club. Galton also was influenced greatly by his own cousin, Charles Darwin.

Galton was a typical eccentric, independently wealthy gentleman scientist. Aside from his work in statistics, he possessed a medical degree, invented glasses for reading underwater, experimented with stereoscopic maps, dabbled in meteorology and anthropology, devised a system for classifying fingerprints that is still in use, and wrote a paper about receiving intelligible signals from the stars.

Above all, Galton was a compulsive counter. Some of his counts are rather infamous. Once while attending a lecture he counted the fidgets of an audience per minute, looking for variations with the boringness of the subject matter. While twice having his picture painted, he counted the artist's brush strokes per hour, concluding that each portrait required an average of 20,000 strokes. While walking the streets of various towns in the British Isles, he classified the beauty of the female inhabitants using a recording device in his pocket to register good, medium, or bad.

Galton's consuming interest, however, was the counting of geniuses, criminals, and other types in families. He wanted to understand how each type was produced so that science could improve the human race by encouraging governments to enforce eugenics—selective breeding for intelligence, proper moral behavior, and other qualities—to be determined, of course, by the eugenicists. (Eugenics has since been generally discredited.) The concept of correlation came directly from his first simple efforts in this area, the study of the relation of the height of children and their parents.

At first, Galton's method of exactly measuring the tendency for "one thing to go with another" seemed almost the same as proving the cause of something. For example, if it could be shown mathematically that most of the brightest people came from a few highborn British families and most of the least intelligent people came from poor families, that seemed at first to "prove" that intelligence was caused by the inheritance of certain genes (provided that you were prejudiced enough to overlook the differences in educational opportunities). Now the study only proves that if you were a member of one of those highborn British families, history would make you a prime example of how easy it is to misinterpret the meaning of a correlation.

You can learn more about Galton on the following Web page: *http://www-history.mcs.st-andrews.ac.uk/Biographies/Galton.html*.

Sources: Peters (1987); Salsburg (2001); Tankard (1984).

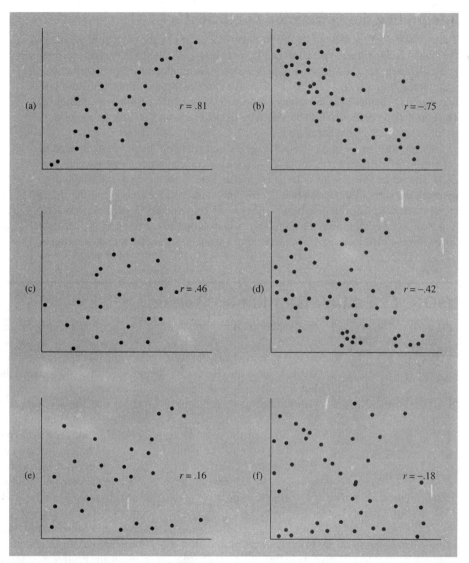

Figure 11 Examples of scatter diagrams and correlation coefficients for different degrees of linear correlation.

this is that, in a scatter diagram, the closer the dots are to falling on a single straight line, the larger the linear correlation. Figure 11 shows the scatter diagrams from Figure 9, with the correlation coefficient shown for each scatter diagram. Be sure that the correlation coefficient for each scatter diagram agrees roughly with the correlation coefficient you would expect based on the pattern of dots.

Formula for the Correlation Coefficient

The correlation coefficient, as we have seen, is the sum of the products of the Z scores divided by the number of people in the study. Put as a formula,

The correlation coefficient is the sum, over all the people in the study, of the product of each person's two Z scores, then divided by the number of people.

$$r = \frac{\sum Z_X Z_Y}{N} \tag{1}$$

r is the correlation coefficient. Z_X is the Z score for each person on the X variable and Z_Y is the Z score for each person on the Y variable. $Z_X Z_Y$ is Z_X multiplied by Z_Y (the cross-product of the Z scores) for each person and $\Sigma Z_X Z_Y$ is the sum of the cross-products of Z scores over all the people in the study. N is the number of people in the study.[1]

Steps for Figuring the Correlation Coefficient

Here are the steps for figuring the correlation coefficient.

❶ **Change all scores to Z scores.** This requires figuring the mean and the standard deviation of each variable, then changing each raw score to a Z score (using the method from *Central Tendency and Variability*).

❷ **Figure the cross-product of the Z scores for each person.** That is, for each person, multiply the person's Z score on one variable by the person's Z score on the other variable.

❸ **Add up the cross-products of the Z scores.**

❹ **Divide by the number of people in the study.**

An Example

Let us try these steps with the sleep and mood example.

❶ **Change all scores to Z scores.** Starting with the number of hours slept last night, the mean is 7 (sum of 42 divided by 6 students), and the standard deviation is 1.63 (sum of squared deviations, 16, divided by 6 students, for a variance of 2.67, the square root of which is 1.63). For the first student, the number of hours slept is 5. The Z score for this person is $(5 - 7)/1.63$, which is -1.23. Thus the first score is a Z score of -1.23. We figured the rest of the Z scores for the number of hours slept in the same way and you can see them in the appropriate column in Table 3. We also figured the Z scores for the happy mood scores and they are also shown in Table 3. For example, you will see that the happy mood Z score for the first student is -1.04.

❷ **Figure the cross-product of the Z scores for each person.** For the first student, multiply -1.23 by -1.04, which gives 1.28. The cross-products for all the students are shown in the last column of Table 3.

TIP FOR SUCCESS

Note, you use the formula for the sample's actual standard deviation, *SD*, not the estimated population standard deviation (*S*).

TIP FOR SUCCESS

If you have drawn a scatter diagram, which we recommend, check that the correlation coefficient you figured is consistent with the pattern of correlation shown in the diagram (that is, it should have the same sign and be very roughly the same degree of correlation).

TIP FOR SUCCESS

When changing the raw scores to Z scores in Step ❶, you will make fewer mistakes if you do all the Z scores for one variable and then all the Z scores for the other variable. Also, to make sure you have done it correctly, when you finish all the Z scores for a variable, add them up—they should add up to 0 (within rounding error).

Table 3 Figuring the Correlation Coefficient for the Sleep and Mood Study (Fictional Data)

\multicolumn{4}{Number of Hours Slept (X)}				\multicolumn{4}{Happy Mood (Y)}				Cross-Products
Deviation		Dev Squared	Z Scores	Deviation		Dev Squared	Z Scores	
X	X − M	(X − M)²	Z_X ❶	Y	Y − M	(Y − M)²	Z_Y ❶	$Z_X Z_Y$
5	−2	4	−1.23	2	−2	4	−1.04	❷ 1.28
7	0	0	0	4	0	0	0	0
8	1	1	.61	7	3	9	1.56	.95
6	−1	1	−.61	2	−2	4	−1.04	.63
6	−1	1	−.61	3	−1	1	−.52	.32
10	3	9	1.84	6	2	4	1.04	1.91
Σ = 42		$\Sigma(X - M)^2 = 16$		Σ = 24		$\Sigma(Y - M)^2 = 22$		❸ $\Sigma Z_X Z_Y = 5.09$
M = 7		$SD^2 = 16/6 = 2.67$		M = 4		$SD^2 = 22/6 = 3.67$		r = 5.09/6 = .85
		$SD = 1.63$				$SD = 1.92$		❹

❸ **Add up the cross-products of the Z scores.** Adding up all the cross-products of Z scores, as shown in Table 3, gives a sum of 5.09.

❹ **Divide by the number of people in the study.** Dividing 5.09 by 6 (the number of students in the study) gives a result of .848, which rounds off to .85. This is the correlation coefficient.

In terms of the correlation coefficient formula,

$$r = \frac{\Sigma Z_X Z_Y}{N} = \frac{5.09}{6} = .85.$$

Because this correlation coefficient is positive and near 1, the highest possible value, this is a very large positive linear correlation.

A Second Example

Suppose that a memory researcher does an experiment to test a theory predicting that the number of exposures to a word increases the chance that the word will be remembered. One research participant is randomly assigned to be exposed to the list of 10 words once, one participant to be exposed to the list twice, and so forth, up to a total of eight exposures to each word. This makes eight participants in all, one for each of the eight levels of exposure. The researchers record how many of the 10 words each participant is able to remember. Results are shown in Table 4. (An actual study of this kind would probably show a pattern in which the relative improvement in recall is less at higher numbers of exposures.) The steps for figuring the correlation coefficient are shown in Table 5.

❶ **Change all scores to Z scores.** The mean number of exposures is 4.50 and the standard deviation is 2.29. The Z score for the first person is −1.53. The mean number of words recalled is 5.00 and the standard deviation is 2.00. The Z score for the first person is −1.00.

Table 4   Effect of Number of Exposures to Words on the Number of Words Recalled (Fictional Data)

Number of Exposures	Number of Words Recalled
1	3
2	2
3	6
4	4
5	5
6	5
7	6
8	9

Table 5   Figuring the Correlation Coefficient for the Effect of Number of Exposures to Each Word on the Number of Words Recalled (Fictional Data)

Number of Exposures (X)				Number of Words Recalled (Y)				Cross-Products
	Deviaition	Dev Squared	Z Scores		Deviation	Dev Squared	Z Scores	
X	X − M	(X − M)²	Z_X ❶	Y	Y − M	(Y − M)²	Z_Y ❶	$Z_x Z_y$ ❷
1	−3.5	12.25	−1.53	3	−2	4	−1.00	1.53
2	−2.5	6.25	−1.09	2	−3	9	−1.50	1.64
3	−1.5	2.25	−.66	6	1	1	.50	−.33
4	−.5	.25	−.22	4	−1	1	−.50	.11
5	.5	.25	.22	5	0	0	.00	.00
6	1.5	2.25	.66	5	0	0	.00	.00
7	2.5	6.25	1.09	6	1	1	.50	.55
8	3.5	12.25	1.53	9	4	16	2.00	3.06
Σ = 36		Σ(X − M)² = 42		Σ = 40		Σ(Y − M)² = 32		❸ $\Sigma Z_X Z_Y$ = 6.56
M = 4.50		SD² = 42/8 = 5.25		M = 5.00		SD² = 32/8 = 4.00		❹ r = 6.56/8 = .82
		SD = 2.29				SD = 2.00		

❷ **Figure the cross-product of the Z scores for each person.** For the first person, multiply −1.53 by −1.00, which gives 1.53. The cross-products for all of the people in the study are shown in the last column of Table 5.

❸ **Add up the cross-products of the Z scores.** Adding up all the cross-products of Z scores, as shown in Table 5, gives a sum of 6.56.

❹ **Divide by the number of people in the study.** Dividing 6.56 by 8 (the number of people in the study) gives a result of .82. This is the correlation coefficient. In terms of the correlation coefficient formula,

$$r = \frac{\Sigma Z_X Z_Y}{N} = \frac{6.56}{8} = .82$$

Because this correlation coefficient is positive and near 1, the highest possible value, this is a very large positive linear correlation.

How are you doing?

1. Give two reasons why we use Z scores for figuring the exact linear correlation between two variables, thinking of correlation as how much high scores go with high scores and lows go with lows (or vice versa for negative correlations).
2. When figuring the correlation coefficient, why do you divide the sum of cross-products of Z scores by the number of people in the study?
3. Write the formula for the correlation coefficient and define each of the symbols.
4. Figure the correlation coefficient for the Z scores shown below for three people who were each tested on two variables, X and Y.

Person	Z_X	Z_Y
K	.5	−.7
L	−1.4	−.8
M	.9	1.5

Answers

1. First, Z scores put both variables on the same scale of measurement so that a high or low score (and how much it is high or low) means the same thing for both variables. Second, high Z scores are positive and low Z scores are negative. Thus, if highs go with highs and lows with lows, the cross-products of the Z scores will all be positive. Similarly, with a negative correlation where highs go with lows and lows with highs, the cross-products will all be negative.
2. You divide the sum of cross-products of the Z scores by the number of people in the study, because otherwise the more people in the study, the bigger the sum of the cross-products, even if the strength of correlation is the same. Dividing by the number of people corrects for this. (Also, when using Z scores, after dividing the sum of the cross-products by the number of people, the result has to be in a standard range of −1 to 0 to +1.)

3. The formula for the correlation coefficient is: $r = (\sum Z_X Z_Y)/N$. r is the correlation coefficient. $\sum$ is the symbol for sum of—add up all the scores that follow (in this formula, you add up all the cross-products that follow). Z_X is the Z score for each person's raw score on one of the variables (the one labeled X) and Z_Y is the Z score for each person's raw score on the other variable (labeled Y). N is the number of people in the study.

4. $r = (\sum Z_X Z_Y)/N = [(.5)(-.7) + (-1.4)(-.8) + (.9)(1.5)]/3 = [-.35 + 1.12 + 1.35]/3 = 2.12/3 = .71$.

Significance of a Correlation Coefficient

The correlation coefficient is a descriptive statistic, like the mean or standard deviation. The correlation coefficient describes the linear relationship between two variables. However, in addition to *describing* this relationship, we may also want to test whether it is statistically significant. In the case of a correlation, the question is usually whether it is significantly different from zero. That is, the null hypothesis in hypothesis testing for a correlation is usually that in the population the true relation between the two variables is no correlation ($r = 0$).[2]

The overall logic is much like that we have considered for the various t test and analysis of variance situations. Suppose for a particular population we had the distribution of two variables, X and Y. And suppose further that in this population there was no correlation between these two variables. The scatter diagram might look like that shown in Figure 12. Thus, if you were to consider the dot for one random person from this scatter diagram, the scores might be $X = 4$ and $Y = 2$. For another random person, it might be $X = 2$ and $Y = 1$. For a third person, $X = 3$ and $Y = 5$. The correlation for these three persons would be $r = .24$. If you then took out another three persons and figured the correlation it might come out to $r = -.12$. Presuming there was no actual correlation in the population, if you did this lots and lots of times, you would end up with a distribution of correlations with a mean of zero. This is a distribution of correlations of

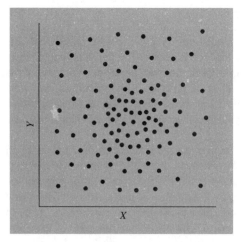

Figure 12   Scatter diagram for variables X and Y for a population in which there is no relationship between X and Y.

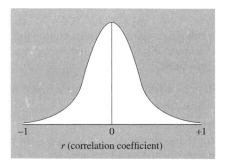

Figure 13 Distribution of correlation coefficients for a large number of samples ($N = 3$) drawn from a population with no correlation between variables X and Y.

three persons' each. As shown in Figure 13, it would have a mean of zero and be spread out in both directions up to a maximum of 1 and a minimum of -1.

It would actually be possible to figure out the cutoffs for significance on such a distribution of correlation coefficients, just as we did for example for the t and the F distributions. Then you could just compare your actual r to that cutoff to see if it was significant. However, we do not need to introduce a whole new distribution with its own tables and such. It turns out that we can figure out a number based on the correlation coefficient that will follow a t distribution. This number is figured using the following formula:

$$t = \frac{r}{\sqrt{(1 - r^2)/(N - 2)}} \qquad (2)$$

> The t score for a correlation coefficient is the result of dividing the correlation coefficient by the square root of what you get when you divide one minus the correlation coefficient squared by two less than the number of people in the study.

Notice that in this formula if $r = 0$, $t = 0$. This is because the numerator would be 0 and the result of dividing 0 by any number is 0. Also notice that the bigger the r, the bigger the t.

If you were to take three persons' scores at random from the distribution with no true correlation, you could figure this t value. For example, for the first three-person example we just considered, the correlation was .24. So, $t = .24/\sqrt{(1 - .24^2)/(3 - 2)} = .24/\sqrt{(.9424)/(1)} = .25$. If you took a large number of such samples of three persons each, computed the correlation and then the t for each, you would eventually have a distribution of t scores. And here is the main point: you could then compare the t score figured in this way for the actual correlation in the study, using the standard t table cutoffs.

As usual with the t statistic, there are different t distributions for different degrees of freedom. In the case of the t test for a correlation, df is the number of people in the sample minus 2. (We subtract 2 because the figuring involved two different means, the mean of X and the mean of Y.) In terms of a formula,

$$df = N - 2 \qquad (3)$$

> The degrees of freedom for the t test for a correlation are the number of people in the sample minus 2.

Finally, note that the t value will be positive or negative, according to whether your correlation is positive or negative. Thus, as with any t test, the t test for a correlation can be either one-tailed or two-tailed. A one-tailed test means that the researcher has predicted the sign ($+$ or $-$) of the correlation. However, in practice, as with other t tests, even when a researcher expects a certain direction of correlation, correlations are most often tested with two-tailed tests.

An Example

In the sleep and mood study example, let's suppose that the researchers predicted a correlation between number of hours slept and happy mood the next day, to be tested at the .05 level, two-tailed.

❶ **Restate the question as a research hypothesis and a null hypothesis about the populations.** There are two populations:

Population 1: People like those in this study.
Population 2: People for whom there is no correlation between number of hours slept the night before and mood the next day.

The null hypothesis is that the two populations have the same correlation. The research hypothesis is that the two populations do not have the same correlation.

❷ **Determine the characteristics of the comparison distribution.** The comparison distribution is a t distribution with $df = 4$. (That is, $df = N - 2 = 6 - 2 = 4$.)

❸ **Determine the cutoff sample score on the comparison distribution at which the null hypothesis should be rejected.** The t table (Table A-2 in the Appendix) shows that for a two-tailed test at the .05 level, with 4 degrees of freedom, the cutoff t scores are 2.776 and -2.776.

❹ **Determine your sample's score on the comparison distribution.** We figured a correlation of $r = .85$. Applying the formula to find the equivalent t, we get

$$t = \frac{r}{\sqrt{(1 - r^2)/(N - 2)}} = \frac{.85}{\sqrt{(1 - .85^2)/(6 - 2)}} = \frac{.85}{\sqrt{.0694}} = 3.23$$

❺ **Decide whether to reject the null hypothesis.** The t score of 3.23 for our sample correlation is more extreme than a cutoff t score of 2.776. Thus, we can reject the null hypothesis and the research hypothesis is supported.

Assumptions for the Significance Test of a Correlation Coefficient

The assumptions for testing the significance of a correlation coefficient are similar to those for the t test for independent means and analysis of variance. In those situations you have to assume the population for each group follows a normal distribution and has the same variance as the population for the other groups. With the correlation you have to assume that:

1. **The population of each variable (X and Y) follows a normal distribution.** Actually you also assume that the relationship *between* the two variables also follows a normal curve. This creates what is called a *bivariate normal distribution* (think of this as a three-dimensional normal curve set on top of a scatter diagram, with a big hill in the middle that spreads out evenly in both directions). In practice, however, we usually check whether we have met the requirement by checking whether the distribution in the sample for each of our variables is roughly normal.

2. **There is an equal distribution of each variable at each point of the other variable.** For example, in a scatter diagram, if there is much more variation at the low end than at the high end (or vice versa), this suggests a problem. In practice, you should look at the scatter diagram for your study to see if it looks like the dots are much more spread out at the low or high end (or both). A lot of dots in the middle are to be expected. So long as the greater number of dots in the middle are not a lot more spread out than those at either end, this does not suggest a problem with the assumptions.

Like the *t* tests you have already learned and like the analysis of variance, the *t* test for the significance of a correlation coefficient is pretty robust to all but extreme violations of its assumptions of normal distributions and an equal distribution of each variable at each point of the other variable.

Also, remember that the correlation coefficient assumes the relationship between the two variables is linear (and not curvilinear). A final assumption is that the people (or cases) are independent. (That is, no one pair of scores can be matched in any particular way with another pair of scores. For example, in a study of doing exciting activities and marital satisfaction, you could not properly figure the significance of a correlation coefficient in the usual way if some of the people in the group were married to each other.)

How are you doing?

1. What is the usual null hypothesis in hypothesis testing with a correlation coefficient?
2. Write the formula for testing the significance of a correlation coefficient, and define each of the symbols.
3. Use the five steps of hypothesis testing to determine whether a correlation coefficient of $r = -.31$ from a study with a sample of 60 people is significant at the .05 level, two-tailed.
4. What are the assumptions for the significance test of a correlation coefficient?

Answers

1. In hypothesis testing with a correlation coefficient, the usual null hypothesis is that in the population the true relation between the two variables is no correlation ($r = 0$).
2. Formula for testing the significance of a correlation coefficient: $t = \dfrac{r}{\sqrt{(1 - r^2)/(N - 2)}}$. *t* is the *t* statistic for testing the significance of the correlation coefficient; *r* is the correlation coefficient; *N* is the number of people in the study.
3. ❶ **Restate the question as a research hypothesis and a null hypothesis about the populations.** There are two populations:

   Population 1: People like those in this study.
   Population 2: People for whom there is no correlation between the two variables.

   The null hypothesis is that the two populations have the same correlation. The research hypothesis is that the two populations do not have the same correlation.
   ❷ **Determine the characteristics of the comparison distribution.** The comparison distribution is a *t* distribution with $df = 58$. (That is, $df = N - 2 = 60 - 2 = 58$.)
   ❸ **Determine the cutoff sample score on the comparison distribution at which the null hypothesis should be rejected.** The *t* table (Table A-2 in the Appendix) shows that for a two-tailed test at the .05 level, with 58 degrees of freedom, the cutoff *t* scores are 2.004 and −2.004 (we used the cutoffs for $df = 55$, the closest *df* in the table below 58).

❹ **Determine your sample's score on the comparison distribution.** The correlation in the study was −.31. Applying the formula to find the equivalent t, we get

$$t = \frac{r}{\sqrt{(1 - r^2)/(N - 2)}} = \frac{-.31}{\sqrt{(1 - (-.31^2))/(58)}} = \frac{-.31}{.125} = -2.48.$$

❺ **Decide whether to reject the null hypothesis.** The t score of −2.48 for our sample correlation is more extreme than a cutoff t score of −2.004. Thus, we can reject the null hypothesis and the research hypothesis is supported.

4. The population of each variable (and the relationship between them) follows a normal distribution, there is an equal distribution of each variable at each point of the other variable, the relationship between the two variables is linear, and the people (or cases) are independent from each other.

Correlation and Causality

If two variables have a significant linear correlation, we normally assume that there is something causing them to go together. However, you can't know the **direction of causality** (what is causing what) just from the fact that the two variables are correlated.

Three Possible Directions of Causality

Consider the example with which we started the chapter, the correlation between doing exciting activities with your partner and satisfaction with the relationship. There are three possible directions of causality for these two variables:

1. It could be that doing exciting activities together causes the partners to be more satisfied with their relationship.
2. It could also be that people who are more satisfied with their relationship choose to do more exciting activities together.
3. Another possibility is that something like having less stress (versus more stress) at work makes people happier in their marriage and also gives them more time and energy to do exciting activities with their partner.

These three possible directions of causality are shown in Figure 14a.

The principle is that for any correlation between variables X and Y, there are at least three possible directions of causality:

1. X could be causing Y.
2. Y could be causing X.
3. Some third factor could be causing both X and Y.

These three possible directions of causality are shown in Figure 14b.

It is also possible (and often likely) that there is more than one direction of causality making two variables correlated.

Ruling Out Some Possible Directions of Causality

Sometimes you can rule out one or more of these three possible directions based on additional knowledge of the situation in which you know that one variable was measured before the other. For example, the correlation between sleep the night before

direction of causality path of causal effect; if X is thought to cause Y then the direction of causality is from X to Y.

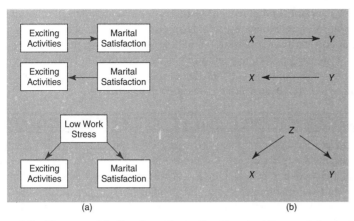

Figure 14   Three possible directions of causality (shown with arrows) for a correlation for (a) the exciting activities and marital satisfaction example and (b) the general principle for any two variables X and Y.

and a happy mood the next day cannot be due to happy mood the next day causing you to sleep more the night before (causality doesn't go backward in time). But we still do not know whether the sleep the night before caused the happy mood or some third factor, such as a general tendency to be happy, caused people both to sleep well and to be happy on any particular day.

Using this principle of the future not causing the past, Tsapelas et al. (2009) conducted a study in which they found that doing exciting activities, measured in a group of people when they were 7 years into their marriages, was strongly correlated with their satisfaction measured 9 years later. But again, this does not rule out the possibility that some third aspect of the marriage, such as absence of conflict, makes for both more exciting activities and more satisfaction at all points. (The researchers actually did some further analyses to get at this.)

Most psychologists would argue that the strongest way we can rule out alternative directions of causality is by conducting a true experiment. In a true experiment, participants are randomly assigned to a particular level of a variable and then measured on another variable. An example of this is the study in which participants were randomly assigned (say, by flipping a coin) to different numbers of exposures to a list of words, and then the number of words they could remember was measured. There was a .82 correlation between number of exposures and number of words recalled. In this situation, any causality has to be from the variable that was manipulated (number of exposures) to the variable that is measured (words recalled). The number of words recalled can't cause more exposures because the exposures came first. And a third variable can't be causing both number of exposures and words recalled because number of exposures was determined randomly; nothing can be causing it other than the random method we used (such as flipping a coin).

Correlational Statistical Procedures versus Correlation Research Methods

Discussions of correlation and causality in psychology research are often confused by there being two uses of the word *correlation*. Sometimes the word is used as the name of a statistical procedure, the correlation coefficient (as we have done in this chapter). At other times, the term *correlation* is used to describe a kind of research design. A **correlational research design** is any research design other than a true experiment. A correlational research design is not necessarily statistically analyzed using the correlation coefficient, and some studies using experimental research designs are most appropriately analyzed using a correlation coefficient. Hence the confusion. We recommend you take one or more research methods courses to learn more about research designs used in research in psychology.

How are you doing?

1. If anxiety and depression are correlated, what are three possible directions of causality that might explain this correlation?
2. If high school and college grades are correlated, what directions of causality can and cannot be ruled out by the situation?
3. A researcher randomly assigns participants to eat zero, two, or four cookies and then asks them how full they feel. The number of cookies eaten and feeling full are highly correlated. What directions of causality can and cannot be ruled out?
4. What is the difference between correlation as a statistical procedure and a correlational research design?

Answers

1. Three possible directions of causality are: (a) being depressed can cause a person to be anxious; (b) being anxious can cause a person to be depressed; and (c) some third variable (such as some aspect of heredity or childhood traumas) could be causing both anxiety and depression.
2. College grades cannot be causing high school grades (causality doesn't go backward), but high school grades could be causing college grades (maybe knowing you did well in high school gives you more confidence), and some third variable (such as general academic ability) could be causing students to do well in both high school and college.
3. Eating more cookies can cause participants to feel full. Feeling full cannot have caused participants to have eaten more cookies, because how many cookies were eaten was determined randomly. Third variables can't cause both, because how many cookies were eaten was determined randomly.
4. The statistical procedure of correlation is about using the formula for the correlation coefficient, regardless of how the study was done. A correlational research design is any research design other than a true experiment.

Issues in Interpreting the Correlation Coefficient

There are a number of subtle cautions in interpreting a correlation coefficient. (And there's the important issue that in daily life we sometimes see correlations when they aren't really there—see Box 2.)

The Correlation Coefficient and the Proportionate Reduction in Error or Proportion of Variance Accounted For

A correlation coefficient tells you the direction and strength of a linear correlation. Bigger rs (values farther from 0) mean a higher degree of correlation. That is, an r of .60 is a larger correlation than an r of .30. However, most researchers would hold that an r of .60 is *more than* twice as large as an r of .30. To compare correlations with each other, most researchers square the correlations (that is, they use r^2 instead of r). This is called

correlational research design   any research design other than a true experiment.

the **proportionate reduction in error** (and also the *proportion of variance accounted for*).

For example, a correlation of .30 is an r^2 of .09 and a correlation of .60 is an r^2 of .36. Thus, a correlation of .60 is actually four times as large as one of .30 (that is, .36 is four times as big as .09).

Restriction in Range

Suppose an educational psychologist studies the relation of grade level to knowledge of geography. If this researcher studied students from the entire range of school grade levels, the results might appear as shown in the scatter diagram in Figure 15a. That is, the researcher might find a large positive correlation. But suppose the researcher had studied students only from the first three grades. The scatter diagram (see Figure 15b) would show a much smaller correlation (the general increasing tendency is in relation to much more noise). However, the researcher would be making a mistake by concluding that grade level is only slightly related to knowledge of geography over all grades.

The problem in this situation is that the correlation is based on people who include only a limited range of the possible values on one of the variables. (In this example, there is a limited range of grade levels.) It is misleading to think of the correlation as if it applied to the entire range of values the variable might have. This situation is called **restriction in range**.

It is easy to make such mistakes in interpreting correlations. (You will occasionally see them even in published research articles.) Consider another example. Businesses sometimes try to decide whether their hiring tests are correlated with how successful the persons hired turn out on the job. Often, they find very little relationship. What they fail to take into account is that they hired only people who did well on the tests. Their study of job success included only the subgroup of high scorers. This example is shown in Figure 16.

Yet another example is any study that tries to correlate intelligence with other variables that uses only college students. The problem here is that college students do not include many lower or below-average intelligence students. Thus, a researcher could find a low correlation in such a study. But if the researcher did the same study with people who included the full range of intelligence levels, there could well be a high correlation.

proportionate reduction in error
(r^2) measure of association between variables that is used when comparing associations. Also called *proportion of variance accounted for*.

restriction in range situation in which you figure a correlation but only a limited range of the possible values on one of the variables is included in the group studied.

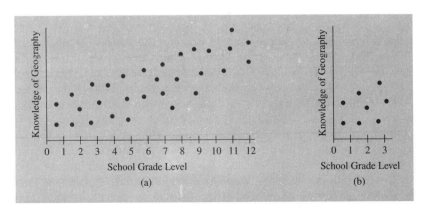

Figure 15 Example of restriction in range comparing two scatter diagrams (a) when the entire range is shown (of school grade level and knowledge of geography) and (b) when the range is restricted (to the first three grades) (fictional data).

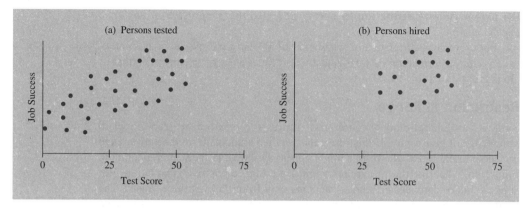

Figure 16 Additional example of restriction in range comparing two scatter diagrams (a) when the entire range is shown (of all persons tested) and (b) when the range is restricted (to just those persons who were hired) (fictional data).

Unreliability of Measurement

Suppose the number of hours slept and mood the next day have a very high degree of correlation. However, suppose also that in a particular study the researcher had asked people about their sleep on a particular night three weeks ago and about their mood on the day after that particular night. There are many problems with this kind

---

BOX 2   Illusory Correlation: When You Know Perfectly Well That If It's Big, It's Fat—and You Are Perfectly Wrong

The concept of correlation was not really invented by statisticians. It is one of the most basic of human mental processes. The first humans must have thought in terms of correlation all the time—at least those who survived. "Every time it snows, the animals we hunt go away. Snow belongs with no animals. When the snow comes again, if we follow the animals, we may not starve."

In fact, correlation is such a typically human and highly successful thought process that we seem to be psychologically organized to see more correlation than is there—like the Aztecs, who thought that good crops correlated with human sacrifices (let's hope they were wrong), and like the following examples from social psychology of what is called *illusory correlation* (Hamilton, 1981; Hamilton & Gifford, 1976; Johnson & Mullen, 1994).

Illusory correlation is the term for the overestimation of the strength of the relationship between two variables (the term has also had other special meanings in the past). Right away, you may think of some harmful illusory correlations related to ethnicity, race, gender, and age. One source of illusory correlation is the tendency to link two infrequent and therefore highly memorable events.

Suppose Group B is smaller than Group A, and in *both* groups one-third of the people are known to commit certain infrequent but undesirable acts. In this kind of situation, research shows that Group B, whose members are less frequently encountered, will in fact be blamed for far more of these undesirable acts than Group A. This is true even though the odds are greater that a particular act was committed by a member of Group A, since Group A has more members. The problem is that infrequent events stick together in memory. Membership in the less frequent group and the occurrence of less frequent behaviors form an illusory correlation. One obvious consequence is that we remember anything unusual done by the member of a minority group better than we remember anything unusual done by a member of a majority group.

Illusory correlation due to "paired distinctiveness" (two unusual events being linked in our minds) may occur because when we first encounter distinctive experiences, we think more about them, processing them more deeply so that they are more accessible in memory later (Johnson & Mullen, 1994). If we encounter, for example, members of a minority we don't see often, or negative acts that we rarely see or hear about, we really think about them. If they are paired, we study them both and they are quicker to return to memory. It also seems that we can continue to process information about groups, people, and their behaviors without any awareness of doing so. Sometime along the way, or when we go to make a judgment, we overassociate the unusual groups or people with the unusual (negative) behaviors (McConnell et al., 1994). This effect is stronger when information about the groups or people is sparse, as if we try even harder in ambiguous situations to make sense of what we have seen (Berndsen et al., 2001).

Indeed, observing a single instance of a rare group showing some unusual behavior, a "one-shot illusory correlation," is sufficient to create the effect (Risen et al., 2007). (There is also some evidence that we can sometimes unlearn the illusion with increased experience; Murphy et al., 2010.)

Most illusory correlations, however, occur simply because of prejudices. Prejudices are implicit, erroneous theories that we carry around with us. For example, we estimate that we have seen more support for an association between two social traits than we have actually seen: driving skills and a particular age group; level of academic achievement and a specific ethnic group; certain speech, dress, or social behaviors and residence in some region of the country. One especially interesting example is that most people in business believe that job satisfaction and job performance are closely linked, when in fact the correlation is quite low. People who do not like their jobs can still put in a good day's work; people who rave about their job can still be lazy about doing it.

By the way, some people form their implicit theories impulsively and hold them rigidly; others seem to base them according to what they remember about people and change their theories as they have new experiences (McConnell, 2001). Which are you?

The point is, the next time you ask yourself why you are struggling to learn statistics, it might help to think of it as a quest to make ordinary thought processes more moral and fair. So, again, we assert that statistics can be downright romantic: it can be about conquering dark, evil mistakes with the pure light of numbers, subduing the lie of prejudices with the honesty of data.

---

of study, but one is that the measurement of hours slept and mood would not be very accurate. For example, what a person recalls about how many hours were slept on a particular night three weeks ago is probably not very close to how many hours the person actually slept. Thus, the true correlation between sleep and mood could be high, but the correlation in the particular study might be quite low, just because there is lots of "random noise" (random inaccuracy) in the scores.

Here is another way to understand this issue: think of a correlation in terms of how close the dots in the scatter diagram fall to a straight line. One of the reasons why dots may not fall close to the line is inaccurate measurement.

Consider another example. Height and social power have been found in many studies to have a moderate degree of correlation. However, if someone were to do this study and measure each person's height using an elastic measuring tape, the correlation would be much lower. Some other examples of not fully accurate measurement are personality questionnaires that include items that are difficult to understand (or are understood differently by different people), ratings of behavior (such as children's play activity) that require some subjective judgment, or physiological measures that are influenced by things like ambient magnetic fields.

Often in psychology research our measures are not perfectly accurate or *reliable*. The result is that a correlation between any two variables is lower than it would be if you had perfect measures of the two variables.

The reduction in a correlation due to unreliability of measures is called *attenuation*. More advanced statistics texts and psychological measurement texts describe formulas for *correction for attenuation* that can be used under some conditions.

However, studies using such procedures are relatively rare in most areas of psychology research.

The main thing to remember from all of this is that, to the extent the measures used in a study are less than perfectly accurate, the correlations reported in that study usually underestimate the true correlation between the variables (the correlation that would be found if there was perfect measurement).

Influence of Outliers

The direction and strength of a correlation can be drastically distorted by one or more individual's scores on the two variables if each pair of scores is a very unusual combination. For example, suppose in the sleep and mood example that an additional person was added to the study who had only 1 hour of sleep and yet was extremely happy the next day (8 on the happiness scale). (Maybe the person was going through some sort of manic phase!) We have shown this situation in the scatter diagram in Figure 17. It turns out that the correlation, which without this added person was a *large positive correlation* ($r = .85$), now becomes a *small negative correlation* ($r = -.11$)!

Extreme scores are called **outliers** (they lie outside of the usual range of scores, a little like "outlaws"). Outliers are actually a problem in most kinds of statistical analyses. However, the main point for now is this: if the scatter diagram shows one or more unusual combinations, you need to be aware that these individuals have an especially large influence on the correlation.

What If There Is Some Curvilinearity? The Spearman Rho

outliers scores with an extreme (very high or very low) value in relation to the other scores in the distribution.

The correlation coefficient, as we have seen, describes the direction and strength of the *linear* relationship between two variables. It shows us how well the dots in a scatter diagram follow a straight line in which highs go with highs and lows go with

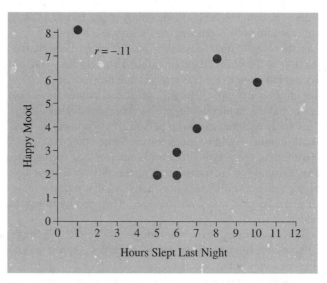

Figure 17 A scatter diagram for the hours slept last night and happy mood example (see Table 1 and Figure 2d) with an outlier combination of scores (1 hour slept and happy mood of 8) for an extra person (correlation is now $r = -.11$ compared to $r = .85$ without the extra person).

lows (a positive correlation) or highs go with lows and lows with highs (a negative correlation). Sometimes however, as you saw earlier in the chapter, the pattern of dots follow a precise pattern, but that pattern is curved. For example, consider Figure 6b. In this example, highs go with highs, middle scores go with lows, and low scores go with highs. It is a kind of U shape. There are methods of figuring the degree to which the dots follow such a curved line; these procedures are considered in advanced textbooks (e.g., Cohen et al., 2003).

Sometimes, however, as shown in Figure 5, highs go with highs and lows with lows, but the pattern is still not quite linear. In these particular kinds of situations we can in a sense straighten out the line and then use the ordinary correlation. One way this can be done is by changing all the scores to their rank order. So, separately for each variable, you would rank the scores from lowest to highest (starting with 1 for the lowest score and continuing until all the scores have been ranked). This makes the pattern more linear. In fact, we could now proceed to figure the correlation coefficient in the usual way, but using the rank-order scores instead of the original scores. A correlation figured in this way is called **Spearman's rho**. (It was developed in the 1920s by Charles Spearman, an important British psychologist who invented many statistical procedures to help him solve the problems he was working on, mainly involving the nature and measurement of human intelligence.)

Some researchers prefer Spearman's rho because it works correctly even if the original scores are not based on true equal-interval measurement. Finally, many researchers like to use Spearman's rho because it is much less affected by outliers.

Spearman's rho the equivalent of a correlation coefficient for rank-ordered scores.

How are you doing?

1. (a) What numbers do psychologists use when they compare the size of two correlation coefficients? (b) What are these numbers called? (c) How much larger is a correlation of .80 than a correlation of .20?
2. (a) What is restriction in range? (b) What is its effect on the correlation coefficient?
3. (a) What is unreliability of measurement? (b) What is its effect on the correlation coefficient?
4. (a) What is the outlier combination of scores in the set of scores below?

X	Y
10	41
8	35
12	46
7	48
9	37

(b) Why are outliers a potential problem with regard to correlation?
5. Give three reasons why a researcher might choose to use Spearman's rho instead of the regular correlation coefficient.

Answers

1. (a) When psychologists compare the size of two correlation coefficients, they use the correlation coefficients squared. (b) The correlation coefficient squared is called the proportionate reduction in error (or proportion of variance accounted for). (c) A correlation of .80 is 16 times larger than a correlation of .20 (for $r = .80$, $r^2 = .64$; for $r = .20$, $r^2 = .04$; and .64 is 16 times larger than .04).

2. (a) Restriction in range is a situation in correlation in which the scores of the group of people studied on one of the variables do not include the full range of scores that are found among people more generally. (b) The effect is often to drastically reduce the correlation compared to what it would be if people more generally were included in the study (presuming there would be a correlation among people more generally).

3. (a) Unreliability of measurement is when the procedures used to measure a particular variable are not perfectly accurate. (b) The effect is to make the correlation smaller than it would be if perfectly accurate measures were used (presuming there would be a correlation if perfectly accurate measures were used).

4. (a) The outlier combination of scores is the fourth pair of scores ($X = 7$ and $Y = 48$). The other pairs of scores all suggest a positive correlation between variables X and Y, but the pair of $X = 7$ and $Y = 48$ is a very low score for variable X and a very high score for variable Y. (b) Outliers have a larger effect on the correlation than other combinations of scores.

5. First, Spearman's rho can be used in certain situations when the scatter diagram suggests a curvilinear relationship between two variables. Second, Spearman's rho can be used in certain situations to figure a correlation when the original scores are not based on true equal-interval measurement. Finally, Spearman's rho is less affected by outliers than the regular correlation coefficient.

Effect Size and Power for the Correlation Coefficient

The correlation coefficient itself is a measure of effect size. (Thus, in the study of sleep and mood, effect size was $r = .85$.) Cohen's (1988) conventions for the correlation coefficient are .10 for a small effect size, .30 for a medium (or moderate) effect size, and .50 for a large effect size.

Power for a correlation can be determined using a power table, a power software package, or an Internet power calculator. Table 6 gives the approximate power for the .05 significance level for small, medium, and large correlations, and one-tailed or two-tailed tests.[3] For example, the power for a study with an expected medium effect size ($r = .30$), two-tailed, with 50 participants, is .57 (which is below the standard desired level of at least .80 power). This means that even if the research hypothesis is in fact true and has a medium effect size (that is, the two variables are correlated at $r = .30$ in the population), there is only a 57% chance that the study will produce a significant correlation.

Planning Sample Size

Table 7 gives the approximate number of participants needed for 80% power for estimated small, medium, and large correlations, using one-tailed and two-tailed tests, all using the .05 significance level.[4]

Table 6 Approximate Power of Studies Using the Correlation Coefficient (*r*) for Testing Hypotheses at the .05 Level of Significance

		Small (r = .10)	Medium (r = .30)	Large (r = .50)
		Effect Size		
Two-tailed				
Total *N*:	10	.06	.13	.33
	20	.07	.25	.64
	30	.08	.37	.83
	40	.09	.48	.92
	50	.11	.57	.97
	100	.17	.86	*
One-tailed				
Total *N*:	10	.08	.22	.46
	20	.11	.37	.75
	30	.13	.50	.90
	40	.15	.60	.96
	50	.17	.69	.98
	100	.26	.92	*

*Power is nearly 1.

Table 7 Approximate Number of Participants Needed for 80% Power for a Study Using the Correlation Coefficient (*r*) for Testing a Hypothesis at the .05 Significance Level

	Small (r = .10)	Medium (r = .30)	Large (r = .50)
	Effect Size		
Two-tailed	783	85	28
One-tailed	617	68	22

How are you doing?

1. What are the conventions for effect size for correlation coefficients?
2. What is the power of a study using a correlation, with a two-tailed test at the .05 significance level, in which the researchers predict a large effect size and there are 50 participants?
3. How many participants do you need for 80% power in a planned study in which you predict a small effect size and will be using a correlation, two-tailed, at the .05 significance level?

Answers

1. The conventions for effect size for correlation coefficients: *r* = .10, small effect size; *r* = .30, medium effect size; *r* = .50, large effect size.
2. Power is .97.
3. The number of participants needed is 783.

Controversy: What Is a Large Correlation?

An ongoing controversy about the correlation coefficient is, "What is a large r?" Traditionally in psychology, a large correlation is considered to be about .50 or above, a moderate correlation to be about .30, and a small correlation to be about .10 (Cohen, 1988). In fact, in many areas of psychology it is rare to find correlations that are greater than .40. Even when we are confident that X causes Y, X will not be the *only* cause of Y. For example, doing exciting activities together may cause people to be happier in their marriage. (In fact, we have done a number of true experiments supporting this direction of causality; Aron et al., 2000.) However, exciting activities is still only one of a great many factors that affect marital satisfaction. All those other factors are not part of our correlation. No one correlation could possibly tell the whole story. Small correlations are also due to the unavoidably low reliability of many measures in psychology.

It is traditional to caution that a low correlation is not very important even if it is statistically significant. (A small correlation can be statistically significant if the study includes a very large number of participants.)

Further, even experienced research psychologists tend to treat any particular size of correlation as meaning more of an association between two variables than it actually does. Michael Oakes (1982) at the University of Sussex gave 30 research psychologists the two columns of numbers shown in Table 8. He then asked them to estimate r (without doing any calculations). What is your guess? The intuitions of the British researchers (who are as a group at least as well trained in statistics as psychologists anywhere in the world) ranged from $-.20$ to $+.60$, with a mean of .24. You can figure the true correlation for yourself. It comes out to .50! That is, what psychologists think a correlation of .50 means in the abstract is a much stronger degree of correlation than what they think when they see the actual numbers (which even at $r = .50$ only *look* like .24).

Oakes (1982) gave a different group of 30 researchers just the X column and asked them to fill in numbers in the Y column that would come out to a correlation of .50 (again, just using their intuition and without any figuring). When Oakes figured the actual correlations from their answers, these correlations averaged .68. In other words, once again, even experienced researchers think of a correlation coefficient as meaning more linkage between the two variables than it actually does.

In contrast, other psychologists hold that small correlations can be very important theoretically. They also can have major practical implications in that small effects may accumulate over time (Prentice & Miller, 1992).

To demonstrate the practical importance of small correlations, Rosnow and Rosenthal (1989) give an example of a now famous study (Steering Committee of the Physicians' Health Study Research Group, 1988) in which doctors either did or did not take aspirin each day. Whether or not they took aspirin each day was then correlated with heart attacks. The results were that taking aspirin was correlated $-.034$ with heart attacks.[5] This means that taking aspirin explains only .1% ($r^2 = -.034 \times -.034 = .001$, which is .1%) of the variation in whether people get heart attacks. So taking aspirin is only a small part of what affects people getting heart attacks; 99.9% of the variation in whether people get heart attacks is due to other factors (diet, exercise, genetic factors, and so on). However, Rosnow and Rosenthal point out that this correlation of "only $-.034$" meant that among the more than 20,000 doctors who were in the study, there were 72 more heart attacks in the group that did not take aspirin. (In fact, there were also 13 more heart attack deaths in the group that did not take aspirin.) Certainly, this difference in getting heart attacks is a difference we care about.

Table 8 Table Presented to 30 Psychologists to Estimate r

X	Y
1	1
2	10
3	2
4	9
5	5
6	4
7	6
8	3
9	11
10	8
11	7
12	12

Source: Based on Oakes (1982).

Another argument for the importance of small correlations emphasizes research methods. Prentice and Miller (1992) explain:

> Showing that an effect holds even under the most unlikely circumstances possible can be as impressive as (or in some cases, perhaps even more impressive) than showing that it accounts for a great deal of variance. (p. 163)

Some examples they give are studies showing correlations between attractiveness and judgments of guilt or innocence in court cases (e.g., Sigall & Ostrove, 1975). The point is that "legal judgments are supposed to be unaffected by such extraneous factors as attractiveness." Thus, if studies show that attractiveness is associated with legal judgments even slightly, we are persuaded of just how important attractiveness could be in influencing social judgments in general.

Finally, you should be aware that there is even controversy about the widespread use of Cohen's (1988) conventions for the correlation coefficient (that is, .10 for a small effect size, .30 for a medium effect size, and .50 for a large effect size). When proposing conventions for effect size estimates, such as the correlation coefficient (r), Cohen himself noted: ". . . these proposed conventions were set forth throughout with much diffidence, qualifications, and invitations not to employ them if possible. The values chosen had no more a reliable basis than my own intuition. They were offered as conventions because they were needed in a research climate characterized by a neglect of issues of [effect size] magnitude" (p. 532). Thus, some researchers strongly suggest that the magnitude of effects found in research studies should not be compared with Cohen's conventions, but rather with the effects reported in previous similar research studies (Thompson, 2007).

Correlation in Research Articles

Scatter diagrams are occasionally included in research articles, most commonly when there are relatively small numbers of individuals involved, such as in many perception and neuroscience studies. But sometimes they are included in larger studies, especially in some applied research areas. For example, Gump and colleagues (2007) conducted a study of the level of lead in children's blood and the socioeconomic status of their family. The participants were 122 children who were taking part in an ongoing study of the developmental effects of environmental toxicants. Between the ages of 2 and 3 years, a blood sample was taken from each child (with parental permission), and the amount of lead in each sample was determined with a laboratory test. The researchers measured the socioeconomic status of each child's family, based on the parents' self-reported occupation and education level. As shown in Figure 18, Gump et al. (2007) used a scatter diagram to describe the relationship between childhood blood levels and family socioeconomic status. There was a clear linear negative trend, with the researchers noting ". . . increasing family SES [socioeconomic status] was significantly associated with declining blood levels" (p. 300). The scatter diagram shows that children from families with a higher socioeconomic status had lower levels of lead in their blood. Of course, this is a correlational result. Thus, it does not necessarily mean that family socioeconomic status directly influences the amount of lead in children's blood. It is possible that some other factor may explain this association or even that the amount of lead in the blood influenced socioeconomic status. The researchers acknowledged this latter notion in the discussion section of their paper: "In addition, perhaps heightened blood lead in children (and their parents) affects cognitive functioning and thereby social and economic selection (failure to reach or keep expected social position) or drift (movement from higher to lower social class) occurs" (p. 302).

Figure 18   Children's family socioeconomic status (Hollingshead Index) as a function of childhood lead levels.

Source: Gump, B. B., Reihman, J., Stewart, P., Lonky, E., Darvill, T., & Matthews, K. A. (2007). Blood lead (Pb) levels: A potential environmental mechanism explaining the relation between socioeconomic status and cardiovascular reactivity in children. *Health Psychology, 26,* 296–304. Published by the American Psychological Association. Reprinted with permission.

Correlation coefficients are very commonly reported in research articles, both in the text of articles and in tables. The result with which we started the chapter would be described as follows: there was a positive correlation ($r = .51$) between excitement of activities done with partner and marital satisfaction. Usually, the statistical significance of the correlation will also be reported; in this example, it would be $r = .51$, $p < .05$.

Tables of correlations are common when several variables are involved. Usually, the table is set up so that each variable is listed down the left and also across the top. The correlation of each pair of variables is shown inside the table. This is called a **correlation matrix**.

Table 9 is a correlation matrix from a study by Gallup and colleagues (2010), who examined the association between temperature and various heat-regulating behaviors among budgerigars (a common kind of pet parakeet). The study was conducted with 16 birds that were exposed to air temperatures varying from 73 °F to 93 °F (a temperature range that these birds commonly experience in their natural habitat) over a period of 20 minutes in a controlled laboratory setting. The birds were video recorded during the study and their behaviors were coded by trained observers.

This example shows several features that are typical of the way correlation matrixes are laid out. First, notice that the correlation of a variable with itself is not given. In this example, a short line is put in instead; sometimes they are just left blank. Also notice that only the lower left triangle is filled in. This is because the upper right triangle would contain exactly the same information. (Sometimes the upper right triangle is filled in and the lower left triangle is left blank.) For example, the correlation

correlation matrix   common way of reporting the correlation coefficients among several variables in a research article; table in which the variables are named on the top and along the side and the correlations among them are all shown.

Table 9 Pearson Correlations Between Temperature and Recorded Behaviors

Variable	Temperature	Panting	Stretching	Wing venting	Yawning
Temperature	—				
Panting	.740**	—			
Stretching	.069	−.059	—		
Wing venting	.214*	.166	.182*	—	
Yawning	.333**	.365**	.175	.312*	—

Note: Yawning and stretching were measured as the number of yawns and stretches recorded for all four birds in a group during each 2-min interval; panting and wing venting were measured as the number of birds observed engaging in these behaviors during each trial.

* $p < .05$. ** $p < .01$.

Source: Gallup, A. C., Miller, M. L., & Clark, A. B. (2010). The direction and range of ambient temperature change influences yawning in budgerigars *(Melopsittacus undulatus). Journal of Comparative Psychology, 124,* 133–138. Published by the American Psychological Association. Reprinted with permission.

of temperature with stretching (which is .069) has to be the same as the correlation of stretching with temperature. Looking at this example, among other results, you can see that there is a large positive correlation between temperature and panting. Also, there is a small to moderate positive correlation between temperature and wing venting (holding the wings out from the body) and a moderate correlation between temperature and yawning. The asterisks—* and **—after some of the correlation coefficients tell you that those correlations are statistically significant. The note at the bottom of the table tells you the significance levels that go with the asterisks.

Learning Aids

Summary

1. Two variables are correlated when they are associated in a clear pattern (for example, when high scores on one consistently go with high scores on the other, and lows on one go with lows on the other).
2. A scatter diagram shows the relation between two variables. The lowest to highest possible values of one variable (the one you are predicting from if one variable can be thought of as predicting the other variable) are marked on the horizontal axis. The lowest to highest possible values of the other variable are marked on the vertical axis. Each individual's pair of scores is shown as a dot.
3. When the dots in the scatter diagram generally follow a straight line, this is called a linear correlation. In a curvilinear correlation, the dots follow a line pattern other than a simple straight line. There is no correlation when the dots do not follow any kind of line. In a positive linear correlation, the line goes upward to the right (so that low scores go with lows, mediums with mediums, and highs with highs). In a negative linear correlation, the line goes downward to the right (so that low scores go with highs, mediums with mediums, and highs with lows). The strength of the correlation refers to the degree to which there is a clear pattern of relationship between the two variables.
4. The correlation coefficient (r) gives the direction and strength of linear correlation. It is the average of the cross-products of the Z scores. The correlation coefficient is highly positive when there is a strong positive linear correlation. This is because positive Z scores are multiplied by positive, and negative Z scores by

negative. The correlation coefficient is highly negative when there is a strong negative linear correlation. This is because positive Z scores are multiplied by negative and negative Z scores by positive. The coefficient is 0 when there is no linear correlation. This is because positive Z scores are sometimes multiplied by positive and sometimes by negative Z scores and negative Z scores are sometimes multiplied by negative and sometimes by positive. Thus, positive and negative cross-products cancel each other out.

5. The sign ($+$ or $-$) of a correlation coefficient tells you the *direction* of the linear correlation between two variables. The actual value of the correlation coefficient (ignoring the sign) tells you the *strength* of the linear correlation. The maximum positive value of r is $+1$. $r = +1$ when there is a perfect positive linear correlation. The maximum negative value of r is -1. $r = -1$ when there is a perfect negative linear correlation.

6. The statistical significance of a correlation coefficient can be tested by changing the correlation coefficient into a t score and using cutoffs on a t distribution with degrees of freedom equal to the number of people in the study minus two. The t score for a correlation coefficient is the result of dividing the correlation coefficient by the square root of what you get when you divide one minus the correlation coefficient squared by two less than the number of people in the study. The null hypothesis for hypothesis testing with a correlation coefficient is that the true relation between the two variables in the population is no correlation ($r = 0$).

7. The assumptions for the significance test of a correlation coefficient are that the population of each variable (and the relationship between them) follows a normal distribution, there is an equal distribution of each variable at each point of the other variable, the relationship between the two variables is linear, and the people (or cases) are independent from each other.

8. Correlation does not tell you the direction of causation. If two variables, X and Y, are correlated, the correlation could be because X is causing Y, Y is causing X, or a third factor is causing both X and Y.

9. Comparisons of the degree of linear correlation are considered most accurate in terms of the correlation coefficient squared (r^2), called the proportionate reduction in error or proportion of variance accounted for.

10. A correlation coefficient will be lower (closer to 0) than the true correlation if it is based on scores from a group selected for study that is restricted in its range of scores (compared to people in general) or if the scores are based on unreliable measures.

11. The direction and strength of a correlation can be drastically distorted by extreme combinations of scores called outliers.

12. Spearman's rho is a special type of correlation based on rank-order scores. It can be used in certain situations when the scatter diagram suggests a curvilinear relationship between two variables. Spearman's rho is less affected than the regular correlation by outliers, and it works correctly even if the original scores are not based on true equal-interval measurement.

13. The correlation itself is a measure of effect size. Power and needed sample size for 80% power for a correlation coefficient can be determined using special power tables, a power software package, or an Internet power calculator.

14. Studies suggest that psychologists tend to think of any particular correlation coefficient as meaning more association than actually exists. However,

small correlations may have practical importance and may also be impressive in demonstrating the importance of a relationship when a study shows that the correlation holds even under what would seem to be unlikely conditions.

15. Correlational results are usually presented in research articles either in the text with the value of r (and usually the significance level) or in a special table (a correlation matrix) showing the correlations among several variables.

Key Terms

correlation	negative correlation	restriction in range
scatter diagram	cross-product of Z scores	outliers
linear correlation	correlation coefficient	Spearman's rho
curvilinear correlation	direction of causality	correlation matrix
no correlation	correlational research design	
positive correlation	proportionate reduction in error	

Example Worked-Out Problems

Making a Scatter Diagram and Describing the General Pattern of Association

Based on the class size and average achievement test scores for five elementary schools in the following table, make a scatter diagram and describe in words the general pattern of association.

Elementary School	Class Size	Achievement Test Score
Main Street	25	80
Casat	14	98
Lakeland	33	50
Shady Grove	28	82
Jefferson	20	90

Answer

The steps in solving the problem follow; Figure 19 shows the scatter diagram with markers for each step.

❶ **Draw the axes and decide which variable goes on which axis.** It seems more reasonable to think of class size as predicting achievement test scores rather than the other way around. Thus, you can draw the axis with class size along the bottom. (However, the prediction was not explicitly stated in the problem; so the other direction of prediction is certainly possible. Thus, putting either variable on either axis would be acceptable.)

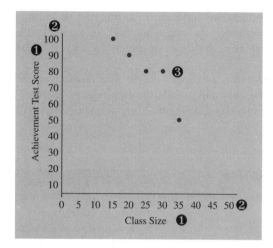

Figure 19   Scatter diagram for scores in Example Worked-Out Problem. ❶ Draw the axes and decide which variable goes on which axis. ❷ Determine the range of values to use for each variable and mark them on the axes. ❸ Mark a dot for each pair of scores.

❷ **Determine the range of values to use for each variable and mark them on the axes.** We will assume that the achievement test scores go from 0 to 100. We don't know the maximum class size; so we guessed 50. (The range of the variables was not given in the problem; thus any reasonable range would be acceptable as long as it includes the values of the scores in the actual study.)

❸ **Mark a dot for each pair of scores.** For example, to mark the dot for Main Street School, you go across to 25 and up to 80.

The general pattern is roughly linear. Its direction is negative (it goes down and to the right, with larger class sizes going with smaller achievement scores and vice versa). It is a quite large correlation, since the dots all fall fairly close to a straight line; it should be fairly close to -1. In words, it is a large, linear, negative correlation.

Figuring the Correlation Coefficient

Figure the correlation coefficient for the class size and achievement test in the preceding example.

Answer

The steps in solving the problem follow; the basic figuring is shown in Table 10 with markers for each of the steps.

❶ **Change all scores to Z scores.** For example, the mean for the class size variable is 24, and the standard deviation is 6.54. Thus, the Z score for the first class size, of 25, is $(25 - 24)/6.54 = .15$.

Table 10 Figuring the Correlation Coefficient Between Class Size and Achievement Test Score for the Example Worked-Out Problem

School	Class Size X	Class Size Z_X ❶	Achievement Test Score Y	Achievement Test Score Z_Y ❶	Cross-Products $Z_X Z_Y$ ❷
Main Street	25	.15	80	.00	.00
Casat	14	−1.53	98	1.10	−1.68
Lakeland	33	1.38	50	−1.84	−2.54
Shady Grove	28	.61	82	.12	.07
Jefferson	20	−.61	90	.61	−.37
Σ:	120		400		−4.52 ❸
M:	24		80		r = −.90 ❹
	$SD = \sqrt{214/5} = 6.54$		$\sqrt{1,328/5} = 16.30$		

❷ **Figure the cross-product of the Z scores for each person** (in this case for each school). For example, for Main Street School, the cross-product is .15 multiplied by 0, which is 0; for Casat School, is −1.53 multiple by 1.10, which equal −1.68.

❸ **Add up the cross-products of the Z scores.** The total is −4.52.

❹ **Divide by the number of people in the study** (in this case, the number of schools). The sum (−4.52) divided by 5 is −.90; that is, $r = −.90$. In terms of the correlation coefficient formula, $r = (\sum Z_X Z_Y)/N = −4.52/5 = −.90$.

Figuring the Significance of a Correlation Coefficient

Figure whether the correlation between class size and achievement test score in the preceding example is statistically significant (use the .05 level, two-tailed).

Answer

❶ **Restate the question as a research hypothesis and a null hypothesis about the populations.** There are two populations:

Population 1: Schools like those in this study.
Population 2: Schools for whom there is no correlation between the two variables.

The null hypothesis is that the two populations have the same correlation. The research hypothesis is that the two populations do not have the same correlation.

❷ **Determine the characteristics of the comparison distribution.** The comparison distribution is a t distribution with $df = 3$. (That is, $df = N − 2 = 5 − 2 = 3$.)

❸ **Determine the cutoff sample score on the comparison distribution at which the null hypothesis should be rejected.** The t table (Table A-2 in the Appendix) shows that for a two-tailed test at the .05 level, with 3 degrees of freedom, the cutoff t scores are 3.182 and −3.182.

❹ **Determine your sample's score on the comparison distribution.** The correlation in the study was $-.90$. Applying the formula to find the equivalent t, we get

$$t = \frac{r}{\sqrt{(1-r^2)/(N-2)}} = \frac{-.90}{\sqrt{(1-(-.90^2))/(3)}} = \frac{-.90}{\sqrt{.0633}} = -3.58.$$

❺ **Decide whether to reject the null hypothesis.** The t score of -3.58 for our sample correlation is more extreme than a cutoff t score of -3.182. Thus, we can reject the null hypothesis and the research hypothesis is supported.

Outline for Writing Essays on the Logic and Figuring of a Correlation Coefficient

1. If the question involves creating a scatter diagram, explain how and why you created the diagram to show the pattern of relationship between the two variables. Explain the meaning of the term *correlation*. Mention the type of correlation (e.g., linear; positive or negative; small, moderate, or large) shown by the scatter diagram.
2. Explain the idea that a correlation coefficient tells you the direction and strength of linear correlation between two variables.
3. Outline and explain the steps for figuring the correlation coefficient. Be sure to mention that the first step involves changing the scores for each variable to Z scores. Describe how to figure the cross-products of the Z scores. Explain why the cross-products of the Z scores will tend to be positive if the correlation is positive and will tend to be negative if the correlation is negative. Mention that the correlation coefficient is figured by taking the mean of the cross-products of the Z scores so that it does not get higher just because there are more cases. Explain what the value of the correlation coefficient means in terms of the direction and strength of linear correlation.
4. Be sure to discuss the direction and strength of correlation of your particular result. As needed for the specific question you are answering, discuss whether the correlation is statistically significant.

Practice Problems

These problems involve figuring. Most real-life statistics problems are done with special statistical software. Even if you have such software, do these problems by hand to ingrain the method in your mind. To learn how to use a computer to solve statistics problems like those in this chapter, refer to the Using SPSS section at the end of this chapter.

All data are fictional unless an actual citation is given.

Set I

1. For each of the following scatter diagrams, indicate whether the pattern is linear, curvilinear, or no correlation; if it is linear, indicate whether it is positive or negative and the approximate strength (large, moderate, small) of the correlation.

2. A researcher studied the relation between psychotherapists' degree of empathy and their patients' satisfaction with therapy. As a pilot study, four patient–therapist pairs were studied. Here are the results:

Pair Number	Therapist Empathy	Patient Satisfaction
1	70	4
2	94	5
3	36	2
4	48	1

(a) Make a scatter diagram of the scores; (b) describe in words the general pattern of correlation, if any; (c) figure the correlation coefficient; (d) figure whether the correlation is statistically significant (use the .05 significance level, two-tailed); (e) explain the logic of what you have done, writing as if you are speaking to someone who has never heard of correlation (but who does understand the mean, standard deviation, Z scores, and hypothesis testing); and (f) give three logically possible directions of causality, saying for each whether it is a reasonable direction in light of the variables involved (and why).

3. An instructor asked five students how many hours they had studied for an exam. Here are the hours studied and the students' grades:

Hours Studied	Test Grade
0	52
10	95
6	83
8	71
6	64

(a) Make a scatter diagram of the scores; (b) describe in words the general pattern of correlation, if any; (c) figure the correlation coefficient; (d) figure whether the correlation is statistically significant (use the .05 significance level, two-tailed); (e) explain the logic of what you have done, writing as if you are speaking to someone who has never heard of correlation (but who does understand the mean, standard deviation, Z scores, and hypothesis testing); and (f) give three logically possible directions of causality, saying for each whether it is a reasonable direction in light of the variables involved (and why).

4. In a study of people first getting acquainted with each other, researchers examined the amount of self-disclosure of one's partner and one's liking for one's partner. Here are the results:

Partner's Self-Disclosure	Liking for Partner
8	7
7	9
10	6
3	7
1	4

(a) Make a scatter diagram of the scores; (b) describe in words the general pattern of correlation, if any; (c) figure the correlation coefficient; and (d) figure whether the correlation is statistically significant (use the .05 significance level, two-tailed).

5. The following have been prepared so that data sets B through D are slightly modified versions of data set A. For each data set, (a) make a scatter diagram, (b) figure the correlation coefficient, and (c) figure whether the correlation is statistically significant (use the .05 significance level, two-tailed).

Data Set A		Data Set B		Data Set C		Data Set D	
X	Y	X	Y	X	Y	X	Y
1	1	1	1	1	5	1	1
2	2	2	2	2	2	2	4
3	3	3	3	3	3	3	3
4	4	4	5	4	4	4	2
5	5	5	4	5	1	5	5

6. For each of the following situations, indicate why the correlation coefficient might be a distorted estimate of the true correlation (and what kind of distortion you would expect):

   (a) Scores on two questionnaire measures of personality are correlated.

   (b) Comfort of living situation and happiness are correlated among a group of millionaires.

7. What is the power of each of the following studies using a correlation coefficient and the .05 significance level?

	Effect Size (r)	N	Tails
(a)	.10	50	2
(b)	.30	100	1
(c)	.50	30	2
(d)	.30	40	1
(e)	.10	100	2

8. About how many participants are needed for 80% power in each of the following planned studies that will use a correlation coefficient and the .05 significance level?

	Effect Size (r)	Tails
(a)	.50	2
(b)	.30	1
(c)	.10	2

9. Chapman et al. (1997) interviewed 68 pregnant inner city women and their male partners twice during their pregnancy, once between three and six months into the pregnancy and again between six and nine months into the pregnancy. Table 11 shows the correlations among several of their measures. ("Zero-Order Correlations" means the same thing as ordinary correlations.) Most important in this table are the correlations among women's reports of their own stress, men's reports of their partners' stress, women's perception of their partners' support at

Table 11 Zero-Order Correlations for Study Variables

Variable	1	2	3	4	5	6	7	8	9	10
1. Women's report of stress	—									
2. Men's report of women's stress	.17	—								
3. Partner Support 1	−.28*	−.18	—							
4. Partner Support 2	−.27*	−.18	.44***	—						
5. Depressed Mood 1	.23*	.10	−.34**	−.17	—					
6. Depressed Mood 2	.50***	.14	−.42***	−.41***	.55***	—				
7. Women's age	.06	.16	.04	−.24*	−.35*	−.09	—			
8. Women's ethnicity	−.19	−.09	−.16	−.14	.11	.13	−.02	—		
9. Women's marital status	−.18	.01	.12	.24*	−.04	−.20	.05	−.34**	—	
10. Parity	.19	.13	−.11	−.17	.10	.16	.26*	.31*	−.12	—

$*p < .05, **p < .01, ***p < .001.$

Source: Chapman, H. A., Hobfoll, S. E., & Ritter, C. (1997). Partners' stress underestimations lead to women's distress: A study of pregnant inner-city women. *Journal of Personality and Social Psychology, 73,* 418–425. Published by the American Psychological Association. Reprinted with permission.

the first and at the second interviews, and women's depression at the first and at the second interviews.

Explain the results on these measures as if you were writing to a person who has never had a course in statistics. Specifically, (a) explain what is meant by a correlation coefficient using one of the correlations as an example; (b) study the table and then comment on the patterns of results in terms of which variables are relatively strongly correlated and which are not very strongly correlated; and (c) comment on the limitations of making conclusions about the direction of causality based on these data, using a specific correlation as an example (noting at least one plausible alternative causal direction and why that alternative is plausible).

Set II

10. For each of the following scatter diagrams, indicate whether the pattern is linear, curvilinear, or no correlation; if it is linear, indicate whether it is positive or negative and the approximate strength (large, moderate, small) of the correlation.

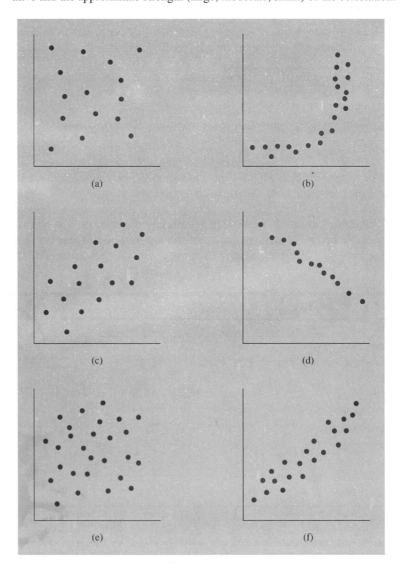

11. Make up a scatter diagram with 10 dots for each of the following situations: (a) perfect positive linear correlation, (b) large but not perfect positive linear correlation, (c) small positive linear correlation, (d) large but not perfect negative linear correlation, (e) no correlation, (f) clear curvilinear correlation.

Instructions for Problems 12 to 14. For problems 12 to 14, do the following: (a) Make a scatter diagram of the scores; (b) describe in words the general pattern of correlation, if any; (c) figure the correlation coefficient; (d) figure whether the correlation is statistically significant (use the .05 significance level, two-tailed); (e) explain the logic of what you have done, writing as if you are speaking to someone who has never heard of correlation (but who does understand the mean, standard deviation, Z scores, and hypothesis testing); and (f) give three logically possible directions of causality, indicating for each direction whether it is a reasonable explanation for the correlation in light of the variables involved (and why).

12. (The instructions for this problem are shown after problem 11.) Four research participants take a test of manual dexterity (high scores mean better dexterity) and an anxiety test (high scores mean more anxiety). The scores are as follows.

Person	Dexterity	Anxiety
1	1	10
2	1	8
3	2	4
4	4	-2

13. (The instructions for this problem are shown after problem 11.) Four young children were monitored closely over a period of several weeks to measure how much they watched violent television programs and their amount of violent behavior toward their playmates. The results were as follows:

Child's Code Number	Weekly Viewing of Violent TV (hours)	Number of Violent or Aggressive Acts Toward Playmates
G3368	14	9
R8904	8	6
C9890	6	1
L8722	12	8

14. (The instructions for this problem are shown after problem 11.) Five college students were asked about how important a goal it is to them to have a family and about how important a goal it is for them to be highly successful in their work. Each variable was measured on a scale from 0, *not at all important goal* to 10, *very important goal.*

Student	Family Goal	Work Goal
A	7	5
B	6	4
C	8	2
D	3	9
E	4	1

Instructions for Problems 15 and 16. For problems 15 and 16, (a) make a scatter diagram of the scores; (b) describe in words the general pattern of correlation, if any; (c) figure the correlation coefficient; and (d) figure whether the correlation is statistically significant (use the .05 significance level, two-tailed).

534   Correlation

15. (The instructions for this problem are shown after problem 14.) The Louvre Museum in Paris is interested in the relation of the age of a painting to public interest in it. The number of people stopping to look at each of 10 randomly selected paintings is observed over a week. The results are as shown:

Painting Title	Approximate Age (Years) (M = 268.40; SD = 152.74)		Number of People Stopping to Look (M = 88.20; SD = 29.13)	
	X	Z_X	Y	Z_Y
The Entombment	480	1.39	68	−.69
Mystic Marriage of St. Catherine	530	1.71	71	−.59
The Bathers	255	−.09	123	1.19
The Toilette	122	−.96	112	.82
Portrait of Castiglione	391	.80	48	−1.38
Charles I of England	370	.67	84	−.14
Crispin and Scapin	155	−.75	66	−.76
Nude in the Sun	130	−.91	148	2.05
The Balcony	137	−.86	71	−.59
The Circus	114	−1.01	91	.10

16. (The instructions for this problem are shown after problem 14.) A developmental psychologist studying people in their eighties was interested in the relation between number of very close friends and overall health. The scores for six research participants follow.

Research Participant	Number of Friends X	Overall Health Y
A	2	41
B	4	72
C	0	37
D	3	84
E	2	52
F	1	49

17. What is the power of each of the following studies using a correlation coefficient and the .05 significance level?

	Effect Size (r)	N	Tails
(a)	.10	30	1
(b)	.30	40	2
(c)	.50	50	2
(d)	.30	100	2
(e)	.10	20	1

18. About how many participants are needed for 80% power in each of the following planned studies that will use a correlation coefficient and the .05 significance level?

	Effect Size (r)	Tails
(a)	.10	1
(b)	.30	2
(c)	.50	1

19. As part of a larger study, Speed and Gangstead (1997) collected ratings and nominations on a number of characteristics for 66 fraternity men from their fellow fraternity members. The following paragraph is taken from their Results section:

> ... men's romantic popularity significantly correlated with several characteristics: best dressed ($r = .48$), most physically attractive ($r = .47$), most outgoing ($r = .47$), most self-confident ($r = .44$), best trendsetters ($r = .38$), funniest ($r = .37$), most satisfied ($r = .32$), and most independent ($r = .28$). Unexpectedly, however, men's potential for financial success did not significantly correlate with romantic popularity ($r = .10$). (p. 931)

Explain these results as if you were writing to a person who has never had a course in statistics. Specifically, (a) explain what is meant by a correlation coefficient using one of the correlations as an example; (b) explain in a general way what is meant by "significantly" and "not significantly," referring to at least one specific example; and (c) speculate on the meaning of the pattern of results, taking into account the issue of direction of causality.

20. Gable and Lutz (2000) studied 65 children, 3 to 10 years old, and their parents. One of their results was "Parental control of child eating showed a negative association with children's participation in extracurricular activities ($r = .34$; $p < .01$)" (p. 296). Another result was "Parents who held less appropriate beliefs about children's nutrition reported that their children watched more hours of television per day ($r = .36$; $p < .01$)" (p. 296). Explain these results as if you were writing to a person who has never had a course in statistics. Be sure to comment on possible directions of causality for each result.

21. Table 12 is from a study by Baldwin and colleagues (2006) that examined the associations among feelings of shame, guilt, and self-efficacy in a sample of 194 college students. Self-efficacy refers to people's beliefs about their ability to be successful at various things they may try to do. (For example, the students indicated how much they agreed with statements such as, "When I make plans, I am certain I can make them work.") Table 12 shows the correlations among the questionnaire measures of shame, guilt, general self-efficacy, social self-efficacy, and total self-efficacy (general self-efficacy plus social self-efficacy).

Explain the results as if you were writing to a person who has never had a course in statistics. Specifically, (a) explain what is meant by a correlation coefficient using one of the correlations as an example; (b) study the table and then comment on the patterns of results in terms of which variables are relatively strongly correlated and which are not very strongly correlated; and (c) comment on the limitations of making conclusions about the direction of causality based

Table 12 Correlations Among Shame, Guilt, and Self-Efficacy Subscales

	1	2	3	4	5
1. Shame					
2. Guilt	.34**				
3. General Self-efficacy	−.29**	.12			
4. Social Self-efficacy	−.18*	−.06	.47**		
5. Total Self-efficacy	−.29**	.07	.94**	.74**	

$*p < .01$, $**p < .001$. For all correlations, n is between 184 and 190.

Source: Baldwin, K. M., Baldwin, J. R., & Ewald, T. (2006). The relationship among shame, guilt, and self-efficacy. *American Journal of Psychotherapy, 60*, 1–21. Copyright © 2006 by The Association for the Advancement of Psychotherapy. Reprinted by permission of the publisher.

on these data, using a specific correlation as an example (noting at least one plausible alternative causal direction and why that alternative is plausible).

22. Arbitrarily select eight people from your class whose name you know. Do each of the following: (a) Make a scatter diagram for the relation between the number of letters in each person's first and last name; (b) figure the correlation coefficient for the relation between the number of letters in each person's first and last name; (c) figure whether the correlation is statistically significant (use the .05 significance level, two-tailed); (d) describe the result in words; and (e) suggest a possible interpretation for your results.

Using SPSS

The ✑ in the following steps indicates a mouse click. (We used SPSS version 19 for Windows to carry out these analyses. The steps and output may be slightly different for other versions of SPSS.)

In the following steps for the scatter diagram and correlation coefficient, we will use the example of the sleep and happy mood study. The scores for that study are shown in Table 1, the scatter diagram is shown in Figure 2, and the figuring for the correlation coefficient and its significance is shown in Table 3.

Creating a Scatter Diagram

❶ Enter the scores into SPSS. Enter the scores as shown in Figure 20.

Figure 20   SPSS data editor window for the fictional study of the relationship between hours slept last night and mood.

❷ ✍ *Graphs.*
❸ ✍ *Legacy/Dialogs,* ✍ *Scatter/Dot.* A box will appear that allows you to select different types of scatter diagrams. You want the "Simple Scatter" diagram. This is selected as the default type of diagram; so you just need to ✍ *Define.*
❹ ✍ the variable called "mood" and then ✍ the arrow next to the box labeled "Y axis." This tells SPSS that the scores for the "mood" variable should go on the vertical (or Y) axis of the scatter diagram. ✍ the variable called "sleep" and then ✍ the arrow next to the box labeled "X axis." This tells SPSS that the scores for the "sleep" variable should go on the horizontal (or X) axis of the scatter diagram.
❺ ✍ *OK.* Your SPSS output window should look like Figure 21.

Finding the Correlation Coefficient

❶ Enter the scores into SPSS. Enter the scores as shown in Figure 20.
❷ ✍ *Analyze.*
❸ ✍ *Correlate.*
❹ ✍ *Options.* Check the box next to "Means and standard deviations". ✍ *Continue.* (Step ❹ is optional, but we strongly recommend that you request such descriptive statistics.)

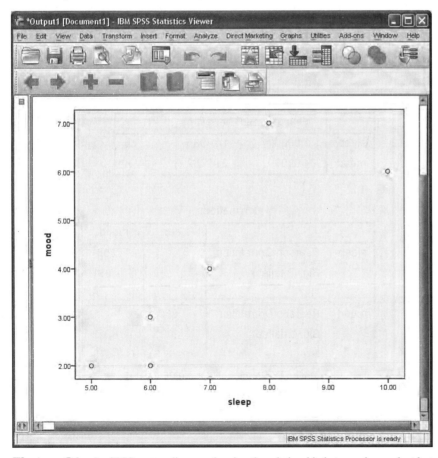

Figure 21 An SPSS scatter diagram showing the relationship between hours slept last night and mood (fictional data).

❺ ✑ *Bivariate.*

❻ ✑ on the variable called "mood" and then ✑ the arrow next to the box labeled "Variables." ✑ on the variable called "sleep" and then ✑ the arrow next to the box labeled "Variables." This tells SPSS to figure the correlation between the "mood" and "sleep" variables. (If you wanted to find the correlation between each of several variables, you would put all of them into the "Variables" box.) Notice that by default SPSS carries out a Pearson correlation (the type of correlation you have learned in this chapter), gives the significance level using a two-tailed test, and flags statistically significant correlations using the .05 significance level. (Clicking the box next to "Spearman" requests Spearman's rho, which is a special type of correlation we briefly discussed earlier in the chapter.)

❼ ✑ *OK.* Your SPSS output window should look like Figure 22.

The first table shown in Figure 22 gives the mean and standard deviation (to be precise, it gives the estimated population standard deviation, *S*)

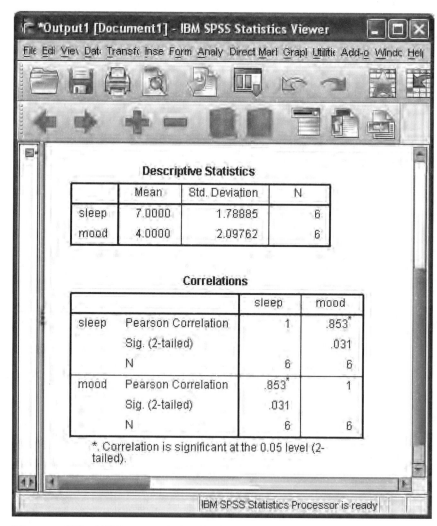

Figure 22   SPSS output window for the correlation between hours slept and mood (fictional data).

for each of the variables. The second table shown in the output is a small correlation matrix (there are only two variables). (If you were interested in the correlations among more than two variables—which is often the case in psychology research—SPSS would produce a larger correlation matrix.) The correlation matrix shows the correlation coefficient ("Pearson Correlation"), the exact significance level of the correlation coefficient ["Sig. (2-tailed)"], and the number of people in the correlation analysis ("N"). Note that two of the cells of the correlation matrix show a correlation coefficient of exactly 1. You can ignore these cells; they simply show that each variable is perfectly correlated with itself. (In larger correlation matrixes all of the cells on the diagonal from the top left to the bottom right of the table will have a correlation coefficient of 1.) You will also notice that the remaining two cells provide identical information. This is because the table shows the correlations between sleep and mood and also between mood and sleep (which are, of course, identical correlations). So you can look at either one. (In a larger correlation matrix, you need only look either at all of the correlations above the diagonal that goes from top left to bottom right or at all of the correlations below that diagonal.) The correlation coefficient is .853 (which is usually rounded to two decimal places in research articles). The significance level of .031 is less than the usual .05 cutoff, which means that it is a statistically significant correlation. The asterisk (*) by the correlation of .853 also shows that it is statistically significant (at the .05 significance level, as shown by the note under the table).

Chapter Notes

1. There is also a "computational" version of this formula that is mathematically equivalent and thus gives the same result:

$$r = \frac{N\Sigma(XY) - (\Sigma X)(\Sigma Y)}{\sqrt{[N\Sigma X^2 - (\Sigma X)^2]}\sqrt{[N\Sigma Y^2 - (\Sigma Y)^2]}}$$

This formula is easier to use when computing by hand (or with a hand calculator) when you have a large number of people in the study, because you don't have to first figure out all the deviation scores. However, researchers rarely use computational formulas like this any more because the actual figuring is done by a computer. As a student learning statistics, it is much better to use the definitional formula (1). This is because when solving problems using the definitional formula, you are strengthening your understanding of what the correlation coefficient means. In all examples in this chapter, we use the definitional formula and we urge you to use it in doing the chapter's practice problems.

2. Statisticians usually use Greek letters for population parameters. The population parameter for a correlation is ρ (rho). However, for ease of learning (and to avoid potential confusion with a term we introduce later in the chapter), and following standard usage in psychology, we use the ordinary letter r for both the correlation you figure from a sample and the correlation in a population.

3. More complete tables are provided in Cohen (1988, pp. 84–95).
4. More complete tables are provided in Cohen (1988, pp. 101–102).
5. To figure the correlation between getting a heart attack and taking aspirin, you would have to make the two variables into numbers. For example, you could make getting a heart attack equal 1 and not getting a heart attack equal 0; similarly, you could make being in the aspirin group equal 1 and being in the control group equal 0. It would not matter which two numbers you used for the two values for each variable. Whichever two numbers you use, the result will come out the same after converting to Z scores. The only difference that the two numbers you use makes is that the value that gets the higher number determines whether the correlation will be positive or negative.

Appendix: Table

Table A-2   Cutoff Scores for the t Distribution

	One-Tailed Tests			Two-Tailed Tests		
df	.10	.05	.01	.10	.05	.01
1	3.078	6.314	31.821	6.314	12.706	63.657
2	1.886	2.920	6.965	2.920	4.303	9.925
3	1.638	2.353	4.541	2.353	3.182	5.841
4	1.533	2.132	3.747	2.132	2.776	4.604
5	1.476	2.015	3.365	2.015	2.571	4.032
6	1.440	1.943	3.143	1.943	2.447	3.708
7	1.415	1.895	2.998	1.895	2.365	3.500
8	1.397	1.860	2.897	1.860	2.306	3.356
9	1.383	1.833	2.822	1.833	2.262	3.250
10	1.372	1.813	2.764	1.813	2.228	3.170
11	1.364	1.796	2.718	1.796	2.201	3.106
12	1.356	1.783	2.681	1.783	2.179	3.055
13	1.350	1.771	2.651	1.771	2.161	3.013
14	1.345	1.762	2.625	1.762	2.145	2.977
15	1.341	1.753	2.603	1.753	2.132	2.947
16	1.337	1.746	2.584	1.746	2.120	2.921
17	1.334	1.740	2.567	1.740	2.110	2.898
18	1.331	1.734	2.553	1.734	2.101	2.879
19	1.328	1.729	2.540	1.729	2.093	2.861
20	1.326	1.725	2.528	1.725	2.086	2.846
21	1.323	1.721	2.518	1.721	2.080	2.832
22	1.321	1.717	2.509	1.717	2.074	2.819

(continued)

Table A-2 (*continued*)

	One-Tailed Tests			Two-Tailed Tests		
df	.10	.05	.01	.10	.05	.01
23	1.320	1.714	2.500	1.714	2.069	2.808
24	1.318	1.711	2.492	1.711	2.064	2.797
25	1.317	1.708	2.485	1.708	2.060	2.788
26	1.315	1.706	2.479	1.706	2.056	2.779
27	1.314	1.704	2.473	1.704	2.052	2.771
28	1.313	1.701	2.467	1.701	2.049	2.764
29	1.312	1.699	2.462	1.699	2.045	2.757
30	1.311	1.698	2.458	1.698	2.043	2.750
35	1.306	1.690	2.438	1.690	2.030	2.724
40	1.303	1.684	2.424	1.684	2.021	2.705
45	1.301	1.680	2.412	1.680	2.014	2.690
50	1.299	1.676	2.404	1.676	2.009	2.678
55	1.297	1.673	2.396	1.673	2.004	2.668
60	1.296	1.671	2.390	1.671	2.001	2.661
65	1.295	1.669	2.385	1.669	1.997	2.654
70	1.294	1.667	2.381	1.667	1.995	2.648
75	1.293	1.666	2.377	1.666	1.992	2.643
80	1.292	1.664	2.374	1.664	1.990	2.639
85	1.292	1.663	2.371	1.663	1.989	2.635
90	1.291	1.662	2.369	1.662	1.987	2.632
95	1.291	1.661	2.366	1.661	1.986	2.629
100	1.290	1.660	2.364	1.660	1.984	2.626
∞	1.282	1.645	2.327	1.645	1.960	2.576

Answers to Set I Practice Problems

Chapter 11

1. (a) Curvilinear; (b) linear, positive, large; (c) linear, negative, large; (d) linear, positive, large; (e) linear, positive, small to moderate; (f) no correlation.
2. (a)

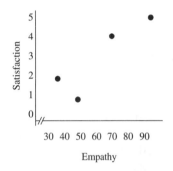

(b) Positive linear correlation—as therapist empathy goes up, so does patient satisfaction.
(c) Therapist empathy $M = 62, SD = 22.14$; patient satisfaction $M = 3, SD = 1.58$.

Therapist Empathy (X)		Patient Satisfaction (Y)		Cross-Product of Z Scores
Raw	Z_X	Raw	Z_Y	$Z_X Z_Y$
70	.36	4	.63	.23
94	1.45	5	1.27	1.84
36	−1.17	2	−.63	.74
48	−.63	1	−1.27	.80
				$\Sigma = 3.61$
				$r = 3.61/4 = .90$

(d) Comparison distribution is a t distribution with $df = N - 2 = 4 - 2 = 2$. The t tables (Table A-2 in the Appendix) shows that for a two-tailed test at the .05 level, with 2 degrees of freedom, the cutoff t scores are 4.303 and −4.303. Using the formula $t = r/\sqrt{(1 - r^2)/(N - 2)} = .90/\sqrt{(.19)/(2)} = 2.92$. This t value is not more extreme than the cutoffs; do not reject the null hypothesis.
(e) The first thing I did was make a graph, called a scatter diagram, putting one variable on each axis; I then put a

dot where each person's pair of scores goes on that graph. This gives a picture of the pattern of relationship between the two variables. In this example, high scores generally go with high scores and lows with lows. The scores are going together in a systematic pattern makes this a *correlation*; that highs go with highs and lows with lows makes this correlation *positive*; that dots fall roughly near a straight line makes this positive correlation *linear*.

Next, I figured the *correlation coefficient*, a number describing the degree of linear correlation (in a positive correlation, how consistently highs go with highs and lows with lows). To do this, I changed all the scores to Z scores because Z scores tell you how much a score is low or high relative to the other scores in its distribution. You figure the correlation coefficient by multiplying each person's two Z score by each other, totaling up these products, and then averaging this total over the number of people. This will be a high number if highs go with highs and lows with lows, because with Z scores, highs are always positive and positive times positive is positive, and with Z scores, lows are always negative and negative times negative becomes positives too. Correlation coefficients can vary from −1 (a perfect negative correlation) to +1 (a perfect positive correlation). In this example, the correlation coefficient (r) of .90 indicates a large positive linear correlation between therapist empathy and patient satisfaction.

To test the statistical significance of a correlation coefficient, you determine a t score for the correlation coefficient and compare that t score to a cutoff t value from a t table. The formula for finding the t score from the correlation coefficient involves dividing the correlation coefficient by the square root of what you get when you divide 1 minus the correlation coefficient squared by 2 less than the number of people in the study. The degrees of freedom for the t test are 2 less than the number of people in the study. In this example, there were 2 degrees of freedom, which gave t cutoffs (from the t table) of 4.303 and −4.303. The t value for the correlation coefficient was 2.92, which was not more extreme than the cutoff values; so the null hypothesis (of no correlation between therapist empathy and patient satisfaction in the population) was not rejected.
(f) (i) If a therapist has more empathy, this causes the patient to feel more satisfied (empathy causes satisfaction); (ii) if a patient feels more satisfied, this causes the therapist to feel more empathic toward the patient (satisfaction causes empathy); or (iii) some third factor, such as a good match of the patient's problem with the therapist's ability, causes patients to be more satisfied and therapists to be

more empathic (third factor causes both satisfaction and empathy).

3. (a) See question 2a for example scatter diagram. (b) Positive linear correlation: as hours studied go up, so do test grades. (c) $r = 4.20/5 = .84$. (d) $df = N - 2 = 5 - 2 = 3$; cutoff t scores are 3.182 and -3.182; $t = 2.69$; do not reject the null hypothesis. (e) Like question 2e. (f) (i) Studying more causes improved test grades; (ii) getting a better test grade causes more hours studied; note that, although this is theoretically possible, in reality it is not possible to have a future event (the score on the test) cause a previous event (hours studied); or (iii) a third factor, such as interest in the subject matter, could be causing the student to study more and also to do better on the test.

4. (a) See question 2a for example scatter diagram. (b) Positive linear correlation: as self-disclosure goes up, so does liking for partner. (c) $r = 2.33/5 = .47$. (d) $df = N - 2 = 5 - 2 = 3$; cutoff t scores are 3.182 and -3.182; $t = .92$; do not reject the null hypothesis.

5. Set A:

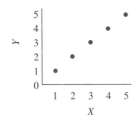

	X			Y		Cross-Product of Z Scores
Raw	Z_X		Raw	Z_Y		$Z_X Z_Y$
1	−1.41		1	−1.41		2.0
2	−.71		2	−.71		.5
3	.00		3	.00		.0
4	.71		4	.71		.5
5	1.41		5	1.41		2.0
For X, M = 3, SD = 1.41						$\Sigma = 5.0$
For Y, M = 3, SD = 1.41						$r = 5.0/5 = 1.00$

$df = N - 2 = 5 - 2 = 3$; cutoff t scores are 3.182 and -3.182; using the formula gives $t = 1/0$, which is undefined (since you can't divide a number by 0). However, any perfect correlation is statistically significant; so we can reject the null hypothesis and the research hypothesis is supported.
Set B: $r = .90$; $t = 3.58$; reject the null hypothesis; the research hypothesis is supported.
Set C: $r = -.60$; $t = -1.30$; do not reject the null hypothesis.
Set D: $r = .60$; $t = 1.30$; do not reject the null hypothesis.

6. (a) The measures may have low reliability, thus reducing (attenuating) the possible correlation between them. (b) There is restriction in range: among millionaires, there may not be a very great range of comfort of living situation (they probably all have quite comfortable situations); so the correlation with any variable (including happiness) is limited.

7. From Table 11-7: (a) .11; (b) .92; (c) .83; (d) .60; (e) .17.

8. From Table 11-8: (a) 28; (b) 68; (c) 783.

9. (a) This table shows the degree of association among scores on several measures given to pregnant women and their partners. (Here continue with an explanation of the correlation coefficient like that in question 2e, except in this problem you also need to explain the mean, standard deviation, and Z scores, which you do in the same way as in answering the problems in Chapters 2 and 3.) For example, the correlation of .17 between women's reports of stress and men's reports of stress indicates that the association between these two measures is quite weak. That is, how much stress a woman is under is not highly related to how much stress her partner believes she is under. On the other hand, the correlation of .50 (near the middle of the first column of correlations) tells you that there is a much stronger association between a woman's report of stress and her depressed mood in the second interview. That is, women who report being under stress are also likely to report being depressed; those reporting being under not much stress are likely to report not being very depressed.
(b) In general, the correlations shown in this table are strongest among the stress, support, and mood items; correlations of these variables with demographics (age, ethnicity, etc.) were fairly weak. Partner support seemed to be strongly correlated with stress and mood, and depressed mood at the second testing was particularly related to the other variables.
(c) Just because two variables are correlated, even strongly correlated, does not mean that you can know the particular direction of causality that creates that association. For example, there is a strong negative correlation between partner support at time 1 and depressed mood at time 2. There are three logically possible directions of causality here: (1) support can be causing lower depression, (2) lower depression can be causing support, or (3) some third factor can be causing both. You can rule out the second possibility, since something in the future (low depression) cannot cause the past (initial support). However, the other two possibilities remain. It is certainly plausible that having her partner's support helps reduce depression, but it is also possible that a third factor is causing both. For example, consider level of income. Perhaps when a couple has more income, the partner has more time and energy to provide support and the greater comfort of living keeps depression down.

Chapter 12

Prediction

In this chapter, we consider a major practical application of statistical methods: making predictions. Psychologists of various kinds are called on to make informed (and precise) guesses about such things as how well a particular job applicant is likely to perform if hired, how much a reading program is likely to help a particular third grader, how likely a particular patient is to commit suicide, or how likely a potential parolee is to commit a violent crime if released. Statistical prediction also plays a major part in helping research psychologists understand how various factors affect outcomes of interest. For example, what factors in people who marry predict whether they will be happy and together 10 years later; what are the factors in childhood that predict depression and anxiety in adulthood; what are the circumstances of learning something that predict good or poor memory for it years later; or what are the various kinds of support from friends and family that predict how quickly or poorly someone recovers from the death of a loved one? Finally,

> **TIP FOR SUCCESS**
> Be sure you have fully mastered the material on correlation in *Correlation* before reading this chapter.

545

learning the intricacies of statistical prediction deepens your insight into other statistical topics and prepares you for central themes in more advanced statistics courses.

The main part of this chapter considers in some detail the logic and procedures for making predictions about one variable, such as predicting college grade point average (GPA), based on information about another variable, such as SAT scores. We then briefly introduce procedures for situations in which predictions about one variable, such as college GPA, are made based on information about two or more other variables, such as using both SAT scores and high school GPA. Finally, as an Advanced Topic, we discuss how to estimate the expected accuracy of the predictions we make using these procedures.

As you learn these new topics, you will find that they are closely linked with the topic of correlation. That is because if two variables are correlated it means that you can predict one from the other. So if sleep the night before is correlated with happiness the next day, this means that you should be able, to some extent, to predict how happy a person will be the next day from knowing how much sleep the person got the night before. But if two variables are not correlated, then knowing about one does not help you predict the other. So if shoe size and income have a zero correlation, knowing a person's shoe size does not allow you to predict anything about the person's income. As we proceed, we will be referring again to the connections of correlation with prediction. But for now let us turn to prediction before we come back to correlation.

Predictor (*X*) and Criterion (*Y*) Variables

One of the ways correlation and prediction look different is this: with correlation it did not matter much which variable was which. But with prediction we have to decide which variable is *being predicted from* and which variable is *being predicted*. The variable being predicted from is called the **predictor variable**. The variable being predicted is called the **criterion variable**. In formulas the predictor variable is usually labeled X, and the criterion variable is usually labeled Y. That is, X predicts Y. In the example we just considered, SAT scores would be the predictor variable or X, and college grades would be the criterion variable or Y (see Table 1).

Prediction Using *Z* Scores Versus Raw Scores

We know that one of the key steps in calculating the correlation coefficient is to change all of the raw scores to Z scores. It turns out that you can do prediction based on either Z scores or raw scores. In other words, you can use Z scores for a predictor variable to predict Z scores for a criterion variable, or you can use raw scores for a predictor variable to predict raw scores for a criterion variable. In real research situations, it is more common to conduct the statistical analyses for prediction using raw scores, so that is what we focus on in this chapter.

The Linear Prediction Rule

predictor variable (usually *X*) in prediction, variable that is used to predict scores of individuals on another variable.

criterion variable (usually *Y*) in prediction, a variable that is predicted.

Suppose we want to predict students' GPA at a particular college from their SAT scores. We could go about predicting college GPA by ignoring the SAT scores and just predicting that everyone will have an average level of college GPA. But we

Table 1	Predictor and Criterion Variables	
	Variable Predicted from	**Variable Predicted to**
	Predictor Variable	**Criterion Variable**
Symbol	X	Y
Example	SAT scores	College GPA

would not be taking advantage of knowing the SAT scores. Another possibility would be to use the information we have about SAT and GPA from recent students at this college to set up a complicated set of rules about what GPA we predict for each possible SAT score. For example, suppose in the past few years that students who came to this college with an SAT of 580 had an average GPA at graduation of 2.62; for students with an SAT of 590 the average GPA was 2.66; for students with an SAT of 600 the average GPA was 2.70; and so forth. We could then use these numbers to set up a rule that, for future students who come in with an SAT of 580, we would predict they would graduate with a GPA of 2.62; for those who come in with an SAT of 590, we would predict they would graduate with a GPA of 2.66; and so forth. This would be a pretty good rule and probably would make reasonably accurate predictions. However, the problem with this kind of rule is that it is quite complicated. Also because some SAT scores may have only a few students, it might not be that accurate for students with those SAT scores.

Ideally, we would like a prediction rule that is not only simpler than this kind of complicated rule but also does not depend on only a few cases for each prediction. The solution that is favored by research psychologists is a rule of the form "to predict a person's score on Y, start with some baseline number, which we will call a, then add to it the result of multiplying a special predictor value, which we will call b, by the person's score on X." For our SAT and GPA example, the rule might be "to predict a person's graduating GPA, start with .3 and add the result of multiplying .004 by the person's SAT score." That is, the baseline number (a) would be .3 and the predictor value (b) is .004. Thus, if a person had an SAT of 600, we would predict the person would graduate with a GPA of 2.7. That is, the baseline number of .3 plus the result of multiplying the predictor value of .004 by 600 gives .3 plus 2.4, which equals 2.7. For a student with an SAT of 700, we would predict a graduating GPA of 3.1 [that is, $.3 + (.004 \times 700) = 3.1$].

This is an example of a **linear prediction rule** (or *linear prediction model*). We will see in the next main section why it is called "linear." For now it is enough just to note that "linear" here means the same thing as it does when we consider correlation: Lows go with lows and highs with highs (or, for a negative correlation, lows with highs and highs with lows). In our SAT score and college GPA example, a low score on the predictor variable (SAT score) predicts a low score on the criterion variable (college GPA), and a high score on the predictor variable predicts a high score on the criterion variable.

In a linear prediction rule the formal name for the baseline number or a is the **regression constant** or just *constant*. It has the name "constant" because it is a fixed value that you always use when making a prediction. *Regression* is another name statisticians use for prediction; that is why it is called the regression constant. The number you multiply by the person's score on the predictor variable, b, is called the **regression coefficient** because a coefficient is a number you multiply by something. Later in the chapter, you will learn how to figure the values of a and b, and you will use them to draw a figure that shows the linear prediction rule, but for now we are focusing on the logic for making predictions about one variable (the criterion variable) based on information about another variable (the predictor variable).

All linear prediction rules have this formula:

$$\hat{Y} = a + (b)(X) \qquad\qquad (1)$$

In this formula, $\hat{Y}$ is the person's predicted score on the criterion variable; a is the regression constant, b is the regression coefficient, and X is the person's score on the predictor variable. The symbol over the Y means "predicted value of" and is called a *hat* (so, $\hat{Y}$ is said "Y hat").

linear prediction rule formula for making predictions; that is, formula for predicting a person's score on a criterion variable based on the person's score on one or more predictor variables.

regression constant (a) in a linear prediction rule, particular fixed number added into the prediction.

regression coefficient (b) number multiplied by a person's score on a predictor variable as part of a linear prediction rule.

A person's predicted score on the criterion variable equals the regression constant, plus the result of multiplying the regression coefficient by that person's score on the predictor variable.

An Example

In the example of using SAT scores to predict college GPA, the regression constant (*a*) was .3 and the regression coefficient (*b*) was .004. So, to predict a person's GPA, you start with a score of .3 and add .004 multiplied by the SAT score. In terms of the linear prediction rule formula,

$$\hat{Y} = a + (b)(X) = .3 + (.004)(X)$$

Or in terms of the variable names,

$$\text{Predicted GPA} = .3 + (.004)(\text{SAT score}).$$

Applying this formula to predicting GPA from a SAT score of 700,

$$\text{Predicted GPA} = .3 + (.004)(700) = .3 + 2.80 = 3.10.$$

You may be interested to know that research studies have consistently shown that SAT scores (as well as high school GPA) predict students' GPA in college (e.g., Schmitt et al., 2009). As you can imagine (and may know from personal experience), SAT scores are not the only factor that predict students' college GPA.

Another Example

In *Correlation* we considered the relationship between the number of hours of sleep and happy mood the next day for six students. In this example, hours of sleep is the predictor variable (*X*) and happy mood is the criterion variable (*Y*). The regression constant (*a*) in this example is -3 and the regression coefficient (*b*) is 1. (You will learn in a later section how to figure these values of *a* and *b*.) So, to predict a person's mood level, you start with a score of -3 and add 1 multiplied by the number of hours of sleep. In terms of the linear prediction rule formula,

$$\hat{Y} = a + (b)(X) = -3 + (1)(X)$$

Or in terms of the variable names,

$$\text{Predicted mood} = -3 + (1)(\text{hours of sleep}).$$

Applying this formula to predicting mood after having 9 hours of sleep,

$$\text{Predicted mood} = -3 + (1)(9) = -3 + 9 = 6.$$

Table 2 shows the worked-out linear prediction rule formula for the predicted mood scores for scores on sleep ranging from 0 to 16 hours. An important thing to notice from Table 2 is that in actual prediction situations it is not a good idea to predict from scores on the predictor variable that are much higher or lower than those in the study you used to figure the original correlation. You can see in this example that when a person sleeps a very small number of hours, you predict negative scores on the mood scale, which is impossible (the scale goes from 0 to 8); and when the person sleeps a great many hours, you predict scores on the mood scale that are higher than the limits of the scale. (In fact, it does not even make sense; sleeping 16 hours would probably not make you incredibly happy.) This is why a prediction rule should be used only for making predictions within the same range of scores for the predictor variable that were used to come up with the original correlation on which the prediction rule is based.

Table 2 Using the Linear Prediction Rule Formula for the Fictional Sleep and Mood Example for 0 to 16 Hours of Sleep

Linear prediction rule: $\hat{Y} = a + (b)(X)$ Predicted mood $= -3 + (1)(\text{hours of sleep})$	
0 hours sleep	$-3 = -3 + (1)(0)$
1 hours sleep	$-2 = -3 + (1)(1)$
2 hours sleep	$-1 = -3 + (1)(2)$
3 hours sleep	$0 = -3 + (1)(3)$
4 hours sleep	$1 = -3 + (1)(4)$
5 hours sleep	$2 = -3 + (1)(5)$
6 hours sleep	$3 = -3 + (1)(6)$
7 hours sleep	$4 = -3 + (1)(7)$
8 hours sleep	$5 = -3 + (1)(8)$
9 hours sleep	$6 = -3 + (1)(9)$
10 hours sleep	$7 = -3 + (1)(10)$
11 hours sleep	$8 = -3 + (1)(11)$
12 hours sleep	$9 = -3 + (1)(12)$
13 hours sleep	$10 = -3 + (1)(13)$
14 hours sleep	$11 = -3 + (1)(14)$
15 hours sleep	$12 = -3 + (1)(15)$
16 hours sleep	$13 = -3 + (1)(16)$

How are you doing?

1. *Fill in the blanks:* The variable being predicted from is called the _____ variable and the variable being predicted is called the _____ variable.
2. What is the linear prediction rule in words?
3. Write the formula for the linear prediction rule and define each of the symbols.
4. In a particular prediction rule, $a = -1.23$ and $b = 6.11$. What is the predicted score on the criterion variable if the score on the predictor variable is (a) 2.00; (b) 4.87; (c) −1.92?
5. Why should the linear prediction rule be used for making predictions only within the same range of scores in the group of people studied that was the basis for forming the particular prediction rule?

Answers

1. The variable being predicted from is called the *predictor* variable and the variable being predicted is called the *criterion* variable.
2. To predict a person's score on a criterion variable (Y), start with a particular regression constant and add to it the result of multiplying the particular regression coefficient by the person's score on the predictor variable (X).
3. Formula for the linear prediction rule: $\hat{Y} = a + (b)(X)$. $\hat{Y}$ is the predicted score on the criterion variable (Y); a is the regression constant; b is the regression coefficient; and X is the score on the predictor variable (X).
4. Predicted scores: (a) $\hat{Y} = a + (b)(X) = -1.23 + (6.11)(2.00) = 10.99$; (b) $-1.23 + (6.11)(4.87) = 28.53$; (c) $-1.23 + (6.11)(-1.92) = -12.96$.
5. Using scores outside the range for the predictor variable may give unrealistic (or even impossible) predicted scores for the criterion variable.

The Regression Line

You can visualize a linear prediction rule as a line on a graph in which the horizontal axis is for values of the predictor variable (*X*) and the vertical axis is for predicted scores for the criterion variable ($\hat{Y}$). (The graph is set up like the scatter diagrams in *Correlation*.) The line is called a **regression line** and shows the relation between values of the predictor variable and the *predicted values* of the criterion variable.

Figure 1 shows the regression line for the SAT scores (predictor variable) and college GPA (criterion variable) example. By following the regression line, you can find the GPA score that is predicted from any particular SAT score. The dotted lines show the prediction for having an SAT score of 700. From the figure, the predicted GPA score for an SAT score of 700 is a little more than 3.0, which is consistent with the precise predicted value of 3.1 we found earlier when using the linear prediction rule formula. So, as you can see, the regression line acts as a visual display of the linear prediction rule formula.

The regression line for the hours slept last night (predictor variable) and happy mood (criterion variable) example is shown in Figure 2. The dotted lines show that having 9 hours of sleep gives a predicted happy mood score of 6, which is the same value we found when using the linear prediction rule formula.

Slope of the Regression Line

regression line   line on a graph such as a scatter diagram showing the predicted value of the criterion variable for each value of the predictor variable; visual display of the linear prediction rule.

slope   steepness of the angle of a regression line in a graph of the relation of scores on a predictor variable and predicted scores on a criterion variable; number of units the line goes up for every unit it goes across.

The steepness of the angle of the regression line, called its **slope**, is the amount the line moves up for every unit it moves across. In the example in Figure 1, the line moves up .004 on the GPA scale for every additional point on the SAT. In fact, the slope of the line is exactly *b*, the regression coefficient. (We don't usually think of SAT scores increasing by as little as 1 point—say, from 600 to 601. So instead of thinking about a 1-point increase in SAT giving a .004-point increase in GPA, it may be easier to think in terms of a 100-point increase in SAT giving a .4-point increase in GPA.)

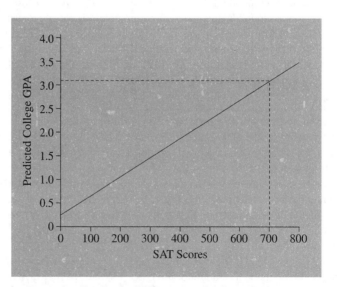

Figure 1   Regression line for the SAT scores and college GPA example, showing predicted college GPA for a person with an SAT score of 700 (fictional data).

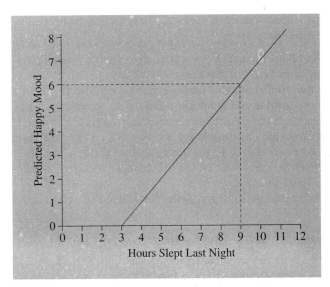

Figure 2 Regression line for the hours of sleep and happy mood example, showing predicted happy mood for a person who slept 9 hours (fictional data).

For the hours of sleep and happy mood example shown in Figure 2, the value of the regression coefficient, b, is 1. So, the line moves up 1 on the happy mood scale for every additional hour of sleep.

The Intercept of the Regression Line

The point at which the regression line crosses (or "intercepts") the vertical axis is called the **intercept** (or sometimes the *Y intercept*). (This assumes you have drawn the vertical axis so it is at the 0 point on the horizontal axis.) The intercept is the predicted score on the criterion variable $(\hat{Y})$ when the score on the predictor variable (X) is 0. It turns out that the intercept is the same as the regression constant. This works because the regression constant is the number you always add in—a kind of baseline number, the number you start with. And it is reasonable that the best baseline number would be the number you predict from a score of 0 on the predictor variable. In Figure 1, the line crosses the vertical axis at .3. That is, when a person has an SAT score of 0, they are predicted to have a college GPA of .3. In fact, the intercept of the line is exactly a, the regression constant. Another way of thinking of this is in terms of the linear prediction rule formula, $\hat{Y} = a + (b)(X)$. If X is 0, then whatever the value of b, when you multiply it by X you get 0. Thus, if b multiplied by X comes out to 0, all that is left of the prediction formula is $\hat{Y} = a + 0$. That is, if X is 0, then $\hat{Y} = a$.

For the hours of sleep and happy mood example, the regression constant, a, was -3. If you were to extend the regression line in Figure 2, it would cross the vertical axis at -3.

How to Draw the Regression Line

The first steps are setting up the axes and labels of your graph—the same steps as in *Correlation* for setting up a scatter diagram. The regression line is a straight line and thus shows a *linear* prediction. Thus, to draw the regression line, you only have

intercept the point where the regression line crosses the vertical axis; the regression constant (a).

552 Prediction

TIP FOR SUCCESS

To help you remember which variable goes on which axis, you can use the mnemonic "what's known forms a stable *basis* for what's predicted or envisioned up *high*."

to figure the location of any two points and draw the line that passes through them. Overall, there are four steps:

❶ **Draw and label the axes for a scatter diagram.** Remember to put the predictor variable on the horizontal axis.

❷ **Figure the predicted value on the criterion variable for a low value of the predictor variable and mark the point on the graph.** You make the prediction using the linear prediction rule you learned earlier: $\hat{Y} = a + (b)(X)$.

❸ **Do the same thing again, but for a high value on the predictor variable.** It is best to pick a value of the predictor variable (X) that is much higher than you used in Step ❷. This is because it will make the dots fairly far apart, so that your drawing will be more accurate.

❹ **Draw a line that passes through the two marks.** This is the regression line.

An Example of Drawing the Regression Line

Here is how you would draw the regression line for the SAT scores and college GPA example. (The steps are shown in Figure 3.)

❶ **Draw and label the axes for a scatter diagram.** Note that we labeled the Y axis "Predicted" college GPA, as the regression line shows the relationship between actual scores of the predictor variable (X) and *predicted scores* of the criterion variable ($\hat{Y}$).

❷ **Figure the predicted value on the criterion variable for a low value of the predictor variable and mark the point on the graph.** Recall from earlier that the linear prediction rule formula for predicting college GPA from an SAT score is $\hat{Y} = .3 + (.004)(X)$. So, for an SAT score of 200 (a low SAT score), the predicted college GPA is $.3 + (.004)(200)$, which is 1.1. Thus, you mark this point $(X = 200, \hat{Y} = 1.1)$ on the graph, as shown in Figure 3.

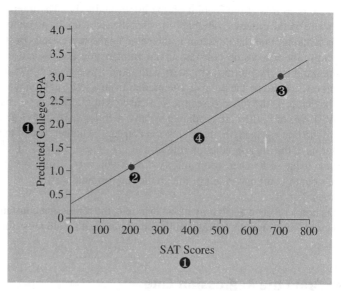

Figure 3 Steps in drawing a regression line for the SAT scores and college GPA example. ❶ Draw and label the axes, ❷ mark a point for a low value of the predictor variable and its predicted value on the criterion variable, ❸ mark a point for a high value of the predictor variable and its predicted value on the criterion variable, and ❹ draw the regression line.

❸ **Do the same thing again, but for a high value on the predictor variable.** We saw earlier that if a person has an SAT score of 700 (a high SAT score), we predict a college GPA of 3.1 [that is, $.3 + (.004)(700) = 3.1$]. Thus, you mark this point ($X = 700$, $\hat{Y} = 3.1$) on the graph, as shown in Figure 3.

❹ **Draw a line that passes through the two marks.** The line is shown in Figure 3.

Another Example of Drawing the Regression Line

Here is how you would draw the regression line for the hours of sleep and happy mood example. (The steps are shown in Figure 4.)

❶ **Draw and label the axes for a scatter diagram.**

❷ **Figure the predicted value on the criterion variable for a low value of the predictor variable and mark the point on the graph.** Recall that the linear prediction rule for predicting happy mood from the number of hours of sleep is $\hat{Y} = -3 + (1)(X)$. So, for 3 hours of sleep (a low amount of sleep), the predicted happy mood is $-3 + (1)(3)$, which is 0. Thus, you mark this point ($X = 3$, $\hat{Y} = 0$) on the graph, as shown in Figure 4.

❸ **Do the same thing again, but for a high value on the predictor variable.** If a person has 10 hours of sleep (a large amount of sleep), we predict a happy mood of 7 [that is, $-3 + (1)(10) = 7$]. Thus you mark this point ($X = 10$, $\hat{Y} = 7$) on the graph, as shown in Figure 4.

❹ **Draw a line that passes through the two marks.** The line is shown in Figure 4.

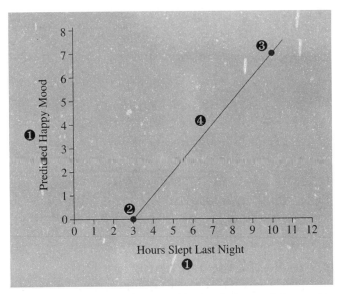

Figure 4   Steps in drawing a regression line for the hours of sleep and happy mood example. ❶ Draw and label the axes, ❷ mark a point for a low value of the predictor variable and its predicted value on the criterion variable, ❸ mark a point for a high value of the predictor variable and its predicted value on the criterion variable, and ❹ draw the regression line.

How are you doing?

1. What does the regression line show?
2. What is the relationship between the regression line and the linear prediction rule?
3. (a) What is the slope of the regression line? (b) What is it equivalent to in the linear prediction rule?
4. (a) What is the intercept of the regression line? (b) What is it equivalent to in the linear prediction rule?
5. Draw the regression line for X and $\hat{Y}$ where $a = 4$ and $b = 1.33$ (put values from 0 to 12 on the X axis and values of 0 to 20 on the Y axis.)

Answers

1. The regression line shows the relationship between the predictor variable (X) and predicted values of the criterion variable ($\hat{Y}$).
2. The regression line is a visual display of the linear prediction rule.
3. (a) The slope of the regression line is the amount the line goes up for every one unit it moves across. (b) In the linear prediction rule, it is equivalent to b, the regression coefficient.
4. (a) The intercept of the regression line is the point at which the regression line crosses the vertical axis (assuming the vertical axis is at 0 on the horizontal axis). (b) In the linear prediction rule, it is equivalent to a, the regression constant.
5. See Figure 5.

Figure 5　Regression line for "How are you doing?" question 5.

Finding the Best Linear Prediction Rule

In any given situation, how do we find the right linear prediction rule, the correct numbers for the regression constant, a, and the regression coefficient, b? Whether we think of it as a rule in words, a formula, or a regression line on a graph, we still have to know these two numbers. Figure 6 shows the scatter diagram for the six students in the hours of sleep and happy mood example. Four different regression

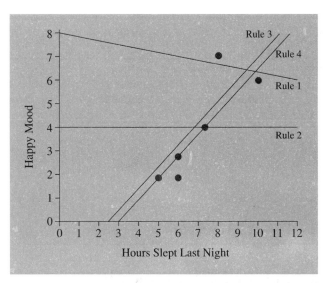

Figure 6 Actual scores from six students (shown as dots) and four prediction rules (shown as regression lines) for predicting happy mood from hours of sleep (fictional data).

lines (each showing a different linear prediction rule) are shown in the figure. In the figure, the dots show the actual scores of the six students, and the lines show different prediction rules for predicting happy mood from hours of sleep. So the closer a line comes to matching the actual results (the dots), the better the job it does as a prediction rule. In reality, there is only *one* best linear prediction rule, but for learning purposes, imagine you have four rules to pick from. Which rule in Figure 6 will do the best job of predicting happy mood scores from the number of hours slept?

Suppose we used Rule 1 as our linear prediction rule. This would be a rule $\hat{Y} = 8 - (.18)(X)$. For example, if we used this rule to make a prediction for a person who had 6 hours of sleep, we would predict a happy mood of 6.92 [that is, $8 - (.18)(6) = 6.92$], which would be way off from the actual scores of the two people in the study who slept for 6 hours (one of whom had a mood score of 2, the other a 3). In fact, you can see from the line that most of the predictions based on Rule 1 would be way off from the actual happy mood scores. Rule 2 is a prediction rule of $\hat{Y} = 4 + (0)(X)$, which more simply is $\hat{Y} = 4$. (Since the mean of the Y values in this example is 4, this rule involves always predicting the mean of Y.) If we used this rule we would make a reasonable prediction for a person with 6 hours of sleep: we would predict a happy mood of 4, which would be pretty close to the true scores. But using this prediction rule would not do so well if we were predicting for a person with 5 hours of sleep or 8 hours of sleep. Overall, Rule 3 does a good job of predicting actual happy mood scores (it is quite close to most of the dots), but Rule 4 does an even better job.

Table 3 summarizes how well each of the four rules predicts the actual happy mood scores of the six students in this example. The table shows the hours slept (X), the actual happy mood score (Y), and the predicted happy mood score ($\hat{Y}$) for each student using each of the four prediction rules. The table shows that Rules 3 and 4 have predicted values of the happy mood criterion variable ($\hat{Y}$) that are much closer to the actual values of the criterion variable (Y) than is the case for Rules 1 and 2.

Table 3 Comparing Actual and Predicted Happy Mood Scores for Six Students Using Four Linear Prediction Rules (shown as Rules 1, 2, 3, and 4 in Figure 6)

		Happy Mood			
		Rule 1 Predicted Mood $\hat{Y} = 8 - (.18)(X)$	Rule 2 Predicted Mood $\hat{Y} = 4 + (0)(X)$	Rule 3 Predicted Mood $\hat{Y} = -2.5 + (1)(X)$	Rule 4 Predicted Mood $\hat{Y} = -3 + (1)(X)$
Hours Slept	Actual Mood				
X	Y	$\hat{Y}$	$\hat{Y}$	$\hat{Y}$	$\hat{Y}$
5	2	7.10	4.00	2.50	2.00
6	2	6.92	4.00	3.50	3.00
6	3	6.92	4.00	3.50	3.00
7	4	6.74	4.00	4.50	4.00
8	7	6.56	4.00	5.50	5.00
10	6	6.20	4.00	7.50	7.00

The Least Squared Error Principle

One way to come up with a prediction rule is by eyeballing and trial and error. Using such a method we might come up with Rule 3 or 4 in Figure 6 or a similar rule (each of which would be a lot better than Rule 1 or Rule 2). However, what we really need is some method of coming up with the precise, very best linear prediction rule (that is, the best regression line); and this method should not be subjective or based on eyeballing (where different researchers may decide on different lines). Remember, we are trying to find the *one best rule;* we considered four rules for the mood and sleep example in Figure 6 to show the logic of linear prediction rules.

Coming up with the best prediction rule means we first have to decide on what we mean by "best." In terms of a regression line, we basically mean the line that comes closest to the true scores on the criterion variable, that makes predictions that are as little off from the true scores as possible. The difference between a prediction rule's predicted score on the criterion variable and a person's actual score on the criterion variable is called **error**.

We, of course, want as little error as possible over the whole range of scores we would predict, so what we want is the *smallest* sum of errors. But there is one more problem here. Sometimes the errors will be positive (the rule will predict too low), and sometimes they will be negative (the rule will predict too high). The positive and negative errors will cancel each other out. So, to avoid this problem, we use *squared errors*. That is, we take each amount of error and square it (multiply it by itself), then we add up the squared errors. Using squared errors also has various other statistical advantages over alternative approaches. For example, this approach penalizes large errors more than small errors; this approach also makes it easier to do more advanced computations.

Thus, to evaluate how good a prediction rule is, we figure the **sum of the squared errors** that we would make using that rule. Table 4 gives the sum of squared errors for each of the four prediction rules shown in Figure 6 and Table 3. To avoid making Table 4 too complex, we show only the actual figuring of the sum of squared errors for Rule 1 and Rule 4. The scores in each "Error" column show the result of subtracting the predicted score on the criterion variable ($\hat{Y}$) using the rule from the actual score on the criterion variable (Y) for each of the six students in the example (error $= Y - \hat{Y}$). We then squared each error score for each rule. The sum

error in prediction, the difference between a person's predicted score on the criterion variable and the person's actual score on the criterion variable.

sum of the squared errors sum of the squared differences between each predicted score and actual score on the criterion variable.

Table 4 The Sum of Squared Errors for Rules 1, 2, 3, and 4 (from Figure 6 and Table 3), Showing the Figuring for Rule 1 and Rule 4

		Rule 1			Rule 4		
		Rule 1 Predicted Mood $\hat{Y} = 8 - (.18)(X)$	Rule 1 Error	Rule 1 Squared Error	Rule 4 Predicted Mood $\hat{Y} = -3 + (1)(X)$	Rule 4 Error	Rule 4 Squared Error
Hours Slept	Actual Mood						
X	Y	$\hat{Y}$	$(Y - \hat{Y})$	$(Y - \hat{Y})^2$	$\hat{Y}$	$(Y - \hat{Y})$	$(Y - \hat{Y})^2$
5	2	7.10	−5.10	26.01	2.00	.00	.00
6	2	6.92	−4.92	24.21	3.00	−1.00	1.00
6	3	6.92	−3.92	15.37	3.00	.00	.00
7	4	6.74	−2.74	7.51	4.00	.00	.00
8	7	6.56	.44	.19	5.00	2.00	4.00
10	6	6.20	−.20	.04	7.00	−1.00	1.00
				$\Sigma = 73.33$			$\Sigma = 6.00$

Rule 1 sum of squared errors = 73.33
Rule 2 sum of squared errors = 22.00
Rule 3 sum of squared errors = 7.50
Rule 4 sum of squared errors = 6.00

of these squared error scores was 73.33 for Rule 1 and 6.00 for Rule 4. We repeated this process for Rules 2 and 3. Overall, the results for the sum of squared errors for Rules 1, 2, 3, and 4 were 73.33, 22.00, 7.50, and 6.00, respectively. Because the goal is to come up with a linear prediction rule—values for a and b in the formula $\hat{Y} = a + (b)(X)$—that creates the *smallest sum of squared errors,* we would in this case pick Rule 4.

In picking this linear prediction rule, we have used what statisticians call the *least squares criterion.* That is, we found the regression line that gave the lowest sum of squared errors between the *actual scores* on the criterion variable (Y) and the *predicted scores* on the criterion variable ($\hat{Y}$). In the next section, you learn how to find the values of a and b for the linear prediction rule that gives the smallest sum of squared errors possible.

TIP FOR SUCCESS
Remember, the regression line is a visual display of the linear prediction rule.

Finding a and b for the Least Squares Linear Prediction Rule

There are straightforward formulas for figuring the values of a (the regression constant) and b (the regression coefficient) that will give the linear prediction rule with the smallest possible sum of squared errors. These formulas give you the linear prediction rule guaranteed to produce less squared error than any other possible prediction rule.
Here are the formulas:

$$b = \frac{\Sigma[(X - M_X)(Y - M_Y)]}{SS_X} \qquad (2)$$

The regression coefficient is the sum, over all the people in the study, of the product of each person's two deviation scores, divided by the sum of everyone's squared deviation scores on the predictor variable.

In this formula, b is the regression coefficient. $X - M_X$ is the deviation score for each person on the X (predictor) variable and $Y - M_Y$ is the deviation score for each person on the Y (criterion) variable; $(X - M_X)(Y - M_Y)$ is the product of deviation scores for each person; and $\Sigma[(X - M_X)(Y - M_Y)]$ is the sum of the products of deviation scores over all the people in the study. SS_X is the sum of squared deviations for the X variable.

$$a = M_Y - (b)(M_X) \tag{3}$$

Notice that you need to know the value of b in order to figure the value of a. So you first use formula (2) to find the value of b and then use formula (3) to figure the value of a.

Here are the steps for figuring the regression coefficient, b:

❶ **Change the scores for each variable to deviation scores.** Figure the mean of each variable. Then subtract each variable's mean from each of its scores.

❷ **Figure the product of the deviation scores for each pair of scores.** That is, for each pair of scores, multiply the deviation score on one variable by the deviation score on the other variable.

❸ **Add up all the products of the deviation scores.**

❹ **Square each deviation score for the predictor variable (X).**

❺ **Add up the squared deviation scores for the predictor variable (X).**

❻ **Divide the sum of the products of deviation scores from Step ❸ by the sum of squared deviations for the predictor variable (X) from Step ❺.** This gives the regression coefficient, b.

Here are the steps for figuring the regression constant, a:

❶ **Multiply the regression coefficient, b, by the mean of the X variable.**

❷ **Subtract the result of Step ❶ from the mean of the Y variable.** This gives the regression constant, a.

Earlier in the chapter, we told you that the regression coefficient, b, for the hours of sleep and mood example was 1, and the regression constant, a, was -3. Now let's see how we figured those values. The figuring for the regression coefficient, b, is shown in Table 5. Using the steps,

❶ **Change the scores for each variable to deviation scores.** Figure the mean of each variable. Then subtract each variable's mean from each of its scores. The deviation scores are shown in the $X - M_X$ and $Y - M_Y$ columns in Table 5.

❷ **Figure the product of the deviation scores for each pair of scores.** That is, for each pair of scores, multiply the deviation score on one variable by the deviation score on the other variable.

❸ **Add up all the products of the deviation scores.** Adding up all the products of the deviation scores, as shown in the final column of Table 5, gives a sum of 16.

❹ **Square each deviation score for the predictor variable (X).**

❺ **Add up the squared deviation scores for the predictor variable (X).** As shown in the $(X - M_X)^2$ column of Table 5, the sum of squared deviations for the sleep variable is 16.

❻ **Divide the sum of the products of deviation scores from Step ❸ by the sum of squared deviations for the predictor variable (X) from Step ❺.** Dividing 16 by 16 gives a result of 1. This is the regression coefficient. In terms of the formula,

$$b = \frac{\sum[(X - M_X)(Y - M_Y)]}{SS_X} = \frac{16}{16} = 1$$

Table 5 Figuring the Regression Coefficient (*b*), Regression Constant (*a*), and the Linear Prediction Rule for Predicting Happy Mood from Hours of Sleep (Fictional Data)

Number of Hours Slept (*X*)			Happy Mood (*Y*)		Products of ❷ Deviation Scores
	Deviation ❶	Deviation Squared ❹		Deviation ❶	
X	*X* − *M*$_X$	(*X* − *M*$_X$)²	*Y*	*Y* − *M*$_Y$	(*X* − *M*$_X$)(*Y* − *M*$_Y$)
5	−2	4	2	−2	4
7	0	0	4	0	0
8	1	1	7	3	3
6	−1	1	2	−2	2
6	−1	1	3	−1	1
10	3	9	6	2	6
Σ = 42		Σ = SS$_X$ = 16	Σ = 24		Σ = 16
M = 7		❺	*M* = 4		❸

$$b = \frac{\Sigma[(X - M_X)(Y - M_Y)]}{SS_X} = \frac{16}{16} = 1 \qquad ❻$$

$$a = M_Y - (b)(M_X) = 4 - (1)(7) = 4 - 7 = -3$$

Linear prediction rule: Using formula $\hat{Y} = a + (b)(X), \hat{Y} = -3 + (1)(X)$

Note: The circled numbers refer to the steps for figuring the regression coefficient, *b*.

The figuring for the regression constant, *a*, is also shown in Table 5. Using the steps,

❶ **Multiply the regression coefficient, *b*, by the mean of the *X* variable.** We just figured the value of *b* to be 1, and 1 multiplied by 7 (the mean of *X*) gives 7.
❷ **Subtract the result of Step ❶ from the mean of the *Y* variable.** Subtracting 7 (the result of Step ❶) from 4 (the mean of *Y*) gives −3. This is the regression constant, *a*. In terms of the formula,

$$a = M_Y - (b)(M_X) = 4 - (1)(7) = -3.$$

So, for the sleep and happy mood example, the (least squares) linear prediction rule for predicting mood from hours of sleep—using our formula $\hat{Y} = a + (b)(X)$—is $\hat{Y} = -3 + (1)(X)$. As we showed earlier in the chapter (see Table 2), you can enter values for *X* (hours of sleep) into this formula to give predicted values of happy mood.

How are you doing?

1. What is the least squared error principle?
2. Give three advantages of using squared errors, as opposed to unsquared errors, when figuring the best linear prediction rule.
3. (a) Write the formula for the regression coefficient, *b*, and define each of the symbols. (b) Write the formula for the regression constant, *a*, and define each of the symbols.
4. (a) Find the linear prediction rule for predicting *Y* scores from *X* scores based on the following numbers. (b) Figure the sum of the squared errors when using the

linear prediction rule from part (a) to predict the scores for the four people in this study. (c) Repeat part (b), this time using the prediction rule $\hat{Y} = 9 - (.7)(X)$. (d) Why *must* your answer to (b) be lower than your answer to (c)?

X	Y
4	6
6	8
7	3
3	7

Answers

1. The least squared error principle is the principle that the best prediction rule is the rule that gives the lowest sum of squared errors between the actual scores on the criterion variable and the predicted scores on the criterion variable.

Table 6 Figuring the Linear Prediction Rule for "How Are You Doing?" Question 4

	X			Y		
	Deviation ❶	**Deviation Squared ❹**			**Deviation ❶**	**Products of ❷ Deviation Scores**
X	$X - M_X$	$(X - M_X)^2$		Y	$Y - M_Y$	$(X - M_X)(Y - M_Y)$
4	−1	1		6	0	0
6	1	1		8	2	2
7	2	4		3	−3	−6
3	−2	4		7	1	−2
$\Sigma = 20$		$\Sigma = SS_X = 10$		$\Sigma = 24$		$\Sigma = -6$
$M = 5$		❺		$M = 6$ ❻		❸

$$b = \frac{\Sigma[(X - M_X)(Y - M_Y)]}{SS_X} = \frac{-6}{10} = -.6$$

$$a = M_Y - (b)(M_X) = 6 - (-.6)(5) = 6 + 3 = 9$$

Linear prediction rule: Using formula $\hat{Y} = a + (b)(X), \hat{Y} = 9 - (.6)(X)$

Note: The circled numbers refer to the steps for figuring the regression coefficient, *b*.

Table 7 Figuring the Sums of Squared Errors for "How Are You Doing?" Questions 4b and 4c

		Prediction Rule from Part (a)			**Prediction Rule from Part (c)**		
		$\hat{Y} = 9 - (.6)(X)$	Error	Squared Error	$\hat{Y} = 9 - (.7)(X)$	Error	Squared Error
X	Y	$\hat{Y}$	$(Y - \hat{Y})$	$(Y - \hat{Y})^2$	$\hat{Y}$	$(Y - \hat{Y})$	$(Y - \hat{Y})^2$
4	6	6.6	−.6	.36	6.2	−.2	.04
6	8	5.4	2.6	6.76	4.8	3.2	10.24
7	3	4.8	−1.8	3.24	4.1	−1.1	1.21
3	7	7.2	−.2	.04	6.9	.1	.01
				$\Sigma = 10.40$			$\Sigma = 11.50$

2. Unlike unsquared errors, squared errors do not cancel each other out. Using squared errors penalizes large errors more than small errors; they also make it easier to do more advanced computations.

3. (a) The formula for the regression coefficient: $b = \dfrac{\Sigma[(X - M_X)(Y - M_Y)]}{SS_X}$. b is the regression coefficient; Σ is the symbol for sum of—add up all the scores that follow (in this formula, you add up all the products of deviation scores that follow); $X - M_X$ is the deviation score for each person on the predictor (X) variable; $Y - M_Y$ is the deviation score for each person on the criterion (Y) variable; SS_X is the sum of squared deviations for the predictor variable.

   (b) $a = M_Y - (b)(M_X)$. a is the regression constant; M_Y is the mean of the criterion variable; b is the regression coefficient; M_X is the mean of the predictor variable.

4. (a) The figuring is shown in Table 6. The linear prediction rule is $\hat{Y} = 9 - (.6)(X)$. (b) As shown in Table 7, the sum of squared errors is 10.40. (c) As shown in Table 7, the sum of squared errors is 11.50. (d) The linear prediction rule figured in part (a) is the rule that gives the *smallest* sum of squared errors; so the sum of squared errors for any other rule will be larger than this sum.

Issues in Prediction

In this section, you will learn about two issues in prediction: the standardized regression coefficient, and hypothesis testing and prediction.[1]

The Standardized Regression Coefficient

The linear prediction rule you have learned provides a useful and practical way of making predictions on a criterion variable from scores on a predictor variable. Recall from the hours of sleep and happy mood example that the prediction rule for predicting mood from sleep was: $\hat{Y} = -3 + (1)(X)$. Now, imagine that another group of researchers carry out the same study and find the prediction rule to be $\hat{Y} = -3 + (2)(X)$. In this new study, the regression coefficient (of 2) is much larger than the regression coefficient (of 1) in the original study. Recall that the regression coefficient tells you the slope of the regression line. That is, the regression coefficient is the predicted amount of increase in units for the criterion variable when the predictor variable increases by one unit. So the original study shows a 1-unit increase in sleep is associated with a 1-unit increase in mood. The new study, however, shows a 1-unit increase in sleep is associated with a 2-unit increase in mood. With this in mind, you might conclude that the larger regression coefficient in the new study shows that sleep has a much stronger effect on mood.

At this point, however, we should note one important difference between the two studies of sleep and happy mood. In the original study, happy mood was measured on a scale going from 0 to 8. However, the researchers in the new study used a scale of 0 to 20. Thus, with the first study, a 1-hour increase in sleep predicts a 1-point increase in mood on a scale from 0 to 8, but in the second study a 1-hour increase in sleep predicts a 2-point increase in mood but on a scale of 0 to 20. Thus, the second study might actually have found a slightly smaller effect of sleep!

Researchers in psychology quite often use slightly different measures or the same measure with a different scale (1 to 5 versus 10 to 100, for example) for the same variable. This can make it hard to compare the linear prediction rule for the same type of effect (such as the effect of sleep on happy mood) across studies. This is because the scale used for the predictor and criterion variables will affect the value of b (the regression coefficient) in the linear prediction rule. (The value of a, the regression constant, will also be affected by the scales used. But researchers in psychology are usually more interested in the actual value of b than a.)

Does this type of problem seem familiar to you? You know how to change a raw score into a Z score, which is a score on a scale of standard deviation units. For example, a Z score of 1.23 is a score that is 1.23 standard deviation units above the mean of the scores, and a Z score of $-.62$ is .62 standard deviation units below the mean. This allows you to compare the score on one variable relative to the score on another variable, even when the two variables use different scales. In the case of the regression coefficient in this chapter, we need a type of regression coefficient that can be compared across studies (that may have used different scales for the same variable).

It turns out that, just as there was a formula for changing a raw score to a Z score, there is a formula for changing a regression coefficient into what is known as a **standardized regression coefficient**. A standardized regression coefficient, which is referred to using the Greek symbol β (beta), shows the predicted amount of change in standard deviation units of the criterion variable if the value of the predicted variable increases by one standard deviation. For example, a standardized regression coefficient of .63 would mean for every increase of 1 standard deviation on X, we predict an increase of .63 standard deviations on Y. The formula for the standardized regression coefficient (β) is

> The standardized regression coefficient is equal to the regular, unstandardized regression coefficient multiplied by the result of dividing the square root of the sum of squared deviations for the predictor variable by the square root of the sum of squared deviations for the criterion variable.

$$\beta = (b)\frac{\sqrt{SS_X}}{\sqrt{SS_Y}} \qquad (4)$$

This formula has the effect of changing the regular (unstandardized) regression coefficient (b), the size of which is related to the specific scales for the predictor and criterion variables, to a standardized regression coefficient (β) that shows the relationship between the predictor and criterion variables in terms of standard deviation units.

An Example

For the sleep and mood example shown in Table 5, $SS_X = 16$. Table 5 doesn't show the value of SS_Y, but we can figure it by squaring each score in the $Y - M_Y$ column and summing the resulting values. Thus, $SS_Y = 0^2 + (-2)^2 + (3)^2 + (-2)^2 + (-1)^2 + 2^2 = 0 + 4 + 9 + 4 + 1 + 4 = 22$. The value of b was 1; so the standardized regression coefficient for the sleep and mood example is

$$\beta = (b)\frac{\sqrt{SS_X}}{\sqrt{SS_Y}} = (1)\frac{\sqrt{16}}{\sqrt{22}} = (1)\frac{4}{4.69} = .85.$$

This means that for every standard deviation increase in sleep, the predicted level of mood increases by .85 standard deviations. You could then compare this value of $\beta = .85$ to the standardized regression coefficient (β) from other studies, such as the study we described earlier that used a 0 to 20 mood scale instead of the 0 to 8 mood in the original study.

Later in the chapter, we will discuss when researchers describe their results in terms of the regular (unstandardized) regression coefficient (b) and when they report the standardized regression coefficient (β).

standardized regression coefficient (β) regression coefficient in standard deviation units. It shows the predicted amount of change in standard deviation units of the criterion variable if the value of the predictor variable increases by one standard deviation.

The Standardized Regression Coefficient (β) and the Correlation Coefficient (*r*)

In the examples we have used so far in this chapter, in which scores on a criterion variable are predicted based on scores from *one predictor variable,* the standardized regression coefficient (β) has the same value as the correlation coefficient (*r*) between the two variables. So, the β of .85 for the sleep and mood example is the same as the *r* of .85 between sleep and mood we figured in *Correlation* (see Table 3 of that text). However, in formula (4), we gave a more general method for figuring a standardized regression coefficient, because the standardized regression coefficient is *not* the same as the correlation coefficient when scores on a criterion variable are predicted based on scores from *more than one predictor variable* (a situation we examine in the next main section).

Hypothesis Testing and Prediction

In *Correlation*, you learned that hypothesis testing with a correlation coefficient meant examining whether the coefficient was significantly different than 0 (no correlation). You learned how to use a *t* test to determine whether a correlation coefficient was statistically significant. Since the standardized regression coefficient is the same as the correlation coefficient (when predicting a criterion variable from one predictor variable), the *t* test for the correlation between the two variables also acts as the *t* test for the prediction of the criterion variable from the predictor variable. The standardized regression coefficient is just another way of presenting the regular regression coefficient; so the *t* test for the correlation applies to both types of regression coefficients. In terms of prediction, the hypothesis test for a regression coefficient (for both *b* and β) tests whether the regression coefficient is significantly different from 0. A regression coefficient of 0 means that knowing a person's score on the predictor variable does not give you any useful information for predicting that person's score on the criterion variable. However, if the hypothesis testing result shows that the regression coefficient is significantly different from 0, then knowing a person's score on the predictor variable gives you useful information for predicting a person's score on the criterion variable.

TIP FOR SUCCESS

If you did not read the section on the significance test of a correlation coefficient in *Correlation*, you should skip this section on hypothesis testing and prediction.

How are you doing?

1. What does a standardized regression coefficient show?
2. (a) Write the formula for the standardized regression coefficient, β, and define each of the symbols. (b) Figure the value of β when $b = -1.21, SS_X = 2.57$, and $SS_Y = 7.21$.
3. When predicting scores on a criterion variable from scores on one predictor variable, the standardized regression coefficient has the same value as what other statistic?
4. How is hypothesis testing carried out with a regression coefficient?

Answers

1. A standardized regression coefficient shows how much of a standard deviation the predicted value of the criterion variable changes when the predictor variable changes by one standard deviation.
2. (a) The formula for the standardized regression coefficient is $\beta = (b)\dfrac{\sqrt{SS_X}}{\sqrt{SS_Y}}$.

β is the standardized regression coefficient; b is the regular, unstandardized regression coefficient; SS_X is the sum of squared deviations for the predictor variable (X); and SS_Y is the sum of squared deviations for the criterion variable (Y).

(b) $\beta = (b)\dfrac{\sqrt{SS_X}}{\sqrt{SS_Y}} = (-1.21)\dfrac{\sqrt{2.57}}{\sqrt{7.21}} = -.72.$

3. The standardized regression coefficient has the same value as r, the correlation coefficient between the two variables.

4. When predicting a criterion variable based on scores on one predictor variable, the hypothesis test for a regression coefficient is the same as the hypothesis test for the correlation between the two variables. The test uses a t statistic and tests whether the regression coefficient is significantly different from 0. A statistically significant regression coefficient means that knowing a person's score on the predictor variable provides useful information for predicting a person's score on the criterion variable.

Multiple Regression

So far, we have predicted a person's score on a criterion variable using the person's score on a single predictor variable. That is, each example so far was for **bivariate prediction** (or *bivariate regression*)—bivariate means two variables—and the prediction rules we used were *bivariate prediction rules*.

Suppose you could use more than one predictor variable. For example, in predicting happy mood, all you had to work with was the number of hours slept the night before. Suppose you also knew how well the person had slept and how many dreams the person had had. With this added information, you might be able to make a much more accurate prediction of mood.

The association between a criterion variable and two or more predictor variables is called **multiple correlation**.[2] Making predictions in this situation is called **multiple regression**.

We explore these topics only briefly here. However, multiple regression and multiple correlation are very frequently used in research articles in psychology, especially in fields like clinical, developmental, personality, and social psychology. So it is valuable for you to have a general understanding of them.

Multiple Regression Prediction Rules

A multiple regression linear prediction rule with three predictor variables goes like this:

$$\hat{Y} = a + (b_1)(X_1) + (b_2)(X_2) + (b_3)(X_3) \tag{5}$$

In this formula, $\hat{Y}$ is the predicted score on the criterion variable; a is the regression constant; b_1, b_2, and b_3 are the regression coefficients for the first, second, and third predictor variables, respectively; and X_1, X_2, and X_3 are the person's scores on the first, second, and third predictor variables, respectively. Notice that there is one regression constant and each predictor variable has its own regression coefficient.

bivariate prediction prediction of scores on one variable based on scores of one other variable. Also called *bivariate regression*.

multiple correlation correlation of a criterion variable with two or more predictor variables.

multiple regression procedure for predicting scores on a criterion variable from scores on two or more predictor variables.

A person's predicted score on the criterion variable is the regression constant, plus the regression coefficient for the first predictor variable multiplied by the person's score on the first predictor variable, plus the regression coefficient for the second predictor variable multiplied by the person's score on the second predictor variable, plus the regression coefficient for the third predictor variable multiplied by the person's score on the third predictor variable.

For example, in the sleep and mood study, a multiple regression linear prediction rule for predicting mood with three predictor variables might be as follows:

$$\text{Predicted mood} = -3.78 + (.87)(\text{hours of sleep}) + (.33)(\text{how well slept}) + (.20)(\text{number of dreams})$$

Suppose a particular person had slept 7 hours the night before, rated how well slept as a 3, and had 1 dream. Their predicted mood would be

$$\begin{aligned}\text{Predicted mood} &= -3.78 + (.87)(7) + (.33)(3) + (.20)(1) \\ &= -3.78 + 6.09 + .99 + .20 = 3.50\end{aligned}$$

An Important Difference Between Multiple Regression and Bivariate Prediction

There is one particularly important difference between multiple regression and bivariate prediction. In ordinary bivariate prediction the standardized regression coefficient is the same as the correlation coefficient. But, as we noted earlier, the standardized regression coefficient (β) for each predictor variable in multiple regression is *not* the same as the ordinary correlation coefficient (r) of that predictor with the criterion variable.

Usually, a β will be closer to 0 than r. The reason is that part of what makes any one predictor successful in predicting the criterion will usually overlap with what makes the other predictors successful in predicting the criterion variable. In multiple regression, both the standardized and the regular regression coefficients are about the unique, distinctive contribution of the variable, excluding any overlap with other predictor variables.

Consider the sleep and mood example. When we were predicting mood using just the number of hours slept, β was the same as the correlation coefficient of .85. Now, with multiple regression, the β for number of hours slept turns out to be .74. It is less because part of what makes number of hours slept predict mood overlaps with what makes sleeping well and number of dreams predict mood. (In this fictional example, people who sleep more hours usually sleep well and have more dreams.)

In multiple regression, the correlation between the criterion variable and all the predictor variables taken together is called the **multiple correlation coefficient** and is symbolized as **R**. However, because of the usual overlap among predictor variables, the multiple correlation is usually smaller than the sum of the individual rs of each predictor with the criterion variable. The squared multiple correlation, r^2 gives the proportionate reduction in error or proportion of variance accounted for in the criterion variable by all the predictor variables taken together. For example, an R of .40 gives an r^2 of .16, which means that the predictor variables together account for 16% (.40 × .40 = .16, which is the same as 16%) of the variation in the scores in the criterion variable. R^2 is a measure of the effect size for multiple regression. Cohen's (1988) conventions for R^2 for multiple regression are .02, a small effect size; .13, a medium effect size; and .26, a large effect size.

In multiple regression, there are a number of possible hypothesis tests. First, you can test the significance of the multiple correlation (and the squared multiple correlation) using a procedure in which the null hypothesis is that in the population the multiple correlation is 0. This tests whether the variables as a whole are associated with the criterion variable. You can also test the significance of each individual predictor variable using a t test in a similar manner for hypothesis testing with bivariate prediction. Each test shows whether the regression coefficient for that variable is

multiple correlation coefficient (R) in multiple regression, the correlation between the criterion variable and all the predictor variables taken together.

significantly different from 0. As with bivariate prediction, a significant regression coefficient for a predictor variable means that knowing a person's score on that predictor variable gives you useful information for predicting a person's score on the criterion variable. However, here the focus is on whether this predictor variable adds more than 0 to the prediction over and above what the other predictor variables already predict. Finally, there is also a hypothesis test for whether the regression constant is significantly different from 0. However, researchers in psychology typically do not pay much attention to this test, because the actual value of the regression constant (and whether it is different from 0) is usually not of great importance in many areas of research.

Assumptions of Prediction

The assumptions of the significance test for prediction are similar to the assumptions for the significance test of a correlation coefficient: there is an equal distribution of each variable at each point of the other variable; the relationship between the variables is linear; and the people (or cases) are independent. Another assumption is that the error scores (that is, the difference between the prediction rule's predicted scores on the criterion variable and people's actual scores on the criterion variable) are normally distributed. Also, for the type of prediction that we focus on in this chapter, we assume that both the predictor and the criterion variable are equal-interval numeric variables. (It is possible to use other types of predictor and criterion variables in prediction; you will likely learn about such types of prediction if you take more advanced statistics classes.)

Limitations of Prediction

All of the limitations for correlation apply to prediction. The procedures we have considered in this chapter are inaccurate if the correlation is curvilinear, the group studied is restricted in range, the measures are unreliable, or there are outliers. That is, in each of these situations the regression coefficients (whether bivariate or multiple) are smaller than they should be to reflect the true association of the predictor variables with the criterion variable. Nor do these prediction procedures by themselves tell you anything about the direction of causality. Even in published articles, researchers sometimes overlook these limitations when considering complex regression results. We will not go in to detail, but prior to doing prediction (and correlation) analyses, researchers often check to see if any of the preceding limitations are relevant in their research situation. For example, a scatter diagram can help to identify outliers. The researcher can then conduct the analysis two ways. In one analysis, the outliers are included in the figuring; and in a separate analysis, the outliers are excluded from the figuring. By doing this, the researcher can see how the outliers influence the overall results.

How are you doing?

1. What is multiple regression?
2. Write the multiple regression linear prediction rule with two predictors and define each of the symbols.
3. In a multiple regression linear prediction rule, the regression constant is 2.19, the regression coefficient for the first variable is −3.16, and the regression

coefficient for the second variable is .99. What is the predicted score on the criterion variable for (a) a person with a score of .40 on the first predictor variable and a score of 10.50 on the second predictor variable, and (b) a person with a score of .15 on the first predictor variable and a score of 5.50 on the second predictor variable?

4. In multiple regression, why are the standardized regression coefficients for each predictor variable often smaller than the ordinary correlation coefficient of that predictor variable with the criterion variable?

5. What are the different hypothesis tests for multiple regression?

6. What are the effect size conventions for multiple regression?

7. What are the assumptions of the significance test for prediction?

8. List four conditions that may lead to regression procedures being inaccurate.

Answers

1. Multiple regression is the procedure for predicting a criterion variable from a prediction rule that includes more than one predictor variable.

2. The multiple regression linear prediction rule is $\hat{Y} = a + (b_1)(X_1) + (b_2)(X_2)$. $\hat{Y}$ is the predicted score on the criterion variable; a is the regression constant; b_1 is the regression coefficient for the first predictor variable; X_1 is the person's score on the first predictor variable; b_2 is the regression coefficient for the second predictor variable; and X_2 is the person's score on the second predictor variable.

3. Predicted scores on the criterion variable:
   (a) $\hat{Y} = 2.19 - (3.16)(.40) + (.99)(10.50) = 2.19 - 1.26 + 10.40 = 11.33$.
   (b) $\hat{Y} = 2.19 - (3.16)(.15) + (.99)(5.50) = 2.19 - .47 + 5.45 = 7.17$.

4. In multiple regression, a predictor variable's association with the criterion variable usually overlaps with the other predictor variables' association with the criterion variable. Thus, the unique association of a predictor variable with the criterion variable (as shown by the standardized regression coefficient) is usually smaller than the ordinary correlation of the predictor variable with the criterion variable.

5. There is a hypothesis test to test the significance of the multiple correlation. Also, a hypothesis test can be carried out for each predictor variable to test whether its regression coefficient is significantly different from 0. Finally, there is a hypothesis test to test whether the regression constant is significantly different from 0.

6. The effect size conventions for multiple regression are .02, a small effect size; .13, a medium effect size; and .26, a large effect size.

7. The assumptions of the significance test for prediction are: there is an equal distribution of each variable at each point of the other variable; the relationship between the variables is linear; the people (or cases) are independent; and the error scores follow a normal distribution.

8. Four conditions that may lead to regression procedures being inaccurate: (i) restriction in range, (ii) curvilinear associations, (iii) unreliable measurement, and (iv) outliers.

Controversy: Unstandardized and Standardized Regression Coefficients; Comparing Predictors

There is some debate in the psychological research literature about whether research studies should present their results in terms of unstandardized regression coefficients (bs), standardized regression coefficients (βs), or both types of coefficients. Some researchers recommend listing only regular unstandardized regression coefficients when the study is purely applied, only standardized regression coefficients when the study is purely theoretical, and both the regular and standardized regression coefficients in all other cases. Although this appears to be a straightforward solution to the issue, researchers do not always agree as to when a study is *purely* applied or *purely* theoretical. This issue is further complicated by the fact that standardized regression coefficients can be less than consistent across different samples because they are influenced by the range (and variance) of the scores in the samples, while unstandardized regression coefficients are not so influenced. Overall, we generally recommend that, unless there is a good reason not to do so, you present the results of your own research studies in terms of both unstandardized and standardized regression coefficients.

Related to these issues, recall from earlier in the chapter that we introduced the standardized regression coefficient as a useful way to compare a regression coefficient from one study with a regression coefficient from another study. Similarly, when comparing the size of the regression coefficients for each of several predictor variables in a multiple regression, you should compare the standardized regression coefficients (the βs), as opposed to the regular unstandardized regression coefficients (the bs). This is because a larger value of b for one predictor variable compared to another predictor variable may simply reflect the different scales for each variable (0 to 10 versus 0 to 100, for example).

However, even assuming we want to focus on standardized values for some purposes, there is an ongoing controversy in multiple regression about how to judge the relative importance of each predictor variable in predicting the criterion variable. The question is whether (i) you should use the standardized regression coefficients (the βs) of the predictor variables from the overall regression equation, or (ii) you should instead use the bivariate correlation coefficients (the rs) of each predictor variable with the criterion variable. Both are standardized in that they adjust for the variation in the variables used, and in bivariate regression they are the same thing. But in multiple regression, as we noted, they are not the same thing. Specifically, a regression coefficient tells you the unique contribution of the predictor variable to the prediction, over and above all the other predictors. When predicting by itself, without considering the other predictors (that is, using its ordinary correlation, r, with the criterion variable), a predictor variable may seem to have a quite different importance relative to the other predictor variables.

For example, if there are three predictors, the standardized regression coefficients (the βs) could be .2, .3, and .4. But in that particular study, the rs for these three predictors might be .6, .4, and .5. Thus, if you looked at the βs, you would think the third predictor was most important; but if you looked at the rs, you would think the first predictor was the most important.

Many approaches to this problem have been considered over the years, but all are controversial. What most experts recommend is to use all the information you have; consider *both* the rs *and* the βs, keeping in mind the difference in what they tell you. The r tells you the overall association of the predictor variable with the criterion variable. The β tells you the unique association of this predictor variable, over and above the other predictor variables, with the criterion variable.

In addition to these and other controversies relating to the statistical aspects, there has been an ongoing controversy for many years about the superiority of statistical prediction over more intuitive, humanistic, or clinical approaches. This issue is addressed in Box 1.

BOX 1 Clinical Versus Statistical Prediction

More than fifty years ago, Paul Meehl (1954) wrote an unsettling little book called *Clinical vs. Statistical Prediction*. He argued that when experts such as clinical psychologists (or business managers, economic forecasters, engineers, or doctors, among others) use the kinds of unspecified internal cognitive processes that are usually called "trained intuitions," they are not very accurate. On the average their decisions are no better than those anybody could make by using very simple, straightforward prediction *formulas*. For example, in psychiatric diagnosing, a supposedly well-trained clinician's interview and diagnosis are less useful than a mere rule such as "if the person has been admitted to the hospital twice before, is over 50, and appears suicidal, then…"—the kind of rule generated by using a multiple regression model.

In the first decade after Meehl questioned the accuracy of experts, considerable efforts were made to disprove him. But on the whole, Meehl's discovery has held up. He noted this himself 30 years later in an article entitled "Causes and Effects of My Disturbing Little Book" (Meehl, 1986). Looking specifically at predictions in clinical psychology, a recent meta-analysis of nearly a hundred research studies (Ægisdóttir et al., 2006) continues to support his basic conclusion, with some caveats. It is important that clinicians be allowed to follow a client model-building process, in which clinicians act like scientists, forming a hypothesis about a patient based on statistical information and then applying it to see if it holds up (Strohmer & Arm, 2006). Perhaps with this client the hypothesis needs revising because new facts have come to light, making other research more relevant. Then the clinician hears some other new aspect that requires the hypothesis to be revised again, on the basis of research on this aspect, and so on. What is important is that this scientific model-building process replace jumping to the wrong conclusion, which could happen either with intuition or a formula.

Further, this issue tends to become polarized between "therapy-as-an-art" and "formulas-beat-clinicians." In fact, "Although the statistical method is almost always the equal of the clinical method and is often better, the improvement is not overwhelming" (Ægisdóttir et al., 2006, p. 367). It amounts in study after study to be about a 13% increase in accuracy. Formulas, therefore, seem most important when making a mistake is especially dangerous. That is in fact how formulas have been most often used so far—to predict suicide, violence, and recidivism.

Remember, this is an issue of prediction, and statistical methods often cannot do all that well at predicting violence or suicide either. Their main advantage is consistency, like a gambler with a system.

Naturally, the focus has turned to how cognition operates, why it is flawed, and what, if anything, can be done to improve it. The flaws are mainly that people make illusory correlations. Or they are overconfident; they do not keep a record of their successes and failures to see whether they are in fact accurate, but instead put too much weight on their remembered successes and forget their failures. Also, overconfidence comes in part from lack of feedback; clinicians may make hundreds of diagnoses without learning whether they were correct. Finally, human memory and cognition may not have the capacity to handle the information and operations required to make certain complex decisions. And that capacity varies. Some people have a high "need for cognition," the desire to think about things. Those with a low need are less consistent and accurate (Ruscio, 2000).

A great deal of research has addressed how to "de-bias" human decisions. People can be shown when they must rely on their intuition—for example, when there is not enough time to apply a formula or when simple averaging will suffice. At other times they need to understand that a formula is more accurate—for example, when rules are complicated.

There is also considerable work on decision aids, such as computer programs with built-in decision rules supplied by experts. Sometimes, more intuitive or subjective information can be added at the last minute by experts knowledgeable about the particular situation

(Holzworth, 1996; Whitecotton, 1996). What cannot be allowed with any decision aid is that it be abandoned when someone has a hunch they can do better without the aid.

The use of decision support systems is on the rise. For example, expert chess players have developed aids that can sometimes outwit their own creators, merely by being thoroughly consistent. Thus, some chess players have become comfortable using decision support systems to keep themselves on track during a game. And as health care is forced to become more cost conscious, it may have to use impartial decision aids about who receives what treatment. And the public may benefit. For example, a decision aid for helping doctors who are not dermatologists decide if something might be skin cancer and require referral to a specialist was found to decrease errors by 64% (Gerbert et al., 1999). Another decision aid reduced serious medication errors by 55% (Bates et al., 1998).

Prediction in Research Articles

It is rare for bivariate linear prediction rules to be reported in psychology research articles; usually, simple correlations are reported. Sometimes, however, you will see regression lines from bivariate predictions. This is usually done when there is more than one group and the researcher wants to illustrate the difference in the linear prediction rule between the two groups.

For example, consider an experiment Oettingen and her colleagues (2001) conducted with German university students. This experiment focused on the students' thoughts about the possibility of studying abroad. First, the students were asked about how much they expected to succeed (that is, how likely it was that they would study abroad). In the next part of the study, participants were divided into one of three groups. Participants in the positive fantasy group were instructed to spend some time thinking about specific positive aspects of studying abroad; those in the negative reality group, were instructed to spend some time thinking about specific obstacles that stand in the way of studying abroad; and those in the contrast group were instructed to spend some time thinking about both positive possibilities and negative realities. Afterward, participants answered questions about how disappointed they would be if they were never able to study abroad.

Figure 7 (from Oettingen et al., 2001) shows a regression line for each of the three experimental groups. Each regression line shows how much expectation of success predicts anticipated disappointment. The major result is shown in the solid blue line: For students in the contrast group (those who thought about both the positive possibilities and realistic obstacles), the greater their initial expectations of success, the more disappointed they would be if they were not able to study abroad.

The researchers see the pattern for the contrast group as what would be expected: that people are most disappointed when they expect to succeed and least disappointed when they don't. But either having positive fantasies or dwelling on negative obstacles interferes with this normal process; so level of disappointment is much less related to expectations of success.

Multiple regression results are common in research articles and are often reported in tables. Usually, the table lays out the regression coefficient for each predictor variable, which can be either the regular unstandardized (b), standardized (β), or both, along with the overall R or R^2 in a note at the bottom of the table. The table may also give the correlation coefficient (r) for each predictor variable with the criterion variable. This is helpful, because it lets you compare the unique association of each predictor to the criterion variable (what the regression coefficient tells you) with the overall association (what the correlation coefficient tells you) (Kashy et al., 2009). As with correlation tables, regression tables also

Figure 7 Regression lines depicting the link of expectation of success to anticipated disappointment as a function of self-regulatory thought.

Source: Oettingen, G., Schnetter, K., and Pak, H. (2001). Self-regulation of goal setting: Turning free fantasies about the future into binding goals. *Journal of Personality and Social Psychology, 80,* 736–753. Published by the American Psychological Association. Reprinted with permission.

usually give the statistical significance for the various statistics reported. Finally, many tables will provide a variety of other statistics that go beyond what we have covered. But if you understand the basics, you should be able to make good sense of the key information in such tables.

Consider an example from a study (Hahlweg et al., 2001) of a treatment method for agoraphobia, a condition that affects about 4% of the population and involves unpredictable panic attacks in public places such as crowded restaurants, buses, or movie theaters. Table 8 (from Hahlweg et al., 2001) shows the correlation coefficients (rs) and standardized regression coefficients (βs) for four variables

Table 8 Multiple Regression Analysis Predicting Average Intragroup Effect Size at Postassessment

Independent Variable	r	β
BDI	.30***	.30***
Age	−.21***	−.20**
No. of sessions	.12*	.08
Duration of disorder	−.13*	−.02

Note: $R = .36$; $R^2 = .13$. BDI = Beck Depression Inventory.

*$p < .05$. **$p < .01$. ***$p < .000$.

Source: Hahlweg, K., Fiegenbaum, W., Frank, M., Schroeder, B., & von Witzleben, I. (2001). Short- and long-term effectiveness of an empirically supported treatment of agoraphobia. *Journal of Consulting and Clinical Psychology, 69,* 375–382. Published by the American Psychological Association. Reprinted with permission.

predicting the effectiveness of the treatment. (The actual criterion variable is labeled "Average Intragroup Effect Size at Postassessment." The article explains that this is each patient's change from before to after treatment, averaged across several measures of mental health.)

Looking at the β column, you can see that the standardized regression coefficients were very small for number of sessions attended and the duration of the disorder. At the same time, age and BDI (a measure of depression at the start of treatment) were much more important unique predictors of the outcome of treatment. Notice from the asterisks and the note at the bottom of the table that the regression coefficients for the number of sessions and duration of disorder were not statistically significant, whereas the coefficients for BDI and age were significant. Also notice (from the bottom of the table) that the overall correlation of the four predictors with treatment outcome had an R of .36 and an R^2 of .13. This is a moderate overall relationship, but not substantial; that is, only 13% of the overall variation in treatment outcome was predicted by these four variables. Notice also the r column. For BDI and for age, the βs and rs are about the same. Note, however, that number of sessions and durations have larger rs than βs. This suggests that these two variables have considerable overlap with each other or other variables in the prediction rule, so that their unique contribution to predicting treatment outcome is rather small.

Advanced Topic: Error and Proportionate Reduction in Error

How accurate are the predictions you make using regression? Normally, you predict the future; so there is no way to know how accurate you are in advance. However, you can estimate your likely accuracy. What you do is figure how accurate your prediction rule would have been if you had used it to make "predictions" for the scores you used to figure the linear regression rule (and correlation coefficient) in the first place. We did this earlier in the chapter when we figured the sum of squared errors for the linear prediction rule for the sleep and mood example. The linear prediction rule for this example was $\hat{Y} = -3 + (1)(X)$. This rule was shown as regression line "Rule 4" in Figure 6. The figuring of the squared error for the rule is shown in Table 4.

Proportionate Reduction in Error

Now, how is knowing the squared errors useful? The most common way to think about the accuracy of a prediction rule is to compare the amount of squared error using your prediction rule to the amount of squared error you would have without the prediction rule.

First, you figure the amount of squared error using the prediction rule. Next, you figure the squared error you would make predicting without the prediction rule. Finally, you compare the two amounts of squared error.

The squared error using the prediction rule is the *sum of the squared errors*. That is, you just add up the squared errors of the individuals in the study. In the sleep and mood example, this is the sum of the last column in Table 4, which is 6.00. The sum of squared errors is abbreviated as SS_{Error}. In our example, $SS_{Error} = 6.00$.

How do you figure the amount of squared error predicting without the prediction rule? If you cannot use the prediction rule, the most accurate prediction for anyone will be the criterion variable's mean. In our example, suppose you knew nothing about how much a person slept the night before. Your best strategy for any student would be to predict that the student will have the mean score on happy mood.

SS_{Error} (sum of the squared errors) sum of the squared differences between each score on the criterion variable and its predicted score.

That is, your best strategy would be to predict a mood score of 4. (Earlier in the chapter we called this particular rule of predicting 4 for each person "Rule 2" and showed the regression line for it in Figure 6.) Consider another example. Suppose you wanted to predict a person's college GPA, but you had no information about any predictor variables. Your best bet here is to predict that the person will have the mean college GPA for students at that college.

Thus, predictions without a prediction rule involve predicting the mean. This tells you that *the amount of squared error when predicting without a rule is the amount of squared error when predicting each score to be the mean.* Error in general is the actual score on the criterion variable minus the predicted score on the criterion variable. When the predicted score is the mean, error is the actual score minus the mean. Squared error is the square of this number. The sum of these squared errors is the **total squared error when predicting from the mean**; we call this number SS_{Total}. (What we are now calling SS_{Total} is the same as what we call SS in *Central Tendency and Variability* when figuring the variance, and is also the same as what we call SS_Y in this chapter and *Correlation*. In *Central Tendency and Variability*, we define SS as the sum of squared deviations from the mean. A deviation from the mean is the score minus the mean. This is exactly the same as the error that results when our prediction is the mean.)

The value of a prediction rule is how much *less* error you make using the prediction rule (SS_{Error}) compared to using the mean (SS_{Total}). With a good prediction rule, SS_{Error} should be much smaller than SS_{Total}.

The key comparison is the *proportionate reduction in error*: The reduction in error ($SS_{Total} - SS_{Error}$), divided by the total amount that could be reduced (SS_{Total}). In terms of a formula,

$$\text{Proportionate reduction in error} = \frac{SS_{Total} - SS_{Error}}{SS_{Total}} \qquad (6)$$

> The proportionate reduction in error is the sum of squared error when predicting from the mean minus the sum of squared error when predicting from the bivariate prediction rule, all divided by the sum of squared error when predicting from the mean.

To put this another way, using the mean to predict is not a very precise method because it leaves a lot of error. So now you are seeing how much better you can do—how much the proportion of the squared error you would make using the mean is reduced by using the prediction rule.

Suppose a prediction rule is no improvement over predicting from the mean. In this situation, SS_{Error} equals SS_{Total} (SS_{Error} can never be worse than SS_{Total}). The prediction rule has reduced zero error ($SS_{Total} - SS_{Error} = 0$), and it has reduced 0% of the total error ($0/SS_{Total} = 0$).

Now suppose a prediction rule gives perfect predictions with no error whatsoever. The prediction rule has reduced the error by 100%. (In terms of the equation, if $SS_{Error} = 0$, then the numerator will be $SS_{Total} - 0$, or SS_{Total}; dividing SS_{Total} by SS_{Total} gives 1, or 100%.)

In most actual situations, the proportionate reduction in error will be somewhere between 0% and 100%.

Steps for Figuring the Proportionate Reduction in Error

❶ **Figure the sum of squared errors using the mean to predict.** Take each score minus the mean, square it, and add these up. This gives SS_{Total}.

❷ **Figure the sum of squared errors using the prediction rule.** Take each score minus the predicted score for this person, square it, and add these up. This gives SS_{Error}.

total squared error when predicting from the mean (SS_{Total}) sum of squared differences of each score on the criterion variable from the predicted score when predicting from the mean.

Table 9 Figuring Proportionate Reduction in Error for the Fictional Sleep and Mood Example

Hours Slept	Actual Mood	Predicted Mood Using Mean ❶			Predicted Mood Using Prediction Rule ❷		
X	Y	Mean Mood M	Error $(Y - M)$	Error^2 $(Y - M)^2$	Predicted Mood $\hat{Y}$	Error $(Y - \hat{Y})$	Error^2 $(Y - \hat{Y})^2$
5	2	4	−2	4	2.00	.00	.00
6	2	4	−2	4	3.00	−1.00	1.00
6	3	4	−1	1	3.00	.00	.00
7	4	4	0	0	4.00	.00	.00
8	7	4	3	9	5.00	2.00	4.00
10	6	4	2	4	7.00	−1.00	1.00
				$\Sigma = SS_{\text{Total}} = 22$			$\Sigma = SS_{\text{Error}} = 6.00$

Proportionate reduction in error $= \dfrac{❸ SS_{\text{Total}} - SS_{\text{Error}}}{SS_{\text{Total}}} = \dfrac{22 - 6}{22} = \dfrac{16}{22} = .73$ ❹

❸ **Figure the reduction in squared error.** This is the sum of squared errors using the mean to predict (from Step ❶) minus the sum of squared errors using the prediction rule (from Step ❷).

❹ **Figure the proportionate reduction in squared error.** This is the reduction in squared error (from Step ❸) divided by the total squared error when using the mean to predict (from Step ❶).

An Example

Table 9 shows the actual scores, predicted scores, errors, squared errors, sums of squared errors, and proportionate reduction in error for the sleep and mood example. Using the steps,

❶ **Figure the sum of squared errors using the mean to predict.** Take each score minus the mean, square it, and add these up. From Table 9, $SS_{\text{Total}} = 22$. (Note that this is the same as SS_Y we figure for happy mood in *Correlation* and again in this one as part of the figuring for the standardized regression coefficient.)

❷ **Figure the sum of squared errors using the prediction rule.** Take each score on the criterion variable (Y) minus the predicted score on the criterion variable ($\hat{Y}$) for this person, square it, and add these up. From Table 9, $SS_{\text{Error}} = 6.00$.

❸ **Figure the reduction in squared error.** This is the sum of squared errors using the mean to predict (from Step ❶) minus the sum of squared errors using the prediction rule (from Step ❷). Reduction in squared error $= 22 - 6 = 16$.

❹ **Figure the proportionate reduction in squared error.** This is the reduction in squared error (from Step ❸) divided by the total squared error when using the mean to predict (from Step ❶). Proportionate reduction in squared error $= 16/22 = .73$.

Thus, when predicting happy mood from sleep the night before, the prediction rule, based on the scores from our group of 6 students, provides a 73% reduction in error over using the mean to predict.

Proportionate Reduction in Error as r^2

The proportionate reduction in error turns out to equal the correlation coefficient squared. That is,

The proportionate reduction in error is equal to the correlation coefficient squared.

$$\text{Proportionate reduction in error} = r^2 \tag{7}$$

Because of this equivalence, r^2 is typically used as the symbol for the proportionate reduction in error with bivariate prediction. (As we noted earlier in the chapter, R^2 is the symbol for the proportionate reduction in error for multiple regression.)

For example, in the sleep and mood study, the correlation coefficient was .85, and .85 squared is .72. That is, $r^2 = .72$. Notice that, within rounding error, this number (.72) is the same as we just figured (.73) by finding predicted scores, errors, squared errors, sums of squared errors, and proportionate reduction in squared error.

We figured the proportionate reduction in error so laboriously in this example only to help you understand this important concept. However, in an actual research situation, you would use the simpler procedure of squaring the correlation coefficient. (Also note that this works in reverse also. If you know the proportionate reduction in error, you can find the correlation coefficient by taking the square root of the proportionate reduction in error. Since a square root can be positive or negative, look at the pattern of numbers to determine if the correlation is positive or negative.)

How are you doing?

1. Explain in words how you figure (a) the sum of squared error predicting from the mean, and (b) the sum of squared error using the prediction rule.
2. Write the formula for figuring the proportionate reduction in error and define each of its symbols in words.
3. Explain why the procedure for figuring the proportionate reduction in error tells you about the accuracy of the prediction rule.
4. The following scores and predicted scores are for four people on a particular criterion variable using a prediction rule based on the scores from these four people. Figure the proportionate reduction in error and correlation coefficient.

Score	Predicted Score
Y	$\hat{Y}$
6	5.7
4	4.3
2	2.9
8	7.1

Answers

1. (a) You figure the sum of squared error predicting from the mean by taking each criterion variable score (Y) minus the mean of the criterion variable scores (M_Y), squaring this difference, then summing up all these squared differences.
   (b) You figure the sum of squared error using the prediction rule by taking each criterion variable score (Y) minus what you would predict for that person's criterion variable score using the prediction rule ($\hat{Y}$), squaring this difference, then summing up all these squared differences.
2. Proportionate reduction in error = $(SS_{Total} - SS_{Error})/SS_{Total}$. SS_{Total} is the sum, over all participants, of the squared difference between each person's criterion variable score and the criterion variable mean; SS_{Error} is the sum, over all participants, of the squared difference between each person's criterion variable score and that person's predicted criterion variable score.
3. The procedure for figuring the proportionate reduction in error tells you about the accuracy of the prediction rule because it tells you the proportion of

total error (the error you would make if just predicting from the mean) you are reducing by using the prediction rule (where your error is based on predicting from the prediction rule). That is, the larger proportion of total error you reduce, the more accurate your prediction rule will be. Perfect prediction would be 100% reduction.

4.

Score	Mean	Error	Error^2	Predicted Score	Error	Error^2
Y	M	$(Y - M)$	$(Y - M)^2$	$\hat{Y}$	$(Y - \hat{Y})$	$(Y - \hat{Y})^2$
6	5	1	1	5.7	.3	.09
4	5	−1	1	4.3	−.3	.09
2	5	−3	9	2.9	−.9	.81
8	5	3	9	7.1	.9	.81
		$\Sigma = SS_{Total} = 20$			$\Sigma = SS_{Error} = 1.80$	

Proportionate reduction in error $= (SS_{Total} - SS_{Error})/SS_{Total} = (20 - 1.80)/20 = 18.20/20 = .91.$ $r = \sqrt{r^2} = \sqrt{.91} = .95.$ (It is a positive correlation, as low scores go with lows and highs with highs.)

Learning Aids

Summary

1. Prediction (or regression) involves making predictions about scores on a criterion variable based on scores on a predictor variable.
2. The linear prediction rule for predicting scores on a criterion variable from scores on a predictor variable is $\hat{Y} = a + (b)(X)$, where $\hat{Y}$ is the predicted score on the criterion variable, a is the regression constant, b is the regression coefficient, and X is the score on the predictor variable.
3. A regression line, which is drawn in the same kind of graph as a scatter diagram, shows the predicted criterion variable value ($\hat{Y}$) for each value of the predictor variable (X). The slope of this line equals b; a is where this line crosses the vertical axis (the intercept). A regression line is a visual display of a linear prediction rule.
4. The best linear prediction rule is the rule that gives the lowest sum of squared errors between the actual scores on the criterion variable and the predicted scores on the criterion variable. There are formulas for figuring the regression constant (a) and the regression coefficient (b) that will give the linear prediction rule with the smallest sum of squared errors.
5. A standardized regression coefficient (β) shows how much of a standard deviation the predicted value of the criterion variable changes when the predictor variable changes by one standard deviation. The standardized regression coefficient can be figured from the regular regression coefficient and the sum of squared deviations for the predictor and criterion variables. When predicting scores on the criterion variable from scores on one other variable (bivariate prediction), the standardized regression coefficient (β) is the same as the correlation coefficient (r) between the two variables.
6. In bivariate prediction, the hypothesis test for a regression coefficient is the same as the hypothesis test for the correlation between the two variables.

7. In multiple regression, a criterion variable is predicted from two or more predictor variables. In a multiple regression linear prediction rule, there is a regression constant, the score for each predictor variable is multiplied by its own regression coefficient, and the results are added up to make the prediction. Each regression coefficient tells you the unique relation of the predictor to the criterion variable in the context of the other predictor variables. The multiple correlation coefficient (R) is the overall degree of association between the criterion variable and the predictor variables taken together. R^2 is the overall proportionate reduction in error for multiple regression.

8. The measure of effect size for multiple regression is R^2. The assumptions for the significance test for prediction are as follows: there is an equal distribution of each variable at each point of the other variable; the relationship between the variables is linear; the people (or cases) are independent; and the error scores follow a normal distribution. Bivariate prediction and multiple regression have the same limitations as ordinary correlation. In addition, in multiple regression there is ambiguity in interpreting the relative importance of the predictor variables.

9. Bivariate prediction results are rarely described directly in research articles, but regression lines are sometimes shown when prediction rules for more than one group are being compared. Multiple regressions are commonly reported in articles, often in a table that includes the regression coefficients and overall proportionate reduction in error (R^2).

10. ADVANCED TOPIC: The proportionate reduction in error, an indicator of the accuracy of a prediction rule, is figured by applying the prediction rule to the scores on which the prediction rule was based. The sum of squared error when using the prediction rule (SS_{Error}) is the sum of the squared differences between each actual score and the predicted score for that individual; the sum of squared error total (SS_{Total}) is the sum of the squared differences between each actual score and the mean; the proportionate reduction in error is the reduction in squared error gained by using the prediction rule $(SS_{Total} - SS_{Error})$ divided by the squared error when predicting from the mean (SS_{Total}). The proportionate reduction in error (or proportion of variance accounted for) in bivariate prediction equals the correlation coefficient squared (r^2).

Key Terms

predictor variable (X)	intercept	multiple regression
criterion variable (Y)	error	multiple correlation coefficient (R)
linear prediction rule	sum of the squared errors	SS_{Error} (sum of the squared
regression constant (a)	standardized regression	errors)
regression coefficient (b)	coefficient (β)	total squared error when predicting
regression line	bivariate prediction	from the mean (SS_{Total})
slope	multiple correlation	

Example Worked-Out Problems

The following bivariate problems are based on the following data set. In this study, the researchers want to predict achievement test score from class size.

Elementary School	Class Size	Achievement Test Score
Main Street	25	80
Casat	14	98
Lakeland	33	50
Shady Grove	28	82
Jefferson	20	90
M	24	80
$r = -.90$		

Using the Linear Prediction Rule

If the regression constant for predicting achievement test scores from class size is 134 and the regression coefficient is -2.25 (you will figure these values for yourself in a later example worked-out problem), what is the predicted achievement test score for a school with a class size of (a) 23, and (b) 14?

Answer

Using the linear prediction rule $\hat{Y} = a + (b)(X)$, $\hat{Y} = 134 - (2.25)(X)$.

(a) If class size is 23, then the predicted achievement test score $= 134 - (2.25)(23) = 82.25$.

(b) Predicted achievement test score $= 134 - (2.25)(14) = 102.50$.

Drawing a Regression Line

Draw the regression line for predicting achievement test scores from class size.

Answer

The result of each step is shown in Figure 8.

❶ **Draw and label the axes for a scatter diagram.**
❷ **Figure the predicted value on the criterion variable for a low value on the predictor variable, and mark the point on the graph.** From the answer to the previous problem, the predicted achievement test score for a school with a class size of 14 is 102.50. Thus, you mark the point $(X = 14, \hat{Y} = 102.50)$.
❸ **Do the same thing again, but for a high value on the predictor variable.** For a class size of 30, the predicted achievement test score is $134 - (2.25)(30)$, which is 66.50. Thus, you mark the point $(X = 30, \hat{Y} = 66.50)$.
❹ **Draw a line that passes through the two marks.**

Finding the Values of *a* and *b*

Earlier we told you that the regression constant (a) for predicting achievement test scores from class size was 134 and the regression coefficient (b) was -2.25. Carry out the figuring for a and b to make sure these are the correct values.

Answer

The figuring for a and b is shown in Table 10.

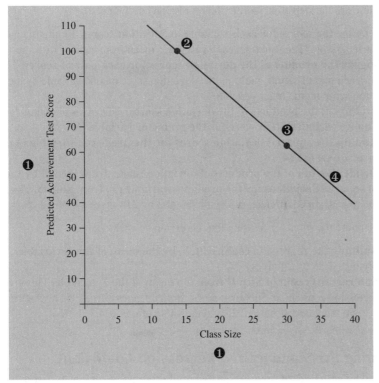

Figure 8 Steps in drawing a regression line for the class size and achievement test score Example Worked-Out Problem. ❶ Draw and label the axes, ❷ mark a point for a low value of the predictor variable and its predicted value on the criterion variable, ❸ mark a point for a high value of the predictor variable and its predicted value on the criterion variable, and ❹ draw the regression line.

Table 10   Figuring the Values of *a* and *b* for the Example Worked-Out Problem

Class Size (X)			Achievement Test Score (Y)		
Deviation ❶		**Deviation Squared ❹**	**Deviation ❶**		**Products of ❷ Deviation Scores**
X	X − M_X	(X − M_X)²	Y	Y − M_Y	(X − M_X)(Y − M_Y)
25	1	1	80	0	0
14	−10	100	98	18	−180
33	9	81	50	−30	−270
28	4	16	82	2	8
20	−4	16	90	10	−40
Σ = 120		Σ = SS_X = 214 ❺	Σ = 400		Σ = −482 ❸
M = 24			M = 80		❻

$$b = \frac{\Sigma[(X - M_X)(Y - M_Y)]}{SS_X} = \frac{-482}{214} = -2.25$$

$$a = M_Y - (b)(M_X) = 80 - (-2.25)(24) = 134$$

Note: The circled numbers refer to the steps for figuring the regression coefficient, *b*.

Here are the steps for figuring the regression coefficient, b:

❶ **Change the scores for each variable to deviation scores.** Figure the mean of each variable. Then subtract each variable's mean from each of its scores.

❷ **Figure the product of the deviation scores for each pair of scores.** That is, for each pair of scores, multiply the deviation score on one variable by the deviation score on the other variable.

❸ **Add up all the products of the deviation scores.** This gives a total of -482.

❹ **Square each deviation score for the predictor variable (X).**

❺ **Add up the squared deviation scores for the predictor variable (X).** This gives a total of 214.

❻ **Divide the sum of the products of deviation scores from Step ❸ by the sum of squared deviations for the predictor variable (X) from Step ❺.** This gives the regression coefficient, b. Dividing -482 by 214 gives a b of -2.25.

Here are the steps for figuring the regression constant, a:

❶ **Multiply the regression coefficient, b, by the mean of the X variable.** Multiplying -2.25 by 24 gives -54.

❷ **Subtract the result of Step ❶ from the mean of the Y variable.** This gives the regression constant, a. Subtracting -54 from 80 gives $80 - (-54)$, which is 134. So the value of b is -2.25 and the value of a is 134.

Figuring the Standardized Regression Coefficient

Figure the standardized regression for predicting achievement test scores from class size.

Answer

The formula for a standardized regression coefficient is

$$\beta = (b)\frac{\sqrt{SS_X}}{\sqrt{SS_Y}}.$$

From Table 10, SS_X is 214. Table 10 doesn't show the value of SS_Y, but we can figure it by squaring each score in the $Y - M_Y$ column and summing the resulting values. Thus, $SS_Y = 0^2 + 18^2 + (-30^2) + 2^2 + 10^2 = 1328$. The value of b was -2.25; so the standardized regression coefficient for predicting achievement test scores from class size is

$$\beta = (b)\frac{\sqrt{SS_X}}{\sqrt{SS_Y}} = (-2.25)\frac{\sqrt{214}}{\sqrt{1328}} = (-2.25)\frac{14.63}{36.44} = -.90.$$

Multiple Regression Predictions

A (fictional) psychologist studied the talkativeness of children in families with a mother, father, and one grandparent. The psychologist found that the child's talkativeness score depended on the quality of the child's relationship with each of these people. The multiple regression linear prediction rule was as follows:

Child's predicted talkativeness $= 2.13 + (1.32)(\text{mother}) + (1.21)(\text{father})$
$+ (1.41)(\text{grandparent}).$

Predict a child's talkativeness score who had scores for relationship quality of 4 with mother, 5 with father, and 3 with grandparent.

Answer

$$\text{Child's predicted talkativeness} = 2.13 + (1.32)(\text{mother}) + (1.21)(\text{father})$$
$$+ (1.41)(\text{grandparent}).$$
$$= 2.13 + (1.32)(4) + (1.21)(5)$$
$$+ (1.41)(3) = 17.69.$$

Advanced Topic: Figuring the Proportionate Reduction in Error

Using the method of finding SS_{Total} and SS_{Error}, find the proportionate reduction in error for predicting achievement test scores from class size.

Answer

We first need to find the predicted achievement score for each school using the linear prediction rule. The rule in this example is $\hat{Y} = 134 - (2.25)(X)$. So, for the first school, Main Street, $\hat{Y} = 134 - (2.25)(25) = 77.75$. Repeating this process for the other schools gives predicted achievement test scores of: Casat, 102.50; Lakeland, 59.75; Shady Grove, 71.00; Jefferson, 89.00.

The figuring for the proportionate reduction of error is shown in Table 11, and the steps follow.

❶ **Figure the sum of squared error using the mean to predict.** Take each score minus the mean, square it, and add these up. From Table 11, $SS_{Total} = 1328$.

❷ **Figure the sum of squared errors using the prediction rule.** Take each score minus the predicted score for this person, square it, and add these up. From Table 11, $SS_{Error} = 242.37$.

❸ **Figure the reduction in squared error.** This is the sum of squared errors using the mean to predict (from Step ❶) minus the sum of squared errors using the prediction rule (from Step ❷). Reduction in squared error $= 1328 - 242.37 = 1085.63$.

Table 11 Figuring Proportionate Reduction in Error for the Example Worked-Out Problem

			Predicted Test Score ❶ Using Mean			Predicted Test Score ❷ Using Prediction Rule		
Class Size	Actual Test Score	Mean Test Score	Error	Error²		Predicted Test Score	Error	Error²
X	Y	M	$(Y - M)$	$(Y - M)^2$		$\hat{Y}$	$(Y - \hat{Y})$	$(Y - \hat{Y})^2$
25	80	80	0	0		77.75	2.25	5.06
14	98	80	18	324		102.50	-4.50	20.25
33	50	80	-30	900		59.75	-9.75	95.06
28	82	80	2	4		71.00	11.00	121.00
20	90	80	10	100		89.00	1.00	1.00
				$\Sigma = SS_{Total} = 1328$				$\Sigma = SS_{Error} = 242.37$

$$\text{Proportionate reduction in error} = \frac{SS_{Total} - SS_{Error}}{SS_{Total}} = \frac{1328 - 242.37}{1328} = \frac{1085.63}{1328} = .82.$$

❹ **Figure the proportionate reduction in squared error.** This is the reduction in squared error (from Step ❸) divided by the total squared error when using the mean to predict (from Step ❶). Proportionate reduction in squared error = $1085.63/1328 = .82$. You can interpret this in terms of 82% of the variation in test scores being accounted for by class size.

Outline for Writing Essays on the Logic and Figuring of Bivariate Prediction

1. Explain the meaning of the term *prediction* as it is used in the context of statistics. Be sure to mention and explain key terms such as *predictor variable* and *criterion variable.*
2. Explain the concept of the linear prediction rule, including its formula. As part of this explanation, be sure to emphasize the meaning of the regression coefficient and regression constant.
3. Explain how the linear prediction rule can be shown as a line on a graph, called a *regression line.* Be sure to describe how to draw the regression line and what it shows.
4. Explain how the regression coefficient and regression constant are each related to the regression line.
5. Explain the idea of the best linear prediction rule in terms of the notion of least squared error.
6. Explain the meaning of the standardized regression coefficient, why it is useful, and how it is figured.
7. In the context of these explanations, describe the meaning of the numeric results of the particular question you are answering.

Practice Problems

These problems involve figuring. Most real-life statistics problems are done with special statistical software. Even if you have such software, do these problems by hand to ingrain the method in your mind. To learn how to use a computer to solve statistics problems like those in this chapter, refer to the Using SPSS section at the end of this chapter.

All data are fictional unless an actual citation is given.

Set I

1. A sports psychologist working with hockey players has found that players' knowledge of physiology predicts the number of injuries received over the subsequent year. The regression constant in the linear prediction rule for predicting injuries from knowledge of physiology is 10.30 and the regression coefficient is $-.70$. (a) Indicate the predictor variable, and (b) the criterion variable. (c) Write the linear prediction rule for this example. Indicate the predicted number of injuries for athletes whose scores on the physiology test are (d) 0, (e) 1, (f) 2, (g) 5, and (h) 6.
2. A professor has found that scores on the midterm exam in her classes predict scores on the final exam. The regression constant in the linear prediction

rule for predicting final exam scores from midterm exam scores is 40 and the regression coefficient is .5. (a) Indicate the predictor variable, and (b) the criterion variable. (c) Write the linear prediction rule for this example. Figure the predicted final exam scores for each of eight students whose scores on the midterm were (d) 30, (e) 40, (f) 50, (g) 60, (h) 70, (i) 80, (j) 90, and (k) 100.

3. For each of the following, (a) through (d), determine the linear prediction rule for predicting criterion variable Y from predictor variable X. Then (e) make a single graph (with values from 0 to 10 on both axes) showing all the regression lines, labeling each by its letter. (Be sure to make your graph large enough so that the lines are clearly separate.)

	Regression Constant *a*	Regression Coefficient *b*
(a)	1.5	.8
(b)	10.0	−.4
(c)	2.0	.2
(d)	9.5	−.8

4. An instructor asked five students how many hours they had studied for an exam. The number of hours studied and their grades, along with the means, are shown here. (a) Determine the linear prediction rule for predicting test grade from hours studied, and (b) draw the regression line. Use the linear prediction rule to figure the predicted test grade of students who studied for each of the following number of hours: (c) 3, (d) 5, and (e) 7. (f) Determine the standardized regression coefficient, and (g) explain what you have done in all the previous parts of this question to someone who understands the mean and deviation scores but does not know any more about statistics. (h) Add the dots for the pairs of scores for the five students to your figure from part (b) and also add a regression line for the linear prediction rule $\hat{Y} = 60 + (5.00)(X)$. (i) Which regression line does a better job of coming close to the dots in your figure for part (h), and why? (j) Figure the sum of squared errors for your linear prediction rule from part (a) and for the prediction rule $\hat{Y} = 60 + (5.00)(X)$. (k) ADVANCED TOPIC: Find the proportionate reduction in error (using SS_{Error} and SS_{Total}).

	Hours Studied	Test Grade
	0	52
	10	95
	6	83
	8	71
	6	64
M	6	73

5. Repeat problem 4, doing parts (a) through (f), but this time predicting hours studied from test grade, and using values of 70, 75, and 80 for parts (c), (d), and (e), respectively.

6. A pilot study of the relation between psychotherapists' degree of empathy and their patients' satisfaction with therapy studies four patient–therapist pairs. The results are presented here, including the means.

Pair Number	Therapist Empathy	Patient Satisfaction
1	70	4
2	94	5
3	36	2
4	48	1
M	62	3

(a) Determine the linear prediction rule for predicting satisfaction from empathy, and (b) draw the regression line. Use the linear prediction rule to figure the predicted satisfaction of patients whose therapist had the following amount of empathy: (c) 50, (d) 64, and (e) 80. (f) Determine the standardized regression coefficient, and (g) explain what you have done in all the previous parts of this question to someone who understands the mean and deviation scores but does not know any more about statistics. (h) ADVANCED TOPIC: Find the proportionate reduction in error (using SS_{Error} and SS_{Total}).

7. Repeat problem 6, doing parts (a) through (f), but this time predicting empathy from satisfaction, and using values of 3, 2, and 1 for parts (c), (d), and (e), respectively.

8. Repeat problem 6, doing parts (a) through (f), but this time adding an additional pair of scores, with a therapist empathy value of 95 and a patient satisfaction value of 1 (this pair of scores can be thought of as an outlier). (g) Discuss how the results from problem 6 compare with the results of this problem.

9. For each of the following, (a) through (d), determine the multiple linear prediction rule for predicting criterion variable Y from predictor variables X_1, X_2, and X_3. Then (e) figure the predicted score on the criterion variable for part (a) for a person with scores on the predictor variables of $X_1 = 2$, $X_2 = 5$, and $X_3 = 9$.

	Regression Constant	Regression Coefficient	Regression Coefficient	Regression Coefficient
	a	b_1	b_2	b_3
(a)	1.5	.8	−.3	9.99
(b)	10.0	−.4	11.0	−8.62
(c)	2.0	.2	6.13	2.12
(d)	9.5	−.8	21.23	1.02

10. In the Oettingen and colleagues (2001) study described earlier (in the "Prediction in Research Articles" section), in addition to studying anticipated disappointment, the researchers conducted an experiment focusing on number of plans and on taking responsibility. Their results are shown in Figure 9. Explain the meaning of each graph to a person who has never had a course in statistics.

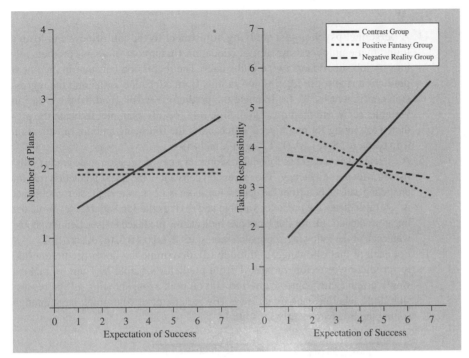

Figure 9 Regression lines depicting the link of expectation of success to formulating plans (left) and to taking responsibility (right) as a function of self-regulatory thought.

Source: Oettingen, G., Schnetter, K., & Pak, H. (2001). Self-regulations of goal setting: Turning free fantasies about the future into binding goals. *Journal of Personality and Social Psychology*, *80*, 736–753. Published by the American Psychological Association. Reprinted with permission.

Set II

11. A personnel psychologist studying adjustment to the job of new employees
found that employees' amount of education (in number of years) predicts ratings by job supervisors two months later. The regression constant in the linear
prediction rule for predicting job ratings from education is 0.5 and the regression coefficient is .40. (a) Indicate the predictor variable, and (b) the criterion
variable. (c) Write the linear prediction rule for this example. Indicate the predicted job rating for employees with each of the following amount of education
(in years): (d) 8, (e) 10, (f) 17, (g) 19, and (h) 21.

12. A clinical psychologist has found that scores on a new depression scale predict satisfaction with psychotherapy. The regression constant in the linear prediction rule for
predicting satisfaction from the depression score is 12 and the regression coefficient
is −.4. (a) Indicate the predictor variable and (b) the criterion variable. (c) Write the
linear prediction rule for this example. Indicate the predicted satisfaction for people
with each of the following depression scores: (d) 8, (e) 6, (f) 5, (g) 3, and (h) 0.

13. For each of the following, (a) through (d), determine the linear prediction rule
for predicting criterion variable Y from predictor variable X. Then (e) make a
single graph (with values from 0 to 100 on both axes) showing all the regression lines, labeling each by its letter. (Be sure to make your graph large enough
so that the lines are clearly separate.)

	Regression Constant a	Regression Coefficient b
(a)	89.0	−.8
(b)	5.0	.7
(c)	50.0	.1
(d)	20.0	.4

14. Four individuals were given a test of manual dexterity (high scores mean better dexterity) and an anxiety test (high scores mean more anxiety). The results are presented here, including the means.

Person	Dexterity	Anxiety
1	1	10
2	1	8
3	2	4
4	4	−2
M	2	5

(a) Determine the linear prediction rule for predicting anxiety from dexterity, and (b) draw the regression line. Use the linear prediction rule to figure the predicted anxiety of people with dexterity scores as follows: (c) 1, (d) 2, and (e) 3. (f) Determine the standardized regression coefficient, and (g) explain what you have done in all the previous parts of this question to someone who understands the mean and deviation scores but does not know any more about statistics. (h) ADVANCED TOPIC: Find the proportionate reduction in error (using SS_{Error} and SS_{Total}).

15. Repeat problem 15, doing parts (a) through (f), but this time predicting dexterity from anxiety, and using values of 0, 4, and 7 for parts (c), (d), and (e), respectively.

16. Repeat problem 15, doing parts (a) through (f), but this time adding an additional pair of scores, with a dexterity value of 4 and an value of 10 (this pair of scores can be thought of as an outlier). (g) Discuss how the results from problem 15 compare with the results of this problem.

17. The results for the amount of violent television watched and the amount of violent behavior toward their playmates for four young children are presented here, including the means.

Child's Code Number	Weekly Viewing of Violent TV (hours)	Number of Violent or Aggressive Acts Toward Playmates
G3368	14	9
R8904	8	6
C9890	6	1
L8722	12	8
M	10	6

(a) Determine the linear prediction rule for predicting violent acts from watching violent television, and (b) draw the regression line. Use the linear prediction rule to figure the predicted number of violent acts for children watching the following number of hours of violent television: (c) 7, (d) 9, and (e) 11. (f) Determine the standardized regression coefficient, and (g) explain what you have done in all the previous parts of this question to someone who understands the mean and deviation scores but does not know any more about statistics. (h) Add the dots for the pairs of scores for the four children to your figure from part (b) and also add a regression line for the linear prediction rule $\hat{Y} = -2 + (.20)(X)$. (i) Figure the sum of squared errors for your linear prediction rule from part (a) and for the prediction rule $\hat{Y} = -2 + (.20)(X)$. (j) Explain why the sum of squared errors for your linear prediction rule from (a) must be lower than the sum of squared errors for any other linear prediction rule. (k) ADVANCED TOPIC: Find the proportionate reduction in error (using SS_{Error} and SS_{Total}).

18. Repeat problem 18, doing parts (a) through (f), but this time predicting the number of hours of watching violent television from violent acts, and using values of 2, 5, and 7 for parts (c), (d), and (e), respectively.

19. For each of the following, (a) through (d), determine the multiple linear prediction rule for predicting criterion variable Y from predictor variables X_1, X_2, and X_3. Then (e) figure the predicted score on the criterion variable for part (a) for a person with scores on the predictor variables of $X_1 = 12$, $X_2 = 8$, and $X_3 = 1$.

	Regression Constant	Regression Coefficient	Regression Coefficient	Regression Coefficient
	a	b_1	b_2	b_3
(a)	3.8	4.1	.9	7.1
(b)	11.2	.9	2.5	3.9
(c)	.8	.1	1.0	1.5
(d)	−3.1	.8	12.4	4.3

20. Nezlek and colleagues (1997) had participants first write self-descriptions and then exchange them with four other students also taking part in the study. Then the students privately ranked the other students on how much they would like to work with them on the next task. One group of participants were then told that they had been selected to work on the next task with the rest of the group; this was the inclusion condition. The remaining participants were told that they had not been chosen to work with the others and would work alone—the exclusion condition. At this point, participants were asked about how accepted they felt. Earlier, at the start of the study, they had completed a self-esteem scale. Figure 10 shows regression lines for the two experimental groups. Explain what these two lines mean to a person who understands correlation but knows nothing about prediction.

21. Social psychologists studying criminal justice issues have long been interested in what influences people's attitudes about punishment of criminal offenders. Graham and her colleagues (1997) took advantage of the very public trial of U.S. football star O. J. Simpson to test some basic issues in this area. In the first few days after Simpson was accused of having murdered his ex-wife, the researchers asked people a series of questions about the case. The researchers were mainly interested in the responses of the 177 individuals who believed Simpson was probably guilty, particularly their belief about retribution—how much they agreed or disagreed with the statement, "The punishment should make O. J. suffer as he made others suffer." The researchers were interested in a number of possible influences on this belief. These included "control" (how much control they believed Simpson had over his actions at the time of the crime), "responsibility" (how much they believed he was responsible for the crime), "anger" they felt toward him, "sympathy" they felt for him, "stability" (how much they believed his actions represented a stable versus temporary way

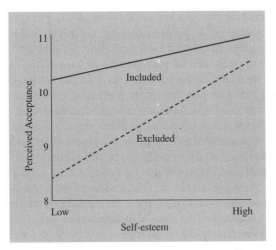

Figure 10   Effects of inclusion/exclusion and traits self-esteem on perceived acceptance.

Source: Nezlek, J. B., Kowalski, R. M., Leary, M. R., Blevins, T., & Holgate, S. (1997). Personality moderators of reactions to interpersonal rejection: Depression and trait self-esteem. *Personality and Social Psychology Bulletin*, *23*, 1235–1244. Copyright © 1997 by Sage Publications, Ltd. Reprinted by permission of Sage Publications, Thousands Oaks, London, and New Delhi.

of behaving), and "expectancy" (if they thought he would commit such a crime again). Graham and her colleagues reported

…Table [12] reveals partial support for our hypotheses. As expected, the strongest predictors of the retributive goal of making Simpson suffer were inferences about responsibility and the moral emotions of anger and sympathy. [S]tability and expectancy…were relatively weak [predictors]. (p. 337)

Explain these results as if you were writing to a person who understands bivariate prediction but does not understand multiple regression. (Refer only to the retribution part of the table. You may ignore the *t* column, which is about the statistical significance of the results.)

Table 12   Multiple Regressions Predicting Punishment Goals from the Attributional Variables, Study 1

| | Punishment Goal | | | | | | | |
| | Retribution | | Rehabilitation | | Protection | | Deterrence | |
Predictors	β	t	β	t	β	t	β	t
Control	−.05	<1	−.05	<1	−.03	<1	.15	1.90
Responsibility	.17	2.07*	−.00	<1	−.04	<1	.19	2.15*
Anger	.30	4.04***	.11	1.54	−.03	<1	−.04	<1
Sympathy	−.30	−3.68***	.39	5.18***	−.07	<1	−.13	−1.54
Stability	−.01	<1	−.34	−4.85***	−.19	2.33*	.04	<1
Expectancy	−.10	−1.33	−.06	<1	−.27	3.36***	.08	1.04
R^2		.27		.37		.17		.18

Note: β = standardized regression coefficient.

*p < .05; ***p < .001.

Source: Graham, S., Weiner, B., & Zucker, G. S. (1997). An attributional analysis of punishment goals and public reactions to O. J. Simpson. *Personality and Social Psychology Bulletin*, *23*, 331–346. Copyright © 1997 by the Society for Personality and Social Psychology, Inc. Reprinted by permission of Sage Publications, Inc.

22. Think of something that you would like to be able to predict and what predictor variable would be useful in predicting it. (This should be different from any example given in class or used for a previous problem. Also, both variables should be measured on a numeric scale.) (a) Write a linear prediction rule, noting the name of the predictor variable and the name of the criterion variable. (b) Estimate numbers for the regression constant and the regression coefficient that you think make some sense based on what you know about the things you are making predictions about. Finally, explain why you picked (c) the regression constant and (d) the regression coefficient size you did.

23. Think of something that you would like to be able to predict and what *two or more* predictor variables would be useful in predicting it. (This should be different from any example given in class or used in a previous problem. All variables should be measured on numeric scales.) (a) Write a linear prediction rule, noting the name of the predictor variables and the name of the criterion variable. (b) Estimate numbers for the regression constant and for the regression coefficients for each predictor variable that you think make some sense based on what you know about the things you are making predictions about. Finally, explain why you picked (c) the regression constant, and (d) the regression coefficient sizes you did.

24. Ask five other students of the same gender as yourself (each from different families) to give you their own height and also their mother's height. Determine the linear prediction rule for predicting a person's height from his or her mother's height, and make a graph showing the regression line. Finally, based on your prediction rule, predict the height of a person of your gender whose mother's height is (a) 5 feet, (b) 5 feet 6 inches, and (c) 6 feet. (*Note:* Either convert inches to decimals of feet or do the whole problem using inches.)

Using SPSS

The ✐ in the following steps indicates a mouse click. (We used SPSS version 19 for Windows to carry out these analyses. The steps and output may be slightly different for other versions of SPSS.)

In the following steps for figuring the bivariate linear prediction rule, we use the example of the sleep and happy mood study. The scores and figuring of the regression constant (a) and the regression coefficient (b) for that study are shown in Table 5.

Figuring the Bivariate Linear Prediction Rule

❶ Enter the scores into SPSS. Enter the scores as shown in Figure 11.

❷ ✐ *Analyze.*

❸ ✐ *Regression.* ✐ *Linear.* This tells SPSS that you are figuring a *linear* prediction rule, as opposed to any one of a number of other types of prediction rules.

❹ ✐ the variable called "mood" and then ✐ the arrow next to the box labeled "Dependent." This tells SPSS that the "mood" variable is the criterion variable (which is also called the *dependent variable* in prediction, because it "depends" on the predictor variable's score). ✐ the variable called "sleep" and then ✐ the arrow next to the box labeled "Independent(s)." This tells SPSS that the "sleep" variable is the predictor variable (which is also called the *independent variable*

Figure 11 SPSS data editor window for the fictional study of the relationship between hours slept last night and mood.

in prediction). (If you were figuring a multiple regression, you would put all of the predictor variables in the "Independent(s)" box.)

❺ ✎ *Statistics, ✎ Descriptives, ✎ Continue.* This requests useful descriptive information on the variables (such as the mean and estimated population standard deviation) and also gives the correlation between the variables. (Step ❺ is optional, but we strongly recommend requesting descriptive statistics for any hypothesis-testing situation.)

❻ ✎ *OK.* Your SPSS output window should look like Figure 12.

SPSS provides six tables in the output. (It provides four tables if you do not select "Descriptives," as shown in Step ❺ above.) The first two tables show descriptive statistics and a correlation matrix. The third table shows which variable was the predictor variable ("variable entered") and which was the criterion variable ("dependent variable"). Always check to see that you used the correct variables. These first three tables are not shown in Figure 12. The fourth table (labeled "Model Summary") gives the correlation coefficient ("R") between the two variables and the proportionate reduction in error ("R square" or R^2), which we discussed in the Advanced Topic section of this chapter. Also, recall that R^2 (shown as "R square" in the SPSS output) is the measure of effect size for prediction. (With bivariate prediction, SPSS uses R and R^2 for what we refer to as r and r^2 in the chapter. Following the usual way of doing this in psychology, we used lower case r and r^2 with bivariate regression, and capital R and R^2 with multiple correlation and the proportionate reduction in error for multiple regression. But SPSS just uses capitals for both.) You can ignore

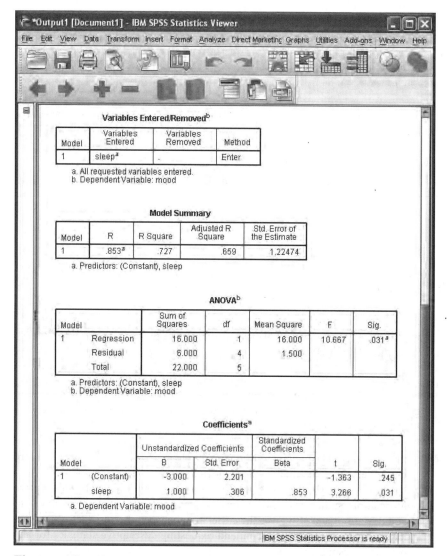

Figure 12 SPSS output window for the bivariate prediction rule predicting mood from hours slept last night (fictional data).

the final two columns of the "Model Summary" table. You can also ignore the table in the output labeled "ANOVA." (However, if you read the Advanced Topic section in this chapter on error and proportionate reduction in error, note that SS_{Error} is shown as the "Sums of Squares" for "Residual" in the second column and the SS_{Total} is the "Sums of Squares Total" shown in the same column. The "Regression" in the "Sums of Squares" column shows the difference between SS_{Total} and SS_{Error}.)

The final table (labeled "Coefficients") gives the information for the linear prediction rule. This is what you want to focus on. The first row of the table gives the regression constant, which in this case is -3.000. (It also gives some other statistics related to the constant, such as a t test of whether the constant is significantly different from 0.) So, using the terminology from this chapter, $a = -3.00$. The regression coefficients are shown in the second row of the table. (In a multiple regression, there would a row of regression coefficients for each predictor variable.) The value of 1.000 in the "B" column ("B" is the same as b you learned in this chapter) is the regular, unstandardized regression coefficient. So, using the terminology from this chapter, $b = 1.000$. We now have the necessary information—a and b—for the linear prediction rule. Thus, the linear prediction rule is Predicted mood $= -3 + (1)$ (hours of sleep). The table also shows the standardized regression coefficient, which is .853. The final two columns for the "sleep" row give the statistical test of whether each regression coefficient is significantly different from 0. The significance level of .031 is less than our usual .05 cutoff, which means that the number of hours slept is a statistically significant predictor of mood the next day. Notice that the t value of 3.226 for the sleep predictor variable is consistent (within rounding error) with the t (of 3.21).

Chapter Notes

1. Psychologists often call the kind of prediction in this chapter *regression*. Regression means, literally, going back or returning. The term *regression* is used here because, for any individual, the predicted score on the criterion variable is closer to the mean of the criterion variable compared to the distance from the person's predictor variable score to the mean of the predictor variable. This would be true in all cases except for a perfect correlation between the two variables. So you can think of this in terms of the predicted value of the criterion variable regressing, or going back, toward the mean of the criterion variable.

2. There are also procedures that allow you to use more than one criterion variable. For example, you might want to know how good a predictor hours slept is for both mood and alertness. Procedures involving more than one criterion variable are called "multivariate statistics" and are quite advanced.

Answers to Set I Practice Problems

Chapter 12

1. (a) Score on knowledge of physiology; (b) number of injuries; (c) linear prediction rule formula is $\hat{Y} = a + (b)(X)$, so predicted number of injuries $= 10.30 - (.70)$ (knowledge of physiology); (d) $10.30 - (.70)(0) = 10.30$; (e) 9.60; (f) 8.90; (g) 6.80; (h) 6.10.

2. (a) Midterm exam score; (b) final exam score; (c) predicted final exam score $= 40 + (.5)$(midterm exam score); (d) $40 + (.5)(30) = 55$; (e) 60; (f) 65; (g) 70; (h) 75; (i) 80; (j) 85; (k) 90.

3. (a) $\hat{Y} = 1.5 + (.8)(X)$; (b) $\hat{Y} = 10.0 - (.40)(X)$; (c) $\hat{Y} = 2.0 + (.2)(X)$; (d) $\hat{Y} = 9.5 - (.8)(X)$.

(e)

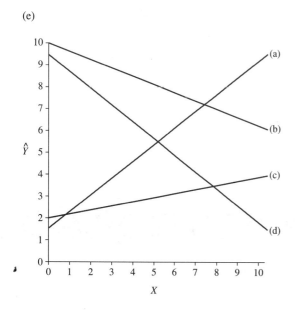

4. (a) Use the formula $b = \sum[(X - M_X)(Y - M_Y)]/SS_X$. $\sum[(X - M_X)(Y - M_Y)] = 210$ and $SS_X = 56$. Thus, $b = 210/56 = 3.75$. $a = M_Y - (b)(M_X) = 73 - (3.75)(6) = 50.50$. Therefore, predicted test grade $= 50.50 + (3.75)$ (hours studied).

(b)

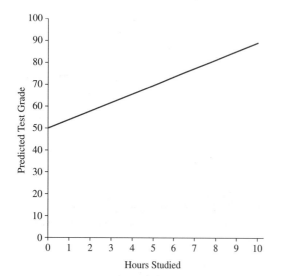

(c) $50.50 + (3.75)(3) = 61.75$; (d) 69.25; (e) 76.75; (f) $\beta = (b)(\sqrt{SS_X}/\sqrt{SS_Y})$. $SS_Y = 1110$. Therefore, $\beta = (3.75)(\sqrt{56}/\sqrt{1110}) = .84$.

(g) Prediction is a statistical procedure used to predict scores on one variable (called a criterion variable) from scores on another variable (called a predictor variable). You use a linear prediction rule to make predictions. The linear prediction rule says that, to predict a person's score on a criterion variable (Y), start with a particular number (called a regression constant) and add to it the result of multiplying a particular number (called a regression coefficient) by the person's score on the predictor variable (X). The regression constant (which is labeled a) is a fixed value that you always add in to the prediction. The regression coefficient (which is labeled b) is called a coefficient because it is a number you multiply by something.

There are formulas for determining the values of a (the regression constant) and b (the regression coefficient) that give the best linear prediction rule. The best linear prediction rule is the one that gives the lowest sum of squared errors between the actual scores on the criterion variable and the predicted scores on the criterion variable. The linear prediction rule can be written as a formula: $\hat{Y} = a + (b)(X)$. $\hat{Y}$ means the predicted value of Y, that is, the predicted value of the criterion variable (the variable you are trying to predict). In this example, the linear prediction rule was predicted test grade $= 50.50 + (3.75)$(hours studied). The linear prediction rule can be shown as a line on a graph. This line is called a regression line. The regression line shows the relationship between values for the X variable and predicted values for the Y variable. You draw the regression line by using the linear prediction rule to predict the value of the Y for a low value of X and marking that point on a graph, then predicting the value of Y for a high value of X and marking that point on a graph, and then finally you draw a line through the two dots. The slope of the regression line is b (the regression coefficient). The regression coefficient is the predicted amount of increase in units for the criterion variable when the predictor variable increases by one unit. So the regression coefficient of 3.75 in this example means that every one-hour increase in the number of hours studied gives a predicted increase of 3.75 points on the test grade. The point where the regression line crosses the vertical axis—which is called the intercept—is a (the regression constant). In this example, the regression line crosses the vertical axis at 50.50 (which is the value of a). I used the linear prediction rule to figure the predicted test grade of the students who studied for different amounts of time.

The scale used for the predictor and criterion variables will affect the value of b (the regression coefficient) in the linear prediction rule. This can make it hard to compare linear prediction rules across studies. You can avoid this problem by figuring a standardized regression coefficient, which is referred to using the Greek symbol β (beta). The standardized regression coefficient shows the predicted amount of change in standard deviation units of the criterion variable if the value of the predicted variable increases by one standard deviation. The standardized regression coefficient can be figured by multiplying the regression coefficient by the result of dividing the square root of the sum of squared deviations for the predictor variable by the square root of the sum of squared deviations for the criterion variable. The standardized regression coefficient of .84 in this example means that, for every standard deviation increase in hours studied, the predicted test grade increases by .84 of a standard deviation.

(h)

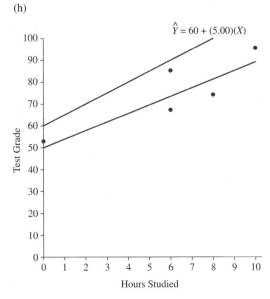

$\hat{Y} = 60 + (5.00)(X)$

Test Grade (y-axis, 0 to 100)

Hours Studied (x-axis, 0 to 10)

$126/1960 = .06.$ $a = M_Y - (b)(M_X) = 3 - (.06)(62) = -.72.$ Therefore, predicted satisfaction $= -.72 + (.06)$ (empathy).

(b)

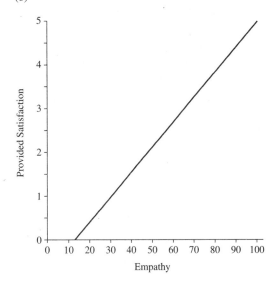

Provided Satisfaction (y-axis, 0 to 5)

Empathy (x-axis, 0 to 100)

(i) The regression line figured in part (b) does a better job of coming close to the dots. The regression line from part (b) is a visual equivalent of the linear prediction rule figured in part (a). Since that linear prediction rule is the best linear prediction rule (in terms of giving the lowest sum of squared errors between actual scores on the criterion variable and the predicted scores on the criterion variable), the regression line equivalent of that rule is the line that does the best job of coming close (in squared units) to the actual scores (shown by the dots).

(j) $\hat{Y} = 50.50 + (3.75)(X)$, the sum of squared errors using the prediction rule from (a) is 322.5. The sum of squared errors using the prediction rule $\hat{Y} = 60 + (5.00)(X)$ is 1855.0.

(k) Proportionate reduction in error $= (SS_{Total} - SS_{Error})/SS_{Total}$. From (j) above, $SS_{Error} = 322.5$. SS_{Total} is the same as SS_Y, which from (c) above was 1110. So, proportionate reduction in error $= (1110 - 322.5)/1110 = .71$.

5. (a) Predicted hours studied $= -7.87 + (.19)(\text{test grade})$; (b) similar to question 4b; (c) 5.43; (d) 6.38; (e) 7.33; (f) $\beta = (b)(\sqrt{SS_X}/\sqrt{SS_Y}) = (.19)(\sqrt{1110}/\sqrt{56}) = .85.$

6. (a) Use the formula $b = \sum[(X - M_X)(Y - M_Y)]/SS_X$. $\sum[(X - M_X)(Y - M_Y)] = 126$ and $SS_X = 1960$. Thus, $b =$

(c) $-.72 + (.06)(50) = 2.28$; (d) 3.12; (e) 4.08; (f) $\beta = (b)(\sqrt{SS_X}/\sqrt{SS_Y})$. Therefore, $\beta = (.06)(\sqrt{1960}/\sqrt{10}) = .84$. (g) Similar to 4g above.

(h) Proportionate reduction in error $= (SS_{Total} - SS_{Error})/SS_{Total}$. Using the same procedure as in 4j above, $SS_{Error} = 1.94$. SS_{Total} is the same as SS_Y, which from part (f) above was 10. So, proportionate reduction in error $= (10 - 1.94)/10 = .81$.

7. (a) Predicted empathy $= 24.2 + (12.6)(\text{satisfaction})$; (b) similar to question 6b; (c) 62.0; (d) 49.4; (e) 36.8; (f) $\beta = (b)(\sqrt{SS_X}/\sqrt{SS_Y}) = (12.6)(\sqrt{10}/\sqrt{1960}) = .9$.

8. (a) Use the formula $b = \sum[(X - M_X)(Y - M_Y)]/SS_X = 73.20/2831.20 = .03.$ $a = M_Y - (b)(M_X) = 2.6 - (.03)(68.6) = .54.$ Therefore, predicted satisfaction $= .54 + (.03)(\text{empathy})$.

(b) Figure like question 6b; (c) 2.04; (d) 2.46; (e) 2.94; (f) $\beta = (.03)(\sqrt{2831.20}/\sqrt{13.20}) = .44$. (g) In this question, we added an extra person to the study. The therapist

Hours Studied	Test Grade	Rule: $\hat{Y} = 50.50 + (3.75)(X)$			Rule: $\hat{Y} = 60 + (5.00)(X)$		
		Predicted Test Grade	Error	Squared Error	Predicted Test Grade	Error	Squared Error
X	Y	$\hat{Y}$	$(Y - \hat{Y})$	$(Y - \hat{Y})^2$	$\hat{Y}$	$(Y - \hat{Y})$	$(Y - \hat{Y})^2$
0	52	50.5	1.5	2.25	60.0	−8.0	64.0
10	95	88.0	7.0	49.00	110.0	−15.0	225.0
6	83	73.0	10.0	100.00	90.0	−7.0	49.0
8	71	80.5	−9.5	90.25	100.0	−29.0	841.0
6	64	73.0	−9.0	81.00	90.0	−26.0	676.0
				$\Sigma = 322.5$			$\Sigma = 1855.0$

empathy value for that person was a very high score (95), and the patient satisfaction was a very low score (1). The best way to compare the relationship between therapist empathy and patient satisfaction in the original case (question 6) and with the addition of the new person is to look at the standardized regression coefficients (βs). In question 6, the β was .84. This tells you that every increase of one standard deviation on therapist empathy is associated with a .84 standard deviation change in patient satisfaction. After adding the new person into the study, the β was .44. This tells you that every one standard deviation increase in therapist empathy is associated with a .44 standard deviation in patient satisfaction. Thus, by adding this new person to the study, the overall association between therapist empathy and patient satisfaction has become weaker. This makes sense because the patient we added to the study was quite different from the other patients. In question 6, there was a very strong tendency for high scores on therapist empathy to be associated with high sores on patient satisfaction (and low scores with low scores). The new patient we added in this question has a very high score on therapist empathy but a very low score on patient satisfaction. So the new patient can be thought of as an outlier, which in this case has the effect of making the association between therapist empathy and patient satisfaction less strong than it was without the outlier.

9. (a) $\hat{Y} = a + (b_1)(X_1) + (b_2)(X_2) + (b_3)(X_3) = 1.5 + (.8)(X_1) - (.3)(X_2) + (9.99)(X_3)$.
(b) $\hat{Y} = 10.0 - (.4)(X_1) + (11.0)(X_2) - (8.62)(X_3)$.
(c) $\hat{Y} = 2.0 + (.2)(X_1) + (6.13)(X_2) + (2.12)(X_3)$.
(d) $\hat{Y} = 9.5 - (.8)(X_1) + (21.23)(X_2) + (1.02)(X_3)$.

10. First, explain prediction as in question 4g and correlation as in Chapter 11. The two graphs show regression lines separately for each experimental group. The left graph shows that Expectation of Success provides little information to predict Number of Plans for either the Positive Fantasy or Negative Reality group, but for the Contrast group, there is a fairly strong positive relation between Expectation of Success and Number of Plans. The right graph, which shows the regression lines for predicting Taking Responsibility from Expectation of Success, indicates that there is a moderate negative relation for the Positive Fantasy group, a small negative relation for the Negative Reality group, and a strong positive relation for the Contrast group.

Chapter 13

Chi-Square Tests

Chapter 13

Chi-Square Tests

Chapter Outline

- ❖ The Chi-Square Statistic and the Chi-Square Test for Goodness of Fit
- ❖ The Chi-Square Test for Independence
- ❖ Assumptions for Chi-Square Tests
- ❖ Effect Size and Power for Chi-Square Tests for Independence
- ❖ Controversy: The Minimum Expected Frequency

- ❖ Chi-Square Tests in Research Articles
- ❖ Learning Aids
  - ❖ Summary
  - ❖ Key Terms
  - ❖ Example Worked-Out Problems
  - ❖ Practice Problems
  - ❖ Using SPSS
- ❖ Chapter Notes

chi-square tests hypothesis-testing procedures used when the variables of interest are nominal variables.

The procedures like *t* tests, analysis of variance, correlation, and prediction are very versatile, but there are certain research situations in which these methods cannot be used. One such situation is hypothesis testing for variables whose values are categories, such as a person's region of the country, religious preference, or hair color. The *t* test, analysis of variance, correlation, and prediction all required that the measured variable or variables have scores that are quantitative, such as a rating on a 7-point scale or number of dreams during a week. This chapter focuses on **chi-square tests**, which are used when the scores are on a *nominal variable* (that is, a variable with values that are categories). (Chi is the Greek letter χ; it is pronounced *ki,* rhyming with high.) Therefore, the scores that you will encounter in this chapter represent *frequencies:* that is, how many people or observations fall into different categories. The chi-square test was originally developed by Karl Pearson (see Box 1) and is sometimes called the Pearson chi-square.

BOX 1 Karl Pearson, Inventor of Chi-Square and Center of Controversy

Topham/The Image Works

Karl Pearson, sometimes hailed as the founder of the science of statistics, was born in 1857. Both his virtues and vices are revealed in what he reported to his colleague Julia Bell as his earliest memory: he was sitting in his highchair, sucking his thumb, when he was told to stop or his thumb would wither away. Pearson silently thought, "I can't see that the thumb I suck is any smaller than the other. I wonder if she could be lying to me." Here we see Pearson's faith in himself and in observational evidence, as well as his rejection of authority. We also see his tendency to doubt the character of people with whom he disagreed.

Pearson studied mathematics at Cambridge. Soon after he arrived, he requested to be excused from compulsory chapel. As soon as his request was granted, however, he appeared in chapel. The dean summoned him for an explanation, and Pearson declared that he had asked to be excused not from chapel "but from *compulsory* chapel."

After graduation, Pearson studied in Germany, becoming a socialist and a self-described "free-thinker." Returning to England, he changed his name from Carl to Karl (in honor of Karl Marx) and wrote an attack on Christianity under a pen name. In 1885 he founded a Men and Women's Club to promote equality between the sexes. In 1892 he published a book titled, *The Grammar of Science*, that subsequently influenced Albert Einstein's theories of relativity.

Most of Pearson's research from 1893 to 1901 focused on the laws of heredity, but he needed better statistical methods, leading to his most famous contribution, the chi-square test. Pearson also invented the method of computing correlation used today and coined the terms *histogram, skew*, and *spurious correlation*. When he felt that biology journals failed to appreciate his work, he founded the famous journal *Biometrika*.

Unfortunately, Pearson was a great fan of eugenics, and his work was later used by the Nazis as justification for their treatment of the Jews. Toward the end of his life, however, he fought back, writing a paper using clear logic and data on Jews and Gentiles from all over the world to demonstrate that the Nazis' ideas were sheer nonsense.

Indeed, throughout his life, Pearson's strong opinions created a long list of enemies, especially as other, younger statisticians passed him by, while he refused to publish their work in *Biometrika*. William S. Gosset was one of his friends. Sir Ronald Fisher was one of Pearson's worst enemies. The kindly Gosset was always trying to smooth matters between them. In 1933, Pearson finally retired, and Fisher, of all persons, took over his chair, the Galton Professorship of Eugenics at University College in London. In 1936, the two entered into their bitterest argument yet; Pearson died the same year.

For more information about Pearson, see *http://en.wikipedia.org/wiki/Karl_Pearson* and *http://www.human-nature.com/nibbs/03/kpearson.html*.

Sources: Peters (1987); Salsburg (2001); Stigler (1986); Tankard (1984); Wright (2009).

An Example

Black, Marola, Littman, Chrisler, and Neace (2009) were interested in the extent to which cereal boxes are likely to show male as opposed to female characters. Previous research has shown that male characters outnumber female characters in various forms of media targeted toward children, including books, video games, and television. The researchers noted that "cereal boxes . . . depict a plethora of characters used to market the products to both children and adults" and that ". . . these boxes are on the kitchen table each morning as people eat their breakfast, and may be more prevalent in households than some other forms of media that have been studied previously. As such, the gender of the characters and manner in which they are depicted

Table 1 Observed and Expected Frequencies for the Gender of Characters on Cereal Boxes (Data from Black et al., 2009)

Gender	Observed Frequency (O)	Expected Frequency (E)	Difference $(O - E)$	Difference Squared $(O - E)^2$	Difference Squared Weighted by Expected Frequency $(O - E)^2/E$
Male	996	693	303	91,809	132.48
Female	390	693	−303	91,809	132.48

on cereal boxes may contribute to people's gender schemas" (pp. 882–883). In order to test their hypothesis that male characters would appear more often than female characters on cereal boxes, the researchers assigned student research assistants the task of coding the gender of the characters on every cereal box in a large grocery superstore in the northeastern United States. The researchers described the coding process as follows: "[F]or gender, coders relied on cues such as clothing (e.g., skirts), hairstyle (e.g., pony tails with ribbons), facial features (e.g., mustache), and name (e.g., Tony the Tiger)" (p. 885). Of the 1,386 characters on cereal boxes whose gender could be determined, 996 were male and 390 were female (in percentage terms, 72% male and 28% female).

Suppose the characters were equally likely to be male or female. If that were the case, then about 693 (half of the 1,386) characters should have been male and another 693 should have been female. This information is laid out in the "Observed Frequency" and "Expected Frequency" columns of Table 1. The Observed Frequency column shows the breakdown of character genders actually *observed*. The Expected Frequency column shows the breakdown you would *expect* if the genders had been exactly equally likely. (Note that it won't always be the case that you expect an *equal breakdown* across the categories. In some situations, the expected frequency for each category may be based on theory, or on a breakdown from another study or circumstance. We will consider some examples of this kind shortly.)

Clearly, there is a discrepancy between what was actually observed and the breakdown you would expect if male and female characters were equally likely. The question is this: Should you assume that this discrepancy is no more than what we would expect just by chance for a sample of this size? Suppose that characters on all cereal boxes (that is, the entire population of cereal boxes, not just the sample the students saw at that supermarket) are equally likely to be male or female. In that case, you would still not expect a perfectly equal gender split for the sample of cereal boxes examined from any single store. But if the breakdown in the sample of cereal boxes is a long way from equal, you would doubt that the gender split in the full population of cereal boxes really is equal. In other words, we are in a hypothesis-testing situation, much like the ones we have been considering all along—but with a big difference, too.

In some situations, the scores can all be *numerical values* on some dimension, such as a score on a standard achievement test, length of time in a relationship, an employer's rating of an employee's job effectiveness on a 9-point scale, and so forth; often we figure means of these numbers. By contrast, the gender of characters on cereal boxes is an example of what can be call a *nominal variable* (or a *categorical variable*). A nominal variable is one in which the information is the number of people or observations in each category. Therefore, the numbers associated with nominal variables are frequencies (and not means at all); the frequency tells you how many people or observations fall into each category of the variable. We use the term *nominal variables* because the different categories or levels of the variable have *names* instead of numbers. Hypothesis testing with nominal variables uses *chi-square tests.*

The Chi-Square Statistic and the Chi-Square Test for Goodness of Fit

The basic idea of any chi-square test is that you compare how well an *observed breakdown* of people over various categories fits some *expected breakdown.* (In the example we just considered, we are comparing how well the observed breakdown of genders of characters on cereal boxes compares to the expected breakdown, if the null hypothesis were true, of an equal, 50-50, breakdown.) In this chapter you will learn about two types of chi-square tests: First, you will learn about the **chi-square test for goodness of fit**, which is a chi-square test involving levels of a *single nominal variable.* Later in the chapter, you will learn about the **chi-square test for independence**, which is used when there are *two nominal variables*, each with several categories.

More specifically, again in terms of the example of characters on cereal boxes—in which there is a single nominal variable with two categories (male and female)—you are comparing the observed breakdown of 996 and 390 to the expected breakdown of about 693 for each gender. A breakdown of numbers expected in each category is actually a frequency distribution. Thus, a chi-square test is more formally described as comparing an **observed frequency** distribution to an **expected frequency** distribution. *Here is the key idea: What this hypothesis testing involves is first figuring a number for the amount of mismatch between the observed frequencies and the expected frequencies, and then seeing whether that number indicates a greater mismatch than you would expect by chance.* This gives an idea as to how the chi-square test for *goodness of fit* came to have that name: the test shows how well an observed frequency distribution fits an expected (or predicted) frequency distribution.

Let's start with how you would come up with that mismatch number for the observed versus expected frequencies. The mismatch between observed and expected for any one category is just the observed frequency minus the expected frequency. For example, consider again the Black and colleagues (2009) study. For male characters, the observed frequency of 996 is 303 more than the expected frequency of 693. For female characters, the difference is -303 (that is, $390 - 693 = -303$). These differences are shown in the Difference column of Table 1.

You do not use these differences directly. One reason is that some differences are positive and some are negative. Thus, they would cancel each other out. To get around this, you square each difference. In our example, the squared difference for male characters is 303 squared, or 91,809. For female characters it is -303 squared, which is also 91,809. These squared differences are shown in the Difference Squared column of Table 1.

However, we need to consider that a particular numerical amount of difference between observed and expected has a different importance according to the size of the expected frequency. For example, a difference of 8 people between observed and expected is a much bigger mismatch if the expected frequency is 10 than if the expected frequency is 1,000. If the expected frequency is 10, a difference of 8 would

chi-square test for goodness of fit hypothesis-testing procedure that examines how well an observed frequency distribution of a nominal variable fits some expected pattern of frequencies.

chi-square test for independence hypothesis-testing procedure that examines whether the distribution of frequencies over the categories of one nominal variable is unrelated to the distribution of frequencies over the categories of a second nominal variable.

observed frequency in a chi-square test, number of individuals actually found in the study to be in a category or cell.

expected frequency in a chi-square test, number of people in a category or cell expected if the null hypothesis were true.

TIP FOR SUCCESS

Note that in situations when you have more than two categories, the squared differences will usually not be the same for all of the categories.

mean that the observed frequency was 18 or 2, frequencies that are dramatically different from 10. But if the expected frequency is 1,000, a difference of 8 is only a slight mismatch. This would mean that the observed frequency was 1,008 or 992, frequencies that are only slightly different from 1,000.

How can you adjust the mismatch (the squared difference) between observed and expected for a particular category? What you need to do is adjust, or weight, the mismatch to take into account the expected frequency for that category. You can do this by dividing your squared difference for a category by the expected frequency for that category. Thus, if the expected frequency for a particular category is 10, you divide the squared difference by 10. If the expected frequency for the category is 1,000, you divide the squared difference by 1,000. In this way, you weight each squared difference by the expected frequency. This weighting puts the squared difference onto a more appropriate scale of comparison.

Let's return to our example. For male characters, you would weight the mismatch by dividing the squared difference of 91,809 by 693, giving 132.48. For female characters, dividing 91,809 by 693 again results in 132.48. These adjusted mismatches (squared differences weighted by expected frequencies) are shown in the right-most column of Table 1.

What remains is to get an overall number for the mismatch between observed and expected frequencies. This final step is done by adding up the mismatch for all the categories. That is, you take the result of the squared difference divided by the expected frequency for the first category, add the result of the squared difference divided by the expected frequency for the second category, and so on. In the Black et al. (2009) example, there are only two categories, so this would be 132.48 plus 132.48, for a total of 264.96. This final number (the sum of the weighted squared differences) is an overall indication of the amount of mismatch between the expected and observed. It is called the **chi-square statistic**. (Remember, the chi-square statistic is basically a fancy way of measuring the mismatch between what you observe and what would be expected.) In terms of a formula,

> Chi-square is the sum, over all the categories, of the squared difference between observed and expected frequencies, divided by the expected frequency.

$$\chi^2 = \sum \frac{(O - E)^2}{E} \tag{1}$$

In this formula, χ^2 is the chi-square statistic. Σ is the summation sign, telling you to sum over all the different categories. O is the observed frequency for a category (the number of people or observations actually found in that category in the study). E is the expected frequency for a category. (In the Black et al. [2009] example, it is based on what we would expect if there were equal numbers in each category.)

Applying the formula to the Black et al. (2009) example,

$$\chi^2 = \sum \frac{(O - E)^2}{E} = \frac{(996 - 693)^2}{693} + \frac{(390 - 693)^2}{693} = 264.96$$

Steps for Figuring the Chi-Square Statistic

Here is a summary of what we've said so far in terms of steps:

❶ Determine the actual, observed frequencies in each category.
❷ Determine the expected frequencies in each category.
❸ In each category, take observed minus expected frequencies.
❹ Square each of these differences.
❺ Divide each squared difference by the expected frequency for its category.
❻ Add up the results of Step ❺ for all the categories.

chi-square statistic (χ^2)   statistic that reflects the overall lack of fit between the expected and observed frequencies; sum, over all the categories or cells, of the squared difference between observed and expected frequencies divided by the expected frequency.

Figure 1   Examples of chi-square distributions for different degrees of freedom.

The Chi-Square Distribution

Now we turn to the question of whether the chi-square statistic you have figured is a bigger mismatch than you would expect by chance. To answer that, you need to know how likely it is to get chi-square statistics of various sizes by chance. As long as you have a reasonable number of people in the study, the distribution of the chi-square statistic that would arise by chance follows quite closely a known mathematical distribution—the **chi-square distribution**.

The exact shape of the chi-square distribution depends on the degrees of freedom. For a chi-square test, the degrees of freedom are the number of categories that are free to vary, given the totals. In the example of the gender of characters on cereal boxes, there are two categories (male and female). If you know the total number of cereal boxes and you know the number in any one category, you could figure out the number in the second category—so only one category is free to vary. That is, in a study like this one (which uses a chi-square test for goodness of fit), if there are two categories, there is one degree of freedom. In terms of a formula,

$$df = N_{\text{Categories}} - 1 \qquad (2) \quad \longleftarrow$$

Chi-square distributions for several different degrees of freedom are shown in Figure 1. Notice that the distributions are all skewed to the right. This is because the chi-square statistic cannot be less than 0 but can have very high values. (Chi-square must be positive because it is figured by adding a group of fractions in each of which the numerator and denominator both have to be positive. The numerator has to be positive because it is squared. The denominator has to be positive because the number of people expected in a given category can't be a negative number; you can't expect less than no one! So if you figure a chi-square and it comes out to be a negative value, you've made an arithmetic mistake somewhere.)

The Chi-Square Table

What matters most about the chi-square distribution for hypothesis testing is the cutoff for a chi-square to be extreme enough to reject the null hypothesis. A **chi-square table** gives the cutoff chi-squares for different significance levels and various degrees of freedom. Table 2 shows a portion of a chi-square table like the one in the Appendix (Table A1). For our example, where there is one degree of freedom, the table shows that the cutoff chi-square for the .05 level is 3.841.

Table 2   Portion of a Chi-Square Table (with Cutoff Value Highlighted for the Black et al. Example)

	Significance Level		
df	.10	.05	.01
1	2.706	3.841	6.635
2	4.605	5.992	9.211
3	6.252	7.815	11.345
4	7.780	9.488	13.277
5	9.237	11.071	15.087

Note: Full table is Table A1 in the Appendix.

The degrees of freedom for the chi-square test for goodness of fit are the number of categories minus 1.

chi-square distribution
mathematically defined curve used as the comparison distribution in chi-square tests; distribution of the chi-square statistic.

chi-square table   table of cutoff scores on the chi-square distribution for various degrees of freedom and significance levels.

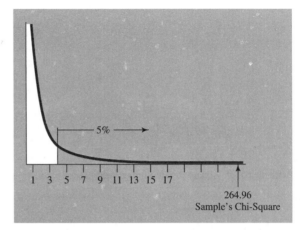

Figure 2   For the Black et al. (2009) example, the chi-square distribution ($df = 1$) showing the cutoff for rejecting the null hypothesis at the .05 level and the sample's chi-square (note that the sample's chi-square would, in reality, be located even further to the right).

(Of course, as with other hypothesis testing procedures, when you carry out a chi-square using a statistics program like SPSS, you will be given an exact probability level, which you then check to see if it is less than the cutoff you set for the study, such as .05 or .01.)

In the Black et al. (2009) example, we figured a chi-square of 264.96. This is clearly larger than the chi-square cutoff for this example (using the .05 significance level) of 3.841 (see Figure 2). Thus, the researchers rejected the null hypothesis. That is, they rejected as too unlikely that the mismatch they observed (between the observed and expected frequencies) could have come about if the entire population of characters on cereal boxes had an equal number of male and female characters. It seemed more reasonable to conclude that there truly were different proportions of male and female characters on cereal boxes.

Steps of Hypothesis Testing

Let us review the chi-square test for goodness of fit using the same example, but this time systematically following the standard steps of hypothesis testing. In the process we also consider some fine points.

❶ **Restate the question as a research hypothesis and a null hypothesis about the populations.** There are two populations:

Population 1: Characters on cereal boxes like those in the study.
Population 2: Characters on cereal boxes who are equally likely to be male and female.

The research hypothesis is that the distribution of observations over categories in the two populations is different; the null hypothesis is that they are the same.

❷ **Determine the characteristics of the comparison distribution.** The comparison distribution here is a chi-square distribution with 1 degree of freedom. (Once you know the total, and the number in one category, there is only one category number still free to vary.)

❸ **Determine the cutoff on the comparison distribution at which the null hypothesis should be rejected.** You do this by looking up the cutoff on the chi-square table for your significance level and the study's degrees of freedom. In the present example, we used the .05 significance level, and we determined in Step ❷ that there was 1 degree of freedom. Based on the chi-square table, this gives a cutoff chi-square of 3.841.

❹ **Determine your sample's score on the comparison distribution.** Your sample's score is the chi-square figured from the sample. In other words, this is where you do all the figuring.

  Ⓐ **Determine the actual, observed frequencies in each category.** These are shown in the first column of Table 1.

  Ⓑ **Determine the expected frequencies in each category.** We figured these each to be 693 based on a null hypothesis of expecting an equal distribution of the 1,386 characters.

  Ⓒ **In each category, take observed minus expected frequencies.** These are shown in the third column of Table 1.

  Ⓓ **Square each of these differences.** These are shown in the fourth column of Table 1.

  Ⓔ **Divide each squared difference by the expected frequency for its category.** These are shown in the fifth column of Table 1.

  Ⓕ **Add up the results of Step Ⓔ for all the categories.** The result we figured earlier (264.96) is the chi-square statistic for the sample. It is shown in Figure 2.

❺ **Decide whether to reject the null hypothesis.** The chi-square cutoff to reject the null hypothesis (from Step ❸) is 3.841 and the chi-square of the sample (from Step ❹) is 264.96. Thus, you can reject the null hypothesis. The research hypothesis that the two populations are different is supported. That is, consistent with their hypothesis, Black et al. (2009) could conclude that the characters on cereal boxes are more likely to be male than female. Now take a look at the cereal boxes you have at home and see if there are more male than female characters on the boxes. Be sure to look at all of the characters on both the front and back of the box!

Another Example

A fictional research team of clinical psychologists want to test a theory that mental health is affected by the level of a certain mineral in the diet, called "mineral Q." The research team has located a region of the United States where mineral Q is found in very high concentrations in the soil. As a result, it is in the water people drink and in locally grown food. The researchers carry out a survey of older people who have lived in this area their whole life, focusing on mental health disorders. Of the 1,000 people surveyed, 138 had at some point in their life experienced an anxiety disorder, 99 had suffered from alcohol or drug abuse, 123 from a mood disorder (such as major chronic depression), and 111 from an impulse-control disorder (such as attention deficit hyperactivity disorder); 529 had never experienced any of these problems. (In this example, we ignore the problem of what happens when a person had more than one of these problems.)

The psychologists then compared their results to what would be expected based on large surveys of the U.S. public in general. In these surveys, 14.6% of adults at some point in their lives suffer from an anxiety disorder, 8.0% from alcohol or drug abuse, 11.0% from a mood disorder, and 12.8% from an impulse-control disorder; 53.6% do not experience any of these conditions (based on Kessler et al., 2005). If their sample of 1,000 is not different from the general U.S. population, 14.6% of them (146) should have had anxiety disorders, 8.0% of them (80) should have suffered from alcohol or drug abuse, and so forth. The question the clinical

Table 3   Observed and Expected Frequencies and the Chi-Square Goodness of Fit Test for Types of Mental Health Disorders in a U.S. Region High in Mineral Q Compared to the General U.S. Population (Fictional Data)

Condition	Observed Ⓐ	Expected Ⓑ
Anxiety disorder	138	146 (14.6% × 1,000)
Alcohol or drug abuse	99	80 (8.0% × 1,000)
Mood disorder	123	110 (11.0% × 1,000)
Impulse-control disorder	111	128 (12.8% × 1,000)
None of these conditions	529	536 (53.6% × 1,000)

Degrees of freedom $= N_{Categories} - 1 = 5 - 1 = 4$ Ⓑ

Chi-square needed, $df = 4$, .05 level: 9.488 Ⓒ

$$\chi^2 = \sum \frac{(O - E)^2}{E} = \frac{(138 - 146)^2}{146} + \frac{(99 - 80)^2}{80} + \frac{(123 - 110)^2}{110} + \frac{(111 - 128)^2}{128} + \frac{(529 - 536)^2}{536} \;Ⓒ$$

$$= \frac{-8^2}{146} + \frac{19^2}{80} + \frac{13^2}{110} + \frac{-17^2}{128} + \frac{-7^2}{536} \;Ⓓ$$

$$= 0.44 + 4.51 + 1.54 + 2.26 + 0.09 \;Ⓔ$$

$$= 8.84 \;Ⓕ$$

Decision: Do not reject the null hypothesis. Ⓖ

Figure 3   For the mineral Q example, the chi-square distribution $(df = 4)$ showing the cutoff for rejecting the null hypothesis at the .05 level and the sample's chi-square.

psychologists posed is, "On the basis of the sample we have studied, can we conclude that the rates of various mental health problems among people in this region are different from those of the general U.S. population?"

Table 3 shows the observed and expected frequencies and the figuring for the chi-square test.

❶ **Restate the question as a research hypothesis and a null hypothesis about the populations.** There are two populations:

Population 1: People in the U.S. region with a high level of mineral Q.
Population 2: People in the U.S. population in general.

The research hypothesis is that the distribution of numbers of people over the five mental health categories is different in the two populations; the null hypothesis is that it is the same.

❷ **Determine the characteristics of the comparison distribution.** The comparison distribution is a chi-square distribution with 4 degrees of freedom (that is, $df = N_{Categories} - 1 = 5 - 1 = 4$). See Figure 3.

❸ **Determine the cutoff sample score on the comparison distribution at which the null hypothesis should be rejected.** We will use the standard 5% significance level and we have just seen that there are 4 degrees of freedom. Thus, Table 2 (or Table A1 in the Appendix) shows that the clinical psychologists need a chi-square of at least 9.488 to reject the null hypothesis. This is shown in Figure 3.

❹ **Determine your sample's score on the comparison distribution.** The chi-square figuring is shown in Table 3.

❹Ⓐ **Determine the actual, observed frequencies in each category.** These are shown in the first column of Table 3.

❹Ⓑ **Determine the expected frequencies in each category.** These are figured by multiplying the expected percentage by the total number. For example, with 14.6% expected to have anxiety disorders, the actual expected number to have anxiety disorders is 146 (that is, 14.6% of 1000). All of the expected frequencies are shown in Table 3.

- **❺ In each category, take observed minus expected frequencies.** The result of these subtractions are shown in the numerators of the second formula line on Table 3.
- **❻ Square each of these differences.** The results of these squarings are shown in the numerators of the third formula line on Table 3.
- **❼ Divide each squared difference by the expected frequency for its category.** The result of these divisions are shown in the fourth formula line on Table 3.
- **❽ Add up the results of Step ❼ for all the categories.** The sum comes out to 8.84. The addition is shown on Table 3; the location on the chi-square distribution is shown in Figure 3.

❹ **Decide whether to reject the null hypothesis.** The sample's chi-square (from Step ❸) of 8.84 is less extreme than the cutoff (from Step ❹) of 9.488. The researchers cannot reject the null hypothesis; the study is inconclusive. (Having failed to reject the null hypothesis with such a large sample, it is reasonable to suppose that, if there is any difference between the populations, it is quite small.)

How are you doing?

1. In what situation do you use a chi-square test for goodness of fit?
2. List the steps for figuring the chi-square statistic, and explain the logic behind each step.
3. Write the formula for the chi-square statistic and define each of the symbols.
4. (a) What is a chi-square distribution? (b) What is its shape? (c) Why does it have that shape?
5. (a) Use the steps of hypothesis testing to carry out a chi-square test for goodness of fit (using the .05 significance level) for a sample in which one category has 15 people, the other category has 35 people, and the first category is expected to have 60% of people and the second category is expected to have 40% of people. (b) Sketch the distribution involved.

Answers

1. You use a chi-square test for goodness of fit when you want to test whether a sample's distribution of people across categories represents a population that is significantly different from a population with a particular expected distribution of people across categories.
2. ❶ **Determine the actual, observed frequencies in each category.** This is the key information for the sample studied.
   ❷ **Determine the expected frequencies in each category.** Having these numbers makes it possible to make a direct comparison of what is expected to the observed frequencies.
   ❸ **In each category, take observed minus expected frequencies.** This is the direct comparison of the distribution for the sample versus the distribution representing the expected population.
   ❹ **Square each of these differences.** This gets rid of the direction of the difference (since the interest is only in how much difference there is).

ⓓ Divide each squared difference by the expected frequency for its category. This adjusts the degree of difference for the absolute size of the expected frequencies.

ⓔ Add up the results of Step ⓓ for all the categories. This gives you a statistic for the overall degree of discrepancy.

3. Formula for the chi-square statistic: $\chi^2 = \Sigma \dfrac{(O - E)^2}{E}$.

   χ^2 is the chi-square statistic; Σ tells you to sum over all the different categories; O is the observed frequency for a category; E is the expected frequency for a category.

4. (a) A chi-square distribution: for any particular number of categories, the distribution you would expect if you figured a very large number of chi-square statistics for samples from a population in which the distribution of people over categories is the expected distribution.

   (b) A chi-square distribution is skewed to the right.

   (c) It has this shape because a chi-square statistic can't be less than 0 (since the numerator, a squared score, has to be positive, and its denominator, an expected number of individuals, also has to be positive), but there is no limit to how large it can be.

5. (a) **❶ Restate the question as a research hypothesis and a null hypothesis about the populations.** There are two populations:

   Population 1: People like those in the sample.
   Population 2: People in general who have a distribution of 60% in the first category and 40% in the second category.

   The research hypothesis is that the distribution of numbers of people over categories in the population is not 60% in the first category and 40% in the second category; the null hypothesis is that the distribution is 60% in the first category and 40% in the second category.

   ❷ Determine the characteristics of the comparison distribution. The comparison distribution is a chi-square distribution with 1 degree of freedom (that is, $df = N_{\text{Categories}} - 1 = 2 - 1 = 1$).

   ❸ Determine the cutoff sample score on the comparison distribution at which the null hypothesis should be rejected. At the .05 level with $df = 1$, cutoff is 3.841.

   ❹ Determine your sample's score on the comparison distribution.

   ⓐ Determine the actual, observed frequencies in each category. As given in the problem, these are 15 and 35.

   ⓑ Determine the expected frequencies in each category. With 50 people total and expecting a 60% to 40% breakdown, the expected frequencies are 30 and 20.

   ⓒ In each category, take observed minus expected frequencies. These come out to −15 (that is, $15 - 30 = -15$) and 15 (that is, $35 - 20 = 15$).

   ⓓ Square each of these differences. Both come out to 225 (that is, $-15^2 = 225$ and $15^2 = 225$).

   ⓔ Divide each squared difference by the expected frequency for its category. For the first category, this comes out to 7.5 (that is, $225/30 = 7.5$). For the second category, this comes out to 11.25 (that is, $225/20 = 11.25$).

❹ Add up the results of Step ❸ for all the categories. 7.5 +
11.25 = 18.75.

❺ Decide whether to reject the null hypothesis. The sample's chi-
square of 18.75 is more extreme than the cutoff of 3.841. Reject the
null hypothesis; people like those in the sample are different from the
expected 60% to 40% breakdown.

(b) See Figure 4.

Figure 4   For "How are
you doing?" question 5, the
chi-square distribution ($df = 1$)
showing the cutoff for rejecting the
null hypothesis at the .05 level and
the sample's chi-square.

The Chi-Square Test for Independence

So far, we have looked at the distribution of *one nominal variable* with several categories, such as the gender breakdown of characters on cereal boxes. In fact, this kind of
situation is fairly rare in research. We began with an example of this kind mainly as
a stepping-stone to a more common actual research situation, to which we now turn.

The most common use of chi-square is one in which there are *two nominal
variables*, each with several categories. Hypothesis testing in this kind of situation is called a *chi-square test for independence*. (You will learn shortly why it has
this name.) For example, in addition to being interested in the gender breakdown
of characters on cereal boxes, Black et al. (2009) were also interested in the age
distribution of the characters (in terms of whether they were children or adults). In
this case, we have two nominal variables. The gender of the characters (that is, male
versus female) is the first nominal variable. The age of the characters (that is, child
versus adult) is the second nominal variable. Based on previous research, Black et
al. hypothesized that male characters would be more likely to be displayed as adults
than female characters. Table 4 shows the results. Notice the two nominal variables:
gender (with two levels) and *age* (with two levels). For this part of their study, the
researchers focused on 222 characters for which the student research assistants carried out detailed coding of both gender and age.

Contingency Tables

Table 4 is a **contingency table**, a table in which the distributions of two nominal
variables are set up so that you have the frequencies of their combinations as well as
the totals. Thus, in Table 4, the 125 in the Male/Adult combination is how many of
the male characters were adults.

contingency table   two-dimensional
chart showing frequencies in each
combination of categories of two
nominal variables.

Chi-Square Tests

Table 4 Contingency Table of Observed Frequencies of Gender and Age of Characters on Cereal Boxes (Data from Black et al., 2009)

		Gender		
		Male	Female	Total
Age	Child	28	30	58 (26.1%)
	Adult	125	39	164 (73.9%)
	Total	153	69	222 (100%)

Table 4 is a 2×2 contingency table because it has two levels of one variable crossed with two levels of the other. It is also possible to have larger contingency tables, such as a 4×7 or a 6×18 table. Smaller tables, such as 2×2 and 3×2 contingency tables, are especially common.

Independence

The question in this example is whether there is any relation between the gender of the characters and whether they are children or adults. If there is no relation, the *proportion* of child and adult characters is the same among male characters and female characters. Or to put it the other way, if there is no relation, the *proportion* of male and female characters is the same for child and adult characters. However you describe it, the situation of no relation between the variables in a contingency table is called **independence**.[1]

Sample and Population

In the survey results in the example, the proportions of child and adult characters vary for male and female characters. For male characters, 18.3% are child characters and 81.7% are adult characters. However, among female characters, 43.5% are child characters and 56.5% are adult characters. Thus, as hypothesized by the researchers, more of the male characters are adults than are the female characters. Still, the sample is only of 222 characters. Thus, it is possible that in the larger population of cereal boxes, the age of characters is independent of the characters' being male or female. The big question is whether the lack of independence in the sample is large enough to reject the null hypothesis of independence in the population. That is, you need to do a chi-square test.

Determining Expected Frequencies

One thing that is new in a chi-square test for independence is that you now have to figure differences between observed and expected for each *combination* of categories—that is, for each **cell** of the contingency table. (When there was only one nominal variable, you figured these differences just for each category of that single nominal variable.) Table 5 is the contingency table for the example of characters on cereal boxes with the expected frequency shown (in parentheses) for each cell.

The key idea to keep in mind when figuring expected frequencies in a contingency table is that "expected" is based on the two variables being independent. If they are independent, then the proportions up and down the cells of each column should be the same. In the example, overall, there are 26.1% child characters and 73.9% adult characters; thus, if a character's gender is independent of being a child

independence situation of no relationship between two variables; term usually used regarding two nominal variables in a chi-square test for independence.

cell in chi-square, the particular combination of categories for two variables in a contingency table.

Table 5 Contingency Table of Observed (and Expected) Frequencies of Gender and Age of Characters on Cereal Boxes (Data from Black et al., 2009)

		Gender		
		Male	**Female**	**Total**
Age	Child	28 (39.9)[a]	30 (18.0)	58 (26.1%)
	Adult	125 (113.1)	39 (51.0)	164 (73.9%)
	Total	153	69	222 (100%)

[a] Expected frequencies are in parentheses.

TIP FOR SUCCESS
Always ensure that you have the same number of expected frequencies as observed frequencies. For example, with a 2 × 2 contingency table, there will be four observed frequencies and four corresponding expected frequencies. In Table 5, we have put in the expected frequency (in parentheses) next to each observed frequency.

or adult character, this 26.1–73.9% split should hold for each column (male and female). First, the 26.1–73.9% overall split should hold for the male characters. This would make an expected frequency in the male cell for child characters of 26.1% of 153 (the total number of male characters), which comes out to 39.9. (Don't worry that 39.9 isn't a whole number; even though you can't have 0.9 of a character, it makes sense because it's an expected, or theoretical, value.) The expected frequency for the male characters that are adults is 113.1 (that is, 73.9% of 153 is 113.1). The same principle holds for the column of female characters: The 69 female characters should have a 26.1–73.9% split, giving an expected frequency of 18.0 child characters (that is, 26.1% of 69 is 18.0) and 51.0 adult characters (that is, 73.9% of 69 is 51.0).

Summarizing what we have said in terms of steps,

❶ **Find each row's percentage of the total.**
❷ **For each cell, multiply its row's percentage by its column's total.**

Applying these steps to the top left cell (child characters who are male),

❶ **Find each row's percentage of the total.** The 58 characters in the child row is 26.1% of the overall total of 222 (that is, $58/222 = .261$, which is 26.1%).
❷ **For each cell, multiply its row's percentage by its column's total.** The column total for the male characters is 153; 26.1% of 153 comes out to 39.9 (that is, $.261 \times 153 = 39.9$).

These steps can also be stated as a formula,

$$E = \left(\frac{R}{N}\right)(C) \tag{3}$$

TIP FOR SUCCESS
Be sure to check that you are selecting the correct row percentage and column total for each cell. Selecting the wrong value is a common mistake when figuring chi-square.

A cell's expected frequency is the number in its row divided by the total, multiplied by the number in its column.

In this formula, E is the expected frequency for a particular cell. R is the number of people observed in this cell's row, and N is the number of people total (thus, R divided by N is the proportion of the total number of people that are in that row). C is the number of people observed in this cell's column. (Thus, for any given column, taking the result of R divided by N—the proportion in that row—and multiplying by C, the number in that column, gives you the number you would expect for that row to be in that column.)

Applying the formula to the same top left cell,

$$E = \left(\frac{R}{N}\right)(C) = \left(\frac{58}{222}\right)(153) = (.261)(153) = 39.9$$

Looking at the entire Table 5, notice that in each column (as well as overall) the expected frequencies add up to the same totals as the observed frequencies.

TIP FOR SUCCESS
As a check on your arithmetic, it is a good idea to make sure that the expected and observed frequencies add up to the same row and column totals.

(This is as it should be because the expected frequencies are just a different way of dividing up the column total.) For example, in the first column (male characters), the expected frequencies of 39.9 and 113.1 add up to 153, just as the observed frequencies in that column of 28 and 125 do. Similarly, in the top row (child characters), the expected frequencies of 39.9 and 18 add up to 57.9, the same total (allowing for rounding error) as for the observed frequencies of 28 and 30. And the total of the four observed frequencies (28 + 30 + 125 + 39 = 222) is the same as the total of the four expected frequencies (39.9 + 18.0 + 113.1 + 51.0 = 222).

Figuring Chi-Square

You figure chi-square the same way as in the chi-square test for goodness of fit, except that you now figure the weighted squared difference for each *cell* and add these up. Here is how it works for our example:

$$\chi^2 = \Sigma \frac{(O - E)^2}{E} = \frac{(28 - 39.9)^2}{39.9} + \frac{(30 - 18)^2}{18}$$
$$+ \frac{(125 - 113.1)^2}{113.1} + \frac{(39 - 51)^2}{51}$$
$$= 3.55 + 8 + 1.25 + 2.82 = 15.62.$$

Degrees of Freedom

A contingency table with many cells may have relatively few degrees of freedom. In our example, there are 4 cells but only 1 degree of freedom. (Recall that the degrees of freedom are the number of categories free to vary once the totals are known.) With a chi-square test for independence, the number of categories is the number of cells; the totals include the row and column totals—and if you know the row and column totals, you have a lot of information.

Consider our example of the gender and age of characters on cereal boxes. Suppose you know the first cell frequency across the top, for example, and all the row and column totals. You could then figure all the other cell frequencies just by subtraction. Table 6 shows the contingency table for this example with just the row and column totals and this one cell frequency. Let's start with the Child/Female cell. There is a total of 58 child characters, and the other child cell (the Child/Male cell) has 28 in it. Thus, only 30 remain for the Child/Female cell. Now consider the two adult character cells. You know the frequencies for all child character cells and the column totals for male and female characters. Thus, each cell frequency for the adult characters is its column's total minus the child characters in that column. For

Table 6 Contingency Table Showing Marginal and One Cell's Observed Frequencies to Illustrate Figuring Degrees of Freedom (Data from Black et al., 2009)

		Gender		
		Male	Female	Total
Age	Child	28	—	58 (26.1%)
	Adult	—	—	164 (73.9%)
	Total	153	69	222 (100%)

example, there are 153 male characters, and 28 of those are child characters. Thus, the remaining 125 must be adult characters.

What you can see in all this is that with knowledge of only one of the cells, you could figure out the frequencies in each of the other cells. Thus, although there are four cells, there is only 1 degree of freedom—only one cell whose frequency is really free to vary once we have all the row and column totals. However, rather than having to think all this out each time, there is a shortcut. In a chi-square test for independence, the degrees of freedom are the number of columns minus 1 multiplied by the number of rows minus 1. Put as a formula,

$$df = (N_{Columns} - 1)(N_{Rows} - 1) \qquad \textbf{(4)} \leftarrow$$

> The degrees of freedom for the chi-square test for independence are the number of columns minus 1 multiplied by the number of rows minus 1.

$N_{Columns}$ is the number of columns and N_{Rows} is the number of rows.

Using this formula for our example,

$$df = (N_{Columns} - 1)(N_{Rows} - 1) = (2 - 1)(2 - 1) = (1)(1) = 1.$$

Hypothesis Testing

With 1 degree of freedom, Table 2 (or Table A1) shows that the chi-square you need for significance at the .05 level is 3.841. The chi-square of 15.62 for our example is larger than this cutoff. Thus, you can reject the null hypothesis that the two variables are independent in the population.

Steps of Hypothesis Testing

Now let's go through the example again, this time following the steps of hypothesis testing.

❶ **Restate the question as a research hypothesis and a null hypothesis about the populations.** There are two populations:

Population 1: Characters on cereal boxes like those in the study.
Population 2: Characters on cereal boxes for which the age distribution of the characters is independent of the gender of the characters.

The null hypothesis is that the two populations are the same—that, in general, the proportion of characters that are children and adults is the same for male characters and female characters. The research hypothesis is that the two populations are different, that for characters on cereal boxes, the proportion of characters that are children and adults is different for male and female characters.

> **TIP FOR SUCCESS**
>
> As in the previous examples in this chapter, Population 2 is a population in which the null hypothesis is true. So if Population 1 and 2 are the same, the null hypothesis is also true of Population 1.

Put another way, the null hypothesis is that the two variables are independent (they are unrelated to each other). The research hypothesis is that they are not independent (that they are related to each other).

❷ **Determine the characteristics of the comparison distribution.** The comparison distribution is a chi-square distribution with 1 degree of freedom (the number of columns minus 1 multiplied by the number of rows minus 1).

❸ **Determine the cutoff sample score on the comparison distribution at which the null hypothesis should be rejected.** You use the same table as for any chi-square test. In the example, setting a .05 significance level with 1 degree of freedom, you need a chi-square of 3.841.

❹ **Determine your sample's score on the comparison distribution.**
  ❹ **Determine the actual, observed frequencies in each cell.** These are the results of the survey, as given in Table 4.

Figure 5 For the Black et al. (2009) example of the age and gender of characters on cereal boxes, the chi-square distribution ($df = 1$) showing the cutoff for rejecting the null hypothesis at the .05 level and the sample's chi-square.

❸ **Determine the expected frequencies in each cell.** These are shown in Table 5. For example, for the bottom right cell (Adult/Female cell):

   ❶ **Find each row's percentage of the total.** The 164 characters in the adult row are 73.9% of the overall total of 222 (that is, $164/222 = 73.9\%$).

   ❷ **For each cell, multiply its row's percentage by its column's total.** The column total for female characters is 69; 73.9% of 69 comes out to 51.0 (that is, $.739 \times 69 = 51.0$).

❹ **In each cell, take observed minus expected frequencies.** For example, for the Adult/Female cell, this comes out to -12 (that is, $39 - 51 = -12$).

❺ **Square each of these differences.** For example, for the Adult/Female cell, this comes out to 144 (that is, $-12^2 = 144$).

❻ **Divide each squared difference by the expected frequency for its cell.** For example, for the Adult/Female cell, this comes out to 2.82 (that is, $144/51 = 2.82$).

❼ **Add up the results of Step ❻ for all the cells.** As we saw, this came out to 15.62.

❺ **Decide whether to reject the null hypothesis.** The chi-square needed to reject the null hypothesis is 3.841 and the chi-square for our sample is 15.62 (see Figure 5). Thus, you can reject the null hypothesis. The research hypothesis that the two variables are not independent in the population is supported. That is, the proportion of characters that are children or adults is different for male and female characters.

A Second Example

Riehl (1994) studied the college experience of students who were the first generation in their family to attend college. These students were compared to other students who were not the first generation in their family to go to college. (All students in the study were from Indiana University.) One of the variables Riehl measured was whether or not students dropped out during their first semester.

Table 7 shows the results along with the expected frequencies (shown in parentheses). Below the contingency table is the figuring for the chi-square test for independence.

❶ **Restate the question as a null hypothesis and a research hypothesis about the populations.** There are two populations:

Population 1: Students like those surveyed.
Population 2: Students whose dropping out or staying in college their first semester is independent of whether or not they are the first generation in their family to go to college.

The null hypothesis is that the two populations are the same—that, in general, whether or not students drop out of college is independent of whether or not they are the first generation in their family to go to college. The research hypothesis is that the populations are not the same. In other words, the research hypothesis is that students like those surveyed are different from the hypothetical population in which dropping out is unrelated to whether or not you are first generation.

❷ **Determine the characteristics of the comparison distribution.** This is a chi-square distribution with 1 degree of freedom.

❸ **Determine the cutoff sample score on the comparison distribution at which the null hypothesis should be rejected.** Using the .01 level and 1 degree of

Table 7 Results and Figuring of the Chi-Square Test for Independence Comparing Whether First-Generation College Students Differ from Others in First Semester Dropouts

	Generation to Go to College		
	First	**Other**	**Total**
	Ⓐ Ⓑ		
Dropped Out	73 (57.7)	89 (103.9)	162 (7.9%)
Did Not Drop Out	657 (672.3)	1,226 (1,211.1)	1,883 (92.1%)
Total	730	1,315	2,045

$df = (N_{Columns} - 1)(N_{Rows} - 1) = (2 - 1)(2 - 1) = (1)(1) = 1.$ ❷

Chi-square needed, $df = 1$, .01 level: 6.635. ❸

$$\chi^2 = \Sigma \frac{(O - E)^2}{E} = \frac{(73 - 57.7)^2}{57.7} + \frac{(89 - 103.9)^2}{103.9} + \frac{(657 - 672.3)^2}{672.3} + \frac{(1,226 - 1,211.1)^2}{1,211.1}$$

Ⓒ $$= \frac{15.3^2}{57.7} + \frac{-14.9^2}{103.9} + \frac{-15.3^2}{672.3} + \frac{14.9^2}{1,211.1}$$

Ⓓ $$= \frac{234.1}{57.7} + \frac{222}{103.9} + \frac{234.1}{672.3} + \frac{222}{1,211.1}$$

Ⓔ $= 4.06 + 2.14 + .35 + .18$

$= 6.73.$ Ⓕ

Decision: Reject the null hypothesis. ❺

Notes: 1. With a 2 × 2 analysis, the differences and squared differences (numerators) are the same for all four cells. In this example, the cells are a little different due to rounding error. 2. Data from Riehl (1994). The exact chi-square (6.73) is slightly different from that reported in the article (7.2), due to rounding error.

freedom. Table A-4 shows that you need a chi-square for significance is 6.635. This is shown in Figure 6.

❹ **Determine your sample's score on the comparison distribution.**

　Ⓐ **Determine the actual, observed frequencies in each cell.** These are the results of the survey, as given in Table 7.

　Ⓑ **Determine the expected frequencies in each cell.** These are shown in parentheses in Table 7.

　For example, for the top left cell ("First Generation/Dropped Out" cell),

　　❶ **Find each row's percentage of the total.** The "Dropped Out" row's 162 is 7.9% of the overall total of 2,045 (that is, 162/2,045 = 7.9%).

　　❷ **For each cell, multiply its row's percentage by its column's total.** The column total for the "First Generation" students is 730; 7.9% of 730 comes out to 57.7 (that is, .079 × 730 = 57.7).

　Ⓒ **In each cell, take observed minus expected frequencies.** These are shown in Table 7. For example, for the "First Generation/Dropped Out" cell, this comes out to 15.3 (that is, 73 − 57.7 = 15.3).

　Ⓓ **Square each of these differences.** These are also shown in Table 7. For example, for the "First Generation/Dropped Out" cell, this comes out to 234.1 (that is, $15.3^2 = 234.1$).

　Ⓔ **Divide each squared difference by the expected frequency for its cell.** Once again, these are shown in Table 7. For example, for the "First Generation/Dropped Out" cell, this comes out to 4.06 (that is, 234.1/57.7 = 4.06).

　Ⓕ **Add up the results of Step Ⓔ for all the cells.** As shown in Table 7, this comes out to 6.73. Its location on the chi-square distribution is shown in Figure 6.

❺ **Decide whether to reject the null hypothesis.** Your chi-square of 6.73 is larger than the cutoff of 6.635. Thus, you can reject the null hypothesis. That

Figure 6 For the example from Riehl (1994), chi-square distribution ($df = 1$) showing the cutoff for rejecting the null hypothesis at the .01 level and the sample's chi-square.

is, judging from a sample of 2,045 Indiana University students, first generation students are somewhat more likely to drop out during their first semester than are other students. (Remember, of course, that there could be many reasons for this result.)

The results of Riehl's (1994) study have been replicated in many other universities. For example, a recent study of this issue among college students across the United States also found that first generation students were more likely to drop out of college than other students (Chen, 2005).

How are you doing?

1. (a) In what situation do you use a chi-square test for independence? (b) How is this different from the situation in which you would use a chi-square test for goodness of fit?
2. (a) List the steps for figuring the expected frequencies in a contingency table. (b) Write the formula for expected frequencies in a contingency table and define each of its symbols.
3. (a) Write the formula for figuring degrees of freedom in a chi-square test for independence and define each of its symbols. (b) Explain the logic behind this formula.
4. Carry out a chi-square test for independence for the following observed scores (using the .10 significance level). (a) Use the steps of hypothesis testing, and (b) sketch the distribution involved.

		Nominal Variable A	
		Category 1	Category 2
	Category 1	10	10
Nominal Variable B	Category 2	50	10
	Category 3	10	10

Answers

1. (a) You use a chi-square test for independence when you know the number of people in each of the various combinations of levels of two nominal variables. (b) The focus is on the independence of *two* nominal variables, whereas in a chi-square test for goodness of fit the focus is on the distribution of people over categories of a *single* nominal variable.
2. (a) ❶ Find each row's percentage of the total.
   ❷ For each cell, multiply its row's percentage by its column's total.
   (b) $E = \left(\dfrac{R}{N}\right)(C)$.

   E is the expected frequency for a particular cell, R is the number of people observed in this cell's row, N is the total number of people, and C is the number of people observed in this cell's column.
3. (a) $df = (N_{\text{Columns}} - 1)(N_{\text{Rows}} - 1)$.
   df are the degrees of freedom, N_{Columns} is the number of columns, and N_{Rows} is the number of rows.

(b) *df* are the number of cell totals free to vary given you know the column and row totals. If you know the totals in all the columns but one (and you know the row totals), you can figure the total in the cells in the remaining column by subtraction. Similarly, if you know the total in all the rows but one (and you know the column totals), you can figure the total in the cells in the remaining row by subtraction.

4. (a) Chi-square test for independence:

❶ **Restate the question as a null hypothesis and a research hypothesis about the populations.** There are two populations:

Population 1: People like those studied.
Population 2: People whose being in a particular category of Nominal Variable A is independent of their being in a particular category of Nominal Variable B.

The null hypothesis is that the two populations are the same; the research hypothesis is that the populations are not the same.

❷ **Determine the characteristics of the comparison distribution.** This is a chi-square distribution with 2 degrees of freedom. That is, $df = (N_{Columns} - 1)(N_{Rows} - 1) = (2 - 1)(3 - 1) = 2$.

❸ **Determine the cutoff sample score on the comparison distribution at which the null hypothesis should be rejected.** From Table A1 (in the Appendix), for the .10 level and 2 degrees of freedom, the needed chi-square is 4.605.

❹ **Determine your sample's score on the comparison distribution.**

  Ⓐ **Determine the actual, observed frequencies in each cell.** These are shown in the contingency table for the problem.

  Ⓑ **Determine the expected frequencies in each cell.**

   ❶ **Find each row's percentage of the total.** For the top row 20/100 = 20%; for the second row, 60/100 = 60%; for the third row, 20/100 = 20%.

   ⓫ **For each cell, multiply its row's percentage by its column's total.** For the top left cell, 20% × 70 = 14; for the top right cell, 20% × 30 = 6; for the middle left cell, 60% × 70 = 42; for the middle right cell, 60% × 30 = 18; for the bottom left cell, 20% × 70 = 14; for the bottom right cell, 20% × 30 = 6.

  Ⓒ **In each cell, take observed minus expected frequencies.** For the six cells, 10 − 14 = −4; 10 − 6 = 4; 50 − 42 = 8; 10 − 18 = −8; 10 − 14 = −4; 10 − 6 = 4.

  Ⓓ **Square each of these differences.** The squared differences are 16, 16, 64, 64, 16, 16.

  Ⓔ **Divide each squared difference by the expected frequency for its cell.** These come out to 16/14 = 1.14; 16/6 = 2.67; 64/42 = 1.52; 64/18 = 3.56; 16/14 = 1.14; 16/6 = 2.67.

  Ⓕ **Add up the results of Step Ⓔ for all the cells.** 1.14 + 2.67 + 1.52 + 3.56 + 1.14 + 2.67 = 12.70.

❺ **Decide whether to reject the null hypothesis.** The sample's chi square of 12.70 is larger than the cutoff of 4.605. Thus, you can reject the null hypothesis: which category people are in on Nominal Variable A is not independent of which category they are in on Nominal Variable B.

(b) See Figure 7.

Figure 7 For "How are you doing?" question 4, chi-square distribution ($df = 2$) showing the cutoff for rejecting the null hypothesis at the .10 level and the sample's chi-square.

Assumptions for Chi-Square Tests

The chi-square tests of goodness of fit and for independence do not require the usual assumptions of normal population variances and such. There is, however, one key assumption: each score must not have any special relation to any other scores. This means that you can't use these chi-square tests if the scores are based on the same people being tested more than once. Consider a study in which 20 people are tested to see if the distribution of their preferred brand of yogurt changed from before to after a recent nutritional campaign. The results of this study could not be tested with the usual chi-square, because the distributions of yogurt choice before and after are from the same people. You may also hear about a rule that, for the results of a chi-square test to be valid, none of the expected frequencies should be less than 5. However, these days most statisticians no longer hold to this idea. We have more to say about this issue in the Controversy section later in this chapter.

Effect Size and Power for Chi-Square Tests for Independence

Effect Size

In chi-square tests for independence, you can use your sample's chi-square to figure a number that shows the degree of association of the two nominal variables.

With a 2 × 2 contingency table, the measure of association is called the **phi coefficient (φ)**.

Here is the formula:

> The phi coefficient (effect size for a chi-square test for independence for a 2 × 2 contingency table) is the square root of the result of dividing the sample's chi-square by the total number of people in the sample.

$$\phi = \sqrt{\frac{\chi^2}{N}} \tag{5}$$

phi coefficient (φ) effect-size measure for a chi-square test for independence with a 2 × 2 contingency table; square root of division of chi-square statistic by N.

The phi coefficient has a minimum of 0 and a maximum of 1, and it can be considered like a correlation coefficient.[2] Cohen's (1988) conventions for the phi coefficient are that .10 is a small effect size, .30 is a medium effect size, and .50 is a large effect size (the same as for an ordinary correlation coefficient).

For example, in the Riehl (1994) study of first generation college students, the sample's chi-square was 6.73 and there were 2,045 people in the study. Thus,

$$\phi = \sqrt{\frac{\chi^2}{N}} = \sqrt{\frac{6.73}{2,045}} = \sqrt{.00329} = .06.$$

This is a very small effect size. The fact that the chi-square of 6.73 was significant in this study tells you that the greater likelihood of first generation students dropping out that you saw in the sample is probably not due to the particular people that were randomly recruited to be in this sample. You can thus have some confidence that there is a pattern of this kind in the population. But the small phi coefficient tells you that this population tendency may not be a very important factor in practice.

You only use phi when you have a 2 × 2 situation. **Cramer's phi** is an extension of the ordinary phi coefficient that you can use for contingency tables larger than 2 × 2 (Cramer's phi is also known as *Cramer's V* and is sometimes written ϕ_C or V_C). You figure Cramer's phi the same way as the ordinary phi coefficient, except that instead of dividing by N, you divide by N times the degrees of freedom of the smaller side of the table. Stated as a formula,

$$\text{Cramer's } \phi = \sqrt{\frac{\chi^2}{(N)(df_{\text{Smaller}})}} \qquad (6) \leftarrow$$

> Cramer's phi coefficient (effect size for a chi-square test for independence) is the square root of the result of dividing the sample's chi-square by the product of the total number of people in the sample multiplied by the degrees of freedom for the smaller side of the table.

In this formula, df_{Smaller} is the degrees of freedom for the smaller side of the contingency table.

For question 4 of the "How are you doing?" section you just completed, the sample's chi-square was 12.70, and the total number of people was 100. There was one degree of freedom for the smaller side of the table (the columns in this example). Cramer's phi is the square root of what you get when you divide 12.70 by 100 multiplied by 1. This comes out to .13. In terms of the formula,

$$\text{Cramer's } \phi = \sqrt{\frac{\chi^2}{(N)(df_{\text{Smaller}})}} = \sqrt{\frac{12.70}{(100)(1)}} = .13.$$

Cohen's conventions for effect size for Cramer's phi depend on the degrees of freedom for the smaller side of the table. Table 8 shows Cohen's (1988) effect size conventions for Cramer's phi for tables in which the smallest side of the table is 2, 3, and 4. Notice that when the smallest side of the table is 2, there is one degree of freedom. Thus, the effect sizes given in the table for this situation are the same as for the ordinary phi coefficient.

Based on the table, for question 4 of the "How are you doing?" section, there is an approximately small effect size (.13), a small amount of relationship between nominal variable A and nominal variable B.

> **Cramer's phi (Cramer's ϕ)** measure of effect size for a chi-square test for independence with a contingency table that is larger than 2 × 2. Also known as *Cramer's V* and sometimes written as ϕ_C or V_C.

Table 8 Cohen's Conventions for Cramer's Phi

Smallest Side of Contingency Table	Effect Size		
	Small	Medium	Large
2 ($df_{\text{Smaller}} = 1$)	.10	.30	.50
3 ($df_{\text{Smaller}} = 2$)	.07	.21	.35
4 ($df_{\text{Smaller}} = 3$)	.06	.17	.29

Total df	Total N	Effect Size		
		Small	Medium	Large
1	25	.08	.32	.70
	50	.11	.56	.94
	100	.17	.85	*
	200	.29	.99	*
2	25	.07	.25	.60
	50	.09	.46	.90
	100	.13	.77	*
	200	.23	.97	*
3	25	.07	.21	.54
	50	.08	.40	.86
	100	.12	.71	.99
	200	.19	.96	*
4	25	.06	.19	.50
	50	.08	.36	.82
	100	.11	.66	.99
	200	.17	.94	*

Table 9 Approximate Power for the Chi-Square Test for Independence for Testing Hypotheses at the .05 Significance Level

*Nearly 1.

Power

Table 9 shows the approximate power at the .05 significance level for small, medium, and large effect sizes and total sample sizes of 25, 50, 100, and 200. Power is given for tables with 1, 2, 3, and 4 degrees of freedom.[3]

Consider the power of a planned 2×4 study ($df = 3$) of 50 people with an expected medium effect size (Cramer's $\phi = .30$). The researchers will use the .05 level. From Table 9 you can find this study would have a power of .40. That is, if the research hypothesis is true, and there is a true medium effect size, there is about a 40% chance that the study will come out significant. Notice from this table two things about power for a chi-square test for independence. First, like all other hypothesis-testing situations, the more participants there are in the study, the more power there will be. Second, the more degrees of freedom there are (the more different categories that are crossed with each other), the less power there is. Thus, for maximum power, you want as many participants as possible with as simple a contingency table (that is, as few categories in each direction) as possible.

Needed Sample Size

Table 10 gives the approximate total number of participants needed for 80% power with small, medium, and large effect sizes at the .05 significance level for chi-square tests for independence of 2, 3, 4, and 5 degrees of freedom.[4] Suppose you are planning a study with a 3×3 ($df = 4$) contingency table. You expect a large effect size and will use the .05 significance level. According to the

| **Table 10** | Approximate Total Number of Participants Needed for 80% Power for the Chi-Square Test for Independence for Testing Hypotheses at the .05 Significance Level | | |

| | Effect Size | | |
Total *df*	Small	Medium	Large
1	785	87	26
2	964	107	39
3	1,090	121	44
4	1,194	133	48

table, you would only need 48 participants. Again, the same principle holds that we emphasized earlier regarding the degrees of freedom when figuring power. In this case, it means that the more degrees of freedom there are (that is, the more categories in each variable being crossed), the more participants you need for the same amount of power.

How are you doing?

1. What are the assumptions for chi-square tests?
2. (a) What is the measure of effect size for a 2×2 chi-square test for independence? (b) Write the formula for this measure of effect size and define each of the symbols. (c) What are Cohen's conventions for small, medium, and large effect sizes? (d) Figure the effect size for a 2×2 chi-square test for independence in which there are a total of 100 participants and the chi-square is 12.
3. (a) What is the measure of effect size for a chi-square test for independence for a contingency table that is larger than 2×2? (b) Write the formula for this measure of effect size and define each of the symbols. (c) What is Cohen's convention for a small effect size for a 4×6 contingency table? (d) Figure the effect size for a 4×6 chi-square test for independence in which there are a total of 200 participants and the chi-square is 20.
4. What is the power of a planned 3×3 chi-square with 50 participants total and a predicted medium effect size?
5. What are two factors that affect the power of a study using a chi-square test for independence?
6. About how many participants do you need for 80% power in a planned 2×2 study in which you predict a medium effect size and will be using the .05 significance level?

Answers

1. The only major assumption for chi-square tests is that the numbers in each cell or category are from separate persons.
2. (a) The measure of effect size for a 2×2 chi-square test for independence is the phi coefficient.

   (b) The formula for the measure of effect size is $\phi = \sqrt{\dfrac{\chi^2}{N}}$.

ϕ is the phi coefficient (effect size for a chi-square test for independence with a 2 × 2 contingency table); χ^2 is the sample's chi-square; and N is the number of participants in the study.

(c) Cohen's conventions: .10 is a small effect size, .30 is a medium effect size, and .50 is a large effect size.

(d) Effect size: $\phi = \sqrt{\dfrac{12}{100}} = .35$.

3. (a) Effect size: Cramer's phi.

(b) Formula: Cramer's $\phi = \sqrt{\dfrac{\chi^2}{(N)(df_{Smaller})}}$

Cramer's ϕ is Cramer's phi coefficient (effect size for a chi-square test for independence); χ^2 is the sample's chi-square; N is the number of participants in the study total; and $df_{Smaller}$ is the degrees of freedom for the smaller side of the contingency table.

(c) Cohen's convention: .06.

(d) Effect size: $\sqrt{20/(200)(3)} = .18$.

4. Power: .36.

5. Two factors that affect the power of a study using a chi-square test for independence: number of participants and degrees of freedom. (Another factor we did not discuss here, but which also affects power for chi-square as it does for any significance test, is the significance level chosen.)

6. Number of participants needed: 87.

Controversy: The Minimum Expected Frequency

Over a half century ago, Lewis and Burke (1949) published a landmark paper on the misuse of chi-square. They listed nine common errors that had appeared in published papers, giving many examples of each. With one exception, their work has held up very well through the years. The errors are still being made, and they are still seen as errors. (If you follow the procedures of this chapter, *you* won't be making them!)

The one exception to this critical picture is the error that Lewis and Burke considered the most common weakness in the use of chi-square: expected frequencies that are too low. Now, it seems that low expected numbers in cells may not be such a big problem after all. Lewis and Burke, like most statistics textbook authors of their time, held that every cell of a contingency table (and every category of a goodness of fit test) should have a reasonable-sized expected frequency. They recommended a minimum of 10, with 5 as the bottom limit. Others recommended figures ranging from 1 to 20. Even Sir Ronald Fisher (1938) previously had his own suggestion, recommending 10 as his minimum. Still others recommended that the minimum should be some proportion of the total or that it depended on whether the expected frequencies were equal or not. (Incidentally, notice that what was being debated were minimum *expected* frequencies, not observed frequencies.)

Since 1949, when Lewis and Burke published their article, there has been some systematic research on just what the effects of low expected frequencies are. (These studies use Monte Carlo methods; for an example of a study focusing on chi-square see Parshall & Kromrey, 1996). And what is the conclusion? As in most areas, the matter is still not completely settled. However, by the early 1980s, a major review of the research on the topic (Delucchi, 1983) and still the definitive word drew two main conclusions:

1. "As a general rule, the chi-square statistic may be properly used in cases where the expected values are much lower than previously considered permissible" (p. 168). Even expected frequencies as low as 1 per cell may be acceptable in terms of Type I error, provided that there are a reasonable number of individuals overall. The most important principle seems to be that there should be at least five times as many individuals as there are cells. For example, a cell with a very low expected frequency would be acceptable in a 2×2 contingency table if there were at least 20 participants in the study overall.[5]

2. However, Delucchi cited one researcher as concluding that, even though using chi-square with small expected frequencies may be acceptable (in the sense of not giving too many Type I errors in the long run), it may still not be a wise approach. This is because the chance of getting a significant result, even if your research hypothesis is true, may be quite slim. That is, with small expected frequencies, power is very low. Thus, you run the risk of Type II errors instead. (There are also more advanced, alternative methods that can be used when sample sizes are very small, which is probably the ideal approach in such cases; for a recent discussion of the issues, see Ruxton & Neuhäuser, 2010).

Chi-Square Tests in Research Articles

In research articles, chi-square tests for goodness of fit usually include the frequencies in each category or cell, as well as the degrees of freedom, number of participants, the sample's chi-square, and significance level. For example, Black et al. (2009) reported their finding for the gender of characters on cereal boxes as follows: "[A] chi-square goodness-of-fit test was conducted on the total number of characters whose gender could be determined ($n = 1,386$). Seventy-two percent ($n = 996$) were male characters and 28% ($n = 390$) were female characters, which represents a significant disparity, $\chi^2 (1) = 264.96, p < .001$" (p. 886).

Here is another example of a chi-square test for goodness of fit. Sandra Moriarty and Shu-Ling Everett (1994) had graduate students go to 55 different homes and observe people watching television for 45-minute sessions. In one part of their results, they compared the number of people they observed who fell into one of four distinct categories:

> Flipping [very rapid channel changing], the category dominated by the most active type of behavior, occurred most frequently in 33% of the sessions ($n = 18$). The grazing category [periods of browsing through channels] dominated 24% of the sessions ($n = 13$), and 22% were found to be in each of the continuous and stretch viewing categories ($n = 12$). These differences were not statistically significant ($\chi^2 = 1.79, df = 3, p > .05$). (p. 349)

Published reports of chi-square tests for independence provide the same basic chi-square information. For example, Durkin and Barber (2002) studied the relationship between playing computer games and positive development (such as being close to one's family, involved in activities, having positive mental health, and low disobedience to parents) among 16-year-old high school students in Michigan. As part of the study, the researchers tested whether male and female students differed in how often they played computer games. Students indicated how often they played computer games with a 7-point scale, from *never* (1) to *daily* (7). Here is how the researchers reported their results:

> The participants were categorized into three groups based on their frequency of play: "None" included participants who did not use computers at all, as well as those who used computers, but never for computer games; "Low" included participants who checked 2, 3, 4, or 5 for frequency of computer use to play computer games; and "High" included participants who checked 6 or 7 for frequency of computer game play. A chi-square test [for independence] indicated that males and females were not evenly distributed across these three categories $[\chi^2(2, N = 1043) = 62.39, p < .001]$. Girls were overrepresented among the nonusers, with a majority never playing computer games (50.6%), compared to 29.4% of boys who never played. Boys were more than twice as likely (23.8%) as girls (9.9%) to be in the high use group. A substantial number of both girls (39.4%) and boys (46.8%) were in the low use group. (p. 381)

You may be interested to read the researchers' conclusions from the overall study: "No evidence was obtained of negative outcomes among game players. On several measures—including . . . [all of the positive development outcomes mentioned earlier]—game players scored more favorably than did peers who never played computer games. It is concluded that computer games can be a positive feature of a healthy adolescence" (Durkin & Barber, 2002, p. 373).

Durkin and Barber (2002) do not give the effect size for their significant result. However, you can figure it out from the chi-square, number of participants, and design of the study (2 × 3 in this example). Using the formula,

$$\phi = \sqrt{\chi^2/[(N)(df_{\text{Smaller}})]} = \sqrt{62.39[(1043)(1)]} = \sqrt{.060} = .24.$$

This suggests that there is something close to a moderate effect size.

Black et al. (2009) reported the result of their chi-square test for independence of the association between the gender and age of characters on cereal boxes as follows: "The . . . hypothesis was that male characters would be more likely than female characters to be displayed as . . . adults. . . . A chi-square [analysis] tested the extent to which gender was associated with . . . age. . . . [F]emale characters were more likely than male characters to be depicted as children. . ., and male characters were more likely than female characters to be depicted as adults $[\chi^2(1) = 15.62, p < .001]$" (p. 886).

Learning Aids

Summary

1. Chi-square tests are used for hypothesis tests with *nominal variables*. A sample's chi-square statistic (χ^2) shows the amount of mismatch between expected and observed frequencies over several categories. It is figured by finding, for each category or combination of categories, the difference between observed frequency and expected frequency, squaring this difference (eliminating positive and negative signs), and dividing by the expected frequency (making the squared differences more proportionate to the numbers involved). The results are then added up for all the categories or combinations of categories. The distribution of the chi-square statistic is known and the cutoffs can be looked up in standard chi-square tables.

2. The chi-square test for goodness of fit is used to test hypotheses about whether a distribution of frequencies over two or more categories of a *single nominal variable* matches an expected distribution. (These expected frequencies are based, for example, on theory or on a distribution in another study or circumstance). In this test, the expected frequencies are given in advance or are based on some expected percentages (such as equal percentages in all groups). The degrees of freedom are the number of categories minus 1.

3. The chi-square test for independence is used to test hypotheses about the relation between *two nominal variables*—that is, about whether the breakdown over the categories of one variable has the same proportional pattern in each of the categories of the other variable. The frequencies are set up in a contingency table in which the two variables are crossed and the numbers in each combination are placed in each of the resulting cells. The frequency expected for a cell if the two variables are independent is the percentage of all the people in that cell's row multiplied by the total number of people in that cell's column. The degrees of freedom for the chi-square test for independence are the number of columns minus 1 multiplied by the number of rows minus 1.

4. Chi-square tests make no assumptions about normal distributions of their variables, but they do require that no individual be counted in more than one category or cell.

5. The estimated effect size for a chi-square test for independence (that is, the degree of association) for a 2×2 contingency table is the phi coefficient; for larger tables, Cramer's phi. Phi is the square root of the result of dividing your sample's chi-square by the number of persons. Cramer's phi is the square root of the result of dividing your sample's chi-square by the product of the number of persons multiplied by the degrees of freedom in the smaller side of the contingency table. These coefficients range from 0 to 1.

6. The minimum acceptable frequency for a category or cell has been a subject of controversy. Currently, the best advice is that even very small expected frequencies do not seriously increase the chance of a Type I error, provided that there are at least five times as many individuals as categories (or cells). However, low expected frequencies seriously reduce power and should be avoided if possible.

7. Chi-square tests are reported in research articles using a standard format. For example, $\chi^2(3, N = 196) = 9.22, p < .05$.

Key Terms

chi-square tests	expected frequency	independence
chi-square test for goodness of fit	chi-square statistic (χ^2)	cell
	chi-square distribution	phi coefficient (ϕ)
chi-square test for independence	chi-square table	Cramer's phi (Cramer's ϕ)
observed frequency	contingency table	

Example Worked-Out Problems

Chi-Square Test for Goodness of Fit

The expected distribution (from previous years) on an exam roughly follows a normal curve in which the highest scoring 2.5% of the students get As; the next highest scoring 14%, Bs; the next 67%, Cs; the next 14%, Ds; and the lowest 2.5%, Fs.

Table 11 Figuring for Chi-Square Test for Goodness of Fit Example Worked-Out Problem

Grade	Observed Ⓐ	Expected Ⓑ
A	10	5 (2.5% × 200)
B	34	28 (14.0% × 200)
C	140	134 (67.0% × 200)
D	10	28 (14.0% × 200)
F	6	5 (2.5% × 200)

Degrees of freedom = $N_{\text{Categories}} - 1 = 5 - 1 = 4$ ❷
Chi-square needed, $df = 4$, .01 level: 13.277 ❸

$$\chi^2 = \Sigma \frac{(O - E)^2}{E} = \frac{(10 - 5)^2}{5} + \frac{(34 - 28)^2}{28} + \frac{(140 - 134)^2}{134} + \frac{(10 - 28)^2}{28} + \frac{(6 - 5)^2}{5}$$

$$= \frac{5^2}{5} + \frac{6^2}{28} + \frac{6^2}{134} + \frac{-18^{2}\,Ⓒ}{28} + \frac{1^2}{5}$$

$$= \frac{25}{5} + \frac{36}{28} + \frac{36\,Ⓓ}{134} + \frac{324}{28} + \frac{1}{5}$$

$$= 5 + 1.29 + .27 + 11.57 + .20 = 18.33.\;Ⓕ$$

Ⓔ

Decision: Reject the null hypothesis. ❺

A class takes a test using a new grading system and 10 get As, 34 get Bs, 140 get Cs, 10 get Ds, and 6 get Fs. Can you conclude that the new system produces a different distribution of grades (using the .01 level)? (a) Use the steps of hypothesis testing, and (b) make a sketch of the distribution involved.

Answers

(a) Table 11 shows the observed and expected frequencies and the figuring for the chi-square test.

❶ **Restate the question as a research hypothesis and a null hypothesis about the populations.** There are two populations:

Population 1: Students like those graded with the new system.
Population 2: Students like those graded with the old system.

The research hypothesis is that the populations are different; the null hypothesis is that the populations are the same.

❷ **Determine the characteristics of the comparison distribution.** The comparison distribution is a chi-square distribution with 4 degrees of freedom ($df = N_{\text{Categories}} - 1 = 5 - 1 = 4$).

❸ **Determine the cutoff sample score on the comparison distribution at which the null hypothesis should be rejected.** Using the .01 level and $df = 4$, Table A1 (in the Appendix) shows a needed chi-square of 13.277.

❹ **Determine your sample's score on the comparison distribution.** As shown in Table 11, this comes out to 18.33.

❺ **Decide whether to reject the null hypothesis.** The sample's chi-square of 18.33 is more extreme than the needed chi-square of 13.277. Thus, you can reject the null hypothesis and conclude that the populations are different; the new grading system produces a different distribution of grades than the previous one.

(b) Figure 8 shows the distribution.

Figure 8 For the chi-square test for goodness of fit Example Worked-Out Problem, chi-square distribution ($df = 4$) showing the cutoff for rejecting the null hypothesis at the .01 level and the sample's chi-square.

Chi-Square Test for Independence

Janice Steil and Jennifer Hay (1997) conducted a survey of professionals (lawyers, doctors, bankers, and the like) regarding the people they compare themselves to when they think about their job situation (salary, benefits, responsibility, status, and so on). One question of special interest was how much professionals compare themselves to people of their own sex, the opposite sex, or both. Here are the results:

	Participant Gender	
	Men	**Women**
Comparison		
Same sex	29	17
Opposite sex	4	14
Both sexes	26	28

Can the researchers conclude that the gender of who people compare themselves to is different depending on their own gender (using the .05 level)? (a) Use the steps of hypothesis testing, and (b) make a sketch of the distribution involved.

Answers

(a) Table 12 shows the figuring for the chi-square test.

❶ **Restate the question as a null hypothesis and a research hypothesis about the populations.** There are two populations:

Population 1: Professionals like those surveyed.
Population 2: Professionals for whom own sex is independent of the sex of those to whom they compare their job situations.

The null hypothesis is that the two populations are the same—that, in general, professional men and women do not differ in the sex of those to whom they compare their job situations. The research hypothesis is that the populations are not the same, that professionals like those surveyed are unlike the hypothetical population in which men and women do not differ in the sex of those to whom they compare their job situations.

❷ **Determine the characteristics of the comparison distribution.** This is a chi-square distribution with 2 degrees of freedom.

❸ **Determine the cutoff sample score on the comparison distribution at which the null hypothesis should be rejected.** Using the .05 level and 2 degrees of freedom, the needed chi-square for significance is 5.992.

Table 12 Figuring for Chi-Square Test for Independence Example Worked-Out Problem

		Participant Gender		
		Men Ⓐ	**Women** Ⓑ	**Total**
Comparison	Same sex	29 (23)	17 (23)	46 (39.0%)
	Opposite sex	4 (9)	14 (9)	18 (15.3%)
	Both sexes	26 (27)	28 (27)	54 (45.8%)
	Total	59	59	118

$df = (N_{Columns} - 1)(N_{Rows} - 1) = (2 - 1)(3 - 1) = (1)(2) = 2.$ ❷

Chi-square needed, $df = 2$, .05 level: 5.992. ❸

$$\chi^2 = \Sigma \frac{(O - E)^2}{E} = \frac{(29 - 23)^2}{23} + \frac{(17 - 23)^2}{23} + \frac{(4 - 9)^2}{9} + \frac{(14 - 9)^2}{9} + \frac{(26 - 27)^2}{27} + \frac{(28 - 27)^2}{27}$$ Ⓒ

$$= \frac{6^2}{23} + \frac{-6^2}{23} + \frac{-5^2}{9} + \frac{5^2}{9} + \frac{-1^2}{27} + \frac{1^2}{27}$$ Ⓓ

$$= \frac{36}{23} + \frac{36}{23} + \frac{25}{9} + \frac{25}{9} + \frac{1}{27} + \frac{1}{27}$$ Ⓔ

$$= 1.57 + 1.57 + 2.78 + 2.78 + .04 + .04 = 8.78.$$ Ⓕ

Decision: Reject the null hypothesis. ❺

Note: Data from Steil and Hay (1997). The chi-square computed here (8.78) is slightly different from that reported in their article (8.76) due to rounding error.

Figure 9 For the chi-square test for independence Example Worked-Out Problem, chi-square distribution ($df = 2$) showing the cutoff for rejecting the null hypothesis at the .05 level and the sample's chi-square. *Source*: Data from Steil & Hay, 1997.

❹ **Determine your sample's score on the comparison distribution.** As shown in Table 12, this comes out to 8.78.

❺ **Decide whether to reject the null hypothesis.** The chi square of 8.78 is larger than the cutoff of 5.992; thus you can reject the null hypothesis: The gender of the people with whom professionals compare their job situations is likely to be different for men and women.

(b) Figure 9 shows the distribution.

Effect Size for a 2 × 2 Chi-Square Test for Independence

Figure the effect size for a study with 85 participants and a chi-square of 14.41.

Answer

$$\phi = \sqrt{\chi^2/N} = \sqrt{14.41/85} = \sqrt{.170} = .41.$$

Effect Size for a Chi-Square Test for Independence with a Contingency Table Greater Than 2 × 2

Figure the effect size for the example shown in Table 12.

Answer

$$\text{Cramer's } \phi = \sqrt{\chi^2/(N)(df_{Smaller})} = \sqrt{8.78/(118)(1)} = \sqrt{.074} = .27.$$

Outline for Writing Essays for a Chi-Square Test for Goodness of Fit

1. Explain that chi-square tests are used for hypothesis testing with nominal variables. The chi-square test for goodness of fit is used to test hypotheses about whether a distribution of frequencies over two or more categories of a single nominal variable matches an expected distribution. Be sure to explain the meaning of the research hypothesis and the null hypothesis in this situation.

2. Describe the core logic of hypothesis testing in this situation. Be sure to mention that the hypothesis testing involves comparing observed frequencies (that is, frequencies found in the actual study) with expected frequencies (that is, frequencies that you would expect based on a particular theory or the results of previous research studies). The size of the discrepancy between the observed and expected frequencies determines whether the null hypothesis can be rejected.

3. Explain that the comparison distribution in this situation is a chi-square distribution. Be sure to mention that the shape of the chi-square distribution depends on the number of degrees of freedom. Describe how to determine the degrees of freedom and the cutoff chi-square value.

4. Describe how to figure the chi-square value for the sample. The key idea is to get a single number that indicates the overall discrepancy between what was found in the study and what would be expected based on some null hypothesis idea (such as the groups all being equal). To get this number you figure, for each group, the difference between the observed frequency and the expected frequency, square it (because otherwise the sign of the differences would cancel each other out when you added them up), and divide the squared difference by the expected frequency (to adjust for the size of the numbers involved). You then add up all of the adjusted squared differences to get an overall number. (This should all be explained using the numbers in the study as an example.)

5. Explain how and why the scores from Steps ❸ and ❹ of the hypothesis-testing process are compared. Explain the meaning of the result of this comparison with regard to the specific research and null hypotheses being tested.

Outline for Writing Essays for a Chi-Square Test for Independence

Follow the preceding general outline for the chi-square test for goodness of fit, noting that the chi-square test for independence is used to test hypotheses about the relation between two nominal variables. Using the actual numbers in your study as examples, be sure also to explain the concept of independence and how and why you figure the expected frequency for each cell (in terms of the cells in each column having the same proportions of the column total as the cell's row total is a proportion of the overall total).

Practice Problems

These problems involve figuring. Most real-life statistics problems are done with special statistical software. Even if you have such software, do these problems by hand to ingrain the method in your mind. To learn how to use a computer to solve

statistics problems like those in this chapter, refer to the Using SPSS section at the end of this chapter.

All data are fictional unless an actual citation is given.

Set I

b

1. Carry out a chi-square test for goodness of fit for each of the following studies (use the .05 level for each):

(a)	Category	Expected	Observed
	A	20%	19
	B	20%	11
	C	40%	10
	D	10%	5
	E	10%	5

(b)	Category	Expected	Observed
	I	30%	100
	II	50%	100
	III	20%	100

(c)	Category	Number in the Past	Observed
	1	100	38
	2	300	124
	3	50	22
	4	50	16

2. Carry out a chi-square test for goodness of fit for each of the following studies (use the .01 level for each). In each situation, the observed numbers are shown; the expected numbers are equal across categories.
   (a) Category A, 10; Category B, 10; Category C, 10; Category D, 10; Category E, 60.
   (b) Category A, 5; Category B, 5; Category C, 5; Category D, 5; Category E, 30.
   (c) Category A, 10; Category B, 10; Category C, 10; Category D, 10; Category E, 160.

3. A director of a small psychotherapy clinic is wondering whether there is any difference in the use of the clinic during different seasons of the year. Last year, there were 28 new clients in the winter, 33 in the spring, 16 in the summer, and 51 in the fall. On the basis of last year's data, should the director conclude that season makes a difference? (Use the .05 level.) (a) Carry out the five steps of hypothesis testing for a chi-square test for goodness of fit. (b) Make a sketch of the distribution involved. (c) Explain your answer to a person who has never taken a course in statistics.

4. Folwell and others (1997) interviewed a group of adults, aged 54 and older, about their relationships with their siblings. One question they asked was whether there had been a change in emotional closeness over the years. They found that 43 of the respondents "perceived changes of emotional closeness in their sibling relationships . . . [and] 14 did not report a change in closeness in their sibling relationships" (p. 846). They also tested whether this difference

was greater than you would expect by chance (which would be a 50-50 split). "A chi-square analysis revealed that respondents perceive changes in closeness in their sibling relationships ($\chi^2 = 14.75$, $df = 1$, $\alpha = .05$)" (p. 846). (a) Figure the chi-square yourself (your results should be the same, within rounding error). (b) Explain this result to a person who has never had a course in statistics.

5. Carry out a chi-square test for independence for each of the following contingency tables (use the .01 level). Also, figure the effect size for each contingency table.

(a)

10	16
16	10

(b)

100	106
106	100

(c)

100	160
160	100

(d)

10	16	10
16	10	10

(e)

10	16	16
16	10	16

(f)

10	16	10
16	10	16

6. A developmental psychologist is interested in whether children of three different ages (5, 8, and 11 years) differ in their liking for a certain kind of music. The psychologist studies 200 children at a local elementary school. The results are shown in the table below. Is there a significant relationship between these two variables? (Use the .05 level.) (a) Carry out the steps of hypothesis testing, (b) make a sketch of the distribution, (c) figure the effect size, and (d) explain your answer to (a) to a person who has never taken a course in statistics.

		Age of Child (Years)		
		5	8	11
Liking for this kind of music	Yes	42	62	26
	No	18	38	14

7. A political psychologist is interested in whether the community a person lives in is related to that person's opinion on an upcoming water conservation ballot initiative. The psychologist surveys 90 people by phone with the following results. Is opinion related to community at the .05 level? (a) Carry out the steps of hypothesis testing, (b) make a sketch of the distribution, (c) figure the effect size, and (d) explain your answer to part (a) to a person who has never taken a course in statistics.

	Community A	Community B	Community C
For	12	6	3
Against	18	3	15
No opinion	12	9	12

8. Figure the effect size for the following studies:

	N	Chi-Square	Design
(a)	100	16	2×2
(b)	100	16	2×5
(c)	100	16	3×3
(d)	100	8	2×2
(e)	200	16	2×2

9. What is the power of the following planned studies using a chi-square test for independence with $p < .05$?

	Predicted Effect Size	Design	N
(a)	Small	2 × 2	25
(b)	Medium	2 × 2	25
(c)	Small	2 × 2	50
(d)	Small	2 × 3	25
(e)	Small	3 × 3	25
(f)	Small	2 × 5	25

10. About how many participants do you need for 80% power in each of the following planned studies using a chi-square test for independence with $p < .05$?

	Predicted Effect Size	Design
(a)	Medium	2 × 2
(b)	Large	2 × 2
(c)	Medium	2 × 5
(d)	Medium	3 × 3
(e)	Large	2 × 3

11. Lydon and his associates (1997) conducted a study that compared long-distance to local dating relationships. The researchers first administered questionnaires to a group of students one month prior to their leaving home to begin their first semester at McGill University (Time 1). Some of these students had dating partners who lived in the McGill area; others had dating partners who lived a long way from McGill. The researchers contacted the participants again late in the fall semester, asking them about the current status of their original dating relationships (Time 2). Here is how they reported their results:

> Of the 69 participants . . . 55 were involved in long-distance relationships, and 14 were in local relationships (dating partner living within 200 km of them). Consistent with our predictions, 12 of the 14 local relationships were still intact at Time 2 (86%), whereas only 28 of the 55 long-distance relationships were still intact (51%), $\chi^2(1, N = 69) = 5.55, p < .02$. (p. 108)

(a) Figure the chi-square yourself (your results should be the same, within rounding error). (b) Figure the effect size. (c) Explain this result to a person who has never had a course in statistics.

12. Wilfley and colleagues (2001), in a study of binge eating disorder, compared 37 women getting treatment in a clinic to a control group of 108 otherwise similar women from the general community. However, before beginning their analysis, they needed to check that the two groups were in fact not different in important ways. For example, they reported the following: "Equivalent proportions of women in the clinic ($N = 32, 87\%$) and the community ($N = 89, 82\%$) samples were obese . . . $\chi^2(1, N = 145) = 0.33, p = .56$" (p. 385).

(a) Figure the chi-square yourself (your results should be the same, within rounding error). (b) Figure the effect size. (c) Explain this result to a person who has never had a course in statistics.

Set II

13. Carry out a chi-square test for goodness of fit for each of the following studies (use the .01 level for each):

(a)	Category	Expected	Observed
	1	2%	5
	2	14%	15
	3	34%	90
	4	34%	120
	5	14%	50
	6	2%	20

(b)	Category	Proportion Expected	Observed
	A	1/3	10
	B	1/6	10
	C	1/2	10

14. Carry out a chi-square test for goodness of fit for each of the following studies (use the .05 level for each). In each situation, the observed numbers are shown; the expected numbers are equal across categories.
    (a) Category I, 20; Category II, 20; Category III, 60.
    (b) Category I, 20; Category II, 20; Category III, 20; Category IV, 60.
    (c) Category I, 20; Category II, 20; Category III, 20; Category IV, 20; Category V, 60.

15. A researcher wants to be sure that the sample in her study is not unrepresentative of the distribution of ethnic groups in her community. Her sample includes 300 whites, 80 African Americans, 100 Latinos, 40 Asians, and 80 others. In her community, according to census records, there are 48% whites, 12% African Americans, 18% Latinos, 9% Asians, and 13% others. Is her sample unrepresentative of the population in her community? (Use the .05 level.) (a) Carry out the steps of hypothesis testing. (b) Make a sketch of the distribution involved. (c) Explain your answer to a person who has never taken a course in statistics. (This problem is a chi-square for a single nominal variable; it is not a chi-square test for independence and does not involve any contingency tables.)

16. Stasser and colleagues (1989) conducted a study involving discussions of three different "candidates," which were described to participants in a way the researchers intended to make the candidates equally attractive. Thus, before analyzing their main results, they wanted to first test whether the three candidates were in fact seen as equally attractive. Of the 531 participants in their study, 197 initially preferred Candidate A; 120, Candidate B, and 214, Candidate C. The researchers described the following analysis:

> The relative frequencies of prediscussion preferences . . . suggested that we were not entirely successful in constructing equally attractive candidates. . . . [T]he hypothesis of equal popularity can be confidently rejected, $\chi^2(2, N = 531) = 28.35, p < .001$. (p. 71)

(a) Figure the chi-square yourself (your results should be the same, within rounding error). (b) Explain this result to a person who has never had a course in statistics.

17. Carry out a chi-square test for independence for each of the following contingency tables (use the .05 level). Also, figure the effect size for each contingency table.

(a)	0	18
	18	0

(b)	0	0	18
	9	9	0

(c)	0	0	9	9
	9	9	0	0

(d)	20	40
	0	40

18. Carry out a chi-square test for independence for each of the following contingency tables (use the .05 level). Also, figure the effect size for each contingency table.

(a)	8	8
	8	16

(b)	8	8
	8	32

(c)	8	8
	8	48

(d)	8	8	8
	8	8	8
	8	8	16

(e)	8	8	8
	8	8	8
	8	8	32

(f)	8	8	8
	8	8	8
	8	8	48

19. The following results are of a survey of a sample of people buying ballet tickets, laid out according to the type of seat they purchased and how regularly they attend. Is there a significant relation? (Use the .05 level.) (a) Carry out the steps of hypothesis testing, (b) make a sketch of the distribution, (c) figure the effect size, and (d) explain your answer to part (a) to a person who has never taken a course in statistics.

Seating Category	Attendance	
	Regular	Occasional
Orchestra	20	80
First balcony	20	20
Second balcony	40	80

20. A comparative psychologist tests rats, chimpanzees, and humans on a particular learning task. The following table shows the numbers of each species that were and were not able to learn the task. Is there a relation between species and ability to learn this task (use the .01 level)? (a) Carry out the steps of hypothesis testing. (b) Make a sketch of the distribution. (c) Explain your answer to a person who has never taken a course in statistics.

		Species		
		Rat	Chimpanzee	Human
Learned Task	Yes	2	4	14
	No	28	16	6

21. Figure the effect size for the following studies:

	N	Chi-Square	Design
(a)	40	10	2 × 2
(b)	400	10	2 × 2
(c)	40	10	4 × 4
(d)	400	10	4 × 4
(e)	40	20	2 × 2

22. What is the power of the following planned studies, using a chi-square test for independence with $p < .05$?

	Predicted Effect Size	Design	N
(a)	Medium	2 × 2	100
(b)	Medium	2 × 3	100
(c)	Large	2 × 2	100
(d)	Medium	2 × 2	200
(e)	Medium	2 × 3	50
(f)	Small	3 × 3	25

23. About how many participants do you need for 80% power in each of the following planned studies, using a chi-square test for independence with $p < .05$?

	Predicted Effect Size	Design
(a)	Small	2 × 2
(b)	Medium	2 × 2
(c)	Large	2 × 2
(d)	Small	3 × 3
(e)	Medium	3 × 3
(f)	Large	3 × 3

24. Everett and colleagues (1997) mailed a survey to a random sample of physicians. Half were offered $1 if they would return the questionnaire (this was the experimental group); the other half served as a control group. The point of the study was to see if even a small incentive would increase the return rate for physician surveys. The researchers report their results as follows:

Of the 300 surveys mailed to the experimental group, 39 were undeliverable, 2 were returned uncompleted, and 164 were returned completed. Thus, the response rate for the experimental group was 63% ($164/[300 - 39] = .63$). Of the 300 surveys mailed to the control group, 40 were undeliverable, and 118 were returned completed. Thus, the response rate for the control group was 45% ($118/[300 - 40] = .45$). A chi-square test comparing the response rates for the experimental and control groups found the $1 incentive had a statistically significantly improved response rate over the control group $[\chi^2(1, N = 521) = 16.0, p < .001]$.

(a) Figure the chi-square yourself (your results should be the same, within rounding error). (b) Figure the effect size. (c) Explain the results to (a) and (b) to a person who has never had a course in statistics.

25. Irving and Berel (2001) compared the effects of four kinds of programs (three actual programs and a control group) designed to make women more skeptical of media portrayals of female body image. After completing each program, the 110 participants were given stamped, addressed postcards that they could mail to a media activism organization ("About Face") if they so chose. Here are some of their results:

> . . . [P]ostcards were sent by approximately twice as many of the participants in the video-only condition (i.e., 36%) than in the internally oriented condition (19% of participants returned postcards) and the externally oriented condition (15% returned postcards). Only 5% of those in the no-intervention control group sent postcards to "About Face." Group differences in the rate of return were significant, $\chi^2(3, N = 110) = 8.79, p < .05$, suggesting that the intervention had a differential impact on intentions to engage in media activism. (p. 109)

(a) Figure the chi-square yourself (your results should be the same, within rounding error). (b) Figure the effect size. (c) Explain the results to a person who has never had a course in statistics.

Using SPSS

The ✐ in the following steps indicates a mouse click. (We used SPSS version 19 for Windows to carry out these analyses. The steps and output may be slightly different for other versions of SPSS.)

It is easier to learn the SPSS steps for chi-square tests using actual numbers. As an example, imagine you are a student in a class of 20 students and want to determine whether the students in the class are split equally among first- and second-year students (the class is not open to students in other year groups). We will use a chi-square test for goodness of fit to answer this question. Each student's year in college is shown in the first column of Figure 10.

TIP FOR SUCCESS

In the examples in this chapter, we typically started with category or cell totals, but in order to use SPSS to carry out chi-square tests, you need to enter the full data for the study into SPSS (for example, see Figure 10).

Chi-Square Test for Goodness of Fit

❶ Enter the scores into SPSS. As shown in Figure 10, the score for each person is listed in a separate row. We labeled the variable "year." (For now, you can ignore the "campus_y1n0" variable.)

❷ ✐ *Analyze.*

❸ ✐ *Nonparametric Tests,* ✐ *Legacy Dialogs,* ✐ *Chi-Square.*

❹ ✐ on the variable called "year" and then ✐ the arrow next to the box labeled "Test Variable List." This tells SPSS that the chi-square test for goodness of fit should be carried out on the scores for the nominal variable called "year." Notice in the "Expected Values" box that the option "All categories equal" is selected by default. This means that SPSS will carry out the chi-square to compare the observed frequency distribution in your sample with an expected frequency distribution based on an equal spread of scores across the categories. If you wish to use a different expected frequency distribution, select the "Values" option and enter the appropriate expected values.

❺ ✐ *OK.* Your SPSS output window should look like Figure 11.

The first table in the SPSS output gives the observed frequencies, the expected frequencies, and the difference between the observed and expected

Figure 10   SPSS data editor window for a fictional study examining the distribution of first- and second-year college students for a particular class and whether the students live on campus.

frequencies (in the "Residual" column). The second table gives the value of chi-square, the degrees of freedom, and the exact significance level. The significance level of .025 (for the chi-square value of 5.00) is less than our .05 cutoff, which means that you can reject the null hypothesis. Thus, you can conclude that the students in the class are not split equally among first- and second-year students.

Chi-Square Test for Independence

Using the same example as for the chi-square test for goodness of fit, let's suppose you are interested in whether the distribution of first- and second-year students in the class is different for students who live on campus versus those who do not live on campus. To answer this question (which involves *two nominal variables*), we will use a chi-square test for independence.

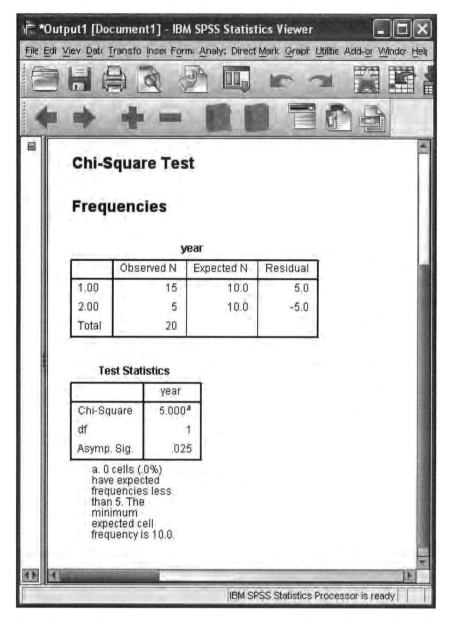

Figure 11 SPSS output window for a chi-square test for goodness of fit for a fictional study examining the distribution of first- and second-year college students for a particular class.

❶ Enter the scores into SPSS. As shown in Figure 10, the score for each person is listed in a separate row. We labeled the variables "year" and "campus_y1n0." (We assigned students who live on campus a value of "1" and students who don't live on campus a value of "0".)

❷ ✐ *Analyze.*

❸ ✐ *Descriptive Statistics,* ✐ *Crosstabs.*

❹ ✐ on the variable called "campus_y1n0" and then ✐ the arrow next to the box labeled "Row(s)." ✐ on the variable called "year" and then ✐ the arrow next to the box labeled "Column(s)." (It doesn't matter which variable is assigned to rows and which is assigned to columns; the result will be the same.)

❺ ✍ *Statistics.* ✍ the box labeled *Chi-square* (this checks the box). ✍ the box
labeled *Phi and Cramer's V* (this checks the box). ✍ *Continue.*

❻ ✍ *Cells.* ✍ the box labeled *Expected* (this checks the box). ✍ *Continue.* This
step requests the expected frequencies to be included in the output. (Although
this step is optional, we recommend that you always do it, as it reinforces the
logic of the chi-square test.)

❼ ✍ *OK.* Your SPSS output window should look like Figure 12.

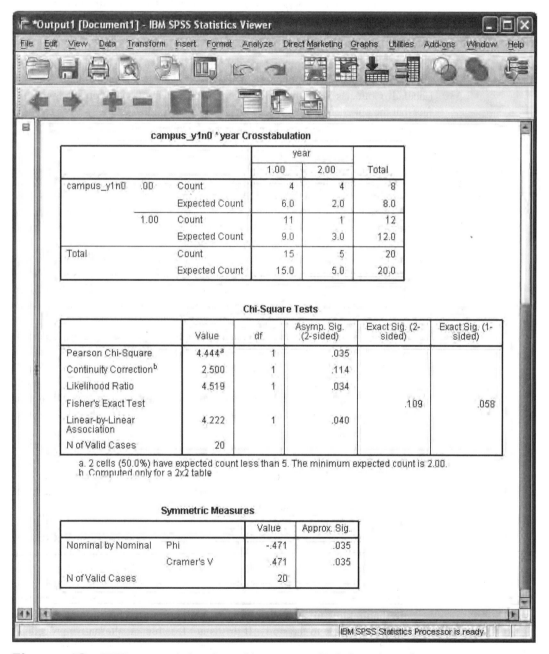

Figure 12 SPSS output window for a chi-square test for independence for a
fictional study examining the distribution of first- and second-year college students for
a particular class and whether the students live on campus.

The first table in the SPSS output (which is not shown in Figure 12) gives the number of individuals in the analysis. The second table (labeled "campus_y1n0 * year Crosstabulation") gives the contingency table of observed and expected values for the two nominal variables ("campus_y1n0" and "year"). The third table (labeled "Chi-Square Tests") shows the actual result of the chi-square test for independence, as well as the results of other tests. The results of the chi-square test for independence are provided in the first row (labeled "Pearson Chi-Square"), which shows the chi-square value, the degrees of freedom, and the exact significance level. The significance level of .035 (for the chi-square value of 4.444) is smaller than our .05 cutoff. Thus, you can reject the null hypothesis and conclude that the distribution of first- and second-year students in the class is different according to whether students live on campus. The final table (labeled "Symmetric Measures") shows the effect size measures, namely the phi coefficient (labeled "Phi" in the table) and Cramer's ϕ (labeled "Cramer's V" in the table). The phi coefficient of .471 (you can ignore the fact that the phi coefficient is a negative value) tells you that there is a large relationship between the year of students in the class and whether students live on campus.

Chapter Notes

1. Independence is typically used to talk about a lack of relation between two nominal variables. However, it may be helpful to think of independence as roughly the same as the situation of no correlation ($r = 0$).

2. Phi is actually identical to the correlation coefficient. Suppose you were to take the two variables in a 2×2 contingency table and arbitrarily make one of the values of each equal to 1 and the other equal to 2 (you could use any two different numbers). And suppose you then figured a correlation coefficient between the two variables. The result would be exactly the same as the phi coefficient. (Whether it was a positive or negative correlation, however, would depend on which categories in each variable got the higher number.)

3. Cohen (1988, pp. 228–248) gives more detailed tables. However, Cohen's tables are based on an effect size called w, which is equivalent to phi but not to Cramer's phi. He provides a helpful conversion table of Cramer's phi to w on page 222. There are also power calculators available on the Internet and power can be calculated using SPSS.

4. More detailed tables are provided in Cohen (1988, pp. 253–267). When using these tables, see Chapter Note 3. Also, Dunlap and Myers (1997) have shown that with a 2×2 table, the approximate number of participants needed for 80% to 90% power is $8/\phi^2$. There are also power calculators available on the Internet, and power can be calculated using SPSS.

5. Suppose you have a table larger than 2×2 with a category or cell that has an extremely small expected frequency (or even a moderately small expected frequency if the number of participants is also small). One solution is to combine related categories to increase the expected frequency and reduce the total number of cells. But this is a solution of last resort if you are making the adjustment based on the results of the experiment. The problem is that you are then taking advantage of knowing the outcome. The best solution is to add more people to the study. If this is not feasible, an alternative procedure, called Fisher's exact test, is sometimes possible. It is described in some intermediate statistics texts.

Appendix: Table

Table A1 Cutoff Scores for the Chi-Square Distribution

	Significance Level		
df	.10	.05	.01
1	2.706	3.841	6.635
2	4.605	5.992	9.211
3	6.252	7.815	11.345
4	7.780	9.488	13.277
5	9.237	11.071	15.087
6	10.645	12.592	16.812
7	12.017	14.067	18.475
8	13.362	15.507	20.090
9	14.684	16.919	21.666
10	15.987	18.307	23.209

Answers to Set I Practice Problems

Chapter 13

1. (a) χ^2 needed ($df = 5 - 1 = 4$, .05 level) $= 9.488$.

Category	O	Expected	$O - E$	$(O - E)^2$	$(O - E)^2/E$
A	19	$(.2)(50) = 10$	9	81	8.10
B	11	$(.2)(50) = 10$	1	1	.10
C	10	$(.4)(50) = 20$	−10	100	5.00
D	5	$(.1)(50) = 5$	0	0	0.00
E	5	$(.1)(50) = 5$	0	0	0.00
Total	50	50	0		$\chi^2 = 13.20$

Conclusion: Reject the null hypothesis

(b) χ^2 needed $= 5.992$; $\chi^2 = 44.45$, reject the null hypothesis; (c) χ^2 needed $= 7.815$; $\chi^2 = 1.23$, do not reject the null hypothesis.

2. χ^2 needed for (a), (b), and (c): ($df = 5 - 1 = 4$, 1%) $= 13.277$;

(a)

Category	O	Expected	$O - E$	$(O - E)^2$	$(O - E)^2/E$
A	10	20	−10	100	5
B	10	20	−10	100	5
C	10	20	−10	100	5
D	10	20	−10	100	5
E	60	20	40	1600	80
Total	100	100	0		$\chi^2 = 100$

Conclusion: Reject the null hypothesis

(b) $\chi^2 = 50$, reject the null hypothesis; (c) $\chi^2 = 450$, reject the null hypothesis.

3. (a) ❶ **Restate the question as a research hypothesis and a null hypothesis about the populations.** There are two populations of interest:
Population 1: Clients like those of this psychotherapy clinic.
Population 2: Clients for whom season makes no difference to when they use the psychotherapy clinic.

The research hypothesis is that the distribution over seasons of when clients use the psychotherapy clinic is different between the two populations. The null hypothesis is that the distributions over seasons of when clients use the psychotherapy clinic is not different between the populations.
❷ **Determine the characteristics of the comparison distribution.** Chi-square distribution with 3 degrees of freedom ($df = 4$ categories $- 1 = 3$).
❸ **Determine the cutoff sample score on the comparison distribution at which the null hypothesis should be rejected.** .05 level, $df = 3$: χ^2 needed $= 7.815$.

❹ **Determine your sample's score on the comparison distribution.**

Season	O	Expected	O − E	(O − E)²	(O − E)²/E
Winter	28	(1/4)(128) = 32	−4	16	.50
Spring	33	(1/4)(128) = 32	1	1	.03
Summer	16	(1/4)(128) = 32	−16	256	8.00
Fall	51	(1/4)(128) = 32	19	361	11.28
Total	128	128	0		$\chi^2 = 19.81$

❺ **Decide whether to reject the null hypothesis.** 19.81 is larger than 7.815; reject the null hypothesis; the research hypothesis is supported.
(b)

(c) If the season makes no difference, you would expect about 25% of clients to use the psychotherapy clinic each season (for last year, 25% of 128 is 32). Are last year's actual numbers in each season so discrepant from these expectations that you should conclude that in general the numbers of new clients are not equally distributed over the seasons? The chi-square statistic reflects the discrepancy between observed and expected results. For each category

(such as the four seasons), you figure that discrepancy, square it, and divide by the expected number; then you add up the results. In the winter, 28 minus 32 is −4, squared is 16, divided by 32 is .50. Doing the same for the other three seasons and adding up the four gives a total chi-square of 19.81. (Chi-square uses squared discrepancies so that the result is not affected by the directions of the differences. You divide by the expected number to reduce the impact of the raw number of cases on the result.)

Statisticians have determined mathematically what would happen if you took an infinite number of samples from a population with a fixed proportion of cases in each category and figured chi-square for each sample. This distribution depends only on how many categories are free to take on different expected values. (The total number expected is the total number of cases; thus, if you know the expected for any three categories, you can just subtract to get the number expected for the fourth). A table of the chi-square distribution when three categories are free to vary shows that there is only a 5% chance of getting a chi-square of 7.815 or greater. Because our chi-square is larger than this, the observed result differs from the expected more than you would reasonably expect by chance; the number of new clients, in the long run, is probably not equal over the four seasons.

4. (a) You should get the same result within rounding error.
(b) Similar to question 3c.
5. For (a), (b), and (c): $df = (N_{Columns} - 1)(N_{Rows} - 1) = (2 - 1)(2 - 1) = 1$; χ^2 needed $= 6.635$.
(a)

10 (13)	16 (13)	26	(50%)
16 (13)	10 (13)	26	(50%)
26	26	52	

$\chi^2 = (10 - 13)^2/13 + (16 - 13)^2/13 + (16 - 13)^2/13 + (10 - 13)^2/13 = 2.76$. Do not reject the null hypothesis: effect size, $\phi = \sqrt{\chi^2/N} = \sqrt{2.76/52} = \sqrt{0.53} = .23$.
(b) $\chi^2 = .36$, do not reject the null hypothesis; effect size, $\phi = .03$.
(c) $\chi^2 = 27.68$, reject the null hypothesis; effect size, $\phi = .23$. For (d), (e), and (f): $df = (N_{Columns} - 1)(N_{Rows} - 1) = (3 - 1)(2 - 1) = 2$; χ^2 needed $= 9.211$.
(d) $\chi^2 = 2.76$, do not reject the null hypothesis; effect size, Cramer's $\phi = \sqrt{\chi^2/[(N)(df_{Smaller})]} = \sqrt{2.76/[(72)(1)]} = \sqrt{.0383} = .20$.
(e) $\chi^2 = 2.76$, do not reject the null hypothesis; effect size, Cramer's $\phi = .18$.
(f) $\chi^2 = 3.71$, do not reject the null hypothesis; effect size, Cramer's $\phi = .22$.

6. (a) ❶ **Restate the question as a research hypothesis and a null hypothesis about the populations.** There are two populations of interest:
Population 1: Children like those surveyed.
Population 2: Children for whom age is independent of whether or not they like this kind of music.

The research hypothesis is that the two populations are different. The null hypothesis is that the two populations are the same.

❷ **Determine the characteristics of the comparison distribution.** Chi-square distribution with two degrees of freedom. $df = (N_{Columns} - 1)(N_{Rows} - 1) = (3 - 1)(2 - 1) = 2$.
❸ **Determine the cutoff sample score on the comparison distribution at which the null hypothesis should be rejected.** .05 level, $df = 2$: χ^2 needed $= 5.992$.
❹ **Determine your sample's score on the comparison distribution.**

		Age of Child (years)			
		5	8	11	
Likes Type of Music	Yes	42 (39)	62 (65)	26 (26)	130 (65%)
	No	18 (21)	38 (35)	14 (14)	70 (35%)
		60	100	40	200

$\chi^2 = (42 - 39)^2/39 + (62 - 65)^2/65 + (26 - 26)^2/26 + (18 - 21)^2/21 + (38 - 35)^2/35 + (14 - 14)^2/14 = 1.06$.
❺ **Decide whether to reject the null hypothesis.** 1.06 is less extreme than 5.992; do not reject the null hypothesis; the study is inconclusive.
(b)

5%

1.06 =
Obtained Chi-Square

(c) Cramer's $\phi = \sqrt{\chi^2/[(N)(df_{Smaller})]} = \sqrt{1.06/[(200)(1)]} = \sqrt{.0053} = .07$.
(d) In this example, 65% of all children liked the particular kind of music. Thus, if age and liking of this kind of music are not related, 65% of the children in each age group should like this kind of music. For example, you would expect 39 of the 60 8-year-olds to like this music. Are the survey results so discrepant from these expectations that you should conclude that age is related to what kind of music children like?

The chi-square statistic reflects the discrepancy between observed and expected results. For each combination of the 2 × 3 arrangement, you figure that discrepancy between observed and expected, square it, and divide by the expected number; then you add up the results. In the yes-8-year-old combination, 42 minus 39 is 3, squared is 9, divided by 39 is .23. Doing the same for the other five combinations and adding them all up gives 1.06. (Chi-square uses squared discrepancies so that the result is not affected by the directions of the differences. It is divided by

the expected number to adjust for the impact of relatively different numbers expected in the combinations.)

The rest is similar to question 3c, except for the following about degrees of freedom. For each age group, if you know the totals and the figure for children who like this kind of music, you can figure the number who do not by subtraction. And of the three age groups, if you know the total and any two of them, you can figure the third by subtraction. So only two combinations are "free to vary."

7. (a) ❶ **Restate the question as a research hypothesis and a null hypothesis about the populations.** There are two populations of interest:
Population 1: People like those surveyed.
Population 2: People for whom the community they live in is independent of their opinion on the upcoming ballot initiative.

The research hypothesis is that the two populations are different (the community people live in is not independent of their opinion on the upcoming ballot initiative). The null hypothesis is that the two populations are the same (the community people live in is independent of their opinion on the upcoming ballot imitative).
❷ **Determine the characteristics of the comparison distribution.** Chi-square distribution with four degrees of freedom. $df = (N_{Columns} - 1)(N_{Rows} - 1) = (3 - 1)(3 - 1) = 4$.
❸ **Determine the cutoff sample score on the comparison distribution at which the null hypothesis should be rejected.** .05 level, $df = 4$: χ^2 needed $= 9.488$.
❹ **Determine your sample's score on the comparison distribution.** $\chi^2 = (12 - 9.8)^2/9.8 + (6 - 4.2)^2/4.2 + (3 - 7)^2/7 + (18 - 16.8)^2/16.8 + (3 - 7.2)^2/7.2 + (15 - 12)^2/12 + (12 - 15.4)^2/15.4 + (9 - 6.6)^2/6.6 + (12 - 11)^2/11 = .49 + .77 + 2.29 + .09 + 2.45 + .75 + .75 + .87 + .09 = 8.55$.
❺ **Decide whether to reject the null hypothesis.** χ^2 in Step ❹ (8.55) is less extreme than Step ❸ cutoff (9.488). Therefore, do not reject the null hypothesis; the study is inconclusive.
(b) Similar to question 6b.
(c) Cramer's $\phi = \sqrt{[8.55/(90)(2)]} = \sqrt{[8.55/180]} = \sqrt{.05} = .22$.
(d) Similar to question 6d but focusing on this study's results.
8. (a) $\phi = \sqrt{\chi^2/N} = \sqrt{16/100} = .40$;
(b) Cramer's $\phi = \sqrt{\chi^2/[(N)(df_{Smaller})]} = \sqrt{16/[(100)(1)]} = .40$;
(c) Cramer's $\phi = .28$;
(d) $\phi = .28$;
(e) $\phi = .28$.
9. From Table 13-9: (a) .08; (b) .32; (c) .11; (d) .07; (e) .06; (f) .06.
10. From Table 13-10: (a) 87; (b) 26; (c) 133; (d) 133; (e) 39.
11. (a) You should get the same results within rounding error.
(b) $\phi = \sqrt{\chi^2/N} = \sqrt{5.55/69} = .28$.
(c) Similar to question 6d but focusing on this study's results.
12. (a) You should get the same results within rounding error.
(b) $\phi = \sqrt{\chi^2/N} = \sqrt{.33/145} = .05$.
(c) Similar to question 6d but focusing on this study's results.

Chapter 14

Overview of the Logic and Language of Psychology Research

This chapter provides an overview of the logic and language of the research process in psychology. Statistical methods are tools used in the research process. You will find the statistical procedures in *Statistics for Psychology* easier to understand if you appreciate the context in which they are used.

Usually, the purpose of a research study in psychology is to test a theory or the effectiveness of a practical application.[1] The strongest research procedures lead to unambiguous conclusions that apply to a wide variety of other situations and people beyond the particular ones included in the study. Weak research designs, even if their results are consistent with your predictions, leave open many alternative interpretations as to why those results were found or apply only to a narrow group of people or situations. (Sometimes, circumstances limit the sort of research procedure that is possible, yet the research may still seem worth pursuing, even if in a less than rigorous way. In fact, especially in the case of applied research, much of the most important work has been done by psychologists using, of necessity, less than perfect methods, but in very creative ways.)

Most psychologists think about the logic of research in terms of a kind of ideal approach. A real-life study is evaluated in terms of the ways it does and does not come close to this ideal. In this chapter, we first discuss this ideal, the "true experiment." We then turn to four key areas in which studies do or do not come close to it: equivalence of participants across experimental groups, equivalence of circumstances across experimental groups, generalizability, and adequacy of measurement.

The Traditionally Ideal Research Approach

The True Experiment

The **true experiment** is the standard against which all other methods are compared. Consider the hypothesis "Changing the level of X causes a change in the score on Y." A true experiment systematically varies the level of X, keeping everything else the same, and looks at the effect on Y. For example, suppose you want to know whether flashing lights in a room affects people's scores on a math test. X is whether or not there are flashing lights in the room, and Y is math test scores. In a true experiment, a group of students might each be tested in a room with flashing lights. Participants in another, initially identical group of students, would each be tested under conditions that are completely identical, except there are no flashing lights in the room. Thus, the only difference between the two groups is the level of X, the presence or absence of flashing lights in the room. If the students tested in the room with flashing lights have lower scores on the math test (Y), it must be due to the lighting. (If they have higher scores, then *that* effect would also have to be due to the flashing lights.)

Basic Terminology of the Experiment

A group in which the level of X is changed is usually called the **experimental group**. The comparison group in which X is kept at normal levels is called the **control group**.[2] The individuals studied in the research are called **participants**. The variable that is systematically changed (X–for example, whether the lights flash or not) is called the **independent variable** (it is also called the variable that divides the groups). The procedure of systematically changing the independent variable is sometimes called an **experimental manipulation** or *manipulating the independent variable*. The variable that is supposed to change as a result of the study (Y, *if X is predicted to* cause Y, for example, a score on the math test) is called the **dependent variable** (it is also called the measured variable). Participants are taken from the **population**—all the people on earth of the type being studied. The particular participants selected to be studied from that population are called the **sample**.

Imagine you have two identical cans of a soft drink and you want to test the hypothesis that heating a can of soft drink will make it explode. (Don't try this at home!) To study this, you could put a match under one can (the experimental can) and not put a match under the other can (the control can). If the experimental can explodes and the control can does not, the hypothesis is confirmed. Each can is a participant, heating or not is the independent variable, whether a can explodes is the dependent variable, and these two cans are samples, respectively, of the populations of all soft drink cans that are and are not heated (see Figure 1).

Figure 1 An ideal experiment: One of two identical soft drink cans is heated, and the researcher observes to see if it will explode while the other does not explode.

Four Characteristics of the Ideal Research Design

There are four key characteristics of an ideal research design:

1. The participants in the experimental and control groups are identical.
2. The experimental and control groups are exposed to identical situations (*except* for the manipulation of the independent variable).

3. The sample studied perfectly represents the intended population.
4. The measurement of the dependent variable is completely accurate and appropriate for what it is supposed to be measuring.

The rest of this chapter examines the various ways that real-life research tries to come close to each of these ideal conditions.

Equivalence of Participants in Experimental and Control Groups

Ordinarily, the equivalence of participants in the experimental and control groups is the main issue in deciding how well a study can give unambiguous conclusions about what is causing what. Suppose the basic math ability of the participants sent to the room with flashing lights was different from those sent to the room without flashing lights. Whatever the difference in math scores you found between the two groups at the end of the study, it would be hard to know what that difference means. The difference could be due either (a) to the manipulation of the independent variable (the presence or absence of flashing lights) or (b) to the initial differences in ability of the two groups. To avoid such ambiguous results, researchers aim for strict equivalence of the experimental and control groups. Five main strategies are employed: random assignment to groups, matched-group designs, repeated measures designs, correlational research designs, and single-subject research.

Random Assignment to Groups

The research procedure that in practice comes closest to creating two identical groups of participants is called **random assignment to groups**. For example, if 100 people were available to be in the experiment, each person could be put in either the experimental group or the control group by flipping a coin. The two groups of 50 created in this way are not identical, but at least there will be no *systematic* difference between them.

It is important to emphasize that "random" means using a strictly random procedure, not just haphazardly picking people to go into the two groups. Any haphazard procedure is likely to create unintended systematic differences. For example, suppose you choose one group from students attending a morning class and the others from students attending an evening class. The two groups might differ because the kinds of people taking classes at these different times of day might differ. Or suppose one group are volunteers willing to participate in a self-esteem enhancement program, and the control group is simply whoever is willing to take a self-esteem test. The kinds of people in the experimental and control groups might be quite different.

Random assignment rules out initial systematic differences between groups. Any actual difference that exists after random assignment will be entirely due to random processes. Thus, if there are differences on the dependent variable after the experiment, they only can be due to either the manipulation of the independent variable or to the random assignment. True random processes follow the laws of probability. Thus, the hypothesis-testing procedures are able to check the probability of whether the difference found in a study could have been due to the random assignment. If the statistical analysis indicates that this is unlikely, the only reasonable remaining explanation is that the manipulation of the independent variable caused the difference. This is the basic logic behind the analysis of results of experiments. And this is why random assignment and statistical methods are so important in psychology research.

Matched-Group Designs

Sometimes random assignment to groups is not practical. For example, ethics would require that all students in a school district who need a certain reading program receive it; some cannot be randomly chosen to miss out. How can the program be shown to be the cause of improvements in the students? One widely used alternative research approach when random assignment can not be used is the **matched-group research design**. For example, you might compare an experimental group of students who have been selected for the program in one school district to a control group of students in another district who also need the program but for whom it is not available. The control group could be matched to the experimental group in terms of age, social class, sex, reading problems, and so forth.

Matched-group designs are much better than having no control group at all. In fact, if both groups are tested before and after, the matched-group design can lead to fairly unambiguous results. This situation, called a *matched-group pretest-posttest design*, is an example of a *quasi-experimental design*. A quasi-experimental design is any approach that reasonably approximates a true experiment but does not use random assignment.

However, no matter how well-matched two groups are, and even when before-and-after testing is used, a researcher can never know for certain that there is no systematic initial difference between the groups. Indeed, in most cases, if you have not used random assignment, you know that there *is* a systematic initial difference—whatever it was that put people into one group or the other. (In the reading program example, the systematic difference might be that one group of students lives in a school district not well-funded enough to offer the reading program.)

Repeated Measures Designs

Another research approach is to create two identical groups by testing the same people twice. This is called a **repeated measures research design** (it is also called a *within-subjects research design*). The students in our example could be tested before and after the reading program.

The simplest repeated measures design is a *single-group pretest-posttest design*. As the name implies, a single group of individuals is tested twice, once before and once after some experimental treatment. This kind of research design, however, is very weak in the sense that, if you found a change, there are many possible alternative explanations for it. Merely being tested the first time can change a participant, so that when tested again, the person is different—different due to the initial testing, not due to the experimental treatment. And time itself produces change. More generally, in this kind of study, any change could be due to the reading program or to whatever else happened to the participants (besides the experimental treatment) during that time period. Or there could be preexisting trends for improvement, or the change could be due to general maturation and experience, or to people starting at a very low point that would naturally improve without the treatment, and so forth.

Because it is such a weak research design, the single-group pretest-posttest design is considered a *preexperimental design*. Research of this kind is often extremely important as a first stage in exploring a research area, but any conclusions from a study of this type are very tentative and should be followed up by a stronger research design (such as a quasi-experimental or true experimental design).

In a laboratory setting, however, a repeated measures design is often used in a way that makes it a true experiment. Consider again our interest in the effect of flashing lights in the room on performance on a math test. The researcher might test the same participant's performance with flashing lights (the experimental condition) and then test that person's performance without flashing lights (the control condition). A problem with this approach, however, is that the participants could be more familiar with the test the second time, creating a *practice effect* or *carry-over effect*, or they could be tired out by the time they get to the second task, creating a *fatigue effect*.

To deal with problems of this kind, researchers use a procedure called **counterbalancing**, in which half the participants are tested first in one condition and the other half first in the other condition. In this way, any practice, carry-over, fatigue, or similar effects are balanced out over the two conditions. Ideally, you use counterbalancing so that the condition a participant experiences first is determined by random assignment. In this situation, the study becomes a true experiment. Indeed, repeated measures designs with counterbalancing and random assignment are among the most powerful research methods psychologists use because they make groups so very equivalent.

Correlational Research Designs

A **correlational research design** tests whether there is an association between two variables as they exist in a group of people, without any attempt at experimental manipulation. Thus, a correlational approach to studying self-esteem and job satisfaction might survey a group of workers on their self-esteem and their job satisfaction. Then you would see whether those scoring high on self-esteem also tended to score high on job satisfaction. (You figure the degree to which there is an association using a statistical technique called a "correlation coefficient.")

The correlational approach is often the best that can be done under the circumstances and is widely used. But it is a fairly weak research design in that its results are open to many alternative explanations besides "X caused Y." For example, suppose you find that self-esteem and job satisfaction are associated in a correlational study. This could be due to high self-esteem causing high job satisfaction. But it could also be that high job satisfaction causes high self-esteem. The association between self-esteem and job satisfaction could even be due to other differences among the workers, such as age—perhaps being older causes workers to have both high self-esteem and high job satisfaction. Thus, one advantage of a true experiment (when it is feasible) over a correlational study is that the true experiment manipulates the independent variable and then sees the effect on the dependent variable, making it quite clear what causes what.

Researchers are well aware of the limits of correlational designs. When possible, they try to rule out some alternative explanations, mainly by using sophisticated statistical procedures such as partial correlation. Still, the correlational approach never produces results as clear as a true experiment or, in most cases, even as clear-cut as a quasi-experiment. However, often, the correlational approach is the strongest method that is practical—for example, you cannot randomly assign people to marry certain other types of people. Even when true experiments are possible, they may be very costly to conduct. Thus, researchers may not be willing or able to test an untried idea experimentally. In these situations, correlational studies often provide a valuable first step in opening up a new area of research.

Single-Subject Research

Finally, some research studies involve an intense examination of a single group, organization, or individual, using the *case study* or *participant observation* approach. Such **single-subject research** is not considered experimental or even correlational. However, in clinical psychology and in some other behavioral and social science fields, such as education, sociology, and anthropology (and the sociological and anthropological approaches to organizational behavior, criminology, communication, and so forth), this kind of research is valuable because it gives a rich understanding of all the complexities of what is being studied rather than forcing attention on a few variables that may or may not be the most critical. In all areas of psychology, as well as other behavioral and social sciences, single-subject research is also considered useful as a precursor to other, more rigorous research approaches.

Single-subject research is also used in a highly systematic way by researchers in the behaviorist tradition developed by B. F. Skinner. A single participant—whether an animal, like a rat or a pigeon, or a client in a behavior therapy program—is studied over time, with the researcher systematically manipulating the conditions that affect the participant and observing the changes that result. Statistics for testing this have been developed, but are not usually used; the pattern of results should be so clear that you don't need statistics.

Summary of Research Designs

Table 1 summarizes the various research designs we have considered, noting their advantages and disadvantages as compared to the ideal of identical experimental and control groups.

Table 1   Major Research Designs and Their Advantages and Disadvantages

Design	Advantages	Disadvantages
True experiment (random assignment to conditions)	Ensures no systematic difference between conditions.	Can be impractical or unethical.
Matched-group (without random assignment)	Controls for obvious differences between conditions; may be most practical with intact groups.	Groups may differ systematically on variables on which they were not matched.
Matched-group pretest-posttest	Controls fairly strongly for initial differences among participants; is often practical where random assignment is not.	Systematic differences between groups may influence impact; pretest measuring procedure can confound results.
Single-group pretest-posttest	Provides some control; is often the only practical approach.	Impossible to know if change would have occurred without the experimental treatment.
Repeated measures true experiment (random assignment)	Ensures no systematic difference; minimizes random differences by making participants their own controls.	Practice or carry-over effects; procedure may be difficult to implement.
Correlational	Is relatively easy to do with existing groups.	Difficult to determine direction of causality.
Single-subject	Permits deep understanding of processes.	Difficult to generalize results.

Equivalence of Circumstances for Experimental and Control Groups

The ideal study involves not only identical groups but also testing them under identical circumstances. In practice, it is quite difficult to test two groups under circumstances where the sole difference is the manipulation of the independent variable. In a chemistry laboratory such equivalence may be possible. But when conducting research with human beings, circumstances are never completely equivalent. One strategy designed to maximize equivalence is to use an isolated location, such as a cubicle in a research laboratory. This minimizes outside influences and interruptions that might make one session of the experiment different from another. A related approach is to standardize the situation as much as possible. For example, experimenters typically try to follow a precise script in interacting with participants; or for even more equivalence, an entire study may be administered by computer.

There are, however, two special problems that plague much psychology research—particularly applied research—with regard to equivalence of circumstances: placebo or Hawthorne effects and experimenter effects.

Placebo and Hawthorne Effects

Placebo effects are the influence of a participant's expectation or motivation to do well. **Hawthorne effects** are the influence of the attention the participant receives and of the participant's reaction to being a participant (the term comes from a 1927 study done at the Hawthorne Works plant of the Western Electric Company in Cicero, Illinois). For example, if one wing of a factory is trained in a new program and one wing is not, there are several differences between the situations the two groups are in. One wing uses the new way of operating resulting from the program, and the other wing does not—this is the manipulation of the independent variable. But another difference is that those in the wing getting the new program know they are getting a new program and may thus expect to get benefits (creating a placebo effect). Yet another is that one wing has received special attention and the other wing has not (creating a Hawthorne effect). These additional differences between groups (different expectations and different attention received) greatly complicate the interpretation of the results.

How can researchers deal with these undesired differences in circumstances? The best solution is to conduct a study in which both groups receive *some* treatment that they believe should be helpful, however, only one group actually receives a treatment consisting of more than mere raised expectations and greater attention. For example, in medical research, both groups would receive pills that look and taste identical, but one group's pills contain the active ingredient and the other group's do not. No one in the experiment knows who is receiving the real drug. A drug that looks and tastes like the real thing but is actually inactive is called a *placebo* (Latin for "I shall please").

In psychology, it is often impossible or unethical to set up a control group condition where a person receives a treatment that is believed to be effective but in fact is not. A situation where it is feasible to use a true placebo control group and also in which the research personnel can be unaware of which participants are in which group is called a *double-blind procedure*.

Placebo and Hawthorne effects are the most common problems in drawing unambiguous conclusions from results of applied research in many areas such as clinical, educational, and organizational psychology.

Experimenter Effects

Experimenter effects, including *experimenter bias*, are the unintended influences of the researcher on the study. For example, consider a study that is testing the effects of a new type of psychotherapy. Suppose that the researcher is a therapist evaluating the mental health of the participants. In this case, it is quite possible that the therapist's desire to see the study work creates an unconscious predisposition to see participants in the experimental group as having improved more. Even if an independent observer rates the two groups but knows who is in which group, a desire for the experiment to come out a particular way may unintentionally influence the observer's evaluations.

The preferred solution to this problem is called *blind conditions of testing*. This means that the experimenter, at the time of interacting with the participant, is not aware of whether the participant is in the experimental or control group. (We already considered above what is called double-blind testing, where neither researcher nor participant knows what condition they are in. There we were emphasizing the importance of the participant not being aware of who was in what condition; here we are emphasizing the importance of the experimenter not knowing who is in which condition at the time of testing.)

Representativeness of the Sample

The third requirement for an ideal study is that the particular sample of participants studied accurately represents the larger population to which the study is supposed to apply. This representativeness is called **generalizability** or *external validity*. (*Internal validity* refers to the equivalence of the experimental and control groups and equivalence of circumstances.)

Participants in psychology research are often university students, and it is assumed that what is discovered about them applies to the larger population of people in general. In a study of the effect of flashing lights on performance, the general pattern of results with students probably applies to most other human beings. However, in many other types of research, who the participants are is very important. For example, university students would probably not be suitable participants for studies of attitudes toward children—their experience does not commonly include parenthood. You cannot study reading skills in suburban schools and generalize to students in all schools; you cannot study job satisfaction in the music industry and generalize to all industries.

Another problem involves how a study's participants are recruited. For example, in a mail survey of knowledge about an issue, some individuals will return the questionnaire and some will not. Presumably there are systematic differences between those who do and do not—it is likely that those who do may know more about the issue being studied. Using only the questionnaires that are returned, the researcher may conclude that people are more knowledgeable about an issue than if the researcher had been able to study the entire population. Similarly, people who respond to a telephone survey that includes land lines may be quite different from the larger population in which many people may have only cell phones. **Random sampling** is considered the optimal method for ensuring that a particular group of people studied is representative of the larger population to which results are intended to apply. Random sampling means that researchers begin with a list of everyone in the population about which they want to generalize their results, such as a list of all psychotherapists in the nation, then use a random procedure (such as a computer-generated random list) to select a sample of psychotherapists to contact from this population. (The reason is that it would be far too expensive to contact all of them.) This produces what is called a *probability sample* because every member of the population being studied has an equal probability of being included in the study's sample.

Do not confuse random sampling with random assignment to groups, which we discussed earlier. Both procedures use true random procedures. However, random sampling is a method of selecting the sample to study; random assignment to groups is a method of deciding which members of the sample will be in the experimental group and which in the control group.

Measurement

The fourth condition we noted for an ideal study is that the measures should be accurate and appropriate. There are three main kinds of measures used in psychology research: **self-report measures**, such as questionnaires or interviews; *observational* or **behavioral measures**, such as rating scales of children's play behavior, number of customers who enter a particular store, number of milliseconds to respond in a reaction time experiment, or number of times a rat presses a bar; and **physiological measures**, such as hormone levels, heart rate, or blood flow in a particular brain area. All three kinds of measurement are evaluated mainly in terms of their reliability and validity.

Reliability

The **reliability** of a measure is its accuracy or consistency. That is, when you apply the same measure to the same thing, under identical circumstances, how similar are the results? In psychology research, the results are not necessarily similar at all. For example, the same person taking the same questionnaires on different days may get a quite different score. Sometimes, questions are worded poorly, so that a person may answer in one way at one time and in another way at another time. Or, people may simply mark some or all of their answers in the wrong place on one or more occasions. Self-report measures are not the only ones that can be unreliable. Observational measures may be unreliable because observers may disagree. Physiological measures are sometimes highly erratic from moment to moment.

There are three types of indicators of degree of reliability: (a) **test-retest reliability**, in which the same group is tested twice; (b) **internal consistency**, in which, for example, scores on half the questions are compared to scores on the other half (*Cronbach's alpha* is the most common approach to internal consistency); and (c) **interrater reliability**, used for observational measures, which is the degree of agreement between observers. These kinds of reliability are summarized in Table 2.

Validity

The **validity** of a measure refers to whether it actually measures what it claims to measure. (The word validity is also applied to entire studies, as in internal validity and external validity, when it refers to the appropriateness and breadth of the conclusions that can be drawn from the results.)

Table 2	Types of Reliability
Test-retest reliability	Correlation of tests administered to the same people on different occasions
Internal consistency	Correlation among the items
Interrater reliability	Correlation among different raters' scores when rating the same group of people or objects

A measure that is not reliable cannot be valid. An unreliable measure does not measure anything. But even if a measure is reliable (accurate and repeatable), it is not necessarily valid for measuring what it is intended to measure. For example, consider a marital satisfaction questionnaire with many items such as, "How likely are you to stay with your spouse over the next several years?" The questionnaire may turn out to be highly reliable (for example, people may answer all the questions on it quite consistently). But instead of measuring marital satisfaction, it might really be measuring commitment to the marriage. And respondents might be committed not because they are satisfied but because they have no alternative to married life or because they feel they are very unattractive and could only do worse if they left their partner.

Another reason that a test may not be valid, even if it is reliable, is that rather than measuring the intended variable, it is actually measuring a tendency for the respondents to try to make a good impression or to say yes or to answer with some other **response bias**. One way to address the problem of trying to make a good impression is to include a *social desirability scale*, sometimes called a *lie scale*. When a participant's score on such a social desirability scale is high, the researcher may simply throw out that participant's data. Alternatively, scores on a social desirability scale may be used in a statistical procedure, such as partial correlation or an analysis of covariance, to adjust the person's score on the regular part of the measure.

Validity of a measure is more difficult to assess than reliability. Several methods are used. **Content validity** results when the content of the measure appears to get at all the different aspects of the things being measured. Usually, this is determined by the judgment of the researcher or other experts.

There are, however, more systematic means of evaluating the validity of a measure. Determining **criterion-related validity** involves doing a special study in which the researcher compares scores on the measure to some other likely indicator of the same variable. For example, a researcher might test the validity of a measure of mental health by comparing scores of people in a mental hospital to people from the general population. One type of criterion-related validity is a measure's *predictive validity*—for example, whether scores on a job skills test taken when applying for a job predict effective performance on the job. Predictive validity is used especially where a measure is designed for predictive purposes, such as job or educational placement. Another type of criterion-related validity is *concurrent validity*. This refers to the procedure of comparing scores on one measure to those on another that directly measures the same thing—for example, a new, short intelligence test compared to an existing, longer intelligence test.

You may also see the term *construct validity*, which is used in a variety of ways. Even textbooks on psychological measurement disagree about it. Sometimes construct validity includes criterion-related validity, and sometimes content validity. Probably the most common usage is that construct validity of a measure means that a study using this measure successfully showed an effect that was predicted by theory. Because the measure used was successful in producing the predicted result, it shows that the idea (or "construct") behind that measure proved itself under the theory. The various ways of assessing validity are summarized in Table 3.

Table 3	Major Types of Validity of a Measure
Content validity	The content of the test appears to experts to accurately represent the full range of what the test claims to measure.
Criterion-related validity	Scores on the test correlate with some other indicator of what the test is supposed to measure.
Predictive validity	The test score predicts scores on another variable that ought to be predicted by the test, given what it is claimed to measure; a type of criterion-related validity.
Concurrent validity	The test score correlates with another variable measured at the same time that is already known to be related to what the test is claimed to measure; a type of criterion-related validity.
Construct validity	There is evidence that what the test measures corresponds to the underlying theoretical variable it is meant to assess.

Learning Aids

Summary

1. A true experiment systematically varies the level of one variable (for example, an independent variable, X) and looks at the effect on another variable (for example, a dependent variable, Y).

2. In an ideal research design: (a) the participants in the experimental and control groups are identical; (b) the experimental and control groups are exposed to identical situations; (c) the sample studied perfectly represents the intended population; and (d) the dependent variable is measured in a completely accurate and appropriate manner for what it is supposed to be measuring.

3. There are several approaches available to researchers in order to maintain the equivalence of experimental and control groups, including: random assignment to groups; matched-group designs; repeated measures designs; correlational research designs; and single-subject research. There are advantages and disadvantages to each of these approaches.

4. In practice, it can be quite difficult to test experimental and control groups under identical circumstances. The most common problems that can affect the equivalence of circumstances are placebo effects, Hawthorne effects, and experimenter effects.

5. Random sampling is the best method for ensuring that a sample is representative of its population.

6. The three types of measures that are used most often in psychology research are self-report, behavioral, and physiological measures.

7. Researchers evaluate a measure in terms of its reliability and validity. A measure's reliability is its accuracy or consistency. The most commonly examined types of reliability are test-retest reliability, internal consistency, and inter-rater reliability. A measure's validity is how well it actually measures what it is intended to measure. A measure has content validity if it gets at all the different

aspects of what it is intended to measure. It has criterion-related validity if the measure correlates with another indicator of what it is intended to measure. Predictive validity and concurrent validity are two different types of criterion-related validity. A measure is often considered to have construct validity if there is evidence that what the test measures corresponds to the underlying theoretical variable it is meant to assess.

Key Terms

true experiment
experimental group
control group
participants
independent variable
experimental manipulation
dependent variable
population
sample
random assignment to groups
matched-groups research design

repeated measures research
    design
counterbalancing
correlational research design
single-subject research
placebo effects
Hawthorne effects
experimenter effects
generalizability
random sampling
self-report measures

behavioral measures
physiological measures
reliability
test-retest reliability
internal consistency
interrater reliability
validity
response bias
content validity
criterion-related validity

Chapter Notes

1. Research is sometimes done for other purposes, such as to explore relationships among measures, to determine the incidence of some characteristic in the population, or to develop a test or technique for use in other research. However, the basic logic of the usual kind of research (the focus of this Web chapter) shapes psychologists' approaches to almost all systematic research.

2. Traditionally psychologists used the term *subject*. However, in keeping with the contemporary practice, we use the word *participant* here.

Chapter 15

Applying Statistical Methods in Your Own Research Project

So you're going to carry out your own research project! This chapter helps you use what you have learned in *Statistics for Psychology* to explore an idea in your own research. You have a fairly clear understanding of the major statistical methods used in psychology, and you can make sense of them when they are used in a research article. However, it will help you to have some additional points to apply this smoothly to your own research. In particular, in this Web chapter we consider the following topics:

❶ Designing your study (determining whether there is an appropriate statistical method and determining needed sample size)

❷ Conducting the study

❸ Entering the scores into the computer

❹ Checking for and dealing with missing scores (for example, where a participant did not answer all the questions on a personality test)

❺ Checking whether the scores on each variable meet the assumptions for the procedure you want to use (and what to do about it if they don't)

❻ Carrying out the analyses

❼ Writing up your results

Designing Your Study: Selecting a Statistical Test

Once you have a possible idea for a research question, the next step is to develop a specific research plan to address that question—one that does as good a job as possible of approximating the ideal research design in terms of equivalence of experimental and control groups, equivalence of circumstances, generalizability, and measurement.

Before starting out on a new study, experienced researchers plan what statistical method they will use when the study is done. Otherwise you may find there are no methods available or the ones that are available will be less than ideal for some reason. You also need to decide in advance what statistical test you will use in order to figure out how many participants you will need (sample size) and the statistical power of your planned study.

What Test to Use in the Usual Situation of Equal-Interval Measurement

In the most common research situation, your scores are measured on an approximately equal-interval scale. Figure 1 shows a decision tree for deciding on an appropriate statistical test in this standard situation. Answering the questions in the decision tree will guide you to the appropriate statistical test. (Figure 1 also assumes you have just one dependent or criterion measured variable; we'll consider what to do when you have more than one at the end of this overall section on selecting an appropriate test.)

The first question in the decision tree is: Are you testing the *difference between means* or *the association among variables*? For example, consider a study comparing the effect of different colors of printing on reading time. This study focuses on the mean reading time for each color; thus, this is a study comparing means of variables. On the other hand, consider a study looking at the relation of mother's age to her oldest child's school grades (or, to put this another way, whether mother's age predicts her oldest child's school grades). This study is about associations among variables.

Suppose your study focuses on *differences between means*. The next question is whether there are two means being compared (for example, if you were looking

Figure 1 Decision tree for identifying statistical tests for studies with an equal-interval dependent or criterion measured variable.

at red printing vs. black printing) or whether there are three or more means (for example, if you were looking at differences among printing in red, black, green, and blue). A *t* test is the appropriate test when there are two means being compared and an analysis of variance is the appropriate test with three or more means. Once you have decided on a *t* test or analysis of variance, you have to make another decision. You next must decide whether this is a between-subjects design or a within-subjects design (also called a repeated measures design). In a between-subjects design different people are in each group (for example, some participants will read a story in black printing and other participants will read the story in red printing). In a within-subjects design the same people will be in each group (for example, each participant will read one story in black printing and another story in red printing).

What if your study focuses on *associations or predictions*? In that case, the next question is whether there is one variable being correlated with or predicting the other (for example, mother's age predicting her oldest child's school grades) or more than one variable being correlated with or predicting the other (for example, mother's age and father's age predicting oldest child's school grades). You use correlation or bivariate prediction when there is one predictor variable. You use multiple regression when there are two or more predictor variables. Notice that in all these situations we are correlating with or predicting about a single variable. In the language of prediction (regression) there is only one criterion variable (in the example it is oldest child's school grades). We will have more to say about this situation shortly.

The decision tree in Figure 1 leads you to the correct statistical test to use in each of these situations.

What Test to Use When Your Scores are Categories

Suppose you are testing a hypothesis with a variable whose scores are categories (that is, it is a nominal variable). Examples of categorical variables are which of several candidates a person most favors, or which major a student is taking. The standard chi-square tests for goodness of fit and for independence cover most such situations. However, you can only use these tests when each person is in a single category on any one nominal variable. So, for example, it would not be appropriate to use a chi-square test in an experiment to examine the change in distribution of men's and women's preferred brand of shampoo from before to after viewing a video clip about hair maintenance (the problem arises because it is the same people tested twice). Also, if you have a three- or more-way contingency table, you need to use procedures that are quite advanced (such as *log-linear chi-square*) and in any case often can not answer very directly the questions you might pose. Thus, if you have designed a study with nominal variables and any one person can be in more than one category on a particular nominal variable, or you have more than a two-way table, we strongly urge you to find a way to re-design your study, perhaps by using a measure that is equal-interval instead.

Incidentally, there is a trick you can use when your nominal variable has only two categories, such as male and female (or if you can combine categories so you end up with only two, as in whether various majors are arts or science). In this situation you can then give the two categories any two arbitrary numbers, such as 1 and 2, and then treat the variable as an ordinary equal-interval variable so you can use *t* tests, correlation, and so on. But this does not work for more than two categories; also you should not use this method if the split between the two categories is quite extreme (say more than 80% in one of the groups).

What Test to Use When You Have Rank-Order Scores

Suppose you are interested in carrying out hypothesis testing with scores for a rank-order variable, such as place finished in a race or birth order in one's family. With rank-order scores, you may want to use one of the special rank-order tests. (You will likely learn more about such tests in intermediate statistics courses.) Most of these are available in SPSS (by selecting *Analyze* and then *Nonparametric Tests*). You can use Figure 1 to find what test you would use if you had equal interval scores, and then find the appropriate equivalent rank-order test using Table 4 of "Strategies When Population Distributions Are Not Normal." However, in most cases you get reasonably accurate results if you just use the ordinary equal-interval statistical procedures, treating the ranks (1, 2, 3, etc.) as if they were equal-interval scores. If you want to be more accurate, you can use the ordinary tests with the adjustment described in Chapter Note 3 of "Strategies When Population Distributions Are Not Normal."

When You Have More than One Criterion or Dependent Measured Variable

Most psychology research studies have a single criterion or dependent measured variable, and the standard methods you know (correlation, regression, *t* test, etc.) are designed for such situations. However, you will sometimes want do to studies that use more than one such variable. For example, an experiment on the effect of color of printing on reading a story might measure both time to read the story and also comprehension of the story. Or a survey might look at how mother's age predicts four criterion variables, her oldest child's grades in elementary school, junior high school, high school, and college. We focus on three potential solutions for handling such research situations: method of separate analyses; method of averaging measures; and multivariate tests.

Method of Separate Analyses   In studies like these, one solution is to use separate ordinary tests for each variable. Thus, you might run one *t* test comparing the effects of different colors of printing on reading time and another *t* test comparing the effect of the different colors on reading comprehension. Similarly, you could conduct one regression analysis with mother's age predicting her oldest child's elementary school grades, another with mother's age predicting her oldest child's junior high school grades, and so on. Keep in mind, however, the kinds of issues having to do with multiple comparisons. For example, if you have four *different* *t* tests you have a better than 5% chance that one of them, by chance, will come out significant at the .05 level. One solution to the problem is to use a Bonferroni procedure.

Method of Averaging Measures   Another solution is to combine the several criterion or dependent measures into a single overall measure. (This is particularly appropriate if there are high correlations among the variables being combined.) For example, you could take the average of the four kinds of grades. However, in some situations, it is not so simple. Consider what would happen if you just did a simple average of each participant's reading time and reading comprehension score. One problem is that shorter reading times are better, but higher comprehension scores are better. So, before averaging, you would need to reverse one of them. For example, if reading times go from 200 to 300 seconds, you can subtract each time from 300; then a high score would mean a better time and a low score would mean a worse reading time. Another problem in this example is that the two variables might be on quite different scales—for example, reading time (after reversing) goes from 0 to 100, comprehension scores might go from 1 to 7. Thus, if you combined them, the reading time would probably have a bigger influence on the mean. A solution to this problem is to convert all the scores on each scale to Z scores, then average the Z scores. (In the reading example, you would still have to reverse one of the measures before figuring the Z scores.) In this way, the different measures are put on the same scale.

Multivariate Tests   Yet another approach would be to carry out an overall analysis that considers all the criterion or dependent variables together. (The advantage of such a procedure over just averaging is that it automatically gives optimal weights to each variable in the context of what you are specifically testing, instead of just evenly combining them.) Such procedures are called *multivariate statistical tests*. You can learn more about multivariate statistical tests in more advanced statistics courses. So, until you take such courses, it is best to use the procedures you know, either doing separate tests for each variable or combining the variables by averaging. (In fact, the general advice even to experienced researchers who are masters of advanced statistical methods, is to use the simplest methods available that are reasonably accurate. The idea is that, with simpler procedures, results will be more understandable to readers, and also the researcher is less likely to make mistakes.)

Figuring Power and Needed Sample Size

A crucial issue when planning a study is deciding if there is sufficient statistical power. That is, power addresses the question, if the research hypothesis is true, what is the probability this study will produce a significant result supporting it? To figure the statistical power of a planned study, first you need to decide what statistical test you will use. Then you have to make some estimate of the expected effect size. You would be aware of estimating effect size—you may have a rough idea of whether the effect will be small, medium, or large based on previous similar research or a minimum effect size that would be important. If your study will use one of the major procedures we cover (*t* tests, analysis of variance, chi-square tests, correlation, and regression) in *Statistics for Psychology*, there are power tables in each chapter. (Table 5 in the Appendix is an index to these power tables.) If you are using a more advanced or unusual procedure that is not covered in the book, you may be able to find the power in Cohen's (1988) book of tables or by using power statistical software or an Internet power calculator. If your planned study has too little power (say, less than 80%), our Table 5 of "Making Sense of Statistical Significance" suggests several ways you can alter the study to increase the power—such as by increasing the number of participants.

You can also start with an expected effect size and use one of the tables that tell you how many participants you need for 80% power. (Table 5 in the Appendix includes an index to such tables.) It often turns out that the number you need is too large to be practical. This happens because participants can be hard to recruit, not everyone you try to recruit will actually qualify for your study, and if you need to test participants on more than one occasion, you are likely to lose some of them after the first testing. Thus, you may need to use one of the other methods listed in Table 5 of "Making Sense of Statistical Significance" to increase power or change the basic study itself.

Conducting the Study

From the point of view of the statistical analyses, there are three main things to keep in mind during the data gathering:

1. When you set up the layout of the questionnaires or data recording sheets, consider how easy it will be to type the scores into the computer (or if you are having participants respond on the computer, by e-mail, or via the Internet, set up the program so that it is easy to move their responses to an SPSS file).
2. Keep all of the questionnaires, data recording sheets, or participant files in a safe place (and if you have computer data, make copies right away).
3. Make sure you have recorded everything important with each participant's data—such as date and time of the study, experimental condition, and anything else that is not filled out by the participants. Now and then a student conducts a study and when it is done discovers that there is no record of which participant was in which experimental condition! It is also important to record anything unusual that happens with a participant.

Entering Scores Into the Computer

As for entering the scores into a computer, here are some suggestions for making the process as straightforward and accurate as possible. (This section assumes the data are not collected directly on the computer.)

Setting Up the Spreadsheet

With SPSS and most statistical programs, you type the scores into a spreadsheet, using one line per participant and one column per variable. Give some thought in advance as to how you will set this up. For example, arrange the columns for the variables in the same order as they are on the original questionnaires or data recording sheets.

Variable Names

It is important to type at the top of each column the descriptive name for each variable (rather than leave the variable named by the column number). Use a name that describes the particular variable—for example, "age" and "gender" are better than "variable1" or "question2." Until a few years ago, SPSS limited variable names to a maximum of 8 characters. Recent versions of SPSS allow longer variable names, but we still recommend that you try not to use variable names that are longer than about 10–12 characters. (Otherwise it gets hard to read the names in the columns and the printouts of results are very lengthy.)

Sums and Codes

To avoid work and errors, enter the scores directly and let the program do any needed combining figuring. For example, if you have a 10-item questionnaire, it is better to enter the person's score on each item and let the program figure the total or average. Similarly, if the program needs number codes for a variable that was originally entered as words or letters, enter the words or letters—for example, "f" or "m" for gender, and then instruct the program to make an additional column with number codes it creates for these. That way you will make fewer mistakes, and you won't forget later which number goes with which letter! Alternatively, you may want to include number codes in your variable name. For example, the variable name "campus_y1n0" could be used to indicate that students who live on campus were coded as "1" and students who do not live on campus were coded as "0."

Typing in the Scores

Have all material organized and at hand. If possible, type in all the data at once. Save often. Keep notes of any irregularities (for example, a participant who answers 8 on a 1 to 7 scale) or any decisions you make (for example, that if a person marks between two scale points, you have decided you will always score it as the higher scale point). When you are done, be sure to save a copy of the data file in more than one location (for example, on the hard drive of your computer and on a flash drive—but, of course, also be sure that any file that includes identifying information about participants is kept in a secure location).

Check Your Work

Accuracy is extremely important. If possible, have someone else double check the entries for at least a few of your participants.

Conducting Research Using Computerized and Internet Methods

Psychologists commonly conduct research studies that use computerized methods (such as examining reaction times to different stimuli presented on a computer monitor) or for which data are collected via the Internet. Just as with data entry of information from paper and pencil questionnaires, it is very important to thoroughly check that the data from a computerized or Internet study are being collected accurately and that the way the results are recorded and will be available to you will be in a form you can easily interpret. Also, be sure that your output is labeled so that it has all the needed information about the time and date and any additional information you need to tie the material on the computer to any other information that participants provided (for example, on paper questionnaires). If you are considering conducting a computerized or Internet study, be sure to consult some of the many helpful resources that are available (e.g., Fielding et al., 2008; Gaiser & Schreiner, 2009; Gosling & Johnson, 2010; Reynolds et al., 2007).

Data Screening

Experienced researchers resist the urge to jump right into the analysis as soon as all the scores are entered. First, they "screen" the data for accuracy, missing values, and whether the assumptions for the planned statistical tests are met. That way, they don't get excited (or depressed) about their conclusions, and then find later that their conclusions had no relation to the real results.

Checks for Accuracy

Even after you have double checked your typing or program entries carefully, errors are still common. With so many numbers, it is just too easy to make mistakes (even big ones that drastically change results—such as holding down the 0 key too long so that you accidentally enter 100 instead of 10, or the program putting numbers into the wrong column). The most important additional check is based on a listing of each variable's number of cases, mean, standard deviation, and maximum and minimum score. (In SPSS, you can get such a listing by selecting *Analyze*, *Descriptive Statistics*, *Descriptives*, then selecting all of your numeric variables and clicking *OK*.) If you have more than one grouping, such as an experimental and a control group, you may want to list the output for each group separately. (In SPSS, you can get separate outputs for each grouping by selecting *Data*, *Split File*, checking "Organize output by groups," selecting the grouping variable, and clicking *OK*.)

Once you have this listing, for each variable you look at (a) the number of cases, to be sure that all or most of the participants have scores on the variable; (b) the maximum, to be sure that none of the scores are higher than is possible (such as a 700 on a scale that goes from 1 to 7); (c) the minimum, to be sure that none of the score are lower than possible (such as a minus value for number of children); and (d) the mean and standard deviation, to be sure they seem reasonable in light of other similar variables in your study and what you know about these measures. For example, consider a study in which you ask 70 people to rate their anxiety level on a scale from 1 (very low) to 10 (very high) after watching a frightening movie. Figure 2 shows the SPSS output for the descriptive statistics of the anxiety variable (this output was obtained by selecting *Analyze, Descriptive Statistics, Descriptives*). The output shows that anxiety scores were obtained from 68 of the 70 people. Thus, you should double check that two people did in fact not indicate their level of anxiety. The "maximum" column shows that the highest score was 100. This cannot be correct, as the scale went from 1 to 10. Even with the incorrect value of 100, the mean of 6.84 (rounding to two decimal places) seems plausible in the context of the study (ratings of anxiety from 1 to 10 after watching a frightening movie). However, hopefully you would question whether the standard deviation for a set of scores ranging from 1 to 10 could really be 11.70. Remember that, roughly speaking, the standard deviation represents the average amount that scores vary around the mean. Thus, it would not make sense for a set of scores ranging from 1 to 10 to vary by an average of 11.70 from the mean of the scores. After realizing that the score of 100 cannot be correct, you go back to the relevant survey and notice that the correct score was 10. You then make the correction in the SPSS spreadsheet and repeat the descriptives analysis. Figure 3 shows the SPSS output. As you see, all of

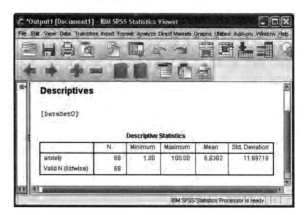

Figure 2   Descriptive statistics for the anxiety variable when one score was incorrectly entered as 100 instead of 10.

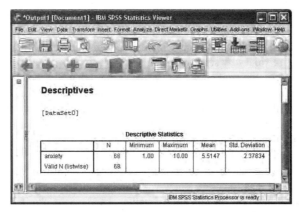

Figure 3   Descriptive statistics for the anxiety variable when all of the scores were entered correctly.

the descriptive statistics (including the maximum value and the standard deviation, both of which previously seemed problematic) now seem plausible.

If you have any nominal variables, you can do a similar check with a listing for each such variable of how many participants fall into each category. This is also a good idea for numeric variables that have only a few possible whole number values, such as a 1 to 5 scale or number of siblings. (In SPSS, you can get such a listing by selecting *Analyze*, *Descriptive Statistics*, *Frequencies*, and then selecting the desired variables and clicking *OK*.) For each variable, check whether the numbers in the different categories seem reasonable.

Missing Values

Often, participants don't answer every question on a questionnaire, observers miss a particular behavior, recording devices fail, there was a glitch in a program, or a participant's results are lost. These kinds of situations create *missing values*. (When entering your data, it is usually best to leave the place blank where a missing value would go. If instead you put in some number like 999 or –1, it could end up being included in the figuring later!)

You can tell how many missing values you have from the number of cases for each variable in the variable listing you make for your accuracy check (as described in the previous subsection). It is also a good idea to look through the data spreadsheet file on the computer or print it out (in SPSS, with the data on the screen, select *File* and then *Print*). You can then see whether any particular participants have most of the missing values or the missing values are spread among different participants.

In general, what you do about missing values depends on whether you think they are missing for some systematic reason or just haphazardly. For example, if the question is about a sensitive topic, those who don't answer might be systematically different in relation to this topic from those who do. In such situations, you have two main choices: You can simply not do any analyses involving that variable, or you can go ahead with just those participants who answered on it, but keeping in mind that your results only apply to the kinds of people who are likely to answer such questions.

Suppose there are only a few missing values and the pattern seems more or less random. In this situation, a common procedure is to substitute, for each missing value, the average of everyone else's score on that variable. (If you were merely to leave them missing, you might exclude any participant who had a missing value on any variable—something SPSS does automatically most of the time—sometimes resulting in losing most of your participants from the analysis.) In SPSS, you can substitute missing values by selecting *Transform, Replace Missing Values,* selecting the appropriate variable, and clicking *OK* (the method that SPSS automatically uses here if you don't select special options is to replace the missing values with the mean of all other participants who had scores for that variable). If the study has groups, you can substitute the value for the average of that group. If a person has a missing value on an item that is part of a multi-item measure (such as one item not answered on a 12-item anxiety questionnaire), you might substitute that person's average on the items of the scale that he or she completed. When you are substituting missing values, it is a good idea to create a new variable (with its own column on the SPSS spreadsheet) that includes the substituted values, keeping the original variable as it was. That way you don't lose track of exactly when you did and did not substitute.

Checking for Normal Distributions

Most statistical tests require that the variables be normally distributed in the population. There are also additional assumptions in many procedures, such as equal population variances, which should be checked before carrying out a particular analysis. But we focus here on normality because it applies to nearly all parametric statistical tests.

Checking for Skewness   Skewness means a distribution is not normal because it is lopsided with a long tail on one side. Thus, as part of data screening, you check each variable for its degree of skewness. First, you figure each variable's numerical skewness value; perfect normality is 0. (In SPSS, you can get skewness by selecting *Analyze, Descriptive Statistics, Descriptives, Options,* checking "Skewness," and then clicking *Continue* followed by *OK*.) Then, for any variable that has a very high or low skewness value—say more extreme than ± 1— you make a histogram and look at it visually to see if it looks seriously skewed. (In SPSS, you make a histogram by selecting *Graphs, Legacy Dialogs, Histogram*.)

What to do About Seriously Skewed Distributions   Presuming skewed distributions are not caused by one or a few very extreme cases (see below), you can go ahead and use one of the strategies that you know, such as transforming the scores or using a rank-order method.

Checking for Outliers (Extreme Scores)   Most statistical tests still give accurate results as long as skewness is not too extreme. The main cause of extreme skewness are outliers, which are problematic for almost all statistical tests. You check for outliers by looking for *very* high skewness values or for very long tails or separated scores in the histograms. Another method is to figure Z scores for your variables. (In SPSS, you can get Z scores by selecting *Analyze, Descriptive Statistics, Descriptives,* checking "Save standardized values as variables," and clicking *OK*. This gives each variable a new column showing the Z scores for that variable. Next, you can look down the columns of Z scores for any scores that appear extreme. For example, unless you have a *very* large sample size, a Z score more than ± 3 is almost surely an outlier.

What to do About Outliers If you find an outlier, look at the raw questionnaire or data record to be sure it is not a typing error. Next, consider whether there is something about the participant that might categorize him or her as outside of the population to which you want to apply your results. (For example, in a college-student sample, this person might be 45 years old when everyone else is age 18 to 22.) In that situation, you can simply exclude the participant from the analysis. If the person really is part of what you consider the relevant population, one option is to use a rank-order test. Another common option is to recode the extreme score so that it is still the most extreme score, but just slightly higher than the next highest score. (For example, if this person's reading time is 300 seconds and the next highest is 141 seconds, you could recode the person as 142.) Some researchers simply make it a practice to exclude participants whose scores are very extreme. Whatever solution you adopt, it is very important to include in your research report a description of what you did and why. (One huge advantage of screening data before analyzing results is that you are in a better position to make such decisions without having to worry that you are unconsciously biasing the outcome of the statistical test in your favor.)

Carrying out the Major Analyses

The most important advice here is, again, be sure you have thoroughly screened your data before you begin. Once you are ready, the next important step is to *look* at your data. Look at the means overall and by groups, at the histograms, at scatter diagrams, at patterns of correlations. Get to know your data.

Next, write out a systematic analysis plan—what analyses you are going to carry out and in what order—and follow it. (Ideally, you laid this out in advance when you designed the study.) Be sure that your plan focuses first and foremost on the hypotheses or research questions with which you began the study. Only then conduct the analyses.

When you look at each output, before looking at the results, be sure that the computer used the variables you intended, that it included all of the participants, and that it did the analysis you intended.

Once you have the major results, then it is a good idea to explore. But even here, it is wise to write out a list of the exploratory analyses you will do. Many of the most important discoveries in psychology came not from what was predicted in advance, but from unexpected findings in these explorations. Remember, however, that findings from exploration are more likely to be chance findings. It is like the problem of too many *t* tests; with many tests a few will come out significant just by chance. Thus, any findings from exploratory analyses need to be labeled as such when you write them up in your report and need to be taken as very tentative until they are replicated in a new study.

Writing Up Your Results

When you come to write up the results of your research study, it will usually be in the form of a paper or report with the following main sections: Abstract, Introduction, Methods, Results, Discussion. Some of your results actually go in the Methods section. These include information on your participants (mean and standard deviations for age and any other relevant background variables, number of each gender, and so on) and any reliability analyses on your measures. The rest of your results go in the Results section. Usually, you begin with descriptive statistics—means and standard deviations of your major variables. Then you describe each analysis in a systematic fashion, starting with those testing your hypotheses and research questions and then turning to exploratory analyses. For each analysis, clarify what hypothesis or research question or exploratory issue it is designed to test; describe the analysis (what kind of analysis it is, such as a correlation or t test for independent means, and what variables are involved); and give the results, including means, standard deviations, significance results (with degrees of freedom and p values), and effect sizes. Wherever it would make results clearer, use tables and graphs.

After the results section, a Discussion section usually summarizes the key conclusions, describes how your results bear on the larger issues the study was designed to address (that is, how is what we know about what you are studying different now than it was before you did the study and how this bears on previous research and theory), and notes the limitations of your study and anomalous results. Here, it is important not to get bogged down in explaining failures to get significance—be brief. And remember, a nonsignificant result means "inconclusive," not "no difference" (unless you had very high power). Finally, consider the implications for future research. Above all, in the Discussion, it is important to stick to the big picture. You will learn more about writing up your results in research methods courses. We strongly recommend that you take one or more such courses. There are also many resources, such as style and writing guides, available to help you improve your writing of research studies (e.g., American Psychological Association, 2009; Landrum, 2012; Nicol & Paxman, 2010a; Nicol & Paxman, 2010b).

Summary

1. Before conducting a research study, it is important to plan what statistical method(s) will be used to analyze the results.
2. When scores are measured on an apparently equal-interval scale, you must first decide whether you are testing the difference between means or the association among variables. If the focus is on differences between means, you have to determine whether you are comparing two means (in which case a t test is the appropriate test) or three or more means (for which an analysis of variance is the appropriate test), and you must also decide whether you have a between-subjects or a within-subjects (repeated measures) design. If the focus is on the association among variables, you must decide whether there is one variable being correlated with or predicting another variable (in which case correlation or bivariate prediction are appropriate tests) or more than one variable correlated with or predicting another variable (for which multiple regression is the appropriate test).
3. Chi-square tests are used when your scores are categories, but they can only be used when each person is in a single category on any one nominal variable. Special rank-order tests are used when your scores are measured on a rank-order scale.
4. When you have scores on one or more criterion or dependent measured variables, you can handle this situation using one of three approaches: (a) conduct separate analyses for each criterion or dependent variable; (b) create a single measure by averaging the scores across the criterion or dependent

variables; (c) use a multivariate test that considers all the criterion or dependent variables together.

5. It is important to estimate a study's statistical power before carrying it out.

6. There are a number of factors you should consider when entering the scores from your study into the computer, including setting up the spreadsheet carefully, using appropriate variable names, letting the computer do any summing or variable coding, typing in the data accurately, and checking your work. If you are collecting your data by computer, be sure to check that the data are being collected accurately and that the results will be available to you in a form you can use.

7. Before carrying out the main statistical analyses, you should screen your data for accuracy, to identify and handle missing values, and to check for normal distributions.

8. After carrying out your plan for the main statistical analyses, you may want to consider conducting some exploratory analyses.

9. When you are writing up the results of a research study, most of the results of the statistical analyses will go in the Results section of your paper or report, although some information about the study participants is usually given in the Methods section. Describe the implications of the study results and conclusions in your Discussion section.

References

American Psychological Association (2009). *Publication manual of the American Psychological Association (6th edition)*. Washington, DC: American Psychological Association.

Cohen, J. (1988). *Statistical power analysis for the behavioral sciences*. Hillsdale, NJ: Erlbaum.

Fielding, N. G., Lee, R. M., & Blank, G. (Eds.) (2008). *The handbook of online research methods*. London: Sage.

Gaiser, T. J., & Schreiner, A. E. (2009). *A guide to conducting online research*. London: Sage.

Gosling, S. D., & Johnson, J. A. (Eds.) (2010). *Advanced methods for conducting online behavioral research*. Washington, DC: American Psychological Association.

Landrum, R. E. (2012). *Undergraduate writing in psychology: Learning to tell the scientific story*. Washington, DC: American Psychological Association.

Nicol, A. A. M., & Paxman, P. M. (2010a). *Displaying your findings: A practical guide for creating figures, posters, and presentations (6th edition)*. Washington, DC: American Psychological Association.

Nicol, A. A. M., & Paxman, P. M. (2010b). *Presenting your findings: A practical guide for creating tables (6th edition)*. Washington, DC: American Psychological Association.

Reynolds, R. A., Woods, R., & Baker, J. D. (Eds.) (2007). *Handbook of research on electronic surveys and measurements*. Hershey, PA: Idea Group.

Appendix: Table

Table 5 Index to Power Tables and Tables Giving Number of Participants Needed for 80% Power

Hypothesis-Testing Procedure	Chapter	Power Table	Number of Participants Table
t test for dependent means	7	p. 253	p. 253
t test for independent means	8	p. 294	p. 295
One-way analysis of variance	9	p. 347	p. 347
Two-way analysis of variance	10	p. 415	p. 416
Correlation coefficient (r)	11	p. 471	p. 471
Chi-square test for independence	13	p. 564	p. 565

Chapter 16

Repeated Measures Analysis of Variance

Repeated Measures Analysis of Variance

TIP FOR SUCCESS

Before starting this chapter, you should have mastered the first ten chapters of *Statistics for Psychology*. It is especially important to have mastered the procedures in "Factorial Analysis of Variance" for working out a two-way analysis of variance.

In all the analysis of variance situations, the different cells or groupings were based on scores from different individuals. Sometimes, however, a researcher measures the same individual in several different situations. (If there are only two such conditions, such as before and after some treatment, you can use a *t* test for dependent means.) Consider a study in which the participants' task is to recognize a syllable when embedded in three word types flashed quickly on a screen: familiar words, unfamiliar words, and nonword sounds. The result is that, for each participant, you have the total number of errors for each word type. Or suppose you do a study of psychotherapy effects testing patients on their depression before, immediately following, and again three months after therapy. In both examples, you have three groups of scores, but all three scores are from the same people. These studies each employ a **repeated measures design**.

Repeated measures designs are often analyzed with a **repeated measures analysis of variance**, so named because the same participants are measured repeatedly. This kind of design and analysis is also called a **within-subjects design** and **within-subjects analysis of variance** because the comparison is within, not between, the different participants or subjects. In this chapter, we cover the following topics:

❶ The logic and figuring for a one-way repeated measures analysis of variance
❷ The assumptions for a one-way repeated measures analysis of variance and how researchers handle situations where the assumptions might not be met

❸ How to expand the basic one-way repeated measures analysis of variance to factorial repeated measures analysis of variance and to analyses of variance that include both repeated measures factors and the usual between-subjects factors

Basic Logic

Ironically, you carry out a *one-way* repeated measures analysis of variance using the procedures for a standard *two-way* between-subjects analysis of variance. But this standard two-way analysis is modified in one crucial respect. Just as with an ordinary two-way analysis of variance, you treat your groupings (conditions) as one factor, usually as columns. The modification is that the rows, instead of another factor, are participants. That is, there is one participant per row, and each participant has a score in each column. (See the example in the top of Table 1.) Thus, one factor is conditions and the other factor is participants; the cells have only one score each. Your main effect for conditions, as in any analysis of variance, uses the population variance estimate based on the deviation of each score's condition's mean from the grand mean. However, what changes is the population variance estimate that is the denominator of the *F* ratio.

In a repeated measures analysis of variance, you cannot use the within-cell variation as your denominator for the *F* ratio. One problem is that there is no within-cell variation. There is only one score per cell, and there cannot be any variation within a single score. An alternative that might seem reasonable at first glance would be to use the average variation within each condition, as you would do in an ordinary one-way between-subjects analysis of variance. This, however, ignores the fact that

Table 1 Scores and Scores Minus Participant's Mean for Four Participants Each Exposed to Target Syllable in Familiar, Unfamiliar, and Nonword-Sound Word Types (Fictional Data)

Actual Scores:

Measure: Number of errors

	Word Type		
	Familiar	*Unfamiliar*	*Nonword*
Participant	*Word*	*Word*	*Sound*
A	9	3	0
B	6	2	1
C	11	6	4
D	10	5	3

Scores minus participant's mean:

Measure: Number of errors

	Word Type		
	Familiar	*Unfamiliar*	*Nonword*
Participant	*Word*	*Word*	*Sound*
A	5	−1	−4
B	3	−1	−2
C	4	−1	−3
D	4	−1	−3

the scores in each condition are from the same participants. Ignoring this is a problem for technical reasons (it violates the requirement that all scores should be independent). More important, however, is that doing so would not take advantage of the fact that you are interested in differences among conditions *over and above individual overall differences among participants*. So how do you take the repeated measures nature of the study into account?

One solution that takes the repeated measures nature of the study into account would be to use, for each score, not the actual score, but its difference from that participant's mean across conditions. For example, consider the scores in the top part of Table 1 showing the number of errors for four participants who each were exposed to the syllable embedded in 30 presentations each of Familiar Words, Unfamiliar Words, and Nonword Sounds. Participant A's average is 4 errors (that is, $9 + 3 + 0$ divided by 3). Thus, A's errors in the Familiar Word condition are 5 above A's average, A's errors in the Unfamiliar Word condition are 1 below A's average, and A's errors in the Nonword Sound condition are 4 below A's average. The bottom part of Table 1 shows these scores (each score minus the participant's own mean) for all four participants.

Suppose you were to figure an ordinary between-subjects one-way analysis of variance using these difference-from-the-participant's-own-mean scores. Your results would come out in a way that takes into account, and properly takes advantage of, the fact that the same participants are in each condition. You can see that there is much less variance within conditions in this lower table than in the original scores in the upper table. This is because we have eliminated the variation due to overall between person tendencies—everyone's scores only vary from their own mean so that any variation among different participants' means is eliminated. The result of there being less variance is that the within-group population variance is smaller, making the overall F larger. (This is the same principle with the t test for dependent means that a repeated measures design in general has more power. Now you can see the reason for this: the repeated measures design removes the variance due to individual overall differences among participants.)

If you were actually to carry out a standard between-subjects one-way analysis of variance with these scores in the bottom table (that is, taking the conditions as groups and figuring the denominator of the F ratio based on the variation within conditions), you would have to correct the degrees of freedom for the fact that you are subtracting out mean scores. You would then get the correct results. But it would also be a tedious process in a larger analysis because you would have to perform all these subtractions of scores from each participant's means. This method also gets complicated in more complex designs.

Thus, in practice, researchers use a slightly different approach that accomplishes the same thing. When figuring the denominator of the F ratio in a repeated measures analysis like this, they take advantage of the two-way set up and use the interaction of participants by conditions. This interaction, like any interaction, is the difference in pattern across one factor according to the level of the other factor. In this situation, it means the average variation in pattern across conditions for different participants. Since we are looking at patterns, we are in effect subtracting out each participant's mean. In fact, using this interaction term gives exactly the same result as using the scores based on differences from each participant's mean that we described in the preceding paragraph (after adjusting the degrees of freedom appropriately).

Here is another way to think of this participant × condition interaction. Like any interaction, its sum of squared deviations is the total squared deviations from the grand mean minus all the other deviations—the deviations within cells and the deviations for each of the factors. In this situation, however, the deviations within cells (the deviation of each score from its cell's mean) are all 0, because there is only one score per cell. This means that, in addition to subtracting out the deviations for the main effect for conditions (each score's condition's mean minus the grand mean), you are *also* subtracting out the deviations of each score's participant's mean from the grand mean. That is, by subtracting out the differences among participant's means, you are subtracting out the overall differences among participants, which is—as we have seen—what gives such an advantage to repeated measures designs.

In sum, you can think of a one-way repeated measures analysis of variance across conditions as a two-way analysis of variance in which one factor is experimental condition and the other factor is participant. Also, your between-conditions population variance estimate is as usual based on the deviations of each score's condition mean from the grand mean, but in which the within-groups population variance estimate is based only on the deviation of scores within conditions after adjusting for each participant's overall mean.

It is important to note that, in order to conduct a repeated measures analysis of variance, each participant in your study must have a score for each condition. Participants who are missing a score from one or more conditions should be dropped from the analysis.

Figuring a One-Way Repeated Measures Analysis of Variance

Following the logic we have just considered, you figure a one-way repeated measures analysis of variance by setting it up as a condition × participant two-way design, figuring the two main effects and interaction in the usual way, and testing the condition main effect with an *F* ratio of the between-condition population variance estimate divided by the interaction population variance estimate.

Here are the steps:

❶ **Set up the scores with groupings across the top** (the conditions factor on which each participant has a score for each condition) **and a row for each participant**.

❷ **Figure the sums of squares in the usual way for total** (squared deviations of each score from the grand mean), **columns** (squared deviations of each score's column's mean from the grand mean), **and rows** (squared deviations of each score's row's mean from the grand mean). Notice that in figuring the sum of squares for rows, the row means are the same as each participant's mean score across conditions.

❸ **Figure the sum of squares for the interaction**, figuring the deviation for each score as its deviation from the grand mean minus the deviation of its column's mean from the grand mean and minus the deviation of its row's mean from the grand mean. (That is, you don't need also to subtract the scores deviation from its cell's mean because all cells only have one score, so this deviation is always 0.)

❹ **Figure the degrees of freedom in the usual way for columns** (the number of columns minus 1), **rows** (the number of rows minus 1), **and interaction** (the number of cells minus the degrees of freedom for rows and columns, minus 1). Notice that the degrees of freedom for rows is the number of participants minus 1.

❺ **Figure the mean squares** (the population variance estimates) **in the usual way for columns and the interaction**. For columns, this means the columns' sum of squares divided by the columns' degrees of freedom; for the interaction, this means the interaction's sum of squares divided by the interaction's degrees of freedom. Notice that you do not figure a population variance estimate based on rows. This would be the variance among participants, which is not usually of interest.

❻ **Figure the F ratio for the repeated measures condition effect**: Divide the mean square for columns by the mean square for the interaction.

To test the significance of the repeated measures condition effect, compare your F to a cutoff F based on the appropriate numerator (columns) and denominator (interaction) degrees of freedom.

Table 2 shows scores, figuring, and an analysis of variance table for the repeated measures analysis of variance for the example we have been considering.

Assumptions and Related Issues

The assumptions for a repeated measures analysis of variance include the usual ones for an ordinary analysis of variance—normal distributions and equal variances of the populations for each condition or condition combination. There is also an additional assumption, called **sphericity**. Sphericity means that not only are the population variances for each condition the same, but the population correlations among the different conditions are the same. A correlation describes the association between scores on two or more variables.) For example, if you have sphericity, the population correlation between errors in the Familiar Word condition and errors in the Unfamiliar Word condition will be the same as the correlation between errors in the Familiar Word condition and errors in the Nonword Sounds condition.

With the small sample size usually used in repeated measures analysis of variance, it is hard to know whether you meet any of the assumptions. For example, regarding sphericity, correlations in small samples can vary quite considerably even if in the population they are equal. And correlations in small samples could be quite similar even if in the population they are different. The difficulty of knowing whether you have met the sphericity assumption is especially a problem because the accuracy of the F test for repeated measures analysis of variance can be strongly affected by violations of this assumption.

There are two widely used solutions for dealing with possible violations of the sphericity assumption. One solution is to estimate how much the assumption is violated and statistically correct for it by using a comparison F distribution with fewer degrees of freedom (so that you need a stronger result to be significant). Thus, when you do a repeated measures analysis of variance with most statistics programs (including SPSS), in addition to the standard results, you get various results with corrected degrees of freedom and the resulting more conservative (less extreme) significance levels.

For example, Figure 1 shows a key section of the SPSS output for the example we have been considering. (The slight difference in the F figured in Table 2 is due to rounding error.) Notice that in addition to the standard output ("sphericity assumed"), you get three other results. These refer to different ways of correcting for violation of the sphericity assumption. The correction is to the degrees of freedom. The Fs all come out the same, but since they are being compared to different F distributions, the p levels are not the same. In this present example, the

Table 2 One-Way Repeated Measures Analysis at Variance for Study of Errors in Recognition for Four Participants Each Exposed to Target Syllable in Familiar, Unfamiliar, and Nonword-Sound Word Types (Fictional Data)

Measure: Number of errors

		Word Type			Row	
		Familiar	Unfamiliar	Nonword		
Participant	❶	Word	Word	Sound	Σ	M
A		9	3	0	12	4
B		6	2	1	9	3
C		11	6	4	21	7
D		10	5	3	18	6
Σ		36	16	8		
M		9	4	2		

$$GM = 5$$

Squared deviations from grand mean

Participant		Familiar Word				Unfamiliar Word				Nonword Sound		
	X	Column	Row	Int	X	Column	Row	Int	X	Column	Row	Int
A	16	16	1	1	4	1	1	0	25	9	1	1
B	1	16	4	1	9	1	4	0	16	9	4	1
C	36	16	4	0	1	1	4	0	1	9	4	0
D	25	16	1	0	0	1	1	0	4	9	1	0
Σ	78	64	10	2	14	4	10	0	46	36	10	2

$SS_{Total} = 78 + 14 + 46 = 138$

❷ $SS_{Columns} = 64 + 4 + 36 = 104$

$SS_{Rows} = 10 + 10 + 10 = 30$

❸ $SS_{Interaction} = 2 + 0 + 2 = 4$

Check: $SS_{Total} = SS_{Columns} + SS_{Rows} + SS_{Interaction} = 104 + 30 + 4 = 138$

$df_{Total} = 12 - 1 = 11$

$df_{Columns} = 3 - 1 = 2$

$df_{Rows} = 4 - 1 = 3$

❹ $df_{Interaction} = 11 - 2 - 3 = 6$

Check: $df_{Total} = df_{Columns} + df_{Rows} + df_{Interaction} = 2 + 3 + 6 = 11$

F needed for repeated measures (columns) effect ($df = 2, 6; p < .05$): 5.14

Analysis of Variance Table

Source	SS	df	❺ MS	F
Between Conditions (Columns)	104	2	52	77.6
Participants (Rows)	30	3		
Error (Interaction)	4	6	.67	
Total	138	11		

Conclusion: Reject the null hypothesis. ❻

uncorrected result (with $df = 2, 6$) has a p that rounds off to .000. But the corrected results (with $dfs = 1, 3$) are all about .003.

In most real data sets, the three different corrected results (that is, their dfs and p values) also differ from each other. The "Lower-bound" correction, as the name

Figure 1 Key section of SPSS output for study of errors in recognition for four participants, each exposed to a target syllable in familiar, unfamiliar, and nonword-sound word types (fictional data).

suggests, is the most conservative, giving the highest p value. The "Greenhouse-Geisser" correction is the next most conservative. The "Huynh-Feldt" correction is the least conservative, but still widely (although not unanimously) agreed to be quite accurate. Thus, most psychologists focus on the Huynh-Feldt correction.

If the results using the **Huynh-Feldt correction** are not much different from the uncorrected (sphericity assumed) results, for simplicity, researchers usually just report the uncorrected results. However, if there is much difference between the corrected and uncorrected results, then the Huynh-Feldt corrected results are usually reported. In the present example, researchers would probably just report significance as $p <$ .01. Another solution to the concern about violating the sphericity assumption is to use an entirely different approach, a special application of *multivariate analysis of variance*. Thus, most computer printouts for a repeated measures analysis of variance also automatically include results of multivariate tests. The results using these tests are typically similar to those using the standard procedures. (In the word-type example we have been considering, the p for the multivariate tests is .003.) Most psychologists use the standard procedures, although there is a strong minority opinion in favor of the multivariate approach. The advantage of the multivariate approach is that you don't have to make the sphericity assumption. On the other hand, with small samples, the multivariate approach usually has lower power and you get around the sphericity assumption in any case by using the Huynh-Feldt correction.

More Complex Repeated Measures Designs and Mixed Designs

So far, we have considered the one-way repeated measures analysis of variance, in which each of several participants are tested under different conditions. In this design, there is one repeated measures variable, such as Word Type. Sometimes, however, a study includes two or more repeated measures variables. For example, Word Type could be crossed with Word Length, so that each participant might have scores in six conditions: Familiar Long Words, Familiar Short Words, Unfamiliar Long Words, and so forth. This would be an example of a **two-way repeated measures design**. The repeated measures two-way analysis of variance would be set up like a three-way between-subjects analysis of variance, with one dimension for Word Type, one dimension for Word Length, and one dimension for Participants. The denominator of the F ratio for each of the two condition main effects (Word Type and Word Length) and their interaction (Word Type $\times$ Word Length) would in each case be the interaction of that term with the Participant factor. For example, you would test the Word Length main effect by figuring an F ratio in which the numerator is the population variance estimate based on the Word Length mean squares and the denominator is the population variance estimate based on the Word Length $\times$ Participant interaction mean squares.

It is also possible to have in the same analysis both repeated measures and ordinary between-subjects factors. For example, in the word recognition study, each participant might have only the three Word Types, but some participants might be college age and other participants might be in their 70s. Thus, you would have one repeated measures factor (Word Type) and one between-subjects factor (Age). This would be an example of a **mixed design**. In this example, the analysis of variance allows you to test the main effect for the repeated measures factor (Word Type), the main effect for the between-subjects factor (Age), and the interaction (Word Type $\times$ Age).

The actual figuring of a mixed design is somewhat complicated, but two main points are of interest. First, the between-subjects part of the analysis would come out the same as if you were doing a one-way analysis for the between subjects factor using each participant's mean across the conditions. That is, in the example, it would be the same result as if you just had two levels of age and the scores within each were each participant's mean number of errors across the three words types. Second, the denominator of the F ratio for the repeated measures main effect and the interaction is based on the interaction of participant with the repeated measures factor, figured separately within each level of the between-subjects factor (for each age group) and averaged. That is, in the example, the main effect for Word Type and the Word Type $\times$ Age interaction would both be figured using as the denominator the Word Type $\times$ Participant interaction figured separately within each age group and then averaged. Thus, the computer output from a mixed analysis of variance, gives two sets of results: one for the between-subjects and one part for the repeated measures aspect.

Learning Aids

Summary

1. A study uses a repeated measures design (or within-subjects design) when each participant is tested more than once. Repeated measures designs are commonly analyzed with a repeated measures analysis of variance.
2. You carry out a one-way repeated measures analysis of variance using a modified two-way between-subjects analysis of variance. Just as with an ordinary two-way analysis of variance, the groupings (conditions) are treated as a factor, usually as columns. The modification is that the rows, instead of another factor, are participants. Thus, one factor is condition and the other factor is participants. This modification has implications for the population variance estimate that is the denominator of the F ratio.
3. In practice, when figuring the denominator of the F ratio in a repeated measures analysis of variance, researchers take advantage of the two-way set up and use the variance of the interaction of condition by participants. Thus, you figure a

one-way repeated measures analysis of variance by setting it up as a condition ✕ participant two-way design, figuring the two main effects and interaction in the usual manner, and then testing the condition main effect with an *F* ratio of the between-condition population variance estimate divided by the interaction population variance estimate.

4. As with the ordinary analysis of variance, the repeated measures analysis of variance assumes that the populations for each condition or condition combination follow a normal distribution and have equal variances. An additional assumption of the repeated measures analysis of variance is called sphericity, which means that not only are the population variances for each condition the same but the population correlations among the different conditions are the same.

5. It is often difficult to know whether the sphericity assumption has been violated. The most common solution to this issue is to use a statistical correction based on an estimate of how much the assumption is violated. This correction involves using a comparison *F* distribution with fewer degrees of freedom. Several different corrections are provided by computer programs, such as SPSS. The Huynh-Feldt correction is often used by researchers. Another solution to the issue of violating the sphericity assumption is to use a special application of multivariate analysis of variance. However, this approach usually has lower power with small samples.

6. Some studies include two or more repeated measures variables. Other studies might include one (or more) repeated measures factor and one (or more) between-subjects factor. This is an example of a mixed design.

Key Terms

repeated measures design
repeated measures analysis of variance

within-subjects design
within-subjects analysis of variance
sphericity
Huynh-Feldt correction

two-way repeated measures design
mixed design

Using SPSS

The ✑ in the following steps indicates a mouse click. (We used SPSS version 19 for Windows to carry out these analyses. The steps and output may be slightly different for other versions of SPSS.) It is easier to learn the SPSS steps for repeated measures analysis of variance using actual numbers, so we will use the example in which four participants were asked to recognize a syllable when it was embedded in three types of word (familiar words, unfamiliar words, and nonword sounds) that were flashed quickly on a screen (see Table 1).

One-Way Repeated Measures Analysis of Variance

❶ Enter the scores into SPSS. As shown in Figure 2, the scores for each person are listed in a separate row. We labeled the variables "familiar", "unfamiliar", and "nonword".

❷ ✑ *Analyze.*

❸ ✑ *General Linear Model,* ✑ *Repeated Measures.*

Figure 2 SPSS data editor window for a fictional study of errors in recognition for four participants, each exposed to a target syllable in familiar, unfamiliar, and nonword-sound word types.

❹ In the "Within-Subject Factor Name" box, type "wordtype" (the default name is "factor1", but we recommend using a name that describes the variables in your study). Enter "3" as the number of levels. ✐ *Add.* ✐ *Define.*

❺ In the new window that opens up, ✐ *familiar* and ✐ the arrow to move it into the box labeled "Within-Subjects Variables". Repeat this process for "unfamiliar" and "nonword". The window should now look like Figure 3.

Figure 3 SPSS repeated measures window for a fictional study of errors in recognition for four participants, each exposed to a target syllable in familiar, unfamiliar, and nonword-sound word types.

❻ ⌖ *Options.* ⌖ the box labeled "Descriptive statistics" (this checks the box). ⌖ *Continue.* (Although this step is optional, we recommend that you always request descriptive statistics when carrying out any statistical test.)

❼ ⌖ *OK.* The SPSS output is quite long, but the most important tables for you to look at are labeled "Descriptive Statistics" and "Tests of Within-Subjects Effects" (see Figure 1). The descriptive statistics include the mean number of errors for each word type. As you learned earlier in the chapter, the tests of within-subjects effects include the standard test (which is used when the sphericity assumption is not violated) as well as three other tests that are used if the sphericity assumption is violated. As shown in Figure 1, all of the tests were statistically significant, indicating that the number of errors made by participants varied according to the type of word they viewed.

Chapter 17

Integration and the General Linear Model

T his chapter is intended to integrate and deepen your knowledge of the major statistical techniques. Equally important, it provides a thorough review of those techniques.

The General Linear Model

The general linear model is a general statement of the influences that make up an individual's score on a particular variable. The general linear model states that the value of a variable for any individual is the sum of a constant, plus the weighted influence of each of several other variables, plus error. Bivariate and multiple correlation and regression (and associated significance tests), the *t* test, and the analysis of variance are all special cases of the general linear model. You also know that bivariate correlation/prediction and analysis of variance are special cases of multiple regression, and that the *t* test can be derived directly from either bivariate correlation/prediction or analysis

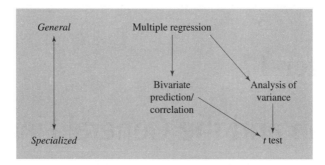

Figure 1   The relationship among the four major statistical techniques.

of variance (for a summary, see Figure 1). We describe these relationships in detail in this Web chapter.

The General Linear Model and Multiple Regression

The link between the general linear model and multiple regression is intimate—they are nearly the same. Traditionally, they have not been equated because the general linear model is understood to be behind other techniques, such as bivariate correlation and the analysis of variance, in addition to multiple regression. However, in recent years psychologists have become increasingly aware that these other techniques can be derived from multiple regression as well as from the general linear model.

Bivariate Prediction and Correlation as Special Cases of Multiple Regression

Bivariate prediction, prediction from one predictor variable to one criterion variable, is a special case of multiple regression, which is prediction from any number of predictor variables to one criterion variable. Similarly, bivariate correlation, the association between one predictor variable and one criterion variable, is a special case of multiple correlation, the association of any number of predictor variables and one criterion variable.

The *t* Test as a Special Case of the Analysis of Variance

Both the *t* test and the analysis of variance test differences between means of groups. You use the *t* test when there are only two groups.[1] You usually use the analysis of variance, with its F ratio, only when there are more than two groups. However, you can use the analysis of variance with just two groups. When there are only two groups, the *t* test and the analysis of variance give identical conclusions.

The strict identity of t and F applies only in this two-group case. You cannot figure an ordinary *t* test among three groups. This is why we say that the *t* test is a *special case* of the analysis of variance. The test is mathematically identical to the analysis of variance in the particular case where there are only two groups.

Intuitive Understanding of the Relationship of the two Procedures

One way to get a sense of the link of the two procedures is through the analogy of signal-to-noise ratio to explain the analysis of variance. The idea is that the analysis of variance F ratio is a measure of how much the signal (analogous to the difference between group means) is greater than the noise (analogous to the variation within each of the groups). The same idea applies to a t test, which is also really about how much the signal (the difference between the two group means) is greater than the noise (the standard deviation of the distribution of differences between means, which is also based on the variation within the groups).

Parallels in the Basic Logic of the Two Procedures

The analysis of variance F ratio is the population variance estimate, based on the variation between the means of the groups divided by the population variance estimate, based on the variation within each of the groups. That is, the F ratio is a fraction in which the numerator is based on the differences among the groups, comparing their means, and the denominator is based on the variation within each of the groups.

The t score is the difference between the means of the two groups divided by the standard deviation of the distribution of differences between means (and this standard deviation is based mainly on a pooled variance estimate that is figured from the variation within each of the two groups). Thus, the t score is a fraction in which the numerator is the difference between the groups, comparing their means, and the denominator is based on the variation within each of the groups.

In other words, as shown in the top sections of Table 1, an F ratio and a t score are both fractions in which the numerator is based on the differences between the group means and the denominator is based on the variances within the groups.

Numeric Relationship of the Two Procedures

The formula for a t score comes out to be exactly the square root of the formula for the F ratio in the situation where there are just two groups. Most of you will not be interested in the precise derivation, but there is an important implication. If you

Table 1   Some Links Between the t Test for Independent Means and the Analysis of Variance

t Test	Analysis of Variance
Numerator of t is the difference between the means of the two groups.	Numerator of F is partly based on variation between the means of the two or more groups.
Denominator of t is partly based on pooling the population variance estimates figured from each group.	Denominator of F is figured by pooling the population variance estimates figured from each group.
Denominator of t involves dividing by number of scores.	Numerator of F involves multiplying by number of scores. (Multiplying a numerator by a number has the same effect as dividing the denominator by that number.)
When using two groups, $t = \sqrt{F}$	When using two groups, $F = t^2$
$df = (N_1 - 1) + (N_2 - 1)$	$df_{Within} = (N_1 - 1) + (N_2 - 1) + \cdots + (N_{Last} - 1)$

figure a t score, it will come out to be exactly the square root of what you would get if you figured an F ratio for the same study. For example, if you figured a t of 3 and then you figured F for the same study, the F would come out to 9. Similarly, consider the cutoffs in a t table. These are exactly the square roots of the cutoffs in the column of an F table for an analysis of variance for two groups (that is, the part of the F table with numerator $df = 1$).

An apparent difference between the two procedures is how they are affected by sample size. In the analysis of variance, the sample size is part of the numerator. The numerator of the F ratio is the population variance estimate using the difference among the means multiplied by the number of scores in each group. That is, $S^2_{\text{Between}} = (S^2_M)(n)$. In the t test, the sample size is part of the denominator. The denominator of the t test uses the pooled population variance estimate divided by the number of scores in each group. That is, $S_{\text{Difference}} = \sqrt{S^2_{\text{Difference}}}$ and $S^2_{\text{Difference}} = S^2_{M_1} + S^2_{M_2}$; $S^2_{M_1} = S^2_{\text{Pooled}}/N_1$; $S^2_{M_2} = S^2_{\text{Pooled}}/N_2$. This apparent contradiction is resolved, however, because multiplying the numerator of a fraction by a number has exactly the same effect as dividing the denominator by that number. For example, take the fraction 3/8. Multiplying the numerator by 2 gives 6/8, or 3/4; dividing the denominator of 3/8 by 2 also gives 3/4.[2]

Worked-Out Example of the Two Procedures

An example with all the figuring makes the equivalence more vivid. Table 2 shows the t and F figuring for a study in which a researcher randomly assigns seven individuals to a new experimental procedure and seven to a control condition. At the end of the study, all 14 are measured. Scores for those in the experimental group were 6, 4, 9, 7, 7, 3, and 6. Scores for those in the control group were 6, 1, 5, 3, 1, 1, and 4. Notice the following: (a) The pooled population variance estimate in the t test ($S^2_{\text{Pooled}} = 4.17$) is the same as the within-group population variance estimate for the analysis of variance ($S^2_{\text{Within}} = 4.17$), both figured as part of the denominator. (b) The degrees of freedom for the t distribution ($df = 12$) is exactly the same as the denominator degrees of freedom for the F distribution ($df_{\text{Within}} = 12$). (c) The cutoff t for rejecting the null hypothesis (2.179) is the square root of the cutoff F for rejecting the null hypothesis ($\sqrt{4.75} = 2.179$). (d) The t for these data (2.73) is the square root of the F ($\sqrt{7.55} = 2.75$, the slight difference being due to rounding error). And (e) the conclusion is the same. With both methods, you reject the null hypothesis (and if you were to get an exact p value using a statistics program, both methods would give exactly the same exact p value).

How are you doing?

1. How is bivariate prediction a special case of multiple regression?
2. When can you use an analysis of variance to do the same thing as a t test?
3. How is the numerator of a t test like the numerator of an F ratio in an analysis of variance?
4. How is the denominator of a t test like the denominator of an F ratio in an analysis of variance?
5. How is S^2_{Pooled} like S^2_{Within}?
6. When figured for the same scores, what is the relation of the t to the F?
7. What is the relation of the t cutoff to the F cutoff for the same study (involving two groups)?

Table 2 *t* Test and Analysis of Variance Computations for the Same Study (Fictional Data)

Experimental Group			Control Group		
X_1	$X_1 - M_1$	$(X_1 - M_1)^2$	X_2	$X_2 - M_2$	$(X_2 - M_2)^2$
6	0	0	6	3	9
4	−2	4	1	−2	4
9	3	9	5	2	4
7	1	1	3	0	0
7	1	1	1	−2	4
3	−3	9	1	−2	4
6	0	0	4	1	1
Σ 42	0	24	21	0	26

$M_1 = 6$ $S_1^2 = 24/6 = 4$ $M_2 = 3$ $S_2^2 = 26/6 = 4.33$

$N_1 = 7$ $df_1 = N_1 - 1 = 6$ $N_2 = 7$ $df_2 = N_2 - 1 = 6$

t test	ANOVA

Numerator

Mean difference = 6.00 − 3.00 = 3.00

$$df_{Between} = N_{Groups} - 1 = 2 - 1 = 1$$

$$GM = (6 + 3)/2 = 9/2 = 4.5$$

$$\Sigma(M - GM)^2 = (6 - 4.5)^2 + (3 - 4.5)^2$$

$$= 1.5^2 + -1.5^2$$

$$= 2.25 + 2.25 = 4.5$$

$$S_{Between}^2 \text{ or } MS_{Between} = \left(\frac{\Sigma(M - GM)^2}{df_{Between}}\right)(n) = \left(\frac{4.5}{1}\right)(7) = 31.5$$

Denominator

$$S_{Pooled}^2 = \left(\frac{df_1}{df_{Total}}\right)(S_1^2) + \left(\frac{df_2}{df_{Total}}\right)(S_2^2) = \left(\frac{6}{12}\right)(4) + \left(\frac{6}{12}\right)(4.33)$$

$$= (.5)(4) + (.5)(4.33) = 2.00 + 2.17 = 4.17$$

$$S_{Within}^2 \text{ or } MS_{Within} = \frac{S_1^2 + S_2^2 + \cdots + S_{Last}^2}{N_{Groups}} = \frac{4 + 4.33}{2}$$

$$= \frac{8.33}{2} = 4.17$$

$$S_{Difference}^2 = S_{M_1}^2 + S_M^2 = (S_{Pooled}^2/N_1) + (S_{Pooled}^2/N_2)$$

$$= (4.17/7) + (4.17/7)$$

$$= .60 + .60 = 1.20$$

$$S_{Difference} = \sqrt{S_{Difference}^2} = \sqrt{1.20} = 1.10$$

Degrees of Freedom

$$df_{Total} = df_1 + df_2 = 6 + 6 = 12$$

$$df_{Within} = df_1 + df_2 \cdots df_{Last} = 6 + 6 = 12$$

Cutoff

Needed *t* with $df = 12$ at 5% level, two-tailed = ± 2.179

Needed *F* with $df = 1, 12$ at 5% level = 4.75

Score on Comparison Distribution

$$t = (M_1 - M_2)/S_{Difference} = (6.00 - 3.00)/1.10 = 3.00/1.10 = 2.73$$

$$F = S_{Between}^2/S_{Within}^2 \text{ or } MS_{Between}/MS_{Within} = 31.5/4.17 = 7.55$$

Conclusions

Reject the null hypothesis; the research hypothesis is supported.

Reject the null hypothesis; the research hypothesis is supported.

Answers

1. Multiple regression predicts the criterion variable from any number of predictor variables; bivariate prediction is the special case in which you are predicting from only one predictor variable.
2. When there are only two groups.
3. Both are about the difference or variation between the groups.
4. Both are about variation within groups.
5. The two are identical.
6. The t is the square root of the F.
7. The t cutoff is the square root of the F cutoff.

The t Test as a Special Case of the Significance Test for the Correlation Coefficient

The relationship of the correlation coefficient to the t test is far from obvious. The correlation coefficient is about the degree of association between two variables; the t test is about the significance of the difference between two population means. What is the possible connection?

One connection is that both use the t distribution to determine significance. As a reminder, the score for a correlation coefficient on the comparison distribution is a t score figured from the correlation coefficient using the formula $t = r/\sqrt{(1 - r^2)/(N - 2)}$. However, knowing about this procedure does not give much insight into *why* the correlation coefficient can be turned into a t score for purposes of hypothesis testing or of the connection between this t based on the correlation coefficient and the t test for the difference between means of two groups. Let's take a look at these issues now.

Group Differences as Associations Among Variables

We usually think of the correlation coefficient as the association between two variables, typically a predictor variable and a criterion variable. Testing the significance of a correlation coefficient asks whether you can reject the null hypothesis that in the population there is no association between the predictor and criterion variable (that in the population, $r = 0$).

The t test for independent means examines the difference between two population means, based on the means of two samples. The sample scores are on a measured variable that is like a criterion variable (you want to know the effect on it). The distinction between the two groups in a t test is like the predictor variable. In our example from the previous section (see Table 2), the variable that divides the two groups was whether participants were in the experimental or control group. Thus, you can think of the t test as about whether there is any association between the variable that divides the groups and the measured variable (see Table 3).

Numerical Predictor Variables Versus Two-Category Nominal Variable that Divides the Groups

"But wait!" you might say. "The predictor variable in a correlation coefficient is a numerical variable, such as number of hours sleep or high school GPA. The variable that divides the groups in a t test for independent means is a variable with exactly

Table 3   Relation between Correlation and *t* Test for Independent Means

	Correlation	***t* Test**
Variable 1	Predictor Variable	Variable that Divides the Groups
Variable 2	Criterion Variable	Measured Variable
Relation tested	High scores on predictor go with high scores on criterion	Those in one group on the variable that divides the groups have higher scores on the measured variable

two values, the two categories, such as experimental group versus control group." You would be quite correct. This is precisely the difference between the situations in which you use a correlation coefficient and those in which you ordinarily use a *t* test for independent means.

How can this gap be bridged? Suppose that you arbitrarily give a number to each level of the two-category nominal variable that divides the groups. For example, you could make the experimental group a "1" and the control group a "2." (Using any other two numbers will, in the end, give exactly the same result. However, which group gets the higher number does determine the plus or minus sign of the final result.) Once you change the two-category nominal variable that divides the groups to a numerical variable, you can then figure the correlation between this two-valued numeric variable and the measured variable.

Example of the Numeric Equivalence of the *t* Test and the Correlation Coefficient Significance Test

Table 4 shows the figuring for the correlation coefficient and its significance using the scores from the same *t* test example we used earlier (see Table 2). Notice that in this correlation setup, each individual has two scores: (a) a 1 or a 2, depending on whether the person is in the experimental group or the control group, and (b) a score on the measured variable.

The resulting correlation is $-.62$. Using the formula for changing a correlation to a *t* score gives a *t* of -2.74. This *t* is the same, within rounding error, that we figured earlier (2.73) using the ordinary *t* test procedures (see Table 2). The difference in sign has to do with which group gets the 1, and which group gets the 2—a decision that is arbitrary. The degrees of freedom, and thus the needed *t* for significance and the conclusion, are also the same as for the *t* test for independent means.

In sum, the significance test of the correlation coefficient gives the same result as the ordinary *t* test. We say that the *t* test is a special case of the correlation coefficient, however, because you can use the *t* test only in the situation in which the predictor variable has exactly two values.

Graphic Interpretation of the Relationship of the *t* Test to the Correlation Coefficient

Figure 2 shows the scatter diagram, including the regression line, for the scores in the example we have been following. The predictor variable (the variable that divides the groups) has just two values, so the dots all line up above these two values. Note that the regression line goes through the middle of each line of dots. In fact, when making a scatter diagram of the scores for a *t* test, the regression line always goes exactly through the mean of each set of dots. This is because the regression line

Table 4   Figuring of the Correlation Coefficient and a Hypothesis Test of the Correlation Coefficient Using the Data from Table 2 and Changing the Variable that Divides the Groups Into a Numeric Variable Having Values of 1 (for the Experimental Group) or 2 (for the Control Group)

Variable that Divides the Groups (Experimental Versus Control) (X)			Measured Variable (Y)				Cross-Products of Z Scores
Deviation	Deviation Squared	Z Score		Deviation	Deviation Squared	Z Score	
X	$X - M_X$	$(X - M_X)^2$	Z_X	Y	$Y - M_Y$	$(Y - M_Y)^2$	Z_Y	$Z_X Z_Y$
1	−.5	.25	−1	6	1.5	2.25	.62	−.62
1	−.5	.25	−1	4	−.5	.25	−.21	.21
1	−.5	.25	−1	9	4.5	20.25	1.87	−1.87
1	−.5	.25	−1	7	2.5	6.25	1.04	−1.04
1	−.5	.25	−1	7	2.5	6.25	1.04	−1.04
1	−.5	.25	−1	3	−1.5	2.25	−.62	.62
1	−.5	.25	−1	6	1.5	2.25	.62	−.62
2	.5	.25	1	6	1.5	2.25	.62	.62
2	.5	.25	1	1	−3.5	12.25	−1.45	−1.45
2	.5	.25	1	5	.5	.25	.21	.21
2	.5	.25	1	3	−1.5	2.25	−.62	−.62
2	.5	.25	1	1	−3.5	12.25	−1.45	−1.45
2	.5	.25	1	1	−3.5	12.25	−1.45	−1.45
2	.5	.25	1	4	−.5	.25	−.21	−.21

$\Sigma = 21$ $\Sigma(X - M_X)^2 = 3.5$ $\Sigma = 63$ $\Sigma(Y - M_Y)^2 = 81.5$ $\Sigma = -8.71$

$M_X = 1.5$ $SD^2 = 3.5/14 = .25$ $M_Y = 4.5$ $SD^2 = 81.5/14 = 5.82$

         $SD = .5$ $SD = 2.41$

$df = N - 2 = 14 - 2 = 12.$ $r = (\Sigma Z_X Z_Y)/N = -8.71/14 = -.62$

t needed with $df = 12$ at 5% level, two-tailed $= \pm 2.179$.

$t = r/\sqrt{(1 - r^2)/(N - 2)} = -.62/\sqrt{(1 - (-.62)^2)/(14 - 2)} = -.62/\sqrt{.0513} = -2.74$

Decision: Reject the null hypothesis; the research hypothesis is supported.

shows the best predicted score at each level of the predictor variable, and for any group of scores, the best predicted score is always the mean.

Figure 3 shows some additional examples. In Figure 3a, the two means are nearly the same. Here, the slope of the regression line is about 0; the correlation is low and not statistically significant. The correlation is .10; thus, with 20 participants, $t = r/\sqrt{(1 - r^2)/(N - 2)} = .10/\sqrt{(1 - .10^2)/(20 - 2)} = .43$. Thinking in terms of a t test for independent means, because there is little difference between the means of the two groups, the t test will not be significant. The mean difference is $7.39 - 7.60 = -.21$. The standard deviation of the distribution of differences between means is .48; thus, $t = (M_1 - M_2)/S_{\text{Difference}} = (7.39 - 7.60)/.48 = -.44$. This is the same result as you get using the correlation approach (within rounding error, and ignoring sign).

In Figure 3b, the means of the two groups are somewhat different, but the dots in each group are even more widely spread out. Once again, the correlation coefficient

Figure 2 Scatter diagram and regression line for the example, originally analyzed with a *t* test for independent means, with a value of 1 for the experimental group and 2 for the control group.

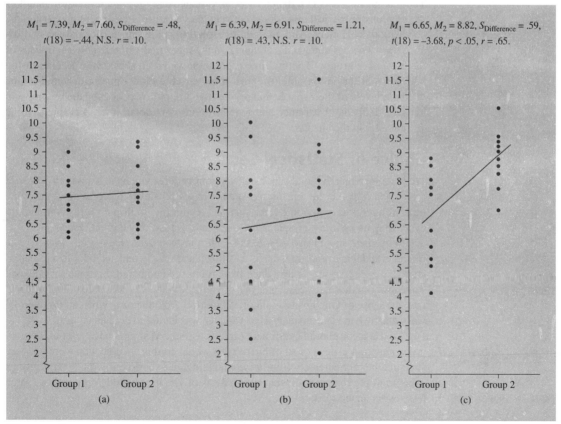

Figure 3 Three possible scatter diagrams of scores analyzed with a *t* test for independent means, in which the means for the two groups are (a) nearly the same, (b) different but the scores are widely spread (large pooled variance and thus large standard deviation of the distribution of differences between means), and (c) very different, with the scores not widely spread.

is low and not statistically significant. In the *t* test for independent means, the spread of the dots makes a large estimated population variance for each group, creating a large pooled variance estimate and a large standard deviation of the distribution of differences between means. In a *t* test, you divide the mean difference by the standard deviation of the distribution of differences between means; thus, the larger this standard deviation, the smaller the *t* score. In the example, the mean difference is .52, and the standard deviation of the distribution of differences between means is 1.21. This gives a *t* of .43, which is clearly not significant.

Finally, in Figure 3c, there is a large difference between the means and less variation among the dots around each mean. Thus, the regression line is a very good predictor. Similarly, the large mean difference and small variance within each group make for a large *t* using a *t* test for independent means.

These figures illustrate the principle that the *t* test for independent means and the significance test for the correlation coefficient give the same results. This is because both are largest when the difference between the two means is large and the variation among the scores in each group is small.

The Analysis of Variance as a Special Case of the Significance Test of Multiple Regression

The relationship between the analysis of variance and multiple regression parallels the relationship we just considered between the *t* test for independent means and the correlation coefficient. And, in both, the solution is the same. The analysis of variance tests whether there is a difference on the measured variable between means of three or more groups. The multiple regression approach sees this as a relationship between a criterion variable (the measured variable) and a predictor variable (the different levels of the variable that divides the groups). We describe the relationship between analysis of variance and regression in more detail in an Advanced Topic section later in the chapter.

Choice of Statistical Tests

We have seen that the four major statistical procedures you have learned in *Statistics for Psychology* can be considered special cases of multiple regression. You may now wonder why you don't learn just one technique, multiple regression, and do everything using it. You could. And you would get entirely correct results.

Why, then, should anyone use, say, a *t* test instead of an analysis of variance? The reason is that it is a procedure that is traditional and widely understood. Most researchers today expect to see a *t* test when two groups are compared. It seems strange, and somehow grandiose, to see an analysis of variance when a *t* test would do—though, in fact, the sense of grandiosity is simply a holdover from the days when all the figuring was done by hand and an analysis of variance was harder to do than a *t* test.

To use a correlation coefficient (and its associated significance test) in the two-group situation instead of an ordinary *t* test would confuse people who were not very statistically sophisticated. Similarly, analyzing an experiment with several groups using multiple regression instead of analysis of variance would confuse those same less sophisticated readers.[3]

There is one advantage in using correlation and regression over the t test or an analysis of variance: The correlational approach automatically gives you direct information on the relationship between the variable that divides the groups and the measured variable as well as permitting a significance test. The t test and the analysis of variance give only statistical significance. (You can figure an effect size for either of these, but with a correlation coefficient or a multiple regression, you get the effect size automatically.)

How are you doing?

1. How can you understand a difference between groups on a measured variable in terms of an association between a predictor and a criterion variable?
2. How can you make a two-level nominal variable that divides the groups into a numeric variable that you can use in correlation or regression?
3. (a) What is the effect of the scores being spread out around their mean, and (b) why, for the t test for independent means?
4. When you make a scatter diagram for the scores in a t test for independent means, (a) what does it look like, and (b) where does the regression line go?
5. How do the variables in an analysis of variance correspond to the variables in a regression?
6. (a) Why do researchers use t tests and analyses of variance when they could use correlation or regression instead? (b) What is an advantage of using regression and correlation over using analysis of variance and the t test?

Answers

1. A difference between groups on a measured variable is the same as an association between the variable that divides the groups (which is like the predictor variable in correlation or regression) and the measured variable (which is like the criterion variable in correlation or regression).
2. Make it into a two-valued numeric variable by giving a score of, say, 1 on this variable to everyone in one group and a score of, say, 2 on this variable to everyone in the other group.
3. (a) It reduces the t.
   (b) The variance of each group will be greater, making the pooled estimate of the population variance greater, making the variance of the distribution of differences between means greater, making the standard deviation of the distribution of differences between means greater. You figure the t by dividing by the standard deviation of the differences between means. Thus, if it is bigger, the t is smaller.
4. (a) The dots are all lined up above the points for the two levels of the variable that divides the groups.
   (b) It goes through the mean of each group.
5. The grouping variable in an analysis of variance is like a predictor variable in regression. The measured variable in an analysis of variance is like a criterion variable in regression.
6. (a) Researchers are familiar with t tests and analysis of variance for testing differences between groups, they are traditional for this purpose, and some researchers are unfamiliar with and would be confused by the use of correlation and regression for this purpose.
   (b) Correlation and regression automatically give you estimates of effect size and not just significance.

Controversy: What is Causality?

The general linear model itself is not very controversial; it is simply a mathematical statement of a relationship among variables. In fact, its role as the foundation of the major statistical techniques has not yet been widely realized among practicing researchers. There is, however, an area of controversy that is appropriate to mention here. It has to do with the role of statistics in science generally, but in practice it is most often raised in the context of the major general linear model-based procedures. This is the issue of causality. We are aware of the problem of inferring a direction of causality from a study that does not use random assignment to groups. But there is a still deeper level to the issue: What does causality mean?

In a classic discussion of the issues, the eminent developmental psychologist Diana Baumrind (1983) outlined two main understandings of causality that are used in science. One, which she calls the *regularity theory of causality*, has its roots in philosophers like David Hume and John Stuart Mill (as well as early scientists, including Galileo). This view holds that we recognize X as a cause of Y if (a) X and Y are regularly associated, (b) X precedes Y, and (c) there are no other causes that precede X that might cause both X and Y. In psychology, we address the (a) part by finding a significant correlation between X and Y. We address the (b) part, if possible, by our knowledge of the situation (for example, in a correlation of whether one is the firstborn in one's family with anxiety later in life, you can rule out the possibility that anxiety later in life caused the person to be firstborn) or designing the study into an experiment (by manipulating X prior to measuring Y). The (c) part has to do with the issue of a correlation between X and Y being due to some third variable causing both. Ideally, we address this by random assignment to groups. But if that is not possible, various statistical methods of equating groups on proposed third factors are used as a makeshift strategy.

As psychologists, we are only sometimes in a position to do the kind of rigorous experimental research that provides a strong basis for drawing conclusions about cause and effect. Thus, much of the criticism and controversy involving research of practical importance, where it is usually least easy to apply rigorous methods, often hinges on such issues. For example, if marriage correlates with happiness, does marriage make people happier, or do happy people get and stay married?

There is another view of causality, a still more stringent view that sees the regularity theory conditions as a prerequisite to calling something a cause, but that these conditions are not sufficient alone. This other view, which Baumrind calls the *generative theory of causality*, has its roots in Aristotle, Thomas Aquinas, and Immanuel Kant. The focus of this view is on just *how* X affects Y. This is the way most nonscientists (and nonphilosophers) understand causality. The very idea of causality may have its roots as a metaphor of experiences, such as willing your own arm to move (Event X) and it moves (Event Y). Scientists also take this view of causality very much to heart, even if it offers much more difficult challenges. It is addressed primarily by theory and by careful analysis of mediating processes. But even those who emphasize this view would recognize that demonstrating a reliable connection between X and Y (by finding statistical significance, for example) plays an important role at least in identifying linkages that require scrutiny for determining the real causal connection.

Finally, there are also those who hold—with some good arguments—that demonstrating causality should not be a goal of scientific psychology at all. But we have already had enough controversy for one chapter.

Advanced Topic: Detailed Examination of the Analysis of Variance as a Special Case of the Significance Test of Multiple Regression

In order to follow the material in this Advanced Topic section, you must have read the Advanced Topic sections in "Introduction to the Analysis of Variance" (on the structural model in the analysis of variance) and "Prediction" (on error and proportionate reduction in error).

Earlier in this chapter, we noted that the relationship between the analysis of variance and multiple regression parallels the relationship between the t test for independent means and the correlation coefficient. Here, we give a detailed analysis of the relationship between the analysis of variance and multiple regression.

Analysis of Variance for Two Groups as a Special Case of the Significance of a Bivariate Correlation

The link between the analysis of variance and multiple regression is easiest to see if we begin with a two-group situation and (a) consider the correlation coefficient in terms of its being the square root of the proportionate reduction in error, and (b) consider the analysis of variance using the structural model approach. Table 5 shows the scores for our experimental versus control group example. However, this

Table 5 Figuring of the Proportionate Reduction in Error With Bivariate Prediction Using the Data From Table 2

Predictor Variable (Experimenal Versus Control)	Criterion Variable			
	Actual Score	Predicted Score	Error	Error^2
	Y	$\hat{Y}$	$Y - \hat{Y}$	$(Y - \hat{Y})^2$
1	6	6	0	0
1	4	6	-2	4
1	9	6	3	9
1	7	6	1	1
1	7	6	1	1
1	3	6	-3	9
1	6	6	0	0
2	6	3	3	9
2	1	3	-2	4
2	5	3	2	4
2	3	3	0	0
2	1	3	-2	4
2	1	3	-2	4
2	4	3	1	1
				$\Sigma = SS_{\text{Error}} = 50$

Sum of squared error using the overall mean as a prediction rule (computation not shown): $SS_{\text{Total}} = 81.5$

Proportionate reduction in error $= \dfrac{SS_{\text{Total}} - SS_{\text{Error}}}{SS_{\text{Total}}} = \dfrac{81.5 - 50}{81.5} = .39$

$r^2 = .39; r = \sqrt{r^2} = \sqrt{.39} = \pm.62.$

Table 6   Figuring of the Proportional Reduction in Error with the One-Way Analysis of Variance Structural Model Approach Using the Data From Table 2

One-way analysis of variance structural model calculation

$GM = 4.5$

	Experimental Group							Control Group						
X	$X - GM$		$X - M$		$M - GM$		X	$X - GM$		$X - M$		$M - GM$	
	Dev	Dev²	Dev	Dev²	Dev	Dev²		Dev	Dev²	Dev	Dev²	Dev	Dev²
6	1.5	2.25	0	0	1.5	2.25	6	1.5	2.25	3	9	−1.5	2.25
4	−.5	.25	−2	4	1.5	2.25	1	−3.5	12.25	−2	4	−1.5	2.25
9	4.5	20.25	3	9	1.5	2.25	5	.5	.25	2	4	−1.5	2.25
7	2.5	6.25	1	1	1.5	2.25	3	−1.5	2.25	0	0	−1.5	2.25
7	2.5	6.25	1	1	1.5	2.25	1	−3.5	12.25	−2	4	−1.5	2.25
3	−1.5	2.25	−3	9	1.5	2.25	1	−3.5	12.25	−2	4	−1.5	2.25
6	1.5	2.25	0	0	1.5	2.25	4	−.5	.25	1	1	−1.5	2.25
Σ:		39.75		24		15.75			41.75		26		15.75

$M = 6$ $M = 3$

Note: Dev = Deviation; Dev² = Squared deviation

Sums of squared deviations:

$\Sigma(X - GM)^2$ or $SS_{Total} = 39.75 + 41.75 = 81.5$

$\Sigma(X - M)^2$ or $SS_{Within} = 24 + 26 = 50$

$\Sigma(M - GM)^2$ or $SS_{Between} = 15.75 + 15.75 = 31.5$

Degrees of freedom:

$df_{Total} = N - 1 = 14 - 1 = 13$

$df_{Within} = df_1 + df_2 + \cdots + df_{Last} = 6 + 6 = 12$

$df_{Between} = N_{Groups} - 1 = 2 - 1 = 1$

Check $(df_{Total} = df_{Within} + df_{Between})$: $13 = 12 + 1$

Population variance estimates:

S^2_{Total} or $MS_{Total} = SS_{Total}/df_{Total} = 81.5/13 = 6.27$

S^2_{Within} or $MS_{Within} = SS_{Within}/df_{Within} = 50/12 = 4.17$

$S^2_{Between}$ or $MS_{Between} = SS_{Between}/df_{Between} = 31.5/1 = 31.5$

F ratio: $F = S^2_{Between}/S^2_{Within}$ or $MS_{Between}/MS_{Within} = 31.5/4.17 = 7.55$

$R^2 = eta^2 = SS_{Between}/SS_{Total} = 31.5/81.5 = .39$

time we show the predicted scores and the errors and squared errors, as well as the figuring for the proportionate reduction in error. Table 6 shows the analysis of variance figuring, using the structural model approach, for the same scores.

There are several clear links. First, the sum of squared error figured in the correlation when using the bivariate prediction rule ($SS_{Error} = 50$) is the same as the within-group sum of squared deviations (SS_{Within}) for the analysis of variance. Why are they the same? In regression, the error is a score's difference from the predicted value, and the predicted value in this situation of only two values for the predictor variable is the mean of the scores at each value (that is, the mean of each group's scores). In other words, in the regression, the sum of squared error comes from squaring and summing the difference of each score from its group's mean. In the analysis of variance, you figure the sum of squared error within groups as precisely the same thing—the sum of the squared deviations of each score from its group's mean.

Second, the sum of squared error total (SS_{Total}) is the same in regression and analysis of variance (in this example they are both 81.5). They are the same because in regression, SS_{Total} is the sum of the squared deviations of each criterion variable score from the overall mean of all the criterion variable scores and in the analysis of variance, SS_{Total} is the sum of the squared deviations of each measured variable score from the grand mean, which is the overall mean of all the measured variable scores.

Third, the reduction in squared error in regression—the sum of squared error using the mean to predict (that is, 81.5) minus the sum of squared error using the bivariate prediction rule (that is, 50)—comes out to 31.5. This is the same as the analysis of variance sum of squared error between groups (that is, $SS_{Between} = 31.5$). The reduction in error in regression is what the prediction rule adds over knowing just the mean. In this example, the prediction rule estimates the mean of each group, so the reduction in squared error for each score is the squared difference between the mean of that score's group and the overall mean. In analysis of variance, you figure $SS_{Between}$ by adding up, for each participant, the squared differences between the participant's group's mean and the grand mean.

Finally, the proportionate reduction in error in the regression ($r^2 = .39$) comes out to exactly the same as the proportionate reduction in error used as an effect size in analysis of variance (R^2 or eta$^2 = .39$). Both tell us the proportion of the total variation in the criterion (or measured) variable that is accounted for by its association with the predictor variable (the variable that divides the groups). That these numbers come out the same should be no surprise by now; we have already seen that the numerator and the proportionate reduction in error are the same for both.

Thus, the links between regression and the analysis of variance are quite deep. In fact, some researchers figure the significance of a correlation coefficient by laying it out as a regression analysis and plugging the various sums of squared error into an analysis of variance table and figuring F. The result is identical to any other way of figuring the significance of the correlation coefficient. If you figure the t for the correlation, it comes out to the square root of the F you would get using this procedure.

Analysis of Variance for More Than two Groups as a Special Case of Multiple Correlation

When considering the t test for independent means or the analysis of variance for two groups, we could carry out a correlation or regression analysis by changing the two categories of the nominal variable that divides the groups into any two different numbers (in the example, we used 1 for the experimental group and 2 for the control group). The problem is more difficult with an analysis of variance with more than two groups because the variable that divides the groups has more than two categories.

In the two-category situation, the particular two numbers you use do not matter (except for the sign). However, when there are three or more groups, making up a predictor variable with arbitrary numbers for the different groups will not work. Whatever three numbers you pick imply some particular relation among the groups, and not all relations will be the same. For example, with three groups, making a predictor variable with 1s, 2s, and 3s gives a different result depending on which groups gets put in the middle. It also gives a different result than using 1s, 2s, and 4s.

Consider an example comparing ratings of a defendant's degree of guilt for participants who believed the defendant had either a criminal record or a clean record or in which nothing was said about the defendant's record. Suppose that we arbitrarily give a 1 to the first group, a 2 to the second, and a 3 to the third. This would imply that we consider these three levels to be equally spaced values on a numerical variable of knowledge about the criminal record. For this particular example, we might want to think of the three groups as ordered from criminal record to clean record, with the no information group in between. However, even then it would not be clear that the groups are evenly spaced on this dimension.

More generally, when you have several groups, you may have no basis in advance for putting the groups in a particular order, let alone for deciding how they should be spaced. For example, in a study comparing attitudes of four different Central American nationalities, nationality is the nominal variable that divides the groups. But you can't make these four nationalities into any meaningful four values of a single numerical variable.

There is a clever solution to this problem. When there are more than two groups, instead of trying to make the nominal variable that divides the groups into a single numerical variable, you can make it into several numerical predictor variables with two levels each.

Here is how this is done: Suppose that the variable that divides the groups has four categories—for example, four Central American nationalities: Costa Rican, Guatemalan, Nicaraguan, and Salvadoran. You can make one predictor variable for whether the participant is Costa Rican—1 if Costa Rican, 0 if not. You can then make a second predictor variable for whether the participant is Guatemalan, 1 or 0; and a third for whether the participant is Nicaraguan, 1 or 0. You could make a fourth for whether the participant is Salvadoran. However, if a participant has 0s on the first three variables, the participant has to be Salvadoran (because there are only the four possibilities).

In this example, you know any participant's nationality by the scores on the combination of the three two-value numerical variables. For example, a Costa Rican participant would have a 1 for Costa Rican and 0s for Guatemalan and Nicaraguan. Each Guatemalan participant would have a 1 for Guatemalan but 0s for Costa Rican and Nicaraguan. Each Nicaraguan participant would have 0s for Costa Rican and Guatemalan. Each Salvadoran participant would have 0s on all three variables. (Incidentally, you can use any two numbers for each two-valued nominal variable; we just used 1 and 0 for convenience.) Table 7 shows this coding for 10 participants.

Table 7	Example of Nominal Coding for Participants of Four Central American Nationalities			
Participant	**Nationality**	**Variable 1** **Costa Rican or Not**	**Variable 2** **Guatemalan or Not**	**Variable 3** **Nicaraguan or Not**
1	Guatemalan	0	1	0
2	Nicaraguan	0	0	1
3	Salvadoran	0	0	0
4	Nicaraguan	0	0	1
5	Costa Rican	1	0	0
6	Costa Rican	1	0	0
7	Salvadoran	0	0	0
8	Nicaraguan	0	0	1
9	Costa Rican	1	0	0
10	Guatemalan	0	1	0

This entire procedure is called **nominal coding** (or *dummy coding*). The result in this example is that the variable that divides the groups, instead of being a nominal variable with four categories, is now three numerical variables but with only two values each. Creating several two-valued numerical variables in this way avoids the problem of creating an arbitrary ranking and distancing of the four levels.

More generally, you can code the nominal variable that divides the groups in an analysis of variance into several two-value numerical variables, exactly one less such two-valued numerical variables than there groups. (Not coincidentally, this comes out the same as the degrees of freedom for the between-group population variance estimate.)

Once you have done the nominal coding (changed the variable that divides the groups into two-value numerical variables), you then want to know the relation of this set of variables to the measured variable. You do this with multiple regression, using the set of two-value numerical variables as predictors and the measured variable as the criterion variable. Consider again the criminal record example. Having done the nominal coding, you can now figure the multiple regression of the two numerical predictor variables taken together with what you now think of as the criterion variable, rating of guilt. The result (in terms of significance level and R^2) comes out exactly the same as the analysis of variance.

The nominal coding procedure is extremely flexible and can be extended to the most complex factorial analysis of variance situations. In practice, researchers rarely actually do nominal coding—usually, a computer does it for you. We wanted you to see the principle so that you can understand how it is possible to make an analysis of variance problem into a multiple regression problem. There are, however, a number of analysis of variance research situations in which there are advantages to using the multiple regression approach (such as in a factorial analysis with unequal cell sizes). In fact, many analysis of variance computer programs do the actual computations—not using the analysis of variance formulas, but by doing nominal coding and multiple regression.

How are you doing?

1. Under what conditions can you use the analysis of variance to find the significance of a bivariate prediction or correlation?
2. When there are only two groups, explain the similarity between the analysis of variance structural model approach and regression in terms of (a) SS_{Total}, (b) SS_{Within} and SS_{Error}, (c) $SS_{Between}$ and $SS_{Total} - SS_{Error}$, and (d) proportionate reduction in error.
3. Based on what you have learned in previous sections, give an argument for why, when there are only two groups, the analysis of variance and correlation should give the same significance.
4. (a) What is nominal coding? (b) How is it done? (c) Why is it done? (d) Why can't you just use a single numeric variable with more than two values? (e) In a particular study, participants 1 and 2 are in Group A, participants 3 and 4 are in Group B, and participants 5 and 6 in Group C. Make a table showing nominal coding for these six participants.

Answers

1. When the predictor variable has only two values.
2. (a) In analysis of variance, SS_{Total} is the sum of squared deviations of each measured variable score from the grand mean, which is the mean of all measured variable scores; in regression, SS_{Total} is the sum of squared deviations of each criterion variable score from the mean of all criterion variable scores. The measured variable in analysis of variance is the same as the criterion variable in regression. Thus, for the same study, SS_{Total} is the same in both.
(b) SS_{Within} in analysis of variance is the sum of squared deviations of each measured variable score from the mean of the measured variable scores of its group. SS_{Error} in regression is the sum of squared deviations of each criterion variable score from the predicted criterion variable score. The mean of the measured variable scores of a particular group in analysis of variance is exactly what would be the predicted score for the criterion variable in regression if there are only two groups. Thus, for the same study, SS_{Within} and SS_{Error} is the same.
(c) In analysis of variance, $SS_{Total} = SS_{Between} + SS_{Within}$. Thus, $SS_{Between}$ has to equal $SS_{Total} - SS_{Within}$. We have already seen that SS_{Total} is the same in analysis of variance and regression, and that SS_{Within} in analysis of variance is the same as SS_{Error} in regression. Thus, for the same study, $SS_{Between}$ and $SS_{Total} - SS_{Error}$ are the same.
(d) Proportionate reduction in error in analysis of variance is $SS_{Between}/SS_{Total}$. The proportionate reduction in error in regression is $(SS_{Total} - SS_{Error})/SS_{Total}$. We have already seen that the terms that make up these numerators

and denominators are the same in analysis of variance and regression. Thus, in the same study, the proportionate reduction in error is the same.

3. In this situation, both the analysis of variance and the significance test of the correlation give the same results as the t test for independent means. Thus, they must give the same result as each other.

4. (a) Changing a nominal variable that divides groups into several two-value numeric variables.

(b) Participants in the first group are given a 1 on the first two-value numeric variable and a 0 on all others; participants in the second group are given a 1 on the second two-value numeric variable and a 0 on the rest; this continues up to participants in the last group, who are given a 0 on all the two-value numeric variables.

(c) It allows you to figure an analysis of variance using the two-value numeric variables as predictors in a multiple regression.

(d) The order of those values and the distance between them would influence the results.

(e)

Participant	Score on Numeric Variable 1	Score on Numeric Variable 2
1	1	0
2	1	0
3	0	1
4	0	1
5	0	0
6	0	0

Learning Aids

Summary

1. The general linear model states that the value of a variable for any individual is the sum of a constant, plus the weighted influence of each of several other variables, plus error. Bivariate and multiple correlation and regression (and associated significance tests), the t test, and the analysis of variance are all special cases of the general linear model.

2. Multiple regression is almost identical to the general linear model, and bivariate correlation and regression are the special cases of multiple regression/correlation in which there is only one predictor variable.

3. The t test for independent means can be mathematically derived from the analysis of variance. It is a special case of the analysis of variance in which there are only two groups. The t score for the same data is the square root of the F ratio. The numerators of both t and F are based on the differences between group means; the denominators of both are based on the variance within the groups; the denominator of t involves dividing by the number of participants, and the numerator of F involves multiplying by the number of participants; and the t degrees of freedom are the same as the F denominator degrees of freedom.

4. The t test for independent means is also a special case of the significance test for the correlation coefficient. A correlation is about the association of a predictor variable with a criterion variable. In the same way, by showing a difference between group means, the t test is about an association of the variable that divides the groups with the measured variable. If you give a score of 1 to each participant in one of the two groups and a 2 to each participant in the other group (or any two different numbers), then figure a correlation of these scores with the measured variable, the significance of that correlation will be the same as the t test. Drawing a scatter diagram of these data makes a column of scores for each group, with the regression line passing through the mean of each group. The more the means are different, the greater the proportionate reduction in error over using the grand mean and the greater the t score based on a comparison of the two groups' means.

5. The relationship between the analysis of variance and multiple regression parallels the relationship between the t test for independent means and the correlation coefficient. The grouping variable in an analysis of variance is like a predictor variable in regression. The measured variable in an analysis of variance is like a criterion variable in regression.

6. The t test, analysis of variance, and correlation can all be done as multiple regression. However, conventional practice leads to these procedures being used in different research contexts, as if they were actually different.

7. The regularity view identifies X as a cause of Y if X and Y are associated, X precedes Y, and no other third factors precede X that could cause them both. The generative view argues that in addition there must be a clear understanding of the mechanism by which X affects Y.

8. ADVANCED TOPIC: The analysis of variance and regression also have many similarities. SS_{Total} in regression and in the analysis of variance are both about the deviations of each score from the mean of all the criterion or measured variable scores. The group means in an analysis of variance are the predicted scores for each individual in regression; thus, SS_{Error} and SS_{Within} are the same. The reduction in squared error $(SS_{Total} - SS_{Error})$ in regression is the same as the sum of squared deviations of scores' group's means from the grand mean $(SS_{Between})$ in the analysis of variance. Finally, regression's proportionate reduction in error $(r^2$ or $R^2)$ is the same as the proportion of variance accounted for $(R^2$ or $eta^2)$ effect size in analysis of variance.

9. ADVANCED TOPIC: An analysis of variance can be set up as a multiple regression using nominal coding to make the categories for the different groups into two-value numerical variables. The analysis of variance is a special case of multiple regression in which the predictor variables are set up in this way.

Key Term

nominal coding

Practice Problems

These problems involve figuring. Most real-life statistics problems are done with special statistical software. Even if you have such software, do these problems by hand to ingrain the method in your mind. To learn how to use a computer to solve

statistics problems like those in this chapter, refer to the Using SPSS section at the end of this chapter.

All data are fictional unless an actual citation is given.

Set I (for Answers to Set I problems, see the end of this Web chapter)

1. (a) Look up and write down the t cutoff at the .05 level (two-tailed) for 5, 10, 15, and 20 degrees of freedom. (b) Square each t cutoff and write it down next to the t. (c) Look up and write down, next to the squared ts, the cutoffs for F distributions with 1 degree of freedom in the numerator and 5, 10, 15, and 20 degrees of freedom as the denominators. (The results should be identical, within rounding error.)

2. Following are two data sets. For the first data set, in addition to the means and estimated population variances, we have shown the t test information. You should figure the second yourself. Also, for each, figure a one-way analysis of variance using the regular method of "Introduction to the Analysis of Variance" (not the structural model approach shown in the Advanced Topic section of that chapter). Make a chart of the similarities of (a) t df to F denominator df, (b) t cutoff to square root of F cutoff, (c) S^2_{Pooled} to S^2_{Within}, and (d) the t score to the square root of the F ratio. (Use the .05 level throughout; t tests are two-tailed.)

| | Experimental Group | | | Control Group | | | | t test | | |
	N	M	S^2	N	M	S^2	df	t needed	S^2_{Pooled}	t
(i)	36	100	40	36	104	48	70	1.995	44	2.56
(ii)	16	73	8	16	75	6				

3. Following is a data set. Figure the t test for this problem. Then, also figure a one-way analysis of variance using the regular method of "Introduction to the Analysis of Variance" (not the structural model approach shown in the Advanced Topic section of that chapter). Make a chart of the similarities of (a) t df to F denominator df, (b) t cutoff to square root of F cutoff, (c) S^2_{Pooled} to S^2_{Within}, and (d) the t score to the square root of the F ratio.

| | Experimental Group | | | Control Group | |
N	M	S^2	N	M	S^2
30	12.0	2.4	30	11.1	2.8

4. Group A includes 10 people whose scores have a mean of 170 and a population variance estimate of 48. Group B also includes 10 people: $M = 150$, $S^2 = 32$. Carry out a t test for independent means (two-tailed) and an analysis of variance (using the regular method of "Introduction to the Analysis of Variance," not the structural model approach shown in the Advanced Topic section of that chapter). Do your figuring on the two halves of the same page, with parallel computations next to each other. (That is, make a table similar in layout to the lower part of Table 2.) Use the .05 level for both.

5. Do the following for the scores in practice problems (a) 6, (b) 7, and (c) 8: (i) Figure a t test for independent means, (ii) figure the correlation coefficient (between the group that participants are in and their scores on the measured

variable), (iii) figure the t for significance of the correlation coefficient (using the formula $t = r/\sqrt{(1 - r^2)/(N - 2)}$) and note explicitly the similarity of results, and (iv) make a scatter diagram. (v) For (a) only, explain the relation of the spread of the means, and the spread of the scores around the means, to the t test result.

6. ADVANCED TOPIC: For the following scores, figure a t test for independent means (two-tailed) and then figure an analysis of variance using the structural model approach from "Introduction to the Analysis of Variance" (use the .05 level for both). Make a chart of the similarities of (a) t df to F denominator df, (b) t cutoff to square root of F cutoff, (c) S^2_{Pooled} to S^2_{Within}, and (d) the t score to the square root of the F ratio.

Group A	Group B
13	11
16	7
19	9
18	
19	

7. ADVANCED TOPIC: For the following scores, figure a t test using the .05 level, two-tailed. Then figure a one-way analysis of variance (also .05 level) using the structural model method from "Introduction to the Analysis of Variance." Make a chart of the similarities of (a) t df to F denominator df, (b) t cutoff to square root of F cutoff, (c) S^2_{Pooled} to S^2_{Within}, and (d) the t score to the square root of the F ratio.

	Ordinary Story		Own-Name Story
Student	Reading Time	Student	Reading Time
A	2	G	4
B	5	H	16
C	7	I	11
D	9	J	9
E	6	K	8
F	7		

8. ADVANCED TOPIC: For the following scores, figure a t test for independent means and then figure an analysis of variance using the structural model approach from "Introduction to the Analysis of Variance." Make a chart of the similarities of (a) t df to F denominator df, (b) t cutoff to square root of F cutoff, (c) S^2_{Pooled} to S^2_{Within}, and (d) the t score to the square root of the F ratio. (Use the .05 level throughout; the t test is two-tailed.)

Group A	Group B
.7	.6
.9	.4
.8	.2

9. ADVANCED TOPIC: Do the following for the scores in practice problems (a) 6, (b) 7, and (c) 8: (i) Figure the analysis of variance using the structural model approach from "Introduction to the Analysis of Variance"; (ii) figure the proportionate reduction in error based on the analysis of variance results; (iii) carry out a regression analysis (predicting the measured variable score from the group that

participants are in); (iv) figure the proportionate reduction in error using the long method of figuring predicted scores, and finding the average squared error using them; and (v) make a chart showing the parallels in the results; for (a), also (vi) explain the major similarities. (Use the .05 level throughout.)

10. ADVANCED TOPIC: Participants 1, 2, and 3 are in Group I; participants 4 and 5 are in Group II; participants 6, 7, and 8 are in Group III; and participants 9 and 10 are in Group IV. Make a table showing nominal coding for these 10 participants.

Set II

11. (a) Look up and write down the F cutoff at the .01 level for distributions with 1 degree of freedom in the numerator and 10, 20, 30, and 60 degrees of freedom in the denominator. (b) Take the square root of each and write it down next to it. (c) Look up the cutoffs on the t distribution at the .01 level (two-tailed) using 10, 20, 30, and 60 degrees of freedom, and write it down next to the corresponding F square root. (The results should be identical, within rounding error.)

12. Following are three data sets. For the first two data sets, in addition to the means and estimated population variances, we have shown the t test information. You should figure the third yourself. Also, for each, figure a one-way analysis of variance using the regular method of "Introduction to the Analysis of Variance" (not the structural model approach shown in the Advanced Topic section of that chapter). Make a chart of the similarities of (a) t df to F denominator df, (b) t cutoff to square root of F cutoff, (c) S^2_{Pooled} to S^2_{Within}, and (d) the t score to the square root of the F ratio. (Use the .01 level throughout; t tests are two-tailed.)

| | Experimental Group | | | Control Group | | | t test | | | |
	N	M	S^2	N	M	S^2	df	t needed	S^2_{Pooled}	t
(i)	20	10	3	20	12	2	38	2.724	2.5	4
(ii)	25	7.5	4	25	4.5	2	48	2.690	3.0	6.12
(iii)	10	48	8	10	55	4				

13. The following are scores from three data sets. Figure the t tests for these using the .01 level, two-tailed. Then, for each, also figure a one-way analysis of variance (also .01 level) using the regular method of "Introduction to the Analysis of Variance" (not the structural model approach shown in the Advanced Topic section of that chapter). Make a chart of the similarities of (a) t df to F denominator df, (b) t cutoff to square root of F cutoff, (c) S^2_{Pooled} to S^2_{Within}, and (d) the t score to the square root of the F ratio.

| | Experimental Group | | | Control Group | | |
	N	M	S^2	N	M	S^2
(i)	10	604	60	10	607	50
(ii)	40	604	60	40	607	50
(iii)	10	604	20	10	607	16

14. Group I consists of 12 people whose scores have a mean of 15.5 and a population variance estimate of 4.5. Group B also consists of 12 people: $M = 18.3, S^2 = 3.5.$ Carry out a t test for independent means (two-tailed) and

an analysis of variance (using the regular method of "Introduction to the Analysis of Variance", not the structural model approach shown in the Advanced Topic section of that chapter), figuring the two on two halves of the same page, with parallel computations next to each other. (That is, make a table similar in layout to the lower part of Table 2.) Use the .05 level.

15. Do the following for the scores in practice problems (a) 16, (b) 17, and (c) 18: (i) Figure a t test for independent means, (ii) figure the correlation coefficient (between the group that participants are in and their scores on the measured variable), (iii) figure the t for significance of the correlation coefficient (using the formula $t = r/\sqrt{(1 - r^2)/(N - 2)}$) and note explicitly the similarity of results, (iv) make a scatter diagram, and (v) explain the relation of the spread of the means and the spread of the scores around the means to the t test results.

16. ADVANCED TOPIC: For the following scores, carry out a t test for independent means (two-tailed) and an analysis of variance using the structural model method from "Introduction to the Analysis of Variance." (Use the .05 level for both.) Make a chart of the similarities of (a) t df to F denominator df, (b) t cutoff to square root of F cutoff, (c) S^2_{Pooled} to S^2_{Within}, and (d) the t score to the square root of the F ratio.

Group A	Group B
0	4
1	5
0	6
	5

17. ADVANCED TOPIC: For the following scores, figure a t test for independent means (.05 level, two-tailed) and an analysis of variance (.05 level) using the structural model method from "Introduction to the Analysis of Variance." Make a chart of the similarities of (a) t df to F denominator df, (b) t cutoff to square root of F cutoff, (c) S^2_{Pooled} to S^2_{Within}, and (d) the t score to the square root of the F ratio.

Group A	Group B
0	0
0	0
0	0
0	0
0	0
0	0
0	1
0	1
0	1
0	1
0	1
0	1
1	1
1	1
1	1
1	1

18. ADVANCED TOPIC: For following scores, figure the t test using the .05 level, two-tailed. Then figure a one-way analysis of variance (also .05 level) using the structural model method from "Introduction to the Analysis of Variance." Make a chart of the similarities of (a) t df to F denominator df, (b) t cutoff to square root of F cutoff, (c) S^2_{Pooled} to S^2_{Within}, and (d) the t score to the square root of the F ratio.

Big Meal Group		Small Meal Group	
Subject	Hearing	Subject	Hearing
A	22	D	19
B	25	E	23
C	25	F	21

19. ADVANCED TOPIC: Do the following for the scores in practice problems (a) 16, (b) 17, and (c) 18: (i) Figure the analysis of variance using the structural model approach from "Introduction to the Analysis of Variance"; (ii) figure the proportionate reduction in error based on the analysis of variance results; (iii) carry out a regression analysis (predicting the measured variable score from the group that participants are in); (iv) figure the proportionate reduction in error using the long method of figuring predicted scores, and finding the average squared error using them; and (v) make a chart showing the parallels in the results.

20. ADVANCED TOPIC: Participants 1 and 2 are in Group A; participants 3, 4, 5, and 6 are in Group B; and participants 7, 8, and 9 are in Group C. Make a table showing nominal coding for these nine participants.

Using SPSS

The ⤏ in the following steps indicates a mouse click. (We used SPSS version 19 for Windows to carry out these analyses. The steps and output may be slightly different for other versions of SPSS.)

For each SPSS analysis that follows, we use the scores from the main example we used in this chapter (see Tables 2 and 4, and also Table 6 if you read this chapter's Advanced Topic section). First, we use SPSS to figure a t test for independent means for the example. We compare the results of this t test with the results of a one-way analysis of variance. Next, we figure the correlation coefficient for the example and compare it with the results for the t test. Finally, in an Advanced Topic Section, we figure the bivariate prediction (regression) for the example and compare the results to the analysis of variance results.

For the results of each of the following tests, we highlight the most important parts of the SPSS output.

t Test for Independent Means

❶ Enter the scores into SPSS as shown in Figure 4. In the first column (labeled "group"), we used the number "1" to indicate that a person is in the

Figure 4   SPSS data editor window Using SPSS examples, showing scores on an equal-interval variable for individuals in an experimental and a control group.

experimental group and the number "2" to indicate that a person is in the control group.

❷ ☞ *Analyze*.

❸ ☞ *Compare means*.

❹ ☞ *Independent-Samples T Test*.

❺ ☞ on the variable called "score" and then ☞ the arrow next to the box labeled "Test Variable(s)".

❻ ☞ the variable called "group" and then ☞ the arrow next to the the box labeled "Grouping Variable." ☞ *Define Groups*. Put "1" in the Group 1 box and put "2" in the Group 2 box. ☞ *Continue*.

❼ ☞ *OK*. Your SPSS output window should look like Figure 5.

The first table in the SPSS output provides information about the two variables. The second table shows the actual results of the t test for independent means. Note the t value of 2.750 in the SPSS output in Figure 5 is consistent (within rounding error) with the value of t (of 2.73) shown in Table 2 earlier in the chapter. The result of the t test is statistically significant, as the significance level of .018 is less than our .05 cutoff significance level.

One-Way Analysis of Variance

We will carry out the analysis of variance using the same set of scores as shown in Figure 4.

❶ ☞ *Analyze*.

❷ ☞ *Compare means*.

❸ ☞ *One-Way ANOVA*.

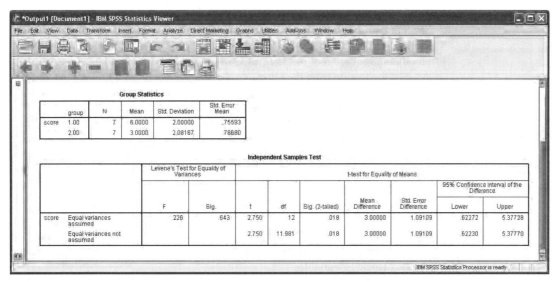

Figure 5 SPSS output window for a *t* test for independent means, using the scores shown in Figure 4.

❹ ✑ on the variable called "score" and then ✑ the arrow next to the box labeled "Dependent List".

❺ ✑ the variable called "group" and then ✑ the arrow next to the the box labeled "Factor."

❻ ✑ *OK*. Your SPSS output window should look like Figure 6.

Note the *F* value of 7.560 in the SPSS output in Figure 6 is consistent (within rounding error) with the value of *F* (of 7.55) shown in Table 2. Also, note that if we figure the square root of the *F* value of 7.560 from the SPSS output, the result is

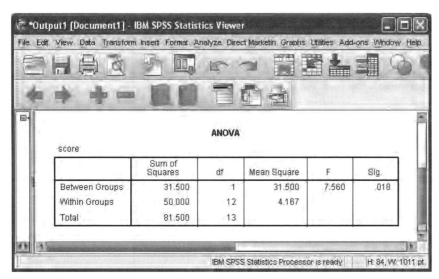

Figure 6 SPSS output window for a one-way analysis of variance, using the scores shown in Figure 4.

2.750. As we would expect, this is exactly the same value as the value of t from the SPSS output shown in Figure 5. Notice also that the F test is statistically significant, as the significance level of .018 is less than our .05 cutoff significance level. The fact that the square root of the F value from this analysis of variance is exactly the same as the t value from the t test for independent means, and the fact that the significance levels of both tests were exactly the same (.018), show that the t test is a special case of the analysis of variance.

Finding the Correlation Coefficient

We will find the correlation coefficient using the same set of scores as shown in Figure 4.

❶ ✑ *Analyze.*

❷ ✑ *Correlate.*

❸ ✑ *Bivariate.*

❹ ✑ on the variable called "group" and then ✑ the arrow next to the box labeled "Variables." ✑ on the variable called "score" and then ✑ the arrow next to the box labeled "Variables."

❺ ✑ *OK.* Your SPSS output window should look like Figure 7.

Note that the correlation coefficient (r) of −.622 shown in the SPSS output in Figure 7 is consistent with the correlation coefficient of −.62 shown in Table 4 earlier in the chapter. As with the t test (and analysis of variance), the correlation coefficient is statistically significant, as the significance level of .018 is less than our .05 cutoff level. Again, the .018 significance level is identical to the .018 significance level found for the t test (and the analysis of variance) SPSS output. This demonstrates that the t test is a special case of the significance test for the correlation coefficient.

Advanced Topic: Bivariate Prediction

We will figure the bivariate prediction using the same set of scores as shown in Figure 4, using "group" as the predictor variable and "score" as the criterion variable.

Figure 7   SPSS output window for a correlation coefficient, using the scores shown in Figure 4.

❶ ⌖ *Analyze.*

❷ ⌖ *Regression.* ⌖ *Linear.*

❸ ⌖ the variable called "score" and then ⌖ the arrow next to the the box labeled "Dependent." ⌖ the variable called "group" and then ⌖ the arrow next to the the box labeled "Independent(s)."

❹ ⌖ *OK.* Your SPSS output window should look like Figure 8.

Note that the values of SS_{Error}, SS_{Total}, R Square, and R in the model summary table of the SPSS output in Figure 8 are the same as the equivalent values in Table 5 earlier in the chapter. Notice also that the values in the "ANOVA" table for the bivariate prediction shown in Figure 8 are identical to the values in the "ANOVA" table for the one-way analysis of variance shown in Figure 6. (The only differences between the two "ANOVA" tables is in their terminology: The "Regression Sums of Squares" and "Residual Sums of Squares" for the table for bivariate prediction in Figure 8 are called "Between Groups Sums of Squares" and "Within Groups Sums of Squares" for one-way analysis of variance in Figure 6.) This shows that analysis of variance is a special case of prediction (regression). This particular example shows the equivalence of analysis of variance and bivariate prediction, which is an example of the more general principle that analysis of variance is a special case of multiple regression.

Overall, the series of analyses in this Using SPSS section show that *t* tests, analysis of variance, correlation, and regression (bivariate prediction and multiple regression) are all based on the same underlying formula provided by the general

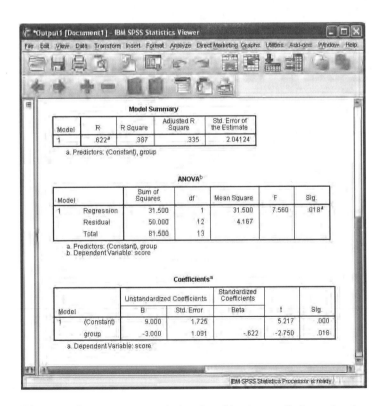

Figure 8 SPSS output window for a bivariate prediction, using the scores shown in Figure 4.

linear model. Your knowledge and understanding of this concept will provide a solid foundation for learning additional statistical procedures in intermediate and advanced statistics courses.

ANSWERS TO SET I PRACTICE PROBLEMS

1.

df		5	10	15	20
(a)	t	2.571	2.228	2.132	2.086
(b)	t^2	6.61	4.96	4.55	4.35
(c)	F	6.61	4.97	4.54	4.35

2. (i)

	(a)	(b)	(c)	(d)
	df	Cutoff	Within-Group Variance	t or F
t	70	1.995	$S^2_{Pooled} = 44$	2.56
F	70	3.980	$S^2_{Within} = 44$	6.55
		($\sqrt{} = 1.995$)		($\sqrt{} = 2.56$)

(ii)

	(a)	(b)	(c)	(d)
	df	Cutoff	Within-Group Variance	t or F
t	30	2.043	$S^2_{Pooled} = 7$	−2.13
F	30	4.170	$S^2_{Within} = 7$	−4.57
		($\sqrt{} = 2.042$)		($\sqrt{} = 2.14$)

3.

	(a)	(b)	(c)	(d)
	df	Cutoff	Within-Group Variance	t or F
t	58	2.004	$S^2_{Pooled} = 2.6$	2.16
F	58	4.020	$S^2_{Within} = 2.6$	4.67
		($\sqrt{} = 2.005$)		($\sqrt{} = 2.16$)

4.

t Test	ANOVA
	Numerator
	$df_{Between} = N_{Groups} - 1 = 2 - 1 = 1$
Mean difference = 170 − 150	$GM = (170 + 150)/2$
= 20	= 160
	$\Sigma(M - GM)^2 = (170 - 160)^2 + (150 - 160)^2$
	= 200

t Test	ANOVA
	$S^2_{Between}$ or $MS_{Between} = \dfrac{\Sigma(M-GM)^2}{df_{Between}}(n)$
	$= (200/1)(10)$
	$= 2,000$

Denominator

$S^2_{Pooled} = (df_1/df_{Total})(S^2_1)$ $\quad + (df_2/df_{Total})(S^2_2)$ $\quad = (.5)(48) + (.5)(32)$ $\quad = 40$	S^2_{Within} or $MS_{Within} =$ $\quad (S^2_1 + S^2_2 + \ldots + S^2_{Last})/(N_{Groups})$ $\quad = (48 + 32)/2 = 40$
$S^2_{Difference}$ $= S^2_{M1} + S^2_{M2}$ $= (S^2_{Pooled}/N_1) + (S^2_{Pooled}/N_2)$ $= (40/10) + (40/10) = 8$	
$S_{Difference}$ $= \sqrt{S^2_{Difference}}$ $= \sqrt{8} = 2.83.$	

Degrees of Freedom

$df_{Total} = df_1 + df_2 = 9 + 9$ $\quad = 18$	$df_{Within} = df_1 + df_2 + \ldots + df_{Last}$ $\quad = 9 + 9 = 18$

Cutoff

Needed *t* ($df = 18, p < .05$, two-tailed): 2.101	Needed *F* ($df = 1, 18; p < .05$): 4.41 ($\sqrt{} = 2.1$)

Score on Comparison Distribution

$t = (M_1 - M_2)/S_{Difference}$ $\quad = 20/2.83$ $\quad = 7.07$	$F = S^2_{Between}/S^2_{Within}$ or $MS_{Between}/MS_{Within}$ $\quad = 2,000/40 = 50$ ($\sqrt{} = 7.07$)

Conclusions

Reject the null hypothesis.	Reject the null hypothesis.

5. (a)(i) $t = \underline{4.60}$ (see question 6); (ii) $r = 15/16.99 = .88$; (iii)
   $t = .88/\sqrt{(1 - .88^2)/6} = 4.54$ (result is same as 4.60 within rounding error).
(iv)

(v) A t test is the difference between the means divided by the standard deviation of the distribution of differences between means. So, the larger the difference between the means, the larger the t test result. The standard deviation of the distribution of differences between means is largely based on the variances in each sample, and the variance in each sample is an indication of how spread out the scores in each sample are around the mean. So, the smaller the variance in each sample (that is, the closer the scores are to the mean of the sample), the larger the t test result (since you will be dividing by a smaller number when figuring the value of t).

(b)(i) $t = -1.73$ (see question 7); (ii) $r = -.50$; (iii) $t = -1.73$; (iv) similar to 5 (a)(iv) above.

(c)(i) $t = 3.1$ (see question 8); (ii) $r = .84$; (iii) $t = 3.10$; (iv) similar to 8 (a)(iv) above.

6.

	(a) df	(b) Cutoff	(c) Within-Group Variance	(d) t or F
t	6	2.447	$S^2_{Pooled} = 5.67$	4.60
F	6	5.99	$S^2_{Within} = 5.67$	21.16

7.

	(a) df	(b) Cutoff	(c) Within-Group Variance	(d) t or F
t	9	2.262	$S^2_{Pooled} = 11.69$	-1.73
F	9	5.99	$S^2_{Within} = 11.69$	3.02

8.

	(a) df	(b) Cutoff	(c) Within-Group Variance	(d) t or F
t	4	2.776	$S^2_{Pooled} = 0.25$	3.1
F	4	7.71	$S^2_{Within} = 0.25$	9.6

9. (a)(v)

Regression	ANOVA
Mean of $Y = 14$	Grand mean $= 14$
$SS_{Total} = 154$	$SS_{Total} = 154$
Predicted Y for Group A $= 17$	Mean of Group A $= 17$
Predicted Y for Group B $= 9$	Mean of Group B $= 9$
$SS_{Error} = 34$	$SS_{Within} = 34$
Reduction in error $= 120$	$SS_{Between} = 120$
$r^2 = .77$	$R^2 = .78$

(vi) You can think of the analysis of variance as about the relationship between the variable on which the groups differ (Group A versus Group B in this problem) and the measured variable. If you think of the variable on which the groups differ as a predictor variable, regression is also about the same thing. In this problem, you can consider those in Group A to have a score of 2 on this predictor and those in Group B to have a score of 1 on it. (Any two numbers would do; these are just examples.) In fact, the underlying mathematics is the same. Here are some of the parallels. In both regression and the analysis of variance, you figure the total squared deviations from the overall mean (in both, this is SS_{Total}). A deeper link is that the best predictor for those in either group is the group's mean, so the linear prediction rule predicts the mean for each group. The result is that the errors of predictions are deviations of the scores from the mean. If you square these and add them up, they are called SS_{Error} in regression and SS_{Within} in ANOVA. In regression, before figuring the proportionate reduction in error, you figure the reduction in error ($SS_{Total} - SS_{Error}$)—the amount of squared error that the prediction rule saves over predicting from the overall mean of the criterion variable. This is the same as $SS_{Between}$ in ANOVA, because when there are only two group means, regression improves on prediction only to the extent that the means of the two groups are different. Finally, because SS_{Total} is the same in both regression and analysis of variance, and because reduction in error $= SS_{Between}$, r^2 in regression has to come out the same as R^2 figured as an effect size in ANOVA.

(b)

Regression	ANOVA
Mean reading time $= 7.64$	Grand mean $= 7.64$
$SS_{Total} = 140.55$	$SS_{Total} = 140.55$
Predicted reading time ordinary story $= 6$	Mean reading time ordinary story $= 6$
Predicted reading time own-name story $= 9.6$	Mean reading time own-name story $= 9.6$
$SS_{Error} = 105.2$	$SS_{Within} = 105.2$
Reduction in error $= 35.35$	$SS_{Between} = 35.35$
$r^2 = .34$	$R^2 = .34$

(c)

Regression	ANOVA
Mean of criterion variable $= .6$	Grand mean $= .6$
$SS_{Total} = .34$	$SS_{Total} = .34$
Predicted score for Group A $= .8$	Mean of Group A $= .8$
Predicted score for Group B $= .4$	Mean of Group B $= .4$
$SS_{Error} = .1$	$SS_{Within} = .1$
Reduction in error $= .24$	$SS_{Between} = .24$
$r^2 = .71$	$R^2 = .71$

10.

Participant	Group	Variable 1 (Group I or not)	Variable 2 (Group II or not)	Variable 3 (Group III or not)
1	I	1	0	0
2	I	1	0	0
3	I	1	0	0
4	II	0	1	0
5	II	0	1	0
6	III	0	0	1
7	III	0	0	1
8	III	0	0	1
9	IV	0	0	0
10	IV	0	0	0

Chapter Notes

1. In this chapter, we focus on the t test for independent means (and also the analysis of variance for between-subject designs). However, the conclusions are all the same for the t test for dependent means. It is a special case of the repeated measures analysis of variance. Also, both the t test for dependent means and the repeated measures analysis of variance are special cases of multiple regression/correlation. However, the link between these methods and multiple regression involves some extra steps of logic that we do not consider here to keep the chapter focused on the main ideas.

2. Other apparent differences (such as the seeming difference that the F ratio numerator is based on a variance estimate and the t score numerator is a simple difference between means) are also actually the same when you go into them in detail.

3. Another reason for the use of different procedures is that the t test and analysis of variance have traditionally been used to analyze results of true experiments with random assignment to levels of the variables that divide the groups, while correlation and regression have been used mainly to analyze results of studies in which the predictor variable was measured in people as it exists, what is called a correlational research design. Thus, using a correlation or regression approach to analyze a true experiment, while correct, might imply to the not-very-careful reader that the study was not a true experiment.

Reference

Baumrind, D. (1983). Specious causal attributions in the social sciences: The reformulated stepping-stone theory of heroin use as exemplar. *Journal of Personality and Social Psychology 45*, 1289–1298.

Index

Page references followed by "f" indicate illustrated figures or photographs; followed by "t" indicates a table.